REFERENCE GUIDE TO
FANTASTIC FILMS

Boris Karloff in <u>The Mummy</u> (1932)

VOLUME 2

G – O

REFERENCE GUIDE TO

fantastic films

SCIENCE FICTION, FANTASY, & HORROR

COMPILED BY WALT LEE

ASSISTED BY BILL WARREN

chelsea-lee books   box 66273   los angeles, 90066   1973

Library of Congress Catalog Card Number: 72-88775.

ISBN 0-913974-02-1

```
*******************************************************
*                                                     *
*   ISBNs for the 3-Volume                            *
*   Reference Guide to Fantastic Films are:           *
*         Volume 1:    ISBN 0-913974-01-3             *
*         Volume 2:    ISBN 0-913974-02-1             *
*         Volume 3:    ISBN 0-913974-03-X             *
*         Volumes 1-3: ISBN 0-913974-04-8.            *
*                                                     *
*******************************************************
```

Printed in the U.S.A.

contents

list of illustrations

introduction

. . . Christopher Lee

"Fantastic:" How many millions of times is that word mentioned during our lifetime, both in conversation and in the literary sense? And what exactly do we mean when we use this adjective?

There is no doubt in my mind. Whenever I read or hear the word, it is always in the context of something unusual and out of the ordinary — something extra special and almost certainly something enjoyable and positive. The word in itself is virtually a compliment even when casually applied. In modern terms, "out of this world" would seem to be the most appropriate parallel.

We are not dealing here with the ordinary or commonplace everyday world. In effect, we are letting our fancies roam freely without the drawback of being shackled by conventional experiences or rules of conduct.

We escape.

And what a joy it is. We are in a literal sense enchanted. The Necromancer waves his wand before our dazzled eyes and immediately we are in a world of mystery, magic and the unknown. We are in a world of Fantasy.

In relation to the Cinema or any other entertainment medium, the French description, "Cinema of the Fantastic" has always seemed to me to be the ideal description. We are not bound by any conventions

Christopher Lee shown above as Lord Summerisle in The Wicker Man (1973).

or restrictions. And the Cinema of the Fantastic covers what is undoubtedly the widest and most detailed area of entertainment now in existence. The literature on the subject is vast and so is the number of films made that lie within this category. I myself do not believe that we have progressed beyond skimming the surface of this enchanted pool. Virtually every writer of note, in every country of the world from the time of the Ancient Egyptians, Greeks and Romans, up to the present day, has contributed to the Fantastic and the results have almost always been fascinating.

Science Fiction, horror, terror, shock, melodrama, the prehistoric, the modern, suspense, action and adventure, the future, the past, the occult, Black Magic, superstition, the weird, the incredible, the unbelievable. All these, in one degree or another, come within the scope of the Cinema of the Fantastic. This has been the case since the first film was made, it is the case today, and it will never change in the future.

I myself have been involved to some degree in this "Secret, black, and midnight" world and I feel most strongly that there is still a great deal of work to be done. I would appeal to writers, producers and directors to concentrate more on an area which possesses this universal appeal and to give the world more of the kind of film that the world so obviously craves.

As I have said before, it is our vocation and duty to make the unbelievable believable. It is a narrow and dangerous line we tread, but your conviction and acceptance is our award.

It is with pleasure and admiration that I commend to you the writer of this book, the work and the diligence of one who has so faithfully and accurately recorded the contribution of the Cinema in this immensely popular field.

He has done a "Fantastic" job.

Christopher Lee

additional acknowledgements

Since Volume I of this Reference Guide went to press, valuable help has been received from persons not previously credited. In addition, some whose help was acknowledged previously have made continuing contributions deserving further acknowledgment.

Special thanks are due Christopher Lee for writing the introduction to this Volume. I doubt that my deadline could have fallen at a more inconvenient time for him, occurring as it did in the middle of a long-term, grueling production schedule on location in Madrid. That he took the time to do the job so well indicates his high regard for the fantastic film genre in which he is one of the top performers.

Bob Pardi has supplied difficult-to-obtain credits on many films by using a very direct and straight-forward approach: he photographs the credits on the screen. His generous help has filled in many blank spots in this work and is much appreciated.

One of Bill Warren's many continuing contributions has been praised in several reviews of Volume I and, I think, deserves special mention here. The brief statements of fantastic content following the classifications are, for the most part, his. Those statements are based on having seen the films, on the references given, or on my notes.

To the long list of film companies that have cooperated on this research project over the years, including practically every major firm, Azteca should now be added. A.M. Enriquez, manager of their Hollywood office has generously supplied stills, press sheets, and other material on many of the Spanish-language fantastic films they release.

The extensive assistance of my wife, Eve, which continues unabated in spite of her rather low regard for most horror films, deserves more thanks than can be conveyed here.

Of the many libraries consulted during this research project, the Margaret Herrick library of the Academy of Motion Picture Arts and Sciences must be singled out for repeated thanks. That library, with its helpful staff, under the capable direction of Mildred Simpson, continues to be indispensable to this project.

Eric Hoffman has continued to provide valuable help. Besides extensive information about sound serials, Eric has supplied data and even pressbooks on several obscure films.

Fantastic films made in the Republic of the Philippines have long been a difficult research problem for me. Considerable information about such films has now been obtained from Fred Chodkowski who lived in the Philippines for a few years and saved local newspaper and magazine articles, reviews, and advertisements. Fred's material, collected in five large scrapbooks, has provided considerable data, and his cooperation is most appreciated.

One of the anticipated advantages of publishing this work was that it would initiate contact with fantastic film authorities all over the world who would be willing to supply additional information. Horácio Higuchi, who is extremely knolwedgable about fantastic films on a world-wide basis, is one such authority. Horácio wrote from Brazil, where he lives, after he had seen Volume I in the Library of the British Film Institute in London. He supplied data on a number of fantastic films previously unknown to me. Several titles are listed in this volume as a result of his knowledge, and other such films will be included in Volume 3.

David Soren, editor of <u>Fantastic Worlds</u>, who spends his summers in Tunisia, has supplied information on a number of obscure films he has seen there. In addition, Hector R. Pessina of Argentina has supplied useful information about space films. Valuable information has also been received from Jean-Claude Romer, co-editor of <u>Midi-Minuit Fantastique</u>, and Luigi Cozzi, editor of <u>Il Mostro Sexy</u>, as well as from Chris Collier (Australia), Benjamen Kunz (Switzerland), Alejandro A. Lerena (Argentina), Gilbert Verschooten (Belgium), and Gary R. Williams (Canada).

In the United States, the following have made useful continuing contributions to this work: Ron Borst, Frank Capra, Don Glut, Bob Greenberg, Greg Grosz, Norman Kagan, Dick Klemensen, Fred Patten, Andy Romanoff, and Don Willis. The assistance my children, Cindy and Steve, have given over the years also deserves special mention here.

Continuing access to Forrest J Ackerman's extensive personal collection of fantastic film material (probably the largest such collection in the world) has contributed much to the realization of this project. It is hoped that this <u>Reference Guide</u> will make a contribution to the serious study of fantastic films and, thus, help repay all those who, like Forry, are devoted to the genre and have themselves contributed so much.

If information continues to be received, as expected, from fantastic film authorities all over the world, every effort will be made to obtain the backing necessary to ensure a revised and expanded second edition of this work several years from now.

abbreviations

```
*****************
*    GENERAL    *
*****************
```

aka
  also known as

ca
  circa: approximately

d
  died

et al.
  et alibi (and others)

etc.
  et cetera (and others, and
  so forth)

pseud
  pseudonym

rn
  real name

sic
  thus (Latin word used to indicate
  a suspected error in quoted matter)

```
************************
*    TITLE VARIANTS    *
************************
```

ad.t.
  advertised title -- one
  used only in advertising
  or other published material.

alt.t.
  alternate title

Aust.t.
  Australian title

Brit.t.
  British title

c.t.
  copyright title

e.t.
  early title -- one used
  before production.

8mm t.
  8-millimeter title -- one
  used for home-movie release.

f.t.
  foreign title -- one in
  English used in other
  countries.

rr.t.
  re-release title

S.E.A. t.
  Southeast Asia title.

s.t.
  shooting title -- one used
  during production.

16mm t.
  16 millimeter title -- one
  used for 16mm prints for
  home or other non-theatrical
  use.

TV t. (tv.t.)
  television release title

trans.t.
  translation of title

```
**************************
*  STUDIOS/DISTRIBUTORS  *
**************************
```

AA
  Allied Artists

ABC
  ABC Films, Inc (a subsidiary
  of American Broadcasting
  Companies)

AI
  See: AIP.

AIP
  American International Pictures.

API
  Associated Producers Inc.

ARC
  American Releasing Corporation.

AsA
  Associated Artists

BV
  Buena Vista

Biog
  American Mutoscope &
  Biograph Co.

CFS
  Creative Film Society.

Cinemat.
  Cinematografica

Co.
  Company

Col
  Columbia Pictures

Corp.
  Corporation

DCA
  Distribution Corporation of
  America

Defu
  Deutsche Film Union

FBO
  Film Booking Offices of
  America, Inc.

Film-makers' Coop
  Film-makers' Cooperative

Fox
  Fox Film Corporation, until
  1935. Later, Twentieth Century
  Fox.
  See also: 20th-Fox.

FN
  First National

Gaum
  Gaumont

IMP
  Independent Motion Picture Co.

Inc.
  Incorporated

Int'l
  International

MGM
  Metro-Goldwyn-Mayer/Loew's Inc.

Mono
  Monogram

NFB
  National Film Board of Canada

NGC
  National General Corp.

NTA
  National Telefilm Associates

NYMP
  New York Motion Picture Co.

PAGU
  Projections-Aktiengesellschaft
  Union.

PRC
  Producers Releasing Corporation

Par
  Paramount

Pics
  Pictures

Prods
  Productions

RKO
  RKO Radio

Rep
  Republic

20th-Fox
  Twentieth Century-Fox.
  See also: Fox.

U
  Universal/Universal-International

UA
  United Artists

UPA
  United Productions of
  America

UFA
  Universum Film Aktiengesellschaft
  (Universal Film Joint-Stock
  Company)

US
  United States

Vit
  Vitagraph

WB
  Warner Brothers

WD
  Walt Disney Productions

W7
  Warner Brothers-7 Arts

```
************************
*   FILM DESCRIPTION   *
************************
```

ani
  animated artwork

ani puppet
  figures made to move by
  stop-motion cinematography

CS
  CinemaScope
  see also: scope.

colored
  see: hand colored.

ft
  feet (0.3048 meters)
  See: EXPLANATORY NOTES.

hand colored
  individual prints colored
  by hand -- each color applied
  by a separate stencil.

live
  live action (used only to
  indicate animation & live
  action in same film)

mins
  minutes

mm
  millimeter
  standard unit for specifying
  film widths; 35mm assumed
  unless otherwise stated

n.d.
  no date available

pixilation
  stop-motion/animation techniques
  applied to live action

pup
  puppet

reels
  standard (1000 foot) 35mm
  reels
  See EXPLANATORY NOTES

scope
  anamorphic wide screen process
  see also: CS.

ser
  serial

sh
  short -- less than feature
  length

sil
  silent

3D
  three dimensional -- provides
  separate image to each eye
  for illusion of depth

tinted
  different sequences printed on film
  with a colored base

VV
  VistaVision -
  nonanamorphic process for
  increasing aspect ratio and
  negative area

wide screen
  aspect ratio greater than 4:3
  achieved by cropping frame
  see also: CS; scope; VV

Adapt

Adaptation by

Ani

Animator(s)

Ani Dir

Animation Director(s)

Art Dir

Art Director(s)

Assist

Assistant

Assoc

Associate

Ass't

See: Assist

BG

Backgrounds by

Choreog

Choreographer(s)

Cin

Cinematography

Dir

Director(s)

Edit

Film Editor(s)

Exec Prod

Executive Producer(s)

FX

Effects

FX Ani

Effects Animation -- non-character animation: water, lightning, bubbles, etc.

Mus

Music Composer(s)

Mus Dir

Music Director(s)

Nar

Narrator(s)

Pres

Presented by
(used often in silent productions; equivalent of today's Prod or Exec Prod).

Prod

Producer(s)

Prod Design

Production Designer(s)

SP

Screenplay by
(scenario & dialogue)

Sc

Scenario by
(scene descriptions; does not include dialogue)

Seq Dir

Sequence Director(s)

Sp Ani FX

Special Animation Effects -- usually animation to be combined with live action

see also: FX Ani.

SpCin FX

Special Cinematography Effects -- usually rear projection and/or optical printing

SpFX

Special Effects

SpFX Cin

Special Effects Cinematography -- filming required for front or rear projection and/or optical printing

Story

For animated films, the "Story" is often prepared in storyboard format and is actually more detailed than an ordinary screenplay.

Sup

Supervisor/supervising

abs

abstract

alleg

allegorical

bor

borderline (opinions differ)

com

comedy

doc

documentary

dream

dream sequence(s)

exp

experimental

F

fantasy

H

horror

hist

historical

mus

musical

myst

mystery

myth

mythological

psy

psychological -- subjective distortions of reality

rel

religious

sat

satire

seq

sequence(s).

SF

science fiction

sur

surrealistic

west

western

(Note: The information given here is intended only to explain the abbreviations used in the References and, consequently, is organized alphabetically by abbreviation. A bibliography is included in Volume 3.)

AFI F2

Munden, Kenneth W., Editor.

The American Film Institute Catalog of Motion Pictures Produced in the United States.

Vol F2: Feature Films 1921-1930.

R.R. Bowker Company, New York & London, 1971.

AHF

Nealon, Jack.

An Historical and Critical Survey of the American Horror Film Since 1930.

Unpublished Master of Arts Thesis.

University of Southern California, Los Angeles, 1953.

ASIFA

Association Internationale du Film d'Animation.

Bulletins and information sheets, notes distributed to members, and programs distributed at the Los Angeles County Art Museum at time of screenings 1966. . .
ASIFA 1 was the 1966 program, ASIFA 2 1967, and so forth.

Acad

Academy of Motion Picture Arts and Sciences, Los Angeles.

Programs, information sheets, and notes, distributed at screenings or as publicity and maintained in the Academy's private library files.

Acad Nom

Nominated for Award by the Academy of Motion Picture Arts and Science.

Ackerman

Ackerman, Forrest J

Editor of Famous Monsters of Filmland, and authority on science fiction and fantastic films.

Agee

Agee, James.

Agee on Film: Reviews and Comments.

McDowell Obolensky, New York, 1958.

LC cat 58-12581.

Am Cin

American Cinematographer.

International Journal of Motion Picture Photography and Production Techniques.

Herb A. Lightman, Editor.

Published by ASC Holding Corp, 1782 N. Orange Dr., Hollywood, CA 90028.

1920. . .

An/Cin Ital

See: Annuario.

Anderson/Richie

Anderson, Joseph L. & Richie, Donald.

The Japanese Film: Art and Industry.

Grove Press, New York, 1960.

Ani/Belgium

Maelstaf, R.

"The Animated Cartoon Film in Belgium."

Ministry of Foreign Affairs & External Trade, Brussels, Belgium, July, 1970.

Ani Chart

Martin, André.

"Origin and Golden Age of the American Cartoon Film 1906-1941."

La Cinematheque Canadienne, Canada, 1967.

Ani/Cin

Stephenson, Ralph.

Animation in the Cinema.

A. Zwemmer Limited, London; A.S. Barnes & Co., New York, 1967.

Ani/NF prog

Animation -- New Facets program.

Animé

Benayoun, Robert.

Le Dessin Animé après Disney.

J.-J. Pauvert, Paris, 1961.

Annecy

International Days of Animated Film, Annecy, France.

Program Notes.

Annuario

Annuario del Cinema Italiano.

1966-1967.

Centro Studi di Cultura, Economia, e Divulgozione del Cinema, Rome, Italy, 1967.

Reviewed by Don Willis.

Arab Cin

Sadoul, Georges, Editor.

Cinema in the Arab Countries.

Inter-Arab Centre of Cinema and Television, Beirut, Lebanon, 1966.

Art/Ani

Thomas, Bob.

The Art of Animation.

Simon and Schuster, New York, 1958.

Art of Ani

See: Art/Ani.

AtMo

Atlantic Monthly.

Audio Film Center Cat

Audio Film Center Catalog, 1971-72.

Audio Film Center/Ideal Pictures 34 MacQuesten Parkway South Mount Vernon, New York 10550.

Aventura

Blanco, Jorge Ayala.

Aventura del Cine Mexicano.

Ediciones Era, Mexico, 1968.

Azteca

U.S. distributor of Spanish-language films, principally Mexican.

Various information sheets, press sheets, posters, synopses, etc.

B

See: Brandon cat.

BB

See: B&B.

B&B

Bardeche, Maurice, and Brasillach, Robert.

The History of Motion Pictures, translated and edited by Iris Barry.

W.W. Norton & Co., and The Museum of Modern Art, New York, 1938.

BFI cat

National Film Archive Catalogue, Part III, Silent Fiction Films, 1895-1930.

The British Film Institute, 81 Dean St., London W.1, England, 1966.

BFI Dist Cat

British Film Institute Distribution Catalogue.

The British Film Institute, London, England, 1962.

BFI list

See: Sadoul/M.

BIB's

TV Feature Film Source Book.

Broadcast Information Bureau, Inc.

B Movies

Miller, Don.

B Movies: An Informal Survey of the American Low-Budget Film, 1933-1945.

Curtis Books, New York, 1973.

BO

Boxoffice.

Weekly motion picture trade publication 1934--

Associated Publications, 825 Van Brunt Blvd, Kansas City, Missouri, 64124.

Balanchine

Balanchine, George.

Balanchine's Complete Stories of the Great Ballets.

Doubleday & Co, Inc, Garden City, New York, 1954.

Bangkok Post

Daily newspaper.

Bangkok, Thailand.

Barbour/T&A

Barbour, Alan G.

Days of Thrill and Adventure.

Collier Books/Collier-Macmillan Limited, London, England, 1970.

See also: SQ; ScF; Ser/Col; Ser/Rep.

Barry, Iris

Museum of Modern Art, New York.

Film Notes.

Distributed at film screenings and maintained in library files.

Baxter/SF

Baxter, John.

Science Fiction in the Cinema.

A.S. Barnes & Co., New York, and A. Zwemmer Ltd., London, 1970. LC cat 69-14896.

Barry/Griffith

Barry, Iris.

D.W. Griffith, American Film Master, by Iris Barry with an annotated list of films by Eileen Bowser.

Museum of Modern Art, New York, & Doublday, Garden City New York, 1940, 1965.

Belgian Experimental Film Festival Program

1958

Beranger

Beranger, Clara.

Writing for the Screen

William C. Brown Co., Dubuque, Iowa 1950.

Bianco

Bianco e Nero.

Centro Sperimentale di Cinematografia, Rome, Italy, 1960-1968.

Researched by Don Willis.

Biograph Bulletins

Press sheets published by Biograph, 1896-1908.

Also compiled by Kemp R. Niver.

Historical Films, Los Angeles, California, 1971.

Bios

The Bioscope.

British motion picture trade magazine.

London, 1909-1914.

Bizarre

Laclos Michel, Editor.

"Cinema Fantastique, l'Epouvante" no. 24-25, July-Sept '62.

"Tarzan" no.29-30, April-June 1963.

J.-J. Pauvert, Paris, France.

Bloch

Bloch, Robert.

Writer and fantastic film authority.

Blum

Blum, Daniel.

A Pictorial History of the Silent Screen.

Grosset & Dunlap, New York, 1953.

A Pictorial History of the Talkies.

Grosset & Dunlap, New York, 1958.

Bodeen, DeWitt

Writer and authority on motion picture history.

Bogdanovich/Dwan

Bogdanovich, Peter

Allan Dwan, The Last Pioneer

Praeger, New York, 1971.

Borst

Borst, Ronald V.

Authority on fantastic films.

Boys Cin

British magazine.

London, 1932-35.

Researched by Don Willis.

Brandon cat

Brandon Films, Inc., catalog No. 27, 1963.

The Audio/Brandon 16mm Collection of International Cinema, 1972-73.

Brisbane Prog

Programs of the Brisbane Cinema Group, Australia.

Brit Cin

Gifford, Denis.

British Cinema, An Illustrated Guide.

A. Zwemmer Ltd., London and A.S. Barnes & Co., New York, 1968.

LC cat 68-24000.

Brit YB

Noble, Peter; Editor.

British Film Yearbook.

British Yearbook Ltd., London. Published annually.

Brownlow

Brownlow, Kevin.

The Parade's Gone By. . .

Alfred A. Knopf, New York, 1968.

Broz

Brož, Jaroslav.

The Path of Fame of the Czechoslovak Film.

Prague, Czechoslovakia, 1965.

Butler/HF

Butler, Ivan.

The Horror Film.

A. S. Barnes & Co., New York; A. Zwemmer Ltd., London. 1967.

CCC

Center Cinema Co-op Catalog 2.

540 North Lake Shore Drive, Chicago, Illinois 60611.

CFC

Classic Film Collector.

(Formerly 8mm Collector.)

Samuel K. Rubin, Editor.

747 Philadelphia St., Indiana, PA 15701.

CFS

Creative Film Society Catalog.

14558 Valerio St., Van Nuys, CA 91405.

C/H

See: C to H.

CNW

Lahue, Kalton C.

Continued Next Week: A History of the Moving Picture Serial.

University of Oklahoma Press, Norman, 1964.

LC cat 64-20767.

CoF

Castle of Frankenstein.

Beck, Calvin T., Editor.

Fantastic film periodical, 1959. . .

Box 43, Hudson Heights Station, North Bergen, New Jersey 07047.

C of F

See: CoF.

CPC

See: Polish Cin.

C-16

Cinema-16 catalog.

Cinema-16 Division, Grove Press, 214 Mercer St., New York, NY 10012.

C to H

Kracauer, Siegfried.

From Caligari to Hitler, A Psychological History of the German Film.

Princeton University Press, London, 1947.

CU

Close Up

British film periodical.

London, 1930-?

Cahiers

Cahiers du Cinema.

French film periodical.

Editions de l'Etoile, Paris, 1956--

Came the Dawn

See: Hepworth.

Capra

Capra, Frank.

Frank Capra, the Name Above the Title.

Macmillan Co, New York, 1971.

LC cat 72-135643.

cat

catalog.

Center Cinema Co-op Cat

See: CCC.

Chilling Monster Tales

M.M. Publishing Ltd., New York, 1966.

Chodkowski

Chodkowski, Fred.

Informed source on Philippine fantastic films with many scrapbooks of Philippine film advertisements and articles.

Cine Argentino

Argentine film periodical.

Instituta Nacional de Cinematografia, Buenos Aires, 1968.

Researched by Don Willis.

Cine Español

See: SpCin.

Cine Nost

Larkin, Frankie, Editor.

Ciné Nostalgia.

15133 1/2 Greenleaf St., Sherman Oaks, CA 91403.

Ciné Nouvelles

Egyptian film periodical.

Cairo, 1953.

Cine YB Japan

Cinema Yearbook of Japan.

CineF

Cinefantastique.

Clarke, Frederick S., Editor.

Periodical devoted to fantastic films.

7470 Diversy, Elmwood Park, Illinois, 60635.

Cinelandia

Mayrink, Geraldo, Editor.

Brazilian film periodical.

Rio de Janeiro.

Monthly.

Cinema, The

Indian film periodical.

Cinema of Fritz Lang, The

Jensen, Paul M.

A.S. Barnes & Co, New York, and A. Zwemmer Ltd., London, 1969.

LC cat 69-14895.

Clarens

Clarens, Carlos.

An Illustrated History of the Horror Film.

G.P. Putnam's Sons, New York, 1967.

LC cat 67-10951.

Clasa-Mohme

Subsidiary of Azteca, distributor of Spanish-language films.

Press sheets, information sheets, synopses, etc.

Classics of the Film

Lenning, Arthur, Editor.

Wisconsin Film Society Press 1312 West Johnson St. Madison, Wisconsin 1965.

Classics/Sil

Franklin, Joe.

Classics of the Silent Screen.

The Citadel Press, New York, 1959.

LC cat 59-14063.

Collier

Chris Collier, film authority living in Australia.

ConBul

Consumers' Bulletin.

Connor, Ed.

Authority on films.

Cont FR

Continental Film Review.

Film periodical.

London.

Contemp

Contemporary Films Inc catalog, 1961.

Now: Contemporary/McGraw-Hill Films.

330 W. 42nd St., New York, NY 10036.

Continental Film Review

See: Cont FR.

Corman

Will, David & Willemen, Paul, Editors.

Roger Corman, the Millenic Vision.

Edinburgh Film Festival 1970, in association with Cinema Magazine, Cambridge, 1970.

Coronet

Rohauer, Raymond.

Coronet Louvre Society of Cinema Arts Program, Los Angeles.

Cowie/70

Cowie, Peter.

Seventy Years of Cinema.

A.S. Barnes & Co., South Brunswick and New York; Thomas Yoseloff Ltd., London, 1960.

Cue

Newman, Stanley, Editor; Wolf, William, Film Editor.

Periodical.

New York.

DdC

Bessy, Maurice, & Chardans, Jean-Louis.

Dictionnaire du Cinema et de la Television.

Jean-Jacques Pauvert, Paris, 1965-67.

Four volumes.

dG

See: de Groot.

DKA program

Programs distributed by DKA fraternity at their screenings.

University of Southern California, Los Angeles.

DTA

Barbour, Alan G.

Days of Thrills and Adventure.

Collier Books. New York, 1970.

Daily Variety

See: Vd.

Danforth, Jim
Authority on and expert in 3D model & puppet animation and special effects.

Danish Film
See: Neergaard.

de Groot
de Groot, Alexander.
Filmographie (1938 - 1961) Science-Fiction, Epouvante, et Fantastique.
Lausanne club Futopia, 1962.

Dean List
Dean, Walter.
"The Feature Motion Picture 1919 to 1929"
in
Classic Film Collector No. 15, Summer 1966

Destiny
Willits, Malcolm & Kemp, Earl, Editors.
"The British Horror Film" by Dennis [sic] Gifford, in amateur science fiction magazine, Destiny, Summer 1954, p 17-18 & 58-59, Portland, Oregon.

Deutscher
Kraatz, Karl L.
Deutscher Filmkatalog 1930 - 1945.
Transit-Film Gesellschaft(?), Frankfurt-am-Main, Germany, 1969.
Researched by Don Willis.

Dimmitt
Dimmitt, Richard Bertrand.
A Title Guide to the Talkies.
Scarecrow Press, New York, 1965; 2 volumes.

Dipali
Indian film periodical.
Calcutta, 1934-41.

Disney Version
See: Schickel/Disney.

Durgnat/Buñuel
Durgnat, Raymond.
Luis Buñuel.
University of California Press, Berkeley, 1968.
LC cat 68-17758.

Dyer, P.J.
Peter John Dyer, British authority on film history.

EK
Edison Kinetogram.
Periodical published by Thomas A. Edison Inc., Orange, New Jersey, 1909-14.

Early Am Cin
Slide, Anthony.
Early American Cinema.
A.S. Barnes & Co., New York, and A.Zwemmer Ltd., London, 1970.
LC cat 71-119639.

Eastern Europe
Hibbin, Nina.
Eastern Europe, An Illustrated Guide.
A.S. Barnes, New York; A. Zwemmer Ltd., London, 1969.
LC cat 69-14898.

Ecran
L'Ecran Fantastique.
French fantastic film periodical.
Alain Schlockoff, Publisher.
9 Rue du Midi.
92200 Neuilly
France.

Ed Film
Educational Films Catalog, International Film Bureau, Chicago, Illinois, 1962.

Edinburgh Fest
Edinburgh, Scotland, Film Festival Programs.

8mm Collector
See: CFC.

Eisner
Eisner, Lotte H.
The Haunted Screen.
Thames and Hudson, London, 1969.

Elements
"Elements d'une Filmographie."
Filmography in
La Dessin Animé après Disney.
See also: Animé.

Encic DS
Enciclopedia dello Spettacolo.
Unione Editoriale, Rome, 1958.

Ency/Op
Ewen, David.
Encyclopedia of the Opera.
Hill and Wang, New York, 1963.
LC cat 55-10884.

Estes, Oscar G.
Authority on film history.

ExCin
Youngblood, Gene.
Expanded Cinema.
E.P. Dutton & Co Inc., New York, 1970.
LC cat 71-87207.

Exhibitors Herald
See: MPH.

Exp in Film
See: Exp/Film.

Exp/Film
Manvell, Roger, Editor.
Experiment in the Film.
Grey Walls Press, London, 1949.

Essoe/Tarzan
Essoe, Gabe.
Tarzan of the Movies.
Citadel Press, New York, 1968.
LC cat 68-28454.

f
following

F/A
Leonard, Harold, Editor.
Film as Art.
Vol I of The Film Index.
The Museum of Modern Art Film Library and the H.W. Wilson Co., New York, 1941.

FACSEA
French American Cultural Services & Education Aids catalog.
New York, n.d.

F&F
Bean, Robin, Editor.
Films and Filming.
British film periodical published by Hansom Brooks, Artillery Mansions, 75 Victoria St., London SW 1.

F&SF
The Magazine of Fantasy and Science Fiction.
Fiction periodical with column on fantastic films by Baird Searles, previously by Charles Beaumont.
Mercury Press, New York.

F as A
See: F/A.

F Assoc
Film Associates catalog.

FC
Mekas, Jonas, Editor.
Film Culture.
Film periodical.
GPO Box 1499, New York, NY, 10001.

FD
Lipton, Edward, Editor.
Film Daily.
Film trade publication 1915-1970.
Reviews indexed in Film Daily Yearbook. (FDY)

FDY
Alicoate, Jack, Editor; later Fordin, Hugh.
Film Daily Yearbook of Motion Pictures.
1920-1970.

FEFN
Far East Film News.
Later Movie/TV Marketing.
See also: MTVM.

F et R
Fantastique et Realism dans le Cinema Allemand 1912-1933.
Musée du Cinéma, Bruxelles, Belgium, 1969.

FF
Parmentier, Ernest, Editor.
Filmfacts.
Compilation of reviews with full credits. Indexed annually, 1958 -- currently.
P.O. Box 213, Village Station, New York, NY 10014.

FFF
Jones, Jack R., Compiler.
Fantasy Films and Their Fiends.
Jones, Oklahoma City, 1964.

F/Future
Martin, Marie.
Films on the Future A Selective Listing.
World Future Society
P.O. Box 30369
Bethesda Branch
Washington, DC 20014 1973

FI
The Film Index.
Motion picture trade periodical
Films Publishing Co., New York, 1906-1910.
Later Views and Film Index.
See also: V&FI; Views.

FIR
Reilly, Charles Phillips, Editor; formerly Hart, Henry.
Films in Review.
Film periodical.
National Board of Review, New York, 1950 --
210 East 68th St., New York, NY 10021.

FM
Ackerman, Forrest J, Editor.
Famous Monsters of Filmland.
Warren Publishing Co, New York, 1958 --

FMC 5
Film-makers' Cooperative, catalog no. 5.
175 Lexington Ave, New York, NY 10016.

FQ
Callenbach, Ernest, Editor.
Film Quarterly.
Formerly Quarterly of Film, Radio, and Television.
University of California Press, Berkeley, 1946 -- 94720

FTN
Rotha, Paul & Griffith, Richard.
Film Till Now, A Survey of World Cinema.
Vision Press & The Mayflower Publishing Co Ltd, London,

F/3rd R
Hull, David Stewart.
Films in the Third Reich, A Study of the German Cinema,1933-1945.
University of California Press, Berkeley, CA 94720, 1969.
LC cat 69-16736.

FW
Film World.
Motion picture trade publication.
See also: Monatgu/FW.

FW Dir
Simonson, Harry C., Editor.
Film World Film and Industry Directory.
C.J. Ver Halen Jr., Hollywood, California, 1951-52.

FXRH
Farino Jr., Ernest D. and Calvin, Sam, Editors.
Special Visual Effects Created by Ray Harryhausen.
Talos Publications, 3030 Ellen St, Irving, Texas 75062.

FanMo
Haydock, Ron, Editor.
Fantastic Monsters of the Films.
Horror film periodical.
Black Shield Publications, Topanga, California, 1962-64.

Fantastic World
See: Soren.

Fernett/NTD
Fernett, Gene.
Next Time Drive Off the Cliff.
Cinememories Publishing Co, Cocoa, Florida, 1968.

Fernsehen
Fernsehen Film.
German film periodical.
Friedrich, Hanover, 1967 --
Researched by Don Willis.

Ficara
Gregorie Ficara, trade paper columnist and free-lance writer.

50 Yrs Ital Cin
Malerba, Luigi and Siniscalco, Carmine, Editors.
Fifty Years of Italian Cinema.
Tudor, New York, 1955.

The Film and the Public
Manvell, Roger.
Penguin Books, Baltimore, Md. 1955.

Film Anthol
Talbot, Daniel, Editor.
Film: An Anthology.
Simon & Schuster, New York, 1959.

Film as Art
See: F/A.

Film Bulletin
Film periodical.
Wax Publications, Philadelphia, 1969--

Film Collectors' Registry
Bi-monthly newspaper.
Blair, Earl, Editor.
10918 Sageburrow
Huston, Texas 77034.

Film Com
Hitchens, Gordon, Editor.
Film Comment.
Periodical on films.
Lorien Productions, 11 St. Luke's Place, New York, NY 10014.

Film Culture
See: FC.

Film Fan Monthly
Maltin, Leonard, Editor.
77 Grayson Place
Teaneck, NJ 07666.

Film Images
Film Images Inc catalog, 1960?
1860 Broadway, New York, NY 10023.

Film Lex
See: Filmlex.

Film Review
Speed, F. Maurice.
Macdonald & Co, London; annual.

Film Weekly
Morrison, Peter, Editor.
The Film Weekly.
Australian film periodical.
Sydney; weekly.

Film World
Ramachandran, T.M., Editor.
Indian film periodical.
Bombay; quarterly.

Filmcritic
Rishi, R.R., Editor.
Indian Film periodical.
Bombay.

Filmex
Los Angeles International Film Exposition program.
I: 1971.
II: 1972.
Filmex
7000 Hollywood Blvd
Hollywood, CA 90028.

Filmfare
Karanjia, B.K., Editor.
Indian film periodical.
The Times of India, Bombay; biweekly.

Filmindia
Patel, Baburao, Editor
Indian film periodical, now called Mother India.
Bombay; monthly.

Filmlex
Filmlexicon degli Autori e delle Opere.
Bianco e Nero, Rome.

Filmmakers
Filmmakers Newsletter.

Films/Dreyer
Bowser, Eilseen.
The Films of Carl Dreyer.
Museum of Modern Art
11 West 53rd St.
New York, NY 10019 1964.

Films of W.C. Fields
Deschner, Donald.
Citadel, New York, 1966.

Focus
Eyles, Allen, Editor.
Focus on Film.
British film periodical.
Tantivy Press, 108 New Bond St., London W1Y OQX; quarterly.

For Monsters Only
Horror film periodical.
Major Magazines, Valley Stream, New York, 1965 --

Ford, Charles
Authority on motion pictures.
Letter dated 20 July 1964, listing films of Ladislas Starevitch.
See also: Jeanne.

Foreign Cinema
See: World Cinema.

Four Aspects of the Film
See: Limbacher/4.

French Exp List
French Experimental Film List (unpublished).

Fritz Lang in America
Bogdanovich, Peter.
Studio Vista Ltd, London, 1967.

GC
Svehla, Gary J., Editor.
Gore Creatures.
Magazine devoted to fantastic films.
5906 Kavon Ave, Baltimore, MD 21206.

GFN
German Film News.

GM Mage
Bessy, Maurice & Duca, Lo.
Georges Méliès Mage.
J.-J. Pauvert, Paris, 1961.

Gala Cat
Gala Film Distributors catalog.
British Film Institute, 81 Dean St., London W1; 1965.

Gasca
Gasca, Luis.
Imagen y Cienca-Ficcion.
Gráficas Izarra, Peña y Goñi, 13, San Sebastian, Spain, 1966.

German Pics 63/64
German Pictures 1963/64.
Spitzenorganisation der Filmwirtschaft ev.

Germany
Bucher, Felix.
A. Zwemmer Ltd., London, 1970.

Ghouls, The
See: Haining/Ghouls.

Gifford/BFC
Gifford, Denis.
The British Film Catalog 1895-1970, A Reference Guide
McGraw-Hill Book Company, 1973.
LC cat 72-7861.

Gifford/Karloff
Gifford, Denis.
Karloff: The Man, The Monster, The Movies.
Curtis Books, New York, 1973.

Gifford/MM
Gifford, Denis.
Movie Monsters.
Studio Vista Ltd & E.P. Dutton & Co, London & New York, 1969.

Gifford/SF
Gifford, Denis.
Science Fiction Film.
Studio Vista Ltd. & E.P. Dutton & Co Inc, London & New York, 1971.

Gilson
Gilson, René.
Jean Cocteau.
Crown, New York, 1969.

Gio
See: Scognamillo.

Glut
Don Glut, authority on fantastic films, principally serials.

Glut/F
Glut, Donald F.
The Frankenstein Legend: A Tribute to Mary Shelley and Boris Karloff.
Scarecrow Press Inc., Metuchen, NJ 1973.
LC cat 73-944.

Gordon, Alex
Film producer and authority on fantastic films.

Gray, Milton
Authority on animated films.

Great Radio Heroes, The
Harmon, Jim.
Doubleday & Company, Inc.
Garden City, NY 1967.
LC cat 67-19803.

Griffith Index
Stern, Seymour.
An Index to the Creative Work of David Wark Griffith.
British Film Index Series.
April, 1944.

HM
Horror Monsters.
Charlton Publications, Inc, Derby, Connecticut, 1961-66.

HQ
Hollywood Quarterly
See: FQ.

HR
Powers, James, Editor.
Hollywood Reporter.
6715 Sunset Blvd, Hollywood, CA 90028; daily.

Haining/Ghouls
Haining, Peter, Editor.
The Ghouls.
Stein and Day, New York, 1971.

Halliwell
Halliwell, Leslie.
The Filmgoer's Companion.
Hill and Wang, New York, 1967.

Harmon & Glut/GSH
Harmon, Jim, & Glut, Donald F.
The Great Serial Heroes.
Doubleday & Company, Inc., Garden City, New York 1972.
LC cat 70-171269.
See also: Great Radio Heroes, The.

Harmon, Jim
See: Great Radio Heroes.

Harrison Reports
Motion picture periodical.
P.S. Harrison, New York, 1932-35.

Henderson/Griffith
Henderson, Robert M.
D.W. Griffith: The Years at Biograph.
Farrar, Straus and Grioux, New York, 1970.

Hepworth
Hepworth, Cecil.
Came the Dawn.
Phoenix House Ltd, London, 1951.

Heraldo
Heraldo del Cinema
Argentine film periodical.
Buenos Aires, 1940 --
Researched by Don Willis.

Higham, Charles
Author and authority on motion pictures.

Higuchi, Horácio
Authority on fantastic films living in Brazil.

Hist/Brit
Low, Rachel.
The History of the British Film 1896-1906.
(with Manvell, Roger)
Allen & Unwin, London, 1948.
1906-1914
Allen & Unwin, London, 1949.
1914-1918
George Allen & Unwin, 1950.
1918-1926
George Allen & Unwin, London, 1972.

Hist US Ani Prog
Kitson, Clare.
A History of American Animation, program notes.
ASIFA/Los Angeles County Museum of Art, 1972.

Hitchcock/Truffaut
Hitchcock, Alfred and Truffaut, François.
Simon and Schuster, New York, 1972.

Hoffman, Eric
Authority on fantastic films.

Houston Chronicle
Newspaper.
Houston, Texas; daily.

IAFF 72
International Animated Film Festival program.
New York, 1972.

IFC cat
International Film Classics, Audio Fiom Center catalog, 1963-64.
1619 North Cherokee, Los Angeles, CA 90028.

Ideal
Ideal Pictures Catalog, 1964.
Kenney's Ideal Pictures, 6514 Selma Ave, Hollywood, CA 90028.

Illustrated Weekly of India
Indian film periodical.

Imagen y CF
See: Gasca.

Imparcial Film
Argentine film periodical, Buenos Aires.
Researched by Don Willis.

IndCin YB
Baruch, B.D., Editor.
Indian Cinematograph Yearbook 1938.
The Motion Picture Society of India, Bombay.

Index
Index de la Cinematographie Francaise.
La Cinématographie Française, Paris, 1951-66.
Researched by Don Willis.

Indian MPA
Indian Motion Picture Almanac & Who's Who.
Film Federation of India, 1953.

Indice
de la Fuente, Maria Isabel, Editor.
Indice Bibliografico del Cine Mexicano (1930-1965).
Talleves de Editorial America, Mexico, 1967.
Researched by Don Willis.

Int Film Cat
See: IFC cat.

Iris Barry Film Notes
See: Barry, Iris.

It
Lee, Walt, Editor.
Amateur science fiction & fantasy magazine (fanzine).
Coos Bay, Oregon; later, Beverly Hills, CA.
1951-56.

Ital Prods
Italian Productions.
Unitalia Film, Rome; annual; 1950--

Iwerks Retrospective
Program notes on showing of films by Ub Iwerks, distributed at the Los Angeles County Museum of Art, 1972.

Japanese Films
Unijapan Film, Tokyo; annual; 1962--

Jeanne
Jeanne, René and Ford, Charles.
L'Histoire Encyclopédique du Cinéma.
Robert Laffont, Paris, 1947-62, 5 volumes.

Jones, Jack
See: FFF.

K'Scope
Shay, Don & Cabana Jr., Ray, Editors.
Kaleidoscope.
Film magazine.
Longmeadow, Massachusetts, 1962-1967; irregular.

Kagan, Norman
Authority on all-Negro-cast films in the USA.

Kinematograph YB
Kinematograph and Television Year Book.
Oldhams, London; annual.

Kinetogram
See: EK.

Kino
Leyda, Jay.
Kino: A History of the Russian and Soviet Film.
Macmillan, New York, 1960.

Korea Cinema
Motion Picture Producers Association of Korea, Inc, Seoul, Korea, 1967.

Kurosawa
Richie, Donald.
The Films of Akira Kurosawa.
University of California Press, Berkeley & Los Angeles, 1965.

Kyrou/Buñuel
Kyrou, Ado, Editor.
Luis Buñuel: An Introduction.
Simon and Schuster, New York, 1963.
LC cat 63-15366.

LA
Knight, Arthur.
The Liveliest Art, a Panoramic History of the Movies.
The Macmillan Company, New York, 1957.
LC cat 57-12222.

LA County Museum
Program notes distributed at screenings.
Los Angeles County Museum of Art.

LA Daily News
Los Angeles Daily News.
Defunct newspaper.
Many film clippings in Motion Picture Academy Library files.

LAFP
Los Angeles Free Press.
Weekly newspaper.
6013 Hollywood Blvd, Hollywood, Calif., 1964--

LA Herald-Ex
Los Angeles Herald-Examiner.
Daily newspaper, Los Angeles, California.

LAT
Los Angeles Times.
Daily newspaper.
Times-Mirror Square, Los Angeles.
Many film clippings in Motion Picture Academy Library files.

LC
Library of Congress, Copyright Office.
Catalog of Copyright Entries; Motion Pictures
1894-1912 (1953)
1912-1939 (1951)
1940-1949 (1953)
1950-1959 (1960)
1960-1969 (1971).

US Government Printing Office, Washington, DC.

LR
See: Richardson, Larry.

LSH
Klemensen, Richard E., Editor.
Little Shoppe of Horrors.
Magazine devoted to fantastic films.
Richard Klemensen, 608 Lakeside St., Waterloo, Iowa 50703.

Laclos
Laclos, Michel.
Le Fantastique au Cinema.
J.-J. Pauvert, Paris, 1958.

Lahue/B&G
Lahue, Kalton C.
Bound and Gagged: The Story of the Silent Serials.
A.S. Barnes & Company, South Brunswick and New York, 1968.

Landers
Jim Landers, information source on Chinese-language films he has seen in Taiwan and the United States.

Lee, Christopher
British actor specializing in fantastic films.

Lighthouse
Indian film magazine.
Bombay, 1936-38.

Limbacher/4
Limbacher, James L.
Four Aspects of the Film.
Brussell & Brussel, New York, 1969.

Locus
Brown, Charles and Dena, Editors.
Bi-weekly newspaper covering the science fiction field.
P.O. Box 3938
San Francisco, CA 94119.

London Times
The Times.
London; daily.

Luna
Dietz, Ann F., Editor.
Luna Monthly.
655 Orchard St, Oradell, New Jersey 07649.

MFB
Dawson, Jan, Editor.
Monthly Film Bulletin.
British Film Institute, 81 Dean St, London WIV 6AA.

MMA
Museum of Modern Art, catalog.
11 West 53rd St, New York, NY 10019, 1963.

MMF
Caen, Michel and Romer, Jean-Claude, Editors.
Midi/Minuit Fantastique.
French periodical devoted to fantasy and horror films.
Le Terrain Vague, 14-16 rue de Verneuil, Paris, 7e, 1962--

MPA
International Motion Picture Almanac.
Quigley Publishing Co; annual.
See also: Indian MPA.

MPH
Quigley Jr, Martin, Editor.
Motion Picture Herald (Exhibitor's Herald)
Motion picture trade periodical.
Quigley Publishing Co, Inc, New York.

MPN
Motion Picture News.
Motion picture trade periodical.
Motion Picture News, Inc, New York, 1914-30.

MPW
Moving Picture World.
Motion picture trade periodical.
Chalmers Publishing Co, New York, 1907-28.

MT
Kane, Joe, Editor.
The Monster Times.
Bi-weekly newspaper.
The Monster Times Publishing Co, Inc, 11 West 17th St, New York, NY 10011, 1971--

MTVM
Ireton, Glenn F., Editor.
Movie/TV Marketing (formerly Far East Film News).
Motion picture & television trade periodical.
Box 30, Central Post Office, Tokyo, 100-91, Japan.

MW
Ackerman, Forrest J, Editor.
Monster World.
Warren Publishing Co, New York, 1964-66.

MadMon
Mad Monsters.
Charlton Publications Inc, Derby, Connecticut, 1961-66.

Magnitude
Stapenhorst, Ralph Jr, Editor.
Amateur science fiction magazine (fanzine).
Glendale, California, 1955.

Maltin/GMS
Maltin, Leonard.
The Great Movie Shorts.
Crown Publishers Inc, New York, 1972.
LC cat 72-168318.

Maltin/MCT
Maltin, Leonard.
Movie Comedy Teams.
Signet, New American Library, New York, 1970.

Maltin/TV
Maltin, Leonard.
TV Movies.
The New American Library, Inc., New York, 1969.

Mamaia
International Festival of Animated Film, Program Notes.
Mamaia, Romania, 1966--
Bi-annual.

Matheson, Richard
Writer specializing in fantastic films.

Mercury folder
Mercury Audio-Visual Center catalog.
1207 33rd Ave, San Francisco, California 94122.

Milne/Dreyer
Milne, Tom.
The Cinema of Carl Dreyer.
A.S. Barnes & Co, New York, and A. Zwemmer Ltd., London, 1971.
LC cat 71-118772.

Mitry
Mitry, Jean.
Filmographie Universelle.
Institute des Hautes Etudes Cinematographiques, Paris, 1964.
Researched by Don Willis.

Modern Czech Film
Modern Czechoslovak Film.
Motion picture periodical.
Artia/Czechoslovak Film Institute, Prague, 1963--

Modern Monsters
Collins, Gunther; later, Glut, Donald F., Editors.
Bi-monthly horror film magazine.
Prestige Publications, Los Angeles, 1965-67?

Monster Mania
Renaissance Productions, New York, 1966-67.

Monsters and Heroes
Ivie, Larry, Editor.
M&H Publications, New York, 1967.

Monsters and Things
Shaw, L.T.
Magnum Publications, New York, 1959.

Montagu/FW
Montagu, Ivor.
Film World, A Guide to the Cinema.
Penguin Books, Baltimore, Maryland, 1964.

Montevideo
Montevideo (Uruguay) Film Festival Program.

Mother India
See: Filmindia.

Motog
Motography.
Motion picture trade periodical.
Chicago, Illinois, 1911-15.

MovPicM
Moving Picture Monthly.
Indian film periodical.
D. Dwivedi, Bombay, 1934-38.

Movie Herald
Indian film magazine.

Movie Marketing
See: MTVM.

Movies, The
Griffith, Richard, and Mayer, Arthur.
Simon and Schuster, New York, 1957.

Movieland
Indian film magazine.

Movies Int'l
Silke, James R., Editor.
Movies International.
Latigo Productions, North Hollywood, 1966.

Moving Pic Annual '39
See: Indian MPA.

NBR
National Board of Review, publishers of Films In Review.
New York.
See also: FIR.

NW
See Newsweek.

NYT
New York Times.
Daily newspaper.
The New York Times Co, 1913--

Neergaard
Neergaard, Ebbe.
The Story of Danish Film.
The Danish Institute, 1963.

Negro in Films, The
Noble, Peter.
Skeleton Robinson, London, 1948.

New Trends
New Trends advertising flyer.

Newsweek
Moregenstern, Joseph, Movies Editor.
Weekly news magazine.
New York.

Niver
Niver, Kemp.
Motion Pictures from the Library of Congress Paper Print Collection, 1894-1912.
University of California, Berkeley, 94720, 1967.

Niver/20

Niver, Kemp.
The First Twenty Years.
Locare Research Group, Los Angeles, 1968.
LC cat 68-58700.

Núbila

Di Núbila, Domingo.
Historia del Cine Argentino.
Buenos Aires, 1959, 2 volumes.

Obaggy, Bill

Authority on the films of Bela Lugosi.

Orient

Holmes, Winifred.
Orient: A Survey of Films Produced in Countries of Arab and Asian Cultures.
British Film Institute, London, 1959.

Orpheus

Johnson, Charles, Editor.
Periodical devoted to fantastic films.
Charles Johnson, Omaha, Nebraska, 1964-66.

Osterr

Walter, Fritz.
Osterreichischen Spielfilme der Stummfilmzeit 1907-1930; 1929-1938 (1967).
Osterreichischen Spielfilme der Tonfilmzeit 1929-1938 (1968).
Osterreichischen Gesellschaft fur Filmwissenschaft, Wien (Vienna).
Researched by Don Willis.

p

page(s).

PB

Press Book -- pamphlet of advertising material and press releases prepared by the studio or distributor for exhibitors' use.

PS

Press Sheet -- similar to press book, only less extensive.

Pardi

Pardi, Bob.
Authority on fantastic films.

Pendulum

Lee, Walt.
"UPA" p42-52, Spring, 1953.
California Institute of Technology, Pasadena.

Pessina, Hector R.

Argentinian expert on space films.

Photo

Photoplay.
Photoplay Publishing Co, Chicago, Illinois, 1924--

Photon

Frank, Mark, Editor.
Periodical devoted to fantastic films.
Mark Frank, 801 Avenue "C", Brooklyn, NY 11218, 1963--

Playboy

Hefner, Hugh, Editor.
Monthly periodical.
The Playboy Press, Chicago, Illinois.

Polish Cin

Various authors.
Contemporary Polish Cinematography.
Polonia Publishing, Warsaw, 1962.

PopCar

Retrospectives of Popular Cartoon Characters.
Zagreb, Yugoslavia, 1972.

Positif

Editions Le Terrain Vague, 1965-1966.

Pyramid

Pyramid Films catalog, 1971-72.
Box 1048, Santa Monica, CA 90406.

Q/FR & TV

See: FQ.

QPH

QP Herald.
Gertner, Richard, Editor.
Motion picture trade periodical.
Quigley Publications
1270 Sixth Ave.
New York, NY 10020
1972-- (weekly)

RAF

Jacobs, Lewis.
The Rise of the American Film, A Critical History.
Harcourt, Brace and Company, New York, 1939.

Reamy, Tom

Authority on fantastic films.

Rel/Cin

Butler, Ivan.
Religion in the Cinema.
A.S. Barnes Co, New York, and A. Zwemmer Ltd., London, 1969.
LC cat 69-14897.

Repertoire General

Répertoire Général des Films.
(Analyse Général des Films)
Central Catholique du Cinéma et de la Radio, Paris, 1944--

Richardson

Larry Richardson, authprity on fantastic films.

Richter Index

Weinberg, Herman G.
An Index to the Creative Works of Hans Richter.
British Film Institute, London, & Film Culture, New York, 1957.

Rider, D.

David Rider, authority on animated films.

RolSt

See: Rolling Stone.

Rolling Stone

Wenner, Jann, Editor.
Biweekly periodical devoted to rock music; some film reviews.
Straight Arrow Publishers Inc, 625 Third St, San Francisco, California, 94107.

S&S

Houston, Penelope, Editor.
Sight and Sound.
Quarterly periodical devoted to films.
British Film Institute, 81 Dean St., London W1V 6AA, 1932--

SF Art Mus Prog

San Francisco Art Museum Program.

SF Chronicle

San Francisco Chronicle.
Daily newspaper, San Francisco, California.

SF Cin

See: Gifford/SF.

SF/Cin

See: Baxter/SF.

SFF

Menville, Douglas.
"A Historical and Critical Survey of the Science Fiction Film."
Unpublished Master of Arts Thesis, University of Southern California, Los Angeles, 1959.

SF Fest '65

San Francisco Film Festival 1965 program.

SF Times

Taurasi, James V., Editor.
Science Fiction Times.
Syracuse, New York, 1921-69.

SM

Ackerman, Forrest J, Editor.
Spacemen.
Warren Publishing Co, New York, 1961-64.

SQ

Barbour, Alan G., Editor.
Serial Quarterly.
Alan G. Barbour/Milton Luboviski, Box 154, Kew Gardens, NW 11415, 1966--

SR

Knight, Arthur, film critic; formerly also Alpert, Hollis.
Saturday Review.
Saturday Review Inc, New York; weekly.

STI

Sherman, Samuel M., Editorial Director.
Screen Thrills Illustrated.
Warren Publishing Co, New York, 1962-65.

Sadoul

Sadoul, Georges.
L'Histoire Générale du Cinema.
Flammarion, Paris, 1946, 5 volumes.

Sadoul/DF

Sadoul, Georges; translated, edited, and updated by Peter Morris.
Dictionary of Films.
University of California Press Berkeley & Los Angeles, 1972.

Sadoul/F

Sadoul, Georges.
French Film.
The Falcon Press, London, 1953.

Sadoul/Film Makers

Sadoul, Georges; translated, edited, and updated by Peter Morris.
Dictionary of Film Makers.
University of California Press Berkeley & Los Angeles, 1972.

Sadoul/M

Sadoul, Georges.
An Index to the Creative Works of Georges Méliès.
British Film Institute.

Salumbides

Salumbides, Vincente.
Motion Pictures in the Philippines.
Vincente Salumbides, 1952.

Sarris

Sarris, Andrew.
The American Cinema Directors and Directions 1929-1968.
E.P. Dutton & Co., Inc., 1968.
LC cat 69-12602.

ScF

Barbour, Alan G., Editor.
Screen Facts.
P.O. Box 154, Kew Gardens, New York 11415, 1963--

Scand Film

Hardy, Forsyth.
Scandinavian Film.
The Falcon Press, London, 1952.

Schickel/Disney

Schickel, Richard
The Disney Version
Simon and Schuster, New York, 1968.

Scognamillo

Giovanni Scognamillo, film authority from Italy, living in Turkey.

Screen Facts

See: ScF.

Ser/Col

Barbour, Alan G.
The Serials of Columbia.
Screen Facts Press, Kew Gardens, New York, 1967.

Ser/Rep

Barbour, Alan G.
The Serials of Republic.
Screen Facts Press, Kew Gardens, New York, 1965.

Seton/Ray

Seton, Mavie.
Portrait of a Director: Satyajit Ray.
Indiana University Press Bloomington, 1971.

70 Years

Cowie, Peter.
70 Years of Cinema.
A.S. Barnes, South Brunswick, New Jersey, 1969.

ShF/J

Short Films of Japan.

Shake/Sil

Ball, Robert Hamilton.
Shakespeare on Silent Film A Strange Eventful History
George Allen and Unwin, Ltd., London, 1968.

Shankar's Weekly

Indian film periodical.
Researched by Don Willis.

Shea

Shea, J. Vernon, authority on fantastic films.

Showmen's

Showmen's Trade Review.
Showmen's Trade Reviews Inc, 1938-57.

Shriek

Periodical devoted to fantasy and horror films.
House of Horror, London, ca 1963-66.

Sightlines

Dick, Mrs. Esme J., Editor.
Educational Film Library Association, 17 West 60th St, New York, NY 10023; bi-monthly.

Sil Cin

O'Lear, Liam.
The Silent Cinema.
Studio Vista Ltd, London, and E.P. Dutton and Co, Inc, New York, 1965.

Singapore Straits-Times

Singaporean newspaper.

Sitges

Gil, Antonio Rafales, Director.
Fantastic and Horror Cinema Festiva, San Isidro 12, Sitges (Barcelona), Spain.

Soren

Soren, David; editor of Fantastic Worlds
22 Chauncy St. #18
Cambridge, Mass 02138.

Sound and Shadow

Indian Film Magazine.
Madras, 1932-36.

Sov Cat

Sovexportfilm Catalog.
1 -- 1962-63.
2 -- 1964-65.
3 -- 1966-67(?).

Soviet Cinema
Dickinson, Thorold, and DeLaRoche, Catherine.
The Falcon Press, London, 1948.

SpCin
The Spanish Cinema.
Uniespaña, Madrid, 1950--
Annual

Straits-Times
See: Singapore Straits-Times.

Stringham, James
Authority on serials.

Subotsky, M.
Subotsky, Milton, film producer and writer, specializing in fantastic films, living in England.

Surrealisme
Kyrou, Adonis.
Le Surréalisme au Cinéma.
Le Terrain Vague, Paris, 1963.

Sus/Cin
Gow, Gordon
Suspense in the Cinema.
A. Zwemmer Limited, London;
A.S. Barnes & Co., New York, 1968.

Sweden 2
Cowie, Peter.
A.S. Barnes & Co., New York;
A. Zwemmer Ltd., London, 1970.
LC cat 69-14905.

Sydney Film Festival Programs
Stratton, David J., Director.
Sydney, Australia.

TBC
Weiss, Ken. & Goodgold, Ed.
To Be Continued.
Crown Publishers Inc, New York, 1972.

T/F
Kracauer, Siegfried.
Theory of Film.
Oxford, New York, 1960.

T of F
See: T/F.

TVG
Panitt, Merrill, Editor.
TV Guide.
Weekly periodical of television viewer information.
Triangle Publications, Radnor, Pennsylvania.

TVK
Scheuer, Steven H.
TV Key Movie Guide.
Bantam Books, 1958, 1961, 1966.

T-W
Trans-World Films, Inc, catalog, 1963.
Chicago, Illinois.

Tabori/Korda
Tabori, Paul.
Alexander Korda.
Oldbourne, London, 1959.

Take One
Lebensold, Peter, Editor.
Periodical devoted to films, published bi-monthly.
Unicorn Publishing Corp, P.O. Box 1778, Station B, Montreal 110, Canada.

Telegraph
Australian newspaper.
Brisbane, Australia.

Television Feature Film Source Book
See: BIB's.

Terror Fantastic
Yoldi, Pedro, Editor.
Periodical devoted to fantastic films.
Dje. Pla, 11-13, 1° B, Barcelona-9, Spain, 1971--

Thought
Indian periodical.
Siddhartha Publications, Delhi, 1954-56.

Time
Weekly news periodical.
Time, Inc., New York.

Times, The
See: London Times; LAT; NYT.

Toho Theater fliers
Toho LaBrea Theater, Los Angeles.

Transit Mix Program
University of California at Los Angeles Student Film Screening, 1971.

Trieste
Cumbat, Edoardo, President.
Festival of Science Fiction Films.
Castello DiS. Giusto, 134121, Trieste, Italy.
1963--
Programs.

Trnka
Boček, Jaroslav.
Jiří Trnka, Artist and Puppet Maker.
Designed and produced by Articia.
Paul Hamlyn, London, 1965.

20 Yrs Venice
Various authors.
Twenty Years of Cinema in Venice.
Edizioni del'Ateneo, Rome, 1952.

Twyman cat
Twyman Films Inc, catalog, 1972-73.
329 Salem Ave, Dayton, Ohio, 45401.

UCLA Programs
University of California at Los Angeles.
Film notes distributed at screenings.

UF
Fraenkel, Heinrich.
Unsterblicher Film, Die Grosse Chronik.
Two volumes:
Von Der Laterna Magica bis Zum Tonfilm.
Kindler, Munich, 1956.
Vom Ersten Ton Dis Zur Farbigen Breitwand.
Kindler, Munich, 1957.

UNESCO cat
"Ten Years of Films on Ballet and Classical Dance."
United Nations Educational, Scientific and Cultural Organization, 1966.

USA Exp List
List of American Experimental Films (unpublished).

USC cat
University of Southern California Film Catalog, Los Angeles, 1965-66.

Undrgnd
Renan, Sheldon.
An Introduction to the American Underground Film.
E.P. Dutton & Co, Inc, New York, 1967.

Uniespaña
See: SpCin.

Unifrance
Unifrance-Film, Paris.

UniJ
Unijapan Quarterly.
Unijapan Film, Tokyo, Japan, 1958--

UniJ Bltn
Unijapan Bulletin.
Special publication of Unijapan Film, Tokyo.
(UniJ Bltn 31 listed ghost films.)

Unitalia
See: Ital Prod.

V&FI
Views and Film Index
(Also called: Views; Film Index)
Films Publishing Co, New York, 1906-10.
See also: FI; Views.

Vd
Pryor, Thomas M., Editor.
Daily Variety.

Verschooten
Verschooten, Gilbert, Belgian fantastic film authority.

Views
(later Views and Film Index)
Motion picture trade publication.
Film Publishing Co, New York, 1906-10.
See also: FI; V&FI.

Views & FI
See: V&FI.

Village Voice
Weekly newspaper.
Village Voice, Inc., New York.

Vogue
Vreeland, Diana, Editor.
Talmey, Allene, Film Reviews.
Monthly periodical devoted to women's fashions.
New York.

Vw
Silverman, Syd, Publisher and Executive Editor. (Abel Green, d1973, former Editor.)
Variety.
Weekly show-business newspaper.
Variety, Inc., New York, 1905--

Warren, B.
Warren, Bill, authority on fantastic films.

Western, The
Fenin, George N., & Everson, William K.
The Western from Silents to Cinerama.
The Orion Press Inc., New York, 1962.

WID's
WID's Weekly.
Hollywood, California, ca 1915--

Willis
Willis, Don.
Horror and Science Fiction Films: A Checklist.
Scarecrow Press, Inc., Metuchen, N.J., 1972.
LC cat 72-3682.
And unpublished notes.

World Cinema
(formerly Foreign Cinema)
Hyberger, Hy, Editor.
Tri-weekly newspaper.
7520 W. Norton Ave.
Los Angeles, CA 90046.

Z/Zagreb
Holloway, Ronald.
Z Is for Zagreb.
A.S. Barnes & Co., New York;
Tantivy Press, London, 1972.
LC 70-38005.

SCIENCE-FICTION,

FANTASY, & HORROR

FILMS

G

G.G. Passion
1966 British, Cadre Films 25 mins.

Prod: Gene Gutowski.

Dir: David Bailey.

SP: Gerard Brach.

Art Dir: Michael Haynes.

Cin: Stanley A. Long.

Edit: John Beaton.

Mus: Phil Dennis & Terry Roberts.

Cast: Eric Swayne, Chrissie Shrimpton, Rory Davis, Janice Hayes.

F (pop music star 'G.G. Passion' is chased by a mysterious organization, machine-gunned to death, then turns into icon of St. Sebastian)

Ref: MFB May '67 p80.

G-Men Never Forget
1947 Rep serial 12 parts 24 reels.

Assoc Prod: Mike Frankovich.

Dir: Fred Bannon & Yakima Canutt.

SP: Franklin Adreon, Basil Dickey, Jesse Duffy, & Sol Shor.

Cin: John MacBurnie.

Edit: Cliff Bell & Sam Starr.

Mus Dir: Mort Glickman.

Cast: Clayton Moore, Roy Barcroft, Ramsay Ames, Drew Allen, Dale Van Sickel, Ken Terrell, Eddie Acuff, Edmund Cobb, Bob Wilke.

bor-SF (perfect plastic surgery makes man look exactly like another person)

Ref: LC; Ser/Rep; Glut.

Also edited to 100 minute feature in 1966 as Code 645.

G-Men vs. the Black Dragon
1943 Rep serial 15 parts 31 reels.

Assoc Prod: W.J. O'Sullivan.

Dir: William Witney.

SP: Ronald Davidson, Joseph Poland, William Lively, & Joseph O'Donnell.

Art Dir: Russell Kimball.

Cin: Bud Thackery.

SpFX: Howard Lydecker.

Edit: Edward Todd & Tony Martinelli.

Mus: Mort Glickman.

Cast: Rod Cameron, Roland Got, Constance Worth, Nino Pipitone, C. Montague Shaw.

SF-seq (ray gun; suspended animation; explosive paint)

Ref: Ser/Rep p29; SQ #5; STI 3:50.

Also edited to 100 minute feature in 1966 as Black Dragon of Manzanar.

Gabby
1941 Fleischer (Par) ani sh series.

F-com

Ref: Ani Chart; LC

See also: Swing Cleaning (1941).

Gabriel Grub the Surly Sexton
1904 British, Williamson sil 400 ft.

Dir: James Williamson.

F-dream (dream of abduction by goblins causes reformation of sexton)

Ref: Gifford/BFC 00953.

Based on portion of novel "The Pickwick Papers" by Charles Dickens.

Gabriel Over the White House
1933 MGM 87 mins.

Prod: Walter Wanger.

Dir: Gregory La Cava.

SP: Carey Wilson & Bertram Bloch.

Cin: Bert Glennon.

Edit: Basil Wrangell.

Mus: William Axt.

Cast: Walter Huston, Karen Morley, Franchot Tone, Dickie Moore, C. Henry Gordon, Samuel Hinds, Jean Parker, David Landow.

F (ineffectual, newly-elected president of U.S. has auto accident, becomes apparently divinely inspired, turns into benevolent dictator, cures all country's, then world's, ills)

Ref: HR 2 March '33; MPH 8 April '33 p26; F/A p519; RAF p516.

Based on the novel by Thomas Frederic Tweed.

Gagamba at si Scorpio
(Spider and the Scorpion)

1969 Philippine, GR.

Prod & Dir: George Rowe.

Story: Nestor Redondo.

Mus: Jimmy Navarro.

Cast: Bernard Bonnin, Eddie Fernandez, Loretta Marquez, Vic Silayan, Bert Olivar, Rolly Aquino, Rodolfo Garcia, Tessie Concepcion.

bor-SF (superhero vs supervillain; probable gadgetry)

Ref: Chodkowski.

Based on the series in Alcala comics.

Gahmlet
See: Hamlet (1964).

Gaj Gouri
1958 (1959) Indian (in Hindi), Prabhat.
Dir: Raja Thakur.

Sc: G.D. Madgulkar.

Dialog: Shrinivas Joshi.

Lyrics: Bharat Vyas.

Cin: E. Mohammed.

Mus: Sudhir Phadke.

Cast: Sulochana, Ratnamala, Shahu (Sahu) Modak, Anant Marathe, Nana Palsikar.

myth-F (lives of gods when they were young; enchanted elephant; arrows form ladder to heaven; one god becomes gigantic)

Ref: Filmindia Jan '59 p64-65; FEFN last '58 issue p55.

Galatée
1910 French sil sh.

Prod: Georges Méliès.

F (statue comes to life)

Ref: Sadoul/M; GM Mage.

Based on the legend of Pygmalion and Galatea.

See also: Pygmalion.

Galathea
1935 German ani silhouette sh.

Prod: Lotte Reiniger.

exp-F (statue comes to life)

Ref: Contemp p65.

Based on the early Greek version of the legend of Pygmalion and Galatea.

See also: Pygmalion.

Galaxie
1965 French color ani sh.

Dir: Piotr Kamler.

F

Ref: Ani/Cin p 172.

Galaxis
1966 German sh.

SF (in future, 3 women choose their collective husband)

Ref: S&S Summer '67 p 124 at Oberhausen Festival.

Galaxy
1964 Australian, Firebird 16mm 4 mins.

Made by: Arthur & Corinne Cantrill.

exp-F ("music related to film image")

Ref: Collier.

Galaxy Criminals, The
See: Wild, Wild Planet (1965).

Gallant Little Tailor
1954 British, Primrose Prods (Contemporary) ani silhouette 10 mins. Originally produced for TV.

Prod: Lotte Reiniger.

Mus: Freddie Phillips.

F (tailor battles giant)

Ref: MFB July '56 p94; Contemp.

Based on fairy tale "The Brave Little Tailor" collected by Jacob & Wilhelm Grimm.

See also: Brave Little Tailor, The (1938).

Gallery
1970 Yugoslavian, Zagreb color ani 10 mins.

Dir, SP, Design: Zlatko Pavlinic.

Bg: Ante Šamanic.

Mus: Andjelko Klobučar.

F-com (jokes centering around an art gallery)

Ref: Z/Zagreb p 104.

Gallery of Horrors
See: Dr. Terror's Gallery of Horrors (1967).

Gallina Vogelbirdae
(Vogel's Specics; Spatne Namalovana Slepice)

1963 Czech, Ceskoslovensky ani 14 mins.

Dir: Jiří Brdečka.

Story: Milos Macourek & J. Brdečka.

Ref: Ani/Cin p 126; ASIFA 1.

Gallopin' Through
See: Galloping Thru (1923).

Galloping Thru
(Gallopin' Through --alt.t.)

1923 Sunset Prods sil 4600 ft (4190 ft).

Dir: Robert North Bradbury.

Cast: Jack Hoxie, Priscilla Brown.

west; F-seq (in opening scenes little girl tells brother a story about a man on a white horse who appears out of the fog to defeat goblins; boy thinks Hoxie is this Fog Man)

Ref: AFI F2.2006 p280; The Western p 157.

Based on story "The Fog Man."

Galvanic Fluid
(More Fun with Liquid Electricity --alt.t.)

1908 Vit sil 500 ft.

Prod & Dir: J. Stuart Blackton.

SF-com

Ref: MPW II:103; Filmlex p682; LC.

See also: Liquid Electricity (1907).

Gambara tai Barugon
See: War of the Monsters (1966).

Gambler and the Devil
See: Devil and the Gambler, The (1908).

Gambler's Luck
See: Dreams of Death (1950).

Gamblers Sometimes Win
(novel by T.H. Bird)

See: March Hare, The (1956).

Gambling with the Gulf Stream
1922 (1923) Bray Prods (Hodkinson) sil 1 reel.

Prod: John R. Bray.

SF (shift in Gulf Stream turns Atlantic coast of US to tropical paradise, England to ice cap)

Ref: MPN 26:3003; LC.

Game, The
(Igra; Play --Brit.t.)

1962 Yugoslavian, Zagreb color ani seq 8 mins.

Dir, Story, Design: Dusan Vukotic.

Ani BG: Zvonimir Lončarić.

Cin: Mihajlo Ostrovidov.

Mus: Tomislav Simović.

Cast: Jelena Verner, Zvonko Pavlis.

F-seq (evil magic bird; anti-war allegory)

Ref: MFB Sept '65 p 140; Z/Zagreb p 38, 71, 45; Acad nom; MTVM Aug '70 p21.

Game of Cards
See: Jeux de Cartes (1959); Juego de Naipes (1969).

Game of Death, A
(Dangerous Adventure --e.t.)

1945 RKO 72 mins.

Prod: Herman Schlom.

Dir: Robert Wise.

SP: Norman Houston.

Art Dir: Albert D'Agostino & Lucius Croxton.

Cin: J. Roy Hunt.

SpFX: Vernon L. Walker.

Edit: J.R. Whittredge.

Mus: Paul Sawtell.

Mus Dir: C. Bakaleinikoff.

Cast: John Loder, Audrey Long, Edgar Barrier, Russell Wade, Jason Robards, Noble Johnson, Robert Clarke.

psy-H (due to a head wound, a big-game hunter becomes a homicidal maniac, hunts people like animals who become stranded on his private island; trophy room with human heads)

Ref: FIR May '58 p282, Jan '63 p20; MFB Jan '47 p5; FDY '46.

Based on short story "The Most Dangerous Game" by Richard Connell.

See also: Most Dangerous Game, The (1932).

Game of Imagination
See: Vaxelspel (1953).

Game of Men
See: Juego des Hombres (1964).

Gamera
See: Gammera the Invincible (1966).

Gamera tai Barugon
See: War of the Monsters (1966).

Gamera tai Daimaju Jaiga
See: Gamera vs. Monster X (1970).

Gamera tai Gyaos
See: Return of the Giant Monsters (1967).

Gamera tai Shinkai Kaijû Jigura
(Gamera vs. Zigra --ad.t.)

1971 Japanese, Daiei color.

Dir: Noriaki Yuasa.

Cast: Ken Utsui, Yûsuke Kawazu, Kayo Matsuo.

SF (Gamera battles a beast like a giant prehistoric fish that shoots rays)

Ref: MPH 8 Sept '71 p5 ad; UniJ 53:33.

Sequel to: Gammera the Invincible (1966).

Gamera tai Uchi Kaiju Bairusu
See: Destroy All Planets (1968).

Gamera tai Viras

See: Destroy All Planets (1968).

Gamera vs. Barugon

See: War of the Monsters (1966).

Gamera vs. Guiron

See: Attack of the Monsters (1969).

Gamera vs. Gyaos

See: Return of the Giant Monsters (1967).

Gamera vs. Jiger

See: Gamera vs. Monster X (1970).

Gamera vs. Monster X

(Gamera tai Daimaju Jaiga: Gamera vs. Jiger; Monsters Invade Expo '70 --S.E. Asia t.)

1970 Japanese, Daiei (AIP-TV) color scope 83 mins.

Dir: Noriaki Yuasa.

SP: Fumi Takahashi.

Art Dir: Sho Inoue.

Cin: Akira Kitazaki.

Mus: Shunsuke Kikuche.

Cast: Tsutomu Takakuwa, Kelly Varis, Katherine Murphy, Kon Omura, Junko Yashiro.

SF (Jiger, a new monster, follows a statue to Expo '70, but Gamera stops him; Jiger lays an egg in Gamera's body, & offspring suck Gamera's blood)

Ref: UniJ 49; Manila Bulletin 20 Dec '70.

Sequel to: Gammera the Invincible (1966).

Gamera vs. Outer Space Monster Virus

See: Destroy All Planets (1968).

Gamera vs. Viras

See: Destroy All Planets (1968).

Gamera vs. Zigra

See: Gamera tai Shinkai Kaijû Jigura (1971).

Games

1967 U color scope 100 mins.

Prod: George Edwards.

Dir: Curtis Harrington.

Story: G. Edwards & C. Harrington.

SP: Gene Kearney.

Art Dir: Alexander Golitzen & William D. DeCinces.

Cin: William A. Fraker.

Edit: Douglas Stewart.

Mus: Samuel Matlovsky.

Cast: Simone Signoret, James Caan, Katherine Ross, Don Stroud, Kent Smith, Estelle Winwood, Ian Wolfe, Florence Marly.

psy-H (plot to drive wife insane includes supposedly walking dead man)

Ref: MFB '68 p50; Vw 20 Sept '67; FF '67 p245.

Games of Angels, The

See: Jeux des Anges, Les (1964).

Gamma People, The

1955 (1956) British, Warwick (Col) 9 reels (79 mins).

Prod: John Gossage.

Dir: John Gilling.

Story: Louis Pollock.

SP: J. Gilling & J. Gossage.

Art Dir: John Box.

Cin: Ted Moore.

SpFX Cin: Tom Howard.

Edit: Jack Slade & Alan Osbiston.

Mus: George Melachrino.

Cast: Paul Douglas, Eva Bartok, Leslie Phillips, Walter Rilla, Martin Miller.

cont.

Gamma People, The cont.

SF-H (in a Ruritanian country, bombarding children with gamma rays unpredictably produces either geniuses or morons)

Ref: MFB March '56 p31; V 12 Sept '56; FDY '57.

Gamma Sango Uchu Daisakusen

See: Green Slime, The (1968).

Gammera the Invincible

(Daikaiju Gamera)

1966 Japanese, Daiei (World Entertainment Corp) 88 mins.

Prod: Yonejiro Saito.

Dir: Noriaki Uyasa (Yuasa).

SP: Fumi Takahashi & Richard Kraft.

Art Dir: (U.S. scenes) Hank Aldrich.

Cin: Nobuo Munekawa.

Edit: Tatsuji Nakashizu.

Cast: Eiji Funakoshi, Harumi Kiritachi, (U.S. scenes) Brian Donlevy, Albert Dekker, Diane Findlay.

SF-H (Gammera [sic] is thawed out of ice, is giant, fire-breathing, jet-propelled, flying, prehistoric turtle)

Ref: Vw 27 Dec '67; MPH 24 Nov '65 p 17 ad.

Sequels: War of the Monsters (1966); Return of the Giant Monsters (1967); Destroy All Planets (1968); Attack of the Monsters (1969); Gamera vs. Monster X (1970); Gamera tai Shinkai Kaijû Jigura (1971).

Gandy Goose

1938-54 Terrytoons ani sh series, some in color.

Prod: Paul Terry.

F-com

Ref: LC.

See also: Gandy Goose. . .; Fortune Hunters (1946).

Gandy Goose in the Ghost Town

(The Ghost Town --alt.t.)

1944 Terrytoons (20th-Fox) color ani 1 reel.

Dir: Mannie Davis.

Story: John Foster.

Mus: Philip A. Scheib.

F-com (Gandy vs ghosts, also Frankenstein's Monster and Dracula)

Ref: LC; D. Glut.

See also: Dracula (1930); Frankenstein (1931).

Ganesh Avatar

● 1922 Indian, Hindustan sil.

Ref: IndCin YB.

● 1925 Indian, Hindustan sil.

Ref: IndCin YB.

myth-F

Ganesh Janma

1930 Indian, Madan sil.

myth-F

Ref: IndCin YB.

Ganesh Mahima

(Supernatural Ganesh; Krishna Vivah: Krishna's Marriage -- alt.t.)

1950 Indian, Besant 121 mins.

Prod & Dir: Homi Wadia.

SP & Mus Dir: S.N. Tripathi.

Art Dir: Babubhai Mistry.

Cin: P.R. Ram Rao.

Edit: Kamlakar.

Cast: Meena Kumari, Mahipal, S.N. Tripathi, Moolchand, Vimal, Mangala, Dalpat.

myth-F

Ref: Indian MPA '53 p26.

Gang Busters

1942 U serial 13 parts 27 reels.

Assoc Prod: Ford Beebe.

Dir: Ray Taylor & Noel Smith.

SP: Morgan Cox, Al Martin, Vic McLeod, & George Plympton.

Cast: Kent Taylor, Irene Hervey, Robert Armstrong, Ralph Morgan, Richard Davies, Grace Cunard, John Gallaudet.

SF (arch-criminal brings dead crooks back to life)

Ref: FIR March '64 p 154; LC; Acad.

Based on the radio show.

Ganga Avataran

(Origin of the Ganges River)

1935 Indian, Kolhapur 142 mins.

Prod, Dir, Story, Dialog, & Songs: D. Phalke.

Art Dir: Shankerrao Shinde.

Cin: Vasudev D. Karnatki.

Mus: Viswanathbuva Jadhav.

Cast: Chitnis, Suresh, Ibrahim, Bhagavat, Ahmed Khan, Shankararao Bhosle.

myth-F (legend of descent of river Ganges from Heaven to remove famine)

Ref: Lighthouse 14 Aug '37, 21 Aug '37; Filmindia Aug '37 p25, 36; Dipali 1 Nov '35.

Ganga Maiya

(Mystery of the Ganges River)

1953 Indian.

Prod: C.M. Trivedi.

Mus: Shankerrao Vyas.

Cast: Sumitra, Prem Adib, Jeevan, Asha Mathur, Bipin Gupta, Sapru.

myth-F (Shiva)

Ref: Filmfare 25 Dec '53 p2 ad; Filmindia April '53.

Ganja and Hess

1973 Kelly-Jordan Enterprises color 110 mins.

Exec Prod: Quentin Kelly & Jack Jordan.

Prod: Chiz Schultz.

Dir & SP: Bill Gunn.

Prod Design: Tom John.

Cin: James E. Hinton.

Edit: Victor Kanefsky.

Mus: Sam Waymon.

Cast: Duane Jones, Marlene Clark, Bill Gunn, Sam Waymon, Leonard Jackson, Candece Tarpley.

F-H (black professor stabbed by germ-laden knife which turns him into a vampire & murderer; he turns girl into vampire; professor commits suicide by standing in shadow of cross; girl continues as vampire)

Ref: Vw 18 April '73 p30 & 32.

Gap, The

1937 British, GB Instructional 38 mins.

Dir: Donald Carter.

Cast: G.H. Mulcaster, Patric Curwen, Carleton Hobbs, Jack Vyvyan, Charles Danville, Norman Wooland, Foster Carlin.

soc-SF; doc (pre-WW II depiction of air-raid on London)

Ref: Gifford/BFC 10246.

Gappa, Frankenstein Fliegend Monster

See: Monster from a Prehistoric Planet (1967).

Gappa -- Triphibian Monster

See: Monster from a Prehistoric Planet (1967).

Garbancito de la Mancha

(Little Bean of La Mancha; The Little Knight --ad.t.)

1946 Spanish color ani feature.

cont.

Garbancito de la Mancha cont.

Dir: Arturo Moreno.

F (boy outwits a wizard)

Ref: Ani/Cin p 157-58. Collier.

Garcon Plein d'Avenir, Un

(A Boy with a Future)

1965 French, Films Europart ani 6 1/2 mins.

Prod: Paul Haim.

Dir: Peter Foldes.

F (graphics derivative of Picasso)

Ref: ASIFA 1.

Garde Fantôme, La

(The Phantom Guard)

1904 French, Pathé sil sh.

Dir: Gaston Velle.

F

Ref: Filmlex p785.

Garden, The

1967? Czech 16 mins.

Dir: Jan Svankmajer.

alleg-F ("garden fenced by live ring of mute, obliging people")

Ref: Edinburgh Fest '68.

Garden Dwarfs, The

See: Gartenzwerge, Die (1962).

Garden Murder Case, The

1936 MGM 61 mins.

Prod: Lucien Hubbard & Ned Marin.

Dir: Edwin L. Marin.

SP: Bertram Millhauser.

Cin: Charles Clarke.

Edit: Ben Lewis.

Mus: William Axt.

Cast: Edmund Lowe, Virginia Bruce, Gene Lockhart, Benita Hume, Nat Pendleton, H.B. Warner, Kent Smith, Grant Mitchell, Frieda Inescort, Douglas Walton, Henry B. Walthall.

bor-F-H (murder by hypnotism)

Ref: Vw 4 March '36; K'Scope 2:3:28-30, 31-32; Acad.

Based on the novel by S.S. Van Dine.

See also: Philo Vance.

Garden of Delights, The

(El Jardin de las Delicias)

1970 Spanish, Elias Querejeta Prod color scope 95 mins.

Prod: Elias Querejeta.

Dir: Carlos Saura.

SP: Rafael Azcona & C. Saura.

Art Dir: Emilio Sanz.

Cin: Luis Quadrado.

Edit: Pablo G. Del Amo.

Mus: Luis de Pablo.

Cast: José Luis Lopez Vazquez, Luchy Soto, Francisco Pierrá, Charo Soriano, Lina Canalejas, Julio Peña, Mayrata (Mairata) O'Wisiedo, Geraldine Chaplin, Esperanza Roy, Alberto Alonso.

psy-F-seqs (crippled man has fantasies; in one, knights climb out of painting & chase him)

Ref: FF '71 p352-54; SpCin '71 p 122-23.

Garden of Fate, The

1910 IMP sil 1000 ft.

F (Father Time gives magic rose)

Ref: MPW 7:830, 834.

Garden of Paradise, The

(story by H.C. Andersen)

See: Daydreamer, The (1966).

Garden of Shadows, The

1916 Laemmle (U) sil 2 reels.

Prod: Lucius Henderson.

Author: Olga Printzlau.

Cast: Mary Fuller.

F ("child's spirit" returns to body for happy ending)

Ref: MPN 14:458; LC.

Garden of the Dead

1972 (1973?) Clover color? 85 mins.

Prod & Story: Daniel Cady.

Dir: John Hayes.

SP: John Jones (possibly Jack Matcha).

Cast: John Dennis, Duncan McCloud, Eric Stern, Marland Proctor.

F-H (killed convicts from chain gang rise from the dead)

Ref: BO 10 Jan '72 pW-1, 22 May '72 p 15; Vw 14 June '72 p22.

Gardul

(The Fence)

1969 Rumanian color ani 10 mins.

Dir & Story: Gelu Muresan.

F

Ref: Mamaia '70.

Gargon Terror, The

See: Teenagers from Outer Space (1958).

Gargoyles

1972 Tomorrow Entertainment Inc. (CBS-TV) color "90 mins."

Exec Prod: Roger Gimbel.

Prod: Robert W. Christiansen & Rick Rosenberg.

Dir: B.W.L. Norton.

SP: Stephen & Elinor Karpf.

Makeup Supervisor: Del Armstrong.

Gargoyle Makeup: Ellis Burman & Stan Winston.

Cin: Earl Rath.

SpFX: Milt Rice & George Peckham.

Edit: Frank P. Keller.

Mus: Robert Prince.

Cast: Cornel Wilde, Jennifer Salt, Grayson Hall, Bernie Casey [head gargoyle], Scott Glenn, William Stevens, John Gruber.

F-H (living gargoyles with 500-year life cycle found in Southwestern U.S. desert; they plan to conquer world)

Ref: CBS; B. Warren.

Garm Coat

(The Clerk and the Coat)

1955 Indian (in Hindi), Cine Co-Operative 129 mins (78 mins).

Prod & SP: Rajindar Singh Bedi.

Dir: Amar Kumar.

Cin: K. Vaikunth.

Edit: Hrishikes Mukherji & Ezra Mir.

Mus: Amar Nath.

Cast: Balraj Sahni, Nirupa Roy, Jayant, Rashid Khan, Baby Chand, Baby Indira.

F (when poor clerk's overcoat is stolen & he dies, his ghost takes coats from the living)

Ref: Orient.

Based on "Shinel" (The Overcoat) by Nikolai Gogol.

Garou-Garou le Passe-Muraille

(novelet by M. Aymé)

See: Mr. Peek-A-Boo (1950); Man Who Walked Through the Wall, The (1960).

Garret in Bohemia, A

1915 British, London sil 2795 ft.

Dir: Harold Shaw.

Cast: Edna Flugrath, Ben Webster, Christine Rayner, Gwynne Herbert, Jeff Barlow [ghost].

F ("ghost of blind fiddler inspires poor composer and enables him to marry art teacher")

Ref: Gifford/BFC 05710.

Gartenzwerge, Die

(The Garden Dwarfs; Gnomes)

1962 W. German, Lux color ani? 8 mins.

Prod: Borris Borresholm.

Dir: Wolfgang Urchs.

F (good gnomes' success turns them into "dwarfs made of burnt earth")

Ref: F&F Nov '64 letters; Ani/Cin p 153, 176.

Garu the Mad Monk

(Guru the Mad Monk --ad.t.)

1970 (1971) Maipix (Nova Int'l) color 57 mins.

Filmed in England?

Dir & Cin: Andy Milligan.

Story: M.A. Isaacs.

Settings: James Fox.

Artistic Dir: Lillian Greneker.

Cast: Neil Flanagan, Jacqueline Webb, Judith Isral, Julia Willis, Ron Keith.

F-H (body snatching; split personality; witch-like vampire; hunchback)

Ref: BO 2 March '71.

Gas House Kids in Hollywood, The

1947 PRC (Eagle Lion) 67 mins.

Exec Prod: Ben Stoloff.

Prod: Sam Baerwitz.

Dir: Edward L. Cahn.

SP: Robert E. Kent.

Art Dir: F. Paul Sylos.

Cin: James Brown.

Edit: W. Donn Hayes.

Mus: Albert Glasser.

Cast: Carl "Alfalfa" Switzer, Benny Bartlett, Rudy Wissler, Tommy Bond, James Burke, Jan Bryant, Michael Whalen, Douglas Fowley.

H-com (haunted house; moving skeletons; mad professor)

Ref: HR & Vd 1 Oct '47; FD 28 Aug '47.

Gas, or It Became Necessary to Destroy the World in Order to Save It

See: Gas-s-s-s! (1970).

Gas-s-s-s!

(Gas, or It Became Necessary to Destroy the World in Order to Save It)

1970 (1971) AIP color 79 mins.

Prod & Dir: Roger Corman.

SP: George Armitage.

Set Decorations: Stephen Graham.

Art Dir: David Nichols.

Cin: Ron Dexter.

Edit: George Van Noy.

Mus: Country Joe McDonald & Barry Melton.

Cast: Robert Corff, Elaine Giftos, Bud Cort, Talia Coppola, Ben Vereen, Cindy Williams, Country Joe McDonald, Pat Patterson, George Armitage, Bruce Karcher [Edgar Allan Poe].

F-sat-com (gas kills everyone over age 25; ending has all dead coming out of crack in the ground -- JFK, Che, Martin Luther King, etc.)

Ref: FF '71 p318-19; NYT 27 March '71; Rolling Stone 1 April '71.

Gaston le Crayon

1957-59 Terrytoons (20th-Fox) color ani scope sh series.

F-com

Ref: LC.

Gasu-Ningen Dai Ichi-go

See: Human Vapor, The (1960).

Gates of the Night, The

See: Portes de la Nuit, Le (1946).

Gato, El

See: Cat Creeps, The (1930, Spanish version).

Gato con Botas, El

See: Puss in Boots (1961).

Gaucho, The

1927 (1928) Elton Corp (UA) sil color seq 10 reels (9358 ft).

Prod: Douglas Fairbanks.

Dir: F. Richard Jones.

Story: Elton Thomas (probably Douglas Fairbanks).

Sc: Lotta Wood.

Supr Art Dir: Carl Oscar Borg.

Cin: Tony Gaudio.

Film Cutter: William Nolan.

Cast: Douglas Fairbanks, Lupe Velez, Eve Southern, Gustav von Seyffertitz, Nigel de Brulier, Geraine Greear, Michael Vavitch, Mary Pickford.

rel-F (vision; miraculous healing)

Ref: AFI F2.2025 p283; MPN 36:1754; FD 27 Nov '27 p6.

Gaucho y el Diablo, El

(The Gaucho and the Devil)

1952 Argentinian color 83 mins.

Dir: Ernesto Remani.

SP: José Maria Fernández Unsain.

Cin: Humberto Corell & Alvaro Duraňona y Vedia.

Cast: Juan José Miguez, Elisa Christian Galvé, Francisco Martinez Allende, Elina Colomer, Raul del Valle.

F (man granted wishes)

Ref: Nubila p300.

Based on short story "The Bottle Imp" by Robert Louis Stevenson.

See also: Bottle Imp, The (1917).

Gaudeamus

(Let Us Rejoice; Vesel'ye Scenki iz Zizni Zivotnych; Happy Scenes of the Life of the Animals)

1912 Russian, Khanzhonkov sil ani puppet 440 ft.

Dir: Ladislas Starevitch.

F (crickets, butterflies, beetles, ants, etc.)

Ref: Kino p416; Filmlex; UF p383.

Gauloises Bleues, Les

See: Les Gauloises Bleues (1968).

Gawain and the Green Knight

1972 British, Anglo-EMI (UA).

Prod: Carlo Ponti.

Dir: Stephen Weeks.

SP: Philip Breen & S. Weeks.

Cast: Murray Head, Ciaran Madden, Nigel Green.

F (magical green knight's head comes off, can be replaced)

Ref: Vw 3 May '72 p26, 27, 3 Jan '73 p 10 ad; BO 13 Nov '72 p20 ad.

Based on the medieval poem.

Gay Ball, The

See: Flicek the Ball (1956).

Gay Purr-ee

1962 UPA (WB) color ani 85 mins.

Exec Prod: Henry G. Saperstein.

Assoc Prod: Lee Orgel.

Dir: Abe Levitow.

SP: Dorothy & Chuck Jones.

Art Dir: Victor Haboush.

Mus: Harold Arlen.

Lyrics: E.Y. Harburg.

Voices: Judy Garland, Robert Goulet, Red Buttons, Hermione Gingold, Paul Frees, Morey Amsterdam, Julie Bennet, Mel Blanc, Joan Gardner.

F-mus-com (cats on a spree in Paris)

Ref: FF '62; FIR Dec '62 p614; MFB June '63 p85.

Gaz Mortels, Les

(The Deadly Gases)

1916 French sil sh?

Prod: Louis Nalpas.

Dir: Abel Gance.

Cin: Léonce Burel & Dubois.

Cast: Léon Mathot, Maud Richard.

bor-SF

Ref: F&F Nov '58; FIR Nov '52 p437.

Gazza Ladra, La

See: Thieving Magpie, The (1964).

Gdzie Jestes Luizo?

(Where Are You, Luizo?)

1964 Polish, Se-Ma-For.

Dir: Janusz Kubik.

Cin: Bousław Lambach.

Mus: Jerzy Groszang.

Cast: Zofia Slaboszewska, Władisław Kowalski.

SF (circus turns out to be a flying saucer)

Ref: Gasca p337.

Ge-Ge-Ge no Kitaro

(Kitro --alt.t.)

1968 Japanese, Toei ani 44 mins.

Dir: Hiroshi Shitara.

F (little boy turns people into monsters)

Ref: UniJ 42.

Géant de Thessalie, Le

See: Giants of Thessaly, The (1960).

Gebissen Wird nur Nachts — Happening der Vampire

(The Vampire Happening --ad.t.)

1971 W. German, Aquila Enterprises color 97 mins.

Exec Prod: H. Klaus Pohlen.

Prod: Pier A. Caminneci.

Dir: Freddie Francis.

Story: Karl Heinz Hummel.

SP: August Rieger.

Art Dir: Hans Zehetner.

Make-up: Fupp Paschke & Helmut Kraft.

Cin: Gerard Vandenberg.

Edit: Fred Srp.

Mus: Jerry Van Rooyen.

Cast: Pia Degermark, Thomas Hunter, Yvor Murillo, Ingrid van Bergen, Lyvia Bauer, Joachim Kemmer, Ferdy Mayne [Dracula].

F-H-com (girl resembles vampire aunt; Dracula rides about in helicopter)

Ref: Vw 4 Aug '71; Photon 21:44.

Based on a character created by Bram Stoker.

See also: Dracula (1930).

Gee Whiz-z-z-z-z-z-z!
1956 WB color ani 7 mins.
Dir: Chuck Jones.
F-com
Ref: LC.
See also: Road Runner & Coyote
(1948...   ).

Geet Govind
(Music of Govind)
1947 (1948) Indian, Kanu
Desai.
Prod & Art Dir: Kanu Desai.
Dir & SP: Ramchandra Thakur.
Cin: Naval Bhatt.
Mus: Gyan Dutt.
Cast: Sulochana Chatterjee,
Prem Adib, Leela Desai, David.
myth-F (miracles)
Ref: Filmindia March '48 p52-53.

Gefahren der Hypnose
See: Verlorene Ich, Das (1923).

Gegner nach Mass
(Rival Made to Measure)
1963 E? German, Defa color
ani 4 1/2 mins.
Dir: Bruno J. Böttge.
Mus: Addy Kurth.
F
Ref: ASIFA sheets.

Geheimnis der Gelben Mönche, Das
(Il Segreto dei Frati Gialli:
The Secret of the Yellow Monks;
Tiro a Segno per Uccidere:
Shooting Gallery for Killing;
Wietoten Man eine Dame?, Come
si Uccide una Signora?: How to
Kill a Lady?; Target for Killing
--Brit.t.)
1966 Austrian/Italian, Inter-
continental/PEA color 102
mins.
Exec Prod: Karl Spiehs.
Prod: Paul Waldherr.
Dir & Edit: Manfred R. Köhler.
SP: Anatol Bratt.
Art Dir: Nino Borghi.
Cin: Siegried Hold.
Mus: Marcello Giombini.
Cast: Stewart Granger, Karin
Dor, Curt (Curd) Jürgens,
Rupert Davies, Adolfo Celi,
Klaus Kinski, Mollie Peters,
Scilla Gabel, Erika Remberg.
bor-SF ("electro-psychic mas-
sage" results in super-brain-
washing)
Ref: MFB Oct '69 p215; MTVM
Oct '66 p 18; Filmkunst.

Geheimnis der Schwarzen Koffer, Das
See: Secret of the Black Trunk,
The (1962).

Geheimnisse des Orients
See: Secrets of the Orient
(1928).

Geheimnisse Einer Seele, Die
See: Secrets of a Soul (1925).

Gekko Kamen
(The Moonbeam Man)
● (The Man in The Moonlight
Mask --ad.t.)
1958 Japanese, Toei 102
mins.
Dir: Tsuneo Kobayashi.
SP: Yasunori Kawauchi.
Cin: Ichiro Hoshijima.
Cast: Fumitake Omura, Junya
Usami, Hiroko Mime, Mitsue
Komiya, Yaeko Wakamizu, Yasushi
Nagata.
bor-SF (super bomb; evil
scientist; masked hero)
Ref: UniJ 2:24; SM 8:5;
FEFN 3 Oct '58 p 13.

cont.

Gekko Kamen cont.
● (The Challenging Ghost --ad.t.)
1959 Japanese, Toei.
Dir: Shoichi Shimazu.
Cast: Fumitake Omura.
bor-SF (masked superhero)
Ref: UniJ 1960 p96.

● (The Last Death of the Devil --
ad.t.)
1959 Japanese, Toei.
Dir: Shoichi Shimazu.
Cast: Fumitake Omura.
bor-SF
Ref: Japanese Films '60.

● (The Monster Gorilla --ad.t.)
1959 Japanese, Toei scope
60 mins.
Dir: Satoru Ainuda.
Cast: Fumitake Kimura, Yaeko
Wakamizu.
SF-H (hero battles monsters)
Ref: FEFN June '59 p56.
See also: Satan no Tsume
(1959).

Gems of the Screen
See: Q-Riosities by 'Q'
(1922).

Gene Autry and the Phantom Empire
See: Phantom Empire, The (1935).

Génération Spontanée
(Spontaneous Generation)
1909 French, Gaum sil sh.
Dir: Emile Cohl.
F
Ref: Filmlex p 1370.

Genesis
(booklets by J. Effel)
See: Creation of the World, The
(1958).

Genesis
● Genesis I
1968 Genesis Films Ltd
120 mins.
Collection of 15 films, some
with fantastic content.
Organized by: Reg Childs.
Ref: Acad.

● Genesis II
1969 Genesis Films Ltd (Filmways) ani & live 119 mins.
Organized by: Reg Childs.
Collections of 16 films, some
with fantastic content. See
also: Bambi Meets Godzilla; Campus
Christi; E Pluribus Unum; Project
I; Unicycle Race; Vicious Cycles
(all 1969).
Ref: LAT 6 Nov '69; LAFP 7 Nov
'69; Vw 26 Nov '69.

● Genesis III
1970 Genesis Films 113 mins.
Organized by: Reg Childs.
Collection of 9 films, some with
fantastic content. See also:
Delineation; Omega; Runs Good
(all 1970).
Ref: LAT 3 Dec '70; Vw 9 Dec
'70.

● Genesis IV
1971 Genesis Films 115 mins.
Collection of 12 films some with
fantastic content. See also:
Appointment Reminder; Marguerite;
Last of the Shcunue; Intermission;
Ass (all 1971).
Ref: Genesis program; Vw 6 Oct
'71.

Genesis II
1973 (CBS-TV) color "90
mins."
Prod & SP: Gene Roddenberry.
Dir: John Llewellyn Moxey.

cont.

Genesis II cont.
Art Dir: Hilyard Brown.
Cin: Gerald Perry Finnerman.
Cast: Alex Cord, Mariette
Hartley, Percy Rodriguez,
Ted Cassidy, Lynn Marta,
Harvey Jason, Titos Vandis.
SF (suspended animation experi-
ment gone awry causes 20th
Century man to wake up in
2133; mutants vs. humans)
Ref: Vw 28 March '73; LAT
23 March '73; Locus 131:3.

General and a Fly, A
1961 Polish color ani sh.
Dir: Jerzy Zitzman.
F
Ref: Ani/Cin p 114, 176.

Genie, The
1953 British, Fairbanks
75 mins.
Three stories; one, the title
story, is fantastic. Credits
for this story follow:
Prod: Douglas Fairbanks Jr.
Dir: Lance Comfort.
SP: Doreen Montgomery.
Cin: Brendan Stafford.
Edit: Francis Beeber.
Mus: Allan Gray.
Cast: Yvonne Furneaux, Martin
Miller, Douglas Fairbanks Jr.
[genie].
F-seq (genie from Aladdin's
Lamp was wished human, can
no longer perform miracles,
until one is needed enough &
he becomes genie again)
Ref: MFB Feb'54 p24.

Genie, The
1957 Unicorn 16mm color
1 reel.
Dir: Al Lewis.
SP: Fritz Leiber & Bjo.
Cast: Forrest J Ackerman,
Fritz Leiber [genie], Bjo.
F-com (genie appears to
indecisive modern man)

Genie de Feu, Le
See: Genii of Fire, The (1908).

Génie des Cloches, Le
(La Fête du Sonneur: The
Spirit of the Bells)
1908 French sil 905 ft.
Prod: Georges Méliès.
F
Ref: Sadoul/M; GM Mage p49,
50.

Genie with the Light Touch, The
1972 U color ani 1 reel.
Prod: Walter Lantz.
Dir: Paul Smith.
Voice of Woody: Grace Stafford.
F-com
Ref: PopCar.
See: Woody Woodpecker
(1940-72).

Genii
(Devils)
1969 Czech, Slovensky Film &
Koliba Film color 90 mins.
Dir: Stefan Uher.
SP: Alfonz Bednar.
Cin: Stanislav Szomolanyi.
Edit: Maximillian Remen.
Mus: Ilja Zeljenka.
Cast: Vilfam Polonyi, Vlado
Muller, Mikulas Ladizinsky,
Elena Zvarikova, Vlasta Fia-
lova.
F-com (devils come from center
of Earth to check on man; devils
turn temporarily into angels)

cont.

Genii of Darkness
(Nostradamus, El Genio de las
Tinieblas: Nostradamus, Genius
from the Dark)
1960? (1962) Mexican, (Clasa-
Mohme; AIP-TV) 77 mins.
Prod: Victor Parra.
Dir: Frederic Curiel.
SP: Charles Taboada & Alfred
Ruanova.
Cin: Ferdinand Colin.
Edit: Joseph J. Mungula.
Eng Lang Version Credits:
Prod: K. Gordon Murray.
Dir: Stim Segar.
Cast: German Robles [vampire],
Julio Aleman, Domingo Soler,
Aurora Alvarado, Fanny Schiller,
Rina Valdarno, Luis Aragon.
F-H (Nostradamus is a vampire,
descendent of the prophet)
Ref: Photon 19:36; FDY '62;
TVG.
Sequel to: Curse of Nostra-
damus (1960).

Genii of Fire, The
(Le Génie de Feu)
1908 French, Star sil 410
ft (310 ft).
Prod: Georges Méliès.
F (man looks at sacred fire &
is blinded; sight restored by
priest)
Ref: Sadoul/M; GM Mage; LC;
Views 99:10.

Genii of the Vase, The
1914 Joker (U) sil 1 reel.
Cast: Ernest Shields.
F-com-dream (man dreams he finds
bottle with genie who grants
wishes)
Ref: MPW 22:1430, 1524; MPN 12
Dec '14 p49.

Genio de las Tinieblas, El
See: Genii of Darkness (1960?).

Genius, The
See: Supersabio, El (1948).

Genius at Work
(Master Minds --e.t.)
1946 RKO 61 mins.
Exec Prod: Sid Rogell.
Prod: Herman Schlom.
Dir: Leslie Goodwins.
SP: Robert E. Kent & Monte
Brice.
Art Dir: Albert D'Agostino &
Ralph Berger.
Cin: Robert de Grasse.
SpFX: Vernon L. Walker.
Edit: Marvin Coil.
Mus Dir: C. Bakaleinikoff.
Cast: Wally Brown, Alan Carney,
Anne Jeffreys, Lionel Atwill,
Bela Lugosi, Ralph Dunn, Robert
Clarke, Forbes Murray.
H-com (Atwill's home has chamber
of horrors & wax museum)
Ref: Vd 1 Aug '46; HR 4 Aug
'46; LC.

Genius from the Dark, The
See: Genii of Darkness (1960?).

Genocide
See: Konchû Daisensô (1968).

Genosse Münchhausen
1961 German, Satir Film 89
mins.
Dir: Wolfgang Neuss.
Cin: Hugo Schott.
Mus: Rudolf Maluck & Johannes
Rediske.
Cast: Wolfgang Neuss, Corny
Collins, Peer Schmidt, Ingrid
van Bergen, Wolfgang Wahl,
Balduin Baas, K.H. Zeitler.
SF-com (manned Soviet rocket
to Venus)
Ref: Gasca p267-68.

Gens Qui Pleurent et Gens Qui Rient

See: Crying and Laughing (1900).

Gentleman from America, A

(story by M. Arlen)

See: Fatal Night, The (1948).

Gentleman in the House, The

See: Herr im Haus, Der (1940).

Gentlemen, Who Threw That?

1970? Czech color ani sh.

Dir: Ivan Urban, Miroslav Stepanek, &? Bretislav Pojar.

F-com (first in series about two bears)

Ref: Czech Films '71.

See also: Something Went Bump (1970?).

Genuine

1920 German, Decla Bioscop sil.

Dir: Robert Wiene.

Sc: Carl Mayer.

Art Dir: César Klein & Walter Reimann.

Cin: Willy Hameister.

Cast: Fern Andra, Hans von Tvardovsky, Harald Paulsen, Ernst Gronau.

F-H (old painter loves his painting of a cruel Oriental princess, "who escapes from her glass cage to destroy him and all other men" --F&F; expressionistic)

Ref: FTN p640; F&F June '58 p34; Eisner p27, 28, 350.

George Pal Puppetoon

See: Puppetoons (1943-47).

George Pal's Madcap Models

See: Madcap Models (1941-43).

George Washington Jones

1916 Edison sil sh.

F-H-com (title character calls on Svengali, scared by ghosts)

Ref: MPW 10 Oct '16.

Georgie and the Dragon

1951 UPA (Col) color ani 7 mins.

Prod: Stephen Bosustow.

Supervision: John Hubley.

Dir: Robert Cannon.

F-cum (baby dragon in Scotland)

Ref: It 6; MFB March '52 p40.

Gerald McBoing-Boing

1950 UPA (Col) color ani 7 mins.

Prod: Stephen Bosustow.

Supervision: John Hubley.

Dir: Robert Cannon.

Story: Dr. Seuss.

SP: Ted Hee & R. Cannon.

Design: T. Hee & J. Hubley.

Color: Jules Engel.

Ani: Frank Smith, Alan Zaslove, & Gerald Ray.

Mus: Gail Kubic.

Nar: Marvin Miller.

F-com (little boy talks only in sound effects)

Ref: Annecy '65; MFB July '51 p301; Acad winner.

Sequels: Gerald McBoing-Boing's Symphony (1952); How Now Boing Boing (1954); Gerald McBoing-Boing on Planet Moo (1955).

Gerald McBoing-Boing on Planet Moo

1955 (1956) UPA (Col) color scope ani 8 mins.

Prod: Stephen Bosustow.

Dir: Robert Cannon.

Story: T. Hee & R. Cannon.

cont.

Gerald McBoing-Boing on Planet Moo cont.

Design: Lew Keller.

Ani: Frank Smith & Alan Zaslove.

Mus: Ernest Gold.

Nar: Marvin Miller.

F-com (Gerald is captured by aliens from Planet Moo)

Ref: MFB June '56 p80; LC; Acad nom.

Based on a character created by Dr. Seuss.

Sequel to: Gerald McBoing-Boing (1950).

Gerald McBoing-Boing's Symphony

1952 (1953) UPA (Col) color ani 7 mins.

Prod: Stephen Bosustow.

Dir: Robert Cannon.

Nar: Marvin Miller.

F-com

Ref: MFB May '53 p77; LC.

Based on a character created by Dr. Seuss.

Sequel to: Gerald McBoing-Boing (1950).

Gergasi

1958 Singapore (in Malayan) Shaw.

SF-H (abominable snowman)

Ref: FEFN 10 Oct '58 p 17.

See also: Abominable Snowman of the Himalayas, The (1957).

Germ, The

1923 Research Pictures sil 6 reels.

Dir: P.S. McGreeney.

Author: Charles Swinton Warnock.

F (eradication of certain germs takes away evil; girl turns into butterfly, later into tarantula)

Ref: AFI F2.2050 p286; LC.

Germ of Mystery, The

1916 Selig sil 3 reels.

Dir: William Robert Daly.

Sc: L.V. Jefferson.

Cast: Guy Oliver, Fritzi (Fritzie?) Brunette, Lillian Hayward.

SF-H ("super-explosive; huge, repulsive spider")

Ref: MPN 14:1101.

Germanic Love

1916 Vogue (Mutual) sil 1 reel.

Dir: Rube Miller.

Sc: Thomas Delmar.

Cast: Artur (Arthur?) Tavares, Henry Kernan, Madge Kirby, Alice Neice.

SF-com (professors test love potion on tramps at a girls' college)

Ref: MPW 28:1394.

Germelshausen

See: Brigadoon (1954).

Gertie on Tour

1917 sil ani sh.

Prod: Winsor McCay.

SF-com

Ref: Hist US Ani Prog.

Sequel to: Gertie the Dinosaur (1909).

Gertie the Dinosaur

1909 McCay sil ani & live 1 reel.

Prod: Winsor McCay.

Cast: Winsor McCay, George McManus.

F-com (man talks to animated dinosaur)

Ref: F/A p626; MPW 22:1863.

Sequel: Gertie on Tour (1917).

Gertie the Dinosaur

1910? sil ani 1 reel.

cont.

Gertie the Dinosaur cont.

Dir: John Bray.

F-com (imitation of the McCay film)

Ref: D. Glut.

Geschichte vom Kleinen Muck, Die

(Little Muck's Treasure; Little Mook --ad.t?)

1954 E. German, DEFA color sh.

Dir: Wolfgang Staudte.

SP: W. Staudte & Peter Podehl.

Cin: Robert Baberske.

SpFX: Ernst Kunstmann.

Edit: Ruth Schreiber.

Mus: Ernst Roters.

Cast: Thomas Schmidt, Johannes Mau, Friedrich Richter, Trude Hesterberg, Alwin Lippsch.

F (fairy tale: hunchbacked boy finds cane & magic slippers that give him superswiftness; one magic fig makes enemy's ears grow, another returns to normal)

Ref: Montevideo '56

Based on the fairy tale by Wilhelm Hauff.

Gestohlene Nase, Die

(The Stolen Nose)

1955 E. German, DEFA color ani puppet sh.

Dir: Kurt Weiler.

Puppets by: Gabriele Otto.

Mus: Hans-Hendrik Wehding.

F (animals steal carrot nose of snowman)

Ref: Montevideo '56.

Getting Up Made Easy

1903 British sil 100 ft.

Prod: Cecil Hepworth.

F-com

Ref: Film & the Public p21; Hist/Brit p82.

Gevatter Tod

(Godfather Death; Death)

1921 Austrian sil.

Dir: Heinz Hanus.

SP: Hans Berger & L. Gunther.

Art Dir: H. Berger.

Cin: Hans Androschin & Eduard Hosch.

Cast: Armin Seydelmann, Artur Ranzenhofer [Death], Erika (Erica?) Wagner, Fritz Strassny, Louis Nerz.

F-H

Ref: Osterr.

Based on "Der Pate des Todes" (Death's Godfather) by R. Baumbach.

Gewissen, Das

(German title BFI cat has for French film)

See: Conscience (1905).

Ghanchakkar

See: Sheikhchilli (1940).

Ghastly Ones, The

1969 JER Pictures color 81 mins.

Prod & Dir: Andy Milligan.

SP: Hal Sherwood & A. Milligan.

Cin: D. Mills.

Edit: Gerald Jackson.

Cast: Eileen Haves, Don Williams, Carol Vogel, Richard Ramos, Anne Linden, Fib LaBlanque, Hal Borski, Neil Flanders, Veronica Radburn, Maggie Rogers, Hal Sherwood.

H (18th century blood & gore; hunchback eats live rabbits)

Ref: MMF 23:60-61; V 15 Jan '69; CoF 16:60; BO 13 March '72.

Ghastly Shadows

See: Sombras Cadavericas (1957).

Ghidorah. . .

See: Ghidrah. . .

Ghidrah, the Three-Headed Monster

(Ghidorah, Sandai Kaiju Chikyu Saidai no Kessan; Monster of Monsters Ghidorah --ad.t.; The Biggest Fight on Earth --ad.t.; The Greatest Battle on Earth --ad.t.)

1965 Japanese, Toho (Continental) color scope 85 mins.

Exec Prod: Tomoyuki Tanaka.

Dir: Inoshiro Honda.

SP: Shinichi Sekizawa.

Cin: Hajime Koizumi.

SpFX: Eiji Tsuburaya.

Edit: Ryohei Fujii.

Mus: Akira Ifukube.

Cast: Yosuke Natsuki, Yuriko Hoshi, Hiroshi Koizumi, Takashi Shimura, Emi Ito, Yumi Ito, Eiji Okada.

SF (Ghidrah, 3-headed, flying, lightning-breathing dragon from outer space, battles Godzilla, Rodan, & Mothra)

Ref: Vw 6 Oct '65; FD 8 Oct '65; MPH 27 Oct '65.

See also: Godzilla, King of the Monsters (1954); Rodan (1956); Mothra (1961); Monster Zero (1965); Destroy All Monsters (1968); Godzilla Tai Gigan (1971).

Ghosks Is the Bunk

1939 Par ani 7 mins.

Prod: Max Fleischer.

Dir: Dave Fleischer.

F-com (phoney ghost; invisibility paint)

Ref: MPH 22 July '39 p53; LC.

See: Popeye (1933-57).

Ghost, The

1911 Biograph sil 481 ft.

F-com (real ghost chases phoney ones)

Ref: MPW 9:93, 140, 292; Bios 13 Nov '13.

Ghost, The

1913 Domino sil 2 reels.

Dir: William H. Clifford.

F-dream (man dreams of himself dead; St. Patrick appears)

Ref: MPW 18:660.

Ghost, The

1914 Pathé sil 3 reels.

Cast: Crane Wilbur, M.O. Penn, William Riley Hatch, Logan Paul, Clare Rea.

H (phoney ghost scares villain to death)

Ref: MPW 20:526, 673.

Ghost

1960 Thailand.

F

Ref: FEFN June '60 p42.

Ghost, The

(Lo Spettro de Dr. Hichcock; The Spectre --Brit.t?)

1963 (1965) Italian, Panda (Magna) color 93 mins.

Prod: Luigi Carpentieri & Ermanno Donati (Louis Mann).

Dir: Riccardo Freda (Robert Hampton).

SP: Oreste Biancoli (Robert Davidson) & R. Freda.

Art Dir: Mario Chiari (Samuel Fields).

Cin: Raffaele Masciocchi (Donald Green).

Edit: Ornella Micheli (Donna Christie).

Mus: Franco Mannino (Frank Wallace), Ennio Morricone, & Roman Vlad.

Cast: Barbara Steele, Peter Baldwin, Elio Jotta (Leonard G. Elliot), Harriet White, Umberto Raho.

cont.

host, The cont.

H (apparent ghost of supposedly murdered man "haunts" his unfaithful wife; gore murders)

Ref: MFB May '64 p78-79; F&F June '64; FM 39:28; Borst.

Sequel to: Horrible Dr. Hichcock, The (1962).

host, The

1970? Hongkong? (in Mandarin).

F

Ref: Singapore Straits-Times 29 Aug '70.

host and Mr. Chicken, The

1965 (1966) U color scope 90 mins.

Prod: Edward J. Montagne.

Dir: Alan Rafkin.

SP: James Fritzell & Everett Greenbaum.

Art Dir: Alexander Golitzen & George Webb.

Cin: William Margulies.

Edit: Sam E. Waxman.

Mus: Vic Mizzy.

Cast: Don Knotts, Joan Staley, Liam Redmond, Dick Sargent, Reta Shaw, Lurene Tuttle, Cliff Norton, Skip Homeier, Charles Lane, Eddie Quillan, Ellen Corby.

H-com (timid man menaced by phoney ghosts)

Ref: MFB June '66 p93; FF '66 p259; FD 18 Jan '66.

host and Mrs. Muir, The

1947 Fox 104 mins.

Prod: Fred Kohlmar.

Dir: Joseph Mankiewicz.

SP: Philip Dunne.

Art Dir: Richard Day & George Davis.

Cin: Charles Lang Jr.

Edit: Dorothy Spencer.

SpFX: Fred Sersen.

Mus: Bernard Herrmann.

Cast: Gene Tierney, Rex Harrison [ghost], George Sanders, Vanessa Brown, Anna Lee, Natalie Wood, Isobel Elsom.

F (ghost of dead sea captain & living woman fall in love)

Ref: Vd 16 May '47; LC; FDY '48.

Based on novel "The Ghost of Captain Gregg and Mrs. Muir" by R.A. Dick.

See also: Stranger in the Night (1955?).

Ghost Appears in Valley

1961 Japanese.

F

Ref: FEFN Nov '61.

Ghost Beauty

See: Kaidan Botan Doro (1968).

Ghost Breaker, The

● 1914 Lasky (Par) sil 60 mins.

Prod: Jesse L. Lasky.

Sc: James Montgomery & Cecil B. de Mille.

Cast: H.B. Warner, Rita Sanwood, Betty Johnson, Theodore Roberts, Jode Mullally, Horace B. Carpenter, Jeanie MacPherson.

H (fake ghosts)

Ref: MPW 22:1692, 1747; MPN 19 Dec '14 p62; FIR April '72 p221.

See also: Ghost Fakir, The (1915).

● 1922 Famous Players-Lasky (Par) sil 5130 ft.

Dir: Alfred Green.

Adapt: Jack Cunningham.

cont.

Ghost Breaker, The cont.

Sc: Walter De Leon.

Cin: William Marshall.

Cast: Wallace Reid, Lila Lee, Walter Hiers, Arthur Carew, J. Farrell MacDonald, Frances Raymond, Snitz Edwards.

H-com (haunted castle; fake ghosts)

Ref: AFI F2.2060 p287; MPW 56:f220; MPN 26:1505.

Based on the play by Paul Dickey and Charles W. Goddard.

See also: Ghost Breakers, The (1940); Scared Stiff (1952).

Ghost Breakers, The

1940 Par 82 mins.

Prod: Arthur Hornblow Jr.

Dir: George Marshall.

SP: Walter De Leon.

Art Dir: Hans Dreier & Robert Usher.

Cin: Charles Lang & Theodore Sparkuhl.

Process Cin: Farciot Edouart.

Edit: Ellsworth Hoagland.

Mus: Ernst Toch.

Cast: Bob Hope, Paulette Goddard, Richard Carlson, Paul Lukas, Willie Best, Anthony Quinn, Pedro de Cordoba, Noble Johnson [zombie], Tom Dugan, Paul Fix, Lloyd Corrigan.

F-H-com (set in Cuba; fake ghosts; one brief real ghost; zombie)

Ref: Photon 20:33; Vd 6 June '40; MPH 24 Aug '40 p47; FDY '41; LC.

Based on play "The Ghost Breaker" by Paul Dickey & Charles W. Goddard.

See also: Ghost Breaker, The: White Zombie (1932).

Ghost Buster

1952 RKO 18 mins.

Cast: Gil Lamb, Carol Hughes, Claire Carleton.

H-com (haunted house; real ghosts?)

Ref: Willis; LC; Maltin/GMS p 199.

Ghost Busters

See: Spook Busters (1946).

Ghost Cat. . .

See: Kaibyo. . .

Ghost Cat Mansion

See: Black Cat Mansion (1958).

Ghost-Cat Mansion of Nabeshima

See: Nabeshima Kaibyoden (1949).

Ghost Catchers, The

1944 U 69 mins.

Prod & SP: Edmund L. Hartmann.

Dir: Edward F. Cline.

Assist Dir: Howard Christie.

Art Dir: John B. Goodman & Richard H. Riedel.

Cin: Charles Van Enger.

SpFX Cin: John P. Fulton.

Edit: Arthur Hilton.

SpFX: Carl Lee & Eddie Robinson.

Mus: Edward Ward.

Cast: Ole Olsen, Chic Johnson, Gloria Jean, Martha O'Driscoll, Leo Carrillo, Andy Devine, Lon Chaney Jr., Kirby Grant, Walter Catlett, Morton Downey, Tor Johnson, Jack Norton, Mel Torme.

F-H-mus-com (real ghosts turn up at times to help Olsen & Johnson)

Ref: MFB Aug '44 p89; Vd & Hr 2 June '44; FDY '45.

Ghost Chasers

1951 Mono 69 mins.

Prod: Jan Grippo.

Dir: William Beaudine.

SP: Bert Lawrence.

Art Dir: David Milton.

Cin: Marcel Le Picard.

Edit: William Austin.

Mus Dir: Edward Kay.

Cast: Leo Gorcey, Huntz Hall, Lloyd Corrigan, Robert Coogan, Jan Kayne, Bernard Gorcey, George Gorcey, Philip Van Zandt, Billy Benedict.

F-H-com (phoney spiritualists; real ghost)

Ref: Hr 3 May '51; LC; FDY '52.

Ghost Crazy

See: Crazy Knights (1944).

Ghost Creeps, The

(Boys of the City --e.t?)

1940 Mono 63 mins.

Assoc Prod: Sam Katzman.

Dir: Joseph H. Lewis.

SP: William Lively.

Cin: Robert Cline.

Edit: Carl Pierson.

Cast: Bobby Jordan, Leo Gorcey, Dave O'Brien, Vince Barnett, Hally Chester, Ina Gest, Minerva Urecal, Dave Gorcey.

H-com (fake ghosts)

Ref: FD 22 July '40; Vw 17 Aug '40; MPH 2 July '40 p31.

See also: Spooks Run Wild (1941).

Ghost Fakirs, The

(episode in Two Boobs series)

1915 Starlight (United Film Service) sil 1 reel.

Cast: James Aubrey, Walter Kendig.

F-H-com (haunted house with real ghosts)

Ref: MPN 1 May '15 p83; MPW 24:1338.

See also: Ghost Breakers, The (1914).

Ghost for Sale, A

1952 British, Bushey 31 mins.

Prod: Gilbert Church.

Dir: Victor M. Gover.

SP: John Gilling.

Cast: Tod Slaughter, Patrick Barr, Tucker McGuire.

F-H (caretaker tells story about mad squire, then vanishes himself)

Ref: Gifford/BFC 11748.

Includes scenes from Curse of the Wraydons, The (1946).

Ghost from the Pond

See: Kaidan Hitotsu-me Jizo (1959).

Ghost Goes Gear, The

1966 British, Associated British-Pathé color 41 mins.

Prod: Harry Field.

Dir: Hugh Gladwish.

SP: Roger Dunton & H. Gladwish.

Choreog: Denys Palmer.

Art Dir: Peter Moll.

Cin: George Stevens.

Edit: Ronald Glenister.

Mus: John & Joan Shakespeare.

Cast: Spencer Davis, Stevie Winwood, Muff Winwood, Peter York, Nicholas Parsons, Lorne Gibson [ghost].

F-mus-com (in their manager's ancestral home, a rock group encounters a ghost)

Ref: MFB Oct '67 p 157.

Ghost Goes West, The

(The Laying of the Glourie Ghost --e.t?)

1936 British, London Films (UA) 85 mins.

Prod: Alexander Korda.

Dir: Rene Clair.

SP: Robert E. Sherwood & Geoffrey Kerr.

Art Dir: Vincent Korda.

Cin: Hal Rosson.

Edit: William Hornbeck.

SpFX: Ned Mann.

Mus: Mischa Spolianski.

Cast: Robert Donat [ghost & descendant of ghost], Eugene Pallette, Jean Parker, Ralph Bunker, Elsa Lanchester, Everly Gregg, Hay Petrie, Patricia Hilliard.

F-sat-com (when a rich American buys an ancient Scottish castle & ships it to America the castle's ghost goes too)

Ref: F/A p357; FDY '37; FTN p528; MPH 4 Jan '36 p48; Pardi.

Based on short story "Sir Tristram Goes West" by Eric Keown.

Ghost Goes Wild, The

1947 Rep 66 mins.

Assoc Prod: Armand Schaefer.

Dir: George Blair.

Story: Randall Faye & Taylor Caven.

SP: R. Faye.

Art Dir: Hilyard Brown.

Cin: John Alton.

Edit: Fred Allen.

SpFX: Howard & Theodore Lydecker.

Mus: Joseph Dubin & Morton Scott.

Cast: James Ellison, Anne Gwynne, Edward Everett Horton, Grant Withers, Lloyd Corrigan, Jonathan Hale.

F-H-com (fake ghost & a real ghost summoned by seance)

Ref: MFB May '47 p64; FD 4 April '47; Vd & HR 14 Feb '47.

Ghost Holiday, The

1907 Williams, Brown & Earle sil sh.

F (ghosts & skeletons play among graves, ride auto, train, etc; cockcrow summons them back to their graves)

Ref: MPW 1:458.

Ghost Hounds

1917 Kalem sil.

Cast: Lloyd V. Hamilton, Bud Duncan, Henry Murdoch, Ethel Teare.

H-com (fake dancing skeleton; haunted house)

Ref: MPW 31:1074, 1035, 1212.

Ghost House, The

1917 Par sil.

Dir: William C. de Mille.

Sc: Beulah Marie Dix.

Cin: Paul P. Perry.

Cast: Eugene Pallette.

bor-H (bank robbers use haunted house)

Ref: MPW 34:169, 397, 444; MPN 16:2772; LC.

Ghost in the Castle

See: Spuk im Schloss (1945).

Ghost in the Invisible Bikini

(Slumber Party in Horror House; Bikini Party in a Haunted House; Beach Party in a Haunted House; Pajama Party in a Haunted House; --all s.t.s)

1966 AIP color scope 82 mins.

Prod: James H. Nicholson & Samuel Z. Arkoff.

cont.

160

Ghost in the Invisible Bikini cont.

Co Prod: Anthony Carras.

Dir: Don Weis.

Story: Louis M. Heyward.

SP: L.M. Heyward & Elwood Ullman.

Art Dir: Daniel Haller.

Cin: Stanley Cortez.

Edit: Fred Feitshans & Eve Newman.

SpFX: Roger George.

Ghost Seq: Ronald & Carol Sinclair.

Mus: Les Baxter.

Cast: Tommy Kirk, Deborah Walley, Aron Kincaid, Quinn O'Hara, Jesse White, Harvey Lembeck, Nancy Sinatra, Francis X. Bushman, Basil Rathbone, Patsy Kelly, Boris Karloff [ghost], Susan Hart [title ghost].

F-H-mus-com (two ghosts try to help true heirs gain fortune & to get their own way into heaven)

Ref: FF 66:380; Vw 6 April '66; FD 27 April '66.

Ghost Jesters, The

See: Fantasmas Burlones, Los (1964).

Ghost Lamp

1971? Hongkong?

F

Ref: B. Warren.

Ghost Love

1956 Hongkong (in Mandarin).

Cast: Li Li Hwa, Chang Yang.

F

Ref: FEFN 27 July '56 p21.

Ghost Music of Shamisen

See: Kaidan Shamisen-bori (1962).

Ghost of a Chance

1971? color.

Cast: Jimmy Edwards.

F (ghosts help kids turn old house into youth club)

Ref: Courier-Mail 29 April '71.

Ghost of a Chance, A

1973 Northlake (Jaguar) color.

Prod: Barry Knight.

Dir & SP: Gorton Hall.

Cast: Roy Clark, Glen Brock, Jimmy Hughes, Toby Willis, Tom Winston, Ralph Martin, Gena Powers.

sex-F-com (ghost comedy about homosexuals)

Ref: Advocate 9 May '73 p24-25 ad.

Ghost of Bragehus, The

See: Spoket pa Bragehus (1936).

Ghost of Captain Gregg and Mrs. Muir, The

(novel by R.A. Dick)

See: Ghost and Mrs. Muir, The (1947); Stranger in the Night (1955?).

Ghost of Chibusa Enoki

See: Kaidan Chibusa Enoki (1958).

Ghost of Chidori-ga-fuchi

See: Kaidan Chidori-ga-fuchi (1956).

Ghost of Dragstrip Hollow

(The Haunted Hotrod --s.t.)

1959 AIP 65 mins.

Prod & SP: Lou Rusoff.

Dir: William Hole Jr.

Art Dir: Daniel Haller.

Cin: Gilbert Warrenton.

Edit: Frank Keller & Ted Sampson.

cont.

Ghost of Dragstrip Hollow cont.

Mus: Ronald Stein.

Cast: Jody Fair, Martin Braddock, Russ Bender, Leon Tyler, Elaine Dupont, Henry McCann, Jack Ging, Paul Blaisdell ["monster"].

F-H-com (title ghost revealed as ex-monster actor; talking, intelligent car; real ghost at climax)

Ref: MFB Sept '61 p 128; HR 4 Aug '59; FF '59 p246.

Ghost of Frankenstein

1942 U 68 mins.

Assoc Prod: George Waggner.

Dir: Erle C. Kenton.

Story: Eric Taylor.

SP: W. Scott Darling.

Art Dir: Jack Otterson.

Make-up: Jack P. Pierce.

Cin: Milton Krasner & Woody Bredell.

Edit: Ted Kent.

Mus: H.J. Salter.

Cast: Cedric Hardwicke, Ralph Bellamy, Lionel Atwill, Bela Lugosi, Evelyn Ankers, Lon Chaney Jr. [Frankenstein's Monster], Barton Yarborough, Olaf Hytten, Dwight Frye, Doris Lloyd, Holmes Herbert, Lionel Belmore, Michael Mark, Dick Alexander, Eddie Parker [stunts].

SF-H (dug out of sulphur pit, Monster is revived by lightning; Ygor's brain put in Monster's body, goes blind; ghost of first Dr Frankenstein speaks to his son)

Ref: HR & Vd 2 March '42; FanMo 5:16; MFB June '42 p72; FD 5 March '42.

Based on a character created by Mary W. Shelley.

Sequel to: Frankenstein (1931).

Ghost of Gojusan-tsugi

See: Kaidan Gojusan-tsugi (1960).

Ghost of Granleigh, The

1913 Edison sil 1000 ft.

Dir: Richard Ridgely.

Sc: Bannister Merwin.

Cast: Bigelow Cooper, Laura Sawyer, Charles Ogle [ghost], Yale Benner, Herbert Prior.

F (a ghost tries to warn living they are in a situation like that which caused his death)

Ref: EK 15 Aug '13 p 15; F/A p421; Bios 13 Nov '13; MPW 17:868, 943, 1175; LC.

Ghost of John Holling, The

(novel by E. Wallace)

See: Mystery Liner (1934).

Ghost of Kagami-ga-fuchi

See: Kaidan Kagami-ga-fuchi (1959).

Ghost of Mudtown, The

1910 Pathé sil 478 ft.

bor-H-com (fake ghost)

Ref: Bios 2 June '10.

Ghost of Oiwa

See: Kaidan Oiwa no Borei (1961).

Ghost of Old Morro, The

1917 Edison-KESE sil 5 reels.

Filmed in Cuba.

Dir: Richard Ridgely.

Story: James Oppenheim.

Cin: George W. Lane.

Cast: Mabel Trunnelle, Robert Conness, Helen Strickland, Herbert Prior, Bigelow Cooper.

H (old castle; hag; murders)

Ref: WID's 28 June '17; MPW 30:408; MPN 16:118; LC.

Ghost of Rashmon Hall, The

See: Night Comes too Soon, The (1947).

Ghost of Sacramento, The

See: Duch Zamczyska Sacramento (1962).

Ghost of Saga Mansion

See: Kaidan Saga Yashiki (1953).

Ghost of Seaview Manor, The

1913 sil 1000 ft.

H (fake ghost)

Ref: MPW 16:1137.

Ghost of Self, The

1913 (1914) Essanay sil 1000 ft.

F (ghost cures cruel man through apparitions of men & women he had wronged)

Ref: MPW 19:289; Bios 19 March '14.

Ghost of Slumber Mountain, The

1919 H.M. Dawley (World Pictures) sil 1000 ft.

Prod, Dir, Sc: Herbert M. Dawley.

SpFX: Willis O'Brien & H.M. Dawley.

Cast: Herbert M. Dawley, Willis H. O'Brien.

F-dream (man dreams ghost of a mad hermit shows him a special telescope which shows land in prehistoric times, with dinosaurs and other primitive animals)

Ref: CineF Winter '71 p 10; FM 12 letters; LC; MPW 40:32, 925.

Ghost of Snake-Girl

See: Kaidan Hebionna (1968).

Ghost of Snow-Girl Prostitute

See: Kaidan Yukijoro (1968).

Ghost of the Girl Diver

See: Kaidan Ama Yurei (1960).

Ghost of the Hunchback

See: Kaidan Semushi Otoko (1965).

Ghost of the Jungle, The

1916 Bison (U) sil 2 reels.

Prod: Jay Hunt.

Sc: Allen Watt & Rex De Rosselli.

Cast: Rex De Rosselli, Edythe Sterling, Bud Chase, T.D. Crittenden.

F (girl's ghost appears to her father when he dies; his ghost joins hers; man who wronged girl led to his death by her ghost)

Ref: MPW 28:2293; LC.

Ghost of the Mine, The

1914 Eclair sil 1 reel.

F (spirit of girl proves her accused murderer innocent)

Ref: MPW 22:1126.

Ghost of the One-Eyed Man

See: Kaidan Katame no Otoko (1965).

Ghost of the Opera

See: Spuk im Opernhaus (1940?).

Ghost of the Rancho, The

1918 Anderson-Brunton Co (Pathé) sil 5 reels.

Dir: William Worthington.

Story: Arthur Henry Gooden.

Sc: Jack Cunningham.

Cast: Bryant Washburn, Rhea Mitchell.

west; F-H seq (posse of ghosts)

Ref: MPW 37:882, 1021; LC.

Ghost of the Strangler, The

See: Espectro del Estrangulador, El (1965).

Ghost of the Twisted Oaks, The

1915 Lubin sil 3 reels.

Prod & Dir: Sidney Olcott.

cont.

Ghost of the Twisted Oaks, The cont.

Sc: Pearl Gaddis.

Cast: Valentine Grant, James Vincent, Florence Wolcott.

F-H (voodoo; real ghost)

Ref: MPW 26:1317, 1500, 1505; LC.

Ghost of Yotsuya, The

See: Shinpan Yotsuya Kaidan (1928); Yotsuya Kaidan I & II (1949); Yotsuya Kaidan (1956 & 1959); Kaidan Bancho Sarayashiki (1957); Tokaido Yotsuya Kaidan (1959); Kaidan Oiwa no Borei (1961); Illusion of Blood (1966); Yotsuya Kaidan -- Oiwa no Borei (1969).

Ghost Parade

1931 Mack Sennett 22 mins.

Prod & Dir: Mack Sennett.

SP: John A. Waldron, Earle Rodney, & Harry McCoy.

Cast: Andy Clyde, Harry Gribbon, Marjorie Beebe, Frank Eastman, Marion Sayers.

F-H-com (ghosts in a haunted house)

Ref: Maltin/GMS p96; LC.

Ghost Patrol

1936 Puritan 58 mins.

Prod: Sig Neufeld & Leslie Simmonds.

Dir: Sam Newfield.

Story: Joe O'Donnell.

SP: Wyndham Gitten.

Cin: John Greenhalgh.

Edit: Jack English.

Cast: Tim McCoy, Claudia Dell, Walter Miller, Wheeler Oakman, Jim Burtis, Lloyd Ingraham, Slim Whitaker.

west; SF-seq (mob brings down planes by means of radium tube controlling electrical impulses)

Ref: Vw 10 Sept '36, 16 Sept '36; FD 10 Sept '36.

Ghost Party

See: Hillbillys in a Haunted House (1967).

Ghost Ship, The

1943 RKO 69 mins.

Prod: Val Lewton.

Dir: Mark Robson.

Story: Leo Mittler.

SP: Donald Henderson Clarke.

Art Dir: Albert S. D'Agostino & Walter E. Keller.

Cin: Nicholas Musuraca.

Edit: John Lockert.

SpFX: Vernon L. Walker.

Mus: Roy Webb.

Mus Dir: C. Bakaleinikoff.

Cast: Richard Dix, Russell Wade, Edith Barrett, Ben Bard, Edmund Glover, Skelton Knaggs, Tom Burton, Steve Winston, Sir Lancelot.

bor-psy-H (psychopathic sea captain commits murders)

Ref: HR & Vd 7 Dec '43; MFB March '44 p29; FD 14 Dec '43.

Ghost Ship

1952 (1953) British, Abtcon Pictures (Lippert) 69 mins (74 mins).

Prod, Dir, SP: Vernon Sewell.

Pres: Herman Cohen.

Art Dir: George Haslan.

Cin: Stanley Grant.

Edit: Francis Bieber.

Mus: Eric Spear.

Cast: Hazel Court, Dermot Walsh, Hugh Burden, John Robinson, Hugh Latimer.

bor-F-H (medium in trance discovers previous murders)

Ref: Vw 23 July '53.

st Ship, [The]
  See: Yurei-Sen (1957); Buque
Fantasma, El (1969).

st Steps Out, The
  See: Time of Their Lives, The
(1946).

st Stories
  See: Kwaidan (1963).

st Story, The
  1907 Vit sil sh.
  Prod & Dir: J. Stuart Blackton.
  F
  Ref: LC; Filmlex p681.

st Story in Passage, A
  See: Kaidan Dochu (1958).

st Story of Booby Trap
  See: Kaidan Otoshiana (1968).

st Story of Broken Dishes
Bancho Mansion
  See: Kaidan Bancho Sarayashiki
(1957).

st Story of Devil's Fire Swamp
  See: Kaidan Onibi no Numa (1963).

st Story of Funny Act in Front
Train Station
  See: Kigeki Ekimae Kaidan
(1964).

st Story of Kakui Street
  See: Kaidan Kakuidori (1961).

st Story of Peonies and Stone
anterns, A
  See: Kaidan Botan Doro (1968).

st Story of Stone Lanterns and
ying in the Night
  See: Kaidan Yonaki-doro (1962).

st Story of Two Travellers
  See: Kaidan Dochu (1958).

st Story of Wanderer at Honjo
  See: Kaidan Honjo Nanfushigi
(1957).

st Tales Retold
  1938 British, A.I.P. sh series.
  Dir: Widgey R. Newman.
  Stories: W.R. & Joan Newman.
  SP: George A. Cooper.
  Cast: Hal Walters, Ian Fleming,
Howard Douglas, W.E. Hodge, Vi
Kaley, D.J. Williams, Claude
Bailey, Jenny Lovelace.
  F-H (various famous ghost
stories)
  Ref: Gifford/BFC 10524-30; Brit
Cin p90.

host Talks, The
  1928 (1929) Fox 9 reels
(61 mins).
  Dir: Lewis Seiler.
  SP: Frederick Hazlitt Brennon &
Harlan Thompson.
  Cin: George Meehan.
  Edit: Ralph Dietrich.
  Cast: Helen Twelvetrees,
Charles Eaton, Carmel Myers,
Earle Fox, Arnold Lucy, Stepin
Fetchit, Bess Flowers.
  myst-com; bor-H (crooks haunt
house)
  Ref: AFI F2.2066 p288; MPN
41:11:82; FD 24 Feb '29.
  Based on play "Badges" by
Max Marcin & Edward Hammond.

Ghost Talks, The
  1949 Col 2 reels.
  Prod & Dir: Jules White.
  Cast: The Three Stooges (Moe
Howard, Shemp Howard, Larry
Fine), Kenneth MacDonald.
  F-H-com (ghost of Peeping
Tom)
  Ref: Maltin/GMS p 136; LC;
Maltin/MCT p217.
  See also: Three Stooges, The
(1934-59).

Ghost Town, The
  See: Gandy Goose in the Ghost
Town (1944).

Ghost Town Law
  1942 Mono.
  Prod: Scott R. Dunlap.
  Dir: Howard Bretherton.
  SP: Jess Bowers.
  Cin: Harry C. Neumann.
  Edit: Carl L. Pierson.
  Cast: Buck Jones, Tim McCoy,
Raymond Hatton, Virginia
Carpenter.
  bor-H-west (fake ghosts)
  Ref: HR 25 March '42.

Ghost Wagon, The
  1915 Bison (U) sil 3 reels.
  Prod: Joseph Franz.
  Sc: Bess Meredyth.
  Cast: Edythe Sterling, Sherman
Bainbridge, Rex de Rosselli,
Warren Ellsworth, A. Emundson.
  F-seq (prairie schooner with
a ghostly driver)
  Ref: MPW 25:1501, 1939, 26:80,
142; LC.

Ghost Walks, The
  1934 (1935) Invincible (Chester-
field) 69 mins.
  Prod: Maury M. Cohen.
  Dir: Frank Strayer.
  SP: Charles S. Belden.
  Cin: M.A. Anderson.
  Edit: Roland Reed.
  Cast: John Miljan, June Collyer,
Richard Carle, Spencer Charters,
Johnny Arthur, Eve Southern,
Henry Kolker, Donald Kirke,
Douglas Gerrard, Jack Shutt.
  myst; bor-H (secret panels;
lunatic kidnaps surgical com-
plex, intends to operate on
victims)
  Ref: HR 23 Jan '35; Vw 3 April
'35; LC; MPH 27 April '35 p54.

Ghostly Inn, The
  See: Halfway House, The (1944).

Ghostly Trap, The
  See: Kaidan Otoshiana (1968).

Ghosts
  1912 British, Hepworth sil
420 ft.
  F
  Ref: Bios 24 Oct '12.

Ghosts, The
  See: Spiritisten (1914).

Ghosts Before Breakfast
  (Vormittagsspuk: Ghosts Before
Noon)
  1928 German, Tobis (Film-makers'
Coop) 9 mins (6 mins).
  Dir: Hans Richter.
  Cin: Reimar Kuntze.
  Mus: Paul Hindemith.
  Cast: Darius Milhaud, Jean
Oser, Walter Gronostay, Werner
Graeff, Paul Hindemith, Hans
Richter.
  exp-F (everyday objects fly
around in the morning)
  Ref: CFS Sept '68; Undrgnd
p59; FMC 5:273; BFI cat p69.

Ghosts in Buenos Aires
  See: Fantasmas en Buenos Aires
(1942).

Ghosts in Rome
  (Fantasmi a Roma; Phantom Lovers
--Brit.t.)
  1960 Italian, Lux & Vides &
Galatea color 101 mins.
  Prod: Franco Cristaldi.
  Dir: Antonio Pietrangeli.
  SP: Ennio Flaiano, A. Pietrangeli,
Sergio Amidei, Ettore Scola, &
Ruggero Maccari.
  Cin: Giuseppe Rotunno.

Ghosts in Rome cont.
  Edit: Eraldo Da Roma.
  Mus: Nino Rota.
  Cast: Marcello Mastroianni,
Vittorio Gassman, Sandra Milo,
Belinda Lee, Eduardo de Filippo,
Tino Buazzelli.
  F-com (ancestral ghosts)
  Ref: Vw 9 Aug '61; FM 12:10 &
12; FIR Dec '61 p616-17.

Ghosts in the Night
  See: Ghosts on the Loose
(1943).

Ghosts -- Italian Style
  (Questi Fantasmi: These Ghosts)
  1967 (1969) Italian/French,
Champion/Corona (MGM) color
(92 mins).
  Prod: Carlo Ponti.
  Dir: Renato Castellani.
  SP: Adriano Baracco, Tonino
Guerra, R. Castellani, & De
Bernardi.
  Art Dir: Piero Poletto.
  Cin: Tonino Delli Colli.
  Edit: Jolande Benevenuti.
  Mus: Luis Enriquez Bakalov.
  Eng Dialog: Ernest Pintoff.
  Cast: Sophia Loren, Vittorio
Gassman, Mario Adorf, Carlo
Giuffre, Francesco Tensi,
Margaret Lee, Marcello Mas-
troianni [ghost].
  com; F-seq (fake ghosts; real
Scottish ghost at end)
  Ref: FF "69 p 14; Vd 22 Jan
'69; FD 24 Jan '69; ItalProds
'67.
  Based on play "Questi Fantasmi"
By Eduardo De Filippo.
  See also: Questi Fantasmi
(1954).

Ghosts of Berkeley Square, The
  1947 British, National 90
mins.
  Dir: Vernon Sewell.
  SP: James Seymour.
  Art Dir: Wilfred Arnold.
  Cin: Ernest Palmer.
  Mus Dir: Hans May.
  Cast: Robert Morley, Felix
Aylmer, Ronald Frankau, Yvonne
Arnaud, Martita Hunt, Ernest
Thesiger, Harry Fine, James
Hayter, Abraham Sofaer, Wilfrid
Hyde-White.
  F-com (ghosts must haunt castle
until it is visited by roy-
alty)
  Ref: MFB Nov '47 p 153; Acker-
man.
  Based on novel "No Nightin-
gales" by S.J. Simon & Caryl
Brahms.

Ghosts of Two Travelers at
Tenamonya
  See: Tenamonya Yurei Dochu
(1967).

Ghosts of Yesterday
  1928 British, British Filmcraft
sil sh series.
  Prod: George J. Banfield.
  Dir: G.J. Banfield & Leslie
Eveleigh.
  Sc: G.J. Banfield, George A.
Cooper, & Anthony L. Ellis.
  hist-F
  Ref: Gifford/BFC 08339-45.

Ghosts on Parade
  See: Yokai Daisenso (1968).

Ghosts on the Loose
  (Ghosts in the Night --Brit.t.)
  1943 Mono 65 mins.
  Prod: Sam Katzman & Jack Dietz.
  Dir: William Beaudine.
  SP: Kenneth Higgins.
  Assoc Prod: Barney Sarecky.
  Set Dir: David Milton.
  Cin: Mack Stengler.

Ghosts on the Loose cont.
  Edit: Carl Pierson.
  Mus: Edward J. Kay.
  Cast: Bela Lugosi, Ava Gardner,
Minerva Urecal, Leo Gorcey,
Huntz Hall, Rick Vallin,
Bobby Jordan, Wheeler Oakman,
Stanley Clements, Jack Mulhall,
Billy Benedict, Frank Moran.
  H-com (spies fake house-haun-
ting to hide counterfeiting)
  Ref: MFB Oct '43 p 112; LC;
HR & Vd 9 June '43; Borst.
  See also: Spooks Run Wild (1941).

Ghost's Story, The
  (novel by B. King)
  See: Earthbound.

Ghost's Sword, The
  1972? Hongkong? HH
color scope.
  Prod: Nan-Hong Kuo.
  Dir: Chang Ping-Han.
  F-seq (mystic martial arts)
  Ref: Collier.

Ghost's Vengeance, A
  1968? Hongkong (In Mandarin).
  F ("world of the super-
natural" --ads)
  Ref: Singapore Straits-Times
5 Oct '68.
  Same film as Ghost's Revenge
in problem list?

Ghost's Warning, The
  1911 Edison sil 1000 ft.
  F (ghost of girl who chose
wrong in love warns modern
girl)
  Ref: MPW 10:494, 725; LC;
Bios 1 Feb '12; EK 15 Nov '11
p3.

Ghosts with Cheese
  See: Fantasmitas con Queso
(1970).

Ghoul, The
  1933 (1934) British, Gaum
85 mins (73 mins).
  Dir: T. Hayes Hunter.
  Adapt: Rupert Downing.
  SP: Roland Pertwee & John
Hastings Turner.
  Art Dir: Alfred Junge.
  Cin: Gunther Krampf.
  Edit: Ian Dalrymple.
  Cast: Boris Karloff, Cedric
Hardwicke, Ernest Thesiger,
Dorothy Hyson, Anthony Bush-
ell, Ralph Richardson.
  bor-F-H (Karloff, as a cata-
leptic Egyptologist, returns
from the grave to reclaim a
sacred stone)
  Ref: Vw 30 Jan '34; MPH 28
Oct '33 p59, 62; FDY '33;
Gore Creatures 19:17.
  Based on the novel by Frank
King & Leonard Hines.
  See also: No Place Like Homi-
cide (1961).

Ghoul in School, The
  See: Werewolf in a Girls'
Dormitory (1961).

Giant Behemoth, The
  (Behemoth, the Sea Monster
--Brit.t.)
  1958 (1959) Diamond (AA)
80 mins.
  Filmed in England.
  Prod: Ted Lloyd.
  Dir: Eugene Lourie & Douglas
Hickok.
  SP: E. Lourie.
  Art Dir: Harry White.
  Make-up: Jimmy Evans.
  Cin: Ken Hodges.
  Edit: Lee Doig.
  SpFX: Jack Rabin, Irving
Block, Louis DeWitt, Willis

cont.   cont.   cont.

Giant Behemoth, The cont.

O'Brien, & Pete Petterson.

Mus: Ted Astley.

Cast: Gene Evans, Andre Morell, Jack MacGowran, Leigh Madison, Henry Vidon.

SF-H (dinosaur revived & made gigantic by radiation attacks London; can kill with its eyes by radiation)
Ref: MFB Dec '59 p 157; LC; FF '59 p 119.

See also: Son of Tor (1964).

Giant Claw, The

(The Mark of the Claw --s.t.)
1957 Clover (Col) 76 mins.
Prod: Sam Katzman.
Dir: Fred F. Sears.
SP: Samuel Newman & Paul Gangelin.
Art Dir: Paul Palmentola.
Cin: Benjamin H. Kline.
Edit: Saul A. Goodkind & Tony Di Marco.
Mus: Mischa Bakaleinikoff.
Cast: Jeff Morrow, Mara Corday, Morris Ankrum, Louis D. Merrill, Edgar Barrier, Robert Shayne, Ruell Shayne, Morgan Jones.
SF-H (interplanetary buzzard attacks New York; bird is protected by force-field)
Ref: MFB Oct '57 p 127; FD 28 June '57; LC; HR 19 June '57.

Giant Devil, The

See: Devil and the Statue, The (1901).

Giant from the Unknown

1958 Screencraft Enterprises Prod (Astor) 77 mins.
Prod: Arthur A. Jacobs.
Dir & Cin: Richard E. Cunha.
SP: Frank Hart Taussig & Ralph Brooke.
Make-up: Jack Pierce.
Edit: Screencraft.
SpFX: Harold Banks.
Mus: Albert Glasser.
Cast: Edward Kemmer, Sally Fraser, Buddy Baer [giant], Morris Ankrum, Bob Steele.
SF-H (giant Spanish conquistador revived from the dead in 20th century by lightning)
Ref: FF '58 p41; FIR March '64 p 151; Borst.

Giant Gila Monster, The

1959 Hollywood Pictures Corp (McLendon Radio Pictures) 74 mins.
Exec Prod: Gordon McLendon.
Prod: Ken Curtis.
Dir: Ray Kellogg.
SP: Jay Sims & R. Kellogg.
Art Dir: Louis Caldwell.
Make-up: Corinne Daniel.
Cin: Wilfred Cline.
Edit: Aaron Stell.
SpFX: Ralph Hammeras & Wee Risser.
Mus: Jack Marshall.
Cast: Don Sullivan, Lisa Simone, Shug Fisher, Jerry Cortwright, Beverly Thurman.
SF-H (monster of title terrorizes New Mexico)
Ref: FF '59 p265; MFB Jan '60 p8; Willis.

Giant Leeches, The

(Attack of the Giant Leeches --s.t.; Attack of the Blood-Leeches --e.t.; Demons of the Swamp --Brit.t.)
1959 Balboa (AIP) 62 mins.
Exec Prod: Roger Corman.
Prod: Gene Corman.
Dir: Bernard L. Kowalski.
SP: Leo Gordon.

cont.

The Ghoul (1933) British

Giant Leeches, The cont.

Art Dir: Dan Haller.
Cin: John M. Nickolaus Jr.
Edit: Tony Magro.
Mus: Alexander Laszlo.
Cast: Ken Clark, Yvette Vickers, Michael Emmet, Bruno Ve Sota, Jan Shepard, Tyler McVey, Gene Roth.
SF-H (man-sized leeches kill people in Florida swamp)
Ref: FF '59 p342; cutting continuity.

Giant of Metropolis, The

(Il Gigante di Metropolis; Metropolis --ad.t.; Il Mistero di Atlantide --s.t?)
1962 (1963) Italian, Centro (Seven Arts) color 92 mins.
Prod: Emimmo Salvi.
Dir: Umberto Scarpelli (R. Nichols?).

cont.

Giant of Metropolis, The cont.

SP: Sabatino Ciuffino, Oreste Palella, Ambrogio Molteni, Gino Stafford, & E. Salvi.
Art Dir: G. Giovannisti.
Cin: Mario Sensi.
Edit: Leo Scuccuglia & Adriana Bellanti.
Mus: Armando Trovajoli.
Cast: Gordon Mitchell, Bella Cortez, Roldano Lupi, Liani Orfei, Furio Meniconi.
SF (in 10,000 BC villainous scientists plan immortality, are destroyed by natural disasters; "magnetic" death ray)
Ref: MFB July '63 p99-100; FF '63 p307; MPH 27 Nov '63; FM 31:74.

Giant of the Lost Tomb

See: Samson vs. the Giant King (1963).

Giant of the Valley of Kings

See: Son of Samson (1960).

Giant Ymir, The

See: Twenty Million Miles to Earth (1957).

Giants of Thessaly, The

(I Giganti Della Tessaglia; Le Géant de Thesalie; Jason and the Golden Fleece --Aust.t.)
1960 Italian/French, Alexandra/ Lyre (Medallion-TV) color 97 mins (86 mins).
Prod: Virgilio De Blasi.
Dir: Riccardo Freda.
SP: Giuseppe Masini, Mario Rossetti, R. Freda, & Ennio De Concini.
Art Dir: Franco Lolli.
Cin: Vaclav Vich & Raffaele Masciocchi.
Edit: Otello Colangeli.
Mus: Carlo Rustichelli.

cont.

Giants of Thessaly, The cont.

Cast: Roland Carey, Ziva Rodann, Massimo Girotti, Alberto Farnese, Luciano Marin, Cathio Caro, Nadine Duca, Moira Orfei.

myth-F (Jason & Orpheus after the Golden Fleece; island witch turns men into animals; marauding monster)

Ref: MFB Oct '63 p 146; Ital Prod 60:180-81.

See also: Jason and the Argonauts (1963); Goldene Ding, Das (1971).

Gibel Sensatsy

(Loss of Sensation)

1935 Soviet.

Dir: A. Andrievski.

SF (robot kills its inventor)

Ref: Musee du Cinema.

Gift, The

(Dárek)

1946 Czech ani.

Dir, Story Idea, SP: Jiří Trnka.

F

Ref: Trnka p261.

Gift

n.d. color ani sh.

Dir: Philip Stapp.

F

Ref: Ani/Cin p 175.

Gift, The

See: Cadeau, Le (1961).

Gift from Santa Claus, A

1909 Edison sil 920 ft.

F

Ref: EK 15 Dec '09 p3-4; LC; MPW 5:900; FI IV-51 p 16-17.

Gift of Oscar, The

See: Cadeau d'Oscar, Le (1965).

Gift of Youth, The

1909 Vit sil 535 ft.

F (spirit of youth makes old woodcutter first young, then restores him to true age)

Ref: FI IV-33 p10, 35 p7; LC.

Gigante di Metropolis, Il

See: Giant of Metropolis, The (1962).

Gigantes Planetarios

(Planetary Giants)

1963 Mexican, America.

Prod: Emilio Gómez.

Dir: Alfredo B. Crevenna.

Cin: Alfredo Uribe.

Cast: Guillermo Murray, Lorena Velazquez, José Galvez, Adriana Roel, Rogelio Guerra, Irma Lozano.

SF (space travel; death ray)

Ref: Gasca p314; FDY '68; Willis p384.

Giganti della Tessaglia, I

See: Giants of Thessaly, The (1960).

Gigantic Marionettes

1914 British, Clarendon sil 370 ft.

F

Ref: Bios 12 Feb '14 p iii.

Gigantis, the Fire Monster

(Gojira no Gyakushyu; Godzilla's Counterattack; Godzilla no Gyakushyu; Counter-Attack of the Monster; Godzilla Raids Again --ad.t.; The Volcano Monster --e.t.)

1955 (1959) Japanese, Toho (WB) 82 mins (78 mins).

Prod: Tomoyuki Tanaka.

Dir: Motoyoshi Odo (Hoda?).

Story: Shigeru Kayama.

cont.

Gigantis, the Fire Monster cont.

SP: Takeo Murata & Sigeaki Hidaka.

Art Dir: Takeo Kita.

Cin: Seiichi Endo.

SpFX Supr: Eiji Tsuburaya.

SpFX: Akira Watanabe, Hiroshi Mukoyama, & Masso Shirota.

Mus: Masaru Sato.

Cast: Hiroshi Koizumi, Yukio Kasama, Setsuko Wakayama, Takashi Shimura, Mayuri Mokusho, Minuro Chiaki, Sonosake Sawamura, Masao Chimizu, Takeo Oikawa, Minosuki Yamada.

SF-H (Godzilla, here called Gigantis, fights another revived dinosaur, Angorus)

Ref: FDY '60; FF '59 p218; Anderson/Richie p263.

Sequel to: Godzilla, King of the Monsters (1954).

See also: Fire Monsters, The (1959); Destroy All Monsters (1968); Godzilla tai Gigan (1971).

Gigue Merveilleuse, La

(The Marvelous Hind Leg)

1909 French sil 130 ft.

Prod: Georges Méliès.

F (dancing boots)

Ref: Sadoul/M; GM Mage p76.

Gilala

See: X from Outer Space, The (1967).

Gildersleeve's Ghost

1943 (1944) RKO 63 mins.

Prod: Herman Schlom.

Dir: Gordon Douglas.

SP: Robert E. Kent.

Art Dir: Albert D'Agostino & Carroll Clark.

Cin: Jack McKenzie.

SpFX: Vernon L. Walker.

Edit: Les Millbrook.

Mus: Paul Sawtell.

Mus Dir: C. Bakaleinikoff.

Cast: Harold Peary, Marian Martin, Richard LeGrand, Amelita Ward, Frank Reicher, Charles Gemora [gorilla].

F-com (invisibility; real ghosts)

Ref: HR 20 June '44; Vw 21 June '44; FDY '45; LC.

Giles Has His Fortune Told

1911 British, Urban sil 343 ft.

Dir: W.R. Booth (?).

F-dream-com ("yokel dreams Devil reduces him in size")

Ref: Gifford/BFC 03130.

Gilgamesh

1972? color ani 4 mins.

Dir: Vincent Collins.

F

Ref: ASIFA 8.

Gill Women, The

See: Voyage to the Planet of Prehistoric Women (1968).

Gimbo ki Beti

(Daughter of Gimbo)

1960 Indian, Rajni Chitra Films 134 mins.

Cast: Naazi, Samar Roy, Majnu.

bor-F (female Tarzan)

Ref: FEFN March '60 p57.

Gina of Chinatown

(story by T. Burke)

See: Dream Street (1921).

Gingerbread Cottage, The

See: Perniková Chaloupka (1951).

Gingerbread House

1951 Czech ani sh.

Dir: Bretislav Pojar.

F

Ref: Ani/Cin p 122-23, 175.

Gingerbread House

See: Whoever Slew Auntie Roo? (1971).

Girdhar Gopal ki Mira

1949 Indian, Shree Bharat Lakshmi Pics 133 mins.

Dir: Prafulla Roy.

Story: Pandit Bhushan.

Cin: V.V. Date.

Edit: Sham Dass.

Mus Dir: Brijlal Varma.

Cast: Ranjit Kumari, Mukhtar, Aruna Das, Kamala Jharia, Sultana.

myth-F

Ref: Indian MPA '53 p8.

Girl and the Devil, The

(Flickan och Djävulen)

1943 (1947) Swedish, Terrafilm (Scandia) 88 mins.

Prod: Lorens Marmstedt.

Dir: Hampe Faustman.

SP: Bertil Malmberg.

Cin: Hilding Bladh.

Cast: Gunn Wållgren, Stig Jarrel [Devil], Sven Miliander, Linnea Hillberg.

F-H (old witch's spirit enters girl; the devil)

Ref: HR & Vd 1 May '47; Sweden I; Scand Film p25-27.

Girl and the Dinosaur

1918 sil ani puppet sh.

SpFX: Willis O'Brien.

SF-com

Ref: CFC 11:33; CineF Winter '71 p9.

Girl and the Gorilla, The

See: Nabonga (1943); Zamba, the Gorilla (1949).

Girl Danced Into Life, The

See: Eletbetancoltatott Lany (1964).

Girl Diver of Spook Mansion

See: Ama no Bakemono Yashiki (1959).

Girl from 5,000 A.D., The

See: Terror from the Year 5000 (1958).

Girl from Frisco

See: Witch of the Dark House (1916).

Girl from Scotland Yard

(End of Adventure --alt.t.)

1937 Par 62 mins.

Prod: Emanuel Cohen.

Dir: Robert Vignola.

Story: Coningsby Dawson.

SP: Doris Anderson & Dore Schary.

Cin: Robert Pittack.

Edit: George McGuire.

Cast: Karen Morley, Eduardo Ciannelli, Robert Baldwin, Katherine Alexander, Milli Monti, Lloyd Crane, Bud Flanagan.

SF-seq (radio death ray)

Ref: LC; Vw 2 June '37.

Based on a character created by Edgar Wallace.

Girl from Sicily, The

See: Witches, The (1965).

Girl in His Pocket

See: Amour de Poche, Un (1957).

Girl in the Kremlin, The

1957 U 71 mins.

Prod: Albert Zugsmith.

Dir: Russell Birdwell.

Story: Harry Rushkin & DeWitt Bodeen.

SP: Gene L. Coon & Robert Hill.

Art Dir: Alexander Golitzen & Eric Orbom.

Edit: Sherman Todd.

Mus Sup: Joseph Gershenson.

Cast: Lex Barker, Zsa Zsa Gabor, Jeffrey Stone, Maurice Manson, William Schallert, Aram Katcher, Natalia Daryll, Michael Fox.

soc-SF (Stalin only thought to have died; changed face completely, later killed in Greece)

Ref: MFB Nov '57 p 139; FD 30 April '57.

Girl in the Moon

See: Frau im Mond, Die (1929).

Girl Next Door, The

1952 (1953) 20th Fox color ani seq 92 mins.

Prod: Robert Bassler.

Dir: Richard Sale.

SP: Isobel Lennart.

Art Dir: Lyle Wheeler.

Cin: Leon Shamroy.

Ani: UPA.

SpFX: Ray Kellogg.

Edit: Robert Simpson.

Cast: June Haver, Dan Dailey, Dennis Day, Billy Gray, Cara Williams, Natalie Schaefer.

F-dream

Ref: MFB Dec '53 p 177; Vd 11 May '53.

Girl of the Water, The

See: Fille de l'Eau, La (1924).

Girl of Tin, The

See: Ragazza de Latta, La (1970).

Girl on the Broomstick, The

(Divka na Kosteti)

1971? Czech.

Dir: Vaclav Vorlicek.

SP: Milos Macourek, V. Vorlicek, & Hermina Frankova.

F-com (parody about witches & witchcraft)

Ref: Vw 2 Aug '72; MTVM 26:12:10.

Girl Scouts vs. the Cookie Creature

1971 Girl Scout Troop 370 sil 8mm color 10 mins.

Advisors: Walt & Eve Lee.

Cast: Susan Rogers, Teri Cousin, Robin Boyarsky, Cindy Fowler, Cindy Lee, Sravanthi Reddy, Karen Bryson, Lori Gotlieb, Cindy Stein, Stevie Lee.

F-com (girl steals Girl Scout cookies, eats too many, turns into monster)

Ref: Program.

Girl Under the Sheet, The

See: Ragazza Sotto il Lenzulo, La (1960).

Girl Who Dared, The

1944 Rep 56 mins.

Assoc Prod: Rudy Abel.

Dir: Howard Bretherton.

SP: John K. Butler.

Art Dir: Russell Kimball.

Cin: Bud Thackery.

Edit: Arthur Roberts.

Mus Dir: Morton Scott.

Cast: Lorna Gray, Kirk Alyn, Veda Ann Borg, Grant Withers, Roy Barcroft, John Hamilton, Willie Best.

H (murders; ghost hunt; secret panels)

cont.

Girl Who Dared, The cont.

Ref: MPH 11 Nov '44; FD 5 Dec '44; Vw 25 Oct. '44.

Based on novel "Blood on Her Shoe" by Medora Field.

Girl Who Stole the Eiffel Tower, The

See: Paris When It Sizzles (1964).

Girls, The

1972 Swedish, Goran Lindgren Prods 100 mins.

Dir: Mai Zetterling.

SP: M. Zetterling & David Hughes.

Cast: Bibi Andersson, Harriet Andersson, Gunnel Lindblom, Gunnar Björnstrand.

F-seqs

Ref: BO 14 Aug '72 Bookinguide.

Girls of Spider Island

See: It's Hot in Paradise (1959).

Girls on the Moon

See: Nature Girls on the Moon (1960).

Girly

(Mumsy, Nanny, Sonny and Girly --Brit.t.)

1969 (1970) British, Brigitte (Cinerama) color 102 mins.

Prod: Ronald J. Kahn.

Dir: Freddie Francis.

SP: Brian Comport.

Art Dir: Maggie Pinhorn.

Cin: David Muir.

Edit: Tristam Cones.

Mus: Bernard Ebbinghouse.

Cast: Michael Bryant, Ursula Howells, Patricia Heywood, Howard Trevor, Vanessa Howard, Michael Ripper.

psy-H (Grand Guignol; head boiled on stove, etc.)

Ref: MFB '70 p57; LAT 24 Sept. '70.

Based on play "Happy Family" by Maisie Mosco.

Giro del Mondo degli Innamorati, Il

(Two Lovers Around the World)

1973? Italian, Italnoleggio Cinemat. color ani feature.

Made by: Raymond Peynet.

sex-F

Ref: Vw 9 May '73 p49 ad.

Giudizio Universale, Il

(The Last Judgement)

1961 French/Italian, De Laurentiis/ Standard.

Prod: Dino De Laurentiis.

Dir: Vittorio de Sica.

SP: Cesare Zavattini.

Cin: Gabor Pogany.

Mus: Alessandro Cicognini.

Cast: Vittorio Gassman, Renato Rascel, Elli Davis, Fernandel, Akim Tamiroff, Franco Franchi, Ciccio Ingrassia, George Rivière, Paolo Stoppa, Anouk Aimée, Jaime de Mora, Melina Mercouri, Nino Manfredi, Vittorio de Sica, Silvana Mangano, Jack Palance, Mike Bongiorno, Eleonora Brown, Elisa Cegani, Lino Ventura, Alberto Sordi, Ernest Borgnine, Jimmy Durante, Domenico Modugno, Marisa Merlini.

F-com (voice is heard coming from Heaven announcing Judgment Day)

Ref: Gasca p268-69; MTVM Aug '61 p46, Sept '61 p9; Acad.

Giuletta Degli Spiriti

See: Juliet of the Spirits (1964).

Giuseppe Venduto dai Fratelli

(Joseph Sold by His Brothers; Sold Into Egypt --Brit.t.)

1960 Italian, Donati & Carpentieri color scope 104 mins.

Prod: Ermanno Donati & Luigi Carpentieri.

Dir: Luciano Ricci & Irving Rapper.

SP: Guglielmo Santangelo, Ennio De Concini, & Oreste Biancoli.

Art Dir: Oscar D'Amico.

Cin: Riccardo Pallottini.

Edit: Mario Serandrei.

Mus: Mario Nascimbene.

Cast: Geoffrey Horne, Robert Morley, Belinda Lee, Vira Silenti, Mario Girotti, Finlay Currie, Carlo Giustini, Robert Reitty, Julian Brooks, Helmut Schneider.

bor-F (Joseph interprets Pharaoh's dream to mean 7 years of plenty followed by 7 years of famine, & it comes to pass)

Ref: MFB May '64 p73; Ital Prods 60:168-69.

Based on a Biblical story.

Give a Dog a Bone

1966 British, Westminster Prods & Moral Re-Armament Prods color 77 mins.

Prod & Dir: Henry Cass.

Art Dir: W. Cameron Johnson.

Cin: S.D. Onions.

Edit: John S. Smith.

Choreog: Bridget Espinosa.

Mus: George Fraser.

Mus Dir: Peter Knight.

Cast: Ronnie Stevens, Ivor Danvers, Richard Warner, Bryan Coleman, Robert Davies, Len Maley, Patricia Callaghan.

alleg-mus-F-com (man from space helps boy & dog defeat King of Rats)

Ref: MFB Jan '72 p7.

Filmed stage play by Peter Howard.

Give Us a Rest

See: Emak Bakia (1926).

Give Us the Moon

1944 British, Gainsborough 95 mins.

Dir & SP: Val Guest.

Cin: Phil Grindrod.

Cast: Margaret Lockwood, Vic Oliver, Peter Graves, Jean Simmons, Roland Culver, Frank Cellier, George Relph, Max Bacon, Irene Handl.

bor-soc-SF (made before end of WW II, story is set 3 years after the war's end)

Ref: MFB '44 p87; FIR Feb '72 p81; Gifford/SF p 142.

Based on novel "The Elephant Is White" by Caryl Brahms & S.J. Simon.

Glace à Trois Faces, La

(The Glass with Three Faces; The Three-Way Mirror; Mirror with Three Faces)

1927 French sil.

Made by: Jean Epstein.

exp-F ("dynamic distortions of reality")

Ref: Scognamillo.

Glackens Cartoons

1916 Bray (Par) 1 reel sil ani series.

Dir: W.L. Glackens.

F-com

Ref: Ani Chart.

Gladiator, The

1938 (Col) 70 mins.

Prod: David L. Loew.

Dir: Edward Sedgwick.

cont.

Gladiator, The cont.

Adapt: James Mulhauser & Earle Snell.

SP: Charlie Melson & Arthur Sheekman.

Addtl Dialog: George Marion Jr.

Art Dir: Albert D'Agostino.

Cin: George Schneiderman.

Edit: Robert Crandall.

Mus Dir: Victor Young.

Cast: Joe E. Brown, June Travis, Dickie Moore, Lucien Littlefield, Robert Kent, Man Mountain Dean.

SF-com (serum makes Brown super-strong)

Ref: HR 4 Aug '38; MPH 13 Aug '38 p59, 62.

Based on novel "Gladiator" by Philip Wylie.

Gladiatorena

See: Gladiators, The (1969).

Gladiators, The

(Gladiatorena; The Peace Game --ad.t.)

1969 (1971) Swedish, Sandrews (New Line) color 105 mins.

Prod: Göran Lindgren.

Dir: Peter Watkins.

SP: Nicholas Gosling & P. Watkins.

Art Dir: William Brodie.

Cin: Peter Suschitsky.

SpFX: Stig Lindberg.

Edit: Lars Hagstrom.

Mus: Mahler & Claes af Geijerstam.

Cast: Arthur Pentelow, Frederick Danner, Kenneth Lo, Björn Franzén, Jeremy Child, Erich Stering.

SF (in future world, international teams are chosen to decide global disputes, rather than warfare)

Ref: MFB April '70 p73; Vw 4 June '69; FF '71 p615-17.

Glamis Castle

(Haunted Castles series)

1926 British sil sh.

Dir: Maurice Elvey.

F-H

Ref: Brit Cin; V 24 Feb '26.

Glass-Bottom Boat, The

1966 Arwin-Reame (MGM) color scope 110 mins.

Prod: Martin Melcher & Everett Freeman.

Dir: Frank Tashlin.

Asst Dir: Al Jennings.

SP: E. Freeman.

Art Dir: George W. Davis & Edward Carfagno.

Cin: Leon Shamroy.

SpFX: J. McMillan Johnson & Carroll L. Sheppird.

Edit: John McSweeney.

Mus: De Vol.

Cast: Doris Day, Rod Taylor, Arthur Godfrey, John McGiver, Paul Lynde, Edward Andrews, Eric Fleming, Dom De Luise, George Tobias, Alice Pearce, Elizabeth Fraser, Robert Vaughn.

SF-com-seq (robot vacuum cleaner; anti-gravity room)

Ref: FF '66 p 158; Time 17 June '66; HR & Vd 20 April '66; MFB July '66 p 108.

Glass of Goat's Milk, A

1909 British, Clarendon sil 377 ft.

F-com (man grows horns after drinking goat's milk)

Ref: BFI cat p87.

Glass Slipper, The

1955 MGM color 94 mins.

Prod: Edwin H. Knopf.

Dir: Charles Walters.

cont.

Glass Slipper, The cont.

SP: Helen Deutsch.

Art Dir: Cedric Gibbons & Daniel B. Cathcart.

Cin: Arthur E. Arling.

Edit: Ferris Webster.

Cast: Leslie Caron, Michael Wilding, Elsa Lanchester, Amanda Blake, Keenan Wynn, Estelle Winwood.

mus-F (the Cinderella story)

Ref: Vd & HR 14 Feb '55; MFB Sept '55 p 136.

Based on the musical play by Herbert & Eleanor Farjeon from the fairy tale collected by the brothers Grimm & Charles Perrault.

See also: Cinderella.

Glass Slipper, The

See: Mighty Mouse in the Glass Slipper (1951).

Glass Sphinx, The

(La Esfinge de Cristal; Una Sfinga Tutta d'Oro; An All-Gold Sphinx)

1967 Spanish/Italian (AIP) color scope 91 mins.

Prod: Fulvio Lucisano.

Dir: Luigi Scattini.

SP: Adalberto Albertino, Camas Gil, & José A. Cascales.

English Dialog: Louis M. Heyward & Adriano Bolzoni.

Art Dir: Luis Arguello.

Cin: Felix Martinez Miran.

Mus (original film): Roberto Pregadio.

Mus (Eng lang version): Les Baxter.

Cast: Robert Taylor, Anita Ekberg, Gianna Serra, Giacomo Rossi-Stuart (Jack Stuart), Angel Del Pozo, José Truchado.

bor-F (longevity serum sought)

Ref: FF '68 p539; SpCin '69 p 176-77; Ital Prod 67:70-71.

Glass Tale, The

1967 Czech ani puppet sh.

Dir: Vaclav Bedrich.

F (bits of glass tell the story of a boy & a dragon)

Ref: MTVM June '67 p 17.

Glass with Three Faces, The

See: Glace à Trois Faces, La (1927).

Glen and Randa

1971 UMC color 94 mins.

Exec Prod: Sidney Glazier.

Dir: Jim McBride.

SP: Lorenzo Mans, Rudolph Wurlitzer, & J. McBride.

Art Dir: Gary Weist.

Cin: Alan Raymond.

Edit: Mike Levine & Jack Baran.

Cast: Steven Curry, Shelley Plimpton, Woodrow Chambliss, Garry Goodrow, Roy Fox, Robert Holmer.

SF (2 youngsters search for imagined city of Metropolis in post WW III Idaho)

Ref: FF '71 p577-78; Newsweek 7 Dec '70; Vw 2 June '71.

Glen or Glenda?

(I Changed My Sex; Transvestite; I Led Two Lives --all alt.ts.)

1952 (1953) Weiss.

Prod: George G. Weiss.

Dir & SP: Edward D. Wood Jr.

Cast: Bela Lugosi, Lyle Talbot, Dolores Fuller, Daniel Davis, Charles Crofts, Conrad Brooks.

bor-F (at climax, literal sex change by magic)

Ref: Ackerman; Bizarre 24-25 p73.

Glens Falls Sequence

1946 sil 16mm color 10 mins.

Made by: Douglas Crockwell.

exp-abs-F

Ref: USA Exp List; C-16 p 14; T/F p 186.

Glimmering

n.d. French · 16mm 36 mins.

Made by: Pierre Tevenard.

exp-psy-F

Ref: C-16 p 14.

Glimpse of Bygone Days, A

n.d. German sil sh.

F

Ref: FM 19:36, 63:28.

Glittering Sword, The

1929 British, Altrincham School sil 1800 ft.

Dir & Sc: Ronald Gow.

Cast: T. Hampson, L. Galloway, H. Mitchell [Death], A. Gregory [Devil].

alleg-F

Ref: Gifford/BFC 08735.

Gloomy

See: Gris (1969).

Glooskap

1972 Holt, Rinehart & Winston color ani? 12 mins.

F (land of giant animals)

Ref: Previews Dec '72.

Based on Algonquin Indian legend.

Gloria Mundi

1969 Hungarian color ani 1.5 mins.

Dir: György Kovásznai.

F (angels sing while sitting on a mushroom cloud)

Ref: Film Parade '70 p 6.

Glorious Days, The

(by R. Nesbitt)

See: Let's Make Up (1955).

Glorious Times in the Spessart

See: Herrliche Zeiten im Spessart (1967).

Gloves of Ptamas, The

1914 British, Martin sil 568 ft.

Dir: Dave Aylott.

F ("tramp dons Egyptian gloves which cause objects to disappear")

Ref: Gifford/BFC 04680.

Glory

1959 Czech color ani 10 mins.

Dir: Bretislav Pojar.

F

Ref: Ani/Cin p 122; Czech films flyer.

Glory of Love, The

(story by Pan)

See: While Paris Sleeps (1920).

Gloves

1914 British, Martin sil 507 ft.

F (magic gloves cause things to vanish)

Ref: BFI cat p98.

Glowing Brasier, The

See: Brasier Ardent, Le (1922).

Gluma Nova cu Fier Vechi

(A New Joke with Old Iron)

1965 Rumanian, Animafilm Studio color ani puppet 6 mins.

Dir & Story: Bob Calinescu.

F-com (3 pairs of tongs start out from scrapheap)

Ref: Collier.

Glutton's Nightmare, The

1901 British, Hepworth sil.

Prod: Cecil M. Hepworth.

F-H-dream

Ref: Sadoul p389; Hist/Brit p82; Brit Cin p57.

Gnome-Mobile, The

1967 WD (BV) color 90 mins.

Prod: Walt Disney & James Algar.

Dir: Robert Stevenson.

SP: Ellis Kadison.

Art Dir: Carroll Clark & William H. Tuntke.

Make-up: Pat McNalley.

Cin: Edward Colman.

SpFX: Eustace Lycett & Robert A. Mattey.

Edit: Norman Palmer.

Mus: Buddy Baker.

Cast: Walter Brennan, Tom Lowell, Matthew Garber, Karin Dotrice, Ed Wynn, Richard Deacon, Sean McClory, Ellen Corby, Jerome Cowan.

F-mus-com (children encounter gnomes in California redwoods)

Ref: FF '67 p216-17; MFB '67 p 124; Vw 10 Nov '65; FD 5 June '67.

Based on the novel by Upton Sinclair.

Gnomes

See: Gartenzwerge, Die (1962).

Gnomes in Spring

1959 Polish ani sh.

Dir: Witold Giersz.

F

Ref: Ani/Cin p 170.

Gnosis

1972 Crocus Prods stop-action 65 mins.

F

Ref: IAFF '72.

Go Among the Birds

See: Go Chez les Oiseaux (1939).

Go and Get It

1920 Marshall Neilan Prods (FN) sil 6300 ft.

Prod: Marshall Neilan.

Dir: M. Neilan & Henry R. Symonds.

Sc: Marion Fairfax.

Art Dir: Ben Carré.

Cin: David Kesson.

Cast: Pat O'Malley, Wesley Barry, Agnes Ayres, J. Barney Sherry, Charles Hill Mailes, Noah Beery, Bull Montana [gorilla], Walter Long.

SF-H (dead convict's brain put in gorilla's body)

Ref: MPN 22:560, 728-29 ad, 1013, 1090-91; LC.

Go Chez les Oiseaux

(Go [?] Among the Birds)

1939 French ani sh.

Dir: Paul Grimault.

F

Ref: Ani/Cin p 170.

Go Down Death

1944 Harlemwood.

Exec Prod: Alfred N. Sack.

Prod & Dir: Spencer Williams.

Story Idea: Jean Ruddy.

SP: Sam Elljay.

Cin: H.W. Kier.

Cast: Myra D. Hemmings, Samuel H. James, Eddy L. Houston, Spencer Williams, Amos Droughan.

psy-F-seq (man imagines he's in Hell with devils, tortures, etc.; all-Negro cast)

Ref: Norman Kagan.

Based on a poem by James Weldon Johnson.

Go Fly a Kit

1957 WB color ani 7 mins.

Dir: Chuck Jones.

F-com (because it is reared by an eagle, a cat can fly)

Ref: LC; David Rider.

Go to Mars

See: Abbott and Costello Go to Mars (1953).

Go to Thy Deathbed

(novel by S. Forbes)

See: Reflection of Fear, A (1971).

Goal Rush, The

1946 Par color ani sh.

F-com

Ref: LC.

See: Noveltoon (1945...).

Goat and the Lion, The

1957 Czech ani sh.

Dir: Vladimir Lehky.

F

Ref: Ani/Cin p 127, 173.

Goblet of Life and Death, The

1912 Russian, Pathé sil.

H

Ref: Kino p60.

Goccia d'Acqua, La

(story by Chekhov)

See: Black Sabbath (1963).

God Bala

See: Dev Bala (1938).

God Bless the Bomb

See: Wild in the Sky (1971).

God Game, The

See: Magus, The (1968).

God Is Love

1913 Pathé sil sh?

rel-F (man is visited by "the hand")

Ref: MPW 16:379.

Based on a story by Leo Tolstoi.

God Lord Krishna

See: Bhagwan Shri Krishna (1950).

God, Man and Devil

1949 (1950) Aaron Prods (in Yiddish) 108 mins.

Dir: Joseph Zeiden.

Cast: Michal Michalesko, Berta Gersten, Gustav Berger [devil].

rel-F

Ref: Vw 28 Jan '50.

Based on the play by Jacob Gordin.

God of Tomorrow, The

1913 Majestic sil sh?

F (statue induces girl to return to her lover; visions)

Ref: MPW 18:1545.

God Selected His Travelers

See: Hora Incognita, La (1964).

God Snake, The

See: Dio Serpente, Il (1970).

Goddess, The

1915 Vit sil serial 15 parts 30 reels.

Dir: Ralph W. Ince.

Sc: Gouverneur Morris & Charles W. Goddard.

Cast: Anita Stewart, Earle Williams, Paul Scardon, William Dangman, Ned Finley.

bor-F (girl raised in isolated innocence; hypnotism)

Ref: MPW 24:1089, 26:314; LC; FIR March '68 p 149, 158; CNW p32, 163.

Goddess, The

See: Devi (1960).

Goddess Durga

See: Chamundeswari (1937).

Goddess of Luck

(Nasibani Devi)

1927 Indian, Victoria Fatma sil.

myth-F

Ref: IndCin YB.

Goddess of the Home

See: Griha Lakshmi (1959).

Goddess of the Sea

1909 French, Le Lion sil 860 ft.

F (goddess from dominion of Father Neptune; Cupid; shepherd drowns while trying to escape from goddess)

Ref: MPW 5:737, 800; Bios 4 Nov '09.

Godfather Death

See: Gevatter Tod (1921).

Gods and the Dead, The

See: Os Deuses e os Mortos (1970).

Gods Hate Kansas, The

(novel by J. Millard)

See: They Came from Beyond Space (1967).

God's Witness

1915 Than-Mutual sil 3000 ft.

Cast: Florence La Badie, Morris Foster, Harris Gordon.

F-seq (lightning prints death scene on windowpane)

Ref: MPN 29 May '15.

Same film as Monsieur Nickola Duprée (1915)?

Godspell

1973 Lansbury-Duncan-Behruh (Col) color 103 mins.

Prod: Edgar Lansbury.

Dir: David Greene.

SP: D. Greene & John-Michael Tebelak.

Prod Design: Brian Eatwell.

Art Dir: Ben Kasazkow.

Cin: Richard G. Heimann.

Edit: Alan Helm.

Mus & Lyrics: Stephen Schwartz.

Cast: Victor Garber, David Haskell, Jerry Sroka, Lynne Thigpen, Katie Hanley, Robin Lamont.

rel-F-mus (modern Christ appears & disappears; evil computerized monster)

Ref: Vw 28 March '73; QPH 6 Jan '73 p8, 31 March '73 p6; Time 9 April '73; BO 2 April '73 p4578.

Based on the rock musical play by John-Michael Tebelak & Stephen Schwartz from the book of Matthew.

See also: Gospel According to St. Matthew, The (1964); King of Kings.

Godzilla Against Mothra

See: Godzilla vs. the Thing (1964).

Godzilla, King of the Monsters

(Gojira)

1954 (1956) Japanese, Toho (Embassy) 98 mins (81 mins).

Prod: Tomoyuki Tanaka.

Dir: Inoshiro Honda & (Eng lang scenes) Terry Morse.

Story: Shigeru Kayama.

SP: Takeo Murata & I. Honda.

Art Dir: Satoshi Chuko.

Cin: Masao Tamai & (Eng lang scenes) Guy Roe.

SpFX: Eiji Tsuburaya, Akira Watanabe, Hiroshi Mukouyama, cont.

Godzilla, King of the Monsters cont.

& Kuichiro Kishida.

Edit: T. Morse.

Mus: Akira Ifukube.

Cast: Raymond Burr , Akira Takarada, Akihiko Hirala, Takashi Shimura, Momoko Kochi.

SF-H (nuclear radiation in Pacific revives 400 ft dinosaur, gives it radioactive breath; it attacks Tokyo, finally dissolved in sea by "oxygen-destroyer" invention)

Ref: FDY '57; V 25 April '56; MFB Feb '57 p 15; Toho.

Sequels: Gigantis, the Fire Monster (1955); King Kong vs. Godzilla (1962); Godzilla vs. the Thing (1964); Ghidrah, the Three-Headed Monster (1965); Monster Zero (1965); Godzilla vs. the Sea Monster (1966); Son of Godzilla (1968); Destroy All Monsters (1968); Godzilla's Revenge (1969); Godzilla vs. the Smog Monster (1971); Godzilla tai Giagan (1971); Godzilla vs. Megalon (1973).

See also: Fire Monsters, The (1959); Son of Godzilla (1963); Son of Tor (1964); Bambi Meets Godzilla (1969).

Godzilla no Musuko

See: Son of Godzilla (1968).

Godzilla no Gyakushu

See: Gigantis, the Fire Monster (1955).

Godzilla Radon Kinggidorah

See: Monster Zero (1965).

Godzilla Raids Again

See: Gigantis, the Fire Monster (1955).

Godzilla tai Giagan

(Godzilla vs. Gigan)

1971 Japanese, Toho color scope.

Dir: Jun Fukuda.

Cast: Hiroshi Ishikawa, Tomoko Umeda.

SF (new outer-space monster Giagan with saw in his stomach & Ghidrah gang up on Godzilla and Angorus; alien monsters controlled by giant alien intelligent cockroaches)

Ref: UniJ 55 15:1:24; Willis.

Sequel to: Godzilla, King of the Monsters (1954).

See also: Gigantis, the Fire Monster (1955); Ghidrah, the Three-Headed Monster (1965).

Godzilla vs Gigan

See: Godzilla tai Giagan (1971).

Godzilla vs. Hedorah

See: Godzilla vs. the Smog Monster (1971).

Godzilla vs. Megalon

1973 Japanese, Toho color scope 82 mins.

Exec Prod: Tomoyuki Tanaka.

Dir & SP: Jun Fukuda.

Story: Shinichi Sekigawa.

Cin: Yuzuru Aizawa.

Cast: Katshuhiko Sasaki, Hiroyuki Kawase, Yutaka Hayashi, Kotaro Tomita.

SF (Godzilla fights two new monsters on alien planet, & giant flying robot)

Ref: MTVM 27:6:1-A ad.

Sequel to: Godzilla, King of the Monsters (1954).

Godzilla vs the Sea Monster

(Nankai no Dai Ketto: Big Duel in the North Sea; Ebirah, Horror of the Deep --Brit.t.; Frankenstein und die Ungeheuer aus dem Meer --German t.)

1966 (1969) Japanese, Toho (Continental) color scope 87 mins.

Prod: Tomoyuki Tanaka.

cont.

NEITHER BEAST NOR MAN
WHAT?

Go and Get It (1920)

Godzilla vs. the Sea Monster cont.

Dir: Jun Fukuda.

SP: Shinichi Sekizawa.

Art Dir: Takeo Kita.

Cin: Kazuo Yamada.

SpFX: Eiji Tsuburaya.

Mus: Masaru Sato.

Cast: Akira Takarada, Toru Watanabe, Hideo Sunazuka, Kumi Mizuno, Jun Tazaki.

SF (Godzilla & Mothra battle evil giant shrimp)

Ref: MFB '69 p 175; UniJ 36 p 18-19; F&F Oct '69 p56.

Sequel to: Godzilla, King of the Monsters (1954); Mothra (1961).

See also: Godzilla's Revenge (1969).

Godzilla vs. the Smog Monster

(Gojira tai Hedora: Godzilla vs. Hedorah)

Godzilla vs. the Smog Monster cont.

1971 (1972) Japanese, Toho (AIP) color scope? 87 mins.

Exec Prod: Tomoyuki Tanaka.

Dir: Yoshimitsu Banno.

SP: Kaoru Mabuchi & Y. Banno.

Art Dir: Yasuyuki Inoue.

Cin: Yôichi Manoda.

SpFX: Shokei Nakano.

Mus: Riichirô Manabe.

Cast: Akira Yamauchi, Toshie Kimura, Hiroyuki Kawase, Keiko Mari.

SF (Godzilla battles monster created from pollution)

Ref: UniJ 52-53 p 12; BO 24 Jan '72 pW-3, 28 Feb '72 Booking-guide.

Sequel to: Godzilla, King of the Monsters (1954).

Godzilla vs. the Thing

(Godzilla tai Mothra: Godzilla Against Mothra; Mosura tai Gojira: Mothra vs. Godzilla)

1964 Japanese, Toho (AIP) color scope? 94 mins (87 mins).

Prod: Tomoyuki Tanaka.

Dir: Inoshiro Honda.

SP: Shinichi Sekizawa.

Art Dir: Takeo Kita.

Cin: Hajime Koizumi.

SpFX: Eiji Tsuburaya, Sadamasa Arikawa, Mototaka Tomioka, & Akira Watanabe.

Edit: Ryohei Fujii.

Mus: Akira Ifkube.

Cast: Akira Takarada, Yuriko Hoshi, Hiroshi Koisumi, Emi Ito, Yumi Ito, Yu Fujiki.

SF (Godzilla kills Mothra, but her giant caterpillar offspring wrap Godzilla in silk & dump him in sea)

cont.

Godzilla vs. the Thing cont.

Ref: MFB Nov '65 p 167; FD 21 Sept '64; Pardi.

Sequel to: Godzilla, King of the Monsters (1954); Mothra (1961).

Godzilla's Counterattack

See: Giantis, the Fire Monster (1955).

Godzilla's Revenge

(Oru Kaiju Daishingeki)

1969 (1971) Japanese, Toho (UPA) color scope 92 mins (70 mins).

Prod: Tomoyuki Tanaka.

Dir: Inoshiro Honda.

SP: Shinichi Sekizawa.

Art Dir: Takeo Kita.

Cin: Mototaka Tomioka.

SpFX: Eiji Tsuburaya.

Edit: Masahira Himi.

Mus: Kunio Miyauchi.

Cast: Kenji Sahara, Tomonori Yazaki, Machiko Naka, Sachio Sakai, Chotaro Togin, Yoshibumi Tujima.

F (child daydreams adventures on Monster Island, with Godzilla's son, who talks to him; also Godzilla, new monster, and other monsters)

Ref: UniJ 48 13:2; Borst.

Sequel to: Godzilla, King of the Monsters (1954).

Includes extensive stock footage from Godzilla vs the Sea Monster (1966), and Son of Godzilla (1968).

Godzira no Musuko

See: Son of Godzilla (1968).

Goe Tam

(A Fantastic Ghost Story -- ad.t?)

1968 S. Korean, Yun Bang Films color scope 90 mins.

Dir: Choe Joemyong.

SP: Hahn Youlim & Kim Kangyoon.

Cin: Chung Woonkyo.

Cast: Nam Chungim, Moon Hee, Nam Kungwon, Nam Jin.

F-H (ghosts; horrible dreams; possibly omnibus film)

Ref: Korea Cinema '68.

Gog

1954 Ivan Tors Prods (UA) color 3D 85 mins.

Prod & Story: Ivan Tors.

Dir & Edit: Herbert L. Strock.

SP: Tom Taggart.

Art Dir: William Ferrari.

Cin: Lathrop B. Worth.

SpFX: Harry Redmond Jr.

Mus: Harry Sukman.

Cast: Richard Egan, Constance Dowling, Herbert Marshall, John Wengraf, Philip Van Zandt, Valerie Vernon, William Schallert.

SF (super-computer taken over by spies, uses Gog & Magog, the two non-humanoid robots it controls, for murder)

Ref: MFB Nov '54 p 162; FIR '54 p362; HR & Vd 7 June '54.

Gogola

1965? Indian, Indradhanush.

Dir: Balwant Dave.

Cast: Azad, Tabassum.

SF (sea monster attacks Bombay)

Ref: MTVM Dec '64 p44, June '65 p29.

Going, Going, Gosh!

1952 WB color ani 7 mins.

Dir: Chuck Jones.

F-com

Ref: LC.

See also: Road Runner & Coyote (1948-).

Going to Bed Under Difficulties

(Le Déshabillage Impossible)

1900 French sil 130 ft.

Prod: Georges Méliès.

F (reverse action)

Ref: Sadoul/M; GM Mage.

Gojira

See: Godzilla, King of the Monsters (1954).

Gojira no Gyakushyu

See: Gigantis the Fire Monster (1955).

Gojira no Musuko

See: Son of Godzilla (1968).

Gojira tai Hedora

See: Godzilla vs. the Smog Monster (1971).

Goké -- Body Snatcher from Hell

See: Kyuketsuki Gokemidoro (1968).

Gokul

(Shepherd)

1947 Indian, Prabhat.

Dir: Vasant Painter.

Story: Shivram Washikar.

SP: Balgovind Shrvastava & Joshi.

Art Dir: S.G. Joshi.

Cin: G. Kale.

Mus: Sudhir Phadke.

Cast: Anant Marathe, Kamla Kotnis, Sapru, Chandrakant, Butt Kashar.

myth-F

Ref: Filmindia Feb '47 p41.

Gokul Cha Raja

(The Shepherd King/Krishna)

1950 Indian, Maharashtra Chitravani 122 mins.

Dir: Bal Gajbar.

Story & Dialog: P.L. Deshpande.

Art Dir: Pandurang Haval.

Cin: I. Bargin.

Edit: Dinkar Jagtap.

Mus Dir: S. Purshottam.

Cast: Dwarkanath, Ratnamala, Chandrakant, Gauri, Hanmath, Angre.

myth-F

Ref: Indian MPA '53 p82.

Gold

1934 German, UFA 120 mins.

Dir: Karl Hartl.

SP: Rolf E. Vanloo.

Sets: Otto Hunte.

Cin: Gunther Rittau, Otto Baecker, & Werner Bohne.

Mus: Hans-Otto Borgmann.

Cast: Hans Albers, Lien Deyers, Michael Bohnen, Brigitte Helm, Ernst Karchow.

Simultaneously filmed in French-language version as L'Or.

Dir: Serge de Poligny.

Cast: Pierre Blanchar, Brigitte Helm, Line Noro, Jacques Dumesnil, Roger Karl.

SF (giant electrical machines used to make artificial gold)

Ref: FD 23 Oct '34; FIR March '65 p 155-56, 166; Laclos p 156.

Gold and Lead

See: Or et le Plomb, L' (1966).

Gold Bug, The

(short story by E.A. Poe)

See: Golden Beetle, The (1911); Raven, The (1912?); Manfish (1956).

Gold Diggers of '49

1935 (1936) Vitaphone (WB) ani 1 reel.

Ani: Chuck (Charles) Jones & Robert Clampett.

F-com

Ref: LC.

Gold Rose, The

See: Rose d'Or, La (1910).

Gold Rush, The

1925 Charles Chaplin Prods (UA) sil 8555 ft.

Prod & Dir: Charles Chaplin.

Cin: Roland H. Totheroh.

Tech Dir: Charles D. Hall.

Cast: Charlie Chaplin, Mack Swain, Georgia Hale, Betty Morissey, Tom Murray, Malcolm Waite, Henry Bergman.

com; psy-F-seq (because they are lost and starving, Mack Swain sees Charlie as a giant chicken)

Ref: BFI cat p259; AFI F2.2162 p 302.

Gold Spider, The

1909 (1910) French, Pathé sil 643 ft.

F (spider spins webs of gold)

Ref: MPW 6:889; Bios 18 Nov '09.

Golden Antelope, The

1954 Soviet color ani sh.

Dir: L. Atamanov.

Story: N. Abramov.

Mus: V. Yourovsky.

F

Ref: MMF 3:48; Ani/Cin p 148, 166.

Based on an Indian fairy tale.

Golden Apples

1952 Czech color ani sh.

Dir: Eduard Hofman.

F

Ref: Ani/Cin p 171.

Golden Arrow, The

(La Freccia d'Oro)

1962 (1964) Italian, Titanus (MGM) color scope 91 mins.

Dir: Antonio Margheriti.

Story & SP: Bruno Vailati, Augusto Frassinetti, Filippo Sanjust, Giorgio Prosperi, & Giorgio Alorio.

Art Dir: Flavio Mogherini.

Cin: Gabor Pogany.

SpFX: Fernando Mazza.

Edit: Mario Serandrei.

Mus: Mario Nascimbene.

Cast: Tab Hunter, Rossana Podesta, Umberto Melnati, Giustino Durano, Mario Feliciani, José Jaspe, Giampaolo Rosmino.

F (monster; magic arrow; flying carpet; genii)

Ref: MFB Aug '65 p 123; Scognamillo; FD 28 April '64.

Golden Axe, The

1952 World TV Corp (Encyclopedia Britannica) 16mm 8 min.

Dir: William Wilder.

F (dwarf rewards honest woodsman)

Ref: Collier; LC.

Based on the tale by Aesop.

Golden Bat

See: Ogon Batto (1966).

Golden Beetle, The

1907 French, Pathé Frères sil 164 ft.

F (winged golden maiden)

Ref: BFI cat p 18.

Golden Beetle, The

(Le Scarabée d'Or)

1911 (1914) Italian, Cines (Kleine-General) sil 4 reels.

Dir: Henri Desfontaines.

bor-F-psy-H (dual personality; murder of best friend)

Ref: MPW 22:458-59; LC; DdC.

Based on short story "The Gold Bug" by Edgar Allan Poe.

Golden Blade, The

1953 U color 80 mins.

Prod: Richard Wilson.

Assoc Prod: Leonard Goldstein.

Dir: Nathan Juran.

SP: John Rich.

Art Dir: Bernard Herzbrun & Eric Orbom.

Cin: Maury Gertsman.

Edit: Ted J. Kent.

Mus Dir: Joseph Gershenson.

Cast: Rock Hudson, Piper Laurie, Gene Evans, George Macready, Kathleen Hughes, Steven Geray, Edgar Barrier, Alice Kelley, Anita Ekberg.

F (magic sword cuts through steel)

Ref: HR & Vd 21 Aug '53; MFB Jan '54 p9.

Golden Claws of Cat Girl

1972? Hongkong?

F

Ref: MTVM 26:7:1:25.

Golden Deer, The

1970 Japanese ani cut-outs 11 mins.

F

Golden Earrings

1947 Par 95 mins.

Prod: Harry Tugend.

Dir: Mitchell Leisen.

SP: Abraham Polonsky, Frank Butler, & Helen Deutsch.

Art Dir: Hans Dreier & John Meehan.

Cin: Daniel L. Fapp.

SpFX: Gordon Jennings.

Edit: Alma Macrorie.

Mus: Victor Young.

Cast: Ray Milland, Marlene Dietrich, Murvyn Vye, Quentin Reynolds, Bruce Lester.

F-seq (after faking as mind-reader, Milland suddenly finds he has genuine precognition)

Ref: HR & Vd 26 Aug '47; LC.

Golden Fern, The

See: Zlate Kapradi (1963).

Golden Fish, The

(Ozlaté Rybee)

1951 Czech color ani 15 mins.

Dir, SP, Art Dir: Jiří Trnka.

F

Ref: Ani/Cin; Trnka p261.

Golden Fish, The

1952 Dutch color ani sh.

F

Ref: FIR Jan '53 p29.

Based on a Chinese legend.

Golden Fish, The

(Histoire d'un Poisson Rouge: Story of a Golden Fish)

1959 (1960) French color 19 mins.

Prod: Jacques Yves Costeau.

Dir: Edmond Sechan.

SP: Roger Mauge.

Cin: Pierre Gonpil.

Mus: Maurice Le Roux.

bor-F (dancing goldfish; cat replaces fish in water)

Ref: HR 27 Jan '60.

Golden Hair, The

1938 Indian, Ram Movietone 162 mins.

Dir: Narottam Vyas.

Cast: Feroze Dastur, Indu Ranj.

myth-F (warrior searches for object in possession of King of Undersea Kingdom to save life of his own king)

Ref: Lighthouse 19 Feb 38.

Golden Key

(The Little Golden Key --alt.t.)

1939 Soviet ani puppet & live.

Dir: A. Ptushko.

F

Ref: Soviet Cinema p76.

Based on a story by Alexei Tolstoi.

Golden Mistress, The

1954 R.K. Prods (UA) color 82 mins.

Filmed in and around Haiti.

Exec Prod: Sam X. Abarbanel.

Prod: Richard Kay & Harry Rybnick.

Dir: Joel Judge.

Story: Lew Hewitt.

SP: L. Hewitt & J. Judge.

Cin: William C. Thompson.

Edit: Howard Smith.

Mus: Raoul Kraushaar.

Cast: John Agar, Rosemary Bowe, Kiki, Abner Biberman, Andre Marcisse.

F-H-seq (stolen idol results in Bowe's father being killed by voodoo)

Ref: MFB Feb '55 p24-25; Vd & HR 18 Oct '54.

Golden Peacock Castle

See: Ogon Kujyaku-jo (1961).

Golden Pomegranates, The

1924 British, Stoll sil 2094 ft.

Prod & Adapt: Fred Paul.

Art Dir: Walter W. Murton.

Cin: Frank Canham.

Cast: Harry Agar Lyons, Fred Paul, Humberston Wright, Dorinea Shirley, Frank Wilson, Julie Suedo.

bor-F-H (Fu-Manchu mystery)

Ref: BFI cat p 130.

Based on characters created by Sax Rohmer.

See also: Further Mysteries of Dr. Fu Manchu (1924).

Golden Rabbit, The

1962 British, Argo (Rank) 64 mins.

Exec Prod: Jack Lamont.

Prod: Barry Delmaine.

Dir: David MacDonald.

SP: Dick Sharples & Gerald Kelsey.

Art Dir: George Provis.

Cin: S.D. Onions.

Edit: Alan Morrison.

Mus: Bill McGuffie.

Cast: Timothy Bateson, Maureen Beck, John Sharp, Willoughby Goddard, Kenneth Fortescue.

F-com (man invents formula for gold transmutation, but the gold turns back into lead)

Ref: MFB Nov '62 p 154.

Golden Superman

1968 S. Korean ani 70 mins.

Dir: Yongil Park.

F (sunlight weapon; cooper [copper?] devil)

Ref: Luna 15, Aug '70 at Trieste; Korea Cinema '68.

Golden Supper, The

1910 Biograph sil sh.

Cast: Dorothy West, Edwin August, Charles H. West.

H (girl in coma buried)

Ref: MPN 13:1923.

Golden Touch, The

1935 Disney (UA) color? ani 1 reel.

Prod: Walt Disney.

F-com (whatever king touches turns into gold)

cont.

Golden Touch, The cont.

Ref: F/A p630; LC.

Based on the legend of King Midas.

See also: King Midas.

Golden Voyage of Sinbad, The

(Sinbad's Golden Voyage --s.t.)

1973 Charles H. Schneer Prods (Col) color.

Prod: Charles H. Schneer.

Assoc Prod & SpFX: Ray Harryhausen.

Dir: Gordon Hessler.

SP: Brian Clemens.

Prod Design: John Stoll.

Cin: Ted Moore.

Mus: Miklos Rozsa.

Cast: John Phillip Law, Caroline Munro, Tom Baker, Martin Shaw, Gregoire Aslan, Douglas Wilmer, Kurt Christian, Takis Emmanuel, John D. Garfield.

F (griffin; living statue; flying demon; centaur-cyclops)

Ref: HR 7 July '72 p8; Vd 14 July '72; QPH 3 Feb '73 p 10; J. Danforth.

See also: Sinbad the Sailor.

Goldene Ding, Das

(The Golden Thing)

1971 W. German, Reitz-Film color 118 mins.

Prod, Dir, SP: Edgar Reitz, Ulla Stoeckl, Alf Brustellin, & Nicos Perakis.

Cin: E. Reitz.

Edit: Hannelore von Ungern-Sternberg.

Mus: Nikos Mamangates.

Cast: Christian Reitz, Oliver Jovine, Colombe Smith, Alf Brustellin, Angela Elsner, Katrin Seybold, Erich Beth.

F (Jason & Golden Fleece story, with sea monsters, superhuman warriors, and the clashing rocks in the Bosporas; all of the Argonauts are played by children 12-14 years old)

Ref: Vw 2 Feb '72 p 16.

Based on Greek legend.

See also: Giants of Thessaly (1960); Jason and the Argonauts (1963).

Goldene See, Die

(The Golden Sea; Die Spinnen [The Spiders] Part I)

1919 German, Decla-Bioscop sil 81 mins.

Dir & Sc: Fritz Lang.

Art Dir: Otto Hunte, Carl Ludwig Kirmse, Hermann Warm, & Heinrich Umlauff.

Cin: Emil Schünemann.

Cast: Carl de Vogt, Ressel Orla, Lil Dagover, Paul Morgan, Georg John, Bruno Lettinger, Paul Biensfeldt, Thea Zander, Friedrich Kühne, Edgar Pauly.

bor-SF (master criminals out to take over the world)

Ref: C to H; Gasca p28; Fritz Lang in America p 120.

Sequel: Brillantenschiff, Das (1920).

Goldface, il Fantastico Superman

(Goldface, the Fantastic Superman)

1967 Italian/Spanish, Unepratuzioni/Balcazar color scope.

Prod: Balcazar.

Dir: Adalberto Albertini (Stanley Mitchell).

SP: Balcazar, Molteni, & Fasan.

Cin: Carlo Fiore.

Mus: Piero Umiliani.

Cast: Spartaco B. Santoni (Robert Anthony), Evy Marandi, Micaela Pignatelli, Manuel Monroy, Hugo Pimentel, Big Mattews, Leontine May.

cont.

Goldface, il Fantastico Superman cont.

bor-SF (superstrong man becomes superhero to battle mysterious organization)

Ref: Ital Prods '67 p230-31

Goldfinger

1964 British, Eon (UA) color 109 mins.

Prod: Albert R. Broccoli & Harry Saltzman.

Dir: Guy Hamilton.

SP: Richard Maibaum & Paul Dehn.

Prod Design: Ken Adam.

Cin: Ted Moore.

SpFX: John Stears & Frank George.

Edit: Peter Hunt.

Mus: John Barry.

Cast: Sean Connery, Gert Fröbe, Honor Blackman, Shirley Eaton, Bernard Lee, Harold Sakata, Cec Linder, Lois Maxwell, Austin Willis, Martin Benson, Bill Nagy.

bor-SF (plot by gold-hungry madman to increase value of his gold by setting off A-bomb in Fort Knox, making U.S. gold reserves unusable; torture by laser beam)

Ref: FF '64 p306-08; MFB Nov '64 p 161; MPH 25 Nov '64; FD 9 Nov '64.

Based on the novel by Ian Fleming.

Sequel to: Dr. No (1962).

See also: Goldwhiskers (1964).

Goldframe

1968 Belgian ani 6 mins.

Dir & Story: Raoul Servais.

Art & Ani: Willy Verschelde.

Mus: Paul Van Gysegem.

F (man fights his own shadow; it becomes independent).

Ref: Ani/Belgium p47-48; Mamaia 70.

Goldilocks

1954 Czech color ani puppet sh.

Dir: Hermina Tyrlova.

F (the fairy tale)

Ref: FIR Oct '56 p390; FEFN July '61 p 13; Ani/Cin p 176.

Based on the fairy tale by K.J. Erben.

Goldilocks and the Jivin' Bears

1944 WB color ani 7 mins.

Dir: Friz (I.) Freleng.

Story: Tedd Pierce.

Ani: Ken Champin.

Mus Dir: Carl W. Stalling.

F-com

Ref: LC.

Goldilocks and the Three Bears

1917 Peter Pan sil puppet 508 ft.

F (little girl finds 3 bears' house in woods, eats their porridge, frightened out of their beds)

Ref: BFI cat p233.

See also: Goldilocks. . .; Teddy Bears, The (1907); Three Bears, The (1911); Mo-Toy Comedies (1917).

Goldstein

1963 (1965) Altura (Montrose) 115 mins (82 mins).

Prod: Zev Braun.

Prod, Dir, SP: Philip Kaufman & Benjamin Manaster.

Cin: Jean-Philippe Carson.

Edit: Adolfas Mekas.

Mus: Meyer Kupferman.

Cast: Lou Gilbert, Ellen Madison, Thomas Erhart, Benito Carruthers, Jack Burns, Severn Darden, Nelson Algren.

cont.

Goldstein cont.

exp-sat-F-com (an old tramp arises from a lake; invisible driver; Gilbert is Hebrew prophet Elijah, disappears when recognized)

Ref: CoF 6:56; MFB '67 p 186; NYT 2 May '65; Time 7 May '65; MPH 9 June '65; MMF 14:124.

Goldtown Ghost Riders

1952 (1953) Gene Autry Prods (Col) sepia 59 mins (57 mins).

Prod: Armand Schaefer.

Dir: George Archainbaud.

SP: Gerald Geraghty.

Art Dir: George Brooks.

Cin: William Bradford.

Edit: James Sweeney.

Mus Dir: Mischa Bakaleinikoff.

Cast: Gene Autry, Smiley Burnette, Gail Davis, Kirk Riley, Carleton Young, Steve Conte.

west; F-seq (fake ghosts; real ghosts at end ensure justice)

Ref: HR 20 May '53; LC.

Goldwhiskers

1964 British, Biographics color ani 8 mins.

Dir & Ani: Keith Learner & Vera Linnecar.

Edit: Peter Hearn.

sat-F-com

Ref: Collier; Ani/Cin p87.

Parody of: Goldfinger (1964).

Goldwyn-Bray Pictographs

1919-21 Goldwyn-Bray 1 reel sil ani series.

F-com

Ref: LC; Ani Chart.

Golem, The

● (Der Golem; The Monster of Fate --alt.t.)

1914 (1917) German, Bioscop (Hawk) sil.

Dir: Paul Wegener & Henrik Galeen.

Sc: H. Galeen.

Art Dir: Robert A. Dietrich.

Costumes: R. Gliese.

Cin: Guido Seeber.

Cast: Paul Wegener [golem], Henrik Galeen, Albert Steinrück, Ernst Deutsch, Lydia Salmanova.

F (Rabbi Loew's living man of clay dug up centuries later, goes on rampage)

Ref: C to H p 31-33; Scognamillo; Clarens; F&F June '58 p 14; MPW 31:2026 ad, 36:1482-83.

Based on the novel by Gustav Meyrink from medieval Jewish legend.

● (Der Golem)

1916 Danish sil.

Dir: Urban Gad.

F-H

Ref: Gasca p26; Film Sept '67.

● (Der Golem, Wie Er in die Welt Kam: The Golem, How He Came Into the World)

1920 (1921) German, PAGU & UFA (Par) sil 6 reels.

Dir: Paul Wegener & Carl Boese.

Sc: P. Wegener & Henrik Galeen.

Dir Sup: Ernst Lubitsch.

Art Dir: Hans Pölzig.

Costumes: Rochus Gliese.

Cin: Karl Freund & Guido Seeber.

Assist Cin: Edgar G. Ulmer.

Cast: Paul Wegener [golem], Albert Steinrück, Ernst Deutsch, Lyda Salmanova, Hanns Sturm, Grete Schröder, Ferdinand von Alten, Henrik Galeen, Lothar Müthel, Otto Gebühr, Max Kronert, Dora Paetzold.

cont.

Golem, The cont.

F-H (to help his enslaved people in medieval Prague, Rabbi Loew creates a living man of clay, but it goes on a rampage)

Ref: MPN 24:271; F/A p421; FD 26 June '21; FTN p641; Eisner p350; FIR Feb '63 p97.

Based on the novel by Gustav Meyrink from medieval Jewish legend.

● (Le Golem; The Legend of Prague --Brit.t; The Man of Stone -- 8mm t)

1936 (1937) French (Metropolis Pictures) 88 mins.

Filmed in Prague, Czechoslovakia.

Prod: Charles Philipp.

Dir: Julien Duvivier.

SP: J. Duvivier & André-Paul Antoine.

Art Dir: A. Andrejeff & S. Kopecky.

Cin: Vaclav Vich & Jan Stallich.

Edit (U.S. version): Martin J. Lewis.

Mus: Joseph Kumok.

Cast: Harry Baur, Germaine Aussey, Roger Karl, Ferdinand Hart [golem], Jany Holt.

sat-F (golem brought to life at climax, rights wrongs, then dissolves into dust)

Based on play by Jan Werich & Jiri Voskovec from medieval Jewish legend.

Ref: FD 24 March '37; HR 3 March '36; Int Film cat p35; MPH 27 March '37, p43, 45.

See also film which included scenes from this: Dr. Terror's House of Horrors (1943).

● (Le Golem; Mask of the Golem --ad.t.)

1966 French, ORTF.

Prod: L. Bureau.

Dir: Jean Kerchbron.

SP: Louis Pauwels & J. Kerchbron.

Art Dir: J. Gourmelin & A. Nègre.

Make-up: R. Simon.

Cin: Albert Schimel.

Edit: G. Fourmond & M. Gourot.

Mus: Jean Wiéner.

Cast: André Reybaz [golem], Pierre Tabard, Michel Etchevery, Marika Green, Francois Vibert, Douking, Robert Etchevery, Magali Noel.

F-H

Ref: MMF 15/16:3-14; Gifford/MM p 146.

Based on the novel by Gustav Meyrink from medieval Jewish legend.

See also: Golem und die Tänzerin (1917); Alraune und der Golem (1919); Golems Letztes Abenteuer, Des (1921); Emperor and the Golem, The (1951); It! (1966); Pražské Noci (1968).

Golem und die Tänzerin

(Golem and the Dancer)

1917 German, Union sil.

Dir: Paul Wegener.

Cast: Paul Wegener, Lyda Salmanova, Rochus Gliese.

com; bor-F (Wegener as himself puts on Golem disguise to impress dancer)

Ref: Gifford/MM p 146, 38; Eisner p 44.

See also: Golem, The.

Golem's Daughter

See: Goulve, La (1971).

Golem's Last Adventure, The

See: Golems Letztes Abenteuer, Des (1921).

Golems Letztes Abenteuer, Des

(The Golem's Last Adventure; Der Dorfgolem)

1921 Austrian, Sascha Film sil.

Dir: Julius Szomogyi.

F

Ref: Osterr.

See also: Golem, The.

Golfers, The

1936 U ani 1 reel.

Prod: Walter Lantz.

Story: W. Lantz & Victor McLeod.

Artists: Laverne Harding, Ed Benedict, & Leo Salkin.

F-com

Ref: LC.

See: Meany, Miny, Moe (1936-37).

Golgotha

See: Ecce Homo (1935).

Goliat Contra los Gigantes

See: Goliath Against the Giants (1962).

Goliath Against the Giants

(Goliath contro i Giganti; Goliat contro los Gigantes)

1960 (1962) Italian/Spanish, Procusa/Filmar (Medallion-TV) color 95 mins (90 mins).

Prod: Cesare Seccia & Manuel Pérez.

Dir: Guido Malatesta.

Story: C. Seccia.

SP: C. Seccia, Gianfranco Parolini, Giovanni Simonelli, Arpad De Riso, & Sergio Sollima.

Art Dir: Ramiro Gómez & Carlo Santonocito.

Art Sup: G. Parolini.

Cin: Alessandro Ulloa.

Edit: Mario Sansoni & Edmondo Lozzi.

Mus: Carlo Innocenzi.

Cast: Brad Harris, Gloria Milland, Fernando Rey, Barbara Carrol, José Rubio, Lina Rosales, Carmen DeLiro.

myth-F (sea monster; valley of giants; amazons)

Ref: MFB May '63 p66; SpCin '63 p66-67; F&F June '63 p35-36; TVG.

Goliath and the Dragon

(La Vendetta de Ercole: The Vengeance of Hercules, The Revenge of Hercules)

1960 Italian/French (AIP) color 90 mins.

Prod: Achille Piazzi & Gianni Fuchs.

Dir: Vittorio Cottafavi.

SP: Mario Piccolo & Archibald Zounds Jr.

Art Dir: Franco Lolli.

Cin: Mario Montuori.

Edit: Maurizio Lucidi.

Mus (U.S. prints): Les Baxter.

Cast: Mark Forest, Broderick Crawford, Eleonora (Leonora) Ruffo, Gaby André, Phillipe Hersent, Sandro Maretti.

F (Hercules, here called Goliath, battles three-headed dog, giant bat, & dragon; Wind Goddess)

Ref: FF '60 p325; MFB Aug '61 p 117; Ital Prods '60 p 140-41.

See also: Hercules.

Goliath and the Golden City

See: Samson and the 7 Miracles of the World (1961).

Goliath and the Sins of Babylon

(Maciste l'Eroe Piu Grande del Mondo: Maciste, the World's Greatest Hero)

Goliath and the Sins of Babylon cont.

1963 (1964) Italian, Leone Film (AIP) color (80 mins).

Prod: Elio Scardamaglia.

Dir: Michele Lupo.

Story & SP: Roberto Gianviti, Francesco Scardamaglia, & Lionello de Felice.

Art Dir: Pier Vittorio Marchi.

Cin: Guglielmo Mancori.

Edit: Alaberto Gallitti.

Mus: Francesco De Masi.

Cast: Mark Forest, Eleanora Bianchi, Scilla Gabel, John Chevron, José Greci, Giuliano Gemma.

bor-F (Maciste, here called Goliath, overcomes obstacles with superhuman strength)

Ref: MFB March '65 p41; FF '64 p 16.

See also: Maciste.

Goliath and the Vampires

(Maciste contro il Vampiro: Maciste vs. the Vampire; The Vampires --tv.t.)

1961 (1964) Italian, Ambrosiana (AIP) color scope 92 mins.

Exec Prod: Dino De Laurentiis.

Prod: Paolo Moffa.

Dir: Giacomo Gentilomo & Sergio Corbucci.

SP: S. Corbucci & Duccio Tessari.

Art Dir: Gianni Polidori.

Cin: Alvaro Mancori.

Edit: Eraldo da Roma.

Mus: Angelo Francesco Lavagnino.

Cast: Gordon Scott, Jacques Sernas, Gianna Maria Canale, Eleanora Ruffo, Annabella Incontrera, Rocco Vitolazzi, Van Aikens, Guido Celano [vampire].

F-H (men turned into mindless slaves; underground race of Blue Men; vampire assumes hero's identity)

Ref: MFB Oct '64 p 150; FF '64 p 131 &257; Photon 19:38.

See also: Maciste.

Goliath Contro i Giganti

See: Goliath Against the Giants (1962).

Goliath II

1960 WD (BV) color ani sh.

Prod: Walt Disney.

F

Ref: FD 28 Feb '61; Acad nom.

Goliath vs. the Giants

See: Goliath Against the Giants (1960).

Gollywog's Motor Accident

(In Gollywog Land --Brit.t.)

1912 British, Natural Colour Kinematograph Co 2-color sil 590 ft.

Dir: F. Martin Thornton & W.R. Booth.

F

Ref: Gifford/BFC 03761.

Goloshes of Fortune

1907 Danish sil 380 ft.

F

Ref: Neergaard p 19.

Based on the story by Hans Christian Andersen.

Golpe de Mil Millones, Un

(A Stroke of a Thousand Millions)

1966 Spanish/Italian/French color 91 mins.

Dir: Paolo Heusch.

Story: Fulvio Gicca.

SP: Pierre Levy, José Jerez, & F. Gicca.

Art Dir: Roman Catatayud.

Cin: Fausto Rossi.

Golpe de Mil Millones, Un cont.

Mus: Piero Umiliani.

Cast: Rick von Nutter, Marilu Tolo, Eduardo Fajardo, Maximo Pietrobon.

bor-SF (attempt to make the Suez Canal radioactive)

Ref: SpCin '67 p304 - 05.

Gonks Go Beat

1965 British, Titan color 92 mins.

Prod & Story: Peter Newbrook & Robert Hartford-Davis.

Dir: R. Hartford-Davis.

SP: Jimmy Watson.

Art Dir: William Constable.

Cin: Peter Newbrook.

Edit: Teddy Darvas.

Mus Dir: Robert Richards.

Cast: Kenneth Connor, Frank Thornton, Barbara Brown, Iain Gregory, Terry Scott.

SF-mus-com (alien sent to settle difficulties between rival music-oriented countries)

Ref: MFB '65 p 136; F&F Sept '65 p28.

Good and Bad Woodcutters, The

See: Kuroi Kikori to Shiroi Kikori (1959?).

Good and Evil

1921 Bohemian (Herz Film Corp & F.B. Warren Corp) sil 6 reels (5 reels).

Prod: Sasch.

Cast: Lucy Doraine, Alphonse Fryland, Madeline Nagy, Antoin Tiller, Ralph Osterman.

alleg-F (fate shows hero the "book of life")

Ref: MPN 24:1669, 1683.

Good Bed, A

See: Midnight Episode, A (1899).

Good Friend, The

1969 Murakami-Wolf color ani sh.

Dir: Jimmy Murakami.

F-H (man with no face given eyes, mouth, nose, etc.)

Ref: ASIFA 5.

Good Glue Sticks

(La Colle Universelle)

1907 French sil 400 ft (311 ft).

Prod: Georges Méliès.

F

Ref: Sadoul/M; GM Mage; LC.

Good Grief

1972 UCLA color ani 4 mins.

Made by: Mike Jittlov.

F-com (little boy's fears of things in night)

Ref: Filmex II; LAT 28 April '72.

Good Joke with My Head, A

See: Tit for Tat (1903).

Good Little Devil, A

1913 Famous Players (Par) sil 5 reels.

Exec Prod: Adolph Zukor.

Prod: Daniel Frohman.

Tech Dir: Edwin S. Porter.

Sc: Austin Strong.

Cast: Mary Pickford, Ernest Truex, William Norris, Wilda Bennett, David Belasco.

F (children helped by fairies)

Ref: MPW 17:407, 19:1050-51, 1249; Blum p52.

Based on a play by Rosemond Gerard & Maurice Rostand.

cont.   cont.

Good Little Monkeys

1935 Harman-Ising (MGM) color ani 9 mins.

Prod: Hugh Harman & Rudolf Ising.

F-com (Satan overpowered by famous personalities)

Ref: Lighthouse 19 Dec '36; LC.

Good Luck Horseshoe, The

See: Podkova pro Štěstí (1946).

Good Morning

1968 Danish color ani sh.

Dir: Flemming Quist Moller.

F

Ref: ASIFA 5.

Good Morning -- and Goodbye!

1967 Eve Prods color 80 mins.

Prod, Dir, Story, Cin: Russ Meyer.

Assoc Prod: Eve Meyer.

Assist Dir: George Costello.

SP: John E. Moran.

Edit: R. Meyer & Richard Brummer.

Mus: Alaina Capri, Stuart Lancaster, Haji [witch], Pat Wright, Karen Ciral.

sex; F-seq (sexual rejuvenation by witchcraft)

Ref: FF '68 p34; Vw 20 Dec '67.

Good Morning, Eve!

1934 Vitaphone (WB 2 reels.

Dir: Roy Mack.

SP: Cyrus Woods, Eddie Moran, & A. Dorian Otvos.

Cast: Leon Errol, June MacCloy, Vernon Dent, Maxine Doyle.

F-com (adventures of Adam & Eve thru the centuries)

Ref: Maltin/GMS p 115, 122; LC.

See also: Leon Errol Comedy; Adam and Eve.

Good Morning, Paris

See: Bonjour Paris (1953).

Good Morning Tales

See: Buna Dimineata Poveste (1969).

Good Night Aliens!

1967 Japanese, Dentsu 16mm color ani puppet 14 mins.

Dir: Tadashige Okamoto.

SF-com (aliens encounter girl robot)

Ref: UniJ '67.

Good Scouts

1938 WD (RKO) color? ani sh.

Prod: Walt Disney.

F-com

Ref: LC; Acad nom.

See also: Donald Duck (1934-61).

Good Sheperdess and the Evil Princess, The

See: Bonne Bergére et la Méchante Princesse, La (1908).

Good Soldier Schweik, The

(Dobry Vojak Sveik)

1929 Soviet sil ani sh?

Dir: B. Antonovsky.

F

Ref: Kino p274.

Based on the novel by Jaroslav Hasek.

See also: Osudy Dobrého Vojáka Svejka (1954).

Good Spirits

1925 Christie (Educational) sil 2 reels.

Dir: Archie Mayo.

Cast: Walter Hiers.

F-com (spirits)

Ref: MPN 31:363, 530.

Le Golem (1966) French

Good, the Bad and the Angel, The

1969 Amateur color 8mm? 12 mins.

Made by: John Lopez.

rel-F (angel battles evil to get halo)

Ref: Luna (Kodak 7th Teenage Movie Awards).

Good Times

1967 Steve Broidy Prod (Col) color 91 mins.

Exec Prod: Steve Broidy.

Prod: Lindsley Parsons.

Dir: William Friedkin.

Story: Nicholas Hyams.

SP: Tony Barrett.

Art Dir: Hal Periera & Arthur Lonergan.

Cin: Robert Wyckoff.

cont.

Good Times cont.

SpFX Cin: Farciot Edouart.

Edit: Melvin Shapiro.

Mus: Sonny Bono.

Cast: Sonny Bono, Cher Bono, George Sanders, Norman Alden, Larry Duran, Lennie Weinrib.

mus-com; F-seq (Sonny imagines himself as Tarzan and other movie heroes)

Ref: Vw 26 April '67; FF '67 p234.

See also: Tarzan.

Good Trick, A

(Le Chevalier Démontable et le Général Boum)

1901 French sil 65 ft.

Prod: Georges Méliès.

F-com

Ref: Sadoul/M; GM Mage.

Good Will to Men

1955 MGM color ani 8 mins.

Prod: Fred Quimby.

Dir: William Hanna & Joseph Barbera.

F (mice ask about men after future war)

Ref: LC; Acad nom.

See also: Peace on Earth (1939).

Goodbye Charlie

1964 Venice Prods (20th-Fox) color scope 117 mins.

Prod: David Weisbart.

Dir: Vincente Minnelli.

SP: Harry Kurnitz.

Art Dir: Jack Martin Smith & Richard Day.

Cin: Milton Krasner.

cont.

Goodbye Charlie cont.

SpFX: L.B. Abbott & Emil Kosa Jr.

Edit: John W. Holmes.

Mus: Andre Previn.

Cast: Tony Curtis, Debbie Reynolds, Pat Boone, Walter Matthau, Joanna Barnes, Laura Devon, Martin Gabel, Donna Michelle.

F-com (spirit of murdered roué takes over the body of a beautiful girl [Reynolds])

Ref: FD 5 Nov '64; MPH 11 Nov '64; FF '64 p349-50; MFB April '65 p51-52.

Based on the play by George Axelrod.

Goodbye Gemini

1970 British, Josef Shaftel Prods color 89 mins.

Prod: Peter Snell.

Dir: Alan Gibson.

SP: Edmund Ward.

Art Dir: Fred Carter.

Cin: Geoffrey Unsworth.

Edit: Ernest Hosler.

Mus: Christopher Gunning.

Cast: Judy Geeson, Martin Potter, Michael Redgrave, Alexis Kanner, Mike Pratt, Freddie Jones.

psy-H (twins have almost incestuous relationship, together commit horror murders)

Ref: MFB Sept '70 p 186.

Based on novel "Ask Agamemnon" by Jenni Hall.

Goodness! A Ghost

1940 RKO 16 mins.

Prod: Lou Brock.

Dir: Harry D'Arcy.

Story: George Jeske & Arthur V. Jones.

SP: Harry Langdon.

Edit: John Lockert.

Cast: Harry Langdon.

F-com (hero's grandfather's ghost inhabits a uniform)

Ref: LC; Maltin/GMS p73.

See also: Harry Langdon Comedy.

Goodrich Dirt

1915 1 reel live & ani sil series.

Dir: Wallace A. Carlson.

F-com

Ref: Ani Chart.

Goody-Goody Jones

1912 Selig sil 500 ft.

F-com (pill makes husband chase other women; tricks)

Ref: MPW 12:1058.

Goofy

1932-53 WD color ani sh series.

Prod: Walt Disney.

Voice: Pinto Colvig.

F-com

Ref: LC; Art/Ani p46.

See also: How to Play Football (1944); Fun and Fancy Free (1947).

Googolplex

1972 Bell Telephone color computer ani 5 1/2 mins.

Made by: Lillian Schwartz & Ken Knowlton.

exp-F

Ref: IAFF '72.

Goon Song, The

1966 Cal Institute of the Arts color ani 10 mins.

Dir: Carl Bell.

Voices: Spike Milligan, Peter Sellers, and others.

abs-F-com

Ref: ASIFA 3.

Goona-Goona

(Love Powder; The Kriss --alt.ts.)

1932 French (First Division) 65 mins.

Filmed in Bali.

Prod: André Roosevelt & Armand Denis.

Edit: Al Friedlander.

bor-F (love potion seems effective)

Ref: LC; Vw; Acad.

Goonland

1938 Par ani 1 reel.

Prod: Max Fleischer.

Dir: Dave Fleischer.

Ani: Seymour Kneitel & Abner Matthews.

F-com

Ref: LC; PopCar.

See also: Popeye (1933-57).

Goons from the Moon

See: Mighty Mouse in Goons from the Moon (1951).

Goopy Gyne Bagha Byne

(The Adventures of Goopy and Bagha)

1969 Indian, Purnima color & B&W 132 mins (120 mins).

Prod: Nepal Dutta & Ashim Dutta.

Dir, SP, Mus: Satyajit Ray.

Art Dir: Bansi Chandragupta.

Choreog: Shamblunath Bhattacherji.

Cin: Soumendu Ray.

Edit: Dulal Dutta.

Cast: Tapen Chatterjee, Robi Gosh, Santosh Dutt, Harindra, Jahar Roy, Durgadas Bannerjee, Santi Chatterjee, Prasad Mukherjee.

F (2 children have magic powers & settle war between two kingdoms; rival ghost hordes dance; invisibility; "King of the Ghosts")

Ref: Vw 2 July '69; Harpers Dec '69; MFB March '72 p51-52.

Based on a story by Upendra Kishore Roychowdhury.

Goose that Laid the Golden Egg, The

See: Felix the Cat and the Goose that Laid the Golden Egg (1936).

Gopal Krishna

1928 Indian, Prabhat sil.

myth-F

Ref: IndCin YB.

See also: Krishna. . .

Gopal Krishna

1938 Indian, Prabhat 132 mins.

Dir: U. Damle & S. Fatehlal.

Story: S.S. Washikar.

Cin: Avadhoot.

Mus: Krisnarao.

Cast: Shanta Apte, Ramchandra Marathe, Parashuram, Pralhad, Ulhas, Shankar.

myth-F (childhood of Krishna)

Ref: Dipali 29 July '38 p27; MovPicM July '38 p40; Filmindia Aug '37 p 19, Sept '38 p7, Feb '38 p 12.

See also: Krishna. . .

Gopher, The

See: Topo, El (1971).

Goulve, La

(Erotic Witchcraft --Brit.t.; Golem's Daughter --ad.t.; Homo Vampire --ad.t.)

1971 French, Welp color 87 mins.

Prod: Bepi Fontana.

Dir: Mario Mercier & B. Fontana.

SP: M. Mercier.

Goulve, La cont.

Cin: Paul Soulignac.

Mus: Guy Boulanger.

Cast: Hervé Hendricks, César Torres, Anne Varèse, Marie-Ange Saint-Clair, Maïka Simon [the Goulve], Manuel Navo.

F-H (elemental snake goddess, the Goulve, takes possession of humans, causes suicide, insanity, etc; Goulve spirit is contained in portrait)

Ref: MFB May '73 p97; Vw 3 May '72 p 167.

Gorakhnath

(Maya Machindra)

1951 Indian, Super Pics 128 mins.

Prod & Dir: Aspi Irani.

SP: S.S. Washikar.

Cin: Vishnu Kumar.

Edit: Narayan Rao.

Mus: Premnath.

Cast: Nirupa Roy, Tirlok Kapur, Surendra, Usha Kiran, Chandni.

myth-F

Ref: Filmcritic Jan '52; Indian MPA '53 p44.

Gorath

(Yosei Gorasu)

1962 Japanese, Toho (Col) color 89 mins.

Dir: Inoshiro Honda.

SP: Takeshi Kimura.

Cin: Hajime Koizumi.

SpFX: Eiji Tsuburaya.

Cast: Ryo Ikebe, Jun Tazaki, Akihiko Hirata, Yumi Shirakawa, Takashi Shimura, Kumi Mizuno.

SF (runaway planet about to hit Earth; Earth moved out of the way by giant rockets; huge prehistoric monster like a walrus released by Earthquake)

Ref: SM 4:2, 8, 9; MMF 7:85; UniJ 17:14.

Gore Gore Girls, The

1971 (1972) Lewis Motion Picture Enterprises color 90 mins.

Prod & Dir: Herschell Gordon Lewis.

SP: Alan J. Dachman.

Asst Dir: Louise Downe.

Cin: Eskandar Ameripoor (Alex Ameri).

Edit: E. Ameripoor.

Mus: H.G. Lewis (Sheldon Seymour).

Cast: Frank Kress, Amy Farrell, Hedda Lubin, Russ Badger, Nora Alexis, Phil Laurensen, Frank Rice, Ray Sager, Henny Youngman.

myst-H (horror murders of dancers)

Ref: PB.

Gorgo

(The Night the World Shook -- s.t.)

1959 (1961) British, King Bros (MGM) color 78 mins.

Exec Prod: Frank & Maurice King.

Prod: Wilfred Eades.

Dir: Eugene Lourie.

Story: E. Lourie & Daniel Hyatt.

SP: John Loring & D. Hyatt.

Art Dir: Elliott Scott.

Cin: F.A. Young.

SpFX Cin: Tom Howard.

Edit: Eric Boyd-Perkins.

Mus: Angelo Francesco Lavagnino.

Cast: Bill Travers, William Sylvester, Vincent Winter, Bruce Seton, Joseph O'Connor, Martin Benson.

SF (prehistoric monster caught in Irish sea taken to London; its enormous mother comes in search of it)

Gorgo cont.

Ref: FF '61 p55; FEFN Feb '60 p 15; MFB Nov '61 p 155; HR 11 Dec '59; Vd 25 June '61.

See also: Son of Tor (1964).

Gorgon, The

1964 (1965) British, Hammer (Col) color 83 mins.

Prod: Anthony Nelson Keys.

Dir: Terence Fisher.

Story: J. Llewellyn Devine.

SP: John Gilling.

Art Dir: Bernard Robinson & Don Mingaye.

Make-up: Roy Ashton.

Cin: Michael Reed.

Edit: James Needs & Eric Boyd-Perkins.

Mus: James Bernard.

Cast: Peter Cushing, Christopher Lee, Richard Pasco, Barbara Shelley, Michael Goodliffe, Patrick Troughton, Jack Watson, Prudence Hyman.

F-H (spirit of one of three gorgon sisters inhabits beautiful girl, turns her hideous & gives her snakes for hair; gaze turns men to stone)

Ref: FD 28 Jan '65; MFB Oct '64 p 149; MMF 14:26.

Gorilla, The

● 1927 FN sil 7133 ft.

Prod & Dir: Alfred Santell.

Adapt: James T. O'Donohoe.

Sc: Al Cohn & Henry McCarty.

Titles: Sidney Lazarus.

Cin: Arthur Edeson.

Cast: Charlie Murray, Fred Kelsey, Alice Day, Tully Marshall, Walter Pidgeon, Claude Gillingwater, Gaston Glass.

Ref: AFI F2.2199 p308; Vw 23 Nov '27; FD 13 Nov '27; MPN 36:1755.

● 1930 FN (WB) 65 mins.

Dir: Bryan Foy.

Adapt: Herman Ruby.

SP: Ralph Spence & B. Harrison Orkow.

Edit: George Amy.

Cin: Sid Hickox.

Cast: Joe Frisco, Harry Gribbon, Walter Pidgeon, Lila Lee, Purnell Pratt, Edwin Maxwell, Roscoe Karnes.

Ref: AFI F2.2200; Vw 25 Feb '31; MPN 42:14:56.

● 1939 20th-Fox 67 mins.

Exec Prod: Darryl F. Zanuck.

Assoc Prod: Harry Joe Brown.

Dir: Allan Dwan.

SP: Rian James & Sid Silvers.

Art Dir: Richard Day & Lewis Creber.

Cin: Edward Cronjager.

Edit: Allen McNeil.

Mus: David Buttolph.

Cast: Jimmy Ritz, Harry Ritz, Al Ritz, Patsy Kelly, Anita Louise, Lionel Atwill, Bela Lugosi, Joseph Calleia.

Ref: HR 18 May '39; MPH 15 April '39 p48, 27 May '39 p32.

H-com (man in gorilla suit is murderer; 1939 version may have "mechanical monster")

Based on the play by Ralph Spence.

Gorilla

See: Nabonga (1943).

Gorilla at Large

1954 Panoramic Prods (20th-Fox) 3D color 93 mins (84 mins).

Exec Prod: Leonard Goldstein.

Prod: Robert L. Jacks.

cont.

cont.

cont.

Gorilla at Large cont.

Dir: Harmon Jones.

SP: Leonard Praskins & Barney Slater.

Cin: Lloyd Ahern.

Edit Sup: Paul Weatherwax.

Edit: George A. Gittens.

Mus Dir: Lionel Newman.

Cast: Cameron Mitchell, Anne Bancroft, Lee J. Cobb, Raymond Burr, Charlotte Austin, Lee Marvin, Warren Stevens.

H (woman commits murders while wearing gorilla suit)

Ref: Vd & HR 30 April '54.

Gorilla of Soho, The

See: Gorilla von Soho, Der (1968).

Gorilla Story, The

1951? Crown Pictures 28 mins.

Prod: Clyde Bruckman.

Dir: Arthur Hilton.

SP: Harold Goodwin, Ben Perry, & Carl K. Hittelman.

Cin: Jackson Rose.

Cast: Buster Keaton.

F-com (explorers after missing link; Buster dreams he finds & talks to gorilla)

Ref: MFB April '54 p62.

Probably episode of TV series released theatrically in England.

Gorilla von Soho, Der

(The Gorilla of Soho)

1968 W. German, Rialto color.

Dir: Alfred Vohrer.

SP: Freddy Gregor.

Cin: Karl Löb.

Cast: Horst Tappert, Uschi Glas, Uwe Friedrichsen, Albert Lieven, Herbert Fux, Inge Langen, Hubert von Meyerinck.

bor-H (man commits murders while wearing gorilla suit)

Ref: Film March '68 p3.

Based on work by Edgar Wallace.

Gorilla's Dance

(Ples Gorilla)

1968 Yugoslavian/U.S., Zagreb/McGraw-Hill color ani 9.1 mins.

Dir. Design, Ani: Milan Blažeković.

Story & Superv: Dusan Vukotić.

Bg: Branko Varadin.

Mus: Andjelko Klobučar.

F-com (dancing gorillas get along better than their trainers)

Ref: Z/Zagreb p21, 34, 50, 95.

Görünmiyen Adam Istanbulda

(Invisible Man in Istanbul)

1956 Turkish, Kemal.

Prod & SP: Osman Seden.

Dir: Lütfü Akad.

Cin: Krito Ilyadis.

Cast: Turan Seyfioglu, Nese Yulac, Atif Kaptan.

SF

Ref: Scognamillo; FM 22:7.

Based on novel "The Invisible Man" by H.G. Wells.

See also: Invisible Man, The (1933).

Gory Creatures, The

See: Terror Is a Man (1959).

Gorycz

1962 Polish color ani collage sh.

Dir: Wajser.

F (anti-drunkenness)

Ref: F&F March '63 p64.

Gorgo (1959) British

Gospel According to Saint Matthew, The

(Il Vangelo Secondo Matteo)

1964 (1966) Italian/French (Continental) 142 mins (135 mins).

Prod: Alfredo Bini.

Dir & SP: Pier Paolo Pasolini.

Cin: Tonino Delli Colli.

Art Dir: Nino Baragli & Luigi Scaccianoce.

Cin: Tonino Delli Colli.

SpFX: E. Catalucci.

Edit: Andrea Fantucci.

Mus: Luis E. Bacalor, Bach, Mozart, Prokofiev, Webern.

Cast: Enrique Irazoqui [Jesus], Marherita Caruso, Susanna Pasolini, Marcello Morante, Mario Socrate, Settimo Di Porto, Otello Sestili, Ferruccio Nuzzo.

Gospel According to Saint Matthew, The cont.

rel-F (many of the miracles of Christ: walking on water, healing of blind, loaves & fishes, resurrection of Lazarus & of Jesus, etc.)

Ref: NYT 1 Aug '65 p E9; MFB '67 p 104; MPH 2 March '66; SR 26 March '66; FF '66 p29; FIR Jan '66 p54-55.

Based on the book of Matthew from "The Bible."

See also: Godspell (1973); King of Kings.

Gospel Road, The

1973 Carter & Johnny Cash (20th-Fox) color 93 mins.

Partly filmed in Israel.

Prod: June Carter Cash & Johnny Cash.

Dir: Robert Elfstrom.

cont.

Gospel Road cont.

SP: J. Cash & Larry Murray.

Cin: R. Elfstrom & Tom Mc-Donough.

Edit: John Craddock.

Mus Sup: Larry Butler.

Nar: J. Cash.

Cast: Robert Elfstrom [Jesus], June Carter Cash, Larry Lee, Paul Smith, Alan Dater, Robert Elfstrom Jr., Gelles LaBlanc, Thomas Leventhal.

mus-doc; rel-F-seqs (tour of Jesus' land, w/scenes of Christ's life; many songs; deliberate anachronisms; some miracles shown)

Ref: 20th-Fox notes; Vw 21 March '73 p 18 & 26; QPH 24 March '73; BO 2 April '73 p4577.

See also: King of Kings.

Gotamah, the Buddha

1956 Indian (in Hindi), Bimal Roy Prods & Government of India 55 mins.

Prod & SP: Bimal Roy.

Dir: Rajbana Khanna.

Cin: Dilip Gupta.

Edit: Hrishikesh Mukherji.

Mus: Salil Chowdhury.

Nar: David Abraham, Uma Anand, Romesh Thapar, Hima Devi, Zul-Vellani, Berkeley Hill.

myth-F-seq (Buddha's life told with statues)

Ref: Orient.

See also: Buddha (1961).

Goto l'Ile d'Amour

(Goto, the Island of Love)

1968 French, Euro-Images & Les Productions René Thévenet color & b&w 93 mins.

Exec Prod: Rene Thévenet & Louis Duchesne.

Dir & Sc: Walerian Borowczyk.

Dialog: W. Borowczyk & Dominique Duvergé.

Cin: Guy Durban & Paul Coteret.

Edit: Bob Wade.

Mus: Georg Friedrich Handel.

Mus Dir: Jean-Francois Paillard.

Cast: Pierre Brasseur, Ligia Branice, Ginette Leclerc, René Dary, Jean-Pierre Andréani, Guy Saint-Jean, Fernand Bercher.

sur-F (bizarre, Kafka-esque society on an island; brief resurrection at end)

Ref: MFB Dec '69 p257-58; S&S Autumn '69 p 166-, 170.

Gourd Fairy, The

1972? Hongkong, Shaw.

Dir: Kuei Chih Hung.

Cast: Karen Yip, Tsung Hua.

F

Ref: MTVM 26:8:23.

Gradanim IM5

(Citizen IM 5)

1962 Yugoslavian, Zagreb color ani 8 mins.

Dir: Boris Kolar.

Story: Vladimir Tadej.

Ani: Milan Blaẑeković.

F (robot; superhero)

Ref: Gasca p286-87.

See also: Inspector Mask (1950-).

Graf von Cagliostro, Der

See: Cagliostro (German, 1920).

Graft

1915-16 U 20 part series sil.

See: Insurance Swindlers, The (1916).

Ref: LC.

Grafting, The

See: Przekladaniec (1972?).

Grain de Bon Sens, Un

1955 French ani sh.

Prod: Jean Image.

F

Ref: Animée.

Gran Amor del Conde Dracula, El

(The Great Love of Count Dracula; Count Dracula's Great Love; Dracula's Great Love --ad.t.)

1972 Spanish/??, Eva Films/ Janus Films color 90 mins.

Prod: F. Lara Polop.

Dir: Javier Aguirre.

Cast: Paul Naschy (r.n. Jacinto Molina) [Dracula], Rossana Yanni, Haydee Politoff, Mirta Miller, Vic Winner, Ingrid Garbo.

F-H (Dracula dies for the love of a woman)

cont.

Gran Amor del Conde Dracula, El cont.

Ref: D. Klemensen; LSH 2.

Based on a character created by Bram Stoker.

See also: Dracula (1930).

Grand Amour, Le

(The Great Love)

1969 French, CAPAC & Madeleine & Productions de la Guéville color 85 mins.

Dir: Pierre Etaix.

SP: P. Etaix & Jean-Claude Carriere.

Design: Daniel Louradour.

Cin: Jean Boffety.

Edit & Mus: Henri Lanoë.

Cast: Pierre Etaix, Annie Fratellini, Nicole Calfan, Ketty France, Louis Maiss, Alain Janey.

com; F-dream (beds cruise down streets like cars in hero's dream; also beds turn into trains, etc.)

Ref: Vw 2 April '69.

Grand Cérémonial, La

(Weird Weirdo -- Brit.t.)

1968 French, Production Alcinter color 110 mins.

Prod: André Cotton.

Dir: Pierre-Alain Jolivet.

SP: P.-A. Jolivet & Serge Ganzi.

Art Dir: Jacques Mawart.

Cin: Bernard Daillencourt.

Edit: Mireille Mauberna.

Mus: Jack Arel.

Cast: Michel Tureau, Marcella Saint-Amant, Ginette Leclerc, Fernando Arrabal, Jean-Daniel Ehrmann.

H (rituals, sado-masochism, etc.)

Ref: MFB June '70 p 128.

Based on the play by Fernando Arrabal.

Grand Depart, Le

(The Big Departure)

1972 French, NEF color 75 mins.

Dir & SP: Martial Raysse.

Cin: Jean-Jacques Florey.

Edit: Monique Giraudy.

Cast: Sterling Hayden, Anna Wiazemsky, Lucienne Hamon.

F (mostly in color negative; man in cat mask has strange adventures, at climax is on raft racing with the world)

Ref: Vw 20 Dec '72 p 18.

Grand Duel in Magic

See: Magic Serpent (1967).

Grand Guignol

1921 British, Screen Plays sil 1 reel series.

Dir: Fred Paul, Jack Raymond.

Sc: F. Paul, George Saxon, Percy Nash, C.E. Dering, Eric Clare, Norman Ramsay, Laurence Theval, Frank King Jr.

Cast: Fred Paul, Jack Raymond, George Foley, Lionel D'Aragon, Annette Benson, Bertram Burleigh, Joan Beverly, Frank Stanmore.

F?-H (macabre short stories)

Ref: Gifford/BFC 07115-20, 07166-74, 07197-204, 07219-23, 07265-69.

See also: Sting of Death, The (1921); Voice from the Dead, A (1921).

Grand Méliès, Le

(The Great Méliès)

1952 French Armor Films 30 mins.

Prod: Fred Orain.

Dir & SP: Georges Franju.

Art Dir: Henri Schmitt.

Cin: Jacques Mercanton.

Mus: Georges Van Parys.

cont.

Grand Méliès, Le cont.

Cast: Georges Méliès, André Méliès.

doc; SF-seq, F-seq (story of the life of Georges Melies with scenes from his films)

Ref: MFB Aug '54 p 123; FIR Oct '53 p396.

Includes Trip to the Moon, A (1902).

Grand Tour, The

1972 Japanese color? ani 6 mins.

Dir: Hal Fukushima.

F

Ref: IAFF '72.

Grand Tour -- Manned Exploration of the Outer Planets

1973 Graphic, San Diego Hall of Science.

doc-SF?

Ref: Graphic Info Sheet.

Grandfather Frost

See: Jack Frost (1965).

Grandfather's Pills

1908 French, Pathé sil 541 ft.

SF-com (pills make grandchild strong & grandfather young)

Ref: MPW 2:532; BFI cat p22.

Grandflapper, The

(story by N.W. Putnam)

See: Slaves of Beauty (1927).

Grandmother

See: Nagymama (1935).

Grandmother Cybernetica

See: Cybernetic Grandmother (1962).

Grandmother's Goat

1963 Soviet, Soyuzmultfilm color ani 18.6 mins.

Dir: L. Amalrik.

Story: F. Krivin.

F (goat leads wolves to grandmother & they eat her)

Ref: Sovexportfilm cat p 132.

Grandmother's Story, A or **To the Land of Toys**

(Conte de la Grand'mère et Rêve de l'Enfant ou Au Pays de Jouets)

1908 French, Star sil 840 ft.

Prod: Georges Méliès.

F-dream (fairies; animated toys)

Ref: LC; Sadoul/M; Views 128:10.

Grandmother's Umbrella

(Babuskin Zontik)

1969 Soviet color ani 9 mins.

Dir: L. Milcin (Milchin?).

Story: I. Iakovlev.

F

Ref: Mamaia '70.

Grandpa Ivan

1939 Soviet ani sh.

Dir: A. Ivanov.

F

Ref: Ani/Cin p 172.

Grandpa Planted a Beet

See: Zasadil Dédek Ǩepu (1945).

Grant, Police Reporter

See: Violet Ray, The (1917).

Graphic Sound

1968? Belgian ani & live 25 mins.

Dir: Jean Antoine & Jean Janssens.

exp-mus-F-seq

Ref: Ani/Belgian p55.

cont.

Grasping Hand, The

See: Max and the Clutching Hand (1915).

Grasshopper and the Ant

● (La Cigale et la Fourmi)

1897 French sil 65 ft.

Prod: Georges Méliès.

Ref: Sadoul/M; GM Mage.

● (Strekoza i Muravej)

1912 Russian ani puppet sil 520 ft.

Prod: Ladislas Starevitch.

Ref: Filmlex; FIR April '58 p 190; Kino p416.

● (La Cigale et la Fourmi)

1954 French (FACSEA) color ani 10 mins.

Prod: Jean Image.

Ref: FACSEA p 11.

● 1954 British, Primrose Prods (Contemporary) ani silhouette 10 mins. Originally produced for TV.

Prod: Lotte Reiniger.

Mus: Freddie Phillips.

F (an industrious ant has an easy time in the winter, while the lazy grasshopper who whiled away the summer does not)

Based on the fable by La Fontaine.

See also: Wandering Minstrel, The (1899); Eva and the Grasshopper (1927); Cigale et la Fourmi, La (1955), and following film.

Grasshopper and the Ants

1934 WD ani 1 reel.

Prod: Walt Disney.

F-com

Ref: LC.

Based on the fable by La Fontaine.

See also: Grasshopper and the Ant, The.

Grateful Badger, The

(Bunbuku Chagama)

1958 Japanese, Dentsu puppet 13 mins.

F

Ref: UniJ 2:40.

Grateful Dead, [The?]

1967 Amateur (Film-makers' Coop; Canyon Cinema; etc.) 16mm color 7.5 mins.

Made by: Robert Nelson.

Mus: The Grateful Dead.

exp-sur-F

Ref: FMC 5:254; FC 48-49:29.

Grausige Nächte

(Horrible Night)

1920 German sil.

Dir: Lupu Pick.

F-H (ghosts)

Ref: DdC III:257; UF p402.

Grave Digger's Ambitions

1913 Welt sil silhouette? 330 ft.

F (deal with the devil -- sells soul to learn how to fly)

Ref: Bios 8 May '13 p vi.

Grave New World

1972 British, Crown Int'l color 29 mins videotape-to-film.

Prod Assoc: Des Cox.

Dir: Steve Turner.

SP: D. Cox & S. Turner.

Cin: Peter Middleton.

Vision Sup: Derry Wood.

Vision Mixer: Ros Storey.

Edit: John Middlewick.

Videotape Edit: Barry Stevens.

cont.

Grave New World cont.

Choreog: Fergus Early.

Mus: The Strawbs.

Cast: The Strawbs (Blue Weaver, Tony Hooper, John Ford, Richard Hudson, David Cousins), Des Cox, Jacqueline Lansley.

mus; F-seq ("the group. . . cloaked & floating in super-imposition above the clouds")

Ref: MFB June '72 p 126.

Grave of the Vampire

1972 (1973) Clover color 95 mins.

Prod: Daniel Cady.

Dir: John Patrick Hayes.

SP: J.P. Hayes & David Chase.

Art Dir: Earl Marshall.

Make-up: Tino Zacchia.

Cin: Paul Hipp.

Edit: Ron Johnson.

Cast: William Smith, Michael Pataki [vampire], Lyn Peters, Diane Holden, Kitty Vallacher, Jay Adler, Jay Scott.

F-H (vampire's son born as a result of rape, spends life hunting for father; kills him, then becomes a vampire himself)

Ref: BO 22 Jan '72; Vw 22 March '72 p34; PB; Eric Hoffman.

Based on novel "The Still Life" by David Chase.

Grave Robbers

See: Ladron de Cadaveres (1957).

Grave Robbers from Outer Space

See: Plan 9 from Outer Space (1956).

Gray Horror, The

1915 Lubin 40 mins sil.

H ("frightful apparition")

Ref: MPN 8 May '15; MPW 24:957.

Gray Lady, The

See: Grey Dame, The (1909).

Greaser's Palace

1972 Greaser's Palace Ltd color 91 mins.

Prod: Cyma Rubin.

Dir & SP: Robert Downey.

Set Design: David Forman.

Cin: Peter Powell.

Edit: Bud Smith.

Mus: Jack Nitzsche.

Cast: Albert Henderson, Allan Arbus [Jesus], Michael Sullivan, Luana Anders, James Antonio, George Morgan, Ron Nealy, Larry Moyer, Elsie Downey, Stan Gottlieb.

west-sat-com-alleg-rel-F (zoot-suited Christ parachutes into Old West; Holy Ghost in a bedsheet; man killed & resurrected repeatedly; walking on water; etc.)

Ref: Vw 26 July '72 p 14, 22.

See also: King of Kings.

Great Adventures on Bottle-Gourd Island

See: Hyokkori Hyôtan Jima (1967).

Great Alaskan Mystery, The

(The Great Northern Mystery -- Brit.t.)

1944 U serial 13 parts 26 reels.

Assoc Prod: Henry MacRae.

Dir: Ray Taylor & Lewis D. Collins.

Story: Jack Foley.

SP: Maurice Tombragel & George H. Plympton.

Cin: William Sickner.

Cast: Ralph Morgan, Marjorie Weaver, Milburn Stone, Fuzzy Knight, Martin Kosleck, Joseph Crehan, Anthony Warde, Jay Novello, Jack Ingram, Gibson Gowland.

cont.

Great Alaskan Mystery cont.

SF ("peratron" machine transmits matter through space)

Ref: MFB Dec '46 p 169; FFF p81; SM 5:11; FDY '56; LC.

Great Bet, The

(Die Grosse Wette)

1916 German sil.

Dir: Harry Piel.

Cast: Mizzi Wirth, Ludwig Hartmann, Harry Piel.

SF (airline cabs; robots; set in year 2000)

Ref: MPW 1 April '16 p71; Gifford/SF p 136; Ackerman.

Great Big Crocodile, The

See: Crocodile Majuscule, Le (1964).

Great Brain Robbery, The

n.d. Amateur (Film-makers' Coop) 16mm color ani 3 mins.

Made by: Charles Plymell.

exp-F

Ref: FMC 5:266.

Great Crooner, The

(story by C.B. Kelland)

See: Mr. Dodd Takes the Air (1937).

Great Fear, The

(Veliki Strah)

1958 Yugoslavian, Zagreb color ani 11.8 mins.

Dir: Dušan Vukotić.

Story: D. Vukotić & Ivo Vrbanic.

Design: Boris Kolar.

Ani: Zlatko Grgić.

Bg: Zlatko Bourek.

Mus: Tomislav Simović.

F-com (spoof of horror films & mysteries)

Ref: Z/Zagreb p56; MFB April '61 p53; MMF 10-11:82, 84.

Great Gabbo, The

1929 (1930) James Cruze Inc. (Sono-Art, World Wide) 111 mins (70 mins) 2-color seq.

Prod & Dir: James Cruze.

SP: F. Hugh Herbert.

Sets: Robert E. Lee.

Choreog: Maurice L. Kusell.

Cin: Ira Morgan.

Cast: Erich von Stroheim, Betty Compson, Don Douglas, Marjorie Kane.

Based on short story "The Rival Dummy" by Ben Hecht.

bor-psy-F-H (insane ventriloquist smashes dummy then realizes it to be his sole object of love)

Ref: AFI F2.2224 p311; MPN 41:11: 83; Vw 18 Sept '29.

Great Gambini, The

1937 Par 71 mins.

Prod: B.P. Schulberg.

Dir: Charles Vidor.

SP: Frank Partos, Howard Young, & Frederick Jackson.

Art Dir: Albert S. D'Agostino.

Cin: Leon Shamroy.

Edit: Robert Bischoff.

Cast: Akim Tamiroff, Reginald Denny, William Demarest, Edward Brophy, Marian Marsh, John Trent, Genevieve Tobin, Lya Lys.

myst; bor-H (magician & mind-reader predicts murder that occurs)

Ref: MPH 24 July '37 p50.

Great German North Sea Tunnel, The

1914 British, Dreadnought sil.

Dir: Frank Newman.

SF

Ref: Gifford/SF p45.

Great Impersonation, The

1935 U 67 mins.

Prod: Carl Laemmle Jr.

Dir: Alan Crosland.

SP: Frank Wead & Eve Greene.

Cin: Milton Krasner.

Edit: Phil Kahn.

Mus: Franz Waxman.

Cast: Edmund Lowe [dual role], Valerie Hobson, Frank Reicher, Brandon Hurst, Lumsden Hare, Spring Byington, Leonard Mudie, Dwight Frye.

myst-H (spy story in old manor house; horror scenes)

Ref: LC; Willis.

Based on the novel by E. Phillips Oppenheim.

Great Jewel Robbery, The

(Kradja Dragulja)

1959 Yugoslavian, Zagreb color ani 9.3 mins.

Dir: Mladen Feman.

Story: Berislav Brkić.

Design: Vladimir Kristl.

Ani: Branislav Nemet.

Bg: Zlatko Bourek.

Mus: Miljenko Prohaska.

F-com

Ref: Z/Zagreb p 59, 16-18; Ani/Cin p 134.

Great Kali's Victory

See: Jai Maha Kali (1951).

Great Love, The

See: Grand Amour, Le (1969).

Great Love of Count Dracula, The

See: Gran Amor del Conde Dracula, El (1972).

Great Lure of Paris, The

1913 Feature Photoplay Co. sil 3 reels.

F (scientist uses superhuman power on girl, raises her to heights of fame)

Ref: MPW 18:783, 920.

Great Magic

See: Maha Maya (1945).

Great Meeting, The

1951 Yugoslavian, Zagreb ani 22 mins.

Dir: Norbert Neugebauer.

Ani: Dusan Vukotić and others.

F

Ref: Ani/Cin p 129-30; AtMo Dec '62 p95-97.

Great Méliès, The

See: Grand Méliès, Le (1952).

Great Mr. Handel, The

1944 British (Midfilm) color 89 mins.

Prod: James B. Sloan.

Dir: Norman Walker.

Story: Gerald Elliott.

SP: L. Du Gerald Peach.

Settings: Sidney Gausden.

Cin: Claude Friese-Greene & Jack Cardiff.

Edit: Sam Simmons.

Mus Dir: Ernest Irving.

Mus: Georg Friedrich Handel.

Cast: Wilfred Lawson, Elizabeth Allan, Malcolm Keen, Michael Shepley, Max Kirby, Hay Petrie.

biog; F-dream (visions of Christ appear to Handel)

Ref: HR 18 June '44; LAT 17 June '44; FD 22 Sept '43.

Based on the life of composer Georg Friedrich Handel.

Great Mono Miracle, The

(by P.B. Kyne)

See: Face in the Fog, A (1936).

Great Monster Yongary, The

See: Yongary, Monster from the Deep (1967).

Great Northern Mystery, The

See: Great Alaskan Mystery, The (1944).

Great Physician, The

1913 Edison sil 950 ft.

Dir: Richard Ridgely.

Sc: Bannister Merwin.

Cast: Mabel Trunnelle, Helen Couglin, Robert Brower, Charles Ogle [Death].

F (death personified takes child in death's third disguise)

Ref: EK 15 Sept '13 p7; MPW 13:1207-08.

Great Pie Mystery, The

1931 Mack Sennett (Educational) 22 mins.

Dir: Del Lord.

SP: John A. Waldron, Earle Rodney, Harry McCoy, & Lew Foster.

bor-H-com (eccentric inventor; eerie house)

Ref: Maltin/GMS p 135; LC.

Remake: Spook Louder (1943).

Great Pumpkin Plot, The

1972? Amateur 16mm? sh.

F (tale of Halloween; film was made by children)

Ref: LATVG 4 June '72.

Great Race, The

1965 WB color scope 150 mins.

Prod: Martin Jurow.

Assoc Prod: Dick Crockett.

Dir: Blake Edwards.

Story: B. Edwards & Arthur Ross.

SP: A. Ross.

Art Dir: Fernando Carrere.

Cin: Russell Harlan.

Edit: Ralph E. Winters.

Mus: Henry Mancini.

Cast: Jack Lemmon, Tony Curtis, Natalie Wood, Peter Falk, Keenan Wynn, Arthur O'Connell, Vivian Vance, Dorothy Provine, Larry Storch, Ross Martin, George Macready, Denver Pyle.

com; SF-seq (villain uses noise-seeking torpedo)

Ref: MFB Nov '65 p 163-64; FDY '66.

Great Radium Mystery, The

(The Radium Mystery --alt.t.)

1919 Pacific Producing Co (U) sil serial 18 parts 36 reels.

Dir: Robert F. Hill & Robert Broadwell.

Sc: Frederick Bennett.

Cast: Cleo Madison, Eileen Sedgwick, Robert Reeves, Edwin Brady, Robert Kortman, Jeff Osborne, Gordon McGregor, Robert Grey.

west; bor-SF (new type of tank, almost indestructible)

Ref: MPN 20:1949; CNW p68, 193-94; LC.

Great Redeemer, The

1920 Maurice Tourneur (Metro) sil 5 reels.

Prod: Maurice Tourneur.

Dir: Clarence Brown.

Story: H.W. Van Loan.

Sc: Jules Furthman & Jack Gilbert.

Cast: House Peters.

rel-F (Christ appears from a sketch on the wall)

Ref: LC; MPH.

Great Reward, The

1921 Burston (National) sil serial 15 parts.

Exec Prod: Louis Burston.

Dir: Francis Ford.

Story: Elsie Van Name.

Cin: Jerome Ash.

Cast: Francis Ford, Ella Hall.

F (little people climb out of glasses, crawl over books, dance on tables)

Ref: MPW 50:325; LC.

Great Romance, The

See: Forever (1921).

Great Rupert, The

1949 (1950) George Pal (Eagle-Lion) 88 mins (79 mins).

Prod: George Pal.

Dir: Irving Pichel.

Story: Ted Allan.

SP: Laslo Vadnay.

Prod Design: Ernest Fegte.

Cin: Lionel Lindon.

Edit: Duke Goldstone.

Mus: Leith Stevens.

Cast: Jimmy Durante, Terry Moore, Tom Drake, Frank Orth, Sara Haden, Chick Chandler.

bor-F-com (trained squirrel [animated puppet] does tricks, dances Highland fling, etc.)

Ref: HR & Vd 30 Dec '49; MFB Oct '50 p 154; FDY '51.

Great Secret, The

1917 Serial Producing Co (Metro, Quality Pictures Corp) sil serial 18 parts 36 reels.

Prod, Dir, Sc: William Christy Cabanne.

Story: Fred de Gresac.

Cast: Francis X. Bushman, Beverly Bayne, Belle Bruce, Fred R. Stanton, Tom Blake, Charles Ripley, Tammany Young.

F-H (vision appears; suspended animation)

Ref: CNW p55-56, 177; MPW 32:325, 493, 635, 681, 851, 1020.

Great Toy Robbery

1963 Canadian, NFB color ani 6.5 mins.

F (Santa Claus defeats out-Taws)

Ref: Pyramid '72 p244.

Great Universe, The

1955 Soviet color 40 mins.

Dir: P. Klushantsev & N. Leschenko.

SF-doc

Ref: F&F May '55 p 18.

Great Unknown, The

See: Velká Neznámá (1971).

Great Walled City of Xan, The

1968? Amateur color ani 10 mins.

Dir: Hal Barwood.

F-com

Ref: ASIFA 4.

See also: Take One (1970).

Great World of Little Children, The

See: Wielka, Wielka i Naj-wieksza (1962).

Greatcoat, The

See: Overcoat, The.

Greater Will, The

1915 Pathé sil 5 reels.

Cast: Cyril Maude, Lois Mere-dith.

F-H (father wills a vision, causes man who wronged his daughter to commit suicide)

Ref: MPN 25 Dec '15 p 121; LC.

Greatest Battle on Earth, The

See: Ghidrah, the Three-Headed Monster (1965).

Greatest Gift, The

(story by P.V.D. Stern)

See: It's a Wonderful Life (1946).

Greatest Power, The

1917 Rolfe (Metro) sil 5 reels.

Dir: Edwin Carewe.

Story: Louis R. Wolheim.

Sc: Albert Shelby Le Vino.

Cast: Ethel Barrymore, William B. Davidson, Harry S. Northrup, Frank Currier, William Black, Cecil Owen.

SF (chemist discovers cancer cure & "exonite," a super-explosive; plans to give it to whole world so all would be afraid to use it; given to U.S. only at end)

Ref: MPW 32:1838; LC.

Greatest Question, The

1919 Griffith sil 6 reels.

Prod & Dir: D.W. Griffith.

Story: William Hale.

Cast: Lillian Gish, Robert Harron.

F (spiritualism; ghost)

Ref: RAF p387, 390; LC; Blum p 188; New Yorker 13 Feb '71.

Greatest Story Ever Told, The

(Jesus --rr.t.)

1965 George Stevens (UA) color 70mm 222 mins (196 mins).

Prod & Dir: George Stevens.

Exec Prod: Frank I. Davis.

Creative Consultant: Carl Sandburg.

SP: G. Stevens & James Lee Barrett.

Art Dir: Richard Day & William Creber.

Cin: William C. Mellor & Loyal Griggs.

SpFX: J. McMillan Johnson, Clarence Slifer, A. Arnold Gillespie, & Robert R. Hoag.

Edit: Harold F. Kress, Argyle Nelson, & Frank O'Neill.

Mus: Alfred Newman.

Cast: Max von Sydow [Jesus], Michael Anderson Jr., Carroll Baker, Ina Balin, Pat Boone, Victor Buono, Richard Conte, Joanna Dunham, José Ferrer, David Hedison, Van Heflin, Charlton Heston, Martin Landau, Angela Lansbury, Robert Loggia, Janet Margolin, David McCallum, Roddy McDowall, Dorothy McGuire, Sal Mineo, Nehemiah Persoff, Donald Pleasence [Devil], Sidney Poitier, Claude Rains, Gary Raymond, Telly Savalas, Joseph Schildkraut, Marian Seldes, Paul Stewart, Michael Tolan, John Wayne, Shelley Winters, Ed Wynn.

rel-F (life of Christ with usual miracles: raises Lazarus from the dead, heals the lame & blind; meets the Devil in the desert)

Ref: FF '65 p63-68; MFB May '65 p69; FIR May '71 p319; F&F June '65 p25-26.

Based on the "Four Gospels" from "The Bible."

Title from the novel by Fulton Oursler.

See also: King of Kings.

Greatest Truth, The

1921? (1922) German, UFA (Par) sil 5257 ft.

Dir: Joe May.

Cast: Mia May.

F (reincarnation from time of Roman Empire)

Ref: MPW 57:450.

Greed of William Hart, The

See: Horror Maniacs (1948).

Greedy Bee, The

1958 Hungarian ani sh.

Dir: Gyula Macskassy.

F

Ref: Ani/Cin p 174.

Greek Mirthology

1954 Par color ani 1 reel.

F-com

Ref: LC; PopCar.

See also: Popeye (1933-57).

Green Archer, The

● 1926 Pathé sil serial 10 parts 20 reels.

Dir: Spencer Gordon Bennet.

Sc: Frank Leon Smith.

Cast: Allene Ray, Walter Miller, Burr McIntosh, Frank Lackteen, Stephen Gratten, Walter P. Lewis, Jack Tanner, Ray Allan, William Randall.

Ref: CNW p 125-26, 135, 246-47; FIR Aug/Sept '55 p329; LC.

● 1941 Col serial 15 parts 31 reels.

Prod: Larry Darmour.

Dir: James W. Horne.

SP: Morgan B. Cox, John Cutting, Jesse A. Duffy, & J.W. Horne.

Cin: James S. Brown Jr.

Edit: Dwight Caldwell & Earl Turner.

Mus: Lee Zahler.

Cast: Victor Jory, Iris Mere-dith, James Craven, Robert Fiske, Dorothy Fay, Forrest Taylor, Jack Ingram, Joseph W. Girard, Fred Kelsey.

Ref: Ser/Col; LC; SQ 5.

● 1961 W. German, Casino 95 mins.

Dir: Jurgen Roland.

SP: Wolfgang Menge.

Cast: Gert Fröbe, Karin Dor, Charles Pallent.

Ref: Willis.

myst; bor-H (murders around an old mansion apparently committed by ghostly green archer)

Based on the novel by Edgar Wallace.

Green Button, The

1966? Soviet, Kiev (Sovex-portfilm) color ani 11 mins.

Dir: I. Gurvich.

Story: L. Kazarov.

Ani: I. Gurvich & N. Churilov.

doc; SF (future exploration of the planets)

Ref: Sovexportfilm cat 3:109.

Green Eye of the Yellow God, The

1913 Edison sil 1020 ft?

Dir: Richard Ridgely.

Cast: Charles Ogle.

bor-F-H (man dies mysterious-ly after stealing eye of Hindu idol)

Ref: EK 1 Sept '13; MPW '13 p 1086; LC.

Based on the poem by J. Milton Hayes.

Green Eyed Monster

1915 (1916) Fox sil 5 reels.

Prod & Dir: J. Gordon Edwards.

Sc: J.G. Edwards & Mary Murillo.

Cast: Robert B. Mantell, Stuart Holmes, Genevieve Hamper, Henry Leone, Charles Davidson.

H (woman dies of shock on seeing husband's body; murderer does same later)

Ref: MPN 13:256; LC.

Green Ghost, The

See: Unholy Night, The (1929); Spectre Vert, Le (1930).

Green Grow the Lilacs

(play by L. Riggs)

See: Oklahoma! (1955).

Green Hornet, The

1939 (1940) U serial 13 parts 26 reels.

Assoc Prod: Henry MacRae.

Dir: Ford Beebe & Ray Taylor.

SP: George H. Plympton, Basil Dickey, Morrison C. Wood, & Lyonel Margolies.

Cin: William Sickner & Jerry Ash.

Cast: Gordon Jones, Keye Luke, Anne Nagel, Wade Boteler, Philip Trent, Walter McGrail, John Kelly, Anne Gwynne, Ann Doran, Selmar Jackson, Ben Taggart, Kenneth Harlan, Guy Usher, Alan Ladd, Lane Chandler.

bor-SF (super-speed car; gas gun)

Ref: LC; Old Movies 2; MPH 2 Dec '39 p45.

Based on the radio serial by Fran Striker.

Sequel: Green Hornet Strikes Again, The (1940).

See also: Adventures of the Spirit, The (1963).

Green Hornet Strikes Again, The

1940 U serial 15 parts 30 reels.

Dir: Ford Beebe & John Rawlins.

SP: George H. Plympton, Basil Dickey, & Sherman Lowe.

Cin: Jerome Ash.

Cast: Warren Hull, Anne Nagel, Keye Luke, C. Montague Shaw, Nestor Paiva, Wade Boteler, Eddie Acuff, James Seay, Eddie Dunn, John Merton, Roy Barcroft, Lane Chandler, Pat O'Malley, Eddie Parker, Ray Teal, Jason Robards, Walter Sande, Tristram Coffin.

bor-SF (super-speed car; gas gun; new type of bomb)

Ref: Old Movies 4; LC; Acad; Willis.

Based on radio serial "The Green Hornet" by Fran Striker.

Sequel to: Green Hornet, The (1939).

Green Mansions

1959 MGM color scope 104 mins.

Prod: Edmund Grainger.

Dir: Mel Ferrer.

SP: Dorothy Kingsley.

Art Dir: William A. Horning & Preston Ames.

Cin: Joseph Ruttenberg.

SpFX: A. Arnold Gillespie, Lee LeBlanc, & Robert R. Hoag.

Edit: Ferris Webster.

Mus: Heitor Villa-Lobos.

Mus Score: Bronislau Kaper.

Cast: Audrey Hepburn, Anthony Perkins, Lee J. Cobb, Sessue Hayakawa, Henry Silva, Nehe-miah Persoff, Michael Pate.

bor-F (Rima is a girl who lives in Amazon jungle & communicates with animals; apparition of Rima appears to her lover at end)

Ref: FF '59 p63-65; LC; FDY '60; FIR '59 p237.

Based on the novel by William Henry Hudson.

Green Mare, The

(La Jument Verte; Bedroom Vendetta --alt.t.)

1959 (1961) French/Italian, Sneg & Sopac/Zebra (Zenith) color scope 93 mins.

Prod & Dir: Claude Autant-Lara.

SP: Jean Aurenche & Pierre Bost.

Art Dir: Max Douy.

Cin: Jacques Natteau.

cont.

Green Mare, The cont.

Edit: Madeleine Gug.

Mus: René Cloerec.

Cast: Bourvil, Sandra Milo, Francis Blanche, Yves Robert, Valerie Lagrange, Mireille Perrey, Marie Dea.

com; F-seq (green horse born at story's beginning)

Ref: FF ;61 p280-81; HR 6 Feb '62; FIR March '62.

Based on the novel by Marcel Aymé.

Green Pastures, The

1936 WB 90 mins.

Prod: Henry Blanke.

Dir: Marc Connelly & William Keighley.

SP: M. Connelly.

Art Dir: Allen Saalburg & Stanley Fleischer.

Cin: Hal Mohr.

SpFX: Fred Jackman.

Edit: George Amy.

Cast: Rex Ingram [de Lawd], Eddie (Rochester) Anderson, Oscar Polk, George Reed.

rel-F-com ("de Lawd" and angels have a fish fry in Heaven)

Ref: HR 27 Jan '36, 16 May '36; FDY '37; LC.

Based on the play by Marc Connelly suggested by Southern sketches "Ol' Man Adam an His Chillun" by Roark Bradford.

See also: Clean Pastures (1937); Grim Pastures (1943).

Green Planet, The

See: Planete Verte, La (1965).

Green Slime, The

(Gamma Sango Uchu Daisakusen; Battle Beyond the Stars --s.t.; Death and the Green Slime --ad.t?)

1968 (1969) U.S./Japanese, Southern Cross/Toei (MGM) color 77 mins. (90 mins.)

Prod: Ivan Reiner & Walter Manley.

Dir: Kinji Fukasaku.

Story: I. Reiner.

SP: Charles Sinclair, William Finger, & Tom Rowe.

Art Dir: Sinichi Eno.

Makeup: Takeshi Ugai.

Cin: Yoshikazu Yamasawa.

SpFX: Akira Watanabe.

Edit: Osamu Tanaka.

Mus: Toshiaki Tsushima.

Cast: Robert Horton, Richard Jaeckel, Luciana Paluzzi, Bud Widom, Ted Gunther.

SF-H (set in future; fast-multiplying alien monsters are loosed aboard a space-station)

Ref: FF '69 p235; MFB '69 p215; Vw 28 May '69; LAT 21 Aug '69.

Green Spot Mystery, The

See: Detective Lloyd (1931-32).

Green Terror, The

1919 British, Gaum sil 6524 ft.

Dir: Will P. Kellino.

Sc: G.W. Clifford.

Cast: Aurele Sydney, Heather Thatcher, W.T. Ellwanger, Cecil du Gue, Maud Yates, Arthur Poole.

bor-SF (doctor schemes to destroy the world's wheat)

Ref: FIR May '67 p314; Gifford/ BFC 06745.

Based on a story by Edgar Wallace.

Greensleeves

n.d. Amateur (CFS) color 4 mins.

Made by: Lynn Fayman.

abs-F

Ref: CFS cat Sept '68.

Greetings, Atom!

1966? Soviet, Soyuzmultfilm (Sovexportfilm) ani 9.5 mins.

Dir: I. Milchin.

Story: A. Peschersky & D. Rodychev.

Ani: G. Brashishkite.

doc; F (atomic structure & uses; power for spaceships, etc.)

Ref: Sovexportfilm cat 3:108.

Greetings, Bait!

1943 WB color ani 7 mins.

Prod: Leon Schlesinger.

Story: Ted Pierce.

Ani: Manuel Perez.

Mus Dir: Carl W. Stalling.

F-com

Ref: LC; Acad nom.

Greetings, Friends

See: Saludos Amigos (1942).

Gregorio and His Angel

1966? Mexican, Valdes Pro-ducciones.

Prod: John Anderson.

Dir: Gilberto Martinez Solares.

Cast: Broderick Crawford, Tin-Tan, Connie Carol.

F-com (graven image turns into little girl)

Ref: MTVM July '66 p32; Collier.

Gremlins, The

1942 WD (RKO) color ani sh.

Prod: Walt Disney.

F-com

Ref: Acad.

Grenouilles Qui Demandent un Roi, Les

See: Frogs Who Wanted a King, The.

Grey Cart, The

See: Stroke of Midnight, The (1920).

Grey Dame, The

(The Gray Lady --Brit.t.)

1909 Danish, Nordisk (Great Northern) sil 972 ft.

bor-F (Sherlock Holmes investi-gates "grey lady," a ghost)

Ref: MPW 5:344, 432; Bios 2 Sept '09.

Based on the character "Sher-lock Holmes" created by Arthur Conan Doyle.

See also: Sherlock Holmes.

Greyskin

See: Sivoushko (1962).

Grief in Bagdad

1925 Roach-Pathé sil sh.

Prod: Hal Roach.

sat-F-com (rope trick; flying donkey; magic carpet; all-chimpanzee cast)

Ref: Willis; LC; D. Glut; B. Warren.

Satire of Thief of Bagdad, The (1924).

Grigori Rasputin i Velikor Russkoi

(Grigori Rasputin and the Great Russian Revolution)

1917 Russian (Soviet?) sil.

bor-F; hist-H (powers of super-hypnotism)

Ref: CineF 4.

See also: Rasputin.

Grigory Rasputin and the Great Russian Revolution

See: Grigori Rasputin i Velikor Russkoi (1917).

Griha Lakshmi

(Goddess of the Home)

1959 Indian (in Hindi), Bombay Movietone 161 mins.

Griha Lakshmi cont.

Dir: Raman B. Desai.

Cast: Pandari Bai, Lalita Pawar, Indira Bansal, Sahu Modak.

rel-F (young wife, subjected to endless toil & trouble, appeals to God who comes & takes her away to heaven)

Ref: FEFN 12:16, 17, 41.

Grim Pastures

1943 Canadian, NFB color ani sh.

Dir: George Dunning.

F

Ref: Ani/Cin p85.

Satire on Green Pastures (1936)?

Grimaces

See: Gyermekbetegsegek (1966).

Grimm's Fairy Tales

1955 (1961?) German color

F (witch; talking wolf)

Ref: Acad.

Based on fairy tales "Little Red Riding Hood" and "Hansel and Gretel" as collected by Jacob & Wilhelm Grimm.

See also: Hansel and Gretel; Little Red Riding Hood.

Grimm's Fairy Tales (for Adults Only)

(Grimm's Märchen -- für Lüsterne Pärchen: Grimm's Fairy Tales for Lusting Couples)

1969 (1971) W. German, Caro (Cinemation) color 90 mins (76 mins).

German version:

Dir & SP: Rolf Thiele.

Cin: Wolf Wirth.

Mus: Brand Kampka.

Eng Lang version:

Dir: Helen Gray.

SP: Tom Baum.

Mus: Joe Beck & Regis Mull.

Cast: Marie Liljedahl, Eva V. Rueber-Staier, Ingrid von Begen, Walter Giller, Peter Hohberger, Gaby Fuchs.

sex-F

Ref: Vw 27 Jan '71; FF '71 p69; NYT 23 March '71.

Grinning Face, The

See: Grinsende Gesicht, Das (1921).

Grinsende Gesicht, Das

(The Grinning Face; The Man Who Laughs --ad.t.)

1921 Austrian, Olympic sil 90 mins.

Dir: Julius Herzka.

Sc: Louis Nerz.

Art Dir: Ladislaus Tuszinsky (Tuszynsky?).

Cin: Eduard Hosch.

Cast: Franz Hobling, Nora Gregor, Lucienne Delacroix, Anna Kallina, Eugen Jensen, Armin Seydelmann, Fritz Strassny.

hist-H (child's face carved permanently into hideous grin; grows up to be clown)

Ref: Osterr.

Based on novel "L'Homme Qui Rit" by Victor Hugo.

See also: Homme Qui Rit, L' (1909).

Grip of Iron, The

• 1913 British, Brightonia sil 3250 ft.

Dir: Arthur Charrington.

Cast: Fred Powell, Nell Emerald, H. Agar Lyons, Frank E. Petley, Gertrude Price, Stanley Bedwell.

Ref: Gifford/H p 195; Gifford/BFC 04208.

• 1920 British, Famous Pictures sil 5000 ft.

Grip of Iron, The cont.

Dir: Bert Haldane.

Sc: Arthur Shirley & B. Haldane.

Cast: George Foley, Malvina Long-fellow, James Lindsay, Laurence Tessier, Ronald Power, Ivy King, Warwick Buckland, John Power, Moore Marriott.

Ref: Gifford/H p 195; Gifford/BFC 06833.

myst; bor-H (strangler is clerk who robs for extravagant daughter

Based on the play by Arthur Shirley from the novel "Les Estrangleurs de Paris" by Belot.

Grip of the Strangler, The

See: Haunted Strangler, The (1958).

Gripoterio, El

(The Gripoterium)

1971 Spanish, Procinsa color ani 12.1 mins.

Dir: José Ramón Sánchez.

F (children, waging war on hunger, meet a prehistoric animal which continues to grow as it eats)

Ref: SpCin '72.

Gripoterium, The

See: Gripoterio, El (1971).

Gris

(Gloomy)

1969 Spanish, Teletecnicine Internacional color scope 14 mins.

Dir: Antonio Gómez Diez.

F (evil spirits frustrate musician)

Ref: SpCin '70 p260.

Gritos en la Noche

See: Awful Dr. Orlof, The (1961).

Grosse Verhau, Der

(The Big Mess)

1971 W. German, Kairos Film color 90 mins.

Dir & SP: Alexander Kluge.

Cin: Thomas Mauch.

SpFX: Bernd Hoeltz.

Edit: Maximilian Mainka & Beate Mainka-Jellinghaus.

Cast: Vinzenz Sterr, Maria Sterr, Sigi Graue, Silvia Forsthofer, Hajo von Zuendt.

SF-com (set in future; 2 astro-nauts try to wreck spaceships to sell to insurance company)

Ref: Vw 22 Sept '71; MTVM Autumn II '71 edition p 14-A.

Based on "The Monopole Capital-ism" by Baran and Sweezy.

Grosse Wette, Die

See: Great Bet, The (1916).

Grosser Grau-Blauer Vogel, Ein

(A Big Gray-Blue Bird)

1970 W. German, T-S Film color 98 mins.

Prod & Dir: Thomas Schamoni.

SP: T. Schamoni, Uwe Brandner, Hans Noever, & Max Zihlmann.

Cin: Dietrich Lohmann & Bernd Fiedler.

Mus: The Can.

Cast: Klaus Lemke, Olivera Vuco, Sylvia Winter, Lukas Ammann, Umberto Orsini.

SF (old man has formula which can alter structure of uni-verse; he gives it to poet who converts it into a poem; metaphysical gangsters; secret hidden hypnotically in minds of scientists)

Ref: GFN 33; Vw 14 July '71.

Grotesques

1908 French, Pathé sil 328 ft.

F (puppets in grotesque cos-tumes change sizes; tricks)

Ref: Views 126:10.

cont.

cont.

Grotte aux Surprises, La
See: Grotto of Surprises, The (1904).

Grotto of Surprises, The
(La Grotte aux Surprises)
1904 French, Star sil 125 ft.
Prod: Georges Méliès.
F
Ref: LC; Sadoul/M; GM Mage.

Grotto of Torture, The
1912 Pathé sil 2 reels.
H (trained leopard; torture)
Ref: MPW 14:682 ad.

Ground Zero
1973 James Flocker Enterprises color.
Prod & Dir: James T. Flocker.
SP: Samuel Newman.
Mus: The Chosen Few.
Cast: Ron Casteel, Melvin Belli, Augie Treibach, Kim Friese, John Waugh, Yvonne D'Angiers.
bor-soc-SF (madman plants bombs on the Golden Gate Bridge in San Francisco)
Ref: SF Chronicle ad from Harold Sommerfeldt.

Gruesome Twosome, A
1945 WB color ani 7 mins.
Dir: Robert Clampett.
Story: Warren Foster.
Ani: Roderick Scribner.
Mus Dir: Carl W. Stalling.
F-com
Ref: LC.

Gruesome Twosome, The
1966 Mayflower.
Exec Prod: Fred M. Sandy.
Prod & Dir & Cin: Herschell Gordon Lewis.
SP: Louise Downe.
Mus Sup: Larry Wellington.
Cast: Elizabeth Davis, Chris Martell, Gretchen Welles, Rodney Bedell.
H-com (mentally defective son of a wigmaker scalps young women for her)
Ref: LAT 12 Oct '68; Photon 15:13.

Grustalni Bashmachok
See: Cinderella (1960).

Gu
1972 Belgian color? ani 5 mins.
Made by: Vivian Missen.
F
Ref: IAFF '72; Vw 20 Sept '72 p6 at Sitges Festival.

Guarding Angel, The
1909 Lubin sil 750 ft.
F (angels; vision of true parents appears to girl living with gypsies)
Ref: LC; FI IV-14:9.

Guepardo, El
(The Cheetah)
1971 Spanish, Estudios Castilla color ani 8.7 mins.
Dir: Armaro Carretero.
Realisation: Vicente Rodriguez.
bor-F-com-doc (the natural history of the cheetah, with some gags)
Ref: SpCin '72.

Guess What Happened to Count Dracula?
1970 Merrick Int'l color 80 mins.
Exec Prod, Dir, SP: Laurence Merrick.
Prod: Leo Rivers.
Art Dir: Michael Minor.
Makeup: Rick Sagliani.

cont.

Guess What Happened to Count Dracula? cont.
Cin: Bob Caramico.
Edit: George Watters.
Mus: Des Roberts.
Cast: Des Roberts [vampire], Claudia Barren, John Londen, Robert Branche, Frank Donato, Sharon Beverly, Damu King.
F-H (Dracula, here called "Count Adrian", in Hollywood)
Ref: Photon 21:30-31; BO 22 Feb '71; FF '71 p756.
Based on a character created by Bram Stoker.
See also: Dracula (1930).

Guest, The
1969? Amateur (Film-makers' Coop) 16mm pixilation 2 1/3 mins.
Made by: Frank Gardner.
F-com (man entertained at tea by two young ladies, in pixilation)
Ref: FMC 5:113.

Gueux au Paradise, Les
See: Hoboes in Paradise (1950).

Gugusse and the Automaton
(Gugusse et l'Automate; Clown and the Automaton --ad.t.)
1897 French sil 65 ft.
Prod: Georges Méliès.
F
Ref: Sadoul/M; GM Mage.

Guguste et Belzébuth
See: Clown vs. Satan, The (1900).

Guillaume Tell et le Clown
See: Adventures of William Tell (1898).

Guillemette Babin
See: Destin Exécrable de Guillemette Babin, Le (1948).

Guilt of Janet Ames, The
1947 Col 82 mins.
Dir: Henry Levin.
Story: Lenore Coffee.
SP: Louella MacFarlane, Allen Rivkin, & Devery Freeman.
Cin: Joseph Walker.
Edit: Charles Nelson.
Mus: George Duning.
Cast: Rosalind Russell, Melvyn Douglas, Sid Caesar, Betsy Blair, Nina Foch, Hugh Beaumont.
bor-psy-F (via hypnosis, woman imagines she enters lives of other survivors)
Ref: Vd 5 March '47; MFB May '47 p64; FD 6 March '47.

Guirlande Merveilleuse, La
See: Marvellous Wreath, The (1903).

Guitar and the Hooter, The
1962? Bulgarian color ani sh.
Dir: Christo Topouzanov.
F
Ref: Bulgarian Films 8.

Gul Bakawli
1960 (1961) Pakistani, Zaman Art Prods color.
Dir: Munshi Dil.
Art Dir: Habib Shah.
Cast: Sudhir, Jamila, Nazar, Rakhshi.
F (ad shows genie or big monster; winged woman; magic flower)
Ref: FEFN March '61 cover; Ackerman.

Gul Sanovar
1928 Indian, Kohinoor sil.
F
Ref: IndCin YB.

cont.

Gul Sanover
(Flower Lake)
1934 Indian, Imperial.
Dir: Homi Masteri.
Cast: Sulochana, Zillo, Zubeda Jr., D. Bilimoria, Gulam Mohammod.
F (tricks; fairy tale)
Ref: Dipali 18 Jan '35 p 19.

Gulbadan
1960? Pakistani, Super-Hit Movies.
Prod: Shabab Kairanvi.
Dir: A. Hameed.
Mus: Akhtar.
Cast: Musarrat, Ejaz Laila, Nasira, Sh. Iqbal, Azad, Nazar.
F (man turned into wooden staff extinguishes evil magician's magic flame & frees princess; evil girl genie)
Ref: FEFN Feb '61 p44, 61.

Gulbakavali
● 1955 Indian, Sharad.
Dir: Dhirubhai Desai.
F
Ref: Filmindia July '55 p58.

● 1947 (1948) Indian, Central.
Dir: Rustom Modi.
Cin: Balwant Dave.
Mus: Firoz Dastur & Bundu Khan.
Cast: Firoz Dastur, Rabab, Sanobar, Jamshedji, Menka.
myth-F
Ref: Filmindia April '48 p43.

Gulliver in Lilliput
1923 French sil ani puppet 3000 ft.
Dir: Albert Mourlan & Raymond Villette.
sat-F (land of tiny people)
Ref: F/A p633.
Based on "Voyage to Lilliput" portion of novel "Gulliver's Travels" by Jonathan Swift.
See also: Gulliver's Travels.

Gulliver Mickey
1934 WD ani 1 reel.
Prod: Walt Disney.
F-com
Ref: LC.
Suggested by novel "Gulliver's Travels" by Jonathan Swift.
See also: Gulliver's Travels; Mickey Mouse (1928 --).

Gulliver's Travels
● (Le Voyage de Gulliver à Lilliput et chez les Géants)
1902 French sil 280 ft.
Prod: Georges Méliès.
Ref: Sadoul/M; GM Mage.

● 1939 Par color ani 77 mins.
Prod: Max Fleischer.
Dir: Dave Fleischer.
Adapt: Edmond Seward.
SP: Dan Gordon, Cal Howard, Ted Pierce, Izzy Sparber, & E. Seward.
Ani: Graham Place, Arnold Gillespie, and others.
Cin: Charles Schettler.
Mus: Victor Young.
Songs (Mus & Lyrics): Ralph Rainger & Leo Robin.
Voices: Jessica Dragonette, Lanny Ross.
Ref: MPH 11 Dec '39 p25; HR 16 Dec '39; FDY '40.

F (English traveler of 18th Century finds land of tiny people; in 1902 version, also land of giants)

cont.

Gulliver's Travels cont.
Based on the novel by Jonathan Swift.
See also: Monsieur Clown chez les Lilliputiens (1909); Gulliver in Lilliput (1923); Gulliver Mickey (1934); New Gulliver, The (1935); 3 Worlds of Gulliver, The (1959); Gulliver's Travels Beyond the Moon (1965); Pripad Pro Zacinajicho Kata (1970).

Gulliver's Travels Beyond the Moon
1965 (1966) Japanese, Toei (Continental Distributing) color ani 85 mins.
Prod: Hiroshi Okawa.
Dir: Yoshio Kuroda.
SP: Shinichi Sekizawa.
Ani Dir: Hideo Furusawa.
Eng Lyrics & Mus: Milton & Anne DeLugg.
F-dream (living toys; Gulliver & little boy go by spaceship to planet beyond moon; friendly & evil robots)
Ref: FD 13 May '66; FF '66 p384; MPH 25 May '66.
Based on a character created by Jonathan Swift.
See also: Gulliver's Travels.

Gumbasia
1955 Amateur (CFS) color ani clay? 4 mins.
Made by: Art Clokey.
abs-F
Ref: CFS cat Sept '68; Undrgnd p91, 273.

Gumby's Adventures on the Moon
1969 Clokey Prods? (Film-makers' Coop) 8mm sil ani puppet? 2 mins.
Made by: Roni Hoffman.
F
Ref: FMC 5:157.

Gunan-Bator
1966? Soviet, Soyuzmultfilm (Sovexportfilm) color ani 20 mins.
Dir: R. Davydov.
Story: L. Belokurov.
Ani: A. Vinokurov.
F (shepherd performs 3 tasks to win princess)
Ref: Sovexportfilm cat 3:106.

Gungala, la Vergine della Giungla
(Gungala, the Virgin of the Jungle)
1967 Italian, Romana color.
Dir: Romano Ferrara (Mike Williams).
SP: L.A. Rolhemann.
Cin: Augusto Tiezzi.
Mus: Francesco Lavagnino.
Cast: Kitty Swan, Linda Veras, Poldo Bendandi, Conrad Loth, Archie Savage.
bor-F (black leopard protects girl raised in the jungle)
Ref: Ital Prods '67 p20-21.
See also: Gungala. . .

Gungala Pantera Nuda
1968 Italian, Samma Cinemat. color.
Dir: Roger Drake.
Cast: Kitty Swan, Micaela Cendali Pignatelli, Angelo Infanti, Tiffany Anderson, Jeff Tangen.
bor-F
Ref: MTVM May '68 p31; Bankok Post 23 July '69; Singapore Straits-Times 5 Oct '70.
See also: Gungala. . .

Gungala the Black Panther Girl
1968? Italian.
Cast: Kitty Swan?

cont.

Gungala the Black Panther Girl cont.

bor-F

Ref: Singapore Straits-Times 5 Oct '70.

Is this the same film as Gungala Pantera Nuda (1968)?

Gungala Vergin [sic] of the Jungle

See: Gungala, la Vergine della Giungla (1967).

Gunnar Hedes Saga

1922 Swedish sil.

Dir & Sc: Mauritz Stiller.

Art Dir: Axel Esbensen.

Cin: J. Julius.

Cast: Einar Hansson, Pauline Brunius, Mary Johnson, Stina Berg, Adolf Olchansky.

F

Ref: Swedish Cin p39-41, 214; UF p412.

Based on novel "En Herrgårdssägen" by Selma Lagerlöf.

Gurgle, Gurgle, Little Brook

1963 Soviet, Soyuzmultfilm color ani 20 mins.

Dir: P. Nosov.

Story: R. Nagornaya.

F (animals save brook)

Ref: Sovexportfilm cat 1:132.

Guru the Mad Monk

See: Garu the Mad Monk (1970).

Gusztáv-Sorozat

(Gustavus --Brit.t.)

1960 Hungarian, Pannonia color ani sh series.

Dir & Story: Miklós Temesi, Marcell Jankovics, Attila Dargay, & József Nepp.

F-com

Ref: MFB Oct '72 p220; MTVM Nov '67 p9; Vw 12 May '71.

Guy Named Joe, A

1943 MGM 120 mins.

Prod: Everett Riskin.

Dir: Victor Fleming.

Story: Chandler Sprague & David Boehm.

SP: Dalton Trumbo.

Art Dir: Cedric Gibbons.

Cin: Karl Freund & George Folsey.

SpFX: Arnold Gillespie, Donald Jahraus, & Warren Newcombe.

Edit: Frank Sullivan.

Cast: Spencer Tracy [ghost], Irene Dunn, Van Johnson, Lionel Barrymore, Ward Bond, James Gleason, Esther Williams.

F (Tracy is dead flyer assigned to help other new flyers)

Ref: MFB March '44 p30; Vd & HR 24 Dec '43; MPH 17 July '43.

Gwangi

See: Valley of Gwangi, The (1968).

Gyermekbetegsegek

(Grimaces)

1966 Hungarian, Studio III Malim color 77 mins.

Dir & SP: Ference Kardos & Janos Rozsa.

Cin: Sandor Sara.

Cast: Istvan Geczy, Tundi Kassai, Gabor Lontay, Judith Halasz.

exp-F ("exaggerated fantasy world" -- Collier)

Ref: Collier; Richardson.

Gypsy Life

See: Mighty Mouse in Gypsy Life (1945).

Gypsy Moon

1953 Reed (MCA-TV) 78 mins.

Prod: Roland Reed.

cont.

Gypsy Moon cont.

Cast: Richard Crane, Scotty Beckett, Sally Mansfield.

SF (adventures of a wandering moon)

Ref: CoF 10:40; Willis.

See also: Rocky Jones, Space Ranger.

Gypsy's Revenge

1907 (1908) Lubin sil sh.

F (man haunted by apparition)

Ref: LC; MPW 1908 p82.

Gyromorphosis

1958 Dutch color 16mm 7 mins.

Prod: Hy Hirsh.

abs-F

Ref: CFS cat Sept '68; BFI Dist Cat p75; Undrgnd p95.

H

H and r

n.d. Amateur (Film-makers' Coop) 16mm color sil 11 mins.

Made by: Tony Siani.

exp-abs-F (painting-on-film)

Ref: FMC 3:57.

H.G. Wells' New Invisible Man

See: New Invisible Man, The (1960).

H-Man, The

(Uomini H; Bijyo To Ekitai-ningen: Beautiful Women and the Hydrogen Man)

1958 (1959) Japanese, Toho (Col) color 87 mins (79 mins).

Prod: Tomoyuki Tanaka.

Dir: Inoshiro Honda.

Story: Hideo Kaijo.

SP: Takeshi Kimura.

Cin: Hajime Koizumi.

SpFX: Eiji Tsuburaya.

Mus: Masaru Sato.

Cast: Yumi Shirakawa, Kenji Sahara, Akihiko Hirata, Koreya Senda, Eitaro Ozawa.

SF-H (radiation from H-bomb turns men into living radio-active water; they dissolve people and eat them)

Ref: FF '59 p200; FDY '60; UniJ 2:16-17.

H2S

1969 Italian, Documento.

Exec Prod: Gianni Hecht Lucari.

Prod: Mario de Biase.

Dir: Roberto Faenza.

Art Dir: Gianni Polidori.

Cin: Giulio Albonico.

Cast: Denis Gilmore, Lionel Stander, Carrol (Carole?) André, Paolo Poli, Giancarlo Cobelli.

sex-alleg-SF (world exploded at climax)

Ref: Ital Prods '68 p 110-11; Revue du Cinema July-Aug '69 p34-35.

Habatales

1960 British, Halas & Batchelor color ani sh series.

Prod: John Halas & Joy Batchelor.

F-com

Ref: Ani/Cin p81, 171.

See also: Cultured Ape, The (1960); Insolent Matador, The (1960); Widow and the Pig, The (1960).

Habeas Corpus

1929 Roach-MGM sil 2 reels.

Story & Sup: Leo McCarey.

Dir: James Parrott.

Edit: Richard Currier.

Cast: Stan Laurel, Oliver Hardy.

H-com (Stanley & Ollie as body snatchers)

Ref: Willis; LC.

Habitant of the Desert Isle, The

(Zitel Neobitajemovo Ostrova: Inhabitant of a Desert Isle)

1915 Russian sil 2800 ft.

Dir, Sc, Art Dir, Cin: Ladislas Starevitch.

Cast: Ladislas Starevitch [faun], A. Gromov, N. Valitzkaja, Yelena (Ielena) Caika.

F

Ref: Filmlex p930; Kino p421.

Habitantes de la Casa Deshabitada, Los

(The Inhabitants of the Uninhabited House)

1959 Spanish, Guión & P.C.

Dir: Pedro L. Ramirez.

SP: Vicente Coello.

Cin: Emilio Toriscot.

Mus: Federico Contreras.

Cast: Tony Leblanc, Luz Marquez, Fernando Rey, Manuel G. Bur.

bor-H-com (plot to drive someone crazy with ghost tricks)

Ref: SpCin '59 p88-89.

Hacha Diabolica, La

(The Diabolical Axe, The Diabolical Hatchet)

1964 (1965) (Col).

Prod: Luis Enrique Vergara.

Dir: José Diaz Morales.

SP: Rafael Garcia Traves & Fernando Oses.

Mus: Jorge Perez Herrera.

Cast: Santo, Lorena Velazquez, Bety Gonzales, Fernando Oses, Mario Sevilla, Colocho.

H (black-hooded axeman is murderer)

Ref: PS.

See also: Santo.

Hacha Para la Luna de Miel, Un

See: Hatchet for the Honeymoon (1969).

Hadschi Murat

(story by L. Tolstoi)

See: White Devil, The (1930).

Haggard's "She" -- The Pillar of Fire

(La Danse du Feu: The Dance of Fire; La Colonne de Feu: The Column of Fire)

1899 French sil 65 ft.

Prod: Georges Méliès.

F (woman dances in pillar of fire)

Ref: Sadoul/M; GM Mage.

Based on idea from novel "She" by H. Rider Haggard.

See also: She.

Hagibis, Mga

1970 Philippine, Virgo.

Prod?: Louise De Mesa.

Dir & SP: Luis Enriquez.

Cin: Ricardo Remias.

Mus: Manuel Franco.

Cast: Eddie Rodriquez, Vic Vargas, Jing Abalos, Renato Robles, Danny Rojo, Eddie Garcia, Lucita Soriano, Rosemarie Gil, Matimtiman Cruz, Joy Del Sol, Larry Silva, Joe Cunanan, Dagul Se.

F ("the Magic Five" have telepathic & superhuman powers, superspeed, invisibility, etc.)

Ref: Chodkowski.

Hail!

1972 Hail Co (Scotia Int'l) color scope 85 mins.

Prod: Roy L. Townsend.

Dir: Fred Levinson.

SP: Larry Spiegel & Phil Dusenberry.

Cin: William Storz.

Edit: Robert DeRise.

Mus: Trade Martin.

Cast: Richard B. Shull, Dan Resin, Dick O'Neill, Joseph Sirola, K. Callan, Gary Sandy, Phil Foster, Lee Meredith.

soc-SF-com-sat (U.S. president establishes concentration camps for young dissenters, sets out to become dictator)

Ref: Vw 3 May '72 p223, 24 May '72 p26; BO 18 Dec '72 BookinGuide.

Hailstones and Halibut Bones

1964 Walter Reade-Sterling color ani 6 mins.

Artist: Robert Curtis.

Nar: Celeste Holm.

exp-F

Ref: Collier.

Based on a book by Mary O'Neill.

Hair Cartoons

1915 sil ani sh.

Dir: Sid Marcus.

F-com

Ref: LA County Museum.

Hair-Raising Episode in One Splash, A

1914 British, Cricks sil 540 ft.

Dir: Edwin J. Collins (?).

SF-com ("prof's hair restorer causes Frenchman to be mistaken for ape")

Ref: Gifford/BFC 04873.

Hair Raising Hare

1945 WB color ani 7 mins.

Dir: Chuck (Charles M.) Jones.

Story: Tedd Pierce.

Voices: Mel Blanc.

F-com

Ref: LC.

See also: Bugs Bunny (1938-63).

Hair Restorer

1907 Williams, Brown & Earle sil sh.

SF-com (grows beard on wife)

Ref: MPW 1:393.

Hair Restorer, The

1909 Pathé sil 8 mins.

SF-com (works instantly)

Ref: Bios 10 Feb '10.

Haiti Moon

(novel by C. Ripley)

See: Black Moon (1934).

Hakuja Den

See: Panda and the Magic Serpent (1958).

Hakusen-Midare Kuro-Kami

(The White Fan)

1956 Japanese, Toei 85 mins.

Cast: Chiyonosuke Azuma, M. Bando, Yuriko Tashiro, Yumika Hasegawa.

F-H (ghosts in period setting)

Ref: FEFN 23 March '56.

Hal Roach Charley Chase Comedy

See: Charley Chase Comedy (1929?--'40).

Hal Roach Comedy Carnival Part I

See: Fabulous Joe, The (1946).

Hal Roach's Our Gang Comedy

See: Our Gang Comedy (1923-44).

Half a Loaf. . .

See: Yoku (1958).

f Human

(Jujin Yukiotoko: Monster
Snowman; Snowman --ad.t.)
1955 (1958) Japanese, Toho
(DCA) 95 mins (70 mins).
Prod: Tomoyuki Tanaka.
Dir: Inoshiro Honda.
Story: Shigeru Kayama.
SP: Takeo Murata.
Art Dir: Tatsuo Kita.
Cin: Tadashi Imura.
SpFX: Eiji Tsuburaya and others.
Mus: Masaru Sato.
Dir U.S. Seqs: Kenneth G. Crane.
Cast: Akira Takarada, Kenji
Kasahara, Momoko Kochi, Noboru
Nakamura, (following in U.S.
seqs only) John Carradine,
Morris Ankrum, Russell
Thorsen, Robert Karnes.
SF-H (monster apeman & child
found in Northern Japan)
Ref: FF '58 p282-83; Toho
Films; Anderson/Richie p263.
See also: Abominable Snowman
of the Himalayas, The (1957).

alf Wit, The

1916 Lubin sil 2 reels.
Dir: Wilbert Melville and/or
Leon Kent.
Sc: Arthur Peterman.
Cast: L.C. Shumway, Helen
Eddy, George Routh.
bor-SF (surgery makes moron
normal)
Ref: MPN 14:457; LC.

alfway House

(The Ghostly Inn --ad.t?)
1944 (1945) British, Ealing
(A.F.E.) 95 mins (72 mins).
Prod: Michael Balcon.
Assoc Prod: A. Cavalcanti.
Dir: Basil Dearden.
SP: Angus MacPhail & Diana
Morgan.
Cin: Wilkie Cooper.
Edit: Sidney Cole.
Mus: Lord Berners.
Cast: Francoise Rosay, Tom
Walls, Mervyn Johns [ghost],
Glynis Johns [ghost], Sally
Ann Howes.
F (house lies between the
ghost world & the real world)
Ref: MFB Feb '44 p 13; HR 8
Oct '46; FDY '46.

Hallelujah the Hills

1963 Vermont 82 mins.
Prod: David C. Stone.
Dir & Sc: Adolfas Mekas.
Cin: Ed Emshwiller.
Edit: A. Mekas & Louis Brigante.
Mus: Meyer Kupferman.
Cast: Peter H. Beard, Sheila
Finn, Marty Greenbaum, Peggy
Steffans, Ed Emshwiller, Taylor
Mead, Jerome Hill.
sur-F-sat-com
Ref: FMC 5:230-31; MMF 9:123-
24; FF '63 p276.

Halley's Comet

1910 French sil 535 ft.
SF (comet destroys city)
Ref: BFI cat p31.

Halloween

1931 Van Beuren (RKO) ani
sh.
Credits: Dick Huemer & Sid
Marcus.
F-com
Ref: LC; Ani Chart.
See also: Toby the Pup
(1930-31).

Hallucinated Alchemist, An

(L'Hallucination de l'Alchimiste)
1897 French sil color 65
ft.
Prod: Georges Méliès.
F (star with five heads; giant
faces spews people out of its
mouth)
Ref: DdC III:350; Willis.

Hallucination de l'Alchimiste, L'

See: Hallucinated Alchemist, An
(1897).

Hallucinationer, Studio 2

(Hallucinations, Studio 2)
1954 Swedish color ani 6
mins.
Dir: Peter Weiss.
exp-F
Ref: Montevideo '56; C-16
p 14; FQ Fall '68.

**Hallucinations of Baron Münchausen,
The**

(Les Hallucinations du Baron de
Münchausen)
1911 French, Star sil
770 ft.
Prod: Georges Méliès.
F-dream (dragon & other wonders)
Ref: Sadoul/M; GM Mage; Bios
21 Sept '11.
Based on the character created
by R.E. Raspe.
See also: Baron Münchausen.

Hallucinations Pharmaceutiques ou
Le Truc du Potard

(Pharmaceutical Hallucinations or
The Trick of Potard)
1908 French sil 850 ft.
Prod: Georges Méliès.
F
Ref: Sadoul/M; GM Mage.

Hallucinations, Studio 2

See: Hallucinationer, Studio
2 (1954).

Haltet Beides Gut Zusammen

(Hold on to Both Things)
1969 E. German, DEFA color
ani 21 mins.
Dir & Story: Bruno J. Bottge.
F (fairy tale)
Ref: Mamaia '70.

Ham and Eggs

1933 U ani 1 reel.
Dir: Walter Lantz & Bill
Nolan.
Ani: Tex Avery & others.
F-com
Ref: Hist US Ani Prog; LC.
See also: Oswald (1927-38).

Ham and Hattie

1957 UPA (Col) color ani
1 reel series.
F-com
Ref: MFB Feb '59 p 19; LC.
See also: Trees and Jamaica
Daddie (1957).

Ham and the Experiments

1915 Kalem sil 1 reel.
Dir: Al Santell.
Cast: Lloyd V. Hamilton, Bud
Duncan.
F-com (love potion injection)
Ref: MPW 25:1832.

Ham and the Sausage Factory

1915 Kalem sil 1000 ft.
Cast: Lloyd Hamilton, Bud
Duncan.
F-com (dogs into sausages;
sausage follows Ham home,
does tricks)
Ref: MPW 23:873; MPN 11:6:52.

Hamelin

1967 Spanish color 85 mins.
Dir: Luis Maria Delgado.
SP: Roberto P. Carpio.
Art Dir: Gil Parrondo.
Cin: Godofredo Pacheco.
Mus: Adolfo Waitzman.
Cast: Miguel Rios, Margaret
Peters, Roberto Camardiel,
Luchy Soto, Miguel Ligero.
F (magic circus; pied
guitarist lures troublesome
rats out of city)
Ref: SpCin '68 p26-27; Vw 8
May '68.
Based on legend and a poem,
"The Pied Piper of Hamelin"
by Robert Browning.
See also: Pied Piper of Hame-
lin, The.

Hamfat Asar

1965 Amateur 16mm color
ani 15 mins.
Made by: Larry Jordan.
exp-F
Ref: FC 52:80, 82-83; Undrgnd
p 155.

Hamlet

● 1907 French, Star sil 720
ft (570 ft).
Prod: Georges Méliès.
Cast: Georges Méliès.
F-seq (Hamlet sees Ophelia's
ghost, his father's ghost, and
other apparitions)
Ref: LC; Sadoul/M; GM Mage;
Shake/Sil p34-35.

● (Amleto)
1908 Italian, Cines sil
855 ft.
In charge: Mario Caserini.
Ref: Scognamillo; Shake/Sil
p96-98.

● (Amleto)
1908 Italian, Comerio sil
sh.
Dir (probable): Luca Comerio.
Ref: Shake/Sil p98.

● 1910 British, Barker Motion
Photography sil 1325 ft.
Prod & Dir: William George
Barker.
Cast: Charles Raymond.
Ref: Shake/Sil p77-78.

● 1910 (1911) Danish, Nordisk
(Great Northern) sil 972 ft.
Prod: Olé Olsen.
Dir: August Blom.
Sc: Oluf Jensen.
Cast: Alwin Neuss, Emilie
Sannom, Aage Hertel, Ella
la Cour, Einar Zangenberg,
Oscar Langkilde, Axel Mattson.
Ref: Shake/Sil p 108-12;
MPW 8:765, 883; Neergaard p20.

● 1910? French, Eclipse? sil
1 reel.
Dir: Henri Desfontaines?
Cast: Jacques Grétillat,
Colonna Romano.
Ref: Shake/Sil p 107.

● 1910 French, Lux sil 950
ft.
Ref: MPW 6:217, 315; Shake/
Sil p 105-107.

● (Amleto)
1910 Italian, Cines sil sh.
Dir: Mario Caserini.
Cast: Dante Capelli.
Ref: Shake/Sil p 107; Scog-
namillo.

● 1912 British, Barker sil 1525 ft.
Dir: Charles Raymond.
Cast: Charles Raymond, Dorothy
Foster, Constance Backner.
Ref: Gifford/BFC 03344.

Hamlet cont.

● 1913 (1915) British, Hepworth/
Gaum (Knickerbocker Star Pic-
tures) sil 5345 ft (3100 ft).
Prod: Cecil Hepworth.
Dir: E. Hay Plumb.
Cast: Johnston Forbes-Robertson,
Gertrude Elliott, S.A. Cooksoon,
Walter Ringham, J.H. Barnes,
Percy Rhodes, Grendon Bentley.
Ref: MPW 25:119, 317-18; Hist
Brit p 180; Shake/Sil p 188-99.

● 1914 Vit sil sh?
Dir: James Young.
Cast: Clara Kimball Young,
Julia Swayne Gordon, James
Young.
Ref: F/A; MPW 21:814.

● (Amleto)
1914 Italian, Ambrosio sil
sh?
Sc: Arrigo Frusta.
Cast: A. Hamilton Revelle.
Ref: Shake/Sil p211.

● 1917 Italian, Rodolfi-Film
sil 3 reels.
Dir: Eleuterio Rodolfi.
Sc: Carlo Chiaves.
Design & Costumes: Ditta
Zamperoni.
Cast: Ruggero Ruggeri, Mercedes
Brignone, Elena Makowska,
Armando Pouget [ghost], Penia,
Martelli.
Ref: Shake/Sil p254-62.

● 1920 (1921) German, Art-Film
(Asta) sil 7723 ft.
Dir & Sets: Svend Gade.
Sc: Erwin Gepard.
Cin: Kurt Courant & Axel
Graatjär (Graatkjär?).
Cast: Asta Nielsen, Eduard
von Winterstein, Mathilde
Brandt, Hans Junkermann,
Heinz Stieda, Paul Conradi
[ghost].
F-seq (Hamlet is girl
raised as man to protect right
of succession; has visions of
dead father)
Ref: Shake/Sil p272-78; MMA
'63 p28; FIR Jan '56 p22,
Oct '64 p513.
In addition to play by William
Shakespeare, based on several
sources including "The Mystery
of Hamlet" by Edward P. Vining.

● (Blood for Blood)
1927 Indian, United Pictures
Syndicate sil.
Ref: IndCin YB.

● (Khun-E-Nahak)
1928 Indian, Excelsior sil.
Ref: IndCin YB.

● (Khoon-ka-Khoon or Khun Kakhun:
Blood for Blood)
1935 Indian (in Urdu), Stage
Film Co 90 mins.
Prod, Dir, SP: Sohrab Modi.
Cast: Sohrab Modi, Naseem,
Shamshad.
Ref: Sound & Shadow 20 Nov '35;
FIR March '73 p 141.

● 1948 British, Two Cities (U)
155 mins.
Prod & Dir: Laurence Olivier.
Adapt: Alan Dent.
Design: Roger Furse.
Art Dir: Carmen Dillon.
Cin: Desmond Dickinson.
SpFX: Paul Sheriff, Henry
Harris, & Jack Whitehead.
Edit: Helga Cranston.
Mus: William Walton.
Mus Dir: Muir Mathieson.
Cast: Laurence Olivier, Jean
Simmons, Eileen Herlie, Basil
Sydney, Felix Aylmer, Norman
Wooland, Terrence Morgan,

cont

Hamlet cont.

Stanley Holloway, Niall MacGinnis, Peter Cushing, Anthony Quayle, Christopher Lee.

Ref: FIR March '73 p 144-45; Vd 1 July '48; MFB May '48 p60.

⦿ (Khoon-e-Nahag)

1953 Indian.

Prod & Dir: Kishore Sahu.

Cast: Kishore Sahu, Mala Sinha, Venus Banerji.

Ref: Filmfare 7 Aug '53 ad; FIR March '73 p 148.

⦿ 1960 (1967?) W. German, Bavaria Atelier G mb H 127 mins.

Produced for tv, also released theatrically in U.S.

Pres: Edward Dmytryk & Sam Weiler.

Prod: Hans Gottschalk.

Dir & SP: Franz Peter Wirth.

Eng Dialog Dir: Fred Brown.

Cin: Kurt Fewissen, Hermann Gruber, Rudolf Jakob, & Boris Goriup.

Mus: Rolf Unkel.

Cast: Maximillian Schell, Dieter Kirchlechner, Karl Michael Vogler, Hans Caninenberg, Wanda Rota (Roth?), Dunja Movar.

Ref: FIR Dec '62 p618, March '73 p 151; Ideal cat '69-70 p79.

⦿ 1964 Theatrofilm (WB) Electronovision -- video tape transferred to film. 204 mins.

Combination of videotape recordings of two live stage presentations shown theatrically.

Exec Prod: Alexander H. Cohen.

Prod: William Sargent Jr. & Alfred W. Crown.

Play Dir: John Gielgud.

Electronovision Dir: Bill Colleran.

Design: Ben Edwards.

Cin: Carl Hanseman.

Edit: Bruce Pierce.

Cast: Richard Burton, Hume Cronyn, Eileen Herlie, Alfred Drake, Linda Marsh, John Gielgud [voice of ghost], William Redfield, George Rose, George Voskovec, Robert Milli, John Cullum.

Ref: MFB Aug '72 p 163; FF '64 p315-17; FIR Aug-Sept '64 p387, Nov '64 p574-75.

⦿ (Gahmlet)

1964 (1966) Soviet, Lenfilm (Lopert) scope 150 mins.

Dir & SP: Grigory Kozintsev.

Art Dir: Evgeny Ene (Enei?) & K. Kropachev.

Cin: Ionas Gritsyus.

Edit: E. Makhankova.

Mus: Dimitri Shostakovitch.

Cast: Innokenty Smoktunovsky, Anastasia Vertinskaya, Elza Radzin-Szolkonis, Mikhail Nazwanov, Yuri Tolubeyev.

Ref: MFB Feb '65 p 19-20; FD 13 Jan '66; Life 24 April '64 p89; FIR March '73 p153-54.

Based on the play by William Shakespeare as translated into Russian by Boris Pasternak.

⦿ (Hamlie)

1965 Ghanian 120 mins.

Prod: Sam Aryeetey.

Dir: Terry Bishop.

Cin: R.O. Fenuku.

Cast: Kofi Middleton-Mends, Joe Akonor, Mary Yirenkyi.

F-seq ("Hamlet" in an African setting; ghost looks like witch doctor)

Ref: LAT 21 Sept '65; Vw 20 Oct '65.

cont.

Hamlet cont.

⦿ 1969 British, Woodfall (Col) color 117 mins.

Exec Prod: Leslie Linder & Martin Ransohoff.

Prod: Neil Hartley.

Dir: Tony Richardson.

Art Dir: Jocelyn Herbert.

Cin: Gerry Fisher.

Edit: Charles Rees.

Mus: Patrick Gowers.

Cast: Nicol Williamson, Anthony Hopkins, Judy Parfitt, Mark Dignam, Marianne Faithfull, Michael Pennington, Gordon Jackson, John Carney, Roger Livesey, Roger Lloyd-Pack, Anjelica Huston.

Ref: MFB May '70 p98; Vw 17 Dec '69; LAT 18 Dec '69; FIR March '73 p 160.

⦿ 1970 NBC-TV (Hallmark Hall of Fame) color 115 mins.

Prod: George LeMaire.

Dir: Peter Wood.

Adapt: John Barton.

Mus: John Addison.

Cast: Richard Chamberlain, Ciaran Madden, Margaret Leighton, Richard Johnson, Michael Redgrave, John Gielgud [ghost], Alan Bennett, Nicholas Jones.

Ref: FIR March '73 p 162-63.

F-seq (in Medieval Denmark, Prince Hamlet is told by his father's ghost that he was murdered by his brother)

Based on the play by William Shakespeare.

See also: Rest Is Silence, The (1960); Hamlet at Elsinore (1964).

Hamlet at Elsinore

1964 British/Danish, BBC/Danish Television Service videotape 180 mins.

Prod: Peter Luke.

Dir: Philip Saville.

Cast: Christopher Plummer, Robert Shaw, Alec Clunes, Jo Maxwell Muller, Michael Caine, June Tobin, Dyson Lovell.

F-seq (in Medieval Denmark, Prince Hamlet is told by his father's ghost that he was murdered by his brother)

Ref: FIR March '73 p 154-55; TVG.

Based on play "Hamlet" by William Shakespeare.

See also: Hamlet.

Hamlie

See: Hamlet (1965).

Hammer for the Witches

See: Kladivo na Carodejnice (1970).

Hammersmith Is Out

1971 (1972) Alex Lucas (J. Cornelius Crean) color 114 mins (108 mins).

Exec Prod: Frank Beetson.

Prod: Alex Lucas.

Dir: Peter Ustinov.

SP: Stanford Whitmore.

Set Dec: Robert Benton.

Cin: Richard H. Kline.

Edit: David Blewitt.

Mus: Dominic Frontiere.

Cast: Elizabeth Taylor, Richard Burton, Peter Ustinov, Beau Bridges, Leon Ames, Leon Akin, John Shuck, George Raft, Anthony Holland.

bor-F-H-com (escaped lunatic Burton may be the Devil, Ustinov may be God; Faustian story)

Ref: F&F March '71 p 16; LAT 24 May '72 IV:12; MFB Nov '72 p212-13; Vw 17 May '72 p28.

Hammond Mystery, The

See: Undying Monster, The (1942).

Hana to Mogura

(Flowers and Moles)

1969 Japanese color ani 16 mins.

Dir & SP: Tadanari Okamoto.

F (mechanical moles grow flowers on desert island)

Ref: Mamaia '70.

Hanakurabe Tanuki Dochu

(Tanuki Vagabonds)

1960? Japanese, Toei color scope.

Dir: Tokuzo Tanaka.

Cast: Raizo Ichikawa, Ayako Wakao, Shintaro Katsu, Yasuko Nakada, Katsuhiko Kobayashi.

F (stairway to the sky)

Ref: FEFN Dec '60 p26 ad.

Hanaori

(Breaking Branches Is Forbidden)

1968 Japanese color? ani puppet 14 mins.

Made by: Kihachiro Kawamoto.

F

Ref: IAFF '72.

Hand, The

1960 (1961) British, Luckwell Prod (AIP) 61 mins.

Prod: Bill Luckwell.

Dir: Henry Cass.

SP: Ray Cooney & Tony Hilton.

Art Dir: John Earl.

Cin: James Harvey.

Mus: Wilfred Burns.

Cast: Derek Bond, Ronald Leigh-Hunt, Reed de Rouen, Ray Cooney, Bryan Coleman, Walter Randell, Tony Hilton.

bor-H (in wartime, man saves his hand by confessing to captors; out of revenge, friends who've lost theirs track him down; his hand is cut off by train)

Ref: FF '61 p372; MFB Nov '60 p 155.

Hand, The

(Ruka)

1965 Czech, Ceskoslovensky. color ani puppet 19 mins.

Dir, SP, Prod Design: Jiří Trnka.

Cin: Jiří Safař.

Mus: Václav Trojan.

sat-F (giant hand forces little man to make sculpture of it; he rebels & is killed)

Ref: MFB '68 p82; CFS cat '69.

Hand, The

See: Main, La (1969).

Hand Bell, The

1909 French, Gaum sil 420 ft.

F (fairy gives magic bell to hero so he can overcome difficulties)

Ref: MPW 5:51, 70; FI IV-27:7.

Hand in the Trap, The

(La Mano en la Trampa)

1962? Argentian, Angel 90 mins.

Dir: Leopoldo Torre Nilsson.

SP: L.T. Nilsson, Ricardo Luna, & Beatriz Guido.

Cin: Alberto Etchebehere.

Mus: A. Stampone.

H ("terrible secret in the family attic")

Ref: BO 5 Aug '63.

Hand of a Dead Man, The

See: Mano de un Hombre Muerto, La (1963).

Hand of a Wizard, The

1909 British, Urban-Eclipse (George Kleine) sil 374 ft.

F (disembodied hands; transformations)

Ref: Views IV-8:9.

Hand of Death

1961 API (20th-Fox) 59 mins.

Prod & SP: Eugene Ling.

Dir: Gene Nelson.

Art Dir: Harry Reif.

Makeup: Bob Mark.

Cin: Floyd Crosby.

Sup Edit: Jodie Copelan.

Edit: Carl Pierson.

Mus: Sonny Burke.

Cast: John Agar, Paula Raymond, Steve Dunne, Roy Gordon, John Alonzo.

SF-H (nerve gas experiments give Agar touch of death; he becomes monstrous-looking)

Ref: MFB June '63 p86; FF '62 p92; FM 38:2.

Hand of Fate, The

1908 Lubin sil 670 ft.

F-seq (lightning kills villain while he's trying to kill heroine)

Ref: Views 111:11.

Hand of Mary Constable, The

(novel by P. Gallico)

See: Daughter of the Mind (1969).

Hand of Night, The

See: Beast of Morocco (1966).

Hand of Peril, The

1916 Paragon (World) sil 5 reels.

Prod, Dir, Sc: Maurice Tourneur.

Cast: House Peters, June Elvidge, Ralph Delmore, Doris Sawyer.

SF (X-ray device makes wall transparent)

Ref: MPW 27:2033; LC; RAF p207.

Based on a story by Arthur Stringer.

Hand of the Artist, The

1906 British ani & live sil sh.

Dir: Walter Booth.

F

Ref: Ani/Cin p28; Brit Cin p 18.

Hand of the Gallows

See: Terrible People, The (1960).

Hand of the Hun, The

1917 Italian (Hary Raver) sil ani puppet seq 4 reels.

Dir: Giovanni Pastrone.

F-dream (boy dreams toy soldiers come to life)

Ref: MPW 34:1957.

Hand of the Skeleton, The

See: Main du Squelette, La (1915).

Hands

(Hände; Ballet of Hands --alt.t.)

1928 German, Fama-Film 20 mins.

Dir: Stella Simon & Miklos Bandy.

Art Dir: Hans Richter.

Cin: Leopold Kutzlub.

Mus: Marc Blitzstein.

exp-F

Ref: MMA Prog.

Hands Invisible

1914 Powers (U) sil 1 reel.

psy-H (hands repeat action of strangling innocent wife)

Ref: MPW 19:1430.

Hands of a Killer

See: Planets Against Us (1961).

Hands of a Stranger

(The Answer --e.t.)

1960 (1962) Glenwood-Neve Prods (AA) 86 mins.

Prod: Newton Arnold & Michael Du Pont.

Dir & SP: N. Arnold.

Art Dir: Theobald Holsopple.

Cin: Henry Cronjager.

Edit: Bert Honey.

Mus: Richard La Salle.

Cast: Paul Lukather, Joan Harvey, Irish McCalla, Ted Otis, Barry Gordon, Sally Kellerman, George Sawaya.

SF-H (when pianist's mutilated hands are replaced surgically, his inability to accept them turns him into a murderer)

Ref: FF '62 p255; MFB Aug '62 p 113; Vw 26 Sept '62.

See also: Hands of Orlac, The.

Hands of Nara, The

1922 Samuel Zierler Photoplay Corp (Metro) sil 6000 ft.

Pres & Dir: Harry Garson.

Cin: L.W. O'Connell.

Cast: Clara Kimball Young, John Orloff, Elliott Dexter, Edwin Stevens, Vernon Steele, John Miltern.

F-seq (faith healing)

Ref: AFI F2.2306 p323; MPW 57:610.

Based on the novel by Richard Washburn Child.

Hands of Orlac, The

● (Orlac Hände; Die Unheimlichen Hände des Dr. Orlak: The Sinister Hands of Dr. Orlak)

1925 (1928) Austrian, Pan Film sil.

Dir: Robert Wiene.

Sc: Louis Nerz.

Art Dir: S. Wessely.

Cin: G. Krampf & Hans Androschin.

Cast: Conrad Veidt, Fritz Kortner, Carmen Cartellieri, Alexandra (Vera) Sorina, Paul Askonas, Fritz Strassny.

Ref: F/A p421; FIR March '64 p 158; Gasca.

● (Les Mains d'Orlac)

1960 (1964) British/French (Continental) 105 mins (95 mins).

Prod: Steven Pallos & Donald Taylor.

Dir: Edmond T. Gréville.

Sc: John Baines & E.T. Gréville.

Dialog: Donald Taylor & Max Montagut.

Art Dir: John Blezard & Eugene Pierac.

Cin: Desmond Dickinson & Jacques Lemare.

Edit: Oswald Hafenrichter & Jean Ravel.

Mus: Claude Bolling.

Cast: Mel Ferrer, Lucile Saint-Simon, Christopher Lee, Dany Carrel, Felix Aylmer, Basil Sydney, Donald Wolfit (Antoine Balpêtré has same role in French-language prints), Donald Pleasence, David Peel.

Ref: Vw 26 April '61; MFB April '62 p53-54; BO 22 June '64.

SF-H (when hands destroyed in accident, those of murderer grafted onto pianist; in 1960 version murderer found innocent)

Based on novel "Les Mains d'Orlac" by Maurice Renard.

See also: Mad Love (1935); Hands of a Stranger (1960).

Hands of the Ripper

1971 (1972) British, Hammer & Rank (U) color 85 mins.

Prod: Aida Young.

Dir: Peter Sasdy.

SP: L.W. Davidson.

Art Dir: Roy Stannard.

Cin: Kenneth Talbot.

SpFX: Cliff Culley.

Edit: Christopher Barnes.

Mus: Christopher Gunning.

Cast: Eric Porter, Angharad Rees, Jane Merrow, Keith Bell, Derek Godfrey, Dora Bryan, Lynda Baron.

F-H (Jack the Ripper's daughter becomes possessed by his spirit, forced to kill)

Ref: MFB Oct '71 p 196; Vw 13 Oct '71; CoF 19:27.

Based on a short story by Edward Spencer Shew.

See also: Jack the Ripper.

Hands Off Gretel!

See: Hänsel und Gretel Verliefen Sich im Wald (1970).

Handwritten

1959 Amateur 16mm 9 mins.

Made by: Charles Boultenhouse.

Mus: Teiji Ito.

exp-F

Ref: FC 31:16; FQ Spring '61 p30.

Hanging Lamp, The

1908 French, Pathé sil 295 ft.

F (wolf-like demon)

Ref: MPW 1908 p402; Views 106:10.

Hangman

1964 Melrose Prods color ani 11 mins.

Prod: Les Goldman.

Dir: L. Goldman & Paul Julian.

SP & Design: P. Julian.

Ani: Margaret Julian.

Edit: Sid Levin.

Mus: Serge Hovey.

Nar: Herschel Bernardi.

sur-F-H (hangman one by one hangs everyone in town without protest)

Ref: MFB '67 p 192.

Hangman of London, The

See: Mad Executioners, The (1963).

Hangover Square

1944 (1945) 20th-Fox 78 mins.

Prod: Robert Bassler.

Dir: John Brahm.

SP: Barré Lyndon.

Art Dir: Lyle Wheeler & Maurice Ransford.

Cin: Joseph LaShelle.

SpFX: Fred Sersen.

Edit: Harry Reynolds.

Mus: Bernard Herrmann.

Cast: Laird Cregar, George Sanders, Linda Darnell, Glenn Langan, Alan Napier, Leyland Hodgson.

psy-H (split-personality psychopathic killer in turn-of-the-century London)

Ref: Vd & HR 17 Jan '45; FM 24:36; Agee p 140.

Based on the novel by Patrick Hamilton.

Hank and Mary Without Apologies

1962-70 Amateur (Film-makers' Coop) 16mm color 17 1/3 mins.

Made by: Dick Higgins.

exp-F

Ref: FMC 5:154.

Hanky Panky Cards

1907 French, Urban-Eclipse sil 247 ft.

F (tricks; transformations)

Ref: MPW 1:428.

Hannah -- Queen of the Vampires

1972 (1973?) American/Turkish? Fine Films Prods & Coast Industries color.

Exec Prod: Wolf Schmidt.

Prod & SP: Lou Shaw.

Dir: Ray Danton.

Cast: Andrew Prine, Mark Damon, Theresa Gimpera, Patty Shepard, Francisco Brana.

F-H (vampires)

Ref: Vw 14 June '72 p24.

Hans Christian Andersen

● (Mr. H.C. Andersen --Brit.t.)

1950 (1952) British (Hoffberg) ani seq 62 mins.

Prod & Dir: Ronald Haines.

Cin: W.R. Hutchinson.

Cast: Ashley Glenn, Kenyon Jervis, Constance Lewis.

biog; F-seq (cartoon versions of some of Andersen's stories)

Ref: MFB Aug '50 p 119; Vd 31 Jan '51; Vw 19 Nov '52.

Based on "The True Story of My Life" by Hans Christian Andersen.

● 1952 Goldwyn (RKO) color 112 mins.

Prod: Samuel Goldwyn.

Dir: Charles Vidor.

Story: Myles Connolly.

SP: Moss Hart.

Art Dir: Richard Day & Clavé.

Cin: Harry Stradling.

SpFX Cin: Clarence Mueller.

Edit: Daniel Mandell.

Mus: Frank Loesser.

Cast: Danny Kaye, Jeanmaire, Farley Granger, Joey Walsh, Erik Bruhn, John Qualen.

biog; ballet-F-seq; mus (some of the stories are depicted)

Ref: FD 28 Nov '52; MFB Feb '53 p 19; FIR Jan '53 p39.

Hans Christian Andersen Fairy Tales

1952 Danish color series 2 reels each.

Prod: Karl Moseby.

Assoc Prod & SP: Malvin Wald.

Dir: Thor Brooks.

Cin: Reginald Wyer.

Nar: Michael Redgrave.

Cast: Joan Vohs, Allyn Smith, John Neville.

F

Ref: HR 18 Nov '52; V 14 April 52; FIR Aug-Sept '53 p378.

Hansel and Gretel

● 1909 Edison sil 630 ft.

Dir: Edwin S. Porter.

F (fairies in addition to usual story)

Ref: MPW 5:499; EK 1 Oct '09 p9-10; FIR June-July '70 p340.

● 1923 Century sil 2 reels.

Cast: Baby Peggy.

Ref: MPN 28:3000; LC.

● 1954 Michael Myerberg Prods (RKO) color ani puppet 78 mins.

Prod: Michael Myerberg.

Dir: John Paul.

SP: Padraic Colum.

Cin: Martin Munkacsi.

Edit: James F. Barclay.

Voices: Anna Russell, Mildred Dunnock.

Ref: MFB Jan '55 p3; FDY '55; FIR '54 p485.

Hansel and Gretel cont.

F-mus

Based on the light opera by Engelbert Humperdinck with libretto by Adelheid Wette from the fairy tale collected by Jacob & Wilhelm Grimm.

● 1954 British, Primrose Prods (Contemporary) ani silhouette 10 mins.

Originally produced for TV.

Prod: Lotte Reiniger.

Mus: Freddie Phillips.

Ref: Contemp p77.

● (Hänsel und Gretel)

1954 (1965) German, Schonger Films (Childhood Prods) color (52 mins).

Eng Lang SP: Christopher Cruise.

Songs: Anne & Milton Delugg.

Nar: Paul Tripp.

Ref: CoF 10:40; DdC I:201; FD 19 Nov '65.

● n.d. (AIP-TV) color 100 mins.

Prod: K. Gordon Murray.

F (living snowman in addition to usual story)

Ref: MTVM Jan '66 p35.

Probably same as 1954 German version.

F (fairy tale: old witch who lives in gingerbread house captures 2 children, plans to eat them)

Based on the story collected by Jacob & Wilhelm Grimm.

See also: Babes in the Woods; Hänsel und Gretel (1924); Puppetry (1947); Story of Hansel and Gretel, The (1951); Grimm's Fairy Tales (1955); Hänsel und Gretel Verliefen Sich im Wald (1970); Whoever Slew Auntie Roo? (1971).

Mighty Mouse in Hansel and Gretel (1952).

Hansel and Gretel Get Lost in the Woods

See: Hänsel und Gretel Verliefen Sich im Wald (1970).

Hänsel und Gretel

(Hansel and Gretel; Story of Hansel and Gretel --Brit.t.)

1924 Austrian sil 6 reels.

F (old witch in gingerbread house holds 2 children captive)

Ref: Osterr; BFI cat p63.

Based on the fairy tale collected by Jacob & Wilhelm Grimm.

See also: Hansel and Gretel.

Hänsel und Gretel Verliefen Sich im Wald

(Hansel and Gretel Get Lost in the Woods; Hands Off Gretel! --Brit.t.)

1970 W. German, Pohland color 82 mins.

Prod: Hans Jürgen Pohland.

Dir: F.J. Gottlieb.

SP: F.J. Gottlieb & Heinz Freitag.

Cin: Petrus Schloemp & Wolfgang Dickan.

Edit: Christa Pohland, Barbara Mondry, & Katerina Kaschewsky.

Mus: Attila Zoller.

Cast: Barbara Klingered, Francy Fair, Dagobert Walter, Herbert Fux, Karl Dall.

sex-F-com (witch)

Ref: MFB May '71 p96.

Suggested by fairy story "Hansel and Gretel" as collected by Jacob and Wilhelm Grimm.

See also: Hansel and Gretel.

Hanuman

See: Hanuman. . .; Jai Hanuman; Lanka Dahan; Rambhakta Hanuman (1948).

cont.

Hanuman Janman
(Birth of Hanuman)
- 1925 Indian, Hindustan sil.
  Ref: IndCin YB.
- 1953 Indian.
  Prod: Mohan Lal Wahai.
  Dir: Raja Nene.
  Cast: Ranjana, Prem Adib, Paro, Meera Devi, Raj Adib, Uma Dutt.
  Ref: Filmfare 18 Sept '53 p39.
  myth-F

Hanuman Patel Vijay
1951 Indian, Basant 139 mins.
Prod & Dir: Homi Wadia.
SP & Mus Dir: S.N. Tripathi.
Art Dir: Babu Bhai Mistry.
Cin: P.R. Ram Rao.
Edit: Kamlakar.
Cast: Meena Kumari, S.N. Tripathi, Mahipal, Shanta Kunwar, Vimal, Dalpat, H. Prakash, Kanta Kumar.
myth-F
Ref: Indian MPA '53 p42; Filmcritic Sept '51 p6 ad.

Hanuman Vijay
(Hanuman's Victory)
1929 Indian, British India Film Co sil.
myth-F
Ref: IndCin YB.
See also: Jai Hanuman (1948).

Happening of the Vampires, The
See: Gebissen wird nu Nachts -- Happening der Vampire (1971).

Happenings
1968? British color ani sh.
Dir: Bob Godfrey.
F-com
Ref: F&F Feb '69.
Also included in Two Off the Cuff (1968).

Happiness Cage, The
See: Mind Snatchers, The (1972).

Happiness Is a Three Legged Dog
1967 Australian 16mm ani? 30 mins.
Prod: Bruce Buchanan.
Dir & SP: Anthony Airey.
Idea: Robert Riddel.
Cin: Darryl Ellwood & A. Airey.
Mus: Ian Clarkson.
SF (set in totalitarian future society)

Happy Birthday, Wanda June
1971 Filmakers Group & Sourdough Ltd & Red Lions (Col) color 105 mins.
Prod: Lester Goldman.
Dir: Mark Robson.
SP: Kurt Vonnegut Jr.
Prod Design: Boris Leven.
Set Dec: Ruby Levitt.
Makeup: Ben Lane.
Cin: Fred Koenenkamp.
Edit: Dorothy Spencer.
Cast: Rod Steiger, Susannah York, George Grizzard, Don Murray, William Hickey, Steven Paul, Pamelyn Ferdin.
sat-com; F-seqs (some scenes set in Heaven where everyone plays shuffleboard)
Ref: Vw 8 Dec '71; SR 11 Dec '71 p60; FF '71 p694-96.
Based on the play by Kurt Vonnegut Jr.

Happy Circus, The
See: Vesely Cirkus (1951).

Happy Days
See: Trouble with 2B, The (1972).

Happy End
1958 Yugoslavian, Zagreb color ani 10.8 mins.
Dir: Vatroslav Mimica.
Story: V. Mimica & Vladimir Tadej.
Design: Aleksandar Marks.
Ani: Vladimir Jutriša.
Bg: Zlatko Bourek.
Mus: Bojan Adamic.
sur-F (A-bomb end of world)
Ref: Z/Zagreb p56; Gasca; MMF 10-11:82, 85.

Happy End
1968 Czech, Barrandov (Continental) 73 mins.
Dir: Oldřich Lipský.
Story: Milos (Miles) Macourek.
SP: O. Lipský & M. Macourek.
Cin: Vladimir Novotny.
Mus: Vlastimil Hala.
Cast: Vladimir Mensik, Jaroslava Obermaierova, Josef Abrham, Bohus Zahorssky (Bohuz Zahorsky), Stella Zazvorkova.
F-com (murder story told backwards w/narration explaining action as if it were forward)
Ref: Vd 12 June '68.

Happy End
1969 Bulgarian color ani 6 mins.
Dir: Donio Donev.
F (little fish chased by big fish, changes to quadruped to bird, but always chased, so returns to water)
Ref: Mamaia '70.

Happy Ever After
See: Tonight's the Night (1954).

Happy Family
(play by M. Mosco)
See: Girly (1969).

Happy Gears, The
1912 Russian sil ani puppet 440 ft.
Prod: Ladislas Starevitch.
F
Ref: Scognamillo.

Happy-Go Lucky Stationmaster, A
See: Nonki Ekicho (1959?).

Happy-Go-Nutty
1944 MGM color ani 668 ft.
Dir: Tex Avery.
Story: Heck Allen.
Ani: Ed Love, Ray Abrams, & Preston Blair.
Mus: Scott Bradley.
F-com (Screwy Squirrel on the loose)
Ref: LC; Hist US Ani Prog.
See also: Screwy Squirrel (1944-45?).

Happy Harmonies
1934-37 MGM color ani sh series.
Prod: Hugh Harman & Rudolf Ising.
F-com
Ref: LC.

Happy Hooligan
- 1917 Hearst Int'l Film Service 1 reel sil ani series.
  Prod: Frank Moser.
  Dir: Jack King, Bill Nolan, Ben Sharpsteen, F. Moser, & others.
  Ani: Walter Lantz & others.
  Ref: Ani Chart; LC.
  See also: New Recruit, The (1917); Three Strikes You're Out (1917); White Hope, The (1917).

cont.

Happy Hooligan cont.
- 1920-21 John Colman Terry & Int'l Film Service (some released by Goldwyn) sil ani 1 reel series.
  Prod: Bill Tytla.
  Dir: Ben Sharpsteen, Bill Nolan, & others.
  Ani: Walter Lantz.
  Ref: Ani Chart; LC.
  See also: Happy Hooligan in Dr. Jekyl and Mr. Zip (1920); Village Blacksmith, The (1920); Roll Your own (1921).
  F-com (adventures of a happy hobo)
  Based on the comic strip by Frederic Burr Opper.
  See also: Hooligan Assists the Magician (1900); Happy Hooligan Turns Burglar (1902); Twentieth Century Tramp, The (1902); Hooligan's Christmas Dream (1903).

Happy Hooligan and His Airship
See: Twentieth Century Tramp, The (1902).

Happy Hooligan in Dr. Jekyl and Mr. Zip
1920 Int'l Film Service sil ani 1 reel.
Dir: Bill Nolan.
F-com
Ref: LC.
See also: Happy Hooligan (1920-21).
See also: Dr. Jekyll and Mr. Hyde.

Happy Hooligan Turns Burglar
1902 Edison sil 118 ft.
Dir: Edwin S. Porter.
F-com (policeman blown up, put back together, comes to life)
Ref: Niver p42.
See also: Happy Hooligan.

Happy Land
1943 20th-Fox 76 mins.
Prod: Kenneth Macgowan.
Dir: Irving Pichel.
SP: Kathryn Scola & Julian Josephson.
Cin: Joseph La Shelle.
Edit: Dorothy Spencer.
SpFX: Fred Sersen.
Cast: Don Ameche, Frances Dee, Harry Carey [ghost], Ann Rutherford, Cara Williams, Richard Crane, Henry Morgan.
F (ghost of grandfather proves son lost in war had full life)
Ref: MFB Feb '44 p 16; HR & Vd 11 Nov '43; Agee p63, 89.
Based on the novel by MacKinlay Kantor.

Happy Man, The
1961 Bulgaria color ani puppet 9.5 mins.
Dir & SP: S. Topaldjikov.
Art Dir: P. Schauer.
F

Happy Now I Go
(novel by T. Charles)
See: Her Paneled Door (1950).

Happy Scenes in the Life of the Animals
See: Gaudeamus (1912).

Happy Squirrels
195? Soviet color ani 20 mins.
F
Ref: MFB Feb '54 p29.

Har Har Mahadev
1950 Indian, Jayant Desai 137 mins.
Prod & Dir: Jayant Desai.

cont.

Har Har Mahadev cont.
Cast: Nirupa Roy, Trilok Kapoor, Durga Khote, Jeevan.
myth-F
Ref: Indian MPA '53 p27; Filmcritic Aug '51.

Hara Gouri
1923 Indian, Lotus sil.
myth-F
Ref: Indian Film p26.

Haram Alek
(Shame on You)
1953 Egyptian, Studio Guiza.
Dir: Issa Karama.
Cast: Ismail Yassine.
F-H-com (Yassine encounters Frankenstein monster, mummy, werewolf)
Ref: Arab Cin p280; Cine Nouvelles Sept '53 p43.
See also: Frankenstein; Mummy, The (1932); Wolf Man, The (1941).

Harap Alb
(The White Moor)
1964 Rumanian, Romfilm color 91 mins (89 mins).
Dir & SP: Ion Popescu Gopo.
Decor & Costumes: Ion Oroveanu.
Cin: Grigore Ionescu.
Mus: Dumitru Capoianu.
Cast: Florin Piersis, C.C. Codrescu, Lica Gheorghiu, Cristea. Avram, Irina Petrescu, George Demetru, Eugenia Popovici.
F-com (lots of fantasy: witch turns into beautiful woman; shivering man turns forest fire into ice)
Ref: Vw 21 July '65.
Based on old Romanian fairy tale by Ion Creangă.

Harbor Lights
See: Havenlichten (1960).

Hard Feelings
1962 Soviet, Soyuzmultfilm color ani puppet 8.3 mins.
Dir: R. Kachanov.
Story: S. Byalkovskaya & A. Sazonova.
F (fickle girl's puppy & doll run away)
Ref: Sovexport cat 1:137.

Hard Times for Dracula
See: Uncle Was a Vampire (1959).

Hard Times for Vampires
See: Uncle Was a Vampire (1959).

Hardrock Dome
1917 Pat Sullivan (U?) sil ani 1/2 reel series.
Prod: Otto Messmer.
Ani: Charles Saxton, George Clardy, W. Anderson, Bill Cause, W.E. Stork, & Ernest Smythe.
F-com
Ref: Ani Chart.

Hare and Hedgehog
1964 Soviet, Kiev (Sovexportfilm) color ani 16 mins.
Dir: I. Gurvich.
Story: A. Snesarov.
F
Ref: Sovexportfilm cat 2:120.
Based on a tale by Ivan Franko.

Hare and the Leopard, The
1935 African.
F
Ref: The African and the Cinema p47-48.
Based on African fable.

Hare Brained Hypnotist, The
1942 WB color ani 7 mins.
Prod: Leon Schlesinger.
Story: Michael Maltese.
Ani: Philip Monroe.
Mus Dir: Carl W. Stalling.
Voices: Mel Blanc.
F-com
Ref: LC.
See also: Bugs Bunny (1938-63).

Hare Brush
1955 WB color ani 7 mins.
Dir: Friz Freleng.
Voices: Mel Blanc.
F-com
Ref: LC; PopCar.
See also: Bugs Bunny (1938-63).

Hare Conditioned
1945 WB color ani 7 mins.
Dir: Chuck (Charles M.) Jones.
Story: Tedd Pierce.
Ani: Robert Cannon.
Mus Dir: Carl W. Stalling.
Voices: Mel Blanc.
F-com
Ref: LC.
See also: Bugs Bunny (1938-63).

Hare Force
1944 WB color ani 7 mins.
Prod: Leon Schlesinger.
Dir: Friz (I) Freleng.
Story: Tedd Pierce.
Ani: Virgil Ross.
Mus Dir: Carl W. Stalling.
Voices: Mel Blanc.
Ref: LC.
See also: Bugs Bunny (1938-63).

Hare Grows in Manhattan, A
1947 WB color ani 7 mins.
Dir: Friz (I.) Freleng.
Story: Michael Maltese & Tedd Pierce.
Voices: Mel Blanc.
F-com
Ref: LC.
See also: Bugs Bunny (1938-63).

Hare-Less Wolf
1958 WB color ani 7 mins.
Dir: Friz Freleng.
Voices: Mel Blanc.
F-com
Ref: LC; PopCar.
See also: Bugs Bunny (1938-63).

Hare Lift
1953 WB color ani 7 mins.
Dir: Friz Freleng.
Voices: Mel Blanc.
F-com
Ref: LC; PopCar.
See also: Bugs Bunny (1938-63).

Hare Remover
1945 WB color ani 7 mins.
Dir: Frank Tashlin.
Story: Warren Foster.
Mus Dir: Carl W. Stalling.
Voices: Mel Blanc.
F-com
Ref: LC.
See also: Bugs Bunny (1938-63).

Hare Ribbin
1944 WB color ani 7 mins.
Prod: Leon Schlesinger.
Dir: Robert Clampett.
Story: Lou Lilly.
Ani: Robert McKimson.
Voices: Mel Blanc.

cont.

Hare Ribbin cont.
F-com
Ref: LC.
See also: Bugs Bunny (1938-63).

Hare Splitter
1948 WB color ani 7 mins.
Dir: Friz (I.) Freleng.
Story: Tedd Pierce.
Voices: Mel Blanc.
F-com
Ref: LC.
See also: Bugs Bunny (1938-63).

Hare Tonic
1945 WB color ani 7 mins.
Dir: Chuck (Charles M.) Jones.
Story: Tedd Pierce.
Ani: Ben Washam.
Mus Dir: Carl W. Stalling.
Voices: Mel Blanc.
F-com
Ref: LC.
See also: Bugs Bunny (1938-63).

Hare Trigger
1945 WB color ani 7 mins.
Dir: Friz (I.) Freleng.
Story: Michael Maltese.
Ani: Virgil Ross.
Mus Dir: Carl W. Stalling.
Voices: Mel Blanc.
F-com
Ref: LC.
See also: Bugs Bunny (1938-63).

Hare Trimmed
1953 WB color ani 7 mins.
Dir: Friz Freleng.
Voices: Mel Blanc.
F-com
Ref: LC; PopCar.
See also: Bugs Bunny (1938-63).

Hare-Way to the Stars
1958 WB color ani 7 mins.
Dir: Chuck Jones.
Bg: Philip de Guard.
Voices: Mel Blanc.
F-com (Bugs vs. Martian in Roman helmet & sneakers)
Ref: LC; David Rider.
See also: Bugs Bunny (1938-63).

Hare We Go
1951 WB color ani 7 mins.
Dir: Friz Freleng.
Voices: Mel Blanc.
F-com
Ref: LC; PopCar.
See also: Bugs Bunny (1938-63).

Haredevil Hare
1947 WB color ani sh.
Dir: Chuck (Charles M.) Jones.
Story: Michael Maltese.
Ani: Ben Washam, Lloyd Vaughan, Ken Harris, & Phil Monroe.
Voices: Mel Blanc.
F-com
Ref: LC.
See also: Bugs Bunny (1938-63).

Hares and the Frogs, The
(La Lievre et les Grenouilles)
1969 French, EDIC color ani 13 mins.
Dir & Story: Victor Antonescu.
F (hare believes he is the most cowardly animal)
Ref: Mamaia '70.
Based on the fable by Aesop?

Hari Darshuan
(Audience with God)
1953 Indian.

cont.

Hari Darshuan cont.
Prod: C.M. Trivedi.
Dir: Raman B. Desai.
Mus: Shankarrao Vyas.
Cast: Leela Chitnis, Roopa Varman, Sapru, Bipin Gupta, Raj Kumar.
myth-F (haloed god figure)
Ref: Filmfare 24 July '53 p38 ad, 7 Aug '53 p39.

Hari-Har Bhakti
(Devotee to the God)
1955 Indian.
Prod & Dir: C. Raghuvir.
Mus: K. Dutta.
Cast: Asha Mathur, Trilok Kapoor, Vivek, Shahu Modak, Ramesh Sinha, Indira, Shravan Kumar, Rajenkapur, Ullhas, Durga Khote.
myth-F
Ref: Filmindia May '55 p53 ad.

Hari ng Ninja
1969 Philippine, RG.
Dir & SP: Solano Gaudite.
Cast: Roberto Gonzalez, Rosanna (Rossana) Ortiz, Rolando Gonzalez, Katsu Harada, Kurosawa Koryo, Kimura Osaka, Okawa Tora, Sato Maru, Marissa Delgado.
F (Philippine hero in Japan vs various magical warriors, whose powers include "Breath of Fire," "Breath of Storm" and "Paralizing [sic] Halitosis")
Ref: Chodkowski.

Harichandra
1932 Indian.
myth-F
Ref: IndCin YB.

Harischandra
● 1951 Indian, Studio X 114 mins.
myth-F
Ref: Indian MPA '53 p93.

● 1959 Indian (in Hindi), Prabha 134 mins.
Dir: Dhirubhai Desai.
Cast: Sulochana, Shahu Modak, Kanhaiyalal, Niranjan Sharma.
myth-F (king loses kingdom because he's truthful; when ordered to kill his wife, gods save him & her)
Ref: FEFN 17 Jan '58 p 19, 12:5-6:48.

Harishchandra
● (Raja Harishchandra --alt.t)
1912 (1913) Indian sil 3700 ft.
Prod & Dir: Dada Phalke.
myth-F
Ref: The Lighthouse 21 Aug '37 p9; Filmindia May '39 p59-60; Dipali 28 April '39 p4.

● 1935 (1936) Indian, Pioneer.
Dir: Prafulla Ghosh.
Cin: Paul Briquet, T. Marconi, D.G. Gune, & Mangloo.
Cast: Bhaskar Deb, Shankar Mukherje, Benoy Goswami, Shanti Gupta, Ganesh.
myth-F
Ref: Dipali 15 Nov '35 p22, 3 Jan '36 ad.
See also: Harichandra (1932); Harischandra.
Based on the play by Amritalal Bose.

Harlequin
1931 German ani silhouette sh.
Prod & Dir: Lotte Reiniger.
Mus Dir: Eric Walter White.
F
Ref: F/A p635.

cont.

Harlequin cont.
Based on original "commedia dell' arte" figures.

Harlequin
See: Arlekin (1960).

Harlequin and Columbine
See: Loves of Zero, The (1928).

Harlequin's Love Story
1907 French, Pathé Frères sil 1111 ft.
F (Harlequin rides wooden horse, uses magic wand)
Ref: BFI cat p 18.

Harm Machine, The
See: Agent for H.A.R.M. (1965).

III-es, A [spelled: Harmas, A]
(The Third; Number III; In No. III; In Room III)
● 1919 Hungarian sil.
Dir: Alexander Korda.
Cast: Antonia Farkas, Gabor Rajnay.
Ref: Sarris; Tabori p54, 60, 312.

● (III-es Szobaban: The Third Room --alt.t.)
1937 Hungarian, Muveszfilm (Danubia) 82 mins.
Dir: Stepen Szekely.
SP: Eugene (Jenö) Heltai & Istvan Mihaly.
Cast: Paul Javor, Jenö Torsz, Maria Lazar, Julus Csortos, Marica Gervay.
Ref: NYT 2 April '38; FD 18 April '38.
myst; bor-F-H (magician uses hypnotism & illusions to avenge dead girl)
Based on the novel by Eugene Heltai.

III-es Szobaban [spelled Harmas Szobaban]
See: III-es, A (1937) [spelled Harmas, A].

Harold and the Purple Crayon
1957 Piel (Brandon) color ani 9 mins.
Dir: David Piel.
Mus: Jimmy Carrol.
F
Ref: Brandon p282.
Based on the book by Crockett Johnson.

Harps and Halos
1917 Bud Fisher sil ani sh.
Ani: Bud Fisher.
F-com (Mutt & Jeff go to Heaven & Hell)
Ref: BFI cat p233.
See also: Mutt and Jeff (1916-28).

Harry Langdon Comedy
193?-4? Various Studios 2 reel series.
See also: Shrimp, The (1930); Shivers (1934); Goodness! A Ghost (1940); Here Comes Mr. Zerk (1943).

Harvey
1950 U 104 mins.
Prod: John Beck.
Dir: Henry Koster.
SP: Mary C. Chase & Oscar Brodney.
Art Dir: Bernard Herzbrun & Nathan Juran.
Makeup: Bud Westmore.
Cin: William Daniels.
Edit: Ralph Dawson.
Mus: Frank Skinner.
Cast: James Stewart, Josephine Hull, Charles Drake, Cecil Kellaway, Peggy Dow, Jesse White, Wallace Ford.

cont.

Harvey cont.

F-com (Elwood P. Dowd's friend is a pooka, a 6-ft tall invisible white rabbit with magical powers)

Ref: Vd & HR 12 Oct '50; MFB Jan '51 p200; FDY '51.

Based on the play by Mary C. Chase.

See also: Mr. Horatio Knibbles (1971).

Harvey's Girls

See: Peeping Phantom, The (1964?).

Hashashin, the Indifferent

(story by G.P. Dillenback)

See: Love Doctor, The (1917).

Hasher's Delirium

1906 French, Gaum sil ani 240 ft.

F-com

Ref: CFS cat; Collier; Film Fan Monthly Feb '64 p9.

Hasty Hare, The

1952 WB color ani 7 mins.

Dir: Chuck Jones.

Voices: Mel Blanc.

F-com (Bugs vs. a Martian)

Ref: LC; David Rider.

See also: Bugs Bunny (1938-63).

Hat, The

1964 Storyboard (CFS) color ani 18 mins.

Prod, Dir, SP, Design: John Hubley & Faith Hubley.

Ani: William Littlejohn, Gary Mooney, & Shamus Culhane.

Mus & Voices: Dizzy Gillespie & Dudley Moore.

F-com (border incident triggered by soldier's hat)

Ref: MFB '68 p62; CFS cat Sept '68; Collier.

Hat, The

(El Sombrero)

1964 Spanish, Estudios Moro S.A. color ani 16mm 9 mins.

Dir: Robert Balser.

Story: Alan Shean.

F-sat (man wants to join society whose members all wear red hats)

Ref: Collier; Ani/Cin p 158.

Hat Parade

See: Parade de Chapeaux (1936).

Hat with Many Surprises, The

(Le Chapeau à Surprises)

1901 French sil 165 ft.

Prod: Georges Méliès.

F

Ref: Sadoul/M, GM Mage 371-72.

Hatch Up Your Troubles

1949 MGM color ani 8 mins.

Prod: Fred Quimby.

Dir: William Hanna & Joseph Barbera.

Ani: Ed Barge, Ray Patterson, Irven Spence, & Kenneth Muse.

Mus: Scott Bradley.

F-com

Ref: LC; Acad nom.

See also: Tom and Jerry (1940--).

Hatchet for the Honeymoon

(Una Hacha para la Luna de Miel: An Axe for the Honeymoon; Il Rosso Segno della Follia: The Red Mark of Madness; Blood Brides --Brit.t.)

1969 (1971) Spanish/Italian, Pan Latina/Mercury (G.G.P. Rel. Co.) color 93 mins (83 mins).

Prod: Manuel Cano Sanciriaco.

Dir & Cin: Mario Bava.

cont.

The Haunted Castle (1896) French

Hatchet for the Honeymoon cont.

SP: Santiago Moncada & M. Bava.

Art Dir: Jesus Maria Herrero.

Edit: Soledad Lopez.

Mus: Sante Romitelli.

Cast: Stephen Forsyth, Dagmar Lassander, Laura Betti, Jesús Puente, Femi Benussi, Antonia Mas, Luciano Pigozzi.

F-H (man obsessed with discovering his past commits cleaver murders of other men's brides; haunted by ghost of his wife; whom he has murdered)

Ref: MFB Feb '73 p29; SpCin '71 p36-37; BO 3 Jan '72 back cover ad.

Hatim Ta

1956 Indian (in Hindi), Basant color.

Cast: Shakila, Jairaj.

F-H (curse threatens to turn girl to stone)

Ref: FEFN 13 April '56.

Hatimtai-ki-Beti

1955 Indian (in Hindi), Vakil Prods.

Cast: Citra, Mahipal.

F-H (evil spirits from devil persecute a princess)

Ref: FEFN 23 Dec '55.

Hatsuharu Tanuki Goten

See: Enchanted Princess (1960).

Hattie, the Hair Heiress

1915 Mutual (Falstaff) sil.

Cast: Frances Keyes, Claude Cooper, Arthur Cunningham.

bor-SF-com (hair tonic grows hair overnight)

Ref: MPN 23 Oct '15.

Hattogol Vijay

(Hattogol's Victory)

1960? Indian (in Hindi), H.S. Dasgupta Prods. ani puppet sh?

Prod: Hari S. Dasgupta.

Dir: Bulu Das Gupta & Raghunath Goswami.

cont.

Hattogol Vijay cont.

Mus Dir: Hari Prasanna Das.

F

Ref: Indian Films '61 p39.

Haunted

1915 Superba sil 7 mins.

F (vision of dead man haunts hero)

Ref: MPN 23 Jan '15.

Haunted, The

See: Curse of the Demon (1956).

Haunted and the Haunters, The

(play by E. Bulwer-Lytton)

See: Night Comes too Soon, The (1947).

Haunted and the Hunted, The

See: Dementia 13 (1963).

Haunted Barn

1931 Australian?

H

Ref: Sidney Cinema Journal Winter '67 p9; Collier.

Haunted Bedroom, The

1913 (1914) Edison sil 939 ft.

Dir: Richard Ridgely.

Cast: Mabel Trunnelle, Jack Strong, Augustus Phillips, Harry Linson, Carlton King, Harry Eytinge, Harry Beaumont, Hebert Prior.

F-H (ghost haunts money it hid in life in haunted bedroom)

Ref: EK 15 Dec '13 p6; BFI cat p 197; MPW 19:48.

Haunted Bedroom, The

1919 Par sil 5 reels.

Prod: Thomas H. Ince.

Dir: Fred Niblo.

Sc: C. Gardner Sullivan.

Cin: George Barnes.

Cast: Enid Bennett, Dorcas Mathews, Jack Nelson, Lloyd Hughes, William Conklin, Harry Archer.

H (fake ghosts)

Ref: MPN 19:4213, 4214; MPW 40:1689; LC; Blum p 171.

Haunted by Conscience

1910 Kalem sil 995 ft.

F (ghost)

Ref: MPW 7:207.

Haunted by the Cops

1909 French, Pathé sil 407 ft.

F-com (sees policemen everywhere: flowers, cabby, etc. turn into cops)

Ref: FI IV-19:9.

Haunted Cafe

1911 German, Messter-Film sil 425 ft.

F-dream (man asleep in restaurant dreams of transformations, disappearances, tricks)

Ref: BFI cat p57.

Haunted Castle, The

(Le Manoir du Diable: The Manor of the Devil, The Devil's Manor)

1896 French sil 195 ft.

Prod: Georges Méliès.

F-H

Ref: Sadoul/M, GM Mage 78-80.

Haunted Castle

1908 French, Pathé sil 688 ft.

F-H (ghosts; imp; wizard)

Ref: MPW 1908; Views 107:11.

Haunted Castle, [The]

See: Schloss Vogelöd (1921); Spukschloss im Spessart, Das (1960); Hiroku Kaibyoden (1969).

Haunted Castle at Dudinci, The

1952 Yugoslavian, Duga Film color? ani sh.

Dir, Design, Ani: Dušan Vukotić.

F-com

Ref: Z/Zagreb p 19.

See also: Kićo (1951-52).

Haunted Castles

1926 British sil sh series.

Dirs: Bert Cann, Maurice Elvey, C.C. Calvert, Hugh Croise, Walter West, Fred Paul, A.V. Bramble.

cont.

Haunted Castle cont.

Series cast: Godfrey Tearle, Isabel Jeans, Isobel Elsom, Gladys Jennings, Madge Stuart, Gabrielle Morton, Betty Faire, Hugh Miller, James Knight.

F-H (depicts the legends & ghosts supposedly inhabiting various British castles)

Ref: Vw 24 Feb '26; Brit Cin.

See also (all 1926): Ashridge Castle; Baddesley Manor; Bodiam Castle; Glamis Castle; Kenilworth Castle; Mistletoe Bough, The; Tower of London; Warwick Castle; Windsor Castle; Woodcroft Castle.

Haunted Cave

See: Ama no Bakemono Yashiki (1959).

Haunted Chateau, The

See: Devil's Castle, The (1897).

Haunted Curiosity Shop, The

1901 British, Paul sil 131 ft.
Prod: Robert W. Paul.
Dir: Walter R. Booth.
F-com (3 gnomes become one; top half of lady crosses room; mummy into skeleton; etc.)
Ref: BFI cat p76; Gifford/H p22; Gifford/MM p146; Hist/Brit p45.

Haunted Gold

1933 WB 58 mins.
Prod: Leon Schlesinger.
Assoc Prod: Sid Rogell.
Dir: Mack V. Wright.
SP: Adele Buffington.
Edit: William Clemens.
Cast: John Wayne, Sheila Terry, Erville Anderson, Harry Woods, Otto Hoffman, Blue Washington.
west; bor-H (abandoned mine in ghost form; phantom guards mine)
Ref: Vw 17 Jan '33; Photo Jan '33.

Haunted Harbor

1944 Rep serial 15 parts 31 reels.
Assoc Prod: Ronald Davidson.
Dir: Spencer Bennet & Wallace Grissell.
SP: Royal Cole, Basil Dickey, Jesse Duffy, Grant Nelson, & Joseph Poland.
Cin: Bud Thackery.
SpFX: Theodore Lydecker.
Mus: Joseph Dubin.
Cast: Kane Richmond, Kay Aldridge, Roy Barcroft, Clancy Cooper, Oscar O'Shea, Forrest Taylor, Hal Taliaferro, George J. Lewis, Kenne Duncan, Dale Van Sickel, Tom Steele, Robert Wilke.
bor-SF (fake sea monster)
Ref: LC; STI 3:15-16; SQ 4.
Based on the novel by Dayle Douglas.

Haunted Hills

1924 Educational sil 1 reel.
Cast: Jim Bemis.
psy-H (mysterious happenings drive villain insane & to his death)
Ref: MPN 29:879.

Haunted Hotel, The

1907 Vit sil 500 ft.
Prod & Dir: J. Stuart Blackton.
F-H-com (objects & whole hotel run about)
Ref: LC; Sadoul p440; MPW 1:62.

Haunted Hotel, The

1918 British, Kinekature sil 1 reel.
Prod: Fred Rains.
Cast: Will Asher, Marion Peake.
H-com

cont.

Haunted Hotel, The cont.

Ref: Hist/Brit p288; DdC III:194; Collier.

Haunted Hotrod, The

See: Ghost of Dragstrip Hollow (1959).

Haunted House, The

1913 Pathé sil 480 ft.
F-com (house spins, fire comes out chimneys, other tricks)
Ref: MPW 17:454; Bios 7 March '12.

Haunted House, The

1918 Frazee Film Prods sil 2 reels.
Dir & Sc: Edwin A. Frazee.
F-H-com (mystical illusions & magic)
Ref: MPW 37:436 ad.

Haunted House, The

1925 Pathé sil ani sh.
Prod: Paul Terry.
F-H-com
Ref: LC.

Haunted House, The

1928 FN sync sound FX 65 mins.
Pres: Richard A. Rowland.
Prod: Wid Gunning.
Dir: Benjamin Christensen.
Sc: Richard Bee & Lajos Biró.
Titles: William Irish.
Cin: Sol Polito.
Edit: Frank Ware.
Cast: Larry Kent, Thelma Todd, Edmund Breese, Sidney Bracy, Barbara Bedford, Flora Finch, Chester Conklin, William V. Mong, Montague Love, Eve Southern.
sat-H-com (mad doctor; fake ghost; apparitions)
Ref: AFI F2.2333 p325; FD 23 Dec '28; MPN 38:17:1261-62.
Based on the play by Owen Davis.

Haunted House, The

1929 (1930) Disney ani 1 reel.
Prod: Walt Disney.
Dir: Ub Iwerks.
F-com
Ref: MPN 41:1;35; LC.
See also: Mickey Mouse (1928-).

Haunted House, [The]

See: Maison Hantée, La (1907; Bhutio Mahal (1932); Rumah Puaka (1957).

Haunted House of Horror, The

See: Horror House (1969).

Haunted Inn, The

1910 Cosmopolitan sil 795 ft.
bor-H-com (phoney ghosts)
Ref: Bios 20 Jan '10 p52, 66.

Haunted Island, The

1911 Powers sil 1000 ft.
H (half-man, half-monkey)
Ref: MPW 8:1532, 1328.

Haunted Life of a Dragon-Tattooed Lass, The

See: Blind Woman's Curse, The (1970).

Haunted Man, The

1909 German, Duskes sil 480 ft.
F-com (man haunted by his doppelgänger or double)
Ref: Gifford/H p46; Bios 9 Dec '09 p45, 58.

Haunted Mouse, The

1941 Vitaphone (WB) ani 1 reel.
Prod: Leon Schlesinger.
Story: Michael Maltese.

cont.

Haunted Mouse cont.

Ani: Sid Sutherland.
Mus Dir: Carl W. Stalling.
F-com
Ref: LC.

Haunted Pajamas, The

1917 Yorke Film Corp (Metro) sil 5 reels.
Dir & Sc: Fred J. Balshofer.
Cin: Tony Gaudio.
Cast: Harold Lockwood, Carmel Myers, Ed Sedgwick, Helen Ware.
F-com (pajamas change personality of whoever wears them)
Ref: MPH 7 Oct '39 p 15; MPN 15:4113; Blum p 141; LC.
Based on the novel by Francis Perry Elliott.

Haunted Palace

1948 British, Nell Gwynn Prods.
Dir & SP: Richard Fisher.
Cin: Stanley Clinton.
Cast: Shaw Desmond.
doc; H (ghost-breaking; restoration of reputedly true legend)
Ref: MFB '49 p96.

Haunted Palace, The

1963 Alta Vista (AIP) color scope 85 mins.
Prod & Dir: Roger Corman.
SP: Charles Beaumont.
Art Dir: Daniel Haller.

Make-up: Ted Coodley.
Cin: Floyd Crosby.
Edit: Ronald Sinclair.
Mus: Ronald Stein.
Cast: Vincent Price, Debra Paget, Lon Chaney Jr., John Dierkes, Leo Gordon, Elisha Cook Jr, Frank Maxwell, Harry Ellerbe, Barboura Morris, Bruno Ve Sota, I. Stanford Jolley, Milton Parsons.
F-H (warlock burned at stake in 1765 takes over descendant's body 200 years later via portrait; his curse when dying causes deformed & monstrous villagers; alien creature in well under house; revival from dead; 250-year-old assistant warlock)
Ref: FF '64 p286; MFB March '66 p44; Corman p98.
Based on the poem by Edgar Allan Poe and short novel "The Case of Charles Dexter Ward" by H.P. Lovecraft.

Haunted Picture Gallery, The

1899 British sil sh.
Dir: G.A. Smith.
F-com
Ref: Brit Cin.

Haunted Planet

See: Planet of the Vampires (1965).

Haunted Room, The

1911 (1912) French, C.G.P.C. sil sh.
F-com (tricks: transformations, disappearances, etc.)
Ref: BFI cat p37-38; MPW 11:62.

Haunted Sentinal Tower, The

1911 Edison sil 980 ft.
Filmed in Cuba.
Cast: Herbert Prior, James Gordon, Mabel Trunnelle.
F (ghosts at Morro Castle)
Ref: EK 15 April '11 p3-4; MPW 8:965-66.

Haunted Spooks

1920 Pathé sil 2 reels.
Prod: Hal Roach.
Dir: Harold Lloyd.
Titles: H.M. Walker.
Cast: Harold Lloyd, Mildred Davis.

cont.

Haunted Spooks cont.

F-H-com (ghosts)
Ref: Photo June '20; LC; MPW 44:140-41.

Haunted Station, The

(#62 in The Hazards of Helen series)
1915 (1916) Kalem (General) sil 1 reel.
Dir: James Davis.
Cast: Helen Gibson, Robin Adair, Clarence Burton.
bor-H (insane man thought to be ghost)
Ref: MPW 27:470; CNW p22-27, 155-56.

Haunted Strangler, The

(The Grip of the Strangler -- s.t.; Stranglehold --Brit.t.)
1958 British, Amalgamated (MGM) 81 mins.
Prod: John Croydon.
Dir: Robert Day.
Story: Jan Read.
SP: J. Read & John C. Cooper.
Art Dir: John Elphick.
Makeup: Jim Hydes.
Cin: Lionel Banes.
SpFX: Les Bowie.
Edit: Peter Mayhew.
Mus: Buxton Orr.
Cast: Boris Karloff, Jean Kent, Elizabeth Allan, Anthony Dawson, Dorothy Gordon, Derek Birch.
psy-H (Karloff plays Jekyll-Hyde type: professor discovering he is insane strangler thought long dead)
Ref: MFB Nov '58 p 143; FF '58 p 129; FDY '59.

Haunted World

See: Planet of the Vampires (1965).

Haunting, The

1963 Argyle Enterprises (MGM) scope 112 mins.
Prod & Dir: Robert Wise.
SP: Nelson Gidding.
Art Dir: Elliott Scott.
Cin: David Boulton.
SpFX: Tom Howard.
Sound FX: A.W. Watkins.
Edit: Ernest Walter.
Mus: Humphrey Searle.
Cast: Julie Harris, Claire Bloom, Richard Johnson, Russ Tamblyn, Lois Maxwell, Valentine Dyall, Fay Compton, Diane Clare.
psy-F-H (old house is evil in itself, causes people to die within it, & their ghosts haunt it)
Ref: FF '63 p 181; MFB Jan '64 p4; FQ 63-64 p44.
Based on novel "The Haunting of Hill House" by Shirley Jackson.

Haunting at Castle Montego

See: Castle of Evil (1966).

Haunting of Hill House, The

(novel by S. Jackson)
See: Haunting, The (1963).

Haunting We Will Go, A

See: A-Haunting We Will Go (1942).

Haunting Winds

1915 Powers (U) sil 100 ft.
Dir: Carl M. Le Viness (Le Vinness?).
Story: G.E. Jenks.
Sc: Earl R. Hewitt.
Cast: Sidney Ayres, Doris Pawn.
bor-psy-F-H (accidental killer haunted by winds which stop when he discovers the dead man was bank robber)
Ref: MPN 14 Aug '15 p91; LC.

Haunts for Hire

(Haunts for Rent --alt.t.)

1916 Bray-Gilbert (Par) sil live & ani sh?

Ani: L.M. Glackens.

Sc: C. Allan Gilbert.

F-H-com (girl agrees to marry one who shows fewest ill effects after night in haunted chamber of roadhouse; she hires spirit expert to frighten one)

Ref: MPW 27:429.

Haunts for Rent

See: Haunts for Hire (1916).

Haunts of the Very Rich

1972 ABC-TV color 73 mins approx.

Prod: Lillian Gallo.

Dir: Paul Wendkos.

Story: T.K. Brown.

SP: William Wood.

Art Dir: Eugene Lourie.

Makeup: Jerry Cash.

Cin: Ben Colman.

Edit: Fredric Steinkamp.

Mus: Dominic Frontiere.

Cast: Lloyd Bridges, Cloris Leachman, Edward Asner, Anne Francis, Tony Bill, Donna Mills, Robert Reed, Moses Gunn.

bor-F (group of people stranded in tropical resort to which they have been mysteriously brought are apparently really dead & in Hell)

Ref: LAT 20 Sept '72 IV:18; B. Warren.

Haus ohne Turen und Funster, Das

(The House Without Windows or Doors)

● 1914 German sil sh?

Dir: Stellan Rye.

Cin: Guido Seeber.

Cast: Theodor Loos.

Ref: Eisner p44, 45, 350; Laclos p 188; DdC I:299, II:308.

● 1921 German sil.

Dir: Friedrich Feher.

Ref: FIR Nov '61 p567; Clarens.

sur-F

Hauser's Memory

1970 U color 104 mins.

Produced for tv.

Prod: Jack Laird.

Dir: Boris Sagal.

SP: Adrian Spies.

Art Dir: Ellen Schmidt.

Cin: Petrus Schloemp.

Sup Edit: Richard Belding.

Mus: Billy Byers.

Cast: David McCallum, Susan Strasberg, Lilli Palmer, Robert Webber, Leslie Nielsen, Helmut Kautner.

SF (man injects RNA from dead scientist into self, has some of dead man's memories)

Ref: CineF Winter '71 p35.

Based on the novel by Curt Siodmak.

Novel but not the film is a sequel to Donovan's Brain (1953).

Havai Khataula

1946 Indian, A.M. Khan.

Prod: A.M. Khan.

Dir: A.M. Khan & Sultan Alam.

Cast: Gohar Karnataki, Devraj, Amina, Chisti, Bashir.

F (flying balcony, other effects)

Ref: Filmindia Oct '46 p48, Nov '46 p44, Dec '46 --all ads.

Have Rocket Will Travel

1959 Col 76 mins.

Prod: Harry Romm.

Dir: David Lowell Rich.

SP: Raphael Hayes.

Art Dir: John T. McCormack.

Cin: Ray Cory.

Edit: Danny Landres.

Mus: Mischa Bakaleinikoff.

Nar: Don Lamond.

Cast: The Three Stooges (Moe Howard, Larry Fine, Joe De Rita), Jerome Cowan, Anna-Lisa, Bob Colbert, Marjorie Bennett, Nadine Datas.

SF-mus-com (Stooges go to Venus, meet robot, unicorn, large spider, are shrunken, etc.; death ray)

Ref: HR 21 July '59; FF '59 p 196; FDY '60.

See also: Three Stooges, The (1934-59); Snow White and the Three Stooges (1961); Three Stooges Meet Hercules, The (1961); Three Stooges in Orbit, The (1962); Outlaws IS Coming, The (1965).

Have You Got Any Castles?

1938 Vitaphone (WB) color ani 7 mins.

Prod: Leon Schlesinger.

Dir: Frank Tashlin.

Story: Jack Miller.

Ani: Ken Harris.

Mus Dir: Carl W. Stalling.

Voices: Mel Blanc.

F-com

Ref: LC.

Havenlichten

(Harbor Lights)

1960 Belgian 16mm color ani 10 mins.

Dir: Raoul Servais.

Mus: L. Van Branteghem.

F

Ref: Ani/Belgium p42-43.

Hawaii

1966 Mirisch Corp (UA) color scope 189 mins.

Prod: Walter Mirisch.

Dir: George Roy Hill.

SP: Dalton Trumbo & Daniel Taradash.

Art Dir: James Sullivan.

Prod Design: Cary Odell.

Cin: Russell Harlan.

SpFX: Paul Bird.

SpCin FX: Linwood G. Dunn & James B. Gordon.

Edit: Stuart Gilmore.

Mus: Elber Bernstein.

Cast: Julie Andrews, Max Von Sydow, Richard Harris, Torin Thatcher, Jocelyn La Garde, Carroll O'Connor.

hist; bor-rel-F (set in days of first white missionaries to Hawaii; prayers to pagan gods answered with storms, etc.; shark guides man)

Ref: FF '66 p229; F&F March '67 p30.

Based on portions of the novel by James A. Michener.

Hawaiian Lullaby

1968 Dutch ani sh?

F

Ref: MTVM Nov '68 p20A.

Hawk of the Wilderness

1938 (1939) Rep serial 12 parts 24 reels.

Also edited to 100 minute TV feature in 1966 as Lost Island of Kioga.

Assoc Prod: Robert Beche.

Dir: William Witney & John English.

Hawk of the Wilderness cont.

SP: Barry Shipman, Rex Taylor, & Norman Hall.

Cin: William Nobles.

Edit: Helene Turner & Edward Todd.

Mus: William Lava.

Cast: Herman Brix (later Bruce Bennett), Jill Martin, Mala, Monte Blue, Noble Johnson, William Royle, Tom Chatterton, George Eldridge.

bor-SF-H (Arctic Island with warm temperature; fake monster; search for land-bridge between Europe & N. America)

Ref: TEMI 15:206-10; Ser/Rep.

Based on the novel by William L. Chester.

Hawks and the Sparrows, The

(Uccellacci e Uccellini: Bad Birds and Good Birds, Ugly Birds and Sweet Birds)

1965 (1967) Italian, Arco (Brandon) 91 mins.

Prod: Alfredo Bini.

Dir & SP: Pier Paolo Pasolini.

Art Dir: Luigi Scaccianoce.

Cin: Mario Bernardo & Tonino Delli Colli.

Edit: Nino Baragli.

Mus: Ennio Morricone.

Cast: Toto, Ninetto Davoli, Femi Benussi, Umberto Bevilacqua, Renato Capogna, Rossana Di Rocco.

F-com-sat (talking crow; time displacement; flying man; man talks to birds)

Ref: FF '67 p230; Vw 4 May '66; Time 23 Sept '66; Ital Prods '65 p86-87.

Hawk's Trail, The

1920 Burston sil serial 15 parts 30 reels.

Prod: Louis Burston.

Dir: W.S. Van Dyke.

Cast: King Baggot, Rhea Mitchell, Grace Darmond, Harry Lorraine, Fred Windermere, Stanton Heck, George Siegmann.

bor-F-H (crook with hypnotic powers; chapter titles: 2: "The Superman," 5: "House of Fear," 8: "The Phantom Melody.")

Ref: MPW 43:666; LC; F/A p512; CNW p78, 205.

Häxan

See: Witchcraft Through the Ages (1921).

Hay Muertos Que No Hacen Ruido

(There Are Dead That Are Silent)

1946 Mexican, AS Films.

Dir: H.G. Landero.

Cin: Victor Herrera.

Mus: A. Rosales.

Cast: Tin Tan, Marcelo Chavez.

F-com (comedy with ghosts)

Ref: Aventura p420.

Hazaar-Raten

1953 Indian.

F (hypnotizes girl into loving; magic; genie)

Ref: Filmfare 20 March '53 p33-35.

Hazards of Helen, The

See: Haunted Station, The (1915).

He Couldn't Dance, But He Learned

1909 Vit sil 400 ft.

F-com-dream (man dreams he learns to dance by hypnotism; everyone he meets dances too)

Ref: FI IV-22:8; LC.

He Danced Himself to Death

1914 Vit sil 2 reels.

Dir: Ralph Ince.

He Danced Himself to Death cont.

Sc: Rube Goldberg.

Cast: Rube Goldberg, Ralph Ince.

F-com (artist assumes characters he has drawn; tricks)

Ref: MPW 21:1082; F/A p358; LC.

He Had to Die

See: Onryo Sakura Dai-Sodo (1957).

He Learns the Trick of Mesmerism

1909 French, Pathé sil 443 ft.

F-com (hypnotism gives hero power over mother-in-law)

Ref: MPW 5:459; FI IV-40:8.

He Made Me Love Him

1916 Hearst Int'l Film Service sil ani sh.

Ani: Frank Moser.

F-com

Ref: Hist US Ani Prog.

Based on characters created by George Herriman.

See also: Krazy Kat (1916-17).

He, She, or It?

See: Poupée, La (1962).

He Wanted to Be Brave

1963 Soviet, Soyuzmultfilm (Sovexportfilm) color ani puppet 16min.

Dir: V. Kurchevsky & N. Serebryakov.

Story: N. Gernet.

F (animals tease tiger cub)

Ref: Sovexportfilm cat 1:140.

Based on the play by G. Yanushevskaya & Ja. Vilkovsky.

He Went to See the Devil Play

1908 (1909) Vit sil 295 ft.

F-com (after seeing a play about the devil, everyone a drunk sees looks like the Devil to him)

Ref: Views IV-2:8; LC.

He Who Died of Love

See: El Que Murio de Amor (1945).

Head, The

(Die Nackte und der Satan: The Naked and Satan; A Head for the Devil --ad.t.; The Screaming Head --ad.t.)

1959 (1963) W. German, Rapid (Trans-Lux) 92 mins.

Prod: Wolfgang Hartwig.

Dir & SP: Victor Trivas.

Story: V. Trivas & Jacques Mage.

Art Dir: Hermann Warm & Bruno Monden.

Cin: Otto Reinwald & Kurt Rendel.

SpFX: Theo Nischwitz.

Edit: Friedl Buckow-Schier.

Mus: Willy Mattes & Jacques Lasry.

Cast: Horst Frank, Michel Simon, Karin Kernke, Paul Dahlke, Helmuth Schmid.

SF-H (Serum-Z which keeps severed portions of human body alive is used by villain on its inventor's head; beautiful head of deformed girl transplanted to perfect body)

Ref: MFB Jan '65 p9; FF '63 p66; HM 5:31

Head

1968 Raybert (Col) color 86 mins.

Exec Prod: Bert Schneider.

Prod & SP: Bob Rafelson & Jack Nicholson.

cont.

cont.

con

Head cont.

Dir: B. Rafelson.

Art Dir: Sydney Z. Litwack.

Cin: Michel Hugo.

SpFX: Butler-Glouner & Chuck Gaspar.

Edit: Mike Pozen.

Mus: Ken Thorne.

Cast: The Monkees (Peter Tork, David Jones, Micky Dolenz, Michael Nesmith), Annette Funicello, Timothy Carey, Abraham Sofaer, Vito Scotti, Victor Mature, T.C. Jones, Percy Helton, Sonny Liston, Carol Doda, Frank Zappa, Jack Nicholson.

F-sat-com (mostly plotless; many F sequences, as when The Monkees are dandruff on Victor Mature's head)

Ref: FF '68 p488; Vw 16 Oct '68; LAT 20 Nov '68.

Head for the Devil, A

See: Head, The (1959).

Head Makes, the Head Draws, The

1970? Bulgarian ani sh.

Dir: Dimiter Todorov.

F

Ref: ASIFA Bltn 2 '71.

Head of Pancho Villa, The

See: Cabeza de Pancho Villa, La (1955).

Head Rag Hop

1970 British, Amateur color & b&w 3 mins.

Made by: Peter Turner.

Mus: Romeo Nelson.

exp-sur-F

Ref: MFB '71 p 151.

Head Scape

1972 Japanese, Amateur color? ani 7.5 mins.

Made by: Taku Furukawa.

exp-F

Ref: IAFF '72.

Head Spoon

1971 Japanese, Amateur color? ani 5.5 mins.

Made by: Taku Furukawa.

exp-F

Ref: IAFF '72.

Head that Wouldn't Die, The

See: Brain that Wouldn't Die, The (1959).

Headless Eyes, The

1971? SR.

H (gore & blood)

Ref: BO 13 March '72 p39.

Headless Ghost, The

1959 AIP 63 mins.

Filmed in England.

Prod: Herman Cohen.

Dir: Peter G. Scott.

SP: Kenneth Langtry.

Art Dir: Wilfred Arnold.

Makeup: Jack Craig.

Cin: John Wiles.

Edit: Bernard Gribble.

Mus: Gerard Schumann.

Mus Dir: Muir Mathieson.

Cast: Richard Lyon, Lilliane Scottane, David Rose, Clive Revill, Jack Ellen, Alexander Archdale.

F-H-com (only by finding a secret potion hidden in the castle can the headless ghost regain his head & find peace; banquet with lots of ghosts)

Ref: FF '59 p82-83.

Headless Horseman, The

1922 Sleepy Hollow Corp. (Hodkinson) sil 6145 ft.

Dir: Edward Venturini.

Adapt: Carl Stearns Clancy.

Cin: Ned Van Buren.

Cast: Will Rogers, Lois Meredith, Ben Hendricks Jr., Mary Foy, Charles Graham.

H-com (in 18th-century New England, Ichabod Crane is scared away by a phoney headless horseman)

Ref: AFI F2.2356 p330; F/A p388; MPN 26:2173, 2619.

Based on short story "The Legend of Sleepy Hollow" by Washington Irving.

See also: Legend of Sleepy Hollow, The.

Headless Horseman, The

1934 Celebrity Prods ani 1 reel.

Dir: Ub Iwerks.

F-com

Ref: LC.

Possibly based on short story "The Legend of Sleepy Hollow" by Washington Irving.

Headless Rider, The

(El Jinete sin Cabeza)

1958 Mexican, Importadora (Clasa-Mohme).

Cast: Luis Aguilar, Flor Silvestre, Crox Alvarado, Jaime Fernandez, Pascual Garcia Peña.

F-H

Ref: PS; TVG.

Heads that Are Cut

See: Cabezas Cortadas (1970).

Heart of a Mermaid, The

1915 (1916) IMP (U) sil 3 reels.

Prod: Lucius Henderson.

Sc: Elaine Stearne.

Cast: Mary Fuller, Glen White, Paul Panzer.

F-com-dream (mermaid from algae taken aboard hero's yacht, assumes human form, returns to sea: all revealed to be dream)

Ref: LC.

Heart of Stone

See: Kalte Herz, Das (1950).

Heart of the Princess Marsari, The

1915 Thanhouser sil 2 reels.

myst; bor-H (man murders someone with liquid air)

Ref: MPW 24:1334.

Heart Trump in Tokyo for O.S.S. 117

See: Atout Coeur à Tokyo pour O.S.S. 117 (1966).

Heartbeat

1949 General Television Enterprises (Post Pictures) 16mm 2 reels.

TV film also distributed theatrically

Dir: William Cameron Menzies.

Cast: Richart Hart.

psy-H (demented killer hounded by imagined sound of heart of man he murdered)

Ref: FIR Oct '61 p470; LC; FW Dir p 193.

Based on short story "The Tell-Tale Heart" by Edgar Allan Poe.

See also: Tell-Tale Heart, The.

Heart's Haven

1922 Benjamin B. Hampton Prods (Hodkinson) sil 5275 ft.

Prod, Dir, Sc: Benjamin B. Hampton.

Heart's Haven cont.

Assist Dir: Eliot Howe & Jean Hersholt.

Cin: Gus Peterson & Friend Baker.

Cast: Robert McKim, Claire Adams, Carl Gantvoort, Claire MacDowell, Betty Brice, Frankie Lee, Jean Hersholt.

rel-F-seq (faith healing)

Ref: AFI F2.2388 p334-35; MPW 57:528.

Based on the novel by Clara Louise Burnham.

Hearts of Age, The

1934 Todd School sh.

Dir: William Vance & Orson Welles.

Cast: William Vance, Virginia Nicholson, Orson Welles.

alleg-F

Ref: FQ Spring '70 p 19-22.

Heating Powder

1908 Lubin sil 410 ft.

SF-com (powder heats whatever it touches)

Ref: Views 127:11.

Heaven, The

See: Paradise (1912).

Heaven Can Wait

1943 20th-Fox color 119 mins (93 mins).

Prod & Dir: Ernst Lubitsch.

SP: Samson Raphaelson.

Art Dir: James Basevi & Leland Fuller.

Cin: Edward Cronjager.

SpFX: Fred Sersen.

Edit: Dorothy Spencer.

Mus: Alfred Newman.

Cast: Don Ameche, Gene Tierney, Laird Cregar [Devil], Charles Coburn, Spring Byington, Allyn Joslyn, Signe Hasso, Louis Calhern, Florence Bates, Michael Ames, Eugene Pallette, Marjorie Main, Dickie Moore.

F-com (late 19th-Century lover tries to explain to genial Devil why he [lover] doesn't belong in Hell)

Ref: MFB Aug '43 p90; Vd 21 July '43; FDY '44; Agee p49-50; Blum p 195.

Based on play "Birthday" by Lazlo Bus-Fekte.

Heaven Can Wait

(play by H. Segall)

See: Here Comes Mr. Jordan (1941).

Heaven on One's Head

See: Sky Above Heaven (1964).

Heaven Only Knows

(Montana Mike --rr.t.)

1947 Nero (UA) 98 mins.

Prod: Seymour Nebenzal.

Dir: Albert S. Rogell.

Story: Aubrey Wisberg.

Adapt: Ernest Haycox.

SP: Art Arthur & Rowland Leigh.

Art Dir: Martin Obzina.

Cin: Karl Struss.

SpFX: Rocky Cline.

SpCin FX: Ray Binger.

Edit: Edward Mann.

Mus: Heinz Roemheld.

Cast: Robert Cummings [Archangel Michael], Brian Donlevy, Marjorie Reynolds, Bill Goodwin, Stuart Erwin, Gerald Mohr, Lurene Tuttle.

F-west (Archangel Michael visits old west to clear up problem of man born with no soul)

Ref: Vd 28 July '47; MFB Dec '47 p 173; FIR Aug-Sept '58 p378.

Heaven Scent

1956 WB color ani 7 mins.

Dir: Chuck Jones.

Voices: Mel Blanc.

F-com

Ref: LC; David Rider.

See also: Pepe le Pew (1947-56?).

Heaven Ship

See: Sky Ship (1917).

Heavenbent

(story by G. Beaumont)

See: Rainmaker, The (1926).

Heavenly Body, The

1943 MGM 93 mins.

Prod: Arthur Hornblow Jr.

Dir: Alexander Hall.

Story: Jacques Thery.

Adapt: Harry Kurnitz.

SP: Michael Arlen & Walter Reisch.

Art Dir: Cedric Gibbons & William Ferrari.

Cin: Robert Planck.

SpFX: Arnold Gillespie.

Edit: Blanche Sewell.

Mus: Bronislau Kaper.

Cast: William Powell, Hedy Lamarr, James Craig, Fay Bainter, Henry O'Neill, Spring Byington, Morris Ankrum.

com; SF-seq (marital misadventures of astronomer features sequence in which comet is shown colliding with the moon)

Ref: Vw; Acad.

Heavenly Daze

1949 Col 17 mins.

Prod & Dir: Jules White.

SP: Zion Myers.

Cin: Allan Siegler.

Edit: Edwin Bryant.

Cast: The Three Stooges (Moe Howard, Shemp Howard, Larry Fine), Vernon Dent, Sam McDaniel.

F-com-dream (Shemp dreams he dies & can't get into Heaven until he reforms the other two Stooges)

Ref: LC; Maltin/GMS p 136; Maltin/MCT P217; B. Warren.

Remake: Bedlam in Paradise (1955).

See also: Three Stooges, The (1934-59).

Heavenly Music

1943 MGM 2 reels.

Assoc Prod: Sam Coslow.

Dir: Josef Berne.

Story: Reginald Le Borg.

SP: Edward James, Paul Gerard Smith, & Michael L. Simmons.

Edit: Albert Akst.

Cast: Fred Brady, Steven Geray.

F

Ref: LC; Acad; Collier.

Heavenly Play, The

See: Road to Heaven, The (1942).

Heavenly Star

1972 UCLA 16mm color sh.

Made by: Alan Holleb.

ballet-F-seq (based on 50s rock 'n' roll)

Ref: UCLA notes; Greg Chalfin.

Heavens Call, The

See: Nebo Zowet (1959); Battle Beyond the Sun (1959).

cont.

Heavy Traffic

1973 Steve Krantz Prods & AIP (AIP) color ani & live 78 mins.

Prod: Steve Krantz.

Dir & SP: Ralph Bakshi.

Voices: Joe Kaufmann, Beverly Hope Atkinson, Frank DeKova, Mary Dean Lauria, Terri Haven.

F (fantasies of an underground cartoonist)

Ref: BO 13 Nov '72 p47; HR 8 Dec '72 p 12; Milt Gray.

Heavy Water

1960 Amateur 16mm color collage 5 mins?

Made by: Larry Jordan & Jess Collins.

exp-F

Ref: FC 52:79.

Heba the Snake Woman

1915 British, Excel sil 1000 ft.

F-H ("Aztec princess changes into snake and kills doctor")

Ref: Gifford/BFC 05794.

Hebimusume to Hakuhatsuma

(The Snake Girl and the Silver-Haired Witch)

1969? Japanese, Daiei.

Dir: Noriaki Yuasa.

Cast: Yachie Matsui, Yûko Hamada, Yoshio Kitahara, Tamami Takahashi.

F-H (girl possessed by snake's spirit)

Ref: Photon 21:8; UniJ 43:32. p32.

Heckle and Jeckle in King Tut's Tomb

1950 Terrytoons (20th-Fox) color ani 1 reel.

F-com (flying carpet; Frankenstein's Monster; ghosts; mummies)

Ref: LC.

See also: Frankenstein.

Heckle and Jeckle, the Talking Magpies

1946-56 Terrytoons (20th-Fox) color ani sh series.

Prod: Paul Terry.

F-com

Ref: LC.

See also: Terrytoons (1930-).

Hector Servadac

(novel by J. Verne)

See: Valley of the Dragons (1961); Na Komete (1971).

Heeza Liar

See: Col. Heeza Liar (1913-23).

Heinzelmännchen

(Brownie)

1956 W. German color 75 mins.

F (tale of the goblins of Cologne)

Ref: Collier.

Heir of Mars, The

See: Pasnyok Marsa (1914).

Heir of the Ages, The

1917 Par sil 5 reels.

Dir: E.J. LeSaint.

Sc: William Addison Lathrop.

Cast: House Peters, Eugene Pallette, Nina Byron, Adele Farrington.

F (2 cave men are reincarnated, relive their earlier story)

Ref: MPN 15:4112; LC.

Heiress of Dracula, The

See: Vampyros Lesbos -- Die Erbin des Dracula (1971).

Heirs

1969 Bulgarian ani sh.

Dir: Ivan Vasslinov.

F

Ref: Vw 6 Jan '71.

Heksen og Cyklisten

See: Witch and the Bicyclist, The (1909).

Helen of Troy

See: Private Life of Helen of Troy, The (1927).

Helena y Fernanda

(Helen and Fernanda)

1970 Spanish/French, Diagonal Films/16-35 Films) color 100 mins.

Dir & SP: Julio Diamante.

Art Dir: Juan Alberto Soler.

Cin: Juan Gelpi.

Edit: María Rosa Ester.

Mus: Georges Garvarentz.

Cast: Gérard Barray, Teresa Gimpera, Valérie Lagrange, Alberto Dalbes, Eduardo Fajardo.

bor-H (man thinks he's killed his wife, then is apparently haunted by her ghost)

Ref: SpCin '70? p96-97.

Helene la Belle

1958 British color ani silhouette 16 mins.

Dir: Lotte Reiniger & Carl Koch.

F

Ref: Ani/Cin p25, 175; Collier.

Based on opera "La Belle Hélène" by Offenbach.

Helicopter Invaders

See: Helicopter Spies, The (1967).

Helicopter Spies, The

(Helicopter Invaders --S.E. Asia t.)

1967 Arena (MGM) color 93 mins.

Exec Prod: Norman Felton.

Prod: Anthony Spinner.

Dir: Boris Sagal.

SP: Dean Hargrove.

Art Dir: George W. Davis & James W. Sullivan.

Cin: Fred Koenekamp.

Edit: Joseph Dervin & John B. Rogers.

Mus: Richard Shores.

Cast: Robert Vaughn, David McCallum, Carol Lynley, Bradford Dillman, Lola Albright, John Dehner, Leo G. Carroll, John Carradine, Julie London.

bor-SF (new secret weapon the "thermal prism")

Ref: MFB '68 p41; MTVM Dec '67 p 1 ad; Singapore Straits-Times 8 June '68.

Made of episodes from TV series "The Man from U.N.C.L.E."

See also: Man from U.N.C.L.E., The.

Helikopter

1962 Polish ani sh.

Dir: Wladyslaw Nehrebecki.

F

Ref: ASIFA info sheet.

Hell

See: Jigoku (1960).

Hell and High Water

1954 20th-Fox color scope 103 mins.

Prod: Raymond A. Klune.

Dir: Samuel Fuller.

SP: Jesse Lasky Jr. & S. Fuller.

Hell and High Water cont.

Art Dir: Lyle Wheeler & Leland Fuller.

Cin: Joe MacDonald.

Edit: James B. Clark.

Cast: Richard Widmark, Bella Darvi, Victor Francen, Cameron Mitchell, Gene Evans, David Wayne, Stephen Bekassy, Richard Loo, Henry Kulky.

bor-soc-SF (Chinese explode A-bomb, American submarine endangered)

Ref: MFB June '54 p85; FD 2 Feb '54.

Based on a work by David Hempstead.

Hell-Bent for Election

1943 (1944) Industrial Films (later UPA) color ani 7 mins.

Prod: Stephen Bosustow.

Dir: Chuck Jones.

Story: Robert Lees.

Design: Zac Schwartz.

Ani: Robert Cannon.

Mus: Earl Robinson.

alleg-F (campaign film for F.D. Roosevelt's re-election; FDR personified as streamline train)

Ref: Annecy '65; Hist US Ani Prog.

Hell Creatures, The

See: Invasion of the Saucer Men (1957).

Hell Diggers, The

1921 Famous Players-Lasky (Par) sil 4277 ft.

Dir: Frank Urson.

Sc: Byron Morgan.

Cin: Charles E. Schoenbaum.

Cast: Wallace Reid, Lois Wilson, Alexander Broun, Frank Geldert, Lucien Littlefield, Clarence Geldert, Buddy Post.

bor-SF (digger machine which "resoils the land" as it digs)

Ref: AFI F2.2404 p336.

Based on the story by Byron Morgan.

Hell-Face

See: Incredible Face of Dr. B, The (1961).

Hell Fighters

1970? Chinese language color.

F (mystic martial arts)

Ref: Bob Greenberg.

Hell Has No Doors

n.d. Amateur (CFS) 16mm? 8 mins.

Made by: Ahmed Lateef.

sur-F

Ref: CFS cat Sept '68.

Hell House

(novel by R. Matheson)

See: Legend of Hell House (1972).

Hell of Frankenstein, The

See: Orlak, el Infierno de Frankenstein (1960).

Hell on Earth

(Niemandsland)

1931 German.

Dir: Victor Trivas.

F-seq (German, French, English, Negro, Jew soldiers die together in WWI, march off as spectres at end)

Ref: C to H p235-36, 271; LA p209-10.

Hellevision

1939 A Roadshow Attraction. Includes stock footage from Dante's Inferno (1909).

Hellevision cont.

SF (scientist's TV invention picks up scenes from Hell)

Ref: Ackerman; FM 67:11.

Hellish Spiders

See: Arañas Infernales (1966).

Hello Down There

1969 Ivan Tors (Par) color 98 mins.

Exec Prod: Ivan Tors.

Prod: George Sherman.

Dir: Jack Arnold.

Underwater Dir: Ricou Browning.

Story: I. Tors & Art Arthur.

SP: Frank Telford & John McGreevey.

Art Dir: Jack Collis.

Cin: Cliff Poland.

Underwater Cin: Lamar Boren & Jordan Klein.

Edit: Erwin Dumbrille.

Mus: Jeff Barry.

Cast: Tony Randall, Janet Leigh, Jim Backus, Roddy McDowall, Ken Berry, Merv Griffin, Bruce Gordon, Arnold Stang.

bor-SF-com (man & family, as part of experiment, live in underwater house, battle "giant" sharks, etc.)

Ref: MFB March '70 p55; FF '69 p317.

Hello God

1958 Cavalcade Pictures 64 mins.

Dir & SP: William Marshall.

Cast: Errol Flynn, Sherry Jackson, Joe Muzzuca, Armando Formica.

rel-F (voices from grave; soldier approaches God's kingdom)

Ref: NYT 22 April '58.

Hello Television

1930 Mack Sennett Inc (Educational) 20 mins.

Prod: Mack Sennett.

Dir: Leslie A. Pearce.

Cast: Andy Clyde, Ann Christy, Nick Stuart, Julia Griffith.

SF-com (set in future; television phone)

Ref: Maltin/GMS p96; LC; E H-W 100:7:56, 100:8:38.

See also: Andy Clyde Comedy (1929-56).

Hell's Bells

1929 Walt Disney (Col) ani 6 mins.

Prod: Walt Disney.

F-com (Hell with grotesque animals)

Ref: FD 17 Nov '29.

Hell's Creatures

See: Frankenstein's Bloody Terror (1968).

Hell's Fire

1934 Iwerks (MGM) ani sh.

F-com

Ref: LC.

See also: Willie Whopper (1933-34).

Hell's 400

1926 Fox color seq sil 5582 ft.

Pres: William Fox.

Dir: John Griffin Wray.

Sc: Bradley King.

Cin: Karl Struss.

Cast: Margaret Livingston, Harrison Ford, Henry Kolker, Wallace MacDonald, Rodney Hildebrand, Amber Norman.

psy-F-seq (society melodrama; girl sees "her sins take the form of monsters" in color seq)

cont.

cont.

cont.

Hell's 400 cont.

Ref: AFI F2.2413 p338.

Suggested by "The Just and the Unjust" by Vaughn Kester.

Hellstrom Chronicle, The

1971 David L. Wolper Prods (Cinema 5) color 90 mins.

Prod & Dir: Walon Green.

SP: David Seltzer.

Cin: Ken Middleham, Vilis Lapenieks, Helmut Barth, & W. Green.

Edit: John Soh.

Mus: Lalo Schifrin.

Cast: Lawrence Pressman.

doc; SF-seq (documentary on insect life features scenes from SF films as illustrative examples)

Ref: FF '71 p259-62; MFB Oct '71 p 197; Time 19 July '71; Vw 16 June '71.

Includes footage from Naked Jungle, The (1953); Them! (1953).

Hellzapoppin'

1941 (1942) Mayfair (U) 84 mins.

Prod: Jules Levey.

Assoc Prod: Glenn Tryon & Alex Gottlieb.

Dir: H.C. Potter.

Story: Nat Perrin.

SP: N. Perrin & Warren Wilson.

Cin: Woody Bredell.

SpFX: John P. Fulton.

Edit: Milton Carruth.

Mus: Frank Skinner.

Mus Dir: Charles Previn.

Cast: Ole Olsen, Chic Johnson, Martha Raye, Mischa Auer, Hugh Herbert, Robert Paige, Shemp Howard, George Chandler, Eddie Acuff, Angelo Rossitto, Elisha Cook Jr., Dale Van Sickel [Frankenstein's Monster].

F-com (many sight gags, including invisibility, Olsen & Johnson carrying on fights with Howard who is projectionist for the film as you watch, Frankenstein's Monster, etc. etc.)

Ref: Agee p335-36; FDY '42; Vd 18 Dec '41, D. Glut.

Based on the stage production.

Help!

1954 Italian 15 mins.

Dir: Glenn Alvey Jr.

Cin: Pier Ludovico Pavoni.

Cast: Giovanna Galletti.

sur-F

Ref: S&S Summer '55 p36; FIR Oct '61 p472.

Based on short story "William Wilson" by Edgar Allan Poe.

Help!

1965 British, Walter Shenson Prods & Subafilms (UA) color 92 mins.

Prod: Walter Shenson.

Dir: Richard Lester.

Story: Marc Behm.

SP: M. Behm & Charles Wood.

Art Dir: Ray Simm.

Cin: David Watkins.

SpFX: Cliff Richardson & Roy Wybrow.

Edit: John Victor Smith.

Mus Dir: Ken Thorne.

Cast: The Beatles (John Lennon, Paul McCartney, Ringo Starr, George Harrison), Leo McKern, Eleanor Bron, Victor Spinetti, Roy Kinnear, Alfie Bass.

mus-com; SF-seqs (Ringo's magic ring is sought by mad scientists & Eastern cult; Paul shrunken; paralyzing ray; much other F & SF)

Ref: MFB Sept '65 p 133; FD 3 Aug '65; MPH 18 Aug '65; FQ Fall '65 p5/-58.

Help!

See: Au Secours! (1923).

Help! My Snowman's Burning Down

1964 Carson Davidson Prods (Pathé Contemporary) color 10 mins.

Prod, Dir, SP: Carson Davidson.

Cin: C. Davidson & Jack Curtis.

Mus: Gerry Mulligan.

Cast: Bob Larkin, Dian Robertson.

exp-sur-F

Ref: MFB April '66 p65; Acad nom.

Help! I'm Invisible

See: Hilfe, Ich Bin Unsichtbar (1951).

Helter Skelter

1949 British, Gainsborough 84 mins.

Dir: Ralph Thomas.

Story: Patrick Campbell.

SP: P. Campbell, Jan Read, & Gerard Bryant.

Cast: Carol Marsh, David Tomlinson, Mervyn Johns, Peter Hammond, Richard Hearne, Terry-Thomas, Wilfrid Hyde-White, Esma Cannon, Jimmy Edwards, Shirl Conway, Glynis Johns, Valentine Dyall, Dennis Price.

com; F-seq (in one seq, cast encounters real ghosts in a castle)

Ref: Collier; Gifford/BFC 11370.

Hen and the Changelings, The

196? E. Germany, DEFA.

Dir: Bruno Boettige.

F

Ref: Ani/Cin p 153.

Hen Hop

1942 Canadian, NFB (Pyramid) color ani 4 mins.

Made by: Norman McLaren.

F-com (includes egg dancing)

Ref: Contemp p70; Pyramid p226; Ed Film.

Hen with the Wrong Chicks, The

See: Henne mit de Flaschen Hühnchen, Die (196?).

Hencrake Witch

1913 Summit sil 720 ft.

F

Ref: Bios 19 June '13.

Henker von London, Der

See: Mad Executioners, The (1963).

Henne mit den Falschen Hühnchen, Die

(The Hen with the Wrong Chicks)

196? E. German, DEFA color ani 7 mins.

Prod: Bruno J. Böttge.

Story: Nils Werner.

Mus: Günter Klein.

F-com

Ref: ASIFA records.

Henpeck's Nightmare

1914 Cosmograph sil 480 ft.

F ("weird apparitions")

Ref: Bios 7 May '14.

Henpecked Hoboes

1946 MGM color ani 8 mins.

Prod: Fred Quimby.

Dir: Tex Avery.

Story: Heck Allen.

Mus: Scott Bradley.

F-com

Ref: Ani/Cin p 166; LC.

Henry Aldrich Haunts a House

(Henry Haunts a House --Brit.t.)

1943 Par 74 mins.

Prod: Michel Kraike.

Dir: Hugh Bennett.

SP: Val Burton & Muriel Roy Bolton.

Art Dir: Hans Dreier & Haldane Douglas.

Cin: Daniel L. Fapp.

Edit: Everett Douglas.

Mus: Gerard Carbonara.

Cast: Jimmy Lydon, Charles Smith, John Litel, Olive Blakeney, Lucien Littlefield, Mike Mazurki.

bor-SF-H-com (spooky old house; serum to give abnormal strength leaves Henry dizzy)

Ref: FDY '44; CoF 10:42; MFB '43 p 123; Vd 5 Nov '43.

Based on a character created by Clifford Goldsmith.

Henry Haunts a House

See: Henry Aldrich Haunts a House (1943).

Henry Nine to Five

1970 British (Audio-Brandon) color ani sh.

Dir: Bob Godfrey.

sex-F-com (the busy executive whiles away the day thinking about sex & having sexual fantasies)

Ref: ASIFA 7; MFB June '73 p 137.

Henry, the Rainmaker

1949 Mono 64 mins.

Prod: Peter Scully.

Dir: Jean Yarbrough.

SP: Lane Beauchamp.

Cin: William Sickner.

Edit: Peter Scully.

Cast: Raymond Walburn, Walter Catlett, William Tracy, Mary Stuart, Barbara Brown, Addison Richards.

bor-SF-com (man makes it start raining, can't make it stop)

Ref: Vd 19 Jan '49; LC; MFB June '49 p 100.

Based on story "The Rainmaker" by D.D. Beauchamp.

Henry's Night Inn (In?)

1969? color feature.

sex-SF-com (invisible man reappears when he sneezes)

Ref: Photon 21:5.

See also: Invisible Man, The (1933).

Her Dangerous Path

1923 Pathé sil series 10 parts 21 reels.

Dir: Roy Clements.

Author: Frank Howard Clark.

Cast: Edna Murphy, Charley Chase.

F-seq (each episode is a separate story told by a Chinese seer predicting the future)

Ref: Film Fan Monthly July-Aug '69; CNW p 109, 235; LC.

Her Dolly's Revenge

1909 Lux sil 300 ft.

F-H-dream (child dreams she is stabbed to death by doll)

Ref: Bios 21 Oct '09.

Her Fairy Godfather

1913 Majestic sil sh.

F-dream (godfather uses club instead of wand to work magic)

Ref: MPW 16:958, 1033, 1144.

Her Father's Gold

1916 Than (Mutual) sil 55 mins.

Cast: Barbara Gilroy, Harris Gordon, William Burt, Louise Bates.

Her Father's Gold cont.

bor-SF (sea monster)

Ref: MPN 13:3092.

Her Flowers

1908 French, Pathé sil colored 475 ft.

F (elixir makes flowers grow; grotesque face in a cabbage; transformations)

Ref: Views 137:9.

Her Greatest Love

See: Suo Piu' Grande Amore, Il (1955).

Her Honor, the Mare

1943 Par color ani 1 reel.

Dir: Isidore Sparber.

Story: Jack Mercer & Jack Ward.

F-com (note: first color Popeye cartoon)

Ref: LC; PopCar.

See also: Popeye (1933-57).

Her Husband's Affairs

1947 Col 86 mins.

Prod: Raphael Hakim.

Dir: S. Sylvan Simon.

SP: Ben Hecht & Charles Lederer.

Art Dir: Stephen Goosson & Carl Anderson.

Makeup: Clay Campbell.

Cin: Charles Lawton Jr.

Edit: Al Clark.

Mus: George Duning.

Mus Dir: M.W. Stoloff.

Cast: Lucille Ball, Franchot Tone, Edward Everett Horton, Mikhail Rasumny, Gene Lockhart, Larry Parks.

SF-com (byproduct of embalming fluid found to first completely removes hair from people, then grows it luxuriantly)

Ref: HR 18 July '47; FD 22 July '47; Film Digest 10:19; LC.

Her Invisible Husband

1916 IMP (U) sil.

Prod: Matt Moore.

Sc: Samuel Greiner.

Cast: Matt Moore, Jane Gail, Frank Smith.

F-dream-com (dreams sorceress gives her magic ring which causes invisibility)

Ref: MPW 27:1498, 1854, 1885; LC.

Her Jungle Love

1938 Par color 78 mins.

Prod: George M. Arthur.

Dir: George Archainbaud.

Story: Gerald Geraghty & Curt (Kurt) Siodmak.

SP: Joseph Moncure March, Lillie Hayward, & Eddie Welch.

Art Dir: Natalie Kalmus, Hans Dreier, & Earl Hedrick.

Cin: Ray Rennahan.

Edit: Hugh Bennett.

Songs: Frederic Holländer & Ralph Reed.

Mus Dir: Boris Morros.

Cast: Dorothy Lamour, Ray Milland, Lynne Overman, J. Carrol Naish, Dorothy Howe, Jonathan Hale, Archie Twitchell.

bor-F (hypnosis; sacrifice to crocodile god)

Ref: Hr & Vd 19 March '38; MPH 26 March '38 p42; LC.

Her Paneled Door

(The Woman with No Name --Brit.t.)

1950 British, A.B.P.C. 84 mins.

Dir: Ladislas Vajda.

cont.

cor

Her Paneled Door cont.

SP: L. Vajda & Guy Morgan.

Art Dir: Wilfrid Arnold.

Cin: Otto Heller.

Mus: Allan Gray.

Cast: Phyllis Calvert, Edward Underdown, Helen Cherry, Richard Burton, James Hayter, Betty Ann Davies.

F-H-dream (dream sequence shot in negative: woman is afraid something horrible is behind the door)

Ref: MFB '50 p 174; TVG.

Based on novel "Happy Now I Go" by Theresa Charles.

Her Surrender

1916 Ivan Film Prods Inc sil 5 reels.

Prod, Dir, Sc: Ivan Abramson.

Cast: Anna Nilsson, Rose Coghland, William H. Tooker, Wilmuth Merkyl, Harry Springler, Frankie Mann.

psy-F (girl gets transfusion, keeps seeing vision of donor, falls in love with him)

Ref: MPW 29:2101, 2167; LC.

Her Temptation

1917 Fox 5 reels sil.

Dir: Richard Stanton.

Story: Ben Cohn.

Sc: Norris Shannon.

Cast: Gladys Brockwell, Bertram Grassby, Ralph Lewis, James Cruze, Beatrice Burnham.

bor-F (hypnosis)

Ref: MPN 15:2689; LC.

Herb Alpert and the Tijuana Brass Band Double Feature

1966 Hubley (Par) color ani 5 mins.

Prod & Dir: John & Faith Hubley.

Mus: Herb Alpert.

F-com

Ref: MFB Sept '67 p 144; Acad nom.

Herbie Rides Again

See: Love Bug Rides Again, The (1972).

Hercules

(Le Fatiche di Ercole: The Labors of Hercules)

1957 (1959) Italian, Oscar (Embassy) color 107 mins.

Prod: Federico Teti.

Dir: Pietro Francisci.

SP: Ennio De Concini, Gaio Frattini, & Pietro Francisci.

Art Dir: Flavio Mogherini.

Cin: Mario Bava.

Mus: Enzo Masetti.

Cast: Steve Reeves [Hercules], Sylva Koscina, Gianna Maria Canale, Ivo Garrani, Arturo Dominici.

myth-F (son of Jupiter & mortal woman, Hercules has super-human strength; he helps Jason find the Golden Fleece; dragon; other magic)

Ref: FF '59 p 155; Ital Prods '57 p50.

Taken from "The Argonauts."

See the following films which feature the character Hercules. Note: not all films with "Hercules" in the title are about Hercules; some are about the character Maciste. See the entry under Maciste.

See also: Douze Travaux d'Hercules, Les (1910); Hercules and the Big Stick (1910); Hercules Unchained (1959); Goliath and the Dragon (1960); Loves of Hercules, The (1960); Fury of Hercules, The (1961); Hercules and the Captive Women (1961); Hercules in the Haunted World (1961);

Hercules cont.

Three Stooges Meet Hercules, The (1961); Ulysses Against the Son of Hercules (1961); Hercules in the Vale of Woe (1962); Conquest of Mycene (1963); Hercules, Samson and Ulysses (1963); Hercules the Invincible (1963); Jason and the Argonauts (1963); Hercules Against Rome (1964); Hercules Against the Sons of the Sun (1964); Hercules and the Tyrants of Babylon (1964); Hercules, Prisoner of Evil (1964); Hercules vs. the Giant Warriors (1964); Samson and the Mighty Challenge (1964); Combate de Gigantes (1966); Hercules in New York (1970); Son of Hercules in the Land of Darkness, The (196?).

Hercules Against Moloch

See: Conquest of Mycene (1963).

Hercules Against Rome

(Ercole contro Roma; Hercule contre Rome)

1964 Italian/French color.

Dir: Piero Pierotti.

SP: Arpad De Riso & Nino Scolaro.

Cin: Augusto Tiezzi.

Mus: Francesco Lavagnino.

Cast: Sergio Ciani (Alan Steel) [Hercules], Wandisa Guida, Domenico Palmara, Daniele Vargas, Livio Lorenzon, Andrea Aureli.

bor-F (Hercules' super-strength)

Ref: Ital Prods '64 p 12-13; Collier.

See also: Hercules (1957).

Hercules Against the Barbarians

(Maciste nell' Inferno di Gengis Khan: Maciste in Gengis Khan's Hell)

1964 (1969) Italian, Jonia Film color scope 97 mins (91 mins).

Prod: Felice Felicioni.

Dir: Domenico Paolella.

SP: D. Paolella & A. Ferraù.

Art Dir: Alfredo Montori.

Cin: Raffaele Masciocchi.

Edit: Otello Colangeli.

Mus: Carlo Savina.

Cast: Mark Forest [Maciste], José Greci, Gloria Milland, Ken Clark, Roldano Lupi, Renato Rossini.

bor-F (superstrength of Maciste, here called Hercules)

Ref: Ital Prods '64 p44-45; MFB '69 p83.

See also: Maciste.

Hercules Against the Moon Men

(Maciste contro gli Uomini della Luna: Maciste vs. the Moon Men)

1964 (1965) Italian/French, Nike/Comptoir Francais du Film (Governor) color (88 mins).

Prod: Luigi Mondello.

Dir: Giacomo Gentilomo.

SP: Arpad De Riso, Nino Scolaro, G. Gentilomo, & Angelo Sangarmano.

Art Dir: Amedeo Mellone.

Cin: Oberdan Tyojani.

SpFX: Ugo Amadoro.

Mus: Carlo Franci.

Cast: Sergio Ciani (Alan Steel) [Maciste], Jany Clair, Anna-Maria Polani, Nando Tamberlani, Jean-Pierre Honore.

F (Maciste, here called Hercules, battles magical moon men trying to conquer world; queen of moon men has slept for centuries, needs blood to revive her, dissolves at climax; Maciste battles "stone robots" --MFB)

Hercules Against the Moon Men cont.

Ref: MFB May '65 p76; Photon 13:1-14; Pardi.

See also: Maciste.

Hercules Against the Sons of the Sun

(Ercole contro i Figli del Sole; Hercules contra los Hijos del Sol)

1964 Italian/Spanish, Wonder/Hispamer color 89 mins (68 mins).

Prod, Dir, Story: Osvaldo Civirani.

SP: O. Civirani & Tannuzzini.

Art Dir: Tadeo Villalba.

Cin: Julio Ortas.

Edit: Nella Nannuzzi.

Mus: Lallo Gori.

Cast: Mark Forest [Hercules], Anna Maria Pace, Giuliano Gemma, Angela Rhu, Ricardo Valle, Giulio Donnini, Andrea Scotti.

bor-F (superstrong Hercules vs. Incas)

Ref: SpCin '66 p 112-13; MFB March '66 p43; Ital Prods '64 p204-05.

See also: Hercules (1957).

Hercules and the Big Stick

1910 French, Gaum (Kleine) sil 505 ft.

myth-F (hydra-headed monster vs Hercules)

Ref: F/A p421; MPW 6:1115.

See also: Hercules (1957).

Hercules and the Captive Women

(Ercole alla Conquista della Atlantide: Hercules and the Conquest of Atlantis)

1961 (1963) Italian/French (Woolner Bros) color 101 mins (93 mins).

Prod: Achille Piazzi.

Dir: Vittorio Cottafavi.

Story: Archibald Zounds Jr.

SP: Alessandro Continenza, V. Cottafavi, & Duccio Tessari.

Art Dir: Franco Lolli.

Cin: Carlo Carlini.

Edit: Maurizio Lucidi.

Mus: Gino Marinuzzi.

Cast: Reg Park [Hercules], Fay Spain, Ettore Manni, Luciano Marin, Laura Atlan.

myth-F (Hercules & friends go to Atlantis; battle monsters & army of identical men; girl imprisoned in stone; Hercules sinks Atlantis)

Ref: FF '63 p 186; MFB Aug '62 p 112.

See also: Hercules (1957); Atlantis the Lost Continent (1961).

Hercules and the Giant Warriors

See: Hercules vs. the Giant Warriors (1964).

Hercules and the Queen of Lidia

See: Hercules Unchained (1959).

Hercules and the Ten Avengers

See: Hercules vs. the Giant Warriors (1964).

Hercules and the Tyrants of Babylon

(Ercole contro i Tiranni di Babilonia)

1964 Italian, Romana color.

Dir: Domenico Paolella.

SP: L. Martino & D. Paolella.

Cin: Augusto Tiezzi.

Mus: Francesco Lavagnino.

Cast: Rock Stevens [Hercules], Helga Line, Mario Petri, Annamaria Polani, Livio Lorenzon, Tullio Altamura.

myth-F (Hercules vs. a sorceress)

Hercules and Tyrants of Babylon cont.

Ref: Ital Prods '64 p 114-15; TVK.

See also: Hercules (1957).

Hercules at the Center of the Earth

See: Hercules in the Haunted World (1961).

Hercules Attacks

See: Conquest of Mycene (1963).

Hercules Challenges Samson

See: Hercules, Samson and Ulysses (1963).

Hercules Contra los Hijos del Sol

See: Hercules Against the Sons of the Sun (1964).

Hercules in New York

1970 (RAF; United Film) color 90 mins.

Dir: Arthur A. Seidelman.

Cast: Arnold Strong [sic; Hercules], Arnold Stang.

F-com (Hercules annoys Zeus on Mt. Olympus, sent to modern-day Earth)

Ref: United Films cat '73-74 p208.

See also: Hercules (1957).

Hercules in the Haunted World

(Ercole al Centro Delle Terra: Hercules at the Center of the Earth --Brit.t.)

1961 (1964) Italian, SPA Cinemat. (Woolner Bros) color 91 mins (83 mins).

Exec Prod: Achille Piazzi.

Dir: Mario Bava.

SP: Alessandro Continenza, M. Bava, Duccio Tessari, & Franco Prosperi.

Art Dir: Franco Lolli.

Cin: M. Bava & Ubaldo Terzano.

Edit: Mario Serandrei.

Mus: Armando Trovajoli.

Cast: Reg Park [Hercules], Christopher Lee, Eleonora Ruffo, Giorgio Ardisson, Franco Giacobini, Marisa Belli, Ida Galli.

myth-F-H (Hercules tries to help a princess under a spell by getting a plant from Hades; rock monster; Goddess of Hades; vampires)

Ref: MFB Feb '63 p21; FF '65 p69; Vd 14 July '64; Photon 19:37.

See also: Hercules (1957).

Hercules in the Regiment

1909 Pathé sil 420 ft.

F ("invulnerable giant" bounces bullets off)

Ref: Bios 18 Nov '09.

Apparently not about the mythological Hercules.

Hercules in the Vale of Woe

(Maciste Against Hercules in the Vale of Woe --alt.t.)

1962 Italian color.

Cast: Kirk Morris [Hercules], Frank Gordon, Bice Valori, Liana Orfei, Franco Franchi.

myth-F; SF-com (2 con men from present day go back to Hercules' time in a time machine)

Ref: BIB's '64; CoF 17:28; TVG; D. Glut.

See also: Hercules (1957); Maciste.

Hercules, Maciste, Samson and Ursus vs. the Universe

See: Samson and the Mighty Challenge (1964).

Hercules of the Desert

(La Valle dell' Eco Tonante: The Valley of the Thundering Echo)

1964 Italian, Cineluxor color.

cont.   cont.   cont.   cont.

Hercules of the Desert cont.

Dir: Tanio Boccia (Amerigo Anton).

SP: Mario Moroni, Alberto De Rossi, & T. Boccia.

Cin: Aldo Giordano.

Mus: Carlo Rustichelli.

Cast: Kirk Morris [Maciste], Hélène Chanel, Alberto Farnese, Spela Rozyn (Rozin?), Furio Meniconi, Rosalba Neri.

bor-myth-F (Maciste, here called Hercules, vs. echo men who cause avalanches)

Ref: Ital Prods '64; MTVM April '67 p54; TVK.

See also: Maciste.

Hercules' Pills

See: Pilloe di Ercole, Le (1960).

Hercules, Prisoner of Evil

(Terror of the Kirghiz --alt.t.)

1964 (1967) Italian, Royale Sodifilm (AIP-TV) color 80 mins.

Prod: Adelpho Ambrosiand.

Dir: Antonio Margheriti (Anthony Dawson).

Cast: Reg Park, Mireille Granelli, Ettore Manni, Maria Teresa Orsini, Furio Meniconi.

F-H (Hercules defeats a monster; witch turns men into werewolves)

Ref: MTVM March '67 p34; Photon 21:45; TVK; Soren.

See also: Hercules; Wolf Man, The (1941).

Hercules, Samson and Ulysses

(Ercole Sfida Sansone: Hercules Challenges Samson)

1963 (1965) Italian, I.C.D. (MGM) color 100 mins (85 mins).

Prod: Joseph Fryd.

Dir & SP: Pietro Francisci.

Art Dir: Giorgio Giovannini.

Cin: Silvano Ippoliti.

Edit: Pietro Francisci.

Mus: Angelo Francesco Lavagnino.

Cast: Kirk Morris [Hercules], Richard Lloyd [Samson], Enzo Cerusico [Ulysses], Liana Orfei, Aldo Giuffré, Fulvia Franco.

myth-F (semi-comic; Hercules, Samson, & Ulysses after a sea monster)

Ref: MFB Nov '66 p 170; F&F Nov '66 p54.

See also: Hercules (1957); Samson.

Hercules, Samson, Maciste and Ursus, the Invincibles

See: Samson and the Mighty Challenge (1964).

Hercules the Invincible

(Ercole l'Invincibile)

1963 Italian, Metheus color 85 mins.

Prod & Dir: Alfredo Mancori (Al World).

SP: Kirk Mayor, Pat Klein, & A. Mancori.

Cin: Claude Haroy.

Edit: Frank Boberston.

Cast: Dan Vadis [Hercules], Spela Rozin, Carla Calo (Caroll Brown), Ken Clark, Jon Simons, Jeanette Barton, Hugo Arden, Red Ross.

myth-F (Hercules fights dragon, floods underground city with lava)

Ref: MFB Jan '65 p7; F&F Jan '65.

See also: Hercules (1957).

Hercules Unchained

(Ercole e la Regina di Lidia: Hercules and the Queen of Lidia)

1959 (1960) Italian/French, Lux Galatea/Lux (Embassy & WB) color scope 101 mins.

cont.

Hercules Unchained cont.

Prod: Bruno Vailati.

Dir: Pietro Francisci.

SP: P. Francisci & Ennio de Concini.

Art Dir: Massimo Tavazzi.

Cin: Mario Bava.

Edit: Mario Serandrei.

Mus: Enzo Masetti.

Cast: Steve Reeves [Hercules], Sylva Koscina, Primo Carnera, Sylvia Lopez, Sergio Fantoni, Carlo D'Angelo, Patrizia Della Rovere, Cesare Fantoni.

myth-F (Hercules drinks from waters of forgetfulness, loses memory; Queen of Lidia embalms discarded lovers; Hercules battles Son of Earth, throws him into sea to prevent his recharging his strength by contact with the earth)

Ref: FF '60 p 150-51.

Sequel to: Hercules (1957).

Hercules vs. Moloch

See: Conquest of Mycene (1963).

Hercules vs. the Giant Warriors

(Il Trionfo di Ercole; The Triumph of Hercules --Brit.t.; Hercules and the Ten Avengers --TV.t.)

1964 (1965) Italian/French, Cinematografica/Jacques Leitienne & Unicite (Alexander) color scope 94 mins.

Prod: Alberto Chimenz.

Dir: Alberto De Martino.

SP: Roberto Gianvita & Allessandro Ferrau.

Cin: Pier Ludovico Pavoni.

Cast: Dan Vadis [Hercules], Moira Orfei, Pierre Cressoy, Piero Lulli (Lupi?), Marilu Tolo, Enzo Fiermonte, Renato Rossini.

myth-F (Zeus first removes Hercules' strength, then restores it when needed; magic dagger; sorceress in Hades; magic power used to call 10 bronze giant warriors)

Ref: MFB April '65 p59-60; BO 23 Aug '65; F&F Nov '65 p31.

See also: Hercules (1957).

Hercules vs. Ulysses

See: Ulysses vs. the Son of Hercules (1961).

Here and There

1961 Japanese ani 30 mins approx.

Dir: Yoji Kuri.

sur-F

Ref: Ani/Cin p 154, 173.

Here Are Some Miracles

See: No Miracle at All (1965).

Here Comes Mr. Jordan

1941 Col 94 mins.

Prod: Everett Riskin.

Dir: Alexander Hall.

SP: Seton I. Miller & Sidney Buchman.

Art Dir: Lionel Banks.

Cin: Joseph Walker.

Edit: Viola Lawrence.

Mus: Frederick Hollländer.

Mus Dir: M.W. Stoloff.

Cast: Robert Montgomery, Evelyn Keyes, Claude Rains [Heavenly messenger], Rita Johnson, Edward Everett Horton, James Gleason, John Emery, Donald MacBride.

F-com (man killed, goes to Heaven, but was taken too soon; since his body was cremated, he is restored to life in body of drowned man; Heavenly messenger Jordan helps him adjust)

Ref: Vd 23 July '41; FDY '42; MFB Nov '41 p 149.

cont.

Here Comes Mr. Jordan cont.

Based on play "Heaven Can Wait" by Harry Segall.

Sequel: Down to Earth (1947).

Here Comes Mr. Zerk

1943 Col 1413 ft.

Dir: Jules White.

SP: Jack White.

Cast: Harry Langdon.

bor-SF-com (scientist & lunatic)

Ref: Maltin/GMS p74; LC.

See also: Harry Langdon Comedy.

Here Comes the Boogie Men

See: You'll Find Out (1940).

Here We Are Again

1913 British, Clarendon sil 489 ft.

F-dream (cop dreams he is chasing Clown, Pantaloon, Harlequin & Columbine, who vanish & reappear)

Ref: BFI cat p95.

Herencia de la Llorona, La

(The Heritage of the Crying Woman)

1946 Mexican, Sonora Films.

Dir & SP: Mauricio Magdaleno.

Cin: Jesús Hernandez.

Mus: R. Ramirez.

Cast: Paquita de Ronda, Florencio Castello, J.J.M. Casado.

F-H (weeping ghost)

Ref: Indice.

Based on Mexican legend.

See also: Curse of the Crying Woman, The (1961); Llorona, La.

Herencia Macabra, La

(The Macabre Legacy)

1939 Mexican.

Prod: Proberto Gallardo.

Dir: José Bohr.

Cast: Miguel Arenas, Roman Armengod, Consuelo Frank.

bor-SF-H (story of famous plastic surgeon; gruesome)

Ref: NYT 4 May '40; Indice.

Here's a Man

See: Devil and Daniel Webster, The (1940).

Heritage of Dracula, The

See: Vampyros Lesbos — Die Erbin des Dracula (1971).

Heritage of the Crying Woman, The

See: Herencia de la Llorona, La (1946).

Herman and Katnip

1953-59 Par color ani sh series.

F-com (smart mouse vs dumb cat)

Ref: LC.

Hermanos Corsos, Los

(The Corsican Brothers)

1955 Argentinian, Sono 94 mins.

Dir: Leo Fleider.

SP: Ariel Cortazzo.

Cin: Anibal Gonzales Paz & Dimas Garrido.

Edit: Jorge Garate.

Mus: Teddy Giorge.

Cast: Antonio Vilar, Analia Gade, Fina Wasserman, Tomás Blanco, Nestor Deval.

bor-F (though twin boys were separated in their youth, while adults one can still experience all the other one's sensations)

Ref: Nubila.

Based on novel "Les Frères Corses" by Alexandre Dumas.

See also: Corsican Brothers, The.

Hermina Tyrlova

n.d. Czech.

doc; F-seq (documentary about lady puppeteer Tyrlova; scenes from some of her films)

Ref: Czech films flyer.

Herncrake Witch, The

1912 British, Heron Films sil 710 ft.

Prod: Andrew Heron.

Dir & Sc: Mark Melford.

Cast: Jakidawdra Melford, Mark Melford.

F ("witch helps grandchild's romance by changing lover's father into woman")

Ref: Gifford/BFC 03845.

Hero and Leander

1910 Italian, Ambrosio sil sh.

myth-F

Ref: F/A p421; MPW 6:186, 217.

Hero of Heroes

1971 Chinese-language (Hongkong or Formosa?), Hsin-Hwa Studios (Mercury) color scope 95 mins.

Dir: Wu Ming-Hsiung.

Cast: Chen Hung-Lieh, Chang Ching-Cing, Ciang Ming, Yi Yuen, Wu Ming-Sha, Ma Chi.

F-seq (mystic martial arts)

Ref: Mercury folder.

Hero of Our Time, A

1969 Amateur (Film-makers' Coop) 16mm 67 mins.

Prod, Dir, SP, Edit: J. Ferrater-Mora.

Cin: James Ferrater.

Cast: Alfonso Gil.

exp-soc-SF (man in future society which is completely totalitarian; escapes to nature at end)

Ref: FMC 5:102.

Herostratus

1967 British, i Films Ltd. ani collage seq 142 mins.

Prod: James Quinn & Don Levy.

Dir, SP, Edit: D. Levy.

Cin: Keith Allams.

Cast: Michael Gothard, Gabriella Licudi, Peter Stephens.

psy-F-seq (poet's imagination juxtaposes slaughterhouse eviscerations with ad temptresses which also appear in animated collage)

Ref: LAT 17 Nov '72; Filmex II.

Herr Arne's Pengingar

(Sir Arne's Treasure)

1954 Swedish color.

Dir: Gustav Molander.

Cast: Ulf Palme, Ulla Jacobsson, Bengt Eklund, Åke Grönberg, Bibi Andersson.

F (curse holds ship in frozen sea)

Ref: Sweden I.

Based on novel "Herr Arnes Pengar" by Selma Lagerlöf.

See also: Sir Arne's Treasure (1919).

Herr im Haus, Der

(The Gentleman in the House)

1940 German, Bavaria Film 88 mins.

Dir: Heinz Helbig.

SP: H. Helbig & Jacob Geis.

Mus: Leo Leux.

Cast: Hans Moser, Leo Slezak, Maria Andergast, Hans Junkermann.

F-com (ghost catcher at seance hit by Napoleon's ghost)

Ref: Deutscher.

Herr von Anderen Stern, Der

(The Man from Another Star)

1948 German.

Dir: Heinz Hilpert.

SP: Werner Illing.

Cin: Georg Bruckbauer.

Cast: Heinz Rühmann, Anneliese Römer, Hilde Hildebrand, Hans Cossy, Bruno Hübner.

SF-com

Ref: UF p419.

Herren der Meere

(Masters of the Sea)

1922 Austrian, Sascha sil.

Dir: Alexander Korda.

Prod Manager: Karl Kartl.

bor-SF (pirates wage war on society with submarines & other undersea equipment)

Ref: Tobori p67-69, 313.

Based on a story by Ernest Vajda.

Herrgårdssägen, En

(novel by S. Lagerlöf)

See: Gunnar Hedes Saga (1922).

Herrn der Welt, Der

(The Master of the World)

1934 (1935) German, Ariel-Film 90 mins.

Dir: Harry Piel.

SP: George Muehlen-Schulte.

Cast: Walter Janssen, Sybille Schmitz, Walter Franck, S. Schuerenberg.

SF (death rays; machines do dangerous work)

Ref: NYT 16 Dec '35; FM 13:30; FD 17 Dec '35.

Herrin der Welt

See: Mistero dei Trei Continenti, Il (1959).

Herrin von Atlantis, Die

See: Atlantide, L' (1932).

Herrliche Zeiten im Spessart

(Glorious Times in the Spessart; Spessart Rockets --ad.t.)

1967 W. German, Independent-Film & Constantin color 105 mins.

Prod: Kurt Hoffmann & Heinz Angermeyer.

Dir: K. Hoffmann.

SP: Guenter Neumann.

Settings: Werner & Isabella Schlichting.

Cin: Richard Angst.

Edit: Gisela Haller.

Mus: Franz Grothe.

Cast: Liselotte (Lilo) Pulver, Harald Leipnitz, Willy Millowitsch, Tatjana Sals, Rudolf Rhomberg, Hans Richter.

mus-com; F-seq (astronauts & rockets, "long ride: through the centuries" --Vw)

Ref: Vw 8 Nov '67; GFN 2.

See also: Spukschloss im Spessart, Das (1960).

He's Got 'Em

1910 British, Warwick sil sh.

psy-F

Ref: Bios 2 June '10 p39; Hist/Brit p260.

Heterodyne

1967 Amateur (Film-makers' Coop) color sil 7 mins.

Made by: Hollis Frampton.

abs-F (flicker films with color)

Ref: FMC 5:108; FC 48-49.

Hex

1973 Max L. Raab Prods (20th-Fox) color.

Exec Prod: Max L. Raab.

Assoc Prod: William McCutchen.

cont.

Hex cont.

Prod: Clark Paylow.

Dir: Leo Garen.

Story: Doran William Cannon & Vernon Zimmerman.

SP: L. Garen & Steve Katz.

Art Dir: Gary Weist & Frank Sylos.

Cin: Charles Rosher Jr.

Edit: Danford B. Greene.

Mus: Pat Williams.

Cast: Keith Carradine, Scott Glenn, Robert Walker Jr., Tina Herazo, Hilarie Thompson, Mike Combs, Doria Cook, Patricia Ann Parker, John Carradine (may not be in finished film).

F-H (turn-of-century motor-cyclists encounter witchcraft; corpses into birds; pyro-kinesis; other occult powers)

Ref: Vw 29 Nov '71 ad; Bob Greenberg.

Hexen

See: Witchcraft Through the Ages (1921).

Hexenlied, Das

(The Witch's Song)

1919 German sil.

F

Ref: UF p400; Eisner p109-10.

Based on story "Elixiere des Teufels" (The Devil's Elixirs) by E.T.A. Hoffmann.

See also: Elixiere des Teufels (1921).

Hexentoter von Blackmoor, Der

See: Proceso de las Brujas, El (1970).

Hexer, Der

See: Mysterious Magician, The (1965).

Hey There, It's Yogi Bear

1964 Hanna-Barbera (Col) color ani 90 mins.

Prod & Dir: Joseph Barbera & William Hanna.

Assoc Prod: Alex Lovy.

SP: J. Barbera, Warren Foster, & W. Hanna.

Art Dir: Richard Bickenbach, William Perez, Willie Ito, Ernest Nordli, Zigamond Jablecki, Iwao Takamoto, Jacques W. Rupp, Tony Sgroi, Jerry Eisenberg, & Bruce Bushman.

Songs: Ray Gilbert & Doug Goodwin.

Mus: Marty Paich.

Cast: Daws Butler, Don Messick, Julie Bennett, James Darren (possibly not used in final print), Mel Blanc, Jean VanderPyl, Hal Smith, J. Pat O'Malley.

F-mus-com (anthropomorphized animals)

Ref: FDY '65.

Hi Hi London

1969 Japanese.

Filmed in London.

mus-F (Japanese pop groups sell souls to the devil)

Ref: F&F Aug '69 p82.

Hiawatha

(poem by H.W. Longfellow)

See: Little Hiawatha (1937).

Hiawatha's Rabbit Hunt

1941 WB color ani sh.

Prod: Leon Schlesinger.

Story: Michael Maltese.

Ani: Gil Turner.

Mus: Carl W. Stalling.

F-com

Ref: LC; Acad nom.

Hibernatus

1969 French/Italian, S.N.E. Gaumont/Rizzoli color scope.

Dir: Edouard Molinaro.

SP: Jean Halain, Jacques Vilfred, Jean-B Luc, & Louis de Funes.

Cast: Louis de Funes, Claude Gensac, Olivier de Funes, Yves Vincent, Paul Preboist, Michel Lonsdale, Bernard Allane, Martine Kelly, Elyette Gensac.

SF (hotel owner's life disrupted when old owner, found frozen in ice, returns to life)

Ref: MTVM April '69 p48, Aug '69 p42; V 24 Sept '69.

Based on the play by Jean-B Luc.

Hicks in Nightmareland

1915 Edison sil ani split reel.

Dir: Raoul Barré.

F-com

Ref: LC.

See also: Animated Grouch Chasers (1915-16).

Hidden Code, The

1920 Sulmac Prods Co (Pioneer Film Corp) sil 5 reels.

Prod: Norman Harsell.

Dir: Richard Lestrange.

Cin: Harry Fischbeck.

Cast: Grace Davidson, Ralph Osborne, Richard Lestrange, Clayton Davis.

bor-SF (powerful new explosive invented; hypnosis)

Ref: MPN 22:1009; LC.

Hidden Dangers

(Moods of Evil --s.t.; The Black Circle --ad.t.; The Vanishing Mask --ad.t.)

1920 Vit sil serial 15 parts.

Dir & Cin: William Bertram.

Story: Albert E. Smith.

Sc: Graham Baker & William B. Courtney.

Cast: Joe Ryan, Jean Page.

H (chapter titles: 1: "The Evil Spirit"; 5: "Hands of Horror")

Ref: CNW p xvi, 82, 95, 205-06; LC.

Hidden Death

1914 Méliès sil 2100 ft.

Prod: Gaston Méliès.

F-H (murderers killed by horrible machine)

Ref: Bios 21 May '14; MPW 21:109.

Hidden Hand, The

1917-18 Pathé sil serial 15 parts 30 reels.

Story: Arthur B. Reeve.

Sc: Charles A. Logue.

Cast: Doris Kenyon, Sheldon Lewis, Arline Pretty, Mahlon Hamilton.

bor-SF-H (poison gases; super-plastic surgery make henchman look like hero)

Ref: MPW 34:1110-11, 1333-34, 1386, 1548, 1677, 1843; LC.

Hidden Hand, The

1942 WB 68 mins.

Prod: William Jacobs.

Dir: Ben Stoloff.

SP: Anthony Coldewey & Raymond Schrock.

Art Dir: Stanley Fleischer.

Cin: Henry Sharp.

Edit: Harold McLeron.

cont.

Hidden Hand, The cont.

Cast: Craig Stevens, Elizabeth Fraser, Julie Bishop, Frank Wilcox, Cecil Cunningham, Ruth Ford, Roland Drew, Milton Parsons, Willie Best, Wade Boteler, Creighton Hale, Monte Blue.

bor-SF-H (suspended animation)

Ref: HR 18 Sept '42; FD 23 Nov '42; LC.

Based on play "Invitation to a Murder" by Rufus King.

Hidden Menace, The

1925 William Steiner Prods sil 5 reels.

Dir: Charles Hutchinson.

Sc: J.F. Natteford.

Cast: Charles Hutchinson.

H (girl captured by mad sculptor is almost sacrificed by him)

Ref: AFI f2.2477 p347.

Hidden Menace

(Star of the Circus -- Brit.t.)

1938 (1940) British, Alliance 56 mins.

Dir: Albert de Courville.

SP: Elizabeth Meehan.

Cin: Claude Friese-Greene.

Cast: John Clements, Gene Sheldon, Otto Kruger, Gertrude Michael, Patrick Barr, Barbara Blair, Norah Howard.

bor-F (magician uses hypnotism to ruin rival's act)

Ref: Brit Cin; Dimmitt; DdC I:426; FD 10 April '40.

Based on book "Program mit Truxa" by Heinrich Seiler.

See also: Truxa (1936).

Hidden Power

1939 Darmour (Col) 60 mins.

Prod: Larry Darmour.

Dir: Lewis D. Collins.

SP: Gordon Rigby.

Cin: James S. Brown Jr.

Edit: Dwight Caldwell.

Cast: Jack Holt, Gertrude Michael, Dickie Moore, Helen Brown, Regis Toomey, Holmes Herbert.

bor-SF (chemist's attempt to discover formula to "ease suffering" instead discovers new explosive)

Ref: Vw 2 Aug '39; HR 18 May '39; MPH 27 May '39 p32, 34.

Hidden Room of 1000 Horrors

See: Tell-Tale Heart, The (1960).

Hidden Treasure, The

See: Dr. Nicola (1909).

Hidden Valley, The

See: Land Unknown, The (1957).

Hideous Sun Demon, The

(Terror from the Sun --s.t.; Blood on His Lips --Brit.t.)

1959 Pacific Int'l 74 mins.

Prod: Robert Clarke.

Dir: R. Clarke & Thomas Cassarino.

Story: R. Clarke & Phil Hiner.

SP: E.S. Seeley Jr. & Doane Hoag.

Production of Monster Seqs: Gianbatista Cassarino.

Cin: John Morrill, Vilis Lapenieks Jr., & Stan Follis.

Edit: T. Cassarino.

Mus: John Seely.

Cast: Robert Clarke [monster], Patricia Manning, Alan Peterson, Patrick Whyte, Fred La Porta.

SF-H (because of scientific accident, sunlight turns man into murderous lizard-like creature)

cont.

Hideous Sun Demon cont.

Ref: FF '59 p344; MFB June '61 p80.

See also: Wrath of the Sun Demon (1965).

Hier, Aujourd'hui, Demain

See: World of Fashion (1968).

High Barbaree

1947 MGM 92 mins.

Prod: Everett Riskin.

Dir: Jack Conway.

SP: Anne Morrison Chapin, Whitfield Cook, & Cyril Hume.

Art Dir: Cedric Gibbons & Gabriel Scognamillo.

Cin: Sidney Wagner.

SpFX: A. Arnold Gillespie & Warren Newcombe.

Edit: Conrad A. Nervig.

Mus: Herbert Stothart.

Cast: Van Johnson, June Allyson, Thomas Mitchell, Marilyn Maxwell, Cameron Mitchell, Claude Jarman Jr, Henry Hull, Paul Harvey, Jimmy Hunt, GiGi Perreau.

psy-F-seq (downed pilot imagines he finds & lands on strange, idyllic island of his boyhood stories)

Ref: MFB May '47 p64; HR & Vd 12 March '47; Scognamillo.

Based on the novel by Charles Nordhoff & James Norman Hall.

High Note

1960 WB color ani 7 mins.

Dir: Chuck Jones.

F-com (drunken musical note creates havoc in score)

Ref: FD 28 Feb '61; David Rider; Acad nom.

High Plains Drifter

1973 Malpaso Co (U) color 105 mins.

Exec Prod: Jennings Lang.

Prod: Robert Daley.

Dir: Clint Eastwood.

SP: Ernest Tidyman.

Art Dir: Henry Bumstead.

Cin: Bruce Surtees.

Edit: Ferris Webster.

Mus: Dee Barton.

Cast: Clint Eastwood, Verna Bloom, Marianna Hill, Mitchell Ryan, Jack Ging, Stefan Gierasch, Ted Hartley, Billy Curtis.

west; bor-F (Eastwood implied to be some type of supernatural avenger of man who was whipped to death; "reincarnation" -- Time; "angel of death" --BO; "archangel of retribution"--Vw)

Ref: LAT 6 April '73; BO 23 April '73; Vw 28 March '73; Time.

High Priestess of Sexual Witchcraft

1973 (Anonymous/Triumvirate) color 90 mins.

Prod: Mona Terry.

Dir & SP: Beau Buchanan.

Cast: Georgina Spelvin, Rick Livermore, Jean Palmer, Harding Harrison, Marc Stevens.

sex-F (sadism; devil worshippers; "incest and the occult")

Ref: Vw 20 June '73.

High Tor

1956 CBS 16mm 90 mins.

TV film given limited theatrical release.

SP: Maxwell Anderson & John Monks Jr.

Cast: Bing Crosby, Julie Andrews [ghost], Everett Sloane, Nancy Olson.

mus-F (along the Hudson River, an idealist encounters ghostly sailors from Dutch ship, and a "phantom girl" --FIR)

High Tor cont.

Ref: FIR April '56 p 179; LC; Collier.

Based on the play by Maxwell Anderson.

High Treason

1929 (1930) British, Gaum (Tiffany) 95 mins (69 mins).

Dir: Maurice Elvey.

SP: L'Estrange Fawcett.

Art Dir: Andrew Mazzei

Mus: Patrick K. Heale & Walter Collins.

Cast: Benita Hume, Basil Gill, Humberston Wright, Jameson Thomas, Milton Rosmer, Henry Vibart, Raymond Massey, Rene Ray.

SF (set in 1940; channel tunnel; television)

Ref: MPN 41:23:134; F/A p549; Vw Oct '29; MMF 14:94.

Based on the play by Pemberton Billing.

Highflyte's Aeroplane

1910 French, Pathé sil 145 ft.

F (flying bicycle)

Ref: BFI cat p32.

Highly Dangerous

1950 (1951) British, Two Cities (Lippert) 88 mins.

Exec Prod: Earl St. John.

Prod: Anthony Darnborough.

Dir: Roy Baker.

SP: Eric Ambler.

Art Dir: Verchinsky.

Cin: Reginald Wyer & David Harcourt.

Edit: Alfred Roome.

Mus: Richard Addinsell.

Cast: Dane Clark, Margaret Lockwood, Marius Goring, Michael Hordern, Naunton Wayne, Wilfred Hyde-White, Olaf Pooley, Anthony Newley.

bor-SF (truth serum; germ warfare via insects)

Ref: Vd & HR 10 Sept '51; MFB Jan '51 p204.

Hija de Frankenstein, La

See: Santo contra la Hija de Frankenstein (1971).

Hilarious Posters, The

(Les Affiches en Goquette)

1906 French, Star sil 200 ft.

Prod: Georges Méliès.

F-com

Ref: Sadoul/M, GM Mage 821-23; LC.

Hilde Warren und der Tod

(Hilda Warren and Death)

1916 German, May Film sil.

Dir: Joe May.

Sc: Fritz Lang.

Art Dir: Siegfried Wroblewsky.

Cin: Carl Hoffmann.

Cast: Mia May, Bruno Kastner, Hans Mierendorff, Ernst Matray, Georg John, Fritz Lang [Death].

F (death personified)

Ref: F et R; UF p401; DdC II:308; Fritz Lang in America p 119.

Hildur and the Magician

1971 (1972) Larry Jordan Prods 16mm 95 mins (90 mins).

Prod, Dir, SP: Larry Jordan.

F (fairy tale with tiny princess, fairy queen, magician; fairy becomes human)

Ref: BO 24 Jan '72; FC 52:87; FQ Summer '70.

Hilfe, Ich Bin Unsichtbar

(Help, I'm Invisible)

1951 German, JFU.

Dir: E.W. Emo.

Cast: Theodor Lingen (Schmitz), Grethe Weiser, Inge Landgut, Arno Assmann.

SF

Ref: DdC III:232; Deustche Filme.

See also: Invisible Man, The (1933).

Hillbillys in a Haunted House

(Ghost Party --s.t.)

1967 Woolner color.

Prod: Bernard Woolner.

Dir: Jean Yarbrough.

SP: Duk Yelton.

Art Dir: Paul Sylos.

Cin: Vaughn Wilkins.

Edit: Roy Livingston.

Mus: Hal Borne.

Mus Dir: Igo Kantor.

Cast: Ferlin Husky, Mamie Van Doren, Lon Chaney Jr., John Carradine, Basil Rathbone, George Barrows [ape], Don Bowman, Sonny James, Merle Haggard, Molly Bee, Richard Webb.

H-mus-com (fake ghosts; sliding panels; ape; etc.)

Ref: Willis; Richardson; PB.

Himlaspelet

See: Road to Heaven, The (1942).

Himmelskibet

See: Sky Ship (1917).

Hindoo Curse, The

See: Hindoo's Curse, The (1912).

Hindoo Fakir

1902 Edison sil 195 ft.

F (trick action; transformations; disappearances)

Ref: Niver p345; LC.

Possibly made in Europe and released by Edison in U.S.

Hindoo's Charm, The

1912 Lubin sil 1058 ft.

F-com (pin in clay figure felt by flirting husband)

Ref: MPW 13:568, 614.

Hindoo's Curse, The

(The Hindoo Curse --Brit.t.)

1912 Vit sil 817 ft.

Cast: Harry Northrup, Herbert L. Barry, Zena Keefe, Tefft Johnson.

bor-H (curse on eye of idol)

Ref: BFI cat p 198 F 1461; MPW 13:998.

Hindrance

1971? Canadian ani sh.

Dir: Pierre Moretti.

F (character caught in trap by calligraphic shape)

Ref: ASIFA Bulletin '71.

Hindu, The

See: Sabaka (1955).

Hindu Tomb, The

See: Indian Tomb, The (1920).

Hindustan Hamara

See: Our India (1950).

Hipnosis

See: Hypnosis (1962).

Hipopótamo, El

(The Hippopotamus)

1971 Spanish, Estudios Castillo color ani 8.7 mins.

Hipopótamo, El cont.

Dir: Amaro Carretero.

Realisation: Vicente Rodriguez.

com-doc; bor-F (natural history of the hippo with gags)

Ref: SpCin '72.

Hippopotamus, The

See: Hipopótamo, El (1971).

Hippopotamus Who Was Afraid of Vaccination, The

1967 Soviet.

Dir: Amalrik.

F

Ref: Vw 6 Dec '67.

Hiram na Kamay

(The Clutching Hand)

1962? Philippine, Sampaguita.

Dir: Tony Cayado.

Cast: Eddie Gutierrez, Josephine Estrada.

H

Ref: MTVM Jan '62 p 14.

Hiroku Kaibyoden

(Haunted Castle)

1969 Japanese, Daiei color scope 83 mins.

Dir: Tokuzo Tanaka.

SP: Shozaburo Asai.

Art Dir: Seiichi Ota.

Cin: Hiroshi Imai.

Mus: Chumei Watanabe.

Cast: Kojiro Hongo, Naomi Kobayashi, Mitsuyo Kamei, Koichi Uenoyama, Akane Kawasaki.

F-H ("cat with supernatural powers becomes female demon [who] drinks the blood of [her] victims" --Willis)

Ref: UniJ 48 p8; Willis.

Based on the famous Japanese legend of the ghost cat of Nabeshima.

See also: Nabeshima Kaibyoden (1949).

His Brother's Ghost

1945 PRC 52 mins.

Prod: Sigmund Neufeld.

Dir: Sam Newfield.

SP: George Milton.

Cin: Jack Greenhalgh.

Edit: Holbrook N. Todd.

Cast: Buster Crabbe, Al "Fuzzy" St. John, Charles King, Karl Hackett, Archie Hall.

west; bor-H-com (gruesome disguise to fake ghost)

Ref: HR 1 Nov '46; MPH 13 Jan '45 p2269.

His Brother's Keeper

1920 (1921) American Cinema Corp (Pioneer) sil 6 reels.

Dir: Wilfrid North.

Sc: N. Brewster Morse.

Cin: Arthur Quinn & W.G. Crolly.

Cast: Albert L. Barrett, Martha Mansfield, Rogers Lytton, Frazer Coulter, Gretchen Harman, Gladden James, Anne Drew.

F (villain uses thought control of other person in order to commit murder)

Ref: AFI F2.2502 p351; MPW 50:431; LC.

His Egyptian Affinity

1915 Nestor (U) sil 1 reel.

Prod & Sc: A.E. Christie.

Cast: Victoria Ford, Eddie Lyons.

F-com (return to life after 3000 years)

Ref: MPW 25:1379, 1481; LC.

cont.

cont.

His Fairy Godmother

1915 Vit sil 1 reel.

Dir: Wally Van Norstrand.

Sc: Mabel Burgess.

Cast: Wally Van (Norstrand?), Nitra Frazer.

F-dream-com (suit vanishes as fairy godmother warned)

Ref: MPW 25:1129.

His Faithful Furniture

1911 French, Lux sil 360 ft.

F (animated furniture returns to owner after being repossessed)

Ref: MPW 8:152, 208, 249.

His First Place

1910 British, Warwick sil 480 ft.

F-com (people become electrified)

Ref: Bios 15 Sept '10.

His Guiding Spirit

1913 (1914) Selig sil 1000 ft.

Prod: E.A. Martin.

F (ghost figure)

Ref: MPW 19:676, 750.

His Hand Slipped

See: Se le Pasó la Mano (1952).

His Last Twelve Hours

(Le Sue Ultime 12 Ore)

1953 (1954) Italian, Cines-Lest Pathe (Independent Film Clearing House) 89 mins.

Prod: Carlo Civallero.

Dir: Luigi Zampa.

SP: Cesare Zavattini.

Cast: Jean Gabin, Antonella Lualdi.

F (after death, angel of justice tells man he was killed 12 hours early, returns him to Earth for 12 hours to expiate sins)

Ref: Acad.

His Loyal Highness

See: His Royal Highness (1932).

His Majesty the Scarecrow of Oz

(The New Wizard of Oz --s.t?)

1914 Oz Film Manufacturing Co. sil 5 reels.

Prod & Sc: L. Frank Baum.

F-com (talking scarecrow, woodsman made of tin, wizard, etc.)

Ref: MPW 20 March '15 p 1781; MPN 6 Feb '15 ad.

Based on book "The Scarecrow of Oz" by L. Frank Baum.

See also: Wizard of Oz, The.

His Phantom Sweetheart

1915 Vit sil 708 ft.

Dir: Ralph W. Ince.

SP: Earle Williams.

Cast: Earle Williams, Anita Stewart, Thomas Mills.

H-dream (lunatic strangler; dream girl becomes "demon of fury" --FIR)

Ref: BFI cat p221; LC; FIR March '68 p 157-58.

His Prehistoric Past

(A Dream --s.t?)

1914 Keystone sil 1157 ft.

Prod: Mack Sennett.

Dir & Sc: Charles Chaplin.

Cast: Charlie Chaplin, Mack Swain, Gene Marsh, Fritz Schade.

bor-SF-com-dream (Charlie dreams he is a caveman)

Ref: BFI cat p211; LC; Collier.

His Royal Highness

(His Loyal Highness --Brit.t.)

1932 Australian, Efftee.

Dir: F.W. Thring.

Cast: George Wallace.

bor-F-dream (man hit on head imagines he is king)

Ref: Collier.

His "Spring Overcoat"

1912 Italian, Cines sil 375 ft.

F-com (overcoat seems alive, protects owner from harm)

Ref: MPW 14:1326.

His Wonderful Lamp

1913 British, Cricks sil 480 ft.

Dir: Edwin J. Collins (?).

Cast: Jack Leigh.

F (rays of lamp stolen by hobo make things vanish)

Ref: Gifford/BFC 04362; Bios 4 Feb '13.

Histoire d'un Poisson Rouge

See: Golden Fish (1959).

Histoires Extraordinaires

(Unusual Tales; Asylum of Horror --alt.t?)

1949 (1950) French, Fred Orain 85 mins.

Dir & SP: Jean Faurez.

Art Dir: René Moulaert.

Cin: Louis Page.

Edit: Suzanne De Trayes.

Cast: Jules Berry, Fernand Ledoux, Suzy Carrier, Olivier Hussenot, Jandeline.

F-H (man imagines he hears heart of man he murdered still beating; man walled up alive; 3rd story)

Ref: FIR Oct '61 p470; Vw 18 Feb '50; FM 11:43.

Based on 3 short stories: "The Tell-Tale Heart" and "The Cask of Amontillado" by Edgar Allan Poe, and "Ecce Homo" by Thomas De Quincy.

See also: Tell-Tale Heart,The.

Histoires Extraordinaires

See: Living Dead, The (1933); Spirits of the Dead (1967).

Historia Natura

1968? Czech color ani sh.

Dir: Jan Svankmajer.

F-doc (story of evolution)

Ref: Kinetic Art Prog 2.

See also: Kinetic Art, The (1970).

History

1970 Amateur (Film-makers' Coop) 16mm sil 40 mins.

Made by: Ernie Gehr.

exp-abs-F

Ref: FMC 5:119.

History of Aladdin, or the Wonderful Lamp, The

See: Aladdin.

History of Ali Baba, and of the Forty Robbers Killed by One Slave, The

See: Ali Baba and the Forty Thieves.

History of Coal, The

1967? Hungarian, Animation Studio ani sh.

Dir: Szabolcs Szabos.

F-doc (past geological ages depicted)

Ref: MTVM Nov '67 p9.

History of Dhruva

See: Dhruva Charita (1921).

History of Inventions, The

See: Story of Inventions, The (1959).

History of Walton, The

1953 British, Kingston and District Cine Club (Amateur) 16mm color ani 15 mins.

Dir: John Daborn.

F (history of British town from stone age to the future)

Ref: BFI Dist cat sup 1 p79.

High Treason (1929) British

Hiwa ng Lagim

(Hiwaga ng Lagim? Mystery and Terror)

1970 Philippine, Viltra.

Prod: Victoria Villanueva.

Dir: José Miranda Cruz.

Mus: D'Romenz.

Cast: Dante Varona, Rossana Ortiz, Etang Discher, Patria Plata, Mar Quijano, Nel Delaysla.

F-H (ghosts? zombies?)

Ref: Borst.

Ho Fatto 13

(I Made 13)

1951 Italian.

Dir: Carlo Manzoni.

Cast: Carlo Croccolo, Antonella Lualdi, Riccardo Billi, Mario Riva.
F-dream

Ref: Ital Prods '50-'51 p98-99.

Hoarder, The

1969 Canadian, NFB color ani 5 mins.

Dir: Evelyn Lambert.

F (bird steals sun)

Ref: ASIF Bltn 2 '71; Mamaia '70.

Based on Indian legend.

Hobby

1968 Polish color ani sh.

Dir: Daniel Szczechura.

F (woman captures birdmen)

Ref: IAFF 1; MTVM Nov '68 p20A, Sept '68 p 23A.

Hoboes in Paradise

(Les Gueux au Paradis)

1950 French, Gaum (Distinguished Films) 86 mins.

Dir: René La Henaff.

Cast: Fernandel, Raimu.

rel-F-com (two men dressed as saints for St Nicholas' day are killed & find themselves in Hell)

cont.

oboes in Paradise cont.

Ref: Acad; FD 19 Oct '50;
deGroot p 115.

Based on the story by G.M.
Maertens.

obo's Dream

1908 Lubin sil 675 ft.

F-dream

Ref: MPW 3:432; Views 137:11.

ocus Pocus

1949 Col 16 mins.

Prod & Dir: Jules White.

SP: Felix Adler.

Edit: Edwin Bryant.

Cast: The Three Stooges (Moe
Howard, Shemp Howard, Larry
Fine), Mary Ainslee, Vernon
Dent, Jimmy Lloyd.

bor-F-com (super-hypnotism)

Ref: LC; GMS p 136.

Remake: Flagpole Jitters
(1956).

See also: Three Stooges,
The (1934-59).

odag

1970? color ani sh.

Dir: Larry Huber.

F-com (hodags are benign
monsters who eat despoilers
of the forest)

Ref: ASIFA 6.

odge Podge

1913 Paul Felton (Pathé)
sil cut-out ani 1/2 reel
series.

Prod: Lyman H. Howe.

F-com

Ref: Ani Chart.

odina Modrych Slonu

(The Hour of the Blue Elephants)

1970? Czech color seq.

Dir: Radim Cvrcek & Zdenek
Rozkopal.

SP: Ota Hofman.

F (land of blue elephants)

Ref: Vw 30 June '71.

Based on a book by Ota Hofman.

Hoffmanns Erzählungen

See: Tales of Hoffmann, The
(1914).

Hoffnung Symphony Orchestra, The

1965 British, Halas & Batchelor
and BBC TV Enterprises color
ani 8 mins.

Prod: John Halas.

Dir: Harold Whitaker.

SP: J. Halas & Derek Lamb.

Art: J. Halas & Tom Bailey.

Mus: Francis Chagrin.

F-com (weird magical musical
instruments wreak havoc at
concert)

Ref: MFB July '66 p 113.

Based on drawings of Gerald
Hoffnung.

Hoichi the Earless

See: Kwaidan (1963).

Hold On!

(There's No Place Like Space --
s.t.)

1966 Four Leaf (MGM) color
scope 85 mins.

Prod: Sam Katzman.

Dir: Arthur Lubin.

SP: James B. Gordon.

Art Dir: George W. Davis &
Eddie Imazu.

Cin: Paul C. Vogel.

SpFX: J. McMillan Johnson
& Carroll L. Shepphird.

Edit: Ben Lewis.

Mus Dir: Fred Karger.

cont.

Hold On! cont.

Cast: Herman's Hermits (Peter
Blair Noone, Karl Green,
Keith Hopwood, Derek Leckenby,
Barry Whitwam), Shelley
Fabares, Sue Ann Langdon,
Herbert Anderson, Bernard
Fox, Harry Hickox, Hortense
Petra, Mickey Deems, Ray
Kellog, John Hart.

mus-com; F-seqs

Ref: CoF 10:6; FF '66 p141-42.

Hold on to Both Things

See: Haltet Beides Gut Zusammen (1969).

Hold That Ghost

1941 U 86 mins.

Assoc Prod: Burt Kelly &
Glenn Tryon.

Dir: Arthur Lubin.

Story: Robert Lees & Fred
Rinaldo.

SP: R. Lees. F. Rinaldo, &
John Grant.

Art Dir: Jack Otterson.

Cin: Elwood Bredell & Joseph
Valentine.

Edit: Philip Cahn.

Mus: H. J. Salter.

Cast: Bud Abbott, Lou Costello,
Richard Carlson, Joan Davis,
Mischa Auer, Evelyn Ankers,
Shemp Howard, Marc Lawrence,
Russell Hicks, Andrews Sisters.

H-mus-com (fake ghosts)

Ref: Vd 28 July '41; Vw 25
June '41; MFB Nov '41 p 149.

Hold That Hypnotist

(Out of This World --s.t.?)

1957 AA 61 mins.

Prod: Ben Schwalb.

Dir: Austen Jewell.

SP: Dan Pepper.

Art Dir: David Milton.

Cin: Harry Neumann.

Edit: George White.

Cast: Huntz Hall, Stanley
Clements, Jane Nigh, David
Condon.

F-com (regression under hypnosis to 1683; treasure found
based on information from
regression)

Ref: FDY '58 p211.

See also: Spooks Run Wild
(1941).

Hold That Line

1952 Mono 64 mins.

Dir: William Beaudine.

Story: Bert Lawrence.

SP: Tim Ryan & Charles R.
Marion.

Art Dir: Martin Obzina.

Cin: Marcel Le Picard.

Mus: Edward J. Kay.

Cast: Huntz Hall, Leo Gorcey,
David Gorcey, Bernard Gorcey,
John Bromfield, Veda Ann
Borg, Gil Stratton Jr, Taylor
Holmes, Mona Knox.

bor-SF-com (elixir of super-
strength)

Ref: FDY; LC; Willis.

See also: Spooks Run Wild
(1941).

Hold Tight to the Satellite

See: Dog, a Mouse and a Sputnik,
A (1958).

Hole, The

1962 Storyboard color 16mm
ani 15 mins.

Dir & SP: John & Faith Hubley.

Voice: Dizzy Gillespie.

sat-SF-com

Ref: Ani/Cin p52-53; Acad
winner.

Hole, The

See: Onibaba (1965); Dupkata
(1967).

Hole in the Ground, A

1963 Australian, Aranda
8 mins.

Dir, SP, Edit: Bruce McNaughton.

Cin: B. McNaughton & John
Scott.

F (ghost of man & ghost of
train; ghost is killed)

Ref: Collier.

Hole in the Moon, A

See: Hor Balevana (1965).

Holiday for Henriette

See: Paris When It Sizzles
(1964).

Holiday Land

1934 Col color ani sh.

Prod: Charles Mintz.

Story: Sid Marcus.

Ani: Art Davis.

Mus: Joe de Nat.

F-com

Ref: LC; Acad nom.

Hollow-My-Weanie, Dr. Frankenstein (...Weenie...?)

(Frankenstein De Sade --ad.t.)

1969.

sex-SF-H (homosexual version:
monster provided with enormous
penis)

Ref: Ackerman; LAPP.

See also: Frankenstein.

Hollowhead as a Magician

1912 French, C.G.P.C. sil
tinted sh?

F-com (tricks)

Ref: MPW 12:830.

Hollywood

1922 Famous Players-Lasky
(Par) sil 8100 ft.

Pres: Jesse L. Lasky.

Dir: James Cruze.

Story: Frank Condon.

Adapt: Tom Geraghty.

Cin: Karl Brown.

Cast: Hope Down, Luke Cosgrave,
George K. Arthur, Ruby Lafayette,
Harris Gordon, Roscoe "Fatty"
Arbuckle, and several dozen
guest stars.

F-dream (hero in dream rows
through streets of Hollywood;
imagines himself as knight;
etc.)

Ref: RAF p304; Bloch; Dyer;
AFI F2.2551 p358.

Hollywood Capers

1935 (1936) WB ani 1 reel.

Ani: Rollin Hamilton & Chuck
(Charles) Jones.

F-com

Ref: LC.

Hollywood Extra, A

See: Life and Death of 9413 --
A Hollywood Extra, The (1928).

Hollywood Revue of 1929, The

1929 MGM sound part color
130 mins.

Prod: Harry Rapf.

Dir: Charles Reisner.

Dialog: Al Boasberg & Robert
E. Hopkins.

Art Dir: Cedric Gibbons &
Richard Day.

Cin: John Arnold, Irving
Ries, Maximilian Fabian,
& John M. Nickolaus.

Edit: William S. Gray &
Cameron K. Wood.

Songs [of interest]: Joe
Goodwin & Gus Edwards.

Mus Arrangers: Arthur Lange,
Ernest Klapholtz, & Ray
Heindorf.

Cast: Conrad Nagel, Jack
Benny, John Gilbert, Norma
Shearer, Joan Crawford,
Bessie Love, Lionel Barry-

cont.

Hollywood Revue of 1929 cont.

more, Cliff Edwards, Stan
Laurel, Oliver Hardy, Anita
Page, Nils Asther, Marion
Davies, William Haines,
Buster Keaton, Marie Dressler,
Gus Edwards.

mus-com; F-seqs (Bessie Love
in miniature crawls out of
Jack Benny's pocket; Gus
Edwards sings "Lon Chaney
Will Get You If You Don't
Look Out" while various
people appear in many of
Chaney's horror makeups,
although Chaney himself is
not in the film)

Ref: AFI F2.2552 p358-59;
NYT 15 Aug '29; FIR Feb &
March '71.

Holy Devil, The

See: Svyatoi Chort (1917).

Holy Mountain, The

1973 US/Mexican, ABKCO color scope
126 mins.

Dir & SP: Alexandro Jodorowsky.

Cin: Rafael Corkidi.

Edit: Frederic Landeros.

Mus: A. Jodorowsky & Ronald Frangipane,
& Don Cherry.

Cast: Alexandro Jodorowsky, Horacio
Salinas, Ramona Saunders.

F (Christ figure is crucified;
search for Holy Mountain with
secret of immortality finds
"empty costumed figures")

Ref: Vw 30 May '73.

Holy Pilgrimage

See: Teerth Yatra (1958).

Holy Wednesday

See: Festin de Satanas, El
(n.d.).

Homage to François Couperin

1964 color ani 2 mins.

Made by: Philip Stapp.

Mus: François Couperin.

mus-F (butterflies dance)

Ref: Annecy '65.

Homage to Tarzan

See: Homenaje a Tarzán
(1970).

Hombre de Puño de Oro, El

See: Uomo dal Pugno d'Oro,
L' (1967).

Hombre Invisible Ataca, El

(The Invisible Man Attacks)

1967 Argentinian, Argentina
Sono Films color 80 mins.

Prod & Dir: Martin Mentasti.

SP: Sergio De Cecco.

Art Dir: L.D. Pedre.

Cin: Ricardo Younis.

Mus: Rodolfo Arizaga.

Cast: Martin Karadagian,
Gilda Lousek, Tristán.

SF

Ref: Cine Argentino; Heraldo
'68.

See also: Invisible Man, The
(1933).

Hombre Lobo, El

See: Frankenstein's Bloody
Terror (1968).

Hombre Que Logro Ser Invisible,
El

See: New Invisible Man, The
(1960).

Hombre Que Vino del Ummo, El

(The Man Who Came from Ummo;
Dracula Jagt Frankenstein;
Dracula Hunts Frankenstein;
Los Monstruos del Terror:
The Monsters of Terror; Dracula
vs. Frankenstein --Brit.t.)

1970 Spanish/W. German/Italian,
Jaime Prades/Eichberg Film/
International Jaguar color
70mm 87 mins.

Prod: Jaime Prades.

cont.

196

Hombre Que Vino del Ummo cont.

Dir: Tulio Demicheli.

SP: Jacinto Molina (Jacinto Molina Alvarez).

Art Dir: Adolfo Cofiño.

Makeup: Francisco R. Ferrer.

Cin: Godofredo Pacheco.

Edit: Emilio Rodriguez.

Mus: Rafael Ferrer.

Cast: Michael Rennie [alien], Karin Dor, Craig Hill, Patty Shepard, Angel del Pozo, Paul Naschy (r.n. Jacinto Molina) [Frankenstein's monster; werewolf].

F-H (alien scientist comes to Earth to conquer it, revives Dracula, Frankenstein's monster, a living mummy and a werewolf to do this, but is foiled by human love)

Ref: SpCin '71 p210; Manila Bulletin 1 Nov '70; Eric Hoffman; Vw 3 Nov '71.

Sequel to: Frankenstein's Bloody Terror (1968).

See also: Dracula (1930); Mummy, The (1932); Wolf Man, The (1941); Frankenstein.

Hombre sin Rostro, El

(The Man Without a Face)

1950 Mexican, Diana y Oro Films (Azteca).

Dir & SP: Juan Bustillo Oro.

Cin: Jorge Stahl (Jr?).

Mus: Raul Lavista.

Cast: Arturo de Córdova, Fernando Galiana (?), Carmen Molino (Molina?), Miguel Arenas, Miguel Angel Ferriz, Matilde Palau, Queta Lavat.

F-H

Ref: Aventura p422; FM 31:22

Hombre y el Fuego, El

(Man and Fire)

1970 Spanish, Castilla color ani 8 mins.

Dir: Amaro Carretero.

F

Ref: SpCin '71.

Hombre y el Monstruo, El

See Man and the Monster, The (1958).

Hombre y la Bestia, El

(The Man and the Beast; El Extraño Caso del Hombre y la Bestia: The Strange Case of the Man and the Beast -- e.t?; Dottor Yekyll --ad.t.)

(Note: erroneously listed in Vol I under Italian title Dottor Jekyll,Il.)

1951 (1956) Argentinian, Sono (Azteca) 80 mins.

Dir: Mario Soffici.

SP: Ulises Petit de Murat, M. Soffici, & Carlos Marin.

Makeup: Alberto Neron & Angel Salerno.

Cin: Gori Munoz & Antonio Merayo.

Edit: Jorge Garate.

Mus: Silvio Vernazza.

Cast: Mario Soffici, Ana Maria Campoy, Olga Zubarry, José Cibrian, Rafael Frontura.

SF-H (in attempt to separate good from evil chemically, man turns himself into monster)

Ref: Nubila II:81, 142, 295-96; Gasca p 136; Scognamillo.

Based on short novel "The Strange Case of Dr. Jekyll and Mr. Hyde" by Robert Louis Stevenson.

See also: Dr. Jekyll and Mr. Hyde.

Home

See: Dom (1958).

Home Made Happy, The

See: Waif and the Wizard, The (1901).

Home of the Muses, The

See: Jupiter's Thunder Bolts (1903).

Home Sweet Home

1972 French, Unite Trois color 83 mins.

Dir: Liliane De Kermadec.

SP: L. De Kermadec & Julien Guiomar.

Cin: Claude Creton.

Edit: Roland Prandini.

Mus: Roland Vincent.

Cast: Julien Guiomar, Coline Deble, Jacques Monory, Denis Gunzbourg, Patrick Dumont.

myst-H (people, chained & bloody, kept in the attic of an old house; suggestions of ghosts)

Ref: Vw 29 March '72 p30.

Note: film is in French language, but title is in English

Homeless Hare

1949 WB color ani 7 mins.

Dir: Chuck Jones.

Voices: Mel Blanc.

F-com

Ref: LC; PopCar.

See also: Bugs Bunny (1938-63).

Homem Lôbo, O

(The Wolf Man)

1971 Brazilian, Pinheiro-Filmes color.

Dir, SP, Edit: Raffaello Rossi.

Cin: Antônio B. Thomé.

Mus: Gabriel Migliori.

Cast: Claudia Cerine, Raffaello Rossi, Lino Braga, Toni Cardi, Osmano Cardoso.

SF-H (scientist, trying to cure crippled son, turns him into werewolf)

Ref: Higuchi.

See also: Wolf Man, The (1941).

Homenaje a Tarzán

(Homage to Tarzan; La Cazadora Inconsciente: The Unconscious Hunter)

cont.

Homenaje a Tarzán cont.

1970 Spanish, X Films color ani 120 mins.

Dir: Rafael Ruiz.

Edit: Elena Jaumandreu.

Homenaje

F (semi-abstract film concerning Tarzan)

Ref: SpCin '71.

See also: Tarzan.

Homer's Odyssey

● (Ulysses --alt.t?)

1909 Special sil 2 reels.

Ref: FW Dir p 196.

● (L'Odissea; The Adventures of Ulysses --ad.t?)

1911 (1912) Italian, Milano (Monopol) sil 3000 ft.

Ref: MPW 11:570-74, 941; LC; F/A p332.

myth-F

Based on epic poem "The Odyssey" by Homer.

See also: Odyssey, The (1963).

Homicidal

1961 Col 87 mins.

Prod & Dir: William Castle.

SP: Robb White.

Art Dir: Cary Odell.

Makeup: Ben Lane.

Cin: Burnett Guffey.

Edit: Edwin Bryant.

Mus: Hugo Friedhofer.

Nar: W. Castle.

Cast: Glenn Corbett, Patricia Breslin, Jean Arless, Eugenie Leontovich, Alan Bunce, Richard Rust, James Westerfield.

psy-H (woman raised as man since birth to gain inheritance pretends to be own wife & commits apparent psycho-murders to protect inheritance)

Ref: FD 22 June '61.

Homnage to Rameau

1967 Amateur 16mm color 7.5 mins.

Made by: John Whitney.

exp-F

Ref: FC 53-55:82.

Homme à la Tête en Caoutchouc, L'

See: Man with the Rubber Head, The (1901).

Homme au Cerveau Greffe, L'

(The Man with the Transplanted Brain; The Man with the Brain Graft --ad.t.)

1972 French/Italian/W. German, Parc Film & UPF &UPG/Verona/Bavaria Atelier color 90 mins.

Prod: Mag Bodard.

Dir & SP: Jacques Doniol-Valcroze.

Art Dir: Claude Pignot.

Cin: Etienne Becker.

Edit: Nicole Berckmans.

Cast: Mathieu Carriere, Jean-Pierre Aumont, Nicoletta Machiavelli, Michel Duchaussoy, Mariane Egerikx, Martine Sarcey.

SF (doctor has own brain transplanted into young patient)

Ref: Vw 19 April '72 p 18; Unifrance Oct '71; FM 99:9.

Based on a novel by Victor Vicas & Alain Franck.

Homme aux Cent Trucs, L'

See: Conjurer with a Hundred Tricks, The (1900).

Homme aux Figures de Cire, L'

(The Man with Wax Faces)

1913 French sil sh?

Dir: Maurice Tourneur.

H

Ref: Laclos p 188; CoF 16:18; Orpheus 2:20; DdC II:308.

Homme aux Mille Inventions, L'

(The Man with a Thousand Inventions)

1910 French sil sh.

El Hombre y la Bestia (1951) Argentinian

Homme aux Mille Inventions cont.

Prod: Georges Méliès.

F

Ref: Sadoul/M, GM Mage 1548-52.

Homme, Cette Dualité, L'

(Man, that Dual Personality)

1958 Belgian drawn on film 4 mins.

Dir: Yvan Lemaire.

abs-F

Ref: Ani/Belgium p48-49.

Homme dans la Lune L'

See: Astronomer's Dream, The (1898).

Homme de Têtes, Un

See: Four Troublesome Heads, The (1898).

Homme Est Satisfait, L'

See: Who Looks, Pays (1906).

Homme Mouche, L'

See: Human Fly, The (1902).

Homme Orchestra, L'

See: One-Man Band, The (1900).

Homme Protée, L'

See: Lightning Change Artist, The (1899).

Homme Qui Rit, L'

(The Man Who Laughs)

1909 French sil sh.

hist-H (boy's face carved into permanent, large grin; becomes clown as adult --plot of novel)

Ref: DdC III:503.

Based on the novel by Victor Hugo.

See also: Grinsende Gesicht, Das (1921); Man Who Laughs, The.

Homme Qui Vendit Son Ame, L'

(The Man Who Sold His Soul)

1943 French 90 mins.

Dir: Jean-Paul Paulin.

Cast: Michèle Alfa, Mona Goya, Dartique, Renée Thorel, Huguette Saint-Arnaud, André Luguet, Pierre Larquey, Robert Le Vigan [Devil].

F (banker sells soul to devil to gain success but must use money to do evil)

Ref: de Groot 54; DdC II:55, III:251.

Based on novel "L'Homme Qui Vendit Son Ame au Diable" (The Man Who Sold His Soul to the Devil" by Pierre Veber.

See also: Homme Qui Vendit Son Ame au Diable, L' (1920).

Homme Quit Vendit Son Ame au Diable, L'

(The Man Who Sold His Soul to the Devil)

1920 French sil.

Dir: Pierre Caron.

Cin: Andre A. Dantan.

Cast: Charles Dullin.

F (banker sells soul to devil to gain success but must use money to do evil)

Ref: Jeanne p458; DdC II:10, 308.

Based on the novel by Pierre Veber.

See also: Homme Qui Vendit Son Ame, L' (1943).

Hommes Veulent Vivre!, Les

(Man Wants to Live!)

1961 French/Italian, Societé Nouvelle/Romana 110 mins.

Prod & Dir: Leonide Moguy.

SP: L. Moguy & Henri Torres.

Art Dir: Rino Mondellini.

Cin: André Villard.

Mus: Joseph Kosma.

cont.

Hommes Veulent Vivre cont.

Cast: Claudio Gora, John Justin, Jacqueline Huet, Yves Massard.

SF (anti-atomic research story; death ray)

Ref: Vd 22 Jan '63.

Homo Sapiens

1959 Rumanian color ani 10 mins.

Prod, Dir, Story: Ion Popescu-Gopo.

Mus: Dumitru Capoianu .

F-doc (evolution of man from protoplasm to interplanetary travel)

Ref: S&S Autumn '60 p 186; ASIFA info sheet

Homo Vampire

See: Goulve, La (1971).

Homunculus

(Die Rache des Homunkulus: The Revenge of Homunculus; Homunkulus der Führer: Homunculus the Leader)

1916 German, Bioscop sil serial 6 parts 24 reels.

Dir: Otto Rippert.

Sc: O. Rippert & Robert Neuss.

Art Dir: Robert A. Dietrich.

Cin: Carl Hoffmann.

Cast: Olaf Fønss [Homunculus, an android], Friedrich (Gustav?) Kühne, Mechtild Their (Thein?), Maria Carmi, Aud Egede Nissen, Lupu Pick.

SF (soulless artificial man of great intellect becomes dictator of large country, plans to conquer the world but is killed by lightning)

Ref: C to H p31-33; Clarens; Neergaard p60; Gasca p 27; Laclos p 188; UF p394.

Based on the novel by Robert Reinert.

Homunculus the Leader

See: Homunculus (1916).

Homunkulus der Führer

See: Homunculus (1916).

Honesty's Strange Reward

1906 French, Pathé sil 393 ft.

F-dream (tramp dreams buildings, trees, etc. are liquor flasks)

Ref: Views & FI 1:23:8.

Honeymoon Bridge

1935 Col 2 reels.

Dir: Del Lord.

SP: Harry McCoy.

Cast: Leon Errol, Geneva Mitchell, Bud Jamison, Bobby Burns, Bess Flowers.

com; F-dream (in frustration Leon shoots everyone playing bridge & himself, goes to heaven --they are angels, still playing bridge; goes with Devil to Hell where there is no bridge; all a dream)

Ref: Maltin/GMS p 115-16, 122; LC.

See also: Leon Errol Comedy.

Honjo Nana Fushigi

(The Seven Wonders of Honjo)

1957 Japanese, Shintoho.

F-H (traditional Japanese ghost -- scarred female seeking revenge)

Ref: Anderson/Richie p262.

Honnête Homme, Un

(An Honorable Man)

1963 French ani 11 mins.

Dir & Story: Ado Kyrou.

Mus: Louise Bessières.

F

Ref: MMF 8:77-78.

Honorable Man, An

See: Honnête Homme, Un (1963).

Hon. Mr. Jap Van Winkle, The

1919 Chester sil 737 ft.

Prod: C.L. Chester.

Edit & Titles: Katherine Hilliker.

F (man lives under sea; visits home on earth & finds parents dead; opens forbidden box & reverts to true, old age)

Ref: BFI cat p242.

Hoo-Ha

n.d. Amateur (Film-makers' Coop) 16mm color 5 mins.

Made by: Monroe Rapaport.

exp-abs-F

Ref: FMC 5:269.

Hoodoo, The

1910 French, Pathé sil 920 ft.

F-com

Ref: MPW 7:762, 768, 934.

Hoodooed

1912 Lubin sil sh?

F-com (breaking mirror brings bad luck passed on by getting Chinaman to break identical mirror)

Ref: MPW 11:1092, 12:41.

Hoofs and Goofs

1957 Col 2 reels.

Prod & Dir: Jules White.

SP: Jack White.

Art Dir: Paul Palmentola.

Cin: Gert Andersen.

Edit: Harold White.

Cast: The Three Stooges (Moe Howard, Larry Fine, Joe Besser), Benny Rubin, Harriette Tarler.

F-com (the Stooges' sister is reincarnated as a horse)

Ref: Maltin/GMS p 140; LC; Pardi.

Sequel: Horsing Around (1957).

See also: Three Stooges, The (1934-59).

Hooligan Assists the Magician

1900 Edison sil 98 ft.

Dir: Edwin S. Porter.

F-com (tricks; transformations; disappearances)

Ref: Niver p345.

See also: Happy Hooligan.

Hooligan's Christmas Dream

1903 Biograph sil 375 ft.

F-com (tricks; Santa Claus)

Ref: Niver p46; LC.

See also: Happy Hooligan.

Hoor-e-Samander

1936 Indian, Vishnu.

Dir: Dhirubhai Desai.

Cast: Ashik Hussein, Kanti, Meher Sultana, Anusuya.

F (magic tricks)

Ref: MovPicM March-April '36 p48.

Hop-Frog

1910 French (Continental Warwick) sil sh.

Dir: Henri Desfontaines.

H (dwarf jester burns several people to death)

Ref: Bios 24 Feb '10; DdC II:68.

Based on the short story by Edgar Allan Poe.

See also: Masque of the Red Death, The (1964).

Hop Harrigan

1946 Col serial 15 parts 31 reels.

Prod: Sam Katzman.

Dir: Derwin Abrahams.

SP: George Plympton & Ande Lamb.

Cin: Ira Morgan.

cont.

Hop Harrigan cont.

Edit: Earl Turner.

Mus: Lee Zahler.

Cast: William Bakewell, Jennifer Holt, Robert "Buzz" Henry, Sumner Getchell, Emmett Vogan, Claire James, John Merton, Wheeler Oakman, Ernie Adams, Anthony Warde, Jackie Moran, Jack Buchanan.

SF (power beam; new source of energy; new motor; death ray)

Ref: Stringham; LC; Acad; Ser/Col; TBC p257.

Based on the radio serial from the comic strip by Jon Blummer.

Hop o' My Thumb

1912 French, Gaum sil tinted 2 reels.

Cast: Jimmie (Bébè), Renée Carl (Carl1?).

F (seven-league boots)

Ref: MPW 25 Jan '13 p351.

Based on fairy tale "Le Petit Poucet" collected by Charles Perrault.

See also: Tom Thumb.

Hopalong Casualty

196? WB color ani 7 mins.

Dir: Chuck Jones.

F-com

Ref: David Rider.

See also: Road Runner & Coyote (1948--).

Hope Diamond Mystery, The

1921 Kosmik Films Ink sil serial 15 parts.

Dir: Stuart Paton.

Cast: Grace Darmond, George Chesebro, Harry Carter, William Marion, Boris Karloff, Carmen Phillips, William Puckley, May Yohe.

myst-bor-F-H (possibly cursed diamond)

Ref: LC; MPW 48:889; CNW p221.

Hope Seems Infinite

1972 UCLA color 16mm ani sh.

Made by: Ron Saks.

abs-F

Ref: UCLA notes; Greg Chalfin.

Hopi Legend, A

(A Pueblo Romance --alt.t.)

1913 Nestor (U) sil.

Prod, Dir, Sc: Wallace Reid.

Cast: Wallace Reid, Dorothy Davenport, Ed Brady, Phil Dunham.

F-seq (lovers unite in Happy Hunting Ground after death)

Ref: FIR April '66 p223; MPW 18:1544, 1590.

See also: Before the White Man Came (1912).

Hoppity Goes To Town

See: Mr. Bug Goes to Town (1941).

Hoppity Pop

1946 Canadian, NFB color ani 3 mins.

Dir: Norman McLaren.

abs-F (hand-drawn on film to Calliope music)

Ref: C-16 p 16; Ani/Cin p 144.

Hor Balevana

(A Hole in the Moon)

1965 Israeli, Navon 80 mins.

Prod: M. Navon.

Dir: Uri Zohar.

SP: Amos Kennan.

Cin: David Gurfinkel.

Edit: Gael Tomarkin.

cont.

Hor Balevana cont.

Cast: Christiane Dancourt, Soshana Lavi, Arieh Lavi, Sai K. Ophir, Uri Zohar, Avraham Heffner.

F-seq (immigrants to Israel have hallucinations, see city spring up; take-off sequences on various film genres, including "King Kong;" Biblical figure with bandaged hand walks on water)

Ref: Vw 19 May '65; MTVM April '67 p6; DdC III:109; Positif 71:45.

See also: King Kong (1933).

Hora Incognita, La

(The Unknown Hour; Dios Eligio Sus Viajeros: God Selected His Travelers)

1964 Spanish.

Dir & SP: Mariano Ozores.

Art Dir: José Antonio de la Guerra.

Cin: Godofredo Pacheco.

Edit: Pedro del Rey.

Mus: Adolfo Waitzman.

Cast: Emma Penella, José Luis Ozores Antonio Ozores, Carlos Ballesteros, Mabel Karr, Fernando Rey.

bor-SF (atomic bomb hits city by accident)

Ref: Gasca p338-39.

Horizontal Lines

See: Lines Horizontal (1962).

Horizontale

1924 German? ani scroll painting.

Made by: Viking Eggeling.

exp-F

Ref: Undrgnd p59.

Horla, The

(story by G. de Maupassant)

See: Diary of a Madman (1962).

Horloge Magique, L'

See: Magic Clock, The (1928).

Horn Blows at Midnight, The

1945 WB 80 mins.

Prod: Mark Hellinger.

Dir: Raoul Walsh.

Story idea: Aubrey Wisberg.

SP: Sam Hellman & James V. Kern.

Art Dir: Hugh Reticker.

Cin: Sid Hickox.

SpFX: Lawrence Butler.

Edit: Irene Morra.

Mus: Franz Waxman.

Cast: Jack Benny [angel], Dolores Moran, Allyn Joslyn, Reginald Gardiner, Guy Kibbee, Paul Harvey, Truman Bradley, Mike Mazurki.

F-com-dream (trumpet player dreams he is angel come to Earth to blow the trumpet of doom, destroying the world)

Ref: Vd & HR 3 April '45; LC; MFB Aug '48 p 114; FDY '46; FIR Aug-Sept '58 p379.

Horoscope September

1972 Project 7 color ani 5 mins.

f

Ref: IAFF '72.

Horrible Cauchemar, Un

(A Horrible Nightmare)

1901 French, Pathé sil sh.

Dir: Ferdinand Zecca.

F-H-com-dream

Ref: Filmlex p 1773.

Horrible Dr. Hichcock, The

(L'Orribile Segreto del Dottor Hichcock: The Horrible Secret of Dr. Hichcock; Raptus; The Terror of Dr. Hichcock -- Brit.t.)

1962 (1965) Italian, Panda

cont.

Homunculus (1916) German Serial

Horrible Dr. Hichcock cont.
(Sigma III) color scope 88 mins (76 mins).

Prod: Luigi Carpentieri & Ermano Donati (Louis Mann).

Dir: Riccardo Freda (Robert Hampton).

SP: Julyan Perry.

Art Dir: Franco Fumagalli (Frank Smokecocks).

Cin: Raffaele Masciocchi (Donald Green).

Edit: Ornella Micheli (Donna Christie).

Mus: Roman Vlad.

Cast: Robert Flemyng, Barbara Steele, Harriet White, Teresa Vianello (Teresa Fitzgerald), Montgomery Glenn.

H (necrophile doctor dopes willing wife to near-death to make love to her; intends to use blood of 2nd wife [Steele] to restore youth of 1st; hallucinations)

Ref: LAT 21 May '65; MFB Nov '63 p 160; BO 30 Nov '64. Sequel: Ghost, The (1963).

Horrible Dr. Orloff, L'

See: Awful Dr. Orlof, The (1961).

Horrible Hyde

1915 Lubin sil 1/2 reel.

Dir: Jerold Hevener.

Sc: Epes W. Sargent.

Cast: Jerold T. Hevener, Eva Bell.

bor-H-com (actor playing Mr. Hyde scares everybody)

Ref: MPN 14 Aug '15 p90; FM 34:55.

Suggested by "The Strange Case of Dr. Jekyll and Mr. Hyde" by Robert Louis Stevenson.

See also: Dr. Jekyll and Mr. Hyde.

Horrible Night

See: Grausige Nächt (1920).

Horrible Nightmare, A

See: Horrible Cauchemar, Un (1901).

Horrible Sexy Vampire, The

(El Vampiro de la Autopista: The Vampire of the Turnpike; Der Vampir von Schloss Frankenstein: The Vampire of Castle Frankenstein)

1970 (1973) Spanish, Cine-films (Paragon) color scope 91 mins.

Prod: Edmondo Amanti.

Dir: José Luis Madrid.

Cin: Francisco Madurga.

Mus: Angel Arteaga.

Cast: Waldemar Wohlfahrt, Patricia Loran, Luis Induni, Barta Barry, Adela Tauler, Anastasio Campoy.

F-H-com? (vampire is reincarnation of a famous baron)

Ref: Vw 12 May '71 p 143; Vw 12 May '71 ad; BO 5 Feb '73 pME-6; CineF 4:44.

Horror, The

1933? F.P. Pictures, Stanley.

Dir: Bud Pollard.

F-H (monster)

Ref: Ackerman.

Horror

1965 Hungarian..

Dir & SP: Gyorgy Hintsch.

Cast: Andrea Drahota, Ferenc Kallai, Antal Pager.

H

Ref: Modern Monsters 3:5; CoF 10:48.

Based on a novel by Laszlo Németh.

Horror

See: Blancheville Monster, The (1963).

Horror and Sex

See: Night of the Bloody Apes (1968?).

Horror at 37,000 Feet, The

(Stones --s.t.)

1973 (CBS) color approx 75 mins.

Prod: Anthony Wilson.

Dir: David Lowell Rich.

SP: Ron Austin & Jim Buchanan.

Art Dir: James Husley.

Makeup: George Lane.

Cin: Earl Rath.

Edit: Bud S. Isaacs.

Mus: Morton Stevens.

Cast: William Shatner, Roy Thinnes, Chuck Connors, Lynn Loring, Buddy Ebsen, Tammy Grimes, Jane Merrow, Paul Winfield, Will Hutchins, France Nuyen, Russell Johnson, Darlene Carr, Brenda Benet, H.M. Wynant.

F-H (druid stone being flown on airliner to US causes 747 to stop dead at 37,000 ft, causes intense cold & other strange happenings)

Ref: B. Warren (credits off screen)

Based on a story by V.X. Appleton

Horror Castle

(Le Vergine di Norimburg: The Virgin of Nuremburg; The Castle of Terror --Brit.t.; Terror Castle --ad.t.)

1963 (1965) Italian, Gladiator (Zodiac) color scope 83 mins.

Prod: Marco Vicario.

Dir: Antonio Margheriti (Anthony Dawson).

SP: A. Margheriti, G. Green, & Edmond T. Greville.

Art Dir: Riccardo Dominici.

Cin: Riccardo Pallottini.

Edit: Angel Coly.

Mus: Riz Ortolani.

Cast: Rossana Podesta, George Riviere, Christopher Lee, Jim Nolan, Anny Delli Uberti.

H (hideously disfigured lunatic, victim of Nazis, kills people in old castle)

Ref: MFB '64 p44; FF '65 p 125; Vw 21 April '65; FM 44:58.

Based on novel "The Virgin of Nuremburg" by Frank Bogart.

Horror Chamber of Dr. Faustus, The

(Yeux sans Visage: Eyes Without a Face --Brit.t.)

1959 (1962) French, Champs-Elysées (Lopert) 95 mins.

Prod: Jules Borkon.

Dir: Georges Franju.

SP: G. Franju, Jean Redon, Claude Sautet, Pierre Boileau, & Thomas Narcejac.

Dialog: Pierre Gascar.

Art Dir: Auguste Capelier.

Cin: Eugen Schüfftan.

Edit: Gilbert Natot.

Mus: Maurice Jarre.

Cast: Pierre Brasseur, Alida Valli, Juliette Mayniel, Edith Scob, Beatrice Altariba, François Guérin.

SF-H (man tries to restore daughter's ruined face by grafting other girls' faces onto hers.

cont.

Horror Chamber of Dr. Faustus   cont.

Ref: UniF 25-26:24; Clarens p241, 154-55; Vw 26 Aug '59.

Horror Creatures of the Pre-historic World

See: Horror of the Blood Monsters (1970).

Horror Express

(Panico en el Transiberiano: Panic on the Transiberian)

1972 Spanish/British?, Granada/Benmar (Scotia Int'l) color scope.

Prod: Bernard Gordon.

Dir: Eugenio Martin.

SP: Arnaud d'Usseau.

Cin: Alejandro Ullea.

Cast: Peter Cushing, Christopher Lee, Telly Savalas, Alberto de Mendoza.

SF-H (trans-Siberian railroad carries a prehistoric creature from China to Moscow; creature's mind takes over bodies of various people)

Ref: Vw 20 Sept '72 p6, 25 Oct '72 p22, 26; BO 5 June '72 p89.

Horror from Beyond, The

See: Blood Thirst (1965).

Horror Hospital

1973 British, Noteworthy Films color 91 mins.

Prod: Richard Gordon.

Assoc Prod: Ray Corbett.

Dir: Antony Balch.

SP: A. Balch & Alan Watson.

Art Dir: David Bill.

Cin: David McDonald.

Edit: Robert Dearberg.

Mus: De Wolfe.

Cast: Michael Gough, Robin Askwith, Vanessa Shaw, Ellen Pollock, Skip Martin, Dennis Price, Kurt Christian, Kenneth Benda, Barbara Wendy, Martin Grace, Colin Skeaping, George Herbert.

SF-H (in 'health hotel' water taps run blood; insane crippled doctor monstrously disfigured, wears disguising mask; controls people's brains by surgery; decapitations)

Ref: MFB June '73 p 126.

Horror Hotel

(City of the Dead --Brit.t.)

1960 (1963) British, Vulcan (Trans-Lux) 76 mins.

Prod: Donald Taylor.

Dir: John Llewellyn Moxey.

Story: Milton Subotsky.

SP: George Baxt.

Art Dir: John Blezard.

Cin: Desmond Dickinson.

SpFX: Cliff Richardson.

Edit: John Pomeroy.

Mus: Douglas Gamley & Ken Jones.

Cast: Patricia Jessel, Betta St. John, Christopher Lee, Dennis Lotis, Venetia Stevenson, Valentine Dyall, Norman MacOwan, Ann Beach.

F-H (250-year-old witch brought back to life in Massachusetts; she & her coven destroyed by shadow of the cross)

Ref: FF '63 p319; NYT 20 June '63; FD 24 June '63.

Horror House

(The Dark --s.t.; Haunted House of Horror --s.t.)

1969 (1970) British, Tigon (AIP) color 92 mins (79 mins).

Prod: Tony Tenser.

Dir: Michael Armstrong.

SP: M. Armstrong & Peter Marcus.

Art Dir: Hayden Pearce.

Cin: Jack Atcheler.

cont.

Horror House   cont.

SpFX: Arthur Beavis.

Edit: Peter Pitt.

Mus: Reg Tilsely.

Cast: Frankie Avalon, Jill Haworth, Dennis Price, Mark Wynter, Julian Barnes, Richard O'Sullivan.

H (psychotic kills friends in supposedly haunted house; gore)

Ref: MFB '69 p266; Vw 29 April '70; CineF Fall '70 p33.

Horror Island

1941 U 60 mins.

Assoc Prod: Ben Pivar.

Dir: George Waggner.

Story: Alex Gottlieb.

SP: Maurice Trombragel & Victor McLeod.

Art Dir: Jack Otterson & Ralph M. DeLacy.

Cin: Elwood Bredell.

Edit: Otto Ludwig.

Mus Dir: Hans J. Salter.

Cast: Dick Foran, Peggy Moran, Foy Von Dolsen, Leo Carrillo, Fuzzy Knight, John Eldredge.

bor-H-com (black-cloaked figure called "the phantom" prowls a supposedly haunted castle)

Ref: Vd & HR 26 March '41; MFB Sept '41 p 116; Pardi.

Horror Maniacs

(The Greed of William Hart -- Brit.t.; Crimes of the Body Snatchers --alt.t?

1948 (1953) British, Eros & Bushey Films (Hoffberg) 79 mins.

Prod: Gilbert Church.

Dir: Oswald Mitchell.

SP: John Gilling.

Cin: D.P. Cooper & S.D. Onions.

Edit: John F. House.

Cast: Tod Slaughter, Henry Oscar, Jenny Lynn, Aubrey Woods, Hubert Woodward, Denis Wyndham, Wilfrid Melville, Patrick Addison, Arnold Bell.

H (men rob graves, then murder to supply bodies)

Ref: MFB April '48 p46; FDY.

See also: Body Snatcher, The (1945).

Horror of a Deformed Man

See: Kyofu Nikei Ningen (1969).

Horror of an Ugly Woman

See: Kaidan Kasanegafuchi (1970).

Horror of Dracula

(Dracula --Brit.t.)

1958 British, Hammer (U) color 82 mins.

Exec Prod: Michael Carreras.

Prod: Anthony Hinds.

Dir: Terence Fisher.

SP: Jimmy Sangster.

Art Dir: Bernard Robinson.

Makeup: Phil Leakey.

Cin: Jack Asher.

Edit: Bill Lenny.

Mus: James Bernard.

Cast: Peter Cushing, Christopher Lee [Dracula], Michael Gough, Melissa Stribling, Carol Marsh, Valerie Gaunt, John Van Eyssen, Charles Lloyd Pack, Miles Malleson, George Woodbridge.

F-H (vampires; Dracula destroyed by exposure to sunlight -- he turns to dust)

Ref: FF '58 p90; FDY '59; Photon 19:33; Classics of the Film p232; F&F July '58 p27.

cont.

Horror of Dracula cont.

Based on novel "Dracula" by Bram Stoker.

Sequels: Brides of Dracula (1960); Dracula, Prince of Darkness (1965); Dracula Has Risen from the Grave (1968); Taste the Blood of Dracula (1970); Scars of Dracula (1970).

See also: Dracula (1930); Ahkea Kkots (1961); Dracula A.D. 1972 (1971); the latter film is not a sequel to Horror of Dracula.

Horror of Frankenstein, The

1970 British, Hammer (Levitt-Pickman) color 95 mins.

Prod & Dir: Jimmy Sangster.

SP: J. Sangster & Jeremy Burnham.

Art Dir: Scott MacGregor.

Makeup: Tom Smith.

Cin: Moray Grant.

Edit: Chris Barnes.

Mus: Malcolm Williamson.

Cast: Ralph Bates, Kate O'Mara, Graham James, Veronica Carlson, Dennis Price, Joan Rice, David Prowse [Monster].

SF-H; bor-com (Dr. Frankenstein brings a turtle back to life, then makes a monster out of dead people and brings it to life)

Ref: Vw 21 Oct '70; MFB Nov '70 p226; FF '71 p266-67.

Based on characters created by Mary Shelley.

See also: Frankenstein; Curse of Frankenstein (1957).

Horror of It All, The

1964 British, English Associated Prods (20th-Fox) 75 mins.

Exec Prod: Robert Lippert.

Assoc Prod: Margia Dean.

Dir: Terence Fisher.

SP: Ray Russell.

Prod Design: Clifford Parkes.

Art Dir: Harry White.

Makeup: Bill Lodge.

Cin: Arthur Lavis.

Edit: Robert Winter.

Mus: Douglas Gamley.

Cast: Pat Boone, Erica Rogers, Dennis Price, Andree Melly, Valentine Dyall, Eric Chitty, Jack Bligh.

H-com (houseful of eccentrics, including vampire-like girl, terrorize American; murders)

Ref: FF '65 p26; MFB Aug '66 p 124; Photon 19:41.

Horror of Malformed Men

See: Kyofu Kikei Ningen (1969).

Horror of Party Beach, The

(Invasion of the Zombies -- s.t.)

1963 (1964) Iselin-Tenney Prods & Inzom (20th-Fox) 82 mins (72 mins).

Prod & Dir: Del Tenney.

Assoc Prod: Allan V. Iselin.

SP & Cin: Richard L. Hilliard.

Art Dir: Robert Verberkmoss.

Edit: Gary Youngman.

Mus: Bill Holmes.

Cast: John Scott, Alice Lyon, Allen Laurel, Eulabelle Moore, Marilyn Clark, Agustin Mayer, Damond Klebroyd, The Del-Aires (Ronny Linares, Bob Osborne, Garry Jones, John Becker).

SF-H-mus (man-killing sea-monsters caused by radioactive waste & plankton)

Ref: FF '64 p68; MFB Oct '64 p 150; Acad; Time.

Horror of the Blood Monsters

(Creatures of the Prehistoric Planet; Horror Creatures of the Prehistoric Planet --both s.t.; Vampire Men of the Lost Planet --tv.t.)

1970 (1971) Tal Prod (Independent-Int'l) color 85 mins.

Exec Prod: Charles McCullen & Zoe Phillips.

Prod & Dir: Al Adamson.

SP: Sue McNair.

Makeup: Jean Hewitt.

Cin: William (Vilmos?) Zsigmond & William G. Troiano.

Edit: Ewing Brown & Peter Perry.

Mus: Mike Velarde.

Nar: Theodore (Theodore Gottlieb, real name).

Cast: John Carradine, Robert Dix, Vicki Volanti, Joey Benson, Jennifer Bishop, Bruce Powers.

SF-H (vampire-plague killings on Earth; Carradine finds source of plague on another planet as virus; planet populated by lobster men, bat men, & two warring tribes, one of which is vampiric)

Ref: FF '71 p 160; Photon 21:32; Vw 12 May '71 p203.

Note: most of the footage of the alien planet is in tinted black and white, and is taken from one (or possibly two) Philippine films, which have not as yet been identified.

Horror on Snape Island

(Tower of Evil --s.t., Brit.t.)

1971 (1972) British, Grenadier (Fanfare) color 89 mins (86 mins).

Exec Prod: Joe Solomon.
Prod: Richard Gordon.

Dir & SP: Jim O'Connolly.

Story: George Baxt.

Art Dir: Disley Jones.

Cin: Desmond Dickinson.

Edit: Henry Richardson.

Mus: Ken Jones.

Cast: Bryan Halliday (Haliday?), Jill Haworth, Anna Palk, Jack Watson, Mark Edwards, Derek Fowlds (Fowles?), John Hamill, Dennis Price, George Coulouris.
H (brutal killings on island, supposedly by maniac)

Ref: MFB Dec '72 p260-61; Vw 26 April '72; FF '72 p 116.

Horror Story

1972 Spanish, Cire.

Dir: Manuel Esteba Gallego.

Cast: Manuel Garcia Lozano, Silvia Solar, Marta May.

H

Ref: Vw 9 May '73 p 137.

Horror That Horrifies

See: Bhoot Bungla (1965).

Horror y Sexo

See: Night of the Bloody Apes (1968?).

Horrores del Bosque Negro, Los

See: Loba, La (1965).

HorroRitual

1972 WB color 3 mins.

Cast: Barry Atwater [vampire].

F-H-com (vampire)

Ref: B. Warren (off screen). Promotion film made to be shown with Dracula A.D. 1972 (1971).

Horrors of Drink, The

(The Drunkard's Conversion --e.t.)

1901 British, Paul sil sh.

Prod: R.W. Paul.

cont.

Horror of Dracula (1958) British

Horrors of Drink   cont.

Dir: W.R. Booth?

psy-F (drunk sees gnome, snake, & Spirit of Temperance)

Ref: Sadoul p467; Gifford/BFC 00433.

Horrors of Frankenstein

1957? Adventure Film Prods (amateur) 8mm sil sh.

Dir: Tony Brzezinski.

Cin: John Mate.

Cast: Ken Carroll [Monster].

SF-H

Ref: CoF 37.

Based on the character created by Mary Shelley.

See also: Frankenstein.

Horrors of Spider Island

See: It's Hot in Paradise (1959).

Horrors of the Black Forest, The

See: Loba, La (1965).

Horrors of the Black Museum

1959 British/US, Herman Cohen (AIP) color scope 95 mins (81 mins).

Filmed in England.

Prod: Herman Cohen.

Dir: Arthur Crabtree.

SP: Aben Kandel & Herman Cohen.

Art Dir: Wilfred Arnold.

Makeup: Jack Craig.

Cin: Desmond Dickinson.

Edit: Georffrey Muller.

Mus: Gerard Schurmann.

Mus Dir: Muir Mathieson.

Cast: Michael Gough, June Cunningham, Graham Curnow, Shirley Ann Field, Geoffrey Keen, Gerald Andersen, Austin Trevor.

H; SF-seq (insane journalist commits horror murders to provide self with copy; uses Dr. Jekyll's Hyde-producing serum to make assistant into fiendish killer)

cont.

Horrors of the Black Museum   cont.

Ref: FF '59 p86; FDY '60; MFB May '59 p59.

See also: Dr. Jekyll and Mr. Hyde.

Horse over Tea Kettle

1962 Amateur (Film-makers' Coop, MMA, Cinema 16, etc.) ani 6 mins.

Made by: Robert Breer.

exp-F

Ref: Undrgnd p 131; FMC 5:44; C-16 p16.

See also: One Man Show (1967?).

Horseman, the Woman, and the Moth, The

1968 Amateur (Film-makers' Coop) 16mm color sil 19 mins.

Made by: Stan Brakhage.

exp-F (film allowed to grow crystals & mold, various objects pasted to it, then printed)

Ref: FMC 5:41.

Horse's Mouth, The

(The Oracle --Brit.t.)

1953 (1954) British, Group 3 (Mayer-Kingsley) 83 mins (77 mins).

Exec Prod: John Grierson.

Prod: Colin Leslie.

Dir: Pennington Richards.

SP: Patrick Campbell.

Art Dir: Michael Stringer.

Cin: Wolfgang Suschitzky.

Edit: John Trumper.

Mus: Temple Abady.

Cast: Robert Beatty, Mervyn Johns, Arthur MacRae, Gillian Lind, Virginia McKenna, Ursula Howells, Louis Hampton, John Charlesworth, Michael Medwin, Joseph Tomelty, Gilbert Harding [voice of the Oracle].

F-com (a spirit, The Oracle, lives at the bottom of a well and foretells the future accurately)

Ref: MFB April '53 p49; Acad; Gifford/BFC 11780.

Based on radio play "To Tell the Truth" by Robert Barr.

Horseshoe, The

1946 Czech ani sh.

Dir: Karel Zeman.

F

Ref: Ani/Cin p 176.

Horsing Around

1957 Col 2 reels.

Prod & Dir: Jules White.

SP: Felix Adler.

Art Dir: Cary Odell.

Cin: Ray Cory.

Edit: William Lyon.

Cast: The Three Stooges (Moe Howard, Larry Fine, Joe Besser), Emil Sitka, Harriette Tarler.

F-com (the Stooges' sister, who has been reincarnated as a horse, tries to rescue her horse-husband)

Ref: Maltin/GMS p 140; LC; Pardi.

Sequel to: Hoofs and Goofs (1957).

See also: Three Stooges, The (1934-59).

Horton Hatches the Egg

1942 (1949--rr) Vitaphone (WB) color ani 7 mins.

Prod: Leon Schlesinger.

Dir: Bob Clampett.

F-com (Horton the elephant sits on an egg for a negligant mother bird; when egg hatches elephant-like chick emerges)

Ref: HR 5 March '42; LC; Ani Chart L41.

Based on the book by Dr. Seuss.

See also: Horton Hears a Who (1970?).

Horton Hears a Who

1970? MGM color ani approx 20 mins. Produced for television.

Dir: Chuck Jones.

Songs: Dr. Seuss & Gene Poddany.

Nar: Hans Conried.

F-com (Horton the elephant protects a group of very tiny people)

Ref: TVG 29 Sept '71.

Based on the book by Dr. Seuss.

See also: Horton Hatches the Egg (1942).

Hospital Hospitality

1939 British, Christy-Bass 25 mins.

Prod: William Christy & George Bass Jr.

Dir: W. Christy.

Cast: George Bass Jr, Wally Patch, Finlay Currie, Charles Penrose, Eve Shelley, June Martin.

SF-com (elixir of life)

Ref: Gifford/BFC 10680.

Host to a Ghost

1941 Col 2 reels.

Dir: Del Lord.

SP: Harry Edwards & Elwood Ullman.

Cast: Andy Clyde.

H-com (haunted house)

Ref: LC; Maltin/GMS p 100.

Host to a Ghost

1947 RKO 17 mins.

Prod: George Bilson.

Dir: Hal Yates.

SP: Charles E. Roberts.

Edit: Edward W. Williams.

Cast: Edgar Kennedy, Florence Lake, Jack Rice, Dot Farley.

F-H-com

Ref: MPH 2 Aug '47 p3759; LC; Maltin/GMS p 113.

Hot Dog

1930 ani 8 mins.

Prod: Max Fleischer.

F-com

Ref: CFS cat '69.

Hot Dog Cartoons

(Pete the Pup --alt.t.)

1926-27 Bray sil ani sh series.

Dir: Walter Lantz & Clyde Geronimi.

F-com

Ref: LC.

Hot Heels

(Patents Pending --e.t.; Painting the Town --e.t.)

1928 U sil 5864 ft.

Dir: William James Craft.

Story: Jack Foley & Vin Moore (credit on screen; AFI says company records disagree)

Sc: Harry O. Hoyt.

Titles: Albert De Mond.

Cin: Arthur Todd.

Edit: Charles Craft.

Cast: Glenn Tryon, Patsy Ruth Miller, Greta Yoltz, James Bradbury Sr., Tod Sloan.

SF-com (mechanical horse wins a race)

Ref: AFI F2.2593 p364.

Hot Scots, The

1948 Col 2 reels.

Prod: Hugh McCollum.

Dir: Edward Bernds.

SP: Elwood Ullman.

Art Dir: Harold MacArthur.

Cin: Allen Siegler.

Edit: Henry De Mond.

Cast: The Three Stooges (Moe Howard, Shemp Howard, Larry Fine), Herbert Evans, Christine McIntyre, Charles Knight, Ted Lorch.

F-H-com (haunted castle with ghosts)

Ref: LC; Maltin/GMS p 136; Pardi.

Remake: Scotched in Scotland (1954).

See also: Three Stooges, The (1934-59).

Hot Stuff

1971 Canadian, NFB color ani 9 mins.

Prod: Robert Verrall & Wolf Koenig.

Dir & Ani: Zlatko Grgic.

Story: Don Arioli.

Mus: Bill Brooks.

Voices: D. Arioli, Gerald Budner, John Howe.

F-com (story of fire and man; safety film with gags)

Ref: ASIFA 7; MFB July '72 p 150.

Hotel de la Muerte

See: Santo en el Hotel de la Muerte (1962).

Hotel Electrico, El

See: Electric Hotel, The (1906).

Hotel for Men

1969 Amateur (Film-makers' Coop) 16mm color live & ani 20 mins.

Made by: John Heinz.

Cast: Tom Palazzolo.

exp-F ("a decaying . . . institution -- inhabited by George Washington, Whistler's Mother, J.P. Morgan, and all the workers of the world" -- FMC)

Ref: FMC 5:146.

Hotel Honeymoon

1912 Solax sil ani seq sh.

Dir: Alice Guy-Blanche (?).

Art Dir: Henri Ménessier.

com; F-seq (moon smiles at lovers)

Ref: S&S Summer '71.

Hothouse

1951-53 Amateur 16mm color computer ani 3 mins.

Made by: John Whitney.

exp-F

Ref: Film Com 53-55 Spring '72 p 82.

Houdini

See: Master Mystery, The (1918).

Hound of Blackwood Castle, The

See: Hund von Blackwood Castle, Der (1968).

Hound of Florence, The

(novel by F. Salten)

See: Shaggy Dog, The (1959).

Hound of the Baskervilles, The

● (Der Hund von Baskerville)

1914 German, sil sh?

Dir: Rudolf Meinert.

Sets: Hermann Warm.

Ref: Eisner p 19; Encic DS.

● (Le Chien des Baskerville)

1914 (1915) French, Pathé (Vitascope) sil 4 reels.

Ref: LC; MPN 6 March '15 p46; DdC II:106; Motog 6 March '15.

● (Der Hund von Baskervilles)

1917 German, Vitascop sil.

Dir: Richard Oswald.

Ref: FIR Aug/Sept '61 p411; UF p394; Germany.

● 1921 British, Stoll (FBO) sil 5091 ft.

Prod: Maurice Elvey.

Sc: William J. Elliott.

Art Dir: Walter W. Murton.

Cin: Germaine Burger.

Cast: Eille Norwood, Hubert Willis, Allan Jeayes, Rex McDougall, Lewis Gilbert, Betty Campbell.

Hound of the Baskervilles cont.

Ref: BFI cat p 111; Photo Nov '22 p 105; MPN 26:1499.

● (Der Hund von Baskervilles)

1929 German, Sudfilm.

Dir: Richard Oswald.

Sc: Herbert Juttke & Georg C. Klaren.

Cast: Carlyle Blackwell, Fritz Rasp, Betty Bird, Alexander Mursky, Livio Pavanelli.

Ref: Vw 2 Oct '29; FIR Aug-Sept '61 p413; UF p433.

● 1931 (1932) British, Gaum (First Division) 72 mins.

Dir: V. Gareth Gundrey.

SP: V.G. Gundrey & Edgar Wallace.

Cin: Bernard Knowles.

Edit: Ian Dalrymple.

Cast: John Stuart, Reginald Bach, Robert Rendel, Fred Lloyd, Heather Angel, Henry Hallett, Wilfred Shine, Sybil Jane.

Ref: FIR Aug-Sept '61 p414; FD 10 April '32; Gifford/BFC 09007.

● (Der Hund von Baskerville)

1936 German, Bavaria Films.

Dir: Carl Lamac.

SP: Gloria von Stackelberg.

Cin: Willi Winterstein.

Mus: Paul Hahn.

Cast: Fritz Rasp, Anneliese Brand, Peter Voss, Fritz Odemar, Friedrich Kayssler.

Ref: HR 10 Oct '36; FIR Aug-Sept '61 p451.

● 1939 20th-Fox 80 mins.

Exec Prod: Darryl F. Zanuck.

Assoc Prod: Gene Markey.

Dir: Sidney Lanfield.

SP: Ernest Pascal.

Art Dir: Richard Day & Hans Peters.

Cin: Peverell Marley.

Edit: Robert Simpson.

Mus Dir: Cyril J. Mockridge.

Cast: Richard Greene, Basil Rathbone, Wendy Barrie, Nigel Bruce, Lionel Atwill, John Carradine, Beryl Mercer, E.E. Clive, Nigel de Brulier.

Ref: HR 23 March '39; MPH 1 April '39 p28, 30; FDY '40.

● 1959 British, Hammer (UA) color 84 mins.

Exec Prod: Michael Carreras.

Prod: Anthony Hinds.

Dir: Terence Fisher.

SP: Peter Bryan.

Art Dir: Bernard Robinson.

Cin: Jack Asher.

Edit: James Needs.

Mus: James Bernard.

Cast: Peter Cushing, Andre Morell, Christopher Lee, Marla Landi, Miles Malleson, David Oxley, Francis de Wolff, John Le Mesurier, Sam Kydd.

Ref: FF '59 p 147; FIR Aug-Sept '61 p418; FDY '60.

● 1971 (1972) U (ABC-TV) color approx 75 mins.

Prod: Stanley Kallis.

Dir: Barry Crane.

SP: Robert E. Thompson.

Art Dir: Howard E. Johnson.

Cin: Harry Wolf.

Edit: Bill Mosher.

Mus Dir: Hal Mooney.

Cast: Stewart Granger, Bernard Fox, William Shatner, Sally Ann Howes, John Williams, Anthony Zerbe, Jane Merrow, Ian Ireland.

cont.

cont

Hound of the Baskervilles cont.

Ref: Vw 16 Feb '72 p43; Borst.

H (Holmes proves supposed phantom killer hound to be elaborate murder weapon)

Based on the novel by Arthur Conan Doyle.

See also: Sherlock Holmes.

Hounds of Zaroff, The

See: Most Dangerous Game, The (1932).

Hour Before Dawn, An

1913 Famous Players sil 3 reels.

Dir & Sc: J. Searle Dawley.

Cast: Laura Sawyer, House Peters.

SF (scientist killed by explosive ray)

Ref: MPW 18:360; F/A p395.

Hour Before the Rendezvous, An

1966? Soviet, Soyuzmultfilm (Sovexportfilm) color ani 17 mins.

Dir: Valentina & Zinaida Brumberg.

Story: B. Laskin & M. Slobodskoi.

Ani: L. Azakh & B. Lalayants.

F-com (comic opera)

Ref: Sovexportfilm cat 3:109.

Hour-Glass Sanatorium, The

See: Sanatorium Pod Klepsydra (1973).

Hour of the Blue Elephants, The

See: Hodina Modrych Slonu (1970?).

Hour of the Wolf

(Vargtimmen)

1967 (1968) Swedish, Svensk Filmindustri (Lopert) 88 mins.

Dir & SP: Ingmar Bergman.

Art Dir: Marik Vos-Lundh.

Cin: Sven Nykvist.

SpFX: Evald Andersson.

Edit: Ulla Ryghe.

Mus: Lars Johan Werle.

Cast: Liv Ullmann, Max von Sydow, Erland Josephson, Gertrud Fridh, Gudrun Brost, Bertil Anderberg, Ingrid Thulin.

psy-F-H (as man goes slowly insane, he imagines demons pursue him, that a dead woman comes back to life, etc.)

Ref: Vw 28 Feb '68; FF '68 p 122; MFB '68 p 115-16; LAT 11 July '68; SR 13 April '68.

Hour When Dracula Comes, The

See: Black Sunday (1960).

House, The

1962 Amateur 16mm sh.

Made by: George Manupelli.

exp-F (doors open & close by themselves)

Ref: FIR Feb '64 p84.

House, The

See: Dom (1958).

House at the End of the World, The

See: Tomb of Ligeia (1964); Die, Monster, Die! (1965).

House Behind the Hedge, The

(by M.S. Vigus)

See: Unknown Treasures (1926).

House Demolished and Rebuilt, A

1901 French, Gaum sil 75 ft.

Dir: Alice Guy.

F (tricks resulting from film being run backwards)

Ref: FIR March '64 p 142.

House Hunting Mice

1947 WB color ani 7 mins.

Dir: Chuck (Charles M.) Jones.

Story: Michael Maltese & Tedd Pierce.

F-com (mice drive cat out of house by sadistic tricks)

Ref: LC.

House in Marsh Road, The

See: Invisible Creature, The (1960).

House in Nightmare Park, The

(Nightmare Park --s.t.)

1973 British, Associated London & Extonation color 95 mins.

Exec Prod: Beryl Vertue.

Prod & SP: Clive Exton & Terry Nation.

Dir: Peter Sykes.

Art Dir: Maurice Carter.

Makeup: Jill Carpenter.

Cin: Ian Wilson.

Edit: Bill Blunden.

Mus: Harry Robinson.

Cast: Frankie Howerd, Ray Milland, Kenneth Griffith, Hugh Burden, John Bennett, Elizabeth MacLennan, Rosalie Crutchley.

H-com (Victorian mansion with pythons & cobras in cellar; family of homicidal maniacs)

Ref: QPH 7 April '73; HR 8 Dec '72 p 13; LSH 2:49-50.

House in the Square, The

See: I'll Never Forget You (1951).

House in the Woods, The

1957? British, Edict (Archway) 62 mins.

Dir & SP: Maxwell Munden.

Mus: Larry Adler.

Cast: Patricia Roc, Ronald Howard, Michael Gough.

F-H (ghost of murdered woman returns)

Ref: FEFN 14 Feb '58; FFF p32; CoF 10:42.

Based on short story "Prelude to Murder" by Walter C. Brown.

House of a Thousand Trembles, The

1922 Star Comedy (U) sil 1 reel.

H-com

Ref: LC.

House of Cards

1947 Amateur 16mm 18 mins.

Made by: Joseph Vogel, & John & James Whitney.

exp-F

Ref: Undrgnd p88, 274; SF Art Mus Prog.

House of Cards, The

1963 Italian color ani sh.

Dir: Giulio Gianini & Emmanuele Luzzati.

F (deck of playing cards comes to life)

Ref: Ani/Cin p 139, 170.

House of Dark Shadows

1970 MGM color 96 mins.

Prod & Dir: Dan Curtis.

SP: Sam Hall & Gordon Russell.

Assoc Prod & Prod Design: Trevor Williams.

Makeup: Robert Layden & Dick Smith.

Cin: Arthur Ornitz.

Edit: Arline Garson.

Mus: Robert Cobert.

Cast: Jonathan Frid [vampire], Joan Bennett, Grayson Hall, Kathryn Leigh Scott, Roger Davis, Thayer David, Nancy Barrett, John Karlen.

cont.

House of Dark Shadows cont.

F-H (vampire Barnabas Collins is released from coffin, makes most of cast into vampires; Barnabas almost cured but reverts to true, ancient age; destroyed by crossbow bolt)

Ref: HR 25 Aug '70; Vw 2 Sept '70; NYT 29 Oct '70; CineF Winter '71 p30; Photon 21:33-34.

Based on ABC-TV series "Dark Shadows."

See also: Night of Dark Shadows (1971).

House of Darkness

1948 (1952) British, Int'l Motion Pictures 77 mins.

Prod: Harry Reynolds.

Dir: Oswald Mitchell.

SP: John Gilling.

Cin: Cyril Bristow.

Mus: George Melachrino.

Cast: Laurence Harvey, Lesley Osmond, Leslie Brooks, John Stuart, George Melachrino.

F-H (murdered man's ghost seeks vengeance on his stepbrother)

Ref: MFB June '48 p73; Acad; Gifford/BFC 11243.

Based on play "Duet" by Betty Davies.

House of Death, The

(story by J.P. Philips)

See: House of Mystery (1931).

House of Dr. Edwardes, The

(novel by F. Beeding)

See: Spellbound (1945).

House of Doom

See: Black Cat, The (1934).

House of Dracula

1945 (U) 8 reels (67 mins).

Exec Prod: Joe Gershenson.

Prod: Paul Malvern.

Dir: Erle C. Kenton.

Story: George Bricker & Dwight V. Babcock.

SP: Edward T. Lowe.

Art Dir: John B. Goodman & Martin Obzina.

Makeup: Jack Pierce.

Cin: George Robinson.

SpFX Cin: John P. Fulton.

Edit: Russell Schoengarth.

Mus Dir: Hans J. Salter.

Cast: Lon Chaney Jr. [Wolfman]; Onslow Stevens; John Carradine [Dracula], Lionel Atwill, Glenn Strange [Frankenstein Monster], Jane Adams, Ludwig Stossel, Martha O'Driscoll, Skelton Knaggs.

F-H (Dracula makes doctor, who is trying to cure him into nocturnal killer by mingling their blood; Wolf Man cured of being werewolf; Frankenstein Monster revived briefly)

Ref: Vd 29 Nov '45; FDY '46.

Sequel to: Dracula (1930); Frankenstein (1931); Wolf Man, The (1941).

House of Evil, The

1968 (1972) Mexican/US, Azteca/Col color.

Prod: Luis Enrique Vergara.

Following two credits for US-filmed scenes only.

Dir & SP: Jack Hill.

Cin: Austin McKinney.

Cast: Boris Karloff.

H (torture dungeon; Karloff dies in flames)

Ref: Vd 23 April '68; FM 51:50; Gifford/Karloff p348.

House of Fear, The

1914 Lubin sil 2100 ft.

F (ghosts)

Ref: Bios 23 April '14.

House of Fear

1939 U 66 mins.

Assoc Prod: Edmund Grainger.

Dir: Joe May.

SP: Peter Milne.

Cin: Milton Krasner.

Edit: Frank Gross.

Cast: Irene Hervey, William Gargan, Walter Woolf King, El Brendel, Dorothy Arnold, Robert Coote, Harvey Stephens, Jan Duggan.

H-com (spooky atmosphere; murders)

Ref: MPH 10 June '39 p29, 32; Vw June '39.

Based on play "The Last Warning" by Thomas F. Fallon from the novel by Wadsworth Camp.

See also: Last Warning, The (1928).

House of Frankenstein

(The Devil's Brood --s.t.; Doom of Dracula --8mm t.)

1944 (1945) U 71 mins.

Prod: Paul Malvern.

Dir: Erle C. Kenton.

Story: Curt Siodmak.

SP: Edward T. Lowe.

Art Dir: John B. Goodman & Martin Obzina.

Makeup: Jack Pierce.

Cin: George Robinson.

SpFX Cin: John Fulton.

Edit: Phillip Cahn.

Mus: H.J. Salter.

Cast: Lon Chaney Jr. [Wolfman], Boris Karloff, John Carradine [Dracula], J. Carrol Naish, George Zucco, Glenn Strange [Frankenstein Monster], Peter Coe, Anne Gwynn, Lionel Atwill, Frank Reicher, Elena Verdugo, Sig Rumann, Philip van Zandt, Julius Tannen, Olaf Hytten, Brandon Hurst, Dick Dickinson, Charles Miller, George Lynn, Michael Mark, Belle Mitchell, Eddie Cobb.

F-H (mad scientist accidentally revives Dracula, who is shortly killed by sunlight; Wolfman is killed by girl who loves him; Frankenstein Monster & mad scientist die in bog; hunchback)

Ref: Vd 15 Dec '44; MFB Aug '46 p 111; Photon 19.

Sequel to: Dracula (1930); Frankenstein (1931); Wolf Man, The (1941).

House of Freaks, The

(Monsters of Frankenstein --alt.t.; Terror Castle --ad.t.)

1973 Italian?

Exec Prod: G. Robert Straub.

Prod: Richard Randall.

Dir: Robert Oliver.

Cast: Rossano Brazzi, Michael Dunn, Edmund Purdom, Christiane Royce, Alan Collins, Xira Papas.

SF-H (ad shows several monsters including "Goliath the Giant" and "Ook the Neanderthal Man")

Ref: Vw 24 Jan '73 p21 ad.

Based on characters created by Mary Shelley.

See also: Frankenstein.

House of Fright

(The Two Faces of Dr. Jekyll -- Brit.t. & tv.t.; Jekyll's Inferno --a.d.t.)

1960 (1961) British, Hammer (AIP) color scope 89 mins.

Prod: Michael Carreras.

Dir: Terence Fisher.

SP: Wolf Mankowitz.

Art Dir: Bernard Robinson & Don Mingaye.

Makeup: Roy Ashton.

Cin: Jack Asher.

cont.

House of Fright   cont.

Edit: James Needs & Eric Boyd-Perkins.

Mus: Monty Norman & David Heneker.

Mus Dir: John Hollingsworth.

Cast: Paul Massie [Jekyll/Hyde], Dawn Addams, Christopher Lee, David Kossoff, Francis De Wolff, Norma Marla, Magda Miller, Percy Cartwright, Oliver Reed.

SF-H (in attempt to separate good from evil in man, elderly Dr. Jekyll becomes younger & more handsome Mr. Hyde)

Ref: FF '61 p 185-86; MMF 1:41.

Based on short novel "The Strange Case of Dr. Jekyll and Mr. Hyde" by Robert Louis Stevenson.

See also: Dr. Jekyll and Mr. Hyde.

House of Fright

See: Black Sunday (1960).

House of Hate

1918 Astra (Pathé) sil serial 20 parts 41 reels.

Prod: Louis J. Gasnier.

Dir: George Brackett Seitz.

Story: Arthur B. Reeve & Charles A. Logue.

Sc: Bertram Millhauser.

Cast: Pearl White, Antonio Moreno, Paul Clerget, J.H. Gilmour, John Webb Dillon, Peggy Shanor.

bor-SF-H (liquid fire; deadly germ used to kill)

Ref: MPW 35:1046f, 1268, 36:434; LC.

House of Horror, The

1929 FN 66 mins.

Dir: Benjamin Christensen.

Sc: Richard Bee.

Dialog: William Irish.

Cin: Ernest Haller & Sol Polito.

Edit: Frank Ware.

Cast: Chester Conklin, Louise Fazenda, Thelma Todd, William V. Mong, Dale Fuller, William Orlamond.

com-myst; bor-H (supposedly haunted house; "weird happenings" --AFI)

Ref: AFI F2.2604 p366; MPN 41:11:85; Clarens p58, 202.

House of Horrors

(Joan Medford Is Missing --Brit.t.)

1946 U 66 mins.

Prod: Ben Pivar.

Dir: Jean Yarbrough.

Story: Dwight V. Babcock.

SP: George Bricker.

Art Dir: John B. Goodman & Abraham Grossman.

Makeup: Jack Pierce.

Cin: Maury Gertsman.

Edit: Philip Cahn.

Mus Dir: Hans J. Salter.

Cast: Martin Kosleck, Rondo Hatton, Kent Taylor, Virginia Grey, Alan Napier, Robert Lowery, Bill Goodwin.

H (mad sculptor rescues deformed, powerful killer from drowning, uses him to get revenge on enemies)

Ref: Vd 4 March '46; LC; AHF p224.

See also: Pearl of Death (1944); Brute Man, The (1946).

House of Incest, The

(poem by A. Nin)

See: Bells of Atlantis (1952).

House of Magic

1937 U ani 1 reel.

Prod: Walter Lantz.

Story: W. Lantz & Victor McLeod.

Ani: Manuel Moreno, George Dane, & Louis Zukor.

F-com

Ref: LC.

See also: Meany, Miny, Moe (1936-37).

House of Mystery, The

1911 Pathé sil 480 ft.

SF-com (mechanical policemen chase burglar)

Ref: Bios 4 April '12.

House of Mystery

1931 U 16 mins.

Dir: Kurt Neumann.

SP: Samuel Freedman.

myst; F-seq

Ref: LC; MPH 2 Jan '32; Great Radio Heroes p56.

Based on story "The House of Death" by Judson P. Philips & radio show "Street & Smith's Detective Story Magazine Hour".

See also: Shadow Detective Series.

House of Mystery

1934 Mono 62 mins.

Prod: Paul Malvern.

Dir: William Nigh.

SP: Albert De Mond.

Edit: Carl Pierson.

Cast: Ed Lowry, Verna Hillie, Mary Foy.

H ("unseen monster seeks vengeance when sacred Indian temple is despoiled" --BIB's)

Ref: CoF 10:44; LC; BIB's Winter-Spring '71.

Based on the play by Adam Hull Shirk.

House of Mystery

(At the Villa Rose --Brit.t.)

1939 (1941) British (Mono) 6 reels (74 mins).

Dir: Walter Summers.

SP: Doreen Montgomery.

Cin: Claude Freise-Greene.

Edit: Lionel Tomlinson.

Cast: Kenneth Kent, Judy Kelly, Walter Rilla, Clifford Evans, Martita Hunt.

myst-F-H (ghosts)

Ref: Brit Cin p68, 113; FD 4 June '41; LC; Collier.

Based on novel & play "At the Villa Rose" by A.E.W. Mason.

See also: At the Villa Rose (1920).

House of Mystery

(The Unseen --e.t.)

1961 British, Independent Artists & Anglo 56 mins.

Prod: Julian Wintle & Leslie Parkyn.

Dir & SP: Vernon Sewell.

Art Dir: Jack Shampan.

Cin: Ernest Steward.

Edit: John Trumper.

Mus: Stanley Black.

Cast: Jane Hylton, Peter Dyneley, Nanette Newman, Maurice Kaufmann, Colin Gordon, John Merivale.

F-H (man electrocuted haunts house via lights going on & off, appearing on TV screen, etc; woman telling whole story turns out to be ghost at end)

Ref: MFB June '61 p82; FM 22:19; FEFN May '61.

House of Mystery

See: Night Monster (1942).

House of Secrets, The

● 1929 Chesterfield 6400 ft.

Dir: Edmund Lawrence.

SP: Adeline Leitzbach.

Cin: George Webber, Irving Browning, George Peters, & Lester Lang.

Edit: Selma Rosenbloom.

Cast: Joseph Striker, Marcia Manning, Elmer Grandin, Herbert Warren, Francis M. Verdi, Richard Stevenson, Harry Southard, Edward Roseman.

Ref: AFI F2.2606 p366.

● 1936 Chesterfield (Batcheller) 70 mins.

Dir: Roland Reed.

SP: John Krafft.

Cin: M.A. Anderson.

Edit: Dan Milner.

Cast: Sidney Blackmer, Holmes Herbert, Leslie Fenton, Syd Saylor, Muriel Evans, Noel Madison, Ian MacLaren.

Ref: MPH 7 Nov '36; Vw 24 Feb '37; LC.

myst-H (mad scientist; dungeons; poison gas; mysterious old mansion)

Based on the novel by Sydney Horler.

House of Seven Gables

See: House of the Seven Gables.

House of Silence, The

1918 Lasky (Par) sil.

Dir: Donald Crisp.

Sc: Margaret Turnbull.

Cast: Wallace Reid, Anna Little, Winter Hall.

myst; bor-H (supposedly haunted house)

Ref: MPH 7 Oct '39 p 17; FIR '66 p 227.

Based on the novel by Elwyn Barron.

House of Storks, The

See: Maison des Cigognes, La (n.d.).

House of Svend Dyring, The

1908 Danish sil sh?

F (ghost of mother aids her daughters against evil stepmother)

Ref: Neergaard p20-21.

House of Terror, The

See: Face of the Screaming Werewolf (1959).

House of Terrors

See: Kaidan Semushi Otoko (1965).

House of the Black Death

(The Widderburn Horror -- e.t.; Night of the Beast --s.t.)

1965 Taurus 80 mins.

Exec Prod: Eldon C. Tollett.

Prod: William White & Richard Shotwell.

Dir: Harold Daniels.

SP: Richard Mahoney.

Makeup: Nicholas Christie.

Cin: Murray DeAtley.

2nd Unit Dir: Reginald Le Borg.

Note: no screen credit for Art Director, Editor, or Music.

Cast: Lon Chaney Jr., John Carradine, Andrea King, Tom Drake, Dolores Faith, Sabrina, Jerome Thor, Sherwood Keith.

F-H (Chaney & Carradine are rival warlocks; werewolf; Chaney has horns like Satan)

Ref: Vw 13 Oct '65; BIB's; Borst; B. Warren; Ackerman.

Based (uncredited) on novel "The Widderburn Horror" by Lora Crozetti.

See also: Wolf Man, The (1941).

House of the Damned

1963 Associated Producers Inc (20th-Fox) scope 63 mins.

Prod & Dir: Maury Dexter.

SP: Harry Spalding.

Set Dec: Harry Reif.

Cin: John Nickolaus Jr.

Edit: Jodie Copelan.

Mus: Henry Vars.

Cast: Ronald Foster, Merry Anders, Richard Crane, Erika Peters, Georgia Schmidt, Dal McKennon, Stacey Winters, Richard Kiel.

H (supposedly haunted house is secretly inhabited by circus freaks)

Ref: FF '63 p338; MFB Nov '63 p 158.

House of the Frights

See: Casa de los Espantos (1963).

House of the Lost Court, The

1915 Edison (Par) sil.

Dir: Charles J. Brabin.

Cast: Gertrude McCoy, Viola Dane, Duncan McRae.

bor-F-H (oriental poison makes man appear)

Ref: MPN 29 May '15; LC.

Based on the novel by (Mrs) C.M. Williamson.

House of the Seven Corpses

1972 Television Corp. of America.

Prod, Dir, SP: Paul Harrison.

Art Dir: Ron Garcia.

Cin: Don Jones.

Edit: Peter Parasheles.

Cast: John Ireland, Faith Domergue, John Carradine, Charles McCauley (Macauley?), Jerry Stricklen (Strickler?).

H (possibly also F)

Ref: Vw 11 Oct '72; HR 8 Dec '72 p 12.

House of the Seven Gables, The

● 1910 Edison sil.

Ref: EK 15 Oct '10 p3-4; MPW 7:862-63, 1004.

● 1940 U 89 mins.

Assoc Prod: Burt Kelly.

Dir: Joe May.

Adapt: Harold Greene.

SP: Lester Cole.

Art Dir: Jack Otterson & Richard Riedel.

Cin: Milton Krasner.

Edit: Frank Gross.

Cast: George Sanders, Margaret Lindsay, Vincent Price, Dick Foran, Nan Grey, Alan Napier, Cecil Kellaway, Gilbert Emery, Charles Trowbridge, Miles Mander.

Ref: HR 1 March '40; FDY '41; FIR April '51 p22; Bloch.

F-H (curse on old house is fulfilled; novel has ghost sequence)

Based on the novel by Nathaniel Hawthorne.

See also: Twice Told Tales (1963).

House of the Tolling Bell

1920 Pathé sil.

Prod & Dir: J. Stuart Blackton.

Sc: Edith Sessions Tupper.

Cast: Bruce Gordon, May McAvoy, William Jenkins.

F-H (ghosts)

Ref: LC; MPH (Willis).

House of Tomorrow, The

1949 MGM color ani 7 mins.

Prod: Fred Quimby.

cont

House of Tomorrow   cont.

Dir: Tex Avery.

Story: Jack Cosgriff & Rich Hogan.

Ani: Walter Clinton, Michael Lah, & Grant Simmons.

Mus: Scott Bradley,

SF-com

Ref: LC; Gasca p 132.

House of Usher

● (The Fall of the House of Usher --title used on some prints & TV.t.)

1960 Alta Vista (AIP) color scope 80 mins.

Prod & Dir: Roger Corman.

SP: Richard Matheson.

Art Dir: Daniel Haller.

Cin: Floyd Crosby.

SpFX: Pat Dinga.

Edit: Anthony Carras.

Mus: Les Baxter.

Cast: Vincent Price, Mark Damon, Myrna Fahey, Harry Ellerbe.

psy-F-H (fearing family tendency to madness; man buries sister while she is in cataleptic trance but she returns and kills him; dream sequence)

Ref: FF '60; FM 9:28-33; Corman p95.

● 1969 Amateur color 8mm? 30 mins.

Made by: Richard Hunter.

F-H (woman buried alive)

Ref: Luna, 7th Annual Kodak Movie Awards.

Based on short story "The Fall of the House of Usher" by Edgar Allan Poe.

See also: Fall of the House of Usher, The.

House of Wax

1953 (1971 --rr) ⅓ color 3D 88 mins.

Prod: Bryan Foy.

Dir: Andre de Toth.

SP: Crane Wilbur.

Art Dir: Stanley Fleischer.

Makeup: Gordon Bau.

Cin: Bert Glennon & J. Peverell Marley.

Edit: Rudi Fehr.

Mus: David Buttolph.

Cast: Vincent Price, Frank Lovejoy, Phyllis Kirk, Carolyn Jones, Paul Picerni, Roy Roberts, Paul Cavanagh, Dabbs Greer, Charles Buchinsky (later Charles Bronson), Ned Young.

H (set in Baltimore at turn of century; man hideously disfigured in fire in wax museum goes insane, makes wax statues out of dead bodies)

Ref: Photon 12:34; Vd 10 April '53; FDY '54.

Based on play "Waxworks" by C.S. Belden.

Remake of: Mystery of the Wax Museum (1932).

See also: Chamber of Horrors (1966).

House of Wild Gramineons, The

See: Ugetsu (1953).

House on Bare Mountain, The

(Night on Bare Mountain --alt.t?)

1962 Olympic Int'l color scope 62 mins.

Prod: David Andrew & Wes Don.

Dir: R.L. Frost.

SP: Denver Scott.

Cin: Greg Sandor.

Edit: Gary Lindsay.

Mus: Pierr Martel.

cont.

House on Bare Mountain   cont.

Cast: Bob Cresse, Laura Eden, Angela Webster, Ann Meyers, Hugh Cannon, Warren Ames [Frankenstein Monster], Jeffrey Smithers [Dracula].

F-H-com: sex (monsters invade party; Dracula & Frankenstein Monster are fakes, but werewolf is real)

Ref: Photon 19:39; LAT July '63 ad; MMF 10-11:86-88; D. Glut.

See also: Dracula; Frankenstein; Wolf Man, The (1941).

House on Haunted Hill

1958 (1959) AA 75 mins.

Prod & Dir: William Castle.

SP: Robb White.

Art Dir: David Milton.

Makeup: Jack Dusick.

Cin: Carl E. Guthrie.

SpFX: Herman Townsley.

Edit: Roy Livingston.

Mus: Von Dexter.

Cast: Vincent Price, Carol Ohmart, Richard Long, Elisha Cook Jr, Alan Marshal, Carolyn Craig, Julie Mitchum, Leona Anderson.

H (woman uses husband's faked haunted-house tricks in effort to kill him, but he kills her with skeleton puppet & vat of acid; implication of real ghosts)

Ref: FF '59 p33; FD 3 Dec '58.

House on Hokum Hill, The

1916 Mutual (Beauty) sil.

Cast: John Sheehan, Carol Holloway, John Steppling, John Gough.

bor-SF-com (machine devises plots for writer of thrillers)

Ref: MPN 13:3934.

House on Skull Mountain

1973 Chocolate Chip & Pinto Co.s color.

Exec Prod: Joe R. Hartsfield.

Prod: Ray Storey.

Dir: Ron Honthaner.

SP: Mildred Pares.

Cast: Victor French, James Michelle, Jean Durand, Zerona Clayton, Ella Woods.

F?-H

Ref: Vw 13 June '73 p 14.

House on the Hill, The

1910 Edison sil sh?

H (fake ghosts)

Ref: EK 1 June '10 p 10-11.

House that Dripped Blood, The

1970 (1971) British, Amicus (Cinerama) color 102 mins.

Prod: Max J. Rosenberg & Milton Subotsky.

Dir: Peter Duffell.

SP: Robert Bloch.

Art Dir: Tony Curtis.

Makeup: Harry & Peter Frampton.

Cin: Ray Parslow.

Edit: Peter Tanner.

Mus: Michael Dress.

Cast: Christopher Lee, Peter Cushing, Denholm Elliott, Nyree Dawn Porter, Chloë Franks, John Pertwee, Tom Adams, Ingrid Pitt [vampire].

F-H; com-seq (4 stories: 1st: wife & lover scare writer husband to death; 2nd: wax statue in museum lures men to their deaths; 3rd: child kills her father via voodoo; 4th: actor buys cloak to play vampire, when he puts cloak on becomes real vampire -- played as comedy)

Ref: MFB March '71 p50; Vw 3 March '71; NYT 22 April '71; Photon 21:42-43; FF '71 p67.

Based on short stories "Method for Murder," "Waxworks," "Sweets to the Sweet," & "The Cloak" by Robert Bloch.

House that Jack Built, The

● 1900 British, G.A. Smith sil 48 ft.

Prod & Dir: G.A. Smith.

F-com (film reversal shows house unbuilding itself)

Ref: BFI cat p73; Filmlex p746.

● 1968? Canadian, NFB (Col) color ani sh.

Prod: Wolf Koenig & Jim McKay.

F

Ref: Acad nom.

Based on the nursery rhyme.

House that Screamed, The

(La Residencia: The Boarding School)

1969 (1971) Spanish, Anabel Films (AIP) color scope 104 mins (94 mins).

Prod: Arturo Gonzalez.

Dir: Narciso Ibañez Serrador.

SP: Luis Verna Penafiel.

Prod Design: Victor Cortezo.

Cin: Manuel Berenguer.

Edit: Reginald Mills.

Mus: Waldo de los Rios.

Cast: Lilli Palmer, Cristina Galbo, John Moulder Brown, Mary Maude, Candida Losada, Tomás Blanco, Pauline Challenor.

H (19th century; domineering mother unknowingly drives son to murder girls to create composite body that looks like her)

Ref: MFB April '72 p77; FF '71 p226-28; BO 19 April '71.

Based on a story by Juan Tebar.

House that Went Crazy, The

1914 Selig sil 1 reel.

SF-com (automatic electric house fouled up by thief)

Ref: MPW 21:1416.

House that Would Not Die, The

1970 (ABC-TV) color 72 mins.

Prod: Aaron Spelling.

Dir: John Llewellyn Moxey.

SP: Henry Farrell.

Art Dir: Tracy Bousman.

Cin: Fleet Southcott.

Sup Edit: Art Seid.

Mus: Laurence Rosenthal.

Cast: Barbara Stanwyck, Richard Egan, Michael Anderson Jr, Katherine Wynn, Doreen Lang, Mabel Albertson.

F-H (haunted house)

Ref: LAT 29 Oct '70; CineF 4:9.

Based on novel "Ammie, Come Home" by Barbara Michaels.

House with Nobody in It, The

1915 Rialto sil.

Dir: Richard Garrick.

Sc: Clarence J. Harris.

Cast: Ivy Troutman, Bradley Barker, Frank Whitson.

bor-H (mysterious flashes from house result in its being thought haunted)

Ref: MPW 18 Sept '15 p2014, 2017, 2036.

House Without Windows or Doors, The

See: Haus ohne Turen und Funster, Das.

How a House Was Built for the Kitten

1963 Soviet, Soyuzmultfilm color ani puppet 11 mins.

Dir: R. Kachanov.

Story: A. Tyurin.

F (bulldozer promises to build house for kitten)

Ref: Sovexport cat 1:135.

How a Mosquito Operates

(The Mosquito --alt.t.)

1910 McCay sil ani sh.

Dir: Winsor McCay.

F-com

Ref: ASIFA; Ani Chart.

How a Sparrow Looked for Brains

1971 Soviet, Alexander Dovzhenko Studio.

F

Ref: MTVM 25:12:13.

Based on Ukrainian fairy tales.

How Awful About Allan

1970 (ABC-TV) color 72 mins.

Exec Prod: Aaron Spelling.

Prod: George Edwards.

Dir: Curtis Harrington.

SP: Henry Farrell.

Art Dir: Tracy Bousman.

Cin: Fleet Southcoat.

Edit: Richard Farrell.

Mus: Lawrence Rosenthal.

Cast: Anthony Perkins, Julie Harris, Joan Hackett, Kent Smith, Robert Harris, Gene Lawrence.

psy-H (semi-blind Perkins tormented by psychotic sister Harris)

Ref: Vw 30 Sept '70; Borst; CineF 4:9.

How Captain Kettle Discovered the North Pole

See: Voyage of the "Arctic" (1903).

How Death Came to the Earth

1972 Canadian, NFB (Contemporary) color ani 14 mins.

myth-F

Ref: Preview March '73.

Based on an ancient folk tale of India.

How Do I Know It's Sunday?

1934 WB ani 1 reel.

Prod: Leon Schlesinger.

Dir: Friz Freleng.

Ani: Frank Tipper & Don Williams.

F (toys in toyshop come to life)

Ref: Hist US Ani Prog; LC.

How DOoo You Do

(How Do You Dooo --Brit.t.)

1945 (1946) PRC 81 mins.

Prod & Story: Harry Sauber.

Dir: Ralph Murphy.

SP: H. Sauber & Joseph Carole.

Art Dir: Edward C. Jewell.

Makeup: Bud Westmore.

Cin: B.H. Kline.

Edit: Thomas Neff.

Mus Dir: Howard Jackson.

Cast: Bert Gordon, Harry von Zell, Cheryl Walker, Ella Mae Morse, Claire Windsor, Frank Albertson, Keye Luke, Charles Middleton.

bor-SF-com (body appears, disappears, comes to life; victim of doctor's experiment for curing heart disease)

Ref: Vw & HR 5 Nov '45; MFB '46 p 111.

How Grandpa Changed till Nothing Was Left

See: Jak Stařecek Měnil Az Vyménil (1952).

How He Missed His Train

(Le Réveil d'un Monsieur Pressé)

1900 French, Star sil 65 ft.

cont.

How He Missed the Train   cont.

Prod: Georges Méliès.

F (tricks)

Ref: Sadoul/M 322; GM Mage 322, p 181.

How I Cook-ed Peary's Record

1909 British, Urban sil 380 ft.

Dir: W.R. Booth.

F (Münchausen tells how he conquered the Pole)

Ref: Gifford/BFC 02407.

Based on the writings of Fritz Raspe.

See also: Baron Münchausen.

How I Won the War

1967 British, Petersham (UA) color 109 mins.

Prod & Dir: Richard Lester.

SP: Charles Wood.

Art Dir: Philip Harrison & John Stoll.

Cin: David Watkin.

SpFX: Eddie Fowlie.

Edit: John Victor Smith.

Mus: Ken Thorne.

Cast: Michael Crawford, John Lennon, Roy Kinnear, Jack MacGowran, Michael Hordern, Lee Montague, Alexander Knox.

F-sat (when soldier in platoon is killed, his ghost[?] rejoins it, and keeps fighting; other F-seqs)

Ref: FF '67 p360; MFB '67 p 168-69; Time 17 Nov '67; SR 18 Nov '67; Life 17 Nov '67.

Based on the novel by Patrick Ryan.

How It Feels to Be Run Over

1900 British, Hepworth sil 50 ft.

Prod: Cecil Hepworth.

F-com (tricks)

Ref: Hist/Brit p83.

How Kicó Was Born

1951 Yugoslavian, Duga Film color? ani sh.

Dir, Design, Ani: Dušan Vukotić.

F-com

Ref: Z/Zagreb p 19.

See also: Kicó (1951-52).

How Love Conquered Hypnotism

See: Strange Case of Princess Khan, The (1914).

How Man Learned to Fly

1957 Czech ani sh.

Dir: Jiří Brdečka.

doc; F-seq

Ref: Ani/Cin p 125-26.

How Now Boing Boing

1954 UPA (Col) color ani 7 mins.

Exec Prod: Stephen Bosustow.

Dir: Robert Cannon.

Story: T. Hee & R. Cannon.

Design: T. Hee.

Mus: George Bruns.

Voices: Marvin Miller.

F-com

Ref: MFB May '55 p77; LC.

Sequel to: Gerald McBoing-Boing (1950).

How One Peasant Supported Two Generals

1966? Soviet, Soyuzmultfilm (Sovexportfilm) color ani puppet 22.6 mins.

Dir: I. Ivanov-Vano & V. Danilevich.

Story: A. Simukov & I. Ivanov-Vano.

Ani: A. Gorabachov & A. Tyurin.

cont.

How One Peasant...... cont.

Cin: I. Golomb.

F (magic wand sends generals to island)

Ref: Sovexportfilm cat 3:111.

How Pretty Cha Cha Cha!

See: ¡Que Lindo Cha Cha Cha! (1958).

How the Cat and Dog Scrubbed the Floor

n.d. Czech ani 10 mins.

F-com

Ref: Czech films.

Based on a story by Josef Capek.

How the Egg Went on a Ramble

1969 Czech ani puppet? sh.

Dir: Josef Kluge.

F-com (egg tries to get out of bottle)

Ref: MTVM Sept '69 p 16.

Sequel: East, West, Home Is Best (1969).

How the Elephant Got His Trunk

1925 Bray (FBO) sil ani 1 reel.

Dir & Sc: Walter Lantz.

F-com

Ref: LC.

See: Unnatural History (1925-27).

How the Grinch Stole Christmas

1966 MGM color ani 25 mins.

Prod: Chuck Jones & Ted Geisel (Dr. Seuss).

Dir: C. Jones.

Mus: Eugene Poddany.

Voices: Boris Karloff and others.

F-com (weird creature comes to small town & steals all Christmas paraphernalia)

Ref: FD 23 Dec '65; HR 19 Dec '66.

Based on the book by Dr. Seuss.

How the Mole Got His Overalls

1957 Czech color ani 15 mins.

Dir: Zdenek Miler.

F-com

Ref: Czech films flyer; Ani/Cin p 174.

See also: Mole, The (1955?-).

How the Old Woman Caught the Omnibus

(Stop That Bus! --Brit.t.)

1903 British, Hepworth sil 175 ft.

Dir: Percy Stow.

F-com (old woman is run over by bus, pulls it back with her umbrella)

Ref: Gifford/BFC 00750.

How the Rhinoceros Got His Skin

1938 Soviet color ani sh.

Dir: V. Sutiev.

F

Ref: Ani/Cin p 148, 175.

Based on the story by Rudyard Kipling.

How the Sun Gave Water Back to the Puppy

See: Příhody Malého Štěňátka (1960).

How They Work in Cinema

1911 French, Eclair sil sh?

SF-com-sat (director uses robots to make movies without people)

Ref: MPW 9:394, 480, 545; F/A.

How to Avoid Friendship

1964 Rembrandt Films ani 7 mins.

cont.

How to Avoid Friendship cont.

Prod: William L. Snyder.

F-com

Ref: Acad sheet, Acad Nom.

How to Be Lucky

1910 Pathé sil 600 ft.

bor-SF (doctor's potion removes hunchback's hunch)

Ref: Bios 21 April '10.

How to Fatten Chickens

See: Pour Epater les Poules (n.d.).

How to Furnish a Flat

See: Jak Zařídit Byt (1960).

How to Have Good Children

(How to Have a Good Child -- alt.trans.)

1966 Czech ani sh.

Dir: Milos Macourek.

F-com

Ref: Ani/Cin p 128; MTVM June '66 p 16.

How to Kill a Lady?

See: Geheimnis der Gelben Mönche, Das (1966).

How to Make a Doll

1967 Argent (Unusual Films) color 81 mins.

Exec Prod: David Chudnow.

Prod, Dir, Special Computer Sounds: Herschell Gordon Lewis.

Assist Dir: Louise Downe.

SP: Bert Ray & H.G. Lewis (Sheldon Seymour).

Set Design: Spyridon Horiatis.

Cin: Roy Collodi.

Sup Edit: Eskandar Ameripoor.

Assoc Edit: Ralph Mullin.

Mus: Larry Wellington.

Cast: Robert Wood, Jim Vance, Bobbi West, Elizabeth Davis, Margie Lester, Delores Johnson [Robot #1].

SF-sex-com (robot girls; man's mind becomes part of computer; ugly girl magically becomes beautiful)

Ref: PB; H.G. Lewis.

How to Make a Monster

1958 AIP color seq 73 mins.

Prod: Herman Cohen.

Dir: Herbert L. Strock.

SP: Kenneth Langtry & H. Cohen.

Art Dir: Leslie Thomas.

Makeup: Philip Scheer.

Cin: Maury Gertsman.

Edit: Jerry Young.

Mus: Paul Dunlap.

Cast: Robert H. Harris, Paul Brinegar, Gary Conway, Gary Clarke, Walter Reed, Morris Ankrum, Malcolm Atterbury, Heather Ames, John Ashley.

SF-H (makeup man goes insane, uses drugged makeup to cause actors playing Teenage Werewolf and Teenage Frankenstein to kill & behave like the real thing; chamber of horrors; makes self up as caveman to commit murders)

Ref: FF '58 p250; MFB Feb '59 p 19.

See also: I Was a Teenage Frankenstein (1957); I Was a Teenage Werewolf (1957).

How to Play Football

1944 WD (RKO) color ani sh.

Prod: Walt Disney.

F-com

Ref: LC; Acad Nom.

See also: Goofy (1932-53).

How to Steal the Crown of England

See: Argoman Superdiabolico (1966).

How to Steal the World

1968 Arena (MGM) color 89 mins.

Exec Prod: Norman Felton.

Prod: Anthony Spinner.

Dir: Sutton Roley.

SP: Norman Hudis.

Art Dir: Fred Carter.

Cin: Robert Hauser.

SpFX: Ted Samuels.

Edit: Peter Tanner.

Cast: Robert Vaughn, David McCallum, Barry Sullivan, Eleanor Parker, Leslie Nielsen, Leo G. Carroll, Tony Bill, Mark Richman, Dan O'Herlihy, Albert Paulsen, Hugh Marlowe, Ruth Warwick.

bor-SF (villain plans to reduce to the world to docile obedience via gas)

Ref: MFB '68 p 119.

Based on TV series "The Man from U.N.C.L.E."

See also: Man from U.N.C.L.E., The.

How to Stop a Motor Car

1902 British, Hepworth sil 89 ft (100 ft?).

Prod: Cecil Hepworth.

Dir: Percy Stow.

Cast: Cecil Hepworth, T.C. Hepworth, Claude Whitten.

F-com (car & rider explode, are reassembled; policeman run over, cut into pieces)

Ref: BFI cat p77; Gifford/BFC 00536.

How to Stuff a Wild Bikini

1965 AIP color scope 90 mins.

Prod: James H. Nicholson & Samuel Z. Arkoff.

Co Prod: Anthony Carras.

Dir: William Asher.

SP: W. Asher & Leo Townsend.

Art Dir: Howard Campbell.

Cin: Floyd Crosby.

Edit: Fred Feitshans Jr & Eve Newman.

Mus: Les Baxter.

Mus Dir: Al Simms.

Cast: Annette Funicello, Dwayne Hickman, Frankie Avalon, Brian Donlevy, Harvey Lembeck, Beverly Adams, Jody McCrea, John Ashley, Irene Tsu, Buster Keaton, Mickey Rooney.

com; F-seq (Keaton as witch doctor makes floating bikini appear; it transports girl to US by magic)

Ref: Vd & HR 23 July '72; FD 16 July '65; CoF 8:6.

How to Succeed with Girls

See: Peeping Phantom, The (1964?).

How War Came

1941 Col ani sh.

Dir: Paul Fennell.

F

Ref: LC; Acad nom.

How We Stole the Atomic Bomb

See: Come Rubammo la Bombe Atomica (1967).

Howdy, Stranger

(play by R. Sloane & L. Pelletier)

See: Two Guys from Texas (1947).

Howl, The

  n.d. Italian, Lion 99 mins.

  Dir & SP: Tinto Brass.

  Cin: Silvano Ippoliti.

  Mus: Florenzo Carpi.

  Cast: Tina Aumont, Luigi
  Proietti, Nino Segurini,
  Tino Scotti.

  sur-F-H (cannibalistic philo-
  sopher crossing a cemetery)

  Ref: Chodkowski.

Hsi, Nou, Ai, Lueh

  See: Four Moods (1970).

Hsi-yu Chi

  See: Monkey (196?).

Huella Macabra, La

  (The Macabre Mark)

  1962? (1963) Mexican, Rosas
  Priego (Clasa-Mohme & Azteca).

  Dir: Alfredo B. Crevenna.

  Cast: Guillermo Murray, Rosa
  Carmina, Carmen Molina, Jaime
  Fernandez, Elsa Cardenas,
  José Luis Jimenez.

  F-H (vampire children)

  Ref: PS; stills.

Huey's Ducky Daddy

  1953 Par color ani 1
  reel.

  F-com

  Ref: LC.

  See also: Noveltoons (1945-).

Huff and Puff

  1956 Canadian color ani
  sh.

  Dir: Gerald Potterton &
  Grant Munro.

  F

  Ref: Ani/Cin p 175.

Hugo the Hunchback

  1910 Selig sil sh.

  bor-H

  Ref: Gifford/H p24.

Huis Clos

  (No Exit; Vicious Circle--
  alt. trans.)

  1954 French, Marceau.

  Dir: Jacqueline Audry.

  SP: Pierre Laroche.

  Art Dir: Maurice Colasson.

  Cin: Robert Juillard.

  Edit: Marguerite Beauge.

  Mus: Joseph Kosma.

  Cast: Frank Villard, Arletty,
  Gaby Sylvia, Nicole Courcel,
  Yves Deniaud, Renaud-Mary,
  Daniele Delorme.

  F (trio of strangers find
  themselves in hotel room
  which they eventually discover is in Hell & where
  they will have to spend
  eternity)

  Ref: Vw 9 Feb '55; MFB Jan
  '60 p3; Unifrance 6:12.

  Based on the play by Jean-
  Paul Sartre.

  See also: No Exit (1962).

8ᵉ Merveille, La (spelled Huitieme)

  (The 8th Wonder)

  1964? Belgian, Studios Misonne.

  Prod: Claude Misonne.

  F

  Ref: Ani/Belgium p20.

Hula-La-La

  1951 Col 2 reels.

  Prod & Dir: Hugh McCollum.

  SP: Edward Bernds.

  Art Dir: Charles Clague.

  Cin: Henry Freulich.

  Edit: Edwin Bryant.

  Cast: The Three Stooges (Moe
  Howard, Shemp Howard, Larry
  Fine), Jean Willes, Joy
  Windsor, Kenneth MacDonald,
  Emil Sitka.

  cont.

La Huella Macabra (1962?) Mexican

Hula-La-La cont.

  com; F-seq (living four-armed
  statue)

  Ref: Pardi; LC; Maltin/GMS
  p 137.

  See also: Three Stooges,
  The (1934-59).

Hullo Hullo

  1961 Rumanian ani sh.

  Dir: Ion Popescu Gopo.

  F-doc (history of communi-
  cation)

  Ref: Ani/Cin p 144, 173.

Human Duplicators, The

  1964 (1965) Hugo Grimaldi
  Prods (Woolner Bros & Crest)
  color 81 mins.

  Prod: Hugo Grimaldi & Arthur
  C. Pierce.

  Dir: H. Grimaldi.

  SP: A.C. Pierce.

  Art Dir: Paul Sylos.

  Makeup: John Chambers.

  Cin: Monroe Askins.

  Edit: Donald Wolfe.

  Mus Dir: Gordon Zahler.

  Cast: George Nader, Barbara
  Nichols, George Macready,
  Dolores Faith, Richard Kiel
  [alien android], Richard
  Arlen, Hugh Beaumont.

  SF (alien android makes
  android duplicates of humans
  as part of plan to conquer
  world; androids destroyed
  by laser beam; blind girl's
  sight restored by alien)

  Ref: LAT 15 May '65; MFB
  March '65 p40-41; FF '65 p 116.

Human Flies, The

  See: Upside Down (1898).

Human Fly, The

  (L'Homme Mouche)

  1902 French sil 130 ft.

  Prod: Georges Méliès.

  F

  Ref: Sadoul/M, GM Mage 415-16.

Human Folly, The

  See: Prostia Omeneasca (1968?).

Human Monster, The

  (Dark Eyes of London --Brit.t.)

  1939 (1940) British, Argyle
  (Mono) 76 mins.

  Prod: John Argyle.

  Dir: Walter Summers.

  SP: Patrick Kirwin, W. Summers,
  & J.F. Argyle.

  Art Dir: Duncan Sutherland.

  Cin: Bryan Langley.

  Edit: E.G. Richards.

  Mus: Guy Jones.

  Cast: Bela Lugosi, Hugh
  Williams, Greta Gynt, Wilfred
  Walter, Edmond Ryan, Alexan-
  der Field.

  myst; bor-H (insurance swindler
  Lugosi uses blind men for
  crime; strong, ugly blind
  killer)

  Ref: Vd 13 March '40; MPH 18
  Nov '39 p49, 52; Gifford/H p204.

  Based on novel "The Dark Eyes
  of London" by Edgar Wallace.

  See also: Dead Eyes of London
  (1961).

Human Soul, The

  1914 Balboa sil 3 reels.

  F (man photographs wife's
  soul leaving her body as
  she dies)

  Ref: MPW 21:838.

Human Sacrifice

  1911 Reliance sil sh?

  F (Egyptian legend)

  Ref: F/A p421; MPW 10:109-10.

Human Torch, The

  1963 Amateur 16mm color
  sil sh.

  Made by: Don Glut.

  Cast: Don Glut.

  SF (superhero covered in
  flame flies, throws fire)

  Ref: D. Glut.

  Based on the comic book
  character.

Human Vapor, The

  (Gasu-Ningen Dai Ichi-Go)

  1960 (1964) Japanese, Toho
  (Brenco-AA) color scope
  80 mins.

  Dir: Inoshiro Honda.

  SpFX: Eiji Tsuburaya.

  Cast: Tatsuya Mihashi, Kaoru
  Yachigusa, Yoshio Tsuchiya
  [vapor man], Keiko Sata.

  SF-H (man capable of turning
  into gas becomes thief & murderer)

  Ref: MMF 9 f32; FEFN Dec '70
  p30 ad.

Human Wreckage

  1923 Ince (FBO) sil 7215
  ft.

  Prod: Thomas H. Ince.

  Dir: John Griffith Wray.

  Sc: C. Gardner Sullivan.

  Cin: Henry Sharp.

  Cast: Dorothy Davenport (Mrs.
  Wallace Reid), Bessie Love,
  James Kirkwood, George Hacka-
  thorne, Claire McDowell,
  Robert McKim, Harry Northrup.

  sur-psy-F-seq (in anti-drug-
  addiction film, sequence with
  world as seen by drug addict)

  Ref: AFI F2.2621 p368; RAF
  p304; FIR Oct '60 p 481.

Human Zoo

  See: Ningen Dobutsuen
  (1962).

Humanettes

  1930-31 RKO ani puppet?
  sh series.

  Prod: Frank L. Newman.

  Dir & Staged: Leigh Jason.

  Story: Al Boasberg, Harold
  Tarshis, Charles Saxton, &
  Buddy Mason.

  Dialog: H. Tarshis & C. Saxton.

  Edit: Archie F. Marshek, Ted
  Cheesman, & Harry B. Schilling.

  F

  Ref: LC.

Humanity Through the Ages
 (La Civilisation à Travers
 les Ages)
 1908 French sil 1200 ft
 (1000 ft).
 Prod: Georges Méliès.
 F-H-seq (Cain & Abel; Druids;
 human sacrifice; Inquisition)
 Ref: Sadoul/M, GM Mage 1050-65;
 LC; Views 101:8.

Humanoids, The
 (novel by J. Williamson)
 See: Creation of the Humanoids,
 The (1962).

Humbug, The
 (play by M. Marcin)
 See: Love Captive, The (1934).

Hummingbird
 1968 Amateur sh.
 Made by: Charles Cueri.
 exp-F
 Ref: Vw 10 Jan '68.

Humor over Strings
 See: Umor pe Sfori (1954).

Humorous Phases of Funny Faces
 1906 Vit sil ani 230
 ft.
 Prod & Dir: J. Stuart Blackton.
 F-com (artist draws faces
 which begin moving)
 Ref: BFI cat p 165; LC;
 Niver p5.

Humpbacked Horse, The
 See: Little Humpbacked Horse,
 The.

Humpty Dumpty Circus
 1908 Kalem sil ani puppet
 sh.
 F (living toys)
 Ref: Views 133:9.

Hunchback, The
 1909 Vit sil.
 bor-H
 Ref: Gifford/H.

Hunchback and the Dancer, The
 See: Bucklige und die Tanzerin,
 Der (1920).

Hunchback and the Infanta, The
 See: Tree Things (1968).

Hunchback Fiddler
 1909 French, Pathé sil sh.
 F (sea spirits)
 Ref: Bios 23 Dec '09.

Hunchback of Cedar Lodge, The
 1914 Balboa sil 3 reels.
 F-H (ghost in a library)
 Ref: MPW 21:838.

Hunchback of Enmei-in
 See: Enmei-in no Semushi
 (1925?).

Hunchback of Notre Dame, The
● 1923 U sil 12000 ft.
 Pres: Carl Laemmle.
 Dir: Wallace Worsley.
 Assist Dir: Jack Sullivan &
 William Wyler.
 Adapt: Perley Poore Sheehan.
 Sc: Edward T. Lowe.
 Art Dir: E.E. Sheeley &
 Sydney Ullman.
 Cin: Robert Newhard & Tony
 Kornman.
 Cast: Lon Chaney [Quasimodo,
 the hunchback], Ernest Torrence,
 Patsy Ruth Miller, Norman
 Kerry, Kate Lester, Brandon
 Hurst, Raymond Hatton, Tully
 Marshall, Nigel De Brulier.
 Ref: AFI F2.2624 p369; MPN
 28:1333; Clarens.
 See also: Enmei-in no Semushi
 (1925?).
 cont.

Hunchback cont.
● 1939 RKO 117 mins.
 Prod: Pandro S. Berman.
 Dir: William Dieterle.
 Adapt: Bruno Frank.
 SP: Sonya Levien.
 Art Dir: Van Nest Polglase.
 Cin: Joseph H. August.
 SpFX: Vernon L. Walker.
 Edit: William Hamilton &
 Robert Wise.
 Mus: Alfred Newman.
 Cast: Charles Laughton [Quasi-
 modo, the hunchback], Maureen
 O'Hara, Edmond O'Brien,
 Thomas Mitchell, Cedric Hard-
 wicke, Alan Marshal, Walter
 Hampden, Harry Davenport,
 George Zucco, Fritz Leiber,
 Arthur Hohl, George Tobias,
 Rod La Rocque.
 Note: Quasimodo & Esmerelda
 do not die in this version.
 Ref: MPH 23 Dec '39 p37, 40;
 FDY '40; HR 15 Dec '39.

● (Notre-Dame de Paris)
 1956 (1957) French/Italian,
 Paris Film Prods (AA) color
 scope 103 mins.
 Prod: Robert & Raymond Hakim.
 Dir: Jean Delannoy.
 SP: Jean Aurenche & Jacques
 Prevert.
 Cin: Michael Kelber.
 Edit: Henri Taverna.
 Mus: Georges Auric.
 Cast: Gina Lollobrigida,
 Anthony Quinn [Quasimodo,
 the hunchback], Alain Cuny,
 Jean Danet, Jean Tissier,
 Robert Hirsch.
 Ref: FDY '58; MFB April '57
 p48; de Groot p261.

 hist-H (ugly hunchbacked
 cathedral bellringer loves
 gypsy girl Esmeralda, protects her from mob, pours
 molten lead on them, etc.
 she is killed, he finds
 her body & dies of grief)
 Based on novel "Notre-Dame
 de Paris" by Victor Hugo.
 See also: Notre-Dame de
 Paris (1911); Notre Dame
 (1913); Darling of Paris,
 The (1916); Dhanwan (1937);
 Nav Jawan (1937); Badshah
 Dampati (1953); Nanbanji
 no Semushi-Otoko (1957).

Hunchback of the Morgue, The
 See: Jorobado de la Morgue, El
 (1972).

Hunchback Pony, The
 See: Little Humpbacked Horse,
 The (1947).

Hund von Baskerville, Der
 See: Hound of the Baskervilles,
 The (German 1914, 1917, 1929,
 1936).

Hund von Blackwood Castle, Der
 (The Hound of Blackwood Castle)
 1968 W. German, Rialto &
 Constantin color.
 Dir: Alfred Vohrer.
 SP: Alex Berg.
 Cin: Karl Löb.
 Mus: Peter Thomas.
 Cast: Heinz Drache, Karin
 Baal, Siegfried Schürenberg,
 Agnes Windeck, Ilse Page.
 H (phantom hound)
 Ref: GFN 12.

Hundred Monsters, The
 See: Yokai Hyaku Monogatari (1968).

Hundred Tricks, A
 1906 French, Pathé sil
 196 ft.
 F (tricks; transformations)
 Ref: Views & FI I.22.9.

Hungarian Dance
 See: Brahm's Hungarian Dance
 (1931).

Hunger
 1972 French, ORTF color
 computer ani sh.
 Dir: Peter Foldes.
 exp-F
 Ref: IAFF '72.

Hunger of the World, The
 See: Faim du Monde, La (1958).

Hungry Country Man, The
 See: Sandwiches, The (1899).

Hungry Kook Goes Bazook
 n.d. Amateur 16mm color
 6 mins.
 F-sat-com (live-action spoof
 of "Road Runner & Coyote"
 animated series)
 Ref: Budget Film Catalog.
 See also: Road Runner and
 the Coyote (1948-).

Hungry Motor-Car, The
 1910 French, Lux sil
 262 ft.
 F-com (car eats objects like
 barrels, lamp posts, men, etc.)
 Ref: Bios 27 Jan '10 p49-50.

Hungry Wives
 (Jack's Wife --s.t.)
 1972 (1973) Latent Image
 (Jack H. Harris) 16mm
 (35mm) color 89 mins.
 Exec Prod: Alvin C. Croft.
 Prod: Nancy M. Romero.
 Dir, SP, Cin, Edit: George
 A. Romero.
 Mus: Steve Gorn.
 Cast: Jan White, Ray Laine,
 Anne Muffly, Joedda McClain,
 Bill Thunhurst, Virginia
 Greenwald.
 F-H (housewife, afraid of
 aging, becomes witch & kills
 husband, is initiated into
 coven at climax)
 Ref: Vw 18 April '73; HR
 13 April '73 p3, 21; CineF
 2:3:8.

Hunky and Spunky
 1938-39 Fleischer (Par)
 color ani 1 reel series.
 Prod: Max Fleischer.
 Dir: Dave Fleischer.
 Ani: Myron Waldman, Graham
 Place, Rudy Zamora, Art
 Davis, Paul Sommers, Manny
 Gould, & Ed Rayberg.
 F-com
 Ref: LC; Ani chart; Acad
 Nom.

Hunter's Dream, The
 1911 Kalem sil 365 ft.
 F-H-dream
 Ref: MPW 8:718.

Hur-e-Baghdad
 1946 Indian, Mohan.
 Cast: Leela Pande, Shiraj,
 Devraj.
 F (magic)
 Ref: Filmindia Aug '46 p
 54 ad.

Hurrah for Adventure!
 See: ¡Viva la Aventura!
 (1970).

Hurricane Island
 1950 (1951) Col color
 74 mins.
 Prod: Sam Katzman.
 Dir: Lew Landers.
 SP: David Mathews.
 cont.

Hurricane Island cont.
 Cin: Lester White.
 Edit: Richard Fantl.
 Mus Dir: Mischa Bakaleinikoff.
 Cast: Jon Hall, Marie Windsor,
 Edgar Barrier, Lyle Talbot,
 Karen Randal, Marshall Reed,
 Rick Vallin, Marc Lawrence,
 Romo Vincent, Don Harvey,
 Alex P. Montoya.
 F (Ponce de Leon finds Fountain
 of Youth; queen becomes old
 crone; hurricane caused by
 evil spirits sinks fountain into
 bottomless pit)
 Ref: MFB April '52 p51; HR
 5 July '51; MPH 7 July '51.
 See also: Fountain of Youth.

Hurry! Kurama!
 See: Shippu! Kurama Tengu
 (1956).

Hurry Up, Please
 1908 French, Pathé sil sh.
 SF-com (speed-controlling invention speeds up cleaning
 girls, bill poster, etc.)
 Ref: Views 134:9.

Hush, Hush, Sweet Charlotte
 (What Ever Happened to Cousin
 Charlotte? --s.t.)
 1964 (1965) Aldrich & Asso-
 ciates (20th-Fox) 134 mins.
 Prod & Dir: Robert Aldrich.
 Story: Henry Farrell.
 SP: H. Farrell & Lukas Heller.
 Art Dir: William Glasgow.
 Edit: Michael Luciano.
 Mus: Frank De Vol.
 Cast: Bette Davis, Olivia
 de Havilland, Joseph Cotten,
 Agnes Moorehead, Cecil Kella-
 way, Victor Buono, Mary
 Astor, Wesly Addy, William
 Campbell, Bruce Dern, Frank
 Ferguson, George Kennedy,
 Ellen Corby.
 psy-H (murder by amputation
 of hand, then decapitation;
 walking corpse faked in
 effort to drive Davis mad)
 Ref: FF '65 p47-48; FD 14
 Jan '65; MFB May '65 p70;
 Vw 23 Dec '64; F&F June '65
 p32.

Hush My Mouse
 1945 WB color ani 10 mins.
 Dir: Chuck (Charles M.) Jones.
 Story: Tedd Pierce.
 Ani: Ken Harris.
 Mus Dir: Carl W. Stalling.
 F-com
 Ref: LC.

Husky
 1951 Soviet, Sovexportfilm
 color ani 19 mins.
 F
 Ref: MFB Jan '52 p8-9.

Husn ka Chor
 1953 Indian, Wadia.
 Dir: J.B.H. Wadia.
 SP: J.B.H. Wadia & Tahir
 Lucknavi.
 Cin: A. Wadadekar.
 Mus: B.C. Rani.
 Cast: Usha Kiron, Sharda,
 B. Raje.
 F (moon fairy; magic mirror;
 flying carpet; magic wish
 box)
 Ref: Filmfare 18 Sept '53.
 Based on "The Arabian Nights."
 See also: Arabian Nights, The.

Hvedza Betlemska
 (The Star of Bethlehem)
 1969 (1970?) Czech color
 ani objects 10 mins.
 Dir & Story: Hermina Tyrlova.
 rel-F
 Ref: Mamaia '70; Czech Films '71.
 See also: King of Kings.

Hyde Park Corner

1935 British, Grosvenor (Pathé) 85 mins.

Prod: Harcourt Templeton.

Dir: Sinclair Hill.

SP: Selwyn Jepson.

Cin: Cyril Bristow.

Assist Cin: Jack Asher.

Cast: Gordon Harker, Eric Portman, Binnie Hale, Gibb McLaughlin, Robert Holmes, Eileen Peel, Donald Wolfit.

F-seq (curse persists 150 years later)

Ref: Vw 11 Dec '35; TVG.

Based on the play by Walter Hackett.

Hydrothérapie Fantastique

See: Doctor's Secret, The (1909).

Hyena of London, The

See: Jena de Londra, La (1964).

Hyena's Laugh

1927 Bray (FBO) sil ani 1 reel.

Dir: Walter Lantz & Clyde Geronimi.

F-com

Ref: LC.

See: Unnatural History (1925-27).

Hyokkori Hyôtan Jima

(Great Adventures on Bottle-Gourd Island; The Madcap Island --ad.t.)

1967 Japanese, Toei color ani scope 61 mins.

Dir: Taiji Yabushita.

SP: Hiroshi Inoue & Morihisa Yamamoto.

Art Dir: Hideo Chiba.

Cin: Miki Shirao.

Mus: Seiichirô Uno.

F-com (floating island drifts to continent with man-hating dogs)

Ref: UniJ 38:20-21.

Hyotan Suzume

(The Sparrow in a Gourd)

1957 Japanese, Otogi-Pro & Toho color ani 55 mins.

Prod, Dir, Story: Ryuichi Yokoyama.

Mus: Koji Taku.

F-com

Ref: Toho Films '59.

Hyp-Nut-Tist, The

1935 Par ani 1 reel.

Prod: Max Fleischer.

Dir: Dave Fleischer.

F-com

Ref: LC; PopCar.

See also: Popeye (1933-57).

Hyperboloid of Engineer Garin, The

1965 Soviet.

Dir: M. Berdicevski.

Sc: I. Manevic & A. Ginzburg.

Cast: E. Evstigneev, V. Safonov, N. Astangov, N. Klimova.

SF (madman tries to conquer world with death ray)

Ref: F&F Nov '66; MMF 15/16 p35; Borst.

Based on novel.

Hypnos

(Massacre Mania --alt.t.)

1971 Italian/Spanish, Record/color scope.

Prod: Frank Yampi.

Dir: Paolo Bianchini (Paul Maxwell).

SP: P. Bianchini (P. Maxwell) & Max Corot.

cont.

Hypnos cont.

Mus: Carlo Savina.

Cast: Giovanni Cianfriglia (Ken Wood), Robert Woods, Fernando Sancho, Rada Rassimov.

bor-SF-H (subliminal messages broadcast by supervillain over public TV brainwashes ordinary people into becoming murderers)

Ref: Soren.

Hypnosis

(Nur Tote Zeugen Schweigen: Only the Dead Are Silent; Hipnosis; Dummy of Death -- Brit.t.)

1962 Italian/German/Spanish, Domiziana/Germania/Procusa 90 mins.

Dir: Eugenio Marten.

SP: Giuseppe Mangione, E. Martin, G. Moreno Burgos, Francis Niewel, & Gerhard Schmidt.

Art Dir: Ramiro Gomez.

Cin: Francisco Sempere.

Edit: Antonio Gimeno Garcia & Edith von Seydewitz.

Mus: Roman Vlad.

Cast: Elonora Rossi-Drago, Götz George, Jean Sorel, Heinz Drache, Massimo Serato, Wenrer Peters, Hildegard Kneff, Mara Cruz.

H (supernatural incidents including dummy coming to life are faked in order to extract confession)

Ref: MFB April '66 p 62; SpCin '63 p72-73.

Hypnotic Chair, The

1912 Majestic sil sh.

SF-com (inventor's chair paralyses by electricity)

Ref: MPW 14:1082.

Hypnotic Cure, The

1909 Lubin sil 385 ft.

F-com (hypnotism cures rheumatism)

Ref: FI 26:8; LC.

Hypnotic Eye, The

1959 AA 77 mins.

Exec Prod: Ben Schwalb.

Prod: Charles B. Bloch.

Dir: George Blair.

SP: Gitta & William Read Woodfield.

Makeup: Emile La Vigne & Tony Lloyd.

Cin: Archie Dalzell.

SpFX: Milton Olsen.

Edit: William Austin.

Mus: Marlin Skiles.

Cast: Jacques Bergerac, Allison Hayes, Marcia Henderson, Merry Anders, Joe Partridge, Guy Prescott, Fred Demara, James Lydon, Lawrence Lipton.

F-H (horrible self-mutilations traced to hideously-scarred wife of super-hypnotist)

Ref: FF /60 p33-34; HR 20 Jan '60.

Hypnotic Hick

1953 U color ani 6 mins.

Prod: Walter Lantz.

Dir: Don Patterson.

Voice of Woody: Grace Stafford.

F-com

Ref: LC; PopCar.

See also: Woody Woodpecker (1940-72).

Hypnotic Monkey, The

1915 Kalem (General) sil 1 reel.

Dir: Al Santell.

Cast: Lloyd V. Hamilton, Bud Duncan.

cont.

Hypnotic Monkey cont.

F-com-dream (in dream hypnotist turns Bud into monkey & back, shows him how to do it -- one way only)

Ref: MPW 25:880, 1316.

Hypnotic Spray, The

1909 British?, Gaum sil 360 ft.

SF-com (boy can control anyone after spraying them with stolen spray)

Ref: Bios 7 Oct '09.

Hypnotic Violinist, The

1914 Warner's Features sil 3 reels.

F (violinist's psychic power steals doctor's wife)

Ref: MPW 22:520 ad, 706.

Hypnotic Wife, The

1909 French, Pathé sil 482 ft.

bor-F (woman hypnotizes her husband & commits him to asylum)

Ref: FI IV-35:6, 37:3.

Hypnotiseur, Der

(Svengali --alt.t.)

1914 Austrian, Wiener Kunst-film sil 3480 ft.

Dir: Luise Kolm & Jakob Fleck.

Cast: Fraulein Nording, Ferdinand Bonn.

bor-F (man's superhypnotic powers make girl into great singer)

Ref: Osterr.

Based on novel "Trilby" by George du Maurier.

See also: Trilby.

Hypnotising the Hypnotist

See: Hypnotist, The (1911).

Hypnotism

1910 French, Lux sil 660 ft.

bor-F (hypnotist forces girl to commit robbery)

Ref: Bios 13 Oct '10.

Hypnotist, The

(Hypnotising the Hypnotist -- alt.t.)

1911 Vit sil 1000 ft.

Cast: Florence Turner.

F-com (hypnotism works as if it were magic)

Ref: BFI cat p 187; MPW 10: 830, 904.

Hypnotist, The

1912 Lubin sil sh.

F-com (hypnotic power from waving arms)

Ref: MPW 13:70; Bios 5 Sept '12.

Hypnotist, The

See: London After Midnight (1927); Scotland Yard Dragnet (1957).

Hypnotist at Work, A

(L' Magnétiseur)

1897 French sil 65 ft.

Prod: Georges Méliès.

F (mesmerist magically strips girl)

Ref: Sadoul/M, GM Mage 129; Gifford/H p 16.

Hypnotist's Revenge, The

1907 Biograph sil 1030 ft.

bor-F-com

Ref: MPW 1:331; LC; Biograph Bulletin 20 July '07.

Hypnotist's Revenge, The

1909 Star sil 380 ft.

Prod: Gaston Méliès.

F (magician vs hypnotist)

Ref: FI IV-44:14, 45:8; LC.

cont.

Hypnotizing the Hypnotist

See: Hypnotist, The (1911).

Hypo-Chondri-Cat, The

1951 WB color ani 7 mins.

Dir: Chuck Jones.

F-com (Claude the neurotic cat vs sadistic mice)

Ref: LC; David Rider.

Hypothesis Beta

(Hypothefe Beta)

1967? French, Films Orzeau (Pathé-Contemporary) ani sh.

Dir: Jean-Charles Meunier.

F (computer card misbehaves)

Ref: Collier; Acad Nom.

Hypothezy

(Hypothesis)

1963 Czech, Popular Science and Instructional Film Studio color 19 mins.

Dir & SP: Vladimir Silhan.

doc; SF-seq (exploration of possibilities of life on other planets)

Ref: Gasca p314-15; Trieste '64.

Hysteria

1964 (1965) British, Hammer (MGM) 85 mins.

Prod & SP: Jimmy Sangster.

Dir: Freddie Francis.

Prod Design: Edward Carrick.

Cin: John Wilcox.

Edit: James Needs.

Mus: Don Banks.

Mus Dir: Philip Martell.

Cast: Robert Webber, Lelia Goldoni, Anthony Newlands, Jennifer Jayne, Maurice Denham, Peter Woodthorpe, Sandra Boize, Sue Lloyd, Kiwi Kingston.

psy-H (attempt to convince amnesiac he is having hallucinations; "macabre" --MFB)

Ref: MFB July '65 p 110; Vw 8 Sept '65; FD 8 Sept '65.

I

I Accuse
See: J'Accusé.

I Am Alladin
See: Main Hoon Alladin (1965).

I Am Curious -- Tahiti
1970 Hollywood Int'l Film Corp. of America color 65 mins.
Prod & Dir: Carlos Tobalina.
Cast: Maria-Pia, William Larra Bure, Leticia Young, Susane Parker, Jay Colonna.
sex-com; bor-SF (girl has gadget which sees & hears through walls)
Ref: Vw 18 Nov '70.

I Am Here
1972 Japanese, Studio T.Y. color? ani 3 mins.
Dir: Ryuji Fujieda.
exp-F
Ref: IAFF '72.

I Am Legend
(novel by R. Matheson)
See: Last Man on Earth, The (1964); Omega Man, The (1971).

I Am Somebody
196? E. German, DEFA ani sh.
Dir: Lothar Barke.
F
Ref: Ani/Cin p 153.

I Am Suzanne
1933 (1934) Jesse L. Lasky (Fox) 115 mins (85 mins).
Dir: Rowland V. Lee.
Story & SP: R.V. Lee & Edwin Justus Mayer.
Cin: Lee Garmes.
Edit: Harold Schuster.
Mus: Frederick Hollander.
Cast: Lilian Harvey, Gene Raymond, Leslie Banks, Lionel Belmore.
mus-F-dream (woman shoots puppet, then dreams she is tried before court of marionettes.
Ref: Vd 16 Dec '33; MPH 27 Jan '34 p44; FDY '35.

I Am the Walrus
n.d. Amateur (Film-makers' Coop) 16mm color sil 4.5 mins.
Made by: Philip Ostrow.
Mus: The Beatles.
exp-F (song of this title given visualization)
Ref: FMC 5 p261.

I Am Thinking of My Darling
(novel by V. McHugh)
See: What's So Bad About Feeling Good? (1968).

IBM Puppet Shows
1965 Eames color puppet 9 mins.
Dir: Charles & Ray Eames.
Cin: C. Eames.
doc; F (2 stories; one is "Sherlock Holmes in the Singular Case of the Plural Green Mustache"; other is "Computer Day at Midvale")
Ref: ΓQ Spring '70 p 18.
See also: Sherlock Holmes.

I Believe
(The Man Without a Soul --Brit.t.)
1916 (1917) British, London (Cosmo-tofilm & Sherman Pictures) sil 7200 ft.
Dir & Sc: George Loane Tucker.

cont.

I Believe cont.
Cast: Milton Rosmer, Edna Flugrath, Barbara Everest, Edward O'Neill, Charles Rock, Frank Stanmore, Kitty Cavendish, Hubert Willis, Kenelm Foss.
rel-F; SF-seq (when scientist restores divinity student to life the student has no soul; he prays & it is restored to him)
Ref: MPN 16:114-15, 2871; LC; Hist/Brit p 176-77; Gifford/BFC 06245.

I Bury the Living
1958 Maxim (UA) 76 mins.
Prod: Albert Band & Louis Garfinkle.
Dir: A. Band.
SP: L. Garfinkle.
Visual Design: E. Vorkapich.
Cin: Frederick Gately.
Edit: Frank Sullivan.
Mus: Gerald Fried .
Cast: Richard Boone, Theodore Bikel, Peggy Maurer, Herb Anderson, Howard Smith, Robert Osterloh, Russ Bender, Cyril Delevanti.
H (when cemetery owner accidentally replaces white pins representing owned but not yet occupied graves in cemetery map with black pins representing occupied graves, the live owners seem to die as a result; all turns out to be a plot)
Ref: FF '58 p264; FDY '59.

I Changed My Sex
See: Glen or Glenda? (1952).

I Discovered Heaven
See: Naan Kanda Swargam (1960).

I Dream of Jeanne
1970 Philippine, Tower Prods.
Prod: Victoria Villanueva.
Dir: Artemio Marquez.
Story: Annavi.
Choreog: Lito Calzado.
Mus: D'Romenz.
Cast: Jeanne Young, Manny DeLeon, Raul Aragon, Angelito Marquez, Bobby Nelson, Mila Del Sol.
mus-F-com
Ref: Chodkowski.

I Drink Your Blood
1971 Cinemation color 80 mins.
Prod: Jerry Gross.
Assoc Prod: Harry Kaplen.
Dir & SP: David Durston.
Art Dir: Charles Baxter.
Cin: Jacques Demarecaux.
Mus: Clay Pitts.
Cast: Bhaskar, Jadine Wong, Ronda Fultz, Riley Mills, George Patterson, Richard Bowler, Tyde Kierney.
H (boy infects gang of murderous hippies with rabies via dog's blood in meat pies; construction workers & hippies gorily kill each other)
Ref: FF '71 p97; LAT 7 May '71.

I Eat Your Skin
(Zombies --s.t.; Voodoo Blood Bath --e.t.)
1964 (1971 --first release) Iselin-Tenney (Cinemation) 82 mins.
Prod, Dir, SP: Del Tenney.
Assoc Prod: Jesse Hartman & Dan Stapleton.
Art Dir: Robert Verberkmoss.
Makeup: Guy Del Russo.
Cin: Francois Farkas.
Edit: Larry Keating.
Mus: Lon E. Norman.
Cast: William Joyce, Heather Hewitt, Betty Hyatt Linton, Dan Stapleton, Walter Coy, Robert Stanton.

cont.

I Eat Your Skin cont.
SF-H (adventurer battles scientifically-created zombies on Atlantic island)
Ref: LAT 7 May '71; FF '71 p96; BO 12 March '71.
See also: White Zombie (1932).

I Have a Stranger's Face
See: Face of Another (1966).

I Have No Mouth But I Must Scream!
See: Fengriffen (1972).
Note: both these were shooting titles; it is listed as Fengriffen in Vol 1, but when it was released in 1973, the final title was --And Now the Screaming Starts!

I Haven't Got a Hat
1934 (1935) Vitaphone (WB) 2-color Technicolor ani 7 mins.
Prod: Leon Schlesinger.
Dir: Friz (Isadore) Freleng.
Story: Bob Clampett.
Ani: Rollin Hamilton & Jack King.
Mus: Bernard Brown.
F-com
Ref: FW 12:15-16; LC.
See also: Porky Pig (1934--).
Note: this was the first Porky Pig cartoon.

I Huvet paa en Gammal Gubbe
See: Out of an Old Man's Head (1968).

I, Justice
See: Ja, Spravedlnost (1968).

I Kill, You Kill
See: Lo Uccido, Tu Uccidi (1965).

I Killed Finstein, Gentlemen
See: Zabil Jsem Einsteina, Panove (1970).

I Killed Rasputin
See: J'Ai Tue Raspoutine (1967).

I Know an Old Lady Who Swallowed a Fly
1962 Canadian, NFB color ani 5 mins.
Prod: Colin Low.
Dir & Story: Derek Lamb.
Ani: Kaj Pindal.
Mus: Alan Mills.
Song Sung By: Burl Ives.
F-com (old lady swallows progressively larger animals to catch those previously swallowed)
Ref: MFB '67 p66.

I Led Two Lives
See: Glen or Glenda? (1952).

I Like Babies and Infinks
1937 Par ani 1 reel.
Prod: Max Fleischer.
Dir: Dave Fleischer.
Ani: Seymour Kneitel & Graham Place.
F-com
Ref: LC; PopCar.
See also: Popeye (1933-57).

I Love a Mystery
1944 (1945) Col 68 mins.
Prod: Wallace MacDonald.
Dir: Henry Levin.
SP: Charles O'Neal.
Art Dir: George Brooks.
Cin: Burnett Guffey.
Edit: Aaron Stell.
Cast: Jim Bannon, Nina Foch, George Macready, Barton Yarborough, Carole Mathews, Lester Matthews, Frank O'Connor.

cont.

I Love a Mystery cont.
myst; bor-F-H (oriental "black magic" is used to cause suicide)
Ref: CoF 11:36; FanMo 3:39; LC.
Based on the radio show.
Sequels: Devil's Mask, The (1946); Unknown, The (1946).

I Love to Singa
1936 Vitaphone (WB) color ani 7 mins.
Prod: Leon Schlesinger.
Dir: Fred (Tex) Avery.
Ani: Chuck (Charles) Jones & Virgil Ross.
Mus: Norman Spencer.
F-com
Ref: LC.

I Love You, I Kill You
(Ich Liebe Dich, Ich Tote Dich)
1971 (1972) W. German, Uwe Brandner (New Yorker Films) color 94 mins.
Prod, Dir, SP: Uwe Brandner.
Cin: André Debreuil.
Edit: Heide Genee.
Mus: Mozart, U. Brandner, Heinz Hetter, & Kid Olanf.
Cast: Ralf Becker, Hannes Fuchs, Helmut Brasch, Thomas Eckelmann, Nikolaus Dutsch, Marianne Blomquist, Monika Hansen, Wolfgang Ebert.
soc-SF (set in near future; police as tools of benevolent totalitarianism use pills to control population)
Ref: FF '72 p 160-62; Village Voice 17 June '71; LAT 7 July '72; Ind Film Journal 8 June '72.

I Love You, I Love You
See: Je T'Aime, Je T'Aime (1968).

I Made 13
See: Ho Fatto 13 (1951).

I Married a Monster from Outer Space
1958 Par 78 mins.
Prod & Dir: Gene Fowler Jr.
SP: Louis Vittes.
Art Dir: Hal Pereira & Henry Bumstead.
Makeup: Charles Gemora.
Cin: Haskell Boggs.
SpFX: John P. Fulton.
Edit: George Tomasini.
Cast: Tom Tryon, Gloria Talbott, Ken Lynch, John Eldredge, Valerie Allen, Maxie Rosenbloom, Jean Carson, Chuck Wassil.
SF-H (in effort to replenish their dying species, aliens make themselves into duplicates of married Earthmen, replace them)
Ref: FF '58 p244; FDY '59.

I Married a Werewolf
See: Werewolf in a Girls' Dormitory (1961).

I Married a Witch
1942 Par (UA) 76 mins.
Prod & Dir: René Clair.
SP: Robert Pirosh & Marc Connelly.
Art Dir: Hans Dreier & Ernst Fegte.
Cin: Ted Tetzlaff.
SpFX: Gordon Jennings.
Edit: Eda Warren.
Mus: Roy Webb.
Cast: Fredric March, Veronica Lake [witch], Robert Benchley, Susan Hayward, Cecil Kellaway [wizard], Elizabeth Patterson, Emory Parnell, Wade Boteler, Chester Conklin, Monte Blue, Billy Bevan.

cont.

I Married a Witch cont.

F-com (lightning frees witch from her imprisonment in tree)

Ref: Vd 19 Oct '42; MFB May '43 p53; FDY '43.

Based on novel "The Passionate Witch" by Thorne Smith & Norman Matson.

I Married an Angel

1942 MGM 84 mins.

Prod: Hunt Stromberg.

Dir: W.S. Van Dyke II.

SP: Anita Loos.

Art Dir: Cedric Gibbons.

Cin: Ray June.

SpFX: Arnold Gillespie & Warren Newcombe.

Edit: Conrad A. Nervig.

Mus: Richard Rodgers.

Lyrics: Lorenz Hart.

Cast: Nelson Eddy, Jeannette MacDonald [angel], Reginald Owen, Mona Maris, Anne Jeffreys, Janis Carter, Inez Cooper, Veda Ann Borg, Edward Everett Horton, Binnie Barnes.

mus-com; F-dream (man dreams a girl is an angel and that they are married)

Ref: HR 20 May '42; FDY '43; FIR Aug'Sept '58 p379, March '65 p143-44; MFB Aug '42 p100.

Based on the musical comedy with music by Richard Rodgers & lyrics by Lorenz Hart from the play by Vaszary Janos.

I, Monster

1971 (1973) British, Amicus (Cannon) color 3D (2D) 75 mins.

Prod: Max J. Rosenberg & Milton Subotsky.

Dir: Stephen Weeks.

SP: M. Subotsky.

Art Dir: Tony Curtis.

Makeup: Harry Frampton & Peter Frampton.

Cin: Moray Grant.

Edit: Peter Tanner.

Mus: Carl Davis.

Cast: Christopher Lee, Peter Cushing, Mike Raven, Richard Hurndall, George Merritt, Kenneth J. Warren, Susan Jameson.

SF-H (in effort to separate good from evil in man, Lee changes from kindly Dr. Marlowe to pure evil Mr. Blake, each transformation makes him uglier than before)

Ref: MFB Dec '71 p241; BO; C. Lee.

Based on short novel "The Strange Case of Dr. Jekyll and Mr. Hyde" by Robert Louis Stevenson.

See also: Dr. Jekyll and Mr. Hyde.

I.N.R.I.

(Crown of Thorns --alt.t.)

1923 (1934) German, Neumann sil 6713 ft.

Prod: Hans Neumann.

Dir: Robert Wiene.

Cast: Gregori Chmara, Henny Porten, Asta Nielsen, Werner Krauss, Emanuel Reicher, Alexander Granach.

rel-F-seq (sequence with life of Christ told in form of a Passion Play)

Ref: C to H p 109; Rel/Cin p37.

See also: King of Kings; Passion Play, The.

I.Q.S.

1967 Spanish color 22 mins.

Dir: Rafael J. Salvia.

F (alchemist steps out of a picture)

Ref: SpCin '67 p223.

I Saw the Shadow

1966 Japanese, Amateur (Film-makers' Coop) 8mm sil 13 mins.

cont.

I Saw the Shadow cont.

Made by: Takahiko Iimura.

Painting by: Jiro Takamatsu.

exp-F (camera's shadow loves a girl's shadow)

Ref: FMC 5:163.

I Saw What You Did

1965 Castle Pictures (U) 82 mins.

Prod & Dir: William Castle.

SP: William McGivern.

Art Dir: William Simonds.

Cin: Joseph Biroc.

Edit: Eddie Bryant.

Mus: Van Alexander.

Cast: Joan Crawford, John Ireland, Leif Erickson, Pat Breslin, Andi Garrett, Sharyl Locke, Sarah Lane, John Archer.

bor-H (children inadvertently make murderer think he knows they are guilty; horror killings in shower)

Ref: MFB Dec '65; Time 30 July '65; FD 14 May '65.

Based on novel "Out of the Dark" by Ursula Curtiss.

I Slept With a Ghost

See: Yo Dormi con un Fantasma (1947)

I-tai Chien-Wang

See: King of Swordmen (1969)

I Taw A Putty Tat

1948 WB color ani 7 mins.

Dir: Friz (I.) Freleng

Story: Tedd Pierce.

Ani: Virgil Ross, Gerry Chiniquy, Manuel Perez, & Ken Champlin.

Mus Dir: Carl Stalling.

Voices: Mel Blanc.

F com

Ref: LC.

See also: Sylvester P. Pussycat.

I, the Body

See: Morianna (1965).

I Videl Sem Daljine Meglene i Kalne

(Far Away I Saw Mist and Mud)

1964 Yugoslavian, Zagreb color ani 12.1 mins.

Dir, Story, Design: Zlatko Bourek.

Bg: Pavao Stalter.

Ani: Vladimir Jutrisa.

Mus: Tomislav Simovic.

F ("horrors of the Turkish-Croatian Wars ";"grotesque figures" --Z/Zagreb)

Ref: Z/Zagreb p26, 33,78.

Based on "The Ballads of Petrica Kerempuh" by Miroslav Krleza.

I Walked with a Zombie

1943 RKO 69 mins.

Prod: Val Lewton.

Dir: Jacques Tourneur.

Story: Inez Wallace.

SP: Curt Siodmak & Ardel Wray.

Art Dir: Albert D'Agostino & Walter Keller.

Cin: J. Roy Hunt.

Edit: Mark Robson.

Mus: Roy Webb.

Mus Dir: C. Bakaleinikoff.

Cast: James Ellison, Frances Dee, Tom Conway, Christine Gordon, Sir Lancelot, Edith Barrett, Darby Jones [zombie].

F-H (nurse goes to Caribbean island to tend semi-zombie woman; voodoo)

Ref: Photon 20:34-38, 31:12; Vd 16 March '43; FDY '44.

I Was a Teenage Apeman

1959 Amateur 16mm sil color sh.

Made by: Don Glut.

Cast: Don Glut.

SF-com

Ref: D. Glut.

I Was a Teenage Birdman

1962 British, Amateur -- Delta SF Film Group 8mm color sound 4 mins.

SF-com

Ref: F&F May '72 p82.

Sequel: Son of Birdman (1969).

I Was a Teenage Caveman

See: Teenage Caveman (1958).

I Was a Teenage Frankenstein

(Teenage Frankenstein --Brit.t.)

1957 Santa Rosa Prod (AIP) color seq 74 mins.

Prod: Herman Cohen.

Dir: Herbert L. Strock.

Story & SP: Kenneth Langtry.

Art Dir: Leslie Thomas.

Makeup: Philip Scheer.

Cin: Lothrop Worth.

Edit: Jerry Young.

Mus: Paul Dunlap.

Cast: Whit Bissell, Phyllis Coates, Robert Burton, Gary Conway [Monster], George Lynn, John Cliff.

SF-H (modern-day descendant of Dr. Frankenstein puts together teenage monster out of dead bodies; at first hideous, he later gives it handsome face)

Ref: FF '58 p29; FDY '58; LC.

Based on ideas from novel "Frankenstein" by Mary Shelley.

See also: How to Make a Monster (1958); Frankenstein; Monster Rumble (1961); Teenage Frankenstein, The (1959); Teenage Frankenstein Meets the Teenage Werewolf, The (1959).

I Was a Teenage Gorilla

See: Konga (1960).

I Was a Teenage Vampire

1959 Amateur 16mm sil sh.

Made by: Don Glut.

Cast: Don Glut.

F-H (son of Dracula)

Ref: D. Glut.

See also: Dracula.

I Was a Teenage Werewolf

(Blood of the Werewolf --s.t.)

1957 Sunset Prods (AIP) 76 mins.

Prod: Herman Cohen.

Dir: Gene Fowler Jr.

SP: Ralph Thornton.

Art Dir: Leslie Thomas.

Cin: Joseph La Shelle.

Edit: George Gittens.

Mus: Paul Dunlap.

Cast: Michael Landon [werewolf], Yvonne Lime, Whit Bissell, Guy Williams, Robert Griffin, Vladimir Sokoloff, Malcolm Atterbury, Eddie Marr, Louise Lewis.

SF-H (in an effort to find guard against radiation, mad scientist retrogresses troubled teenager to primitive, werewolf-like state; being startled thereafter causes transformations)

Ref: FDY '58; Pardi; Willis.

See also: Wolf Man, The (1941); How to Make a Monster (1959); Return of the Teenage Werewolf (1959); Revenge of the Teenage Werewolf (1959);

cont.

I Was a Teenage Werewolf cont.

Teenage Frankenstein Meets the Teenage Werewolf, The (1959); Teenage Werewolf, The (1959); Monster Rumble (1961).

I Yam What I Yam

1933 Par ani 1 reel.

Prod: Max Fleischer.

Dir: Dave Fleischer.

F-com

Ref: LC.

See also: Popeye (1933-57).

I, You, They

See: Je, Tu, Elles (1969).

Ib and Little Christina

1908 British, Clarendon sil 590 ft.

Dir: Percy Stow.

Sc: Langford Reed.

F

Ref: Gifford/BFC 02108.

Based on the story by Hans Christian Andersen.

Ibong Adarna

1941 Philippine, LVN Pictures.

Dir & SP: Vicente (Vincente?) Salumbides.

Art Dir: Teodorico Carmona.

Cast: Mila del Sol, Fred Cortez, Vicente Oliver, Deana Prieto, Ben Rubio, Ester Magalona.

F (princes turn to stone)

Ref: Salumbides.

Ibulong Mo Sa Hangin

See: Curse of the Vampires (1966).

Icaria XB-1

See: Voyage to the End of the Universe (1963).

Icarus

1967 Polish, Cartoon Film Studio ani sh.

Dir: Jerzy Afanasjew & Jerzy Zitzman.

F (tailor makes himself wings)

Ref: MTVM Oct '67 p 12.

See also: Fall (1971?).

Icarus Montgolfier Wright

1962 Format Films (UA) color ani 23 mins? (18 mins).

Prod: Herb Klynn.

Dir: Jules Engel.

SP: Ray Bradbury & George Clayton Johnson.

Art Dir: Joe Mugnaini.

SF-dream (I.M. Wright is destined to be a spaceman)

Ref: Trieste I:26; SM 7:13; Acad nom.

Based on the work by Ray Bradbury.

Ice

1969 Monument Film Corp & AFI 132 mins.

Prod: David C. Stone.

Dir: Robert Kramer.

Cin: Robert Machover.

Cast: Robert Kramer, Tom Griffin.

bor-soc-SF (young revolutionaries in the near future)

Ref: MFB June '71 p 121; FMC 5:179-80.

Ich Liebe Dich, Ich Tote Dich

See: I Love You, I Kill You (1971).

Ichabod and Mr. Toad

See: Adventures of Ichabod and Mr. Toad, The (1949).

I'd Rather Be Rich

1964 U color 96 mins.

Prod: Ross Hunter.

Dir: Jack Smight.

SP: Oscar Brodney, Norman Krasna, & Leo Townsend.

Art Dir: Alexander Golitzen & George Webb.

Cin: Russell Metty.

Edit: Milton Carruth.

Mus: Percy Faith.

Mus Dir: Joseph Gershenson.

Cast: Sandra Dee, Robert Goulet, Andy Williams, Maurice Chevalier, Gene Raymond, Charles Ruggles, Hermione Gingold, Hayden Rorke, Milton Frome.

com; F-dream (dream seq with Sandra Dee as angel, Goulet as the devil, Williams as a knight in shining armor)

Ref: FF '64 p208-10; Shea.

Idea, The

See: Idee, L' (1934).

Ideal

1963 Czech color ani 15 mins.

Dir & Story: Bretislav Pojar.

Ani: Stanislava Prochazkova, Boris Masnik, & Pavel Prochazka.

Mus: Wiliam Bukovy.

F

Ref: Annecy '65.

Idee, L'

(The Idea)

1934 French ani 27 mins.

Dir: Berthold Bartosch.

Mus: Arthur Honegger.

bor-F

Ref: F/A p627; BFI Dist cat p21; C-16 p 16.

Based on woodcuts by Frans Masereel.

Ideology, The

See: Estranho Mundo de Ze do Caixao, O (1969).

Idiot of Xeenemunde, The

1964 Czech 45 mins.

Dir: Jaroslav Balik.

SP: Josef Balik & Josef Nesvadba.

Cin: Josef Hanus.

Mus: Evzon Illin.

Cast: Rudolf Hrusinsky, Jan Pivec, Vladimir Sloup.

bor-SF (idiot-savant uses missiles to attack those for whom he holds grudges)

Ref: Cineaste March '69.

Idle Roomers

1944 Col 17 mins.

Prod: Hugh McCollum.

Dir: Del Lord.

SP: D. Lord & Elwood Ullman.

Art Dir: Charles Clague.

Cin: Glen Gano.

Edit: Henry Batista.

Cast: The Three Stooges (Jerry "Curly" Howard, Moe Howard, Larry Fine), Christine McIntyre, Duke York, Vernon Dent.

F-H-com (wolfman-like beastman scares the Stooges)

Ref: Maltin/MCT p215; MPW 9 Sept '44 p2090; Pardi.

See also: Three Stooges, The (1934-59); Wolf Man, The (1941).

Ido Zero Daisakusen

See: Latitude Zero (1969).

Idol, The

(story by M. Brown)

See: Mad Genius, The (1931).

Idu Dani

(Passing Days; The Day Comes; The Days Elapse)

1968 Yugoslavian/Italian, Zagreb/Corono Cinemat. color ani 10 mins.

Dir, SP, Design, Ani: Nedeljko Dragic.

Bg: Rudolf Borosak.

F (man terrorized by objects & people)

Ref: Z/Zagreb p43, 44, 46, 98; ASIFA 5; Mamaia '70.

Idyll, The

1947 Amateur (C-16) 16mm color ani objects 10 mins.

Made by: Francis Lee.

exp-abs-F (animated costume jewelry)

Ref: Undrgnd p91; C-16 p 17; USA Exp List.

If--

1916 British, London sil 4800 ft.

Dir: Stuart Kinder.

Cast: Iris Delaney, Ernest Leicester, Judd Green.

bor-SF (plan to destroy London with giant guns & fake airships)

Ref: Gifford/BFC 06242.

If. . .

(Crusaders --e.t.)

1968 (1969) British, Memorial Ent (Par) color seqs 111 mins (110 mins).

Prod: Michael Medwin & Lindsay Anderson.

Dir: L. Anderson.

Story: David Sherwin & John Howlett.

SP: D. Sherwin.

Prod Design: Jocelyn Herbert.

Cin: Miroslav Ondricek.

Edit: David Gladwell.

Mus: Mark Wilkinson.

Cast: Malcolm McDowell, David Wood, Richard Warwick, Robert Swann, Christine Noonan, Hugh Thomas.

psy-F-seqs (several F sequences, as when man previously killed sits up in a morgue drawer in office of headmaster of British boys' school were story is set; much other psy-F)

Ref: MFB Feb '69 p25-26; FF '69 p73.

If All the Women in the World

See: Kiss the Girls and Make Them Die (1966).

If One Could See Into the Future

1911 Italian, Ambrosio sil sh.

F (after woman's son dies the Angel of Life guides mother to Death who shows her what the dead child's future would have been)

Ref: MPW 9:310, 465; F/A p421-22.

See also: Angel of Death, The (1913).

If the Hun Comes to Melbourne

1916 Australian sil sh?

soc-SF (Germans invade Australia)

Ref: Collier.

If William Penn Came to Life

1907 (1908) Lubin sil sh.

F (statue comes to life)

Ref: Views 91:10; LC.

Igra

See: Game, The (1962).

Ikaria XB-1

See: Voyage to the End of the Universe (1963).

Il Était une Chaise

See: Chairy Tale, A (1957).

Il Ne Faut Jamais Parier Sa Tête avec le Diable

See: Spirits of the Dead (1967).

Il Suffit d'Aimer

See: Bernadette of Lourdes (1960).

Ile de Calypso, L'

See: Ulysses and Giant Polyphemus (1905).

Ilê d'Epouvante

(Island of Terror)

1913 French, Eclipse sil 3000 ft.

SF-H (mad doctor engages in experiments in grafting)

Ref: Bios 4 Dec '13; Gifford/ H p30.

Idea similar to novel "The Island of Dr. Moreau" by H.G. Wells.

See also: Island of Lost Souls (1932).

Ilê Mystérieux, L'

(novel by J. Verne)

See: Mysterious Island; 20,000 Leagues Under the Sea (1916).

I'll Be Seeing You

(play by G. Seaton)

See: Cockeyed Miracle, The (1946).

I'll Never Forget You

(The House in the Square--Brit.t.; Man of Two Worlds; Journey to the Past --s.t?)

1951 20th-Fox color, b&w seq 91 mins.
Filmed in England.

Prod: Sol C. Siegel.

Dir: Roy Baker.

SP: Ranald MacDougall.

Cin: Georges Périnal.

Edit: Alan Osbiston.

Mus: William Alwyn.

Cast: Tyrone Power, Ann Blyth, Michael Rennie, Dennis Price, Beatrice Campbell.

F (20th Cent. man drawn magically back to 18th cent; falls in love with girl, drawn back to 20th cent, meets her reincarnation)

Ref: MFB Nov '51 p357-58; Vd 7 Dec '51; FDY '52; SFF p87.

Based on play "Berkeley Square" by John Lloyd Balderston and John Collins Squire from unfinished novel "The Sense of the Past" by Henry James.

See also: Berkeley Square (1933).

I'll Wait for You in Hell

See: Ti Aspettero' all' Inferno (1960).

Illiac Passion, The

1968 Gregory Markopoulos Films (Film-makers' Coop) color 90 mins.

Made by: Gregory Markopoulos.

Cast: Gregory Markopoulos, Richard Beauvais, Taylor Mead, Jack Smith, Andy Warhol, John Dowd.

F (Prometheus meets Mother Muse, his own conscience, Narcissus, Echo, other Greek gods and goddesses)

Ref: FF '68 p 170; BO 9 Sept '68; Vw 17 Jan '68.

Based on play "Prometheus Bound" by Aeschylus.

Illuminations, Les

See: Metropolitan (1958).

Illusion of Blood

(Yotsuya Kaidan: The Ghost of Yotsuya)

1966 (1968) Japanese, Tokyo Eiga & Toho (Frank Lee Int'l) color scope 109 mins (107 mins).

Prod: Ichiro Sato.

Dir: Shiro Toyoda.

Story: Nonboku Tsuruya.

SP: Toshiro Yazumi.

Illusion of Blood cont.

Cin: Hiroshi Murai.

Mus: Toru Takemitsu.

Cast: Tatsuya Nakadai, Mariko Okada [ghost], Junko Ikeuchi, Kanzaburo Nakamura, Mayumi Ozora.

F-H (murdering samurai haunted by ghost of first wife, driven to madness & death)

Ref: Vw 9 March '66, 27 Nov '68; FF '68 p504.

Based on a Kabuki Play.

See also: Ghost of Yotsuya, The.

Illusion Travels by Streetcar, The

See: Ilusion Viaja en Tranvia, La (1953).

Illusionniste Double et la Tete Vivante

See: Triple Conjurer with the Living Head, The (1900).

Illusionniste Fin de Siècle

See: Up-to-Date Conjuror, An (1899).

Illusionniste Mondain, L'

(The Mundane Illusionist)

1901 French, Pathé sil sh.

Dir: Ferdinand Zecca.

F-com

Illusionniste Renversant

1903 French, Gaum sil 150 ft.

Dir: Alice Guy.

F

Ref: Sadoul; DdC II:480.

Illusionniste Toqué, L'

See: Addition and Subtraction (1899).

Illusions

(Threshold 9 Illusions --ad.t.)

1972 feature color.

Compilation film, including the following individually listed films with fantastic content:

Trendsetter, The (1969?); Steel (1970); Birth of Aphrodite, The (1971); She Is Like a Rainbow (1971?); Theta (1971?); Threshold (1971?); Wheel Dealer (1971?).

F-seqs

Ref: LAT 27 Sept '72; ad flyer.

Illusions Fantaisistes, Les

(Whimsical Illusions)

1909 French, Star sil 328 ft.

Prod: Georges Melies.

Cast: Georges Meliès.

F (tricks)

Ref: Sadoul/M, GM Mage 1508-12.

Illusions Fantasmagoriques

See: Famous Box Trick, The (1898).

Illusions Funambuleques

See: Extraordinary Illusions (1903).

Illustrated Man, The

1968 (1969) SKM Prods (W7) color 103 mins.

Prod: Howard B. Kreitsek & Ted Mann.

Dir: Jack Smight.

SP: H.B. Kreitsek.

Art Dir: Joel Schiller.

Makeup: Gordon Bau.

Cin: Philip Lathrop.

SpFX: Ralph Webb.

Edit: Archie Marshek.

Mus: Jerry Goldsmith.

cont.   cont.

Illustrated Man cont.

Cast: Rod Steiger, Claire Bloom, Robert Drivas, Don Dubbins, Jason Evers, Tim Weldon, Christie Matchett.

F; SF-seqs (intricate tattoos placed on man by witch show stories: Earthmen lost on planet of eternal rain; children make playroom lions come to life & kill parents; family of distant future faces prospect of world's end)

Ref: FF '69 p 150-53; SR 5 April '69; MFB '69 p 163; LAFP 11 April '69; Time 4 April '69.

Based on the book and 3 short stories from the book by Ray Bradbury: "The Long Rains," "The Veldt" and "The Last Night of the World."

Ils

(Them)

1970 French, COFCI & ORTF & Co Studios de Boulogne color 100 mins.

Dir: Jean-Daniel Simon.

SP: J.-P. Petrolacci & J.-D. Simon.

Cin: Patrice Pouget.

Edit: M. Tornes.

Cast: Michel Duchaussoy, Charles Vanel, Alexandra Stewart, Vernon Potchess, Pierre Massimi.

bor-SF (old man has machine which enables artist to realize his unconscious dreams)

Ref: Vw 23 Dec '70.

Based on the novel by Andre Hardellet.

Ilusion Viaja en Tranvia, La

(The Illusion Travels by Streetcar; The Streetcar --ad.t.)

1953 (1954) Mexican, Clasa Filmas Mundiales.

Dir: Luis Buñuel.

SP: Mauricio de la Serna & José Revueltas.

Decor: Edward Fitzgerald.

Cin: Raul Martinez Solares.

Mus: Luis Hernandez Solares.

Cast: Lilia Prado, Carlos Navarro, Domingo Soler, Fernando Soto, Agustin Isunza, Miguel Manzano.

F-dream

Ref:FC 21; S&S Spring '55 p 183; Buñuel/Durgnat.

Ilya Mourometz

See: Sword and the Dragon, The (1956).

Ilyich Zastava

1963 Soviet.

Dir: Khutsiyev.

Art Dir: Sergei Gerasimov.

F-seq (23 year old man asks advice of his father who died at age 21)

Ref: S&S Summer '63 p 122.

I'm a Monkey's Uncle

1948 Col 16 mins.

Prod & Dir: Jules White.

SP: Zion Myers.

Art Dir: Charles Clague.

Cin: George F. Kelley.

Edit: Edwin Bryant.

Cast: The Three Stooges (Moe Howard, Shemp Howard, Larry Fine), Dee Green, Virginia Hunter.

bor-SF-com (the Stooges as cavemen)

Ref: LC; Pardi ; Maltin/ GMS p 136.

Remake: Stone Age Romeos (1955).

See also: Three Stooges, The (1934-59).

I Walked with a Zombie (1943)

I'm an Explosive

1933 British, George Smith 50 mins.

Prod: Harry Cohen.

Dir & Sc: Adrain Brunel.

Cast: Billy Hartnell, Gladys Jennings, Eliot Makeham, D.A. Clarke-Smith, Sybil Grove, Harry Terry, George Dillon, Blanche Adele.

bor-SF-com (boy drinks liquid explosive)

Ref: Gifford/BFC 09293.

Based on the novel by Gordon Phillips.

I'm from the City

1938 RKO 66 mins.

Prod: William Sistrom.

Dir & Story: Ben Holmes.

SP: Nicholas T. Barrows, Robert St. Clair, & John Grey.

Art Dir: Van Nest Polglase.

Cin: Frank Redman.

Edit: Ted Cheesman.

Songs: Hal Raynor.

Mus Dir: Roy Webb.

Cast: Joe Penner, Richard

cont.

I'm from the City cont.

Lane, Lorraine Krueger, Paul Guilfoyle, Kay Sutton, Kathryn Sheldon.

F-mus-com (man caused by hypnosis to be great rider; magic acorn)

Ref: FD 28 June '38; Vw, reviewed 8 Aug '38; LC.

I'm Glad My Boy Grew Up to Be a Soldier

1915 Selig (V-L-S-E) sil 4 reels.

Dir: Frank Beal.

cont.

I'm Glad My Boy... cont.

Sc: Gilson Willets.

Cast: Harry Mestayer, Eugenie Besserer, Guy Oliver.

soc-SF (foreign power invades the US)

Ref: MPW 26:2090; LC.

I'm Just Wild About Jerry

196? MGM color ani 7 mins.

Dir: Chuck Jones.

F-com

Ref: David Rider.

See also: Tom and Jerry (1942-).

Im Schloss der Blutigen Begierde

See: Castle of Lust, The (1968).

Im Schatten des Meeres

(In the Shadow of the Sea)

1912 German, Messter sil 1962 ft.

Dir: Kurt Stark.

Cast: Henny Porten, Kurt Stark, Fran Retzlag, Lizzy Krüger.

F (shadow of the sea chooses suicide victim)

Ref: UF p387; f et R d Cin A.

Im Stahlnetz des Dr. Mabuse

See: Return of Dr. Mabuse, The (1961).

Image

1964 Pegasus Prods (Film-makers' Coop) 10.5 mins.

Made by: Robert Shaye.

Mus: Walter J. Carlos.

exp-F ("girl phoenix is raised from filmic ashes" -- FMC)

Ref: FMC 3:56.

Image by Images I-IV

1954-56 Amateur 16mm sh series.

Made by: Robert Breer.

exp-F

Ref: Undrgnd p 129, 131.

Image, Flesh and Voice

1969 Amateur (Film-makers' Coop) 16mm 77 mins.

Made by: Ed Emshwiller.

Dancers: Carolyn Carlson, Emery Hermans.

exp-F

Ref: FMC 5:98.

Image Maker, The

1916 (1917) Thanhouser (Pathé) sil 5 reels.

Sc: Emmett Mixx.

Cast: Valkyrien, Harris Gordon, Arthur Bauer, Inda Balmer, Morgan Jones.

F (reincarnation)

Ref: MPW 31:330G ad, 541, 588; Photo April '17.

Image Wife

See: Riko na Oyome-San (1958).

Images

1972 British, Hemdale & Lionsgate (Col) color scope 101 mins.

Prod: Tommy Thompson.

Dir & SP: Robert Altman.

Art Dir: Leon Ericken.

Cin: Vilmos Zsigmond.

Sounds: Stomu Yamash'ta.

Edit: Graeme Clifford.

Mus: John Williams.

Cast: Susannah York, Rene Auberjonois, Marcel Bozzuffi, Hugh Millais, Cathryn Harrison.

psy-F-H (woman going insane has hallucinations: evil alter ego, dead lover appears, gore murders, phantom dog, etc.)

Ref: Vw 10 May '72 p21; MFB Nov '72 p235; F&F Dec '72 p49.

Images en Negatif

1956 French negative projection 9 mins.

Made by: Eugene Deslaw.

exp-F (shot in negative, shows black snow, doves like ravens, etc.)

Ref: MFB Sept '57 p 117.

Images por Bach

1972 French color? ani 6 mins.

Dir: Jean Jabley.

F

Ref: IAFF '72.

Imaginary Voyage, An

1964 Rumanian, Romfilm sh.

Dir: Mircea Popesco.

SF (trip based on Einstein's theory)

Ref: Gasca p349.

Imaginary Voyage, The

See: Voyage Imaginaire, Le (1925).

Imagination

1943 Col color ani 732 ft.

Prod: Dave Fleischer.

Dir: Bob Wickersham.

Story: Dun (Dan?) Roman.

Ani: Ben Lloyd & Basil David-ovick.

Mus: Paul Worth.

F

Ref: LC; Acad nom.

Imagination

See: Kalpana (1946).

Imago

(To Be Free --rr.t.)

1970 (1973) Joe Magarac Inc. (Emerson --1970; Magarac -- 1973) color scope (83 mins --rr. length)

Producer recut the film in 1973 to de-emphasize the sexual aspects and to rein-force the fantasy scenes.

Exec Prod (rr only): Ruby M. Summers.

Prod, Dir, SP: Ned Bosnic.

Cin: Gregory Sandor.

Mus: Lalo Schifrin.

Cast: Barbara Douglas, Morgan Evans, Victoria Wales, Dick DeCoit, Jenie Jackson, Robert Webb, Buddy Arett.

sex; F-seqs; com-seqs (frigid girl goes to psychiatrist, tells of her dream of being chased by three penis-less men; they become real at story's climax, try to kill her; whole story is dream)

Ref: SF Chronicle 8 Dec '70; BO 30 April '73 BookinGuide.

Immediate Disaster

(A Visitor from Venus --alt.t.?; Stranger from Venus --Brit.t.; The Venusian --alt.t?)

1954 (1956?) British, Princess Pictures & Rich and Rich Prods 75 mins.

Prod: Burt Balaban & Gene Martel.

Dir: B. Balaban.

SP: Hans Jacoby.

Cin: Kenneth Talbot.

Edit: Peter Hunt.

Mus: Eric Spear.

Cast: Patricia Neal, Helmut Dantine [Venusian], Derek Bond, Cyril Luckham, Marigold Russell, Arthur Young.

SF (man from Venus wants A-bomb tests stopped; flying saucer ambushed at climax)

Ref: MFB Nov '54 p 164; FIR May '64 p317; deGroot p225.

Immoral Mr. Teas, The

1958 PAD Prods.

Prod: Peter A. DeCenzie.

Dir & Cin: Russ Meyer.

sex-SF-com (anaesthetic gives photographer X-ray eyes, can see women without clothes)

Ref: Playboy Nov '60.

Immortal, The

1969 Par (ABC-TV) color 74 mins.

Prod: Lou Morheim.

Dir: Joseph Sargent.

SP: Robert Specht.

Art Dir: Bill Ross & William L. Campbell.

Cin: Howard Schwartz.

Edit: David Wages.

Mus: Dominic Frontiere.

Mus Sup: Leith Stevens.

Cast: Christopher George, Jessica Walter, Barry Sulli-van, Carol Lynley, Ralph Bellamy.

SF (man has super-resistant blood making him virtually immortal; millionaire seeks total transfusion by criminal means)

Ref: CineF 4:9.

Based on the novel by James Gunn.

Immortal Goose, The

1909 British, Warwick sil sh.

Dir: Charles Raymond (?).

F-com (goose proves unkillable)

Ref: Gifford/BFC 02178.

Immortal Woman, The

See: Immortelle, L' (1962).

Immortelle, L'

(The Immortal Woman)

1962 (1969) French/Italian/Turkish (Grove Press) 100 mins.

Prod: Samy Halfon & Michel Fano.

Dir & SP: Alain Robbe-Grillet.

Art Dir: Konnell Melissos.

Cin: Maurice Barry.

Edit: Robert Wade.

Mus: Georges Delerue.

Cast: Françoise Brion, Jacques Doniol-Valcroze, Guido Celano, Catherine Carayon, Ulvi Uraz.

psy-F (some elements of pre-destination; confusion of time)

Ref: MFB '67 p88; V 8 May '63; FD 12 Nov '69; NYT 8 April '62.

Imp Abroad, The

1913 (1914) Victor (U) sil 1 reel.

F-com (devil's son)

Ref: MPW 19:216, 290.

Imp in the Bottle, The

1950 Pyramid Prods 16mm 2 reels.

F (wishes granted)

Ref: LC.

Based on short story "The Bottle Imp" by Robert Louis Stevenson.

See also: Bottle Imp, The.

Imp in the Bottle, The

See: Liebe, Tod und Teufel (1934).

Imp of the Bottle, The

1909 Edison sil 750 ft.

F (imp in bottle grants any wish except long life; if you die with bottle in possession you go to hell; it must be sold for less than it cost you)

Ref: MPW 5:729, 759; LC; EK 15 Nov '09 p3-4.

Based on short story "The Bottle Imp" by Robert Louis Stevenson.

See also: Bottle Imp, The.

Impaling Voivode, The

(book by R. Seyfi)

See: Drakula Istanbulda (1953).

Imperceptible Transmutations, The

(Les Transmutations Imper-ceptibles)

1904 French, Star sil 125 ft.

Prod: Georges Méliès.

F

Ref: Sadoul/M, GM Mage 566-67; LC.

Imperio de Dracula, El

(The Empire of Dracula; Las Mujeres de Dracula: The Women of Dracula --e.t?)

1966 (1967) Mexican, Vergara (Col) color.

Prod: Luis Enrique Vergara.

Dir: Federico Curiel.

SP: Ramon Obon.

Cin: Alfredo Uribe.

Cast: Luch Villa, Cesar del Campo, Eric del Castillo, Ethel Carrillo, Fernando Oses, Rebeca Iturbide, Victor Alcocer, Altia Michel.

F-H (beautiful women form court of Dracula)

Ref: PB; Photon 19:44.

Based on a character created by Bram Stoker.

See also: Dracula.

Impossible Blancing Feat, An

(L'Equilibre Impossible)

1902 French sil 82 ft.

Prod: Georges Méliès.

F

Ref: Sadoul/M, GM Mage 419.

Impossible Dinner, The

(Le Diner Impossible)

1904 French sil 133 ft.

Prod: Georges Méliès.

F-com

Ref: Sadoul/M, GM Mage 591-92.

Impossible Meal, The

See: Repas Impossible, Le (1902).

Impossible on Saturday

(Pas Question le Samedi; No Questions on Saturday --Brit.t.)

1964 (1966) Israeli/French, Meros/Athos (Magna) 105 mins (120 mins).

Assoc Prod: Jacques Steiner & Itzhak Agadati.

Dir: Alex Joffe.

SP: Jean Ferry, Pierre Levy-Corti, Shabatai-Tevet, & A. Joffe.

Set Decorations: Joe Carl.

Cin: Jean Bourgoin.

Edit: Eric Plumet.

Mus: Sacha Argov.

Cast: Robert Hirsch, Dahlia Friedland, Mischa Asherov, Teddy Bilis, Geula Nuni, Yona Levi.

F-com (man is told by dead father that he must pay atten-tion to neglected children in order to enter Heaven; Hirsch plays 8 roles)

Ref: FF '66 p39; MFB Feb '66 p25-26; FD 15 Feb '66.

Impossible Voyage, An

(Le Voyage à Travers l'Impos-sible: The Voyage Across the Impossible)

1904 French, Star sil 1414 ft.

Prod: Georges Méliès.

Cast: Georges Méliès.

F (space trip to the sun)

Ref: Sadoul/M, GM Mage 641-61; LC.

Impracticable Journey, A

1905 French, Pathé Frères sil 230 ft.

F-com (man finds each conveyance he tries to ride in turns into a miniature)

Ref: BFI cat p 13.

Impression

1970 Finnish ani objects sh.

Dir: Seppo Suo-Anttila.

F (bottles duel)

Ref: ASIFA 6; Mamaia 70.

Improvisations in Black and White

1952 Danish 4 mins.

Prod: Axel Bruel.

abs-F

Ref: IFC cat p75.

Improvisations No. 1

1948 Amateur 16mm sh.

Made by: Jordan Belson.

exp-abs-F

Ref: USA Exp List; Undrgnd p 116.

Belson's second film; all prints were destroyed by him.

Impulses

1965 Amateur 16mm? sh.

Made by: James Davis.

exp-abs-F

Ref: Undgrnd p96.

Impulsos Ópticos en Progresión Geométrica

(Optical Impulses in Geometric Progression)

1971 Spanish, Actual Films color 9 mins.

Dir: Javier Aguirre.

Edit: J.J. Casenave.

exp-F

Ref: SpCin '72.

In a Box

n.d. Canadian, NFB color ani 4 mins.

Dir, SP, Ani: Eliot Noyes Jr.

alleg-F (man in box gets out, doesn't like it, gets back in)

Ref: MFB Oct '70 p209.

In a Glass Darkly

See: Carmilla.

In a Trap

See: W Matni (1965).

In an Old Man's Head

See: Out of an Old Man's Head (1968).

In Between

1955 Amateur (Film-makers' Coop, Grove) 16mm color 10 mins.

Made by: Stan Brakhage.

Mus: John Cage.

sur-F-dream ("a daydream nightmare in the surrealist tradition" --FMC)

Ref: FMC 5:34; IFC cat p75; Undrgnd p 119, 275.

In Cupid's Realm

1908 Vit sil 600 ft.

F-seq (Cupid appears)

Ref: MPW 2:272; Views 101:2, 8.

In Dreamland

(Nel Paese dei Sogni)

1906 (1908) Italian, Cines sil 387 ft.

Dir: Gaston Velle.

F-dream

Ref: Filmlex p785; MPW 1:622; Scognamillo.

In Gollywog Land

See: Gollywog's Motor Accident (1912).

In India

1967? Hungarian ani sh.

Dir: Zsolt Richly.

F

Ref: MTVM Nov '67 p9.

Based on a poem by Attila Jozsef.

In Like Flint

1967 20th-Fox color scope 114 mins.

Prod: Saul David.

Dir: Gordon Douglas.

SP: Hal Fimberg.

Art Dir: Jack Martin Smith & Dale Hennesy.

Cin: William Daniels.

SpFX: L.B. Abbott, Emil Kosa Jr., & Art Cruickshank.

Edit: Hugh S. Fowler.

Mus: Jerry Goldsmith.

Cast: James Coburn, Lee J. Cobb, Jean Hale, Andrew Duggan, Anna Lee, Hanna Landry, Steve Ihnat, Herb Edelman, Yvonne Craig, Erin O'Brien, Thordis Brandt.

SF (secret society of women intends to conquer the world, begins by kidnapping US President & replacing w/double; suspended animation; gadgets)

Ref: FF '67 p67-69; MFB '67 p 106; Vw 15 March '67.

Sequel to: Our Man Flint (1965).

In Number III

See: III-es, A [spelled Harmas, A].

In Padurea lui Ion

See: In the Forest of Ion (1969).

In Paradise

See: W Raju (1962).

In Passing

See: En Passant (1943).

In Payment of the Past

1916 (1917) Selig (General) sil 1 reel.

Prod: Burton L. King.

Sc: Marc E. Jones.

Cast: E.J. Brady, Robyn Adair, Virginia Kirtley, Eugenie Forde.

F (reincarnation: past & present lives shown)

Ref: MPW 31:131, 546; LC.

In Prehistoric Days

See: Brute Force (1913).

In Room Three

See: III-es, A [spelled Harmas, A].

In Search of Dracula

1972 Swedish, Aspekt color 60 mins approx.

Dir: Calvin Floyd.

SP: Yvonne Floyd.

Cast & Nar: Christopher Lee.

F-H-doc (explores life of historical Dracula, also fictional Dracula, with scenes from some films)

Ref: Vw 3 May '72 p 159; D. Glut.

Based on the book by Raymond T. McNally & Radu Florescu.

See also: Dracula.

In Search of the Miraculous

1967 Amateur (Film-makers' Coop) 16mm color/b&w 30 mins.

Made by: Gerard Malanga.

Cast: Benedetta Barzini, Mario Anniballi, Gerard Malanga.

exp-F ("present and past [of famous Italian family] all intermingled. . ." "the modern-day Dante" --FMC)

Ref: FMC 5:226.

In Slumberland

1917 Triangle Ince sil 5 reels.

Dir: Irvin Willat.

Story: L.V. Jefferson.

Cast: Thelma Salter, J.P. Lockney, Laura Sears, Jack Livingston.

F-dream (fairy advises dreamer)

Ref: MPN 16:865.

In the Barber Shop

(Salon de Coiffure)

1908 French sil 180 ft.

Prod: Georges Méliès.

F (Negro turns white)

Ref: Sadoul/M, GM Mage 1102-03; LC; Views 107:13.

In the Bogie Man's Cave

(La Cuisine de l'Ogre)

1908 French, Star sil 492 ft (350 ft).

Prod: Georges Méliès.

F (bogie man eats boy; fairies; gnomes; seven-league boots)

Ref: MPW 4 Jan '08 p45; LC; Sadoul/M, GM Mage 1035-39.

In the Castle of Bloody Lust

See: Castle of Lust, The (1968).

In the Clutch of the Spider

See: In the Spider's Grip (1920).

In the Clutches of the Hindu

1920 Gaum sil serial.

F

Ref: MPN 22:4015.

In the Diplomatic Service

1916 Quality-Metro sil 5 reels.

Dir & Sc: Francis X. Bushman.

Story: John C. Clymer & Hamilton Smith.

Cast: Francis X. Bushman, Beverly Bayne, William Davidson.

bor-SF (electrical anti-aircraft gun)

Ref: MPN 14:2713; LC.

In the Forest of Ion [John?]

(In Padurea lui Ion)

1969 Rumanian color ani 10 mins.

Dir & SP: Petringenaru Adrian.

F (peasant outwits ogre)

Ref: Mamaia 70.

In the Grip of a Charlatan

1913 Kalem sil 1020 ft.

bor-F-H (fakir with hypnotic powers keeps girl prisoner)

Ref: Bios 12 June '13.

In the Grip of the Maniac

See: Diabolical Dr. Z, The (1965).

In the Grip of the Spider

See: Nella Stretta Morsa del Ragno (1971).

In the Grip of the Vampire

1912 French, Gaum sil 3 reels.

Story: Leonce Perret.

bor-SF (villain called "The Vampire" has drug which turns heroine to idiot; she is restored by movie)

Ref: MPW 14:1252, 1308; LC.

In the Jungle

1957 Polish ani sh.

Dir: Witold Giersz.

F

Ref: Ani/Cin p 170.

In the Kingdom of Dreams

(Nel Regno dei Sogni)

n.d. Italian (Vit) sil sh.

F

Possibly the same film as In Dreamland (1906).

In the Kingdom of Fairyland

1903 Lubin sil sh.

F

Ref: LC.

In the Labyrinth

1966 Amateur (Film-makers' Coop) 16mm 5 mins.

Made by: Bob Liikala.

exp-F

Ref: FMC 5:209.

Based on the book by Alain Robbe-Grillet.

In the Land of Nod

1908 British sil sh.

Dir: Arthur Melbourne Cooper.

F

Ref: Brit Cin p28-29.

In the Land of Nod

1909 French, Pathé sil colored 606 ft.

F-dream (doll turns into fairy; friendly polar bears; Jack Frost)

Ref: F Index IV-14:5.

In the Land of the Frogs

1942 Italian ani sh.

Dir: Antonio Rubino.

F

Ref: Ani/Cin p 137.

In the Land of the Gold Mines

(Nel Paese del Oro --Italian t.)

1908 French, Pathé sil colored 574 ft.

F (imps; fairies)

Ref: MPW 2:402; BFI Cat p22.

In the Long Ago

1913 Selig sil 1 reel.

Dir: Colim Campbell.

Sc: Lanier Bartlett.

Cast: Wheeler Oakman, Bessie Eyton, Frank Clark, Harry W. Otto, Tom Santschi.

F (magic wind pipe restores person from deep, long sleep)

Ref: MPW 16:575; F/A p422.

In the Picture

(story by R. Wilkinson)

See: Three Cases of Murder (1955).

In the Power of the Hypnotist

1913 Gauntier (Warner's) sil 3 reels.

Dir: Sidney Olcott.

Cast: Gene Gauntier, Jack J. Clark, Sidney Olcott.

F (influence of villainous hypnotist broken by his death)

Ref: MPW 17:1398, 18:499.

In the Shadow of the Past

See: Shadows of Our Forgotten Ancestors (1964).

In the Shadow of the Sea

See: Im Schatten des Meeres (1912).

In the Spider's Grip

(Dans les Griffes de l'Araignée: In the Clutch of the Spider)

1920 (1925) French, Pathé Consortium Cinema (Educational) sil colored ani puppets 22 mins (10 mins).

Prod: Ladislas Starevitch.

Rhymes: Morris Ryskind (for 1925 release).

F-com

Ref: MPN 31:1515, 1664; Filmlex p930.

In the Steel Net of Dr. Mabuse

See: Return of Dr. Mabuse (1961).

In the Summertime

See: Durante l'Estate (1971).

In the Toils of the Devil

1913 Italian, Milano sil 3000 ft (2500 ft).

F (pact with the Devil)

Ref: MPW 16:777, 876, 993.

In the Valley of Lions

See: Ursus nella Valle dei Leoni (1961).

In the Void

1969 Dutch color ani 7 mins.

Dir & SP: Ronald Bijlsma.

F (reds vs blues)

Ref: Mamaia 70.

In the Woods

(by R. Akutagawa)

See: Rashomon (1950).

In the Year 2889

(2889; Year 2889 --ad.ts.)

1966? (1968) Azalea (AIP-TV) color 80 mins.

Prod & Dir: Larry Buchanan.

Story: Lou Rusoff.

SP: Harold Hoffman.

Cin: Robert C. Jessup.

SpFX: Jack Bennett.

Cast: Paul Petersen, Quinn O'Hara, Charla Doherty, Neil Fletcher, Billy Thurman.

SF-H (post A-war survivors in valley menaced by cannibalistic human mutants with telepathic powers)

Ref: MTVM Oct '68 p7A; Pardi; B. Warren.

Uncredited remake of Day the World Ended, The (1956).

In the Year 2000

1912 Solax sil sh?

Dir: Alice Guy-Blanché (?).

SF-com-sat (spoof of trend in women's rights)

Ref: MPW 12:660, 832; S&S Summer '71 p 154.

In the Year 2014

1914 Joker (U) sil 1 reel.

Cast: Max Asher.

SF-com (women in charge)

Ref: MPW 19:466, 545.

In Zululand

1915 sil.

Cast: Mattie & John Edwards..

bor-H (daughters disguise as ghosts to frighten man out of marrying their mother; ruse leads to man's execution)

Ref: MPW 25 Sept '15 p2233.

Inafferabile Mr. Invisible, L'

See: Invencible Hombre Invisible, El (1970).

Inakappe Taishò

1971 Japanese, Toho color ani 25 mins.

F

Ref: UniJ 53:36.

Inauguration

1971? Hungarian, Pannonia (Learning Corp of America) color ani sh.

Dir: Marcell Jankovics.

F-com (can't cut ribbon to open bridge)

Ref: ASIFA 7.

Inauguration of the Pleasure Dome

1954 (1957; revised 1966) Amateur (Film-makers' Coop) 16mm color 40 mins.

cont.

Inauguration of Pleasure Dome cont.

Made by: Kenneth Anger.

Mus: (first version) Harry Partch; (second version) Janacek.

Cast: Samson De Brier, Cameron, Katy Kadell, Anais Nin, Curtis Harrington [Cesare, the Somnambulist], Kenneth Anger, Peter Loome.

exp-F (celebration of "magick" with Pan and other figures from mythology)

Ref: FMC 5:15; MFB June '55 p94; Undrgnd p 108-09; FC 31:9, 44:71.

Inazuma Kotengu

See: Scroll's Secret, The (1958).

Inbad the Sailor

1915 (1916) Bray-Gilbert (Par) sil ani & live silhouette.

Prod: J.R. Bray.

Sc: C. Allan Gilbert.

F (genii; magic ring; etc.)

Ref: MPW 27:429, 528, 791.

See also: Arabian Nights, The.

Incantesimo Tragico

(Tragic Spell)

1950 Italian, Epic.

Prod: Toni Roma.

Dir: Mario Sequi.

Story: M. Sequi & Luigi Bonelli.

Cin: Piero Portalupi.

Edit: Guido Bertoli.

Mus: Roman Vlad.

Cast: Maria Felix, Rossano Brazzi, Charley Vanel, Massimo Serato.

bor-F (curse on treasure gives bad luck to finders)

Ref: Vw 23 Jan '52; Ital Prods '50-51 p30-31.

Incanto della Foresta, L'

(Song of the Forest --Brit.t.)

1958 Italian color 65 mins.

Prod: Alberto Ancilotto, Pino Donizetti, Guido Rosada, & Giuseppe Tortorella.

Dir: A. Ancilotto.

SP: P. Donizetti, G. Rosada, G. Tortorella, Enzo Di Guida, & Marcello Piccardo.

Edit: Mario Serandrei & Kenneth Baker.

English Version Prod: J. Henry Piperno.

F (raccoon after magic ring)

Ref: MFB March '59 p37.

Incarnation

(Punarjanma)

1926 Indian, Indian Kinema Arts sil.

myth-F

Ref: IndCin YB.

Incarnation of Krishna

See: Shree Krishnavatar (1922); Krishnavatar (1932).

Incarnation of Vishnu

See: Vishnu Avatar (1921).

Incense for the Damned

See: Bloodsuckers (1971).

Incident at Owl Creek

See: Occurrence at Owl Creek Bridge, An (1961).

Incident from Don Quixote

1908 French, Star sil 355 ft.

Prod: Georges Méliès.

F-dream (armor assumes fantastic shapes, including a spider)

Ref: LC; MPW 3:304; F/A p310.

cont.

Incident in a Glass Blower's Shop

n.d. Amateur (CFS) color 13 mins.

Made by: Byron Bauer.

psy-F (deals with split personality)

Ref: CFS cat '69.

Incindiary of Europe, The

See: Brandstifter Europas, Die (1926).

Incomplete, The

1967 Bulgarian ani sh.

Dir: Zdenka Doycheva.

F

Ref: MTVM June '67 p24.

Inconnu de Shandigor, L'

(The Unknown of Shandigor; The Unknown Man of Shandigor --ad.t.)

1967 Swiss, Frajea 90 mins.

Dir: Jean-Louis Roy.

SP: J.-L. Roy & Gabriel Arout.

Cin: Roger Bimpage.

Mus: Alphonse Roy.

Cast: Marie-France Boyer, Ben Carruthers, Daniel Emilfork, Howard Vernon, Jacques Dufilho.

spy-SF (villain has way to make atomic weapons unworkable; he is devoured by his sea monster at climax)

Ref: Vw 3 May '67; Film Society Review Sept '67 p23.

Inconnue, L'

(The Unknown)

1966 French, Films Gilbert Pascaud 17 mins.

Dir & SP: Claude Weisz.

Cast: Gerard Blain, Paloma Matta.

F (ghost)

Ref: Collier.

Incredible Face of Dr. B, The

(Rostro Infernal: Hell Face)

1961 (1963), Mexican, TEC (Clasa-Mohme & Azteca) 82 mins.

Cast: Jaime Fernandez, Erick del Castillo, Elsa Cardenas, Rosa Carmina.

F-H (automaton; immortal man; black magic)

Ref: CoF 10:46; BIB's Winter-Spring '71; FM 29:46; Azteca.

Incredible, Fantastic, Extraordinary

See: Increvel, Fantastico, Extraordinario (1969).

Incredible Invasion

See: Invasion Sinitestra (1968).

Incredible Mr. Limpet, The

1963 (1964) WB color live & ani 102 mins (99 mins).

Prod: John C. Rose.

Dir: Arthur Lubin.

SP: Jameson Brewer & J.C. Rose.

Art Dir: LeRoy Deane.

Cin: Harold Stine.

Ani: Vladimir Tytla, Gerry Chiniquy, Hawley Pratt, Robert McKimson, Maurice Noble, & Don Peters.

Edit: Donald Tait.

Songs: Sammy Fain & Harold Adamson.

Mus: Frank Perkins.

Cast: Don Knotts, Carole Cook, Jack Weston, Andrew Duggan, Larry Keating, (following voices only:) Elizabeth MacRae, Paul Frees.

F-mus-com (Knotts falls into sea, is turned into (cartoon) dolphin, becomes WWII hero)

cont.

Incredible Mr. Limpet cont.

Ref: MFB Oct '65 p 150; FD 27 Jan '64; FF '64 p48-49.

Based on novel "Be Careful How You Wish" by Theodore Pratt.

Incredible Paris Incident

1968 Italian? color 98 mins.

Filmed in France, Italy, & England.

Cast: Roger Browne, Dick Palmer, Dominque Boschero.

SF (Argoman has superhuman powers)

Ref: United Films Cat '73-74 p80.

Sequel to: Argoman Superdiabolico (1967).

Incredible Petrified World, The

1959 G.B.M. (Governor Films) 70 mins.

Prod & Dir: Jerry Warren.

SP: John W. Sterner (Steiner?).

Art Dir: Marvin Harbert.

Cin: Victor Fisher.

Underwater Cin: Mel Fisher.

Edit: James Sweeney & Harold McKenzie.

Mus Dir: Josef Zimanich.

Cast: John Carradine, Robert Clarke, Phyllis Coates, Allen Windsor, Sheila Noonan, George Skaff, Harry Raven, Maurice Bernard.

SF (diving bell finds strange new set of caves; volcano destroys it at climax)

Ref: FF '60 p354-55; MPH 23 April '60.

Incredible Sexy Vampire, The

See: Horrible Sexy Vampire, The (1971).

Incredible Shrinking Man, The

1957 U 81 mins.

Prod: Albert Zugsmith.

Dir: Jack Arnold.

SP: Richard Matheson.

Art Dir: Alexander Golitzen & Robert Clatworthy.

Cin: Ellis W. Carter.

SpFX: Clifford Stine.

Edit: Al Joseph.

Mus: F. Carling & E. Lawrence.

Mus Dir: Joseph Gershenson.

Cast: Grant Williams, Randy Stuart, April Kent, Paul Langton, Raymond Bailey, William Schallert, Frank Scannell, Diana Darrin, Billy Curtis.

SF (radiation combined with insecticide causes man to shrink, little by little, to microscopic size; battles with cat & spider)

Ref: FM 13:40; LC; FDY '58.

Based on novel "The Shrinking Man" by Richard Matheson.

Incredible Transplant, The

See: Incredible Two-Headed Transplant, The (1970).

Incredible Two-Headed Transplant, The

(The Incredible Transplant --s.t.)

1970 (1971) John Lawrence & Mutual General (AIP) color 87 mins.

Exec Prod: Nicholas Wowchuck.

Prod: John Lawrence.

Dir & Edit: Anthony Lanza.

SP: J. Lawrence & James Gordon White.

Art Dir: Ray Markham.

Special Makeup: Barry Noble.

Cin: Jack Steely, Glen Gano, & Paul Hipp.

SpFX: Ray Dorn.

Special Costumes: Bjo Trimble.

cont

Incredible Two-Headed Transplant cont.

Mus: John Barber.

Cast: Bruce Dern, Pat Priest, Casey Kasem, Berry Kroeger, Albert Cole, John Bloom, Larry Vincent.

SF-H (head of homicidal maniac grafted onto body of giant idiot; horror murders)

Ref: LAT 16 April '71; BO 19 April '71; FF '71 p233-34; MFB Oct '71 p 198.

Incredible Werewolf Murders, The

See: Maltese Bippy, The (1969).

Incredibly Strange Creatures Who Stopped Living and Became Mixed-Up Zombies, The

(Teenage Psycho Meets Bloody Mary --rr.t.)

1963 Morgan-Steckler Prods (Fairway Int'l) color 82 mins.

Prod & Dir: Ray Dennis Steckler.

Story: E.M. Kevke.

SP: Gene Pollock & Robert Silliphant.

Art Dir: Mike Harrington.

Makeup: Lilly.

Special Makeup: Tom Scherman.

Cin: Joseph V. Mascelli.

Edit: Don Schneider.

Mus: Libby Quinn & Henry Price.

Cast: Carolyn Brandt, Toni Camel, Erina Enyo, Ray D. Steckler (Cash Flagg), Atlas King, Brett O'Hara, Gene Pollock.

F-H-mus-com (fortune-teller uses hypnosis to cause man to kill woman who discovered the fortune-teller keeps hideously disfigured old boyfriends prisoners)

Ref: Vw 7 July '66; FanMo 6:18-19; Pardi; Borst.

Incrível, Fantástico, Extraordinário

(Incredible, Fantastic, Extraordinary)

1969 Brazilian, C. Adolpho Chadler Prods scope color seq 190 mins.

Prod & Dir: Cícero Adolpho Chadler.

SP: C.A. Chadler & René Martin.

Cin: Roberto Pace.

Edit: João Romiro Mello.

Nar: Mário Lago.

Cast: Glauce (Glauche?) Rocha, Cyll Farney, Fábio Sabag, Sônia Clara, Walda Oliveira, Paula Priestch, María Tânia.

F-H (4 stories: ghost of mother calls truck driver to save her son; hooded figure accurately predicts deaths; woman who murdered husband haunted by his ghost; corpse grabs grave robber)

Ref: Higuchi; Vw 29 April '70 p 167.

Based on Brazilian radio series.

Incubus

1965 Daystar & Contempo III (in Esperanto) 78 mins.

Prod: Anthony M. Taylor.

Dir & SP: Leslie Stevens.

Cin: Conrad Hall.

Edit: Richard K. Brockway.

Mus: Dominic Frontieri.

Cast: William Shatner, Allyson Ames, Ann Atmar, Eloise Hart, Robert Fortier, Milos Milos [demon].

F-H (good & evil demons)

Ref: Vw 2 Nov '66; MMF 15/16 p 106-07.

Indestructible Man, The

1956 C.G.K. Prods (AA) 70 mins.

Prod & Dir: Jack Pollexfen.

SP: Sue Bradford & Vy Russell.

Art Dir: Ted Holsopple.

cont.

Indestructible Man cont.

Cin: John Russell Jr.

Edit: Fred Feitshans Jr.

Mus Dir: Albert Glasser.

Cast: Lon Chaney Jr, Marian Carr, Robert Shayne, Ross Elliott, Kenneth Terrell, Marvin Ellis, Stuart Randall.

SF-H (murderer brought back to life by electricity; now has super-strength, is indestructible by bullets; overdose of power kills him)

Ref: FDY '57; FIR March '64 p 152; Acad.

Indestructible Mr. Jenks, The

1913 Kalem sil split reel.

Cast: Ruth Roland, John Brennan.

SF-com (man made indestructible survives explosion, being run over by steam roller, bludgeoning, etc, but is knocked out by biscuits)

Ref: MPW 16:82, 380; Bios 29 May '13.

India Rubber Head, The

See: Man with the Rubber Head, The (1901).

India Rubber Man, The

(story by E. Wallace)

See: Return of the Frog, The (1938).

Indian Chief and Seidlitz Powder, The

1901 British, Hepworth sil 115 ft.

Prod: Cecil Hepworth.

F-com (tricks; Indian chief grows to huge size)

Ref: BFI cat p 76.

Indian Legend, An

1912 Broncho (Mutual) sil sh.

F (spirit of betrayed Indian girl who committed suicide returns to haunt lake)

Ref: MPW 14:69, 344.

Indian Scarf, The

(Das Indische Tuch)

1963 W. German, Constantin 90 mins.

Dir: Alfred Vohrer.

SP: H.G. Peterson & George Hurdalek.

Cin: Karl Lob.

Mus: Peter Thomas.

Cast: Heinz Drache, Corny Collins, Ady Berber, Klaus Kinski, Hans Nielsen, Siegfried Schurenberg.

myst-H; bor-F ("fantasy touches" - Willis)

Ref: German Pictures; FIR '66 p240, '67 p82; Willis.

Based on novel "The Frightened Lady" by Edgar Wallace.

See also: Criminal at Large (1932); Frightened Lady, The.

Indian Signs

1943 RKO 2 reels.

Prod: Bert Gilroy.

Dir & SP: Charles E. Roberts.

Edit: Robert Swink.

Cast: Edgar Kennedy, Irene Ryan, Dot Farley, Jack Rice.

bor-F-com (occult; medium)

Ref: Maltin/GMS p 112; LC.

Indian Sorcerer, The

(Le Fakir de Singapoore)

1908 French, Star sil 345 ft.

Prod: Georges Méliès.

F

Ref: LC; Views 120:11; GM Mage, Sadoul/M 1444-66.

Indian Tomb, The

(Das Indische Grabmal; Mysteries of India; Above All Law; The Hindu Tomb --alt.ts.)

1920 (1922) German, May-Film (Par) sil 7505 ft.

Prod & Dir: Joe May.

Sc: Thea von Harbou & Fritz Lang.

Art Dir: Martin Jacoby-Boy & Otto Hunte.

Cin: Werner Brandes.

Cast: Mia May, Conrad Veidt, Erna Morena, Bernhard Götzke, Lya de Putti, Olaf Fønss, Paul Richter.

bor-F-H (hero rescued by yogi-magic; prince intends to entomb wife alive)

Ref: F et R 23; Eisner p350; Fritz Lang in America p 122; MPW 57:449; MPN 26:660.

Based on the novel by Thea von Harbou.

Indigestion, Une

See: Up-to-Date Surgery (1902).

Indische Tuch, Das

See: Indian Scarf, The (1963).

Indiscreet Letters

1909 French?, Le Lion sil 360 ft.

SF (x-rays show contents of envelope)

Ref: Bios 7 Oct '09.

Indra Leela

(Drama of God)

1954 Indian, Mirnal.

Dir: Rajendra Sharma.

SP: Deepak.

Cin: Zamir.

SpFX: Shri Dayabhai Patel, & Shri Kanchanbhai Patel.

Mus: Ajit Merchant.

Cast: Trilok Kapoor, Kuldip, Leela Misra, S.N. Tripathi, Rajendra Singh, Raj Kumar, Indu Paul, Shree Nath.

myth-F (head & body separate)

Ref: Filminda July '54 p93; Am Cin June '57.

Indra Sabha

1932 Indian, Madan.

Cast: Kajjan, Nissar.

mus-myth-F (court of immortals)

Ref: Sound & Shadow June '32 p29.

Inexperienced Ghost, The

(short story by H.G. Wells)

See: Dead of Night (1945).

Infernal Caldron, The

(Le Chaudron Infernal)

1903 French sil 117 ft.

Prod: Georges Méliès.

F (devils; woman explodes; ghost-like figures)

Ref: Sadoul/M, GM Mage; Niver 22; LC.

Infernal Meal, The

See: Repas Infernal, Le (1902).

Infernal Ray, The

See: Nido de Espias (1967).

Inferno

1920 Austrian sil.

F (the Devil)

Ref: Osterr.

Inferno

See: Dante's Inferno.

Inferno in Space

1954 Reed (MCA-TV) 78 mins.

Prod: Roland Reed.

Cast: Richard Crane.

SF

cont.

Inferno in Space cont.

Ref: Willis.

See also: Rocky Jones, Space Ranger.

Infierno de Frankenstein, El

See: Orlak, el Infierno de Frankenstein (1960).

Inflation

1928 German, UFA (Filmmakers' Coop) 16mm 2.5 mins.

Made by: Hans Richter.

exp-sur-F (study of monetary inflation)

Ref: FMC 5:273.

Influential Agent, The

See: Agent à le Bras Long, L' (1908).

Information Machine, The

1957 Eames color ani 10 mins.

Dir: Charles & Ray Eames.

Drawings: Dolores Cannata.

Cin: C. Eames.

Mus: Elmer Bernstein.

doc; F-seq

Ref: FQ Spring '70 p 17.

Ingagi

1930 Congo Pictures 80 mins.

Prod: Hubert Winstead.

Dir: Grace McKee.

Story: Nathan H. Spitzer.

Adapt: Adam Hull Shirk.

Cin: Joyce, Dillingham, & Webster.

Edit: G. McKee & A.H. Shirk.

Sup Edit: William Campbell.

Mus: Edward Gage.

Cast: Charles Gemora [gorilla].

bor-SF (supposedly African documentary, but faked in Los Angeles)

Ref: FD 15 March '31; MPN 26 April '30 p43-44; LC; MPH 13 May '33 p 14.

See also: Son of Ingagi (1939).

Ingmarssönerna

(The Sons of Ingmar)

1919 Swedish sil 2 parts.

Dir & Sc: Victor Sjöström.

Cast: Victor Sjöström, Harriet Bosse, Tore Svennberg.

F-dream (sees Jacob's Ladder in dream, climbs it to Heaven)

Ref: FIR May '60 p270, 271.

Based on first chapter of novel "Jerusalem" by Selma Lagerlöf.

Inhabitant of a Desert Isle

See: Habitant of the Desert Isle, The (1915).

Inhabitants of the Uninhabited House, The

See: Habitantes de la Casa Deshabitada, Los (1959).

Inheritance, The

(Uncle Silas --Brit.t.)

1947 (1951) British, Rank (Fine Arts) 103 mins.

Dir: Charles Frank.

SP: Ben Travers.

Art Dir: Ralph Brinton.

Cin: Robert Krasker.

Mus: Alan Rawsthorne.

Cast: Jean Simmons, Katina Paxinou, Derrick De Marney, Esmond Knight, John Lourie, Derek Bond, George Curzon, Guy Rolfe.

psy-H (sinister uncle plots to kill his terrified niece)

Ref: MFB '47 p 154; FIR Dec '58; FD 6 March '51.

Based on novel "Uncle Silas" by J. Sheridan Le Fanu.

See also: Misterioso Tio Sylas, El (1947).

Inhuman Woman, The

See: Inhumaine, L' (1923).

Inhumaine, L'

(The Living Dead Man --alt.t?;
The Inhuman Woman --Brit.t.)

1923 (1924) French, Ciné-
graphic sil.

Dir: Marcel L'Herbier.

Sc: Georgette Le Blanc &
M. L'Herbier.

Art Dir: Fernand Léger,
Robert Mallet-Stevens,
Claude Autant-Lara, & Alber-
to Cavalcanti.

Cin: Georges Specht & Roche.

Mus: Darius Milhaud.

Cast: Eve Francis, Georgette
LeBlanc, Jaques Catelain,
Philippe Hériat.

SF (opera star revived after
death)

Ref: F/A p409; S&S Summer
'63 p 151; Baxter/SF p 18.

Initiation

1971 Australian 16mm 20 mins.

Dir: Garry Shead.

Cast: Gordon Shead.

F ("ghost story with. . .integrated
New Testament concept")

Ref: Collier.

Injun Trouble

1938 Vitaphone (WB) ani
1 reel.

Prod: Leon Schlesinger.

Dir: Robert Clampett.

Ani: Charles (Chuck) Jones
& T. Ellis.

Mus Dir: Carl W. Stalling.

Voices: Mel Blanc.

F-com

Ref: LC.

Inki

(Little Inki --alt.t?)

1941-4? WB color ani
series.

Dir: Chuck Jones.

Story: Michael Maltese, Dave
Monahan, Rich Hogan.

F-com

Ref: Ani Chart; LC.

See also: Inki. . .

Inki and the Lion

1941 WB color ani
1 reel.

Prod: Leon Schlesinger.

Dir: Chuck Jones.

Story: Rich Hogan.

Ani: Philip Monroe.

Mus Dir: Carl W. Stalling.

F-com

Ref: LC; Ani chart.

See also: Inki.

Inki and the Mynah Bird

1942 WB color ani
7 mins.

Dir: Chuck Jones.

F-com

Ref: LC.

See also: Inki.

Inki at the Circus

1947 WB color ani
7 mins.

Dir: Chuck Jones.

F-com

Ref: LC.

See also: Inki.

Inkwell Imps

See: Ko-Ko the Clown
(1922-29).

**Inn Where No Man Rests,
The**

(L'Auberge du Bon Repos)

1903 French sil 345
ft.

(cont.)

Inn Where No Man Rests cont.

Prod: Georges Méliès.

F-com (drunken guest
sees picture come to life
& objects move)

Ref: Niver/20 p31; LC;
Sadoul/M, GM Mage.

Inner and Outer Space

1960 Amateur (Cinema-
16, Film-makers' Coop)
16mm ani 7 mins (4
mins).

Made by: Robert Breer.

exp-F

Ref: FMC 5:43; Undrgnd
p 131; FQ Spring '61 p34.

Inner Brute, The

1915 Essanay sil 2
reels.

F-H (woman is scared by
tiger; her son inherits
the characteristics of
a tiger)

Ref: LC; MPN 3 July '15.

Inner Mind, The

1911 Selig sil 1000 ft.

F (hypnotist detective)

Ref: MPW 10:549, 312.

Inner Sanctum

1948 Film Classics 62
mins.

Prod: Samuel Rheiner &
Walter Shenson.

Dir: Lew Landers.

SP: Jerome Todd Gollard.

Cin: Allen Siegler.

Edit: Fred Feitshans Jr.

Cast: Charles Russell,
Mary Beth Hughes, Billy
House, Fritz Leiber.

F (a clairvoyant tells
a girl on a train about
a murder which will take
place in the town the
train is approaching,
then it all comes true)

Ref: LC; MPA; FIR Feb
'57 p50; TVG.

Inner Sanctum Mysteries

See: Calling Dr. Death
(1943); Dead Man's Eyes
(1944); Frozen Ghost,
The (1944); Weird Woman
(1944); Pillow of Death
(1945); Strange Con-
fession (1945).

Innverview, The

1973 Amateur color 90 mins.

Made by: Richard Beymer.

Cast: Joanna Bochco.

exp-psy-F (personalized exploration
of consciousness, emphasizing how
movies shape lives, with scenes of
Dracula and Frankenstein's Monster)

Ref: Acad; LAT 29 June '73.

See also: Dracula; Frankenstein.

Innocent Sinner, An

1915 Kalem sil 2400
ft.

Cast: Katherine La Salle,
Guy Coombs.

bor-F-H (woman doctor
villain is hypnotist)

Ref: MPN 8 May '15.

Innocent Witch, An

See: Osorezan no Onna
(1966).

Innocents, The

1961 British, Achilles
(20th-Fox) scope 99 mins.

Exec Prod: Albert Fennell.

Prod & Dir: Jack Clayton.

SP: William Archibald &
Truman Capote.

Art Dir: Wilfred Shingleton.

Makeup: Harold Fletcher.

Cin: Freddie Francis.

Edit: James Clark.

(cont.)

Innocents, The cont.

Mus: Georges Auric.

Cast: Deborah Kerr, Martin
Stephens, Pamela Franklin,
Michael Redgrave, Megs
Jenkins, Peter Wyngarde
[ghost], Clytie Jessop
[ghost].

psy-F-H (in old house
in Victorian England,
new governess becomes
convinced two charming
children are possessed
by malevolent ghosts;
film is ambiguous as
to the existence of
the ghosts)

Ref: FQ Summer '62 p21-
27; FF '61 p337-41; SR
23 Dec '61; NYT 26 Dec
'61; Time 5 Jan '62;
MFB Jan '62 p5.

Based on the play by
William Archibald from
short story "The Turn
of the Screw" by Henry
James.

Insane Chronicle

See: Jester's Tale, A
(1964).

Insect to Injury

1956 Par color ani
sh.

F-com

Ref: LC; PopCar.

See also: Popeye (1933-
57).

Insects, The

(Aviacionnaja Nedelja
Nasekomych: Aviation Week
Among the Insects; Up
to Date Flyers --alt.t?)

1912 Russian sil ani
puppet sh.

Prod: Ladislas Starevitch.

F

Ref: Filmlex p928; Kino
p416; Scognamillo.

Insects, The

1963 British, T.V.C.
color ani 5 mins.

Prod, Dir, Story: Teru
(Jimmy) Murakami.

Edit: Alex Rayment.

Nar: Paul Whitsun Jones.

F

Ref: MFB June '64 p96.

Insel der Seeligen, Die

(The Isle of the Blessed)

1913 German, Union sil.

Dir: Max Reinhardt.

Sc: Arthur Kahane.

Cin: Friedrich Weimann.

Cast: Wilhelm Diegelmann,
Willy Prager, Marie
Dietrich, Gertrud Hackel-
berg, Erika de Planque,
Lore Wagner, Greta Schröder,
Leopoldin Konstantin.

F (island where Greek gods
interfere in lives of mortals)

Ref: F et R.

Inside Daisy Clover

1965 WB color scope 128
mins.

Prod: Alan J. Pakula.

Dir: Robert Mulligan.

SP: Gavin Lambert.

Art Dir: Robert Clatworthy.

Cin: Charles Lang.

Edit: Aaron Stell.

Mus: Andre Previn.

Lyrics: Dory Previn.

Cast: Natalie Wood, Christopher Plummer, Robert Red-
ford, Roddy McDowall, Ruth
Gordon.

mus-F-seq (lengthy sequence
in which new child movie star
leaps from star to star in
the sky, dances on Saturn's
rings, and shoots thru sky
like comet)

(cont.)

Inside Daisy Clover cont.

Ref: FD 27 Dec '65.

Based on the novel by Gavin
Lambert.

Inside the Earth

1910 French, Pathé sil
518 ft.

SF

Ref: MPW 7:142.

See also: Journey to the
Center of the Earth.

Insolent Matador, The

1960 British, Halas & Batchelor
color ani sh.

Prod: John Halas & Joy
Batchelor.

F-com

Ref: Ani/Cin p 170.

See also: Habatales (1960).

Insomniac, The

1971 British, Auriga color
45 mins.

Prod, Dir, SP: Rodney Giesler.

Cin: Tony Richmond.

Edit: Michael Pavett.

Mus: James Stevens.

Cast: Morris Perry, Valerie
Van Ost, Patricia Leventon,
Neville Marten, Sarah Nicholls,
Darren Burn, Reggie Winch.

F-dream (man enters his
children's dream world)

Ref: MFB April '72 p73.

Insomnie

(Insomnia)

1965 French color seq sh.

Dir: Pierre Etaix.

F-H-com-seq (man reading book
about vampires -- we see what
he is reading about; at end
wife turns out to be a vampire)

Ref: CoF 8:47; Photon 19:42.

Inspector Calls, An

1954 British, Watergate Prods
(Associated Artists) 79 mins.

Prod: A.D. Peters.

Dir: Guy Hamilton.

SP: Desmond Davis.

Cin: Ted Scaife.

Edit: Alan Osbiston.

Mus: Francis Chagrin.

Cast: Alastair Sim, Eileen
Moore, Bryan Forbes, Olga
Lindo, Arthur Young, Jane
Wenham.

F (inspector shows how
all at party contributed to
girl's suicide; turns out
the inspector did not exist)

Ref: MFB April '54 p53; Acad.

Based on the play by J.B.
Priestley.

Inspector Mask

1950--6? Yugoslavian, Zagreb
color ani sh series.

Dir: Boris Kolar, Nicola
Kostelac, Ivo Vrbanic,
Vatroslav Mimica.

F-com

Ref: Ani/Cin p 131, 172,
176.

See also: Inspektor se Vratio
Kuci (1959); Gradanim IM5
(1962).

Inspector Returns Home, The

See: Inspektor se Vratio Kuci
(1959).

Inspektor se Vratio Kuci

(The Inspector Returns Home)

1959 Yugoslavian, Zagreb
color ani 10 mins.

Dir & Sc: Vatroslav Mimica.

Design: Aleksandar Marks.

BG: Zlatko Bourek.

Ani: Vladimir Jutriša.

Mus: Kurt Grieden.

(cont.)

Inspektor se Vratio Kuci cont.

F-com (inspector chases fingerprint)

Ref: Z/Zagreb p37, 60; MMF 10/11:82, 84; MFB Aug '60 p 117.

See also: Inspector Mask.

Inspirace

See: Inspiration.

Inspiration

(Inspirace)

1949 Czech, Gottwaldov Studios color ani puppet 12 mins.

Prod: R. Brejcha.

Dir & SP: Karel Zeman.

Mus: A. Liska.

F (artist sees tiny ballerina in rain drop; thistledown clown dances with her; artist makes glass figures of them)

Ref: MFB July '55 p 112; CFS cat Sept '68.

Based on story of Pierrot & Columbine.

Inspiration

(Inspirace)

1958 Czech.

Dir: Karel Zeman & Alfred Radok.

Choreog: Zora Semberova.

Cast: Miroslav Kura.

dance-F

Ref: UNESCO cat p25-26.

Note: preceding two films are possibly the same.

Inspirations of Harry Larrabee, The

1917 General sil 4 reels.

Dir: Bertram Bracken.

Cast: Clifford Gray, Margaret Landis, Winifred Greenwood, William Ehfe, Frank Brownlee.

bor-SF (girl restored to life with new machine)

Ref: MPN 15:2030.

Instantaneous Nerve Powder

1909 French, Pathe sil 282 ft.

SF-com (powder makes everyone happy)

Ref: F Index IV-19·9.

Based on novelette by Howard Fielding.

Insurance Swindlers, The

(#9 in Graft series)

1916 U sil 2 reels.

Dir: Richard Stanton.

Story: Hugh C. Weir & Joe Brandt.

Sc: Walter Woods.

Cast: Hobart Henley, Harry D. Carey, Nanine Wright, Richard Stanton, Hayward Mack, Jane Novak.

bor-SF-H (suspended animation)

Ref: MPW 27:979, 1016; CNW p36, 163; LC.

Interesting Story, An

1905 British, Williamson sil 232 ft.

F-com (man very absorbed in book is run over by roller, reinflates, & continues)

Ref: BFI cat p79.

Intergalactic Zoo

1964 Goldsholl Associates color ani 2.5 mins (5 mins?).

Made by: Morton & Mildred Goldsholl.

F-com

Ref: Ani/Cin p66; IAFF '72; Annecy '65.

Interim

(radio play by T.E. O'Connell)

See: Face Behind the Mask (1941).

Interlude by Candlelight

1960 Dutch (Go Pictures) color ani puppet seq sh.

Prod & Dir: Charles Huguenot van der Linden.

Puppets by: Harry van Tussenbroek.

F

Ref: FIR Oct '59 p482.

Intermission

1971 Farquahar Prods color 16mm 3 mins.

Prod: Marshall Harvey, Bob Rogers, & Steve Boyd.

F-com ("gastronomic orgies with ghouls in ptomaine pantomime" --Genesis)

Ref: Genesis 4.

International House

1933 Par 70 mins.

Dir: Edward Sutherland.

Story: Neil Brent & Louis E. Heifetz.

SP: Francis Martin & Walter De Leon.

Cin: Ernest Haller.

Mus & Lyrics: Ralph Rainger & Leo Robin.

Cast: W.C. Fields, Peggy Hopkins Joyce, Rudy Vallee, George Burns, Gracie Allen, Stuart Erwin, Sari Martiza, Bela Lugosi, Sterling Holloway, Edmund Breese, Lumsden Hare, Cab Calloway, Franklin Pangborn, Baby Rose Marie, Stoopnagle & Budd.

SF-com (eccentric guests in large Chinese hotel watch radio shows projected on wall-sized TV screen)

Ref: Vw 30 May '33; MPH 20 May '33; LC; FDY '33.

Interplanetary Revolution

See: Mezhplanetnaya Revolutsiya (1924).

Interplanetary Tourists

See: Turistas Interplanetarios (1960?).

Interplanetary Wedding, An

See: Matrimonio Interplanetario, Un (1910).

Interrupted Nap, An

1914 Lubin sil sh.

com-F-dream (live statue, etc.)

Ref: MPW 22:536.

Into the Light

(by C.J. Williams)

See: Things Men Do (1921).

Intolerance

1916 Wark Producing Co. sil tinted seqs 14 reels.

Dir & Sc: D.W. Griffith.

Cin: G.W. Bitzer & Karl Brown.

Edit: Rose & James Smith.

Cast: Modern Story: Mae Marsh, Fred Turner, Robert Harron, Sam de Grasse, Vera Lewis, Miriam Cooper, Walter Long, Tom Wilson, Ralph Lewis, Lloyd Ingraham, Max Davidson, Monte Blue, Marguerite Marsh, Tod Browning; The Judean Story: Howard Gaye [Jesus], Lillian Langdon, Olga Grey, Erich von Stroheim, Bessie Love, George Walsh; French Story: Margery Wilson, Eugene Pallette, Spottiswoode Aiken, Ruth Handforth, A.D. Sears, Frank Bennett, Maxfield Stanley, Josephine Crowell, Constance Talmadge; Babylonian Story: Elmer Clifton, C. Talmadge, Alfred Paget, Seena Owen, Carl Stockdale, Tully Marshall, George Seigmann, Elmo Lincoln, George Fawcett (Robert Lawler), Ruth St. Denis; Lillian Gish. Reputed to have been extras: Carol Dempster, Douglas Fairbanks, Herbert Beerbohm Tree, DeWolf Hopper, Wallace Reid, Donald Crisp, Nigel de Brulier, Wilfred Lucas, Owen Moore.

cont.

Intolerance cont.

rel-F-seqs (the Christ story; angels)

Ref: RAF p 191; F/A p521; Barry/Griffith p50. See also: Fall of Babylon, The (1919); King of Kings.

Intrigue, The

1916 Pallas sil 5 reels.

Dir: Frank Lloyd.

Sc: Julia Crawford Ivers.

SF (death ray gun)

Ref: MPN 14:2056; MPW 29:2101; Gifford/SF p70; LC.

Introspection

1947 sh.

Prod: Sarah Arledge.

exp-dance-F

Ref: Exp/Film p 142-43; Undrgnd p91.

Invaders from Mars

1953 National Pictures Corp (20th-Fox) color 78 mins. Probably filmed in 3D.

Prod: Edward L. Alperson.

Dir & Design: William Cameron Menzies.

SP: Richard Blake.

Art Dir: Boris Leven.

Makeup: Gene Hibbs & Anatole Robbins.

Cin: John Seitz.

SpFX: Jack Cosgrove.

Edit: Arthur Roberts.

Mus: Raoul Kraushaar.

Cast: Helena Carter, Arthur Franz, Jimmy Hunt, Leif Erickson, Hillary Brooke, Morris Ankrum, Max Wagner, Janine Perreau, Milburn Stone.

SF-dream (boy dreams of Martian invasion; people controlled electronically; giant green androids; Martian lives in glass sphere; heat rays; flying saucer; note: British prints lacked "all-a-dream" explanation)

Ref: MFB Nov '54 p 163; Vd 8 April '53; Photon 21:22-24.

Invaders from Outer Space, The

See: Invasores del Espacio, Los (1967).

Invaders from Space

See: Super Giant 5 & 6.

Invaders from Space

See: Prince of Space (1959).

Invaders from the Planets

English-dubbed, 51 minute version of Super Giant 3 (1957), which see.

Invaders from the Spaceship

See: Prince of Space (1959).

Invasion

1966 British, Merton Park (AIP-TV) 82 mins.

Prod: Jack Greenwood.

Dir: Alan Bridges.

SP: Roger Marshall.

Art Dir: Scott MacGregor.

Cin: James Wilson.

SpFX: Ronnie Whitehouse, Jack Kine, & Stan Shields.

Edit: Derek Holding.

Mus: Bernard Ebbinghouse.

Cast: Edward Judd, Valerie Gearson, Yoko Tani [alien], Lyndon Brook, Tsai Chin, Eric Young [alien], Barrie Ingham.

SF (alien police & prisoner crash-land on Earth; force-field around hospital)

Ref: MFB June '66 p87; F&F Oct '66; Willis.

Based on a story by Robert Holmes.

Invasion

See: Inwazja (1970).

Invasion, The

See: Invasione, L' (1964).

Invasión de los Muertos, La

(The Invasion of the Dead)

1972 Mexican.

Dir: Rene Cardona.

Cast: Blue Demon, Crista Linder, Zorek, Jorge Mistral, Cesar Silva [Dracula], Luis Mariscal [zombie], Tarzán Moreno [Frankenstein's Monster].

F-H

Ref: Azteca log; MTVM 25:11:11; Arena 9 Sept '72 p20.

See also: Blue Demon; Dracula; Frankenstein; White Zombie (1932).

Invasión de los Vampiros, La

See: Invasion of the Vampires, The (1962).

Invasion Earth 2150 A.D.

See: Daleks — Invasion Earth 2150 A.D. (1966).

Invasion from a Planet

See: Invasion of the Neptune Men (1961).

Invasion from the Moon

See: Mutiny in Outer Space (1964).

Invasion of Astro-Monsters

See: Monster Zero (1965).

Invasion of Mars

See: Angry Red Planet, The (1959).

Invasion of the Animal People

(Terror in the Midnight Sun --Brit. t.; Space Invasion of Lapland --ad.t.)

1960 (1962) Swedish/US, A.D.P. (Favorite Films) 73 mins (55 mins).

Filmed in Lapland.

Prod: Bertil Jernberg.

Art Dir: Nils Nilsson.

Cin: Hilding Bladh.

English language version:

Prod: Jerry Warren.

Dir: Virgil Vogel & J. Warren.

SP: Arthur C. Pierce.

Mus: Allan Johannson & Harry Arnold.

Cast: Barbara Wilson, Robert Burton, Sten Gester, Bengt Blomgren, Ake Grönberg.

SF-H (aliens land in Lapland, their monster escapes from spaceship; after terrorizing some people it is recaptured & spaceship leaves)

Ref: FF '62 p362; MFB Jan '60 p 10; Borst; Pardi.

Invasion of the Astro-Monsters

See: Monster Zero (1965).

Invasion of the Bee Girls

1973 Sequoia Pics Inc (Centaur Pics) color.

Dir: Denis Sanders.

SP: Nicholas Meyer.

Cast: William Smith, Anitra Ford, Victoria Vetri, and The Bee Girls.

SF-H (ads: "ordinary housewives turn into ravishing creatures;" "they'll love the very life out of your body")

Ref: BO 9 July '73 pW-3 ad, 16 July '73 p 14.

Invasion of the Astros

See: Monster Zero (1965).

Invasion of the Blood Farmers

1971 (1972) NMD color.

Dir: Ed Adlum.

SP: E. Adlum & Ed Kelleher.

SF-H

Ref: BO 24 Jan '72, 7 Feb '72.

Invasion of the Body Snatchers

(Sleep No More --e.t.; They
Came from Another World --
s.t.)

1955 (1956) AA scope 80 mins.

Prod: Walter Wanger.

Dir: Don Siegel.

SP: Daniel Mainwaring & (uncredited) Sam Peckinpah.

Art Dir: Edward Haworth.

Cin: Ellsworth Fredricks.

SpFX: Milt Rice.

Edit: Robert S. Eisen.

Mus: Carmen Dragon.

Cast: Kevin McCarthy, Dana
Wynter, Carolyn Jones, King
Donovan, Larry Gates, Pat
O'Malley, Richard Deacon
(uncredited), Whit Bissell
(uncredited), Virginia Chris-
tie, Sam Peckinpah, Dabbs
Greer, Jean Willes.

SF-H (pods from outer space
can duplicate any living
thing; they duplicate people
who then try to duplicate
others in same fashion)

Ref: FDY '57; LC; FM 15:40;
CineF 2:3:16-23.

Based on novel "The Body
Snatchers" by Jack Finney.

Invasion of the Body Stealers

(The Body Stealers --ad.t.;
Thin Air --s.t., Brit.t., tv.t.)

1969 (1970) British, Tigon
(AA) color 91 mins.

Prod: Tony Tenser.

Dir: Gerry Levy.

SP: Mike St. Clair & Peter
Marcus.

Art Dir: Wilfred Arnold.

Cin: Johnny Coquillon.

Edit: Howard Lanning.

Mus: Reg Tilsley.

Cast: George Sanders, Maurice
Evans [alien], Patrick Allen,
Neil Connery, Hilary Dwyer,
Robert Flemyng, Lorna Wilde.

SF (aliens kidnap parachutists
by enveloping them in red
mists, send back non-human
duplicates; suspended animation)

Ref: MFB '69 p 170; LAT 11
Dec '70; CineF Winter '71 p27.

Invasion of the Dead, The

See: Invasión de los Muertos, La (1972).

Invasion of the Flying Saucers

See: Earth vs. the Flying
Saucers (1956).

Invasion of the Gargon

See: Teenagers from Outer
Space (1958).

Invasion of the Hell Creatures

See: Invasion of the Saucer Men
(1957).

Invasion of the Neptune Men

(Uchu Kaisoku-sen: Invasion
from a Planet; Space Greyhound --ad.t.)

1961 Japanese, Toei (Manley-
TV) scope 74 mins.

Prod: Hiroshi Okawa.

Dir: Koji Ota.

SP: Shin Morita.

Cin: Shizuka Fujii.

Cast: Shinichi Chiba, Kappei
Matsumoto, Shinjiro Ebara,
Mitsue Komiya, Ryuko Minakami.

SF (space invaders from Neptune
try to conquer Earth, are de-
feated by alien with superpowers)

Ref: UniJ 14:24; MTVM July
'61 p44; Gasca p301-02.

Invasion of the Saucer Men

(Invasion of the Hell Creatures
-- Brit.t.; The Hell Creatures
--ad.t.; Spacemen Saturday
Night --s.t.)

1957 Malibu (AIP) 68 mins.

Invasion of Saucer Men cont.

Exec Prod: Samuel Z. Arkoff.

Prod: James H. Nicholson &
Robert Gurney Jr.

Dir: Edward L. Cahn.

SP: R. Gurney Jr. & Al Martin.

Art Dir: Don Ament.

Makeup: Carlie Taylor & Paul
Blaisdell.

Cin: Frederick E. West.

SpFX: P. Blaisdell & Howard
A. Anderson.

Edit: Ronald Sinclair & Charles
Gross Jr.

Mus: Ronald Stein.

Cast: Steve Terrell, Gloria
Castillo, Frank Gorshin, Ray-
mond Hatton, Lyn Osborn, Russ
Bender.

SF-H-com (little green men
from Mars have alcohol in
their veins, can inject it
via hypodermic nails; crawling disembodied hand; flying saucer; aliens illumin-
ated to death with hotrod
headlights)

Ref: MFB Nov '57 p 140; FDY
'58; cutting continuity.

Based on short story "The
Cosmic Frame" by Paul W.
Fairman.

See also uncredited remake:
Eye Creatures, The (1965).

See also: Adventures of the
Spirit, The (1963).

Invasion of the Star Creatures

(The Star Creatures --e.t.)

1962 AIP 81 mins.

Prod: Berj Hagopian.

Dir: Bruno Ve Sota.

SP: Jonathan Haze.

Art Dir: Mike McCloskey.

Makeup: Joseph Kinder.

Cin: Basil Bradbury.

Edit: Lew Guinn.

Electronic Mus: Jack
Cookerly & Elliott Fisher.

Cast: Bob Ball, Frankie Ray,
Gloria Victor, Dolores Reed,
Mark Ferris.

SF-com (beautiful alien girls'
plot to conquer Earth with
plant monsters is foiled when
they fall in love with zany
soldiers)

Ref: FF '62 supplement.

Invasion of the Thunderbolt Pagoda, The

n.d. Amateur (Film-makers'
Coop) 16mm color 21.3 mins.

Prod & Dir: Ira Cohen.

Makeup & Costumes: Robert
La Vigne.

Cin: Bill Devore, Diane
Rochlin, & Sheldon Rochlin.

Edit: I. Cohen & Marty Topp.

Mus: Angus & Henry MacLise
and others.

Cast: Rosalind, Robert La
Vigne, Hakim Khan, Pedro
Arbol de Pera, Fan Fan
Sheba, and others.

exp-F (LSD trip film)

Ref: FMC 5:66.

Invasion of the Vampires

(La Invasion de los Vampiros)

1962 (1963) Mexican, Tele
Talia (Clasa-Mohme & Azteca)

Prod: Raphael Grovas.

Dir & SP: Miguel Morayta.

Art Dir: Manuel Fontanales.

Cin: Raul Martinez Solares.

Mus: Luis Breton.

English language version:

Prod: K. Gordon Murray.

Cast: Erna Martha Bauman,
Rafael del Rio, Tito Junco,
Carlos Agosti [vampire],
Bertha Moss.

F-H (Count Frankenhausen
is a vampire)

Invasion of Vampires cont.

Ref: Photon 19:39; TVG; FDY;
PS.

Sequel to: Bloody Vampire,
The (1961).

Invasion of the Zombies

(Santo contra los Zombies:
Santo vs. the Zombies)

1961 Mexican, Tec & Pan-
americana (Azteca) 85 mins.

Prod: Fernando Osés.

Dir & SP: Benito Alzraki.

Story: F. Osés & Antonio
Orellana.

Cin: José O. Ramos.

Mus: Raul Lavista.

Cast: Santo, Lorena Velazquez,
Armando Silvestre, Jaime
Fernandez, Irma Serrano,
Carlos Agosti, Dagoberto
Rodriguez, Ramon Bugarini.

SF-H (masked wrestler & crime-
fighter vs. a mad scientist
who tries to conquer the world
with an army of zombies)

Ref: Gasca p300; FM 33:23;
FDY '63; Heraldo 7 Feb '68.

See also: White Zombie (1932);
Santo.

Invasion of the Zombies

See: Horror of Party Beach
(1963).

Invasion Sinitestra

(The Incredible Invasion --s.t.)

1968 (1971) Mexican/US,
Azteca/Col color.

Prod: Luis Enrique Vergara.

Dir: Juan Ibañez & Jack Hill.

SP: Karl Schanzer & L.E.
Vergara.

Cin: Raul Dominguez & Austin
McKinney.

SpFX: (US seqs) James Tanenbaum.

Mus: Enrico C. Cabiati.

Cast: Boris Karloff, Enrique
Guzman, Christa Linder, Maura
Monti, Yerye Beirute, Tene
Valez, Sergio Kleiner.

SF-H (death ray; gadgets;
invasion by energy aliens; man
into semi-monster)

Ref: PB; Vd 23 April '68;
FM 51:50; B. Warren.

Note: this was Boris Karloff's
last film. His scenes were shot
in Los Angeles in 1968.

Invasion U.S.A.

1952 (1953) American Pictures
Corp (Col) 74 mins (70 mins).

Exec Prod: Joseph Justman.

Prod: Albert Zugsmith & Robert
Smith.

Dir: Alfred E. Green.

Story: R. Smith & Franz Spencer.

SP: R. Smith.

Art Dir: James Sullivan.

Cin: John L. Russell.

Sup Edit: W. Donn Hayes.

Mus: Albert Glasser.

Cast: Dan O'Herlihy, Gerald
Mohr, Peggie Castle, Robert
Bice, Phyllis Coates, Aram
Katcher, Edward G. Robinson
Jr, Noel Neill.

F (mysterious stranger hypnotizes
people in bar into thinking US
engaged in nuclear war)

Ref: Vd 3 Dec '52; MFB June
'53 p84; deGroot p213.

Invasione, L'

(The Invasion)

1964 Italian, Roby sh.

Dir: Camillo Bazzoni.

Cast: Pier Paolo Capponi.

SF (set in 1970; aliens have
invaded & substituted themselves
for people)

Ref: Gasca p339; F&F Oct '66;
S&S Autumn '65 p 174.

Invasores del Espacio, Los

(The Invaders from Outer
Space)

1967 Spanish, Acra 71 mins.

Dir: Guillermo Ziener.

SP: Carlos Serrano & Rafael
Henriquez.

Art Dir: Pablo Gago.

Cin: José Luis Alcaine.

Mus: Luis d' Pablo.

Cast: Angel Aranda, José Maria
Prada, Mairata O'Wisiedo,
Manuel Fernandez Aranda, Inma
de Santi.

SF (Martians put everyone to
sleep then invade Earth; boy
& girl survive, chase invaders
away, helped by chimpanzee)

Ref: SpCin '68 p238-39.

Invencible Hombre Invisible, El

(The Invincible Invisible Man;
L'Inafferrabile Mr. Invisible;
Mister Unsichtbar: Mr. Invisi-
ble; Mr. Super Invisible --
S.E.Asia t.; Super Invisible
Man; Invincible Mr. Invisible)

1969 (1970?) Spanish/Italian/
W.German, P.C. Dia/Edo Cinemat./
Peter Carsten color scope
115 mins (98 mins).

Dir: Antonio Margheriti (Anthony M. Dawson).

SP: M. Eller & Luis Marquina.

Art Dir: Adolfo Cofiño & Aurelio
Crugnola.

Cin: Alejandro Ulloa

Edit: Otello Colangeli.

Mus: Carlo Savina.

Cast: Dean Jones, Gastone
Moschin, Ingeborg Schoener,
Roberto Camardiel, Rafael Alonso,
Peter Karstein.

SF-com (young researcher uses
invisibility "filter" to rescue girl he loves from villains)

Ref: SpCin '71; Trieste '70.

See also: Invisible Man, The
(1933).

Inventeur Acharne, Un

See: Original Locataire, Un
(n.d.).

Invention of Destruction, An

See: Fabulous World of Jules
Verne, The (1958).

Invention of Dr. Wright

See: Dr. Wright's Invention
(1909).

Invention of the Door, The

1972 UCLA 16mm color ani
sh.

Made by: Oscar Pittman.

F-com

Ref: UCLA notes; Greg Chalfin.

Inventions of an Idiot

1909 Lubin sil 295 ft.

SF-com (hair removed & restored; "flymobile" --200
mph flying machine)

Ref: F Index IV-18:10; LC.

Inventor, The

1910 Pathe sil 900 ft.

SF (impenetrable material)

Ref: Bios 29 Sept '10.

Inventor Crazybrains and His Wonderful Airship

(Le Dirigeable Fantastique ou
Le Cauchemar d'un Inventeur)

1906 French sil 197 ft.

Prod: Georges Melies.

F-dream

Ref: Sadoul/M, GM Mage 786-88.

Inventor of Shoes

(Izumitelj Cipela)

1967 Yugoslavian, Zagreb
color ani 9.1 mins.

Dir & Ani: Zlatko Grgic.

cont.   cont.   cont.

Inventor of Shoes cont.

F-com

Ref: Film Com Fall '68; MTVM Summer '68; Z/Zagreb.

See also: Professor Balthasar (1967-69).

Inventors, The

1918 Fisher sil ani sh.

Ani: Bud Fisher.

F-com (peculiar inventions)

Ref: BFI cat p238.

See also: Mutt and Jeff (1916-28).

Inventors, The

1934 Educational 2 reels.

Prod: Al Christie.

Story: William Watson & Sig Herzig.

Edit: Barney Rogan.

Cast: Col. Lemuel Q. Stoopnagle (rn F. Chase Taylor) & Budd (rn Wilbur Budd Hulick).

SF-com (robot "Frankenstein" made out of car parts; it gets out of control)

Ref: LC; MPA '37-38 p 162, 788.

Inventor's Galvanic Fluid, The

See: Liquid Electricity (1907).

Inventor's Peril, The

1915 Lubin sil 2000 ft.

Dir: Joseph Smiley.

Author: Adrian Gil-Spear.

Cast: Lulu Leslie, Jack Standing.

bor-SF (wireless telephone)

Ref: MPN 5 June '15; Motog 5 June '15; LC.

Inventor's Secret, The

1911 Biograph sil 468 ft.

SF-com (automatic doll)

Ref: MPW 10:226; LC.

Inventor's Secret, The

1911 Italian, Cines sil 2100 ft.

bor-SF (super-explosive)

Ref: Bios '12 p61.

Inventor's Son, The

1911 British, Kinemacolor color sil sh.

Dir: David Miles.

SF (diamond manufacturing)

Ref: Gifford/SF p 11.

Invincibili Fratelli Maciste, Gli

(The Invincible Maciste Brothers; The Maciste Brothers)

1964 Italian, IFESA color scope.

Dir: Roberto Mauri.

SP: R. Mauri & Mulargia.

Cin: Romolo Garroni.

Mus: Felice Di Stefano.

Cast: Richard Lloyd, Claudie Lange, Tony Freeman, Antonio De Teffe (Anthony Steffen), Pier Ana Quaglia (Ursula Davis), Gia Sandri.

F (underground city; will-destroying potion; fountain of youth; superstrength elixir)

Ref: Ital Prods '64 p 128-29; MMF 12:37.

See also: Maciste.

Invincibili Tre, Gli

(The Invincible Three; The Three Avengers --ad.t.)

1964 Italian color.

Dir: Gianfranco Parolini.

SP: De Felice, Marrosu, & G. Parolini.

Cin: Francesco Izzarelli.

Mus: Francesco Lavagnino.

Cast: Sergio Ciani (Alan Steel), Mimmo Palmara, Carlo Tamberlani, Lisa Gastoni, Rosalba Neri.

cont.

Invincibili Tre cont.

F (Ursus has superstrength; potion causes Ursus' blindness, another restores his sight)

Ref: Ital Prods '64 p54-55; MFB June '65 p92; F&F Oct '65 p31.

See also: Ursus.

Invincible Invisible Man, The

See: Invencible Hombre Invisible, El (1969).

Invincible Maciste Brothers, The

See: Invincibili Fratelli Maciste, Gli (1964).

Invincible Masked Rider, The

1965 Italian/French, SNC color scope 94 mins.

Dir: Umberto Lenzi.

SP: Gino de Sanctis, Luciano Martino, & Guido Malatesta.

Cast: Pierre Brice, Helene Chanel, Daniele Vargas, Massimo Serato, Aldo Bufilandi, Romano Ghini.

west-F (Zorro-like character who disintegrates at will)

Ref: F&F Jan '66 p30.

Invincible Mr. Invisible

See: Invencible Hombre Invisible, El (1969).

Invincible Sleuth, A

n.d. Italian, Cines sil 470 ft.

F-com (tricks)

Ref: MPW 15:779.

Invincible Spaceman

See: Atomic Rulers of the World (1957).

Invincible Three, The

See: Invincibili Tre, Gli (1964).

Invincible Watari

1970? Hongkong? (in Cantonese) color scope.

Cast: Fung Poh Poh, Chang Kong.

F

Ref: Singapore Straits Times 14 Dec '70.

Invisibility

1909 British, Hepworth sil 650 ft.

Dir: Cecil Hepworth & Lewin Fitzhamon.

Cast: Lewin Fitzhamon.

F ("man buys magic powder which makes him invisible")

Ref: Gifford/BFC no2253.

Invisible Agent

1942 Frank Lloyd Prods (U) 81 mins.

Prod: Frank Lloyd.

Assoc Prod: George Waggner.

Dir: Edwin L. Marin.

SP: Curt Siodmak.

Art Dir: Jack Otterson.

Cin: Lester White.

SpFX: John P. Fulton.

Edit: Edward Curtiss.

Mus Dir: Charles Previn.

Cast: Ilona Massey, Jon Hall, Peter Lorre, Cedric Hardwicke, John Litel, Albert Basserman, Holmes Herbert, J. Edward Bromberg, Keye Luke.

SF (man who inherited formula for invisibility from father becomes secret agent in Germany during WWII)

Ref: HR & Vd 30 July '42; PB; MFB Nov '42 p 144; LC.

Suggested by novel "The Invisible Man" by H.G. Wells.

Sequel to: Invisible Man, The (1933).

Invisible Assassin, The

See: Asesino Invisible, El (1964).

Invisible Avenger

1958 Rep 60 mins.
Filmed in New Orleans.

Prod: Eric Sayers & Emanuel Demby.

Dir: James Wong Howe & John Sledge.

SP: George Bellak & Betty Jeffries.

Cin: Willis Winford & Joseph Wheeler.

Edit: John Hemel.

Cast: Richard Derr, Mark Daniels, Helen Westcott, Jeanne Neher, Dan Mullin.

F (Lamont Cranston can make himself invisible, battles dictator)

Ref: FF '58 p296; FDY '59.

Based on character "The Shadow" from the radio series and Street and Smith Magazine Stories by Maxwell Grant.

See also: Shadow, The (1940).

Invisible Boy, The

1957 Pan Prods (MGM) 89 mins.

Prod: Nicholas Nayfack.

Dir: Herman Hoffman.

Story: Edmund Cooper.

SP: Cyril Hume.

Art Dir: Merrill Pye.

Cin: Harold Wellman.

SpFX: Jack Rabin, Irving Block, & Louis DeWitt.

Edit: John Faure.

Mus: Les Baxter.

Cast: Richard Eyer, Philip Abbott, Diane Brewster, Harold J. Stone, Robert H. Harris, Dennis McCarthy, Gage Clark.

SF (boy reassembles Robby the Robot who has been brought from the future before story starts; evil super-computer wants to rule the world, takes control of Robby; boy made invisible briefly; space station)

Ref: LC; FD 25 Oct '57; SFF p 139; Acad.

Semi-sequel to Forbidden Planet (1956).

See also: Invisible Man, The (1933).

Invisible Claws of Dr. Mabuse, The

See: Invisible Dr. Mabuse, The (1961).

Invisible Creature, The

(The House in Marsh Road -- Brit.t.)

1960 (1966) British, Eternal (AIP-TV) 70 mins.

Prod & SP: Maurice J. Wilson.

Dir: Montgomery Tully.

Story: L. Meynell.

Art Dir: John G. Earl.

Cin: James Harvey.

Edit: Jim Connock.

Mus: John Veale.

Cast: Tony Wright, Patricia Dainton, Sandra Dorne, Derek Aylward, Sam Kydd, Olive Sloane, Geoffrey Denton.

F (poltergeist interferes with murder plot, saves intended victim)

Ref: MFB Jan '61 p9; TVG; MTVM June '66 p37.

Invisible Cyclist

1912 French, Pathé sil 280 ft.

F-com (cyclist while being chased by police becomes invisible with no explanation)

Ref: Bios 1 Aug '12 p iii.

Invisible Dr. Mabuse, The

(Die Unsichtbaren Krallen des Dr. Mabuse: The Invisible Claws of Dr. Mabuse; The Invisible Horror --ad.t.)

1961 W. German, CCC (Manley-TV) 89 mins.

Prod & Story Idea: Artur Brauner.

Dir: Harald Reinl.

SP: Ladislas Fodor.

Art Dir: Gabriel Pellon & Oskar Pietsch.

Cin: Ernst W. Kalinke.

Edit: Hermann Haller.

Mus: Peter Sandloff.

Cast: Lex Barker, Karin Dor, Siegfried Lowitz, Werner Peters, Wolfgang Preiss.

SF (invisible mad scientist)

Ref: MFB Oct '65 p 153; MMF 6:79-80; Gasca p303.

Based on characters created by Norbert Jacques.

See also: Dr. Mabuse...

Invisible Fluid, The

1908 Biograph sil 662 ft.

SF (fluid sprayed from atomizer causes temporary invisibility)

Ref: Biograph Bulletin 16 June '08; MPW 2:531; LC.

Invisible Ghost, The

(The Phantom Killer --e.t.)

1941 Banner (Mono) 64 mins.

Prod: Sam Katzman.

Assoc Prod: Peter Mayer.

Dir: Joseph H. Lewis.

SP: Helen & Al Martin.

Art Dir: David Milton.

Cin: Marcel Le Picard.

Edit: Robert Golden.

Mus: Lange & Porter.

Cast: Bela Lugosi, Polly Ann Young, John McGuire, Betty Compson, Jack Mulhall, Ottola Nesmith.

F-H (Lugosi thinks his wife is dead; she isn't, causes him to kill by appearing, unknown to him, at a widow; he murders in a trance; no ghosts)

Ref: Vd 11 April '41; FDY '42; AHF p92; Borst; LC.

Invisible Hands, The

1913 Lux sil 225 ft.

F-com

Ref: MPW 16:520.

Invisible Horror, The

See: Invisible Dr. Mabuse, The (1961).

Invisible Host, The

(novel by G. Bristow & B. Manning)

See: Ninth Guest, The (1934).

Invisible Ink

1921 Out of the Inkwell Films, Inc. sil ani sh.

Prod: Max Fleischer.

Dir: Dave Fleischer.

F-com

Ref: LC; LA County Museum.

See also: Out of the Inkwell (1919-23).

Invisible Invaders

1959 Premium (UA) 67 mins.

Prod: Robert E. Kent.

Dir: Edward L. Cahn.

SP: Samuel Newman.

Art Dir: William Glasgow.

Makeup: Phil Scheer.

Cin: Maury Gertsman.

Edit: Grant Whytock.

cont.

Invisible Invaders cont.

Cast: John Agar, Jean Byron, Robert Hutton, John Carradine, Paul Langton, Hal Torey, Eden Hartford.

SF-H (invisible invaders from the bodies of dead people and use them to attack the living; invaders destroyed by sound)

Ref: FF '59 p 116; FDY '60; MFB Jan '60 p8.

See also: Invisible Man, The (1933); Plan 9 from Outer Space (1956); Earth Dies Screaming, The (1964); Night of the Living Dead (1968).

Invisible Killer, The

1940 PRC 61 mins.

Assoc Prod: Sigmund Neufeld.

Dir: Sherman Stout.

Story: Carter Wayne.

SP: Joseph O'Donnell.

Cin: Jack Greenhalgh.

Edit: H.N. Todd.

Cast: Grace Bradley, Roland Drew, William Newell, Ernie Adams.

bor-SF-H (telephone used to kill by sound)

Ref: FD 9 Feb '40; FDY '41; Showmen's 10 Feb '40.

Invisible Man, The

1933 U 71 mins (56 mins).

Prod: Carl Laemmle Jr.

Dir: James Whale.

SP: R.C. Sherriff.

Art Dir: Charles D. Hall.

Cin: Art Edeson.

Additional Cin & Miniature Cin: John Mescall.

SpFX: John P. Fulton.

Edit: Maurice Pivar & Ted Kent.

Cast: Claude Rains [the Invisible Man], Gloria Stuart, Henry Travers, William Harrigan, Una O'Connor, Holmes Herbert, Dudley Digges, E.E. Clive, Forrester Harvey, John Carradine, Dwight Frye, Walter Brennan.

SF-H-com (man discovers way to make himself invisible but cannot find a way back; drug used slowly drives him mad)

Based on the novel by H.G. Wells.

Ref: Vd & HR 27 Oct '33; MPH 4 Nov '33 p37-38; FD 18 Nov '33; GC 20:3-12; Photon 23:10-23, 35.

Sequels: Invisible Man Returns, The (1940); Invisible Agent (1942); Invisible Man's Revenge, The (1944); Abbott and Costello Meet the Invisible Man (1951).

See also the following films, based on the concept of scientifically-based invisibility:

Invisible Thief (1905); Unseen, The (1914); Unknown Purple, The (1923); Unsichtbarer Geht Durch die Stadt, Ein (1933); Porky's Movie Mystery (1939); Body Disappears, The (1941); Dick Tracy vs Crime, Inc. (1941); Invisible Woman, The (1941); Abbott and Costello Meet Frankenstein (1947); Batman and Robin (1949); Tomei Ningen Arawaru (1949); Invisible Monster, The (1950); Hilfe, Ich Bin Unsichtbar (1951); Tomei Ningen (1954); Görünmiyen Adam Istandbulda (1956); Invisible Boy, The (1957); Tomei-Ningen to Hai-Otoko (1957); Ramadal (1958); Tomei Kaijin (1958); Day I Vanished, The (1959); Invisible Invaders (1959); Invisibles, Los (1959?); New Invisible Man, The (1960); Invisible Teenager, The (1962); Invisible Terror, The (1963); Asesino Invisible, El (1964); Flashman (1925); Hombre Invisible Ataca, El (1967);

cont.

Invisible Man cont.

Mad Monster Party? (1967); Henry's Night Inn (1969?); Invencible Hombre Invisible, El (1969); Now You See Him, Now You Don't (1971); Orloff y el Hombre Invisible (1971).

Invisible Man Attacks, The

See: Hombre Invisible Ataca, El (1967).

Invisible Man Goes Through the City, An

See: Unsichtbarer Geht Durch die Stadt, Ein (1933).

Invisible Man in Istanbul

See: Görünmiyen Adam Istanbulda (1956).

Invisible Man in Mexico

See: New Invisible Man, The (1960).

Invisible Man Returns, The

1939 (1940) U 81 mins.

Assoc Prod: Kenneth Goldsmith.

Dir: Joe May.

Story: J. May & Curt Siodmak.

SP: Lester Cole & C. Siodmak.

Art Dir: Jack Otterson & Martin Obzina.

Cin: Milton Krasner.

SpFX: John Fulton.

Edit: Frank Gross.

Mus: Hans J. Salter.

Cast: Cedric Hardwicke, Vincent Price [Invisible Man], John Sutton, Nan Grey, Cecil Kellaway, Alan Napier, Forrester Harvey, Harry Stubbs, Ivan Simpson, Billy Bevan.

SF (invisibility drug given to brother of original Invisible Man when he has been wrongly condemned to death; he escapes & brings true villain to justice)

Ref: FDY '41; HR 10 Jan '40; AHF p89.

Suggested by novel "The Invisible Man" by H.G. Wells.

Sequel to: Invisible Man, The (1933).

Invisible Man's Revenge, The

1944 U 78 mins.

Prod & Dir: Ford Beebe.

SP: Bertram Millhauser.

Art Dir: John B. Goodman & Harold H. MacArthur.

Cin: Milt Krasner.

SpFX: John Fulton.

Edit: Saul Goodkind.

Mus: H.J. Salter.

Cast: Jon Hall [The Invisible Man], Lester Matthews, Gale Sondergaard, John Carradine, Evelyn Ankers, Alan Curtis, Leon Errol, Leyland Hodgson, Doris Lloyd, Ian Wolfe, Billy Bevan.

SF-H (criminal forces man who has rediscovered original Invisible Man's formula to make him invisible to carry out revenge)

Ref: Vd 29 May '44; AHF p90; MFB Dec '45 p 152; HoH 1:14.

Suggested by novel "The Invisible Man" by H.G. Wells.

Sequel to: Invisible Man, The (1933).

Invisible Men, The

See: Invisibles, Los (1961).

Invisible Monster, The

(Phantom Ruler --s.t?)

1950 Rep serial 12 parts 24 reels. Also edited to 100 min. TV feature in 1966 as Slaves of the Invisible Monster.

Assoc Prod: Franklin Adreon.

Dir: Fred Brannon.

SP: Ronald Davidson.

Cin: Ellis W. Carter.

SpFX: Howard & Theodore Lydecker.

cont.

Invisible Monster cont.

Edit: Cliff Bell & Sam Starr.

Mus: Stanley Wilson.

Cast: Richard Webb, Aline Towne, Lane Bradford, Stanley Price, John Crawford, Eddie Parker (stunts), Dale Van Sickel, Tom Steele, Frank O'Connor, George Meeker, Bud Wolfe.

SF-H (invisible villain)

Ref: Acad; LC; Willis.

See also: Invisible Man, The (1933).

Invisible Mouse, The

1947 MGM color ani 7 mins.

Prod: Fred Quimby.

Dir: William Hanna & Joseph Barbera.

Ani: Ed Barge, Richard Bickenbach, Don Patterson & Irven Spence.

Mus: Scott Bradley.

F-com

Ref: Elements; LC.

See also: Tom and Jerry (1940-).

Invisible Power, The

1914 Kalem sil 4 reels.

Prod: Melford.

Cast: William H. West, Paul C. Hurst, Cleo Ridgeley, Thomas Gillette, James W. Horne, Frank Jonasson, Jane Wolfe.

F (thought transference; two wills clash for control of girl)

Ref: MPW 22:842.

Invisible Ray, The

1920 Frohman Amusement Corp (Joan Film Sales Co) sil serial 15 parts 31 reels.

Prod: Jesse J. Goldburg.

Dir: Harry A. Pollard.

Sc: Guy McConnell.

Cast: Ruth Clifford, Jack Sherrill, Edward Davis, Sidney Bracey, Corinne Uzzell.

F (new, extremely potent power force from atom; palmistry; hypnotism; magic; spiritualism)

Ref: MPW 43:427; CNW p83-84, 206; MPN 22:1749; Collier.

Invisible Ray, The

1935 (1936) U 82 mins (75 mins).

Prod: Edmund Grainger.

Dir: Lambert Hillyer.

Story: Howard Higgins & Douglas Hodges.

SP: John Colton.

Art Dir: Albert D'Agostino.

Cin: George Robinson.

SpFX Cin: John P. Fulton.

Edit: Bernard Burton.

Mus Dir: Franz Waxman.

Cast: Boris Karloff, Bela Lugosi, Frances Drake, Frank Lawton, Beulah Bondi, Frank Reicher, Walter Kingsford, Nydia Westman, George Renavent, Violet Kemble Cooper.

SF-H (Karloff uses ray from space to locate meteor that fell to Earth centuries before; meteor provides powerful new source of energy & healing rays; touching meteor makes Karloff glow & gives him touch of death; kills enemies by touching them; disintegrates at climax)

Ref: MPH 25 Jan '36 p39; HR 11 Jan '36; SFF p52; AHF p91; Vw 15 Jan '36.

Invisible Revenge, The

1925 Fox sil ani 1 reel.

F-com (solution causes invisibility)

Ref: MPW 76:722.

Invisible Revenge cont.

Based on the comic strip "Mutt and Jeff" by Bud Fisher.

See also: Mutt and Jeff (1916-28).

Invisible Sabre, The

1968? Hongkong? (in Mandarin) color scope.

Cast: Chen Man-Ling, Kim Chun, Yen Howe.

F

Ref: Singapore Straits-Times 21 Aug '68.

Invisible Siva, The

(Siva l'Invisible)

1904 French sil 95 ft.

Prod: George Méliès.

F

Ref: Sadoul/M, GM Mage 546.

Invisible Swordsman

See: Tomei Kenshi (1970).

Invisible Teenager, The

1962 Amateur 16mm sil sh.

Made by: Don Glut.

Cast: Don Glut.

SF

Ref: D. Glut.

See also: Invisible Man, The (1933).

Invisible Terror, The

(Der Unsichtbare: The Invisible Man)

1963 W. German, Aero (R&B) 102 mins (90 mins).

Dir: Raphael Nussbaum.

SP: R. Nussbaum & Wladimir Semitjof.

Cin: Michael Marszalek.

Mus: Jean Thomé.

Cast: Hanaes Hauser, Ellen Schwiers, Herbert Stass, Hans von Borsody, Hannes Schmidhauser, Ivan Desny, Ilse Steppat, Harry Fuss, Christiane Nielsen.

SF (crook obtains scientist's invisibility drug)

Ref: Gasca p349; MTVM June '63 p 15; CoF 11:38.

Invisible Thief

(Les Invisibles)

1905 (1909) French, Pathé sil 377 ft.

Dir: Gaston Velle & Gabriel Moreau.

Cast: Charles Lépire.

SF-com (invisible thief plays pranks, undressing people; gets away at end)

Ref: FI IV-29 p7; BFI cat p27; Filmlex p784-85.

See also: Invisible Man, The (1933).

Invisible Woman, The

1940 U 72 mins.

Assoc Prod: Burt Kelly.

Dir: A. Edward Sutherland.

Story: Curt Siodmak & Joe May.

SP: Robert Lees, Fred Rinaldo, & Gertrude Purcell.

Art Dir: Jack Otterson.

Cin: Elwood Bredell.

SpFX: John Fulton.

Edit: Frank Gross.

Mus Dir: Charles Previn.

Cast: Virginia Bruce, John Barrymore, John Howard, Charlie Ruggles, Oscar Homolka, Donald MacBride, Margaret Hamilton, Shemp Howard, Anne Nagel, Maria Montez, Edward Brophy, Thurston Hall.

SF-com (Barrymore's machine makes Bruce invisible; machine & girl sought by spies)

Ref: MFB June '41 p70; Vd 30 Dec '40; FDY '42.

See also: Invisible Man, The (1933).

Invisible Wrestler, The
1911 Lux sil 340 ft.
F (small challenger becomes invisible repeatedly)
Ref: MPW 9:648.

Invisibles, Les
See: Invisible Thief (1905).

Invisibles, Los
(The Invisible Men)
1959? (1966) Mexican, Chapultepec (Clasa-Mohme & Azteca).
Dir: Jaime Salvador.
SP: R.G. Bolaños.
Art Dir: R.G. Granada.
Cin: Jose O. Ramos.
Mus: Antonio Diaz Conde.
Cast: Viruta, Capulina, Eduardo Fajardo, Martha Elena Cervates, José Jasso, Rosa María Gallardo, Chucho Salinas.
SF-com
Ref: Gasca p237; FDY '67; PS.
See also: Invisible Man, The (1933).

Invitation to a Murder
(play by R. King)
See: Hidden Hand, The (1942).

Invitation to the Dance
1954 (1956) MGM color live & ani 93 mins.
Includes 30 minute fantasy sequence "The Magic Lamp" also released separately.
Prod: Arthur Freed.
Dir & Choreog: Gene Kelly.
Ani Dir: Fred Quimby, William Hanna, & Joseph Barbera.
SpFX Ani: Tom Howard & Irving G. Reis.
Cin: Joseph Ruttenberg.
Edit: Raymond Poulton.
Mus: Rimsky-Korsakoff.
Cast: Gene Kelly, Carol Haney, David Kasday [genie].
F-mus-seq (Kelly as Sinbad in a cartoon world)
Ref: FIR June-July '56 p287; MFB Oct '56 p 126; Acad; FD 15 May '56.
See also: Sinbad the Sailor; Aladdin.

Invitation to the Enchanted Town
See: Sennin Buraku (1960).

Invités de M. Latourte, Les
See: Simple Simon's Surprise Party (1904).

Invocation
n.d. S. Korean.
dance-F (woman marries her dead lover but demons take him away.
Ref: Collier.

Invocation of My Demon Brother
1969 Amateur (Film-makers' Coop) color 12 mins.
Made by: Kenneth Anger.
Mus: Mick Jagger.
Cast: Kenneth Anger, Bobby Beausoleil [Lucifer], Anton Szandor La Vey [the Devil], Speed Hacker, Lenore Kandel, Van Leuven.
exp-sur-F (Black Mass)
Ref: FC 48:1-6; CFS cat sup I; FMC 5:16.

Inwazja
(Invasion)
1970 Polish color ani 7 mins.
Dir: Sefan Schabenbeck.
F
Ref: Film Parade '70 p10-11.

Inyah, the Jungle Goddess
See: Forbidden Adventure (1934).

Ipnosi
See: Hypnosis (1962).

Iradiddio, Lo
1963 Italian color ani sh.
Dir: Pino Zac.
F (all letters of the alphabet transformed into letter "I")
Ref: Ani/Cin p 139-40.

Iro
1962 Japanese, Amateur (Film-makers' Coop) 8mm (16mm) color sil (sound) 12 mins (10 mins).
Made by: Takahiko Iimura.
exp-abs-F
Ref: FMC 5:161.

Iron Claw, The
1916 Pathé sil serial 20 parts 40 reels.
Dir: Edward José.
Sc: George Brackett Seitz.
Cast: Pearl White, Creighton Hale, Sheldon Lewis, Harry Fraser, J.E. Dunn.
F-H (ghosts; electric ray projector sets building on fire; face branded; bacillus rapidly ages villain)
Ref: MPW 27:1491, 1894-95, 2084, 28:1351; NYT 1 March '36; CNW p42, 169-70; LC.

Iron Claw, The
1941 Darmour (Col) serial 15 parts 31 reels.
Prod: Larry Darmour.
Dir: James W. Horne.
Story: Arthur Stringer.
SP: Basil Dickey, George H. Plympton, Jesse A. Duffy, Charles R. Condon, & Jack Stanley.
Cin: James S. Brown Jr.
Edit: Dwight Caldwell & Earl Turner.
Mus: Lee Zahler.
Cast: Charles Quigley, Joyce Bryant, Forrest Taylor, Walter Sande, Norman Willis, Alex Callam, James Metcalfe, James Morton.
bor-H (villain has grotesque steel hook for hand)
Ref: Acad; LC; Stringham; D. Glut.

Based on story by Arthur Stringer.

Iron Crown, The
See: Corona di Ferro, La (1941).

Iron Fan and Magic Sword
1970 Hongkong (in Mandarin) Shaw color scope.
F
Ref: Singapore Straits-Times 16 Oct '70; LAT 28 July '71.

Iron Helmet, The
(Zelezný Klobouk: The Tin Hat)
1960 Czech 16mm color ani 10 mins.
Dir, Sc, Ani: Josef Kábrt.
Story: Slavomir Mrozek.
Mus: Jan Bedrich.
F (hen lays eggs in War's helmet; he tries to get it back, turns into moth & eagle)
Ref: MFB Nov '63 p 164; Ani/Cin p 128.

Iron Horse, The
1968 Hongkong, Cathay (Mercury) color scope 102 mins.
Dir: Yuan Chiu-Feng.
Cast: Chao Lei, Chiang Hung, Kelly Kai Chen.
F-seqs (mystic martial arts)
Ref: Mercury folder.

Is Conan Doyle Right?
1923 Pathé sil 2 reels.
Dir: John J. Harvey.
Sc: Cullom Holmes Ferrell.
doc; F-seqs (shows how to fake spiritualism)
Ref: MPN 28:1661; NYT 3 Oct '23 p26.

Is There a Lion in Your House?
See: Do You Keep a Lion at Home? (1963).

Is There Sex After Death?
1971 Abel-Child (U-M Film) color 97 mins.
Prod, Dir, SP: Jeanne & Alan Abel.
Assoc Prod: Michael Rothschild.
Cin: Gerald Cotts.
Edit: J. Abel.
Cast: Buck Henry, Alan Abel, Marshall Efron, Holly Woodlawn, Robert Downey, Jim Moran, Rubin Carson, Larry Wolf [ghost].
sex-com; F-seq (title question answered in affirmative by ghost; magician makes women's clothes disappear)
Ref: Vw 3 Nov '71 p 16; FF '71 p570-72.

Is This Trip Really Necessary?
(Blood of the Iron Maiden --s.t.)
1969? Dorn-Thor (Hollywood Star) color.
Exec Prod: Ray Dorn & Lynn Steed.
Prod & Dir: Ben Benoit.
SP: Lee Kalcheim.
Art Dir: Ray Markham.
Makeup & Costumes: Dodie Warren.
Cin: Austin McKinney.
SpFX: Bob Beck.
Edit: Fred Brown.
Mus: Paul Norman, Ron Blackmer, & Bob Page.
Cast: Marvin Miller, Carol Kane, Peter Duryea, John Carradine, Barbara Mallory, Pat Heider.
sex-H (torture chamber; death in iron maiden; mad scientist; LSD trips)
Ref: Eric Hoffman from PB.

Isabel
1968 Canadian, Quest Prod. (Par) color 108 mins.
Prod, Dir, SP: Paul Almond.
Makeup: Michel Duruelle.
Cin: Georges Dufaux.
Edit: George R. Appleby.
Mus: Harry Freedman.
Cast: Genevieve Bujold, Mark Strange, Gerald Parkes, Elton Hayes, Albert Waxman.
psy-F-seqs (neurotic woman sees apparitions)
Ref: SR 17 Aug '68; FF '68 p310; Vw 24 July '68.

Isabell, a Dream
1958? Italian.
Dir: Luigi Cozzi.
F-H-dream (women rule; hunt Mummy, Dracula, & Frankenstein Monster in forest)
Ref: FM 54:8; Photon 21:29; D. Glut.
See also: Dracula (1930); Frankenstein; Mummy, The (1932).

Ishimatsu Travels with Ghosts
See: Mori no Ishimatsu Yurei Dochu (1959).

Ishwar Bhakti
(Devotee to Ishwar)
1951 Indian, Shree Shyama Chitra 148 mins.
Prod: R.B. Haldia.
Dir & SP: Dada Gunjal.

cont.

Ishwar Bhakti cont.
Cin: D.K. Ambre.
Edit: Narayan Rao.
Mus Dir: Sonik Girdhar.
Cast: Nirupta Roy, Trilok Kapur, Urvashi, Shalini, Nandkishore.
myth-F
Ref: Indian MPA '53 p42.

Isidro el Labrador
(Isidro the Peasant)
1963 Spanish.
Dir: Rafael J. Salvia.
SP: Jaime G. Herranz.
Art Dir: Sigfrido Burman.
Mus: Salvador Ruiz de Luna.
Cast: Javier Escriva, Maria Mahor, Roberto Camardiel, Rafael Duran.
rel-F (God rewards Isidro by causing his wheat to yield an enormous amount of flour, & rescues his son from a well; Isidro made saint 500 years later)
Ref: SpCin '64 p94-95.

Isis
1910 French, Pathé sil sh.
F (when man rejects girl chosen for him by Isis the Moon Goddess, she assumes human form, causes him to fall in love with her, and leaves him)
Ref: MPW 7:1247; F/A p422.

Isla de la Muerte, La
See: Island of the Doomed (1966).

Isla de los Dinosaurios, La
(Dinosaur Island, The Island of the Dinosaurs)
1966 (1967) Mexican, Cinemitografica Calderon & Hal Roach (Azteca).
Uses extensive stock footage from One Million B.C. (1940).
Prod: G. Calderon Stell.
Dir: Rafael Lopez Portillo.
SP: Alfredo Salazar.
Cast: Armando Sivestre, Alma Delia Fuentes, Elsa Cardenas, Jenaro Moreno, Manolo Fabregas, Crox Alvarado, Regina Torne, Roberto Canedos (Canedo?), Tito Junco.
SF (island with dinosaurs & cave men on it discovered by modern-day explorers)
Ref: PS A1312; MMF 18-19:15; FDY '68; MTVM July '66 p32.
See also: One Million B.C. (1940).

Island at the Top of the World, The
1973? WD (BV) color.
Prod: Winston Hibler.
Dir: Robert Stevenson.
SP: John Whedon & Harry Spalding.
Art Dir: John Mansbridge, Walter Tyler, & Al Roelofs.
Cin: Frank Phillips.
Cast: David Hartman, Donald Sinden, Jacques Marin, Agneta Eckemyr.
SF (3 explorers discover lost tribe of Vikings on volcanic island at the North Pole)
Ref: BO 27 Sept '71; HR 11 May '73 p 18.
Based on novel "The Lost Ones" by Ian Cameron.

Island of Dr. Moreau, The
(novel by H.G. Wells)
See: Ilê d'Epouvante (1913); Island of Lost Souls (1932).

Island of Lost Souls

(The Island of Dr. Moreau
--e.t.)
1932 (1933) Par 8 reels
(72 mins).

Dir: Erle C. Kenton.

SP: Waldemar Young & Philip
Wylie.

Art Dir: Hans Dreier.(?)

Makeup: Wally Westmore. (?)

Cin: Karl Struss.

SpFX: Gordon Jennings. (?)

Cast: Charles Laughton,
Richard Arlen, Leila Hyams,
Kathleen Burke [panther
woman], Arthur Hohl, Stanley
Fields, Robert Kortman, Tetsu
Komai, Hans Steinke, Paul
Hurst, George Irving; [the
following played beast-men]
Bela Lugosi, Duke York, John
George, Alan Ladd, Randolph
Scott.

SF-H (mad scientist Laughton
is trying to surgically turn
wild animals into human beings;
tries to get Arlen to fall in
love with Burke, a former
panther; beast-men turn on
Laughton at end)

Ref: FDY '33, '34; MPH 10
Dec '32 p48, 50; Ackerman.

Based on novel "The Island
of Dr. Moreau" by H.G. Wells.

See also: Ilê d'Epouvante
(1913); Terror Is a Man
(1959); Twilight People
(1971).

Island of Lost Women

1959 Jaguar (WB) 71 mins
(66 mins).

Exec Prod: Alan Ladd.

Prod: Albert J. Cohen.

Dir: Frank W. Tuttle.

Story: Prescott Chaplain.

SP: Ray Buffum.

Art Dir: Jack Collis.

Cin: John Seitz.

Edit: Roland Gross.

Mus: Raul Kraushaar.

Cast: Jeff Richards, Venetia
Stevenson, John Smith, Diane
Jergens, June Blair, Alan
Napier, Gavin Muir, George
Brand.

bor-SF (men find island with
scientist & his daughters;
super-radar; long-distance
flame-throwing pistol; deadly
rays)

Ref: BO 20 April '59; FF
'59 p 109; FD 10 April '59.

Island of Surprise, The

1916 Vit sil 5 reels.

Dir: Paul Scardon.

Sc: Cyrus Townsend Brady.

Cast: Eleanor Woodruff,
William Courtenay, Anders
Randolf, Julia Swayne Gordon.

F-seq (being struck by lightning gives man amnesia)

Ref: MPN 13:718; LC.

Island of Terror

(The Creepers; Night of the
Silicates; Night the Creatures
Came; Night the Silicates Came;
The Silicates --all e.ts or s.ts)
1966 (1967) British, Planet (U)
color 89 mins.

Exec Prod: Richard Gordon.

Prod: Tom Blakeley.

Dir: Terence Fisher.

SP: Alan Ramsen & Edward
Andrew Mann.

Art Dir & SpFX: John St. John
Earl.

Cin: Reg Wyer.

Edit: Thelma Connell.

Electronic FX: Barry Gray.

Mus: Malcolm Lockyer.

cont.

Island of Terror cont.

Cast: Peter Cushing, Edward
Judd, Carole Gray, Eddie
Byrne, Sam Kydd, Niall
MacGinnis, James Caffrey,
Liam Caffney, Roger Heathcote.

SF-H (cancer research spawns
crawling, tentacled & nearly
indestructible creatures which
eat bones out of people)

Ref: FF '67 p 143; MFB '66
p 109; FM 42:4; F&F Aug '66
p 10g; FD 24 Aug '66.

Island of Terror
See: Ilê d'Epouvante (1913).

Island of the Burning Damned

(Night of the Big Heat --
Brit.t.; Island of the Burning Doomed --tv.t.)
1967 (1971) British, Planet
color 94 mins.

Prod: Tom Blakeley.

Dir: Terence Fisher.

SP: Ronald Liles, & Pip &
Jane Baker.

Art Dir: Alex Vetchinsky.

Cin: Reg Wyer.

Edit: Rod Keys.

Mus: Malcolm Lockyer.

Cast: Christopher Lee, Peter
Cushing, Patrick Allen, Sarah
Lawson, Jane Merrow, William
Lucas, Percy Herbert.

SF-H (globular alien creatures
cause heatwave on British
island during winter, kill
people by burning)

Ref: MFB '67 p 190; FM
48:7; F&F Feb '68 p27.

Based on novel "Night of
the Big Heat" by John
Lymington.

Island of the Burning Doomed
See: Island of the Burning
Damned (1967).

Island of the Dead
See: Isle of the Dead (1913).

Island of the Dead, The
See: Island of the Doomed
(1966).

Island of the Dinosaurs, The
See: Isla de los Dinosaurios,
La (1966).

Island of the Doomed

(La Isla de la Muerte: Island
of the Dead; Man Eater of
Hydra --tv.t.; The Blood
Suckers --Brit.t.)
1966 (1968) Spanish/W.German,
Orbita/Theumer (AA) color
scope 88 mins.

Prod: George Ferrer.

Dir: Mel Welles.

Assist Dir: F. Wessling.

Story: Ira Meltcher & F.V.
Theumer.

SP: Stephen Schmidt.

Art Dir: Francisco Canet.

Cin: Cecilio Paniagua.

Edit: Antonio Canovas.

Mus: Anton Garcia Abril.

Cast: Cameron Mitchell, Elisa
Montes, Jorge Martin (George
Martin), Kai Fischer (Kay
Fischer), Rolf V. Naukoff
(Ralph Naukoff), Matilde
Munoz.

SF-H (mad scientist on island
has created a vampire tree
with long, tentacle-like
branches that suck blood
from people)

Ref: FF '68 p22; Vw 31 Jan
'68; SpCin '67 p 168-69.

Island of the Fay, The

(story by E.A. Poe)
See: Isle of Oblivion (1917).

Island of the Twilight People
See: Twilight People (1971).

Isle of Lost Ships, The

● 1923 M.C. Levee (FN) sil
7425 ft.

Pres: M.C. Levee.

Prod: Ned Marin.

Dir: Maurice Tourneur.

Sc: Charles Maigne.

Sets: Milton Menasco.

Cin: Arthur L. Todd.

Edit: Frank Lawrence.

Cast: Anna Q. Nilsson, Milton
Sills, Frank Campeau, Walter
Long, Bert Woodruff, Aggie
Herring, Herschel Mayall.

Ref: AFI F2.2757 p387-88;
MPN 27:1454; LC.

● 1929 FN released in sil &
sound versions 7576 ft.

Pres: Richard A. Rowland.

Dir: Irvin Willat.

Sc: Fred Myton.

Titles & Dialog: Paul Perez
& F. Myton.

Cin: Sol Polito.

Edit: John Rawlins.

Cast: Jason Robards (Sr),
Virginia Valli, Clarissa
Selwynne, Noah Beery, Robert
E. O'Connor, Harry Cording,
Margaret Fielding, Sam Baker.

Ref: AFI F2.2758 p388; Vw
30 Oct '29; MPN 41:11:88.

SF (shipwreck caught in
Sargasso Sea; battle with
band of survivors who live
on the wrecks; escape via
submarine)

Based on novel "The Isle
of Dead Ships" by Crittenden
Marriott.

See also: Lost Continent,
The (1968).

Isle of Oblivion

(Ostrov Zabvenya)
1917 Russian, Biofilm sil
5 reels.

Dir: Vyacheslav Turzhansky.

Sc: Lev Nikulin.

Art Dir: V. Rakovsky.

Cin: F. Verigo-Darovsky.

Cast: Vyacheslav Turzhansky,
Y. Chaika, V. Elsky.

F

Ref: Kino p422; FIR Oct '61
p466.

Based on a story, possibly
"The Island of the Fay," by
Edgar Allan Poe.

Isle of the Blessed, The
See: Insel der Seeligen, Die
(1913).

Isle of the Dead [, The]

● (The Island of the Dead --
ad.t.; De Dodes O)
1913 Danish, Danmark Studios
sil.

Dir: Wilhelm Gluckstadt.

Sc: Palle Rosenkrantz.

F

Ref: Neergaard p45-46; DdC
II:315; Hardy/Scan p2.

● 1945 RKO 72 mins.

Exec Prod: Jack Gross.

Prod: Val Lewton.

Dir: Mark Robson.

SP: Ardel Wray & Josef
Mischel.

Art Dir: Albert D'Agostino
& Walter E. Keller.

Cin: Jack MacKenzie.

Edit: Lyle Boyer.

Mus: Leigh Harline.

Mus Dir: C. Bakaleinikoff.

Cast: Boris Karloff, Ellen
Drew, Marc Cramer, Katherine
Emery, Helene Thimig, Alan
Napier, Jason Robards (Sr).

cont.

Isle of the Dead cont.

psy-H (plague borne by wind
exiles group to island; girl
believed to be "vrykolaka;"
woman buried in cataleptic
state escapes, goes insane)

Ref: Vd 7 Sept '45; AHF p233;
Agee p175, 187; FDY '46.

Suggested by the painting
by Arnold Böcklin.

See also: Little Phantasy
on a 19th Century Painting,
A (1946).

Isle of the Snake People
See: Snake People (1968).

Ismail Yassine as Tarzan
See: Ismail Yassine Tarazane
(1958).

Ismail Yassine Tarazane

(Ismail Yassine as Tarzan)
1958 Egyptian.

Dir: Niazi Mustapha.

bor-F

Ref: Arab Cin p282.

See also: Harem Alek (1953);
Tarzan.

Isolated House, The

1915 British?, Victory Films
(Pathe) sil 3 reels.

bor-SF (pocket wireless;
submersible house)

Ref: MPN 17 July '15 p 118;
MPW 25:904; LC.

Based on character Sherlock
Holmes created by Arthur
Conan Doyle.

See also: Sherlock Holmes.

Isotope Man, The

(novel by C.E. Maine)
See: Atomic Man, The (1956).

Issun Boshi

(The Mighty Dwarf;
Issumboshi?)
1959 Japanese, Toei ani
15 mins.

F (tiny knight in Kyoto saves
people from monster)

Ref: FEFN 12:16-17:45; Collier.

It!

(The Curse of the Golem --s.t.)
1966 (1967) British/US, Gold-
star/7 Arts color 97 mins.

Filmed in England.
Exec Prod: Robert Goldstein.

Prod, Dir, SP: Herbert J. Leder.

Art Dir: Scott MacGregor.

Cin: David Boulton.

Edit: Tom Simpson.

Mus: Carlo Martelli.

Cast: Roddy McDowall, Jill
Haworth, Paul Maxwell, Aubrey
Richards, Ernest Clark, Oliver
Johnston, Noel Trevarthen,
Alan Sellers [Golem].

F-H (insane museum curator
McDowall, who keeps mummified
body of his mother at home,
discovers that new statue is
the Golem, uses it to destroy
London Bridge; summons Golem
by telepathy; A-Bomb destroys
McDowall but not Golem, which
walks into the sea)

Ref: MFB '67 p 157-58; FF '67
p366; Vw 20 Sept '67.

See also: Golem, The.

It
See: It! The Terror from
Beyond Space (1958).

It Came from Beneath the Sea

1955 Col 77 mins.

Exec Prod: Sam Katzman.

Prod: Charles H. Schneer.

Dir: Robert Gordon.

Story: George Worthing Yates.

SP: G.W. Yates & Hal Smith.

Art Dir: Paul Palmentola.

cont

Island of Lost Souls (1932)

It Came from Beneath the Sea cont.

Cin: Henry Freulich.

SpFX: Ray Harryhausen & Jack Erickson.

Edit: Jerome Thoms.

Mus Dir: Mischa Bakaleinikoff.

Cast: Kenneth Tobey, Faith Domergue, Donald Curtis, Ian Keith, Harry Lauter, R. Peterson, Dean Maddox Jr, Del Courtney.

SF-H (gigantic octopus has become radioactive, can't eat usual prey, goes after men; destroys Golden Gate Bridge & other San Francisco landmarks; destroyed by electronic torpedo)

Ref: MFB July '55 p 107; FDY '56; F&SF Dec '55 p69; LC.

It Came from Outer Space

1953 U 3D 80 mins.

Prod: William Alland.

Dir: Jack Arnold.

SP: Harry Essex.

Art Dir: Bernard Herzbrun & Robert Boyle.

Makeup: Bud Westmore.

Cin: Clifford Stine.

SpFX Cin: David S. Horsley.

Edit: Paul Weatherwax.

Mus: Herman Stein.

Mus Dir: Joseph Gershenson.

Cast: Richard Carlson, Barbara Rush, Charles Drake, Russell Johnson, Kathleen Hughes,

cont.

It Came from Outer Space cont.
Joe Sawyer, Alan Dexter, Dave Willock, George Eldridge, Morey Amsterdam.

SF (ugly aliens land to repair ship; they have power to make themselves look like any person; one is ruthless, uses ray gun)

Ref: Vd 21 May '53; FDY '54; MFB Oct '53 p 143; SFF p97.

Based on screen treatment "The Meteor" by Ray Bradbury.

It Conquered the World

(It Conquered the Earth --s.t.)

1956 Sunset (AIP) 71 mins.

Exec Prod: James Nicholson.

Prod & Dir: Roger Corman.

SP: Lou Rusoff.

Cin: Frederick West.

SpFX: Paul Blaisdell.

Edit: Charles Gross.

Mus: Ronald Stein.

Cast: Peter Graves, Beverly Garland, Lee Van Cleef, Sally Fraser, Charles B. Griffith, Russ Bender, Jonathan Haze, Richard Miller, Karen Kadler, Paul Blaisdell [monster].

SF-H (monster arrives from Venus in flying saucer, guided by Earthman; takes over minds of Earth people by having its batlike flying things sting them in the neck)

Ref: MFB Nov '56 p 141; Corman p92; F&SF March '57 p74; PB.

cont.

It Conquered World cont.

See also uncredited remake: Zontar, the Thing from Venus (1966).

It Fell from the Flame Barrier
See: Flame Barrier, The (1958).

It Grows on Trees

1952 U 84 mins.

Prod: Leonard Goldstein.

Dir: Arthur Lubin.

SP: Leonard Praskins & Barney Slater.

Art Dir: Bernard Herzbrun & Alexander Golitzen.

Cin: Maury Gertsman.

Edit: Milton Carruth.

Mus: Frank Skinner.

Cast: Irene Dunne, Dean Jagger, Les Tremayne, Joan Evans, Richard Crenna, Sandy Descher.

F-com (family discovers trees in their backyard grow money; this money dries up like leaves at end)

Ref: MFB Oct '52 p 143; Vd & HR 31 Oct '52.

It Had To Be You

1947 Col 98 mins.

Prod: Don Hartman.

Dir: D. Hartman & Rudolph Maté.

Story: D. Hartman & Allen Boretz.

cont.

It Had to Be You cont.

SP: Norman Panama & Melvin Frank.

Art Dir: David Goosson & Rudolph Sternad.

Cin: R. Maté & Vincent Farrar.

Edit: Gene Havlick.

Mus: M.W. Stoloff.

Cast: Ginger Rogers, Cornel Wilde, Percy Waram, Spring Byington, Ron Randell, Thurston Hall, Charles Evans, Frank Orth, Harry H. Morgan, Anna Q. Nilsson.

psy-F-com (Indian from dream becomes real, vanishes at end except for moccasins)

Ref: MFB June '48 p76-77; Acad; deGroot p 128.

It Happened
See: Little Train (1960).

It Happened Here

1963 (1966) British, Rath (Lopert) 99 mins (93 mins).

Prod, Dir, SP: Keven Brownlow & Andrew Mollo.

Story, Addt'l Cin, Edit: K. Brownlow.

Cin: Peter Suschitsky.

Mus: Jack Beaver.

Cast: Pauline Murray, Sebastian Shaw, Fiona Leland, Honor Fehrson, Percy Binns, Frank Bennett.

cont.

It Happened Here cont.

soc-SF (depicts alternate ending to WWII: Nazis occupy England)

Ref: MFB '66 p88; FD 8 Aug '66; FF '66 p224.

It Happened Tomorrow

1944 Arnold Prods (UA) 84 mins.

Prod: Arnold Pressburger.

Dir: René Clair.

Story: Hugh Wedlock, Howard Snyder, & Lewis R. Foster.

SP: R. Clair & Dudley Nichols.

Art Dir: Erno Metzner.

Tech Dir: Eugen Schüfftan.

Cin: Archie Stout.

Edit: Fred Pressburger.

Mus: Robert Stolz.

Cast: Dick Powell, Linda Darnell, Jack Oakie, Eddie Acuff, Marian Martin, Edgar Kennedy, John Philliber [ghost].

F-com (Powell gets copies of tomorrow's newspaper for several days from ghost; finally reads one predicting his own death)

Ref: FDY '45; Vd 20 March '44; MFB Oct '44 p 117; Agee p 92, 346.

Based on idea from playlet by Lord Dunsany.

It Happens Every Spring

1949 20th-Fox 87 mins.

Prod: William Perlberg.

Dir: Lloyd Bacon.

Story: Shirley W. Smith & Valentine Davies.

SP: V. Davies.

Art Dir: Lyle Wheeler & J. Russell Spencer.

Cin: Joe MacDonald.

SpFX: Fred Sersen.

Edit: Bruce Pierce.

Mus: Leigh Harline.

Mus Dir: Lionel Newman.

Cast: Ray Milland, Jean Peters, Paul Douglas, Ted de Corsia, Ray Collins, Ed Begley, Jessie Royce Landis, Alan Hale Jr, Bill Murphy, Gene Evans.

SF-com (Milland's formula makes baseballs dodge wood; becomes famous big-league pitcher)

Ref: HR & Vd 5 May '49; LC.

It Is Enough to Love

See: Bernadette of Lourdes (1960).

It Is for England

(The Hidden Hand --rr.t.)

1916 British, Union Jack sil 10,000 ft.

(1918 reissue by Gaum, 5 reels cut)

Prod, Dir, Sc: Lawrence Cowen.

Cast: Helene Gingold, Percy Moran, Marguerite Shelley, Gilbert Esmond, Gilbert Parker, William Bull, Kinloch-Cooke, Arthur Collins, Willie Clarkson.

F ("reincarnated Saint unmasks baronet as German spy")

Ref: Gifford/BFC 06351.

It Stalked the Ocean Floor

See: Monster from the Ocean Floor (1954).

It! The Terror from Beyond Space

(It --e.t.; It, the Vampire from Outer Space --s.t.)

1958 Vogue (UA) 69 mins.

Prod: Robert E. Kent.

Dir: Edward L. Cahn.

SP: Jerome Bixby.

Art Dir: William Glasgow.

Makeup: Lane Britton.

cont.

It! Terror from Beyond Space cont.

Special Makeup: Paul Blaisdell.

Cin: Kenneth Peach Sr.

Edit: Grant Whytock.

Mus: Paul Sawtell & Bert Shefter.

Cast: Marshall Thompson, Shawn Smith, Ray "Crash" Corrigan [monster], Ann Doran, Kim Spalding, Dabbs Greer, Paul Langton.

SF-H (blood-drinking Martian stows away on spaceship returning from Mars to Earth)

Ref: FF '58 p226; FDY '59; MFB Oct '58 p 128.

It, the Vampire from Outer Space

See: It! The Terror from Beyond Space (1958).

It Was Not in Vain

See: Nije Bilo Uzalud (1967?).

Italia 61

1961 Polish ani sh.

Dir: Jan Lenica & Zamecznic.

F

Ref: Ani/Cin p 173.

Italian in Algiers, The

1969 Italian, Texture color? ani 10 mins.

Dir: Lusatti (&?) Genini.

F

Ref: IAFF '72.

Italian Transplant

See: Transplant (1970).

It's a Dog's Life

(The Bar Sinister --alt.t.)

1955 MGM color scope 58 mins.

Prod: Henry Berman.

Dir: Herman Hoffman.

SP: John Michael Hayes.

Art Dir: Cedric Gibbons & Daniel B. Cathcart.

Cin: Paul C. Vogel.

Edit: John Dunning.

Mus: Elmer Bernstein.

Cast: Jeff Richards, Jarma Lewis, Edmund Gwenn, Dean Jagger, Willard Sage, Sally Fraser, Richard Anderson, Vic Morrow [voice of dog].

com; bor-F (dogs act as smart as people; film narrated by lead dog)

Ref: HR & Vd 23 Aug '55; FDY '56; MFB '56 p 19-20.

Based on story "The Bar Sinister" by Richard Harding Davis.

It's a Gift

1923 Hal Roach (Pathé) sil 1 reel.

Prod: Hal Roach.

Cast: Snub Pollard.

SF-com (flying car; super gasoline substitute)

Ref: LC.

It's a Wonderful Life

(The Greatest Gift --e.t.)

1946 Liberty Films (RKO) 129 mins.

Prod & Dir: Frank Capra.

SP: Frances Goodrich, Albert Hackett, & F. Capra.

Art Dir: Jack Okey.

Cin: Joseph Walker & Joseph Biroc.

Edit: William Hornbeck.

Mus: Dimitri Tiomkin.

Cast: James Stewart, Donna Reed, Lionel Barrymore, Beulah Bondi, Thomas Mitchell, Henry Travers [angel], Frank Faylen, Ward Bond, H.B. Warner, Gloria Grahame, Samuel S. Hinds, Frank Albertson, Sheldon Leonard.

cont.

It's a Wonderful Life cont.

F-com (guardian angel shows disillusioned small-town businessman what his town would have been like had he never been born)

Ref: Vd 19 Dec '46; MFB April '47 p50; Agee p233-34.

Based on story "The Greatest Gift" by Philip Van Doren Stern.

It's a Wondrous, Wondrous, Wondrous, Wondrous World

See: Jack and the Witch (1967).

"It's Alive!"

1968? Azalea (AIP-TV) color 80 mins.

Prod, Dir, SP, Edit: Larry Buchanan.

Assoc Prod: Edwin Tobolowsky.

Prod Coord: Joreta Cherry.

Cin: Robert Alcott.

SpFX: Jack Bennett.

Cast: Tommy Kirk, Shirley Bonne, Billy Thurman, Corveth Osterhouse, Annabelle Macadams.

SF-H (man imprisons 3 people in cave to feed to his pet monster, supposedly a dinosaur)

Ref: B. Warren; Pardi.

Based on novelet "Being" by Richard Matheson.

It's All Einstein's Fault

See: Man in Outer Space (1961).

It's Got Me Again

1931 WB ani sh.

Prod: Leon Schlesinger.

F-com

Ref: Acad nom.

It's Great To Be Alive

1933 Fox 69 mins.

Dir: Alfred Werker.

SP: Paul Perez & Arthur Kober.

Cin: Robert Planck.

Edit: Barney Wolf.

Cast: Paul Roulien, Gloria Stuart, Edna May Oliver, Herbert Mundin, Edward Van Sloan, Robert Greig, Emma Dunn.

SF-mus-com (most of men of world killed in epidemic; governments become matriarchy, battle over last man)

Ref: Vw 11 July '33; LC; SFF p48.

Based on a story by John D. Swain.

Remake of: Last Man on Earth, The (1924).

See also simultaneously-filmed Spanish-language version: Ultimo Varon Sobre la Tierra, El (1933).

It's Hard to Recognize a Princess

n.d. Canadian, NFB color ani puppet sh.

Dir: Bretislav Pojar.

F

Ref: Ani/Cin p 123.

It's Hot in Paradise

(Ein Toter Hing im Netz: Body in the Web; The Spider's Web --ad.t.; Girls of Spider Island --ad.t.; Horrors of Spider Island --rr.t.)

1959 (1963; 1966-rr) German/ Yugoslavian, Rapid Film (Gaston Hakim Prods; Pacemaker --rr) 86 mins (75 mins --rr)

Dir: Fritz Böttger (Jamie Nolan)

Mus: Willy Mattes & Karl Bette.

Cast: Alex D'Arcy, Barbara Valentin (Valentine), Helga Frank, Harald Maresch, Reiner Brand, Helga Neuner.

SF-H (people on tropical island encounter large spiders; after being bitten, man becomes hairy monster)

cont.

It's Hot in Paradise cont.

Ref: BO 29 Nov '65; FF '63 p345; Gasca p233; LAT 29 April '67; FD 12 March '65.

Its Name Was Robert

See: Call Me Robert (1967?).

It's the Natural Thing to Do

1939 Par ani 1 reel.

Prod: Max Fleischer.

Dir: Dave Fleischer.

Ani: Tom Johnson & Lod Rossner.

Voices: May Questall and others.

F-com

Ref: LC; Hist US Ani prog.

See also: Popeye (1933-57).

It's Time for Everybody

1954 UPA (Col) color ani 16 mins.

Dir: Robert Cannon.

Design: Ted Hee & Sterling Sturtevant.

Color: Jules Engel, Robert McIntosh, & Michi Kataoko.

Ani: Frank Smith, Rudy Larriva, Tom McDonald, Alan Zaslove, & Gerald Ray.

Mus: David Brdexman.

Voices: George Brian & Joe Ripley.

F

Ref: Annecy '65.

It's Tough to Be a Bird

1969 WD (BV) ani & live color 22 mins.

Prod & Dir: Ward Kimball.

SP: W. Kimball & Ted Berman.

Ani: Art Stevens & Eric Larson.

Edit: Lloyd L. Richardson.

Mus: George Bruns.

Voices: Richard Bakalyan, Ruth Buzzi.

Cast: John Emerson, Hank Schloss, Jim Swain, Ward Kimball, Walter Perkins.

F-com; doc-seqs (bird shows scenes of man's inhumanity to birds)

Ref: MFB Aug '70 p 172; Vw 24 Dec '69, 1 April '70; Acad nom.

Ivan and the Witch Baba-Yaga

193? Soviet ani sh.

F-H

Ivanna

See: Scream of the Demon Lover (1970).

I've Lived Before

1956 U 82 mins.

Prod: Howard Christie.

Dir: Richard Bartlett.

SP: Norman Jolley & William Talman.

Art Dir: Richard H. Riedel & Alfred Sweeney.

Cin: Maury Gertsman.

Edit: Milton Carruth & Fred MacDowell.

Mus: Herman Stein.

Mus Dir: Joseph Gershenson.

Cast: Jock Mahoney, Leigh Snowden, Ann Harding, John McIntire, April Kent, Jerry Paris, Raymond Bailey, Vernon Rich.

psy-F (modern-day airline pilot discovers he seems to be reincarnation of WWI pilot)

Ref: MFB Dec '56 p 155; FD 19 July '56; FIR March '72 p 152-53.

See also: Search for Bridey Murphy, The (1956).

Ivory Trail, The

(by T. Mundy)

See: Jungle Mystery (1932).

Izmedju Usanai Ćase

(Between the Glass and the Lip)

1968 Yugoslavian/Italian, Zagreb/Corona Cinemat. color ani 9.9 mins.

Dir & SP: Dragutin Vunak.

Design & Bg: Zvonimir Locaric.

Ani: Zlatko Sacer.

Mus: Tomislav Simovic.

F ("life as one long funeral procession" --Z/Zagreb)

Ref: Z/Zagreb p96; Mamaia '70.

Based on poem by Frano Alfirević.

Izumitelj Cipela

See: Inventor of Shoes (1967).

Izvor Zivota

(The Spring of Life)

1969 Yugoslavian color ani 10 mins.

Dir: Nikola Majdak & Borislav Sajtinac.

F (beverage restores youth)

Ref: Mamaia '70.

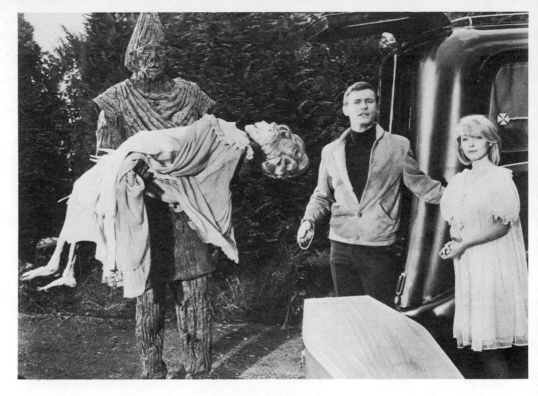

It! (1966) British/US

J

J.S. Bach, Fantasy in G Minor

See: Johann Sebastian Bach — Fantasy in G Minor (1964).

J'Accuse

(I Accuse)

● 1919 French (UA) sil color seq 8 reels.

Prod, Dir, Sc: Abel Gance.

Cin: Léonce Burel, André Bayard, & Forster.

Cast: Séverin-Mars, Romuald Joubé, Marise Daouvray, Desjardins, Angele Guys.

Ref FIR March '64 p 157; MPW 50:327; Photo Aug '21 p58, 82; F/A p350; LC.

● (That They May Live --alt.t.)

1938 (1939) French, G.F.F.C. (Mayer & Burstyn).

Dir: Abel Gance.

Dialog: Steve Passeur.

Cin: Roger Hubert.

Cast: Victor Francen, Line Noro, Marie Lou, Reneé Devillers, Jean Louis Barrault.

Ref: FD 10 Nov '39; HR 26 June '37, 17 Jan '40; FTN p537; FM 1:23.

psy-F-H-seq (anti-war film; at climax, protagonist calls on the dead of WWI to rise from their graves and march on the living, stopping them from fighting again; real WWI casualties, greatly disfigured, were used as the walking dead)

J'Ai Tué Raspoutine

(I Killed Rasputin; Tonnerre sur Saint-Petersbourg: Thunder Over St. Petersburg --s.t?)

1967 French/Italian, Les Films Copernic/Compagnia Generale Cinemat. color scope 102 mins.

Prod: Raymond Danon.

Dir: Robert Hossein.

J'Ai Tué Raspoutine cont.

SP: R. Hossein, Alain Decaux, & Claude Desailly.

Art Dir: Leon Barsacq.

Cin: Henri Persin.

Edit: Jacqueline Thiedot.

Mus: André Hossein.

Cast: Gert Fröbe [Rasputin], Peter McEnery, Geraldine Chaplin, Robert Hossein, Ira Fürstenberg, Patrick Balkany.

bor-F-hist-H (Rasputin keeps control over Czarina and child by hypnosis; he is very hard to kill at climax)

Ref: Vw 10 May '67; MFB '69 p32; CineF Fall '70 p20.

Based on book "Avant l'Evil" by Felix Youssopov.

See also: Rasputin.

Ja, Spravedlnost

(I, Justice)

1968 Czech, Sebor-Bor (Filmexport) 90 mins.

Dir: Zbynek Brynych.

SP: Z. Brynych & Miroslav Hanus.

Cin: Josef Vanis.

Cast: Karel Hoger, Fritz Diez, Angelica Dormrose, Jiri Vrstala.

bor-soc-SF (what happened to Hitler after WWII when he fell into the hands of German soldiers; Hitler is mercy-killed by doctor)

Ref: MTVM Oct '67 p 12; Vw 1 May '68 p 17; S&S p 184.

Based on the novel by Miroslav Hanus.

Jabberwock

(poem by L. Carroll)

See: Three: Les Poissons, Jabberwock, Opus 5 (1962?).

Jabuka Zvana Ljubav

See: Apple of Love, The (1961).

Jack and His Dog

1968 Polish color ani puppet? 11 mins.

F

Ref: LA County Museum.

Jack and Jim

(Jacques et Jim)

1903 French, Star sil 188 ft.

Prod: Georges Méliès.

F (tricks, transformations)

Ref: LC; Sadoul/M, GM Mage.

Jack and the Beanstalk

● 1902 Edison sil colored 625 ft.

Dir: Edwin S. Porter.

Ref: MPW 14:961; Niver p 196; LC; Niver/20 p26-28.

● 1903 Lubin sil sh.

Ref: LC.

● 1912 Edison sil 1000 ft.

Cast: Gladys Hulette, Miriam Nesbitt, Harry Eytinge [giant], Gertrude Clarke, Gertrude McCoy [fairy].

F (in addition to usual story, ogre's wife, fairy)

Ref: MPW 11:140, 303; EK 1 Jan '12 p 13.

● 1912 British, Kinemacolor sil.

Cast: Thomas Carnahan Jr.

Ref: MPW 14:555.

● 1913 Thanhouser sil 1.5 reels.

● 1917 Fox sil 10 reels.

Dir & Story: C.M. & S.A. Franklin.

Sc: Mary Murillo.

Cast: Virginia Lee Corbin, Jim Tarvers, Francis Carpenter, Violet Radcliff.

Ref: Blum p 144; MPW 32:1811; MPN 16:1151; FIR Aug-Sept '72 p398-99; NYT 31 July '17.

Note: giant played by adult, rest of cast by children.

● 1924 Century (U) sil 2 reels.

Dir & Sc: Alf Goulding.

Cast: Albert Williams, Jack Earle, Baby Peggy.

Jack and the Beanstalk cont.

Ref: Blum p265; MPN 29:2555.

● 1931 Par ani 1 reel.

Prod: Max Fleischer.

Dir: Dave Fleischer.

Ref: LC.

● 1933 Celebrity Prods 1 reel.

Ref: LC.

Same as following film?

● 1933 P.A. Powers ani 6 mins.

Prod: Ub Iwerks.

Ref: MPH 14 Oct '33.

Same as preceding film?

● 1952 Exclusive Prods (WB) color; b&w seq 78 mins.

Exec Prod & Story: Pat Costello.

Prod: Alex Gottlieb.

Dir: Jean Yarbrough.

SP: Nat Curtis.

Art Dir: McClure Capps.

Cin: George Robinson.

Edit: Otho Lovering.

Mus: Heinz Roemheld.

Cast: Bud Abbott, Lou Costello, Buddy Baer [giant], William Farnum, Dorothy Ford, Barbara Brown, David Stollery, Shaye Cogan, James Alexander.

F-com-dream (Costello reads children the nursery story, falls asleep & dreams himself & Bud Abbott in it)

Ref: HR & Vd 3 April '52; MFB Dec '52 p 173; Maltin/MCT.

● 1954 British, Primrose Prods color ani silhouette 12 mins.

Prod: Vivian Milroy & Louis Hagan.

Design: Lotte Reiniger.

Ani: L. Reiniger & Carl Koch.

Mus: Freddie Phillips.

Nar: Deryck Guyler.

Ref: MFB July '56 p94; Contemp p77.

cont.

Jack and the Beanstalk cont.

F (boy's magic bean seeds grow into gigantic beanstalk; climbing it, he discovers a giant's castle; he steals giant's treasure, usually including a goose that lays golden eggs & a magical singing harp, escapes to earth; cuts down beanstalk, killing the giant)

Based on the fairy tale.

See also: Fève Enchantée, La (1905?); Magic Beans, The (1939); Jasper and the Beanstalk (1945); Fun and Fancy Free (1947); Woody and the Beanstalk (1966).

Jack and the Witch

(Shōnen Jack to Mahotsukai; It's a Wondrous, Wondrous, Wondrous, Wondrous World --ad.t.)

1967 (1972?) Japanese, Toei color ani 80 mins.

Dir: Taiji Yabushita.

SP: Shinichi Sekizawa & Susumu Takahisa.

Art Dir: Reiji Koyama.

Cin: Hideaki Sugawara.

Mus: Seiichiro Uno.

F (witch; dragon; demon; crystal ball is source of magic)

Ref: UniJ p29-30; UniJ 37 p26-27; TVG.

Jack Armstrong

1947 Col serial 15 parts 31 reels.

Prod: Sam Katzman.

Dir: Wallace Fox.

SP: Arthur Hoerl, Lewis Clay, Royal Cole, & Leslie Swabacker.

Cin: Ira H. Morgan.

Edit: Earl Turner.

Mus: Lee Zahler.

Cast: John Hart, Rosemary La Planche, Joe Brown Jr, Claire James, Pierre Watkin, Wheeler Oakman, Jack Ingram, Eddie Parker, Hugh Prosser, John Merton, Charles Middleton, Gene Stutenroth.

SF (ray gun aimed at world from spaceship in orbit)

Ref: Ser/Col; FDY '56; LC; Acad.

Based on the radio serial.

Jack, el Destripador de Londres

(Jack, the Mangler of London; Jack the Ripper --ad.t.)

1971 Spanish/Italian, Cine Int'l/Apollo color scope 86 mins.

Dir: José Luis Madrid.

SP: Tito Carpi, J.L. Madrid, Jacinto Molina, & Sandro Continenza.

Art Dir: Juan Alberto Soler.

Cin: Diego Ubeda.

SpFX: Antonio Molina.

Edit: Luis Puigvert.

Mus: Piero Piccioni.

Cast: Paul Naschy (rn: Jacinto Molina), Patricia Loran, Renzzo Marignaro, Andres Resino, Irene Mir, Orquidea de Santis.

H (mad killer of prostitutes in London of 1888)

Ref: Vw 27 Oc '71; SpCin '72 p 114-15.

See also: Jack the Ripper.

Jack Frost

(Morozko: Grandfather Frost)

1965 Soviet, Gorky (Embassy) color (79 mins).

Dir: Alexander Rou.

SP: Mikhail Volpin & Nikolai Erdman.

Art Dir: Arseni Klopotovsky.

cont.

Jack Frost cont.

Cin: Dmitri Surensky.

Edit: A. Ovcharova.

Mus: Nikolai Budashkin.

Cast: Alexander Khvylya, Natasha Sedykh, Eduard Izotov, P. Pavlenko, Inna Churikova, Yuri Millyar [witch].

F (gremlin changes hero's head into a bear's; old witch Baba Yaga; walking tree; Jack Frost's scepter changes girl into ice, tear changes her back)

Ref: FF '66 p368; Vw 19 Oct '66; MPH 9 Nov '66; Pardi.

Based on a Russian folk tale.

Jack in the Box

1912 Majestic sil 1 reel.

Cast: Virginia Westbrook.

F-dream (dream of trip to toyland led by Jack-in-the-Box; Santa Claus)

Ref: MPW 14:1232, 1293, 1339.

Jack Jaggs and Dum Dum

(Tom Tight et Dum Dum)

1903 French sil 167 ft.

Prod: Georges Méliès.

Cast: Georges Méliès.

F-com (bundle shaped into mannequin comes to life; tricks; transformations)

Ref: LC; Sadoul/M, GM Mage; Niver p53-54.

Jack le Ramoneur

See: Chimney Sweep (1906).

Jack O'Lantern

(play by G. Goodchild)

See: Condemned to Death (1932).

Jack Spratt and the Scales of Love

1915 Essanay sil 1 reel.

Cast: Victor Potel, Margaret Joslin.

SF-com (drugs make wife fat & husband thin very rapidly)

Ref: MPN 4 Dec '15; LC.

Jack the Giant Killer

1962 Edward Small (UA) color 94 mins.

Prod: Edward Small.

Assoc Prod: Robert E. Kent.

Dir: Nathan Juran.

SP: Orville H. Hampton & Nathan Juran.

Art Dir: Fernando Carrere & Frank McCoy.

Makeup: Charles Gemora.

Cin: David S. Horsley.

SpFX: Howard A. Anderson, Jim Danforth, & David Pal.

Edit: Grant Whytock.

Mus: Paul Sawtell & Bert Shefter.

Cast: Kerwin Mathews, Judi Meredith, Torin Thatcher [sorcerer], Walter Burke, Roger Mobley, Don Beddoe [leprechaun], Barry Kelley, Dayton Lummis, Anna Lee, Helen Wallace, Tudor Owen.

F (much fantasy: black magician; cloak of invisibility; flying dragon; leprechaun; transformations; dragon's-tooth soldiers; demons; two-headed giant; sea monster; horned giant; etc.)

Ref: FF '62 p 180-81; MFB '67 p 125; Photon 20:11+.

Based on the fairy tale.

This film was a deliberate imitation of Seventh Voyage of Sinbad, The (1958), which see.

See also: Woody the Giant Killer (1948).

Jack the Man-Ape

See: Evolution of Man, The (1920).

Jack the Ripper

1959 (1960) British, Mid-Century Film Prod (Par) color seq 88 mins.

Prod, Dir, Cin: Robert S. Baker & Monty Berman.

Story: Peter Hammond & Colin Craig.

SP: Jimmy Sangster.

Edit: Peter Benzencenet.

Mus (British version): Stanley Black.

Mus (US prints): Jimmy McHugh & Pete Rugolo.

Cast: Lee Patterson, Eddie Byrne, Betty McDowall, Ewen Solon [the Ripper], John Le Mesurier, George Rose, Barbara Burke, George Woodbridge.

psy-H (insane surgeon kills prostitutes in an effort to get the one who drove his son to suicide)

Ref: FF '60 p22; FDY '61; HR 4 Feb '60

Based on the true and unsolved series of murders of prostitutes in London, late 1888.

See also: Lodger, The; Three Wax Men (1924); Pandora's Box (1928); Room to Let (1949); Man in the Attic, The (1953); Santo en el Hotel de la Muerte (1961); Lulu (1962); Monster of London City, The (1964); Study in Terror, A (1965); Dr. Jekyll and Sister Hyde (1971); Hands of the Ripper (1971); Jack, el Destripador de Londres (1971); Terror in the Wax Museum (1972).

Jack's Wife

See: Hungry Wives (1972).

Jacques et Jim

See: Jack and Jim (1903).

Jade Box, The

1930 U sil & sound versions serial 10 parts 20 reels.

Dir: Ray Taylor.

Story: Fred Jackson.

Cast: Louise Lorraine, Jack Perrin, Francis Ford, Eileen Sedgwick, Monroe Salisbury.

F-H (hero & heroine haunted by evil spirits of the Oriental cult in search of the jade box)

Ref: MPN 41:8:41; CNW p275.

Jade Mask, The

1944 (1945) Mono 64 mins.

Prod: James S. Burkett.

Dir: Phil Rosen.

SP: George Callahan.

Art Dir: Dave Milton.

Cin: Harry Neumann.

Edit: Dick Carrier.

Cast: Sidney Toler, Mantan Moreland, Edwin Luke, Hardie Albright, Ralph Lewis, Frank Reicher, Dorothy Granger, Jack Ingram, Lester Dorr, Henry Hall.

bor-SF-H (formula for making wood durable as steel; supposedly dead men walk; mysterious house)

Ref: HR & Vd 21 Feb '45.

Based on the character "Charlie Chan" created by Earl Derr Biggers.

See also: Charlie Chan.

Jadu-I-Kangan

1940 Indian, Mohan.

Dir: Nanubhoy Vakil.

Cast: Shiraz, Sarojini, Indurani, Bacha, Jaydev, Gadagkar, Khalilkhan, Garibsha Sadik, Jethalal.

F (magic)

Ref: Filmindia March '40 p51 ad.

Jadu-I-Kismet

1944 Indian.

F ("chills and magic" -- Filmindia)

Ref: Filmindia April '44.

Jadui-Angoothi

(Magic Ring)

1948 Indian, Mohan.

Dir: A.M. Khan.

Cast: Husnara, Anil Kumar, Devraj, Kesari Singh, Yar Mohamud.

F

Ref: Filmindia May '48 p24 ad, June '48 p40.

Jadui Bansari

(Magic Flute)

1948 Indian, Mohan.

Cast: Prakash.

F

Ref: Filmindia March '48 p71.

Jadui-Chitra

(Magic Picture)

1948 Indian, Prabha.

Dir: Jaswant C. Zaveri.

Cast: Anil Kumar, Shanta Patel, Bachcha, Leela Pande, Devraj, Rafique, Ansari.

F

Ref: Filmindia May '48 p24.

Jadui-e-Putli

(Magic Doll)

1946 Indian, Mohan.

F

Ref: Filmindia Aug '46 ad.

Jadui-Shehanai

(Magic Orchestra)

1948 Indian, Mohan.

Dir: Naseem Siddiqui.

Cast: Prakash, Amir, Karnatki, Bachcha, Shanta Patel, Leela Pande, Devraj, Rafique, Ansari.

mus-F

Ref: Filmindia May '48 p24 ad, June '48 p40 ad.

Jadui-Sindoor

(Magic Mark)

1948 Indian, Mohan.

Dir: Naseem Siddiqi.

F

Ref: Filmindia May '48 p24 ad, June '48 p40.

Jagga Daku

(The Bandit)

1960? Indian (In Hindi), Chitra Bharati 153 mins.

Dir: Chandrakant.

Cast: Jabeen, Krishna Kumari, Jairaj, Chandrasekhar.

F (man with supernatural powers & the help of a witch subdues the usurper-princess of the nether world)

Ref: FEFN Feb '60 p50.

Jai Bhim

(Bhim's Victory)

1949 Indian, Navu Zankar Prods 120 mins.

Dir: Anant Mane.

Mus Dir: Sudhir Phadke.

Cast: Vishwas, Vasant Thengdi, Gramopadye, Jivaji Kulkarni, Uma Devi.

myth-F

Ref: Indian MPA '53 p9; Filmindia May '49 p58 ad.

Jai Hanuman

(Hanuman's Victory)

● 1944 Indian, Prafulls Pics.

myth-F (the son of the wind is immortal)

Ref: Filmindia Feb '44 p30 ad.

● 1948 Indian, Ranjit.

Dir: Ramchandra Thakur.

Story: Indra.

Mus: B.C. Rani.

cont.

Jai Hanuman cont.

Cast: P. Kailas, Keshav Purohit, Nirupa Roy, Babu Raje, S.N. Tripathi.

myth-F (deals with early life of great monkey-warrior)

Ref: Filmindia Sept '48 p62 ad, Oct '48 p59 ad, Dec '48 p59.

Jai Mahadev

(Mahadev's Victory)

1953 Indian, K Pics color.

Prod: Ratilal Vora.

Dir: Ramchandra Thakur.

Mus: Manna Dey.

Cast: Nalini Jaywant, Mahipal, Trilok Kapur, Meenaxi, S.N. Tripathi, Jeevan.

myth-F

Ref: Filmfare 18 Sept '53, 25 Dec '53 p37.

Jai Mahakali

(Great Kali's Victory)

1951 Indian, Vikram Vaital 162 mins.

Prod: Dhirubhai Desai & Ravjibhai Patel.

Dir & Sc: D. Desai.

Dialog: V. Mehrotra.

Art Dir: M.H. Palnitkar.

Cin: Babubhai Udeshi.

Edit: B.K. Mistry.

Mus Dir: Kumar.

Cast: Nirupa Roy, Sahu Modak, Ullhas, Vimal, Lalita Pawar, Niranjan Sharma, S.N. Tripati.

myth-F

Ref: Indian MPA '53 p42.

Jai Shankar

(Shankar's Victory)

1951 Indian, Latika 124 mins.

Prod & Dir: Ishwarla.

Story & Dialog: Ambikesh Kuntul.

Art Dir: Baburao Jadhav.

Cin: S. Vasant.

Edit: H. Morey.

Mus: Khemchandra Prakash.

Cast: Iswarla, Ranjana, Niranjan Sharma, Hira Sawant, Shakuntala, Vijaya, Babu Raje.

myth-F

Ref: Indian MPA '53 p43.

Jaje

See: Egg, The (1959).

Jak Stařecek Měnil Az Vyměnil

(How Grandpa Changed till Nothing Was Left)

1952 Czech ani sh.

Dir & Art Dir: Jiří Trnka.

F

Ref: Trnka p261.

Jak Zařídit Byt

(How to Furnish a Flat)

1960 Czech color ani puppet sh.

Dir & Story: Břetislav Pojar.

Art Dir: Svatopluk Pitra & B. Šiška.

Mus: Wiliam Bukový.

F

Ref: Czech An '61; Ani/Cin p 122.

Jalim Jadugarin

See: Enchantress, The (1929).

Jalopy

1953 AA 62 mins.

Dir: William Beaudine.

SP: Tim Ryan, Jack Crutcher, & Bert Lawrence.

Cin: Harry Neumann.

Mus: Marlin Skiles.

Cast: Leo Gorcey, Huntz Hall, Bernard Gorcey, Bob Lowry, Richard Benedict.

SF-com (new formula acts as either a love potion or a super-powered auto fuel)

Ref: CoF 11:40; V 25 March '53.

See also: Spooks Run Wild (1941).

Jalousie du Barbouillé, La

(The Jealousy of the Scribbler --?)

1927 French sil.

Dir: Alberto Cavalcanti.

F (cuckold hatches gigantic eggs)

Ref: B&B p236; Sadoul/Film Makers p40.

Based on a play by Molière.

Jamboree

See: Son of Kong (1933).

James Batman

1967 Philippine, Sampaguita.

Dir & SP: Artemio Marquez.

Story: Pepito Vera Perez.

Mus: Carding Cruz.

Cast: Dolphy, Boy Alano, Shirley Moreno, Bella Flores, Diane Balen, Elsa Bouffaro, Nori Dalshay, Lynn D'Arce.

bor-SF

Ref: Chodkowski; Borst.

See also: Batman; James Bond.

James Bond

(British spy character created by Ian Fleming)

See: Dr. No (1962); Goldfinger (1964); Thunderball (1965); Casino Royale (1967); You Only Live Twice (1967); On Her Majesty's Secret Service (1969); Diamonds Are Forever (1971); Live and Let Die (1973).

See also: James Tont, Operazione U.N.O. (1965); Superdiabolici, I (1965); James Tont, Operation D.U.E. (1966); Bonditis (1967); James Batman (1967); Operation Kid Brother (1967).

James Tont, Operation D.U.E.

1966 Italian/French, Panda/Cineurop.

Prod: Ermanno Donati & Luigi Carpentieri.

Dir: Bruno Corbucci.

Cin: Sandro D'Eva.

Cast: Landro Buzzanca, France Anglade, Furio Meniconi, Claudie Lange, Loris Gizzi, Mirko Valentin.

bor-SF (hormones make people young or old)

Ref: Ital Prods '66.

See also: following title; and James Bond.

James Tont, Operazione U.N.O.

1965 Italian, Panda color.

Prod: Ermano Donati & Luigi Carpentieri.

Dir & SP: Bruno Corbucci & Gianni Grimaldi.

Cin: Alessandro D'Eva & Raffaele Masciocchi.

Mus: Marcello Giombini.

Cast: Lando Buzzanca, Evi Marandi, Loris Gizzi, Gina Rovere, George J. Wang, Alighiero Noschese.

bor-SF (laser beam spectacles)

Ref: Ital Prods '65 p32-33.

See also: James Bond.

Jamestown Baloos

1957 Amateur (Film-makers' Coop) 16mm color seq photos & ani 6 mins.

Prod: Robert Breer.

exp-F

Ref: FQ Spring '59 p57; FC 37 cat p 18; FMC 5:43.

See also: One Man Show (1967?).

Jamuna Puliney

1933 Indian, East India Film Co.

Dir: P.N. Ganguly.

myth-F

Ref: Sound & Shadow Feb '33 p54

Jan of the Jungle

(novel by O.A. Kline)

See: Call of the Savage, The (1935).

Janak Nandini

(Birth of Nandini)

1938 Indian, Radha.

Dir: Phani Burma.

Cin: Probodh Das.

Cast: Ahindra Chowdhury, Manoranjan Bhattacharyya, Susil Roy, Savitri, Devabala Chhaya, Rajlakshmi, Jahar Ganguly, Roby Roy.

myth-F (birth of Sita to her marriage with Rama; woman turned to stone for infidelity, back to life by touch)

Ref: Dipali 25 Nov '38 p 18, p29, 13 Jan '39 p 19, 3 Feb '39 p20.

Based on story from "Ramayan."

Janam Janmake Phere

1957 Indian (in Hindi), Nukti 170 mins.

Dir: Manu Desai.

Cast: Nirupa Roy, Manhar Deasi, B.M. Vyas, Mahipal.

myth-F

Ref: FEFN 9 Aug '57 p 15.

Jane Eyre

● 1914 IMP (U) sil 2 reels.

Prod: Frank H. Crane.

Cast: Irving Cummings, Ethel Grandin.

Ref: MPW 19:810; Bios 7 May '14.

● 1944 20th-Fox 95 mins.

Prod: Kenneth Macgowan.

Dir: Robert Stevenson.

SP: R. Stevenson, John Houseman, & Aldous Huxley.

Cin: Robert Planck.

Art Dir: James Basevi & Wiard B. Ihnen.

Edit: Walter Thompson.

Mus Dir: Bernard Herrmann.

Cast: Orson Welles, Joan Fontaine, John Sutton, Agnes Moorehead, Peggy Ann Garner, Sara Allgood, Margaret O'Brien, Elizabeth Taylor.

Ref: Vd 2 Feb '44; FIR March '63 p 157, Oct '63 p487.

psy-H-seq (mysterious hero keeps insane wife locked in the attic)

Based on the novel by Charlotte Brontë.

Note: the other film versions of the novel are not considered to be significantly psy-H.

Janko the Musician

1961 Polish ani sh.

Dir: Jan Lenica.

F

Ref: Ani/Cin p 106, 108.

Janmashtami

(Birth of Ashtanni [Krishna])

1950 Indian, Hindustan Chitra 122 mins.

Prod: Kishore Sahu.

Dir: Nanabhoy Bhatt.

SP: Pandit Girish.

Art Dir: Yusuf Dhala.

Cin: P. Isaac.

Edit: Kantilal B. Shakla.

Songs: Bharat Vyas.

Mus Dir: Shyam Babu Pathak.

Cast: Nirmala, Shobhana Samarth, Bharat Bhushan, Jeevan, Raj Kumar, Sampson, Ramesh Sinha.

myth-F

Ref: Indian Screen Nov '50 p46; Indian MPA '53 p28.

See also: Krishna.

Janne Vängman och den Stora Kometen

(Johnny Vegman and the Big Comet)

1955 Swedish, Europa.

Dir: Bengt Palm.

Cin: Ingvar Borlid.

Cast: Adolf Jahr, Karl-Erik Flens, Sten Gester, Carl-Gustaf Lindstedt, Märta Dorff, Birgitta Olzon, Lasse Krantz.

SF-com (space travel?, robot)

Ref: FM 12:20, 15:3. 20, 16:43, 17:17.

Januskopf, Der

(Janus-Faced; Love's Mockery --possible US release title)

1920 German, Lipow sil.

Dir: F.W. Murnau.

Sc: Hans Janowitz.

Art Dir: Heinrich Richter.

Cin: Carl Weiss.

Assist Cin: Karl Freund & Karl Hoffmann.

Cast: Conrad Veidt, Bela Lugosi, Margarete Schlegel.

F-H (doctor's formula turns him into monster)

Ref: F&F June '58 p34; Gasca p29-30; S&S '68 p213.

Based on short novel "The Strange Case of Dr. Jekyll and Mr. Hyde" by Robert Louis Stevenson.

See also: Dr. Jekyll and Mr. Hyde.

Jap the Giant Killer

1904 British, Cricks & Sharp sil 140 ft.

F-dream (in dream Japanese soldier decapitates Russian giant)

Ref: Gifford/BFC 00830.

Japan of Fantasy

See: Japon de Fantaisie (1909).

Japanese Butterflies

1908 French, Pathé sil colored 344 ft.

F (painting of silkworm comes to life, spins cocoon, becomes first butterfly then girl; many butterflies ascend to Heaven)

Ref: Views 108:10.

Japanese Mask, The

1915 French, Pathé sil 3 reels.

bor-F-H (looking at a mask causes people to die unnatural deaths)

Ref: MPN 5 June '15 p78; LC; Motog 12 June '15.

Japanese Peach Boy, A

1910 Edison sil 940 ft.

Sc: Pilar Morin.

Cast: Pilar Morin.

F (baby found in peach; ogres; transformations)

Ref: EK 1 Feb '10 p3; MPW 6:179, 216.

Japon de Fantaisie

(Japan of Fantasy)

1909 French, Gaum sil ani.

Dir: Emile Cohl.

F

Ref: Filmlex p 1370.

Japonaiseries

1904 French, Pathé sil 183 ft.

Dir: Gaston Velle.

F-com (woman in Japanese costume materializes from a box)

Ref: BFI cat p 11; Filmlex p785.

Jardin de las Delicias, El

See: Garden of Delights, The (1970).

Jasei no In

(Obscenity of the Viper; Lasciviousness of the Viper; The Maliciousness of the Snake's Evil)

1920 Japanese, Taikatsu sil.

Dir: Thomas Kurihara.

Cast: Tokihiko Okada, Yoko Benizawa.

F

Ref: Anderson/Richie p40.

Based on a story by Akinari Ueda.

See also: Ugetsu (1953).

Jason and the Argonauts

(Jason and the Golden Fleece --s.t.)

1963 British, Morningside & Worldwide (Col) color 103 mins.

Filmed in England & Italy.

Prod: Charles H. Schneer.

Assoc Prod & SpFX: Ray Harryhausen.

SP: Jan Read & Beverly (Beverley?) Cross.

Prod Design: Geoffrey Drake.

Cin: Wilkie Cooper.

Edit: Maurice Rootes.

Mus: Mario Nascimbene.

Cast: Todd Armstrong, Nancy Kovack, Gary Raymond, Laurence Naismith, Michael Gwynn, Niall MacGinnis, John Crawford, Honor Blackman, Douglas Wilmer, Nigel Green [Hercules].

myth-F (Jason's quest for the Golden Fleece, with much fantasy: Greek gods in Mount Olympus, giant bronze statue that comes to life, Neptune, harpies, skeleton army from teeth of seven-headed hydra, etc.)

Ref: MFB Sept '63 p 131; FF '63 p 159-60; FD 5 June '63.

See also: Hercules; Giants of Thessaly, The (1960); Goldene Ding, Das (1971).

Jason and the Golden Fleece

See: Giants of Thessaly, The (1960); Jason and the Argonauts (1963).

Jasper

1942-46 Pal (Par) color ani puppet 1 reel series.

Prod: George Pal.

F-com

Ref: LC.

See also: Jasper. . .; Madcap Models (1941-43); Puppetoons (1943-47).

Jasper and the Beanstalk

1945 George Pal Prods (Par) color ani puppet sh.

Prod & Dir: George Pal.

F-com

Ref: LC; Acad nom.

Based on the nursery tale, "Jack and the Beanstalk."

Jasper and the Beanstalk cont.

See also: Jack and the Beanstalk; Jasper (1942-46); Puppetoons (1943-47).

Jasper and the Haunted House

1942 Par color ani puppet 1 reel.

Prod: George Pal.

F-com

Ref: LC.

See also: Jasper (1942-46).

Jasper and the Watermelons

1942 George Pal (Par) ani puppet 1 reel.

Prod: George Pal.

F-com (little Negro boy Jasper & his friend the talking scarecrow end up in world of watermelons)

Ref: Time 9 March '42.

See also: Jasper (1942-46; Madcap Models (1941-43).

Jassy

1947 (1948) British, Gainsborough (U) color 11 reels.

Prod: Sydney Box.

Dir: Bernard Knowles.

SP: Dorothy Campbell & Geoffrey Kerr.

Art Dir: George Provis & Maurice Carter.

Cin: Jack Asher & Geoffrey Unsworth.

Edit: Charles Knott.

Mus Dir: Louis Levy.

Cast: Margaret Lockwood, Patricia Roc, Dennis Price, Basil Sydney, Dermot Walsh, Cathleen Nesbit, Linda Travers, Ernest Thesiger, Alan Wheatley, Torin Thatcher.

F-seq (wild gypsy girl has psychic powers when needed, can predict future, reduces men to drooling idiots, can sense disaster)

Ref: HR & Vd 5 Feb '48; LC; Acad.

Based on the novel by Norah Lofts.

Jay Walker, The

1956 UPA (Col) color ani 7 mins.

Prod: Stephen Bosustow.

F-com

Ref: LC; Acad nom.

Jazz #1

n.d. Amateur (CFS) color 3 mins.

Made by: Abe Gurvin.

abs-F (collage film)

Ref: CFS cat Sept '68.

Je T'Aime, Je T'Aime

(I Love You, I Love You)

1968 (1973) French, 20th-Fox color scope 94 mins (82 mins).

Prod: Mag Bodard.

Dir: Alain Resnais.

SP: A. Resnais & Jacques Sternberg.

Art Dir: Jacques Dugied & August Pace.

Cin: Jean Boffety.

Edit: Albert Jurgenson & Colette Leloup.

Mus: Krzysztof Penderecki.

Cast: Claude Rich, Olga Georges-Picot, Anouk Ferjac, Van Doude, Annie Fargue.

SF (in an experiment in time-travel, man is sent back in time one year; overpowered by his past emotions, he begins oscillating in time)

Ref: Vw 15 May '68; Time 21 Sept '70; LAT 12 April '73.

Je, Tu, Elles

(I, You, They)

1969 French, ORTF color ani & live 62 mins.

Prod: Pierre Braunberger.

Dir, SP, Ani: Peter Foldes.

Cin: Andre Germain.

Edit: Janine Martin.

Mus: Bernard Parmeggiani.

Cast: Henri Piegay, Jacqueline Coue, Monique Lejeune.

sur-F (artist's life seen in animation, live action -- surrealistically; keeps tiny wife in refrigerator, etc.)

Ref: Vw 3 Sept '69.

Jealous of Myself

See: Wager Between Two Magicians, A (1904).

Jealous Professors, The

1910 Lux sil 420 ft.

F (man turned into monkey, another turned into toad)

Ref: Bios 10 Feb '10.

Jealousy

1963 Bulgarian color ani 8 mins.

Dir: Todor Dinov.

Story: D. Chalkash.

Mus: Simeon Pironkov.

F (spoof on westerns using musical motif: treble clef used as lasso, etc.)

Ref: MFB Dec '66 p 190; Edinburgh '65.

Jealousy of the Scribbler, The

See: Jalousie du Barbouille, La (1927).

Jean Taris, Swimming Champion

(Jean Taris, Champion de Natation; Taris --alt.t.)

1932 (1972) French (Contemporary) sh (10 mins).

Dir, SP, Edit: Jean Vigo.

Cin: Boris Kaufman.

Cast: Jean Taris.

exp-F-seq

Ref: Sadoul p474; Previews March '73.

Jeanne au Bucher

(Joan of Arc at the Stake)

1954 French/Italian, Franco London/Ste' de Productions Cinemat. color.

Dir: Roberto Rossellini

Poem by: Paul Claudel.

Art Dir: Cristini.

Cin: Gabor Pogany.

Mus: Arthur Honegger.

Cast: Ingrid Bergman, Tullio Carminatti.

rel-F-mus (film of symphonic poem about Joan of Arc, full of visions, sourceless voices, etc.)

Ref: UniF 8:15.

See also: Joan of Arc.

Jeanne d'Arc

See: Joan of Arc (1900).

Jeannie

(play by A. Stuart)

See: Let's Be Happy (1957).

Jeannot l'Intrepide

See: Johnny the Giant Killer (1950).

Jedda the Uncivilized

(Jedda --ad.t.)

1956 Australian, DCA color 88 mins.

Prod & Dir: Charles Chauvel.

SP: C. Chauvel & Elsa Chauvel.

Art Dir: Ronald McDonald.

Cin: Carl Kayser & Eric Porter.

cont.

Jedda the Uncivilized cont.

Edit: Alex Ezard, Jack Gardiner, & Pam Bosworth.

Mus: Isador Goodman.

Cast: Narla Kunogh, Robert Tudewali, Betty Suttor, Paul Reynall, George Simpson-Little.

bor-F-H (native magic calls woman to man; chant drives warrior mad; death curse)

Ref: FDY '57; FEFN 22 June '56 p29; PB.

Jedermann

See: Everyman (1961).

Jeep, The

1938 Par ani 1 reel.

Prod: Max Fleischer.

Dir: Dave Fleischer.

Ani: Seymour Kneitel & Graham Place.

F-com (Popeye gets a new pet: a strange animal that can disappear at will)

Ref: LC; Pardi.

See also: Popeye (1933-57).

Jeepers Creepers

1939 Vitaphone (WB) ani 1 reel.

Prod: Leon Schlesinger.

Dir: Robert Clampett.

Story: Ernest Gee.

Ani: Vive Risto.

Mus Dir: Carl W. Stalling.

F-com

Ref: LC; FD Oct '39.

Jeepers Creepers' Car Chase

1965 Amateur 16mm sil sh.

Prod: Don Glut.

bor-F-com

Ref: D. Glut.

Jekyll and Hyde

See: Dr. Jekyll and Mr. Hyde.

Jekyll and Hyde Cat

See: Mighty Mouse Meets Jekyll and Hyde Cat (1944).

Jekyll and Hyde Portfolio, The

1971 (1972) Xerxes Prods (H.M.S. Releasing) color 85 mins.

Prod & Dir: Eric Jeffrey Haims.

Assoc Prod: Shelley Haims.

Story: E.J. Haims & S. Haims.

SP: Don Greer.

Cin: Arch Archambault.

Edit: Schlomo Bina.

Mus: Randy Scott.

Cast: Gray Daniels, Mady Maguire, Sebastian Brook, John Terry, Don Greer, Rene Bond, Bonnie Jean.

psy-H-sex (psychotic killer with split personality)

Ref: HR 24 Jan '72 p3.

Note: this film, possibly a satire, has nothing to do with Dr. Jekyll and Mr. Hyde per se.

Jekyll's Inferno

See: House of Fright (1960).

Jena de Londra, La

(The Hyena of London)

1964 Italian, Geos Film.

Dir & SP: Gino Mancini (Henry Wilson).

Cin: (Griffith Hugh).

Mus: Francesco de Masi (Frank Mason).

Cast: Bernard Price, Diana Martin, Luciano Stella (Tony Kendall), Anthony Wright.

bor-SF (man injects fluid from brain of dead criminal into his own & becomes a criminal himself)

Ref: Ital Prods '64.

Jenkins and the Donkey

1912 Italian, Cines (Kleine)
sil 362 ft.

F (donkey & rider fly thru air after buying balloons)

Ref: MPW 11:512, 690.

Jenseits des Strom

(Beyond the River)

1922 German, Noto Films
sil 3614 ft.

Dir, Sc, Art Dir: Ludwig Czerny.

Settings: Fritz Kränke.

Cin: Ernst Daub.

Mus: Ferdinand Hummel.

Cast: Walter Janssen, Ada Svedin, Ilka Grüning, Lyda Salmonova, Rudolf Laubenthal, Hermann Bachmann.

F (on deathbed wife makes man promise he won't marry wife's friend, but he does; when he tries to make love to her, first wife appears; dead wife taken to the Goddess of Forgetfulness)

Ref: BFI cat p60.

Jerbo, El

(The Jerboa)

1971 Spanish, Estudios Castilla
color ani 8.6 mins.

Dir: Amaro Carretero.

Realisation: Vicente Rodriguez.

bor-F-com-doc (natural history of the jerboa treated for gags)

Ref: SpCin '72.

Jerboa, The

See: Jerbo, El (1971).

Jerry and the Vampire

1917 Cub (Mutual) sil.

Prod: Charles Bartlett.

Sc: Jason Dayton.

Cast: George Ovey, Claire Alexander, Roy Watson.

F-com-dream (in dream man finds magic ring, gets money etc, vamp tries to get his money)

Ref: MPW 34:913.

Note: vampire of title is seductress, not sanguinary ghost.

Jerry on the Job

1916-17 Int'l Film Service
sil ani sh series (mostly 1/2 reel)

Prod & Dir: Gregory La Cava & W.C. Hoban.

Ani: Walter Lantz, Burt Gillett, F.M. Follett, Grim Natwick, George Stallings, George H. Rufle, Nat Collier, Will Powers.

F-com

Ref: LC; Ani chart.

See also: Jerry Ships a Circus (1916); Love and Lunch (1917); Quinine (1917).

Jerry Ships a Circus

1916 Int'l Film Service
sil ani 1/2 reel.

Dir?: W.C. Hoban.

Ani: Will Powers.

F-com

Ref: LC.

See also: Jerry on the Job (1916-17).

Jerry's Cousin

1950 MGM color ani 6 mins.

Prod: Fred Quimby.

Dir: William Hanna & Joseph Barbera.

F-com

Ref: LC; Acad nom.

See also: Tom and Jerry (1940-).

Jersey Skeeter, A

1902 Biograph sil 38 ft.

F-com (giant insect model flies away with man)

Ref: LC; Niver p54.

Jason and the Argonauts (1963) British

Production sketch by Ray Harryhausen.

Jerusalem

(novel by S. Lagerlöf)

See: Ingmarssönerna (1919).

Jesse James Meets Frankenstein's Daughter

1965 (1966) Circle Prods (Embassy) color 82 mins.

Prod: Carroll Case.

Dir: William Beaudine.

SP: Carl Hittleman.

Art Dir: Paul Sylos.

Cin: Lothrop Worth.

Mus: Raoul Kraushaar.

Cast: Narda Onyx, John Lupton, Cal Bolder [Monster], Nestor Paiva, Jim Davis, Estelita, Steven Geray.

west-SF-H (Frankenstein's daughter, living in Mexico, makes outlaw's friend into monster)

Ref: FF '66 p382; HR 9 July '65; CoF 10:6; Gifford/MM p 146.

See also: Frankenstein.

Jessie and Superman

See: Kdo Chce Zabit Jessii? (1965).

Jess's Didactic Nickelodeon

See: Forty and One Nights, The (1963).

Jester's Tale, A

(Bláznova Kronika: Insane Chronicle; Dua Mosketyri: 2 Musketeers)

1964 Czech, Barrandov 85 mins.

Dir: Karel Zeman.

SP: K. Zeman & Pavel Jurácek.

Art Dir: Zdenek Rozkopal.

Cin: Vaclav Huňka.

Edit: Miroslav Hajek.

Mus: Jan Novak.

Cast: Petr Kostica, Miloslav Holub, Emilia Vasaryova, Bohus Zahorsky, Valentina Thielova.

F

Ref: Broz p87; Filmlex p 1789; Ani/Cin p 124.

Jesus

See: King of Kings.

Jesus Christ Superstar

1972 (1973) U color.

Prod: Norman Jewison & Robert Stigwood.

Dir: N. Jewison.

SP: N. Jewison & Melvyn Bragg.

Cast: Ted Neely [Jesus], Carl Anderson, Yvonne Ellimun, Barry Dennen, Joshua Mostel.

rel-F-mus (deliberate anachronisms in rock-opera retelling of Christ story)

Ref: BO 6 Sept '71; Vw 11 Oct '72.

Based on the stage show adapted from the record album.

See also: King of Kings.

Jesus of Nazareth

1928 Ideal Pictures sil
5700 ft.

Titles & Edit: Jean Conover.

Cast: Philip Van Loan [Jesus], Anna Lehr, Charles McCaffrey.

rel-F (standard life of Christ)

Ref: AFI F2.2801 p394-95.

See also: King of Kings.

Jesus of Nazareth

See: From the Manger to the Cross (1912).

Jetée, La

(The Runway; The Jetty; The Pier)

1962 French, Argos (Arcturus Films) composed of still photographs 29 mins (27 mins).

Dir & SP: Chris Marker.

Cin: Jean Chiabaud.

SpFX: C.S. Olaf.

Edit: Jean Ravel.

Mus: Trevor Duncan.

Nar: Jean Negroni.
Cast: Hélène Chatelain, Jacques Ledoux, Davos Hanich, André Heinrich, Jacques Branchu, Pierre Joffroy.

SF (after WWIII, group of scientists experimenting with time travel send man back to pre-WWIII, but he becomes fouled with his own past, tries to flee the seekers from the future, & is killed on an airport runway)

Ref: MFB July '65 p 114; FQ Winter '65-66 p50-52.

Jet Pink

1967 Mirisch-Geoffrey (UA)
color ani sh.

Prod: David DePatie & Friz Freleng.

Dir: Gerry Chiniquy.

Story: Tony Benedict.

Layout: Lin Larsen.

Bg: Tom O'Loughlin.

Ani: Don Williams, Bob Matz, Warren Batchelder, Manny Perez, & Art Leonardi.

Mus: Walter Greene.

F-com

Ref: PopCar.

See also: Pink Panther, The (1964-72).

Jetty, The

See: Jetée, La (1962).

Jeux de Cartes

(Game of Cards)

1959 French color ani sh.

Dir: Henri Lamam.

F

Ref: Ani/Cin p98, 173.

Jeux des Anges, Les

(The Games of Angels)

1964 French, Les Cinéastes Associés (Pyramid) 16mm color ani 13 mins.

Prod: Jacques Forgeot.

Dir & SP: Walerian Borowczyk.

Edit: Claude Blondel.

Mus: Bernard Parmeggiani.

sur-F

Ref: MFB '68 p 13; Ani/Cin p 167; S&S Winter '68-69 p22.

Jeux Sont Fait, Les

See: Chips Are Down, The (1947).

Jewel, The

1960 Hungarian ani sh.

F

Ref: FIR Dec '61 n613.

Jewel, The

See: Bijou, Le (1947).

Jewel of Allah, The

1914 Eclair sil 1 reel.

Cast: Edna Payne, Stanley Walpole.

F (mystic jewel from meteorite heals blindness)

Ref: MPW 22:1681, 1738.

Jewel of Death, The

1916 (1917) Big U (U) sil 2 reels.

Dir: Milton J. Fahrney.

Sc: James Dayton.

Cast: William Clifford, Paul Machete, Belle Bennett, Edna Maison, Louis Fitzroy, Henry Schaum, Bud Osborne.

F (emerald eye of Buddha flashes fire, floats in air, settles on chest of thief)

Ref: MPW 31:416; LC.

Jewel of the Seven Stars

(novel by B. Stoker)

See: Blood from the Mummy's Tomb (1971).

Jig Is Up, The

See: Chips Are Down, The (1947).

Jigoku

(Hell; Sinners to Hell --ad.ts?)

1960 Japanese, Shintoho color 100 mins.

Prod & SP: Nobuo Nakagawa & Ichiro Miyagawa.

Dir: N. Nakagawa.

Cin: Mamoru Morita.

Cast: Shigeru Amachi, Yoichi Numata, Torahiko Nakamura, Utako Mitsuya.

psy-F-H (before dying, person has vision of Hell: people being sawed in half, drowned in blood, turned into skeletons, etc.)

Ref: UniJ 10:26; MW 3:6; Japanese Films '61 p44-45.

Jigokuhen

See: Portrait of Hell (1969).

Jim

1914 American sil 2 reels.

Dir: Thomas Ricketts.

Sc: Douglass Mallock.

Cast: Ed Coxen, Winnifred Greenwood, George Field, John Steppling.

F (the Muses)

Ref: MPW 20:1596, 1613, 1830.

Jim the Man

n.d. Amateur (Film-makers' Coop) 16mm color 77 mins.

Dir: Max Katz.

SP: Herbert Gold.

Cast: Scott Beach.

exp-F (man tries to reconcile his fantasies, depicted, with reality)

Ref: FMC 5:174.

Jimmie as a Hypnotist

1912 French, Gaum sil sh.

Cast: Jimmie.

F-com (sister identifies thief under hypnosis)

Jinete sin Cabeza, El

See: Headless Rider, The (1958).

Jinetes de la Bruja, Los

(The Witch's Riders; The Riders of the Witch; The Bewitched Riders)

1966? (1967) Mexican (Clasa-Mohme/Azteca) color.

Cast: Kitty de Hoyos, Fernando Almada, Dagoberto Rodriguez, Roberto Canedo, Blanca Sanchez.

H

Ref: FDY '68; LAT; PS.

Jinetes del Terror, Los

See: Knights of Terror (1964).

Jinko Eisen to Jinruino Hametsu

See: Super Giant 5 (1958).

Jirí Trnka's Puppets

See: Loutky Jiriho Trnky (1955).

Jitterbugs

1943 20th-Fox 74 mins.

Prod: Sol M. Wurtzel.

Dir: Mal St. Clair.

SP: W. Scott Darling.

Cin: Lucien Andriot.

SpFX: Fred Sersen.

Art Dir: Chester Gore.

Edit: Allen McNeil.

Mus: Charles Newman.

Mus Dir: Emil Newman.

Cast: Stanley Laurel, Oliver Hardy, Vivian Blaine, Bob Bailey, Douglas Fowley, Noel Madison, Jimmy Conlin.

SF-com ("gas pills" cause people to inflate & float in the air)

Ref: Willis; FD 25 June '43.

Joachim's Dictionary

See: Dictionnaire de Joachim, Le (1965).

Joan Medford Is Missing

See: House of Horrors (1946).

Joan of Arc

● (Jeanne d'Arc)

1900 French sil 813 ft.

Prod: Georges Méliès.

rel-F-seq

Ref: Sadoul/M, GM Mage 264-75.

● 1909 French, Pathé sil 853 ft.

rel-F (Joan sees visions which give her information)

Ref: F Index IV-26:9.

Based on legends.

See also: Joan the Woman (1916); Destinees (1953); Jeanne au Bucher (1954).

Joan of Arc at the Stake

See: Jeanne au Bucher (1954).

Joan of the Angels?

(Matka Joanna od Aniolow: Mother Joanna and Angels; Mother Joan of the Angels; The Devil and the Nun -- Brit.t.)

1960 (1962) Polish, Kadr 108 mins.

Dir & SP: Jerzy Kawalerowicz.

Sets & Costumes: Roman Mann & Tadeusz Wybult.

Cin: Jerzy Wojcik.

Mus: Adam Walacinski.

Cast: Lucyna Winnicka, Mieczyslaw Voit, Anna Ciepielewska, Zygmunt Zintel, Kazimierz Fabisiak.

bor-rel-psy-F-H (in 17th century, young priest brought to drive devils out of possessed nuns believes he himself has become possessed, kills innocent people)

Ref: MFB April '62 p47-48; Vw 17 May '61; FQ Winter '63-64 p28; FD 8 May '62.

Based on the novel by Jaroslaw Iwaszkiewicz.

See also: Devils, The (1971).

Joan the Woman

1916 (1917) Cardinal Film Corp (Lasky & Par) tinted seqs sil.

Prod & Dir: Cecil B. DeMille.

Sc: Jeanie MacPherson.

Cast: Wallace Reid, Geraldine Farrar, Raymond Hatton, Theodore Roberts, Tully Marshall, Hobart Bosworth, Charles Clary.

Joan the Woman cont.

F (the betrayer of Joan of Arc is reincarnated, gives his life for France)

Ref: SF 10 p46, 51; LC.

See also: Joan of Arc.

Joconde, La

1958 French color ani & live sh.

Dir: Henri Gruel.

F-com

Ref: Ani/Cin p 101, 170.

Based on the "Mona Lisa" painting by Leonardo Da Vinci.

Joe and Petunia

1968? British, British Board of Trade color ani 1.5 mins.

Dir: Nicholas Spargo.

F

Ref: ASIFA 4; MTVM Nov '68 p20A.

Joe Boko

1915-16 Essanay & U sil ani sh series.

Prod: Wallace A. Carlson & J.R. Bray.

F-com (hero asphyxiates villain with cigar -- title short in series)

Ref: LC; F/A p464; Ani chart.

Joe Egg

(play by P. Nichols)

See: Day in the Death of Joe Egg, A (1971).

Joe MacBeth

1955 (1956) Film Locations (Col) 90 mins.

Filmed in England.

Prod: Mike J. Frankovich.

Assoc Prod: George Maynard.

Dir: Ken Hughes.

SP: Philip Yordan.

Art Dir: Alan Harris.

Cin: Basil Emmett.

Edit: Peter Rolfe Johnson.

Mus Dir: Richard Taylor.

Cast: Paul Douglas, Ruth Roman, Bonar Colleano, Gregoire Aslan, Sidney James, Philip Vickers, Minerva Pious, Bill Nagy.

F-seq (instead of witch, old fortune-teller; ghost of Banquo-character appears)

Ref: MPH 21 Jan '56; MFB Dec '55 p 175; FDY '57.

Based on play "Macbeth" by William Shakespeare.

See also: Macbeth.

Johanes Doktor Faust

1958 Czech ani puppet sh.

F

Ref: Czech An '61.

See also: Faust.

Johann Mouse

1952 MGM color ani 8 mins.

Prod: Fred Quimby.

Dir: William Hanna & Joseph Barbera.

BG: Robert Gentle.

Ani: Kenneth Muse, Ray Patterson, Ed Barge, & Irven Spence.

Nar: Hans Conried.

Piano Music Composed & Played by: Jakob Gimpel.

F-com

Ref: LC; Acad winner.

See also: Tom and Jerry (1940-).

Johann Sebastian Bach — Fantasy in G Minor

1964 Polish scope 15 mins.

Dir: Jan Svankmajer.

Cin: Svatopluk Maly.

mus-F

Ref: Collier.

Johann, the Coffin Maker

See: Coffin Maker, The (1928).

John and Marsha

n.d. Amateur (Center Cinema) 16mm color ani 2 mins.

Made by: Peter Weiner.

Written by: Stan Freberg.

F-com

Ref: CCC 2.

John Dough and the Cherub

1910 Selig sil 1000 ft.

F (Land of Oz; Princess Ozma; magic elixir)

Ref: MPW 7:1488-89, 1538.

Based on characters created by L. Frank Baum.

See also: Wizard of Oz, The.

John Henry and the Inky-Poo

1946 Par color ani puppet 1 reel.

Prod & Dir: George Pal.

SP: Latham Ovens & Robert Monroe.

Nar: Rex Ingram.

F (the American legend)

Ref: LC; Acad nom.

See also: Puppetoons (1943-47).

John, the Hero

1972 (1973) Hungarian, Pannonia color ani 90 mins.

Dir: Marcell Jankovics, Jozsef Nepp, & Bela Ternovszky.

SP: M. Jankovics.

Nar Written by: Sandor Weores.

Mus: Janos Gyulai-Gal.

F-mus

Ref: MTVM 27:3:11.

Based on the epic by Sandor Petofi.

Johnny Doesn't Live Here Any More

(And So They Were Married -- e.t?)

1944 Mono 9 reels (79 mins).

Exec Prod: Maurice King.

Prod: Franklin King.

Dir: Joe May.

SP: Philip Yordan & John H. Kafka.

Art Dir: Paul Palmentola & George Moskov.

Cin: Ira Morgan.

SpFX: Ray Mercer.

Edit: Martin Cohn.

Mus: Franke W. Harling.

Cast: Simone Simon, James Ellison, William Terry, Minna Gombell, Chick Chandler, Alan Dinehart, Gladys Blake, Robert Mitchum, Janet Shaw, Jerry Maren [pixie].

F-com (man spills salt & thereby acquires a bad-luck gremlin)

Ref: MFB Nov '44 p 128; FIR May '64 p274; Vd 15 June '44 p6-7 ad.

Based on the story by Alice Means Reeve.

Johnny Got His Gun

1971 Bruce Campbell Prod (Cinemation) color & b&w 111 mins.

Prod: Bruce Campbell.

Dir & SP: Dalton Trumbo.

Prod Design: Harold Michelson.

Cin: Jules Brenner.

Edit: William P. Dornisch.

Mus: Jerry Fielding.

Cast: Timothy Bottoms, Kathy Fields, Marsha Hunt, Jason Robards (Jr), Donald Sutherland [Jesus], Diane Varsi, Charles McGraw, Eduard Franz, Donald Barry, Bruce Morrow.

cont.

cont

Johnny Got His Gun cont.

psy-F-H (after WWI, a deaf, mute & blind quadruple amputee remembers his past, and has several varieties of fantasies, including conversations with Jesus)

Ref: FF '71 p582-85; F&F Dec '72 p46-48; Vw 19 May '71.

Based on the novel by Dalton Trumbo.

Johnny the Giant Killer

(Jeannot l'Intrepide)

1950 (1953) French, Jean Image (Lippert) color ani 77 mins (60 mins).

Prod & Dir: Jean Image.

Story: J. & Eraine Image.

SP: Paul Colline.

Eng lang SP: Charles Frank & Nesta MacDonald.

Mus: Rene Cloerec.

F (ogre; city of insects; villainous wasps; boy reduced to miniature size)

Ref: Vd 24 June '53; MFB June '52 p80; UniF B 26; LC.

Based on characters from Charles Perrault.

Johnny Vengman and the Big Comet

See: Janne Vångman och den Storen Kometen (1955).

Johnstown Monster, The

1971 British, Sebastion Prods for the Children's Film Foundation color 54 mins.

Filmed in Ireland.

Prod: Gabrielle Beaumont.

Dir & SP: Olaf Pooley.

Art Dir: Arnold Chapkis.

Cin: Clive Tickner & Ray Sturgess.

Mus: Harry Robinson.

Cast: Connor Brennan, Simon Tully, Rory Baily, Kim McDonald, Amanda Jane Tully, Seamus Kelly, Michael Goodliffe.

com; SF-seq (children create a hoax lake monster; the real one turns up at the end briefly)

Ref: MFB Nov '71 p222; TVG.

Joie de Vivre

(Joy of Living)

1934 French ani sh.

Made by: Hector Hoppin & Anthony Gross.

exp-F

Ref: F/A p627.

Joining Out

See: Splitttttttt (n.d.).

Jokai Senhime Goten

1970? Japanese, Leo Production color ani sh?

sex-F (erotic cartoon produced from woodcuts)

Ref: MTVM Nov '69 p20.

Jolly Bad Fellow, A

See: They All Died Laughing (1964).

Jolly Genie, The

1962 (1964) Emerson Film Enterprises ani & live.

Dir & SP: Wesley E. Barry.

F-com

Ref: HR 15 June '62; BO 26 Oct '64.

Jolly Little Elves

1934 U color ani sh.

Prod: Walter Lantz.

Ani: Manuel Marino, Lester Kline, & Fred Kopietz.

F-com

Ref: LC; Acad nom.

Jolly Trio's Dream

1909 French, Pathé sil 417 ft.

F-com-dream (woman flies into air, comes down in pieces; men disappear; all turns out to be a dream)

Ref: Views IV-8:8.

Jonah Man, The or
The Traveler Bewitched

1904 British, Hepworth sil 246 ft.

Prod: Cecil Hepworth.

F-com (tricks; appearances & disappearances)

Ref: BFI cat p79.

Jonathan Livingston Seagull

1973 Hall Bartlett Prods (Par) color.

Prod & Dir: Hall Bartlett.

Assoc Prod & SP: Richard Bach.

Prod Design: Boris Leven.

Cin: Jack Couffer.

Bird Trainer: Ray Berwick.

Ani & SpFX: Bob Clampett.

Matte Paintings: Jim Danforth.

F-com (adventures of a seagull that wants to be the fastest bird in the air)

Ref: Vw 15 Nov '72 p38; SR March '73 p 12, 14; QPH 24 Feb '73.

Based on the novel by Richard Bach.

Jonathan

(Jonathan, Vampire Sterben Nicht)

1970 (1972) W. German, Beta & Iduna-Film (New Yorker) color 110 mins (103 mins).

Dir & SP: Hans W. Geissendörfer.

Art Dir: Hans Gailling.

Cin: Robby Müller &? Fred Zenker.

Edit: Wolfgang Hedinger.

Mus: Roland Kovac.

Cast: Jürgen Jung, Ilse Künkele, Oskar von Schab, Hans-Dieter Jendreyko, Paul Albert Krumm [vampire].

F-H (vampire [Dracula?] is oppressor of peasants; the man who overthrows him becomes just as bad as the vampire)

Ref: Atlas Feb '71; BO 11 Sept '72 BookinGuide; press booklet on film.

Based on characters created by Bram Stoker.

See also: Dracula.

Jones' Nightmare

(The Lobster Still Pursued Him --alt.t?)

1911 British, Acme sil 435 ft.

Dir: Fred Rains.

Cast: Fred Rains.

F-H-dream-com (man pursued by giant lobster & demons, & shot to moon in his dream)

Ref: Bios 16 Feb '11; Gifford/BFC 02913.

Jones' Patent Motor

1906 British, Cricks & Sharp sil sh.

Dir: Arthur Cooper.

SF-com

Ref: Gifford/SF p34.

Jorinde and Joringel

1922 German sil ani silhouette 634 ft.

Dir: Toni Raboldt.

F (girl into bird; seven-league boots)

Ref: F/A p635; BFI cat p59.

Based on the fairy tale collected by Jacob & Wilhelm Grimm.

Jorobado de la Morgue, El

(The Hunchback of the Morgue)

1972 Spanish, Eva & Janus color 90 mins.

Prod: F. Lara Polop.

Dir: Javier Aguirre.

Cin: Raul Perez Cubero.

SpFX: Pablo Perez.

Edit: Petra de Nieva.

Mus: Carmelo Bernaola.

cont.

Jorobado de la Morque cont.

Cast: Paul Naschy (rn: Jacinto Molina) [hunchback], Rossana Yanni, Vic Winner, Elena Arpon, Manuel De Blas, Antonio Pica, Alberto Dalbes, Maria Perschy.

SF-H (hunchback keeps body of dead girl he loves in dungeon, fights rats which try to eat it; also supplies bodies for mad scientist who feeds them to a globular monster; monster & hunchback fight, fall into acid vat)

Ref: Vw 16 May '73 p32; Dick Klemensen.

Josef Killian

(Postava k Podpriani: Order and Disorder)

1963 Czech 16mm 38 mins.

Dir: Pavel Juracek & Jan Schmidt.

SP: P. Juracek.

Cin: Jan Curík.

Mus: Wiliam Bukovy.

Cast: Karel Vasicek, Pavel Bertl.

sur-F (Kafkaesque: man rents a cat from a state cat shop, but can't return it as the shop never existed)

Ref: CoF 6:56; Czech films clipping.

Joseph and His Brethren

1962 Israeli color ani puppet feature.

Prod & Dir: Alina & Yoram Gross.

rel-F

Ref: Ani/Cin p 158.

Based on the story of Joseph from the Bible.

Joseph Killian

See: Josef Killian (1963).

Joseph Sold by His Brothers

See: Giuseppe Venduto dai Fratelli (1960).

Joseph the Dreamer

1967? Israeli color ani puppet.

Prod & Dir: Yoram Gross.

rel-F

Ref: MTVM April '67 p6.

Based on the story of Joseph from the Bible.

Joshua and the Blob

1972 Lange & Greenberg Co (Jack H. Harris) color ani 6 mins.

Dir & Ani: John Lange.

Assist Ani: Bob Greenberg.

Mus: Larry Wolff & Maxine Sellers.

F-com (little man encounters pink blob that eventually becomes a little woman)

Ref: Bob Greenberg.

See also: Joshua in a Box (1970).

Joshua in a Box

1970 John Lange (Stephen Bosustow) color ani 4 mins.

Dir, Story, Ani: John C. Lange.

Mus: Matt Andes.

F-com

Ref: Bob Greenberg.

See also: Joshua and the Blob (1972).

Jouets Vivants, Les

(The Living Toys)

1908 French, Pathé sil sh.

Dir: Segundo de Chomon.

F

Ref: DdC 404.

Joueur d'Echecs, Le

See: Chess Player, The.

Journal Animé, Le

(The Animated Journal)

1908 French, Gaum sil ani sh.

Dir: Emile Cohl.

F

Ref: Filmlex p 1370.

Journal of Albion Moonlight, The

(novel by K. Patchen)

See: Plague Summer (1951).

Journey, The

1970 Polish color? ani 6 mins.

Dir: Daniel Szczechura.

F

Ref: IAFF '72.

Journey, The

See: Putovanje (1972?).

Journey Around My Skull

See: Journey Inside My Brain (1971?).

Journey Back to Oz

1971 Filmation color ani 88 mins.

Prod: Norman Prescott & Lou Scheimer.

Assoc Prod: Fred Ladd & Preston Blair.

Dir: Hal Sutherland.

SP: F. Ladd, N. Prescott, & Bernard Evslin.

Seq Dir: Rudy Larriva & Don Towsley.

Art Dir: Christensen.

Ani: Amby Paliwoda.

Mus & Lyrics: Sammy Cahn & Jimmy Van Heusen.

Mus Dir: Walter Scharf.

Voices: (alphabetical) Milton Berle, Herschel Bernardi, Mel Blanc, Paul Ford, Margaret Hamilton, Jack E. Leonard, Paul Lynde, Ethel Merman, Liza Minnelli, Mickey Rooney, Rise Stevens, Danny Thomas.

F-mus-com (Dorothy back in Oz meets the Scarecrow, the Tin Woodsman, and the Lion again, as well as Jack Pumpkinhead, Woodenhead, and a new witch with a horde of magic green elephants)

Ref: MFB Jan '73 p 10-11; Vw 17 Feb '71.

Based on characters created by L. Frank Baum.

Sequel to: Wizard of Oz, The.

Journey Beneath the Desert

See: Atlantide, L' (1960).

Journey Beyond the Stars

See: 2001: A Space Odyssey (1968).

Journey Inside My Brain

(Journey Around My Skull -- alt.t.)

1971? Hungarian, Mafilm 84 mins.

Dir & SP: Gyorgy Revesz.

Cin: Gyorgy Illes.

Mus: Gyorgy Ranki.

Cast: Zoltan Latinovits, Eva Ruttkay, Mari Toroscik, Imre Sinkovits.

psy-F-H ("nightmares, memories, and fantasies of a man about to be operated on for a brain tumor" --F&F)

Ref: Chodkowski; F&F Nov '71 p35-36.

Based on a novel by Frigyes Karinthy.

Journey that Shook the World, The

See: Those Fantastic Flying Fools (1967).

Journey to a Primeval Age

See: Journey to the Beginning of Time (1954/1966).

Journey to the Beginning of Time

(Cesta do Pravĕku: Journey to a Primeval Age)

1954/1966 (1967) Czech/US (New Trends) color ani puppet & live 93 mins (87 mins).

Dir: Karel Zeman.

SP: K. Zeman & J.A. Novotny.

Art Dir: K. Zeman, Zdenĕk Rozkopal, & Ivo Mrdzek.

Cin: Vaclav Pazdernik & Antonin Horak.

Mus: E.F. Burian.

English language version:

Prod, Dir, SP: William Cayton.

Addit Dialog: Fred Ladd.

Cast: James Lucas, Victor Betral, Peter Hermann, Charles Goldsmith.

SF-doc-dream (boys dream they drift backwards down the river of time, encountering increasingly primitive life: mammoths, dinosaurs, pterodactyls, etc.)

Ref: FF '67 p38; Gasca p 168-69; Broz p74, 88; S&S Autumn '55 p98-99.

Journey to the Center of the Earth

● (Voyage au Centre de la Terre)

1909 French, Pathé sil 540 ft.

Dir: Segundo de Chomon.

Ref: DdC p404; Gasca p21.

● 1959 20th-Fox color scope 132 mins.

Prod: Charles Brackett.

Dir: Henry Levin.

SP: Walter Reisch & C. Brackett.

Art Dir: Lyle R. Wheeler, Franz Bachelin, & Herman A. Blumenthal.

Makeup: Ben Nye.

Cin: Leo Tover.

SpFX: L.B. Abbott, James B. Gordon, & Emil Kosa Jr.

Edit: Stuart Gilmore & Jack W. Holmes.

Mus: Bernard Herrmann.

Cast: Pat Boone, James Mason, Arlene Dahl, Diane Baker, Alan Napier, Thayer David, Peter Ronson, Alan Caillou.

Ref: FF '59 p314-15; FDY '60; Focus March-April '70 p30, 41.

SF; com-seq (explorers in 19th century find way to the center of the Earth; many wonders encountered, including ruins of ancient city [Atlantis?] and dinosaurs)

SF (trip to Earth's center)

Based on novel "Voyage au Centre de la Terre" by Jules Verne.

Journey to the Center of Time

1968 Borealis & Dorad color 82 mins.

Prod: Ray Dorn & David L. Hewitt.

Dir: D.L. Hewitt.

SP: David Prentiss.

Prod Design: Edward D. Engoron.

Cin: Robert Caramico.

SpFX: Modern Film Effects.

Edit: Bill Welburn.

Cast: Scott Brady, Gigi Perreau, Anthony Eisley, Abraham Sofaer, Austin Green, Andy David, Lyle Waggner.

SF (people in time machine first go to future, encountering totalitarian society battling with mutants, then to past with dinosaurs, back to future: they oscillate in time)

Ref: MFB March '73 p53; Borst; Pardi.

Journey to the Far Side of the Sun

(Doppelgänger --s.t.)

1969 British, Century 21 Prods (U) color 101 mins (94 mins).

Prod & Story: Gerry & Sylvia Anderson.

Dir: Robert Parrish.

SP: G. & S. Anderson, & Donald James.

Art Dir: Bob Bell.

SpFX Dir: Derek Meddings.

Cin & SpFX: Harry Oakes.

Edit: Len Walter.

Mus: Barry Gray.

Cast: Ian Hendry, Roy Thinnes, Patrick Wymark, Lynn Loring, Loni von Friedl, Herbert Lom.

SF (planet discovered in the same orbit as Earth on the opposite side of the Sun; identical to Earth, only everything is reversed)

Ref: MFB '69 p240; Vw 15 Aug '69; LAT 8 July '68.

See also: Stranger, The (1973).

Journey to the 4th Planet

See: Angry Red Planet, The (1959).

Journey to the Past

See: I'll Never Forget You (1951).

Journey to the Seventh Planet

1961 (1962) Cinemagic (AIP) color 83 mins.

Filmed in Sweden.

Prod, Dir, Story: Sidney Pink.

SP: Ib Melchior & S. Pink.

Cin: Age Wiltrup.

SpFX: Bent Barfod Films.

Mus: Ib Glindemann.

Cast: John Agar, Greta Thyssen, Ann Smyrner, Mimi Heinrich, Carl Ottosen, Ove Sprogoe.

SF-H (in year 2001, expedition to Neptune encounters huge brain capable of creating matter to deceive & combat spacemen; features various monsters & menaces, including giant rat and giant spider)

Ref: MFB Aug '62 p114; MMF 9:39; FDY '63 p197.

Journey to the Stars

1961 Fine Arts color 80 mins.

Prod & Dir: John Wilson.

SF-doc

Ref: Trieste I.

Journey to the West

See: Monkey (1960?).

Journey with Ghost Along Tokkaido Road

See: Along with Ghosts (1969).

Joy and the Dragon

1916 Pathé sil.

Dir: Henry King.

Sc: Will M. Ritchey.

Cin: William Beckway.

Cast: Marie Osborne, Henry King, Mollie O'Connell.

F

Joy of Living

See: Joie de Vivre (1934).

Joyeux Microbes, Les

See: Magic Cartoons (1909).

Joyeux Prophète Russe, Le

See: Fake Russian Prophet, The (1904).

Joyous Microbes, The

See: Magic Cartoons (1909).

Juan y Junior en un Mundo Diferente

(Juan and Junior in a Different World)

1970 Spanish, Cinematográfica Ronte color 89 mins.

cont.

Juan y Junior... cont.

Dir: Pedro Olea.

Story: Juan G. Atienza, P. Olea, & Juan A. Porto.

SP: P. Olea & J.A. Porto.

Art Dir: Wolfgang Burman.

Cin: Manuel Rojas.

Edit: José Antonio Rojo.

Mus: Juan (rn Juan Pardo) & Junior (rn Antonio Morales).

Cast: Juan Pardo, Antonio Morales, Maribel Martin, Francisco Merino, Luis Peña, Conchito Rabal.

SF-mus (aliens from planet Nigro sent to Earth to kill famous singing duo & take their places)

Ref: SpCin '71 p42-43.

Juanita Banana

(Ang Magkaibang Daidig ni Juanita Banana --ad.t.)

1968 Philippine, Sampaguita.

Dir: José De Villa.

Story & SP: Pablo S. Gomez.

Sets: Honorato de la Paz.

Cin: Felipe Santiago & Tommy Marcelino.

Mus: Danny Holmsen.

Cast: Rosemarie, Pepito Rodriquez, Ricky Belmonte, Bella Flores, Boy Alano, German Moreno, Matimtiman Cruz, Eddie Miller.

F (fairy tale with magic, elf-like tiny people, etc.)

Ref: Chodkowski.

Based on the Continental Komics serial.

Jubilee

1965 Soviet, Gruziafilm (Sovexportfilm) color ani 20 mins.

Dir: O. Andronikashvili.

Story: G. Yeristavi.

Ani: A. Shalikashvili.

F (clay pot honored by dishes and cups)

Ref: Sovexportfilm cat 3:116, 2:128.

Judex

● 1916-17 French sil serial 12 parts.

Dir: Louis Feuillade.

Cast: René Cresté, Yvette Andreyor.

bor-F-H (hero vs masked criminals in Paris)

Ref: S&S Summer '63 p149, Winter '63-64 p242; Laclos p189; LC.

See also: New Mission of Judex, The (1917).

● 1933 French.

Dir: Maurice Champreux.

Cin: Georges Raulet.

Mus: Francois Gailhard.

Cast: Rene Ferte, Marcel Vallee, Mihalesco, Jean Lefebvre, Rene Navarre, Costantini.

Ref: CoF 9 p39; Willis p263.

● (L'Uomo in Nero --alt.t. [possibly L'Uomo en Negro?])

1963 French/Italian, Comptoir Francais du Film/Filmes scope 95 mins (91 mins).

Dir: Georges Franju.

SP: Jacques Champreux & Francis Lacassin.

Art Dir: Robert Giordani.

Cin: Marcel Fradétal.

Edit: Gilbert Natot.

Mus: Maurice Jarre.

Cast: Channing Pollock, Francine Berge, Edith Scob, Michel Vitold, Jacques Jounneau, Sylva Koscina.

bor-SF-H (masked heroes vs masked criminals; video-spy techniques)

cont.

Judex cont.

Ref: Vw 18 Dec '73; FD 25 April '66; MFB '67 p89.

Based on the silent serial.

Judge Rummy

1920-21 Bray (Int'l Film Service Co) sil ani sh series.

Dir: Gregory La Cava, Grim Natwick, Jack King, Burton Gillett.

F-com

Ref: LC.

See also: Smokey Smokes (1920).

Jueces de la Biblia, Los

(The Judges of the Bible)

1966 Spanish/Italian color 110 mins.

Dir: Francisco Perez Dolz.

Story: P. Emilio Cordero.

SP: Ottavio Jemma, Flavio Nicolini, Marcello Baldi, & Tonino Guerra.

Cin: Marcello Masciocchi.

Mus: Teo Usuelli.

Cast: Anton Geesink, Ivo Garrani, Fernando Rey, Maruchi Fresno, Rosalba Neri.

rel-F (the story of Samson and Delilah; at climax he destroys a temple with his super-strength)

Ref: SpCin '67 p208.

Based on the Book of Judges from "The Bible."

See also: Samson and Delilah.

Juego de Hombres

(Game of Men)

1964 Spanish, Alfyega & Gasset.

Dir: José Luis Gamboa.

SP: J. L. Gamboa & Laura Olmo.

Art Dir: L.P. Espinosa.

Cin: Miguel F. Mila.

Mus: José A. Buenagu.

Cast: P.M. Sanchez, Antonio Brañas, Frank Latimore, Laura Granados, Roberto Camardiel.

SF (satellite fails to land on a space station)

Ref: SpCin '64.

Juego de Naipes

(Game of Cards)

1969 Spanish, Deborja Films color scope ani puppet 10.5 mins.

Dir & Cin: Salvador Gijón.

Edit: Pablo G. del Amo.

F (dog & bird, helped by beings from space, save friends from the King of Gambling)

Ref: SpCin '71.

Juego Diabolico

(Diabolic Game)

1964 (1965) Mexican (Azteca).

Cast: Beto El Boticario, Raul Farell, Freddy Fernandez.

F (the devil)

Ref: FDY '65.

Jueves, Milagro, Los

(On Thursdays, a Miracle)

1957 Spanish.

Dir & SP: Luis G. Berlanga.

rel-F (fake miracle becomes real)

Ref: FIR Aug-Sept '58 p354; S&S Summer '58 p58.

Juez Sangriento, El

See: Night of the Blood Monster (1970).

Jug of Bread, a Loaf of Wine, and Lewis Carroll in a Barrel, A

1968 Amateur 16mm color 27 mins.

Made by: John Dentino.

exp-F

Ref: SF Times Dec '68.

Jugendrausch

See: Eva and the Grasshopper (1927).

Juggernaut

1936 (1937) British, Twicken-ham (Grand National) 70 mins.

Prod: Julius Hagen.

Dir: Henry Edwards.

SP: Cyril Campion, H. Fowler Mear, & H. Fraenkel.

Cast: Boris Karloff, Joan Syndham, Arthur Margetson, Gibb McLaughlin, Morton Selten, Anthony Ireland.

bor-H (Karloff at climax poisons self, lectures to group on symptoms of dying)

Ref: HR 17 Nov '36; MPH 17 Oct '36 p51; FDY '38.

Based on a novel by Alice Campbell.

Juggler of Our Lady, The

1957 Terrytoons (20th-Fox) color scope ani 9 mins.

Prod: Paul Terry.

Dir & Ani: Al Kouzel.

Assist: Gene Deitch.

Design: R.O. Blechman.

Nar: Boris Karloff.

exp-F-com (the skill of a Juggler pleases the Virgin Mary)

Ref: MFB Nov '58 p 147; LC.

Based on the book with art by R.O. Blechman.

Juif Errant, Le

See: Wandering Jew, The (1904).

Juif Polonais, Le

(The Polish Jew)

1937 French 79 mins.

Prod: Jacques Haik.

Dir: Jean Kemm.

Cast: Harry Baur, Maddy Berry.

psy-F-H (murderer haunted by his conscience)

Ref: FD 24 Sept '37; Vw 29 Sept '37, Acad.

Based on the novel by Emile Erckmann & Alexandre Chatrian.

See also: Bells, The; Burgo-meister, The (1935).

Jujin Yukiotoko

See: Half Human (1955).

Jujiro

(Crossroads)

1928 Japanese sil.

Dir: Teinosuke Kinugasa.

psy-F-H-seq (time confused; hero imagines arrows coming at him, water turning to steam, cat attracted by his open wounds)

Ref: Anderson/Richie p55.

Juke Box Jamboree

1942 U color ani sh.

Prod: Walter Lantz.

Dir: Alex Lovy.

Story: Ben Hardaway & C. Cough.

Ani: Verne Harding.

Mus: Darrell Calker.

F-mus-com

Ref: LC; Acad nom.

Jules Verne as a Child

See: Petit Jules Verne, Le (1907).

Jules Verne's Mysterious Island

See: Mysterious Island (1950).

Jules Verne's Rocket to the Moon

See: Those Fantastic Flying Fools (1967).

Juliet of the Spirits (1964) Italian

Juliana do Amor Perdido

(Lost Love Juliana)

1970 Brazilian, Entre Films & Vera Cruz & Bras & Continental (MGM?) color 94 mins.

Dir & Mus: Sergio Ricardo.

SP: S. Ricardo & Roberto Santos.

Art Dir: Carmelia Cruz.

Cin: Dib Lufti.

Edit: Silvio Renoldi.

Cast: Mario do Rosario, Francisco Di Franco, Macedo Neto, Itala Nandi, Antonio Pitanga.

F ("voodoo Cinderella")

Ref: Vw 14 Oct '70.

Juliet of the Spirits

(Giulietta degli Spiriti)

1964 (1965) Italian, Federiz (Rizzoli) color 148 mins (137 mins).

Prod & Dir: Federico Fellini.

Story: F. Fellini & Tullio Pinelli.

cont

Juliet of the Spirits cont.

SP: F. Fellini, T. Pinelli, Ennio Flaiano, & Brunello Rondi.

Art Dir: Piero Gherardi.

Cin: Gianni di Venanzo.

Edit: Ruggero Mastroianni.

Mus: Nino Rota.

Cast: Giulietta Masina, Sandra Milo, Sylva Koscina, Fredrich Ledebur, Mario Pisu, Valentina Cortese, Genius, Lou Gilbert.

psy-F-seqs (married woman sees visions of all kinds: pirates, giant grandfather, elfin creatures, etc. etc.)

Ref: FD 3 Nov '65; MPW 22 Dec '65; Time 12 Nov '65; MFB March '66 p37; Vw 7 Nov '66.

Juliette ou la Clef des Songes

(Juliette or the Key to the Dreams)

1950 French, Sacha Gordine 95 mins.

Dir: Marcel Carné.

cont

Juliette... cont.

SP: Jacques Viot.

Art Dir: Alexander Trauner & Auguste Capelier.

Cin: Henri Alekan.

Mus: Joseph Kosma.

Cast: Gérard Philipe, Suzanne Cloutier.

F-dream (in dream, all in village have lost identity; youth in prison escapes to a dream world)

Ref: Vw 16 May '51; deGroot p 156; Sadoul p443; S&S Feb '51 p386, June '51 p39.

Based on a play by Georges Neveux.

Julius Caesar

● 1909 Italian, Itala sil 836 ft.

Ref: Shake/Sil p98-101.

● 1950 Avon 16mm 96 mins.

Dir & Adapt: David Bradley.

Cin: Louis McMahon.

cont.

Julius Caesar cont.

Mus: John Becker.

Mus Dir: Grant Fletcher.

Cast: Charlton Heston, Harold Tasker, David Bradley, Grosvenor Glenn, William Russell, Helen Ross, Mary Darr.

Ref: FIR March '73 p 146.

● 1970 (1971) British, Commonwealth United (AIP) color scope 117 mins.

Exec Prod: Henry T. Weinstein & Anthony B. Unger.

Prod: Peter Snell.

Dir: Stuart Burge.

Adapt: Robert Furnival.

Prod Design: Julia Trevelyan Oman.

Makeup: Cliff Sharpe.

Cin: Ken Higgins.

Edit: Eric Boyd-Perkins.

Mus: Michael Lewis.

Cast: Charlton Heston, Jason Robards (Jr), John Gielgud, Richard Johnson, Robert Vaughn, Richard Chamberlain, Diana Rigg, Jill Bennett, Christopher Lee, Alan Browning, Derek Godfrey, Michael Gough, Andre Morell, Damien Thomas.

Ref: FF '71 p94-96.

hist; F-seqs (prophecy of Caesar's death is fulfilled; Calpurnia has prophetic dream; Caesar's ghost visits Brutus)

Based on the play by William Shakespeare.

See also: Shakespeare Writing Julius Caesar (1907).

Note: the other film versions of this play do not have significant fantasy content.

Jument Verte, La

See: Green Mare, The (1959).

Jump

1972 UCLA 16mm ani sh.

Made by: Jim Keeshen.

F-com (comedy adventures of a fireman)

Ref: UCLA notes; Greg Chalfin.

Jumpin' Jupiter

1955 WB color ani 7 mins.

Dir: Chuck Jones.

Voices: Mel Blanc.

F-com (Porky Pig & Sylvester are kidnapped by a flying saucer)

Ref: LC; David Rider.

See also: Porky Pig (1934-); Sylvester P. Pussycat (194?-).

Jungfrukallan

See: Virgin Spring, The (1960).

Jungle, The

1952 Voltaire Prods (Lippert) sepia 74 mins.

Filmed in India.

Prod & Dir: William Berke.

SP: Carroll Young.

Addit Dialog: Orville Hampton.

Art & Settings: A.J. Dominic & P.B. Krishnan.

Cin: Clyde DeVinna.

Edit: L. Balu.

Mus: Dakshinamoorthy & G. Ramanathan.

Cast: Marie Windsor, Rod Cameron, Cesar Romero, Sulochana, M.N. Nambiar, David Abraham, Ramakrishna, Chutra Devi.

SF (hunters find vicious mammoths alive in India)

Ref: Pardi; Vd 7 Aug '52; LC; Capra p434, 435.

Jungle Book

● 1942 Alexander Korda Films (UA) color 109 mins.

Prod: Alexander Korda.

Dir: Zoltan Korda.

SP: Laurence Stallings.

Prod Design: Vincent Korda.

Cin: Lee Garmes & W. Howard Green.

SpFX: Lawrence Butler.

Mus: Miklos Rozsa.

Cast: Sabu, Joseph Calleia, Patricia O'Rourke, John Qualen, Frank Puglia, Rosemary De Camp, Ralph Byrd, Noble Johnson.

F (boy raised by wolves can communicate with animals; fights giant talking white cobra; other F)

Ref: HR 25 March '42; FDY '43; MFB June '42 p72; LC.

Based principally on story "The King's Ankus."

● (Jungle Book, The)

1967 WD (BV) color ani 78 mins.

Prod: Walt Disney.

Dir: Wolfgang Reitherman.

SP: Larry Clemmons, Ralph Wright, Ken Anderson, & Vance Gerry.

Ani Dir: Milt Kahl, Ollie Johnston, Frank Thomas, & John Lounsbery.

Layout Sup: Don Griffith.

BG Styling: Al Dempster.

FX Ani: Dan MacManus.

Mus: George Bruns.

Voices: George Sanders, Phil Harris, Sebastian Cabot, Louis Prima, Sterling Holloway, David Bailey, Verna Felton.

F-mus-com (Mowgli lives in the jungle with talking animals)

Ref: FF '67 p419-20; MFB Jan '68 p 10; LAT 18 Oct '67; Vw 4 Oct '67.

Based on the book by Rudyard Kipling.

See also: Omar and the Ogres (n.d.).

Jungle Captive

(Wild Jungle Captive -- rr.t.)

1944 (1945) U (Realart --rr) 64 mins.

Exec Prod: Ben Pivar.

Assoc Prod: Morgan B. Cox.

Dir: Harold Young.

Story: Dwight V. Babcock.

SP: M. Coates Webster & D.V. Babcock.

Art Dir: John B. Goodman & Robert Clatworthy.

Cin: Maury Gertsman (or Charles Van Enger?).

Edit: Fred R. Feitshans Jr.

Mus Dir: Paul Sawtell.

Cast: Otto Kruger, Rondo Hatton, Amelita Ward, Phil Brown, Jerome Cowan, Eddie Acuff, Vicky Lane [ape woman].

SF-H (ape woman revived from the dead)

Ref: HR & Vd 13 June '45; FDY '46; MFB Dec '46 ;p 169.

Sequel to: Captive Wild Woman (1943).

Jungle Gents

1954 (1955) AA 64 mins.

Prod: Ben Schwalb.

Dir: Edward Bernds & Austen Jewell.

SP: Elwood Ullman & E. Bernds.

Art Dir: David Milton.

Cin: Harry Neumann.

Edit: Sam Fields.

Mus: Marlin Skiles.

Jungle Gents cont.

Cast: Leo Gorcey, Huntz Hall, Laurette Luez, Bernard Gorcey, David Condon, Bennie Bartlett, Eric Snowden.

bor-F-com (Hall can locate diamonds by smell)

Ref: Vd & HR 10 Feb '55; FDY '55.

See also: Spooks Run Wild (1941).

Jungle Girl

1941 Rep serial 15 parts 31 reels.

Assoc Prod: Hiram S. Brown Jr.

Dir: William Witney & John English.

SP: Ronald Davidson, Norman S. Hall, William Lively, Joseph O'Donnell, Joseph F. Poland, & Alfred Batson.

Cin: Reggie Lanning.

Edit: Edward Todd & William Thompson.

Mus: Cy Feuer.

Cast: Frances Gifford, Tom Neal, Frank Lackteen, Trevor Bardette, Gerald Mohr, Eddie Acuff.

bor-F

Ref: Ser/Rep p23; LC; FDY '58.

Loosely based on the novel by Edgar Rice Burroughs.

Sequel: Perils of Nyoka (1942).

Jungle Goddess

1922 Selig sil serial 15 parts 31 reels.

Dir: James Conway.

Sc: Agnes Johnston & Frank Dazey.

Cast: Elinor Field, Truman Van Dyke, Lafe McKee, Vonda Phelps, Marie Pavis, Olin Francis, William Platt, H.G. Wells, George Reed.

bor-F (girl raised in jungle by savages as goddess; idol with beams from eyes?)

Ref: CNW p102-103, 228-29; MPW 54: 16-17, 427; LC.

See also: Queen of the Jungle (1935).

Jungle Hell

1956 Taj Mahal Prods (Medallion TV).

Prod, Dir, SP: Norman A. Cerf.

Exec Prod: J. Manning Post.

Mus: Michael Carras.

Cast: Sabu, K.T. Stevens, David Bruce, George E. Stone.

SF (radioactive rock menace; it is destroyed by death ray from passing flying saucer)

Ref: Richardson.

Jungle Jim

(white hunter character created by Alex Raymond in the comic strip of the same name)

See: Lost Tribe, The (1948); Fury of the Congo (1951); Jungle Jim in the Forbidden Land (1951); Jungle Manhunt (1951); Voodoo Tiger (1952); Killer Ape (1953).

Jungle Jim in the Forbidden Land

(Jungle Jim in the Land of the Giants --e.t?).

1951 (1952) Katzman (Col) 65 mins.

Prod: Sam Katzman.

Dir: Lew Landers.

SP: Samuel Newman.

Art Dir: Paul Palmentola.

Cin: Fayte Browne.

Edit: Henry Batista.

Mus Dir: Mischa Bakaleinikoff.

Cast: Johnny Weissmuller, Angela Greene, Jean Willes, Lester Matthews.

SF ("giant" beast-people)

Ref: MFB May '52 p66; Vd 29 Feb '52; FM 13:68, 14:27.

Jungle Jim in Forbidden Land cont.

Based on the comic strip "Jungle Jim" by Alex Raymond.

See also: Jungle Jim.

Jungle Jive

1944 U color ani 1 reel.

Prod: Walter Lantz.

Dir: James Culhane.

Story: Ben Hardaway & Milt Schaffer.

mus-F-com (musical gags centered around jungle island, e.g. crab plays boogie-woogie)

Ref: LC; B. Warren.

See also: Swing Symphony (1941-46).

Jungle King

1939 Indian, Wadia.

Prod: Homi Wadia.

Dir: Nari Ghadiali.

Cast: Pramilla, John Cavas, Agha, Nazir, Mehru [gorilla].

bor-F

Ref: MovPicM Annual '39 p59.

See also: Jungle Queen (1956).

Jungle Lovers, The

1915 Selig sil 3 reels.

Dir: Lloyd B. Carleton.

Story: James Oliver Curwood.

Cast: Bessie Eyton, Edward J. Peil, Richard Morris, Tom Bates, Edwin Wallock, Cash Darrel.

bor-SF (eccentric scientist creates new super-explosive)

Ref: MPW 25:2059, 2062; LC.

Jungle Madness

1967 Amateur (Film-makers' Coop) 16mm color collage ani & liquid ani 5 mins.

Made by: Don Duga.

exp-abs-F

Ref: FMC 5:95; ASIFA 3.

Jungle Manhunt

1951 Katzman (Col) sepia 66 mins.

Prod: Sam Katzman.

Dir: Lew Landers.

SP: Samuel Newman.

Cin: William Whitley.

Edit: Henry Batista.

Mus Dir: Mischa Bakaleinikoff.

Cast: Johnny Weissmuller, Sheila Ryan, Bob Waterfield, Rick Vallin, Lyle Talbot.

SF (synthetic diamonds; battle of huge reptiles)

Ref: MFB Dec '51 p376; Vd 3 Oct '51.

Based on the King Features Syndicate comic strip "Jungle Jim" by Alex Raymond.

See also: Jungle Jim.

Jungle Moon Men

1954 (1955) Katzman (Col) 69 mins.

Prod: Sam Katzman.

Dir: Charles S. Gould.

Story: Jo Pagano.

SP: Dwight V. Babcock & J. Pagano.

Art Dir: Paul Palmentola.

Cin: Henry Freulich.

SpFX: Jack Erickson.

Edit: Henry Batista.

Mus: Mischa Bakaleinikoff.

Cast: Johnny Weissmuller, Jean Byron, Helene Stanton, Myron Healey, Bill Henry, Ed Hinton.

SF (Weissmuller as himself vs. woman who is thousands of years old; formula for eternal life; tribe of pygmies called "Moon Men")

Ref: HR & Vd 30 March '55; MFB March '55 p40.

Note: not part of Jungle Jim series.

cont.

cont.

Jungle Mystery

1932 U serial 12 parts
24 reels.

Dir: Ray Taylor.

SP: Ella O'Neill, George Plympton, Basil Dickey, & George Morgan.

Cast: Tom Tyler, Noah Beery Jr, Cecilia Parker, William Desmond, Carmelita Geraghty, Sam Baker [ape-man].

bor-F (half-man, half-ape creature)

Ref: LC; Willis; Eric Hoffman.

Based on "The Ivory Trail" by Talbot Mundy.

Jungle Princess

1936 Par 85 mins.

Exec Prod: William Le Baron.

Prod: E. Lloyd Sheldon.

Dir: William Thiel.

Story: Max Marcin.

SP: Cyril Hume, Gerald Geraghty, Gouverneur Morris, M. Marcin, Frank Partos, & Charles Brackett.

Cin: Harry Fischbeck.

Edit: Ellsworth Hoagland.

Mus: Frederick Hollander.

Cast: Dorothy Lamour, Ray Milland, Akim Tamiroff, Lynne Overman, Molly Lamont.

bor-F (girl grows up with tiger; her animal friends rout attackers in the Malay jungle; huge ape)

Ref: HR 17 Nov '36; Vw 30 Dec '36; MPH 28 Nov '36 p66, 68.

Jungle Queen

1944 U serial 13 parts
26 reels.

Assoc Prod: Ray Taylor & Morgan B. Cox.

Dir: R. Taylor & Lewis D. Collins.

SP: George H. Plympton, Ande Lamb, & M.B. Cox.

Edit: Norman A. Cerf, Alvin Todd, Edgar Zane, Irving Birnbaum, Jack Dolan, & Ace Herman.

Cast: Edward Norris, Eddie Quillan, Douglass Dumbrille, Lois Collier, Ruth Roman, Clarence Muse, Lumsden Hare, Napoleon Simpson.

F-seqs (Roman is supernatural guardian of a tribe -- appears & disappears magically, walks through a flaming wall, etc.)

Ref: LC; Acad; Eric Hoffman.

Jungle Queen

1956 Indian, Chitra.

Dir: Nari Ghadiali.

SP: P. Dehlvi.

Art Dir: I.M. Sheikh.

Cin: Suleman & Manzoor.

Mus: N. Bazmi.

Cast: Nadia, John Cavas, Habib.

SF-com-seq (weapon causes hysterical laughter)

Ref: FEFN 13 July '56.

See also: Jungle King (1939).

Jungle Raiders

1945 Esskay Prods (Col)
15 parts 31 reels.

Prod: Sam Katzman.

Dir: Lesley Selander.

SP: Ande Lamb & George H. Plympton.

Cin: Ira Morgan.

Edit: Earl Turner.

Mus: Lee Zahler.

Cast: Kane Richmond, Eddie Quillan, Veda Ann Borg, Carol Hughes, Janet Shaw.

bor-SF (fungus proves to be cure-all drug)

Ref: Stringham; SQ 6; LC; Acad.

Jungle Tales of Tarzan

See: Tarzan the Mighty (1928).

Jungle Trail of the Son of Tarzan

See: Son of Tarzan (1920).

Jungle Treasure

(Old Mother Riley's Jungle Treasure --s.t?)

1951 British 75 mins.

Dir: Maclean Rogers.

SP: Val Valentine.

Cast: Arthur Lucan, Kitty McShane, Sebastian Cabot, Garry Marsh.

Cast: Arthur Lucan, Kitty McShane.

F-com (Old Mother Riley meets the ghost of a pirate)

Ref: Halliwell p216; CoF 11:43; Brit Cin p 103; Collier.

See also: Old Mother Riley's Ghosts (1941); My Son, the Vampire (1952).

Jungle Woman

1944 U 54 mins.

Exec Prod: Ben Pivar.

Prod: Will Cowan.

Dir: Reginald Le Borg.

Story: Henry Sucher.

Art Dir: John B. Goodman & Abraham Grossman.

Cin: Jack McKenzie.

Edit: Ray Snyder.

Mus Dir: Paul Sawtell.

Cast: Evelyn Ankers, J. Carrol Naish, Lois Collier, Samuel S. Hinds, Douglass Dumbrille, Acquanetta, Milburn Stone, Alec Craig, Pierre Watkin, Heinie Conklin.

SF-H (dead ape brought back to life & turned back into a woman & reverts to part-ape stage after death)

Ref: Vd 22 May '44; FDY '45; Acad; LC.

Sequel to: Captive Wild Woman (1943).

Jungle Goddess (1922) Serial

Jungle Woman, The

See: Nabonga (1943).

Junior G-Men

1940 U serial 12 parts
24 reels.

Dir: Ford Beebe & John Rawlins.

SP: George H. Plympton & Basil Dickey.

Cast: The Dead End Kids (Billy Halop, Huntz Hall, Gabriel Dell, Bernard Punsley, Roger Daniels), Phillip Terry, Kenneth Lundy, Russell Hicks, Cy Kendall, Kenneth Howell.

bor-SF (aerial torpedo; wireless device detonates explosives from a distance; new high explosive)

Ref: DTA p 166; TBC p 167-68; LC; Stringham.

See also: Spooks Run Wild (1941).

Junior "G" Men of the Air

1942 U serial 12 parts
25 reels.

Assoc Prod: Henry MacRae.

Dir: Ray Taylor & Lewis D. Collins.

SP: Paul Huston, George H. Plympton, & Griffin Jay.

Addit Dialog: Brenda Weisberg.

Cin: William S. Sickner.

Cast: Billy Halop, Gene Reynolds, Lionel Atwill, Frank Albertson, Richard Lane, Huntz Hall, Bernard Punsley, Frankie Darro, Gabe Dell, Noel Cravat, David Gorcey, Jack Arnold, Jay Novello, J. Pat O'Malley.

bor-SF (gadgetry; airplane muffler and other devices)

Ref: Showmen's 30 May '42; SQ 3:41-50.

See also: Spooks Run Wild (1941).

Jr. Star Trek

1969 Amateur (Film-makers' Coop) 16mm color 8 mins.

Made by: Peter Emshwiller.

Cast: Ed Emshwiller [monster].

SF

Ref: FMC 5:99.

Junket 89

1970 British, Balfour for Children's Film Foundation color 56 mins.

Prod: Carole K. Smith.

Dir: Peter Plummer.

SP: David Ash.

Art Dir: Chris Cook.

Cin: Tony Imi.

Edit: Peter K. Smith.

Mus: Harry Robinson.

Cast: Stephen Brassett, John Blundell, Linda Robson, Mario Renzullo, Freddy Foote, Gary Sobers.

SF-com (boy tampers with instantaneous transportation device)

Ref: MFB May '71 p99.

Sequel: Trouble with 2B, The (1972).

See also: Super Saturday (1972).

Jupiter

1971 French?

Dir: Jean-Pierre Prevóst.

F-H (vampires)

Ref: MMF 24:63; FM 91:35.

Jupiter Smitten

1910 French, Gaum (Kleine) sil 648 ft.

myth-F (Greek gods; transformations)

Ref: MPW 5:153, 158.

See also: Amphitryon (1935).

Jupiter's Thunder Bolts or The Home of the Muses

(Le Tonnerre de Jupiter)

1903 French, Star sil 230 ft.

Prod: Georges Méliès.

F (Jupiter conjures lightning & thunder; dancing girls disappear; fire on pedestals)

Ref: Sadoul/M, GM Mage; LC.

Jusqu'au Coeur
(Right to the Heart)
1969 Canadian, NFB (Col)
color 92 mins.
Prod: Clement Perron.
Dir & SP: Jean Pierre Lefebvre.
Ani: Pierre Hebert.
Cin: Thomas Vamos.
SpFX: Andre Roy.
Edit: Margurite Duparc.
Mus: Robert Charlebois.
Cast: Robert Charlebois, Claudine Monfette, Claudette Robitaille, Paul Berval, Denis Drouin, Pierre Dufresne.
F
Ref: Vw 4 June '69.

Just and the Unjust, The
(by V. Kester)
See: Hell's 400 (1926).

Just for Fun
1961? (1963) British, Amicus (Col) 85 mins.
Prod & SP: Milton Subotsky.
Dir: Gordon Flemyng.
Art Dir: Bill Constable.
Cin: Nicolas Roeg.
Edit: Raymond Poulton.
Incidental Mus: Tony Hatch.
Mus Dir: Franklyn Boyd.
Nar: Alan Freeman.
Cast: Mark Wynter, Cherry Roland, Richard Vernon, Reginald Beckwith, Jeremy Lloyd, Edwin Richfield, Bobby Vee, Irene Handl, The Crickets, Hugh Lloyd, Freddy Cannon, Mario Fabrizi.
mus-com; bor-SF ("about England in the future when the teenagers have the vote" -- M. Subotsky)
Ref: M. Subotsky; MFB May '63 p66; ГГ '63 p285.

Just Imagine
1930 Fox 113 mins.
Assoc Prod, Story, Lyrics, Mus: Ray Henderson, B.G. DeSylva, & Lew Brown.
Dir: David Butler.
SP: D. Butler, R. Henderson, B.G. DeSylva, & L. Brown.
Art Dir: Stephen Goosson & Ralph Hammeras.
Choreog: Seymour Felix.
Cin: Ernest Palmer.
Edit: Irene Morra.
Cast: El Brendel, Frank Albertson, Maureen O'Sullivan, John Garrick, Marjorie White, Hobart Bosworth, Kenneth Thomson, Wilfred Lucas, Mischa Auer, Ivan Linow, J.W. Girard.
SF-mus-com (man from 1930 wakes up in 1980; airplane travel within city; gadgetry of all kinds; trip to Mars; twin Martians: one set good, one set evil)
Ref: AFI F2.2833 p399; MPN 42:16:61; FDY '31; LC.

Justice
See: Pravda (1962).

Justine de Sade
(Sade's Justine)
1972 French, Pierson & ICAR color 110 mins.
Dir: Claude Pierson.
SP: Huguette Boisvert.
Cin: Jean-Jacques Tarbes.
Mus: Francoise & Rober Cotte.
Cast: Alice Arno, Yves Arcanel, Diana Leperier, Dominique Santarelli, Mauro Parenti.
H; bor-F (innocent girl tortured & subjected to sexual abuse, finally killed by lightning)
Ref: Vw 22 March '72 p20.
Based on the book by the Marquis de Sade.

Juve contre Fantomas
1913 French sil.
Dir: Louis Feuillade.
myst; bor-H (fake haunted villa)
Ref: CoF 9:40; DdC II: 339, 379.

Juvenile Drama
See: Sand Castle, The (1961).

Juvenile Dreams
See: Sueños Juveniles (1968).

Jyrtdan
1970? Soviet, Azerbaidjanfilm ani.
SP: Alla Akhundova.
Drawn by: Elchin Aslanov.
F (3 children outwit an ogre)
Ref: MTVM 25:3:15.

K

K-9000: A Space Oddity
1968? The Haboush Co color ani 9.5 mins.
Dir: Robert Mitchell & Robert Swarthe.
SF-sat-com (dog shot into space first lands on planet of cats, then in strange room where he sees himself age)
Ref: ASIFA 4.
See also: 2001: A Space Odyssey (1968).

Kaathavaraayan
1959 Indian (in Tamil), R.R. Pictures 170 mins.
Dir: Ramanna.
Cast: Shivaji Ganesan, T.S. Balaish, Thangavelu, M.N. Rajam, E.V. Saroja.
myth-F (consort god & son are born on Earth; he is born with supernatural powers)
Ref: FEFN 12:5-6:48.

Kabinett des Dr. Caligari, Das
See: Cabinet of Dr. Caligari, The (1919).

Kabir, Devotee to the God
See: Bhatka Kabir (1935).

Kaczka-Plotka
1954 Polish ani sh.
Dir: Wladyslaw Nehrebecki.
F
Ref: ASIFA info sheet.

Kadoyng
1972 British, Shand, for Children's Film Foundation color 60 mins.
Prod: Roy Simpson.
Dir: Ian Shand.
SP: Leo Maguire.
Art Dir: Peggy Gick.
Cin: Mark McDonald.
Edit: Alvin Bailey.
Mus: Edwin Astley.
Cast: Teresa Codling, Adrian Hall, David Williams, Stephen Bone, Andrew Mussell, Leo Maguire [alien], Jean Dallas, Gerald Sim.
SF-com (alien, with powers of teleportation, comes to Earth & helps family)
Ref: MFB Oct '72 p215.

Kaguyahime
See: Mysterious Satellite (1956).

Kaibyo Arima Goten
(Ghost-cat of Arima Palace)
1953 Japanese, Daiei.
Dir: Ryohei Arai.
Cast: Takako Irie, Kotaro Bando.
F-H (ghost; cat woman)
Ref: UniJ Bltn 31.

Kaibyo Gojusan-tsugi
(Ghost-cat of Gojusan-tsugi)
1956 Japanese, Daiei.
Dir: Bin Kado.
Cast: Shintaro Katsu, Tokiko Mita.
F-H (ghost; cat woman)
Ref: UniJ Bltn 31.

Kaibyo Karakuri Tenjo
(Ghost-cat of Karakuri Tenjo)
1958 Japanese, Toei.
Dir: Kinnosuke Fukada.
Cast: Ryunosuke Tsukigata, Kyonosuke Nango.
F-H (ghost; cat woman)
Ref: UniJ Bltn 31.

Kaibyo Koshinuke Daisodo
(Weak-kneed from Fear of Ghost-cat)
1954 Japanese, Toei.
Dir: Torajiro Saito.
Cast: Achako Hanabishi, Michiko Hoshi.
F-H-com (ghostly cat-woman)
Ref: UniJ Bltn 31.

Kaibyo Noroi no Kabe
(Ghost-cat Wall of Hatred)
1958 Japanese, Daiei.
Dir: Kenji Misumi.
Cast: Shintaro Katsu, Yoko Uraji.
F-H (ghost; cat woman)
Ref: UniJ Bltn 31.

Kaibyo Noroi no Numa
(Ghost-cat Swamp of Hatred; The Cursed Pond --ad.t.)
1968 Japanese, Okura 87 mins.
Dir: Yoshihiro Isikawa.
Cast: Kotaro Satomi, Royhei Uchida.
F-H (murdered family returns from grave en masse; ghost; cat woman)
Ref: UniJ Bltn 31; UniJ 42.

Kaibyo Okazaki Sodo
(Terrible Ghost-cat of Okazaki)
1954 Japanese, Daiei.
Dir: Bin Kado.
Cast: Takako Irie, Kotaro Bando.
F-H (ghost; cat woman)
Ref: UniJ Bltn 31.

Kaibyo Oma-ga-tsuji
(Ghost-cat of Oma-gatsuji)
1954 Japanese, Daiei.
Dir: Bin Kado.
Cast: Takako Irie, Shintaro Katsu.
F-H (ghost; cat woman)
Ref: UniJ Bltn 31.

Kaibyo Otama-ga-Ike
(Ghost-cat of Otama-ga-Ike)
1960 (1961) Japanese, Shintoho.
Dir: Yoshihiro Ishikawa.
SP: Y. Ishikawa & Jiro Fujishima.
Cin: Kikuzo Kawasaki.
Cast: Shozaburo Date, Yoichi Numata, Noriko Kitazawa, Namiji Matsura.
F-H (ghost; cat woman)
Ref: UniJ Bltn 31; Japanese Films '61 p36-37; Scognamillo.

Kaibyo Ranbu
(Many Ghost-cats; The Phantom Cat -- ad.t.)
1956 Japanese, Toei 73 mins.
Dir: Masamitsu Igayama.
Cast: Ryunosuke Tsukigata, Shinobu Chihara, H. Tomiya.
F-H (cat turns into ghost woman)
Ref: FEFN 17 Aug '56; UniJ Bltn 31.

Kaibyo Yonaki Numa
(Ghost-cat of Yonaki Swamp; Necromancy --ad.t.)
1957 Japanese, Daiei 89 mins.
Prod: Shin Sakai.
Dir: Katsuhiko Tasaka.
SP: Toshio Tamikado.
Cin: Senkichiro Takeda.
Cast: Shintaro Katsu, Toshio Chiba, Toshio Hosokawa, Tokiko Mita, Michiko Ai.
F-H (ghost; cat woman)
Ref: UniJ Bltn 31; FEFN 28 June '57 p 14.
Based on a work by Akiro Yamazaki.

Kaidan
See: Kwaidan (1963).

Kaidan Ama Yurei
(Ghost of the Girl Diver)
1960 Japanese, Shintoho.
Dir: Goro Katono.
Cast: Juzaburo Akechi, Shinsuke Mikimoto.
F-H (ghost)
Ref: UniJ Bltn 31.

Kaidan Bancho Sarayashiki
(Ghost Story of Broken Dishes at Bancho Mansion; The Ghost of Yotsuya)
1957 Japanese, Toei.
Dir: Juichi Kono.
Cast: Chiyonosuke Azuma, Hibari Misora.
F-H (maid breaks 13 dishes & her head is cut off; her ghost counts the dishes)
Ref: UniJ Bltn 31.
Based on the well-known Japanese ghost legend of Yotsuya.
See also: Ghost of Yotsuya.

Kaidan Barabara Yurei
(Dismembered Ghost)
1968 Japanese, Okura.
Dir: Kinya Ogawa.
Cast: Reiko Akikawa, Miki Hayashi.
F-H (ghost)
Ref: UniJ Bltn 31.

Kaidan Botan Doro
(A Ghost Story of Peonies and Stone Lanterns; A Tale of Peonies and Stone Lanterns; The Bride from Hades; The Bride from Hell; Botandoro; Ghost Beauty -- ad.ts; My Bride Is a Ghost --S.E. Asia t.)
1968 Japanese, Daiei color scope 89 mins.
Dir: Satsuo Yamamoto.
SP: Yoshitaka Yoda.
Art Dir: Yoshinobu Nishioka.
Cin: Chichi Makiura.
Mus: Shiegero (Shigera) Ikeno.
Cast: Kojiro Hongo, Miyoko Akaza, Michiko Otsuka, Akira (Ko) Nishimura, Mayume Ogawa, Takeshi (Takashi?) Shimura.
F (two female ghosts; man falls in love with one, learns she is a ghost, dies to be with her at end)
Ref: Vw 24 July '68; UniJ 42:18; Chodkowski.
See also: Botan-Doro (1955).

Kaidan Chibusa Enoki

(Ghost of Chibusa Enoki)

1958 Japanese, Shintoho.

Dir: Goro Katono.

Cast: Katsuko Wakasugi, Keiko Hasegawa.

F-H (ghost)

Ref: UniJ Bltn 31.

Kaidan Chidori-ga-fuchi

(Ghost of Chidori-ga-fuchi; The Swamp --ad.t.)

1956 Japanese, Toei 66 mins.

Dir: Eiichi Koishi.

Cast: Kinnosuke Nakamura, Yoshiko Wakamizu.

F-H (man & his prostitute lover attempt suicide but only she is successful; years later she comes back as ghost and lures him into swamp & death)

Ref: FEFN 29 June '56; UniJ Bltn 31.

Kaidan Dochu

(A Ghost Story in Passage; Ghost Story of Two Travellers; The Lady Was a Ghost --ad.t.)

1958 Japanese, Toei 85 mins.

Dir: Tadashi Sawashima.

SP: Tadashi Ogawa.

Cin: Makoto Tsuboi.

Cast: Kinnosuke Nakamura, Keiko Ohkawa, Kazuo Nakamura, Hibari Misora, Satomi Oka.

F-com (two princes are pursued by a ghost)

Ref: FEFN 11/18 July '58 p36; Japanese Film '59 p52-53.

Kaidan Fukagawa Jowa

(Tragic Ghost Story of Fukagawa)

1952 Japanese, Daiei.

Dir: Minoru Inuzuka

Cast: Mitsuko Mito, Yuji Hori.

F-H (ghost)

Ref: UniJ Bltn 31.

Kaidan Gojusan-tsugi

(Ghost of Gojusan-tsugi)

1960 Japanese, Daini-Toei.

Dir: Kokichi Uchide.

Cast: Kokichi Takada, Hiromi Hanazono.

F-H (ghost)

Ref: UniJ Bltn 31.

Kaidan Hebionna

(Ghost of Snake-girl; Fear of the Snake Woman --ad.t.)

1968 Japanese, Toei 83 mins.

Dir: Nobuo Nakagawa.

Cast: Akira Nishimura, Reiko Ohara.

F-H (murdered young woman returns as snake)

Ref: UniJ Bltn 31; UniJ 42.

Kaidan Hitotsu-me Jizo

(Ghost from the Pond)

1959 Japanese, Toei.

Dir: Kinnosuke Fukuda.

Cast: Tomisaburo Wakayama, S. Chihara.

F-H (ghost)

Ref: Japanese Films '60 p96.

Kaidan Honjo Nanfushigi

(Ghost Story of Wanderer at Honjo; Seven Mysteries --ad.t.)

1957 Japanese, Shintoho 57 mins.

Dir: Goro Katono.

Story: Akira Sagawa.

SP: Otoya Hayashi & Nagayoshi Akasaka.

Cin: Hiroshi Suzuki.

Cast: Juzaburo Akechi, Shigeru Amachi, Hiroshi Hayashi, Uraji Matsuura, Akiko Yamashita, Michiko Tachibana.

cont

Kaidan Honjo Nanfushigi cont.

F-H (ghost becomes a badger to help hero avenge his lover's rape)

Ref: FEFN 12 July '57 p5; UniJ Bltn 31.

Kaidan Ijin Yurei

(Caucasian Ghost)

1963 Japanese, Okura.

Dir: Satoru Kobayashi.

Cast: Miyako Ichijo, Kyoko Ogimachi.

F-H (ghost)

Ref: UniJ Bltn 31.

Kaidan Iro-Zange-Kyoren Onna Shisho

(Dancing Mistress --ad.t.)

1957 Japanese, Shochiku.

Prod: Akira Koito.

Dir: Ryosuke Kurahashi.

SP: Shinichi Yanagawa.

Cin: Mikio Hattori.

Cast: Hiroshi Nawa, Yataro Kitagami, Jun Tazaki, Achako Hanabishi, Machiko Mizukara, Michiko Saga.

F-H (dancer's ghost gets revenge on her robber lover who murdered her)

Ref: FEFN 26 July '57 p 15.

Kaidan Kagami-ga-fuchi

(Ghost of Kagami-ga-fuchi)

1959 Japanese, Shintoho.

Dir: Masaki Mori.

Cast: Noriko Kitazawa, Fumiko Miyata.

F-H (ghost)

Ref: UniJ Bltn 31.

Kaidan Kakuidori

(Ghost Story of Kakui Street)

1961 Japanese, Daiei.

Dir: Issei Mori.

Cast: Eiji Funakoshi, Katsuhiko Kobayashi.

F-H (ghost)

Ref: UniJ Bltn 31.

Kaidan Kasane-ga-fuchi

(Ghost of Kasane-ga-fuchi)

● (The Depths --ad.t.)

1957 Japanese, Shintoho 57 mins.

Dir: Nobuo Nakagawa.

Story: Katsuji Tsuda.

SP: Yasunori Kawauchi.

Cin: Yoshimi Hirano.

Cast: Katsuko Wakasugi, Takashi Wada, Tetsuro Tamba, Noriko Kitazawa, Kikuko Hanaoka.

F-H (warrior kills blind man whose ghost causes the warrior to kill his own wife, then himself; years later, the son of the warrior & the daughter of the blind man fall in love, die horribly)

Ref: UniJ Bltn 31; FEFN 2 Aug '57.

● 1960 Japanese, Daiei.

Dir: Kimiyoshi Yasuda.

Cast: Ganjiro Nakamura, Yataro Kitagami.

F-H (ghost; probably the same story as the preceding film)

Ref: UniJ Bltn 31.

Based on a famous Japanese legend and a play.

See also: Kaidan Kasanegafuchi (1970?)

Kaidan Kasanegafuchi

(Masseur's Curse --ad.t.; Horror of an Ugly Woman --ad.t.)

1970? Japanese, Daiei color scope 82 mins.

cont

Kaidan Kasanegafuchi cont.

Dir: Kimiyoshi Yasuda.

SP: Shozaburo Asai.

Art Dir: Akira Naito.

Cin: Tsuchitaro Hayashi.

Mus: Hajime Kaburagi.

Cast: Ritsu Ishiyama, Maya Kitajima, Kenjiro Ishiyama, Reiko Kasahara, Ryuko Minagami, Akane Kawasaki, Matsuko Oka.

H; bor-F (man kills his wife and a debtor -- she seems to turn into a monster, and their ghosts seem to pursue him)

Ref: UniJ 50; MTVM 24:11:43.

See also: Kaidan Kasane-ga-fuchi.

Kaidan Katame Otoko

(Ghost of the One-eyed Man; Curse of the One-eyed Corpse --ad.t.)

1965 Japanese, Toei.

Dir: Tsuneo Kobayashi.

Cast: Akira Nishimura, Sanae Nakahara, Yusuke Kawazu.

F-H (ghost)

Ref: UniJ Bltn 31; MTVM Aug '65 p21.

Kaidan Noboriryu

See: Blind Woman's Curse, The (1970).

Kaidan Oiwa no Borei

(Ghost of Oiwa; The Ghost of Yotsuya)

1961 Japanese, Toei.

Dir: Tai Kato.

Cast: Tomisaburo Wakayama, Hiroko Sakuramachi.

F-H (ghost of maid must count the 13 dishes she broke which caused her to be beheaded)

Ref: UniJ Bltn 31; MTVM April '70 p44.

See also: Ghost of Yotsuya.

Kaidan Onibi no Numa

(Ghost Story of Devil's Fire Swamp)

1963 Japanese, Daiei.

Dir: Bin Kado.

Cast: Kenzaburo Jo, Mieko Kondo.

F-H (ghost; cold fires from bones of dead)

Ref: UniJ Bltn 31.

Kaidan Otoshiana

(Ghost Story of Booby Trap; The Ghostly Trap --ad.t.)

1968 Japanese, Daiei.

Dir: Koji Shima.

Cast: Mikio Narita, Mayumi Nagisa, Eiji Funakoshi.

F-H (man kills his lover, a typist, then is haunted by a ghostly-operated typewriter)

Ref: MTVM Sept '69 p38; UniJ Bltn 31.

Kaidan Saga Yashiki

(Ghost of Saga Mansion)

1953 Japanese, Daiei.

Dir: Ryohei Arai.

Cast: Takako Irie, Kotaro Bando.

F-H (ghost)

Ref: UniJ Bltn 31.

Kaidan Semushi Otoko

(Ghost of the Hunchback; House of Terrors --ad.t.)

1965 Japanese, Toei 81 mins.

Dir: Hajime Sato.

SP: Hajime Takaiwa.

Cin: Shoe Nishikawa.

Cast: Akira Nishimura, Yuko Kusunoki, Yoko Hayama, Masumi Harukawa.

F-H (haunted house; man gets compulsion to murder)

Ref: UniJ '66.

Kaidan Shamisen-bori

(Ghost Music of Shamisen)

1962 Japanese, Toei.

Dir: Kokichi Uchide.

Cast: Ryuji Shinagawa, Norko Kitazawa.

F-H (ghost)

Ref: UniJ Bltn 31.

Kaidan Yonaki-doro

(Ghost Story of Stone Lanterns and Crying in the Night)

1962 Japanese, Daiei.

Dir: Katuhiko Tasaka.

Cast: Ganjiro Nakamura, Katsuhiko.

F-H (ghost)

Ref: UniJ Bltn 31.

Kaidan Yukijoro

(Ghost of Snow-girl Prostitute; Snow Ghost --ad.t.; Yukionna: Woman of the Snow --alt.t.)

1968 Japanese, Daiei color 80 mins.

Dir: Tokuzo Tanaka.

SP: Fuji Yahiro.

Art Dir: Akira Naito.

Cin: Chishi Makiura.

Mus: Akira Ifukube.

Cast: Shiho Fujimura, Akira Ishihama, Machiko Hasegawa, Taketoshi Naito, Mizuho Suzuki, Fujio Suga, Sachiko Murase.

F-H (snow-ghost kills an old sculptor and returns in human form to marry his son)

Ref: UniJ Bltn 31; MTVM April '68 p42, p 18 ad.

See also: Kwaidan (1963).

Kaidan Zankoku Monogatari

(Cruel Ghost Legend; Curse of the Blood --ad.t.)

1968 Japanese, Shochiku.

Dir: Kazuo Hase.

Cast: Masakazu Tamura, Shaeda Kawaguchi, Yusuke Kawazu.

F-H (ghost)

Ref: UniJ Bltn 31; UniJ 41:3.

Kaii Utsunomiya Tsuritenjo

(Weird Death Trap at Utsunomiya)

1956 Japanese, Shintoho.

Dir: Nobuo Nakagawa.

Cast: Ryuzaburo Ogasawara, Akemi Tsukushi.

F-H (ghost)

Ref: UniJ Bltn 31.

Kaiju Daisenso

See: Monster Zero (1965).

Kaijû Ôji

(Monster Prince)

1968 Japanese, Toei 25 mins.

Dir: Keinosuke Tsuchiya.

F (boy fights dinosaur)

UniJ 41:39.

Kaijû Sôshingeki

See: Destroy All Monsters (1968).

Kairyu Daikessen

See: Magic Serpent (1967).

Kaiseijn no Majyo

See: Super Giant 3 (1957).

Kaiser's Shadow, The or The Triple Cross

1918 Ince sil 5 reels.

Prod: Thomas H. Ince.

Dir: R. William Neill.

Sc: Octavus Roy Cohen & J.H. Giesy.

Cast: Dorothy Dalton, Thurston Hall, Edward Cecil.

bor-SF (German spies try to steal ray-gun rifle)

Ref: FIR May '66 p285; LC.

Kaitei Daisenso

See: Terror Beneath the Sea (1966).

Kaitei Gunkan

See: Atragon (1963).

Kaitei 30,000 Mairu

(30,000 Miles Under the Sea)

1970 Japanese, Toei color scope ani 60 mins.
Story: Shotaro Ishimori.

SP: Katsumi Okamoto.

Art Dir: Makoto Yamazaki.

Ani: Sadahiro Okuda.

Mus: Takeo Watanabe.

F (young hero overcomes monsters, robots, & dragons; underwater kingdom)

Ref: UniJ 49:34; 50.

Kalabog En Bosyo

1959 Philippine, Sampaguita.

Dir: Tony Cayado.

Cast: Dolphy, Barbara Perez, Panchito Alba, Eddie Arenas, Tito Galla, Greg Martin.

bor-SF-com (potion created by mad scientist makes men hate women)

Ref: FEFN June '59 p 55.

Kaleidoscope

1935 British, P.W.P. Prods color ani 4 mins.

Dir: Len Lye.

exp-abs-F

Ref: F/A p627; Undrgnd p82, 276.

Kalevala

See: Day the Earth Froze, The (1959).

Kali

1967 Amateur (Film-makers' Coop) 16mm color 4 mins.

Made by: Cassandra M. Gerstein.

Mus: Calo Scott & Ahmed Abdul Malik.

exp-F

Ref: FMC 5:122.

Kalia Mardan

● 1919 Indian, Hindustani Film Co sil 7000 ft.

Prod & Dir: Dada Phalse.

Ref: Lighthouse 21 Aug '37.

● (Muraliwala: Krishna's Flute --alt.t?)

1934 Indian, Kolhapur color.

Dir: Rajopadhyaya.

Cast: Leela.

Ref: MovPicM July '34 p51, Oct '34 p32.

myth-F

Kalkoot or Kismat-ki-Bhul-Sudha

1935 Indian, Sudha.

Dir: D.K. Kale.

Cin: Sirpotdar.

Cast: Nyampally, Godse, Lobo.

F-H (prince turned into leper by supernatural power; sparks fly from body; hypnotic powers)

Ref: MovPicM June '35 p 16; Oct '35 p31.

Apparently imitation of: Mummy, The (1932).

Kalosze Szczescia

(Lucky Galoshes)

1958 Polish, Film Polski 100 mins.

Dir: Antoni Bohdziewicz.

SP: A. Bohdziewicz, Stanislaw Brochowiak, Janusz Majewski, & Andrzej Szczepkowski.

Cin: Stanislaw Wohl.

Mus: Stefan Kisielewski.

Cast: Maria Gella, Teofila Grochowiak, Janusz Majewski, Zygmunt Zintel, Czeslaw Roszkowski, cont.

Kalosze Szczescia cont.

F (magic boots carry those who wear them across time and space)

Ref: Polish Cin p 145; Film Polski '58-59.

Kalpana

(Imagination)

1946 (1965) Indian (122 mins).

Prod, Dir, SP: Uday Shankar.

Cin: K. Rammoth.

Edit: N.K. Gopal.

Mus: Vishnudas Shirali.

Cast: Amla Shankar, Uday Shankar.

sur-F

Ref: Filminda Oct '46; Vw 20 Oct '65.

Kalte Herz, Das

(The Cold Heart)

● (Der Pakt mit dem Satan -- alt.t.)

1923 German, Hermes sil.

Dir: Fred Sauer.

Sc: F. Sauer & W. Wassermann.

Cast: Fritz Schultz, Grete Reinwald, Frieda Richard.

Ref: Deutsche I.

● (Das Wirtshaus im Spessart: The Tavern in Spessart)

1923 German, Orbis sil.

Dir: Adolf Wenter.

Sc: M.M. Langen.

Cast: Fritz Berger, Ellen Kurti, Dary Holm, Hans Staufen.

Ref: Deutsche I.

● 1929 German, Mercedes sil?

Ref: Deutsche II.

● (Heart of Stone --Brit.t?)

1950 E.German color ani puppet & live 103 mins.

Dir: Paul Verhoeven.

SP: P. Verhoeven & Wolf von Gordon.

Cin: Bruno Mondi.

Mus: Herbert Trantow.

Cast: Hanna Rucker, Lutz Moik, Paul Bildt, Paul Esser, Georg Laubenthal, Lotte Lobinger, Erwin Gschonneck [giant], Alexander Engell, Karl Hellmer.

exp-F-dream

Ref: MFB '58 p 14; Collier; Positif '70 p41.

F (fairy tale: man wastes 2 of 3 wishes, but for 3rd trades his heart with that of Dutch Michael, a stone giant)

Based on fable by N. Wilhelm Hauff.

Kama Sutra Rides Again

1972? British color ani 9 mins.

Dir: Bob Godfrey.

F-sex-com (very unusual sexual positions demonstrated by middle-class couple)

Ref: Filmex II; Acad nom.

Kamenni Tsvetok

See: Stone Flower, The (1946).

Kamla

1946 Indian (in Hindustani), Laxmi.

Dialog: M. Nazir.

Cin: Jal Mistry.

Mus: G. Dutt.

Cast: Lila Desai, Agha, Gulab.

F (evil spirit turns hero into madman)

Ref: Filmindia Jan '47.

Kamlata

1935 Indian, Kumar.

Dir: A.R. Kabuli.

Cin: Baburao.

Cast: Miss Swaruparani, Ashraffkhan, Kabuli, Chonker, Kanij.

F (supernatural powers in Arabian Nights setting)

Ref: MovPicM June '35 p32, 49.

See also: Arabian Nights.

Kammená Tetka

(The Stone Auntie)

1960 Czech color ani puppet sh.

Dir & Art Dir: Jan Karpaš.

SP: J.S. Kubín.

Mus: Ladislav Simon.

F (fairy tale: living, grandmotherly cliff; gnomes; magic)

Ref: Czech An '61; FEFN July '61.

Kampon ni Satanas

(Disciple of Satan)

1970 Philippine, Tamaraw color.

Dir & SP: Mar B. Isidro.

Mus: Manuel Franco.

Cast: Jimmy Morato, Eva Montes, Marion Douglas, Alex Froilan, Johnny Monteiro [Devil], Mary Walter, Joe Garcia, Gil De Leon, Venchito Galvez, Luis Florentino.

F-H (girl makes pact with the Devil to bring her dead mother back to life)

Ref: Borst; Chodkowski.

Kanchanamala

See: Vali Sugriva (1950).

Kane

See: Brother John (1971).

Kapetan Arbanas Marko

See: Captain Arbanas Marko (1967).

Kappa no Pataro

(Adventures of a Water Imp)

1957 Japanese, Toei Doga ani 14 mins.

F

Ref: ShF/J '58-59 p30; FEFN 12:18-19:67.

Kappa no Yomei-tori

(Kappa Takes a Bride)

1958 Japanese, National Farm Cinema puppet color 27 mins.

F

Ref: UniJ 4:40.

Karate in Tangiers for Agent Z-7

See: Z 7 Operation Rembrandt (1967).

Karate Killers, The

1967 Arena (MGM) color (92 mins).

Exec Prod: Norman Felton.

Prod & Story: Boris Ingster.

Dir: Barry Shear.

SP: Norman Hudis.

Art Dir: George W. Davis & James W. Sullivan.

Cin: Fred Koenekamp.

Edit: William B. Gulick & Ray Williford.

Mus: Gerald Fried.

Title Theme: Jerry Goldsmith.

Cast: Robert Vaughn, David McCallum, Curt (Curd) Jurgens, Joan Crawford, Herbert Lom, Telly Savalas, Terry-Thomas, Kim Darby, Diane McBain, Jill Ireland, Leo G. Carroll.

bor-SF (gold extracted from seawater; miniature planes)

Ref: MFB Sept '67 p 141-42.

Feature version of episodes from TV series "The Man from U.N.C.L.E."

See also: Man from U.N.C.L.E.,The.

Karlstein

See: Terror in the Crypt (1963).

Karpathian Castle, The

See: Château des Carpathes, Le (1965).

Kartune

1952-53 Par color ani sh series.

F-com

Ref: LC.

Karzan, il Favoloso Uomo della Giungla

(Karzan, the Fabulous Jungle Man; Most Fantastic and Marvelous Adventure in the Jungle [Tarzan] --e.t.)

1971 Italian, Prodimex color scope.

Dir: Miles Deem.

SP: M. Deem & M. Vitelli.

Cin: Franco Villa.

Mus: Lallo Gori.

Cast: Johnny Kismuller Jr, Ettore Manni, Simone Blondell.

bor-F (white man living in jungle is hero)

Ref: Ital Prods '72.

See also: Tarzan.

Kashi to Kodomo

(The Pitfall --ad.t.)

1962 Japanese, Teshigahara.

Dir: Hiroshi Teshigahara.

SP: Kobo Abe.

Cin: Hiroshi Segawa.

Mus: T. Takemitsu.

Cast: Hisashi Igawa, K. Miyahara.

F-H-seq (murdered miner comes back as ghost)

Ref: S&S '63 p 124; MTVM Sept '62.

Kashtanka

1952 Soviet color ani 32 mins.

Dir: M. Tzekhanovsky.

F-com (little dog and his animal friends)

Ref: MFB Dec '54 p 182; Brandon cat p283.

Based on a story by Anton Chekhov.

Katzenjammer Kids

1917-18 Hearst Int'l Film Services (Educational) sil ani sh series.

Dir: John Foster, Gregory La Cava, & others.

Ani: George Stallings & others.

F-com

Ref: LC; MPW 36:1455; Funny-world 14:29-30; Comic Art in America.

Based on the comic strip originated by Rudolph Dirks, later done by H.H. Knerr.

See also: Mysterious Yarn (1917); Sharks Is Sharks (1917); 20,000 Legs Under the Sea (1917).

Kausalya Parinayam

1937 Indian.

Dir: C.S.V. Iyer.

myth-F

Ref: Movie Herald May '37 p43 ad.

Kdby Tisic Klarinetv

(A Thousand Clarinets)

1963 Czech.

Dir: Jan Rohac & Vladimir Svitacek.

SP: Jiri Suchy & Jiri Slitr.

Cin: Rudolf Stahl.

F-mus-com (Johann Sebastian Bach and the mystery of the weapons which have turned into musical instruments)

Ref: Collier.

Kdo Chce Zabit Jessii?

(Who Killed Jessie? --ad.t.; Who Wants to Kill Jessie? --ad.t.; Jessie and Superman --ad.t.)

1965 (1970) Czech, State Film 80 mins.

Dir & SP: Milos Macourek & Vaclav Vorlicek.

Cin: Jan Nemecek.

Mus: Savatopluk Havelka.

Cast: Jiri Sovak, Dana Medricka, Olga Schoberova, Karl Effa, Juraj Visny [Superman].

F-com (middle-aged couple uses machine which materializes comic-book characters, who pursue heroine, Jessie)

Ref: Vw 3 Aug '66; S&S Autumn '66.

See also: Superman.

Keechak Vadh

1951 Indian, Manik.

myth-F

Ref: Filmcritic Sept '51 ad.

Keeler Affair, The

1963 (1964) Danish 88 mins (in Australia).

Prod: John Nasht.

Dir: Robert Spafford.

Cast: Yvonne Buckingham, John Drew Barrymore.

F-dream (Christine Keeler relives her life in a nightmare which has elements of fantasy)

Ref: Collier; Richardson.

Keep Cool

197? Amateur? color? ani 3 mins.

Made by: Barrie Nelson.

exp-F

Ref: IAFF '72.

Keepers, The

See: Brain Eaters, The (1958).

Keepers of the Earth, The

See: Brain Eaters, The (1958).

Keeping Up with the Joneses

1915 H.J. Palmer & Gaum (Mutual) sil ani sh series.

Prod: H.J. Palmer.

F-com

Ref: Ani chart.

Kejklovacka

1968? Czech color 16mm ani 4 mins.

F

Kemek

1970 GHM color 90 mins. Possibly Italian/German.

Dir & SP: Theodore Gershuny.

Cin: Enzo Barboni.

Settings: Flavio Mogherini.

Edit: Sidney Levin.

Mus: John Lewis & the Modern Jazz Quartet.

Cast: Helmut Scheider (Schneider?), Alexandra Stewart, David Hedison, Herbert Weissbach, Robert Wolders, Mary Worondov.

bor-SF (somewhat futuristic; search for special drug)

Ref: Vw 16 Sept '70.

Kenilworth Castle

(Haunted Castles series)

1926 British sil sh.

Dir: Maurice Elvey.

doc-F-H

Ref: V 24 Feb '26; Brit Cin.

See also: Haunted Castles.

Ketbors Okrockske

(Two Little Magic Oxen; Magic Oxen)

1955 Hungarian color ani sh.

cont.

Ketbors Okrockske cont.

Prod: Anny Kamaras.

Dir: Gyula Macskassy.

Mus: György Ranki.

F

Ref: MTVM Nov '67 p9; Montevideo '56.

Based on a Transylvanian folk tale.

Key, The

n.d. Israeli, Amateur (in Hebrew) (Film-makers' Coop) 16mm 14 mins.

Made by: Menakhein Shuval.

SP: Gabriel Dagan.

Cast: Gabriel Dagan.

exp-F (lost key looking for its owner)

Ref: FMC 3:56.

Key of Life, The

1910 Edison sil 975 ft.

Cast: Pilar Morin.

F (reincarnation: cat into woman)

Ref: EK 1 Nov '10 p3-4; LC; MPW 7:1118, 1125.

Khoon-e-Nahag

See: Hamlet (1953).

Khoon-Ka-Khoon

See: Hamlet (1935).

Khorda

See: Deathmaster (1972).

Khubsurat Bala

(Beautiful Girl)

1934 Indian, Sansar.

Dir: D.N. Madhok.

SP: M.R. Kapur.

Cin: Dwarka Khosla

Cast: Madhav Kale, Ekbal.

F (girl suicide brought back to life by the supernatural powers of a Sadhu)

Ref: Dipali 11 May '34 p 15.

Khun-E-Nahak

See: Hamlet (Indian, 1928).

Khun ka Khun

See: Hamlet (1935).

Khwab-E-Hasti

See: Magic Flute (1934).

Kiberneticka Babicka

See: Cybernetic Grandmother (1962).

Kickapoo Juice

1945 Col color ani 644 ft.

Dir: Howard Swift.

Story: Sid Marcus.

Ani: Volus Jones & Grant Simmons.

Mus: Eddie Kilfeather.

F-com

Ref: LC.

Based on the comic strip "Li'l Abner" by Al Capp.

See also: Li'l Abner (1944-45).

Kićo

1951-52 Yugoslavian, Duga Film ani sh series color?

Dir, Design, Ani: Dušan Vukotić.

F-com

Ref: Z/Zagreb p 19.

See also: How Kićo Was Born (1951); Haunted Castle at Dudinci, The (1952).

Kid, The

1919 (1920) FN sil 5300 ft.

Prod, Dir, Sc: Charles Chaplin.

Cast: Charlie Chaplin, Jackie Coogan, Carl Miller, Edna Purviance, Tom Wilson.

F-dream; com (Kid dreams of Paradise, with everyone having wings, including his dog)

Ref: RAF p239; LC; Vw 21 Jan '21.

Kid Colossus, The

See: Roogie's Bump (1954).

Kid for Two Farthings, A

1956 British, London Films (Lopert) color 96 mins.

Prod & Dir: Carol Reed.

SP: Wolf Mankowitz.

Art Dir: Wilfred Shingleton.

Cin: Edward Scaife.

Edit: A.S. Bates.

Mus Dir: Benjamin Frankel.

Cast: Celia Johnson, Diana Dors, David Kossoff, Joe Robinson, Jonathan Ashmore, Brenda De Banzie, Primo Carnera, Lou Jacobi, Irene Handl, Sidney James.

bor-F (when a boy is told about unicorns, he thinks his one-horned goat is a unicorn; it seems to work magic)

Ref: MFB June '55 p83-84; FD 16 April '56.

Based on the novel by Wolf Mankowitz.

Kid from Mars, The

1961 Par color ani 7 mins.

SF

Ref: BO 8 May '61.

Kiddies' Christmas, The

1911 Lubin sil 2 reels.

F (Santa Claus summons gnomes and fairies to open letters)

Ref: MPW 10:924.

Kidnaping in the Stars

See: Rapto en las Estrellas (1971).

Kidnapping of the Sun and Moon, The

(A Nap es a Hold el Rablasa)

1969 (1971) Hungarian color ani 13 mins.

Dir & Story: Sandor Reisenbuchler.

F (demon eats Sun & Moon; hero slays the demon & releases them)

Ref: Vw 12 May '71; ASIFA 6; F&F June '71; LAFP 26 Nov '71.

Based on a poem by Ferenc Juhász.

Kid's Clever, The

1928 (1929) U sil 5792 ft.

Sup: Harry Decker.

Prod & Dir: William James Craft.

Sc: Jack Foley.

Titles: Albert De Mond.

Art Dir: Charles D. Hall.

Cin: Al Jones.

Edit: Charles Craft.

Cast: Glenn Tryon, Kathryn Crawford, Russell Simpson, Lloyd Whitlock, George Chandler, Joan Standing, Max Asher, Stepin Fetchit.

SF-com (boy invents fuelless auto & boat)

Ref: AFI F2.2867 p404; MPN 41:11:88; LC.

Note: according to AFI, some sources credit Sc to Ernest S. Pagano.

Kiganjo no Boken

(Adventure in the Strange Stone Castle --trans?; Adventure in Taklamakan; Adventures of Takla Makan ad.ts)

1965 Japanese, Toho scope 105 mins.

Dir: Senkichi Taniguchi.

SP: Kaoru Mabuchi.

Cin: Kazuo Yamada.

Mus: Akira Ifukube.

Cast: Toshiro Mifune, Mie Hama, Tadao Nakamaru, Yumi Shirakawa, Tatsuya Mihashi, Makoto Sato.

F-seq (priest searches for Buddha's bones; wizards; giant birds; strange castle)

Ref: Vw 25 May '66.

Kigeki Ekimae Kaidan

(Ghost Story of Funny Act in Front of Train Station)

1964 Japanese, Toho.

Dir: Kozo Saeki.

Cast: Fankie Sakai, Hisaya Morishige.

F-H-com (ghost)

Ref: UniJ Bltn 31.

Kiko the Kangaroo

1936-37 Terrytoons (20th-Fox) 1 reel ani series.

Pres: E.W. Hammons.

Made by: Paul Terry, Mannie Davis, George Gordon.

Mus: Philip A. Scheib.

F-com

Ref: LC.

See also: Skunked Again (1936); Red Hot Music (1937).

Kill Baby Kill

(Operazione Paura: Operation Fear; Curse of the Dead -- Brit.t.; Curse of the Living Dead --rr.t., 1972)

1966 (1967; 1972 --rr) Italian, F.U.L. Film (Europix Consolidated) color 85 mins (83 mins; 75 mins, 1972 rr).

Prod: Nando Pisani & Luciano Catenacci.

Dir: Mario Bava.

SP: Romano Migliorini, Roberto Natale, & M. Bava.

Art Dir: Sandro Dell' Orco.

Cin: Antonio Rinaldi.

Edit: Romana Fortini.

Mus: Carlo Rustichelli.

English Version: John Hart.

Cast: Erika Blanc, Giacomo Rossi-Stuart, Fabienne Dali, Gianna Vivaldi, Piero Lulli.

F-H (witch-woman magically drives gold coins into hearts of people, killing them to save them from the worse peril of the ghost of a little girl who is seeking revenge)

Ref: MFB '67 p 104; FF '67 p436; GC 13:30-31; Vw 30 Oct '68; Pardi.

Killer Ape

1953 Col sepia 68 mins.

Prod: Sam Katzman.

Dir: Spencer G. Bennet.

SP: Carroll Young & Arthur Hoerl.

Art Dir: Paul Palmentola.

Cin: William Whitley.

Edit: Gene Havlick.

Mus Dir: Mischa Bakaleinikoff.

Cast: Johnny Weissmuller, Nestor Paiva, Carol Thurston, Max Palmer, Nick Stuart, Ray Corrigan.

bor-SF-H (giant man-ape creature menaces natives; villains developing serum to destroy the will to resist)

Ref: Vd & HR 20 Nov '53; MFB May '54 p75; FDY '54.

Based on the King Features syndicate comic strip "Jungle Jim" by Alex Raymond.

See also: Jungle Jim.

Killer Bats

See: Devil Bat, The (1940).

Killer Lacks a Name, The

(Two Boys for a Murder --alt.t?)

1966 (1970) Italian color scope 104 mins.

Dir: Tullio Domichelli.

Cast: Lang Jeffries, Barbara Nelli, Olga Omar.

bor-SF-H (madman can electrify his steel hand and electrocute foes)

Ref: GC 20:20.

Killer 77, Alive or Dead

See: Sicario 77, Vivo o Morte (1966).

Killer Shrews, The

1959 Hollywood Pictures Corp (McLendon Radio Pictures) 70 mins.

Filmed in Texas.

Exec Prod: Gordon McLendon.

Prod: Ken Curtis.

Dir: Ray Kellogg.

SP: Jay Sims.

Art Dir: Louis Caldwell.

Makeup: Corinne Daniel.

Cin: Wilfred Cline.

Edit: Aaron Stell.

Mus: Harry Bluestone & Emil Cadkin.

Cast: James Best, Ingrid Goude, Ken Curtis, Baruch Lumet, Gordon McLendon.

SF-H (scientist on isolated island develops shrews the size of greyhound dogs)

Ref: FF '59 p260.

Killer with the Third Eye, The

See: Terzo Occhio, Il (1965).

Killers Are Challenged

(A 077, Sfida Ai Killers)

1965 Italian/French, Zenith & Flora/Regina color scope 93 mins.

Prod: Mino Loy & Luciano Martino.

Dir: Antonio Margheriti (Anthony Dawson).

SP: Ernesto Gastaldi (Julian Berry).

Art Dir: Riccardo Dominici (Dick Sanders).

Cin: Riccardo Pallottini (Richard Thierry).

Edit: Renato Cinquini (Jack Quintly).

Mus: Carlo Savina.

Cast: Richard Harrison, Susy Andersen, Wandisa Guida, Mitsouko, Marcel Charvey.

bor-SF (super energy source; electronic gadgets including ring that lights up when death threatens)

Ref: MFB '68 p75.

Killers from Space

1954 Planet Filmplays Inc (RKO) 3-D? 71 mins.

Prod & Dir: W. Lee Wilder.

Story: Myles Wilder.

SP: Bill Raynor.

Cin: William Clothier.

Optical FX: Consolidated Film Industries.

Edit: William Faris.

Mus: Manuel Compinsky.

Cast: Peter Graves, Barbara Bestar, James Seay, Frank Gerstle, Shep Menken, John Merrick.

SF-H (man brought back from dead by pop-eyed aliens who plan to take over Earth by means of giant insects and other creatures)

Ref: Vd 22 Jan '54; FD 15 Feb '54; PB; FIR March '64 p 157.

Killers of the Castle of Blood

See: Scream of the Demon Lover (1970).

Killing Bottle, The

See: Zettai Zetsumei (1967).

Killing the Devil

See: Vrazda Inzenyra Certa (1970).

Killman

n.d. Amateur (Film-makers' Coop; Canyon Cinema) 16mm sil 15 mins.

Made by: Herbert Jean de Grasse.

cont.

Killman cont.

Cast: John Burton, Marsha Dachochlager, Francis Pang, others.

exp-psy-H ("last hours of a homicidal maniac" --FMC)

Ref: FMC 5:129-30.

Kind-Hearted Ant, The

(Mrav Dobra Srca)

1965 Yugoslavian, Zagreb ani 9.6 mins.

Dir, Design, Ani: Aleksandar Marks and Vladimir Jutrisa.

Story: Brana Crnčević.

Bg: Pavao Štalter.

Mus: Miljenko Prohaska.

F-com (ant's good intentions wreak havoc)

Ref: Z/Zagreb p81-82; Film Com Fall '68.

Based on a poem by Brana Crnčević.

Kindar, the Invulnerable

1965 Italian, Copro & Wonder color 98 mins.

Dir & Cin: Osvaldo Civirani.

Cast: Mark Forest, Mimmo Palmara, Rosalba Neri, Dea Flowers.

F (hero is vulnerable only to "red flower")

Ref: Willis; BIB's 17:A332.

Kinegraffiti

1964 Australian, Firebird 16mm 4 mins.

Made by: Arthur & Corinne Cantrill.

exp-F

Ref: Collier.

Kinemacolour Puzzle

1909 British, Natural Colour Kinematograph Co sil 195 ft.

Dir: G.A. Smith.

abs-F (revolving, kaleidoscopic discs)

Ref: Gifford/BFC 02416.

Kinetic Art, The

1968 Collection of 26 short films, some fantastic.

See also: Sophie et les Gammes (1964); Phenomena (1965); Two Grilled Fish (1968); Vita, La (1967?).

Kinetic Art, The (series 2)

1970 Collection of short films, some fantastic.

See also: Re-Entry (1964); See Saw Seems (1965-66); Au Fou (1966); Ego (1968?); Historia Natura (1968?); Divina, La (1969?); Momentum (1969); Poemfield (1969?); Room, The (1969?); Rough Sketch for a Proposed Film Dealing with the Powers of Ten and the Relative Size of Things in the Universe, A (1969?); Unknown Reasons (1969?); Wall, The (1969?).

Kinetic Catalog

1965-69 Amateur (Film-makers' Coop) 16mm color & b&w sil 14.5 mins.

Made by: Michael Mideke.

exp-abs-F

Ref: FMC 5:242.

King and the Jester, The

(François Ier et Triboulet)

1908 French, Star sil 187 ft.

Prod: Georges Melies.

F (model turns to jester in king's arms)

Ref: MPW 4:63; LC; Sadoul/m, GM Mage 1040-43.

King and the Lion, The

n.d. Puppet Films color ani puppet 13 mins.

F (king saved by grateful lion)

cont.

King and the Lion cont.

Ref: Contemp cat p 115.

Based on the fable of Androcles and the Lion.

See also: Androcles and the Lion.

King Ape

See: King Kong (1933).

King Dinosaur

1955 Zimgor (Lippert) 63 mins.

Prod & Story: Bert I. Gordon & Al Zimbalist.

Dir: B.I. Gordon.

SP: Tom Gries.

Cin: Gordon Avil.

SpFX: Howard A. Anderson Co.

Sup Edit: John Bushelman.

Edit: Jack Cornwall.

Nar: Marvin Miller.

Cast: Bill Bryant, Wanda Curtis, Douglas Henderson, Patricia Gallagher.

SF (rocketship to planet which has wandered into the solar system discovers dinosaurs and other primitive life forms)

Ref: HR 27 Sept '55; LC; Pardi; MFB Dec '55 p 181.

King Klunk

1933 U ani 9 mins.

Dir: Walter Lantz & William Nolan.

F-com

Ref: Gasca p59; MPH 23 Sept '33 p35; LC.

Satire on King Kong (1933).

See also: Pooch the Pup (1932-33).

King Kong

(King Ape --e.t.; The Eighth Wonder of the World --s.t.; Kong --ad.t.)

1933 RKO 100 mins.

Exec Prod: David O Selznick.

Prod & Dir: Merian C. Cooper & Ernest B. Schoedsack.

Story: M.C. Cooper.

Adapt: M.C. Cooper & (signed by) Edgar Wallace.

SP: James Creelman & Ruth Rose.

Art Dir: Carroll Clark & Al Herman.

Set Dec: Mario Larrinaga & Byron L. Crabbe.

Cin: Edward Lindon, Vernon L. Walker, & J.O. Taylor.

Technical Dir & SpFX: Willis O'Brien.

Technical Equipment: Marcel Delgado, E.B. Gibbons, Fred Reefe, Orville Goldner, & Carroll Shepphird.

Edit: Ted Cheeseman.

Mus: Max Steiner.

Cast: Fay Wray, Robert Armstrong, Frank Reicher, Bruce Cabot, Sam Hardy, Noble Johnson, Steve Clemento, James Flavin, Victor Wong.

SF-H (documentary film crew finds lost island with dinosaurs & gigantic ape; ape taken back to New York, escapes, shot by biplanes off top of Empire State Building)

Ref: MPH 18 Feb '33 p27, 25 Feb '33 p37, 40; F/A p422; FM 10:26, 27:22-31; Gasca p59-61; MFB Feb '47 p23.

Sequels: Son of Kong (1933); King Kong vs Godzilla (1962); King Kong Escapes (1965).

See also the following films, featuring giant apes, or making use of stock footage from King Kong: King Klunk (1933); Parade of the Wooden Soldiers (1933); African Screams (1949); Mighty Joe Young (1949); Time Monsters, The (1959); Konga (1960);

cont.

King Kong cont.

Tor, King of Beasts (1962); Hor Balevana (1965); Morgan! (1966); Mad Monster Party? (1967); Yellow Submarine (1968); Mighty Gorga, The (1970); Necropolis (1970).

King Kong Escapes

(Kingu Kongu no Gyakushu: King Kong's Counterattack, King Kong's Revenge)

1967 (1968) Japanese, Toho (U) color scope 104 mins (96 mins).

Prod: Tomoyuki Tanaka.

Dir: Inoshiro Honda.

SP: Kaoru Mabuchi.

Art Dir: Takeo Kita.

Cin: Hajime Koizumi.

SpFX: Eiji Tsuburaya.

Mus: Akira Ifukube.

English Language Version:

Prod & Dir: Arthur Rankin Jr.

SP: William J. Keenan.

Cast: Rhodes Reason, Mie Hama, Linda Miller, Akira Takarada, Eisei Amamoto.

SF (Kong battles giant dinosaur, Gorosaurus; also fights robot duplicate of himself, Mechanikong, created by evil mad scientist)

Ref: FF '68 p268; Vw 26 June '68; MFB '69 p 11; UniJ 39:34.

Sequel to: King Kong (1933).

See also: Destroy All Monsters (1968).

King Kong vs Godzilla

(Kingu Kongu tai Gojira)

1962 (1963) Japanese, Toho (U) color scope 99 mins (91 mins).

Prod: John Beck.

Dir: Inoshiro Honda & Thomas Montgomery.

SP: Shinichi Sekizawa, Paul Mason, & Bruce Howard.

Cin: Hajime Koizumi.

SpFX: Eiji Tsuburaya.

Sound FX: William Stevenson.

Edit & Mus: Peter Zinner.

Cast: Michael Keith, James Yagi, Mie Hama, Kenji Sahara, Akihiko Hirata.

SF (Kong fights giant octopus as well as Godzilla)

Ref: FF '63 p 120; MFB Nov '63 p 159; FD 11 June '63.

Based on a story by Willis O'Brien.

Sequel to: King Kong (1933); Godzilla, King of the Monsters (1954).

King Kong's Counterattack

See: King Kong Escapes (1967).

King Kong's Revenge

See: King Kong Escapes (1967).

King Lavra

(Král Lávra)

1950 Czech ani puppet sh.

Dir & SP: Karel Zeman.

F

Ref: FIR '51.

Based on poem by Havolicek Borovsky.

King Midas

n.d. Polish ani puppet sh.

Dir: Edward Sturlis.

F (when his wish is granted, king's touch turns anything to gold, including his food, so he cannot eat)

Ref: Ani/Cin p 117.

See also: Golden Touch, The (1935); King Midas Jr. (1942); King Midas and the Golden Touch (1949); Story of King Midas, The (1953).

King Midas and the Golden Touch

1949 Coronet 16mm 11 mins.

F

Ref: Collier.

See also: King Midas.

King Midas Jr.

(A Color Rhapsody)

1942 Screen Gems (Col)
color ani 622 ft.

Prod: Dave Fleischer.

Dir: Paul Sommer & John
Hubley.

Story: Jack Cosgriff.

SP: Volus Jones.

Mus: Paul Worth.

F-com

Ref: LC.

See also: Color Rhapsody
(1934-51); King Midas.

King Neptune

1932 WD (UA) ani 7 mins.

Prod: Walt Disney.

F (Neptune has denizens of
the sea rout pirate ship &
save mermaid)

Ref: MPH 29 Oct '32 p37; LC.

King of Illusionists, The

1911 British, Gaum sil
540 ft.

F (spirit materialized, grows
huge)

Ref: Bios 9 March '11.

King of Kings

● 1927 De Mille Pictures (Producers Dist Corp) sil 2-color
seq 18 reels (13500 ft)

Prod & Dir: Cecil B. DeMille.

Sc: Jeanie Macpherson (& Henry
MacMahon?).

Art Dir: Mitchell Leisen &
Anton Grot.

Makeup: Fred C. Ryle.

Cin: Peverell Marley, Fred
Westerberg, & Jacob A. Badarocco.

Edit: Anne Bauchens, Harold
McLernon, & Clifford Howard.

Technical Engineering: Paul
Sprunck & Norman Osunn.

Cast: H.B. Warner [Jesus],
Dorothy Cumming, Ernest
Torrence, Joseph Schildkraut,
Joseph Striker, Robert Edeson,
Jacqueline Logan, Rudolph
Schildkraut, Sam DeGrasse,
Victor Varconi, Montagu Love,
William Boyd, Theodore Kosloff,
George Siegmann, Julia Faye,
Kenneth Thompson, Alan Brooks
[Satan], James Mason, May
Robson, Richard Alexander,
Lionel Belmore, Sally Rand,
Noble Johnson, Joe Bonomo,
Brandon Hurst, Edna Mae
Cooper.

rel-F (the life and miracles
of Jesus of Nazareth)

Ref: AFI F2.2874; F/A p490;
MPN 41:11:88; FD 8 April '66.

● (Jesus --s.t.)

1961 MGM 70 mm color
168 mins.
Filmed in Spain.

Prod: Samuel Bronston.

Assoc Prod: Alan Brown & Jaime
Prades.

Dir: Nicholas Ray.

SP: Philip Yordan.

Nar Written by: Ray Bradbury.

Sets & Costumes: Georges
Wakhevitch.

Set Dec: Enrique Alarcon.

Makeup: Mario Van Riel &
Charles Parker.

Cin: Franz F. Planer, Milton
Krasner, & Manuel Berenguer.

SpCin FX: Lee LeBlanc.

SpFX: Alex C. Weldon.

Edit: Harold Kress & Renee
Lichtig.

Mus: Miklos Rozsa.

cont

King Kong (1933)

King of Kings cont.

Nar: Orson Welles.

Cast: Jeffrey Hunter [Jesus],
Siobhan McKenna, Robert Ryan,
Hurd Hatfield, Ron Randell,
Viveca Lindfors, Rita Gam,
Carmen Sevilla, Brigid Bazlen,
Harry Guardino, Rip Torn,
Frank Thring, Guy Rolfe,
George Coulouris, Royal Dano.

rel-F (the life and miracles of
Jesus of Nazareth, with the
miracles somewhat de-emphasized)

Ref: FDY '62; FF '61 p251-54;
Time 27 Oct '61; SR 28 Oct '61;
Vw 11 Oct '61; NYT 12 Oct '61.

Based on the early books of
"The New Testament" portion
of "The Bible."

See also the following films
based on the life of Jesus
or adapted from it:
Passion Play, The; Star of
Bethlehem, The; From the
Manger to the Cross (1912);
Intolerance (1916); I.N.R.I.
(1923); Man Nobody Knows,
The (1925); Jesus of Nazareth (1928); Day of Triumph
(1954); Gospel According
to St. Matthew, The (1964);
Greatest Story Ever Told,
The (1965); Redeemer, The
(1965?); Hvezda Betlemska
(1969); Greaser's Palace
(1972); Godspell (1973);
Gospel Road, The (1973);
Jesus Christ Superstar
(1973).

King of Life, The

See: Picture of Dorian Grey,
The (1917).

King of Sharpshooters, The

(Le Roi des Tireurs)

1905 French sil 225 ft.

Prod: Georges Mélies.

F

Ref: LC; Sadoul/M, GM Mage
680.

King of Swordsmen

(I-tai Chien-wang: Swordsman
of All Swordsmen)

1969 Hongkong, Int'l Motion
Picture Co (Mercury) color
scope 90 mins.

cont

King of Swordsmen cont.

Prod: Sha Yung-fong.

Dir: Kwok Nan-hung.

Story: Hsu (?) Tien-yung.

Art Dir: Lee Lin-cha.

Cin: Ling Chang-ting.

Edit: Chiang Ping Han.

Mus: Lee Szu.

Cast: Hsankuan (Shang Kuan)
Ling-Feng, Tien Peng, Yang
Mon-hua, Chiang Nan, Tsao
Chien, Hsueh Han.

F-seq (mystic martial arts)

Ref: Mercury Folder.

King of the Congo

(The Mighty Thunda --s.t.)

1952 Col serial 15 parts
30 reels.

Prod: Sam Katzman.

Dir: Spencer G. Bennet &
Wallace A. Grissell.

SP: George H. Plympton, Royal
K. Cole, & Arthur Hoerl.

Cin: William Whitley.

Edit: Earl Turner.

Mus: Mischa Bakaleinikoff.

Cast: Buster Crabbe, Gloria
Dea, Leonard Penn, Jack Ingram,
Rusty Westcoatt, Nick Stuart,
Rick Vallin, Alex Montoya,
William Roberts, Frank Ellis.

SF (magnetic rocks that attract
& hold people; cave men; rock
people; man-eating plant; more F)

Ref: LC; Willis; DTA; D. Glut.

Based on the "Thunda" comic book.

King of the Criminals

See: Superargo and the Faceless
Giants (1967).

King of the Jungle

1927 Rayart sil serial
10 parts 20? reels.

Dir: Webster Cullison.

Cast: Sally Long, Elmo Lincoln,
Gordon Standing, True Boardman.

bor-F (apes as menaces)

Ref: FDY '58 p294; CNW p 137,
260.

King of the Jungle

1933 Par 73 mins (65 mins).

Dir: H. Bruce Humberstone &
Max Marcin.

Adapt: M. Marcin.

SP: Philip Wylie & Fred Niblo
Jr.

Cin: Ernest Haller.

Cast: Buster Crabbe, Frances
Dee, Douglass Dumbrille,
Irving Pichel, Robert Adair.

bor-F (boy raised by pride of
lions comes to the US as a
circus attraction)

Ref: Acad; FDY '34; LC.

Based on novel "The Lion's
Way" by C.J. Stoneham.

See also: Tarzan.

King of the Jungleland

1949 Re-release of Darkest
Africa (1936).

King of the Kongo

1929 Mascot sil & sound
versions serial 10 parts
20 reels.

Dir: Richard Thorpe.

Mus: Lee Zahler.

Cast: Jacqueline Logan, Walter
Miller, Richard Tucker, Boris
Karloff.

SF-seq (gorilla menace;
dinosaur?)

Ref: FD 25 Aug '29; CNW
p 147-48, 272-73.

King of the Mounties

1942 Rep serial 12 parts
25 reels.

Assoc Prod: W.J. O'Sullivan.

Dir: William Witney.

SP: Taylor Caven, Ronald
Davidson, William Lively,
Joseph O'Donnell, & Joseph
Poland.
Cin: Bud Thackery.

SpFX: Howard Lydecker.

Edit: Edward Todd & Tony
Martinelli.

Cast: Allan Lane, Gilbert
Emery, Russell Hicks, Peggy

cont.

Drake, George Irving, Abner
Biberman, Nestor Paiva, Jay
Novello, Duncan Renaldo,
Douglass Dumbrille, William
Bakewell, Francis Ford,
Anthony Warde.

SF (flying wing-type plane
without props or jets, un-
detectible on radar)

Ref: LC; FDY; Acad; Stringham.

Suggested by the novel "King
of the Royal Mounted" by
Zane Grey.

See also: King of the Royal
Mounted (1940).

King of the Rocket Men

1949 Rep serial 12 parts
25 reels.

Feature version Lost Planet
Airmen released in 1951.

Assoc Prod: Franklin Adreon.

Dir: Fred Brannon.

SP: Royal Cole, William Lively,
& Sol Shor.

Cin: Ellis W. Carter

SpFX: Howard & Theodore Lydecker.

Edit: Cliff Bell & Sam Starr.

Mus: Stanley Wilson.

Cast: Tristram Coffin, Mae Clarke,
Don Haggerty, James Craven, I.
Stanford Jolley, Douglas Evans,
Stanley Price, Ted Adams, Dale
Van Sickel, Tom Steele, David
Sharpe, Eddie Parker, Buddy
Roosevelt.

SF (rocket-propelled flying suit;
"Sonutron;" "decimator" disintegrates rocks; tidal wave in New
York harbor; volcano destroys
island)

Ref: Ser/Rep p50; TBC p291-
92; STI 5:33; SM 7:40;
FDY '58.

See also: Radar Men from the
Moon (1951); Zombies of the
Stratosphere (1952); Commando
Cody (1953); Adventures of
the Spirit, The (1963);
Rocketman Flies Again (1966).

King of the Royal Mounted

(The Yukon Patrol --ad.t?)

1940 Rep serial 12 parts
25 reels.

Assoc Prod: Hiram S. Brown Jr.

Dir: William Witney & John
English.

SP: Franklyn Adreon, Norman
S. Hall, Joseph Poland,
Barney A. Sarecky, & Sol
Shor.

Cin: William Nobles.

Mus: Cy Feuer.

Cast: Allan Lane, Robert
Kellard, Robert Strange,
Herbert Rawlinson, John
Davidson, John Dilson, Lucien
Prival, Norman Willis.

bor-SF ("Compound X" has
magnetic qualities)

Ref: FDY '56; MPH 29 Aug '36;
Ser/Rep; SQ 3; HR 15 Oct '42.

Title from novel by Zane Grey.

Sequel: King of the Mounties
(1942).

King of the Swordsmen Kings

1970 Hongkong?, Lien Hsin
Film Co (Mercury) color
scope 110 mins.

Dir: Kwok Nan-Hung.

Cast: Yang Chun, Chang
Ching-Ching.

F-seq (mystic martial arts)

Ref: Mercury folder.

King of the Wild

1930 Mascot serial 12
parts 24? reels.

Also released as feature
Bimi.

Dir: Reeves Eason.

SP: Wyndham Gittens & Ford
Beebe.

Cin: Ben Kline & Edward Kull.

cont.

King of the Wild cont.

Mus: Lee Zahler.

Cast: Walter Miller, Boris
Karloff, Dorothy Christy,
Nora Lane, Tom Santschi,
Victor Potel, Mischa Auer,
Arthur McLaglen [ape man].

bor-SF (people menaced by
ape-man creature)

Ref: STI 2:33; FIR Aug'Sept
'65 p462; FDY '56.

King of the Zombies

1941 Mono 67 mins.

Prod: Lindsley Parsons.

Dir: Jean Yarbrough.

SP: Edmund Kelso.

Art Dir: Charles Clague.

Cin: Mack Stengler.

Edit: Richard Currier.

Mus: Edward Kay.

Cast: Dick Purcell, Joan
Woodbury, Mantan Moreland,
Henry Victor, John Archer.

SF-H (doctor creates zombies
which are used by foreign agents;
black magic?)

Ref: MFB Sept '41 p 116; Photon
20:33-34; Vd & HR 7 May '41.

See also: White Zombie (1941).

King of Thule, The

See: Lured by a Phantom (1910).

King Robot

See: My Son, the Vampire
(1952).

King Scatterbrain's Troubles

1908 French, Pathé sil sh.

F (because of wizard's curse,
ghosts attack king whenever
a clock strikes)

Ref: V&FI 25 July '08.

King-Size Canary

1947 MGM color ani 8 mins.

Prod: Fred Quimby.

Dir: Tex Avery.

Story: Heck Allen.

Ani: Robert Bentley, Walter
Clinton, & Ray Abrams.

Mus: Scott Bradley.

F-com

Ref: LC; Ani/Cin p58.

King Solomon's Mines

1937 British (Gaum) 8 reels
(80 mins).

Dir: Robert Stevenson.

SP credit mixed; either
Michael Hogan & Roland Pertwee,
or A.R. Rawlinson, Ralph
Spence, & Charles Bennett.

Cin: Bernard Knowles & Geoffrey
Barkas.

Cast: Cedric Hardwicke, Paul
Robeson, Roland Young, John
Loder, Anna Lee, Arthur Sinclair,
Sydney Fairbrother, Robert
Adams.

F-seq (witch woman causes
volcanic eruption; she also
puts curse on warriors)

Ref: HR 6 July '37; MPH 3
July '37 p44; FD 2 July '37.

Based on the novel by H. Rider
Haggard.

King Tut-Ankh-Amen's Eighth Wife

(The Mystery of Tut-Ankh-Amen's
Eighth Wife --alt.t.)

1923 Max Cohen sil 4100 ft.

Dir & Story: Andrew Remo.

Sc: Max Cohen & George M.
Merrick.

Cin: John Bitzer.

bor-F (concerns the curse on
King Tut's tomb)

Ref: AFI F2.2883.

King Vampire

See: Dr. Terror's Gallery
of Horrors (1967).

Kingdom in the Clouds

(Tinerete Fara Batrinete:
Youth Without Age)

1968 (1971) Rumanian, Bucha-
rest (Xerox) color 87 mins.

Prod: Nicolae Codrescu.

Dir & SP: Elisabeta Bostan.

Story Idea: Petre Ispirescu.

Art Dir: Liviu Popa & Ioana
Cantuniari Marcu.

Cin: Julius Druckman.

Mus: Temistocle Popa.

Mus Dir: Sile Diniou.

English Language Version:

Exec Prod & Lyrics: Robert
Braverman.

SP: Janet Waggener.

Cast: Mircea Breazu, Ana
Szeles, Ion Tugearu, Carmen
Stanescu [witch], Emanoil
Petrut, Nicolae Secareanu,
Margareta Pogonat, Mihai
Paladescu.

F (Father Time; boy on successful
quest for immortality; flower
becomes beautiful girl; magic
bugle; magic feather; fire-
breathing witch; fountain takes
away immortality)

Ref: BO 11 Oct '71; FF '72
p87; NYT 15 Jan '72.

Kingdom in the Sand

See: Conquistatore dell'
Atlantida, Il (1965).

Kingdom of Human Hearts, The

1921 Wilbert Leroy Cosper
(Christian Philosophical
Institute) sil 10 reels.

Dir & Sc: Wilbert Leroy Cosper.

Cast: (in the allegorical
prolog) Hugh Metcalfe, Lona
Good, Geoffrey Bell.

alleg-F-seq (prolog set in
land of title with such characters as Innocence, Love, Temptation, Fear, Truth, etc.)

Ref: AFI F2.2884 p407.

Kingdom of Nosey Land, The

1915 Rex (U) sil 3 reels.

Dir: H.C. Matthews.

Cast: Elsie Albert, Johnnie
Cooke, Seymour Hastings, C.
Norman Hammond.

F (fairy kingdom in which
a big nose is a sign of beauty;
magical spring; imitation
animals)

Ref: MPW 26:1666, 1896; LC.

Kingdom of Poison Moth

See: Super Giant 9 (1959).

Kingdom of the Fairies, The

See: Fairyland, The (1903).

Kingdom Within, The

1922 Producers Security Corp
(W.W. Hodkinson Corp) sil
7 reels.

Dir: Victor Schertzinger.

Story: Kenneth B. Clarke.

Cin: John S. Stumar.

Cast: Russell Simpson, Z. Wall
Covington, Gaston Glass, Pau-
line Starke, Hallam Cooley,
Ernest Torrence, Gordon Russell.

F-seq (good man's crippled
arm miraculously becomes
cured)

Ref: AFI F2.2885 p407.

King's Ankus, The

(story by R. Kipling)

See: Jungle Book (1942).

King's Breakfast, The

1937 British ani silhouette
sh.

Dir: Lotte Reiniger.

F

Ref: Ani/Cin p 175.

Based on a story by A.A.
Milne.

King's Row

(TV series)

See: Man from 1997, The (1957).

Kingukongu no Gyakushu

See: King Kong Escapes (1967).

Kingukongu tai Gojira

See: King Kong vs. Godzilla
(1962).

Kiri the Clown

n.d. French, Films Jean Image
color ani 15 mins.

Dir: Jean Image.

F

Ref: IAFF '72.

Kismat-ki-Bhul-Sudha

See: Kalkoot (1935).

Kiss, The

197? Yugoslavian, Zagreb
color ani 1 min.

Dir: Zlatko Pavlinic.

F

Ref: IAFF '72.

Kiss and Kill

(Blood of Fu Manchu --Brit.t.;
Fu Manchu y el Beso de la
Muerte: Fu Manchu and the
Kiss of Death; Against All
Odds --ad.t.)

1968 (1969) Spanish/German/
US & British, Ada Films/Terra
Filmkunst/Ustadex (Commonwealth United) color scope
91 mins (86 mins).

Partially filmed in Brazil.

Prod: Harry Alan Towers.

Dir: Jesús Franco.

Story & SP: H.A. Towers (Peter
Welbeck), Manfred Köhler, &
J. Franco.

Art Dir: Peter Gasper.

Cin: Manuel Merino.

Edit: Angel Serrano & Allan
Morrison.

Mus: Gert Wilen & Daniel
White.

Cast: Christopher Lee [Fu
Manchu], Goetz George, Ri-
cardo Palacios, Richard
Greene, Tsai Chin, Howard
Marion Crawford, Shirley
Eaton.

bor-SF-H (girls transmit
poison by kiss; torture)

Ref: SpCin '70 p 137; MFB
March '69 p56; FDY '70;
Vw 8 May '68.

Based on characters created
by Sax Rohmer.

Sequel to: Face of Fu Manchu,
The (1965).

Kiss for Cinderella, A

1926 Par sil 9686 ft.

Pres: Adolph Zukor & Jesse
L. Lasky.

Prod & Dir: Herbert Brenon.

Sc: Willis Goldbeck & Townsend
Martin.

Art Dir: Julian Boone Fleming.

Cin: J. Roy Hunt.

Cast: Betty Bronson, Tom
Moore, Esther Ralston [fairy
godmother], Henry Vibart,
Dorothy Cumming, Ivan Simpson,
Dorothy Walters.

F-dream (in contemporary
setting, poor girl dreams she
is Cinderella)

Ref: AFI F2.2892 p408; MPW
78:138; F/A p293; Blum p293.

Based on the play by James
M. Barrie.

See also: Cinderella.

Kiss from Beyond the Grave, The

See: Beso de Ultratumba, El
(1961).

Kiss Kiss, Kill Kill

(Kommissar X: Jagd auf Unbekannt:
Commissar X -- Hunter of the
Unknown)

cont.

1965 (1966) W. German/Italian/
Yugoslavian, Parnass/Metheus/
Avala color scope 92 mins
(87 mins).

Prod: Hans A. Pflüger & Theo
M. Werner.

Dir: Gianfranco Parolini (Frank
Kramer).

SP: Giovanni Simonelli (Sim
O'Neill).

Art Dir: Niko Matul.

Cin: Francesco Izzarelli.

Edit: Edmondo Lozzi

Mus: Mladen Gutesha.

Cast: Luciano Stella (Tony
Kendall), Brad Harris, Maria
Perschy, Christa Linder,
Nicola Popovic, Pino Mattei.

bor-SF (zombie-producing
drug; underground complex)

Ref: MFB '68 p202; F&F Dec
'68 p43-44; TVG.

Based on a novel from the
"Kommissar X" series by
Bert F. Island.

Kiss Me!

1904 Biograph sil 65 ft.

F-com (real girl is poster)

Ref: Niver p57.

Kiss Me Cat

1953 WB color ani 7 mins.

Dir: Chuck Jones.

F-com (Marc Anthony the bull-
dog and his kitten friend)

Ref: David Rider; LC.

Kiss Me Deadly

1955 Parklane Pictures (UA)
105 mins.

Prod & Dir: Robert Aldrich.

SP: A.I. Bezzerides.

Art Dir: William Glasgow.

Cin: Ernest Laszlo.

Edit: Michael Luciano.

Mus: Frank Devol (De Vol?).

Cast: Ralph Meeker, Albert
Dekker, Paul Stewart, Juano
Hernandez, Wesley Addy, Marian
Carr, Maxine Cooper, Cloris
Leachman, Jack Elam, Leigh
Snowden (?), Percy Helton,
Robert Cornthwaite, James Seay.
bor-SF (Mike Hammer after
suitcase full of fissionable
material; when exposed it
burns up woman like torch,
then explodes like A-bomb)

Ref: MFB Aug '55 p 120;
Vd 20 April '55; FD 12 May
'55; B. Warren.

Based on the novel by Mickey
Spillane.

Kiss Me, Monster

See: Besame, Monstruo (1968).

Kiss Me Quick

1963 Fantasy color.

Prod & Dir: Russ Meyer.

Cin: Lester Kovac (Laszlo
Kovacs?).

Cast: Jackie DeWit, Althea
Currier, Fred Coe [Franken-
stein Monster], Claudia Banks.

sex-F-H-com (with Frankenstein
Monster, Dracula, a mummy,
extraterrestrial alien)

Ref: Ackerman; Photon 21:27;
MW 5:20; Gifford/MM p 145.

See also: Dracula; Frankenstein;
Mummy, The (1932).

Kiss of Death

See: Death Kiss, The (1916).

Kiss of Evil

See: Kiss of the Vampire (1963).

Kiss of the Vampire

(Kiss of Evil --TV.t.)

1963 British, Hammer (U)
color 87 mins.

Added scenes were filmed in the
US for TV showing; also used scenes
from Evil of Frankenstein (1964).

King of the Wild (1930) Serial

Kiss of the Vampire cont.

Prod: Anthony Hinds.

Dir: Don Sharp.

SP: John Elder (Anthony
Hinds?).

Prod Design: Bernard Robinson.

Art Dir: Don Mincaye.

Makeup: Roy Ashton.

Cin: Alan Hume.

SpFX: Les Bowie.

Edit: James Needs.

Mus: James Bernard.

Cast: Clifford Evans, Noel
Willman [vampire], Edward
De Souza, Jennifer Daniel,
Barry Warren, Isobel Black,
Carl Esmond (tv version only).

F-H (in 1900's Bavarian, couple
encounter cult of vampires; at
climax, devil invoked to destroy
vampires with hundreds of vicious
bats)

Ref: Photon 19:40; MFB Feb '64
p26; FF '63 p204; TVG; HR
30 July '63; FD 1 Aug '63.

Kiss the Girls and Make Them Die

(Operazione Paradiso: Operation
Paradise; Se Tutte Te Donne del
Mondo: If All the Women in
the World --s.t?)
1966 (1967) Italian, De Laurentiis
(Col) color 106 mins.

Filmed in Brazil.

Prod: Dino De Laurentiis.

Dir: Henry Levin & Dino
Maiuri.

Story: D. Maiuri.

SP: Jack Pulman & D. Maiuri.

Art Dir: Mario Garbuglia.

Cin: Aldo Tonti.

SpFX: Augie Lohman.

Edit: Ralph Kemplen.

Mus: Mario Nascimbene.

cont.

Kiss the Girls cont.

Cast: Michael Connors, Dorothy
Provine, Raf Vallone, Margaret
Lee, Terry-Thomas, Nicoletta
Machiavelli, Beverly Adams,
Jack Gwillim, Senya Seyn,
Marilu Tolo.

SF (satellite can emit rays
which will sterilize mankind;
mad industrialist who wants
to conquer the world keeps
girls in suspended animation
in large plastic blocks)

Ref: FF '67 p20-21; MFB May
'67 p79; Vw 11 Jan '67.

Kisses for My President

1964 WB 113 mins.

Prod & Dir: Curtis Bernhardt.

SP: Claude Binyon & Robert
G. Kane.

Art Dir: Herman Blumenthal.

Cin: Robert Surtees.

Edit: Sam O'Steen.

Mus: Bronislau Kaper.

Cast: Fred MacMurray, Polly
Bergen, Arlene Dahl, Edward
Andrews, Eli Wallach, Donald
May, Anna Capri.

bor-soc-SF; com (set in advance
of 1964 when a woman is elected President of the US)

Ref: BO 16 Nov '64; FM 27:9;
CoF 6:56.

Kissing Pills

1912 Lubin sil 1020 ft.

SF-com (pills make people
kiss)

Ref: MPW 1912 p 144; Bios
22 Feb '12.

Kit the Whale and Kot the Cat

1970? Soviet ani.

Dir: Irina Gurvich.

F

Ref: MTVM 25:3:15.

Kitchen Maid's Dream, The

1907 Vit sil 400 ft.

Prod & Dir: J. Stuart Blackton.

F-dream

Ref: MPW 1:622; LC; Filmlex
p681.

Kite, The

1915 Kay-Bee sil 2 reels.

SF (electric kite detects
approaching storms --Willis)

Ref: MPW 24:981.

Kite from Across the World, The

See: Magic of the Kite, The
(1957).

Kite from the End of the World,
The

See: Magic of the Kite, The
(1957).

Kitro

See: Ge-Ge-Ge no Kitaro (1968).

Kitten, The

n.d. Czech ani puppet &
live 10 mins.

F

Ref: Czech An '61.

Kitty Foiled

1948 MGM color ani 7
mins.

Prod: Fred Quimby.

Dir: William Hanna & Joseph
Barbera.

Ani: Irven Spence, Kenneth
Muse, Irving Levine, & Ed
Barge.

Mus: Scott Bradley.

F-com

Ref: LC; Hist US Ani Prog.

See also: Tom and Jerry
(1941-).

Kitty in Dreamland

1912 French, Eclipse (Klein)
sil 575 ft.

F (fairies, witches, etc.)

Ref: MPW 11:582.

Kladivo na Carodejnice

(Hammer for the Witches)

1970 Czech, Barrandov
scope 110 mins.

Dir & SP: Otakar Vavra.

Story: Vaclav Kaplicky.

Settings: Karel Skvor.

Cin: Josef Illik.

Mus: Jiri Srnka.

Cast: Vladimir Smeral, Elo
Romantcick, Sonia Valentova,
L. Skrbkova, Jirina Stepnickva.

H (realistic & brutal treatment of 17th Century Czech
witchcraft trials)

Ref: Vw 8 April '70.

Klaun Ferdinand a Raketa

(Clow Ferdinand and the Rocket;
Rocket to Nowhere --ad.t?)

1962 Czech 79 mins.

Dir: Jindřich Polák.

SP: Ota Hofman & J. Polák.

Cin: Jan Kališ.

Mus: Evzen Illin.

Cast: Jiri Vrstala, E. Hrabetova,
V. Horka, Hanus Bor.

SF-com (friendly robot captures
clown & some children)

Ref: Broz p78, 95; Gasca.

Kleine Schrause, Eine

See: Little Screw, The (1927).

Kleptomania Tablets

1912 British, HB Films sil
575 ft.

Dir & Sc: Ernest G. Batley.

Cast: Dorothy Balley, Dert
Wynne.

F-com ("girl gives grandfather's
magic pills to curate, soldier,
policeman")

Ref: Gifford/BFC 03556.

Klizi-Puzi

(Twiddle-Twaddle)

1968 Yugoslavian/German,
Zagreb/Rinco color ani
8.1 mins.

Dir, SP, Design, Ani: Zlatko
Grgić.

Mus: Tomislav Simović.

sur-F-com

Ref: Z/Zagreb p43, 96.

Knife in the Body, The

See: Murder Clinic, The
(1966).

Knight-Mare Hare

1955 WB color ani 7 mins.

Dir: Chuck Jones.

Voices: Mel Blanc.

F-com (Bugs vs Merlin)

Ref: LC; David Rider.

See also: Bugs Bunny (1938-63).

Knight Mystery, The

See: Chevalier Mystère, Le
(1907).

Knight of Black Art, The

(Le Tambourin Fantastique
Illusion Fantastique)

1907 (1908) French sil
colored 525 ft (371 ft).

Prod: Georges Méliès.

F

Ref: Sadoul/M, GM Mage
1030-34; Views '08 91:11; LC.

Knight of the Night, The

See: Chevalier de la Nuit, Le
(1953).

Knight of the Snows, The

(Le Chevalier des Neiges)

1912 (1913) French, Star
(Pathé) sil 1310 ft.

Prod: Georges Méliès.

F (Alcofribas conjures up
the devil; man sells his
soul)

Ref: Sadoul/M, GM Mage;
Bios 2 Jan '13.

Knights, The

1963 Polish ani sh.

Dir: Wladyslaw Nehrebecki.

ani-F

Ref: ASIFA info sheet.

Knights of Terror

(Los Jinetes del Terror)

1964 Spanish/Italian/French,
Hispamer/Tibre/Radius color
scope 86 mins.

Dir: Mario Costa.

SP: N. Lillo & E. Fallete.

Art Dir: Tadeo Villalba.

Cin: Julio Ortas.

Cast: Tony Russell, Scilla
Gabel, Yves Vincent, Pilar
Clemens.

bor-SF; H-seqs (super-type
explosives in tiny pellets
in story set before introduction of gunpowder; horrifying masks)

Ref: CoF 12:36; MTVM Feb '65;
SpCin '65; D. Glut.

Knights of the Round Table

1953 MGM color scope 115 mins.
Filmed in England.

Prod: Pandro S. Berman.

Dir: Richard Thorpe.

SP: Talbot Jennings, Jan
Lustig, & Noel Langley.

Art Dir: Alfred Junge & Hans
Peters.

Cin: F.A. Young & Stephen
Dade.

Edit: Frank Clarke.

Mus: Miklos Rozsa.

Cast: Robert Taylor, Ava
Gardner, Mel Ferrer, Anne
Crawford, Stanley Baker,
Felix Aylmer, Maureen Swanson,
Gabriel Woolf, Robert Urquhart,
Niall MacGinnis.

F-seqs (Arthur pulls the sword
from the stone, becomes King
of England; Sir Percival sees
the Holy Grail)

Ref: Vd 23 Dec '53; FIR Feb
'54 p90; MFB July '54 p 100;
Acad.

Based on "Le Mort d'Arthur"
by Thomas Malory.

Knighty-Knight Bugs

1958 WB color ani sh.

Prod: John W. Burton.

Dir: Friz Freleng.

Voices: Mel Blanc.

Mus Dir: Carl W. Stalling.

F-com

Ref: Ani/Cin p 170; Acad
winner.

See also: Bugs Bunny (1938-63).

Knitting Pretty

See: Tetke Pletke (1969).

Knives of the Avenger

(Raffica di Coltelli; Shower
of Knives)

1965 (1968) Italian, Sider
(World Entertainment Corp)
color scope 86 mins.

Prod: P. Tagliaferri.

Dir: Mario Bava (John Hold).

SP: Alberto Liberati, George
Simonelli, & M. Bava.

Cin: Antonio Rinaldi.

Edit: Otello (Othello) Colangeli.

Mus: Marcello Giambini.

cont.

Knives of the Avenger cont.

Cast: Cameron Mitchell, Fausto
Tozzi, Luciano Polletin,
Elissa Picelli (Elisa Mitchell),
Giacomo Rossi-Stuart (Jack
Stewart).

bor-H; F-seqs (brutal life of
Vikings, with decapitations;
soothsayer makes prophecies
which are fulfilled)

Ref: FF '68 p 121-22; Ital
Prods '65 p94-95.

Knock Knock!

1940 U color ani 1 reel.

Prod & Dir: Walter Lantz.

Story: Ben Hardaway & Lowell
Elliot.

Artists: Alex Lovy & Frank
Tipper.

Mus: Frank Marsales.

Voice of Woody: Grace Stafford.

F-com (first Woody Woodpecker
cartoon)

Ref: LC; PopCar.

See also: Andy Panda (1939-5?);
Woody Woodpecker (1940-72).

Knockabout Kelly, Magician

1914 French, Star sil 400 ft.

Prod: Gaston Méliès.

F-com (magic wand produces
water)

Ref: MPW 20:820.

Knocking on the Door, The

1923 British, Stoll sil
2 reels.

Dir: A.E. Colby.

Cast: Harry Agar Lyons, Fred
Paul, H. Humbertson Wright,
Joan Clarkson, Frank Wilson.

bor-F-H

Ref: MMF 14:34; BFI cat.

Based on characters created
by Sax Rohmer.

See also: Mystery of Dr.
Fu Manchu, The (1923).

Knockout Drops

See: Tokyo no Tekisasu-Jin
(1957).

Ko-Ko in 1999

1924 Red Seal sil ani &
live 653 ft.

Ani: Max Fleischer.

Cast: M. Fleischer.

F-com (arriving in 1999, the
clown finds everything automated)

Ref: BFI cat p256.

See also: Ko-Ko the Clown
(1922-29).

Ko-Ko Lamps Aladdin

1928 Par sil ani 1 reel.

Prod: Max Fleischer.

F-com

Ref: LC.

See also: Aladdin; Ko-Ko
the Clown (1922-29).

Ko-Ko the Clown

1922-29 Out of the Inkwell
Films, Red Seal, Famous Players-
Lasky (Par) sil ani & live
1 reel series.

Some in series later had sound
added and were released under
the series title Inkwell Imps.

Prod: Max Fleischer, Alfred
Weiss, others.

Dir: M. Fleischer, Dave Fleischer,
others?

Ani: M. Fleischer & others.

Cast: Max Fleischer, others.

F-com

Ref: BFI cat p250, 256, 262,
263, 265, 267, 268, 271; LC;
MPW 76:567.

See also: Ko-Ko. . .; Out of
the Inkwell; Snow White (1933);
Betty Boop's Penthouse (1933).

Ko-Ko's Haunted House

1928 Par sil ani & live
478 ft.

Prod & Ani: Max Fleischer.

Cast: Max Fleischer.

F-H-com

Ref: BFI cat p268; LC.

See also: Ko-Ko the Clown
(1922-29).

Ko-Ko's Hypnotism

1929 Par sil ani & live
603 ft.

Prod: Alfred Weiss.

Ani: Max Fleischer.

Cast: Max Fleischer.

F-com

Ref: LC; BFI cat p271.

See also: Ko-Ko the Clown
(1922-29).

Kobito to Aomushi

(The Dwarf and the Caterpillar)

1950 Japanese, Toei Doga
ani 17 mins.

F (dwarf helps caterpillar; later
helped by butterfly)

Ref: FEFN 12:16-17, 45; ShF/J '58-59
p32.

Kobutori

(The Old Man and His Hen)

1958 Japanese ani puppet
21 mins.

F

Ref: ShF/J '58-59 p34.

Based on a famous Japanese
legend.

Kod Fotografa

(In the Photograph; At the
Photographer's)

1959 Yugoslavian, Zagreb
color ani 9.5 mins.

Dir & Story: Vatroslav Mimica.

Design: Aleksandar Marks.

Ani: Vladimir Jutriša.

Bg: Zlatko Bourek & Zvonimir
Lončarić.

Mus: Aleksandar Bubanović.

F-com

Ref: Z/Zagreb p60; Film Com
Fall '68; Ani/Cin p 131-33.

Kogan no Misshi

(Mission to Hell)

1959 Japnese, Toei color
100 mins.

Dir & SP: Tai Kato.

Cin: Hashizo Okawa.

Cast: Hashizo Okawa, Yoshio
Yoshida, Jun Tazaki, Sentaro
Fushimi, Yumi Ichijo, Yoyoi
Furusato.

F-seqs (goddess of fortune
sends 2 beautiful girls to
help hero)

Ref: UniJ 6:30.

Koguma no Korochan

(Korochan the Little Bear)

1958 Japanese, Kyohai-T.C.J.
ani 14 mins.

F

Ref: ShF/J '58-59 p33.

Kohraa

1964 Indian, Geetanjali
Pictures.

Dir: Biren Naug.

Cast: W. Rehman.

F-H (dead woman still casts
shadow; witch phantom voices)

Ref: MTVM June '64; Shankar's
Weekly 19 April '64.

Koiya Koi Nasuna Koi

(Love, Thy Name Be Sorrow
--ad.t.; Love Not Again --
ad.t.; The Mad Fox --ad.t.)

1962 Japanese, Toei color
109 mins.

Dir: Tomo Uchida.

cont.

Koiya Koi Nasuna Koi cont.

SP: Yoshitaka Yoda.

Cin: Teiji Yoshida.

Cast: Hashizo Okawa, Michiko Saga, Sumiko Hidaka.

F (strange rainbows in the sky; white fox turns into a woman & gives birth to a boy)

Ref: UniJ '63; FIR Oct '62 p474; MTVM July '62 p63.

Kokakola en la Sangre

See: Fórmula Secreto, La (1965).

Koko the Clown

See: Ko-Ko the Clown (1922-29).

Kokon

See: Cocoon (1965).

Kolchack Tapes, The

(story by J. Rice)

See: Night Stalker, The (1971).

Kommissar X: Jagd auf Unbekannt

See: Kiss Kiss, Kill Kill (1965).

Kon

1968? Polish color ani sh.

Dir: Witold Giersz.

F (animated oil)

Ref: F&F Feb '69.

Koncert za Masinsku Pusku

See: Concerto for Sub-Machine Gun (1958).

Konchu Daisenso

(Genocide --ad.t.; War of Insects --ad.t.)

1968 Japanese, Shochiku color scope 84 mins.

Dir: Kazui Nihonmatsu.

SP: Susumu Takahisa.

Art Dir: Tadataka Yoshino.

Cin: Shizuo Hirase.

Mus: Shunsuke Kikuchi.

Cast: Yusuke Kawazu, Emi Shindo, Keisuke Sonoi, Cathy Horan.

SF (girl survivor of Ausch-witz can scientifically con-trol huge swarms of insects; they crash a plane carrying an H-Bomb)

Ref: UniJ 43:28; MTVM Nov '68 p41.

Konec Srpna V Hotelu Ozon

See: End of August at the Hotel Ozone, The (1965).

Koneko no Rakugaki

(The Scribbling Kitten)

1957? Japanese, Toei Poga ani 14 mins.

F-com (kitten's drawings of rats come to life & pursue her)

Ref: FEFN 12:18-19:67; ShF/J '58-59.

Konflikty

See: Conflict (1960).

Kong

See: King Kong (1933).

Konga

(I Was a Teenage Gorilla --e.t.)

1960 (1961) British/US, Merton Park/Herman Cohen (AIP) color 90 mins.

Prod: Herman Cohen.

Dir: John Lemont.

SP: Aben Kandel & H. Cohen.

Art Dir: Wilfred Arnold.

Makeup: Jack Craig.

Cin: Desmond Dickinson.

Edit: Jack Slade.

cont.

Konga cont.

Mus: Gerard Schürmann.

Mus Dir: Muir Mathieson.

Cast: Michael Gough, Margo Johns, Jess Conrad, Claire Gordon, Austin Trevor, Jack Watson, George Pastell, Leonard Sachs.

SF-H (mad biologist raises man-eating plants; turns chimpanzee into killer go-rilla; later chimp becomes gigantic in size)

Ref: FF '61 p209; MFB April '61 p48-49; FFF p38.

See also: King Kong (1933).

Kongo

1932 MGM 86 mins.

Dir: William Cowen.

SP: Leo Gordon.

Cin: Harold Rosson.

Edit: Conrad A. Nervig.

Cast: Walter Huston, Lupe Velez, Conrad Nagel, Virginia Bruce, C. Henry Gordon, Forrester Harvey.

bor-F; H (crippled sadist holds natives in his sway by using their superstitions; possibly fake monster)

Ref: Vw 22 Nov '32; FDY '33; MPH 29 Nov '32 p31; FIR Feb '60 p82.

Based on the play by Chester DeVonde & Kilbourn Gordon.

Remake of: West of Zanzibar (1928).

Kongress Amuesiert Sich, Der

(The Congress of Love --ad.t.)

1966 German/Austrian 70mm color 98 mins.

Prod: Aldo von Pinnelli, Peter Schaeffers, & Wiener Stadthalle.

Dir: Geza von Radvanyi.

SP: Fred Denger, A. von Pinnelli, & G. von Radvanyi.

Art Dir: Otto Pischinger & Herta Hareiter.

Cin: Heinz Hoelscher.

Mus: Peter Thomas, Johann Strauss, & Robert Stolz.

Cast: Lilli Palmer, Curt Jurgens, Paul Meurisse, Walter Slezak, Hannes Messemer, Anita Hoefer, Brett Halsey.

F-seq (wax figures come to life)

Ref: Vw 1 June '66.

Koniok Gorbunok

See: Little Humpbacked Horse, The (1961).

Konti-Skan

1965 Danish ani sh.

Dir: Bent Barfod.

F

Ref: Ani/Cin p 166.

Korbuda

1965 Soviet, Georgia-Film (Sovexportfilm) color ani 21 mins.

Dir: A. Khintibdze.

Story: R. Tabukashvili.

F (deer given magic antlers by lightning saves doe from wolves)

Ref: Sovexportfilm cat 2:122.

Korean Alphabet

1968 Canadian, NFB color ani 8 mins.

Prod: Robert Verrall.

Dir & SP: Kim in Tae.

Design & Mus: Norman McLaren.

F-doc (Korean alphabet ani-mated)

Körkarlen

(The Phantom Carriage; The Phantom Chariot)

1958 Swedish, Nordisk.

Dir: Arné Mattsson.

cont.

Körkarlen cont.

SP: Rune Lindström.

Cast: George Fant, Ulla Jacobsson, Anita Björk, Edvin Adolphson, Bengt Brun-skog.

F (ghostly wagon; spirit leaves body)

Ref: FF Oct '58; Beranger p331.

Based on a novel by Selma Lagerlöf.

See also: Stroke of Midnight, The (1920); Phantom Wagon, The (1939).

Korochan the Little Bear

See: Koguma no Korochan (1958).

Koshikei

See: Death by Hanging (1968).

Kosice

1963 Argentinan sh.

Dir: Alejandro Vignati.

SF

Ref: Trieste '64; Gasca p317.

Kosmitchesky Reis

(Cosmical Passage; Cosmic Vessel --ad.t.?)

1936 Soviet.

Dir: V. Jouravliav.

SP: Z. Filimonova.

Cin: M. Galperin.

SF

Ref: Soviet Cinema; Musee du Cinema.

Kostimirani Rendez-Vous

(Meeting at the Fashion Show)

1965 Yugoslavian, Zagreb color ani 2 parts; Part I: 13.4 mins; Part II: 13.4 mins.

Dir, Design, Ani: Borivoj Dovnikovic.

SP: B. Dovniković.

Bg: Rudolf Borosak & Pavao Stalter.

Mus: Tomislav Simović.

doc; F-seqs (history of fashion in animation)

Ref: Z/Zagreb p81.

Kotetsu No Kyojin

See: Super Giant 3 & 4 (1957).

Kousagi Monogatari

(The Baby Bunny)

1954 Japanese, Toei Doga ani 19 mins.

F

Ref: FEFN 12:16-17:45; ShF/J '58-59 p30.

Kovačev Šegrt

See: Blacksmith's Apprentice, The (1961).

Koziotoeczek

(Little Goat; Stubborn Little Goat --ad.t?)

1953 Polish color ani 9 mins.

Dir: Lechoslaw Marszalek.

Story: Jan Brzechwa & Jerzy Nel.

Mus: Grzegorz Sielski.

F-com (goat taught to mind)

Ref: MFB April '57 p50-51; Montevideo Festival '56.

Kradja Dragulja

See: Great Jewel Robbery, The (1959).

Krakatit

1948 (1951) Czech (Artkino) 110 mins (97 mins).

Prod, Dir, SP: Otakar Vávra.

Cin: Václav Hanuš.

Mus: Jiří Srnka.

Cast: Florence Marly, Karek (Karel?) Hoger.

SF; F-seq (atomic explosion set off by radio beams; am-bassador from Hell)

cont.

Krakatit cont.

Ref: Vw 2 May '51; FIR April '59 p251; Czech film list; Broz p40; Brandon cat p 152.

Based on the novel by Karel Capek.

Král Lávra

See: King Lavra (1950).

Krasnaya Palatka

See: Red Tent, The (1969).

Krava na Granici

See: Cow on the Frontier (1964).

Krava na Mjesecu

See: Cow on the Moon (1959).

Krazy Kat

● 1916-17; Hearst Int'l Film Service ani sil 1 reel series.

Ani Dir: Bert Green, Frank Moser, Leon Searle, William C. Nolan, & Edward Grinham

Ref: LC; F/A; MPN 15:2683.

See also: He Made Me Love Him (1916).

● 1926-27 Winkler Pictures (R-C Pictures) sil ani 1 reel series.

Ani Dir: Bill Nolan.

Ref: BFI cat; F/A.

● 1927-29 Par ani sil 1 reel series.

Prod: Charles B. Mintz.

Ani Dir: Ben Harrison, Manny Gould, William C. Nolan.

Ref: BFI cat; FD 5 March '28.

● 1929-39 Col ani 1 reel series some in color.

Prod: Charles Mintz.

Ani Dir: Ben Harrison & Manny Gould.

Mus: Joe De Nat, Rosario Bourdon.

Ref: LC.

See also: Krazy's Magic (1938); Krazy's Race of Time (1937).

F-com

Based on (later ones very loosely) the comic strip by George Herriman.

Krazy's Magic

1938 Screen Gems (Col) ani 1 reel.

Prod: Charles Mintz.

Story: Allen Rose.

Ani: Harry Love.

Mus: Joe De Nat.

F-H-com (mad magician; old house; etc,)

Ref: LC; FD 25 May '38.

See also: Krazy Kat (1929-39).

Krazy's Race of Time

1937 Screen Gems (Col) ani 1 reel.

Prod: Charles Mintz.

Story: Allen Rose.

Ani: Harry Love.

Mus: Joe De Nat.

F-com (newsreel of 1999)

Ref: FD 3 June '37; LC.

See also: Krazy Kat (1929-39).

Křeček

(The Sluggard)

1946 Czech puppet sh.

Dir & SP: Karel Zeman.

F

Ref: Filmlex p 1788.

Krek

(The Sergeant)

1967 Yugoslavian, Zagreb color ani 9.6 mins.

cont.

Krek cont.

Dir, Design, Ani: Borivoj
Dovniković (Bordo).

Story: B. Dovniković & Zlatko
Grgić.

Bg: Rudolf Borošak.

F-com (young recruit's human-
like pet frog annoys a sergeant)

Ref: Z/Zagreb p88; Film Com
Fall '68.

Kriemhild's Dream of Hawks

1923 German, Decla Bioscop
sil.

Sequence from Siegfried also
shown separately.

exp-F-dream

Ref: F/A p642.

See also: Siegfried (1923).

Kriemhilds Rache

See: Kriemhild's Revenge (1924).

Kriemhild's Revenge

(Kriemhilds Rache; Niebelungen
Saga Part II)

1924 (1925) German, UFA sil
9000 ft.

Dir: Fritz Lang.

Sc: F. Lang & Thea von Harbou.

Art Dir: Otto Hunte, Erich
Kettelhut, & Karl Vollbrecht.

Cin: Carl Hoffman & Günther
Rittau.

Mus: Gottfried Huppertz.

Cast: Margarete Schön, Hanna
Ralph, Rudolf Klein-Rogge,
Paul Richter, Theodor Loos,
Bernard Goetzke, Hans von
Schlettow.

F-seq (in flashback, Siegfried
slays dragon)

Ref: C to H; FD 28 Oct '28;
Vw 17 Oct '28; FIR '59 p465.

Sequel to: Siegfried (1923).

Based on Teutonic legend.

Krishna

Hindu diety.

See: Krishna. . . .: Radha
Krishna; Shree Krishna Janma
(1918); Shree Krishna Bhakta
Pipaji (1922); Shree Krish-
navtar (1922); Krishnavatar
(1932); Kalia Mardan (1934);
Lakharani (1935); Shree Krishna
Bhagwan (1935); Pritvi Putra
(1938); Rukmini (1939);
Krishnabhakta Bodana (1944);
Krishnarjun Yuddha (1945);
Shree Krishnarjun Yuddha
(1945); Meerabai (1946);
Gokul (1947); Krishavijayam
(1949); Ganesh Mahima (1950);
Gokul Cha Raja (1950); Janmash-
tami (1950); Shree Krishna
Darshan (1950).

Krishna Arjun

1935 Indian, Royal Talkie
Distributors.

myth-F

Ref: Ind Cin YB.

Krishna Arjun Yuddha

1922 Indian sil

myth-F

Ref: Ind Cin list.

See also: Krishnarjun Yuddha
(1945); Shree Krishnarjun
Yuddha (1945).

Krishna/Argun Fight

See: Krishnarjun Yuddha (1945).

Krishna Kumar

(Master Krishna)

1924 Indian, Krishna sil.

Prod: Manecklal Patel.

myth-F

Ref: MovPic M May '38 p 17.

Krishna Kumari

1930 Indian, Young India
Pictures sil.

myth-F

Ref: Ind Cin YB.

Krishna Leela

(Drama of Krishna)

● 1935 (1936) Indian, Vel
Pics color.

Dir: Ch. Narasimba Rao.

Cast: Sri Ranjini, Vemuri
Gaggeah, Parupalli Subba Rau,
P. Styanarayan, Rajeswara
Rau, Ramathilakam, Kamsa,
Sriranjini.

Ref: Sound & Shadow 5 Dec '35
p25-27, March '36 p24.

● 1945 (1946) Indian, Lakhmidas
Anand.

Prod: Lakhmidas Anand.

Dir & SP: De Vaki Bose.

Art Dir: Charu Roy.

Mus: Kamalda Gupta.

Cast: Kananbala.

Ref: Filmindia Dec '45 p 10
ad; Film Pictorial Dec '45
p58, March '46.

myth-F

Krishna Maya

1920 Indian, Kohinoor sil.

myth-F

Ref: Ind Cin YB.

See also: Madari Mohan (1940).

Krishna Naradi

● 1926 Indian, Krishna sil.

Ref: IndCin YB.

● 1936 Indian, Sundaram Talkies.

myth-F

Krishna Sakha

1925 Indian, Aurora sil.

myth-F

Ref: IndCin YB.

Krishna Sambhav

(The Eighth Incarnation --ad.t?)

1926 Indian, United Pictures
Syndicate sil.

myth-F

Ref: IndCin YB.

Krishna Satyabhama

● 1921 Indian sil.

Ref: IndCin YB.

● 1951 Indian, Manik.

Ref: Filmcritic Sept '51.

myth-F

Krishna Sudama

1936 Indian, Radha.

Dir: Phani Barma.

Cin: Biren Dey.

Cast: Ahindra Chowdhury, Kana
Bala, Shanti Gupta, Dhiraj
Bhattacharjee, Mrinal Ghose,
Purnima.

myth-F

Ref: Dipali 15 Nov '35 p6, 30,
24 Jan '36 p20, 28; 6 March '36.

Krishna Tula

1922 Indian, Bharat sil.

myth-F

Ref: IndCin YB.

Krishna Tulabaram

(Krishna Weighed)

1937 Indian, Murugan.

Cast: T.M. Saradambal, T.S.
Ramamani Bai, Lakshmanan.

myth-F

Ref: Movie Herald May '37 p36,
49.

Krishna Under Charge of Theft

1925 Indian, sil.

myth-F

Ref: IndCin YB.

Krishna Vivah

See: Ganesh Mahima (1950).

Krishna Weighed

See: Krishna Tulabaram (1937).

Krishnabhakta Bodana

(Teacher of Krishna's Devotee)

1944 Indian, Wadia Movietone.

Prod & Dir: J.B.H. Wadia.

Songs: Pandit Indra.

SP: J.B.H. Wadia & Munshi.

Cin: Kadam & Balkrishna.

Cast: Vasant Amrit, Rani
Premlata, Sheikh Mukhtar,
Mira, Badriprasad, Ranjitkumari.

myth-F (one scene: sword becomes
embedded in air)

Ref: Filmindia Sept '44 p36.

See also: Krishna.

Krishnarjun Yuddha

(Krishna/Arjun Fight)

1945 Indian, Murari.

Dir & Story: Mohan Sinha.

Cin: V.N. Reddi.

Mus: Jagannath Prakash.

Cast: Prithviraj, Shobhana,
Samarth, Shahu Modak, Kanhai-
yalal, Trilok Kapoor, Menaka,
Ratanbai.

myth-F

Ref: Filmindia Sept '45 p51,
53, Dec '45 p72.

See also: Krishna; Krishna
Arjun Yuddha (1922); Shree
Krishnarjun Yuddha (1945).

Krishna's Flute

See: Kalia Mardan (1934).

Krishna's Marriage

See: Ganesh Mahima (1950).

Krishna's Victory

See: Krishnavijayam (1949).

Krishnavatar

(Incarnation of Krishna)

1932 Indian, Krishnatone.

Cast: Santukumari, Bhole,
Hyder Shah, Kasinath, Dass.

myth-F

Ref: Sound & Shadow June '45
p30.

See also: Krishna.

Krishnavijayam

(Krishna's Victory)

1949 Indian, Jupiter 172
mins.

Dir, Story, Sc, Edit: Sundarao
Nadkarni.

Dialog: Velavani.

Art Dir: P.P. Chaudhri.

Cin: A. Govindaswami.

Mus Dir: S.M. Subaiyya Naidu.

Cast: A.L. Raghavan, M. Rama-
krishnan, K. Rajamanikkam,
Baby Sukumar, P.V. Narasimha
Bharati.

myth-F

Ref: Indian MPA '53 p67.

See also: Krishna.

Kriss, The

See: Goona-Goona (1932).

Kriss Romani

1962 French, Les Films du
Fleuve.

Prod: Sacha Gordine.

Dir & SP: Jean Schmidt.

Art Dir: Roger Briaucourt.

Mus: Adapted from Gypsy folk
music.

Cast: Catherine Rouvel,
Germaine Kerjean, Lila Kedrova,
Gregori Chmara, François Darbon,
Charles Moulin, Gérard Darriey.

F-dream-seq (2 gypsy children
dream of finding root which
bears God's curse on the gypsies, & with it unknowingly
work miracle which frees 2
lovers from tribal punishment)

Ref: UniF 39.

Kronos

1957 Regal (20th-Fox) scope
78 mins.

Exec Prod: E.J. Baumgarten.

Prod & Dir: Kurt Neumann.

Assoc Prod & SpFX: Jack Rabin,
Irving Block, & Louis DeWitt.

Story: I. Block.

Art Dir: Theobold Holsopple.

Cin: Karl Struss.

Edit: Jodie Copelan.

Mus: Paul Sawtell.

Cast: Jeff Morrow, Barbara
Lawrence, John Emery, George
O'Hanlon, Morris Ankrum,
Kenneth Alton, John Parrish,
Richard Harrison, Robert
Shayne.

SF-H (flying saucer brings
giant cubical robot to Earth;
it sucks up & stores energy,
also stomps on people; man
possessed by liquid living-
energy creature)

Ref: FD 15 April '57; Acad;
LC.

Kronos

(Captain Kronus — Vampire
Hunter --e.t.)

1972 British, Hammer color.

Prod: Albert Fennell & Brian
Clemens.

Dir & SP: B. Clemens.

Prod Design: Robert Jones.

Makeup: Jim Evans.

Cin: Ian Wilson.

Edit: James Needs.

Cast: Horst Janson, John
Carson [vampire], John Cater,
Shane Briant, Caroline Munro,
Ian Hendry, Wanda Ventham,
William Hobbs, Susanna East,
Lisa Collings, Joanna Ross,
Caroline Villiers, Olga
Anthony.

F-H (variation on vampirism:
when blood is drained, victim
dies of old age & vampire gets
younger; swashbuckling hero
fights vampires)

Ref: Vw 19 April '72 p16,
3 May '72 p28; LSH 1:61-62.

Krotitelj

(The Lion Tamer)

1961 Yugoslavian, Zagreb
color ani 10 mins.

Dir: Darko Gospodnetic.

Idea: Nasko Frndić.

SP: Dušan Vukotic.

Design & Ani: Martin Pintaric.

Bg: Srdjan Matic.

Mus: Miljenko Prohaska.

F-com (usher dreams of being
lion tamer)

Ref: Z/Zagreb p71.

Krotitelj Divlijh Konja

See: Tamer of Wild Horses
(1966).

Krtek a Zelena Hvezda

See: Mole and the Green
Star, The (1969).

Kuchela, Devotee to the God

See: Bhaktha Kuchela (1935,
1936).

Kuei-wu Li-jen

See: Beautiful Ghost (1969).

Kuldipak

See: Pahadi Heera (1938).

Kulicka

(The Little Ball)

1963 Czech color ani
(puppet?) 9 mins.

Dir & Ani: Hermina Tyrlova.

SP: H. Tyrlova & Miroslav
Simek.

Mus: Evgen Illin.

F-com

Ref: Annecy '65.

Kumonosu-jo

See: Throne of Blood (1957).

Kundelek

See: Bastard, The (1969).

Kunwari

(Unmarried Girl; Widhwa: Widow --alt.t?)

1937 (1938) Indian, Bharat Luxmi.

Dir: Pandit Sudarshan & Profalla Roy.

Cast: Zerina Khatoon, R.P. Kapoor, Bijoy Sukla, Leela, Shajadi, Indubula.

F (magician mesmerizes girl in her sleep & calls her to his apartment)

Ref: Dipali 21 Jan '38 p23.

Kurfürstendamm

1919 German sil.

Prod & Dir: Richard Oswald.

Cast: Conrad Veidt, Asta Nielsen.

F (Satan is assigned to Earth but finds it too rough for him, is glad to return to Hell)

Ref: FIR Jan '56 p22; FIR Oct '58 p445.

See also: Satan in Sofia (1921).

Kuro Hime Dragon, The

n.d. Japanese color ani puppet.

F (young man is actually a dragon that can become a white snake)

Kurobarano Yakata

(The Black Rose Inn)

1969? Japanese, Shochiku.

Dir: Kinji Fukasaku.

Cast: Akihiro Maruyama.

H

Ref: MTVM Nov '68 p38.

Kuroi Kikori to Shiroi Kikori

(The Good and Bad Woodcutters)

1959? Japanese, Toei color ani 15 mins.

F (good man befriended by snow witch)

Ref: FEFN 12:18-19:67.

Kurokami

(The Black Hair)

See: Kwaidan (1963).

Kuroneko

(The Black Cat; Yabu no Naka no Kuroneko)

1968 Japanese, Toho 99 mins.

Exec Prod: Nobuyo Horiba, Setsuo Noto, & Kazuo Kuwahara.

Dir & SP: Kaneto Shindo.

Art Dir: Takashi Marumo.

Makeup: Shigeo Kobayashi.

Cin: Kiyomi Kuroda & Shoichi Tabata.

Mus: Hikaru Hayshi.

Cast: Kichiemon Nakamura, Nobuko Otowa, Kiwako Taichi, Kei Sato, Hideo Kanze, Rokko Toura, Taiji Tonoyama.

F-H (woman & daughter killed, return as ghosts and vampire cats; one loses arm & it turns into black cat's leg)

Ref: MFB '69 p78; Vw 22 May '68; Photon 19:46; UniJ 41.

Kurukshetra

1946 Indian, Unity.

Dir: Rameshwar Sharma.

SP: Kamala & Kant Varma.

Art Dir: Charu Roy.

Cin: G.K. Mehta.

Mus: Ganpat Rao.

Cast: Saigal, Nawab Kashmiri, Agha Muhamad, Kashmiri, Shamli, Udwadia, Biman Banerjee.

myth-F

Ref: Filmindia Aug '46 p53-55.

Kurutta Ippeiji

(A Page of Madness, A Crazy Page)

1926 Japanese, Shin Kankaku-ha Eiga Renmei sil (music added in 1973) (60 mins).

Prod & Dir: Teinosuke Kinugasa.

Sc: Yasunari Kawabata.

Art Dir: Chiyo Ozaki.

Cin: Kohei Sugiyama.

Mus: Minoru Muraoka & Toru Kurashima.

Cast: Masao Inoue, Yoshie Nakagawa, Ayako Iijima, Hiroshi Nemoto, Misao Seki, Minoru Takase.

psy-F-seqs (impressionistic; point-of-view of the insane; domestic drama set in insane asylum with sequences showing inmate's deliriums)

Ref: Anderson/Richie p54-55; BFI cat p 15-16; MFB April '73 p77-78; Vw 23 May '73.

Kut'ásek a Kutilka

(Kut'ásek and Kutilka)

1952 Czech ani puppet sh.

Dir, SP, Collaborator: Jiří Trnka.

F

Ref: Trnka p261.

Kutije

(Boxes)

1967 Yugoslavian, Zagreb color ani 7.9 mins.

Dir, SP, Design: Pavao Stalter.

Ani: Zlatko Grgić.

Mus: Andjelko Klobučar.

F (two little men live in matchboxes)

Ref: Z/Zagreb p92.

Kwaidan

(Weird Tales)

1963 (1965) Japanese, Ninjin Club & Toho (Walter Reade-Sterling) color 164 mins (125 mins).

cont.

Kwaidan (1963) Japanese

Kwaidan cont.

Prod: Shigeru Wakatsuki.

Dir: Masuki Kobayashi.

SP: Yoko Mizuki.

Art Dir: Shigemasa Toda.

Cin: Giyu Miyajima.

Mus: Toru Takemitsu.

Cast: Renato Mikuni, Michiyo Aratama, Tatsuya Nakadai, Keiko Kishi, Tetsuro Tamba, Katsuo Nakamura, Kanyemon Nakamura.

F (four stories, "Yuki-Onna" deleted in general US release prints; "Kurokami" (Black Hair): seeking wealth, young samurai leaves wife, returns to her years later, but awakens in morning to discover she is a skeleton; "Yuki-Onna" (Woman of the Snow): man is haunted by beautiful snow-witch; "Mimihashi Hoichi" (Hoichi the Earless) ghosts lure blind musician to them to sing songs of their battle; his friends paint him with magic symbols, forgetting his ears, which the ghosts rip off; "Chawan no Naka" (In the Cup of Tea): man sees reflection of another in his tea; when he meets him later, tries to stab him but the stranger vanishes)

Ref: Vw 26 May '65; FD 12 Nov '65; MFB Sept '67 p 135-36; F&F March '63; MPH 24 Nov '65.

Based on stories by Lafcadio Hearn.

See also Yuki-Onna, episode released separately.

Kwaidan. . .

See: Kaidan. . .

Kyberneticka Babicka

See: Cybernetic Grandmother (1962)

Kyofu Nikei Ningen

(Horror of Malformed Men; Horror of a Deformed Man --ad.t.)

1969 Japanese, Toei color scope 99 mins.

cont.

Kyofu Nikei Ningen cont.

Dir: Teruo Ishii.

SP: T. Ishii & Masahiro Kakefuda.

Art Dir: Akira Yoshimura.

Cin: Shigeru Akatsuka.

Mus: Masao Yagi.

Cast: Teruo Yoshida, Minoru Oki, Asao Koike, Yukie Kagawa, Mitsuko Aoi, Teruko Yumi, Tatsumi Hijikata.

bor-SF-H (surgical horror story: madman plans to make babies as ugly as he is)

Ref: UniJ 47:20; MTVM Jan '70 p57; Gifford/H p24-25.

Based on story by Rampo Edogawa.

Kyojin Yukiotoko

See: Half-Human (1955).

Kyokanoko Musume Dojoji

(Dojoji Temple)

1956 Japanese, Shochiku color 80 mins.

Cast: Utaemon Nakamura.

F (man turned into white snake by gods)

Ref: FEFN 22 June '56.

Kyrkoherden

(The Lustful Vicar --Brit.t.)

1970 Swedish, Swedish Film-production color scope 90 mins.

Prod: Inge Ivarson.

Dir & SP: Torgny Wickman.

Cin: Lars Bjorne.

Edit: Carl-Olaf Skeppstedt.

Mus: Mats Olsson.

Cast: Jarl Borssen, Magali Noel, Cornelis Vreeswijk, Margit Carlqvist, Anne Grete Nissen, Diana Kjaer.

sex-F (witch's curse on ancestor gives vicar permanent erection; spell removed by alchemists, replaced by another witch)

cont.

Kyrkoherden cont.

Ref: MFB June '72 p 117, Dec '72 p267.

Based on the short story by Bengt Anderberg.

Kyuketsu Dokurosen

(The Living Skeleton)

1968 Japanese, Shochiku scope 81 mins.

Dir: Hiroki Matsuno.

SP: Kikuma Shimoiizaka & Kyuzo Kobayashi.

Art Dir: Kyohei Morita.

Cin: Masayuki Kato.

Mus: Noboru Nishiyama.

Cast: Kikko Matsuoka, Akira Nishimura, Masumi Okada, Nobuo Kaneko, Yasunori Irikawa.

H (vengeance story with cannibalism set on abandoned ship)

Ref: UniJ 43:30; Singapore Straits-Times 16 Jan '71.

Kyuketsu Ga

(The Vampire Moth --ad.t?)

1956 Japanese, Toho 90 mins.

Cast: Ryo Ikebe, Akio Kobori, Asami Kuji, Kinuko Ito.

H (series of killings in which bodies are found with teeth marks on them; a blood-stained moth)

Ref: FEFN 13 April '56 p 17; Photon 21:26.

Based on a novel by Seishi Yokomizo.

Kyûketsuki Gokemidoro

(Goké, Body Snatcher from Hell --ad.t.)

1968 Japanese, Shochiku color scope 84 mins.

Dir: Hajime Sato.

SP: Susumu Tahaku & Kyuzo Kobayashi.

Art Dir: Tadataka Yoshino.

Cin: Shizuo Hirase.

Mus: Shunsuke Kikuchi.

Cast: Hideo Kô, Teru Yoshida, Tomomi Satô, Eizô Kitamura, Masaya Takahashi, Cathy Horan.

SF-H (flying saucers; killer's body taken over by creature from the flying saucer & he is transformed into a vampire killer)

Ref: MFB '69 p216; UniJ 42:8; Photon 19:46; MTVM Nov '68 p22 ad.

L

LA 2017

1970 (1971) U (NBC) color "90 mins."

Episode of TV series "Name of the Game" also shown as feature.

Exec Prod: Richard Irving.

Prod: Dean Hargrove.

Dir: Steven Spielberg.

SP: Philip Wylie.

Art Dir: William Tuntke.

Cin: Richard A. Kelley.

Edit Sup: Richard Belding.

Edit: Frank Morriss.

Title theme: Dave Grusin.

Cast: Gene Barry, Barry Sullivan, Edmond O'Brien, Severn Darden, Paul Stewart, Louise Latham, Sharon Farrell.

SF-dream (newspaper publisher falls asleep, dreams he is in polluted future with almost entire population living underground)

Ref: LC; Universal credit sheet.

LSD I Hate You

See: Movie Star, American Style (1966).

LSD Wall

1965 Amateur (Film-makers' Coop) 16mm color clay ani & live 6.5 mins.

Made by: John H. Hawkins.

exp-F

Ref: FMC 5:143.

La-Haut sur Ces Montagnes

(Up There on Those Mountains)

1946 Canadian, NFB color ani sh.

Dir: Norman McLaren.

F

Ref: Ani/Cin p69-70, 174.

Laast Oordeel, Het

(The Last Judgment)

1972 Belgian sh.

SF (deadly gas ravages the Earth)

Ref: CineF 2:3:39.

Labirynt

See: Labyrinth (1962).

Laboratory of Mephistophéles

(Le Cabinet de Mephistopheles)

1897 French sil 195 ft.

Prod: Georges Méliès.

F

Ref: Sadoul/M, GM Mage 118-20.

Labors of Hercules, The

See: Hercules (1957).

Labyrinth

(Labirynt)

1962 Polish color ani 15 mins.

Dir: Jan Lenica.

Mus: Wlodzimierz Kotonski.

F-H (animated steel engravings; dinosaur skeleton)

Ref: MFB Dec '64 p 181; Ani/Cin p 108-09; MMF 9:26.

Labyrinth

See: Reflection of Fear, A (1971).

Lac Enchanté, Le

See: Fée Libellule, La (1908).

Lacemaker's Dream, The

1910 French, Lux sil 462 ft.

F (dreams supernatural forces cause him to make rare lace; dream is fulfilled)

Ref: F/A p422; MPW 6:803, 816, 943.

Lad an' a Lamp, A

1932 Roach (MGM) 2 reels.

Prod: Hal Roach.

Dir: Robert McGowan.

Cast: Our Gang (Dickie Moore, Matthew Beard, George McFarland, Bobby Hutchins, Bobbie Beard), James C. Morton, Harry Bernard, Lillian Rich.

F-com (Spanky turns Cotton into a monkey with the aid of a magic lamp)

Ref: Maltin/GMS p41.

See also: Aladdin.

Lad and the Lion, The

1917 Selig sil 5 reels.

Dir: Alfred Green.

Cast: Vivian Reed, Will Machin, Charles LaMoyne, Cecil Holland, Frank Clark.

bor-F (adventures of a boy and his pet lion lost in Africa)

Ref: MPW 32:1339, 1456; LC; WID's 24 May '17; FD 24 May '17.

Based on the novel by Edgar Rice Burroughs.

See also: Lion Man, The (1936).

Lad in His Lamp, A

1948 WB color ani 7 mins.

Dir: Robert McKimson.

Story: Warren Foster.
Ani: Phil DeLara, Manny Gould, John Carey, & Charles McKimson.

F-com

Ref: LC.

See also: Aladdin; Bugs Bunny (1938-63).

Ladder, The

1964 Czech ani sh.

Dir: Eduard Hofman.

F

Ref: Ani/Cin p 171.

Ladies and Gentlemen

1964 Polish ani 6 mins.

Dir: Witold Giersz.

F-com

Ref: Ani/Cin p 113; Edinburgh '65?

Ladies and Gentlemen

See: Signore e Signori (1965).

Ladies in Retirement

1941 Col 92 mins.

Prod: Lester Cowan & Gilbert Miller.

Dir: Charles Vidor.

SP: Garrett Fort & Reginald Denham.

Art Dir: Lionel Banks.

Cin: George Barnes.

Edit: Al Clark.

Mus Dir: M.W. Stoloff.

Cast: Ida Lupino, Louis Hayward, Elsa Lanchester, Evelyn Keyes, Edith Barrett, Isobel Elsom.

bor-psy-H (lady kills her victims by putting them in ovens ; feeble-minded sisters)

Ref: MFB April '42 p45; LC; FD 9 Sept '41; FIR '59 May p273.

Based on the play by Reginald Denham & Edward Percy.

See also: Mad Room, The (1969).

Ladro di Bagdad, Il

See: Thief of Bagdad, The (1960).

Ladron de Cadaveres

(Thief of Corpses, Body Snatchers, Grave Robbers)

1956 Mexican, Internacional Cinematografica (Col).

Dir: Fernando Méndez.

SP: F. Méndez & Alessandro Verbitsky.

cont.

Ladron de Cadaveres cont.

Art Dir: Gunther Gerszo.

Cin: Victor Herrera.

Edit: Jorge Bustos.

Mus: Federico Ruiz.

Cast: Wolf Rubinskis, Carlos Riquelme, Arturo Martinez, Eduardo Alcaraz, Guillermo Hernandez.

F-H (brain exchange between gorilla and a man results in super-wrestler)

Ref: PS; Gasca; Acad; FM 9:18.

See also: Neutron.

Lady and Death, The

See: Dama de la Muerte, La (1946).

Lady and Her Luggage, The

See: Vezla Dama Zavazadla (1965).

Lady and the Dragon, The

See: Bijo to Kairyu (1955).

Lady and the Monster, The

(The Monster and the Lady -- alt.t?; Tiger Man --rr.t.)

1944 Rep 86 mins.

Assoc Prod & Dir: George Sherman.

SP: Dane Lussier & Frederick Kohner.

Art Dir: Russell Kimball.

Cin: John Alton.

SpFX: Theodore Lydecker.

Edit: Arthur Roberts.

Mus: Walter Scharf.

Cast: Vera Ralston, Richard Arlen, Erich von Stroheim, Sidney Blackmer, Helen Vinson, Mary Nash, Lola Montez.

SF-H (disembodied brain telepathically dominates the scientist who is keeping it alive)

Ref: Vd 15 March '44; FD 24 March '44; Agee p93; SFF p65; AHF p 103; LC.

Based on novel "Donovan's Brain" by Curt Siodmak.

See also: Donovan's Brain (1953); Brain, The (1962).

Lady and the Tramp

1955 WD (BV) color scope ani 76 mins.

Prod: Walt Disney.

Assoc Prod & SP: Erdman Penner.

Ani Dir: Les Clark, Ollie Johnston, Milt Kahl, Eric Larson, John Lounsbery, Wolfgang Reitherman, & Frank Thomas.

Seq Dir: Clyde Geonimi, Wilfred Jackson, & Hamilton Luske.

Story: Don Da Gradi, Joe Rinaldi, & Ralph Wright.

Layout: Ken Anderson, Tom Codrick, Don Griffith, Victor Haboush, Hugh Hennesy, Jacques Rupp, McLaren Stewart, & Al Zinnen.

Ani: Edwin Aardal, Hal Ambro, Jack Campbell, Robert Carlson, Eric Cleworth, Hugh Fraser, John Freeman, Jerry Hathcock, George Kreski, Hal King, Don Lusk, Dan MacManus, George Nicholas, Cliff Nordberg, Ken O'Brien, George Rowley, John Sibley, Harvey Toombs, & Marvin Woodward.

Bg: Dick Anthony, Claude Coats, Al Dempster, Eyvind Earle, Brice Mack, Jimi Trout, & Thelma Witmer.

Sp Process: Ub Iwerks.

Mus: Oliver Wallace.

Songs: Peggy Lee and others.

Orchestration: Edward Plumb & Sidney Fine.

Voices: Peggy Lee, Barbara Luddy, Larry Roberts, Bill Thompson, Bill Baucon, Stan Freberg, Verna Felton, Allan Reed, George Givot, Dallas McKennon, Lee Millar.

cont

Lady and the Tramp cont.

F-mus-com (1910s story of family seen from point of view of pet dog & her friends)

Ref: Vd 19 April '55; LC; MTD Oct '55 p 149; FD 19 April '55; FIR '55 p244.

Based on a story by Ward Greene.

Lady Baffles and Detective Duck

1915 Powers sil 1 reel series.

See episodes with fantastic content: At the Signal of the Three Socks (1915); Saved by a Scent (1915).

Lady Called Andrew, A

See: Señora Llamada Andres, Una (1970).

Lady Frankenstein

(La Figlia di Frankenstein: The Daughter of Frankenstein; Madame Frankenstein --e.t.)

1971 (1972) Italian, Condor Int'l (New World) color 99 mins (85 mins).

Exec Prod: Umberto Borsato & Gioele Centanni.

Prod: Harry Cushing.

Dir: Mel Welles.

Story: Dick Randall.

SP: Edward Di Lorenzo.

Art Dir: Francis Mellon.

Cin: Riccardo Pallotini (Richard Pallotin).

SpFX: Cipa.

Edit: Cleo Converse.

Mus: Alessandro Alessandroni.

Cast: Joseph Cotten, Sara Bay, Mickey Hargitay, Paul Muller, Paul Whiteman, Herbert Fux.

SF-H (Dr. Frankenstein's monster kills him; his daughter puts brain of her deformed servant into better-looking body & the new and the old monsters fight)

Ref: MFB May '72 p94-95; PB; Photon 21:6; BO 7 June '71 p86; Ital Prods '72 p 122-23.

Apparently based on comic magazine story "For the Love of Frankenstein" by Bill Warren.

See also: Frankenstein.

Lady in a Cage

1964 American Entertainments Corp (Par) 100 mins.

Prod & SP: Luther Davis.

Dir: Walter Grauman.

Art Dir: Hal Pereira.

Cin: Lee Garmes.

SpFX: Paul K. Lerpae.

Edit: Leon Barsha.

Mus: Paul Glass.

Cast: Olivia De Havilland, Ann Sothern, James Caan, Jeff Corey, Jennifer Billingsley, Rafael Campos.

psy-H (crippled woman trapped in private elevator tormented by gang of sadists; man has eyes stabbed out, then head run over by car)

Ref: MFB '67 p 121; FIR May '64 p305-06; FF '64 p 182.

Lady in the Dark

1944 Par color 98 mins.

Prod: B.G. DeSylva.

Assoc Prod: Richard Blumenthal.

Dir: Mitchell Leisen.

SP: Frances Goodrich & Albert Hackett.

Art Sup: Hans Dreier.

Cin: Ray Rennahan.

SpFX: Gordon Jennings & Paul Lerpae.

Edit: Alma Macrorie.

Mus: Kurt Weill.

Lyrics: Ira Gershwin.

cont.

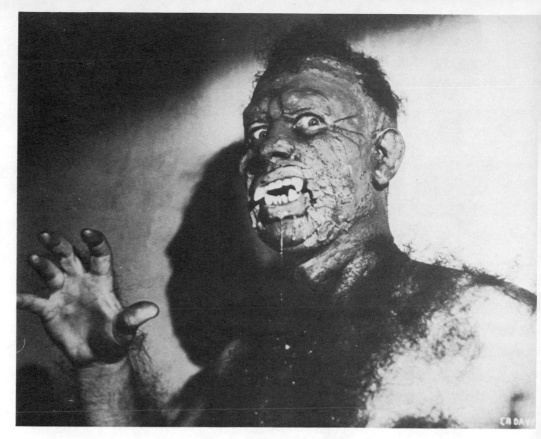

Ladron de Cadaveres (1956) Mexican

Lady in the Dark cont.

Mus Dir: Robert Emmett Dolan.

Cast: Ginger Rogers, Ray Milland, Jon Hall, Warner Baxter, Mischa Auer, Barry Sullivan, May Phillips, Gail Russell.

psy-F-dream-mus (musical-comedy star undergoes psycho-analysis & we see her dreams as elaborate production numbers)

Ref: DeGroote p73; LC; MFB June '44 p70; Acad.

Based on the play by Moss Hart, with music by Kurt Weill and lyrics by Ira Gershwin.

Lady Luna(tic)'s Hat, The

1908 British, R.W. Paul sil 185 ft.

Dir: Jack Smith (?).

F (wind carries lady with large hat to the Moon)

Ref: Gifford/BFC 02123.

Lady Morgan's Revenge

See: Vendetta di Lady Morgan, La (1966).

Lady of Spirits, A

1914 Edison sil sh.

Prod: C. Jay Williams.

Cast: William Wadsworth, Kathleen Humphrey, Harry Gripp [ghost].

F-com (ghost comedy; portrait makes faces, etc.)

Ref: MPW 20:1146, 1540.

Lady of the Camellias, The

See: Camille (1927).

Lady of the Shadows

See: Terror, The (1963).

Lady Possessed

1951 Portland Pictures (Rep) 86 mins.

Prod: James Mason.

Dir: William Spier & Roy Kellino.

SP: J. & Pamela Mason.

cont.

Lady Possessed cont.

Art Dir: Frank Arrigo.

Cin: Karl Struss.

Edit: Arthur Roberts.

Mus: Nathan Scott.

Cast: James Mason, June Havoc, Stephen Dunne, Pamela Mason, Diana Graves.

psy-F (mystic interchange & affinity of personalities)

Ref: MFB Jan '52 p3.

Based on novel "Del Palma" by Pamela Mason.

Lady Was a Ghost, The

See: Kaidan Dochu (1958).

Lagartija con Piel de Mujer, Una

See: Schizoid (1971).

Lake of Dracula

(Chiosu Me: Bloodthirsty Eyes; Dracula's Lust for Blood --ad.t.)

1971 (1972) Japanese, Toho color scope 82 mins.

Exec Prod: Fumio Tanaka.

Dir: Michio Yamamoto.

SP: Masaru Takesue & Ai Ogawa.

Art Dir: Shigekazu Ikuno.

Cin: Rokuro Nihsigaki.

Mus: Riichiro Manabe.

Cast: Midori Fujita, Sanae Emi, Choei Takahashi, Mori Kishida [vampire].

F-H (descendent of Dracula living in Japan dies and becomes a white-faced, golden-eyed vampire)

Ref: MTVM Summer '71 p 19; LAT 8 July '72 II:6; B. Warren; UniJ 54: 12-13.

Based on a character created by Bram Stoker.

See also: Dracula.

Lakharani

1935 Indian, Prabhat.

Dir & Story: Vishram Bedekar.

SP: Pandit Sudarshan.

Cin: Pandurang Naik.

Mus: Krisnarao.

Cast: Durga Khote, Monica Desai, Azurie, Sapru.

myth-F (Krishna seduced out of his stone image)

Ref: Filmindia Dec '35 p51, 53.

See also: Krishna.

Lal-e-Yaman

1934 Indian, Wadia.

Prod & Dir: Homi Wadia.

F (magic)

Ref: MovPicM Annual '39 p21.

See also: Noor-e-Yaman (1935).

Lama nel Corpo, La

See: Murder Clinic, The (1966).

Lambert, the Sheepish Lion

1951 WD (RKO) color ani 8 mins.

Prod: Walt Disney.

F-com (placid lion lives with flock of sheep)

Ref: LC; Acad nom.

Lambeth Walk, The

See: Swinging the Lambeth Walk (1940).

Lame Devil, The

See: Diablo Conjuelo, El (1970).

Lamp in the Window, The

(story by T. Burke)

See: Dream Street (1921).

Lamp that Smokes, The

See: Lampe Qui File, La (1908).

Lampe Qui File, La

(The Lamp that Smokes)

1908 (1909) French sil
ani sh.

Dir: Emile Cohl.

F (tiny genie)

Ref: Jeanne 1:4 144-45;
Ani/Cin p 168; Sadoul.

Lampes Mazda, Les

(The Mazda Lamps)

1940? French (Mazda) ani sh.
Dir: Paul Grimault.

F

Ref: Sadoul p 125.

Lampoons

1920-2? Goldwyn-Bray sil
ani 1/2 reel series.

Dir: Burton Gillett, Grim
Natwick, others.

F-com

Ref: Ani chart.

Land of Love's Dreams, The

See: Enchanted City, The
(1921).

Land of Miracles

1945? Soviet.

Dir: Andrei Vinnitsky.

SF (two explorers are shrunken
to tiny size)

Ref: Penguin Film Review
5:78.

Land of Nowhere, The

1916 (1917) Vogue (U) sil
2 reels.

Cast: Rube Miller, Lillian
Hamilton.

com; F-dream (unconscious man
imagines his spirit leaves
his body, meets wood nymphs,
St. Peter at the Pearly
Gates, etc.)

Ref: MPW 31:134, 177.

Land of Oz, The

1910 Selig sil 1000 ft.

F

Ref: MPW 6:848, 941; FW.

Based on book "The Marvelous
Land of Oz" by L. Frank Baum.

See also: Wizard of Oz, The.

Land of the Lost, The

1948 Par color? ani 8
mins.

Dir: Izzy Sparber.

Story: Isabel Manning Hewson.

Ani: Myron Tafuri.

Mus: Winston Sharples.

F-com (talking fish shows
children where all lost objects
go; lost knife rescues a
lady knife)

Ref: LC; MFB June '50 p92
See also: Noveltoons (1945-67?).

Land of Toys

1940 Soviet sh.

Dir: Obratsov.

F

Ref: FTN p578.

Land Unknown, The

(The Hidden Valley --e.t?)

1957 U scope 78 mins.

Prod: William Alland.

Dir: Virgil Vogel.

Story: Charles Palmer.

Adapt: William N. Robson.

SP: Laszlo Gorog.

Art Dir: Alexander Golitzen
& Richard Riedel.

Makeup: Bud Westmore.

Cin: Ellis W. Carter.

SpFX Cin: Clifford Stine.

SpFX: Fred Knoth, Orien
Ernest, Jack Kevan, & Roswell A. Hoffman.

Edit: Fred MacDowell.

cont.

Land Unknown cont.

Mus Dir: Joseph Gershenson.

Cast: Jock Mahoney, Shawn
Smith, William Reynolds,
Douglas Kennedy, Phil Harvey.

SF (explorers discover
Antarctic tropical oasis
with dinosaurs, man-eating
plants, etc.)

Ref: HR 18 June '57; FD 19
June '57; FM 2:17, 19:33.

Landscape

1972? ani 3 mins.

Made by: Jules Engel.

F

Ref: Filmex II.

Lanka Dahan

(Burning of Dahan/Ceylon)

● 1917 Indian sil 3 reels.

Prod & Dir: Dada Phalke.

Ref: Lighthouse 21 Aug '37
p9.

● 1935 Indian, Radha.

Dir: Sadasiva Rau.

SP: Kesavadas.

Cast: C.S. Nateshan, Bhimraj
Gurumurthi, Koteratnam.

Ref: Filmindia Oct '48 p57;
Dipali 15 Nov '35.

myth-F (Hindu monkey-god
Hanuman burns Ceylon)

See also: Hanuman;
Lankadahan.

Lankadahan

(Burning of Dahan/Ceylon)

● 1933 Indian, Shree Krishna.

Ref: IndCin YB.

● 1936 Indian.

Ref: IndCin YB.

myth-F (Hindu monkey-god
Hanuman burns Ceylon)

See also: Hanuman;
Lanka Dahan.

Laokoon

1970 Czech cut-out ani
sh.

Dir, Story, Art: Vaclav Mergl

Ani: Boris Masnik, Jaroslav
Pojar, & Kristina Tichá.

Mus: Jiří Kolafa.

SF (space explorers discover
strange eggs which hatch
into tentacled monsters)

Ref: MTVM Aug '69 p22; Czech
Films '71.

Lapis

1963/66 Amateur (CFS) color
16mm computer ani 10 mins.

Made by: James Whitney.

exp-abs-F

Ref: CFS cat Sept '68; Undrgnd
p94, 276; F& F Feb '69.

Largo

1970 Yugoslavian, Zagreb
color ani 7 mins.

Dir, SP, Design: Milan
Blažekovic & Bronko Ilic.

Bg: Branko Varadin & Srdjan
Matic.

F-com (series of gags built
around castaway-on-desert-
island theme)

Ref: Z/Zagreb p 102-03.

Larks in Toyland

1913 British sil sh?

Dir: A.M. Cooper.

F

Ref: Brit Cin p28-29.

Lasciate Ogni Speranza

(Leave All Hope, Abandon
All Hope)

1937 Italian, Juventus.

cont.

Lasciate Ogni Speranza cont.

Dir: Gennaro Righelli.

Cin: Mario Montuori.

Cast: Antonio Gandusio,
Maria Denis, Rosina Anselmi.

com-F-dream (man dreams Dante
gives him winning lottery
numbers & predicts death)

Ref: Vw 27 Oct '37; Scog-
namillo.

Lasciviousness of the Viper, The

See: Jasei no In (1920);
Ugetsu (1953).

Last Adventures of Sherlock Holmes

1923 British, Stoll sil
2 reel series.

Based on characters created
by Arthur Conan Doyle.

See also: Cardboard Box,
The; Sherlock Holmes.

Last Call, The

1908 (1909) Lubin sil
485 ft.

rel-F-seq (vision of angels
blowing call for dying man)

Ref: View IV:10:7; LC.

Last Child, The

1971 Spelling (ABC-TV)
color 75 mins.

Prod: Aaron Spelling.

Dir: John L. Moxey.

SP: Peter S. Fischer.

Art Dir: Paul Sylos.

Cin: Arch Dalzell.

Mus: Laurence Rosenthal.

Cast: Van Heflin, Michael
Cole, Harry Guardino, Janet
Margolin, Edward Asner,
Kent Smith.

soc-SF (set in near-future
US with dictatorially-con-
trolled population; couple
has baby, which is illegal)

Ref: LAT 5 Oct '71; TVG.

Last Czar, The

See: Night They Killed Rasputin, The (1960).

Last Death of the Devil, The

See: Gekko Kamen #3 (1959).

Last Flower, The

(by J. Thurber)

See: War Between Men and
Women, The (1971).

Last Generation, The

1971 B&S Film Ent.

Prod: Luther Davis.

Dir: William Graham.

SP: Earl Hamner Jr.

Cast: Stuart Whitman, Vera
Miles, Lew Ayres, Mercedes
McCambridge, Pearl Bailey,
Lee Grant, Connie Stevens,
Cesar Romero, Estelle Winwood,
Phil Harris, Michael Rennie.

SF (deals with overpopulation
in the 21st Century)

Ref: CineF 4:44; MPA.

Possibly not yet released.

Last Golem, The

See: Prazske Noci (1968).

Last Hour, The

1930 British, Nettleford
75 mins.

Prod: Archibald Nettleford.

Dir: Walter Forde.

SP: H. Fowler Mear.

Cast: Stewart Rome, Richard
Cooper, Kathleen Vaughan,
Alexander Field, Wilfred Shine,
James Raglan, George Bealby,
Frank Arlton, Billy Shine.

SF ("crooked prince uses death
ray to force down airships and
steal cargo")

Ref: Gifford/BFC 08856; Gifford/
SF p70.

Based on the play by Charles
Bennett.

cont.

Last Judgment, The

See: Giudizio Universale,
Il (1961); Laast Oordeel,
Het (1972).

Last Look, The

1909 French, Pathé sil
600 ft.

bor-SF (murder victim's eye
retains image of killer)

Ref: Bios 23 Sept '09.

Last Man, The

See: Dernier Homme, Le
(1969).

Last Man on Earth, The

1924 Fox sil tinted seq
7 reels.

Prod & Dir: Jack G. Blystone.

Sc: Donald W. Lee.

Cin: Allan Davey.

Cast: Earle Foxe, Derelys
Perdue, Grace Cunard, Gladys
Tennyson, Maryon Aye, Clarissa
Selwynne, Marie Astaire,
Jean Johnson, Buck Black.

SF-com (disease kills all men
over 14 but one, in 1954;
government of women; 2 sena-
tors fight over hero)

Ref: AFI F2.2975 p421; Photo
Feb '25; FD 28 Dec '24; MPN
30:3893-96, 3365; SFF p32.

Based on a story by John
D. Swain.

See also: It's Great to
Be Alive (1933); Ultimo
Varon Sobre la Tierra, El
(1933).

Last Man on Earth, The

(Vento di Morte: Wind of
Death; The Night Creatures
- ad.t.)

1963 (1964) Italian/US,
La Regina/Alta Vista (AIP)
86 mins.

Prod: Robert L. Lippert.

Dir: Sidney Salkow & Ubaldo
Ragona.

SP: Logan Swanson & William
P. Leicester.

Art Dir: Giorgio Giovannini.

Makeup: Piero Mecacci.

Cin: Franco Delli Colli.

Edit: Gene Ruggiero.

Mus: Paul Sawtell & Bert
Shefter.

Cast: Vincent Price, Franca
Bettoia, Emma Danieli,
Giacomo Rossi-Stuart, Umberto
Rau.

SF-H (wind-borne plague turns
everyone on Earth but one man
into night-walking zombie-like
monsters; he is killed at end
by new society of the night
people)

Ref: MFB Feb '67 p27; Photon
19:40; FF '64 p229.

Based on novel "I Am Legend"
by Richard Matheson.

See also: Omega Man, The (1971).

Last Moment, The

1923 J. Parker Read Jr. Prods
(Goldwyn) sil 6 reels.

Prod & Dir: J. Parker Reed Jr.

Story: Jack Boyle.

Sc: J. Clarkson Miller.

Cin: J.O. Taylor.

Cast: Henry Hull, Doris
Kenyon, Louis Wolheim, Louis
Calhern, William Nally,
Mickey Bennett, Harry Allen,
Jerry Peterson [monster].

SF-H (ape-like monster menaces
hero, kills several people,
in turn killed "with the aid
of a large abalone" --AFI)

Ref: AFI F2.2976 p421.

Last Moment, The

1928 Fejos, Shamroy, & Matiesen
(Zakoro) sil 6 reels (5600
ft).

Dir, Sc, Edit: Paul Fejos.

Cin: Leon Shamroy.

cont.

Last Moment cont.

Cast: Otto Matiesen, Julius Molnar Jr, Lucille La Verne, Anielka Elter, Georgia Hale, Isabelle Lamore, Vivian Winston.

exp-F (man drowning -- his life flashes before him)

Ref: AFI F2.2977 p421; Undrgnd p75; USA Exp List.

Last Moments of Anne Boleyn, The

See: Tower of London, The (1905).

Last Newsreel: 1999, The

1972? Amateur 16mm color approx 700 ft.

Dir, SP, Cin, Edit: Ray Craig.

Nar: Bob Breeding.

Cast: Don Barden, Bette Davis [sic], Ladonna Muleski.

SF (people in 2295 watch a newsreel from 1999)

Ref: B. Warren; D. Glut.

Last Night of the World, The

(short story by R. Bradbury)

See: Illustrated Man, The (1968).

Last of the Secret Agents?, The

1966 Par color 92 mins.

Prod & Dir: Norman Abbott.

Story: N. Abbott & Mel Tolkin.

SP: M. Tolkin.

Art Dir: Hal Pereira & Roland Anderson.

Cin: Harold Stine.

SpFX: Paul K. Lerpae.

Edit: Otho Lovering.

Mus: Pete King.

Cast: Marty Allen, Steve Rossi, John Williams, Nancy Sinatra, Lou Jacobi, Harvey Korman, Theo Marcuse, Ben Lessy, Sig Ruman, Ed Sullivan.

mus-com; bor-SF (trick umbrella used as multi-weapon; at climax Statue of Liberty is stolen)

Ref: FF '66 p 168-69.

Last of the Shcunue

1971 UCLA 16mm 12 mins.

Dir: Mark Griffiths.

bor-SF-com (cave-man spoof)

Ref: LAT 28 April '72; Vw 6 Oct '71; Greg Chalfin.

Last Performance, The

(Erik the Great --s.t.)

1927 U sound fx 6171 ft (silent: 5999 ft).

Prod: Carl Laemmle Jr.

Dir: Paul Fejos.

Sc: James Ashmore Creelman.

Titles: Walter Anthony & Tom Reed.

Cin: Hal Mohr.

Edit: Edward Cahn, Robert Carlisle, & Robert Jahns.

Cast: Conrad Veidt, Mary Philbin, Leslie Fenton, Fred Mackaye, Gustav Partos, William H. Turner, Anders Randolf.

psy-F-H (super-hypnotist controls girl)

Ref: AFI F2.2983 p422.

Last Prey of the Vampire, The

See: Playgirls and the Vampire (1960).

Last Quarter Hour, The

See: OSS 117 — Mission for a Killer (1965).

Last Street Boy, The

194? Italian ani sh.

Dir: Gibba.

F

Ref: Ani/Cin p 137-38.

Last Supper, The

1914 American Film Manu-facturing Co sil sh?

Sc: Lorimer Johnston.

rel-F (part II of story of modern-day Christ, with Last Supper; he walks on the water)

Ref: BFI cat p212; LC.

Last Supper, The

(painting by L. Da Vinci)

See: Passion Play, The (1924).

Last to Go

1971 Canadian, NFB(?) color ani sh.

Dir: Geral Ootterton (Otterson?).

sat-F-com

Ref: Vw 30 June '71.

Based on a short play by Harold Pinter.

Last Tomb of Ligeia

See: Tomb of Ligeia (1964).

Last Trick of Schwarzwald and Mr Edgar, The

(Messrs. Schwarzwalde and Edgar's Last Trick --alt. trans.)

1965? Czech ani puppet? sh.

Dir: Jan Svankmajer.

F (life-size mannikins dis-member each other)

Ref: MTVM May '67 p40; Ani/Cin p 124.

Last War, The

(Senkai Dai Senso; The Final War)

1961 Japanese, Toho (Medallion-TV) color 110 mins (81 mins).

Prod: Sanezumi Fujimoto & Tomoyuki Tanaka.

Dir: Shue Matsubayashi.

SP: Toshio Yazumi & Takeshi Kimura.

Cin: Rokuro Nishigaki.

SpFX: Eiji Tsuburaya.

Cast: Frankie Sakai, Nobuko Otowa, Akira Takarada, Yuriko Hoshi, Yumi Shirakawa.

SF-H (misunderstanding causes nuclear missiles to be fired & war brings end to the world)

Ref: Gasca p278; UniJ 15:12; MPH 27 Sept '61; SM 7:14.

Last Warning, The

1928 (1929) U 88 mins.

Prod: Carl Laemmle Jr.

Dir: Paul Leni.

Adapt: Alfred A. Cohn, Robert F. Hill, & J.G. Hawks.

SP: A.A. Cohn & Tom Reed.

Art Dir: Charles D. Hall.

Cin: Hal Mohr.

Mus: Joseph Cherviavsky.

Cast: Laura La Plante, Montagu Love, Roy D'Arcy, Margaret Livingston, John Boles, Burr McIntosh, Mack Swain, Slim Summerville.

H-com (supposedly ghosts haunt old theater)

Ref: AFI F2.2987 p422-23; Vw 9 Jan '29; FD 13 Jan '29.

Based on novel "House of Fear" by Wadsworth Camp, and the play by Thomas F. Fallon.

See: House of Fear (1939).

Last Will of Dr. Mabuse, The

See: Testament of Dr. Mabuse, Das (1932).

Last Woman on Earth, The

(World Without Women --e.t.)

1960 Filmgroup color scope 71 mins.

Prod & Dir: Roger Corman.

Assist Dir: Jack Bohrer.

SP: Robert Towne.

cont.

Last Woman on Earth cont.

Art Dir: Daniel Haller.

Cin: Jack Marquette.

Edit: Anthony Carras.

Mus: Ronald Stein.

Cast: Antony Carbone, Betsy Jones-Moreland, Edward Wain.

SF (three people on tropical island are only survivors of world-wide disaster)

Ref: Corman p95; FF '60 p339; MFB Nov '62 p 155; Borst.

Last Year at Marienbad

(L'Année Derniere à Marien-bad)

1961 French/Italian, Terra-Film & Tamara & Cormoran & Précitel & Como-Films & Argos & Cinetel & Silver Films/Cineriz (Astor) scope 94 mins.

Prod: Pierre Courau & Raymond Froment.

Dir: Alain Resnais.

SP: Alain Robbe-Grillet.

Art Dir: Jacques Saulnier.

Edit: Henri Colpi & Jasmine Chasney.

Mus: Francis Seyrig.

Cast: Delphine Seyrig, Giorgio Albertazzi, Sacha Pitoëff.

sur-psy-F (surrealistic sets & dialog; repetition; confusion of time)

Ref: FF '62 p47-49; FD 14 March '62; MFB March '62 p30; Acad.

Late August at the Ozone Hotel

U.S. release title of End of August at the Hotel Ozone (1965).

Lately

196? UCLA 7 mins.

Made by: Charles Wurst.

sur-psy-F

Ref: CFS cat '69.

Laterne Magique, La

See: Magic Lantern, The (1903).

Latest Style Airship

1908 French, Pathé sil.

Dir: Ferdinand Zecca.

F-com (bicycle flies)

Ref: Views 116:10; F/A p422; MPW 3:34.

Latin Quarter

1945 British 80 mins.

Dir & SP: Vernon Sewell.

Cin: Gunther Krampf.

Cast: Joan Greenwood, Derrick de Marney, Frederick Valk, Lilly Kann, Martin Miller, Valentin Dyall, Joan Green-wood.

F (seance; spirit tells how it was murdered & encased in statue)

Ref: MFB Jan '46 p2; Destiny.

Based on play "L'Angoise" by Pierre Mills & C. Villars.

See also: Medium, The (1934).

Latitude Zero

(Ido Zero Daisakusen)

1969 Japanese/US, Toho/ Don Sharpe Prods (National General) color 106 mins.

Dir: Inoshiro Honda.

Story: Ted Sherdeman.

SP: T. Sherdeman & Shinichi Sekizawa.

Art Dir: Takeo Kita.

Cin: Taiichi Kankura.

SpFX: Eiji Tsuburaya.

Mus: Akira Ifukube.

Cast: Joseph Cotten, Cesar Romero, Akira Takarada, Tetsu Nakamura, Masumi Okada, Richard Jaeckel, Linda Haynes, Patricia Medina.

cont.

Latitude Zero cont.

SF (two captains of super-submarines; evil one [Romero] makes various sorts of monsters; rays, other SF material)

Ref: CineF Fall '70 p37; UniJ 46:16; Vw 9 Sept '69.

Based on the radio series.

Latset Mizeh

See: Splitttttt (n.d.).

Laugh-O-Grams

1922-23 Laugh-O-Gram sil ani series 7 mins each.

Prod: Walt Disney.

Ani: Ub Iwerks.

F-com

Ref: Schickel/Disney p79.

Based on fairy tales, "Four Musicians of Bremen," "Little Red Riding Hood," "Puss 'n' Boots," etc.

See also: Newman's Laugh-O-Grams (1920).

Laughing at Danger

1924 Carlos Prods (FBO) sil 6 reels.

Dir: James W. Horne.

Story: Frank Howard Clark.

Cin: William Marshall.

Stunts: Richard Talmadge.

Cast: Richard Talmadge, Joe Girard, Joe Harrington, Eva Novak, Stanhope Wheatcroft.

SF-com (death ray invented by patriot is stolen by foreign agents)

Ref: AFI F2.2991 p423; LC; MPN 30:3185.

Laughing Powder

1911 Italian?, Aquila sil 420 ft.

SF-com (powder makes people laugh)

Ref: Bios 16 March '11.

Laundry Blues

1930 Pathé ani 1 reel.

Prod: Paul Terry.

Dir: Mannie Davis.

Story: John Foster.

F-com

Ref: LC; Hist US Ani Prog.

See also: Aesop's Fables (1929-31).

Laurel and Hardy Murder Case, The

1930 Roach (MGM) 30 mins.

Dir: James Parrott.

Dialog: H.M. Walker.

Edit: Richard Currier.

Cast: Stanley Laurel, Oliver Hardy.

myst; bor-H-com (old mansion; fake ghosts; murders)

Ref: BFI Dist cat '62 p42; LC.

Lav Kush

1951 Indian, Shree Bhanu 126 mins.

Prod: Babubhai Shukla.

Dir: Nanabhai Bhatt.

SP: Pandit Anuj.

Art Dir: Yusuf Dhala.

Cin: Haren Bhatt.

Edit: Baburao Barodkar.

Mus Dir: Shanker Rao Vyas.

Cast: Nirupa Roy, Prem Adib, Umarkant, Badri Prasad, Amribai Karnatki.

myth-F

Ref: Indian MPA '53 p44.

Lava-Kusa

1963 Indian, Lalitha Siva-jyothi color.

Cast: S. Varalaxmi, Anjali Devi.

myth-F (twin sons of Rama and Sita).

Ref: Movieland 22 March '63.

Laxmi Narayan

(Laxmi the Guard)

1951 Indian, Basant 139 mins.

Prod: Homi Wadia.

Dir: Nanabhai Bhatt.

Story & Dialog: Pt. Girish.

Sc: Jaisukh Anand.

Art Dir: Babubhai Mistry.

Cin: Anant Wadadekar.

Edit: Kamlakar.

Mus Dir: S.N. Tripathi.

Cast: Meena Kumari, Mahipal, S.N. Tripathi, Vasantrao, Babu Raje, Dalpat Urmilla.

myth-F

Ref: Indian MPA '53 p44.

Laxmi the Guard

See: Laxmi Narayan (1951).

Laying of the Glourie Ghost, The

See: Ghost Goes West, The (1936).

Lead Shoes, The

1950 Amateur (C-16) 16mm 18 mins.

Made by: Sidney Peterson.

exp-F (mother tries to get dead son out of a diving suit)

Ref: Undrgnd p88; C-16 p 18-19.

Based on English ballads "Edward" and "The Three Ravens".

Leap Year

1920 sil ani sh.

Dir: Rube Goldberg.

F-com

Ref: LA County Museum.

Leave All Hope

See: Lasciate Ogni Speranza (1937).

Leave Me Alone

See: Emak Bakia (1926).

Leaves from Satan's Book

(Blade am Satans Bog)

1920 Danish, Nordisk sil.

Dir: Carl Theodore Dreyer.

Sc: Elgar Hojer & Carl T. Dreyer.

Art Dir: C.T. Dreyer, Axel Bruun, & Jens G. Lund.

Cin: George Schneevoigt.

Cast: Helge Nissen [Satan], Halvard Hoff, Jacob Texiere, Erling Hansson, Ebon Strandin, Tenna Kraft, Clara Pontoppidan, Hallander Hellemann, Carlo Wieth.

F (satan enters into each of 4 villains; set during time of Christ, Spanish In- quisition, etc.)

Ref: FC 35:9; Clarens p 178; Rel/Cin p37; MMA '63 p24; FIR Feb '59 p76.

Based on a novel by Marie Corelli.

Lebedinoye Ozero

(ballet by P.I. Tchaikovsky)

See: Swan Lake.

Lebende Buddhas

See: Living Buddhas (1924).

Lecture on Man, A

1962 British ani 4 mins.

Prod & Dir: Richard Williams.

Story: Christopher Logue.

Mus: Tristram Cary.

F-sat

Ref: ASIFA info sheet.

Leda and the Elephant

1946 Soviet, Soyuzdetfilm 18 mins.

Dir: Ilya Frez.

Cin: Grigori Yegiazarov.

Mus: Lev Schwartz.

mus-F-dream

Ref: Brandon cat p283.

Leech Woman, The

(The Leech --e.t?)

1960 U 77 mins.

Prod: Joseph Gershenson.

Dir: Edward Dein.

Story: Ben Pivar & Francis Rosenwald.

SP: David Duncan.

Art Dir: Alexander Golitzen & Robert Clatworthy.

Makeup: Bud Westmore.

Cin: Ellis Carter.

Edit: Milton Carruth.

Mus: Irving Gertz.

Cast: Coleen Gray, Phillip Terry, Grant Williams, Gloria Talbott, John Van Dreelen, Estelle Hemsley, Chester Jones.

SF-H (jungle formula rejuven- ates evil American woman; the serum requires male pineal gland & she murders to get them; turns to dust at end)

Ref: FF '60 p 181.

Left-Handed Fate

See: Fata Morgana (1966).

Left-Handed Smith, The

1964 Soviet, All-Union (Sovexportfilm) color ani 45 mins.

Dir & Story: I. Ivanov-Vano.

F (left-handed Russian black- smith forges shoes for a steel flea)

Ref: Sovexportfilm cat 2:122.

Based on a story by Leskov.

Legacy of Blood

1972? Studio West.

Exec Prod: Ben Rombouts.

Prod & Dir: Carl Monson.

SP: Eric Norden.

Prod Design: Mike McCloskey.

Cin: B. Rombouts & Jack Beckett.

Cast: John Carradine, Faith Domergue, Mary Anders, Jeff Morrow, Richard Davalas, Roy Engle.

H

Ref: HR 11 June '71.

Legacy of Satan

1973 Damiano Film Prods (Film Productions).

Dir & SP: Gerard Damiano.

sex?-F-H ("unholy feast of the damned" --BO)

Ref: LSH 2:66; BO 30 July '73 back cover ad.

Legally Dead

1923 U sil 6076 ft.

Pres: Carl Laemmle (Sr).

Dir: William Parke.

Story: Charles Furthman.

Sc: Harvey Gates.

Cin: Richard Fryer.

Cast: Milton Sills, Claire Adams, Margaret Campbell, Edwin Sturgis, Faye O'Neill, Brandon Hurst.

bor-SF (scientist uses adren- alin to restore life to wrongly hanged man)

Ref: AFI F2.3029; LC; Wid's 4 Aug '23.

Legato

1950 Danish, Dansk Kulturfilm & Minerva 16mm ani 3 mins.

Made by: Henning Bendtsen.

abs-F

Ref: BFI Dist Cat Sup 1 p75.

Legend

1970 Canadian, NFB (Pyramid) 16mm color 15 mins.

F (beings from a mystic world)

Ref: Pyramid cat p 115.

Based on Western Canadian Indian legend.

Legend About the Death and Resurrection of Two Young Men

See: Meztelen Vagy (1972?).

Legend for Today, A

(play by K. Munk)

See: Ordet.

Legend of a Ghost

(La Légende du Fantôme)

1907 (1908) French, Pathé sil 1016 ft.

Dir: Segundo de Chomon.

F (ghost returned to life using Water of Life from Satan's kingdom; dragon; vampire? [doubtful])

Ref: Photon 21:25; MPW 2:463; View 109:10.

Legend of Boggy Creek, The

1972 P & L Prods color scope 90 mins.

Exec Prod: L.W. Ledwell Jr.

Prod, Dir, Cin: Charles B. Pierce.

Assoc Prod & SP: Earl E. Smith.

Edit: Thomas F. Boutross.

Mus & Post-Production Sup: Jaime Mendoza-Nava.

Nar: Vern Stearman.

Cast: Willie E. Smith, John P. Hixon, John W. Oates, Jeff Crabtree, Buddy Crabtree, Herb Jones, and other non-profession- al actors and inhabitants of Fouke, Arkansas.

bor-SF; H-doc (dramatized en- counters of residents of small Arkansas town with shaggy, man-sized ape-monster that purportedly lives in a nearby swamp)

Ref: BO 18 June '73; Producer's fact sheet.

Legend of Cagliostro, The

1912 French, Gaum sil sh.

F (painting of Christ opens eyes; ghost of wife; walls open; other miracles)

Ref: MPW 14:278.

See also: Cagliostro.

Legend of Coyote Rock, The

1945 WD (RKO) color ani 1 reel.

Prod: Walt Disney.

Dir: Charles Nichols.

Story: Eric Gurney.

Ani: John Lounsbery, Norman Tate, George Nicholas, & Edwin Aardal.

Mus: Oliver Wallace.

F-com (dog vs. coyote)

Ref: LC; B. Warren.

See also: Pluto (1940-51).

Legend of Hell House, The

1972 (1973) British/US, Pilgrim/Academy (20th-Fox) color 94 mins.

Exec Prod: James H. Nicholson.

Prod: Albert Fennell & Norman T. Herman.

Dir: John Hough.

SP: Richard Matheson.

Set Design: Robert Jones.

Makeup: Linda Devetta.

Cin: Alan Hume.

Cin FX: Tom Howard.

cont.

cont.

Legend of Hell House cont.

SpFX: Roy Whybrow.

Edit: Geoffrey Foot.

Mus: Brian Hodgson & Delia Derbyshire.

Cast: Pamela Franklin, Roddy McDowall, Clive Revill, Gayle Hunnicutt, Roland Culver, Peter Bowles, Michael Gough (unbilled).

F-H (house haunted by evil spirit; mediums, trances, seances, ectoplasmic material- izations, ghosts, etc.)

Ref: 20th-Fox notes; HR 29 May '73; Vw 30 May '73 p 13.

Based on novel "Hell House" by Richard Matheson.

Legend of Hillbilly John, The

(Who Fears the Devil? --s.t.)

1972 (1973) Two's Company (Jack H. Harris) color 89 mins.

Prod: Barney Rosenzweig.

Dir: John Newland.

SP: Melvin Levy.

Cin: Flemming Olsen.

SpFX: Gene Warren.

Edit: Russell Schoengarth.

Mus: Roger Kellaway.

Cast: Hedge Capers, Severn Darden, Susan Strasberg, Percy Rodrigues, Sharon Henesy, Sidney Clute, Denver Pyle, Harris Yulin, Alfred Ryder, R.G. Armstrong.

F (wandering ballad singer encounters black magic & super- natural evil in the Appala- chians; demon bird)

Ref: Vw 19 July '72 p5; BO 14 May '73 pW-1.

Based on book "Who Fears the Devil?" by Manly Wade Wellman.

Legend of Horror

1972? General Film Corp (Ellman) 80 mins.

Prod: Ricky Torres Tudela.

Dir: Bill Davies.

Cast: Karin Field.

H (mad murderer thinks beating of victim's heart is giving him away)

Ref: BO 11 Sept '72 Bookinguide; Photon 21:6.

Based on short story "The Tell-Tale Heart" by Edgar Allan Poe.

See also: Tell-Tale Heart, The.

Legend of Jimmy Blue Eyes, The

1964 Robert Clouse Assocs (Topaz Film Corp) color 22 mins.

Prod, Dir, SP: Robert Clouse.

Art: Mario Casetta.

Cin: John Aloneo.

Mus: Teddy Buckner.

Cast: Isabelle Cooley, Garland Thompson.

F (blue-eyed Negro musician sells soul to Devil for ability to hit a certain high note)

Ref: Edinburgh '65 p 19; Ideal '69-70 cat p211; Acad nom.

Based on the poem by Edmund Brophy.

Legend of Lake Desolation

1911 Pathé sil 1000 ft.

F (white girl leaves Indians who raised her & river freezes, Sun goes out, leaves die)

Ref: MPW 9:306.

Legend of Lylah Clare, The

1968 Associates & Aldrich Co (MGM) color 130 mins.

Prod & Dir: Robert Aldrich.

SP: Hugo Butler & Jean Rouverol.

Art Dir: George W. Davis & William Glasgow.

Cin: Joseph Biroc.

Edit: Michael Luciano.

cont

254

Legend of Lylah Clare cont.

Mus: Frank De Vol (DeVol).

Cast: Kim Novak, Peter Finch, Ernest Borgnine, Milton Selzer, Rosella Falk, Sidney Skolsky, Vernon Scott.

bor-F (girl trained to imitate dead actress perfectly becomes possessed by the dead one's spirit)

Ref: FF '68 p344; Acad.

Based on the teleplay by Robert Thom and Edward De Blasio.

Legend of Orpheus

1909 French, Pathé sil hand colored 705 ft.

myth-F (descent into Hades; Cupid intervenes, provides happy ending)

Ref: MPW 5:811, 842, 820; F/A p422; FI IV-49:16.

See also: Orpheus (1950); Black Orpheus (1959).

Legend of Prague, The

See: Golem, The (1936).

Legend of Rockabye Point, The

1955 U color ani 6 mins.

Prod: Walter Lantz.

F-com

Ref: LC; Acad nom.

Legend of St. Nicholas, The

See: Legende de Saint-Nicolas, La (1904?); Leggenda di S. Nicola, La (1908).

Legend of Scar Face, The

1910 Kalem sil 875 ft.

Cast: Frank Lanning.

F (Great Spirit has scarred brave wash away the scars in magic water)

Ref: MPW 7:293, 311, 8:245; F/A p422.

Legend of Sleepy Hollow,[The]

◐ 1912 Eclair sil sh?

Ref: MPW 12:427.

◐ 1908 Kalem sil 825 ft.

Ref: Views 105:11; MPW 2:467.

◐ 1972 color ani sh.

Prod: Stephen Bosustow.

Mus: Larry Wolff.

Nar: John Carradine.

Ref: LAT 17 Aug '72 IV:16; Bob Greenberg.

H-com (nervous school-teacher pursued by possibly fake ghost)

Based on the short story from the collection "The Sketch Book" by Washington Irving.

See also: Adventures of Ichabod and Mr. Toad, The (1949); Headless Horseman, The.

Legend of the Amulet, The

1914 Kalem sil sh?

F (ghostly chief leads person to sacred amulet which ends a plague)

Ref: MPW 22:92, 336.

Legend of the Bear's Wedding

See: Marriage of the Bear, The (1926).

Legend of the Boy and the Eagle,The

1968 WD color 48 mins.

Exec Prod: Ron Miller.

Assoc Prod: Hamilton S. Luske & Joe Strick.

Dir & SP: Jack Couffer.

Cin: J. Couffer & Ed Durdon.

Edit: Lloyd L. Richardson & Verna Fields.

Mus: Franklyn Marks.

Nar: Frank de Kova.

cont

Legend of Boy and Eagle cont.

Cast: Stanford Lomakema.

F (persecuted Hopi boy becomes eagle at the climax)

Ref: MFB Jan '68 p 11; Vd 17 Sept '68.

Legend of the Chrysanthemum

1912 Italian, Ambrosio sil sh?

F (fairy story set in Japan)

Ref: MPW 13:44.

Legend of the Cross, The

See: Leggenda della Croce, La (1909).

Legend of the Forget-Me-Nots

1909 French, Pathé sil colored 541 ft.

F-seq (lover sings to pool, floating flowers spell out "do not forget me")

Ref: F Index IV:17:8.

Legend of the Icy Heart

See: Legenda o Ledyanom Serdtze (1958).

Legend of the Lake, The

1911 Italian?, Cines sil 600 ft.

bor-F (man sees fairy seemingly come to life)

Ref: Bios 28 March '12.

Legend of the Lighthouse, The

1909 French, Gaum (Kleine) sil 770 ft.

F (woman turns into lighthouse at the end, after using one in life to wreck ships & rob bodies)

Ref: MPW 5:423; FI IV-39:7.

Legend of the Lilacs, The

1914 French, Eclair sil sh?

F (lilacs put on grave of murder victim turn black)

Ref: MPW 19:716.

Legend of the Lone Tree, The

1914 Vit sil 1 reel.

Dir: Ulysses Davis.

Sc: Archie R. Lloyd.

Cast: Myrtle Gonzalez, Alfred D. Vosburgh.

F (Indian tribe's curse turns murderer into a tree)

Ref: LC; MPN 16 Jan '15.

Legend of the Phantom Tribe, The

1914 Bison (U) sil 2 reels.

F (whole tribe resurrected; brave turned into a bear via witchcraft)

Ref: MPW 19:1090.

Legend of the Pied Piper, The

1949 Coronet 16mm 11 mins.

F (piper lures rats)

Ref: Collier; LC.

See also: Pied Piper of Hamelin, The.

Legend of the Skylark, The

1967 Romanian color sh.

Dir: Aurel Miheles.

Set Design: Nicolae Nobilescu.

Cin: Stefan Horvath.

Mus: Dumitru Capolanu.

Dancers: Rodica Simon, Maria Traila, Petre Cioreta.

ballet-F (beautiful girl who fell in love with Sun turned into skylark)

Ref: MTVM June '67 p 16.

Legend of the Snow Child, The

1914 Thanhouser sil sh?

F (snow child becomes real)

Ref: MPW 20:1302.

Legend of the Three Axes

1910 French, Pathé Frères sil 328 ft.

F (Pierrot & Columbine; the god Mercury offers him two axes; nymphs and fairies)

Ref: BFI cat p32.

Legend of the Undines, The

See: Légende des Ondines, La (1910).

Legend of the White Serpent, The

Famous Japanese folk tale.

See: Byakufujin no Yoren (1956); Panda and the Magic Serpent (1958); Madam White Snake (1965).

Legend of the Witches

1969 British, Negus-Fancey 87 mins.

Dir & SP: Malcolm Leigh.

Cin: Robert Webb.

Edit: Judith Smith.

H-doc (study of witchcraft)

Ref: MFB April '70 p87; F&F March '70 p89.

Legenda o Ledyanom Serdtze

(Legend of the Icy Heart)

1958 Soviet, Mosfilm color 75 mins.

Prod: Alexei Sakharov & Eldar Mongolai.

SP: V. Bitkovich & G. Yagdfeld.

Art Dir: V. Kamsky & C. Stepanov.

Cin: C. Brovin.

Mus: Y. Levitan.

Cast: D. Ibragimova, A. Oumouraliev, C. Boktenov, S. Ryskulov.

mus-F (old man who invented music helps young lover thaw actress' icy heart by use of magic flute which grew from grave of lovers)

Ref: Orient.

Based on Kirghiz legend.

Légende de Rip Van Winkle, La

See: Rip Van Winkle (1905).

Légende de Saint-Nicolas, La

(The Legend of St. Nicholas)

1904? French, Gaum sil sh.

Dir: Alice Guy-Blanche.

F

Ref: S&S Summer '71 p 152.

Légende des Ondines, La

(The Legend of the Undines)

1910 French, Pathe sil 480 ft.

F (knight lured into sea by siren)

Ref: Bios 11 May '11; Mitry II:139.

See also: Undine.

Légende du Fantome, La

See: Legend of a Ghost (1907).

Leggenda della Croce, La

(The Legend of the Cross)

1909 Italian, Ambrosio sil sh.

rel-F

Ref: Scognamillo.

Leggenda di Faust, La

See: Faust and the Devil (1948).

Leggenda di S. Nicola, La

(The Legend of St. Nicholas)

1908 Italian, Itala sil sh.

F

Ref: Scognamillo.

Légumes Vivants, Les

(The Living Vegetables)

1910 French, Pathé sil ani.

Dir: Emile Cohl.

F-com

Ref: Filmlex p 1371.

Leiningen vs. the Ants

(short story by C. Stephenson)

See: Naked Jungle, The (1953).

Lemon Grove Kids Meet the Green Grasshopper and the Vampire Lady from Outer Space, The

196? Steckler color 16mm (35mm) approx 30 mins.

Prod: Ray Dennis Steckler & Keith A. Wester.

Dir: Ted Rotter.

Story: R.D. Steckler.

SP: E.M. Kevke.

Cast: R.D. Steckler (Cash Flagg) [two roles; one as alien], Carolyn Brandt [vampire], Mike Kannon, Coleman Francis.

F-H-com (group of middle-aged idiots vs alien insect man and vampire woman who arrive in flying saucer)

Ref: B. Warren.

See also: Lemon Grove Kids Meet the Monsters, The (1966?).

Lemon Grove Kids Meet the Monsters, The

1966? Morgan-Steckler color approx 30 mins.

Prod & Dir: Ray Dennis Steckler.

SP: Ron Haydock & Jim Harmon.

Cin: Jack Cooperman.

Edit: Keith A. Wester.

Cast: Ray Dennis Steckler (Cash Flagg), Mike Kannon, Larry Byrd, Jim Harmon, Ron Haydock, Gary Collins, Bob Burns [gorilla; fake mummy].

com; H-com-seq (group of middle-aged idiots stage a race; dumbest of group encounters amateur film with mummy, gorilla, & superhero in production, thinks they are all real)

Ref: D. Glut; J. Harmon; Borst; B. Warren.

See also: Lemon Grove Kids Meet the Green Grasshopper and the Vampire Lady from Outer Space, The (196?); Superman vs. the Gorilla Gang (1967).

Lemon Hearts

1960 Amateur (Film-makers' Coop) 16mm 26 mins.

Made by: Vernon Zimmerman.

Cast: Taylor Mead.

exp-F (man becomes dislocated in time)

Ref: FMC 5:344.

Lemonade Joe

◑ 1940 Czech ani sh.

Story: Jiří Brdecka.

F

Ref: Ani/Cin p 167.

◑ (Limonádový Joe)

1964 (1967) Czech, Barrandov (AA) color (b&w) 95 mins (90 mins).

Dir: Oldřich Lipský.

Story: Jiří Brdecka.

SP: J. Brdecka & O. Lipsky.

Cin: Vladimir Novotny.

Mus: Jan Rychlik & Vlastimil Hala.

Cast: Karel Fiala, Olga Schoberova, Xveta Fialova, Milos Kopecky, Rudolf Deyl (Rudy Dale), Joseph Nomaz.

west-sat; F-seq (resurrection serum used at climax)

Ref: FF '67 p366; Broz p55, 96; Vw 5 Aug '64.

Lend a Paw
1941 WD (RKO) color ani sh.
Prod: Walt Disney.
F-com
Ref: LC; Acad winner.
See also: Mickey Mouse (1928-).

Lenin in Poland
1968? Soviet/Polish.
Dir: Youtkevitch.
Cast: Maxim Straukh.
hist; F-seq (Lenin has comic vision of bloated, monstrous capitalists)
Ref: Collier.

Lenora
1949 Czech ani sh.
Dir: Eduard Hofman.
F
Ref: Ani/Cin p 171.

León, El
(The Lion)
1971 Spanish, Estudios Castilla color ani 7.9 mins.
Dir: Amaro Carretero.
Realisation: Vicente Rodriguez.
bor-F-doc (the natural history of the lion with gags)
Ref: SpCin '72.

Leon Errol Comedy
various studios 2 reel series.
See: Good Morning, Eve! (1934); Service with a Smile (1934); Honeymoon Bridge (1935).

Leopard Avenger, The
1913 French, Lux sil 1320 ft.
bor-SF (artificial diamonds; pet leopard kills villain)
Ref: MPW 16:208; Bios 6 Feb '13.

Leopard Lady, The
1927 (1928) De Mille (Pathé) sil 6650 ft.
Prod: Bertram Millhauser.
Dir: Rupert Julian.
Sc: Beulah Marie Dix.
Cin: John J. Mescall.
Edit: Claude Berkeley.
Cast: Jacqueline Logan, Alan Hale, Robert Armstrong, Hedwig Reicher, James Bradbury Sr, Dick Alexander.
bor-F-H (murders by gorilla)
Ref: Vw 29 Feb '28; AFI F2.3036 p429; FD 1 Feb '28, 11 March '28; MPN 37:824.
Based on the play by Edward Childs Carpenter.
See also: Murders in the Rue Morgue.

Leopard Man, The
1943 RKO 66 mins.
Prod: Val Lewton.
Dir: Jacques Tourneur.
SP: Ardel Wray.
Art Dir: Albert D'Agostino & Walter Keller.
Cin: Robert Grasse.
Edit: Mark Robson.
Mus: Roy Webb.
Mus Dir: C. Bakaleinikoff.
Cast: Dennis O'Keefe, Margo, Jean Brooks, Isabel Jewell, James Bell, Abner Biberman, Tula Parma.
psy-H (insane killer puts blame for his crimes on escaped leopard)
Ref: Vd 4 May '43; MFB Nov '43 p 125; FD 11 May '43.
Based on novel "Black Alibi" by Cornell Woolrich.

Leopard Queen, The
1909 Selig sil 1000 ft.
bor-F (orphaned girl becomes able to command jungle animals)
Ref: FI IV-33 p8, IV-34 p 10; LC.

Leopard's Foundling, The
1914 Selig sil 2 reels.
Dir & Sc: Kathlyn Williams.
Cast: Kathlyn Williams, Charles Clary, Thomas Santschi.
F (girl raised by leopard)
Ref: MPW 20:1516-17, 1559, 1864; LC; F/A p341.

Leopold the See-Through Crumbpicker
1970 (1971) Firebird Films (Weston Woods) color ani 9 mins.
F
Based on the book by James Flora.

Leprechaun, The
1908 Edison sil 1000 ft.
F (fairies; leprechaun; magic)
Ref: Views 127:11; LC; FI 26 Sept '08.

Leprechaun's Gold
1949 Par color ani 7 mins.
Dir: Bill Tytla.
Story: I. Klein.
Ani: George Germanetti & Steve Muffatti.
Mus: Winston Sharples.
F-com
Ref: LC.
See also: Noveltoons (1945-).

Les Gauloises Bleues
(correct alphabetization: name of brand of cigarettes)
1968 (1969) French, Les Films Ariane & Les Films 13 & Les Productions Artistes Associes (Lopert) color 93 mins.
Prod: Alexandre Mnouchkine, Georges Danciger, & Claude Lelouch.
Dir & SP: Michel Cournot.
Art Dir: Guy Littaye.
Cin: Alain Levent.
Edit: Agnes Guillemot.
Mus: Monteverdi, Krzysztof Penderecki, & others.
Cast: Annie Girardot, Jean-Pierre Kalfon, Nella Bielski, Bruno Cremer, Henri Garcin, Jean Lescot, Georges Demestre, Anne Wiazemski, Tanya Lopert [Death].
sur-F-seqs
Ref: FF '69 p270-71; FDY '70; MFB Jan '69 p5-6; BO 16 June '69.

Lesbian Vampires — the Heiress of Dracula
See: Vampyros Lesbos — Die Erbin des Dracula (1971).

Lesson to Fathers, A
(novel by F. Anstey)
See: Vice Versa (1947).

Let There Be Light
1915 American-Flying A sil 2 reels.
Dir: William Bertram.
Cast: Helen Rosson, Charles Newton, E. Forrest Taylor.
bor-SF (illuminating electric ray)
Ref: MPN 23 Oct '15.

Let Us Rejoice
See: Gaudeamus (1912).

Letecí Fabijan
(Flying Fabian)
1968 Yugoslavian, Zagreb & Windrose Dumont Time color ani 12 mins.
Dir & Story: Zlatko Grgić, Boris Kolar, & Ante Zaninović.
cont.

Letecí Fabijan cont.
Mus: Tomislav Simovic.
F (birds teach man to fly; flying streetcar)
Ref: Trieste '69; Z/Zagreb p97, 109.
See also: Professor Balthasar.

Let's Be Happy
1957 British (AA) color scope 93 mins.
Prod: Marcel Hellman.
Dir: Lenry Levin.
SP: Diana Morgan & Dorothy Cooper.
Art Dir: Terrence Verity.
Cin: Erwin Hillier.
Edit: E.B. Jarvis.
Mus: Nicholas Brodszky.
Cast: Vera-Ellen, Tony Martin, Robert Flemyng, Zena Marshall, Guy Middleton.
bor-SF bor-F-ballet-dream; mus
Ref: HR & Vd 24 May '57; MPA; Irving Glassman.
Based on play "Jeannie" by Aimee Stuart.

Let's Go to the Movies
See: Vamos al Cine (1970).

Let's Live Again
1947 (1948) Frank Seltzer Prod (20th-Fox) 68 mins.
Prod: Frank N. Seltzer.
Dir: Herbert I. Leeds.
Story: Herman Wohl & John Vlahos.
SP: Rodney Carlisle & Robert Smalley.
Art Dir: Jerome Pycha Jr.
Cin: Mack Stengler.
Edit: Bert Jordan.
Mus: Ralph Stanley.
Mus Sup: David Chudnow.
Cast: John Emery, Hillary Brooke, Taylor Holmes, Diana Douglas, James Millican.
F-com (atomic scientist's brother reincarnated as a dog)
Ref: Vd 27 Feb '48; Gasca p 127.

Let's Make Up
1955 (1956) British, Wilcox (UA) color 62 mins.
Prod & Dir: Herbert Wilcox.
SP: Harold Purcell.
Art Dir: William C. Andrews.
Cin: Max Greene.
Edit: Reginald Beck.
Mus Dir: Robert Farnon.
Cast: Errol Flynn, Anna Neagle, David Farrar, Kathleen Harrison, Peter Graves, Helen Haye, Scott Sanders, Alma Taylor.
mus; F-dream
Ref: MPH 18 Feb '56.
Based on "The Glorious Days" by Robert Nesbitt.

Let's Not Lose Our Heads
See: Non Perdiamo la Testa (1959).

Let's Scare Jessica to Death
1971 Jessica Co (Par) color 89 mins.
Prod: Charles B. Moss Jr & William Badalto.
Dir: John Hancock.
SP: Norman Jonas & Ralph Rose.
Set Decorations: Norman Kenneson.
Cin: Bob Baldwin.
Edit: Murray Solomon & Joe Ryan.
Mus: Orville Stoeber.
Electronic Mus: Walter Sear.
cont

Let's Scare Jessica... cont.
Cast: Zohra Lampert, Barton Heyman, Kevin O'Connor, Gretchen Corbett [vampire-ghost], Alan Manson, Mariclare Costello.
F-H (woman recently released from insane asylum encounters ghost returned as vampire; all in cast vampirized except protagonist Lampert)
Ref: Vw 18, 25 Aug '71; MFB Feb '72 p32; FF '71 p480-82.

Letter, The
See: Litera (1962).

Letter M, The
See: Slowce M (1964).

Letter to Father Christmas
1910 French, Eclair sil 606 ft.
F (angels deliver the letter)
Ref: BFI cat p32.

Letters from My Windmill
(Lettres de Mon Moulin)
1956 French (Tohan Pictures) 180 mins (116 mins).
Prod, Dir, SP: Marcel Pagnol.
Art Dir: Robert Giordani & Mandaroux.
Cin: Willy Factorouitch (Faktorovitch).
Edit: Jacqueline Gaudin.
Mus: Henri Tomas.
Cast: Henry Vilbert, Daxely [Devil], René Sarvil, Viviane Mery, Rellys, Robert Vattier, Arius, Pierrette Bruno, Roger Crouzet, Edouard Delmon, Sarvil.
F-seqs (4 stories; 2 F: "Le Cure de Cucugnon" -- parish priest searches for the faithful in Heaven & Purgatory, finds them in Hell; "L'Elixir du Pere Gaucher" -- elixir rebuilds an abbey from its ruins)
Ref: UniF 6:16; FD 22 Dec '55; FIR April '59 p251.
Based on four short stories by Alphonse Daudet; "Le Cure de Cucugnon" & "L'Elixir du Pere Gaucher" are fantasies.

Lettres de Mon Moulin
See: Letters from My Windmill (1956).

Lewie, My Brother Who Talked to Horses
(story by M. Thompson)
See: My Brother Talks to Horses (1946).

Leycha
1964 Soviet, Soyouzmultfilm color ani 45 mins.
Dir & Story: Ivan Ivanov-Vano.
Decor: A. Tiourine, M. Sokolova, & A. Kouritsine.
Ani: Y. Norchtein, K. Maliantovitch, L. Jdanov, G. Zolotovskaia, & M. Batov.
Mus: A. Alexandrov.
F
Ref: Annecy '65.

Libellule, La
See: Dragon Fly, The (1901).

Liberation
See: Frigorelse (1954).

Liberation of the Mannique Mechanique, The
1967 Amateur (Film-makers' Coop) 16mm 15 mins.
Made by: Steven Arnold.
sur-F
Ref: FMC 5:17; Underground Cinema 12 '71 prog.

Liberator

197? Yugoslavian/US, Zagreb/BFA Educational color ani 1 min.

Dir: Borivoj Dovnikovic.

F

Ref: IAFF '72.

Liberty Bond Short

1918 Par-Artcraft sil sh.

Dir: D.W. Griffith.

Cast: Lillian Gish, Kate Bruce, Carol Dempster, George Fawcett.

F-dream (Gish prefers clothes to Liberty Bonds, until she dreams her family is attacked & killed by Germans invading the US)

Ref: FIR Dec '62 p600.

Liberty for Us

See: A Nous la Liberté (1931).

Liberxina 90

1971 Spanish, Film Di Formentera & Nova Cinematografica color 100 mins.

Dir: Carlos Duran.

SP: Joaquin Jorda & C. Duran.

Art Dir: Juan Alberto Soler.

Cin: Juan Amoros.

Edit: Maricel.

Mus: Luis de Pablo.

Cast: Serena Vergano, William Pirie, Edward Meeks, Romy.

bor-SF (anarchist groups have control of a chemical capable of wiping a man's mind clean)

Ref: Vw 8 Sept '71; MTVM Autumn-II '71 p 14-A.

Libesquelle, Die

See: Fountain of Love, The (1969).

License to Kill

(Nick Carter Va Tout Casser)

1964 French, Chaumaine & Filmstudio (Florida Films) 95 mins.

Dir: Henri Decoin & Philippe Senné.

Story: Jean Marcillac.

SP: J. Marcillac, Andre Haguet, & Andre Legrand.

Cast: Eddie Constantine, Daphne Dayle (Dazle?), Paul Frankeur, Charles Belmond, Yvonne Monlaur, Vladimir Inkijinoff.

bor-SF (new weapons)

Ref: TVG; FIR Aug '68.

Based on character "Nick Carter" created by John R. Corryell.

Licht Spiel Nur I

n.d. Amateur (Center Cinema) color sil 4 mins.

Made by: Robert Stiegler.

abs-F

Ref: Center Cin Coop Film Cat 2:26.

Liebe, Tod und Teufel

(Love, Death and the Devil; The Devil in a Bottle; The Imp in the Bottle --ad.ts?)

1934 German, UFA 101 mins.

Dir: Heinz Hilpert & Reinhart Steinbicker.

SP: Kurt Heuser, P. von Felinan, & L. Gravenstein.

Mus: Theo Mackeben.

Cast: Käthe von Nagy, Brigitte Horney, Rudolf Platte, Albin Skoda, Erich Ponto, Klaus Hellmer.

F-H (imp in bottle grants wishes at cost of owner's soul unless he can sell the bottle at a lower price than he paid for it)

Ref: Deutscher; FD 31 May '35 p7; Vw 29 May '35; F/3rd R p67.

cont.

Liebe, Tod un Teufel cont.

Based on short story "The Bottle Imp" by Robert Louis Stevenson.

See also: Bottle Imp, The.

Lieut. Rose R.N. and His Patent Aeroplane

1912 British, Clarendon sil 1032 ft.

bor-SF ("patent wireless controlled monoplane" --BFI)

Ref: BFI cat p93.

Lievre et la Tortue, Le

See: Tortoise and the Hare, The (n.d.).

Life

See: Zendegui (1969).

Life and Death of a Sphere

1948 Amateur (C-16) 16mm color sil sh.

Made by: Dorsey Anderson.

exp-abs-F

Ref: Undrgnd p91; C-16; USA Exp List.

Life and Death of 9413 — A Hollywood Extra, The

(Suicide of a Hollywood Extra --alt.t.)

1928 Amateur (C-16) sil sh.

Prod, Dir, Sc: Robert Florey.

Art Dir & Edit: Slavko Vorkapich.

Cin: Gregg Toland & S. Vorkapich.

Cast: Jules Raucourt, Voya Georges.

exp-sat-F (expressionistic; rides to Heaven on bicycle)

Ref: Vw 20 June '28; F/A p642; C-16 p 19.

Life and Miracles of Blessed Mother Cabrini, The

1946 Italian, Roma (Elliot) (60 mins).

Dir: Aurelio Battistoni.

Cast: La Cheduzzi, Mila Lanza, Luigi Badolati.

rel-F

Ref: FD 17 July '46.

Life and Passion of Christ

● (La Passion de Notre-Seigneur Jésus-Christ; La Vie et la Passion de Jesus Christ)

1905 French, Pathé sil 2122 ft.

Dir: Ferdinand Zecca & Lucien Nonguet.

Ref: V & FI 1:1:12; Filmlex p 1773; Rel/Cin p33; Sadoul p48, 55, 59, 76, 128.

● 1908 (1914; 1921 --rr) French, Pathe sil colored 3114 ft (7 reels in 1914).

Ref: View 89:16 ad; BFI cat p47; Rel/Cin p33.

Expanded to 7 reels in 1914; modern prolog added in 1921.

rel-F (the Passion Play treatment of the life of Jesus)

See also: Passion Play, The.

Life for a Life, A

See: Necromancy (1971).

Life Hesitates at 40

1935 Roach (MGM) 2 reels.

Prod: Hal Roach.

Dir: Charley Chase (Charles Parrott) & Harold Law.

Edit: William Ziegler.

Cast: Charley Case, Joyce Compton, James Finlayson, Brooks Benedict, Carl Switzer.

F ("Charley has strange spells during which everything around him seems to stop" --Maltin)

Ref: Maltin/GMS p68; LC.

See also: Charley Chase Comedy.

Life in a Tin

See: Vita, La (1967?).

Life in Halves

1966? Soviet, Kiev (Sovexportfilm) color ani 11 mins.

Dir: I. Lazarchuk.

Story: V. Slavkin.

Ani: E. Sivokon.

F (divorcing couple divide literally everything)

Ref: Sovexportfilm cat 3:108.

Life in the Next Century

1909 French, Lux sil 300ft.

Dir: Gerard Bourgeois.

SF (electrically-powered chairs and other wonders of year 2010).

Ref: Gifford/SF p 136; Bios 24 Feb '10.

Life Is a Circus

1958 British, Vale scope 84 mins.

Prod: E. Michael Smedley-Aston.

Dir: Val Guest.

SP: V. Guest, John Warren, & Len Heath.

Cast: Bud Flanagan, Jimmy Nervo, Teddy Knox, Charlie Naughton, Jimmy Gold, Eddie Gray, Shirley Eaton, Michael Holliday, Lionel Jeffries [genie], Joseph Tomelty, Eric Pohlmann, Chesney Allen, Maureen Moore.

F-com (circus uses genie from Aladdin's lamp & other magic to defeat rivals)

Ref: Collier; Gifford/BFC 12589.

See also: Aladdin.

Life Line in Space

n.d. Graphic (Pyramid) 16mm color ani 14 mins.

Prod: Les Novros.

Dir: Con Pederson & Ben Jackson.

doc; SF

Ref: Les Novros.

Life of an American Fireman, The

1903 Edison sil 425 ft.

Dir: Edwin S. Porter.

bor-F-dream

Ref: Early Am Cin p9-13; Niver/20 p30; LC.

Life of Christ

1907 Biograph sil 2164 ft.

rel-F (the Passion Play treatment of the life of Jesus)

Ref: Biograph Bulletin 91, 10 Jan '07.

See also: Passion Play, The; Life of Our Savior, The (1914).

Life of John Bunyan — Pilgrim's Progress

1912 Hochstetter Utility Co sil 5 reels.

Cast: Warner Oland.

biog; rel-F-seqs (unholy monsters confront pilgrim)

Ref: MPW 14:538; F/A p443.

Sequences based on narrative "The Pilgrim's Progress" by John Bunyan.

See also: Pilgrim's Progress (1912).

Life of Lord Buddha

1922 Indian sil.

myth-F

Ref: IndCin YB.

See also: Buddha (1961).

Life of Moses

1909 (1910) Vit sil hand tinted 5 reels.

Dir: J. Stuart Blackton.

rel-F (pillar of fire; parting of Red Sea; giving of the Ten Commandments)

cont.

Life of Moses cont.

Ref: F/A p491; MPW 5:839, 853-55, 6:49; FI IV:48:5, IV:49:18.

See also: Ten Commandments, The.

Life of Our Savior, The

(La Passion; The Life of Christ; The Passion Play)

1914 French, Pathé sil hand colored 7 reels.

Cast: M. & Mme. Moreau, M. Normand, M. Jacquinet.

rel-F (the Passion Play treatment of the life of Jesus)

Ref: AFI F2 p48; MPW 20:188-89; F/A p491; Limbacher/4 p4.

Based on Passion Play, The (1908).

See also: Passion Play, The; Life of Christ (1907); Behold the Man (1921).

Life of Robin Beckett

See: Ordinary Hour in the Extraordinary Life of Robin Beckett, An (1963).

Life of Shri Krishna Bhagwan

See: Shree Krishna Bhagwan (1935); Shri Krishna Bhagwan (1944).

Life of William Shakespeare: His Intrigues and Romances, The

(The Loves, Adventures and Life of William Shakespeare --alt.t.)

1914 British, British Colonial (Trans-Oceanic) sil 5 reels.

Co-Prod: Frank Rawlings.

Managing Dir: J.B. McDowell.

Cast: Albert Ward, Eva Bayley, Sybil Hare, Miss Bennett, Aimee Martinek, Gray Murray, George Foley.

biog; F-seq (at end Shakespeare dreams of scenes from his plays which are superimposed on the scene)

Ref: Shake/Sil p202-06.

Life Returns

1934 (1935; 1938--rr) U 60 mins.

Prod: Lou Ostrow.

Dir: Eugen Frenke.

Story: E. Frenke & James Hogan.

SP: Arthur Horman & John F. Goodrich.

Cin: Robert Planck.

Edit: Harry Marker.

Cast: Onslow Stevens, Lois Wilson, Valerie Hobson, George Breakston, Richard Quine, Robert E. Cornish.

bor-SF-doc-seq (dead dog brought back to life)

Ref: FD 2 Jan '35; MPH 12 Jan '35; V 4 Jan '39.

Based on Dr. Robert E. Cornish's 22 May '34 experiemnt restoring life to a dog.

Life Saving Up-to-Date

(Le Système du Docteur Souflamort)

1905 French, Star sil 304 ft.

Prod: Georges Méliès.

F-com

Ref: Sadoul/M, GM Mage 780; LC.

Life with Feathers

1945 WB color ani 7 mins.

Prod: Eddie Selzer.

Dir: Friz Freleng.

Story: Tedd Pierce.

Ani: Virgil Ross.

Mus Dir: Carl W. Stalling.

F-com

Ref: LC; Acad nom.

257

Life with Video

1971 video tape to film.

sex-F (young girl seduced by announcer who crawls out of TV set)

Ref: LAFP 27 Aug '71 p30.

Life Without Soul

1915 Ocean Film Corp sil 5 reels.

Prod: George DeCarlton.

Dir: Joseph W. Smiley.

Sc: Jesse J. Goldburg.

Cast: Percy Darrell Standing [Frankenstein Monster], William A. Cohill, Jack Hopkins, Lucy Cotton, George DeCarlton, Pauline Curley, David McCauley, Violet DeBiccari.

SF-H (Dr. Frankenstein makes a living man-like monster from parts of dead bodies; it pursues him all over Europe)

Ref: MPN 11 Dec '15 p92; MPW 20 Nov '15 p 1422-23, 4 Dec '15 p 1846.

Based on novel "Frankenstein" by Mary Shelley.

See also: Frankenstein.

Lifelines

1960 Amateur (Film-makers' Coop; Canyon Cinema; Grove) 16mm color ani & live 7 mins.

Made by: Ed Emshwiller.

Mus: Teiji Ito.

Dancer: Barbara Kersey.

exp-abs-F (abstract lines accompany dancer)

Ref: FMC 3:24, 5:97; FQ Spring '61 p34; Undrgnd p 143.

Lifted Veil, The

(play by H.A. Jones)

See: Beyond (1921).

Ligeia

(by E.A. Poe)

See: Tomb of Ligeia, The (1964).

Light Fantastic, The

(Watts Up Doc? --s.t.)

1972 USC 16mm 5 mins.

Dir & Story: Alan Bayersdorfer.

Cin & Mus: Greg Grosz.

Edit: Pete Rothenberg.

Cast: Steven Lee, Hugh Gillin, Maggie Kent.

F-com (talking light bulb competes with TV set)

Light in the Dark, The

1922 Hope Hampton Prods (Associated First National) sil 7 reels.

Dir: Clarence Brown.

Sc: C. Brown & William Dudley Pelley.

Cin: Alfred Ortlieb & Ben Carre.

Cast: Hope Hampton, E.K. Lincoln, Lon Chaney (Sr), Theresa Maxwell Conover, Dorothy Walters, Charles Mussett, Edgar Norton, Dore Davidson.

rel-F (Holy Grail works miracles, cures illnesses)

Ref: AFI F2.3067 p433; Ackerman; Focus May'Aug '70 p37.

Based on the story by William Dudley Pelley.

Light in the Night, A

1968 Dutch color ani 9 mins.

F (mermaid)

Ref: LA County Museum.

Light of Asia

1925 Indian sil.

Cast: Himansu Rai [Buddha].

myth-F

Ref: Filmindia June '40 p4-5.

Light Rhythms

1930 Belgian, Amateur sh.

Made by: Francis Brugiere.

exp-F

Ref: Undrgnd p71.

Light that Kills, The

1913 Gaum sil sh?

SF ("A"-rays heal ; too much use causes inventor's hand to wither, & eventually kills him)

Ref: MPW 16:1072.

Light Within

See: Destiny (1921).

Lighter Burden, A

1913 British, Big Ben Films sil 1900 ft.

Dir: George Pearson.

F-dream ("city man who cannot pay electric bill dreams advertisements come to life")

Ref: Gifford/BFC 04192.

Lightning Bolt

(Operazione Goldman; Operacione Goldman: Operation Goldman)

1966 (1967) Italian/Spanish, 7 Films/Balcazar (Woolner Bros) color scope 100 mins (96 mins).

Prod & Story: Alfonso Balcazar.

Dir: Antonio Margheriti (Anthony Dawson).

SP: A. Balcazar & José Antonio De La Loma.

Art Dir: Juan Alberto Soler.

Cin: Riccardo Pallottini.

Edit: Otello Colangeli & Juan Oliver.

Mus: Riz Ortolani.

Cast: Anthony Eisley, Wandisa Leigh, Diana Lorys, Ursula Parker, Folco Lulli, Paco Sanz, José Maria Caffarell.

SF (laser cannons explode US Moon rockets on takeoff; woman frozen in chamber)

Ref: FF '67 p278; MFB '68 p42-43; Vw 31 May '67; Sp Cin '67 p232-33; Ital Prods 66 I:70-71.

Lightning Bryce

1919 National Film Corp (Arrow) sil serial 15 parts 30 reels.

Dir: Paul C. Hurst.

Story: Joe Brandt.

Sc: Harvey Gates.

Cast: Jack Hoxie, Ann Little.

west; F-seq (fluid from herb induces hypnotic state; mystery woman's touch breaks spell on heroine)

Ref: LC; CNW p72-73, 194.

Lightning Change Artist, The

(L'Homme Protée)

1899 French sil 130 ft.

Prod: Georges Méliès.

F

Ref: Sadoul/M, GM Mage 228-29.

Lightning Conductor, The

(The Lightning Rod)

1962 Bulgarian color ani sh.

Dir: Tudor Dinov.

Story: Valerie Petrov.

Art Dir: Stoyan Doukov.

F

Ref: Ani/Cin p 142, 168; Bulgarian Films 1, 8.

Lightning Paper Hanger, The

1912 C.G.P.C. sil sh?

F-com

Ref: MPW 13:669.

Lightning Raider

1918-19 Astra sil serial 15 parts.

Dir: George B. Seitz.

Sc: Bertram Millhauser & G.B. Seitz.

Cast: Pearl White, Warner Oland, Henry G. Sell.

bor-F-H (villain Wu Fang keeps octopus under his den)

Ref: MPW 18:3453, 19:91, 145; CNW p 194-95; MPN 41:145.

Lightning Rod, The

See: Lightning Conductor, The (1962).

Lightning-Rod Thief, The

See: Voleur de Paratonnerres, Le (1945).

Lightning Sketches

1907 Vit sil ani & live 579 ft.

Prod & Dir: J. Stuart Blackton.

Cast: J. Stuart Blackton.

F (artist's sketches become animated)

Ref: Filmlex; BFI cat p 165.

Lightning Woman

See: Babaing Kidlat (1964).

Lights of New York, The

1922 (1923) Fox sil tinted seq 6 reels (5581 ft).

Pres: William Fox.

Dir & Sc: Charles J. Brabin.

Cin: George W. Lane.

Cast (fantastic episode only): Clarence Nordstrom, Margaret Seddon, Frank Currier, Florence Short, Charles Gerard (Gerrard?).

F-dream (dream sequence shocks hero back into reality)

Ref: AFI F2.3084 p436; LC.

Lignes Horizontales

See: Lines Horizontal (1962).

Like a Bird

See: Como un Pájaro (1969).

Like Babes in the Woods

1917 Victor (U) sil 2 reels.

Dir: George Cochrane.

Sc: Karl R. Coolidge.

Cast: Violet MacMillan, Fred Woodward.

F (wishing bracelet; bear rug comes to life; Woodward turns into donkey)

Ref: MPN 16:613 ad; LC.

Li'l Abner

● 1940 Vogue Pictures (RKO) 78 mins.

Assoc Prod: Herman Schlom.

Dir: Albert S. Rogell.

Story: Al Capp.

SP: Charles Kerr & Tyler Johnson.

Art Dir: Ralph Berger.

Cin: Harry Jackson.

Edit: Otto Ludwig & W. Donn Hayes.

Mus Dir: Lud Gluskin.

Cast: Granville Owen, Martha O'Driscoll, Mona Ray, Buster Keaton, Johnnie Morris, Billie Seward, Kay Sutton, Maude Eburne, Johnny Arthur, Walter Catlett, Edgar Kennedy, Bud Jamison, Frank Wilder, Chester Conklin, Dick Elliot, Doodles Weaver.

F-com

Ref: HR & Vd 4 Nov '40; LC.

● 1944-45 Screen Gems (Col) color ani 1 reel series.

Prod: Dave Fleischer.

Dir: Bob Wickersham, Sid Marcus, Howard Swift.

F-com

Ref: LC.

cont.

Li'l Abner cont.

See also: Pee-kool-yar Sit-chee-ay-shun, A (1944); Porkyliar Piggy (1944); Sadie Hawkins Day (1944); Kickapoo Juice (1945).

● 1959 Par VV color 114 mins.

Prod: Norman Panama.

Dir: Melvin Frank.

SP: N. Panama & M. Frank.

Art Dir: Hal Pereira & J. MacMillan Johnson.

Makeup: Wally Westmore.

Cin: Daniel L. Fapp.

Sp Cin FX: John P. Fulton.

Edit: Arthur P. Schmidt.

Mus: Gene De Paul.

Lyrics: Johnny Mercer.

Mus Dir: Joseph J. Lilley & Nelson Riddle.

Cast: Peter Palmer, Leslie Parrish, Stubby Kaye, Howard St. John, Julie Newmar, Stella Stevens, Bern Hoffman, Billie Hayes, Joe E. Marks, Robert Strauss, Al Nesor [Evil-Eye Fleagle].

F-mus-com (Dogpatch to be used as A-bomb testing area; Evil-Eye Fleagle can put "the whammy" on people -- paralyze them with his gaze; Mammy Yokum has precognitive visions; Yokumberry tonic makes men super-powerful but eliminates their sex drive)

Ref: FF '59 p3-6-08; HR 4 Nov '59; FD 6 Nov '59.

Based on the play by Norman Panama and Melvin Frank.

Based on the comic strip created by Al Capp.

Lil' Eightball

1939 Lantz (U) ani 1 reel series.

Prod: Walter Lantz.

F-com

Ref: LC; Ani chart.

Lila de Calcutta

(novel by J. Bruce)

See: Shadow of Evil (1964).

Lili

1953 MGM color 80 mins.

Prod: Edwin H. Knopf.

Dir: Charles Walters.

SP: Helen Deutsch.

Art Dir: Cedric Gibbons & Paul Groesse.

Cin: Robert Planck.

Edit: Ferris Webster.

Mus: Bronislau Kaper.

Cast: Leslie Caron, Mel Ferrer, Jean Pierre Aumont, Zsa Zsa Gabor, Amanda Blake, Kurt Kasznar.

mus-F-dream (girl dreams crippled puppeteer's puppets come to life and dance with her)

Ref: MFB April '53 p47; Vd 11 March '53; FD 11 March '53.

Based on novel "Love of Seven Dolls" by Paul Gallico.

Liliom

● 1930 Fox 94 mins.

Pres: William Fox.

Dir: Frank Borzage.

SP: S.N. Behrman & Sonya Levien.

Art Dir: Harry Oliver.

Cin: Chester Lyons.

Edit: Margaret Clancy.

Mus: Richard Fall.

Cast: Charles Farrell, Rose Hobart, Estelle Taylor, Lee Tracy, James Marcus, Walter Abel, Mildred Van Dorn, Guinn Williams, H.B. Warner, Dawn O'Day.

cont.

Liliom cont.

Ref: AFI F2.3093 p437; FD 14 Sept '30; FIR March '64 p 157.

● 1934 (1935) French, Fox-Europa 120 mins (85 mins).

Prod: Erich Pommer.

Dir: Fritz Lang.

Assist Dir: Jacques P. Feydeau.

SP: F. Lang, Robert Liebmann, & Bernard Zimmer.

Art Dir: Paul Colin & Rene Renoux.

Cin: Rudolph Mate & Louis Nee.

Mus: Jean Lenoir & Franz Waxman.

Cast: Charles Boyer, Madeleine Ozeray, Florelle, Robert Arnoux, Roland Toutain, Alexandre Regnault, Henri Richaud, Richard Darencet.

Ref: HR 10 July '34; FDY '36; Vw 15 May '34, 20 March '35; Fritz Lang in America p 128-29.

F (carnival barker briefly turns criminal, commits suicide [1930 version], goes to Heaven [Hell, 1930]; granted time on Earth after ten years, but errs again and returned to afterlife) Based on the play by Ferenc Molnar.

See also: Trip to Paradise, A (1921); Carousel (1956).

Lilliputian Minuet, The

(Le Menuet Lilliputien)

1905 French, Star sil 200 ft.

Made by: Georges Mélies.

F (tiny dancers)

Ref: LC; Sadoul/M, GM Mage 690.

Lilliputians in a London Restaurant

See: Cheesemites (1901).

Lily of Life, The

See: Lys de la Vie, Le (1920).

Limonádový Joe

See: Lemonade Joe (1964).

Lindy Leigh

(story by A. Mazure)

See: Bizarre (1969).

Line, The

See: Linea, La (1971).

Line of Apogee

n.d. Amateur (Film-makers' Coop; Canyon Cinema) 16mm color & b&w 60 mins.

Made by: Lloyd Michael Williams.

Electronic Mus: Vladimir Ussachevsky.

exp-sur-F

Ref: FMC 5:338; S&S Spring '68.

Linea, La

(The Line)

1971 Italian, RAI color six ani shorts totalling 29 mins.

Prod: Brunetto del Vita.

Dir, Story, Ani: Osvaldo Cavandoli.

F-com

Ref: MFB Sept '72 p 199.

Lines Horizontal

(Lignes Horizontales)

1962 Canadian, NFB (Pyramid) color ani 7 mins.

Dir: Norman McLaren & Evelyn Lambert.

Mus: Pete Seeger.

abs-F

Ref: Ani/Cin p 174; Pyramid cat p227; CFS cat.

Lines Vertical

(Vertical Lines)

1960 Canadian, NFB (Pyramid) color ani 7 mins.

cont

Lines Vertical cont.

Dir: Norman McLaren & Evelyn Lambert.

Mus: Maurice Blackburn.

abs-F

Ref: Ani/Cin p70, 174; Pyramid cat p227.

Linge Turbulent, Le

(The Turbulent Linen)

1909 French, Gaum sil ani sh.

Dir: Emile Cohl.

F

Ref: Sadoul p445; Filmlex p 1370.

Lion, The

See: León, El (1971).

Lion and the Ditty, The

1960? Czech ani puppet sh.

F

Ref: Czech An '61.

Lion and the Gnat, The

(Le Lion et le Moucheron)

1932 French sil ani puppet sh.

Made by: Ladislas Starevitch.

F

Ref: Filmlex p930; FIR April '58; Scognamillo.

Lion and the Goat, The

n.d. Czech color ani puppet 10 mins.

F

Ref: Czech films flyer.

Lion and the Song

1958 Czech color ani puppet sh.

Dir: Bretislav Pojar.

F

Ref: Ani/Cin p 122-23, 175.

Lion Devenu Vieux, Le

See: Aged Lion, The (1932).

Lion et le Moucheron, Le

See: Lion and the Gnat, The (1932).

Lion Hunt

1955 Amateur color computer ani 3 mins.

Made by: John Whitney.

exp-F

Ref: Film Com 53-54-55 Spring '72 p82.

Lion Man, The

1936 (1937) Normandy Pictures 67 mins.

Dir: John P. McCarthy.

SP: Richard Gordon & John Williams.

Cin: Robert Cline.

Cast: Jon Hall, Kathleen Burke, Eric Snowden, Richard Carlyle, Ted Adams, Lal Chand Mehra, Virginia Barton, Bobby Fairy, Jimmy Aubrey, Henry Hale.

bor-F

Ref: Goodrich; MFB Jan '46 p6; FDY.

Based on novel "The Lad and the Lion" by Edgar Rice Burroughs.

See also: Lad and the Lion, The (1917).

Lion Man

See: Curse of the Voodoo (1964).

Lion Tamer, The

See: Krotitelj (1961); Dressura (1970).

Lion, the Lamb, the Man, The

1914 Rex (U) sil 2 reels.

Dir: Joseph de Grasse.

Cast: Lon Chaney (Sr), Pauline Bush, Millard K. Wilson.

bor-F-seq (stone-age flashback)

Ref: Focus May-Aug '70 #3:32.

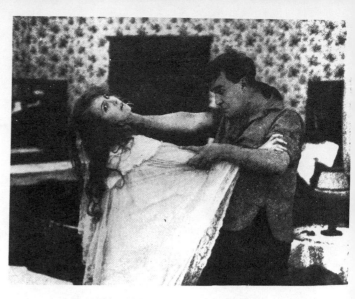

Life Without Soul (1915)

Lion, the Witch and the Wardrobe, The

1972? British, Pathé serial 10 parts 20 reels.

Prod: Pamela Lonsdale.

SP: Trevor Preston.

Design: Nevil Greene.

Nar: Jack Woolgar.

Cast: Elizabeth Crowther, Zuleika Robson, Paul Waller, Edward McMurray, Angus Lennie [faun].

F

Ref: Mythprint Aug '73 p7 & credits off screen; Vanessa Schnatmeier; Ed Finkelstein.

Lion Tonic, The

1912 Italian, Cines sil 350 ft.

SF-com (chemist invents tonic which enlarges wife, turns son into adult, dog into lion)

Ref: MPW 14:1002; Bios 17 Oct '12.

Lion's Breath, The

1916 Nestor (U) sil 1 reel.

Dir: Horace Davey.

Story: Ruth Snyder.

Sc: Al E. Christie.

Cast: Neal Burns, Billie Rhodes, Jean Hathaway, George French, Ray Gallagher.

SF-com (scientist using ultraviolet rays switches attributes of meek hero & lion)

Ref: MPW 27:1532; LC.

Lion's Bride, The

1913 Vit sil 1000 ft.

Cast: Julia Swayne Gordon, Tefft Johnson, Harry Morey.

bor-F (lion kills girl out of jealousy rather than be separated)

Ref: MPW 16:1270, 17:48.

Lion's Holiday, The

1966 Soviet color ani sh.

Dir: Feodor Khitrouk.

F-com

Ref: F&F March '68; Ani/Cin p 149.

Lion's Tale, A

n.d. Amateur (Film-makers' Coop) 16mm color 12 2/3 mins.

Made by: Walter Ungerer.

exp; psy-F-seq (girl's beauty inspires boy "to create a surrealistic world in his own mind" --FMC)

Ref: FMC 5:320; Center Cin Coop Cat 2:27.

Lion's Way, The

(novel by C.T. Stoneham)

See: King of the Jungle (1933).

Lips of Blood

See: Sang des Autres, Les (1972).

Liquéfaction des Corps Durs

(Liquefaction of Solid Bodies)

1909 French, Pathé sil sh.

Dir: Segundo de Chomon.

SF-com

Ref: DdC.

Liquid Air, The

1909 French, Gaum (Kleine) sil 450 ft.

SF-com (liquid air freezes people solid but they thaw out all right)

Ref: MPW 5:539, 548, 569; FI IV-42:6.

Liquid Electricity or The Inventor's Galvanic Fluid

1907 Vit sil 455 ft.

Prod & Dir: J. Stuart Blackton.

F-com (makes people move fast)

Ref: BFI cat p 165; LC; Filmlex p681; MPW '08 p 103.

Sequel: Galvanic Fluid (1908).

Liquid Love

1913 British, Cricks & Martin sil 420 ft.

F-com (love potion)

Ref: Bios 11 Sept '13.

Liska a Džbán

See: Fox and the Jug, The (1947).

Litera

(The Letter)

1962 Polish color ani sh.

Dir: Daniel Szczechura.

F

Ref: ASIFA info sheet.

Little and Big

(Mali i Veliki)

1966 Yugoslavian, Zagreb color ani 8.3 mins.

Dir, Design, Story, Ani: Zlatko Grgić.

Bg: Rudolf Borošak.

Mus: Davor Kajfeš.

F-com

Ref: Z/Zagreb p87; F&F March '68; Film Com Fall '68.

Little Ark, The
1971 Robert B. Radnitz (20th-Fox) color scope ani seq 86 mins.
Prod: Robert B. Radnitz.
Dir: James B. Clark.
SP: Joanna Crawford.
Art Dir: Massimo Cotz.
Cin: Austin Dempster & Denys Coop.
Ani: Fred Calvert Studios.
Edit: Fred A. Chulack.
Mus: Fred Karlin.
Cast: Theodore Bikel, Philip Frame, Genevieve Ambas, Max Croiset, Johan De Slaa.
F-seq (tug captain tells flood-orphaned children in Holland a story about ghosts and a mermaid)
Ref: MFB Aug '72 p 166-67.

Little Artists, The
1911 British, Cricks & Martin sil 325 ft.
F (animated thread forms pictures)
Ref: Gifford/BFC 03059.

Little Audrey Riding Hood
1955 Par color ani 1 reel.
F-com
Ref: LC.
See also: Noveltoons (1945-); Little Red Riding Hood.

Little Ball, The
See: Kulicka (1963).

Little Bean of La Mancha
See: Garbancito de la Mancha (1946).

Little Bear and He Who Lives in the Water, The
1969 Soviet color ani 10 mins.
F (little bear scared by his own reflection tries, on the advice of a porcupine, smiling at it)
Ref: LA County Museum.

Little Bear's Journey
n.d. Soviet color ani puppet sh.
Dir: Rasa Strautman.
F
Ref: Ani/Cin p 149.

Little Beau Pepe
1952 WB color ani 7 mins.
Dir: Chuck Jones.
Voices: Mel Blanc.
F-com (amorous skunk joins the Foreign Legion)
Ref: LC; David Rider.
See also: Pepe le Pew (1947-56?).

Little Bell
1964 Chinese color ani puppet & live 52 mins.
Dir & SP: Hsieh Tien.
Cin: Chang Ching-Hua.
Mus: Chiao Ku.
F
Ref: Collier.

Little Big Man
1970 Cinema Center Films (National General) color scope 150 mins.
Prod: Stuart Millar.
Dir: Arthur Penn.
SP: Calder Willingham.
Prod Design: Dean Tavoularis.
Special Makeup: Dick Smith.
Cin: Harry Stradling Jr.
SpFX: Logan Frazee.
Edit: Dede Allen.
Mus: John Hammond.
Cast: Dustin Hoffman, Faye Dunaway, Martin Balsam, Chief Dan George, Richard Mulligan, Jeff Corey, Amy Eccles.
cont.

Little Big Man cont.
west-sat; bor-F-seq (121-year-old man; old Indian has genuine ESP powers, including precognition)
Ref: Theater flyer; MFB April '71 p78-79.
Based on the novel by Thomas Berger.

Little Black Sambo Hunts the Tiger
See: Chibikuro Sambo no Tora Taiji (1957).

Little Blue and Little Yellow
n.d. Hilberman (Contemporary Films) color ani 10 mins.
Prod & Dir: David Hilberman.
SP & Art Dir: Leon Lionni.
F
Ref: Contemp Art Sup.

Little Brave Heart
1952? Soviet color ani 20 mins.
F (boy overcomes dangers & magic to save brother)
Ref: MFB Feb '54 p29; UCLA.

Little Brother Rat
1939 Vitaphone (WB) color ani 7 mins.
Prod: Leon Schlesinger.
Dir: Chuck (Charles M.) Jones.
Story: Rich Hogan.
Ani: Bob McKimson.
Mus Dir: Carl W. Stalling.
Voices: Mel Blanc.
F-com
Ref: LC.

Little Cheeser
1936-3? Harman-Ising (MGM) color ani 1 reel series.
Prod: Hugh Harman & Rudolf Ising.
F-com (adventures of a little boy mouse)
Ref: LC; Ani chart.

Little Chimney Sweep
1933 German ani silhouette sh.
Dir: Lotte Reiniger.
F
Ref: Ani/Cin p25.

Little Chimney Sweep, The
See: Water Babies (1907).

Little Clown, the Pup and the Moon, The
1960 Polish ani sh.
Dir: Wladyslaw Nehrebecki.
F
Ref: ASIFA info sheet.
See also: Clown and the Little Dog, The (1959).

Little Cock's Diamond Halfpenny, The
1951 Hungarian color ani sh.
Dir: Gyula Macskassy.
F (first color Hungarian cartoon)
Ref: MTVM Nov '67 p9.

Little Diver
See: Small Diver, The (n.d.).

Little Doll, The
1973 Cartoon Film (Contemporary) color ani 8 mins.
F (toys in nursery come alive; spider kidnaps ballerina doll)
Ref: Previews March '73 p 13.

Little Easter Fairy, The
1908 Lubin sil sh.
F-dream
Ref: MPW 2:351; LC.

Little Girl Who Did Not Believe in Santa Claus, A
● 1907 (1908) Edison sil 860 ft.

Little Girl Who... cont.
Ref: MPW 1:692; Views 89:7.
● 1949 William Marion Riddick 2 reels.
Ref: LC.
F (girl meets the real Santa Claus)

Little Goat, The
See: Kozioteczek (1953).

Little Golden Key, The
See: Golden Key (1939).

Little Grandma Charleston
See: Abuelita Charlestón (1961).

Little Gray Hen, The
See: Poulette Grise, La (1947).

Little Grey Neck
1951 Soviet, Sovexportfilm color ani 20 mins.
F
Ref: MFB Jan '51 p8-9; Ideal '69-70 p207.

Little Guardian Angel, The
1956 Bulgarian color ani sh.
Dir: Todor Dinov.
F (angel returns bomb to plane)
Ref: Ani/Cin p 142, 168.
Inspired by French cartoons of Jean Effel.

Little Hiawatha
1937 WD (UA) color ani 1 reel.
Prod: Walt Disney.
F-com
Ref: LC.
Spoof of poem "Hiawatha" by Henry Wadsworth Longfellow.

Little Humpbacked Horse, The
● 1939 Soviet color 78 mins.
Dir: Alexander Rou.
Cast: I. Aleynikov, M. Koval-yova.
Ref: MFB April '43 p44; FTN p578; Limbacher/4 p272.
● (The Magic Horse; The Hunch-back Pony --alt.ts)
1948 Soviet, Soyuzmultfilm color ani 57 mins.
Dir: I. Ivanov-Vano.
SP: E. Pomeschikov & P. Pozhkov.
Ref: Limbacher/4; Acad; Brandon cat p221.
● (Koniok Gorbunok)
1961 (1962) Soviet color 90 mins. (85 mins.)
Dir: Alexander Radunsky & Zoya Tulubiyeva.
Choreog & Libretto: A. Radunsky.
Mus: Rodion Schedrin.
Cin: Mikhail Silenko & Yevgeny Yatsun.
Dancers: Maya Plisetskaya, Vladimir Vasilyev, Anya Scherbinina, Alexander Radunsky, The Bolshoi Ballet.
ballet-F
Ref: UNESCO cat p71; MFB Dec '62 p 172; Brandon cat sup 1.
F (magic horse)
Based on the Russian folk story.

Little Inki
See: Inki (1941-4?).

Little Island, The
1958 British, Richard Williams color ani scope & normal ratio 33 mins.
Prod, Dir, Story: Dick Williams.
Mus: Tristram Cary plus parts of overture to the opera "William Tell" by Rossini.
cont.

Little Island cont.
exp-alleg-F-com (3 men on tiny island have separate visions of Truth, Goodness, and Beauty)
Ref: MFB Feb '59 p22; Ani/Cin p88; FTN p736; FQ Fall '58 p50-52.

Little Jim
1909 British, Cricks & Martin sil 375 ft.
Dir: A.E. Coleby.
F (angels take soul of miner's son to Heaven)
Ref: Gifford/BFC 02241.
Based on the contemporary song.

Little Jimmy
1917 Int'l Film Service sil ani sh series.
Prod: Frank Moser.
F-com
Ref: Ani chart.

Little Joe's Luck
See: Mid-Winter Night's Dream, A (1906).

Little Johnny Jet
1952 MGM color ani 7 mins.
Prod: Fred Quimby.
F-com
Ref: LC; Acad nom.

Little Jules Verne, The
See: Petit Jules Verne, Le (1907).

Little Kate and the Big Wolf
1963 Polish ani sh.
Dir: Wladyslaw Nehrebecki.
ani-F
Ref: ASIFA info sheet.

Little King, The
1933-34 Van Beuren ani sh series.
Dir: George Stallings.
Ani: Jim Tyer.
F-com
Ref: LC; Ani chart.
Based on the King Features comic strip character created by O. Soglow.

Little Knight, The
See: Garbancito de la Mancha (1946).

Little Lame Soldier, The
1927 French sil ani puppet & live sh.
Made by: Ladislas Starevitch.
Cast: Nina Star.
F
Ref: Estes; CFC 17.

Little Liar, The
1956 Rumanian.
Cast: Violeta Marinescu.
F (nose grows like Pinocchio's)
Ref: F&F Dec '56 p31.

Little Lillian, Toe Danseuse
1903 Edison sil 143 ft.
Dir: Edwin S. Porter.
F (tricks)
Ref: Niver 347.

Little Lion Hunter
1939 Vitaphone (WB) ani 1 reel.
Prod: Leon Schlesinger.
Dir: Chuck (Charles M.) Jones.
Story: Robert Givens.
Ani: Philip Monroe.
Mus Dir: Carl W. Stalling.
Voices: Mel Blanc.
F-com
Ref: LC.

Little Lulu
1946-48 Par color ani sh series.
F-com
Ref: LC.
See also: Musicalulu (1946); Loose in the Caboose (1947); Super Lulu (1947).

Little Magician, The
1908 French, Pathé sil 606 ft.
F (boy animates food and utensils)
Ref: View 119:10.

Little Masha and the Swans
1952? Soviet color ani 20 mins.
F (evil swans carry boy to witch for her to eat; stream & apple tree save him)
Ref: MFB Feb '54 p29.

Little Match Girl, The
● 1902 British, Williamson sil sh.
Prod: James A. Williamson.
Ref Sadoul p390.
● 1919 Soviet sil.
Ref: Kino p 133.
● (La Petite Marchande d' Allumettes)
1927 (1928) French sil (40 mins).
Prod & Dir: Jean Renoir & Jean Todesco.
Sc: J. Renoir.
Cin: Jean Bachelet.
Cast: Catherine Hessling, Manuel Raaby, Jean Storm, Amy Wells.
Ref: FTN p 118, 302, 310; MMA '63 p56; F/A p346; Vw 18 July '28.
● 1936 Col color ani 8.5 mins.
Prod: Charles Mintz.
Story: Sid Marcus.
Ani: Art Davis.
Mus: Joe de Nat.
Ref: LC; MPH 27 Nov '37; Acad nom.
● 1953 Danish (Omnibus TV show) sh.
Made for TV; also shown theatrically.

● 1968 Japanese, Gakken 16mm color ani puppet 18 mins.
Dir: Kazuhiko Watanabe.
Ref: UniJ '68.
F (impoverished match seller dies on Christmas, goes to Heaven & becomes bright star)
Based on the story by Hans Christian Andersen.
See also: Mid-Winter Night's Dream, A (1906); Little Matchseller's Christmas, The (1910); Match Girl (1966); Fables from Hans Christian Andersen (1968).

Little Matchseller's Christmas, The
1910 French, Urban-Eclipse (Kleine) sil 749 ft.
F-dream (little matchseller visited in dream by angel; happy ending)
Ref: MPW 7:1427, 1478.
Based on story "The Little Match Girl" by Hans Christian Andersen.
See also: Little Match Girl, The.

Little Mermaid, The
(story by H. C. Andersen)
See: Daydreamer, The (1966); Fantasia...3 (1966); Mala Sirena (1968).

Little Miss Devil
1952 Egyptian (Oriental Film Co) (95 mins).
Prod: Farid El Atrache.
Dir: Mojammed Ragaky.
SP: V.W. Barakat.
Cast: Samia Gamal [djinn], Farid El Atrache.
F-com (girl genie comes from lamp)
Ref: Acad; Exhibitor 19 Dec '51 p3208.

Little Mook
See: Geschichte von Kleinen Muck, Die (1954).

Little Muck
1938 Soviet.
Dir: O. Hodatyev.
F
Ref: Ani/Cin p 147.
Based on an Arabian story.

Little Muck's Treasure
See: Geschichte vom Kleinen Muck, Die (1954).

Little Murmur
1967 Japanese, Kuri Jikken Manga Kobo color ani 12 mins.
Dir: Yoji Kuri.
F (view of world supposedly drawn by child)
Ref: UniJ '67.

Little Nemo
1909 Vit sil ani & live sh.
Tech Dir: J. Stuart Blackton.
Art: Winsor McCay.
Cast: Winsor McCay & John Bunny.
F
Ref: F/A p627; MPW 8:900; Ani chart; Hist US Ani Prog.
Based on the newspaper cartoon by Winsor McCay.

Little Norse Prince Valiant
See: Taiyo no Ôji Horusu no Daibôken (1968).

Little Old Lonesome Little Circle Sound Film, The
197? Amateur 16mm color ani sh.
Mus: John Hartford.
abs-F
Ref: B. Warren.

Little Old Men of the Woods, The
1910 Kalem sil 945 ft.
F
Ref: MPW 6:258; FW.
Based on the fairy tale "Snow White" as collected by Jacob and Wilhelm Grimm.
See also: Snow White.

Little Orphan, The
1948 MGM color ani 8 mins.
Prod: Fred Quimby.
Dir: William Hanna & Joseph Barbera.
Ani: Irven Spence, Kenneth Muse, Ed Barge, & Ray Patterson.
Mus: Scott Bradley.
F-com
Ref: LC; Acad winner.
See also: Tom and Jerry (1940-).

Little Orphan Airedale
1947 WB color ani 7 mins.
Dir: Chuck (Charles M.) Jones.
Story: Michael Maltese & Tedd Pierce.
F-com
Ref: LC.

Little Orphan Annie
1932 RKO ani seq 61 mins.
Dir: John Robertson.
SP: Wanda Tuchock & Tom McNamara.
Cin: Jack McKenzie.
Cast: Mitzi Green, May Robson, Matt Moore, Edgar Kennedy.
F-dream (cartoon nightmare sequence)
Ref: VW 14 Oct '32, 27 Dec '32; MPH 29 Oct '32 p31, 34.
Based on the comic strip by Harold Gray.

Little Painter and the Mermaid, The
See: Petit Peintre et la Sirène, Le (1959).

Little Parade, The
(La Petite Parade)
1930 French sil ani puppet & live 1480 ft.
Made by: Ladislas Starevitch.
Cast: Nina Star.
F
Ref: Charles Ford; Filmlex p930; Scognamillo.
Based on the fairy tale by Hans Christian Andersen.

Little Phantasy on a 19th Century Painting, A
1946 Canadian, NFB ani 4 mins.
Dir: Norman McLaren.
exp-F
Ref: Ani/Cin p69-70, 174; C-16; FIR Feb '58 p 104.
Based on painting "Isle of the Dead" by Arnold Böcklin.

Little Prince, The
1973? Stanley Donen Enterprises (Par) color.
Prod & Dir: Stanley Donen.
SP & Lyrics: Alan Jay Lerner.
Art Dir: Norman Reynolds.
Makeup: Ernie Gasser.
Cin: Christopher Challis.
Edit: Archie Ludski.
Mus: Frederic Loewe.
Cast: Richard Kiley, Steven Warner, Robert Fosse, Gene Wilder, Donna MacKechnie.
mus-F (little prince from Asteroid B-612 visits Earth)
Ref: BO 8 Jan '73 p9; Vw 7 Feb '73 p24; HR 13 April '73 p 10.
Based on the novel by Antoine De Saint-Exupery.

Little Prince and the Eight-Headed Dragon, The
(Wanpaku Oji no Orochitaiji; Prince in Wonderland --e.ad.t.; Rainbow Bridge --e.ad.t.)
1963 Japanese, Toei (Col) color scope ani 86 mins (78 mins).
Dir: Yugo Serikawa.
SP: Shin Yoshida & Isamu Takaheshi.
Ani Dir: Yasuji Mori.
Mus: Akira Ifukube.
F (giants; King of the Sea; Fire God; Sun Goddess; magic crystal; magic horse; etc.)
Ref: MFB Jan '65 p 11-13; MTVM June '62 p 14.

Little Princess, A
1917 Artcraft sil 5 reels.
Dir: Marshall Neilan.
Sc: Frances Marion.
Cast: Mary Pickford, Norman Kerry, Katherine Griffith, Anne Schaefer, Theodore Roberts, ZaSu Pitts, Gustav von Seyffertitz.
F-seq (Pickford tells people the story of Ali-Baba, & it is depicted)
Ref: FIR April '72 p225; MPW 34:1332, 1341; LC.

Little Princess cont.
Based on the novel by Frances Hodgson Bennett.
See also: Ali Baba and the Forty Thieves.

Little Quartet, A
1966? Polish ani puppet 8 mins.
Dir: Edward Sturlis.
F (figures on candlesticks come to life & dance on piano)
Ref: Ani/Cin p 117; F&F March '68 at Cambridge.

Little Queen, The
See: Petite Reine, La (1959).

Little Red Riding Hood
● 1907 French, Pathé sil 328 ft.
Ref: MPW 1:622.
● 1911 Essanay sil 600 ft.
Cast: Eva Prout.
Ref: MPW 10:556, 654, 903; F/A p345; Blum p24.
● 1911 Majestic sil sh.
Cast: Mary Pickford.
F-dream
Ref: MPW 10:926, 993; F/A p344.
● 1917 Edison (K-E-S-E) sil ani silhouette 500 ft.
Ref: MPW 34:127; LC.
● 1921 Blanton sil 1 reel.
Prod: Elma Osborn Blanton.
● 1922 Selznick sil feature.
Ref: FDY '70.
● 1922 British, Hepworth Picture Plays live & ani sil sh.
Ani: Anson Dyer.
F-seq (little girl envisions the fairy tale in cartoon form)
Ref: BFI cat p 117; Hist/Brit p284.
● 1923 Laugh-O-Gram sil ani sh.
Prod: Walt Disney.
Story: Ben Hardaway.
F-com
See also: Laugh-O-Gram (1922-23).
● 1925 Century (U) sil hand colored seq 2 reels.
Prod: Julius Stern.
Dir: Alf Goulding.
Cast: Baby Peggy, Louise Lorraine, Johnny Fox.
Ref: MPW 77:459; LC; MPN 26:2110.
● 1925 Standard sil ani 1 reel.
Dir & Story: Walter Lantz.
Ref: LC; LA County Museum.
● (Le Petit Chaperon Rouge)
1928 French sil.
Dir & Sc: Alberto Cavalcanti.
Cast: Catherine Hessling, Jean Renoir, Odette Talazac, William Aguet, Pola Illéry, Raymond Guérin.
exp-F
Ref: F/A p345; Sadoul; Jeanne 2:447; DdC I:337; Sil Cin p97.
● 1949 U sh.
Prod: Burgess Meredith & Charles MacArthur.
Ref: LC.
● 1949 Wahmann Hand Puppets 16mm puppet 16 mins.
Ref: LC.
● 1954 Yugoslavian color ani sh.
Ref: Ani/Cin p 130.
First Yugoslavian color cartoon.

cont.

cont.

Little Red Riding Hood cont.

● (La Caperucita Roja)

1959 (1962) Mexican, Peliculas-Rodriguez (Azteca; K. Gordon Murray, dubbed version) color.

Dir: Roberto Rodriguez.

Story: Fernando Morales Ortiz.

SP: F.M. Ortiz & R. Garcia Traves.

Cin: Alex Phillips.

Cast: Maria Garcia, Manuel "Loco" Valdez, El Enano Santanon.

Ref: Vw 15 June '60; MTVM Jan '66 p35; FDY '63.

Sequels: Little Red Riding Hood and Her Friends (1959); Little Red Riding Hood and the Monsters (1960?).

F (although individual films will differ, inasmuch as some are comedies, the basic plot involves a little girl en-countering a talking wolf who, in order to eat her, later pretends to be the girl's grandmother)

Based on a story included in "Contes des Temps" collection by Charles Perrault, and collected also by Jacob and Wilhelm Grimm. The story is probably of Italian origin.

See also: When Lillian Was Little Red Riding Hood (1913); Mo-Toy Comedies (1917); Dizzy Red Riding Hood (1931); Little Red Riding Hood (1937); Little Rural Riding Hood (1949); Grimm's Fairy Tales (1955); Little Audrey Riding Hood (1955); Our Red Riding Hood (1960); Alta Schufita Rosie (1969); Red Riding Hood.

Little Red Riding Hood and Her Friends

(Caperucita y Sus Tres Amigos)

1959 (1962; 1965) Mexican, Peliculas-Rodriguez (Azteca; K. Gordon Murray, English-dubbed release) color 90 mins.

Dir & Story: Roberto Rodriguez.

SP: R. Rodriguez & Rafael A. Perez.

Art Dir: Gunther Gerzso.

Cin: Jose Ortiz Ramos.

Edit: José W. Bustos.

Mus: Sergio Guerrero.

English-language version Prod: K. Gordon Murray.

Cast: Maria Garcia, "Loco" Valdez, El Enano Santanon, Prudencia Griffel, Beatriz Aguirre.

F

Ref: Azteca; MTVM Jan '66 p35.

Sequel to: Little Red Riding Hood (1959).

Little Red Riding Hood and the Monsters

(Capurcita y Pulgarcito contra los Monstruos: Little Red Riding Hood and Tom Thumb vs the Monsters)

1960? (1962; 1965) Mexican, Peliculas-Rodriguez (Azteca; K. Gordon Murray, English-dubbed release) color 90 mins.

Prod & Dir: Roberto Rodriguez.

SP: Fernando Morales Ortiz & Adolfo Torres Portillo.

Cin: Rosalio Solano.

Mus: Raul Lavista.

English Language version: Prod: K. Gordon Murray.

Dir: Manuel San Fernando.

Cast: Maria Garcia, Cesarea Quezadas, José Elias Moreno, Manuel "Loco" Valdez, El Enano Santanon.

F (among monsters encountered is a Dracula-style vampire)

Ref: Vw 31 Oct '62; PS; Indice; MTVM Jan '66 p65; FM 33:10.

Sequel to: Little Red Riding Hood (1959).

See also: Dracula; Tom Thumb.

Little Red Riding Hood and the Time Bomb

1968 sh.

Made by: Guido Henderick.

sex-F (girl does strip-tease before bandaged boy; when bandages ripped off boy's crotch, mushroom cloud erupts)

Ref: Foreign Cinema 5 Sept '69.

Little Red Riding Hood and Tom Thumb vs the Monsters

See: Little Red Riding Hood and the Monsters (1960?).

Little Red Schoolhouse, The

1923 Martin J. Heyl (Arrow) sil 5760 ft.

Dir: John G. Adolfi.

Sc: James Shelley Hamilton.

Cin: George F. Webber.

Cast: Martha Mansfield, Harlan Knight, Sheldon Lewis, E.K. Lincoln, Edmund Breese, Florida Kingsley, Paul Everton.

F-seq (at climax a bolt of lightning draws the killer's face on a schoolhouse window)

Ref: AFI F2.3127 p443.

Based on the play by Hal Reid.

Little Red Walking Hood

1937 Vitaphone (WB) ani 1 reel.

Prod: Leon Schlesinger.

Dir: Tex (Fred) Avery.

Story: Cal Howard.

Ani: Irven Spence.

Mus: Carl W. Stalling.

F-com

Ref: LC.

Little Roquefort

1950-55 Terrytoons (20th-Fox) color ani 1 reel series.

Prod: Paul Terry.

F-com

Ref: LC.

Little Rural Riding Hood

1949 MGM color ani 6 mins.

Prod: Fred Quimby.

Dir: Tex Avery.

Story: Rich Hogan & Jack Cosgriff.

Ani: Grant Simmons, Walter Clinton, Bob Cannon, & Michael Lah.

Mus: Scott Bradley.

F-com

Ref: LC; Hist US Ani Prog.

See also: Little Red Riding Hood.

Little Screw, The

1927 Soviet sil ani sh.

Dir: Angivstev.

F

Ref: Coronet Prog.

Little Shego

1957? Soviet, Soyuzmultfilm color ani 11 mins.

Dir: D. Babichenko.

Story: Y. Semyonov.

F (goat, wicked hyena, sick lion; parrot commentator)

Ref: MFB Oct '58 p 133.

Based on Afghan fairy tales.

Little Shop of Horrors, The

(The Passionate People Eater --e.t.)

1960 (1961) Santa Clara (Film-group 70 mins.

Prod & Dir: Roger Corman.

SP: Charles Griffith.

Art Dir: Daniel Haller.

Cin: Archie Dalzell.

Edit: Marshall Neilan Jr.

cont.

Little Shop cont.

Mus: Fred Katz.

Cast: Jonathan Haze, Jackie Joseph, Mel Welles, Dick Miller, Myrtle Vail, Leola Wendorff, Jack Nicholson, Lynn Storey, Tammy Windsor, Toby Michaels, Jack Warford.

SF-H-com (doltish florist's assistant raises a talking, carnivorous plant; eventually he has to kill people to feed it as it grows larger)

Ref: FF '60 p357; Vd 21 April '61; MFB April '73 p78-79; Corman p95.

Little Singing Tree, The

See: Singende Klingende Baumchen, Das (1965).

Little Smarty

n.d. Soviet ani puppet sh.

F

Little Snowdrop

(Little Snow-White --Brit.t.)

1910 French, Pathé sil tinted 1000 ft.

F (Snow White is rescued by 7 dwarfs)

Ref: MPW 7:1427, 1429, 1538; F/A; BFI cat p32.

Based on the fairy tale "Snow White" as collected by Jacob and Wilhelm Grimm.

See also: Snow White.

Little Soldier, The

See: Petit Soldat, Le (1947).

Little Star, The

1965 Bulgarian color ani sh.

Dir: Radka Buchvarova.

F

Ref: Ani/Cin p 167.

Little Street Singer, The

(La Petite Chanteuse des Rues)

1924 French sil ani puppet & live 1150 ft.

Made by: Ladislas Starevitch.

Cast: Nina Star.

F

Ref: Filmlex; Charles Ford; Scognamillo.

Little Train

(Pulnocni Príhoda: It Happened; Midnight Adventure)

1960 Czech (Ideal) color ani puppet & live 14 mins.

Dir & SP: Břetislav Pojar.

Art Dir: Jiří Trnka.

Mus: Wiliam Bukový.

F (at Christmas boy pays more attention to his new train than his old wooden one, which feels resentful, but it saves him from a real train)

Ref: Czech An '61; Ani/Cin p 122, 175; Ideal cat p44.

Little Train, The

(Mali Vlak)

1959 (1972) Yugoslavian, Zagreb (Film Images) Color ani 11 mins.

Dir & SP: Dragutin Vunak.

Design: Borivoj Dovnikovic.

Ani: Vladimir Jutriša.

Bg: Pavao Stalter.

Mus: Aleksandar Bubanović.

F-com (little train runs through the countryside without tracks)

Ref: Z/Zagreb p61; Previews Dec '72.

Little Umbrella, The

See: Paraplícko (1956).

Little Western

(The Small Western --alt.trans) 1960 Polish color ani sh.

Dir: Witold Giersz.

F

Ref: Ani/Cin p 112-13; Polish Cin p82.

Little Zizi, The

See: Petit Zizi, Le (197?).

Littlest Angel, The

1950 Coronet Films (United) color ani 14 mins.

Prod: David A. Smart.

rel-F

Ref: Collier; LC; United Films '73-74 cat p 170.

Based on the story by Charles Tazwell.

Littlest Warrior, The

(Anju to Zushio-mara: The Orphan Brother)

1961 Japanese, Toei color scope ani 70 mins.

Prod: Hiroshi Okawa.

Dir: Taiji Yabushita & Yugo Arikawa.

SP: Sumie Tanaka.

Art: Akira Daikubara & Yasuji Mori.

F (giant spider; other magic)

Ref: UniJ 13:24-25; Collier; MTVM Aug '61 p24.

Based on medieval legend "Sansho Dayu."

Live and Let Die

1973 British, Broccoli & Saltzman (UA) color 121 mins.

Prod: Albert R. Broccoli & Harry Saltzman.

Dir: Guy Hamilton.

SP: Tom Mankiewicz.

Art Dir: Syd Cain & Stephen Hendrickson.

Cin: Ted Moore.

Edit: Bert Bates, Raymond Poulton, & John Shirley.

Title Song: Paul & Linda Mc Cartney.

Mus: George Martin.

Cast: Roger Moore [James Bond], Yaphet Kotto, Jane Seymour, Clifton James, Julius W. Harris, Georffrcy Holder, David Hedison, Gloria Hendry, Bernard Lee, Lois Maxwell.

F (voodoo; heroine "Solitaire" has precognition as long as she remains a virgin; Baron Samedi [Holder] apparently supernatural)

Ref: Vw 27 June '73; UA production notes.

Based on the novel by Ian Fleming.

Sequel to: Dr. No (1962).

See also: James Bond.

Liver Eaters, The

See: Spider Baby; or: the Maddest Story Ever Told (1965?).

Living Buddhas

(Lebende Buddhas)

1924 (1929) German, Paul Wegener sil.

Prod & Dir: Paul Wegener.

Story: P. Wegener & Hans Sturm.

Art Dir: Walter Ruttmann.

Cast: Paul Wegener, Asta Nielsen, Hans Sturm, Grigori Khmara, Max Pohl, Carl Ebert, K. Haack.

F

Ref: F/A p422; FIR Jan '56 p24.

Living Coffin, The

See: Scream of Death (1965).

Living Dead, The

(Funf Unheimliche Geschichten: Five Sinister Stories; Histoires Extraordinaires --French t?)

1933 (1940) German (Hoffberg).

Prod: Gabriel Pascal.

Dir: Richard Oswald.

Cast: Paul Wegener, Eugen Klöpfer, Roma Bohn, Harold Paulsen, Roger Wisten.

bor-F-H

Ref: NYT 17 Dec '40; FIR Dec '61 p634; Laclos p42.

cont.

Living Dead cont.

Based on short stories "The Black Cat" and "The System of Dr. Tarr and Professor Fether" by Edgar Allan Poe, and "The Suicide Club" by Robert Louis Stevenson.

See also: Fünf Unheimliche Geschichten (1919).

See also film which included scenes from this film: Dr. Terror's House of Horrors (1943).

Living Dead, The

(Scotland Yard Mystery --Brit. t?)
1934 (1936) British, Alliance Films (First Division) 65 mins.
Dir: Thomas Bentley.
SP: Frank Miller.
Art Dir: David Raunsley.
Cin: James Wilson.
Edit: Walter Stokvis.
Cast: Gerald Du Maurier, George Curzon, Leslie Perrins, Belle Chrystal, Grete Natzler, Henry Victor, Frederick Peisley.
bor-SF (serum produces catalepsy)
Ref: FD 4 June '35; HR 9 Jan '36; MPH 11 Jan '36 p50-51.
Based on a play by Wallace Geoffrey.

Living Dead, The

See: Snake People (1968); Psychomania (1971).

Living Dead Man, The

See: Inhumaine, L' (1923).

Living Doll, The

(La Poupée Vivante)
1909 French, Star sil partly tinted 1000 ft.
Made by: Georges Méliès.
F-dream (in dream: Santa Claus, angels, etc.)
Ref: MPW 5:879, 889; LC; Sadoul 1442; FI IV-51:11.

Living Ghost, The

1942 Mono 61 mins.
Prod: A.W. Hackel.
Dir: William Beaudine.
Story: Howard Dimsdale.

SP: Joseph Hoffman.
Cin: Mack Stengler.
Edit: Jack Ogilvie.
Mus Dir: Frank Sanucci.
Cast: James Dunn, Joan Woodbury, Paul McVey, J. Farrell MacDonald, Minerva Urecal, George Eldredge, Jan Wiley.
bor-SF-H (fluid paralyses brain, leaving living corpse in zombie-like state)
Ref: FD 27 Oct '42; HR & Vd 22 Oct '44; MPH 31 Oct '42.

Living Head, The

(La Cabeza Viviente)
1959 (1964) Mexican (Clasa-Mohme & Azteca).
Prod: Abel Salazar.
Dir: Chano Urueta.
SP: Frederick Curiel & A. Lopez Portillo.
Cin (on screen) Joseph Ortiz Ramos; (in Ref source) Jorge Stahl Jr.
Edit: Alfred Rosas Priego.
Mus: Gustavo Cesar Carrion.
Cast: Ana Luisa Peluffo, Abel Salazar, Mauricio Garces, German Robles, Antonio Raxel.
F-H (head casts spell over archaeological expedition)
Ref: Indice; PS C1174; Ackerman; FDY; TVG.

Living Idol, The

1957 Albert Lewin Prods (MGM) color scope 101 mins.
Filmed in Mexico.
Prod: Albert Lewin & Gregorio Walerstein.
Dir & SP: A. Lewin.

Assoc Dir: Rene Cardona.
Art Dir: Edward Fitzgerald.
Cin: Jack Hildyard & Victor Herrera.
Edit: Rafael Ceballos.
Mus: Manuel Esperon & Rudolfo Halffter.
Cast: Steve Forrest, Liliane Montevecchi, James Robertson Justice, Sara Garcia, Eduardo Noriega.
F-H (girl is reincarnation of Mayan princess; stone idol of Jaguar god becomes possessed by the god & kills people)
Ref: MFB Feb '58 p22; Vw 24 April '57; MPA 27 April '57.
Based on a novel by Albert Lewin.

Living Playing Cards, The

(Les Cartes Vivantes)
1905 French, Star sil 160 ft.
Made by: Georges Méliès.
Cast: Georges Méliès.
F
Ref: LC; Sadoul/M, GM Mage 678-79.

Living Skeleton, The

See: Kyuketsu Dokurosen (1968).

Living Soap Bubbles, The

See: Soap Bubbles, The (1906).

Living Statue, The

See: Drawing Lesson, The (1903).

Living Sword, The

1971 Hongkong, Cathay (Mercury) color scope 88 mins.
Dir: Wang Ping.
Cast: Melinda Chen Man Ling, Paul Chang Chung, Chin Hsiang Lin.
F-seqs (mystic martial arts)
Ref: Mercury folder.

Living Toys, The

See: Jouets Vivants, Les (1908).

Living Vegetables, The

See: Légumes Vivants, Les (1910).

Livre Magique, Le

See: Magic Book, The (1900).

Lizard in a Woman's Skin, A

See: Schizoid (1971).

Lizzie

1957 Bryna (MGM) 82 mins.
Prod: Jerry Bresler.
Dir: Hugo Haas.
SP: Mel Dinelli.
Art Dir: Rudi Feld.
Cin: Paul Ivano.
Edit: Leon Barsha.
Mus: Leith Stevens.
Cast: Eleanor Parker, Richard Boone, Joan Blondell, Hugo Haas, Johnny Mathis, Michael Mark.
bor-psy-F-H (girl has triple personality)
Ref: deGroote p281; HR & Vd 25 Feb '57.
Based on novel "The Bird's Nest" by Shirley Jackson.

Ljubov i Film

(Love and Film)
1961 Yugoslavian, Zagreb color ani 11 mins.

cont.

Ljubov cont.

Dir: Ivo Vrbanić.
Idea: Slbodan Petković.
Story: Vladimir Tadej & I. Vrbanić.
Design & Ani: Zlatko Grgić.
Bg: Ismet Voljevica.
Mus: Davor Kajfeš.
sat-F-com ("romantic love scenes common to various national movies are parodied" --Z/Z)
Ref: Z/Zagreb p70.

Ljubitelji Cvijeća

(The Flower Lovers)
1970 Yugoslavian/Italian, Zagreb/Corona Cinemat. color ani 10.6 mins.
Dir, SP, Design, Ani: Borivoj Dovniković.
Bg: Nedeljko Dragić.
Mus: Ozren Depolo.
F-com (man makes exploding flowers which become a fad, eventually levelling city)
Ref: Z/Zagreb p 101.

Llán ki Shaokat

(Symphony of Life)
1954 Indian sh.
Prod: V. Shantaram.
Cin: T.A. Abraham.
Edit: N.D. Keluskar.
Mus: V. Shirali.
mus-F
Ref: Montevideo '56.

Llegaron los Marcianos

(The Martians Arrived; I Marziani Hanno Dodici Mani; Martians Have Twelve Hands; Siamo Quattro Marziani --alt.t?)
1964 Spanish/Italian, Epoca/Dario 95 mins.
Dir: Pipolo (r.n.: Giuseppe Moccia) & Franco Castellano.
SP: F. Castellano, G. Moccia, & Leonardo Martin.
Art Dir: Ramiro Gómez.
Cin: Alfio Contini.
Mus: Ennio Morricone.
Cast: Paolo Panelli, Alfredo Landa, Carlo Croccolo, Raimondo Vianello, José Calvo, Enzo Garinei, Magali Noel, Umberto D'Orsi, Margaret Lee, Franco Franchi, Cristina Gajoni.
SF-com (Martians arrive in flying saucers, decide to stay here)
Ref: SpCin '66 p 174-75; Ital Prods '64 p52-53; MTVM 15 May '64 p 11.

Llorona, La

(The Crying Woman)
● 1933 Mexican, Eco.
Dir: Ramon Peon.
Story: Guz Aguila.
SP: C.N. Hope & G. Aguila.
Cin: G. Baqueriza.
Mus: Max Urban.
Cast: Ramon Pereda, Carlos Orellana, María Luisa Zea, Antonio R. Frausto, Paco Martinez, Virginia Zuri.
Ref: Indice; Cine Universal 10 Feb '68.

● 1959 Mexican, Bueno (Clasa-Mohme & Azteca).
Dir: René Cardona.
Story: C. Torres de M. Sanchez.
SP: Adolfo T. Portillo.
Cin: Jack Draper.
Mus: Luis Mendoza López.
Cast: Maria Elena Marqués, Carlos López Moctezuma, Eduardo Fajardo, Mauricio Garces, Emma Roldan, Erna Martha Bauman.
Ref: Aventura p426; PS; Indice; Cine Universal 10 Feb '68.

cont.

Llorona cont.

F-H (weeping ghost)
Based on a well-known Mexican legend.
See also: Herencia de la Llorona, La (1946); Curse of the Crying Woman, The (1961).

Lloyd of the C.I.D.

See: Detective Lloyd (1931-32).

Lo Iradiddio

See: Iradiddio, Lo (1963).

Lo Uccido, Tu Uccidi

(I Kill, You Kill)
1965 Italian/French, Metropolis/Gulliver.
Dir: Gianni Puccini.
SP: G. Puccini, Filippo Sanjust, Ennio De Concini, & Boschi.
Cin: Marcello Gatti.
Cast: E. Riva, Jean-Louis Trintignant, Dominique Boschero, Margaret Lee, Luciana Paluzzi.
bor-F-H (possibly several stories: woman suffers from 'sexual lycanthropy'; three children cause all the bad people they know to die mysteriously)
Ref: Ital Prods (Willis).

Loba, La

(The She-Wolf; Los Horrores del Bosque Negro: The Horrors of the Black Forest --s.t?)
1965 (1966) Mexican, Sotomayor (Col).
Prod: Jesús Sotomayor.
Dir: Rafael Baledon.
SP: Ramón Obón.
Cin: Raul M. Solares.
Mus: Raul Lavista.
Cast: Kitty de Hoyos, Joaquin Cordero, José Elias Moreno, Noe Murayama, Adriana Roel.
F-H (girl werewolf; possibly also male one)
Ref: Vw '65; Ackerman; Col PS 66216.
See also: Wolf Man, The (1941).

Lobo, El

(The Wolf)
1971 Spanish, Estudios Castilla color ani 8.7 mins.
Dir: Amaro Carretero.
Realisation: Vicente Rodríguez.
bor-F-doc (natural history of the wolf in cartoon form)
Ref: SpCin '72.

Lobster Nightmare, The

1910 (1911) British, Walturdaw sil 480 ft.
F-H-dream (imps & lobster torment man in Hell)
Ref: Bios 2 Feb '11.

Lobster Still Pursued Him, The

See: Jones' Nightmare (1911).

Locataire Diabolique, Le

(The Diabolic Tenant)
1909 French, Star sil 384 ft.
Made by: Georges Méliès.
F
Ref: Sadoul/M, GM Mage 1495-1501.

Locataires d'a Coté, Les

(The Tenants Next Door)
1909 French, Gaum sil ani sh.
Dir: Emile Cohl.
F
Ref: Sadoul p445; Filmlex p 1369.

Loch Ness Monster, The

See: Secret of the Loch (1932).

Loch Ness Mystery, The

See: Secret of the Loch (1932).

Lock Up Your Daughters

1956 New Realm 51 mins.

Prod: Sam Katzman.

Cast: Bela Lugosi.

F-H-seqs (extracts from 6 Lugosi films with new footage of Lugosi, who also narrated)

Ref: Collier; MFB May '59.

Lock Your Doors

See: Ape Man, The (1943).

Locura del Terror

(Terror Madness, Madness from Terror)

1960 Mexican, Sotomayor (Col).

Prod: Jesús Sotomayor.

Dir: Julian Soler.

SP: J.M.F. Unsain & A. Varela Jr.

Cin: Raul M. Solares.

Mus: C. Zarzosa.

Cast: Tin Tan, Sonia Furio, "Loco" Valdes, Veronica Loyo, David Silva, Andres Soler.

F-H-com (monsters; large spider; head on skeleton)

Ref: FM 33:22; Indice; Col.

Locus

1963 Japanese ani sh.

Dir: Yoji Kuri.

F

Ref: Ani/Cin p 173.

Lodger, The

● 1927 British, Gainsborough (Amer Anglo) sil 7500 ft.

Prod: Michael Balcon.

Dir: Alfred Hitchcock.

Sc: A. Hitchcock & Eliot Stannard.

Art Dir: C.W. Arnold & Bertram Evans.

Cin: Hal Young (&? Baron Ventimiglia).

Edit: Ivor Montagu.

Cast: Ivor Novello, Malcolm Keen, Arthur Chesney, June, Marie Ault.

bor H (mysterious young lodger wrongly thought to be unknown Ripper-like killer, "The Avenger")

Ref: FIR '66 p233; AHF p 197; LC; CoF 6:43; Gifford/BFC 08115.

● (The Phantom Fiend --1935 rr.t.)

1932 (1935 --55) British, Twickenham (Olympic) 85 mins (67 mins).

Prod: Julius Hagan.

Dir: Maurice Elvey.

Adapt: H. Fowler Mear.

SP: Paul Rotha & Miles Mander.

Cin: Sidney Blythe, Basil Emmott, & William Luff.

Edit: Jack Harris.

Cast: Ivor Novello, Elizabeth Allan, Jack Hawkins, W.E. Bascomb, Kynaston Reeves, Barbara Everest.

H (Ripper-like "Avenger" is revealed as double for the mysterious lodger)

Ref: HR 29 April '35; Vw 20 Sept '32, 24 April '35; MPH 15 Oct '32 p66, 27 April '35.

● 1943 (1944) 20th-Fox 84 mins.

Prod: Robert Bassler.

Dir: John Brahm.

SP: Barré Lyndon.

Art Dir: James Basevi & John Ewing.

Cin: Lucien Ballard.

SpFX: Fred Sersen.

Edit: J. Watson Webb Jr.

Mus: Hugo W. Friedhofer.

Cast: Merle Oberon, George Sanders, Laird Cregar [Jack the Ripper], Cedric Hardwicke, Sara Allgood, Doris Lloyd, Colin Campbell, Aubrey Mather,

Lodger cont.

Queenie Leonard, Lumsden Hare, Billy Bevan, Skelton Knaggs, Forrester Harvey.

H (mysterious lodger is proved to be Jack the Ripper; note: this is set in 1888, the first two were contemporary in setting)

Ref: HR & Vd 5 Jan '44; FIR Jan '65 p23, Jan '66 p60; FD 17 Jan '44; Agee p77.

Based on the novel by Marie Belloc-Lowndes.

See also remake: Man in the Attic (1953).

See also: Jack the Ripper.

Logos

1957 Amateur (CFS) color 2 mins.

Made by: Jane Belson Conger.

Mus: Henry Jacobs.

abs-exp-F

Ref: Undrgnd p95.

Lohengrin

● 1916 German sil.

Ref: DdC III:427.

● 1936 Italian.

Cast: Antonio Cassinelli, Jacqueline Plessis, Ing Borg.

Ref: DdC II:73.

opera-F (magic knight; swan into boy, etc.)

Based on the opera by Richard Wagner.

Lokis

(The Bear)

1969 Polish, Tor color 100 mins.

Dir & SP: Janusz Majewski.

Cin: Stefan Matyjaskiewicz.

Cast: Josef Duriasz, Edmund Fetting, Gustav Lutkiewicz, Malgorzata Braunek, Zofia Mrozowska.

bor-F-H (man apparently turns into bear off-screen on his wedding night)

Ref: Vw 9 Sept '70, 6 Oct '71; MMF 23:62.

Based on the short story by Prosper Mérimée.

See also: Marriage of the Bear, The (1926).

Lola

(play by O. Davis)

See: Without a Soul (1916).

London After Midnight

(The Hypnotist --Brit.t.)

1927 MGM sil 5687 ft.

Prod, Dir, Story: Tod Browning.

Sc: Waldemar Young.

Titles: Joe Farnham.

Art Dir: Cedric Gibbons & Arnold Gillespie.

Cin: Merritt B. Gerstad.

Edit: Harry Reynolds.

Cast: Lon Chaney, Marceline Day, Henry B. Walthall, Percy Williams, Conrad Nagel, Polly Moran, Edna Tichenor, Claude King.

bor-F-H (in order to expose a murderer, a Scotland Yard inspector arranges for two fake vampires to appear)

Ref: Vw 14 Dec '27; FD 18 Dec '27; LC; Photon 19; AFI F2.3147; Gifford/H p68, 71.

See also remake: Mark of the Vampire (1935).

Lonely Man, The

See: Five Bloody Graves (1970).

Lonesome Ghosts

1940 WD (RKO) color ani sh.

Prod: Walt Disney.

Voices: Walt Disney, Clarence Nash, Pinto Colvig.

Lonesome Ghosts cont.

F-H-com (Mickey, Donald & Pluto as ghost exterminators in haunted house)

Ref: HR 9 Oct '37.

See also: Donald Duck (1934-61); Mickey Mouse (1928-); Pluto (1940-51).

Long Bodies, The

1947 Amateur (Museum of Modern Art) 16mm wax block ani sh.

Made by: Douglas Crockwell.

exp-abs-F

Ref: MMA p57; Undrgnd p81.

Long Distance Wireless Photography

(La Photographie Electrique a Distance)

1908 French, Star sil 454 ft (366 ft).

Made by: Georges Méliès.

SF

Ref: Sadoul/M, GM Mage 1091=95; LC; Views 103:5.

Long Ears

(Longears --alt.spelling)

1962 (1965) Bulgarian (Polish?) ani sh.

Dir: Radka Buchvarova.

F (bunnies hung on line by Grandma Bear)

Ref: NYT 28 March '65; Bulgarian Films 8.

Long Green Stocking, The

1962 Italian color ani sh.

Dir: Roberto & G. Gavioli.

F

Ref: Ani/Cin p 138-39.

Long Hair of Death, The

See: Lunghi Capelli della Morte, I (1964).

Long-Haired Hare

1949 WB color ani 7 mins.

Dir: Chuck Jones.

Voices: Mel Blanc.

F-com

Ref: LC; David Rider.

See also: Bugs Bunny (1938-63).

Long Live the Republic!

See: At Zije Republika! (1966).

Long Night of Terror, The

See: Castle of Blood (1964).

Long Night of Veronica, The

See: Lunga Notte de Veronique, La (1966).

Long Rains, The

(short story by R. Bradbury)

See: Illustrated Man, The (1968).

Long, Swift Sword of Siegfried, The

(Siegfried und das Sagenhafte Liebesleben der Nibelungen; The Erotic Adventures of Siegfried --Brit.t.)

1971 W.German/US, Atlas/Entertainment Ventures (Entertainment Ventures) color 92 mins.

German language version:
Dir: Adrian Hoven.

SP: Al de Ger.

Cin: Hannes Staudinger.

Edit: Robert Freeman.

Mus: Richard Wagner & Daniele Patucchi.

English language version:
Prod, Dir, SP: David F. Friedman.

Cast: Raymond Harmstorf (Lance Boyle), Sybill Danning (Sybelle Denninger), Heidi Bohlen (Heidi Ho), Carl H. Heitmann (Peter B. Hard), Celine Berner, Fred Coplan, Peter Berling.

sex-F-com (invisibility; magic cap; wall of fire; invulnerability)

Long Swift Sword... cont.

Ref: FF '71 p755; MFB July '72 p 146; BO 13 Dec '71; Ackerman.

See also: Siegfried.

Longears

See: Long Ears (1962).

Look at the Root

1929 Soviet sil ani.

Dir: B. Antonovsky.

F

Ref: Kino p274.

Look Out!

1960? Czech color ani sh.

Dir: Jiří Brdecka.

F

Ref: Czech An '61.

Looking for John Smith

(Si Jones Looking for John Smith)

1906 Biograph sil ani & live 740 ft.

F (wanted poster moves; 2 men talk with conversation in balloons like comic strip)

Ref: Niver 5.

Looking Forward

1910 Thanhouser sil 1000 ft.

SF-com (man takes potion & sleeps for 100 years; wakes to find women dominant)

Ref: MPW 7:1490, 1539, 1554; F/A p422.

Looney Tunes

1933-6? Vitaphone, released through WB; later produced by WB ani 1 reel series in color from late 1930s.

Prod: Leon Schlesinger.

Dir: Chuck (Charles M.) Jones, Robert Clampett, Arthur Davis, Friz (Isadore) Freleng, others.

Mus: Carl W. Stalling, Frank Marsales, Norman Spencer.

F-com

Ref: LC; Ani chart.

Loonies on Broadway

See: Zombies on Broadway (1945).

Loon's Necklace, The

1948 Canadian, Crawley Films color 12 mins.

Dir: Budge Crawley.

Cin: Grant Crabtree.

F

Ref: MFB Aug '54 p 123; Collier; FIR Oct '51 p 13.

Based on British Columbian Indian legend.

Loops

1940 Amateur (Pyramid) color ani 3 mins.

Dir: Norman McLaren.

abs-F

Ref: CFS cat; Pyramid cat p227.

See also: Dots (1940); Pen Point Percussion (1951).

Loopy de Loop

1959- Hanna-Barbera (Col) color ani 1 reel series.

Prod & Dir: Joseph Hanna & William Barbera.

F-com

Ref: MFB Sept '60 p 133.

Loose in the Caboose

1947 Par color ani 8 mins.

Dir: Seymour Kneitel.

Story: Bill Turner & Larry Riley.

F-com

Ref: LC.

See also: Little Lulu (1946-48).

cont. cont. cont.

Lord Arthur Saville's Crime

● 1919 Hungarian sil.

<u>Dir</u>: Paul Fejos.

<u>Ref</u>: Willis; DdC.

● (Le Crime de Lord Arthur
Saville)

1921 French sil.

<u>Dir</u>: René Hervil.

<u>Ref</u>: DdC III:38.

bor-F-H (fortune-teller's
prediction of death comes
true)

Based on the story by
Oscar Wilde.

See also: <u>Flesh and Fantasy</u>
(1943).

Lord Feathertop

1908 Edison sil sh.

F (witch brings scarecrow
to life)

<u>Ref</u>: FI 5 Dec '08; LC.

Based on story "Feathertop"
by Nathaniel Hawthorne.

See also: <u>Feathertop</u>.

Lord Montdrago

(story by W.S. Maugham)

See: <u>Three Cases of Murder</u>
(1955).

Lord of the Flies

1963 British, Allen-Hodgdon
Prods & Two Arts (Walter Reade-
Sterling) 91 mins.

<u>Exec Prod</u>: Al Hine.

<u>Prod</u>: Lewis Allen.

<u>Dir</u> & <u>SP</u>: Peter Brook.

<u>Cin</u>: Tom Hollyman & Gerald
Feil.

<u>Edit</u>: P. Brook, G. Feil, &
Jean-Claude Lubtchansky.
<u>Mus</u>: Raymond Leppard.

<u>Cast</u>: James Aubrey, Tom Chapin,
Hugh Edwards, Roger Elwin,
Tom Gaman.

bor-SF-H (planeload of British
schoolboys fleeing a nuclear
war crashlands on tropical
island; children revert
to savagery)

<u>Ref</u>: MFB Sept '64 p 131; FF
'63 p 175; FQ Winter '63-64 p31.

Based on the novel by William
Golding.

Lord of the Jungle

1935 Indian.

<u>Cast</u>: Chandrarao, Kadam, Lalita
Pawar, Shyamroa, Bhagwan.

bor-F ("Tarzan thriller" --
MovPicM)

<u>Ref</u>: MovPicM June '35 p64.

Lords of Creation

1967 Amateur?, Canadian ani
9 mins.

<u>Made by</u>: Gerald Robinson.

F (history of the world from
beginning to the end)

<u>Ref</u>: CCC 2:23; Richardson.

Lorelei, The

1913 Edison sil 1 reel.

<u>Cast</u>: Charles Sutton, Laura
Sawyer, Benjamin Wilson,
Jessie McAllister.

F-dream (heartless girl toys
with man's affection, dreams
she sees old painting come
to life & depict the legend
of the Lorelei of the Rhine)

<u>Ref</u>: MPW 15:292, 572; LC;
EK 15 Jan '13; F/A p331.
Based on poem, "Die Lorelei," by
Heinrich Heine.

Lorelei of the Sea, The

See: <u>Modern Lorelei, A</u> (1917).

Lorraine of the Lions

1925 U sil 6700 ft.

<u>Dir</u>: Edward Sedgwick.

<u>Sc</u>: Isadore Bernstein & Karl
Krusada.

<u>Cin</u>: Virgil Miller.

cont.

London After Midnight (1927)

Lorraine of the Lions cont.
<u>Cast</u>: Norman Kerry, Patsy
Ruth Miller, Fred Hume [go-
rilla], Doreen Turner, Harry
Todd, Philo McCullough.

bor-F (fortune-telling; where-
abouts divined; girl lives with
lions)

<u>Ref</u>: AFI F2.3186 p451; LC.

Loss of Sensation

See: <u>Gibel Sensatsy</u> (1935).

Lost Angel

1943 MGM 90 mins.

<u>Prod</u>: Robert Sisk.

<u>Dir</u>: Roy Rowland.

<u>Story Idea</u>: Angna Enter.

<u>SP</u>: Isobel Lennart.

<u>Art Dir</u>: Cedric Gibbons &
Lynden Sparhawk.

<u>Cin</u>: Robert Surtees.

<u>Edit</u>: Frank E. Hull.

<u>Mus</u>: Daniele Amfitheatrof.

<u>Cast</u>: Margaret O'Brien, James
Craig, Marsha Hunt, Philip

cont.

Lost Angel cont.
Merivale, Henry O'Neill, Donald
Meek, Keenan Wynn, Alan Napier.

bor-SF (foundling reared by
child psychologists at age 6
speaks & thinks like college
professor)

<u>Ref</u>: Films Inc p31; Vd 5 Nov '43.

Lost Atlantis

See: <u>Atlantide, L'</u> (1921; 1932).

Lost Charter

1945 Soviet color ani
5 parts.

F

<u>Ref</u>: Sov Cin.
Based on the story by Nikolai
Gogol.

Lost Chord, The

(poem by A.A. Proctor)

See: <u>Trail of the Lost Chord, The</u> (1913).

Lost City, The

(City of Lost Men --feature t.;
The Lost City of the Ligurians
--ad.t.)

1935 Super-Serial Prods (Regal)
cont.

Lost City cont.
serial 12 parts 24 reels.

Also released as 74 min feature.

<u>Prod</u>: Sherman S. Krellberg.

<u>Dir</u>: Harry Revier.

<u>Story</u>: Zelma Carroll, George
M. Merrick, & Robert Dillon.

<u>SP</u>: Pereley Poore Sheehan,
Eddie Graneman, & Leon d'Usseau.

<u>Set Design</u>: Ralph Berger.

<u>Cin</u>: Roland Price & Ed Linden.

<u>Mus Dir</u>: Lee Zahler.

<u>Cast</u>: William ("Stage") Boyd,
Kane Richmond, Claudia Dell,
George F. Hayes, Josef Swickard,
Ralph Lewis, Billy Bletcher,
Eddie Fetherson.

SF (death ray; mad scientist;
no-transmitter TV; tides reversed;
rejuvenation; men into giants;
frozen electricity; thoughts
read; black into white men; etc.)

<u>Ref</u>: Stringham; Vw 6 March '35;
MPH 9 March '35; FD 21 Feb '35.

Lost City of the Jungle

1946 U serial 13 parts 26 reels.

cont.

Lost City of the Jungle cont.

Exec Prod: Morgan B. Cox.

Assoc Prod: Joseph O'Donnell.

Dir: Ray Taylor & Lewis D. Collins.

SP: Joseph F. Poland, Paul Huston, & Tom Gibson.

Cin: Gus Peterson.

Cast: Russell Hayden, Lionel Atwill, Jane Adams, Keye Luke, John Eldredge, John Gallaudet, John Miljan, Gene Roth (Stutenroth), Arthur Space, Frank Lackteen.

SF (metal defense against A-bomb)

Ref: MFB Nov '47 p 157; LC; FIR March '64 p 166; Stringham.

Lost City of the Ligurians, The

See: Lost City, The (1935).

Lost Collar Stud, The

1914 British, Natural Colour Kinematograph Co color sil 1140 ft.

Dir: F. Martin Thornton.

F-com (live collar stud eludes capture)

Ref: Gifford/BFC 04580.

Lost Continent

1951 Lippert green tinted seq 83 mins.

Exec Prod: Robert L. Lippert.

Prod: Sigmund Neufeld.

Dir: Samuel Newfield.

Story: Carroll Young.

SP: Richard H. Landau.

Art Dir: F. Paul Sylos.

Cin: Jack Greenhalgh.

SpFX: Augie Lohman.

Edit: Phil Cahn.

Mus: Paul Dunlap.

Cast: Cesar Romero, Hillary Brooke, John Hoyt, Acquanetta, Whit Bissell, Hugh Beaumont, Chick Chandler, Sid Melton.

SF (atomic rocket gone astray traced to island mountain in South Seas where uranium deposits have preserved primitive atmosphere including brontosaurs, triceratops, pterodactyls, etc.)

Ref: HR & Vd 20 July '51; MFB March '52 p36; FDY '52.

Lost Continent, The

(The People of Abrimes -- European t.)

1968 British, Hammer & 7 Arts (20th-Fox) color 98 mins (89 mins).

Prod & Dir: Michael Carreras.

SP: Michael Nash.

Art Dir: Arthur Dawson.

Cin: Paul Beeson.

SpFX: Robert A. Mattey & Cliff Richardson.

Sup Edit: James Needs.

Edit: Chris Barnes.

Mus: Gerard Schurmann.

Cast: Eric Porter, Hildegard Kneff, Suzanna Leigh, Tony Bentley, Nigel Stock, Neil McCallum, Victor Maddern, Michael Ripper, Eddie Powell.

SF (area of sea choked with seaweed captures ships; giant crabs; giant jellyfish; colony of descendants of lost Spanish conquistadores)

Ref: Vw 18 Oct '67, 3 July '68; FF '68 p236; MFB '68 p 119-20.

Based on novel "Uncharted Seas" by Dennis Wheatley.

See also: Isle of Lost Ships, The.

Lost Doll, The

n.d. Czech ani puppet? 18 mins.

F (lost rag doll comes to life & tries to return home)

Ref: Ideal cat p44.

Lost Empress

(novel by S. Ornitz)

See: Secrets of the French Police (1932).

Lost Face, The

See: Ztracena Tvar (1965).

Lost Horizon

● 1936 (1937) Col 133 mins.

Prod & Dir: Frank Capra.

SP: Robert Riskin.

Art Dir: Stephen Goosson.

Cin: Joseph Walker.

Aerial Cin: Elmer Dyer.

SpFX: E. Roy Davidson & Ganahl Carson.

Edit: Gene Havlick & Gene Milford.

Mus: Dimitri Tiomkin.

Mus Dir: Max Steiner.

Cast: Ronald Colman, Jane Wyatt, Sam Jaffe, Edward Everett Horton, H.B. Warner, Thomas Mitchell, John Howard, Isabel Jewell, Margo, Noble Johnson.

Ref: HR 20 Feb '37; Vw 10 March '37; MPH 30 May '36 p 16-17.

● 1972 (1973) Col color scope 150 mins.

Prod: Ross Hunter.

Dir: Charles Jarrott.

SP: Larry Kramer.

Prod Design: Preston Ames.

Cin: Robert Surtees.

SpCin FX: Butler-Glouner.

Edit: Maury Winetrobe.

Choreog: Hermes Pan.

Lyrics: Hal David.

Mus: Burt Bacharach.

Cast: Peter Finch, Liv Ullman, Sally Kellerman, George Kennedy, Charles Boyer, Michael York, Olivia Hussey, Bobby Van, James Shigeta, John Gielgud, Kent Smith.

mus-F
Ref: Time 2 April '73; Vw 7 March '73 p 18; LAT 17 Feb '72; New Yorker 17 March '73.
F (lost travelers brought to Shangri-La, valley in the Himalayas where no one ages; man several centuries old; when young-looking girl is taken out of the valley she reverts to her true, hundred-year-old age & dies)

Based on the novel by James Hilton.

Lost in a Harem

1944 MGM 10 reels.

Prod: George Haight.

Dir: Charles Riesner.

SP: Harry Ruskin, John Grant, & Harry Crane.

Art Dir: Cedric Gibbons & Daniel Cathcart.

Cin: Lester White.

Edit: George Hively.

Mus Arr: Sonny Burke.

Mus Dir: David Snell.

Cast: Bud Abbott, Lou Costello, Marilyn Maxwell, John Conte, Douglass Dumbrille, Lottie Harrison.

com; F-seq (hypnotic cat's-eye rings make people do anything; Bud & Lou think they are termites & eat furniture)

Ref: HR & Vd 29 Aug '49; LC; D. Glut.

Lost Island of Kioga

See: Hawk of the Wilderness (1938).

Lost Jungle, The

1934 Mascot serial 12 parts 24 reels.

Also released as feature.

Sup: Nat Levine.

cont

Lost Jungle cont.

Dir: Armand Schaefer & David Howard.

Story: Sherman Lowe & Al Martin.

SP: Barney Sarecky, D. Howard, A. Schaefer, & Wyndham Gittens.

Edit: Earl Turner.

Cast: Clyde Beatty, Cecelia Parker, Syd Saylor, Warner Richmond, Wheeler Oakman, Maston William, J. Crawford Kent, Mickey Rooney.

bor-F (explorers find ancient underground, Rome-like city)

Ref: MPH 5 May '34 p49; TBC p48; FD 9 May '34; LC; Barbour/T&A.

Lost Kingdom, The

See: Atlantide, L' (1960).

Lost Love Juliana

See: Juliana do Amor Perdido (1970).

Lost Marzipan Cracknel, The

1965? E. German, Deutscher Fernsehfunk ani puppet 32 mins.

F (treasure-hunting puppet finds a small box in the forest)

Ref: MTVM July '65 p21.

Lost Missile, The

1958 US/Canadian, Wm Berke Prods (UA) 70 mins.

Prod: Lee Gordon.

Dir & Story: Lester W. Berke.

SP: John McPartland & Jerome Bixby.

Art Dir: William Ferrari.

Cin: Kenneth Peach.

Edit: Ed Sutherland.

Mus: Gerald Fried.

Cast: Robert Loggia, Ellen Parker, Larry Kerr, Philip Pine, Marilee Earle, Joe Hyams.

SF (extremely hot missile from outer space orbits Earth at low altitude, incinerating all in its path)

Ref: FD 10 Dec '58; FF '58 p289; LC; FDY '59.

Lost Moment, The

1947 Walter Wanger Pictures Inc. (U) 89 mins.

Prod: Walter Wanger.

Dir: Martin Gabel.

SP: Leonardo Bercovici.

Makeup: Bud Westmore.

Cin: Hal Mohr.

Edit: Milton Carruth.

Mus: Daniele Amfitheatrof.

Cast: Robert Cummings, Susan Hayward, Agnes Moorehead, John Loring, Eduardo Ciannelli, John Archer, Frank Puglia, Minerva Urecal, William Edmunds.

bor-psy-F-H (woman imagines she is living the late 19th century life of her aunt; woman over 100 years old)

Ref: LC; MFB Feb '49 p25; Vd 13 Oct '47; FIR Dec '69 p641.

Based on novel "The Aspern Papers" by Henry James.

Lost One, The

See: Verlorene, Der (1951).

Lost Ones, The

See: Olvidados, Los (1950).

Lost Ones, The

(novel by I. Cameron)

See: Island at the Top of the World, The (1973).

Lost Pilgrim, The

See: Pelerin Perdu, Le (1962)..

Lost Planet, The

(Planet Men --s.t.)

1953 Col serial 15 parts 30 reels.

Prod: Sam Katzman.

Dir: Spencer G. Bennet.

SP: George H. Plympton & Arthur Hoerl.

Cin: William Whitley.

SpFX: Jack Erickson.

Edit: Earl Turner.

Mus Dir: Mischa Bakaleinikoff.

Cast: Judd Holdren, Vivian Mason, Ted Thorpe, Forrest Taylor, Michael Fox, Gene Roth, Karl Davis, I. Stanford Jolley, Pierre Watkin.

SF (aliens attempt to invade the Earth; many gadgets)

Ref: Ser/Col; SM 3:34; LC; FDY; Acad.

Lost Planet Airmen

See: King of the Rocket Men (1949).

Lost Shadow, The

(Der Verlorene Schatten)

1921 (1928) German, Wegener-Union sil (5175 ft).

Dir: Paul Wegener.

Sc: Carl Mayer.

Art Dir: Kurt Richter.

Cin: Karl Freund.

Cast: Paul Wegener, Grete Schröder, Lyda Salmanova, Hannes Sturm, Werner Schock.

F-H (violinist sells his shadow to "evil one" for magic violin; chased out of town for lacking shadow)

Ref: F et R p26; FD 8 April '28; FC 15 p 19.

Based on the story by E.T.A. Hoffmann.

Lost Shoe, The

See: Cinderella (1923).

Lost Soul, The

See: Verlorene Ich, Das (1923).

Lost Tribe, The

1949 Col 72 mins.

Prod: Sam Katzman.

Dir: William Berke.

Story: Arthur Hoerl.

SP: A. Hoerl & Don Martin.

Art Dir: Paul Palmentola.

Cin: Ira H. Morgan.

Edit: Aaron Stell.

Mus Dir: Mischa Bakaleinikoff.

Cast: Johnny Weissmuller, Myrna Dell, Elena Verdugo, Joseph Vitale, Ralph Dunn, Paul Marion, Nelson Leigh.

bor-SF (lost tribe of white natives; rites in ancient city)

Ref: Vd & HR 5 March '49; LC; MPH 30 April '49.

Based on the King Features syndicate comic strip "Jungle Jim."

See also: Jungle Jim.

Lost Valley, The

See: Valley of Gwangi, The (1968).

Lost Weekend, The

1945 Par 101 mins.

Prod: Charles Brackett.

Dir: Billy Wilder.

SP: C. Brackett & B. Wilder.

Art Dir: Hans Dreier & Earl Hedrick.

Cin: John F. Seitz.
SpFX: Gordon Jennings.

Edit: Doane Harrison.

Mus: Miklos Rozsa.

Cast: Ray Milland, Jane Wyman, Howard da Silva, Philip Terry, Doris Dowling, Frank Faylen.

cont

Lost Horizon (1936)

Lost Weekend cont.

psy-F-H-seq (an alcoholic
suffers from the DTs, has
hallucinations)

Ref: MFB Oct '45 p 121; FDY
'46; FIR March '60 p 138.

Based on the novel by Charles
Jackson.

Lost Women of Zarpa

See: Mesa of Lost Women, The
(1952).

Lost World, The

Ⓞ 1925 FN sil tinted seqs
10 reels (9700 ft).

Prod: Earl Hudson & Watterson
R. Rothacker.

Dir: Harry O. Hoyt.

Sc: Marion Fairfax.

Chief Technician: Fred W.
Jackman.

Research & SpFX: Willis O'Brien.

Architecture: Milton Menasco.

Models built by: Marcel Delgado.

Cin: Arthur Edeson.

Edit: George McGuire.

Cast: Wallace Beery, Lewis
Stone, Bessie Love, Lloyd Hughes,
Arthur Hoyt, Bull Montana [ape-
man].

SF (explorers find plateau with
dinosaurs of all kinds on it;
ape-man; volcanic destruction;
brontosaurus taken to London
where it escapes)

cont

Lost World cont.

Ref: AFI F2.3201 p453; MPN
30:2764-65; Photo; Blum p277;
FM 19:30; FD 15 Feb '25.

Ⓞ (The Origin of Man --Chicago
drive-in t.)

1960 20th-Fox color scope
97 mins.

Prod & Dir: Irwin Allen.

SP: I. Allen & Charles Bennett.

Art Dir: Duncan Cramer &
Walter M. Simonds.

Makeup: Ben Nye.

Cin: Winton Hoch.

SpFX: L.B. Abbott, Emil
Kosa Jr, & James B. Gordon.

Edit: Hugh S. Fowler.

Mus: Bert Shefter & Paul
Sawtell.

Cast: Claude Rains, Michael
Rennie, Jill St. John, David
Hedison, Fernando Lamas,
Ray Stricklyn, Jay Novello,
Ian Wolfe.

SF (explorers find plateau
with dinosaurs; giant spider;
man-eating plants)

Ref: FF '60 p 176; FD 1 July
'60; de Groote 371.

Based on the novel by
Arthur Conan Doyle.

See also: Buddy's Lost
World (1935).

Lost World, A

1948 Encyclopedia Britannica
Films Inc 16mm 10 mins.

Ref: Films Inc cat p 124; LC.

Stock footage from Lost World,
The (1925).

Based on novel "The Lost World"
by Arthur Conan Doyle.

Lost World of Sinbad, The

(Daitozoku: Samurai Pirate)

1963 (1965) Japanese, Toho
(AIP) color scope (94 mins).

Prod: Yuko Tanaka.

Dir: Senkichi Taniguchi.

SP: Takeshi Kimura.

Cin: Shinichi Sekizawa.

SpFX: Eiji Tsuburaya.

Mus: Masaru Sato.

Cast: Toshiro Mifune, Makoto
Satoh, Jun Fanado, Ichiro
Arishima.

F (not really about Sinbad,
but a Japanese pirate renamed
Sinbad in English-dubbed prints
only; wizard; witch changes
into flying insect; her gaze
turns people to stone & she
is turned to stone when she
looks in a mirror; man-carrying
kite)

Ref: HR & Vd 17 March '65;
MPH 31 March '65.

See also: Sinbad the Sailor.

Lost Zeppelin, The

1929 Tiffany 6882 ft.

Dir: Edward Sloman.

Story: Frances Hyland & John
F. Natteford.

SP: F. Hyland & Charles Kenyon.

Cin: Jackson Rose.

Edit: Martin G. Cohn & Donn
Hayes.

Cast: Conway Tearle, Virginia
Valli, Ricardo Cortez, Duke
Martin, Kathryn McGuire,
Winter Hall.

bor-SF (first zeppelin to
reach the South Pole crashes)

Ref: AFI F2.3202 p453.

Lot in Sodom

1933 Amateur (Audio-Brandon;
CFS) 27 mins.

Made by: James Sibeley Watson
& Melville Webber.

Mus: Louis Siegel.

Cast: Frederick Haak, Hildegarde
Watson, Louis Whitbeck Jr.

exp-rel-F (angel; woman turns
into pillar of salt; the story
of Lot from "The Bible")

Ref: F/A p642; Undrgnd p76.

Lotna

1959 Polish color & sepia seq.

Dir: Andrzej Wajda.

SP: A. Wajda & Wojciech Żukrowski.

Cin: Jerzy Lipman.

cont.

Lotna cont.

Mus: Tadeusz Baird.

Cast: Jerzy Pichelski, Adam Pawlikowski, Jerzy Moes, Bozena Kurowska.

bor-F (horse brings death to each of its owners)

Ref: FQ Spring '61 p24, 27.

Based on the novel by Wojciech Zukrowski.

Lotus Blossom

1921 Wah Ming Motion Picture Co (Nat'l Exchange) sil 7 reels.

Dir: Frank Grandon.

Story: James B. Leong.

Sc: George Yohalem & Charles Furthman.

Cin: Ross Fisher.

Cast: Lady Tsen Mei, Tully Marshall, Noah Beery, Jack Abbe, Goro Kino, James Wang, Chow Young.

F-seq (bell metals will fuse only with addition of human sacrifice)

Ref: AFI F2.3205 p454.

Lotus Wing

1967? Amateur (Film-makers' Coop) 16mm color & b&w 16.5 mins.

Made by: Jerry Abrams.

exp-F ("ejaculatory delusions, military erections, and the animated virility of Krazy Kat" --FMC)

Ref: FMC 5:7.

Lou Costello and His 30-Foot Bride

See: Thirty Foot Bride of Candy Rock, The (1958).

Louisiana

(play by J.A. Smith)

See: Drums o' Voodoo (1934).

Loup des Malveneurs, Le

(The Wolf of the Malveneurs)

1942 French 85 mins.

Dir: Guillaume Radot.

Cin: Pierre Montazel.

Mus: Maurice Thiriet.

Cast: Madeleine Solonge, Pierre Renoir, Gabrielle Dorziat, Michel Marsay, Louis Salou, Yves Furet, Marcelle Genieat.

F-H (ancestor of hero was cursed & became a wolf)

Ref: DdC III:403; Rep Gen '47; Dyer; de Groote 49.

See also: Wolf Man, The (1941).

Loup et l'Agneau, Le

(The Wolf and the Lamb)

1955 French, Image-Armorial color ani 10 mins.

Dir: Jean Image.

Nar: Francois Périer.

F

Ref: FACSEA p 13.

Based on the fable by La Fontaine.

Loup-Garou, Le

(The Werewolf)

1923 (1924) French sil.

Cast: Jean Marau, Madeleine Guitty.

F-H (priest curses his murderer who becomes werewolf; begs forgiveness & is killed by lightning bolt)

Ref: DdC II:479; Ackerman.

See also: Wolf Man, The (1941).

Loutch Smerti

(The Death Ray; Luch Smerty)

1925 Soviet sil 9800 ft.

Dir: Lev Kuleshov.

Assist Dir: Vsevolod Illarion-ovich Pudovkin, Alexandra Kokhlova (Khkhlova), Sergei Komarov, & Leonid Obolenski.

cont.

Loutch Smerti cont.

Sc: V.I. Pudovkin.

Art Dir: V.I. Pudovkin & Vasili Rakhals.

Cin: Aleksandar Levitski.

Cast: Vsevolod Illarionovich Pudovkin, Alexandra Irena Kokhlova, Sergei Komarov, Porfiri Podobed, Andrei Gorchilin, Vladimir Fogel, Piotr (Pyotr) Galadzhev, Leonid Obolenski.

SF (death ray)

Ref: Kino p429; Gasca p38-39; FTN p227-28; Scognamillo.

Loutky Jiriho Trnky

(Jiří Trnka's Puppets)

1955 Czech ani puppet & live sh.

Dir & SP: Bruno Sefranko.

Cin: Jiří Kolin.

Seq Dir: Jiří Trnka.

Mus: Lubos Sluka.

Cast: Jiří Trnka.

doc; F-seq (shows Trnka at his work with scenes from some of his films)

Ref: Montevideo '56.

Includes sequences from Prince Bayaya (1950); Staré Pověsti Ceske (1952); Osudy Dobrého Vojaka Svejka (1954).

Love

See: Ai (1963).

Love After Death

1969? Mexican (Abrams & Parisi)

Dir: Glauco del Mar.

SP: Antonio Valasques.

Cin: Peter Palian.

sex-F-H (man buried alive comes back to wreak vengeance; at climax he vanishes in flash)

Ref: Photon 21:29; Borst; Eric Hoffman.

Love and Anger

See: Amore e Rabbia (1969).

Love and Film

See: Ljubav i Film (1961).

Love and Goodfellowship Pills

1910 French, Pathé sil 600 ft.

Cast: Max Linder.

SF-com (love pills)

Ref: Bios 7 July '10.

Love and Hypnotism

1912 Italian, Cines sil.

Cast: Amelia Cattaneo.

bor-F (doctor learns of wife's love affair by hypnosis)

Ref: MPW 12:135, 230.

Love and Lunch

1917 Int'l Film Service sil ani 1/2 reel.

F-com

Ref: LC.

See: Jerry on the Job (1916-17).

Love and Marriage in Poster Land

1910 Edison sil sh.

F-com (posters come to life)

Ref: EK 1 May '10 p6-7; F/A p423; MPW 6:832; LC.

Love and Science

1912 French?, Eclair sil 1020 ft.

SF (invention allows you to see who is on the other end of the phone)

Ref: Bios 23 May '12.

Love and the Zeppelin

1948 Czech, Prague Cartoon Film Studios color ani 8 mins.

Dir & SP: Jiří Brdečka.

cont.

Love and the Zeppelin cont.

Design: Kamil Lhotak.

Mus: J. Rychlik.

F (lover rescues his girl friend via airship)

Ref: MFB Dec '56 p 157; Ani/Cin p 125.

Love and War in Toyland

1913 Kinemacolor sil 2 color sh.

F (living toys)

Ref: MPW 17:246.

Love at Chrystie St.

See: One Man Show (n.d.).

Love Birds

1934 U 6 reels.

Prod: Carl Laemmle Jr.

Dir: William A. Seiter.

Story: Clarence Marks & Dale Van Every.

SP: Doris Anderson.

Cin: Norbert Brodine.

Edit: Daniel Mandell.

Cast: ZaSu Pitts, Slim Summer-ville, Mickey Rooney, Emmett Vogan, Maude Eburne, Dorothy Christy, Clarence Wilson.

com; F-seq (ghost)

Ref:FD 4 May '34; MPH 21 April '34; LC.

Love Box, The

1972 British, Short Circuit color 89 mins.

Exec Prod: Barry Jacobs.

Prod, Dir, SP, Lyrics: Billy White & Teddy White.

Cin: Grenville Middleton.

Edit: Rex Graves.

Mus: Mike Vickers.

Cast (SF seq only) Emmett Hennessy, Laurie Goode, Sue Bowen, Jeanette Marsden, Liz Carlson, Rena Brown.

sex; SF-seq (one of eleven sequences is SF: "The Love Camp": "love camp of the future, where graduates are presented with diplomas in the art of love" --MFB)

Ref: MFB Nov '72 p236-37.

Love Bug, The

1968 (1969) WD (BV) color 107 mins.

Prod: Bill Walsh.

Dir: Robert Stevenson.

Story: Gordon Buford.

SP: Bill Walsh & Don DaGradi.

Art Dir: Carroll Clark & John B. Mansbridge.

Cin: Edward Coleman.

SpFX Cin: Eustace Lycett, Alan Manley, & Peter Ellenshaw.

SpFX: Robert A. Mattey, Howard Jensen, & Dan Lee.

Edit: Cotton Warburton.

Mus: George Bruns.

Cast: Dean Jones, Michele Lee, David Tomlinson, Buddy Hackett, Joe Flynn, Joe E. Ross, Iris Adrian.

F-com (Volkswagen with mind of its own moves by itself; wins race for hero)

Ref: FF '69 p80; Vw 11 Dec '68; MFB '69 p 126; Time 4 April '69.

Sequel: Love Bug Rides Again, The (1972).

Love Bug Rides Again, The

(Herbie Rides Again --e.t.)

1972 (1973) WD (BV) color.

Prod & SP: Bill Walsh.

Dir: Robert Stevenson.

Art Dir: Walter Tyler.

Cin: Frank Phillips.

Edit: Cotton Warburton.

Cast: Helen Hayes, Keenan Wynn, Ken Berry, Stephanie

cont.

Love Bug Rides Again cont.

Powers, John McIntire, Huntz Hall, Edward Ashley, Alan Carney, Beverly Carter, Rod McCary.

F-com (Herbie the living Volkswagen has a new owner)

Ref: HR Dec '72 p 12; BO 27 Sept '71 p5, 6 Nov '72 p 18.

Sequel to: Love Bug, The (1968).

Love by the Light of the Moon

1901 Edison sil 65 ft.

Dir: Edwin S. Porter.

F-com (painted face in moon spies on lovers, smiles)

Ref: Niver/20 p 18; LC.

Love Captive, The

(The Humbug --s.t.)

1934 U 65 mins.

Pres: Carl Laemmle.

Assoc Prod: E.M. Asher.

Dir: Max Marcin.

SP: Karen de Wolf.

Cin: Gilbert Warrenton.

Edit: Ted Kent.

Cast: Nils Asther, Gloria Stuart, Paul Kelly, Alan Dinehart, Renee Gadd, Addison Richards, John Wray.

bor-F (hypnosis influences love; murder under hypnosis)

Ref: FD 7 June '34; V 19 June '34; MPH 16 June '34 p79, 82.

Based on play "The Humbug" by Max Marcin.

Love Charm

1914 Columbus sil sh?

F-com (gypsy sells love potion & hate potion)

Ref: MPW 22:410.

Love, Death and the Devil

See: Liebe, Tod und Teufel (1934).

Love Doctor, The

1917 Vit sil 5 reels.

Dir: Paul Scardon.

Cast: Earle Williams, Corinne Griffith, Patsy De Forest, Adele De Garde, Webster Camp-bell, Evart Overton, Frank McDonald.

SF (brain transplant from girl who loves doctor into body of girl he loves)

Ref: MPW 34:396; LC; MPN 16:2949.

Based on story "Hashashin, the Indifferent" by George P. Dillenback.

Love Doctor, The

1969 Sigma III.

Dir: Bon Ross.

SP: Louis Garfinkle.

Cast: Ann Jannin, Frank Mahalan.

sex-SF (robot provides sexual satisfaction)

Ref: Film Bulletin Dec '69.

Love Dope, The

1917 Rolma Films (Metro) sil 1 reel.

SF-com (tablets are love potion)

Ref: MPN 15:2863; LC.

Love Drops

1910 Edison sil 230 ft.

F-com (love potion eaten by mistake)

Ref: EK 1 March '10 p 10.

Love Eternal

See: Eternel Retour, L' (1943).

Love from a Stranger
1936 (1937) British, Trafalgar (UA) 86 mins.

Prod: Max Schach.

Dir: Rowland V. Lee.

SP: Frances Marion.

Cin: Philip Tannura.

Cast: Basil Rathbone, Ann Harding, Binnie Hale, Bruce Seton, Jean Cadell, Bryan Powley.

bor-H (woman marries wife-murderer)

Ref: Vw 27 Jan '37; Bloch.

Based on the play by Frank Vosper from a story by Agatha Christie.

Love from Out of the Grave
1913 French?, Film d'Art sil 1500 ft.

F (ghost of wife's lover haunts artist)

Ref: Bios 6 Nov '13.

Love Germs
1908 (1909) Lubin sil 460 ft.

SF-com (scientist discovers the germs which cause love)

Ref: Views IV-5:7-8; LC.

Love Italian Style
See: Superdiabolici, I (1965).

Love Life of the Inventor of a Torpedo, The
See: Airship Destroyer, The (1909).

Love Magnet, The
1916 Kalem (General) sil 1 reel.

Dir: Al Santell.

Cast: Lloyd V. Hamilton, Bud Duncan, Ethel Teare, A. Edmondson.

F-com (magnet attracts pretty girls, old maids, mermaids)

Ref: MPW 30:224, 568, 746.

Love Me Darling
See: Med Kaerlig Hilsen (1971).

Love Me, Love Me, Love Me
1962 British, ani color 8 mins.

Prod & Dir: Richard Williams.

SP: Stan Hayward.

F-com (one character can do no wrong & is hated; another does things wrong & is loved)

Ref: MFB Feb '63 p26; TVG; F&F Dec '62.

Love Microbe, The
1907 (1908) Biograph sil 670 ft.

SF-com (scientist discovers the germs which cause love)

Ref: Biograph Bulletin 110, 19 Oct '07; LC; MPW 1:526.

Love Not Again
See: Koiya Koi Nasuna Koi (1962).

Love of a Hunchback, The
1910 British, Butcher's Films sil sh?

bor-H

Ref: Gifford/H p24.

Love of a Siren, The
1911 Italian, Cines sil 600 ft.

F (boy lured to death by siren)

Ref: Bios 29 Feb '12.

Love of Seven Dolls
(novel by P. Gallico)
See: Lili (1953).

Love of Sunya, The
1927 Swanson (UA) sil 7311 ft.

Dir: Albert S. Parker.

Sc: Earle Brown.

Art Dir: Hugo Ballin.

Cin: Robert Martin.

Cast: Gloria Swanson, John Boles, Anders Randolf, Flobelle Fairbanks, Ian Keith, Hugh Miller, Raymond Hackett, Ivan Lebedeff.

F (crystal ball shows three alternate futures; ancient Eqyptian girl has several reincarnations & has same love affair in each incarnation)

Ref: AFI F2.3241 p459; LC; MPW 85:212; FIR April '65 p204, 215.

Based on play "Eyes of Youth" by Charles Guernon & Max Marcin.

See also: Eyes of Youth (1919).

Love on the Wing
1937 British, GPO color ani sh.

Dir: Norman McLaren.

F

Ref: Ani/Cin p69.

Love Park, The
See: Love Box, The (1972).

Love Pill, The
1971 British, Mayfair color 82 mins.

Prod: Lawrence Barnett & John Lindsay.

Dir: Kenneth Turner.

Story: J. Lindsay.

Cin: John Mackey.

Edit: David Lane & Mike Campbell.

Mus: Paris Rutherford.

Cast: Toni Sinclair, Melinda Churcher, Henry Woolf, David Pugh, Kenneth Waller, John Stratton.

cont.

The Lost World (1925)

Love Pill cont.
sex-com; bor-SF (grocer's sugar balls are an instant contraceptive & turn women into nymphomaniacs)

Ref: MFB March '72 p52.

Love Potion, The
1911 Powers sil sh.

F-com

Ref: MPW 8:1532, 9:125.

Love Powder
See: Goona-Goona (1932).

Love Requited
1957 Polish ani sh.

Dir: Jan Lenica & Walerian Borowczyk.

F

Ref: Ani/Cin p 106, 167, 173.

Love Slaves of the Amazon
1957 U color 81 mins.

Prod, Dir, SP: Curt Siodmak.

Assoc Prod & Edit: Terry Morse.

Art Dir: Pierino Massenzi.

Cin: Mario Pages.

Mus Dir: Joseph Gershenson.

Cast: Don Taylor, Gianna Segale, Eduardo Ciannelli, Harvey Chalk, John Herbert, Wilson Vianna, Eugenia Carlos.

bor-F (men captured by tribe of women warriors)

Ref: MFB Jan '59 p7; MPH 30 Nov '57 p626; FD 26 Nov '57.

Love Spots
1914 British?, Planet sil 600 ft.

F-com (love potion)

Ref: Bios 23 April '14.

Love Takes His Vengeance
See: Terrible Vengeance, The (1913).

Love Through the Centuries
See: Oldest Profession, The (1967).

Love, Thy Name Be Sorrow
See: Koiya Koi Nasuna Koi (1962).

Love Tyrant, The
1911 Powers sil sh.

F (Cupid)

Ref: MPW 9:127.

Love Wanga
1941 (1942) (Hoffberg) 61 mins.

F (black magic; love charm; zombies)

Ref: Vw 7 Jan '42.

See also: White Zombie (1932); Drums of the Jungle (1935).

Love War, The
1970 Par (ABC-TV) color "90 mins."

Prod: Aaron Spelling.

Dir: George McCowan.

SP: Guerdon Trueblood & David Kidd.

Art Dir: Tracy Bousman.

Cin: Paul Uhl.

Edit: Bob Lewis.

Mus: Dominic Frontiere.

Cast: Lloyd Bridges, Angie Dickinson, Harry Basch, Dan Tavantry, Bill McClean, Allen Jaffe.

SF (mysterious stranger reveals self as alien, one of two small groups using Earth as their battlefield)

Ref: CineF 4:9; B. Warren.

Love Without Question
1920 Jans-Rolfe sil 6 reels.

Prod & Dir: B.A. Rolfe.

Adapt: Violet Clark.

Cast: Olive Tell, James W. Morrison, Mario Manjaroni, Ivo Dawson, Charles Mackay, Gordon Hamilton, Peggy Parr, George S. Stevens, Floyd Buckley.

myst-bor-H (spiritualism; ghostly happenings)

Ref: LC; MPW 44:141.

Based on novel "The Abandoned Room" by C. Wadsworth Camp.

Lover of the Moon
See: Rêve à la Lune (1905).

Lovers Beyond the Tomb
See: Nightmare Castle (1965).

Lovers' Charm, The
1907 Williams, Brown & Earle sil sh.
F (gypsy sells magic stone which grants wishes; transformations; appearances & disappearances; tricks)
Ref: MPW 1:542.

Lovers' Mill, The
1910 French, Gaum (Kleine) sil 292 ft.
F-com (lovers reformed by passing through wheat mill)
Ref: MPW 7:936, 948.

Lovers of Teruel, The
(Les Amants de Teruel)
1962 French, Societé Monarch (Continental Distributing) color scope 90 mins.
Dir & Sc: Raymond Rouleau.
Dialog: R. Rouleau & René-Louis Lafforgue.
Scenery & Costumes: Jacques Dupont.
Cin: Claude Renoir.
Choreog: Milko Sparemblek.
Edit: Marinette Cadix.
Mus: Mikis Theodorakis.
Mus Dir: Kresimir Sipush.
Cast: Ludmilla Tcherina, Rene-Louis Lafforque (Lafforgue?), Milko Sparemblek, Milenko Banovitch, Stevan Grebel, Jean-Pierre Bras, Antoine Marin.
sur-psy-F (ballerina realizes her own life is repeating story of the ballet she is starring in but is helpless to stop it; surrealistic scenes --riderless bicycles, violins which ignite, etc.)
Ref: FF '62 p346-47; Time 18 Jan '63; FD 17 Dec '62.

Loves, Adventures, and Life of William Shakespeare, The
See: Life of William Shakespeare: His Intrigues and Romances, The (1914).

Love's Mockery
See: Januskopf, Der (1920).

Loves of Count Iorga — Vampire, The
See: Count Yorga — Vampire (1970).

Loves of Franistan
1952 Amateur 16mm 9 mins.
Made by: Jules Schwerin.
exp-F-com
Ref: Contemp '67, '73; IFC cat p76.

Loves of Hercules, The
(Gli Amori di Ercole)
1960 Italian/French, Grandi Schermi Italiani/Contact 98 mins.
Dir: Carlo Ludovico Bragaglia.
SP: Continenza & Doria.
Cin: Enzo Serafin.
Cast: Jayne Mansfield, Mickey Hargitay, Massimo Serato, Rossella Como, Moira Orfei.
myth-F (3-headed giant; giant cyclops; trees that were men)
Ref: Unitalia '60 p224-25; Willis.
See also: Hercules.

Loves of Zero, The
(Sad Love of Zero --alt.t?)
1928 Florey-Menzies Prods sil 1200 ft.
Dir & Sc: Robert Florey.
Art Dir: William Cameron Menzies.

cont.

Loves of Zero cont.
Cin: Edward Fitzgerald.
Cast: Josef Marievsky, Tamara Shavrova, Anielka Elter.
exp-F
Ref: FIR April '60 p216-18; F/A p642; FTN; BFI cat.
Based on the story of Harlequin and Columbine.

Love's Potion
1911 Powers sil 360 ft.
F
Ref: Bios 5 Oct '11.

Low Midnight
See: Tačno u Ponoč (1960).

Luana, la Figlia della Foresta Vergine
(Luana, Daughter of the Virgin Forest; Luana Virgin of the Jungle --ad.t.)
1968 Italian, Primex Italiana color scope 88 mins.
Prod: Claude V. Coen.
Dir: Bob Raymond.
SP: Louis Road.
Cin: Mario Capriotti.
Mus: Stelvio Cipriani.
Cast: Mei Chin, Evi Marandi, Glenn Saxon, Pietro Tordi, Raf Baldassare.
SF-H-seq (villain is devoured by man-eating plant; serum made from the plant)
Ref: MFB '69 p 174; Ital Prods '68 p 136-37; F&F Nov '69 p52.

Lucerna
192? Czech sil.
F (sprites)
Ref: Collier.

Lucertola con la Pelle di Donna, Una
See: Schizoid (1971).

Luch Smerti
See: Loutch Smerti (1925).

Luchadoras, Las
"The Wrestling Women" --stars of series of Mexican films.
See: Doctor of Doom (1962); Mujeres Panteras, Las (1966?); Luchadoras. . .; Wrestling Women. . .

Luchadoras contra el Medico Asesino, Las
See: Doctor of Doom (1962).

Luchadoras contra el Robot Asesino, Las
(The Wrestling Women vs the Murdering Robot; El Asesino Loco y el Sexo: The Mad Murderer and Sex --alt.t.; Sex Monster --ad.t?)
1969 Mexican color.
Dir: René Cardona.
Cast: Joaquin Cordero, Regina Torne, Hector Lechuga, Carlos Agosti, Pascual Garcia Pena.
SF-H (hideously disfigured man; robot?)
Ref: MTVM March '69; Cahiers 228; MMF 24:57.
See also: Luchadoras, Las.

Luchadoras contra la Momia, Las
See: Wrestling Women vs the Aztec Mummy, The (1964).

Luck Comes Out of the Clouds
See: Amphytrion (1935).

Luck of the Irish, The
(The Shamrock Touch --e.t?; That Shamrock Touch --e.t?)
1948 20th-Fox green tinted seq 100 mins.
Prod: Fred Kohlmar.
Dir: Henry Koster.
SP: Philip Dunne.
Art Dir: Lyle Wheeler & J. Russell Spencer.

cont.

Luck of the Irish cont.
Cin: Joe La Shelle.
SpFX: Fred Sersen.
Edit: J. Watson Webb Jr.
Mus: Cyril Mockridge.
Mus Dir: Lionel Newman.
Cast: Tyrone Power, Anne Baxter, Cecil Kellaway [leprechaun], Lee J. Cobb, James Todd.
F-com (man-sized leprechaun follows person who caught him from Ireland to America)
Ref: Vd & FD 1 Sept '48; MFB Jan '49 p8; LC.
Based on novel "There Was a Little Man" by Guy and Constance Jones.

Lucky Ducky
1948 MGM color ani 8 mins.
Prod: Fred Quimby.
Dir: Tex Avery.
Story: Rich Hogan.
Mus: Scott Bradley.
F-com
Ref: Ani/Cin p 166; LC.

Lucky Galoshes
See: Kalosze Szczescia (1958).

Lucky Ghost, The
1936 (1942) Toddy-Dixie Nat'l (Consolidated Nat'l).
Prod & Dir: Jed Buell.
Cast: Mantan Moreland, F.E. Miller.
F?-H-com
Ref: Collier; MPA; Norman Kagan.

Lucky Luke
1971 French/Belgian, Dargaud/ R. Leblanc-UA (UA) color ani 75 mins.
Dir & Conceived: Morris.
SP: Morris, René Goscinny, & Pierre Tcherina.
Ani: José Dutillux, Claude Lambert, Henri Gruel, and others.
Edit: R. Chanceux.
Mus: Claude Bolling.
English Language version Voices: Rich Little. (Note: no US release to date)
west-F-com (cowboy Lucky Luke has a super-intelligent horse)
Ref: Vw 22 Dec '71 p6; MFB July '72 p 142.
Based on the comic strip by René Goscinny & Morris.

Lucky Star
(novel by O. Rutter)
See: Once in a New Moon (1935).

Lucky Wishbone, The
1905 Paley & Steiner sil 48 ft.
F-com (tricks)
Ref: Niver 63.

Lucretia Borgia
(novel by V. Hugo)
See: Eternal Sin, The (1917).

Lucy Comes to Stay
(short story by R. Bloch)
See: Asylum (1972).

Luda Noga
(Crazy Leg)
1965 Yugoslavian, Zagreb color ani 9.1 mins.
Dir: Branko Ranitovic.
Story: Dušan Radović.
Design: Zvonimir Lončarić.
Bg: Pavao Stalter.
Ani: Branislav Nemet.
Mus: Boško Petrović.
sat-F-com (spoof on conformity)
Ref: Z/Zagreb p45, 84.

Ludo Srce
(A Crazy Heart)
1959 Yugoslavian, Zagreb color ani 9.9 mins.
Dir: Nikola Kostelac.
Story: Vatroslav Mimica.
Design: Vjekoslav Kostanjšek.
Bg: Zlatko Bourek.
Ani: Leo Fabijani.
Mus: Aleksandar Bubanović.
F-com (second in brief series about a robot)
Ref: Z/Zagreb p62.
See also: Nestašni Robot (1956).

Ludot Vornimac
See: Magic Sword, The (1949).

Luft-Torpedo, Das
See: Air Torpedo, The (1913).

Lui
1904? French, Gaum sil sh.
Dir: Alice Guy-Blanché.
F
Ref: S&S Summer '71 p 152.

Lullaby
1948 Czech, Zlin (Gottwaldov) ani puppet 7 mins.
Dir & Story: Hermina Tyrlova.
Design: R. Prokop.
Mus: Z. Liska.
F
Ref: MFB Dec '56 p 157; FEFN July '61 p 13.

Lulu
(No Orchids for Lulu --Brit.t.)
1962 Austrian, Vienna Film-produktion 100 mins.
Prod: Otto Dürer.
Dir: Rolf Thiele.
SP: Herbert Reinecker.
Art Dir: Fritz Mögle & Heinz Ockermüller.
Cin: Michel Kelber.
Edit: Eleonore Künze.
Mus: Carl de Groof.
Cast: Nadja Tiller, Hildegarde Neff (Kneff), O.E. Hasse, Mario Adorf, Rudolf Forster, Leon Askin, Charles Regnier [Jack the Ripper].
H-seq (at climax heroine is killed by Jack the Ripper)
Ref: FIR Oct '62 p510; GC 21:23.
Based on plays "Erdgeist" and "Der Büchse der Pandora" by Frank Wedekind.
See also: Pandora's Box (1928); Jack the Ripper.

Lum 'n' Abner
(radio show)
See: Two Weeks to Live (1942).

Lumber Jack-Rabbit
1954 WB color ani 3D 7 mins.
Dir: Chuck Jones.
Voices: Mel Blanc.
F-com (Bugs discovers Paul Bunyan's garden, battles his dog)
Ref: LC; David Rider.
See also: Bugs Bunny (1938-63).

Lumigraph I
1955/1969 color sh.
Sound: Oskar Fischinger.
Images: Elfriede Fischinger.
Mus: Katchaturian.
exp-abs-F
Ref: Hist US Ani Prog.
Note: sound recorded by Oskar Fischinger in 1955; images added by his widow in 1969.

Luminis-2

1970 Spanish, Estudios Castilla color ani 10 mins.

Dir: Amaro Carretero.

F-com (spaceman uses magic to steal jewels from an alien planet)

Ref: SpCin '70.

Luminous Procuress

1971 Paramour color 80 mins.

Prod, Dir, SP, Cin: Steven Arnold.

Mus: Warner Jepson.

Cast: Pandora, Steven Solberg, Ronald Farrell, Doro Franco, Cherel Fitzpatrick.

sex-F (trans-sexual fantasy scenes)

Ref: BO 18 Oct '71 p 10; Vw 8 March '72 p20; SF Chronicle 11 July '71.

Lumpaci Vagabundus

(Lumoaci the Vagabond)

◉ 1922 German, Carl Wilhelm sil.

Prod & Dir: Carl Wilhelm.

Cast: Hans Albers, Otto Laubinger, Fritz Hirsch.

Ref: UF p409; FIR March '65 p 165.

◉ 1937 German.

Dir: Geza von Bolvary.

Cin: Werner Brandes.

Cast: Paul Hörbiger, Heinz Rühmann, Hans Holt, Hilde Krahl.

Ref: UF p397.

F (ghost)

Based on the operetta by Motiven von Nestroy.

Luna de Tobalito, La

(The Moon of Tobalito)

1968 Spanish, Zuniga color ani puppet 11 mins.

Dir: Salvador Gijon.

F (dog dreams he goes to the Moon with a bull calf)

Ref: SpCin '69 p242.

Lunatic Asylum

1925? Lupino Lane (Educational Film Exchanges) sil 1365 ft.

Cast: Lupino Lane.

F-com (man floats in the air in an asylum)

Ref: BFI cat p259 F.1882.

Lunatico, El

South American title of Conquistador de la Luna, El (1960).

Lunatics, The

(Dr. Goudron's System --ad.t? Le Système du Dr. Goudron et du Professeur Plume)

1909 (1914) French, Eclair (Leading Players) sil 1310 ft.

Dir: Robert Saidreau.

Cin: Victorin Jasset.

Cast: Henri Gouget.

psy-H (unknown to a reporter & his wife who have come to write an article, the inmates have taken over the asylum)

Ref: F/A p396; Gifford/H p30; FIR Oct '61 p463; LC; MPW 20:1703.

Based on the play by André de Lorde from the short story "The System of Dr. Tarr and Professor Fether" by Edgar Allan Poe.

See also: System of Dr. Tarr and Professor Fether, The.

Lunatics in Power

1909 Edison sil sh.

Dir: J. Searle Dawley. (?)

cont.

Lunatics in Power cont.

H-com (the inmates have taken over the asylum)

Ref: LC; Haining/Ghouls p28.

Based on short story "The System of Dr. Tarr and Professor Fether" by Edgar Allan Poe.

See also: System of Dr. Tarr and Professor Fether, The.

Lune à un Mètre, La

See: Astronomer's Dream, The (1898).

Lune dans Son Tablier, La

(The Moon in His Apron)

1909 French, Gaum sil ani sh.

Dir: Emile Cohl.

F

Ref: Filmlex p 1370.

Lunettes Féeriques, Les

(The Fairy Spectacles)

1909 French, Gaum sil ani sh.

Dir: Emile Cohl.

F

Ref: Filmlex p 1370.

Lung-ch'ang Shih-jih

See: City Called Dragon, A (1969?).

Lung-men K'e-chan

See: Dragon Inn (1968).

Lunga Notte del Terrore, La

See: Castle of Blood (1964).

Lunga Notte di Veronique, La

(The Long Night of Veronica; But You Were Dead --Brit.t.)

1966 Italian, Mercurfin color 79 mins.

Prod: Oscar Righini.

Dir, Cin, Edit: Gianni Vernuccio.

SP: G. Vernuccio & Enzo Ferraris.

Mus: Giorgio Gaslini.

Cast: Alba Rigazzi [ghost], Alex Morrison, Walter Pozzi, Cristina Gajoni, Jeanine, Tony Bellami, Gianni Ruben.

F (1916: cousins in love kept from marriage form suicide pact but only girl dies; 1966: ghost of the girl lures man's descendant to same death her lover avoided)

Ref: Ital Prods '66 II:22-23; MFB June '69 p 127.

Lunghi Capelli della Morte, I

(The Long Hair of Death)

1964 Italian, Cinegai 100 mins.

Prod: Felice Testa Gay.

Dir: Antonio Margheriti (Anthony Dawson).

Story: Ernesto Gastaldi (Julian Berry).

SP: Robert Bohr.

Art Dir: "George Greenwood" (real name: Giorgio Cerioni?).

Cin: Riccardo Pallottini (Richard Thierry).

Edit: Mario Serandrei (Mark Sirandrews).

Mus: Carlo Rustichelli (Evirust).

Cast: Barbara Steele, Giorgio Ardisson, Halina Zalewska, Robert Rains, Jean Rafferty.

F-H (woman under suspicion of murder burned alive; her curse brings plague; later, freed by bolt of lightning, she returns from grave to seek revenge & save daughter from marrying the real killer; killer trapped in effigy which is burned)

Ref: MFB Sept '67 p 142-43; F&F April '68 p28; MMF 12:37, 13:36, 17:6.

Lunyland Pictures

1914 Bray (Pathé) sil ani sh series.

Dir: Leighton Budd.

F-com

Ref: Ani chart.

Lure of Millions

1914 Danish (Prometheus Film) sil 4 reels.

bor-F-dream (suicide pact from swapping lives turns out to be dream)

Ref: MPW 20:799.

Lured by a Phantom or The King of Thule

(Roi de Thule)

1910 French, Gaum (Kleine) sil 712 ft.

F (king follows wife's ghost into the sea)

Ref: MPW 7:1367; Bios 15 Sept '10.

Lurk

1965 Amateur (Film-makers' Coop; Canyon Cinema) 16mm 38 mins.

Made by: Rudy Burckhardt.

SP & Nar: Edwin Denby.

Mus Selected by: Frank O'Hara.

Cast: Red Grooms [monster], Mimi Grooms, Edwin Denby, Yvonne Burckhardt, Jacob Burckhardt, Neil Welliver, others.

exp-SF-H-com (doctor creates a monster)

Ref: FMC 5:52; Undrgnd p34, 102, 134, 135.

Based on ideas from novel "Frankenstein" by Mary W. Shelley.

Satire of Frankenstein (1931).

Lurking Vampire, The

See: Vampiro Acecha, El (1959?).

Lust for a Vampire

(To Love a Vampire --s.t.)

1970 (1971) British, Hammer (Levitt-Pickman) color 95 mins.

Prod: Harry Fine & Michael Style.

Dir: Jimmy Sangster.

SP: Tudor Gates.

Art Dir: Don Mingaye.

Makeup: George Blackler.

Cin: David Muir.

Edit: Spencer Reeve.

Mus: Harry Robinson.

Cast: Ralph Bates, Barbara Jefford, Suzanna Leigh, Michael Johnson, Yutte Stensgaard, Mike Raven.

F-H (man falls in love with descendant & reincarnation of Carmilla the vampire; lesbian vampirism; vampire killed by falling, blazing beam)

Ref: MFB Feb '71 p25-26; FF '71 p417-18; Vw 15 Sept '71.

Based on characters created by J. Sheridan Le Fanu.

Sequel to: Vampire Lovers, The (1970).

Lust of Dracula, The

1971?

sex-F-H

Ref: Ackerman.

See also: Dracula.

Lust of the Ages, The

1917 Ogden Studios sil 5 reels.

Dir: Harry Revier.

Sc: Aaron Hoffman.

Cast: Lillian Walker, Jack Mower.

SF (story within the story: liquid fire destroys any metal)

Ref: MPN 16:1665.

Lust of the Vampire

See: Devil's Commandment, The (1956).

Lustful Vicar, The

See: Kyrkoherden (1970).

Lutkica

(A Doll)

1961 Yugoslavian, Zagreb color ani 10 mins.

Dir, Design, Ani: Borivoj Dovnikovic.

Story & Sup: Dušan Vukotić.

Bg: Ismet Voljevica.

Mus: Tomislav Simovic.

F-com

Ref: Z/Zagreb p70.

Luttes Extravagantes

See: Extraordinary Wrestling Match, An (1899).

Lycanthropus

See: Werewolf in a Girls' Dormitory (1961).

Lys de la Vie, Le

(The Lily of Life)

1920 French sil.

Dir: Loie Fuller.

Cast: Loie Fuller, René Clair.

F (princess pursued by bodiless hands; fairy tale)

Ref: FIR Nov '60 p 515; B&B p 150.

Lyudi Grekha i Krovi

(People of Sin and Blood)

1917 Russian (Soviet?) sil.

Prod: Pobeda.

Dir: A. Chargonin.

Cast: L. Terek, A. Sorin, Ye. Kestler, L. Prebenshikon, A. Gromov (Gromoff), Litin.

bor-F; hist-H (super-hypnotic monk Rasputin proves very difficult to kill)

Ref: CineF 4:4.

See also: Rasputin.

M

M

● 1931 (1933) German, Nerofilm
(Par) 114 mins (92 mins).

Prod: Seymour Nebenzal.

Dir: Fritz Lang.

Story: Thea von Harbou.

SP: F. Lang & T. von Harbou.

Art Dir: Karl Vollbrecht &
Emil Hasler.

Cin: Fritz Arno Wagner,
Gustav Rathje, & Karl Vash.

Cast: Peter Lorre, Ellen
Widmann, Inge Landgut, Gustaf
Gründgens, Herta von Walter,
Theodor Loos, Otto Wernicke,
Fritz Gnass, Fritz Odemar,
Paul Kemp.

Ref: HR 15 April '33; C to H
p218-22; F/A p397.

● 1951 CoI 90 mins.

Prod: Seymour Nebenzal.

Dir: Joseph Losey.

SP: Norman Reilly Raine &
Leo Katcher.

Addit Dialog: Waldo Salt.

Art Dir: Martin Obzina.

Cin: Ernest Laszlo.

Edit: Edward Mann.

Mus: Michel Michelet.

Mus Dir: Bert Shefter.

Cast: David Wayne, Howard
Da Silva, Luther Adler, Karen
Morley, Steve Brodie, Raymond
Burr.

Ref: MFB Aug '51 p307-08; Vd
5 March '51; FD 5 March '51; LC.

Based on the 1931 German film,
with a contemporary US setting.

bor-psy-H (psychopathic
child murderer is hunted
by the police and by other
criminals)

M.A.R.S.

See: Radio-Mania (1922).

MGM's Big Parade of Comedy

1964 MGM 91 mins.

Prod & Written: Robert Youngson.

Nar: Les Tremayne.

Cast (of bor-F seq): Jimmy
Durante [Tarzan], Lupe Velez.

com; bor-F-sat-seq

Ref: CoF 6:50; FF '64 p360-61;
FD 26 Aug '64.

See also: Tarzan.

Ma and Pa Kettle Back on the Farm

1951 U 80 mins.

Prod: Leonard Goldstein.

Dir: Edward Sedgwick.

SP: Jack Henley.

Art Dir: Bernard Herzbrun &
Emrich Nicholson.

Cin: Charles Van Enger.

Edit: Russel Schoengarth.

Mus: Joseph Gershenson.

Cast: Marjorie Main, Percy
Kilbride, Richard Long, Meg
Randall, Ray Collins, Barbara
Brown, Emory Parnell, Peter
Leeds.

SF-com-seq (Pa's overalls
become radioactive, provide
power for kitchen appliances)

Ref: Vd & HR 23 March '51;
B. Warren.

Based on characters created
by Betty MacDonald.

Ma Femme Est une Panthère

(My Wife Is a Panther)

1961 French, UFA Comacuco -
Francis Lopez 85 mins.

Dir: Raymond Bailly.

SP: Gerard Carlier.

cont.

Ma Femme cont.

Cin: Walter Wottitz.

Mus: Francis Lopez.

Cast: Jean Richard, Jean
Poiret, Serault, Silvana
Blasi, Jean-Max, Marcel
Lupovici.

F-H (woman's soul has trans-
migrated into a panther's
body, can become human at
will)

Ref: Rep Gen '61.

See also: Cat People, The
(1942).

Maangalya Bhaagyam

1958 Indian (in Tamil),
Krishna 185 mins.

Dir: T.R. Raghunath.

Cast: Ragini, Kuchalakumari,
M. Saroja, M.N. Rajam, Balaji,
Thangavelu.

F (gods & goddesses rescue
young girl & her lover from
persecution)

Ref: FEFN year-end issue '58
p55.

MacNab Visits the Comet

1910 French, Lux sil
900 ft.

F-dream (girls found on Halley's
comet in dream)

Ref: MPW 6:1067; Bios 26 May '10.

Macabre

1958 Susina Assocs (AA)
73 mins.

Prod & Dir: William Castle.

SP: Robb White.

Art Dir: Jack T. Collis &
Robert Kinoshita.

Makeup: Jack Dusick.

Cin: Carl E. Guthrie.

SpFX & Titles: Jack Rabin,
Louis DeWitt & Irving Block.

Edit: John F. Schreyer.

Mus: Les Baxter.

Cast: William Prince, Jim
Backus, Jacqueline Scott,
Christine White, Susan Morrow,
Philip Tonge, Ellen Corby.

H (plot to kill a man with
fear by making him believe
his young daughter has been
buried alive)

Ref: FF '58 p 120; FD 13 March
'58; LC; de Groote p304A.

Based on novel "The Marble
Forest" by Theo Durrant (pseudonym
of Terry Adler, Anthony Boucher,
Eunice Mays Boyd, Florence
Austern Faulkner, Allen Hymson,
Cary Lucas, Dana Lyon, Lenore
Glen Offord, Virginia Rath,
Virginia Shattuck, Darwin L.
Teilhet, & William Worley).

Macabre Concert

See: Concierto Macabro (n.d.).

Macabre Dr. Scivano, The

See: Macabro Dr. Scivano, O
(1971).

Macabre Legacy, The

See: Herencia Macabra, La
(1939).

Macabre Mark, The

See: Huella Macabra, La
(1962?).

Macabre Trunk, The

See: Baul Macabro, El (1936).

Macabro Dr. Scivano, O

(The Macabre Dr. Scivano)

1971 Brazilian, Natus 72
mins.

Prod: Faustino Correia Campos,
Raul Calhado, & Laércio Silva.

Dir: R. Calhado & Rosalvo
Caçador.

SP: R. Calhado.

Art Dir: Napoleao Resende.

Makeup: Darcy Silva.

Cin: Wanderley Silva & R.
Calhado.

cont.

Macabro Dr. Scivano cont.

SpFX: Josef Reindl.

Mus: Grieg, Dvorak, Carlos
Gomes, Gounod, Liszt,
Beethoven, & Dick Hyam.

Cast: Raul Calhado, Luiz
Leme, Oswaldo de Souza,
Henricao, Lauro Sawaya,
Genésio Aladim.

F-H (Dr Scivano seeks help
of voodoo witch doctor; ghostly
figure gives him some gold
nuggets; in return, Dr S
becomes a vampire; crucifix
turns him into ashes at climax)

Ref: Horácio Higuchi.

Macadam Flowers, The

(Les Fleurs de Macadam)

1969 Canadian, NFB color
ani 2 mins.

Dir & Story: Laurent Coderre.

F

Ref: Mamaia '70; Filmex II.
Based on the song.

Macario

1959 (1960) Mexican, Clasa
Films Mundiales (Azteca) 90
mins.

Exec Prod: José Luis Celis.

Prod: Armando Orive Alba.

Dir: Roberto Gavaldón.

SP: Emilio Garballido & R.
Gavaldon.

Art Dir: Manuel Fontanals.

Cin: Gabriel Figueroa.

SpFX: Juan Munoz Ravelo.

Mus: Raul Lavista.

Cast: Ignacio López Tarso,
Pina Pellicer, Enrique Lucerno
[Death], Mario Alberto Rodriguez,
Jose Galvez [Devil], José
Luis Jiménez [God], Sonia
Infante, Eduardo Fajardo,
Consuelo Frank.

F (hungry peasant refuses to
share food with God & the
Devil, does share with Death,
who gives him a fluid which
cures the dying if Death is
willing; peasant arraigned
by Inquisition as a wizard;
finds Death's cave with one
candle burning for each soul
on Earth, tries in vain to
save his own candle)

Ref: FF '61 p331-32; NYT 28
Sept '61; Vw 22 March '61;
Time 13 Oct '61; Azteca.

Based on story "The Third Guest"
by B. Traven (rn Traven Torsvan).

Macbeth

● 1908 Vit sil tinted
835 ft.

Prod: J. Stuart Blackton.

Dir: William V. Ranous.

Cast: William V. Ranous, Paul
Panzer, Charles Kent.

Ref: Shake/Sil p40-42; Views
104:10; LC.

● 1909 (1910) French, Film
d'Art sil 1 reel.

Dir: André Calmettes.

Cast: Paul Mounet, Jeanne
Delvair.

Ref: Shake/Sil p91.

● 1909 Italian, Cines sil
1443 ft.

Dir: Mario Caserini.

Cast: Dante Capelli, Maria
Gasperini.

Ref: MPW 5:857; Scognamillo;
Shake/Sil p 101.

● 1910 French, Pathé sil 997 ft.
ft.

Ref: MPW 6:955.

Note: possibly the same film
as the 1909 French production.

● 1911 British, Co-operative
Cinematograph sil 1360 ft
(1260 ft).

Prod: G.W. Jones.

cont.

Macbeth cont.

Cast: F.R. Benson, Mrs. F.R.
Benson, Guy Rathbone, Murray
Carrington, Eric Maxim, Nora
Lancaster.

Ref: Hist/Brit p 187, 287;
Collier; Shake/Sil p84.

● 1913 (1916) British/German,
??/Film Industry Gesellschaft
(Big A Film Corporation) sil
4700 ft (4200 ft?).

Cast: Arthur Bourchier, Violet
Vanbrugh.

Ref: MPW 29:269, 471; LC;
Shake/Sil p 183-88.

● 1916 Reliance & Fine Arts
(Triangle) sil 7500 ft.

Exec Prod: D.W. Griffith.

Dir: John Emerson.

Cin: George Hill.

Cast: Herbert Beerbohm Tree,
Constance Collier, Ralph
Lewis, Spottiswoode Aitken,
Wilfred Lucas, Erich von
Stroheim (?).

Ref: MPW 27:228, 28:2258;
FD 8 June '16; Shake/Sil
p229-235; Blum p 116.

Note: no mention of von
Stroheim in Shake/Sil.

● 1916 French sil.

Ref: Shake/Sil p216.

● 1922 British, Master sil
1175 ft.

Prod & Dir: H.B. Parkinson.

Sc: Frank Miller.

Cast: Russell Thorndike,
Sybil Thorndike.

Ref: Gifford/BFC 07439, 07440.

#1 in "Tense Moments from
Great Plays" series.

● 1946 Amateur (Films Inc)
16mm 80 mins.

Prod, SP, Cin, Edit: David
Bradley.

Dir: Thomas A. Blair.

Costume Design: Charlton Heston.

Cast: David Bradley, Jain
Wilimovsky, William Bartholomay,
J. Royal Mills, Louis Northrop,
Ralph Beebe.

Ref: Acad; FIR March '73
p 143-44.

● 1948 Mercury Prods (Rep)
107 mins (86 mins).

Exec Prod: Charles K. Feldman.

Prod & Dir: Orson Welles.

Art Dir: Fred Ritter.

Dialog Dir: William Alland.

Cin: John L. Russell.

SpFX: Howard & Theodore
Lydecker.

Edit: Louis Lindsay.

Mus: Jacques Ibert.

Cast: Orson Welles, Jeanette
Nolan, Roddy McDowall, Edgar
Barrier, Dan O'Herlihy, Erskine
Sandford, Alan Napier, Peggy
Webber, William Alland, John
Dierkes.

Ref: FD & Vd 11 Oct '48;
MFB June '51 p275-76; LC;
FIR '51 p35, '56 p255, '73
p 145.

● 1950 Bob Jones University
(Unusual Films) 16mm color
78 mins.

Prod Sup: Melvin Stratton.

Dir: Katherine Stenholm.

Mus: Richard Girvin.

Cast: Barbara Hudson Sowers,
Bob Jones Jr.

Ref: FIR March '73 p 146;
LC; HR 29 Oct '51; Acad.

● 1954 NBC-TV kinescope 120
mins.

Cast: Maurice Evans, Judith
Anderson.

Ref: FIR March '73 p 148.

cont.

Macbeth cont.

● 1960 (1963; 1966 -rr) British/American, Grand Prize Films Ltd (Prominent) color 107 mins.

Filmed in England and Scotland.

TV film also given theatrical and 16mm release.

Exec Prod: Sidney Kaufman.

Prod: Phil C. Samuel.

Dir: George Schaefer.

Technical Dir: Anthony Squire.

SP: G. Schaefer & A. Squire.

Art Dir: Edward Carrick.

Cin: Freddy Young.

Edit: Ralph Kemplen.

Mus: Richard Addinsell.

Mus Dir: Muir Mathieson.

Cast: Maurice Evans, Judith Anderson, Michael Hordern, Ian Bannen, Felix Aylmer, Malcolm Keen, Megs Jenkins, Jeremy Brett, William Hutt, Michael Ripper, Barry Warren, Douglas Wilmer.

Ref: MFB June '61 p76; Vd 29 Oct '63; FD 28 Sept '66; FIR March '73 p 151-52.

● 1971 British/US, Caliban/Playboy (Col) color scope 140 mins.

Exec Prod: Hugh M. Hefner.

Prod: Andrew Braunsberg.

Dir: Roman Polanski.

SP: R. Polanski & Kenneth Tynan.

Prod Design: Wilfred Shingleton.

Art Dir: Fred Carter.

Makeup: Tom Smith.

Cin: Gil Taylor.

Edit: Alastair McIntyre.

Mus: The Third Ear Band.

Cast: Jon Finch, Francesca Annis, Martin Shaw, John Stride, Nicholas Selby, Terence Bayler, Stephan Chase, Paul Shelley, Noel Davis.

Ref: FF '71 p730-32; MFB March '72 p53; CineF 2:3:35; F&F April '72 p53-54.

hist; F-H-seqs (man meets witches who make prophecies which are fulfilled; ghost of friend haunts murderer; phantom dagger; medieval Scottish setting)

Based on the play by William Shakespeare.

See also: Real Thing at Last, The (1916); Joe MacBeth (1955); Throne of Blood (1957).

Machine

(Die Maschine)

1966 German (Pyramid) color ani 10 mins.

Dir: Wolfgang Urchs.

F (allegorical effects of industrialization)

Ref: ASIFA 3; SF Times Sept '68.

Machine

See: Maszyna (1961).

Machiné a Retrouver le Temps, La

See: Mister Wister the Time Twister (1956).

Machine that Thinks, A

1924 Bray sil ani 1 reel.

Prod: John R. Bray.

F

Ref: LC.

Macht der Finsternis, Die

See: Power of Darkness, The (1922).

Maciste

1915 Italian, Itala sil.

F (strong man created by G. D'Annunzio in his novel "Cabiria")

Ref: FD 9 Sept '15.

cont.

Maciste cont.

Note: the following films all feature Maciste as a character, either as one hero among others, or by himself. Since the name Maciste is not well-known in the US, some distributors have redubbed & retitled Maciste films to seem to be featuring Hercules or Samson, or another better-known hero.

See also Cabiria (1914); Marvelous Maciste, The (1915); Maciste in Hell (1926); Son of Samson (1960); Witch's Curse, The (1960); Atlas Against the Cyclops (1961); Goliath and the Vampires (1961); Molemen vs. the Son of Hercules (1961); Samson and the Seven Miracles of the World (1961); Colossus and the Headhunters (1962); Death in the Arena (1962); Fire Monsters Against the Son of Hercules (1962); Triumph of the Son of Hercules (1962); Goliath and the Sins of Babylon (1963); Samson and the Slave Queen (1963); Samson vs the Giant King (1963); Hercules Against the Barbarians (1964); Hercules Against the Moon Men (1964); Hercules Against Maciste in the Vale of Woe (1964); Hercules of the Desert (1964); Invicibili Fratelli Maciste, Gli (1964); Maciste e la Regina di Samar (1964); Maciste, Gladiatore di Sparta (1964); Samson and the Mighty Challenge (1964); Samson in King Solomon's Mines (1964); Combate de Gigantes (1966).

Maciste Against Hercules in the Vale of Woe

See: Hercules Against Maciste in the Vale of Woe (1964).

Maciste all Corte dello Zar

See: Samson vs. the Giant King (1963).

Maciste all' Inferno

See: Maciste in Hell (1926); Witch's Curse, The (1960).

Maciste alla Corte del Gran Khan

See: Samson and the Seven Miracles of the World (1961).

Maciste and the King of Samar

See: Maciste e. la Regina di Samar (1964).

Maciste and the Night Queen

See: Molemen vs. the Son of Hercules (1961).

Maciste at the Court of the Czar

See: Samson vs. the Giant King (1963).

Maciste Brothers, The

See: Invicibili Fratelli Maciste, Gli (1964).

Maciste contro gli Uomini della Luna

See: Hercules Against the Moon Men (1964).

Maciste contro i Mostri

See: Fire Monsters Against the Son of Hercules (1962).

Maciste contro il Cacciatori di Teste

See: Colossus and the Headhunters (1962).

Maciste contro il Vampiro

See: Goliath and the Vampires (1961).

Maciste contro le Cyclope

See: Atlas Against the Cyclops (1961).

Maciste e la Regina di Samar

(Maciste et la Reine de Samar: Maciste and the King of Samar)

1964 Italian/French color.

Dir: Giacomo Gentilomo.

SP: Arpad De Riso, Nino Scolaro, G. Gentilomo, & Sangermano.

Cin: Oberdan (Obadan?) Troiani.

Mus: Carlo Franci.

Cast: Sergio Ciani (Alan Steel), Jany Clair, Jean-Pierre Honoré,

cont.

Macario (1959) Mexican

Maciste e la Regina... cont.

Annamaria Polani, Delia D'Alberti, Mario Tamberlani.

F (stone men)

Ref: Ital Prods '64 p 132-33.

See also: Maciste.

Maciste, Gladiatore di Sparta

(Maciste, Spartan Gladiator)

1964 Italian/French color.

Dir: Mario Caiano.

SP: Amendola & Alfonso Brescia.

Cin: Pierludovico Pavoni.

Mus: Carlo Franci.

Cast: Mark Forest, Marilu Tolo, Elisabeth Fanti, Claudio Undari (Robert Hundar), Ferruccio Amendola, Ugo Attanasio.

bor-F (super-human strength; gorilla)

Ref: Ital Prods '64 p74-75.

See also: Maciste.

Maciste il Gladiatore Piu Forte del Mondo

See: Death in the Arena (1962).

Maciste in Gengis Khan's Hell

See: Hercules Against the Barbarians (1964).

Maciste in Hell

(Maciste all' Inferno)

1926 (1931) Italian (Olympia) sil (synchronized music & FX) 90 mins (85 mins).

Dir: Guido Brignone.

Cin: Ubaldo Arata & Massimmo Terzano.

SpFX: Segundo de Chomon.

Cast: Umberto Guarracino, Mario Salo, Pauline Polaire, Domenico Serra, Bartolomeo Pagano.

F (Pluto sends one of his demons to Earth to get new subjects & he captures the super-strong Maciste)

cont.

Maciste in Hell cont.

Ref: Vw 29 & 30 June '31; MPH 11 July '31 p35; FD 28 June '31; Scognamillo.

Based on the epic poem "Divina Commedia" by Dante with engravings by Gustav Dore.

See also: Divine Comedy, The; Maciste; Witch's Curse, The (1960).

Maciste in King Solomon's Mines

See: Samson in King Solomon's Mines (1964).

Maciste in the Land of the Cyclops

See: Atlas Against the Cyclops (1961).

Maciste in the Valley of Kings

See: Son of Samson (1960).

Maciste, l'Eroe Piu Grande del Mondo

See: Goliath and the Sins of Babylon (1963).

Maciste, l'Uomo Più Forte del Mondo

See: Molemen vs. the Son of Hercules (1961).

Maciste Magnificent

See: Marvelous Maciste, The (1915).

Maciste nell' Inferno di Gengis Khan

See: Hercules Against the Barbarians (1964).

Maciste nella Terra dei Ciclopi

See: Atlas Against the Cyclops (1961).

Maciste nella Valle dei Re

See: Son of Samson (1960).

Maciste nelle Miniere di Re Salomone

See: Samson in King Solomon's Mines (1964).

Maciste, Spartan Gladiator

See: Maciste, Gladiatore di Sparta (1964).

Maciste, the Giant

See: Son of Samson (1960).

Maciste the Mighty

See: Son of Samson (1960).

Maciste, the Strongest Man in the World

See: Molemen vs the Son of Hercules (1961).

Maciste, the World's Greatest Hero

See: Goliath and the Sins of Babylon (1963).

Maciste vs. the Cyclops

See: Atlas Against the Cyclops (1961).

Maciste vs. the Moon Men

See: Hercules Against the Moon Men (1964).

Maciste vs. the Vampire

See: Goliath and the Vampires (1961).

Macumba Love

1960 (UA) color 86 mins. Filmed in Brazil.

Exec Prod: M.A. Ripps & Steve Barclay.

Prod & Dir: Douglas Fowley.

SP: Norman Graham.

Art Dir: Pierino Massinzi.

Cin: Rudolfo Icsey.

Mus: Enrico Simonetti.

Cast: Walter Reed, Ziva Rodann, June Wilkinson, William Wellman Jr, Ruth De Souza.

cont.

Macumba Love cont.

F-H (voodoo; snake worship; spell cast over Rodann)

Ref: FF '60 p 175; FD 19 March '60; de Groote p372.

Macunaima

1969 Brazilian, Filmes de Serro & K.M. Ekstein & Grupo Filmes & Condor Filmes color 100 mins.

Dir & SP: Joaquim Pedro De Andrade.

Art Dir: Anisio Mederios.

Cin: Guido Cosulich.

Edit: Eduardo Escorel.

Cast: Grande Otelo, Paulo Jose, Milton Goncalves, Rodolfo Arena, Dina Sfat.

sex-F-com (poor black Brazilian from jungles bathes in spring & turns white; cannibalism)

Ref: Vw 17 Sept '69.

Mad About Men

1954 British, Group Film Prods color 90 mins.

Prod: Betty E. Box.

Dir: Ralph Thomas.

SP: Peter Blackmore.

Art Dir: George Provis.

Cin: Ernest Steward.

Edit: Gerald Thomas.

Mus: Benjamin Frankel.

Cast: Glynis Johns [2 roles; one, mermaid], Donald Sinden, Anne Crawford, Margaret Rutherford, Noel Purcell.

F-com (Miranda the mermaid encounters a human look-alike)

Ref: MFB Dec '54 p 178; Pardi; Vw 1 Dec '54; TVG.

Sequel to: Miranda (1948).

Mad About Money

1937 British, Morgan color seq 78 mins.

Dir: Melville Brown.

Design: Len Lye.

Cast: Ben Lyon, Wallace Ford, Harry Langdon, Lupe Velez, Jean Collin.

mus-com; F-seqs (musical numbers include rocketship voyage to Saturn & trial by ghosts)

Ref: MFB '38 (Willis); Gifford/SF.

Mad as a Mars Hare

1963 WB color ani 7 mins.

Dir: Chuck Jones.

Voices: Mel Blanc.

F-com (Bugs stows away on a rocket to Mars, is turned into an ape-like "cave rabbit")

Ref: David Rider; LC.

See also: Bugs Bunny (1938-63).

Mad Baker, The

1972 The Crunch Bird Co (Regency) color ani 9.5 mins.

Prod: Len Maxwell, Ted Petok, & Joe Petrovich.

Voices: L. Maxwell.

F-H-com-sat (Dracula-like mad baker has created a chocolate cake monster which is killed in an old windmill)

Ref: ASIFA 8; Vw 8 March '72.

See also: Dracula (1930); Frankenstein (1931).

Mad Butcher, The

(The Mad Butcher of Vienna; The Vienna Strangler --e.ts)

1971? (1972) Universal Entertainment (Ellman) color.

Prod: Harry Hope.

Dir: Guido Zurli.

SP: Charles Ross.

Cast: Victor Buono, Karin (Karen) Field, Brad Harris, John Ireland.

cont.

Mad Butcher cont.

H (butcher stuffs ground-up victims into sausages which are sold to the police)

Ref: Photon 21:8; Vw 19 Jan '72 ad; Vw 30 June '71; BO 5 June '72 p89 Barometer.

Mad Clouds, The

See: Nuages Fous, Les (1962).

Mad Doctor, The

(A Date with Destiny --e.t?)

1940 (1941) Par 90 mins.

Prod: George Arthur.

Dir: Tim Whelan.

SP: Howard J. Green.

Cin: Ted Tetzlaff.

SpFX: Gordon Jennings.

Mus: Victor Young.

Cast: Basil Rathbone, Ellen Drew, John Howard, Vera Vague (Barbara Allen), Ralph Morgan, Martin Kosleck, Henry Victor.

psy-H (doctor marries wealthy women then murders them)

Ref: Vd 5 Feb '41; HR 3 Feb '41; LC; AHF p 192; FD 4 March '41.

Mad Doctor of Blood Island

1969 Philippine, Hemisphere color 85 mins.

Exec Prod: Kane W. Lynn & Eddie Romero.

Prod: E. Romero.

Dir: E. Romero & Gerardo de Leon.

SP: Reuben Conway.

Cin: Justo Paulino.

Mus Dir: Tito Arevalo.

Cast: John Ashley, Angelique Pettyjohn, Eddie Garcia, Ronald Remy, Alicia Alonzo.

SF-H (chlorophyll monster made by mad scientist)

Ref: LAT 9 Jan '70; Richardson.

Sequel: Beast of Blood (1970).

See also: Brides of Blood (1968).

Mad Doctor of Market Street, The

1941 (1942) U 60 mins.

Assoc Prod: Paul Malvern.

Dir: Joseph H. Lewis.

SP: Al Martin.

Art Dir: Jack Otterson.

Cin: Jerome Ash.

Edit: Ralph Dixon.

Mus Dir: Hans J. Salter.

Cast: Lionel Atwill, Una Merkel, Nat Pendleton, Claire Dodd, Anne Nagle, Hardie Albright, Richard Davies, Noble Johnson.

bor-SF-H (experiments with raising the dead; suspended animation)

Ref: MFB April '42 p46; LC; HR & Vd 2 Jan '42.

Mad Executioners, The

(Der Henker von London: The Hangman of London)

1963 (1965) W. German, CCC & Omnia & Vogel (Par) 92 mins.

Prod: Arthur Brauner.

Dir: Edwin Zbonek.

SP: Robert A. Stemmle.

Sets: Hans Jürgen Kiebach & Ernst Schomer.

Cin: Richard Angst.

Edit: Walter Wischniewsky.

Mus: Raimund Rosenberger.

Cast: Wolfgang Preiss, Chris Howland, Harry Riebauer, Rudolph Fernau.

H (group of hangman-vigilantes right "wrongs" by killing the wrong-doer themselves)

Ref: Pardi; Willis; CoF 8:6.

Based on story "White Carpet" by Bryan Edgar Wallace.

Mad Fox, The

See: Koiya Koi Nasuna Koi (1962).

Mad Gardener's Song, The

See: Chanson du Jardinier Fou, Le (1962).

Mad Genius, The

1931 WB 81 mins.

Dir: Michael Curtiz.

SP: J. Grubb Alexander & Harvey Thew.

Art Dir: Anton Grot.

Cin: Barney McGill.

Edit: Ralph Dawson.

Mus Dir: David Mendoza.

Cast: John Barrymore, Marian Marsh, Boris Karloff, Donald Cook, Louis Alberni, Frankie Darro, Carmel Myers.

bor-H (mad, club-footed ballet teacher dominates young dancer)

Ref: FD 25 Oct '31; AHF p 163; Vw 27 Oct '31; Pardi.

Based on "The Idol" by Martin Brown.

Mad Ghoul, The

1943 U 64 mins.

Assoc Prod: Ben Pivar.

Dir: James P. Hogan.

Story: Hans Kräly.

SP: Brenda Weisberg & Paul Gangelin.

Art Dir: John B. Goodman & Martin Obzina.

Makeup: Jack P. Pierce.

Cin: Milton Krasner.

Edit: Milton Carruth.

Mus Dir: Hans J. Salter.

Cast: George Zucco, Evelyn Ankers, David Bruce, Robert Armstrong, Turhan Bey, Milburn Stone, Charles McGraw, Rose Hobart, Addison Richards.

SF-H (Zucco's gas induces "death-in-life", makes Bruce wrinkled-face zombie-like character; to maintain his life becomes necessary to place fresh heart in his body periodically; grave-robbing & murder)

Ref: HR & Vd 29 Oct '43; LC; MFB Feb '46 p 17; AHF p 132.

Mad House, The

1934 Educational (Fox) ani 7 mins.

F-com (invisibility formula; haunted house)

Ref: FD 11 May '34.

Mad Love

1935 MGM 85 mins.

Prod: John W. Considine Jr.

Dir: Karl Freund.

Adapt: Guy Endore & K. Freund.

SP: P.J. Wolfson & John L. Balderston.

Art Dir: Cedric Gibbons.

Cin: Chester Lyons & Gregg Toland.

Edit: Hugh Wynn.

Mus: Dimitri Tiomkin.

Cast: Peter Lorre, Frances Drake, Colin Clive, Henry Kolker, Isabel Jewell, Keye Luke, Ian Wolfe, Charles Trowbridge, Rollo Lloyd.

SF-H (insane surgeon grafts murderer's hands onto arms of pianist who has lost his own hands; new hands seem to want to kill; surgeon impersonates decapitated man who has had his head replaced & who has steel hands)

Ref: FD 1 July '35; MPH 6 July '35 p74, 76; HR 27 June '35; FM 9:21.

Based on novel "Les Mains d'Orlac" by Maurice Renard.

See also: Hands of Orlac, The.

Mad Love Life of a Hot Vampire, The

1971.

Cast: Jim Parker [Dracula], Jane Bond, Kim Kim.

sex-F-H (Dracula has his girls draw blood from men's penises; hunchback; Dracula killed by sunlight)

Ref: Soren.

Based on a character created by Bram Stoker.

See also: Dracula.

Mad Magician, The

1954 Col color (b&w) 3D 73 mins.

Prod: Bryan Foy.

Dir: John Brahm.

SP: Crane Wilbur.

Art Dir: Frank Sylos.

Cin: Bert Glennon.

Edit: Grant Whytock.

Mus: Emil Newman & Arthur Lange.

Cast: Vincent Price, Mary Murphy, Eva Gabor, Patrick O'Neal, Jay Novello, John Emery, Lenita Lane.

H (illusion-inventor Price kills famous magicians by decapitation with buzz-saw, cremation, etc.)

Ref: Vd 26 March '54; FD 14 April '54; MFB Aug '54 p 121.

Mad Monk, The

See: Rasputin — The Mad Monk (1965).

Mad Monster, The

1942 PRC 77 mins.

Prod: Sigmund Neufeld.

Dir: Sam Newfield.

SP: Fred Myton.

Makeup: Harry Ross.

Cin: Jack Greenhalgh.

SpFX: Gene Stone.

Edit: Holbrook N. Todd.

Mus: David Chudnow.

Cast: Johnny Downs, Anne Nagel, George Zucco, Glenn Strange [monster], Henry Hall, Robert Strange, Sarah Padden, Mae Busch.

SF H (scientist Zucco's serum turns farmhand Strange into a wolf-man throwback)

Ref: HR 6 May '42; FDY '43.

See also: Wolf Man, The (1941).

Mad Monster Party?

1967 Videocraft-Embassy color ani puppet feature.

Probably filmed in Japan.

Exec Prod: Joseph E. Levine.

Prod: Arthur Rankin Jr.

Dir: Jules Bass.

SP: Len Korobkin & Harvey Kurtzman.

Mus & Lyrics: Maury Laws & J. Bass.

Voices: Boris Karloff, Phyllis Diller, Alan Swift, Gale Garnett.

F-H-mus-com (mad scientist invites Dracula, Frankenstein & Monster & Mrs. Monster, Jekyll/Hyde, a sea monster, the Invisible Man, a werewolf, and others to his island for a party; King Kong crashes the party)

Ref: Photon 19:45; Vd 25 Oct '66 p95.

See also: Dracula; Frankenstein; Dr. Jekyll and Mr. Hyde; Invisible Man, The (1933); King Kong (1933); Wolf Man, The (1941).

Mad Murderer and Sex, The

See: Luchadoras contra el Robot Asesino, Las (1969).

Maciste in Hell (1926) Italian

Mad Nest

n.d. Amateur (CFS) 16mm sil 4 mins.

Made by: Hy Hirsch.

exp-abs-F

Ref: Undrgnd p95, 278.

Mad People, The

See: Crazies, The (1972).

Mad Room, The

1969 Col color 93 mins. Filmed in British Columbia.

Prod: Norman Maurer.

Dir: Bernard Girard.

SP: R. Girard & A.Z. Martin.

Art Dir: Sidney Litwack.

Cin: Harry Stradbury Jr.

Edit: Pat Somerset.

Mus: David Grusin.

Cast: Stella Stevens, Shelley Winters, Skip Ward, Carole Cole, Severn Darden, Beverly Garland, Michael Burns.

H (supposedly psychotic children discover their older sister committed the horror murders, including that of their parents, of which they were accused; dog carries human hand around)

Ref: FF '69 p 196-98; F&F Feb '70 p44; Pardi.

Based on screenplay of Ladies in Retirement (1941) by Garrett Fort and Reginald Denham from the play "Ladies in Retirement" by Reginald Denham and Edward Percy.

See also: Ladies in Retirement (1941).

Mad Scientist, The

See: Fou du Labo 4, Le (1967).

Madam White Snake

(Pai-she Chuan; The Magic White Serpent)

1965 Hongkong, Shaw (Frank Lee) color 124 mins (105 mins).

Prod: Run Run Shaw.

Madam White Snake cont.

Dir: Yueh Feng.

SP: Ka Jui-Fan.

Cin: T. Nishimoto.

Mus: Wang Fu-Ling.

Cast: Lin Dai, Chao Lei.

mus-F (goddess; 1000-year old white snake)

Ref: Vw 3 Nov '65; MPH 10 Nov '65.

Based on an old Chinese fairy tale.

See also: Chinese Shadow Play (n.d.); Byakufujin no Yoren (1956); Panda and the Magic Serpent (1958).

Madame Frankenstein

See: Lady Frankenstein (1971).

Madame Jealousy

1918 Famous Players (Par) sil 5 reels.

Dir: Robert G. Vignola.

Story: George V. Hobart.

Sc: Eve Unsell.

Cast: Pauline Frederick, Thomas Meighan, Frank Losee.

alleg-F

Ref: FD 7 Feb '18; LC; MPW 35:91, 871.

Madame Sin

1971 British/US, ITC/ABC-TV color 90 mins.

Prod: Julian Wintle & Lou Morheim.

Dir: David Greene.

Idea: L. Morheim & Barry Shear.

SP: Barry Oringer & D. Greene.

Prod Design: Brian Eatwell.

Cin: Tony Richmond.

Edit: Peter Tanner.

Mus: Michael Gibbs.

Cast: Bette Davis, Robert Wagner, Denholm Elliott,

cont.

Madam Sin cont.

Gordon Jackson, Dudley Sutton, Catherine Schell, Pik-Sen Lim, Alan Dobie, Roy Kinnear, Charles Lloyd-Pack.

SF (Chinese superscientific female mastermind; "sonic guns"; mind-controlling drug; many other gadgets; underground super-laboratory)

Ref: F&F June '72 p49-50; MFB June '72 p 117-18; TVG.

Madan Manjari

1934 Indian, Kala Kinetone.

Dir & SP: Dhani Ram Prem.

Cast: Zohra, Manohar Ghatwai, Dalpatrai, Rajababu, Sunderrao, Patker, Shanta, Mukund.

myth-F

Ref: MovPicM Oct '34 p55.

Madari Mohan

(Krishna Maya)

1940 Indian, Nootan.

Mus: Deodhar.

Cast: Satyarani, Rooprani, Sunita Devi, Krishna Hukeri, Tara, Ramchandra Varde, Surve, Vasant Kanse, Onkar, Kashinath.

myth-F

Ref: Filmindia Feb '40 p 15 ad, May '40 p 16.

Madcap Island, The

See: Hyokkori Hyôtan Jima (1967).

Madcap Models

1941-43 George Pal (Par) color? sh ani puppet series.

Prod: George Pal.

F-com

Ref: LC.

See also: Jasper and the Watermelons (1942); Rhythm in the Ranks (1941).

See also: Puppetoons (1943-47); Jasper (1942-46).

Maddalena
1970 (1971) Italian/Yugoslavian, Unitas/Bosna (Int'l Co-Prods) color 105 mins.
Prod: Joseph Fryd & Alfred Piccolo.
Dir: Jerzy Kawalerowicz.
SP: J. Kawalerowicz & Sergio Bazzini.
Cin: Gabor Pogani.
Edit: Franco Arcalli.
Mus: Ennio Morricone.
Cast: Lisa Gastoni, Eric Woofe, Ivo Garrani, Lucia Alberti.
F-seqs (woman sees blonde version of herself chase priest she loves; other fantasy)
Ref: FF '71 p724-25; BO 20 Dec '71 p 11-12.

Made for Love
1926 Cinema Corp of America (Producers Distributing Corp) sil 6703 ft.
Prod: Cecil B. DeMille.
Dir: Paul Sloane.
Sc: Garrett Fort.
Art Dir: Max Parker.
Cin: Arthur C. Miller.
Edit: Elmer Harris.
Cast: Leatrice Joy, Edmund Burns, Ethel Wales, Bertram Grassby, Brandon Hurst, Frank Butler, Lincoln Stedman.
bor-F (curse on tomb seems to kill man)
Ref: AFI F2.3329 p472.

Made in Japan
1972 Japanese, Studio Lotus & ADB Co color ani 8 mins.
Made by: Ren-Zo Kinoshita.
F
Ref: IAFF '72.

Made in Paradise
1970 Dutch.
Dir: Frans Weisz.
rel-F-com (comedy about the Creation; Adam & Eve)
Ref: V annual '70 p 112.

Madeline
1952 UPA (Col) color ani 1 reel.
Exec Prod: Stephen Bosustow.
Dir: Robert Cannon.
Color: Jules Engel.
Design: Heinz Harneman.
Ani: Bill Melendez & Frank Smith.
Mus: Dave Raksin.
Nar: Gladys Holland.
bor-F-com
Ref: LC; Hist US Ani Prog; Annecy '65; Acad nom.
Based on the book by Ludwig Bemelmans.

Madeline and the Bad Hat
(story by L. Bemelmans)
See: Alice of Wonderland in Paris (1966).

Madeline and the Gypsies
(story by L. Bemelmans)
See: Alice of Wonderland in Paris (1966).

Mademoiselle
See: Story of Three Loves, The (1953).

Mademoiselle de Scudéry
(story by E.T.A. Hoffmann)
See: Dreams of Death (1950).

Madhumati
1958 Indian (in Hindi), Bimal Roy Prods 170 mins.
Dir: Bimal Roy.
Cast: Vyjayantimala, Dilip Kumar, Pran, Jagdish.

cont.

Madhumati cont.
F (reincarnation love story; eventually 2 lovers become one)
Ref: FEFN Oct 17 & 24 '58 p 16.

Madman of Lab 4, The
See: Fou du Labo '4, Le (1967).

Madmen of Mandoras
(The Amazing Mr H; The Return of Mr H --e.ts)
1963 (1964) Sans-S (Crown Int'l) 74 mins.
Prod: Carl Edwards.
Dir: David Bradley.
SP: Richard Miles & Steve Bennett.
Cin: Stanley Cortez.
Cast: Walter Stocker, Audrey Caire, Carlos Rivas, Nestor Paiva, Scott Peters, Marshall Reed.
SF (group of fanatics on island have kept head of Hitler alive since WWII)
Ref: FD 6 Feb '64; FM 27:44.

Madmen's Trial
1962 Soviet, Mosfilm color scope 115 mins.
Dir & SP: Grigori Roshal.
Cast: Irina Skobtseva, Vasili Livanov, Victor Jorjriakov.
SF-mus-com (scientist develops method of paralyzing wills for miles around)
Ref: Gasca p290; FEFN April '61.

Madness
1971? Italian.
Dir: Cesare Rau.
Cast: Thomas Hunter.
psy-H
Ref: Photon 21:8.

Madness from Terror
See: Locura del Terror (1966).

Madness of Dr. Tube, The
See: Folie du Docteur Tube, La (1914).

Madonna in Schnee
See: Wandernde Bild, Das (1920).

Madonna in the Snow
See: Wandernde Bild, Das (1920).

Madonna of the Seven Moons
1944 (1946) British, Gainsborough (U) 109 mins (87 mins).
Prod: R.J. Minney.
Assoc Prod: R.E. Dearing.
Dir: Arthur Crabtree.
SP: Roland Pertwee.
Art Dir: Andrew Mazzei.
Cin: Jack Cox.
Mus & Lyrics: Louis Levy.
Addit Mus: Hans May.
Cast: Phyllis Calvert, Stewart Granger, Patricia Roc, Peter Glenville, John Stuart, Reginald Tate, Peter Murray-Hill.
bor-psy-F-H (woman has split personality; neither "self" is aware of the other)
Ref: Vd 18 Jan '46; MFB Dec '44 p 140; FD 28 Jan '46.
Based on the novel by Margery Lawrence.

Madrid en el Año 2000
(Madrid in the Year 2000)
1925 Spanish, Madrid Film sil.
Dir & SP: Manuel Noriega.
Cin: Antonio Macasoli.
Cast: Roberto Iglesias, Roberto Rey, Javier Rivera, Amelia Sanz Cruzado, Juan Nada.
doc; bor-SF (projection of future development of Madrid)
Ref: Gasca p41.

Maestro, Il
See: Teacher and the Miracle, The (1957).

Maestro Do-Mi-Sol-Do, The
(Le Maestro Do-Mi-Sol-Do)
1906 French, Star sil 225 ft.
Made by: Georges Méliès.
F-com
Ref: Sadoul/M, GM Mage 807-09; LC.

Maestro e Margherita, Il
(The Master and Margherite)
1972 Yugoslavian/Italian, Dunav/Euro Int'l color 101 mins.
Prod: Giorgio Papi & Arrigo Colombo.
Dir: Aleksandar Petrovic.
SP: A. Petrovic, Amadeo Pagani, & Barbara Alberti.
Art Dir: Vlastimir Gavrik.
Cin: Roberto Gerardi.
Edit: Mihajlo Ilic.
Mus: Ennio Morricone.
Cast: Ugo Tognazzi, Mimsy Farmer, Alain Cuny [Devil], Bata Zivojinovic, Ljuba Tadic, Pavle Vujisic.
F (functionaries in Moscow in 1925 are thwarted by the Devil, disguised as a master of Black Magic)
Ref: Vw 13 Sept '72 p20 at Venice fest.
Based on the novel by Mikhail Bulgakov.

Maestro Koko
1969 Yugoslavian, Zagreb color ani 9 min.
F-com (Koko is elephant musician who gets a cold in his trunk)
Ref: Z/Zagreb p 110.
See also: Professor Balthasar (1967-69).

Magia
(Magic)
1917 Hungarian, Corvin sil.
Dir: Alexander Korda.
Sc: Kálmàn Sztrokay & Frigyes Karinthy.
Cast: Mihály Várkonyi.

F-H (Baron Merlin's castle has magic mirror; hero learns of ancient magician who must drink blood of young man every thousandth full moon to live, sees this magician's deeds enacted throughout history in mirror; hero is reincarnation of each of the murdered young men & Baron Merlin is the ancient magician)
Ref: Tabori/Korda p50, 312; Pozitron '72 p75-76.

Magic
1908? French, Pathé sil 221 ft.
F (tricks)
Ref: BFI cat p22.

Magic
See: Magia (1917).

Magic à Travers les Âges, La
See: Olden and New Style Conjuring (1906).

Magic Adventure
See: Magica Aventura (1968).

Magic Album, The
1908 French, Pathé sil colored 278 ft.
Dir: Ferdinand Zecca.
F (wizard's magic fluid makes beautiful girls & grotesque people; drawings come to life)
Ref: MPW 3:366; Views 133:8.

Magic Aster
1964? Chinese.
F
Ref: MTVM 15 April '64 p31.

Magic Beans, The
1939 U ani 7 mins.
(A Walter Lantz Nertsery Rhyme)
Prod: Walter Lantz.
Dir: Lester Kline.
Story: Vic McLeod.
Ani: George Dane & Fred Kopietz.
F (Jack & the beanstalk; giant cat)
Ref: LC; Willis.
See also: Jack and the Beanstalk.

Magic Bird, The
(Putiferio Va alla Guerra: Putiferio Goes to War)
1968 (1971?) Italian, Saba Cinematograficaue & Rizzoli Film & Gamma Film (Cinemation) color ani feature.
Prod: Bruno (Paolo) Paolinelli.
Dir: Roberto Gavioli.
SP: Luciano Doddoli & B. Paolinelli.
Mus: Beppe Moraschi.
English language version
Prod: Jerry Gross.
F (insect warfare story with little owls)
Ref: Vw 2 Sept '70; BO 7 June '71; Ital Prod '68 p 180-81.
Suggested by "The White Warrior" by Mario Gluerighin.

Magic Bon-Bons, The
1915 Victor (U) sil 1 reel.
Cast: Violet MacMillan.
F-dream (fairy tale)
Ref: MPW 26:621.

Magic Book, The
(Le Livre Magique)
1900 French, Star sil 195 ft.
Made by: Georges Méliès.
Cast: Georges Méliès.
F
Ref: Sadoul/M, GM Mage 289-91.

Magic Bottle
1907 British, Urban (Kleine Optical Co) sil 214 ft.
Prod: Charles Urban.
F
Ref: MPW 1:62, 172.

Magic Bottles
1905? French, Pathé sil stenciled color sh.
F
Ref: BFI Dist Cat p28.

Magic Boy, The
(Shonen Sarutobi Sasuke; Adventures of Little Samurai --ad.t.)
1959 (1961) Japanese, Toei (MGM) color ani 83 mins (75 mins).
Prod: Hiroshi Okawa.
Assoc Prod: Hideyuki Takahashi & Sanae Yamamoto.
Dir: Akira Daikubara.
Story: Kazuo Dan.
SP: Dohei (Michihei) Muramatsu.
Ani Dir: Chigao Tera.
Art Sup: Seigo Shindo.
Mus: Toru Funaura.
F (boy uses magic to defeat forces of evil; sea monster; animal friends; witch)
Ref: HR & FD 7 Aug '61; MFB Jan '62 p 14; UniJ 7:28.

Magic Bricks
1905? French, Pathé sil stenciled color sh.
F
Ref: BFI Dist cat p28.

Magic Brush, The

1970 Soviet 40 mins.

Cast: Popov.

F (brush paints whatever is wanted into reality; magic eraser can wipe out anything except the magic brush)

Ref: LA County Museum.

Magic Canvas, The

1948 British ani color 10 mins.

Made by: John Halas & Joy Batchelor.

Mus: Matyas Seiber.

exp-F

Ref: Contemp cat p51; S&S Summer '48 p93.

Magic Car, The

See: Wielka, Wielka i Najwieksza (1962).

Magic Carpet

1909 British, Urban Eclipse (Kleine) sil 357 ft.

F.

Ref: FI IV-23:7.

Magic Carpet, The

1913 Lux sil sh.

F-com

Ref: MPW 15:573.

Magic Carpet, The

1948 Soviet color? ani sh.

Dir: A.L. Atamanov.

F

Ref: Ani/Cin p 166.

Magic Carpet, The

1951 Col color 90 mins(82 mins).

Prod: Sam Katzman.

Dir: Lew Landers.

SP: David Mathews.

Art Dir: Paul Palmentola.

Cin: Ellis W. Carter.

Edit: Edwin Bryant.

Mus Dir: Mischa Bakaleinikoff.

Cast: Lucille Ball, Raymond Burr, John Agar, Patricia Medina, Rick Vallin, George Tobias.

F-com (flying carpet in old Bagdad)

Ref: Vd 26 Sept '51; FD 1 Oct '51; MFB April '52 p52.

See also: Arabian Nights.

Magic Cartoons

(Les Joyeux Microbes: The Joyous Microbes)

1909 French, Gaum (Kleine) sil ani seq 340 ft.

Dir: Emile Cohl.

F (man discovers secret of spontaneous generation & makes germ which grows people)

Ref: FI IV:36:6, 37:5; F/A p627; MPW 5:319, 379, 396.

Magic Cat

1969? Hongkong? (in Cantonese) color scope.

Cast: Chan Poh Choo, Lui Khay, Nancy Sit Kar Yin.

mus-F

Ref: Singapore Straits-Times 27 Sept '69.

Magic Christian, The

1969 British, Commonwealth United color 95 mins.

Prod: Denis O'Dell.

Dir: Joseph McGrath.

SP: J. McGrath, Terry Southern, & Peter Sellers.

Prod Design: Asheton Gorton.

Cin: Geoffrey Unsworth.

SpFX: Wally Veevers.

Edit: Kevin Connor.

Songs: Paul McCartney, Noel Coward, others.

cont.

Magic Christian cont.

Mus: Ken Thorne.

Cast: Peter Sellers, Ringo Starr, Isabel Jeans, Caroline Blakiston, Wilfrid Hyde-White, Richard Attenborough, Leonard Frey, Laurence Harvey, Christopher Lee [vampire], Spike Milligan, Roman Polanski, Yul Brynner (unbilled), Raquel Welch, Patrick Cargill, John LeMesurier, Victor Maddern, Ferdy Mayne, Dennis Price.

com-sat; H-seq (outlandish gags; fake vampire on ship; Welch as literal slave-driver; etc.)

Ref: Vw 17 Dec '69; F&F Feb '70 p43; Photon 19:47.

Based on the novel by Terry Southern.

See also: Dracula.

Magic Christmas Tree, The

1964? Holiday Pictures Inc. color.

SP: Vaughn Taylor.

Cast: Chris Kroesen, Valerie Hobbs, Dick Parish, Charles Nix, Robert Maffei.

F

Ref: Vw 7 April '65; PB.

Magic City, The

(Mayavi Nagari)

1928 Indian, Young India Pictures sil.

F

Ref: IndCin YB.

Magic Cloak of Oz, The

1914 Oz Film Manufacturing Co (Nat'l Film Corp) sil 5 reels.

Prod & Sc: L. Frank Baum.

Cast: Violet MacMillan, Mildred Harris, Juanita Hansen, Fred Woodward.

F

Ref: MPW 21:1466 ad; MPN 16:524 ad; FIR Aug-Sept '56 p331.

Based on book "Queen Zixi of Oz" by L. Frank Baum.

See also: Wizard of Oz, The.

Magic Clock, The

(Die Wunderuhr; L'Horloge Magique)

1928 German & French versions sil ani puppet & live 1970 ft.

Made by: Ladislas Starevitch.

Cast: Nina Star.

F

Ref: FTN p 118; Filmlex p930; Scognamillo.

Magic Coiffeur

1961 French, Celia color 16 mins.

Dir: Louis Cuny.

Cin: Jacques Ledoux.

Mus: Yves Claoue.

Cast: Tessa Beaumont, Jean Guélis, Danièle Darmance, Janine Moulin.

F-com (hair becomes multi-colored)

Ref: Collier.

Magic Dice

1908 French, Gaum (Kleine Optical co) sil colored 187 ft.

F (dice enlarge & open, & women get out)

Ref: MPW 2:549.

Magic Dice

1908 French, Pathé sil colored 459 ft.

F (woman climbs out of dice & returns; dice fly around)

Ref: Viws 127:11, 15 ad.

Magic Doll

See: Jadui-e-Putli (1946).

Magic Donkey, The

See: Peau d'Ane (1970).

Magic Eggs

1909 French, Gaum (Kleine) sil colored 384 ft.

F (transformations)

Ref: FI IV.

Magic Elixir, The

1912 Italian, Cines sil 350 ft.

F-com (elixir makes man immune to all weapons)

Ref: MPW 14:692.

Magic Extinguisher, The

1901 British, Williamson sil 90 ft.

F-com (tricks; transformations)

Ref: BFI cat p76.

Magic Eye

1918 Bluebird (U) sil 5 reels.

Dir: Rea Berger.

Story: Norris Shannon.

Sc: Frank H. Clark.

Cast: H.A. Barrows, Claire DuBrey, Zoe Rae, Charles H. Mailes.

F (daughter has 6th sense: has vision of ship sinking but father being rescued, & it happens that way)

Ref: FD 25 April '18; MPW 36: 289, 431, 434.

Magic Face, The

1951 Col 88 mins.

Prod & SP: Mort Briskin & Robert Smith.

Dir: Frank Tuttle.

Art Dir: Eduard Stolba.

Makeup: Serge Glebof.

Cin: Tony Braun.

Sup Edit: Arthur H. Nadel.

Edit: Henrietta Brunsch.

Mus: Herschel Burke Gilbert.

Nar: William L. Shirer.

Cast: Luther Adler, Patricia Knight, William L. Shirer, Ilka Windish, Heinz Moog, Peter Preses, Manfred Inger, Charles Koenig.

soc-SF (impersonator kills Hitler & takes his place)

Ref: Vd 1 Aug '51; HR 8 Aug '51; MPH 11 Aug '51.

Magic Fiddle, The

1957? Norwegian color 15 mins.

Prod: Jan Mathisen.

Dir: Michael Forlong.

Cast: The Norwegian Ballet Company.

ballet-F

Ref: Contemp cat '58.

Magic Fish, The

1938 Soviet 50 mins.

Dir: Alexander Rou.

F (fairy tale; talking fish grants wish)

Ref: MFB Jan '43 p7; FTN p578.

Magic Flower, The

1909 Kalem sil sh.

F (fairies; magic flower grants wishes)

Ref: MPW 6:103.

Magic Fluke, The

1949 UPA (Col) color ani 7 mins.

Prod: Steve Bosustow.

Dir: John Hubley.

Story: Sol Barzman.

Art Dir: William Hurtz.

Ani: Robert Cannon and others.

Mus: Del Castillo.

cont.

Magic Fluke cont.

F-com (fox accidentally uses a magic wand to conduct an orchestra with disastrous results)

Ref: LC; MFB Jan '57 p 11; Acad nom.

See also: Fox and the Crow, The (1948-49).

Magic Flute, The

(La Flûte Magique --French t?)

1906 French, Pathé sil 557 ft.

F (fairy; magic wand)

Ref: Views & FI 1:21:5, 9.

Magic Flute, The

1910? French, Pathé sil.

F (flute makes dead man rise & people dance)

Ref: Bios 22 Sept '10 p27.

Magic Flute, The

1927 Indian, Imperial sil.

F

Ref: IndCin YB.

Magic Flute

(Khwab-E-Hasti)

1934 Indian, Imperial.

Dir: Homi Master.

Cast: Sulochana, D. Billimoria, Rustom Irani, Ghory, Hadi, W. Khan.

F (magic flute makes everyone spin round & round until they faint)

Ref: MovPicM March '34 p24; Dipali 17 Aug '34 p24 ad, 15 March '35 p 19.

Based on an Arabian tale.

Magic Flute, The

1962 UAR, UAR Info. Dept. 16mm? 18 mins.

dance-F (boy with magic flute can make anyone dance whether they want to or not)

Ref: Collier.

Magic Flute [, The]

See: Papageno (1935); Flûte Magique, La (1946); Jadui Bansari (1948).

Magic Fountain, The

1961 (1964) Allan David (Classic World & Davis Film Distributors) color 85 mins (78 mins).

Prod & Dir: Allan David.

SP: John Lehman.

Cin: Wolf Schneider.

Edit: Richard Hertel.

Cast: Cedric Hardwicke, Buddy Baer, Peter Nestler, Catherine Hansen, Hans Conried [voice of owl].

F (curse on castle; dwarf that changes men to ravens)

Ref: Vw 16 Aug '61; BO 27 April '64.

Based on fairy tale "The Water of Life" by Jacob & Wilhelm Grimm.

Magic Fountain, The

(La Fuente Magica)

1962 Spanish/US, Aguila/Medina.

Dir: Fernando Lamas.

Cast: Esther Williams, Fernando Lamas.

bor-F

Ref: SpCin '63 p92-93.

Magic Fountain Pen, The

(Birth and Adventures of a Fountain Pen --e.t?)

1909 Vit sil ani 475 ft.

Made by: J. Stuart Blackton.

F (pen draws by itself; drawings change)

Ref: BFI cat p 168; MPW 5:67; LC; FI IV-29:9; Sadoul p440.

Magic Game, The
1927 Bray sil ani 2 reels.
Made by: J.R. Bray.
F-com
Ref: MPN 36:1756.

Magic Garden, The
(Pennywhistle Blues)
1951 South African, Swan Film Prods (Arthur Mayer & Edward Kingsley) 63 mins.
Prod & Dir: Donald Swanson.
SP: Ferdinand Webb, D. Swanson, & C. Pennington-Richards.
Cin: C. Pennington-Richards.
Edit: Gerald Ehrlich.
Cast: Tommy Ramokgopa, Dolly Rathbe.
bor-F (money used for good miraculously returns to priest)
Ref: FD 4 March '52; Vw 6 Feb '52; MFB Aug '51 p325-26.
Based on a short story by James Brown.

Magic Glass, The
1914 British, Hepworth sil 691 ft.
Prod: Cecil Hepworth.
Cast: Eric Desmond.
F-com (fluid causes reading glass to get X-ray properties)
Ref: BFI cat p98.

Magic Guitar
1968 Philippine, VP.
Dir: Mar S. Torres.
SP: Tony De Lumen & M.S. Torres.
Art Dir: Honorato de la Paz.
Cin: Tommy Marcelino, Ricardo Marcelino, & Pete Carreon.
Mus: Danny Holmsen.
Cast: Rosemarie, Ricky Belmonte, Alicia Alonzo, Victor Wood, German Moreno, Bella Flores, Bessie Barredo, Hermina Carranza, Naty Mallares, Pablo Raymundo.
F (fairies give houseboy a magical guitar & he becomes a famous singer)
Ref: Borst.
Based on the Kislap Magazine serial by Mars Ravelo.

Magic Handkerchief, The
1908 French, Pathé sil 492 ft.
F (professor uses handkerchief which causes invisibility to get revenge)
Ref: Views 137:9.

Magic Hat, The
(Le Chapeau Magique)
1903 French, Pathé sil sh.
Dir: Gaston Velle.
F

Magic Hat, The
See: Rabiha — Takiet el Ekhfaa (1943/44).

Magic Hood, The
(Fushigina Zukin)
1958 Japanese, Toei 32 mins.
F
Ref: UniJ 1:40.
Based on Japanese fairy tale.

Magic Hoop, The
See: Cerceau Magique, Le (1908).

Magic Horse
1935 Indian, Jayant.
Dir: Kanubhai Shukla & Raja Yagnik.
Mus: Santi Kumar Desai.
Cast: Navin Chandra, Alakananda, Maruti Rao Pahelwan, Bachu (Bachoo), Haridas Trikamlal.
F (flying horse)
Ref: MovPicM Oct '34 p48; Dipali 7 Dec '34 p 15, 15 March '35 p4, 27.

Magic Horse
(Mayakudarai)
1949 Indian, Sobhanachala 221 mins.
F
Ref: Indian MPA '53 p67.

Magic Horse, The
1954 British, Primrose Prods (Contemporary) ani silhouette 10 mins.
Made for TV.
Made by: Lotte Reiniger.
Mus: Freddie Phillips.
F
Ref: FIR '58 p 104; Contemp cat.

Magic Horse, The
See: Little Humpbacked Horse, The (1947).

Magic Hour, The
1925 Cranfield & Clark (Red Seal) sil 1 reel.
F (boy captured by teddy bear; living toys; witch)
Ref: MPW 26 Dec '25 p780.

Magic Island
(book by W. Seabrook)
See: White Zombie (1932).

Magic Jazz Bo, The
1917 Joker (U) sil 1 reel.
Prod & Story: Albert A. Sautell.
Sc: A.F. Statler.
Cast: Gladys Tennyson, Dave Morris.
SF-com (gas makes people go slowly)
Ref: MPW 34:402, 435; LC.

Magic Laboratory, The
1962 Italian.
Dir: Elio Gagliardo.
doc; F (digestive system shown as factory)
Ref: Ani/Cin p 140.

Magic Lamp, The
See: Invitation to the Dance (1954); Fanous el Sehri, El (1959/60).

Magic Lantern, The
(La Lanterne Magique)
1903 French, Star sil 315 ft.
Made by: George Méliès.
F (box projects "moving pictures" which are actually real people)
Ref: Sadoul/M, GM Mage 420-24; Niver/20 p43-44; LC; Niver 63.

Magic Lighter
(Fyrtøjet)
1946 Danish color ani feature.
Dir: Allan Johnsen.
F
Ref: Ani/Cin p 157.

Magic Lotus Lantern
1959 Chinese color 83 mins.
Dancers: Central Experimental Opera Company.
opera-ballet-F (goddess leaves spirit kingdom to marry a mortal)
Ref: Contemp cat; FEFN March '60 p44.

Magic Makinilya
(Magic Typewriter)
1970 Philippine, Lea.
Dir: Armando de Guzman.
SP: José Flores Sibal.
Cin: Conrado Baltazar.
Mus: Dominic Valdez.
Cast: Dante Rivero, Roger Calvin, Blanca Gomez, Chichay Caridad Sanchez, José Morelos, Eva Marie, German Moreno, Eddie Mercado, Larry Silva.
cont.

Magic Makinilya cont.
F-com (magic typewriter makes a man famous; elves & fairies)
Ref: Borst.
Based on the comic strip serial by Mars Ravelo.

Magic Mako
See: Mahô no Makochan (1971).

Magic Marble, The
1951 British, GB Instructional 13 mins.
Dir: Darrell Catling.
F (live marble plays tricks)
Ref: Gifford/BFC 11564.
Sequel: Marble Returns, The (1951).

Magic Mark
See: Jadui-Sindoor (1948).

Magic Melody, The
1909 Essanay sil 431 ft.
F-dream-com (wooden Indian comes to life & waltzes off)
Ref: MPW 5:501, 529; FI IV-40 p6, 42 p4.

Magic Mill, The
195? Soviet color ani 20 mins.
F (magic mill produces unending cakes & pies)
Ref: MFB Feb '54 p29.

Magic Mirror
1908 French, Pathé sil 475 ft.
Dir: Ferdinand Zecca.
F-dream (fluid placed on mirror makes image come to life & imitate the original -- all a dream)
Ref: MPW 3:287; Views 129:11; F/A p360.

Magic Mirror, The
1915 Joker sil sh.
Cast: Ernest Shields.
F-com
Ref: MPN 30 Jan '15 p51.

Magic Mummy
1933 Van Beuren Corp (RKO) ani 645 ft.
Credits: John Foster, George Stallings.
F-com
Ref: LC.
See: Tom and Jerry (1931-33).

Magic Music
1911 French, Eclair sil 330 ft.
F (musical notes form scenery)
Ref: MPW 9:730.

Magic Nickel, The
1913 Powers (U) sil sh.
Prod: Harry Pollard.
Sc: H.C. Griffith.
F-dream

Magic of Méliès
n.d. French (CFS) sil 45 mins.
Ref: CFS cat Sept '68.
Compilation of some of the films of Georges Méliès.

Magic of Music, The
1935 Par 1 reel.
Dir: Fred Waller.
Cast: Richard Himber.
mus-F (miniature orchestra; singer comes out of cigarette container)
Ref: LC; Sound & Shadow 5 Nov '35 p 19.

Magic of the Kite, The
(Le Cerfvolant du Bout du Monde: The Kite from Across the World, The Kite from the End of the World)
1957 (?1971) French/Chinese, Garance & Touraine & Cocinor/ Studio de Pekin (Xerox) color 90 mins.
cont.

Magic of the Kite cont.
Filmed partially in China.
Prod: M. Garance.
Dir & Story: Roger Pigaut.
Assoc Dir: Wang-Kai-Yi.
SP: R. Pigaut, Antoine Tudal, & Wang-Kai-Yi.
Art Dir: Pierre Prevert.
Cin: Henri Alekan.
Edit: Marinette Cadix.
Mus: Louis Bessieres & Tuan-Se-Tchung.
Mus Dir: Georges Derveaux.
Cast: Patrick De Bardine, Sylviane Rozenberg, Gerard (Gerald?) Szymanski, Tchen-Ming-Tchen, Monique Hoa, Lou P'Ung, Alan Astie, (Hsieh Tien, Chang Chun-Hua, Souan Won Kong.
F-dream (Chinese kite lands in Paris; in dream children are wafted to China; Monkey King with magic powers)
Ref: FF '71 p663; Vw 7 May '58; FIR Aug-Sept '58 p354, Feb '71 p 108.

Magic Orchestra
See: Jadui-Shehanai (1948).

Magic Oxen
See: Ketbors Okrockske (1955).

Magic Paintbrush, The
1954 Chinese ani sh.
Dir: Tsin Si.
F
Ref: French Ani book p 153.

Magic Pear Tree, The
1968 Murakami-Wolf color ani 7 mins.
Prod: Jimmy Teru Murakami.
Voices: Keenan Wynn, Agnes Moorehead.
bor-F-com
Ref: ASIFA 8; Acad nom.

Magic Picture
See: Jadui-Chitra (1948).

Magic Pipes, The
1910 British, Gaum sil sh.
F (pipes cause visions of dryads, mermaids, will-o-the-wisps)
Ref: Bios 13 Jan '10 p45.

Magic Pot, The
1955 Italian.
Dir: Roberto & G. Gavioli.
F
Ref: Ani/Cin p 138, 170.

Magic Ring, The
1906 British, Hepworth sil 500 ft.
Dir: Lewin Fitzhamon.
Cast: Dolly Lupone.
F ("youth uses magic ring to save maiden from witch's castle")
Ref: Gifford/BFC 01501.

Magic Ring, The
1911 British, Natural Colour Kinematograph Co color sil 525 ft.
Dir: Theo Bouwmeester.
F (ring makes wearers fall in love)
Ref: Gifford/BFC 03202.

Magic Ring
See: Jadui-Angoothi (1948).

Magic Roses
1906 French, Pathé sil colored 196 ft.
F
Ref: Views & FI 1:33:2.

Magic Roundabout, The
See: Pollux et le Chat Bleu (1970).

Magic Samurai, The

1969? Philippine, Barangay Prods & RFJ Brothers.

Dir: Leody M. Díaz.

SP: Consuelo P. Osorio.

Mus: Paquito Toledo.

Cast: Roberto Gonzalez, Johnny Monteiro, Dencio Padilla, Mario Escudero, Rocco Montalban, Jessette, Angela Montes, Matimtiman Cruz.

F (mystic martial arts)

Ref: Chodkowski.

Magic Screen

1912 French, Pathé sil 259 ft.

F-com (trick film)

Ref: BFI cat p42.

Magic Seed

1942 Soviet.

Sup: S.M. Eisenstein.

Dir: V. Kadochnikov.

F (fairy tale)

Ref: SovCin p72; F&F May '69 p27, 30.

Magic Serpent

(Kairyu Daikessen; Grand Duel in Magic --ad.t.; Froggo and Droggo --ad.t.)

1966 Japanese, Toei (AIP-TV) color 86 mins.

Dir: Tetsuy Yamauchi.

Story: Mokuami Kawatake.

SP: Masaru Igami.

Art Dir: Seiji Yada.

Cin: Motonari Washio.

Mus: Toshiaki Tsushima.

Cast: Hiroki Matsukata, Tomoko Ogawa, Ryûtaro Ōtomo, Bin Amatsu.

F (spider woman; dragon; giant eagle; occult arts; wizards get monsters to fight)

Ref: MTVM Dec '66 p40, Feb '67 p44; BIB's; UniJ 36:32-33; MMF 18/19:15.

Magic Shaving Powder

1909 (Walturdaw) sil 565 ft.

F-com (magic powder removes hair -- kids puff it at people)

Ref: Bios 9 Dec '09 p45.

Magic Shoes, The

1913 Lubin sil 400 ft.

Cast: Clarence Elmer, Jennie Nelson.

F-dream (man dreams fairy gives him magic shoes which cause the wearer to vanish)

Ref: MPW 16:80, 222, 379.

Magic Shoes, The

1935 Australian 3 reels.

F

Ref: Collier.

Magic Skin, The

● 1913 (1914) Victor (U) sil 2 reels.

Cast: J. Warren Kerrigan.

Ref: MPW 19:50, 84.

● 1915 Edison (Kleine-Edison) sil 5 reels.

Dir & Sc: Richard Ridgely.

Cast: Sally Crute, Everett Butterfield, Mabel Trunnelle, Bigelow Cooper, Frank A. Lyon, William West.

F (usual story, plus Devil)

Ref: MPW 26:626, 692, 751; LC.

● (Desire --e.t.)

1920 British sil 6000 ft.

Dir: George Ridgewell.

Cast: Yvonne Arnaud, Dennis Neilson-Terry, Austin Leigh, Christine Maitland, Saba Raleigh, Pardoe Woodman.

cont.

Magic Skin cont.

Ref: Hist/Brit p406.

F (man acquires skin which grants wishes, but shrinks with each wish; when it vanishes, the owner dies)

Based on novel "La Peau de Chagrin" by Balzac.

See also: Wild Ass's Skin, The (1909); Dream Cheater, The (1920); Slave of Desire (1923); Unheimlichen Wünsche, Die (1939); Sagrenska Koža (1960).

Magic Skis

1960? Czech ani puppet 12 mins.

F (spirit of mountains teaches skiing)

Ref: Czech An '61; Czech film flyer.

Magic Slipper, The

See: Cinderella (1912).

Magic Spectacles

(Tickled Pink --e.t?)

1961 Fred Krueger (Fairway-Int'l) color 73 mins (65 mins).

Exec Prod: Fred Krueger.

Prod, SP, Nar: Arch Hall.

Dir: A.H. Mehling.

Cast: Tommy Holden, Margo Mehling, June Pari, Kay Kramer.

sex-F-com (x-ray glasses enables man to see women in the nude)

Ref: BO 21 Nov '64; LA Examiner 26 June '61; Acad.

Magic Squares

1914 British, B&C ani paper sil 498 ft.

Dir & Story: Louis Nikola.

F ("paper squares animated into people, monsters, etc.")

Ref: Gifford/BFC 04981.

Magic Strength

(A Phantasy Cartoon)

1944 Screen Gems (Col) color? ani 1 reel.

Dir: Bob Wickersham.

Story: Dan Roman.

F-com

Ref: LC.

See: Phantasy Cartoon (1939-49).

Magic Strings

1955 British, Stewart Films Malvern color marionettes sh.

Dir & Cin: John R.F. Stewart.

Art Dir: William Foulkes.

Edit: Michael Seligman.

Mus: Tobert Gordon.

F

Ref: Montevideo '56.

Magic Sword, The

1900 British, Paul sil 180 ft.

Prod: R.W. Paul.

Dir: Walter Booth.

F (ghost; witch; ogre; man into giant; good fairy)

Ref: Hist/Brit p98; Filmlex p420; Sadoul p38, p467; Gifford/H p22.

Magic Sword, The

(Cudotvorni Mac; Ludot-Vornimac: The Miraculous Sword)

1949 (1952) Yugoslavian, Zvezda & Avala (Ellis) 97 mins.

Dir & SP: Voislav Nanovich.

Cin: Milenko Stoyanovich.

Mus: Kresimir Baranovich.

Cast: Rade Markovich, Milvoye Zhivanovich, Vera Ilich Djukovich, Marko Marinkovitch.

cont.

Magic Sword cont.

F (talking fish; witch; demon of evil terrorizes the region around his castle; shepherd defeats giant with a magic sword)

Ref: MPH 15 March '52; Vd 10 Sept '52; MMF 10/11:81, 84.

Based on Yugoslavian legends of Bash Chelik (The Steel Giant).

Magic Sword, The

(St. George and the 7 Curses; St. George and the Dragon -- s.ts)

1962 Bert I. Gordon (UA) color 80 mins.

Prod, Dir, Story: Bert I. Gordon.

SP: Bernard Schoenfeld.

Art Dir: Franz Bachelin.

Makeup: Dan Striepeke.

Cin: Paul Vogel.

SpFX: B.I. Gordon, Flora Gordon & Milt Rice.

Edit: Harry Gerstad.

Mus: Richard Markowitz.

Cast: Basil Rathbone, Estelle Winwood, Anne Helm, Gary Lockwood, Liam Sullivan, Jack Kosslyn, Vampira, Richard Kiel, Angelo Rossito.

F-H (to free princess, St. George & his magic sword battle ogre, firedrake, vampire, sorcerer, & two-headed dragon; George's aunt is a witch)

Ref: FF '62 p346; FM 13:22; FD 23 April '62; MMF 1:57.

Magic Sword, The

1970? Hongkong? color scope.

F

Ref: Manila Bulletin 24 Aug '70.

Magic Table, The

n.d. Hungarian 27 mins.

F (3 brothers on quest have fantastic adventures)

Ref: Ideal cat p44.

Magic Table, The

See: Table Magique, La (1908).

Magic Thief

1969? Hongkong? (in Cantonese) color scope.

Cast: Choa Chun, Pai Yin.

F

Ref: Singapore Straits-Times 27 Sept '69.

Magic Town

1947 Robert Riskin Prods Inc (RKO) 103 mins.

Prod & SP: Robert Riskin.

Dir: William A. Wellman.

Story: R. Riskin & Joseph Krumgold.

Prod Design: Lionel Banks.

Cin: Joseph F. Biroc.

Edit: Sherman Todd & Richard G. Wray.

Mus: Roy Webb.

Mus Dir: C. Bakaleinikoff.

Cast: James Stewart, Jane Wyman, Wallace Ford, Ann Doran, Kent Smith, Ned Sparks.

bor-soc-SF (poll of the typical US town predicts results for the rest of the US)

Ref: FD 27 Aug '47; LC.

Magic Treasure, The

195? Soviet color ani 20 mins.

F (good fairy; chest duplicates anyone or anything put in it)

Ref: MFB Feb '54 p29.

Magic Tree, The

1970 Amateur? color ani 10 mins.

Made by: Gerald McDermott.

exp-F

Ref: IAFF '72.

Magic Twig, The

1955 Soviet, Soyuzmultfilm color ani 20 mins.

Dir: I. Axenchuk.

SP: G. Grebner.

Cin: N. Voinov.

Mus: E. Kolmanovsky.

F (fairy tale: magic twig enables girl to find her lost brother)

Ref: MFB April '56 p51.

From a story by Kelin-Gruya.

Magic Typewriter

See: Magic Makinilya (1970).

Magic Umbrella, The

190? Pathé sil sh.

F (when opened, umbrella makes everyone dance)

Ref: Collier.

Magic Vest, The

1917 United States Motion Picture Corp (Par) sil 1 reel.

Sc: James O. Walsh, Rex Taylor, & Joseph A. Richmond.

F-com (tricks)

Ref: MPW 32:34; LC.

Magic Violin, The

See: Ukare Baiorin (1955).

Magic Voyage of Sinbad, The

See: Sadko (1952).

Magic Wand

1935 Indian, Par.

Dir: Dwarka Khosla.

Cin: Gulab Gopal.

Cast: Champa, Shiraz, Pandit, Adam, Razak, Bibi.

F

Ref: MovPicM May '35 p7.

Magic Weaver, The

(Maria, the Wonderful Weaver --ad.t.)

1960 (1965) Soviet, Mosfilm (AA) color 87 mins.

Dir: Alexander Rou.

Cast: Nellie Myshkova, Mikhail Kuzentsov.

F (evil king of the water)

Ref: FEFN July '60 p55.

Magic White Serpent, The

See: Byakufujin no Yoren (1956); Panda and the Magic Serpent (1958); Madam White Snake (1965).

Magic World of Karel Zeman, The

1963 Czech color sh.

Prod: Zdenek Rozkopal.

doc; F-seq (how K. Zeman works, with scenes from some of his films)

Magic World of Topo Gigio, The

1964 (1965) Italian (Col) color ani puppet & live 75 mins.

Created by: Maria Perego.

Dir: Luca de Rico.

SP: Mario Faustinelli, Guido Stagnaro, & M. Perego.

Ani: Annabella Spadon, Grazia Curti, Emanuele Pagani, Emy Ricciotti, & Mario Perego.

Cin: Giorgio Battilana.

Mus: Aldo Rossi.

Voice of Topo Gigio: Peppino Mazzulo.

Cast: Ermanno Roveri, Ignazio Colnaghi, Federica Milani, Armando Benetti, Ignazio Dolci.

F-com (magic hat; magic flute; magician; talking mouse)

Ref: MPH 28 April '65, 5 Jan '66; Ideal cat '69-70 p 114; FD 16 Dec '65.

See also: Topo Gigio i la Guerra Missile (1967).

Magic World of Watari, The

1970 Transocean color scope.

Cast: Kaneko Yoshinobu, Wong Pin Pin.

F (giant man; giant snake)

Ref: Manila Bulletin 24 Dec '70.

This is possibly the same film as Watari and the Seven Monsters (1969), which see.

Magica Aventura

(Magic Adventure)

1968 Spanish, Delgado 15 mins.

Dir: Cruz Delgado.

F (magician)

Ref: SpCin '69 p243.

Magical Matches

1912 British, Urbanora sil ani objects 330 ft.

Prod: Charles Urban.

F

Magical Mystery Tour

1967 British color feature.

Mus & Lyrics: The Beatles (John Lennon, Paul McCartney, George Harrison, Ringo Starr).

Cast: John Lennon, Paul McCartney, George Harrison, Ringo Starr, George Claydon, Ivor Cutler, Shirley Evans, Nat Jackley, Jessie Robins, Derek Royle, Victor Spinetti, Mandy Weet, Maggie Wright.

sur-F

Ref: LAFP 8 Dec '67, 10 May '68, 21 June '68.

Magician, The

(Le Magicien)

1898 French, Star sil 65 ft.

Made by: Georges Méliès.

F (transformations)

Ref: GM Mage, Sadoul/M 153.

Magician, The

1900 Edison sil 55 ft.

F (appearances & disappearances; transformations)

Ref: Niver p347; LC.

Magician, The

1926 MGM sil 8 reels (6960 ft).

Filmed in France.

Dir & Sc: Rex Ingram.

Cin: John Seitz.

Edit: Grant Whytock.

Cast: Alice Terry, Paul Wegener, Ivan Petrovitch, Firmin Gemier, Gladys Hamer. bor-F-H (magician intends to create life through magic by killing girl; hypnosis makes her imagine a faun statue comes to life)

Ref: AFI F2.3342 p474; FD 31 Oct '26; MPW 83:41; RAF fp365, 382; Vw 27 Oct '26.

Based on the novel by W. Somerset Maugham inspired by the career of Aleister Crowley.

Magician, The

(Ansiktet: The Face)

1958 (1959) Swedish, Svensk Filmindustri (Janus) 102 mins.

Prod: Carl-Henry Cagarp.

Dir & SP: Ingmar Bergman.

Art Dir: P.A. Lundgren.

Cin: Gunnar Fischer.

Edit: Oscar Rosander.

Mus: Erik Nordgren.

Cast: Max Von Sydow, Ingrid Thulin, Gunnar Björnstrand, Bibi Andersson, Birgitta Pettersson, Ake Fridell, Naima Wifstrand [witch], Bengt Ekerot.

psy-H: com-seq (phoney magician apparently comes back from dead, terrifies man)

Ref: FF '59 p203; Classics of the Film p 175; FD 25 Aug '59; Contemp p 107.

Magician, The

196? Czech ani sh.

Dir: Ivan Renc & Pavel Hobl.

F

Ref: Kinetic Art prog.

Magician, The

See: Czarodziej (1962); Mysterious Magician, The (1965).

Magician of Bengal, The

1925 Indian, Royal Art Studio sil.

F

Ref: IndCin YB.

Magician of Dreams, The

See: Mago de los Sueños, El (1967?).

Magicians, The

See: Double Deception (1960).

Magician's Cavern, The

(L'Antre des Esprits: Den of Spirits)

1901 French, Star sil 195 ft.

Made by: Georges Méliès.

F

Ref: Sadoul/M, GM Mage 345-47.

Magician's Love Test

1909 Italian, Cines sil colored sh.

F (tricks)

Ref: MPW 5:490.

Magicien, Le

See: Magician, The (1898).

Magiciennes, Les

See: Double Deception (1960).

Magie Diabolique

See: Black Art (1898).

Magie Moderne

1959 French ani sh.

Prod: Jean Image.

F

Ref: Animée.

Magkaibang Daidig ni Juanita Banana, Ang

See: Juanita Banana (1968).

Magnetic Eye, The

1908 Lubin sil 305 ft.

F-com (glance attracts objects and people)

Ref: MPW 25 Jan '08 p83, 481; Views 94:10.

Magnetic Fluid

1912 French, Pathé sil 510 ft.

F-com (man learns hypnosis, has power over other people)

Ref: Bios 15 Feb '12 p iii.

Magnetic Flute, The

1912 French?, Pathé sil 300 ft.

F-com (flute makes people & objects spin)

Ref: Bios 2 May '12.

Magnetic Influence, A

1912 British sil 480 ft.

bor-F (hypnotism)

Ref: Bios 2 May '12.

Magnetic Kitchen

(Cuisine Magnetique; Electric Kitchen --alt.t.)

1908 French, Pathé sil sh.

Dir: Segundo de Chomon.

F-com

Ref: Gasca p21; DdI I:404.

Magnetic Monster, The

1953 A-Men Prods (UA) 76 mins. Includes stock footage from German film Gold (1934), which see.

Magnetic Monster cont.

Prod: Ivan Tors.

Dir: Curt Siodmak.

SP: C. Siodmak & I. Tors.

Prod Design: George Van Marter.

Cin: Charles Van Enger.

SpFX: Jack Glass.

Mus: Blaine Sanford.

Cast: Richard Carlson, King Donovan, Jean Bryon, Harry Ellerbe, Kathleen Freeman, Strother Martin.

SF (new isotope grows by sucking in energy, gives off great deal of radiation & magnetizes metal when it grows; destroyed in cyclotron)

Ref: HR & Vd 9 Feb '53; Vd 11 March '53; MFB April '53 p54; FD 4 March '53.

Magnetic Moon, The

1954 Reed (MCA-TV) 78 mins.

Prod: Roland Reed.

Cast: Richard Crane, Sally Mansfield.

SF

Ref: Willis.

See also: Rocky Jones, Space Ranger.

Magnetic Personality, A

1912 French?, Lux sil 1/2 reel.

F-com (man steals case of magnets which attract metal)

Ref: MPW 14:596, 660.

Magnetic Removal

1908 French, Pathé sil 672 ft.

SF-com (invention magnetically moves household goods)

Ref: Views 114:10; MPW 2:547.

Magnetic Squirt, The

1909 French?, Le Lion sil 480 ft.

SF (fluid makes the lame walk again)

Ref: Bios 15 July '09.

Magnetic Umbrella, The

1911 French, Pathé sil 355 ft.

F-com (umbrella, covered with potion, attracts all kinds of things)

Ref: BFI cat p38; Bios 30 Nov '11.

Magnetic Vapor

1908 French?, Lubin sil 345 ft.

SF (henpecked husband's use of magnetic vapor puts others in his power)

Ref: 2:497; LC.

Magnétiseur, Le

See: Hypnotist at Work, A (1897).

Magnificent Adventure

See: Passport to Destiny (1943).

Magnificent Andrew, The

(novel by D. Trumbo)

See: Remarkable Andrew, The (1942).

Magnificent Bakya

1965 Philippine, Sampaguita.

Dir: Octavio Silos.

Assoc Dir & SP: Chito Tapawan.

Mus: Dick Zamora.

Cast: Gina Pareño, Ramil Rodriguez, Edgar Salcedo, Sarah Calvin, Maria Victoria, Ven Medina, José Morelos.

F (magical shoes enable girl to water-ski without boat, walk on ceiling, fly, dodge cars, etc.)

Ref: Chodkowski.

Based on the Alcala Komix serial by Amado S. Castrillo.

cont.

Mago de los Sueños, El

(The Magician of Dreams; The Dream Maker --ad.t.)

1966 Spanish, Studios Macian ani & live.

Dir: Francisco Macian.

Mus: José Sola.

Cast: Andy Russell, Pinocho, Chicho Gordillo, Tito Mora.

F (story-teller from the skies; flying saucer; Martian)

Ref: MTVM May '67 p52; SpCin '67 p 110-11.

Mago Perforza

(Compelled to be a Magician)

1951 Italian, ATA.

Prod: Antonio Mambretti.

Dir: M. Marchesi, V. Metz, & Marino.

Story: M. Marchesi & V. Metz.

SP: M. Marchesi.

Art Dir: Flavio Mogherini.

Cin: Mario Albertelli.

Cast: Tino Scotti, Isa Barzizza, Aroldo Tieri, Dorian Gray, Adriano Rimoldi, Mirella Uberti, Mario Pisu.

F-com (magician helps win race; travel backward in time)

Ref: Unitalia '50-51 p92-93.

Magoo at Sea

1964 (1967) UPA color ani 112 mins.

Feature re-edited from TV series.

Voices: Jim Backus and others.

F-com

Ref: Ideal cat '69-70 p 105.

Based on the Biblical story of Noah, the life of Captain Kidd, "Moby Dick" by Herman Melville, and "Treasure Island" by Robert Louis Stevenson.

Magoo in the King's Service

1964 (1967) UPA color ani 93 mins.

Feature re-edited from TV series.

Voices: Jim Backus and others.

F-com (Magoo as Merlin)

Ref: Ideal '69-70 p 106.

Based on the legend of King Arthur, "Cyrano de Bergerac" by Edmund Rostand, and "The Three Musketeers" by Alexandre Dumas.

Magoo Meets Frankenstein

1961 UPA 16mm color ani 6 mins.

Voices: Jim Backus and others.

F-H-com (mad scientist tries to transfer Magoo's mind into his monster or his chicken)

Ref: LC; Borst.

See also: Frankenstein; Mister Magoo.

Magoo's Puddle Jumper

1956 UPA (Col) color scope ani 1 reel.

Exec Prod: Stephen Bosustow.

Dir: Pete Burness.

Story: Dick Shaw.

Design: Robert Dranko.

Color: Bob McIntosh.

Ani: Rudy Larriva, Gil Turner, Cecil Surry, & Barney Posner.

Mus: Dean Elliott.

Voice: Jim Backus.

F-com

Ref: LC; PopCar; Acad winner.

See also: Mister Magoo (1949-).

Magritte: the False Mirror

1970 British, BFI color 22 mins.

cont.

Magritte, cont.

Prod & Cin: Bruce Beresford.

Dir & SP: David Sylvester.

Edit: Peter Heelas.

Mus: Johannes Brahms.

Nar: E.L.T. Mesens, Andrew Forge, & Robin Campbell.

sur-F-seqs

Ref: MFB June '71 p 129.

Based on paintings & writings of E.L.T. Mesens, Louis Scutenaire, René Magritte.

Magus, The

(The God Game --s.t.)

1968 British, Blazer Films (20th-Fox) color scope 117 mins.

Prod: John Kohn & Jud Kinberg.

Dir: Guy Green.

SP: John Fowles.

Prod Design: Don Ashton.

Cin: Billy Williams.

Edit: Max Benedict.

Mus: John Dankworth.

Cast: Michael Caine, Anthony Quinn, Candice Bergen, Anna Karina, Paul Stassino, Julian Glover, Corin Redgrave.

sur-F-seq (young man encounters mysterious older man who may be magician; Diana, the Greek goddess, appears; Egyptian god Anubis appears; inexplicable happenings, for which several contradictory explanations within the film are offered)

Ref: FF '69 p525-27; MFB '69 p269; Vw 11 Dec '68; Time Dec 20 '68.

Based on the novel by John Fowles.

Maha Maya

(Great Magic)

1945 Indian, Jupiter.

myth-F

Ref: Filmindia Dec '45 p72.

Mahabharat

● 1919? Indian, Mandan sil.

Prod: J.F. Mandan.

Ref: IndCin YB.

● 1936 Indian, Tamil Nadu Talkies.

Ref: IndCin YB.

myth-F

See also: Akashwani (1934); Matsya Gandha (1934); Nand Kumar (1937); Savitri (1937); Pritvi Putra (1938); Maharathi Karna (1944).

Mahadev's Victory

See: Jai Mahadev (1953).

Maharana Pratap

1948 Indian.

myth-F

Ref: Filmindia Aug '48 p70.

Maharathi Karna

1944 Indian, Prabhakar.

Prod & Dir: Bhal G. Pendharkar.

Cast: Prithvi Raj, Durga Khote, Prithviraj Leela.

myth-F

Ref: Filmindia Dec '45 p72.

Based on "Mahabharat."

Mahasati Anasuya

1944 Indian, Sunrise.

Prod & Dir: Vishnu Vyas.

Story: Mohanlal G. Dave.

SP & Songs: Ehsan Razvi.

Cin: Saju Naik & Keki Mistry.

Mus: Avinash Vyas & Alarakha.

Cast: Durga Khote, Shobhana Samarth, Shahu Modak.

myth-F

Ref: Filmindia April '44 p72, June '44 p67.

Mahasati Savitri

1956 Indian (in Hindi), Shree Om Kareshwar Prods 160 mins.

Prod: R.N. Mandloi.

Dir & SP: Ramnik Vaidya.

Dialog: S.N. Tripathi.

Art Dir: Hiralal Patel.

Cin: Haren Bhatt.

Edit: Kantilal Shukhla.

Mus Dir: Chitragupta.

Songs: G.S. Nepali.

Choreog: Sharud.

Cast: Nirupa Roy, Mahipal, S.N. Tripathi, B.M. Vyas.

F (woman brings her husband back from the kingdom of the dead)

Ref: FEFN 31 Aug '56 p 17.

Mahatma

1936 Indian, Prabhat.

Dir: Shanta Ram.

Cast: Bal Gandharva, Ratna Prabha, Vasanti, Chandra Mohan.

myth-F

Ref: Dipali 31 Jan '36 p23.

Mahô no Makochan

(Magic Mako)

1971 Japanese, Toei color? ani? 24 mins.

Dir: Yugo Serikawa (Serizawa).

F (mermaid becomes human)

Ref: UniJ 53:36-37.

Mahotsukai Sari

(Sally, the Witch)

1968 Japanese, Toei ani 24 mins.

Dir: Hiroshi Shitara.

F (little girl uses magic to do good)

Ref: UniJ 42.

Mai East

1968 Amateur (Film-makers' Coop) 16mm color & b&w 5 mins.

Made by: Cassandra M. Gerstein.

Songs sung by: Mick Jagger.

exp-abs-F

Ref: FMC 5:122.

Maid and the Martian, The

See: Pajama Party (1964).

Maid from Heaven, A

1964 Taiwan, Shaw.

Cast: Ivy Lin Po.

F-mus

Ref: MTVM 15 April '64 p23.

See also: Seven Fairies (1964).

Maiden's Paradise, A

(Le Chimiste Repopulateur: The Chemist Repopulator)

1901 French, Star sil 165 ft.

Made by: Georges Méliès.

F

Ref: Sadoul/M, GM Mage 348-49.

Maidstone

1971 Supreme Mix & Norman Mailer color 110 mins.

Prod: Buzz Farber & Norman Mailer.

Dir & SP: N. Mailer.

Cin: Jim Desmond, Richard Leacock, D.A. Pennebaker, Nick Proferes, Sheldon Rochlin, Diane Rochlin, & Jan Pieter Welt.

Edit: J.P. Welt, Lana Jokel, & N. Mailer.

Mus: Isaac Hayes, Wes Montgomery, & The Modern Jazz Quartet.

Cast: Norman Mailer, Rip Torn, Beverly Bentley, Joy Bang, Jean Campbell, Buzz Farber, Leo Garen, Ultra Violet, Michael McClure,

cont.

Maidstone cont.

José Torres, Harris Yulin and others.

doc; soc-SF (Mailer & friends make a movie about near future when all political leaders have been assassinated & there are 50 presidential candidates; the film is both this story and a documentary about making it)

Ref: FF '71 p656-58.

Mail

1930 Soviet, Soyuzkino ani sh.

Dir: M.M. Tsekhanovsky.

F

Ref: F/A p627; Film Society of London Program 15 April '34.

Based on the children's poem by S. Marshak.

Main, La

(The Hand)

1969 French, Progefi & PECF & Onris Films & PIC (WB) color 85 mins.

Dir: Henri Glaeser.

SP: H. Glaeser & Paul Parisot.

Cin: Sacha Vierny.

Cast: Nathalie Delon, Henri Serre, Michel Duchaussoy, Roger Hanin, Pierre Dux.

bor-F-H (disposal of body -- hand must be chopped off; revealed to be a script being related, then it happens in real life; crawling hand?)

Ref: Vw 31 Dec '69; Soren.

Main du Diable, La

See: Devil's Hand, The (1942).

Main du Squelette, La

(The Hand of the Skeleton)

1915 French sil.

Dir: George Schneevoigt.

F-H (ghost)

Ref: DdC II:315.

The Magician (1926)

Main Enchantée, La

(by A. de Musset)

See: Devil's Hand, The (1942).

Main Hoon Alladin

(I Am Alladin)

1965 Indian, Ramakrishna Films color.

Dir: Ramkishen Sippy.

Cast: Ajit, Sayeeda Khan.

F (magic lamp; genie)

Ref: MTVM March '65 p 19.

See also: Aladdin.

Main Qui Entreint, La

See: Max and the Clutching Hand (1915).

Main Street Kid, The

1947 (1948) Rep 64 mins.

Assoc Prod: Sidney Picker.

Dir: R.G. Springsteen.

SP: Jerry Sackheim.

Addit Dialog: John K. Butler.

Art Dir: Frank Hotaling.

Cin: John MacBurnie.

Edit: Tony Martinelli.

Mus Dir: Morton Scott.

Cast: Al Pearce, Janet Martin, Alan Mowbray, Adele Mara, Arlene Marris, Byron S. Barr, Roy Barcroft.

F-com (amateur student of telepathy is struck by lightning, finds he really can read minds)

Ref: LC; Acad; FD 15 Jan '48.

Based on a radio play by Caryl Coleman.

Mains d'Orlac, Les

(novel by M. Renard)

See: Hands of Orlac, The; Mad Love (1935); Hands of a Stranger (1960).

. . . Mais les Monstres Étaient Muselés

(But the Monsters Were Muzzled)

1956? French, Cinematographique d'Actualites Gaumont Actualites marionnettes 10 mins.

Dir, SP, Design: André Rigal.

Mus: Marc Lanjean.

F (monsters of yesterday are cowed by monsters of today)

Ref: UniF 18:61.

Maison des Cigognes, La

(The House of Storks)

n.d. Belgian sh?

F-H ("the mystery of the House of Storks which nourishes itself on human flesh" -- Annuare du Film Belge)

Ref: Annuaire du Filme Belge p 181.

Maison Hantée, La

(The Haunted House)

1907 French sil sh.

Dir: Segundo de Chomon.

F-H-com

Ref: DdC I:403.

Maison Tranquille, La

See: What Is Home Without the Boarder? (1900).

Maître

(Master)

1962? French ani sh.

Dir: Manuel Otero & Jacques Leroux.

F (secret desires of man are depicted)

Ref: F&F March '63 p64.

Maître de Temps, Le

(The Master of Time)

1970 French/Brazilian, Films 13/Barreto.

Prod: Claude Lelouch & Luis-Carlos Barretto.

Dir: Jean-Daniel Pollet.

SP: J.-D. Pollet & Pierre Kast.

Cast: Dura Cavalcanti, Jean-Pierre Kalfon, Minicius de Moraes.

SF

Ref: MTVM Dec '69 p28; Vw 29 April '70 p73; Borst.

Majin

(Daimajin; Majin the Monster of Terror --rr.t.; Majin the Hideous Idol --ad.t.; The Devil Got Angry --ad.t.; The Vengeance of the Monster --S.E. Asia t.)

1966 (1968) Japanese, Daiei (AIP-TV?) color scope 86 mins.

Prod: Masaichi Nagata.

Dir: Kimiyoshi Yasuda & Yoshiyuki Kuroda.

SP: Tetsuo Yoshida.

Art Dir: Hisashi Okuda.

Cin: Fujio Morita.

SpFX: Y. Kuroda.

Edit: Hirochi Yamada.

Mus: Akira Ifukube.

Cast: Miwa Takada, Yoshihiko Aoyama, Jun Fujimaki, Ryutaro Gomi, Tatsuo Endo.

F (giant stone idol, Majin, comes to life & helps prince & princess regain their thrones)

Ref: FF '68 p362; Vw 14 Aug '68; CineF 3:11; MPH 8 June '66.

Sequels: Return of Majin, The (1966); Majin Strikes Again (1966).

Majin no Tsume

See: Satan no Tsume (1958).

Majin Strikes Again

(Daimajin Gyakushu)

1966 Japanese, Daiei (AIP-TV?) color 80 mins.

Prod: Masaichi Nagata.

Dir: Issei Mori & Yoshiyuki Kuroda.

SP: Tetsuo Yoshida.

Cin: Hiroshi Imai & Fujio Morita.

Mus: Akira Ifukube.

Cast: Hideki (Nideki?) Ninomiya, Masahide Kizuka (Iizuka?), Shinji Hori, Shiei Ilzuka (Iizuka?), Muneyuki Nagatomo.

SF (living stone idol walks again)

Ref: Vw 25 Jan '67.

Sequel to: Majin (1966).

Make Love

197? Japanese ani 1 min.

Dir: Takehito (Takehiko?) Kamei.

F

Ref: IAFF '72.

Make Love, Not War

1972 Yugoslavian, Zagreb color ani 1 min.

Dir: Zlatko Grgić.

F-com

Ref: IAFF '72.

Make Mine Music!

1946 WD (RKO) color ani 75 mins.

Prod: Walt Disney.

Prod Sup: Joe Grant.

Seq Dir: Robert Cormack, Clyde Geronimi, Jack Kinney, Hamilton Luske, & Josh Meador.

Story: James Bodrero, Homer Brightman, T. Hee, Sylvia Holland, Dick Huemer, Dick Kelsey, Jesse Marsh, Tom Oreb, Charles Palmer, Erdman

cont.

Make Mine Music! cont.

Penner, Dick Shaw, John Walbridge, & Roy Williams.

Layout: Don Da Gradi, Hugh Hennesy, John Niendorff, Lance Nolley, Kendall O'Connor, Charles Payzant, Charles Philippi, & Al Zinnen.

Art Sup: Mary Blair, John Hench, & Elmer Plummer.

Ani: Hal Ambro, Jack Boyd, Jack Campbell, Brad Case, Les Clark, Philip Duncan, Andrew Engman, Hugh Fraser, Ollie Johnston, Bill Justice, Milt Kahl, Ward Kimball, Hal King, Eric Larson, John Lounsbery, John McManus, Tom Massey, Fred Moore, Cliff Nordberg, Ken O'Brien, Don Patterson, George Rowley, Harvey Toombs, & Judge Whitaker.

Bg: Claude Coats, Merle Cox, Al Dempster, Art Riley, Jimi Trout, & Thelma Witmer.

Sp Processes: Ub Iwerks.

Color: Mique Nelson.

Voices: Nelson Eddy, Dinah Shore, Sterling Holloway, Jerry Colonna, Andrews Sisters.

F; com-seq; mus (sequences: "Martins & Coys;" "Casey at the Bat;" "The Whale Who Wanted to Sing at the Met;" "Johnny Fedora and Alice Blue Bonnet"; "All the Cats Join In"; "After You've Gone;" "Peter & the Wolf"; "Two Silhouettes"; "Without You;" "Blue Bayou")

Ref: FD 17 April '46; LC; Vd 17 April '46; Art/Ani.

See also: Willie the Operatic Whale.

Make Room, Make Room

(novel by H. Harrison)

See: Soylent Green (1973).

Maker of Diamonds, The

See: Diamond Maker, The (1909).

Making a Welsh Rabbit

1903 Biograph sil 63 ft.

Cast: Kathryn Osterman.

F-com

Ref: Niver 107.

See also: Welsh Rabbit, A (1903).

Making Sausages

(The End of All Things --alt.t.)

1897 British, G.A. Smith sil 50 ft.

Dir: G.A. Smith.

F-com (cats, dogs, ducks, & old boots turned into sausages)

Ref: Gifford/BFC 00074.

Mala Kronika

See: Everyday Chronicle (1962).

Mala Sirena

(A Small Mermaid)

1968 Yugoslavian, Zagreb color ani 10 mins.

Dir, Design, Ani: Aleksandar Marks & Vladimir Jutriša.

Story: Ranko Munitić & A. Marks.

Bg: Rudolf Borošak.

Mus: Andjelko Klobučar.

F (mermaid falls in love with prince she saved from shipwreck)

Ref: Z/Zagreb p96-97.

Based on story "The Little Mermaid" by Hans Christian Andersen.

Malachite Casket, The

See: Stone Flower, The (1946).

Malade Hydrophope, Le

See: Man with Wheels in His Head, The (1900).

Malatesta's Carnival

1972 Windmill Films.

Prod: Richard Grosser & Walker Stuart.

Malatesta's Carnival cont.

Dir & SP: Christopher Speeth.

Story: Werner Liepholt.

Set Design: Alan Johnson, Woody Strange, & Lance Sims.

Sound FX: Sheridan Speeth.

Cast: Janine Carazo, Jerome Dempsey, William Preston, Lenny Baker, Herve Villechaize, Daniel Dietrich, Paul Hostetler, Elizabeth Henn.

F-H-com (cannibalism; gore; mutilations; "flesh-eating ghouls" --PB)

Ref: Vw 6 Dec '72 ad; PB.

Maldicion de la Llorona, La

See: Curse of the Crying Woman, The (1961).

Maldicion de la Momia, La

See: Curse of the Aztec Mummy, The (1959).

Maldicion de los Karnsteins, La

See: Terror in the Crypt (1963).

Maldicion de Nostradamus, La

See: Curse of Nostradamus, The (1960).

Male and Female Since Adam and Eve

1961 All American (William Mishkin) 74 mins.

Cast: Bill Kennedy, Alice Gardner.

sex; F-seq (nude film with Adam & Eve sequence)

Ref: PB.

See also: Adam and Eve.

Male Vampire

See: Onna Kyuketsuki (1959).

Malediction de Belphegor, La

(The Curse of Belphegor)

1966 French, Radius.

Dir: Georges Combret.

Cast: Dominique Boschero, Maurice Sarfati, Raymond Souplex, N. Noblecourt.

H; F?

Ref: MMF 18-19:16; MTVM April '66 p30.

Malefices

See: Where the Truth Lies (1961).

Maleficio

(Witchcraft)

1954 Spanish/Mexican/Argentinian 103 mins.

Dir: Leon Klimovsky, Fernando de Fuentes, & Florian Rey.

Cast: Narciso Ibanez Menta, Olga Zubarry, Santiago Gomez Cou, Jorge Mistral, Antonio Vilar, Amparito Rivelles.

F (3 episodes)

Ref: Sadoul p303.

Malenka

(La Nipote del Vampiro: The Niece of the Vampire; The Vampire's Niece --ad.t.; Fangs of the Living Dead -- U.S. release title)

1968 (1972) Spanish/Italian, Victory/Cobra (Europix) color scope 94 mins.

Prod: Aubrey Ambert & Rossana Yanni.

Dir & SP: Amando de Ossorio.

Art Dir: Lega-Michelena.

Cin: Fulvio Testi.

Mus: Carlo Savina.

Cast: Anita Ekberg, Julian Ugarte, John Hamilton, Diana Lorys, Carlos Casaravilla, Rossana Yanni, Keith Kendal.

F-H (girl resembles portrait of aunt who was burned at stake for witchcraft; Count of Wolduck castle possesses the secret of immortality; vampires?)

Ref: Vw 1 Sept '71; SpCin '69 p220-21; Photon 21:29.

Malheurs d'un Aéronaute, Les

  See: Balloonist's Mishap, The (1900).

Mali i Veliki

  See: Little and Big (1966).

Mali Vlak

  See: Little Train, The (1959).

Malice in Slumberland

  1942 Screen Gems (Col) color? ani 582 ft.

  Prod: Dave Fleischer.

  Dir: Alec Geiss.

  Ani: Ray Patterson.

  Mus: Eddie Kilfeather.

  F-com

  Ref: LC.

  See also: Phantasy Cartoon (1939-49).

Maliciousness of the Snake's Evil, The

  See: Jasei no In (1920); Ugetsu (1953).

Malika Salomi

  1953 Indian, Comedy Pictures.

  Dir & SP: Mohamed Hussein.

  Cin: V. Kamat.

  Mus: Iqbal & K. Dayal.

  Cast: Rupa Varman, Krishna Kumari, Kamran, Sheikh, Shafi, Nanda, Kamal Mohan.

  F (immortal queen rules a lost city; reverts to her true age at climax, turns to dust)

  Ref: Filmfare 15 May '53 p 17.

  Based on novel "She" by H. Rider Haggard.

  See also: She.

Malikmata

  1967? Philippine, Palaris.

  Prod: Fernando Poe.

  Dir: Richard Abelardo.

  Cast: Sylvia Rosales.

  F ("exciting vampire story")

  Ref: Ackerman (Willis).

Malombra

  1942 Italian.

  Dir: Mario Soldati.

  sur-F ("ghosts")

  Ref: deGroote p53A; Laclos p 193; Surrealisme p79.

Malpertius

  1972 French/Belgian/W. German, Societe d'Expansion du Spectacle & Le Productions Artistes Associes/Sofidoc/Artemis (UA -- in Europe) color.

  Exec Prod: Paul Laffargue.

  Prod: Pierre Levie.

  Dir: Harry Kumel.

  SP: Jean Ferry.

  Art Dir: Pierre Cadiou.

  Cin: Gerry Fisher.

  Edit: Richard Marden.

  Mus: Georges Delerue.

  Cast: Orson Welles, Susan Hampshire [Gorgon], Michel Bouquet, Mathieu Carriere, Jean-Pierre Cassel, Walter Rilla, Dora Van Der Groen, Sylvie Vartan, Daniel Pilon.

  F-H (dying Greek gods sewn into human skins live in haunted house; Gorgon turns hero to stone; maybe-a-dream ending)

  Ref: Vw 3 May '72 p 119 ad, 17 May '72.

  Based on the novel by Jean Ray.

Maltese Bippy, The

  (Who Killed Cock Rubin? --e.t.; The Incredible Werewolf Murders --e.t.; The Strange Case of . . .!#*%? --s.t.)

  1969 MGM color scope 92 mins.

  Prod: Everett Freeman & Robert Enders.

  Dir: Norman Panama.

          cont.

Maltese Bippy cont.

  SP: E. Freeman & Ray Singer.

  Art Dir: George W. Davis & Edward Carfango.

  Makeup: William Tuttle.

  Cin: William H. Daniels.

  Edit: Ronald Sinclair & Homer Powell.

  Mus: Nelson Riddle.

  Cast: Dan Rowan, Dick Martin, Carol Lynley, Julie Newmar, Mildred Natwick, Fritz Weaver, Robert Reed, Dana Elcar.

  H-com; F-H-dream (phoney werewolf who dresses & acts like Dracula; Martin dreams he is a werewolf; everyone except Rowan & Martin killed at end, & they make up several endings)

  Ref: FF '69 p284; Vw 11 June '69; FM 58:46; Photon 19:46.

  See also: Dracula; Wolf Man, The (1941).

Mama's Little Pirates

  1934 Roach (MGM) 2 reels.

  Prod: Hal Roach.

  Dir: Gus Meins.

  Edit: Bert Jordan.

  Cast: Our Gang (George McFarland, Scotty Beckett, Matthew Beard, Jerry Tucker, Billie Thomas, Mary Ann Breckell), Claudia Dell.

  com; F-dream (in dream, Our Gang goes after a treasure guarded by a giant; kids swim in gold coins; Spanky has "devilish alter ego" --Maltin)

  Ref: LC; Maltin/GMS p35, 42.

  See also: Our Gang Comedy (1923-44).

Mambo

  1952 Amateur color ani sh.

  Made by: Jordan Belson.

  exp-F

  Ref: FC 48/49:14; Undrgnd p 116.

Mammy's Rose

  1916 American (Mutual) sil 1 reel.

  Cast: Neva Gerber, Frank Borzage.

  F-seq (reunion in "land of spirits")

  Ref: MPN 13:726, 733.

Man

  1911 Yankee sil sh?

  F (reincarnation from stone age implied by vision)

  Ref: MPW 9:914.

Man

  1967 Amateur (Film-makers' Coop) 16mm color collage ani 1 min.

  Made by: Don Duga.

  exp-F

  Ref: FMC 5:95.

Man, The

  1971 (1972) Lorimar & ABC-Circle (Par) color 93 mins.

  Prod: Lee Rich.

  Dir: Joseph Sargent.

  Story & SP: Rod Serling.

  Art Dir: James G. Hulsey.

  Cin: Edward C. Rosson.

  Edit: George Nicholson.

  Mus: Jerry Goldsmith.

  Cast: James Earl Jones, Martin Balsam, Burgess Meredith, Lew Ayres, William Windom, Barbara Rush, Janet MacLachlan, Georg Stanford Brown, Jack Benny, Patric Knowles.

  soc-SF (the accidental death of the US president causes the first black man to become president)

  Ref: NYT 13 Aug '72 D:9; Vw 19 July '72 p 14; BO 12 June '72 p9.

  Filmed for television, but first released theatrically.

Man, The

  See: Aadmi (1968).

Man About Town

  1927? Fox? sil sh.

  Cast: Bob Randall (later Robert Livingston).

  SF-com (belt gives man super-strength)

  Ref: D. Glut; LC.

Man Amplifiers

  1970 U of Calif. Extension Media Center color 30 mins.

  doc; bor-SF (space manipulator to service satellites)

  Ref: F/Future p51.

Man and Beast

  1917 Butterfly (U) sil 5 reels.

  F (animals played by people)

  Ref: MPW 32:2148; LC.

Man and Fire

  See: Hombre y el Fuego, El (1970).

Man and His Dog Out for Air, A

  1957 Amateur (C-16; Film-makers' Coop) ani 3 mins.

  Made by: Robert Breer.

  exp-abs-F

  Ref: C-16 p20; FMC 5:43; Undrgnd p 131; FC 37:18.

Man and His Mate

  See: One Million B.C. (1940).

Man and His Shadow, The
(Čovjek i Sjena)

  1960 Yugoslavian, Zagreb color? ani 10.2 mins.

  Dir & Story: Dragutin Vunak.

  Design & Bg: Aleksandar Srneć.

  Ani: Vladimir Jutriša.

  Mus: Branimir Sakač.

  sur-F

  Ref: Z/Zagreb p65.

Man and His Soul

  1915 (1916) Quality Pictures (Metro) sil 5 reels.

  Dir: John W. Noble.

  Cast: Francis X. Bushman, Beverly Bayne, Edward Brennan, Charles H. Prince, John Davidson, Helen Dunbar.

  alleg-F (creation of world; Adam & Eve; conscience personified)

  Ref: MPW 27:265, 536, 1150-51, 1198; LC; FD 24 Feb '16.

  See also: Adam and Eve.

Man and the Beast, The

  See: Hombre y la Bestia, El (1951).

Man and the Machine

  1969 Canadian, NFB? color ani 1 min.

  Made by: Al Sens.

  exp-F

  Ref: Pyramid cat p 125.

Man and the Monster, The
(El Hombre y el Monstruo)

  1958 (1949) Mexican, A.B.S.A. (Clasa-Mohme theatrical, AIP-TV television release) feature.

  Prod: Abel Salazar.

  Dir: Rafael Baledon.

  Story: Raul Zenteno.

  SP: Alfredo Salazar.

  Cin: Raul M. Solares.

  Mus: Gustavo Cesar Carrion.

  Cast: Enrique Rambal, Martha Roth, Abel Salazar, Anita Blanch, Ofelia Guilman, José Chavez, Carlos Suarez, Mary Vela.

  F-H (man sells soul to the Devil to be pianist; but whenever he plays certain melody, turns into hairy monster)

  Ref: Gasca p220; FDY; MMF 2:46; Azteca; TVG.

Man and the Moon

  1955 WD (BV/Ideal) color ani & live 20 mins.

  Dir: Ward Kimball.

  Cast: Ward Kimball, Wernher von Braun.

  doc-SF

  Ref: LC; Ideal '69-70 p203.

Man and the Snake, The

  1972 British, Jocelyn Films color 26 mins.

  Prod: Elizabeth McKay.

  Dir: Sture Rydman.

  SP: Brian Scobie & S. Rydman.

  Prod Design: Bryan Graves.

  Cin: Gerry Fisher.

  Edit: Peter Musgrave.

  Mus: Marc Wilkinson.

  Cast: John Fraser, André Morell, Clive Morton, Madge Ryan, Damaris Hayman, Brenda Cowling, Stephen Waller.

  psy-H (susceptible man thinks he is mesmerized by cobra & dies of fright, but it is revealed to a toy snake)

  Ref: MFB Dec '72 p264.

  Based on the short story by Ambrose Bierce.

Man Beast

  1955 Jerry Warren (Favorite Films) 67 mins.

  Prod & Dir: Jerry Warren.

  Assoc Prod & 2nd Unit Dir: Ralph Brooke.

  SP: Arthur Cassidy.

  Art Dir: Ralph Tweer.

  Cin: Victor Fisher.

  Edit: James R. Sweeney.

  Mus Dir: Josef Zimanich.

  Cast: Rock Madison, Virginia Maynor, George Skaff, Tom Maruzzi, Lloyd Nelson (Cameron?), Wong Sing.

  SF-H (expedition in Himalayas, searching for the Yeti or Abominable Snowman, finds them, also discovers that one of their expedition members is half-Yeti, seeking to breed with human women to raise intelligence of Yetis)

  Ref: Vd 5 Dec '56; PB; Borst; B. Warren.

  See also: Abominable Snowman of the Himalayas, The (1957).

Man by the Roadside, The

  See: Mensch am Wege, Der (1923).

Man Called Dagger, A

  1967 MGM color 86 mins.

  Exec Prod: M.A. Ripps.

  Prod: Lewis M. Horowitz.

  Dir: Richard Rush.

  SP: James Peatman & Robert S. Weekley.

  Art Dir: Mike McCloskey.

  Cin: Laszlo (Leslie) Kovacs, Kovacs.

  Edit: Len Miller.

  Mus: Steve Allen.

  Cast: Terry Moore, Jan Murray, Sue Ane Langdon, Paul Mantee, Eileen O'Neill, Leonard Stone, Richard Kiel.

  bor-SF (secret agent Mantee vs mad scientist Murray; hypnotic control via device in teeth; gadget-laden wheelchair)

  Ref: Vw 20 Dec '67; FF '68 p323; FD 19 Dec '67.

Man Called Flintstone, The

  1965 Hanna-Barbera (Col) color ani 90 mins (87 mins).

  Prod & Dir: Joseph Barbera & William Hanna.

  SP: Harvey Bullock & Ray Allen.

  Art Dir: Bill Perez.

          cont

Man Called Flintstone cont.

Ani Dir: Charles A. Nichols.

SpFX: Brooke Linden.

Edit Sup: Warner Leighton.

Mus: Marty Paich & Ted Nichols.

Voices: Alan Reed, Mel Blanc, Jean Vanderpyl, Gerry Johnson, Janet Waldo, Don Messick, Paul Frees, June Foray.

F-com (caveman super-spy)

Ref: Fd 20 June '66; Vw 10 Aug '66; MFB Jan '67 p 11; FF '66 p370-71.

Based on the Hanna-Barbera TV series "The Flintstones."

Man Eater of Hydra

See: Island of the Doomed (1966).

Man from Another Star, The

See: Herr von Anderen Stern, Der (1948).

Man from Beyond, The

1921 (1922) Houdini Pictures Corp sil 7 reels.

Dir: Burton King.

Story: Harry Houdini.

Sc: Coolidge Streeter.

Cin: Frank Zucker, Irving B. Ruby, Harry A. Fischbeck, A.G. Penrod, Louis Dunmyre, & L.D. Littlefield.

Cast: Harry Houdini, Jane Connelly, Arthur Maude, Albert Tavernier, Erwin Connelly, Frank Montgomery, Luis Alberni, Nita Naldi.

F (man encased in ice in Arctic for 100 years is thawed out alive, seeks & wins his reincarnated fiancee)

Ref: AFI F2.3369 p478; FIR Nov '61 p573, Dec '61 p635; MPW 55:759; LC.

Man from Button Willow, The

1965 United Screen Arts color ani 84 mins.

Prod: Phyllis Bounds Detiege.

Dir & SP: David Detiege.

Edit: Ted Baker & Sam Horta.

Mus: Dale Robertson, George Bruns, & Mel Henke.

Mus Dir: George Stoll.

Voices: Dale Robertson, Edgar Buchanan, Barbara Jean Wong, Herschell Bernardi, Ed Platt, Howard Keel.

F-com-west (superintelligent animals help cowboy hero)

Ref: Ideal '69-70 p 116; BO 8 Feb '65; FDY '66.

Man from Mars, The

See: Radio-Mania (1922).

Man from 1997, The

1957 WB-TV 56 mins.

Episode of "Kings' Row" TV series shown on TV as feature.

Cast: James Garner, Gloria Talbott, Jacques Sernas, Charles Ruggles.

SF (man from the future brings book which tells the future)

Ref: BIB's; CoF 17:30.

Man from Planet Alpha, The

1967? Japanese, Toho.

SF-mus-com

Ref: LAT '67; Acad.

Man from Planet X, The

1950 (1951) Mid Century Films (UA) 70 mins.

Prod & SP: Aubrey Wisberg & Jack Pollexfen.

Dir: Edgar G. Ulmer.

Art Dir: Angelo Scibetti.

Cin: John L. Russell.

SpFX: Andy Anderson & Howard Weeks.

cont

Man from Planet X cont.

Edit: Fred R. Feitshans Jr.

Mus: Charles Koff.

Cast: Robert Clarke, Margaret Field, Raymond Bond, William Schallert, Roy Engel, Charles Davis.

SF-H (alien invader lands on Earth; becomes hostile when confronted with evil man, uses mind-controlling ray)

Ref: HR & Vd 9 March '51; FD 10 April '51; MFB Oct '51 p343.

Man from Space, A

1967 Greek ani.

SF

Ref: Vw 11 Oct '67.

Man from the First Century

See: Man in Outer Space (1961).

Man from U.N.C.L.E., The

Television series; some episodes edited together to form features; the following are those features which have fantastic content:

Spy with My Face (1965); One of Our Spies Is Missing (1966); One Spy too Many (1966); Spy in the Green Hat (1966); Helicopter Spies, The (1967); Karate Killers, The (1967); How to Steal the World (1968).

Man from Yesterday

1949 British, Int'l Motion Pictures 68 mins.

Dir: Oswald Mitchell.

SP: John Gilling.

Cin: Cyril Bristow.

Cast: John Stuart, Henry Oscar, Marie Burke, Laurence Harvey, Gwyneth Vaughan.

bor-F-H-dream (supposed spiritualistic powers; reincarnation; all-a-dream ending)

Ref: MFB '49 p97; Collier.

Man Goes Through the Wall, A

See: Man Who Walked Through the Wall, The (1960).

Man in Flight

1957 WD (BV/Ideal) color ani & live 31 mins.

Exec Prod: Walt Disney.

doc; F (history of flight from Greek myths to the present)

Ref: Ideal '69-70 p203; LC.

Man in Gray, A

1960 Italian ani sh.

Dir: Pino Zac.

F

Ref: Ani/Cin p 176.

Man in Half Moon Street, The

1943 (1944) Par 92 mins.

Prod: Walter MacEwen.

Dir: Ralph M. Murphy.

Adapt: Garrett Fort.

SP: Charles Kenyon.

Art Dir: Hans Dreier & Walter Tyler.

Makeup: Wally Westmore.

Cin: Henry Sharp.

Edit: Tom Neff.

Mus: Miklos Rozsa.

Cast: Nils Asther, Helen Walker, Reinhold Schünzel, Paul Cavanagh, Edmond Breon, Morton Lowry, Brandon Hurst, Reginald Sheffield, Forrester Harvey.

SF-H (man replaces a gland in his own body with a new one every few years to look 35 for years; misses a transplant, ages 60 years in minutes & dies)

Ref: Vd & HR 17 Oct '44; Agee p 131; MFB Nov '44 p 129.

Based on the play by Barré Lyndon.

Remake: Man Who Could Cheat Death, The (1959).

Man in Outer Space

(Muzz Prvního Století: Man from the First Century; Zavinil to Einstein: It's All Einstein's Fault --s.t.)

1961 (1964) Czech (AIP-TV) scope 96 mins (85 mins).

Prod: Rudolf Wolf.

Dir: Oldřich Lipsky.

SP: O. Lipsky & Zdenek Blaha.

Sets: Jan Zazvorka.

Cin: Vladimir Novotny.

Electronic FX: Zdeněk Liška.

Edit: Jan Kohout.

Mus: Ladislav Simon.

Cast: Milos Kopecky, Radovan Lukavsky, Anita Kajlichova, Vit Olmer, Otomar Krejca.

English Dubbing Dir: William Hole Jr.

English Dialog: Munroe Manning.

SF-com (man of today accidentally rocketed to alien planet; returns to Earth 2500 years in future with alien who can make himself invisible)

Ref: MTVM May '62 p61; Collier; MMF 2:46; FIR June-July '62 p327.

Man in Rue Noir, The

See: Man Who Could Cheat Death, The (1959).

Man in Space

1955 (1957) WD (BV) color ani & live 33 mins.

Exec Prod: Walt Disney.

Prod & Dir: Ward Kimball.

SP: W. Kimball & William Bosche.

SpFX: Ub Iwerks & Robert Ferguson.

Mus: George Bruns.

Cast: Wernher von Braun, Willy Ley, Heinz Haber.

doc; SF-seq (scenes from Méliès films, other SF sequences)

Ref: Ideal '69-70 p203; Menville p38; SFF p 117; MFB Jan '57 p 12.

Man in the Attic

1953 Panoramic Prods (20th-Fox) 81 mins.

Exec Prod: Leonard Goldstein.

Prod: Robert L. Jacks.

Dir: Hugo Fregonese.

SP: Robert Presnell Jr. & Barré Lyndon.

Art Dir: Lyle Wheeler & Leland Fuller.

Cin: Leo Tover.

Edit Sup: Paul Weatherwax.

Edit: Marjorie Fowler.

Mus Dir: Lionel Newman.

Cast: Jack Palance [Jack the Ripper], Constance Smith, Sean McClory, Lillian Bond, Frances Bavier, Rhys Williams.

psy-H (the new lodger turns out to be Jack the Ripper)

Ref: HR & Vd 18 Dec '53; FD 11 Jan '54; MFB June '54 p88-89.

Based on novel "The Lodger" by Marie Belloc-Lowndes.

See also: Jack the Ripper; Lodger, The.

Man in the Dark

(The Man Who Lived Twice --e.t.)

1953 Col 3D 67 mins.

Prod: Wallace MacDonald.

Dir: Lew Landers.

Story: Tom Van Dycke & Henry Altimus.

Adapt: William Sackheim.

SP: George Bricker & Jack Leonard.

Art Dir: John Meeham.

cont

Man in the Dark cont.

Edit: Viola Lawrence.

Mus Dir: Ross DiMaggio.

Cast: Edmond O'Brien, Audrey Totter, Ted de Corsia, Horace McMahon, Nick Dennis, Dayton Lummis.

bor-SF-H (operation on criminal removes his criminal tendencies & his memory; face altered)

Ref: Vd & HR 8 April '53; MFB June '53 p85-86; deGroote p210.

Remake of: Man Who Lived Twice, The (1936).

Man in the Golden Mask vs. the Invisible Assassin, The

See: Asesino Invisible, El (1964).

Man in the Mirror

1936 (1937) British, Twickenham Studios (Grand National) 85 mins (75 mins).

Prod: Julius Hagen.

Dir: Maurice Elvey.

SP: F. McGrew Willis & Hugh Mills.

Cin: Curt Courant.

Cast: Edward Everett Horton, Genevieve Tobin, Ursula Jeans, Garry Marsh, Alistair Sim, Felix Aylmer.

F-com (Horton's other, wilder self appears in mirror, & steps out to replace him from time to time)

Ref: Vw 28 Oct '36; MPH 16 Jan '37 p32; LC.

Based on the novel by William Garrett.

Man in the Moon, The

1909 French, Gaum (Kleine) sil 317 ft.

F (lover lifted to heaven by balloon; Moon, stars, comet all personified)

Ref: MPW 5:99, 162; FI IV-30 p6.

Man in the Moon

1960 (1961) British, Allied & Excalibur (Trans-Lux) 99 mins.

Prod: Michael Relph.

Dir: Basil Dearden.

SP: M. Relph & Bryan Forbes.

Prod Design: Don Ashton.

Art Dir: Jack Maxted.

Cin: Harry Waxman.

Edit: John Guthbridge.

Mus: Philip Green.

Cast: Kenneth More, Shirley Anne Field, Michael Hordern, Norman Bird, John Glyn-Jones, Charles Gray, John Phillips, Noel Purcell.

bor-SF-com (extremely healthy & lucky man chosen to be 1st British astronaut, but attempt to land him on Moon only puts him into wilds of Australia)

Ref: FF '61 p 165-66; Vw 16 Nov '60; FD 12 June '61.

Man in the Moon, The

See: Astronomer's Dream, The (1898).

Man in the Moonlight Mask, The

See: Gekko Kamen (1958).

Man in the Rue Noir, The

See: Man Who Could Cheat Death, The (1959).

Man in the Trunk, The

1942 20th-Fox 70 mins.

Exec Prod: William Goetz.

Prod: Walter Morosco.

Dir: Malcolm St. Clair.

SP: John Larkin.

Art Dir: Richard Day & Albert Hogsett.

Cin: Glen MacWilliams.

Edit: Alexander Troffey.

cont

Man in the Trunk cont.

Mus: Cyril J. Mockridge.

Cast: J. Carrol Naish, Lynne Roberts, Raymond Walburn [ghost], George Holmes, Matt McHugh, Theodore Von Eltz, Douglas Fowley.

F-com (when trunk containing his skeleton is opened, ghost follows those investigating his murder)

Ref: HR & Vd 18 Sept '42; MFB July '43 p79; LC.

Man in the White Cloak, The

1913 Danish, Great Northern sil 3 reels.

F (ghosts)

Ref: MPW 16:945.

Man in the White Suit, The

1951 (1952) British, Ealing Studios (U) 97 mins.

Prod: Michael Balcon.

Dir: Alexander Mackendrick.

SP: Roger MacDougall, John Dighton, & A. Mackendrick.

Art Dir: Jim Morhan.

Cin: Douglas Slocombe.

Edit: Bernard Gribble.

Sound Edit: Mary Hubberfield.

Mus: Benjamin Frankel.

Cast: Alec Guinness, Joan Greenwood, Cecil Parker, Michael Gough, Ernest Thesiger, Howard Marion Crawford, Duncan Lamont, Harold Goodwin, Colin Gordon.

SF-sat-com (man invents fabric that won't get dirty or wear out, makes a suit of it, wreaks havoc in fabric industry)

Ref: Vw 22 Aug '51; MFB Aug '51 p326; FDY 7 April '52.

Based on a play by Roger MacDougall.

Man, Inc.

1970 Canadian, NFB sh?

Dir: Jacques Languirand.

Cast: Don Francks, Patricia Collins.

SF ("story of man from Genesis to the year 2001" --MTVM)

Ref: MTVM June '70 p41.

Man Is a Social Being

See: Clověk Je Tvor Společenský (1960).

Man Is Satisfied, The

See: Who Looks, Pays (1906).

Man Made Monster

(Mysterious Dr. R --s.t.; The Atomic Monster --rr.t.)

1941 U 68 mins (59 mins?).

Assoc Prod: Jack Bernhard.

Dir: George Waggner.

SP: Joseph West.

Art Dir: Jack Otterson.

Makeup: Jack Pierce.

Cin: Elwood Bredell.

SpFX: John P. Fulton.

Edit: Arthur Hilton.

Mus Dir: Charles Previn.

Mus Conductor: H.J. Salter.

Cast: Lionel Atwill, Lon Chaney Jr, Anne Nagel, Frank Albertson, Samuel S. Hinds, William Davidson, Frank O'Connor, Byron Foulger, Russell Hicks, Ben Taggart.

SF-H (mad scientist Atwill discovers that sideshow performer Chaney has tolerance for electricity, charges him up like dynamo so that he glows & touch electrocutes; arrested for murder, Chaney in electric chair only becomes charged up & escapes)

Ref: Vd 24 March '41; LC; MFB Sept '41 p 114; FDY '42.

Based on story "The Electric Man" by H.J. Essex, Sid Schwartz, & Len Golos. Published?

Man Monkey, The

1909 French, Pathé sil 394 ft.

SF (man goes mad; brain replaced with that of monkey & so he acts like one)

Ref: Views FI IV:10:6.

Man Monkey, The

(A Bag Full of Monkey Nuts --alt.t?)

1911 (1912) Cricks & Martin (National) sil 405 ft.

F-com ("monkey nuts" turn a man into an ape)

Ref: MPW 11:430; Bios 12 Nov '11.

Man Next Door, The

1965 Japanese color ani 9.5 mins.

Prod: Kuri Jikken & Manga Kobo.

Dir, Story, Design: Yoji Kuri.

Ani: Masamichi Hayashi & Tadaiku Hurukawa.

Mus: Kuniharu Akiyama.

F

Ref: Collier.

Man Nobody Knows, The

1925 Pictorial Clubs sil 6 reels.

Filmed in Palestine.

Dir & Cin: Errett LeRoy Kenepp.

Titles: Bruce Barton.

Mus Arr: Alexander Savine.

rel-F (the life & miracles of Jesus)

Ref: AFI F2.3406 p482-83.

Based on "The Man Nobody Knows; a Discovery of Jesus" by Bruce Barton.

See also: King of Kings.

Man of a Thousand Faces

1957 U scope 122 mins.

Prod: Robert Arthur.

Dir: Joseph Pevney.

SP: Ivan Goff, R. Wright Campbell, & Ben Roberts.

Art Dir: Alexander Golitzen & Eric Orbom.

Cin: Russell Metty.

SpFX Cin: Clifford Stine.

Edit: Ted J. Kent.

Mus: Frank Skinner.

Mus Dir: Joseph Gershenson.

Cast: James Cagney [Lon Chaney], Dorothy Malone, Jane Greer, Jim Backus, Robert J. Evans, Roger Smith [Lon Chaney Jr], Celia Lovsky.

doc; H-seqs (life of Lon Chaney, recreating scenes from some of his films)

Ref: FD 16 July '57; LC; MFB Oct '57 p 123.

Man of La Mancha

1972 Italian/US, PEA/UA (UA) 70mm color 140 mins.

Exec Prod: Alberto Grimaldi.

Prod & Dir: Arthur Hiller.

Assoc Prod: Saul Chaplin.

SP: Dale Wasserman.

Sets & Costumes: Luciano Damiani.

Cin: Giuseppe Rotunno.

Edit: Robert J. Jones.

Lyrics: Joe Darion.

Mus: Mitch Leigh.

Mus Adapt & Dir: Laurence Rosenthal.

Cast: Peter O'Toole, Sophia Loren, James Coco, Harry Andrews, John Castle, Brian Blessed, Ian Richardson, Julie Gregg, Rosalie Crutchley.

mus; F-seqs (the prisoners to whom Cervantes tells the story of Don Quixote become characters in the story;

Man of La Mancha cont.

Quixote encounters windmills which he mistakes for giants)

Ref: MFB Feb '73 p31; BO 1 Jan '73; FIR March '73 p 175-77.

Based on the play by Dale Wasserman from novel "Don Quixote" by Miguel de Cervantes.

See also: Don Quixote.

Man of Mystery, The

1917 Vit sil 5 reels (4400 ft).

Dir: Frederick A. Thompson.

Adapt: H.C. Bergman.

Cast: E.H. Sothern, Charlotte Ives, Vilda Varesi.

F (fumes from Mt. Vesuvius make man grow 20 years younger & lose a deformity)

Ref: MPN 15:274; LC.

Based on a novel by A.C. Gunter.

Man of Stone

See: Golem, The (1936).

Man of Two Worlds

See: I'll Never Forget You (1951).

Man on the Flying Trapeze, The

1934 Par ani 1 reel.

Prod: Max Fleischer.

Dir: Dave Fleischer.

Ani: Willard Bowsky & Dave Tendlar.

F-com

Ref: LC; PopCar.

See also: Popeye (1933-57).

Man or Gun

1958 Albert C. Gannaway Prod (Rep) scope 79 mins.

Exec Prod & Dir: Albert C. Gannaway.

Prod: Vance Skarstedt.

cont.

Man in Outer Space (1961) Czech

cont

285

Man or Gun cont.

SP: V. Skarstedt & James J. Cassity.

Art Dir: Ralph Oberg.

Cin: Jack Marta.

Edit: Merrill White.

Mus: Gene Garf & Ramez Idriss.

Cast: MacDonald Carey, Audrey Totter, James Craig, James Gleason, Warren Stevens, Harry Shannon, Robert Burton, Ken Lynch.

west; bor-F (a cowboy finds a set of guns belonging to a famous gunfighter; he instantly is a crack shot & great gunfighter -- the guns make whoever owns them into expert gunfighter)

Ref: FF '58 p295; MFB Feb '59 p 19-20; Linda Glut.

Man, that Dual Personality

See: Homme, Cette Dualite, L' (1958).

Man They Could Not Hang, The

1939 Col 72 mins.

Prod: Wallace MacDonald.

Dir: Nick Grinde.

Story: Leslie T. White & George W. Sayre.

SP: Karl Brown.

Cin: Benjamin Kline.

Edit: William Lyon.

Mus Dir: M.W. Stoloff.

Cast: Boris Karloff, Lorna Gray, Robert Wilcox, Roger Pryor, Don Beddoe, Ann Doran, Charles Trowbridge, James Craig, Byron Foulger.

SF-H (executed for experimenting with life, scientist Karloff is restored to life by his own mechanical heart invention; captures judge & jurors who convicted him, starts to kill them one by one; daughter intervenes & is killed; Karloff restores her to life then dies)

Ref: MPH 30 Sept '39; Vw; FFF p43; FD 28 Sept '39.

Man They Couldn't Arrest, The

1931 (1933) British, Gainsborough (Gaum) 72 mins.

Dir: T. Hays Hunter.

SP: T.H. Hunter, Angus MacPhail, & Arthur Wimperis.

Cin: Leslie Rowson.

Edit: Ian Dalrymble.

Cast: Hugh Wakefield, Gordon Harker, Renée Clama, Nicholas Hannen, Garry Marsh, Dennis Wyndham.

bor-SF (scientist invents eavesdropping machine -- can listen in on any conversation anywhere)

Ref: FD 13 March '33; NYT 14 March '33; FIR May '67 p315; Acad.

Based on the story by "Seamark."

Man Wants to Live!

See: ¡Hommes Veulent Vivre!, Les (1961).

Man Who Benefits by Being Invisible, The

See: New Invisible Man, The (1960).

Man Who Came from Ummo, The

See: Hombre Que Vino del Ummo, El (1970).

Man Who Changed His Mind, The

See: Man Who Lived Again, The (1936).

Man Who Cheated Death, The

See: Man Who Could Cheat Death, The (1959).

Man Who Cheated Life, The

See: Student von Prague, Der (1926).

Man Who Collected Poe, The

(short story by R. Bloch)

See: Torture Garden (1967).

Man Who Could Cheat Death, The

(The Man in Rue Noir --ad.t.)

1959 British, Hammer (Par) color 83 mins.

Prod: Michael Carreras.

Dir: Terence Fisher.

SP: Jimmy Sangster.

Prod Design: Bernard Robinson.

Makeup: Roy Ashton.

Cin: Jack Asher.

Edit: James Needs.

Mus: Richard Bennett.

Cast: Anton Diffring, Hazel Court, Christopher Lee, Arnold Marle, Delphi Lawrence, Francis de Wolff.

SF-H (man replaces a gland in his own body with a new one every few years to look 35 for years; misses a transplant, ages 60 years in minutes & dies)

Ref: FF '59 p 182; LC; FDY '60.

Based on play "The Man in Half Moon Street" by Barré Lyndon.

Remake of: Man in Half Moon Street, The (1943).

Man Who Could Not Lose

1914 Favorite Players sil 5 reels.

Dir: Carlyle Blackwell.

F (man dreams names of winning horses)

Ref: MPW 22:1237; F/A p316; LC.

Based on the short story by Richard Harding Davis.

Man Who Could Work Miracles, The

1936 (1937) British, London Films (UA) 90 mins.

Prod: Alexander Korda.

Dir: Lothar Mendes.

SP: H.G. Wells..

Cin: Harold Rosson.

SpFX Cin: E. Cohen.

SpFX: Ned Mann & Laurence Butler.

Edit: Philip Charlot Hornbeck.

Mus: Mischa Spoliansky.

Cast: Roland Young, Ralph Richardson, Joan Gardner, Ernest Thesiger, Sophie Stewart, George Zucco, Bernard Nedell, George Sanders, Torin Thatcher.

F-com (capricious gods give meek man the power to do anything by simply thinking of it; at climax he stops world from rotating & causes cataclysmic destruction; gods put everything back the way they were before giving him power)

Ref: F/A p316; MPH 22 Aug '36 p40; FD 24 Feb '37; Borst; LC; FIR Aug'Sept '58 p379.

Based on the short story by H.G. Wells.

Man Who Had to Sing, The

(Čovjek Koji Je Morao Pjevati)

1970 US/Yugoslavian, Mass Media Associates/Zagreb color ani 9.6 mins.

Dir & Design: Milan Blažeković.

Story: Nedeljko Dragić.

Bg: Rudolf Borošak.

Mus: Tomislav Simović.

F-com (man sings inane song from cradle to grave & afterwards)

Ref: Z/Zagreb p 101-02.

Man Who Haunted Himself, The

1970 (1971) British, Excalibur (Levitt-Pickman) color 94 mins.

Prod: Michael Relph.

Dir: Basil Dearden.

SP: M. Relph & B. Dearden.

Man Who Haunted... cont.

Art Dir: Albert Witherick.

Cin: Tony Spratling.

SpFX: Thomas (Tommy) Howard & Charles Staffel.

Edit: Teddy Darvas.

Mus: Michael Lewis.

Cast: Roger Moore, Hildegard Neil, Olga Georges-Picot, Anton Rodgers, Freddie Jones, Thorley Walters, Charles Lloyd-Pack.

F-H (man pursues & is pursued by other, extrovert self released mystically by operation; ending ambiguous as to which one dies)

Ref: MFB Aug '70 p 166; Vw 29 July '70; FF '71 p485-86.

Based on story "The Case of Mr. Pelham" by Anthony Armstrong.

Man Who Laughs, The

● 1927 (1928) U sil w/syc sound FX & mus 10195 ft.

Prod: Carl Laemmle.

Dir: Paul Leni.

Prod Sup: Paul Kohner.

Story Sup: Bela Sekely.

Adapt: Charles E. Whittaker, Marion Ward, & May McLean.

Sc: J. Grubb Alexander.

Titles: Walter Anthony.

Tech & Art Dir: Charles D. Hall, Joseph Wright, & Thomas F. O'Neill.

Cin: Gilbert Warrenton.

Cast: Conrad Veidt, Mary Philbin, Olga Baclanova, Josephine Crowell, George Siegmann, Brandon Hurst, Sam De Grasse, Stuart Holmes, Edgar Norton, Julius Molnar Jr, Frank Puglia.

hist-H (circus performer whose face was carved into permanent grin as a child is discovered to be a member of English aristocracy)

Ref: AFI F2.3432 p486; Vw 2 May '28; FD 6 May '28; LC.

● (L'Uomo Che Ride)

1965 (1971) Italian/French, Sanson/C.I.P.R.A. color.

Prod: Joseph Fryd.

Dir: Sergio Corbucci.

SP: S. Cobucci, Rosetti, Filippo Sanjust, Issaverdens, & Bertolotto.

Art Dir: Allessandro Dell' Orco.

Cin: Enzo Barboni.

Edit: Mario Serandrei.

Mus: Piero Piccioni.

Cast: Jean Sorel, Ilaria Occhini, Edmond Purdom, Lisa Gastoni.

hist-H (circus performer with grin permanently cut into face; super-disguise makes him look ordinary & like someone else)

Ref: Ital Prods '65 p54-55; Pardi.

Based on novel "L'Homme Qui Rit" by Victor Hugo.

See also: Homme Qui Rit, L' (1909); Grinsende Gesicht, Das (1921).

Man Who Learned to Fly, The

1908 British, Hepworth sil 300 ft.

Dir: Lewin Fitzhamon.

F-dream ("inventor dreams he is flattened by roller and flown as a kite")

Ref: Gifford/BFC 01924.

Man Who Lived Again, The

(The Man Who Changed His Mind --Brit.t.; The Brainsnatcher -- rr.t.; Dr. Maniac --rr.t.)

1936 British, Gainsborough (Gaum) 68 mins.

Dir: Robert Stevenson.

SP: L. du Garde Peach, Sidney Gilliat, & John L. Balderston.

Man Who Lived Again cont.

Makeup: Roy Ashton.

Cin: Jack Cox.

Edit: R.E. Dearing.

Cast: Boris Karloff, Anna Lee, John Loder, Frank Cellier, Lynn Harding, Cecil Parker, Donald Calthrop.

SF-H (Karloff can switch minds with electrical apparatus; exchanges own mind with that of young man so he can have girl who loves the young man, but minds switched back at climax)

Ref: HR 26 Sept '36; LC; Vw 23 Sept '36, 23 Oct '36; LSH 1:10; FD 16 Dec '36.

Man Who Lived Twice, The

1936 Col 73 mins.

Prod: Ben Pivar.

Exec Prod: Irving Briskin.

Dir: Harry Lachman.

Story: Tom Van Dycke & Henry Altimus.

SP: T. Van Dycke, Fred Niblo Jr, & Arthur Strawn.

Cin: James Van Trees.

Edit: Byron Robinson.

Cast: Ralph Bellamy, Marian Marsh, Thurston Hall, Isabel Jewell, Nana Bryant, Ward Bond.

bor-SF (operation on criminal removes his criminal tendencies & his memory; face altered from ugly to handsome, becomes famous doctor)

Ref: HR 19 Oct '36; Vw 14 Oct '36; FD 13 Oct '36.

See also remake: Man in the Dark (1953).

Man Who Made Diamonds, The

1937 British, First Nat'l 73 mins.

Prod: Irving Asher.

Dir: Ralph Ince.

SP: Frank A. Richardson.

Cast: Noel Madison, Lesley Brook, George Galleon, Wilfrid Lawson, Renee Gadd.

bor-SF (great deal of electricity required to make artificial diamonds)

Ref: MFB '37; Gifford/BFC 10270.

Man Who Reclaimed His Head

1934 (1935) U 80 mins.

Prod: Carl Laemmle Jr.

Assoc Prod: Henry Henigson.

Dir: Edward Ludwig.

SP: Jean Bart & Samuel Ornits.

Cin: Merritt Gerstad.

Edit: Murray Seldeen.

Cast: Claude Rains, Lionel Atwill, Joan Bennett, Baby Jane, Henry O'Neill, Wallace Ford, Gilbert Emery, Henry Armetta, Lawrence Grant, Rollo Lloyd, F. Gottschalk.

bor-H (at climax Rains decapitates Atwill, carries his head in bag)

Ref: HR 1 Dec '34; AHF p225; MFB '49 p213; FD 8 Jan '35.

Based on the play by Jean Bart.

See also remake: Strange Confession (1945).

Man Who Saw Tomorrow, The

1922 Famous Players (Par) sil 7 reels.

Pres: Adolph Zukor.

Dir: Alfred E. Green.

Sc: Will Ritchey & Frank Condon.

Cin: Alvin Wyckoff.

Cast: Thomas Meighan, Theodore Roberts, Leatrice Joy, Albert Roscoe, Alec Francis, June Elvidge, Eva Novak.

cont.   cont.   cont.   cont.

Man Who Saw Tomorrow cont.

psy-F (man sees future through hypnotism)

Ref: AFI F2.3437 p487; LC; Photo Jan '23; MPN 26:2433.

Based on novel ("The Prophet"?) by Perley Poore Sheehan.

Man Who Sold His Soul, The
See: Homme Qui Vendit Son Ame, L' (1943).

Man Who Sold His Soul to the Devil, The
(novel by P. Veber)
See: Homme Qui Vendit Son Ame au Diable, L' (1920); Homme Qui Vendit Son Ame, L' (1943).

Man Who Stole the Moon, The
See: Sky Ranger, The (1921).

Man Who Thought Things, The
See: Mandem der Taenkte Ting (1969).

Man Who Turned to Stone, The
(The Petrified Man --e.t.)
1956 (1957) Clover (Col) 80 mins.

Prod: Sam Katzman.

Dir: Leslie Kardos.

SP: Raymond T. Marcus.

Art Dir: Paul Palmentola.

Cin: Benjamin H. Kline.

Edit: Charles Nelson.

Mus: Ross DiMaggio.

Cast: Victor Jory, Ann Doran, Charlotte Austin, William Hudson, Paul Cavanagh, Frederick Ledebur, Barbara Wilson.

SF-H (group of 18th-century scientists keep themselves alive into 20th century by taking energy from young women, which kills women; without treatment, the men's skin turns to stone & they die)

Ref: FD 21 Feb '57; MFB Oct '57 p 128; HR & Vd 15 Feb '57.

Man Who Wagged His Tail, The
(Un Angel Paso Sobre Brooklyn: An Angel Passed Over Brooklyn; Un Angelo E Sceso a Brooklyn; An Angel Has Come to Brooklyn)
1957 (1961) Spanish/Italian, Chamartin/Falco (Continental Distributing) 91 mins.

Prod & Dir: Ladislao Vajda.

SP: Istvan Bekeffi, L. Vajda, O. Alessi, & Ugo Guerra.

Cin: Enrique Guerner.

Edit: Juan Penas.

Mus: Bruno Camfora.

Cast: Peter Ustinov, Pablito Calva, Aroldo Tieri, Silvia Marco, Maurizio Arena, José Isbert, Caligola (the dog).

F-com (meanest man in Brooklyn has curse placed on him by magical seller of fairy tales: he is turned into large mongrel dog, turned back into human when little boy he saved as dog tells him he loves him)

Ref: FF '61 p269-70; Vw 25 Sept '57; NYT 19 Sept '61.

Man Who Walked Through the Wall, The
(Ein Mann Geht Durch die Wand: A Man Goes Through the Wall)
1960 (1964) German (Shawn Int'l) 98 mins.

Prod: Kurt Ulrich.

Dir: Ladislao Vajda.

SP: Istvan Bekeffi & Hans Jacoby.

Cin: Bruno Mondi.

Cast: Heinz Rühmann, Nicole Courcel, Anita V. Ow, Rudolf Rhomberg, Peter Vogel.

F-com (man finds he can walk through walls)

Ref: Vw 2 March '60; BO 2 Nov '64; FIR Dec '60 p605.

Man Who Walked Through Wall cont.

Based on novel "Le Passe Muraille" by Marcel Aymé.

See also: Mr. Peek-A-Boo (1950).

Man Who Walked Through Walls, The
See: Mr. Peek-A-Boo (1950).

Man Who Wanted to Live Forever, The
(The Only Way Out Is Dead --Brit.t.)
1970 Canadian, Palomar (ABC-TV) color 88 mins (75 mins).

Exec Prod: Edgar J. Scherick & Henry Denker.

Prod: Terence Dene.

Dir: John Trent.

SP: H. Denker.

Art Dir: Jack McAdam.

Cin: Marc Champion.

Mus: Dolores Claman.

Cast: Stuart Whitman, Sandy Dennis, Burl Ives, Tom Harvey, Robert Goodier, Jack Creley.

bor-SF (Ives plays billionaire invalid capturing young men to use as future sources for transplants)

Ref: TVG; MFB Feb '71 p27.

Man Who Wouldn't Die, The
1942 20th-Fox 73 mins (65 mins).

Exec Prod: Sol M. Wurtzel.

Dir: Herbert I. Leeds.

SP: Arnaud d'Usseau.

Art Dir: Lewis Creber.

Cin: Joseph P. MacDonald.

Edit: Fred Allen.

Mus Dir: Emil Newman.

Cast: Lloyd Nolan, Marjorie Weaver, Helene Reynolds, Henry Wilcoxon, Richard Derr, Jeff Corey, Francis Ford.

bor-F-H (yogi simulates death, comes out of grave; chair prolongs life)

Ref: HR & Vd 16 April '42; MFB July '42 p88; FD 17 April '42; LC.
Based on novel "No Coffin for the Corpse" by Clayton Rawson and the character "Michael Shayne" created by Brett Halliday.

Man Whose Price Went Up, The
1968 Czech, Filmexport.

Dir: Jan Moravec & Zdenek Podskalsky.

Cast: Jozef Kroner, Jana Ticha, Otakar Janda.

alleg-F (wife of man who has permitted a picture to be painted on his back for public exhibition gives birth to twins who each have the same painting on their backs)

Ref: MTVM June '68 p28.

Man with a Camera
See: Man with the Camera (1928).

Man with a Thousand Inventions, The
See: Homme aux Mille Inventions, L' (1910).

Man with Nine Lives, The
(Behind the Door --Brit.t.)
1940 Col 73 mins.

Dir: Nick Grinde.

Story: Harold Shumate.

SP: Karl Brown.

Art Dir: Lionel Banks.

Edit: Al Clark.

Cast: Boris Karloff, Jo Ann Sayers, Roger Pryor, Hal Taliaferro, Byron Foulger, Charles Trowbridge, Ernie Adams.

SF-H (scientist Karloff, missing several years, is found frozen alive in his ice-encased lab; revived, he attempts to do the same thing to hero)

Man with Nine Lives cont.

Ref: FD 3 May '40; LC; AHF p 176; FIR March '64 p 155.

Man with the Brain Graft, The
See: Homme au Cerveau Greffe, L' (1972).

Man with the Camera
(Chelovek Kinoapparatom: Man with a Camera, The Man with the Movie Camera)
1928 (1929) Soviet, Vufku (Amkino) sil 6000 ft.

Prod, Dir, Sc: Dziga Vertov.

Cin: Mikhail Kaufman.

Edit: E. Svilova.

Cast: Mikhail Kaufman.

doc; F-seq (at one point camera comes to life & walks on its tripod)

Ref: LA p86; FTN p245, 7, 681; MPN 41:11:92; C to H p 185.

Man with the Electric Voice, The
See: Fifteen Wives (1934).

Man with the Gadget, The
See: Mann mit dem Objektiv, Der (1963).

Man with the Golden Fist
See: Uomo dal Pugno d'Oro, L' (1967).

Man with the Iron Head, The
1912 British, Cricks & Martin sil 420 ft.

F-com (man has invulnerable head)

Ref: Bios 9 May '12.

Man with the Iron Heart, The
1915 Selig sil 3 reels.

Dir: George O. Nicholls Jr.

Author: Henry Kolker.

F (death is personified)

Ref: LC; MPN 4 Sept '15.

Man with the Limp, The
1923 British, Stoll sil 2 reels.

Dir: A.E. Colby.

Cast: Harry Agar Lyons, Fred Paul, H. Humbertson Wright, Joan Clarkson, Frank Wilson.

bor-F-H

Ref: MMF 14:34; BFI cat.
Based on characters created by Sax Rohmer.

See also: Mystery of Dr. Fu Manchu, The (1923).

Man with the Movie Camera
See: Man with the Camera (1928).

Man with the Puppets, The
1912 Danish, Nordisk (Great Northern) sil sh.

F (puppets come to life by violin playing)

Ref: MPW 11:336, 483.

Man with the Rubber Head, The
(L'Homme à la Tête en Caoutchouc; The India Rubber Head --alt.t.?)
1901 French, Star sil 165 ft.

Made by: Georges Méliès.

F (man puts his head on table, inflates it)

Ref: Sadoul/M, GM Mage 382-83.

Man with the Transplanted Brain, The
See: Homme au Cerveau Greffe, L' (1972).

Man with the Whistling Nose, The
See: Seventh Floor, The (1966).

Man with the X-Ray Eyes, The
See: "X" the Man with X-Ray Eyes (1963).

Man with the Yellow Eyes
See: Planets Against Us (1961).

Man with Two Faces
(The Mysterious Mr. Chautard --e.t.?)
1934 FN 72 mins.

Dir: Archie Mayo.

SP: Tom Reed & Niven Busch.

Cin: Tony Gaudio.

Edit: William Holmes.

Cast: Edward G. Robinson, Mary Astor, Ricardo Cortez, Louis Calhern, John Eldredge, Arthur Byron, Mae Clarke, Henry O'Neill.

bor-F-H (man holds wife under hypnotic spell)

Ref: Vd 24 May '34; LC; Photo Aug '34 p51.

Based on play "The Dark Tower" by George S. Kaufman and Alexander Woolcott.

Man with 2 Heads, The
(Dr. Jekyll and Mr. Blood --s.t.)
1971 (1972) British/US, Constitution/Wm. Mishkin color 80 mins.

Prod: William Mishkin.

Dir, SP, Cin: Andy Milligan.

Cast: Denis DeMarne, Julia Stratton, Gay Feld, Jacqueline Lawrence, Berwick Kaler, Bryan Southcombe.

SF-H (in effort to separate man's good side from his evil, Jekyll takes potion which instead brings out only his evil nature, Mr. Blood)

Ref: Vd 24 Sept '69, 29 Dec '71; BO 29 May '72 Booking Guide.

Based on short novel "The Strange Case of Dr. Jekyll and Mr. Hyde" by Robert Louis Stevenson.

See also: Dr. Jekyll and Mr. Hyde.

Man with Two Heads
See: Thing with 2 Heads, The (1972).

Man with Two Lives, The
1942 Mono 65 mins.

Prod: A.W. Hackel.

Dir: Phil Rosen.

SP: Joseph Hoffman.

Cin: Harry Neumann.

Edit: Martin G. Cohn.

Mus Dir: Frank Sanucci.

Cast: Edward Norris, Marlo Dwyer, Eleanor Lawson, Frederick Burton, Addison Richards, Hugh Sothern, Anthony Warde, Kenne (Kenneth) Duncan.

F-H-dream (Norris is killed, then returned to life by scientist; but soul of gangster, electrocuted at same moment, takes over Norris' mind)

Ref: Vd & HR 9 March '42; MFB Aug '42 p 101; FDY '43.

Man with Wax Faces, The
See: Homme aux Figures de Cire, L' (1913).

Man with Wheels in His Head, The
(Le Malade Hydrophope)
1900 French, Star sil 65 ft.

Made by: Georges Méliès.

F-com

Ref: Sadoul/M, GM Mage 315.

Man with Yellow Eyes, The
See: Planets Against Us (1961).

Man Within, The
See: Andere, Der (1930).

Man Without a Body, The
1957 (1958) British, Filmplays Ltd. (Budd Rogers) 80 mins.

Prod: Guido Coen.

cont.

Man Without a Body cont.

Dir: W. Lee Wilder & Charles Saunders.

SP: William Grote.

Art Dir: Harry White.

Makeup: Jim Hydes.

Cin: Brendan Stafford.

Edit: Tom Simpson.

Mus: Robert Elms.

Cast: Robert Hutton, George Coulouris, Julia Arnall, Nadja Regin, Sheldon Lawrence, Kim Parker, Tony Quinn, Michael Golden [Nostradamus].

SF-H (scientist brings disembodied head of Nostradamus back to life, it makes accurate predictions; head eventually attached to headless body)

Ref: MFB June '57 p73; PB; Dyer; Pardi.

Man Without a Face, The

See: Hombre sin Rostro, El (1950).

Man Without a Soul, The

See: I Believe (1916).

Man Without Desire, The

1922 (1924) British, Atlas-Biograph sil 7000 ft.

Prod: Miles Lander.

Dir: Adrian Brunel.

Idea: Monckton Hoffe.

Sc: Frank Fowell.

Cin: Henry Harris.

Cast: Ivor Novello, Nina Vanna, Sergio Mari, Christopher Walker, Adrian Brunel, Jane Dryden, Dorothy Warren.

F (suspended animation by hypnosis for centuries; reincarnation of lost love)

Ref: Destiny p224; BFI cat p 124; Vw 12 March '24.

Man Woman and Dog

1964 Japanese ani sh.

Dir: Yoji Kuri.

F

Ref: Ani/Cin p 173.

Manassa Devi

1937 Indian, Madras.

Dir: Jayagopal Pillai.

Cast: A. Sundaram, Bhanumathi, Saraswathi, Shanti Anand.

myth-F

Ref: Movie Herald May '37 p48 ad.

Manbeast

See: Man Beast (1955).

Manchurian Candidate, The

1962 An M.C. Prod. (UA) 126 mins.

Exec Prod: Howard W. Koch.

Prod: George Axelrod & John Frankenheimer.

Dir: J. Frankenheimer.

SP: G. Axelrod.

Prod Design: Richard Sylbert.

Cin: Lionel Lindon.

SpFX: Paul Pollard.

Edit: Ferris Webster.

Mus: David Amram.

Cast: Frank Sinatra, Laurence Harvey, Janet Leigh, Angela Lansbury, Henry Silva, James Gregory, Leslie Parrish, John McGiver, Khigh Dhiegh, James Edwards, Albert Paulsen, Lloyd Corrigan, Whit Bissell, William Thourlby, Robert Burton.

bor-psy-SF-H (patrol of US soldiers in Korea captured & elaborately brainwashed; one is programmed to assassinate US presidential candidate)

Ref: FF '62 p243-45; MFB Dec '62 p 168; Vw 17 Oct '62; NYT 25 Oct '62; Time 3 Nov '62; SR 27 Oct '62.

Based on the novel by Richard Condon.

See also: Psycho Lover, The (1971).

Mandala

1953 Amateur 16mm color ani 3 mins.

Made by: Jordan Belson.

exp-F

Ref: FC 48/49:14; Undrgnd p 116.

Mandala

1968 BYM Prods (Center Cinema) 16mm color ani 4 mins.

exp-F

Ref: CFS cat Sept '68; CCC cat 2:7.

Mandem der Taenkte Ting

(The Man Who Thought Things)

1969 Danish, Asa Film (Palladium) 97 mins.

Dir: Jens Ravn.

SP: Henrik Stangerup.

Cin: Witold Leszczynski.

Mus: Per Noergaard.

Cast: Preben Neergaard, John Price, Lotte Tarp.

F (man can will things into existence; asks doctor for operation so he can keep things alive; doctor refuses so man makes double of doctor; double operates on man, who then dies)

Ref: Vw 21 May '69.

Based on novel by Valdemar Holst.

Mandir

1937 Indian, Shri Shanka 144 mins.

Dir: A.R. Kardar.

Cast: Agha Mahomed Shah, Rajkmari, Dhiraj Bhattacharji.

myth-F (virgin birth; child found in riverbed, grows into manhood after being adopted by king whose arrogance the gods are trying to correct)

Ref: Lighthouse 6 Nov '37 p7.

Mandragora

See: Alraune.

Mandrake

See: Alraune.

Mandrake the Magician

1939 Col serial 12 parts 25 reels.

Exec Prod: Irving Briskin.

Prod: Jack Fier.

Dir: Sam Nelson & Norman Deming.

SP: Joseph F. Poland, Basil Dickey, & Ned Dandy.

Cin: Benjamin Kline.

Edit: Richard Fantl.

Mus: Lee Zahler.

Cast: Warren Hull, Doris Weston, Al Kikume, Rex Downing, Edward Earle, Don Beddoe, Ernie Adams, George Chesebro, George Turner.

SF (deadly machine creates radium energy)

Ref: Ser/Col; LC; MPH 13 May '39 p43; TBC.

Based on the King Features syndicate comic strip by Lee Falk and Phil Davis.

See also: Witches, The (1965).

Manfish

1956 UA color 76 mins.

Prod & Dir: W. Lee Wilder.

Story: Myles Wilder.

SP: Joel Murcott.

Cin: Charles S. Wellborn.

Edit: C. Turnley Smith.

Mus: Albert Elms.

Cast: John Bromfield, Lon Chaney (Jr), Victor Jory, Barbara Nichols, Tessa Predergas, Eric Coverly, Vincent Chang.

myst; bor-H (bubbles give away location of murdered diver)

Ref: FDY '57; Pardi.

Manfish cont.

Loosely based on short stories "The Tell-Tale Heart" and "The Gold Bug" by Edgar Allan Poe.

See also: Tell-Tale Heart, The.

Mangala

1950 Indian, Gemini 175 mins.

Prod & Dir: S.S. Vasan.

Dialog & Songs: Pandit Indra.

Art Dir: Syed Ahamed.

Cin: Kamal Ghosh.

Edit: Chandru.

Mus Dir: M.D. Parthasarathy.

Cast: Bhanumati, Ranjan, Suryaprabha, Aga, David, Narayana Rao.

myth-F

Ref: Indian MPA '53 p30.

Mangayarakarasi

1949 Indian, Bhaghya 172 mins.

Prod: F. Nagor & S.N. Ahmad.

Dir: Jiten Banerji.

Story & Songs: Kambadasan.

Dialog: Surada.

Art Dir: F. Nagoor.

Cin: P.S. Selvaraj.

Edit: Nataraja Mudaliar.

Mus Dir: Kunnapoodi Venketramayya Iyer.

Cast: P.D. Chinnappa, N.S. Krishnan, Kambadasan, Puthukottai Seenu, P.A. Kumar.

myth-F

Ref: Indian MPA '53 p67.

Mangu

1955 Indian (in Hindustani), Sheikh Muhhtar Prods.

Dir: N.A. Ansari.

SP: Tahir Luckowi.

Cin: S. Srivastava.

Lyrics: Majrooh Sultanpuri.

Cast: Nigar Sultana, Mukhtar, Sheila Ramani, Mukri, Ansari.

bor-F (serum causes person to be another's total slave for a short time)

Ref: Filmindia April '55.

Manhandling Ethel

(story by F.R. Adams)

See: Enchantment (1921).

Manhunt in Space

1954 Reed (MCA-TV) 78 mins.

Prod: Roland Reed.

Cast: Richard Crane, Sally Mansfield.

SF (invisible spaceship)

Ref: Willis.

See also: Rocky Jones, Space Ranger.

Manhunt in the African Jungle

See: Secret Service in Darkest Africa (1943).

Manhunt of Mystery Island

1945 Rep serial 15 parts 31 reels.

Also edited to 100 minute TV version in 1966 under the title Captain Mephisto and the Transformation Machine.

Assoc Prod: Ronald Davidson.

Dir: Spencer Bennet, Wallace A. Grissell, & Yakima Canutt.

SP: Albert DeMond, Basil Dickey, Jesse Duffy, Alan James, Grant Nelson, & Joseph Poland.

Cin: Bud Thackery.

SpFX: Howard & Theodore Lydecker.

Mus: Richard Cherwin.

Cast: Richard Bailey, Linda Sterling, Roy Barcroft, Kenne Duncan, Forrest Taylor, Forbes Murray, Jack Ingram, Lane

cont.

Manhunt of Mystery Island cont.

Chandler, Russ Vincent, Dale Van Sickel, Tom Steele, Eddie Parker.

SF (with the aid of a "transformation chair" a man can turn himself into exact replica of pirate ancestor; pocket TV camera; "radium detector;" "radatomic power transmitter;" rays)

Ref: Ser/Rep; STI 3:10, 17, 51; TBC; LC; FDY '58.

Mania

(The Flesh and the Fiends; The Fiendish Ghouls --title of shorter 1965 rr)

1960 (1961; 1965 --Pacemaker) British, Triad (Valiant; Pacemaker) scope 97 mins (84 mins --1965 rr).

Prod: Robert S. Baker & Monty Berman.

Dir: John Gilling.

SP: J. Gilling & Leon Griffiths.

Art Dir: John Elphick.

Cin: Monte Berman.

Edit: Jack Slade.

Mus: Stanley Black.

Cast: Peter Cushing, June Laverick, Donald Pleasence, Dermot Walsh, Renee Houston, George Rose, Billie Whitelaw, John Cairney, George Woodbridge.

hist-H (Burke & Hare are body snatchers who deliver their wares to Dr. Knox; they turn to murder when needed)

Ref: FF '61 p321; Vw 10 Feb '60; FD 12 March '65.

Based on the actual case of Burke, Hare and Knox, tried in Scotland in the early 19th Century.

See also: Body Snatcher, The (1945).

Maniac

(Sex Maniac --alt.t?)

1934 Roadshow Attractions 6 reels.

Prod & Dir: Dwain Esper.

SP: Hildegarde Stadie.

Cast: Horace Carpenter, Phyllis Diller.

bor-SF-H (rapist-murderer; black cat gives away crime; mad scientist)

Ref: FIR Jan '62 p62; LC; Ackerman; Willis.

Partly based on short story "The Black Cat" by Edgar Allan Poe.

See also: Black Cat, The.

Maniac Barber, The

1902 Biograph sil 115 ft.

F-com (barber removes customer's head, shaves it, replaces it, & customer leaves)

Ref: Niver 63.

Manifesto

n.d. Amateur (Film-makers' Coop) 16mm? color 4 mins.

Made by: Richard Preston.

Sound by: Max Roach.

exp-abs-F

Ref: FMC 5:267.

Mankinda

1957 Amateur (Film-makers' Coop; Grove) 16mm ani painting 10 mins.

Made by: Stan VanDerBeek.

exp-F

Ref: FMC 5:321.

Mann Geht Durch die Wand, Ein

See: Man Who Walked Through the Wall, The (1960).

Mann mit dem Objektiv, Der

(The Man with the Gadget)

1963 E. German, DEFA feature.

Dir: Frank Vogel.

cont.

Mann mit dem Objektiv cont.

SP: Paul Wiens.

Cin: Horst Hardt.

Cast: Rolf Ludwig, Christine Laszar, Otto Stark, Helga Labudda, Erik S. Klein.

SF (man from future sent to 1960 brings a mind-reading device with him)

Ref: LSH 2:68; Pessina.

Mannen Unan Ansikte

See: Face of Fire (1959).

Mannikins of Horror

(story by R. Bloch)

See: Asylum (1972).

Mano de un Hombre Muerto, La

(The Hand of a Dead Man)

1963 Spanish, Albatross.

Dir: Jesus Franco.

Story: David Kuhne.

SP: Juan Cobos, G.S. de Erice, J. Franco, & P. Ballesteros.

Art Dir: Andres Vallve.

Cin: Godofredo Pacheco.

Mus: Daniel J. White.

Cast: Howard Vernon, Paula Martel, Fernando Delgado, Ana Castor, Georges Rollin, Gogo Robins.

F-H (present day crimes seem to have been committed by a ghost)

Ref: SpCin '64 p 115; CoF 4:48; MW 1:10.

Mano en la Trampa, La

See: Hand in the Trap, The (1962?).

Manoir de la Terreur, Le

See: Blancheville Monster, The (1964).

Manoir du Diable, Le

See: Haunted Castle, The (1896).

Manor of the Devil, The

See: Haunted Castle, The (1896).

Manos the Hands of Fate

1966? color 92 mins.

Cast: Tom Neyman, John Reynolds.

H (cult defaces women with a burning hand)

Ref: Ideal cat '69/70 p 112.

Man's Genesis

1912 Biograph sil 1035 ft.

Dir & Sc: D.W. Griffith.

Cin: G.W. (Billy) Bitzer.

Cast: Robert Harron, Mae Marsh, Wilfred Lucas, Walter Chrystie Miller.

bor-SF (story of cavemen in the Stone Age; invention of the axe)

Ref: MPW 13:72, 343; Niver/20 p 164; RAF p 113; LC; Blum p32.

See also: Brute Force (1913).

Manster, The

(The Split --s.t.)

1959 (1962) US/Japanese, Breakston/Shaw (Lopert) 72 mins (67 mins).

Prod: George P. Breakston.

Dir: G.P. Breakston & Kenneth G. Crane.

SP: Walter J. Sheldon.

Art Dir: Nobori Miyakuni.

Cin: David Mason.

Edit: K.G. Crane.

Mus: Hirooki Ogawa.

Cast: Peter Dyneley, Jane Hylton, Satoshi Nakamura, Terry Zimmern, Van Hawley, Toyoko Takeichi, Jerry Ito.

cont.

Manster cont.

SF-H (man gradually grows 2nd monstrous head while his own head becomes monstrous as well; finally splits into normal self & hairy monster, which is knocked into volcano; deformed women)

Ref: FF '62 p362; MFB May '61 p67; FEFN 12:16/17:25.

Based on story "Nightmare" by George P. Breakston.

Mantel, Der

See: Overcoat, The (1955).

Mantis in Lace

1968 Boxoffice Int'l color 73 mins.

Exec Prod: Harry H. Novak.

Prod & SP: Sanford White.

Dir: William Rotsler.

Set Design: Frank Borass.

Makeup: Mike Weldon.

Cin: Leslie (Laszlo) Kovacs.

Edit: Peter Perry.

Mus: Frank Coe.

Cast: Susan Stewart, Steve Vincent, M.K. Evans, Vic Lance, Pat Barrington.

psy-H (gory, brutal murders by girl undergoing LSD hallucinations, including vision of giant insect)

Ref: PB; BO 2 Sept '68; MMF 22:23.

Manugang ni Drakula, Mga

(The Secrets of Dracula)

1964 Philippine.

F-H (vampires)

Ref: MTVM 15 Feb '64 p41; Photon 21:27.

Based on a character created by Bram Stoker.

See also: Dracula.

Manuscript Found in Saragossa, The

See: Saragossa Manuscript, The (1964).

Manutara

See: Vulture, The (1966).

Many Days Have Passed

See: Bahut Din Huwe (1954).

Many Ghost Cats

See: Kaibyo Ranbu (1956).

Many Headed Man

See: Four Troublesome Heads, The (1898).

Many Moons

(story by J. Thurber)

See: Alice of Wonderland in Paris (1966).

Mara of the Wilderness

1965 (1966) Unicorn (AA) color 90 mins.

Filmed in Alaska.

Exec Prod: Lindsley Parsons.

Prod: Brice Mack.

Dir: Frank McDonald.

Story: Rod Scott.

SP: Tom Blackburn.

Art Dir: Michael Haller.

Cin: Robert Wyckoff.

Edit: Harold M. Gordon.

Mus: Harry Bluestone.

Cast: Adam West, Linda Saunders, Theo Marcuse, Denver Pyle, Sean McClory, Eve Brent, Ed Kemmer.

bor-F (girl, orphaned in wilds of Alaska, grows up cared for by wolves)

Ref: Vw 22 Feb '66; FF '66 p348.

Marat/Sade

(The Persecution and Assassination of Jean-Paul Marat as Performed by the Inmates of the Asylum of Charenton Under the Direction of the Marquis de Sade --alt.t.)

cont.

Marat/Sade cont.

1967 British, A Marat Sade Prod. (UA) color 116 mins.

Prod: Michael Birkett.

Dir: Peter Brook.

Adapt: Adrian Mitchell.

Prod Design: Sally Jacobs.

Art Dir: Ted Marshall.

Cin: David Watkin.

Edit: Tom Priestley.

Mus: Richard Peaslee.

Cast: Patrick Magee, Glenda Jackson, Freddie Jones, Ian Richardson, Clifford Rose, Brenda Kempner, Ruth Baker, Michael Williams, Hugh Sullivan, Jonathan Burn, Jeanette Landis, Robert Lloyd, Susan Williamson.

H (scenes of insanity; set in 19th-century French insane asylum; torture)

Ref: FF '67 p23-25; Vw 8 Feb '67.

Based on play "The Persecution and Assassination of Jean-Paul Marat as Performed by the Inmates of the Asylum of Charenton Under the Direction of the Marquis de Sade" by Peter Weiss as translated by Geoffrey Skelton.

Marble, The

1966? Amateur color 16mm? sh.

Made by: John Primm.

rel-F (miracle in modern times)

Ref: CineF July '67.

Marble Forest, The

(novel by T. Durrant)

See: Macabre (1958).

Marble Returns, The

1951 British, GB Instructional 11 mins.

Dir: Darrell Catling.

F ("marble changes boy into fairy and father into midget, Indian and Sherlock Holmes")

Ref: Gifford/BFC 11565.

Sequel to Magic Marble, The (1951).

Marc Mato, Agente S. 077

See: Espionage in Tangiers (1963).

Marca de Satanas, La

(The Mark of Satan)

1958 Mexican (Clasa-Mohme).

Dir: Chano Urueta.

Cast: Luis Aguilar, Flor Silvestre, Crox Alvarado, America Martin, Pascual Garcia Peña.

F-H (headless rider; monster)

Ref: PS 815; FM 31:22.

Marca del Hombre Lobo, La

See: Frankenstein's Bloody Terror (1968).

Marca del Muerto, La

(The Mark of Death)

1961? (1962) Mexican, Alameda (Clasa-Mohme & Azteca).

Dir: Fernando Cortes.

Story: José M. Fernandez Unsain.

SP: F. Cortes & Alfredo Varela Jr.

Cin: José Ortiz Ramos.

Mus: Gustavo Cesar Carrion.

Cast: Fernando Casanova, Sonia Furio, Pedro de Aquillón, Aurora Alvarado, Rosa María Gallardo, E. Espino.

F-H (revived corpse?)

Ref: PS C1145; FM 33:10, 12, 38:39; FDY '63; Ackerman.

See also: Creature of the Walking Dead (1965).

Marcelino

(Marcelino Pan y Vino: Marcelino Bread and Wine; The Miracle of Marcelino --alt.t?)

1954 (1956) Spanish, Chamartin (United Motion Picture Organization) 90 mins.

Dir: Ladislao Vajda.

SP: L. Vajda & José María Sanches-Silva.

Cin: Enrique Guerner.

Edit: Julio Peña.

Mus: Pablo Sorozabal.

Cast: Pablito Calvo, Rafael Rivelles, Antonio Vico, Juan Calvo, José Marco Davo, Adriano Dominguez, Juan José Menendez, José Prada, Fernando Rey.

rel-F (the story of St. Marcelino: foundling grows to boyhood; innocently offers life-size crucifix bread & wine, & the statue comes down from the cross to accept the food; medieval setting)

Ref: FD 16 Oct '56 p6; Vw 1 June '55; PB; MFB Dec '55 p 176; Time 26 Nov '56.

Based on the novel by José María Sanches-Silva.

Marcello, I'm So Bored

1966? USC color ani 8 mins.

Made by: John Strawbridge & John Milius.

F

Ref: ASIFA 3.

See also: Take One (1970).

March Hare, The

1956 British, Achilles color scope 85 mins.

Prod: Bertram Ostrer & Albert Fennell.

Dir: George More O'Ferrall.

SP: Allan Mackinnon, Gordon Wellesley, & Paul Vincent Carroll.

Cast: Peggy Cummins, Terence Morgan, Wilfrid Hyde White, Martita Hunt, Cyril Cusack, Derrick de Marney, Charles Hawtrey, Maureen Delany, Ivan Samson, Macdonald Parke, Reginald Beckwith.

F-com (in Ireland, fairy gives trainer a magic word that enables his horse to win the derby)

Ref: Gifford/BFC 12202.

Based on novel "Gamblers Sometimes Win" by T.H. Bird.

March of the Machines, The

(La Marche des Machines)

1928 French sil sh.

Made by: Eugène Deslaw.

Cin: Boris Kaufman.

exp-abs-F

Ref: MMA '63 p56; T/F p 186; F/A p643.

March of the Wooden Soldiers

See: Babes in Toyland (1934).

Marchand des Notes, Le

1942 French ani sh.

Dir: Paul Grimault.

F

Ref: Sadoul p 125; Elements.

Marchand d'Images, Le

See: Fairy Bookseller, The (1910).

Marche des Machines, La

See: March of the Machines, The (1928).

Marche Funèbre de Chopin, La

See: Chopin's Funeral March (1907).

Marching the Colors

1942 Canadian, NFB 16mm color ani 3 mins.

Made by: Guy Glover.

abs-F

Ref: BFI dist cat sup 1:75; Ed Films p9.

Mare Nostrum

1926 Metro-Goldwyn sil
11000 ft (9894 ft.)

Prod & Dir: Rex Ingram.

Sc: Willis Goldbeck.

Cin: John F. Seitz.

Edit: Grant Whytock.

Cast: Alice Terry, Antonio
Moreno, Hughie Mack, Kithnou,
Paquerette, Fernand Mailly,
Andre von Engleman, Michael
Brantford, Uni Apollon [The Triton].

psy-F-seq (man joins Amphitrite
in death; gruesome symbolism)

Ref: Vw 17 Feb '26; MPW 78:
785-86; LC; Acad; AFI F2.3472.

Based on the novel by Vincente
Belasco Ibanez.

Margaritka

1965 Bulgarian color ani
7 mins.

Dir, Story, Design: Todor Dinov.

Decor: Gloria Hristova.

Ani: Gueorgui Stoianov,
Hristina Novakova, Emil
Abadjiev, & Anton Traianov.

Mus: Simeon Pironkov.

F

Ref: Annecy '65.

Margem, A

(The Margin)

n.d. Brazilian (Film-makers'
Coop) 16mm 65.5 mins.

Made by: Ouzualdo R. Candeias.

Mus: Luis Chaves.

Cast: Mario Benvenuti, Valeria
Vidal, Bentinho, Lucy Rangel.

F (big white barge & woman
appear on a river; 4 people
are "marked;" when they later
die because of love the barge
& woman appear again & take
them away)

Ref: FMC 5:55.

Margin, The

See: Margem, A (n.d.).

Marguerite

1971 Amateur color ani 4 mins.

Made by: Betty Yao-Jung Chen.

F

Ref: Vw 6 Oct '71; Genesis IV
Program.

See also: Genesis IV (1971).

Marguerite de la Nuit

(Marguerite of the Night)

1955 French/Italian color
126 mins.

Prod: León Carré.

Dir: Claude Autant-Lara.

SP: Ghislaine Autant'Lara &
Gabriel Arout.

Cin: Jacques Natteau.

Edit: Madeleine Gug.

Mus: René Cloërec.

Cast: Michèle Morgan, Yves
Montand [Devil], Jean-Françoise
Calve, Palau, Massimo Girotti,
Jean Delaucourt,Louis Seigner,
Fernand Sardou.

F (Dr. Faust is descendant of
the 15th Century Faust, becomes
infatuated with Marguerite &
forms pact with the Devil)

Ref: MFB Aug '57 p97-98;
Laclos p5; deGroote p261.

Based on the novel by Pierre
MacOrlan from the Faust legend.

See also: Faust.

Maria Marten

● (Maria Martin [sic] or The Murder in
the Red Barn)

1902 British, Harrison sil
400 ft.

Dir & Sc: Dicky Winslow.

Cast: A.W. Fitzgerald, Mrs.
Fitzgerald.

myst; F-seq (murderer exposed by
cont.

Maria Marten cont.

dream of his victim's mother)

Ref: Gifford/BFC 00602.

Based on the play of unknown
authorship.

Maria Marten; or
The Murder in the Red Barn

● 1913 British, Motograph sil
2850 ft.

Dir & Sc: Maurice Elvey.

Cast: Elizabeth Risdon, Fred
Groves, Douglas Payne, Nessie
Blackford, A.G. Ogden, Mary
Mackenzie, Maurice Elvey.

Ref: Gifford/BFC 04526.

● 1928 British, QTS sil 7430 ft.

Prod: Harry Rowson.

Dir: Walter West.

Cast: Trilby Clark, Warwick
Ward, James Knight, Charles
Ashton, Vesta Sylva, Frank
Perfitt, Dora Barton, Margot
Armand, Judd Green, Tom Morriss.

Ref: Gifford/BFC 08319.

myst; F-seq (in 1820s England
squire kills pregnant mistress
to wed heiress and is exposed
by her mother's dream)

Based on the play of unknown
authorship.

See also: Murder in the Red Barn,
The (1936).

Maria, the Wonderful Weaver

See: Magic Weaver, The (1960).

Mariage de Babylas, Le

See: Marriage of Babylas,
The (1921).

Mariage de l'Amour

See: Marriage of Cupid, The
(1914).

Marianne of My Youth

(Marianne de Ma Jeunesse)

1954 (1959) French/German,
Francinex & Royal/Filmsonor &
Regina (United) (105 mins).

Prod: Andre Daven.

Dir & SP: Julien Duvivier.

Sets: Jean D'Eaubonne.

Cin: L.H. Burel.

Edit: Marthe Poncin.

Mus: Jacques Ibert.

Cast: Marianne Hold, Pierre
Vaneck, Isabella Pia, Gil
Vidal, Jean Galland, Jean
Yonnel, Jacques De Feraudy,
Adi Berber.

bor-F (young man can charm
animals; falls in love with
phantom-like girl)

Ref: MFB July '69 p 155;
FIR Feb '59 p 112; FF '59 p 13;
IFC p41; deGroote 250.

Based on novel "Douloureuse
Arcadie" (Sorrowful Arcadia)
by Peter De Mendelssohn.

Marie Chantal contre Dr. Kha

1965 French/Spanish/Italian/
Moroccan, Dia/Mega/Uni/Maghreb
color 110 mins.

Prod: Georges De Beauregard.

Dir: Claude Chabrol.

SP: Christian Yve, Daniel
Boulanger, & C. Chabrol.

Cin: Jean Rabier.

Edit: Jacques Gaillard.

Cast: Marie Laforet, Francisco
Rabal, Akim Tamiroff, Serge
Reggiani, Charles Denner,
Roger Hanin, Stephane Audran.

F (quest for gem which gives
power over all mankind)

Ref: Vw 6 Oct '65; F&F April
'72 p44.

Based on the character created
by Jacques Chazot.

Marinetti

1965 Australian, Amateur
color 80 mins approx.

Prod, Dir, SP: Albie Thoms.

Cin: David Perry.

Mus: John Sangster.

Cast: Deborah Allard; Charlie
Brown; Lee, Marcus, & Nick
Casey; Brian Fitzpatrick;
Susan Howe; Pete Jackson;
Faith, Ian, & Sam Lightfoot;
Abigayl & David Perry; Judith
Rich; Clemency, Dickie, &
Toby Weight.

exp-F

Ref: Collier.

Inspired by F.T. Marinetti,
the founder of "Futurism."

Marinica

1953 Rumanian color ani
& live sh.

Dir: Ion Popescu Gopo.

Cin: C. Rad.

Mus: H. Malineanu.

Cast: Virginia Romanovschi,
Mircia Buciu.

F

Ref: Montevideo '56.

Based on the song.

Marinica's Bodkin

1955 Rumania ani & live
sh.

Dir: Ion Popescu Gopo.

F

Ref: Ani/Cin p 175.

Mario-Cartoons

1914 British, Bamforth &
Co. sil marionette series.

F

Ref: Hist/Brit p 101.

Based on drawings by A.K.
Hazelden appearing in the
"Daily Mirror," London.

Marionette

1963 Yugoslavian color
ani sh.

Dir: Borivoj Dovnikovic.

F

Ref: Ani/Cin p 169.

Marionetten

See: Marionettes (1958).

Marionettes

1939-48 British, Ace [amateur]
16mm 21 mins.

Made by: Ben Carleton.

F (puppeteer falls in love
with a puppet)

Ref: BFI Dist cat sup 1:79.

Marionettes

(Marionetten)

1958 German puppet sh.

Made by: Dieter H. Lemmel.

exp-F

Mariposas Negras

(Black Butterflies, Dark
Butterflies)

1953 Mexican.

Dir: Carlos Hugo Christensen.

SP: Guillermo Meneses, A. Naeza,
C.H. Christensen.

Cast: Arturo de Cordova,
Virginia Luque, Americo
Barrios.

F (voodoo love potion)

Ref: LAT 8 Dec '53; LA Daily
News 9 Dec '53.

Mark Donen Agente 27

(Mark Donen Agente Zet)

1966 Italian/Spanish/W. German,
CA.PI./Agata/Planet 90 mins.

Dir: Giancarlo Romitelli.

SP: G. Romitelli, Ennio De
Concini, & Robert Veller.
cont.

Mark Donen... cont.

Cin: Guglielmo Mancori.

Cast: Lang Jeffries, Laura
Velanzuela, Carlo Hinterman,
Mitsouko.

bor-SF (weapon uses sunlight)

Ref: Annuario (Willis).

Mark of Death, The

See: Marca del Muerto, Lo (1961?).

Mark of Satan, The

See: Marca de Satanas, La (1958).

Mark of Terror

See: Drums of Jeopardy (1931).

Mark of the Claw, The

See: Giant Claw, The (1957).

Mark of the Devil

(Brenn; Hexe, Brenn: Burn,
Witch, Burn)

1970 (1972) W.German/British,
Hi Fi Stereo 70/Adrian Hoven
(Hallmark) color 95 mins.

Prod: Adrian Hoven.

Dir: Michael Armstrong.

SP: Sergio Cassner.

Sets: Max Melin.

Cin: Ernst W. Kalinke.

Edit: Siegrun Jäger.

Mus: Michael Holm.

Cast: Herbert Lom, Olivera
Vuco, Udo Kier, Herbert Fux,
Reggie Nalder, Michael Maien,
Ingeborg Schoener.

hist-sex-H (sadistic tortures
in story of 17th-Century
witchfinder)

Ref: Vw 20 May '70; LAT 5
May '72; Pardi.

Mark of the Vampire

1935 MGM 60 mins.

Prod: E.J. Mannix.

Dir: Tod Browning.

Adapt: Guy Endore.

SP: G. Endore & Bernard
Schubert.

Art Dir: Cedric Gibbons.

Cin: James Wong Howe.

Edit: Ben Lewis.

Cast: Bela Lugosi, Lionel
Barrymore, Elizabeth Allan,
Jean Hersholt, Lionel Atwill,
Donald Meek, Carol (Carroll)
Borland, Holmes Herbert.

bor-F-H (murder made to look
like work of vampire; Dracula-
like fake vampire & flying
lady vampire -- actors hired
by police inspector)

Ref: HR 23 March '35; FD 28
March '35; AHF p 128; FM 19:22;
Photon 19; MPH 6 April '35 p48.

Based on film London After
Midnight (1927).

See also: Dracula.

Mark of the Vampire

See: Vampire, The (1957).

Mark of the West

See: Curse of the Undead (1959).

Mark of the Whistler

1944 Col 61 mins.

Prod: Rudolph C. Flothow.

Dir: William Castle.

Story: Cornell Woolrich.

SP: George Bricker.

Art Dir: John Datu.

Cin: George Meehan.

Edit: Reg Browne.

Mus: Wilbur Hatch.

Cast: Richard Dix, Janis Carter,
Porter Hall, Paul Guilfoyle,
John Calvert, Matt Willis.

myst; psy-F seqs ("The Whistler"
appears throughout film as the
voice of Fate)

Ref: VD 3 Oct '44; NY Herald
Tribune 11 Nov '44.

Based on the CBS radio show
"The Whistler."

See also: Whistler, The (1940).

Mark of the Witch

1972 (Favorite Films of Calif.)

Prod: Mary Davis & Tom Moore.

Dir: T. Moore.

Cast: Robert Elston, Anitra Walsh, Darryl Wells.

F-H ("a college campus terrorized by a killer witch --dead 300 years" --ad)

Ref: BO 8 May '72 pW2; Richardson.

Mark of the Wolf Man, The

See: Frankenstein's Bloody Terror (1968).

Mark Twain

(play by H.M. Sherman)

See: Adventures of Mark Twain, The (1944).

Markers of the Dead Lost Souls

Chicago drive-in ad retitling of Devil's Partner, The (1958).

Ref: D. Glut.

Market of Souls, The

1919 Ince sil 6 reels.

Prod: Thomas H. Ince.

Dir: Joseph De Grasse.

Story: John Lynch.

Sc: C. Gardner Sullivan.

Cin: John S. Stumar.

Cast: Dorothy Dalton, H.E. Herbert, Philo McCullough, Dorcas Mathews.

F-seq (spiritualism; ghost)

Ref: MPN 20:2467; LC.

Marley's Ghost

See: Scrooge (1901).

Marma Yogi

1951 Indian, Jupiter 174 mins.

Prod: Somasundaram.

Dir: K. Ramnoth.

SP: A.S.A. Samy.

Art Dir: A.K. Sekar.

Cin: M. Masthan.

Edit: M.A. Thirumugam.

Mus Dir: C.G. Subbaraman.

Cast: Anjali Devi, M.G. Ramachandran, S.V. Sahasranaman, Mathuri Devi.

bor-F (king escapes being drowned through yogi powers; fake ghost?)

Ref: Indian MPA '53 p72; Picturepost Feb '51 p33-35.

Marmite Diabolique, La

(The Diabolical Pot)

1903 French, Pathé sil sh.

Dir: Gaston Velle.

F

Ref: Filmlex p785.

Marooned

1969 Col color scope 134 mins.

Prod: M.J. Frankovich.

Assoc Prod: Frank Capra Jr.

Dir: John Sturges.

SP: Mayo Simon.

Prod Design: Lyle R. Wheeler.

Cin: Daniel Fapp.

SpFX: Lawrence W. Butler, Donald C. Glouner, & Robie Robinson.

Edit: Walter Thompson.

Cast: Gregory Peck, Richard Crenna, David Janssen, James Franciscus, Gene Hackman, Lee Grant, Nancy Kovack, Mariette Hartley, Scott Brady, Craig Huebing, John Carter, George Gaynes.

bor-SF (US manned satellite trapped in orbit; rescue craft launched through eye of hurricane)

Ref: FD 19 Nov '69; MFB '70 p48; Capra p492-93.

Based on the novel by Martin Caidin.

Marriage, The

1968 Italian ani sh.

Dir: Paul Campani.

F

Ref: ASIFA 5.

Marriage Chance, The

1922 Hampton Del Ruth Prods (American Releasing Corp) sil 5840 ft.

Dir & Sc: Hampton Del Ruth.

Cin: Dal Clawson.

Cast: Alta Allen, Milton Sills, Henry B. Walthall, Tully Marshall, Irene Rich, Mitchell Lewis.

com; H-dream (in dream: girl put in cataleptic trance, then taken from coffin by mad vivisectionist)

Ref: AFI F2.3479 p493.

Marriage Maker, The

1923 Famous Players-Lasky (Par) sil 7 reels (6295 ft).

Prod & Dir: William B. DeMille.

Sc: Clara Beranger.

Cin: L. Guy Wilky.

Cast: Agnes Ayres, Jack Holt, Charles de Roche [Faun], Robert Agnew, Mary Astor, Ethel Wales, Bertram Johns.

F (faun arranges various marriages, then returns to animal world)

Ref: MPN 28:1078, 1553; LC; F/A p423; AFI F2.3485 p494.

Based on play "The Faun" by Edward Knobloch.

Marriage of Babylas, The

(Le Mariage de Babylas)

1921 French, Polichinei-Film-Serie ani puppet & live sil 1150 ft.

Made by: Ladislas Starevitch.

Cast: Nina Star.

F-dream (in dream, dolls come to life)

Ref: BFI cat p49; Filmlex p930; Charles Ford; Scognamillo.

Marriage of Cupid, The

(Mariage de l'Amour; The Marriage of Psyche and Cupid --ad.t.)

1914 French, Pathé sil 1800 ft.

myth-F (Cupid, Venus, Psyche, other mythological figures played by dancers)

Ref: MPW 20:710, 944, 1117; LC.

Marriage of Mrs. Marcipan

See: Zenidba Gospodina Marcipana (1963).

Marriage of Psyche and Cupid, The

See: Marriage of Cupid, The (1914).

Marriage of the Bear, The

(Lokis: The Bear; Legend of the Bear's Wedding; The Bear's Wedding --ad.ts; Medvezhya Svadba: Wedding of the Bear)

1926 (1928) Soviet, Mezhrab-pom-Russ (Amkino) sil 7350 ft.

Dir: Vladimir Gardin & Konstantin V. Eggert.

Sc: Georgi Grebner & Anatol Lunacharsky.

Art Dir: Vladimir Yegorov.

Cin: Eduard Tisse & Pyotr Ermolov (Yermolov).

Cast: K.V. Eggert, Vera Malanovskaya, Natalya Rosenel, Yuri Zavadsky, A. Geirot.

F-H (man turns into bear at his wedding)

Ref: F/A p315; Vw 1 Aug '28; FD 23 Dec '28; FTN p227; Kino p430; Acad.

Based on the short story "Lokis" by Prosper Merimee.

See also: Lokis (1969).

Marriage of the Pens

See: Noces de Plumes (1968).

Mars

1908 French, Pathé sil sh.

Dir: Segundo de Chomon.

F

Ref: DdC I:404.

Mars

1931 U ani 1 reel.

Prod: Walter Lantz.

Dir: W. Lantz & William Nolan.

F-com

Ref: LC.

See also: Oswald (1927-38).

Mars

1931 Vit ani 7 mins.

F

Ref: MPH 31 Jan '31 p55.

Mars

1947 Amateur 16mm 20 mins.

Made by: Reginald McMahon.

Mus: Moussorgsky.

SF

Ref: Coronet; SF Art Mus Prog.

Mars and Beyond

1957 WD (BV) color ani 30 mins.

Exec Prod: Walt Disney.

Dir: Ward Kimball.

SF

Ref: Ideal cat '69-70 p203.

Mars and Beyond

1967 CBS/Union Carbide (Modern Talking Picture) color 30 mins.

doc; SF (films of life possible on other planets, space vehicles)

Ref: F/Future p45; LC.

Mars at Easter

See: Ne Jouez Pas avec les Martians (1967).

Mars Attacks Puerto Rico

See: Frankenstein Meets the Spacemonster (1965).

Mars Attacks the World

See: Flash Gordon's Trip to Mars (1938).

Mars Calling

See: Radio-Mania (1922).

Mars en Careme

See: Ne Jouez Pas avec les Martians (1967).

Mars, God of War

See: Venus Against the Sons of Hercules (1962).

Mars Invades Puerto Rico

See: Frankenstein Meets the Spacemonster (1965).

Mars Needs Women

1966 Azalea (AIP-TV) color 80 mins.

Prod, Dir, SP, Edit: Larry Buchanan.

Assoc Prod: Edwin Tobolowsky.

Makeup: Annabelle Weenick.

Prod Coordinator: Joreta Cherry.

Cin: Robert C. Jessup.

Cast: Tommy Kirk [Martian], Yvonne Craig, Byron Lord, Roger Ready, Warren Hammack, Pat Delany, Anthony Houston, Neil Fletcher, Bill Thurman.

SF; bor-com (Martians come to Earth to seek mates)

Ref: TVG; MTVM Jan '67 p7A; Richardson; Pardi.

Mars Project

(book by W. von Braun)

See: Conquest of Space, The (1955).

Mars Ravelo

See: Diyosa (1957).

Marsyas

1962? Amateur (Film-makers' Coop) 16mm 12 mins.

Dir: Arnold Gassan.

Cast: Don Crawford.

exp-F ("a snakelike farce about Negroes shedding their color" --film program)

Ref: FMC 5:114.

Marta

1971 Spanish/Italian, Atlantida/Cinemar color 100 mins.

Dir: José Antonio Nieves Conde.

SP: J.A.N. Conde, J.J.A. Millan, & Lopez Aranda.

Art Dir: Román Calatayud.

Cin: Ennio Guarnieri.

Mus: Piero Piccione.

Cast: Marisa Mell, Stephen Boyd, Jesús Puente, Isa Miranda.

H (torture chamber; dead wife kept in suit of armor)

Ref: V (Willis).

Based on "Estado Civil: Marta" by J.J.A. Millan.

Marte a Invade Puerto Rico

See: Frankenstein Meets the Spacemonster (1965).

Marte, Dio Della Guerra

See: Venus Against the Sons of Hercules (1962).

Martian in Paris, A

See: Martien à Paris, Un (1961).

Martian Magoo

1960 UPA 16mm color ani 5 mins approx.

Voice: Jim Backus.

SF-com

Ref: LC.

See also: Mister Magoo (1949-).

Martian Space Party

1972 Firesign Theater color 30 mins.

Cast: David Ossman, Philip Proctor, Peter Bergman, Phil Austin.

SF-com-sat (includes spoof of Japanese space movies)

Ref: CoF 19:4.

Martians, The

See: Disco Volante, Il (1964).

Martians Arrived, The

See: Llegaron los Marcianos (1964).

Martians Come Back

1956 color ani sh.

Dir: Ernest Pintoff.

F

Ref: Ani/Cin p 174.

Martians Have Twelve Hands

See: Llegaron los Marcianos (1964).

Martien à Paris, Un

(A Martian in Paris)

1960 French.

Dir: Jean-Daniel Daninos.

SP: J.-D. Daninos & Jacques Vilfrid.

Cast: Darry Cowl, Nicole Mirel, Henri Vilbert, Gisèle Grandré, Rolande Ségur, Michèle Verez.

SF-com (a Martian lands his flying saucer in Paris to study the disease called love)

Ref: Gasca p259; deGroote p376.

Martien de Noel, Le

(The Christmas Martian)

1971 Canadian (in French), Faroun & Les Cineastes Associes color 66 mins.

Dir: Bernard Gosselin.

SP: Roch Carrier.

Cin: Alain Dostie.

Mus: Jacques Perron.

SF (children find friendly Martian in Canadian forest at Christmas time)

Ref: Vw 9 June '71.

Martin et Gaston

(Martin and Gaston)

1950 French ani children's drawings sh.

Dir: Henri Gruel.

F

Ref: Ani/Cin p 101, 170.

Martirio di S. Stefano

(The Martyr of St. Stefano)

1912 Italian, Latium sil sh.

rel-F

Ref: Scognamillo.

Maruthanad Elavarsee

1950 Indian, G. Govindan 172 mins.

Prod: G. Muthuswami.

Dir: G. Kashilingam.

Story & Dialog: M. Karunanithi.

Art Dir: O.R. Embharaiyya.

Cin: G. Dorai.

Mus Dir: M.S. Gnanmani.

Cast: M.G. Ramchandra, Puli-mootai, C.S.D. Singh, M.G. Chakrapani, P.S. Veerappa, Lalita, Padmini.

myth-F

Ref: Indian MPA '53 p70.

Marvelous Cure, A

1909? Danish, Nordisk sil 420 ft.

SF-com ("hair restorer" -- Willis)

Ref: Bios 10 Feb '10.

Marvelous Fountain, The

See: Fontaine Merveilleuse, La (1908).

Marvelous Hen, The

See: Poule Merveilleuse, La (1902).

Marvelous Hind Leg, The

See: Gigue Merveilleuse, La (1909).

Marvelous Hive, The

See: Ruche Merveilleuse, La (1905)..

Marvelous Invention, A

1911 French?, Gaum sil 300 ft.

SF-com

Ref: Bios 28 Dec '11.

Marvelous Journey of Nils Holgersson, The

See: Wonderful Adventures of Nils, The (1962).

Marvelous Land of Oz, The

(book by L.F. Baum)

See: Land of Oz, The (1910).

Marvelous Maciste, The

(Maciste Magnificent --ad.t.)

1915 (1918) Italian, Itala (Hanover) sil 6 reels.

Cast: Ernesto Pagano, Arline Costello, Louise Farnsworth, Robert Ormand.

bor-F (super-strong Maciste)

Ref: MPW 26:2077, 36:1041.

See also: Maciste.

Marvelous Pearl, The

1909 Italian, Cines sil 720 ft.

F (spell on pearl causes man to drown)

Ref: Bios 9 Sept '09.

Marvelous Suspension and Evolution

(La Femme Volante)

1902 French, Star sil 130 ft.

Made by: Georges Méliès.

F

Ref: Sadoul/M, GM Mage 417-18.

Marvelous Transformations

1911 French, Pathé sil 210 ft.

F

Ref: MPW 10:208.

Marvelous Wreath, The

(La Guirlande Merveilleuse)

1903 French, Star sil 260 ft.

Made by: Georges Méliès.

F

Ref: Sadoul/M, GM Mage 445-48; BFI dist cat p59.

Mary Jane's Mishap

1903 British sil 260 ft.

Dir: G.A. Smith.

F (ghost)

Ref: HQ 1:253-54; Gifford/BFC 00631.

Mary Poppins

1964 WD (BV) color ani & live 139 mins.

Prod: Walt Disney.

Co Prod: Bill Walsh.

Dir: Robert Stevenson.

SP: Bill Walsh & Don DaGradi.

Art Dir: Carroll Clarke & William H. Tuntke.

Cin: Edward Colman.

Ani Dir: Hamilton S. Luske.

SpFX: Peter Ellenshaw, Eustace Lycett, & Robert A. Mattey.

Edit: Cotton Warburton.

Mus & Lyrics: Richard & Robert Sherman.

Mus Dir: Irwin Kostal.

Cast: Julie Andrews, Dick Van Dyke, David Tomlinson, Glynis Johns, Hermione Badderly, Karen Dotrice, Matthew Garber, Elsa Lanchester, Arthur Treacher, Reginald Owen, Ed Wynn, Reta Shaw, Jane Darwell.

mus-com-F (much fantasy: flying, magical nanny comes to 1900s British household; adventure in animated world entered by jumping into sidewalk chalk drawing; laughing makes people float; etc.)

Ref: FF '64 p 188; MFB Feb '65 p20-21; MPH 16 Sept '64.

Based on the books by P.L. Travers.

Mary's Birthday

1949 British color ani (silhouette?) 11 mins.

Dir: Lotte Reiniger.

F (flower fairies' advice enables children to chase insect pests away)

Ref: Ani/Cin p 175.

Marziani Hanno Dodici Mani, I

See: Llegaron los Marcianos (1964).

Marzipan of the Shapes

1920 British, Alliance Film Corp sil sh?

Dir: A.C. Hunter.

Cast: Ray Forrest, Irene Tripod, Frank Stanmore.

bor-F-com-sat (lampoon of Tarzan)

Ref: Gifford/BFC 07092.

See also: Tarzan.

Maschera del Demonio, La

See: Black Sunday (1960).

Maschine, Die

See: Machine (1966).

Mascot, The

1934 French ani puppet sh.

Made by: Ladislas Starevitch.

F

Ref: French Exp List.

Mask, The

1913 Rex (U) sil.

psy-F (man with dual personality, one evil, about to marry, loses control of muscles in face & real character is revealed)

Ref: MPW 18:1153, 1206.

Mask, The

(Eyes of Hell --rr.t, 16 mm t.)

1961 Canadian, Roffman-Taylor & Beaver-Champion Attractions (WB) 3D seqs 83 mins.

Prod & Dir: Julian Roffman.

SP: Frank Taubes & Sandy Haber.

Art Dir: David S. Ballou & Hugo Wuehtrich.

Cin: Herbert S. Alpert.

SpFX: Herman S. Townsley.

SpFX Cin: James B. Gordon.

Edit: Stephen Timar & Robert Schultz.

Mus: Louis Applebaum.

Cast: Paul Stevens, Claudette Nevins, Bill Walker, Anne Collings, Martin Lavut, Jim Moran, Rudi Linschoten, Paul Nevins.

psy-F-H (man gets ancient mask which, when worn, causes psychotic hallucinations [shown in 3D] and drives him to attempt murder)

Ref: FF '61 p272-73; PB; FD 2 Nov '61; FM 16:34.

Mask of Destiny, The

(Shuzenji Monogatari)

1955 (1957) Japanese, Shochiku (Stratford) color 105 mins.

Prod: Kiyoshi Takamura.

Dir: Noboru Nakamura.

SP: Kido Okamoto.

Art Dir: Kisaku Ito.

Cin: Toshio Ubukata.

Mus: Toshiro Mazuzumi.

Cast: Teiji Takahashi, Chikaga Awashima, Minosuke Bando, Keiko Kishi.

bor-F (mask seems to foretell death)

Ref: HR 2 Jan '57; Orient.

Based on play "Shuzenji Monogatari" by Kido Okamoto.

Mask of Diijon, The

1945 (1946) PRC 70 mins.

Prod: Max Alexander & Alfred Stern.

Dir: Lew Landers.

Story: Arthur St. Clair.

SP: A. St. Clair & Griffin Jay.

Art Dir: Edward Jewell.

Cin: Jack Greenhalgh.

SpFX: Ray Mercer.

Edit: Roy Livingston.

Mus Dir: Karl Hajos.

Cast: Erich Von Stroheim, Jeanne Bates, William Wright, Denise Vernac, Edward Van Sloan, Hope Landin, Mauritz Hugo.

bor-F-H (magician uses hypnotism to cause suicide & murder)

Ref: HR & Vd 25 Jan '46; FD 4 Feb '46; MFB Dec '46 p 170; Pardi.

Mask of Fortune, The

1916 Laemmle (U) sil 1 reel.

Dir: George Cochrane.

Sc: Calder Johnstone.

Cast: Marjorie Ellison, Jack Connolly, Malcolm Blevins, Bert Law.

F (girl can foretell stock market's future)

Ref: MPW 29:836; LC.

Mask of Fu Manchu, The

1932 MGM 72 mins (67 mins).

Prod: Irving Thalberg (un-credited).

Dir: Charles Brabin & Charles Vidor.

Adapt: Sax Rohmer.

SP: Irene Kuhn, Edgar Allan Woolf, & John Willard.

Art Dir: Cedric Gibbons.

Cin: Gaetano Gaudio.

Edit: Ben Lewis.

Cast: Boris Karloff [Fu Manchu], Lewis Stone, Karen Morley, Jean Hersholt, Myrna Loy, Gertrude Michael, Charles Starett, Herbert Bunston.

bor-F; H (mind-controlling drugs; electrical ray machine; owner of Ghengis Khan's mask & sword will rule the Oriental world)

Ref: MPH 15 Oct '32 p9; LC; Vw 6 Dec '32; Borst.

Based on the novel by Sax Rohmer.

See also: Fu Manchu.

Mask of Fu Manchu, The

See: Face of Fu Manchu, The (1965).

Mask of Horror, The

See: Masque d'Horreur, Le (1911?).

Mask of the Demon

See: Black Sunday (1960).

Mask of the Golem

See: Golem, Le (1966).

Mask of the Red Death, The

1911 Italian, Ambrosio sil sh.

rel-F (prayer saves mother & children when rest of city dies of the plague)

Ref: MPW 9:994; F/A p492.

Loosely based on the short story by Edgar Allan Poe.

See also: Masque of the Red Death.

Maska Crvene Smrti

See: Masque of the Red Death, The (1969).

Masked Marvel, The

1943 Rep serial 12 parts 25 reel.

Also edited to 100 minute TV feature in 1966 under the title Sakima and the Masked Marvel.

Assoc Prod: W.J. O'Sullivan.

Dir: Spencer G. Bennet.

SP: Royal K. Cole, Ronald Davidson, Basil Dickey, Jesse Duffy, Grant Nelson, George Plympton, & Joseph Poland.

Cin: Reggie Lanning.

SpFX: Howard Lydecker.

Edit: Earl Turner & Wallace Grissell.

Mus: Mort Glickman.

Cast: Tom Steele, William Forrest, Louise Currie, Anthony Warde, Kenneth Harlan, Eddie Parker, Dale Van Sickel, Robert Wilke, Roy Barcroft, Edward Van Sloan, Ernie Adams.

bor-SF (new explosive; super-periscope with TV attachment)

Ref: Ser/Rep; D. Glut; LC.

Masked Terror

See: Dokuro Kyojo (1957).

Masken Erwin Reiners, Die

(novel by J. Wassermann)

See: Masks of the Devil (1928).

Maskerade

1966? Bulgarian ani puppet sh.

Dir: Christo Topouzanov.

sat-F (person with different face for every occasion)

Ref: FIR June/July '67 p372.

Masks

1968? British color ani sh.

Dir: Bob Godfrey.

Ani: Billy Sewell.

F-com

Ref: F&F Feb '69.

Also included in: Two Off the Cuff (1968).

Masks

See: Persona (1966).

Masks of the Devil, The

1928 MGM sil w/sound FX & mus 5575 ft.

Prod & Dir: Victor Seastrom.

Adapt: Sven Gade.

Continuity: Frances Marion.

Titles: Marian Ainslee & Ruth Cummings.

Sets: Cedric Gibbons.

Assist Dir: Harold S. Bucquet.

Cin: Oliver Marsh.

Edit: Conrad A. Nervig.

Cast: John Gilbert, Alma Rubens, Theodore Roberts, Frank Reicher, Eva Von Berne, Ralph Forbes, Ethel Wales, Polly Ann Young.

psy-F-seq (sees himself as devil in mirror)

Ref: Vw 28 Nov '28; LC; MPN 38:22:1698; FD 2 Dec '28; AFI F2.3515 p409.

Based on novel "Die Masken Erwin Reiners" by Jakob Wassermann.

Masque d'Horreur, Le

(The Mask of Horror)

1911? French sil sh?

Dir: Abel Gance.

Cast: Edouard de Max.

H (Grand Guignol-type story)

Ref: F&F Nov '69 p34; S&S Summer '63 p 151.

Masque of the Red Death, The

● 1964 US/British, Alta Vista/ Anglo Amalgamated (AIP) color scope 89 mins.

Prod: George Willoughby.

Dir: Roger Corman.

SP: Charles Beaumont & R. Wright Campbell.

Setting Design: Robert Jones.

Cin: Nicholas Roeg.

SpFX: George Blackwell.

Edit: Ann Chegwidden.

Mus: David Lee.

Cast: Vincent Price, Hazel Court, Jane Asher, David Weston, Patrick Magee, Nigel Green, Skip Martin, John Westbrook [Red Death].

F-H (dissipated 12th-Century Italian nobleman is sadistic Satanist; the Red Death personified visits his castle, has face of the nobleman; dwarf burns enemy alive; torture & sacrifice dream seq; falcon slashes woman to death)

Ref: MFB Aug '64 p 116; Corman p98; Vw & HR 24 June '64; FD 15 June '64.

Based on the story of the same title and "Hop Frog" by Edgar Allan Poe.

● (Maska Crvene Smrti: Mask of the Red Death)

The Mask of Fu Manchu (1932)

Masque of the Red Death cont.

1969 Yugoslavian/US, Zagreb/ Contemporary color ani 10 mins.

Dir: Pavao Stalter & Branko Ranitović.

Story: Zdenko Gašparović & B. Ranitović.

Design & Bg: P. Stalter.

Ani: P. Stalter & Vladimir Jutriša.

Mus: Branimir Sakač.

F-H (Prince Prospero pursues beautiful woman who is revealed to be the plague, personified)

Ref: Mamaia '70; Z/Zagreb p99.

Based on the short story by Edgar Allan Poe.

See also: Mask of the Red Death (1911); Prizak Brodit po Yevrope (1923).

Masques

1953 French color ani sh.

Dir: Alexandre Alexeieff & George Violet.

F

Ref: Ani/Cin p95.

Mass

1964 Amateur (Center Cinema) 16mm? 20 mins.

Made by: Bruce Baillie.

exp-F

Ref: CCC cat 2:4.

Massacre Mania

See: Hypnos (1971).

Masseur's Curse

See: Kaidan Kasanegafuchi (1970).

Master

See: Maître (1962?).

Master and Margherite, The

See: Maestro e Margherita, Il (1972).

Master Key, The

1945 U serial 13 parts 26 reels.

Prod: Morgan Cox.

Dir: Ray Taylor & Lewis D. Collins.

Story: Jack Natteford & Dwight V. Babcock.

SP: Joseph O'Donnell, George H. Plympton, & Ande Lamb.

Cin: William Sickner & Maury Gertsman.

Cast: Milburn Stone, Jan Wiley, Dennis Moore, Addison Richards, Maris Wrixon, Byron Foulger, Russell Hicks, Roland Varno, Ernie Adams, Gene Stutenroth (later Gene Roth), Dick Alexander, John Merton, Alfred LaRue (later "Lash" LaRue).

cont.

cont.

Master Key cont.

bor-SF (machine extracts gold from sea water)'
Ref: MPH 21 April '45; LC; FDY '56.

Master Krishna
See: Krishna Kumar (1924).

Master Magician Alcrofrisbas
(L'Enchanteur Alcrofrisbas)
1903 French, Star sil 230 ft.
Made by: Georges Méliès.
F (vase turns into woman, flies about; transformations; etc.)
Ref: Sadoul/M, GM Mage; LC; Niver p31.

Master Mind, The

◐ 1914 Jesse L. Lasky sil sh?
Cast: Edmund Breese.
Ref: MPW 20:947, 1312; LC; FIR April '62 p221.

◐ 1920 Whitman Bennett (FN) sil 6 reels.
Prod: Whitman Bennett.
Dir & Sc: Kenneth Webb.
Cin: T.L. Griffith & R.R. Schellinger.
Cast: Lionel Barrymore, Gypsie O'Brien, Ralph Kellard, Bradley Barker, Charles Brandt, Marie Shotwell.
Ref: MPN 22:2839; LC; FD 19 Sept '20; FIR April '62 p221.

F (telepathic power)
Based on the play by Daniel D. Carter.

Master Minds
1949 Mono 64 mins.
Prod: Jan Grippo.
Dir: Jean Yarbrough.
SP: Charles R. Marion & Bert Lawrence.
Art Dir: Dave Milton.
Makeup: Jack Pierce.
Cin: Marcel Le Picard.
Edit: William Austin.
Sup Edit: Otho Lovering.
Mus Dir: Edward J. Kay.
Cast: Leo Gorcey, Huntz Hall, Glenn Strange [apeman], Minerva Urecal, William Benedict, Gabriel Dell, Alan Napier, Jane Adams, Bernard Gorcey, David Gorcey, William Benedict, Bennie Bartlett.

SF-H-com; F-seq (mad scientist Napier converted Strange from ape into man but he needs a brain for the monster; person- alities switched from one char- acter to another & back; Hall can predict future when tooth aches)
Ref: MFB Aug '50 p 119; FDY '50; Vw 11 Jan '50; LC.
See also: Spooks Run Wild (1941).

Master Minds
See: Genius at Work (1946).

Master Mystery, The
(Houdini --ad.t.)
1918 (1919) B.A. Rolfe Prods (Octagon Films) sil serial 15 parts 31 reels.
Dir: Burton King.
Story: Arthur B. Reeve & Charles A. Logue.
Cast: Harry Houdini, Marguerite Marsh, Ruth Stonehouse, William Pike, Floyd Buckley ["robot"], Charles Graham, Edna Britton.
bor-SF ("the Automaton" is supposedly a robot with a human brain, but is revealed to be a fake)
Ref: MPN 18:3251; Photo Feb '19 p 101; SBI March '62.
Novelized by Arthur B. Reeve & John Grey.

Master of Existence
1932 Soviet ani puppet sh.
Dir: Alexander Ptushko.
F
Ref: Kino p309.

Master of Horror
(Obras Maestras del Terror: Masterworks of Terror)
1960 (1966) Argentinian, Sono (US Films) color 115 mins (61 mins).
Exec Prod: Rickey Torres & James C. Gates.
Prod: Nicolas Carreras.
Dir: Enrique Carreras.
SP: Luis Penafiel.
Art Dir: Mario Vanarelli.
Cin: Americo Hoss.
Edit: José Gallego.
Mus: Victor Schlichter.
English Language Version
Exec Prod: Jack H. Harris.
Cast: Narciso Ibanez Menta, Inez Moreno, Carlos Estrada, Narciso Ibanez Serrador, Mercedes Carreras, Lilian Valmar.
F-H (3 stories: "The Case of Mr. Valdemar" --doctor hypnotizes man at point of death; when brought out of spell man instantly decom- poses; "The Cask of Amontillado" --man drowns adulterous wife in vat of wine, then walls her lover up alive in niche with vat of wine; "The Tell-Tale Heart" --psychotic murderer confesses when he thinks he hears heartbeat of his victim)
Ref: FF '66 p382, 382A; FM 38:45; CoF 9:6; BO 25 July '66; FIR Oct '61 p473.
Based on short stories "The Facts in the Case of M. Val- demar," "The Cask of Amontillado," and "The Tell-Tale Heart" by Edgar Allan Poe.
Note: "The Tell-Tale Heart" sequence not included in US prints.
See also: Cask of Amontillado, The; Tell-Tale Heart, The; Tales of Terror (1961).

Master of Terror
See: 4D Man, The (1959).

Master of the World, The
1914 Karl Werner (Film Releases of America) sil 3 reels.
SF (process for making gold)
Ref: MPW 20:1691, 1744; LC.

Master of the World
1961 AIP color 104 mins.
Exec Prod: Samuel Z. Arkoff.
Prod: James H. Nicholson.
Co Prod & Edit: Anthony Carras.
Dir: William Witney.
SP: Richard Matheson.
Art Dir: Daniel Haller.
Cin: Gil Warrenton.
SpFX: Ray Mercer, Tim Barr, Wah Chang, & Gene Warren.
Mus: Les Baxter.
Mus Dir: Albert Harris.
Cast: Vincent Price, Charles Bronson, Henry Hull, Mary Webster, David Frankham, Vito Scotti, Wally Campo, Ken Terrell.
SF (in 19th Century, Robur has built an enormous flying machine, like a giant heli- copter, constructed from compressed paper & electrically powered; he intends to use it to end all warfare)
Ref: FF '61 p208-09; MFB Oct '61 p 143; HR 26 April '61.
Based on two novels, "Master of the World" and "Robur the Conqueror" by Jules Verne.

Master of the World, The
See: Herr der Welt, Der (1934).

Master of Time, The
See: Maître de Temps, Le (1970).

Master Physician, The
1915 (1916) Danish, Nordisk (Great Northern) sil 2400 ft.
Cast: Gunner Tolnaes, George Weith.
F (a modern Faust story)
Ref: Pictures & the Picturegoer 15 July '16; LC.
See also: Faust.

Masters of the Sea
See: Herren der Meere (1922).

Masters of Venus
1962 British, Wallace Prods serial 8 parts 16 mins each.
Originally made for TV .
Prod: A. Frank Bundy.
Dir: Ernest Morris.
Story: H.B. Gregory.
Adapt: Mary Cathcart Borer.
SP: Michael Barnes.
Art Dir: Norman Arnold.
Cin: Reg Wyer.
Edit: John S. Smith.
Mus: Eric Rogers.
Cast: Norman Wooland, Amanda Coxell, Robin Stewart, Robert Hunter, Patrick Kavanagh, Ferdy Mayne.
SF (spaceship lands on Venus, finds civilization populated by human survivors of Atlantis)
Ref: MFB May '63 p67; Ideal cat '69-70 p 185; STI 7:4.

Masterworks of Terror
See: Master of Horror (1960).

Maszyna
(Machine)
1961 Polish color ani sh.
Dir: Daniel Szczechura.
F
Ref: Ani/Cin p 114, 175; ASIFA info sheet.

Mat and the Fly
1930 French sil marionette sh.
F
Ref: F/A p633; CU 7:394-95.

Match de Prestidigitation
See: Wager Between Two Magicians, A (1904).

Match Girl
◐ 1966 Amateur (Film-makers' Coop) 16mm color 26 mins.
Made by: Andrew Meyer.
Mus: The Rolling Stones.
Cast: Vivian Kurz.
exp-psy-F ("the fantasy ex- periences of an aspiring young actress" --FMC)
Ref: Undrgnd p 102, 285; FMC 5:241.
Suggested by story "The Little Match Girl" by Hans Christian Andersen.

◐ 1968 Rumanian, Bucuresti color 18 mins.
Dir: Aurel Miheles.
Cast: Ana Szeles.
F
Ref: MTVM March '68 p39.
Based on fairy tale "The Little Match Girl" by Hans Christian Andersen.

See also: Little Match Girl, The.

Match Master, The
See: Streichholzkünstler, Der (1913).

Matches
See: Zviendhoelzer (1962)

Matchless
1966 (1967) Italian, DeLaurentiis (UA) color scope 104 mins.
Exec Prod: Dino De Laurentiis.
Prod: Ermanno Donati & Luigi Carpentieri.
Dir: Alberto Lattuada.
SP: Dean Craif, Jack Pulman, Luigi Malerba, & A. Lattuada.
Art Dir: Vincenzo Del Prato.
Cin: Sandro D'Eva.
SpFX: Guy Delecluse.
Edit: Franco Fraticelli.
Mus: Piero Piccioni & Gino Marinuzzi Jr.
Cast: Patrick O'Neal, Ira Furstenberg, Donald Pleasence, Henry Silva, Nicoletta Machiavelli, Howard St. John, Sorrell Booke.
F-seq (secret agent given magic ring that makes him invisible; villain's castle staffed by robots)
Ref: FF '67 p357; MFB '70 p 131; FD 26 Sept '67.

Matchless Conqueror, The
1972? Hongkong, Hong Hua color scope.
Prod: Nan-Hong Kuo.
Dir: Chang Ping-Han.
F-seqs (mystic martial arts)
Ref: Collier.

Matchseller, The
See: Little Match Girl, The.

Matchstick Pals, The
See: Přátelé na Sirkách (1960).

Mate Doma Iva?
See: Do You Keep a Lion at Home? (1963).

Matka Joanna od Aniolów
See: Joan of the Angels? (1960).

Matrimonio Interplanetario, Un
(An Interplanetary Wedding)
1910 Italian, Latium sil sh.
Dir & Sc: Yambo (real name: Enrico Novelli).
SF-com
Ref: Scognamillo; DdC III:483.

Matrix
1970 Amateur (Pyramid) color ani 6 mins.
Made by: John Whitney.
exp-F
Ref: FC 53/54/55:79-80.

Matsya Gandha or Bhishma Pratignya
1934 Indian, New Era.
Dir: Dakubhai Mehta.
SP: R.K. Rele.
Cin: Rajnikant Pandya.
Cast: Shahazadi, Malat, Nirmali, Maruthi Pehelwan, Inamdar, Baburao Savare.
myth-F
Ref: Dipali 22 June '34.
Based on the Mahabharat.

Matt Helm
Spy character created by Donald Hamilton.
See: Silencers, The (1965); Murderer's Row (1966); Ambushers, The (1967).

Matter of Life and Death, A
See: Stairway to Heaven (1946).

Max and the Clutching Hand
(La Main Qui Entreint: The Grasping Hand)

1915 French, Pathé sil sh.

Dir: Louis Gasnier.

Cast: Max Linder.

F-H-com (ghost)

Ref: DdC II:315, III:230; FIR May '65 p282.

Max Ernst — Entdeckungsfahrten ins Unbewusste
(Max Ernst — Journeys of Discovery into the Unconscious)

1962 W. German color 11 mins.

Dir & SP: Peter Schamoni & Carl Lamb.

Nar: Max Ernst.

doc; F-seqs

Ref: MFB June '65 p97-98.

Max Hypnotized
1910 French sil 540 ft.

Dir: Max Linder.

Cast: Max Linder.

bor-F-H-com (hypnotized man ordered to kill)

Ref: Bios 1 Dec '10, 23 Oct '13; DdC III:230; FIR May '65 p276.

Maxi Cat
1970 Yugoslavian, Zagreb color ani 5.5 mins.

Also series, 1970 --

Dir, SP, Design, Ani: Zlatko Grgić.

Mus: Tomislav Simović.

F-com

Ref: Z/Zagreb p 105.

Maxwell's Demon
1968 Amateur (Film-makers' Coop) 16mm color 4 mins.

Made by: Hollis Frampton.

exp-abs-F

Ref: FMC 5:108; FC 48/49:7-8, 11.

May We Come In
(story by H. & D. Segall)

See: For Heaven's Sake (1950).

Maya Bazar
(Fantasy Bazaar)

● 1939 Indian (in Marathi), Prabha

Dir: G.P. Powar.

SP: N.V. Kulkarni.

Cin: Machave.

Mus: Sarang.

Cast: Indukumari, Kurwalikar, Sandoo, Shyamabai, Surya Mohan, Sakwal.

Ref: MovPicM March '39 p4; Filmindia May '39 p77.

● 1949 Indian (in Marathi), Manick 133 mins.

Prod: P.K. Pathak.

Dir: Dhatta Dharamadhikari.

SP & Songs: G.D. Madgulkar.

Art Dir: A. Mahat.

Cin: E. Mohammad.

Edit: Vasantrao Giri.

Mus Dir: Sudhir Phadke.

Cast: Sahu Modak, Durga Khote, Baby Shakuntala, Balakram, Kusum, Vasant Thengdi.

Ref: Indian MPA '53 p 13, 80.

● 1959 Indian (in Hindi), Basant Pictures 150 mins.

Dir: Rabhubhai Mistry.

Cast: Anita Guha, Krishna Kumari, Mahipal, Raj Kumar.

Ref: FEFN 12:7/9:25.

myth-F (marriage to Krishna's sister averted when he makes demons' disguises vanish)

Maya Kajal
1937 (1938) Indian (in Bengali), Bharat Lakshmi sh.

Dir & SP: Tulsi Lahiri.

Cast: Tulsi Lahiri, Ushabati, Ganesh Roy.

F-com (a spirit gives a suicide-bent henpecked husband secret which amasses the husband great fortune)

Ref: Dipali 19 Feb '37 p27.

See also: Sheikh Chilli (1937).

Maya Machindra
See: Gorakhnath (1951).

Maya Manidhan (...Manithan?)
1958 Indian (in Tamil), Southern Movies.

Cast: Sriram.

F (in dispensary, criminal finds invisibility potion)

Ref: FEFN 13 June '58.

Maya Mohini
1928 Indian sil.

F

Ref: IndCin YB.

Mayakudarai
See: Magic Horse (1949).

Mayavathi
1949 Indian (in Tamil), Ganapathi 145 mins.

Dir: T.R. Sundaram.

SP: P. Kannappa.

Mus Dir: G. Ramanathan.

Cast: T.R. Mahalingam, Anjali Devi, Kali N. Ratnam, Subbiah, Perumal.

myth-F

Ref: Indian MPA '53 p67.

Mayavi Nagari
See: Magic City, The (1928).

Maytime
1937 MGM 132 mins.

Prod: Hunt Stromberg.

Dir: Robert Z. Leonard.

SP: Noel Langley.

Art Dir: Cedric Gibbons.

Cin: Oliver T. Marsh.

Edit: Conrad A. Nervig.

Mus: Sigmund Romberg & Herbert Stothart.

Cast: Jeanette MacDonald, Nelson Eddy, John Barrymore, Herman Bing, Tom Brown, Lynn Carver, Paul Porcasi, Sig Rumann, Walter Kingsford.

operetta; F-seq (ghosts of two lovers meet at the end)

Ref: Vw 24 March '37; Acad.

Based on the play by Rida Johnson Young.

Mazda Lamps, The
See: Lampes Mazda, Les (1940?).

Maze, The
1953 AA 3D 80 mins.

Filmed in England.

Exec Prod: Walter Mirisch.

Prod: Richard Heermance.

Dir & Prod Design: William Cameron Menzies.

SP: Dan Ullman.

Cin: Harry Neumann.

Edit: John Fuller.

Mus: Marlin Skiles.

Cast: Richard Carlson, Veronica Hurst, Michael Pate, Hillary Brooke, Lillian Bond, Robin Hughes.

SF-H (eerie old castle; baronet born in form of large frog is 200 years old)

Ref: Vd 3 July '53; AHF p237; FD 8 July '53.

Based on the novel by Maurice Sandoz.

Meany, Miny, Moe
1936-37 U ani sh series.

Prod & Co-Story: Walter Lantz.

F-com (adventures of 3 chimpanzees)

Ref: LC.

See also: Golfers, The (1936); House of Magic (1937); Stevedores, The (1937).

Measure for Measure
1909 Lubin sil 900 ft.

bor-SF-com (new explosive submarine mine)

Ref: Bios 7 Oct '09; LC.

Mechanical Ballet, The
See: Ballet Mécanique, Le (1924).

Mechanical Butcher
1898 French, Lumiere sil sh.

F (pig turned into ham, bacon, etc. automatically)

Ref: Gifford/SF.

Mechanical Flea, The
1964 Soviet ani cardboard puppet feature.

Dir: Ivanov-Vano.

F

Ref: Ani/Cin p 149, 172.

Mechanical Handy Man, The
1937 U ani 7 mins.

Prod: Walter Lantz.

Story: Charles Bowers.

Artists: Ted Dubois & Ed Benedict.

F-com (Oswald invents a robot)

Ref: MPH 30 Oct '31 p51; LC.

See also: Oswald (1927-38).

Mechanical Husband, The
1910 LCC sil sh.

SF-com (girl falls in love with a robot)

Ref: Gifford/SF p53.

The Master Mystery (1918) Serial

Mechanical Legs, The

1908 French, Gaum sil sh.

SF-com (legless cripple equipped with mechanical legs)

Ref: Gifford/SF p 16.

Mechanical Man, The

1915 Joker (U) sil 1 reel.

Dir: Allen Curtis.

Sc: Clarence Badger.

Cast: Max Asher, Phroso.

SF-com (mechanical life-sized doll with controls on his back; when broken, man impersonates it)

Ref: MPW 24:2118, 2163, 25:65; LC.

Mechanical Man

1932 U ani 1 reel.

Prod: Walter Lantz.

F-com

Ref: LC.

See also: Oswald (1927-38).

Mechanical Mary Anne

1910 British, Hepworth sil sh.

Dir: Lewin Fitzhamon.

SF (robot servant goes berserk)

Ref: Gifford/SF p51.

Mechanical Statue and the In-genious Servant, The

1907 Vit sil 450 ft.

Prod & Dir: J. Stuart Blackton.

SF

Ref: MPW 1:62; LC; Filmlex p681.

Med Kaerlig Hilsen

(Love Me Darling --Brit.t.)

1971 Danish, Gabriel Axel color 88 mins (84 mins).

Prod: Gabriel Axel & Henning Karmark.

Dir & SP: G. Axel.

Art Dir: Erik Bjoric.

Cin: Rolf Rønne.

Edit: Anders Refn.

Mus: B. Fabricius Bjerre (aka Bent Fabric).

Cast: Buster Larsen, Birte Tore, Christian Sarvig, Lone Helmer, Lily Broberg, Grethe Holmer, Annie Birgit Garde, Birgit Bruel.

F (Satanic magician transports 2 lovers to Garden of Eden, then thru several stops in time back to present)

Ref: MFB May '73 p 104.

Medea

1970 (1971) Italian/W.German/French, San Marco/Janus/Films #1 (New Line Cinema) color 118 mins.

Prod: Franco Rossellini & Marina Cicogna.

Dir & SP: Pier Paolo Pasolini.

Art Dir: Dante Ferretti & Nicola Tamburro.

Cin: Ennio Guarnieri.

Edit: Nino Baragli.

Traditional Mus Adapt & Arranged: P.P. Pasolini & Elsa Morante.

Cast: Maria Callas, Massimo Girotti, Laurent Terzieff [centaur], Giuseppi Gentile, Margareth Clementi.

F (magic clothes burst into flame; centaur, Golden Fleece; magic; cannibalism; & other elements of the Medea legend)

Ref: FF '71 p698-700; Vw 11 March '70.

Based on a work by Euripedes.

Medicine of the Future, The

1912 French?, Lux sil 420 ft.

SF-com (machine energizes people)

Ref: Bios 6 Feb '13.

Meditation

1968 B.Y.M. Prods (Film-makers' Coop; Center Cinema) 16mm color 5 mins.

Made by: Peter D. Spoecker.

Mus: Mickie Zekley.

exp-abs-F

Ref: FMC 5:308.

Meditation on Violence

1948 Amateur (C-16) 16mm 12 mins.

Made by: Maya Deren.

exp-dance-F

Ref: USA Exp List; Undrgnd p84, 279.

Medium, The

1934 British, MGM.

Dir: Vernon Sewell.

F-H (psychic power)

Ref: Destiny.

Based on a play by José Levy.

See also: Latin Quarter (1945).

Medium, The

1951 Italian, Transfilm (Lopert).

Prod: Walter Lowendahl.

Dir & SP: Gian-Carlo Menotti.

Co-Dir & Edit: Alexander Hammid.

Art Dir: George Wakhevitch.

Cin: Enzo Serafin.

Cast: Marie Powers, Anna Maria Alberghetti, Leo Coleman, Belva Kibler, Beverly Dame.

opera; F-H (phoney spiritualist ruined by her fear of the supernatural)

Ref: MFB May '53 p69; Vd 12 Sept '51, 11 Jan '52.

Based on the opera by Gian-Carlo Menotti.

Medusa vs. the Son of Hercules

(Perseo l'Invincible: Perseus the Invincible; El Valle de los Hombres de Piedra: The Valley of the Stone Men; Perseus Against the Monsters --Brit.t.)

1962 Italian/Spanish, Bris-tolfi/Copercines color scope 95 mins.

Prod: José Antonio & Emo Bistolfi.

Dir: Alberto de Martino.

SP: Mario Guerra, Luciano Martino, & José Mallorqui.

Cin: Dario Di Palma & Eloy Mella.

Edit: Otello Colangeli.

Mus: Carlo Franci & Manuel Parada.

Cast: Richard Harrison, Anna Ranalli, Leo Anchóriz, Arturo Dóminici, Elisa Cegani.

myth-F-H (Perseus rescues Andromeda from the dragon; prophecy is fulfilled; Medusa not a woman, but a bush-like creature with one large eye which turns men to stone; when Medusa is killed men revive)

Ref: MFB May '64 p76; SpCin '64 p745; BIB's; TVG; MMF 7:84, 8:71.

Medvezhya Svadba

See: Marriage of the Bear, The (1926).

Meerabai

(Mirabai --alt. spelling)

1946 Indian, Shalimar.

Dir: W.Z. Ahmed.

Cast: Arun, Baby Hamida.

myth-F (childhood of Krishna)

Ref: Filmindia Oct '46 p 11.

See also: Krishna.

Meet Dr. Jekyll and Mr. Hyde

See: Abbott and Costello Meet Dr. Jekyll and Mr. Hyde (1953).

Meet Frankenstein

See: Abbott and Costello Meet Frankenstein (1947).

Meet John Doe

1941 Frank Capra Prods (WB) 125 mins.

Prod & Dir: Frank Capra.

Story: Richard Connell & Robert Presnell.

SP: Robert Riskin.

Art Dir: Stephen Goosson.

Cin: George Barnes.

Montage FX: Slavko Vorkapich.

SpFX: Jack Cosgrove.

Edit: Daniel Mandell.

Mus: Dimitri Tiomkin.

Cast: Gary Cooper, Barbara Stanwyck, Edward Arnold, Walter Brennan, Spring Byington, James Gleason, Gene Lockhart, Rod LaRocque, Irving Bacon, Regis Toomey, J. Farrell MacDonald, Sterling Holloway, Mike Frankovich.

bor-soc-SF (industrialist uses "John Doe" clubs & their national hero in an attempt to seize political power in the US)

Ref: HR & Vd 13 March '41; Willis p315; LC.

Note: several different endings were filmed, and some were shown in various parts of the US.

Meet Me, Jesus

n.d. Amateur (Center Cinema) color ani & live 15 mins.

Made by: Walter Ungerer.

Tech Assist: Henry Savage III.

exp-F

Ref: CCC 2:27.

Meet Mr. Kringle

(Miracle on 34th Street --Brit.t.)

1956 20th-Fox 56 mins.

Originally made for TV, shown theatrically in England, on TV as feature.

Prod: Jules Bricken.

Dir: Robert Stevenson.

SP: John Monks Jr.

Cin: Lloyd Ahern.

Edit: Art Seid.

Cast: Thomas Mitchell, Mac-donald Carey, Teresa Wright, Sandy Descher, Hans Conreid, Ray Collins.

bor-F-com (court trial "proves" old man is Santa Claus; seems like he might really be Santa Claus)

Ref: MFB Jan '57 p8; D. Glut; TVG 20 Dec '70; BIB's.

Based on film Miracle on 34th Street, with a screenplay by George Seaton from the story by Valentine Davies.

See also: Miracle on 34th Street (1947).

Meet Mr. Lucifer

1953 British, Ealing 83 mins.

Dir: Anthony Pelissier.

SP: Monja Danischevsky.

Art Dir: Wilfred Shingleton.

Cin: Desmond Dickinson.

Edit: Bernard Gribble.

Mus: Eric Rogers.

Cast: Stanley Holloway [Devil], Peggy Cummins, Jack Watling, Barbara Murray, Joseph Tomelty, Kay Kendall, Gordon Jackson, Ernest Thesiger.

F-dream-com-sat (Mr. Lucifer, the Devil, asks man who looks like him to help him cause TV viewing to make people miserable)

Ref: Vw 9 Dec '53; MFB Jan '54 p5; FIR Feb '59 p77.

Based on play "Beggar My Neighbour" by Arnold Ridley.

Meet the Ghosts

See: Abbott and Costello Meet Frankenstein (1947).

Meet the Invisible Man

See: Abbott and Costello Meet the Invisible Man (1950).

Meet the Killer

See: Abbott and Costello Meet the Killer: Boris Karloff (1949).

Meet the Mummy

See: Abbott and Costello Meet the Mummy (1955).

Meeting at the Fashion Show

See: Kostimirani Rendez-Vous (1965).

Meeting in the Forest, The

See: Rendez-Vous en Forêt, Le (1972).

Mefistofele

(opera by A. Boito)

See: Faust and the Devil (1948).

Melhor da Rua

1966? Portugese, Telecine-Moro color ani 35 seconds.

Dir: Artur Correia.

F

Ref: ASIFA 3.

Melodic Inversion

1958 Amateur (Film Images) 16mm color 10 mins.

Made by: Ian Hugo.

Cast: Anais Nin.

exp-abs-F

Ref: Film Images S-3; FC 31:14.

Melodie der Welt

(Melody of the World)

1929 German (Tobis) 30 mins.

Dir: Walter Ruttman.

Ani: Oskar Fischinger.

Mus: Wolfgang Zeller.

doc; F-seqs (travel film with some animated abstract forms)

Ref: MPH 24 Oct '31 p34; Undrgnd.

Melody

1953 WD (RKO) color 3D ani 10 mins.

Prod: Walt Disney.

Dir: C. August Nichols & Ward Kimball.

Story: Dick Huemer.

Mus: Joseph S. Dubin.

F-com

Ref: MFB Jan '55 p 13; Vd 18 May '53; LC.

See also: Toot, Whistle, Plunk and Boom (1953).

Melody in the Dark

1948 British, Advent (Adelphi) 67 mins.

Dir: Robert Jordan Hill.

SP: R.J. Hill & John Guillermin.

Cin: Jo Jago.

Cast: Ben Wrigley, Eunice Gayson, Richard Thorpe.

bor-H-com ("haunted" mansion)

Ref: MFB '49 p60.

Melody of Doom, The

1915 Selig sil 2 reels.

Dir: Frank Beal.

Author: W.E. Wing.

Cast: Eugenie Besserer, William Sheerer, Fred Huntley.

bor-F-H (woman frightened & later killed by melody on violin)

Ref: MPN 7 Aug '15; LC.

Melody of the World

See: Melodie der Welt (1929).

Melody Time

1948 WD (RKO) color ani & live 75 mins.

Prod: Walt Disney.

Prod Sup: Ben Sharpsteen.

Seq Dir: Clyde Geronimi, Wilfred Jackson, Jack Kinney, & Hamilton Luske.

Ani Dir: Les Clark, Ollie Johnston, Milt Kahl, Ward Kimball, Eric Larson, & John Lounsbery.

Story: Ken Anderson, Homer Brightman, William Cottrell, Winston Hibler, Jesse Marsh, Bob Moore, Erdman Penner, Harry Reeves, Joe Rinaldi, Art Scott, Ted Sears, & John Walbridge.

Layout: Robert Cormack, Don Da Gradi, Don Griffith, Hugh Hennesy, Lance Nolley, Kendall O'Connor, Thor Putnam, McLaren Stewart, & Al Zinnen.

Ani: Edwin Aardal, Hal Ambro, Jack Boyd, Hal King, Rudy Larriva, Don Lusk, Dan MacManus, Josh Meador, Cliff Nordberg, Ken O'Brien, George Rowley, Harvey Toombs, Marvin Woodward, & Judge Whitaker.

BG: Dick Anthony, Merle Cox, Brice Mack, Art Riley, & Jimi Trout.

Color & Style: Mary Blair, Claude Coats, & Dick Kelsey.

Sp Process: Ub Iwerks.

Edit: Don Halliday & Thomas Scott.

Mus Dir: Eliot Daniel & Ken Darby.

Voices include: Dennis Day.

Cast: Roy Rogers, Luana Patten, Bobby Driscoll, the Sons of the Pioneers.

mus-F-com (7 seqs, largely built around American legends: "Once Upon a Wintertime;" "Bumble Boogie;" "Johnny Appleseed" -- ghost of old pioneer urges Johnny to plant apple trees over American frontier; "Little Toot;" "Trees;" "Blame It on the Samba" -- Donald Duck & José Carioca dance with live girls; "Pecos Bill" -- child raised by coyotes becomes super-cowboy, can rope tornadoes, tame anything, etc.; girlfriend bounced to Moon on her bustle)

Ref: Art/Ani; LC; Vd 19 May '48; Acad.

See also: Pecos Bill, sequence released separately.

Melomaniac, The

(Le Mélomane)

1903 French, Star sil 170 ft.

Made by: Georges Méliès.

Cast: Georges Méliès.

Ref: Sadoul/M p 18; LC; GM Mage p 134-37; Niver 347.

Melomaniac, The

1966? Rumanian color ani sh.

Dir: Horia Stefanescu.

F

Ref: Ani/Cin p 113.

Memo to Mars

1954 U.S. Rubber & Wilding 16mm 24 mins.

doc; SF-seq (how the Martians would look upon us)

Ref: LC.

Mémoires d'un Médecin

(novel by A. Dumas)

See: Black Magic (1949).

Memories of the Future

See: Erinnerungen an die Zukunft (1969).

Memories of the Stars

See: Wycieczkaw Kosmos (1961).

Men in the Park, The

1972? Canadian, NFB ani 6 mins.

Made by: George Geertsen.

bor-F

Ref: Filmex II.

Men Must Fight

1933 MGM 72 mins.

Dir: Edgar Selwyn.

SP: C. Gardner Sullivan.

Cin: George Folsey.

Edit: William S. Gray.

Cast: Diana Wynyard, Lewis Stone, Phillips Holmes, May Robson, Ruth Selwyn, Robert Young, Hedda Hopper, Mary Carlisle.

SF (set in 1940; world war; US bombarded; Empire State Bldg destroyed; rocket ship)

Ref: Vw 14 March '33; MPH 18 March '33 p34, 36; FD 11 March '33; LC.

Based on the play by Reginald Lawrence & S.K. Lauren.

Men of Action Meet Women of Drakula

1969 Philippine.

Prod: Victoria Villanueva.

Dir: Artemio Marquez.

SpFX: Totoy Torrente.

Mus: Britz.

Cast: Dante Varona, Eddie Torrente, Ruben Obligacion, Norman Henson, Ernesto Beren, Angelito Marquez, Martin Marfil, Liza Melmonte, Marco Antonio, Nemia Velasco, Silvio (Sylvio?) Ramiro, Miniong Alvarez, Menggay.

F-H (tumblers vs. vampire women & Dracula)

Ref: Chodkowski; MTVM Aug '69 p35.

See also: Dracula.

Men with Steel Faces

See: Phantom Empire, The (1935).

Menace from Outer Space

1954 Reed (MCA-TV) 78 mins.

Prod: Roland Reed.

Cast: Richard Crane, Maurice Cass.

SF

Ref: Willis.

See also: Rocky Jones, Space Ranger.

Mendelism

1971 Canadian cut-out ani sh.

Dir: Pierre Hébert.

F

Ref: ASIFA Bltn 2.

Mensch am Wege

(The Man by the Roadside)

1923 German, Asmania-Film sil.

Dir & Sc: Wilhelm (later William) Dieterle.

Cast: William Dieterle, Marlene Dietrich, Alexander Granach, Heinrich George.

F (man revealed to be an angel)

Ref: FIR April '57 p 149, Jan '71 p 19; UF p 190, 291.

Based on a short story by Leo Tolstoi.

Menuet Lilliputien, Le

See: Lilliputian Minuet, The (1905).

Mephisto and the Maiden

1909 Selig sil 900 ft.

F (Friar Hugo trades his soul to the Devil for two hours with a girl)

Ref: FI IV-18:9.

Mephisto Waltz, The

1971 20th-Fox color 115 mins.

Prod: Quinn Martin.

Dir: Paul Wendkos.

SP: Ben Maddow.

Art Dir: Richard Y. Hamen.

Cin: William W. Spencer.

SpFX: Howard A. Anderson Co.

Edit: Richard K. Brockway.

Mus: Jerry Goldsmith & Franz Liszt.

Cast: Alan Alda, Jacqueline Bisset, Barbara Parkins, Brad Dillman, Curt Jurgens, William Windom, Kathleen Widdoes, Pamelyn Ferdin, Khigh Dhiegh, Berry Kroeger.

F-H (Devil-worshiping elderly pianist transfers his mind into body of younger pianist through black magic; younger pianist's wife transfers her mind into the body of lover of older pianist; murder by black magic)

Ref: Vw 3 Feb '71; FF '71 p76-78; MFB '71 p 167.

Based on the novel by Fred Mustard Stewart.

Mephisto's Affinity

1908 Lubin sil 635 ft.

F-com (with wife's permission the Devil has a good time on Earth; brings statue to life)

Ref: MPW '08 p547; LC; Views.

Mephisto's Son

(The Devil's Son Makes a Night of It in Paris --ad.t?)

1906 French, Pathé sil 1148 ft.

F (Mephisto's son has fun in Paris; scenes in Hell)

Ref: Views 1:25:5, 8-9.

Mera, the Medium

1914 French, Luna Film Industrie (Film Releases of America) sil 3 reels.

F (future predictions)

Ref: MPW 21:482; LC.

Meraviglie di Aladino, Le

See: Wonders of Aladdin, The (1961).

Merbabies

1938 WD (BV) ani 1 reel.

Prod: Walt Disney.

F-com

Merchant of Venice, The

1919 British, Hepworth ani sil sh.

Dir & Ani: Anson Dyer.

F-com

Ref: Shake/Sil p264-65.

Parody of the play by William Shakespeare.

Merle, Le

(The Blackbird)

1958 Canadian, NFB color cut-out ani 5 mins.

Made by: Norman McLaren.

F

Ref: Ani/Cin p72, 174; Ed Film cat p20; Pyramid cat p227.

Based on the old French-Canadian folk song "Mon Merle."

Mermaid, The

(La Sirène)

1904 French, Star sil 233 ft.

Made by: Georges Méliès.

Cast: Georges Méliès.

F

Ref: Sadoul/M, GM Mage; LC; Niver 64; Niver/20 p53.

Mermaid, The

1966 Hongkong, Shaw color 99 mins.
cont.

Mermaid cont.

Prod: Runme Shaw.

Dir: Kao Li.

Sp & Lyrics: Chang Chien.

Art Dir: Chen Chi-ruey.

Cin: Tung Shao-yung.

Edit: Chang Shing-Loong.

Mus: Wang Fu-ling.

Cast: Ivy Ling Po, Li Ching, Ching Miao, Au-Yang Sha-fei, Yang Tse-Chin.

mus-F (fairy; turtle fairy; lobster fairy -- magical creatures beneath the Blue Lake; human embodiment of 1000-year old carp)

Ref: Vw 2 Feb '66; HR 22 Feb '67.

Based on Chinese folklore.

Mermaid, The

1973 (Freeway Films) color.

sex-F

Ref: BO 30 July '73 pNE 3 ad.

Mermaid

See: Sirène (1968).

Mermaids and Sea Robbers

See: Ningyo Shoten (1959).

Mermaids of Tiburon, The

1962 Pacific Prods & Aquasex Inc (Filmgroup) color 77 mins.

Prod, Dir, SP: John Lamb.

Assoc Prod: Ron Graham.

Cin: J. Lamb, Hal McAlpin, & Brydon Baker.

Edit: Bert Honey.

Mus: Richard La Salle.

Cast: George Rowe, Diane Webber [mermaid], Timothy Carey, José Gonzales-Gonzales, John Mylong, Gil Baretto.

F (bevy of mermaids)

Ref: FF '62 p 162; HR & Vd 14 June '62; Pardi.

See also: Aquasex (1964).

Mermaid's Love, A

1971? Taiwanese?, Great Wall color scope.

Cast: Fu Che, Hsia Meng.

F

Ref: Singapore Straits-Times 4 March '71.

Merry Frolics of Satan, The

(Les 400 Farces du Diable; The 400 Blows of the Devil)

1906 French, Star colored sil 1050 ft.

Made by: Georges Méliès.

Cast: Georges Méliès.

F (engineer trying to achieve 400 mph tricked into selling soul to Devil; people walk on ceiling; demons come out of clock; women fall out of umbrella; etc.)

Ref: Views 1:25:5, 8; Sadoul/M, GM Mage 849; LC; Collier.

Based on stage presentation by Victor de Cottens & G. Méliès.

Merry Go Round in the Jungle

1957 UPA color ani 10 mins.

F-com

Ref: CFS cat '69; UPA.

Based on paintings by Henri Rousseau.

Merry Night, A

1914 British, Martin sil 680 ft.

Dir: Dave Aylott.

F-com ("drunkard beset by animated objects takes flight in bed")

Ref: Gifford/BFC 04909.

Merry Old Soul, The
1931 U ani sh.
Prod: Walter Lantz.
F-com
Ref: LC; Acad nom.
See also: Oswald (1927-38).

Merry Widow Waltz, The
1908 French, Pathé sil sh.
Dir: Ferdinand Zecca.
F (objects come to life)
Ref: Willis.

Merry Wives of Windsor
See: Composition in Blue (1933).

Merveilleux Eventail Vivant, Le
See: Wonderful Living Fan, The (1904).

Mesa of Lost Women, The
(Lost Women of Zarpa --ad.t.)
1952 (1953; 1956) Howco (White-Houck --1956 rr) 69 mins.
Prod: G. William Perkins & Melvin Gale.
Dir: Herbert Tevos & Ron Ormond.
SP: H. Tevos.
Cin: Karl Struss & Gilbert Warrenton.
Edit: Hugh Winn & Ray Lockert.
Mus: Hoyt Curtin.
Cast: Jackie Coogan, Allan Nixon, Richard Travis, Mary Hill.
SF-H (mad scientist creates giant tarantulas & superwomen)
Ref: Vd 2 July '52; MFB June '54 p88; Vw 17 Oct '56.

Mésaventures d'un Aéronaute
See: Balloonist's Mishap, The (1900).

Mesdames, Messieurs
See: Opening Speech (1960).

Meshes of the Afternoon
1943 (1958) Amateur (C-16) sil (sound added in 1958) 16mm 14 mins.
Made by: Maya Deren.
Cin: Alexander Hammid.
Mus: Teiji Ito.
Cast: Maya Deren.
exp-psy-F-dream (girl sees man who has mirror face; knife appears everywhere; etc.)
Ref: Undrgnd p84; Agee p 191; T/F p 190; C-16 cat p21.

Mesmerian Experiment, A
(Le Baquet de Mesmer)
1905 French, Star sil 200 ft.
Made by: Georges Méliès.
F
Ref: Sadoul/M, GM Mage 693-95.

Mesmerist, The
1898 British, G.A. Smith sil 75 ft.
Made by: G.A. Smith
F (spirit taken from girl's body & returned)
Ref: Sadoul p361, 471; Filmlex p745; Gifford/BFC 00140.

Mesmerist, The
1908 French, Pathé sil 606 ft.
F (hypnotized widow leads police to where husband was killed, mentally sees the crime, then leads to murderer)
Ref: Views 126:10.

Mesmerist and Country People
1899 Edison sil 103 ft.
F-com (tricks)
Ref: LC; Niver p64.

Message from Beyond, A
1912 Solax sil sh.
Prod: Alice Guy-Blanché.
F (spirit points to portrait where hero finds money)
Ref: MPW 12:768, 770, 864, 946.

Message from Mars, A
● 1909 New Zealand sil sh?
Prod: Franklyn Barrett.
Ref: Collier.

● 1913 British, United Kingdom Films sil 4000 ft.
Prod: Nicholson Ormsby-Scott.
Dir & Sc: J. Wallett Waller.
Cast: Charles Hawtrey, E. Holman Clark, Crissie Bell, Frank Hector, Hubert Willis, Kate Tyndale, Evelyn Beaumont, Eileen Temple, R. Crompton, B. Stanmore, Tonie Reith.
Ref: Gasca p24; MPW 18:287, 1342; Gifford/BFC 04253.

● 1921 Metro sil 5187 ft.
Prod & Dir: Maxwell Karger.
Sc: Arthur Zellner & Arthur Maude.
Cin: Arthur Martinelli.
Cast: Bert Lytell, Raye Dean, Gordon Ash, Maude Milton, Aphonz Ethier [Martian], Leonard Mudie.
F-dream (selfish young man has dream in which a messenger from Mars shows him the poverty and suffering of the world)
Ref: AFI F2.3571 p507; MPN 22:3564; FD 27 March '21.

F (God of Mars commands messenger to Earth to reclaim selfish mortal; crystal globe reveals happenings on Earth)
Based on the play by Richard Ganthony.

Message to the Future
1970? Hungarian serial.
Dir: Jozsef Nepp.
SF (family meets descendants from the 30th Century)
Ref: F&F June '71.

Messages, Messages
n.d. Amateur.
Made by: Steve Arnold.
exp-F
Ref: California Living Magazine of San Francisco Sunday Chronicle & Examiner 11 July '71.

Messe Nere della Contessa Dracula, Le
(The Black Harvest of Countess Dracula)
1972? Italian.
Cast: Paul Naschy (real name: Jacinto Molina).
F-H (vampires)
Ref: LSH 2:69.
See also: Dracula.

Messenger Boy Magician, The
1910 Lubin sil 715 ft.
F
Ref: MPW 6:848.

Messiah, The
(poem by F. Klopstock)
See: Satan (1911).

Messrs. Schwarzwalde and Edgar's Last Trick
See: Last Trick of Mr. Schwarzwalde and Mr. Edgar (1965?).

Mest' Kinematograficeskogo Operatora
See: Revenge of the Kinematograph Cameraman (1912).

Meta
1947 Amateur sh.
Made by: Robert Howard.
Ref: USA Exp List; Undrgnd p96; SF Art Mus Prog 31 Oct'47.

Metamorfeus
1969 Czech, Kratky color ani 14 mins.
Dir & Story: Jiří Brdečka.
myth-F
Ref: Mamaia '70.
Based on the Greek myth of Orpheus and Eurydice.

Metamorfosis
1971 Spanish, Filmscontacto color 90 mins.
Dir: Jacinto Esteva.
SP: José M. Nunes & J. Esteva.
Cin: Jaime Deu Casas.
Edit: Ramon Quadreny.
Mus: Carlos Maleras.
Cast: Romy, Julian Ugarte, Carlos Otero, Marta May, Alberto Puig, Luis Ciges.
SF-H (scientists turn "abnormal being" into an "extraordinarily perfect being" but she slowly reverts to her "primitive state" --SpCin)
Ref: SpCin '72 p 144-45.

Metamorfoza
See: Metamorphosis (1964).

Metamorphoses
1912 French, C.G.P.C. sil tinted 1/2 reel.
F (magician turns toys into animals, flowers into girls)
Ref: MPW 14:1112; F/A p423.

Metamorphoses
1968 Canadian, NFB color ani sh.
Dir: Laurent Coderre.
abs-F
Ref: ASIFA 6.

Métamorphoses du Papillon, Les
(The Metamorphosis of the Butterfly)
1906 French, Pathé sil sh.
Dir: Gaston Velle.
F
Ref: Filmlex p784, 785.

Métamorphoses du Roi de Pique, Les
(The Metamorphosis of the King of Spades)
1903 French, Pathé sil sh.
Dir: Gaston Velle.
F
Ref: Filmlex p785; Sadoul.

Metamorphosis
1914 American sil 2 reels.
Prod: M.R. McKinstry.
Cast: Sydney Ayres, Vinnie Rich, Jack Richardson, Harry Von Meter, Charlotte Burton.
F (spirit leaves body, performs deeds at distance)
Ref: MPW 20:1275, 1300, 1542;LC.

Metamorphosis
● 1951 University of Michigan 16mm 75 mins.
Prod, Dir, Edit: William J. Hampton.
SP: W.J. Hampton, William Wiegland, & Richard Kraus.
Sets & Props: Chuck Elliott.
Cin: Paul Meagher.
Mus: Edward Chudacoff.
Cast: Dana Elcar, Ted Heusel, Bette Ellis.
Ref: FIR Dec '51 p28-33.

● 1953 British, Amateur 28 mins.
Dir: Lorenza Mazzetti.
Ref: BFI Dist Cat Sup 1:79.
exp-sur-F (Gregor Samsa awakes one morning to find he has turned into a large cockroach)
Based on short story "The Metamorphosis" by Franz Kafka.

Metamorphosis
(Metamorfoza)
1964 Yugoslavian, Zagreb 16mm color ani 8 mins.
Dir, Design, Ani: Aleksandar Marks & Vladimir Jutriša.
SP: Fedor Vidas.
Bg: Srdjan Matić.
Mus: Davor Kajfes.
F-com-sat (satire of US pop cults, rock music in particular; sequence with Tarzan)
Ref: Collier; Z/Zagreb p79.
See also: Tarzan.

Metamorphosis
1970 Czech ani sh.
Dir: Jiří Brdečka.
Design: Vladimir Kladiva.
F-com
Ref: Czech Films '71.

Metamorphosis
1971 (Film Images) color ani 5 mins.
F
Ref: Previews Dec '72.

Metamorphosis of the Butterfly, The
See: Métamorphoses du Papillon, Les (1906).

Metamorphosis of the King of Spades, The
See: Métamorphoses du Roi du Pique, Les (1903).

Metamorphosis USA or The Soul of White Folk: A Racial Fantasy
n.d. Amateur (Film-makers' Coop) 16mm 30 mins.
Dir: Dexter Kelly.
Cin: D. Kelly, John Palmer, Norris Eisenbrey, & Ed Nielsen.
Mus: Max Steiner, Miklos Rozsa, Alfred Newman, and others.
exp-F
Ref: FMC 5:176-77.

Metanoia
n.d. Amateur (C-16) 16mm negative projection 10 mins.
Made by: Ilya Bolotowsky.
exp-F
Ref: C-16 p22.

Metanomen
1966 San Francisco State College (Film-makers' Coop) 16mm 8 mins.
Made by: Scott Bartlett.
Cast: Mark Bravo, Nan Schleiger.
exp-abs-F
Ref: FMC 5:28; MFB April '71 p86; CCC p5; FQ Summer '67 p73-74.

Metempsicosi
1913 Italian sil sh?
Cast: Hesperia.
F (transfer of souls at death)
Ref: DdC III:38.

Metempsychosis II
n.d. Amateur (Film-makers' Coop) 16mm 8 3/4 mins.
Made by: Larry Betts.
F-seq (the journey of an emotionless young boy through 4 internal levels; in 4th, the transference of the life force from the dying to the living)
Ref: FMC 5:31.

Métempsycose
1907 French sil sh.
F (reincarnation; souls change bodies)
Ref: DdC II:383.

Métempsycose
See: Tomb of Torture (1963).

Meteor, The

(screen treatment by R. Bradbury)

See: It Came from Outer Space (1953).

Meteor Monster

See: Teenage Monster (1957).

Meter Man, The

(play by C.S. Forbes)

See: Penthouse, The (1967).

Method for Murder

(story by R. Bloch)

See: House that Dripped Blood, The (1970).

Metrographic

1960 Martin Toonder (C-16) 16mm color 3 mins.

Dir: Vittorio Speich.

Cin: Antei Bolchorst.

Mus: Jan Walhoben.

exp-F (transformations)

Ref: C-16 p22; FQ Spring '61 p34.

Metropolis

1926 (1927) German, UFA (Par) sil 10,400 ft (8 reels).

Prod: Erich Pommer.

Dir: Fritz Lang.

Sc: F. Lang & Thea von Harbou.

Art Dir: Otto Hunte, Erich Kettelhut, & Karl Vollbrecht.

Costumes: Anne Willkomm.

Cin: Karl Freund & Günther Rittau.

SpFX: Eugen Shuftan.

Mus: Gottfried (Gothfried) Happertz.

Mus, 2nd Cutting: Konrad Elfers.

Cast: Brigitte Helm, Alfred Abel, Gustav Fröhlich, Rudolf Klein-Rogge, Heinrich George, Fritz Rasp, Theodor Loos.

SF (in gigantic city of distant future, ruler of the city has mad scientist turn robot into duplicate of girl trusted by downtrodden masses to enable ruler to crush their rebellion once and for all)

Ref: Vw 16 March '27; FD 13 March '27; Gasca p42-43; MPW 85:135; F/A p423; LC.

Based on the novel by Thea von Harbou.

Metropolis

See: Giant of Metropolis (1962).

Metropolis II

1969 Amateur 8mm 13.5 mins.

Made by: Paul Hasse.

Sc: Forrest J Ackerman.

SF (dinosaur threatens city of Metropolis, routed by Rotwang the scientist)

Ref: Luna -- 7th Kodak Teenage Movie Awards.

Metropolitain

(Les Illuminations)

1958 French, Armor Films (FACSEA) color ani 10 mins.

Dir: Henri Gruel.

Artwork: Laure Garcia.

Nar: Jean Marc Tennberg.

abs-F

Ref: FACSEA.

Based on the poem by Arthur Rimbaud.

Metroscopix

1953 MGM 3D (anaglyph) 20 mins.

F-seq

Ref: MFB May '53.

Includes Third Dimensional Murder.

Metzengerstein

(story by E.A. Poe)

See: Spirits of the Dead (1967).

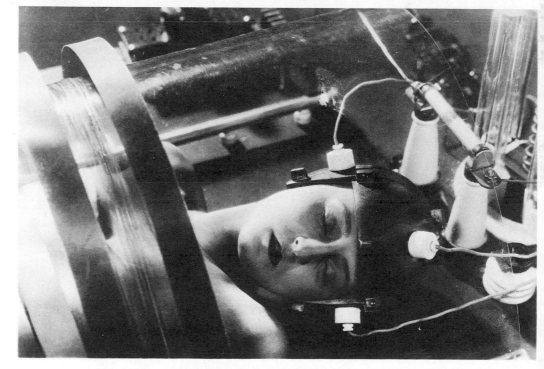

Metropolis (1926) German

Meurtre

(Murder)

1964 French, O.R.T.F. color 3 mins.

Made by: Piotr Kamler.

abs-F

Ref: Annecy '65.

Meurtre en 45 Tours

See: Murder at 45 R.P.M. (1960).

Mexicali Shmoes

1959 WB color ani sh.

Prod: John W. Burton.

F-com

Ref: Acad nom.

Mexican Spitfire Sees a Ghost

1942 RKO 70 mins.

Prod: Cliff Reid.

Dir: Leslie Goodwins.

SP: Charles E. Roberts & Monte Brice.

Art Dir: Albert D'Agostino & Carroll Clark.

Cin: Russell Metty.

Edit: Theron Warth.

Mus Dir: C. Bakaleinikoff.

Cast: Lupe Velez, Leon Errol, Charles "Buddy" Rogers, Elisabeth Rison, Donald MacBride, Minna Gombell, Mantan Moreland.

bor-H-com (ghosts are really saboteurs)

Ref: Vd & HR 5 May '42; MFB June '42 p73; MPH 9 May '42.

Mezga Family, The

See: Message to the Future (1970?).

Mezhplanetnaya Revolutsiya

(Interplanetary Revolution)

1924 Soviet, Stat Film Technicium sil ani 1150 ft.

Art Dir: E. Komissarenko, Y. Merkulov, & N. Khodatayev.

Cin: V. Alexeyev.

SF-com

Ref: Kino p274, 429.

Parody of Aelita (1924).

Meztelen Vagy

(Legend About the Death and Resurrection of Two Young Men)

1972?

alleg-F

Ref: Vw 26 July '72 p22.

Mga Manugang ni Drakula
See: Manugang ni Drakula, Mga (1964).

Mi Adorable Esclava
(My Adorable Slave)
1961 Spanish.
Dir: José M. Elorrieta.
SP: J.M. Elorrieta & Augustin Navarro.
Art Dir: Augusto Lega.
Cin: Alejandro Ulloa.
Cast: Ethel Rojo [genie], Antonio Casal, Licia Calderón, C. González Ruano.
F-com (man's encounter with brass lantern brings forth a girl genie)
Ref: SpCin '62 p87; MMF 9:16, 20.

Mi Adorada Clementina
(My Adored Clementine)
1953 Mexican, Filmex.
Dir: Rafael Baledon.
SP: Ramón Obón.
Cin: Agustín Martinez Solares.
Mus: Antonio Díaz Conde.
Cast: Marga López, Tony Aguilar, Joaquin Pardavé, Elda Peralta, Pedro D'Aguillon.
F-com (ghosts)
Ref: Aventura p429.
Based on a story by Alejandro Verbitzky & Emilio Villalta.

Mi Novia Es una Fantasma
(My Bride Is a Ghost)
1944 Argentine, Lumiton 75 mins.
Dir: Francisco Mugica.
Story: Pondal Rios & Carlos Olivan.
SP: Francisco Oyarzábal.
Cin: R. Connord, R. Rodriguez Remy, & Alfredo Traverso.
Edit: Antonio Rampoldi.
Mus: Bert Rosé.
Cast: Mirtha Legrand, Pepe Iglesias, Nuri Montsé, Osvaldo Miranda, Benita Puértolas, Susana Campos.
F-com
Ref: Nubila II:40, 282.

Miasto
(The Town)
1963 Polish ani sh.
Dir: Miroslaw Kijowicz.
F

Michael Shayne
Detective character created by Brett Halliday.
See: Man Who Wouldn't Die, The (1942).

Michaels in Africa, The
(book by G. Michaels)
See: Drums of Destiny (1962).

Mickey and the Beanstalk
See: Fun and Fancy Free (1947).

Mickey and the Seal
1948 WD (RKO) color ani 1 reel.
Prod: Walt Disney.
Dir: Charles Nichols.
Story: Nick George & Milt Schaffer.
Ani: Phil Duncan, George Nicholas, Hugh Fraser, & Dan MacManus.
Mus: Oliver Wallace.
F-com
Ref: LC; Acad nom.
See also: Mickey Mouse (1928--); Pluto (1940-51).

Mickey Mouse
1928--6? WD (Col, later UA, later RKO, later BV) sh ani series, in color from mid-30s.
Prod: Walt Disney.
F-com
Ref: LC; ScF 5:29-30.
See also: Plane Crazy (1928); Steamboat Willie (1928); Haunted House, The (1929); Mickey's Orphans (1931); Mickey's Gala Premier (1933); Mickey's Mechanical Man (1933); Gulliver Mickey (1934); Orphan's Benefit, The (1934); Band Concert, The (1935); Worm Turns, The (1936); Brave Little Tailor, The (1938); Pointer, The (1939); Fantasia (1940); Lonesome Ghosts (1940); Lend a Paw (1941); Squatter's Rights (1946); Fun and Fancy Free (1947); Mickey and the Seal (1948); Mickey Mouse Anniversary Show, The (1968).

Mickey Mouse Anniversary Show, The
1968 WD color ani & live 89 mins.
Prod & SP: Ward Kimball.
Dir: W. Kimball & Robert Stevenson.
Edit: Ernie Milano.
Mus: George Bruns.
Nar: Dean Jones.
F-seqs (expansion for theatrical release of US TV show, with sequences from various Mickey Mouse cartoons)
Ref: MFB July '71 p 144.
See also: Mickey Mouse (1928-6?).

Mickey's Gala Premier
1933 WD (UA) ani 7 mins.
Prod: Walt Disney.
F-com-dream (Mickey Mouse dreams he is movie star; at premier of his new movie, every star in Hollywood shows up, including Dracula and Frankenstein's Monster)
Ref: MPH 29 July '33 p33; MMF 4/5:147; FIR Nov '66 p581.
See also: Mickey Mouse (1928-6?); Dracula; Frankenstein.

Mickey's Mechanical Man
1933 WD (UA) ani 1 reel.
Prod: Walt Disney.
F-com
Ref: LC; Dipali 21 May '37 p27.
See also: Mickey Mouse (1928-6?).

Mickey's Orphans
1931 WD (Col) ani sh.
Prod: Walt Disney.
F-com
Ref: LC; Acad nom.
See also: Mickey Mouse (1928-6?).

Microscopia
See: Fantastic Voyage (1966).

Microsecond
1969 UCLA color ani sh.
Dir: Dan McLaughlin.
F
Ref: ASIFA 5.

Microspook
1949 Col 16 mins.
Prod: Hugh McCollum.
Dir & SP: Edward Bernds.
Edit: Henry DeMond.
Cast: Harry Von Zell.
H-com (haunted house; real & fake gorilla; fake ghosts)
Ref: LC.

Mid-Winter Night's Dream, A or Little Joe's Luck
1906 Vit sil 600 ft.
Prod & Dir: J. Stuart Blackton.

cont.

Mid-winter Night's Dream cont.
F-dream (toys come to life in dream)
Ref: V & FI 1:35:5, 9; LC.
See also: Little Match Girl, The.

Midget and Giant
See: Dwarf and the Giant, The (1901).

Midi-Minuit
(Noon to Midnight)
1970 French, Albertine color 105 mins.
Dir & SP: Pierre Philippe.
Cin: Pierre Willemin.
Edit: Helene Arnat.
Cast: Sylvie Fennec, Beatrice Arnac, Daniel Emilfork, Jacques Portet, Laurent Vergez, Patrick Jouanne.
H (torture; killer who rips victims apart with iron-clawed gloves; hints of vampirism)
Ref: Photon 21:31; Vw 6 Oct '71; Ecran 2:41-42.

Midnight
1916 (1917) IMP (U) sil 1 reel.
Dir: Allen J. Holubar.
Story: Frank H. Spearman.
Sc: E.J. Clawson.
Cast: Allan J. Holubar, Zoe Rae.
F (ghost of little girl)
Ref: MPW 31:246, 275; LC.

Midnight Adventure
See: Little Train (1960).

Midnight at Madame Tussaud's
1936 British 62 mins.
Dir: George Pearson.
Cast: Charles Oliver, James Carew, Bernard Miles, William Hartnell.
H
Ref: BiB's; Brit Cin (Willis).

Midnight Bell, A
1921 Charles Ray Prods (FN) sil 6140 ft.
Pres: Arthur S. Kane.
Dir: Albert Ray.
Adapt: Richard Andres.
Titles: Edward Withers.
Tech Dir: Robert Bennett.
Cin: George Rizard.
Edit: Harry Decker.
Cast: Charles Ray, Donald MacDonald, Van Dyke Brooke, Doris Pawn, Clyde McCoy, Jess Herring.
H-com (supposedly haunted church; ghosts which may or may not be crooks)
Ref: AFI F2.3583 p508; MPH (Willis).
Based on the play by Charles Hay Hoyt.

Midnight Cafe, The
n.d. Amateur (Film-makers' Coop) 16mm 15 mins.
Dir & SP: Frederic Martin.
Story: Theodore (real name: Theodore Gottlieb).
Mus: Herbert Fauerstein.
Cast: Theodore.
exp-H
Ref: FMC 5:228.

Midnight Episode, A
(Un Bon Lit: A Good Bed)
1899 French, Star sil 65 ft.
Made by: Georges Méliès.
F-com (gigantic bugs are destroyed by fire)
Ref: Sadoul/M, GM Mage 190; Gifford/H p 19.

Midnight Frolic
See: Mo-Toy Comedies (1917).

Midnight in the Graveyard
See: At Midnight in the Graveyard (1909).

Midnight Menace
1937 British, Grosvenor (ABFD) 78 mins.
Dir: Sinclair Hill.
Story: Roger MacDougall & Alexander Mackendrick.
SP: G.H. Moresby-White.
Cin: Cyril Bristow.
Cast: Charles Farrell, Fritz Kortner, Margaret Vyner, Danny Green, Billy Bray.
SF (fleet of pilotless radio-controlled planes bomb London)
Ref: MFB '37; Vw 14 July '37; Gifford/SF.

Midnight Mess
(comic book story by W.M. Gaines & A.B. Feldstein)
See: Vault of Horror, The (1972).

Midnight Parasites, The
1972 Japanese ani 10 mins.
Dir: Yoji Kuri.
F
Ref: IAFF '72.

Midnight Phantasy, A
1903 Biograph sil 38 ft.
F-com (cigar store Indian comes to life, scalps man)
Ref: LC; Niver 65.

Midnight Phantom
See: Fantasma della Mezzanotte (1911).

Midnight Specter, The
See: Spettro di Mezzanotte, Lo (1915).

Midnight Warning
1932 (1933) Mayfair 60 mins (57 mins).
Sup: Cliff Broughton.
Dir: Spencer G. Bennet.
Story: Norman Battle.
SP: John Thomas Neville.
Cin: Jules Cronjager.
Edit: Byron Robinson.
Cast: Claudia Dell, William Boyd, John Harron, Huntley Gordon, Hooper Atchley, Lloyd Ingraham, Henry Hall, Art Winkler.
myst; bor-H (woman's brother vanishes from hotel, seems to have never existed; turns out he died of plague & hotel owner is covering up; treated as horror)
Ref: Vw 20 Jan '33, 14 March '33; Photo April '33; LC.
Note: the same story was filmed as the non-horror So Long at the Fair (1950).

Midstream
1929 Tiffany-Stahl part-talking & silent versions 6337 ft (7472 ft, silent).
Dir: James Flood.
Story: Bernice Boone.
Sc: Frances Guihan.
Dialog & Titles: Frederick Hatton & Fanny Hatton.
Cin: Jackson Rose.
Edit: Desmond O'Brien.
Mus: Hugo Riesenfeld.
Cast: Ricardo Cortez, Claire Windsor, Montagu Love, Larry Kent, Helen Jerome Eddy. "Faust" singers: Leslie Brigham, Louis Alvarez, Genevieve Schrader.
SF (to win a girl, an aging industrialist has a rejuven-ation operation, but during a performance of "Faust" reverts to his real age)
Ref: AFI F2.3610 p512.
See also: Faust.

Midsummer Madness

1964 British, Halas & Batchelor
color ani sh.

F

Ref: Acad; NYT 14 June '64.

Based on play "A Midsummer
Night's Dream" by William
Shakespeare.

See also: Midsummer Night's
Dream, A.

Midsummer Night's Dream, A

● 1909 Vit sil 991 ft.

Prod: J. Stuart Blackton.

Dir: Charles Kent.

Cast: Maurice Costello, Gladys
Hulette, Billy Ranous, Charles
Chapman, Walter Ackerman,
Julia Swayne Dordon, John
Bunny (? doubtful).

Ref: Shake/Sil p52-56; MPW
5:933, 6:10-11; Filmlex p684.

● 1909 French, Le Lion sil
1 reel.

Cast: Footit, Stacia Napierkowska.

Ref: Shake/Sil p 105.

● 1913 German, Deutsche Bioscop
sil.

Prod: Jacques Greenzweig.

Dir: Stellan Rye.

Sc: Hanns Heinz Ewers &
S. Rye.

Cin: Guido Seeber.

Cast: Grete Berger [Puck],
Carl Clewing.

F-dream (man dreams the fantastic
characters from Shakespeare's
play, including a satyr, frolic
on his lawn)

Ref: Shake/Sil p 176-77; LC.

Based on play "Ein Sommer-
nachtstraum" by Hanns Heinz
Ewers from the play by
William Shakespeare.

● 1913? Italian sil 800 ft
(incomplete).

Cast: Socrate Tommasi, Bianca
Maria Hübner.

Ref: Shake/Sil p 168-69.

● (Elfenszene aus dem Sommernachtstraum)

1917 German, Harmonie-Film
sync sound sh.

Choreog: Mary Zimmerman.

Mus: Felix Mendelssohn.

Dancers: Ballet of the Deutschen
Opernhauses Berlin.

ballet-F

Ref: Shake/Sil p221.

Based on the ballet by
Mendelssohn from the play
by William Shakespeare.

● (Ein Sommernachtstraum;
Wood Love --Brit.t.)

1925 (1928) sil 8292 ft.

Prod & Dir: Hans Neumann.

Sc: Hans Behrendt & H. Neumann.

Titles (German version): Klabund
(real name: Alfred Henschke).

Sets & Costumes: Ernö.

Cin: Guido Seeber & Reimar
Kuntze.

Cast: Werner Krauss, Valeska
Gert, Tamara, Theodor Becker,
Paul Günther, André Mattoni,
Wilhelm Bendow, Hans Albers,
Ernst Gronau, Fritz Rasp,
Alexander Granach.

Ref: Shake/Sil p297-99.

● 1935 WB 132 mins.

Prod: Max Reinhardt.

Dir: M. Reinhardt & William
Dieterle.

SP: Charles Kenyon & Mary
McCall Jr.

Design: Anton Grot.

Makeup: Perc Westmore.

Cin: Hal Mohr.

SpFX: Fred Jackman, Byron
Haskin, & H.F. Koenekamp.

cont.

Production Scene from Metropolis

Metropolis (1926) German

Midsummer Night's Dream, A cont.

Edit: Ralph Dawson.

Choreog: Bronislawa Nijinska.
Mus: Felix Mendelssohn.

Mus Adapt & Arranged: Erich
Wolfgang Korngold.

Cast: James Cagney, Olivia
de Havilland, Dick Powell, Joe
E. Brown, Jean Muir, Hugh
Herbert, Ian Hunter, Frank
McHugh, Victor Jory, Ross
Alexander, Grant Mitchell,
Mickey Rooney [Puck], Anita
Louise, Otis Harlan, Nini
Theilade, Arthur Treacher,
Hobart Cavanaugh, Dewey
Robison, Billy Barty.

cont.

Midsummer Night's Dream, A cont.

Ref: HR 9 Oct '35; MPH 21
Sept '35 p20-21, 12 Oct
'35 p38; FIR March '73 p
140-41; LC; FDY '36.

● 1958 British, BBC-TV 16mm
kinescope 104 mins.

Dir: Rudolph Cartier.

Mus: Felix Mendelssohn.

Cast: Paul Rogers, Gillian
Lynne, Miles Malleson, Natasha
Perry, John Justin, Ronald
Fraser, Peter Sallis.

Ref: FIR March '73 p 150.

cont.

Midsummer Night's Dream, A cont.

● (Sen Noci Svatjoanske)

1959 (1961) Czech (Show-
corporation) color ani puppet
scope 80 mins (74 mins).

Dir, SP, Art Dir: Jiří Trnka.

Cin: Jiří Vojta.

Edit: Hana Walachova.

Mus: Václav Trojan.

English Language Credits:

Eng Lang Text Adapt & Dir:
Howard Sackler.

Dialog Production Sup: Len
Appelson.

cont

cont.
cont.
cont.

Milky Way cont.

Edith Scob, Michel Piccoli, Bernerd Verley [Jesus], Georges Marchal, Claudio Brook, Pierre Clementi.

sur-rel-F-com-sat (while 2 20th-Century pilgrims journey to a shrine, they have visions, are transplanted in time, meet the Virgin Mary, etc.; scenes with Jesus; the Marquis De Sade)

Ref: MFB Dec '69 p36-37; Vw 5 March '69; SR 13 Dec '69; FD 2 Dec '69.

Mill, The

1971 Polish color? ani 11 mins.

Dir: Miroslaw Kijowicz.

F

Ref: IAFF '72.

Mill of the Stone Women

(Il Mulino Delle Donne di Pietra; Le Moulin des Supplices; Drops of Blood --Brit.t.)

1960 (1963) Italian/French, Wanguard & Faro & Explorer/ C.E.C. (Parade) color scope 94 mins.

Prod: Gianpaolo Bigazzi.

Dir: Giorgio Ferroni.

SP: Remigio Del Grosso, Ugo Liberatore, Giorgio Stegani, & G. Ferroni.

Art Dir: Arrigo Equini.

Cin: Pierludovico Pavoni.

Edit: Antoninetta Zita.

Mus: Carlo Innocenzi.

Cast: Pierre Brice, Scilla Gabel, Dany Carrel, Wolfgang Preiss, Herbert Boehme, Marco Guglielmi, Liana Orfei, Olga Solbelli.

SF-H (in 1912 in a Dutch windmill, a scientist keeps bringing his daughter back to life with the blood of young women; this turns the women to stone & they are mounted in a mechanical parade of famous beauties)

Ref: FF '63 p341; MFB July '63 p 102; FM 12:13, 14; 23:15.

Miller's Daughter, The

1934 WB ani 1 reel.

Prod: Leon Schlesinger.

Dir: Friz (Isadore) Freleng.

Ani: Rollin Hamilton & Chuck (Charles M.) Jones.

Mus: Norman Spencer.

F-com

Ref: LC.

Million Dollar Duck

1971 WD (BV) color 92 mins.

Prod: Bill Anderson.

Dir: Vincent McEveety.

SP: Roswell Rogers.

Cin: William Snyder.

Art Dir: John B. Mansbridge & Al Roelofs.

Edit: Lloyd L. Richardson.

Mus: Buddy Baker.

Cast: Dean Jones, Sandy Duncan, Joe Flynn, Tony Roberts, James Gregory, Jack Kruschen, Sammy Jackson, Arthur Hunnicutt, Edward Andrews.

SF-com (irradiated duck lays eggs with golden yolks)

Ref: HR 11 June '71; MFB Aug '71 p 167-68; FF '71 p445-46.

Based on a story by Ted Key.

Million Eyes of Su-Muru, The

(Sumuru --s.t.)

1967 British, Sumuru (AIP) scope color 95 mins.

Prod: Harry Alan Towers.

Dir: Lindsay Shonteff.

Story: H.A. Towers (Peter Welbeck).

SP: Kevin Kavanagh.

Art Dir: Scott MacGregor.

cont.

Million Eyes cont.

Cin: John Von Kotze.

Edit: Allan Morrison.

Mus: Johnny Scott.

Cast: Frankie Avalon, George Nader, Shirley Eaton [Su-Muru], Wilfrid Hyde-White, Klaus Kinski.

bor-SF (villainess Su-Muru heads global organization of women intent on conquering world; raygun turns people to stone)

Ref: FF '67 p318; Vw 14 June '67; MFB Jan '68 p 12.

Based on characters created by Sax Rohmer.

See also: Rio 70 (1970).

Millionaire Who Stole the Sun, The

1948 Czech ani 10 mins.

Dir: Zdenek Miler.

F

Ref: Ani/Cin p 126, 176; Czech Film flyer.

Mills of the Gods, The

(poem by E. Madden)

See: Devil's Toy, The (1916).

Mimetism

1964 Rumanian, Bucharesti ani 11 mins.

F

Ref: SF Festival '65.

Miminashi Hoichi

See: Kwaidan (1963).

Miminashi Hacchi

1970 Japanese, Toho ani 26 mins.

F (adventures of a motherless baby bee)
Ref: UniJ 52.

See also following title.

Minashigo Hacchi Otsukisamano Mama

1971 Japanese, Toho color ani 25 mins.

F

Ref: UniJ 53:36.

See also preceding title.

Mince Meet

1968 Amateur (Film-makers' Coop) 16mm ani 5 mins.

Made by: James Douglas.

sur-F

Ref: FMC 5:92.

Mind Benders, The

(The Pit --s.t.)

1963 British, Novus (AIP) 113 mins (99 mins).

Prod: Michael Relph.

Dir: Basil Dearden.

SP: James Kennaway.

Art Dir: James Morahan.

Cin: Denys Coop.

Edit: John D. Guthridge.

Mus: Georges Auric.

Cast: Dirk Bogarde, Mary Ure, John Clements, Michael Bryant, Wendy Craig, Harold Goldblatt, Geoffrey Keen, Norman Bird, Robin Hawdon.

bor-psy-SF (man undergoes personality change for the worse when subject in sensory-deprivation experiments)

Ref: MFB March '63 p31-32; FD 19 March '63; F&F March '63.

Mind-Detecting Ray, The

1918 Hungarian, Star sil.

Dir: Alfred Désy.

Sc: István Lázár.

SF (man's invention of mind-reading machine stolen from him by villainous scientist, whose wrongdoings are revealed at the end by the machine)

Ref: Pozitron '72 p74.

Mind of Mr. Soames, The

1969 (1970) British, Amicus (Col) color 98 mins.

Prod: Max J. Rosenberg & Milton Subotsky.

Dir: Alan Cooke.

SP: John Hale & Edward Simpson.

Art Dir: Bill Constable.

Cin: Billy Williams.

Edit: Bill Blunden.

Mus: Michael Dress.

Cast: Terence Stamp, Robert Vaughn, Nigel Davenport, Donal Donnelly, Christian Roberts, Vickery Turner.

bor-SF (man who has been in a coma since birth is brought out of it in his 20s)

Ref: MFB Nov '70 p229; CineF Winter '71 p25; NYT 13 Oct '70, 16 Oct '70; LAT 11 Nov '70.

Based on the novel by Charles Eric Maine.

Mind Reader, The

1908 French, Pathé sil 567 ft.

F

Ref: Views 130:90.

Mind Snatchers, The

(The Happiness Cage --s.t.)

1972 Int'l Film Ventures (Cinerama) color 94 mins. Filmed in Denmark.

Exec Prod: Richard Lewis.

Prod: George Goodman.

Dir: Bernard Girard.

SP: Ron Whyte.

Art Dir: William Molyneux.

Cin: Manny Wynn.

Edit: Sidney Katz.

Mus: Phil Ramone.

Cast: Christopher Walken, Joss Ackland, Ralph Meeker, Ronny Cox, Marco St. John, Tom Aldredge.

bor-SF-H (army scientists experiment in secret location on volunteers & one incorrigible prisoner: they have electrodes installed in their pleasure centers & can stimulate the centers themselves)

Ref: Vw 12 July '72 p24; BO 24 July '72 BookinGuide.

Based on play "The Happiness Cage" by Dennis Reardon.

Minerva Looks Out into the Zodiac

1960 Amateur 16mm color collage 6 mins.

Made by: Larry Jordan.

exp-abs-F

Ref: FC 52:79; Undrgnd p 155.

Mingling Spirits

1916 Nestor sil 1 reel.

Prod & Sc: Al E. Christie.

Story: Robert McGowan.

Cast: Lee Moran, Eddie Lyons, Betty Compson.

bor-H-com (phoney devil scares off man's spiritualistically-inclined mother-in-law)

Ref: MPN 13:406; LC.

Mini-Midi

See: World of Fashion (1968).

Miniature Circus, The

1908 French, Pathé sil colored 639 ft.

F-dream (person dreams that a toy circus comes to life)
Ref: View 138:9.

Minions

n.d. Amateur (Center Cinema) color 16mm? 4 mins.

Made by: John Heinz.

exp-F ("Lunar free forms invaded by Earthly square forms" --CCC)

Ref: CCC cat 2:12.

Minnie

1922 Marshal Neilan Prods (Associated First Nat'l Pictures) sil 6696 ft.

Pres & Sc: Marshall Neilan.

Dir: M. Neilan & Frank Urson.

Story: George Patullo.

Titles: Frances Marion.

Cin: David Kesson & Karl Struss.

Edit: Daniel J. Gray.

Cast: Leatrice Joy, Matt Moore, George Barnun, Josephine Crowell, Helen Lynch, Raymond Griffith.

bor-SF-com (extremely ugly girl made beautiful by surgery; wireless transmission of power invention)

Ref: AFI F2.3636 p515-16.

Minotaur, The

● 1910 Vit sil 983 ft.

Ref: MPW 6:703, 785.

● (Teseo Contro il Minotauro; Theseus Against the Minotaur; The Wild Beast of Crete --ad.t.; The Warlord of Crete --Brit.t.)

1960 (1961) Italian, Illiria (UA) color 98 mins.

Prod: Dino Mordini, Giorgio Agliani, & Rudolphe Solmsen.

Dir: Silvio Amadio.

SP: Alessandro Continenza & Gian Paolo Callegari.

Art Dir: Piero Poletto.

Cin: Aldo Giordani.

Edit: Nella Nannuzzi.

Mus: Carlo Rustichelli.

English SP: Daniel Mainwaring.

Cast: Bob Mathias, Rosanna Schiaffino, Alberto Lupo, Rik Battaglia, Nico Pepe, Carlo Tamberlani, Suzanne Loret [Goddess of Sea].

myth-F (in addition to Minotaur, Theseus is befriended by Amphitrite, Goddess of the Sea, who gives him a magic sword)

Ref: Vd & HR 2 April '61; MFB Dec '61 p 172; FF '61 p258.

myth-F (the Minotaur is man-eating monster, half-man, half-bull, that lives in Cretan caverns)

Based on the legends of Theseus.

Minotaur

See: Vulture, The (1966).

Minotauramachy

(painting by P. Picasso)

See: Mr. Frenhofer and the Minotaur (1949).

Minstrel's Song

See: Slowce M (1964).

Minuet by Mozart

1931 German ani 5 mins.

Made by: Oskar Fischinger.

abs-F

Ref: Collier.

Mio Amico, Jekyll, Il

(My Friend, Dr. Jekyll)

1960 Italian, MG Cinemat.

Dir: Marino Girolami.

SP: M. Girolami, Scarnicci, & Tarabusi.

Cin: Luciano Trasatti.

Cast: Ugo Tognazzi, Raimondo Vianello, Abbe Lane, Carlo Croccolo, Helene Chanel.

SF-com (professor can switch minds from body to body: trades his ugly one for a handsome one, ends up in chimpanzee's body)

Ref: Gasca p253-54; Unitalia '60 p 154-55; Gifford/MM p 156.

See also: Dr. Jekyll and Mr. Hyde.

Mirabai
See: Meerabai (1946).

Miracle, The
1911 French, Eclipse (George Kleine) sil 1040 ft.
rel-F (baby brought back to life by Jesus)
Ref: MPW 10:918, 1072; F/A p492; FIR March '64 p 158.

Miracle, The
● 1912 Austrian, Continental Kunstfilm (New York Film Co.) sil 4200 ft.

Filmed in Germany.
Prod: Joseph Menchen.
Stage Presentation Prod: Max Reinhardt.
Ref: MPW 14:377, 675, 809, 15:868; F/A p296; LC.

● 1959 WB color scope 121 mins.
Prod: Henry Blanke.
Dir: Irving Rapper.
SP: Frank Butler.
Art Dir: Hans Peters.
Cin: Ernest Haller.
Edit: Frank Bracht.
Mus: Elmer Bernstein.
Cast: Carroll Baker, Roger Moore, Walter Slezak, Vittorio Gassman, Katrina Paxinou, Carlos Rivas, Dennis King, Gustavo Rojo, Isobel Elsom.
Ref: Vd & HR 11 Nov '59; FD 28 Oct '59; FIR '59 p623.

rel-F (when young nun forsakes her vows, a statue of the Virgin Mary comes to life & takes place of young nun until she returns repentant to the convent)

Based on the play or panto-mime by Karl Vollmöller.

Miracle, The
1923 British, Stoll sil 1712 ft.
Prod: A.E. Coleby.
Sc: A.E. Coleby & Frank Wilson.
Cin: D.P. Cooper.
Cast: Harry Agar Lyons, Joan Clarkson, Stacey Gaunt, Frank Wilson, Humberston Wright, Fred Paul.

bor-F-H
Ref: BFI cat p 124.
Based on characters created by Sax Rohmer.
See also: Mystery of Dr. Fu Manchu, The (1923).

Miracle, A
1954 Amateur (Film-makers' Coop) 16mm ani 30 seconds.
Made by: Robert Breer.
Assist: Pontus Hulten.
F
Ref: Undrgnd p 131; FMC 5:42-43.

Miracle de la Madone, Le
See: Devil and the Statue, The (1901).

Miracle de Saint Hubert, Le
See: Forester Made King, A (1907).

Miracle des Roses, Le
(The Miracle of the Roses)
1908 French, Gaum sil ani sh.
Dir: Emile Cohl.
F
Ref: Filmlex p 1370.

Miracle du Brahmine, Le
See: Miracles of Brahmin, The (1899).

Miracle for the Cowards
1962 Spanish.
Dir: Manuel Mur Oti.
Cast: Javier Escrivá, Ruth Roman.
rel-F (characters raised from the dead; lighting, earthquake, beam of light to cross on Calvary)
Ref: Filmespania 4.

Miracle from Mars
See: Red Planet Mars (1952).

Miracle in 49th Street
See: Scoundrel, The (1935).

Miracle in Milan
(Miracolo a Milano)
1951 (1952) Italian, Enic (Joseph Burstyn) 101 mins (96 mins).
Prod & Dir: Vittorio de Sica.
Adapt: Cesare Zavattini, V. de Sica, Adolfo Franci, & Mario Chiari.
SP: C. Zavattini & V. de Sica.
Art Dir: Guido Fiorino.
Cin: Aldo Graziati.
SpFX: Ned Mann.
Edit: Eraldo Da Roma.
Mus: Alessandro Cicognini.
Cast: Francesco Golisano, Emma Gramatica, Paolo Stoppa, Erminio Spalla, Alba Arnova, Virgilio Riento.
rel-F-com (angel gives Toto power to work miracles when dove is rubbed)
Ref: FD 4 March '52; HR 15 Feb '52; MFB Dec '52 p 166-67; FIR Oct '57 p376; LC.
Based on novel "Toto il Buono" (Toto the Good) by Cesare Zavattini.

Miracle in the Rain
1956 WB 110 mins.
Prod: Frank P. Rosenberg.
Dir: Rudolph Maté.
SP: Ben Hecht.
Art Dir: Leo K. Kuter.
Cin: Russell Metty.
Edit: Thomas Reilly.
Mus: Franz Waxman.
Mus Dir: Leonid Raab.
Cast: Jane Wyman, Van Johnson, Peggy Castle, Fred Clark, Eileen Heckart, Barbara Nichols, Alan King, Minerva Urecal, Roxanne Arlen.
F-seq (girl believes dead soldier has returned -- he gives her coin, which later proves to be one he was wearing at his death)
Ref: Vd & HR 1 Feb '56; FD 9 March '56.
Based on the novel by Ben Hecht.

Miracle of Fatima, The
See: Miracle of Our Lady of Fatima, The (1952).

Miracle of Marcelino, The
See: Marcelino (1954).

Miracle of Our Lady of Fatima, The
1952 WB color 104 mins.
Prod: Bryan Foy.
Dir: John Brahm.
Art Dir: Edward Carrere.
Cin: Edwin Du Par.
SpFX: Robert Burks.
Edit: Thomas Reilly.
Mus: Max Steiner.
Cast: Gilbert Roland, Frank Silvera, Angela Clark, Jay Novello, Richard Hale, Sherry Jackson, Sammy Ogg.
rel-F (3 Spanish peasant children see Virgin Mary in a bush; to prove they saw her miracle
cont.

Miracle of Our Lady... cont.
happens: Sun seems to come close to the Earth blind woman regains sight, cripple walks, etc.)
Ref: HR & Vd 21 Aug '52; MFB April '53 p 55; FIR '52 p378.

Miracle of St. Anthony
1931 Italian, Vitullo Films 95 mins.
Dir: Nicola Fausto Neroni.
SP: Floria Vitullo.
Cin: Arturo Gallea.
Cast: Ellen Meis, Maurizo D'Ancora, Evelina Paoli.
rel-F (eyesight restored at shrine)
Ref: FD 17 April '32.

Miracle of the Bells, The
1948 Jesse L. Lasky Prods. (RKO) 120 mins.
Prod: Jesse L. Lasky & Walter McEwen.
Dir: Irving Pichel.
SP: Ben Hecht & Quentin Reynolds.
Art Dir: Ralph Berger.
Cin: Robert De Grasse.
Edit: Elmo Williams.
Mus: Leigh Harline.
Mus Dir: C. Bakaleinikoff.
Cast: Fred MacMurray, Valli, Frank Sinatra, Lee J. Cobb, Harold Vermilyea, Charles Meredith, Jim Nolan, Philip Ahn.
rel-F (at death of self-sacri-ficing actress, bells in church of her home town ring for 3 days and nights by themselves)
Ref: HR & Vd 2 March '48; MFB Sept '48 p 129.
Based on the novel by Russell Janney.

Miracle of the Blind Beggar
n.d. Loyola Film 16mm 30 mins.
rel-F
Ref: Ideal cat '43 p 107.

Miracle of the Necklace
1909 French, Lux sil.
rel-F (Virgin Mary appears)
Ref: MPW 5:842.

Miracle of the Roses, The
1913 Patheplay sil sh.
rel-F (when woman who steals food is caught, the food has turned into roses)
Ref: MPW 16:1394.

Miracle of the Roses, The
See: Miracle des Roses, Le (1908); Rosas del Milagro, Las (1960).

Miracle of Tomorrow, The
1923 German, Piel sil.
Dir: Harry Piel.
Cast: Harry Piel.
SF (robot)
Ref: Gifford/SF p51, 53.

Miracle on 34th Street
1947 20th-Fox 96 mins.
Prod: William Perlberg.
Dir & SP: George Seaton.
Story: Valentine Davies.
Art Dir: Richard Day & Richard Irvine.
Cin: Charles Clarke & Lloyd Ahern.
Edit: Robert Simpson.
Mus Dir: Alfred Newman.
Cast: Edmund Gwenn, Maureen O'Hara, John Payne, Gene Lockhart, Natalie Wood, James Seay.
bor-F-com (Gwenn believes he is Santa Claus, is "proved" to be in court; ending indi-cates he may very well be)
cont.

Miracle on 34th Street cont.
Ref: Agee p274; Vd 2 May '47; LC; FD 2 May '47.
See also remake: Meet Mr. Kringle (1956).

Miracle Rider, The
1935 Mascot serial 15 parts 33 reels.
Pres: Nat Levine.
Prod: Victor Zobel.
Dir: Armand Schaefer & Reeves Eason.
Story: Barney Sarecky, Wellyn Totman, & Gerald Geraghty.
SP: John Rathmell.
Edit: Joseph Lewis.
Cast: Tom Mix, Joan Gale, Charles Middleton, Jason Robards (Sr), Edward Earle, Ernie Adams, George Chesebro.
west-SF (contemporary Western with oil baron vs. Indians over rights to super-explosive X-94 which also acts as super-fuel; "sunray con-densers" send out heat rays; "rocket glider" disguised as legen-dary Firebird)
Ref: Collier; Stringham; FIR Oct '57 p396; LC.

Miracle sous l'Inquisition, Un
See: Miracle Under the Inquisition, A (1904).

Miracle Under the Inquisition, A
(Un Miracle sous l'Inquisition)
1904 French, Star sil 147 ft.
Made by: Georges Méliès.
F
Ref: Sadoul/M, GM Mage 558-59.

Miracle Window, The
(Das Wunderfenster)
1952 W. German, Schengerfilm color 15 mins.
Dir: Gerda Otto, Hedwig Utto, & Marian Krauss.
F (little girl sees toys come to life through toy-shop window)
Ref: Collier.

Miracles Do Happen
1939 British, George Smith Enterprises 59 mins.
Dir: Maclean Rogers.
Story: Con West & Jack Marks.
SP: Kathleen Butler.
Cast: Jack Hobbs, Bruce Seton, Marjorie Taylor, Aubrey Mallalieu, George Carney.
bor-SF-com (artificial milk)
Ref: Collier; Gifford/BFC 10567.

Miracles of Brahmin, The
(Le Miracle du Brahmine)
1899 French, Star sil 260 ft.
Made by: Georges Méliès.
F
Ref: Sadoul/M, GM Mage 237-40.

Miracles of Creation
See: Our Heavenly Bodies (1925).

Miracles of St. Margaret
(1959 --US release date) Italian (Crown Pics) 100 mins.
Exec Prod: Alberto Manca.
Dir: Mario Bonnard.
SP: Cesare Vico Ludovici, Edoardo Nulli, Nino Scolaro, & M. Bonnard.
Cast: Maria Frau, Isa Pola, Mario Pisu.
rel-F (girl accused of witch-craft is saved by appearance of the sign of the cross)
Ref: MPH 30 May '59.

Miracles of the Jungle

1921 WB (Federated Exchanges) sil serial 15 parts 31 reels.

Dir & Sc: E.A. Martin & James Conway.

Cast: Ben Hagerty, Wilbur Higgins, Irene Wallace, Genevieve Burte, Al Ferguson, John George ["See'er of All"].

F ("See'er of All" uses magic pool to call up visions of what is happening or has happened)

Ref: MPW 49:881; LC; CNW p96-97, 222.

Miracolo a Milano

See: Miracle in Milan (1951).

Miraculous Sword, The

See: Magic Sword, The (1949).

Miraculous Virgin

See: Panna Zazracnica (1967).

Miranda

1948 (1949) British, Gainsborough (Eagle-Lion) 80 mins.

Exec Prod: Sydney Box.

Prod: Betty E. Box.

Dir: Ken Annakin.

SP: Peter Blackmore.

Art Dir: George Paterson.

Cin: Ray Elton.

Edit: Gordon Hales.

Mus: Temple Abady.

Mus Dir: Muir Mathieson.

Cast: Glynis Johns [Miranda the mermaid], Googie Withers, Griffith Jones, John McCallum, Margaret Rutherford, David Tomlinson, Yvonne Owen.

F-com (man is rescued by mermaid who wants to visit London)

Ref: Vd 10 Jan '49; HR 11 Jan '49; MFB April '48 p 47.

Based on the play by Peter Blackmore.

Sequel: Mad About Men (1954).

See also: Mr. Peabody and the Mermaid (1948).

Miranda, ang Lagalag na Sirena

(Miranda, the Wandering Mermaid)

1966 Philippine, Lea.

Dir: Richard Abelardo.

SP: Maria Saret.

Mus: Tony Maiquez.

Cast: Marifi, Gloria Romero, Van De Leon, Bella Flores, Matimtiman Cruz, Menchu Morelli, Jing Abalos, Roger Calvin.

F (mermaid)

Ref: Borst.

Based on the Universal Komiks serial by Pablo S. Gomez.

Miranda, the Wandering Mermaid

See: Miranda, ang Lagalag na Sirena (1966).

Miriam

(story by T. Capote)

See: Trilogy (1969).

Mirko the Invisible

1960? Bulgarian color ani puppet sh?

Dir: Stefan Topaldjikov.

Artists: Boika Mavrodinova & G. Slavov.

F (puppet frees friends from captivity by becoming invisible)

Ref: FEFN Feb '61 p46.

Miroir de Cagliostro, Le

See: Cagliostro's Mirror (1899).

Mirror and Markheim, The

1954 British, Motley 28 mins

Prod: Norman Williams.

Dir & SP: John Lamont.

Nar: Marius Goring.

cont.

Miranda (1948) British

Mirror and Markheim cont.

Cast: Philip Saville, Arthur Lowe, Christopher Lee [figure in mirror], Lloyd Lamble, Ruth Sheil.

F ("Period. Mirror figure shows man what would happen if he stabbed an antique dealer")

Ref: Gifford/BFC 11903.

Based on the short story by Robert Louis Stevenson.

Mirror Death Ray of Dr. Mabuse

See: Secret of Dr. Mabuse (1964).

Mirror of Cagliostro, The

See: Cagliostro's Mirror (1899).

Mirror of Life, The

1909 French, Pathé sil 300 ft.

F (mirror shows couple how they will look when they are old)

Ref: Bios 20 Jan '10.

Mirror of the Future

1910 French, Pathé sil 311 ft.

F-com (magic mirror from street vendor reveals the future)

Ref: MPW 6:900, 995; F/A p424.

Mirror of the Witch, The

See: Witch's Mirror, The (1961).

Mirror with Three Faces

See: Glace à Trois Faces, La (1927).

Mis-Takes

1972 Bell Telephone color computer ani 3.5 mins.

Made by: Lillian Schwartz & Ken Knowlton.

exp-F

Ref: IAFF '72.

Misadventures of Merlin Jones, The

1963 (1964) WD (BV) color 91 mins (88 mins).

Prod: Walt Disney.

Assoc Prod: Ron Miller.

Dir: Robert Stevenson.

Story: Bill Walsh.

SP: Tom & Helen August.

Art Dir: Carroll Clark & William H. Tuntke.

Cin: Edward Colman.

Edit: Cotton Warburton.

Mus: Buddy Baker.

Cast: Tommy Kirk, Annette Funicello, Leon Ames, Stuart Erwin, Alan Hewitt, Connie Gilchrist, Norman Grabowski.

SF-com (college student's machine gives him power to read thoughts; he hypnotizes judge into being a thief)

Ref: MFB Sept '64 p 135-36; FD 13 Jan '64; FF '64 p38.

Sequel: Monkey's Uncle, The (1965).

Mischa the Bear

1947 Czech color ani puppet 10 mins.

Dir: Jiří Trnka.

F-com

Ref: MFB Oct '52 p 147.

Mischievous Elf, The

1909 Edison sil 540 ft.

F-com (magic; elf; witch)

Ref: EK 15 Dec '09; Bios 10 Feb '10; MPW 5:961.

Mischievous Puck

1911 British, Natural Colour Kinematograph Co color sil 425 ft.

Dir: W.R. Booth (?) & Theo Bouwmeester.

F-com (Puck plays pranks)

Ref: Gifford/BFC 03172.

Mischievous Sketch, A

(Le Carton Fantastique)

1907 French, Star sil 243 ft.

Made by: Georges Méliès.

F

Ref: Sadoul/M, GM Mage 906-08; MPW 1:126; LC.

Miser Punished, The

See: Moonlight Serenade, A (1903).

Miser's Doom, The

1899 British, Robert Paul sil 45 ft.

Prod: Robert Paul.

Made by: Walter Booth.

F-H (spirit of female victim haunts a miser)

Ref: Gifford/H p 19, 21.

Miser's Dream of Gold, The

(Le Songe d'Or de l'Avare)

1900 French, Star sil 230 ft.

Made by: Georges Méliès.

F

Ref: Sadoul/M, GM Mage 295-97.

Miser's Reversion, The

1914 Thanhouser sil.

Cast: Sidney Bracy, Harry Benham.

SF (youth treatment fails, causes extreme reverse evolution, back to "missing link")

Ref: Gifford/MM p 153; Bios 25 June '14; Gifford/H p37.

Misfit, The

See: Nepovedeny Panacek (1951).

Misguided Missile

1958 U color ani 1 reel.

Prod: Walter Lantz.

Dir: Paul Smith.

cont.

Misguided Missile cont.

Voice of Woody: Grace Stafford.

F-com

Ref: PopCar.

See also: Woody Woodpecker (1940-72).

Mishaps of the New York-Paris Race

(Le Raid Paris New York en Automobile: The Endurance Contest Paris-New York by Automobile; New York Paris en Automobile --alt.t?)

1908 French, Star sil colored 1250 ft.

Made by: Georges Méliès.

F

Ref: Sadoul/M, GM Mage 1199-1217; LC.

Mishka and Mashka

1964 Soviet, Kiev (Sovexportfilm) color ani 9.7 mins.

Dir: E. Lazarchuk.

Story: A. Kanevsky.

F

Ref: Sovexportfilm cat 2:123.

Mislayed Genie, The

1972 Xerxes Prods color.

Prod: Shelley Haims.

Dir: Eric Haims.

SP & Art Dir: Tom Reamy.

Edit: Schlomo Bina.

sex-F-com (instead of intended lamp, genie ends up in hero's penis, so whenever it is rubbed the genie appears)

Ref: Reamy.

Miss Death

See: Diabolical Dr. Z, The (1965).

Miss Faust

1909 French, Pathé sil colored 623 ft.

sat-F-com (Miss Faust sells her soul to Satan to become young & beautiful)

Ref: FI IV-22:7.

Miss Gentibelle

(short story by C. Beaumont)

See: Ursula (1961?).

Miss Hold's Puppets

1908 French, Pathé sil hand colored 524 ft.

F (6" people; appearances & disappearances)

Ref: Views 120:9.

Miss Jekyll and Madame Hyde

1915 Vit sil 3 reels.

Dir & Sc: Charles L. Gaskill.

Cast: Helen Gardner, Paul Scardon [Devil].

F (Satan claims the soul of the villain)

Ref: MPW 24:1830, 25:65.

Note: not a legitimate Jekyll & Hyde story.

Miss Kemeko

1968? Japanese color ani 3.5 mins.

Dir: Yoji Kuri.

F-com-sat

Ref: ASIFA 4.

Miss Leslie's Dolls

1973 World-Wide color 85 mins.
Produced in the Philippines?

Exec Prod: Carlos A. Lopez & J.A. Pina Jr.

Prod: Ralph J. Remy.

Assoc Prod: Eddy A. Lopez.

Dir: Joseph G. Prieto.

SP: J.G. Prieto & R.J. Remy.

Art Dir: Jerry Remy.

Cin: Gregory Sandor.

cont.

Miss Leslie's Dolls cont.

Mus: Imer Leaf.

Cast: Salvador Ugarte, Terry Juston, Marcelle Bichette, Kitty Lewis, Charles W. Pitts.

sex-H; F-seq (hideously disfigured matricidal transvestite homosexual in isolated house kills & embalms girls; at end his spirit enters a girl's body while is own head decays)

Ref: MFB June '73 p 128; BO 12 March '73.

Miss Muerte

See: Diabolical Dr. Z, The (1965).

Miss Shumway Jette un Sort

(Miss Shumway Casts a Spell; Une Blonde Comme Ca! --alt.t?)

1962 French, Metzger & Woog, & Paris Elysées & Standard color scope 91 mins.

Dir: Jean Jabely.

SP: Jacques Robert, Félicien Marceau, & J. Jabely(?).

Cin: Marcel Grignon.

Mus: N. Glanzberg.

Cast: Taina Béryll, Harold Kay, Jess Hahn, René Lefèbvre, Robert Manuel.

F-com (Miss Shumway has a dual personality, one of them mean; she can make animals talk)

Ref: MMF 3:35; Gasca p291; Unifrance '66.

Miss Trillie's Big Feet

1915 Novelty sil 1000 ft.

Cast: Edith Thronton, Joe Burke, Max Ulrich, W.G. Don, Will Browning.

bor-F-com (hypnotist trying to mesmerize Miss Trillie hypnotizes instead everyone else in the restaurant)

Ref: MPN 16 Oct '15 p97.

See also: Trilby.

Misses Stooge, The

Hal Roach (MGM) 2 reels.

Prod: Hal Roach.

Dir: James Parrott.

Edit: William Terhune.

Cast: Thelma Todd, Patsy Kelly, Herman Bing, Esther Howard, Rafael Storm.

bor-F-com (Patsy & Thelma are magician's assistants; Thelma flies out window, has to be tethered to stage by rope)

Ref: Maltin/MCT; LC.

Missile Base at Taniak

See: Canadian Mounties vs Atomic Invaders (1953).

Missile Monsters

See: Flying Disc Man from Mars (1950).

Missile to the Moon

1958 (1959) Astor 78 mins.

Prod: Marc Frederic.

Dir: Richard Cunha.

SP: H.E. Barrie & Vincent Fotre.

Set Dec: Harry Reif.

Makeup: Harry Thomas.

Cin: Meredith Nicholson.

SpFX: Ira Anderson & Harold Banks.

Mus: Nicholas Carras.

Cast: Richard Travis, Cathy Downs, K.T. Stevens, Tommy Cook, Nina Bara, Gary Clarke, Michael Whalen, Laurie Mitchell.

SF (gangsters stow away aboard Moon rocket; on Moon, explorers encounter rock creatures, giant spiders, & lost tribe of women)

Ref: FF '58 p253; MFB Sept '61 p 130; MPH 17 Jan '59.

Based on film Cat Women of the Moon (1953).

Missing Guest, The

1938 U 68 mins.

Assoc Prod: Barney A. Sarecky.

Dir: John Rawlins.

SP: Charles Martin & Paul Perez.

Art Dir: Jack Otterson.

Cin: Milton Krasna.

Edit: Frank Gross.

Mus Dir: Charles Previn.

Cast: Paul Kelly, Constance Moore, William Lundigan, Edwin Stanley, Selmer Jackson, Harlan Briggs, Guy Usher.

myst-H-com (old dark house; pianos & organs play by themselves; fake ghost)

Ref: HR 15 Aug '38; Vw 14 Sept '38; FD 9 Sept '38.

Based on novel "Secret of the Blue Room" by Erich Philippi.

See also: Murder in the Blue Room (1944).

Missing Head, The

See: Strange Confession (1945).

Missing Husbands

See: Atlantide, L' (1921).

Missing Link, The

1926 (1927) WB sil 6485 ft.

Dir: Charles F. Reisner.

Sc: Darryl Francis Zanuck.

Cin: Dev Jennings.

Cast: Syd Chaplin, Ruth Hiatt, Tom McGuire, Crauford Kent, Nick Cogley, Sam Baker [the Missing Link].

SF-com (search for missing link complicated by romance & a chimpanzee, but real missing link finally captured)

Ref: MPW 86:133, 156 ad; LC; AFI F2.3649 p517-18.

Mission Apocalypse

See: 087 "Missione Apocalisse" [spelled Nulla Otto Sette...] (1966).

Mission from Mars

1968 Amateur 8mm color ani 14 mins.

Made by: John Lopez.

SF

Ref: SF Times #461.

Mission Impossible

(Chien-nü Yu-hu: Soul of a Swordsman)

1970? Hongkong, Shaw.

Cast: Ching Li.

F (mystic martial arts; arm stretches to 10 feet; girl restored to life by magic sword; ghost; 130 year-old man kept magically young ages rapidly)

Ref: Jim Landers.

Mission Mars

(Red Planet Mars --ad.t.; Destination Mars --s.t.)

1968 Red Ram Prods & Sagittarius (AA) color 87 mins.

Exec Prod: Morton Fallick.

Prod: Everett Rosenthal.

Dir: Nick Webster.

Story: Aubrey Wisberg.

SP: Mike St. Clair.

Prod Design: Hank Aldrich.

Cin: Cliff Poland.

SpFX: Haberstroh Studios.

Sup Edit: Michael Calamari.

Edit: Paul Jordan.

Mus: Berge Kalajian & Gus Pardalis.

Cast: Darren McGavin, Nick Adams, George De Vries, Heather Hewitt, Michael De Beausset.

SF (expedition to Mars encounters living, glowing

cont.

Mission Mars cont.

spheres, mechanical objects called "polarites")

Ref: FF '68 p521; MFB Nov '69 p 174; Vw 25 Sept '68; F&F Nov '69 p50.

Mission Stardust

(Orbita Mortal: Mortal Orbit; You Only Live Once --S.E. Asia t.)

1968 Spanish/Italian/W.German, Aitor/P.E.A./Theumer (Times Film Corp) color 95 mins.

Dir: Primo Zeglio.

Story: Karl H. Volgeman.

SP: K.H. Volgeman & Federico d'Urrutia.

Art Dir: Jaime Perez Cubero.

Cin: Manuel Merino.

Mus: Antón Garcia Abril.

Cast: Lang Jeffries, Essy Persson, Luis Dávila, Daniel Martin, Gianni Rizzo, Joachim Hansen.

SF (private space ship lands on Moon, finds alien spaceship with young girl commander)

Ref: FD 9 Dec '68; MPH 20 Nov '68 p64; Vw 2 July '69; SpCin '69 p52-53.

Based on the W. German "Perry Rhodan" novels series begun by Walter Ernsting, using the name Clark Darlton.

Mission to Hell

See: Kogan no Misshi (1959).

Mission Wandering Planet

See: War Between the Planets (1965).

Missione Pianeta Errante

See: War Between the Planets (1965).

Mississippi Hare

1949 WB color ani 7 mins.

Dir: Chuck Jones.

Story: Michael Maltese.

Voices: Mel Blanc.

F-com

Ref: LC; David Rider.

See also: Bugs Bunny (1938-63).

Mr. Biddle's Crime Wave

1959? U-Hope (NBC-TV) 49 mins.

Cast: Roddy McDowall, Pat Crowley, Shari Lewis.

bor-SF ("chemical that eats everything")

Ref: BIB's (Willis).

Mr. Bisbee's Princess

(story by J.L. Street)

See: So's Your Old Man (1926); You're Telling Me (1934).

Mr. Bug Goes to Town

(Hoppity Goes to Town -- Brit.t.)

1941 Par color ani 78 mins.

Prod: Max Fleischer.

Dir: Dave Fleischer.

Story: D. Fleischer, Dan Gordan, Ted Pierce, & Isidore Sparber.

SP: D. Gordon, T. Pierce, I. Sparber, William Turner, Carl Meyer, Graham Place, Bob Wickersham, & Cal Howard.

Sound FX: Maurice Manne.

Mus: Hoagy Carmichael, Frank Loesser, & Sammy Timberg.

Incidental Mus: Leigh Harline.

Voices: Pauline Loth, Stan Freed, Ted Pierce, Jack Mercer, Carl Meyer, Kenny Gardner.

F-com (adventures of a grass-hopper & other anthropomorphized insects)

Ref: HR & Vd 5 Dec '41; FD 5 Dec '41; MFB Feb '42 p 18.

Mr. Cinderella

1914 Thanhouser sil sh.

cont.

306

Mr. Cinderella cont.

F (fairy godfather changes
Jimmy's clothes to a uniform
a cigar into a car, etc.)

Ref: MPW 22:548.

See also: Cinderella.

Mister Clown among the Lilliputians

See: Monsieur Clown chez les
Lilliputiens (1909).

**Mr. Dauber and the Mystifying
Picture**

(Le Peintre Barbouillard et
Tableau Diabolique)

1905 French, Star sil 233
ft.

Made by: Georges Méliès.

F

Ref: Sadoul/M, GM Mage 696-98;
LC.

Mr. Dodd Takes the Air

1937 FN (WB) 85 mins.

Prod: Mervyn Le Roy.

Dir: Alfred E. Green.

SP: William Wister Haines &
Elaine Ryan.

Art Dir: Robert M. Haas.

Cin: Arthur Edeson.

Edit: Thomas M. Richards.

Mus & Lyrics: Harry Warren &
Al Dubin.

Cast: Kenny Baker, Frank
McHugh, Alice Brady, Gertrude
Michael, Jane Wyman, John
Eldredge, Harry Davenport.

bor-Sf-mus-com (device "cures"
broken radios; operation turns
baritone into tenor)

Ref: LC; FDY '38; NYT 12
Aug '37.

Based on story "The Great
Crooner" by Clarence Budington
Kelland.

Mr. Drake's Duck

1950 (1951) British, Dougfair
Corp (UA) 85 mins (77 mins).

Prod: Daniel M. Angel.

Dir & SP: Val Guest.

Story: Ian Messiter.

Art Dir: Maurice Carter.

Cin: Jack Cox.

Edit: Sam Simmonds.

Mus: Bruce Campbell.

Cast: Douglas Fairbanks Jr,
Wilfred Hyde-White, Yolande
Donlan, Howard Marion Crawford,
Reginald Beckwith, Jon Pertwee,
A.E. Matthews.

F-com (duck lays radioactive,
explosive eggs)

Ref: MFB March '51 p235;
Vd 10 Aug '51; FD 14 Aug '51.

Mr. Fantomas

1937 Belgian, Les Films
Hagen-Tronje sil 20 mins.

Dir & SP: Ernst Moerman.

Cin: Roger Norbert
Vanpeperstraete.

Mus: Robert Ledent.

Cast: Jean Michel, Trudi
Vantonderen, Françoise Bert,
Jacqueline Arpé, Susan Samuel,
Mary, E. Miecret, Léa Dumont,
Ginette Samuel, A. Hubner.

sur-F

Ref: MMF 24:68-71.

Based on the character created
by Pierre Souvestre & M. Allain.

See also: Fantomas.

Mister Freedom

1968 (1969) French, O.P.E.R.A.
& Les Films du Rond-Point
color 110 mins (95 mins).

Prod: Guy Belfond, Michel
Zemer, & Christian Thivat.

Dir & SP: William Klein.

Art Dir: Jacques Dugied.

Cin: Pierre Lhomme.

Edit: Anne-Marie Cotret.

Mus: Serge Gainsbourg.

cont.

The Mischievous Elf (1909)

Mister Freedom cont.

Cast: John Abbey, Delphine
Seyrig, Jean-Claude Drouot,
Philippe Noiret, Catherine
Rouvel, Samy Frey, Serge
Gainsbourg, Donald Pleasence,
Rufus, Yves Montand.

F-sat (Mr. Freedom, super-
powered & costumed represen-
tative of American Way of
Life, goes to France, battles
Super-French-Man, Moujik-Man,
Red-China-Man; destroys himself
& all of France with Ultimate
Weapon; international leaders
shown as giant, inflatable
puppets; aerosol defoliant;
etc.)

Ref: MFB March '69 p51-52;
Vw 12 Feb '69; F&F Feb '69
p42-43; MMF 20:1.

Mr. Frenhofer and the Minotaur

1949 Workshop 20, California
School of Fine Arts (C-16)
21 mins.

Made by: Sidney Peterson.

sur-F

Ref: Undrgnd p88, 279; C-16
p23.

Based on story "The Unknown
Masterpiece" by Honoré Balzac
and painting "Minotauramachy"
by Pablo Picasso.

Mr. Fuller Pep

1916-17 Follett (U) sil
ani 1/2 reel series.

Prod: P.A. Powers.

F-com

Ref: LC; Ani Chart.

Mr. Fuzz

1908 French, Pathé sil
colored 951 ft.

F (fairy promises to turn
Fuzz into handsome man if he
wins love of princess, who
will become intelligent &
witty)

Ref: View 123:10.

Mr. H.C. Andersen

See: Hans Christian Andersen (1950).

Mr. Hare and Mr. Hedgehog

1963? color ani silhouette
10.5 mins.

Made by?: Albert Rauer.

F

Ref: NY Public Library cat
'63-64 p41.

Mr. Head

See: Monsieur Tête (1959).

Mr. Hex

1946 Mono 63 mins.

Prod & Story: Jan Grippo.

Assoc Prod & SP: Cyril Endfield.

Dir: William Beaudine.

Art Dir: David Milton.

Cin: James Brown.

Sup Edit: Richard Currier.

Edit: Seth Larsen.

Mus Dir: Edward J. Kay.

Cast: Leo Gorcey, Huntz Hall,
Ian Keith, Bobby Jordan,
Gabriel Dell, Gale Robbins,
Billy Benedict, David Gorcey,
Bernard Gorcey.

F-com (hypnotism makes Hall
into great boxer)

Ref: HR & Vd 5 Dec '46; FD
12 Dec '46; LC.

See also: Spooks Run Wild
(1941).

Mr. Horatio Knibbles

1971 British, Anvil for
the Children's Film Foun-
dation (CBS-TV) color 60
mins.

Prod: Hugh Steward.

Dir: Robert Hird.

Story: Wally Bosco.

SP: Peter Blackmore.

Cin: Adrian Jeakins.

SpFX: Sally Long & Frank
George.

Edit: Rhonda Small.

Mus Dir: Muir Mathieson.

cont.

Mr. Horatio Knibbles cont.

Cast: Lesley Roach, Gary
Smith, Rachel Brennock,
John Ash, Nigel Chivers,
Anthony Sheppard [giant
rabbit].

F-com (at first only a
little girl can see giant,
clothed, magical rabbit,
later everyone can)

Ref: MFB Oct '71 p200.

See also: Harvey (1950);
Super Saturday (1972).

Mr. Hurry-up of New York

1907 Biograph sil 663 ft.

Cin: Billy Bitzer.

F-com (furniture moves, appears,
disappears; circular staircase
revolves; bed spins & flies;
etc.)

Ref: Niver 67; Niver/20
p 111-12.

Mr. Invisible

See: Invencible Hombre Invisible,
El (1970).

Mr. Jarr's Magnetic Friend

1915 Vit sil 1 reel.

Dir: Harry Davenport.

Sc: Roy L. McCardell.

Cast: Harry Davenport, Rose
Tapley, Paul Kelly, Audrey
Berry, Frank Bunny, Charles
Eldridge.

SF-com (man magnitized by
dynamo)

Ref: MPW 24:280, 902; LC;
MPN 17 April '15.

Based on characters created
by Roy L. McCardell.

**Mr. Jones' Comical Experience
with a Ghost**

See: Apparition, The (1903).

Mr. Joseph Young of Africa

See: Mighty Joe Young (1949).

Mr. Korek

1958 Polish ani puppet sh?

Mus: Henryk Zyzk.

F (angel loses heart to girl)

Ref: Collier.

Mr. Koumal Carries the Torch

1968 Czech color ani sh.

Dir: Gene Deitch.

F

Ref: ASIFA 5.

Mr. Krane

1957 NBC-TV 54 mins.

Originally telecast as episode of "Matinee Theater" series, later shown separately on TV as feature.

Cast: Cedric Hardwicke [alien], John Hoyt, Peter Hansen.

SF (in 1962, alien race gives Earth an ultimatum; alien has force-field)

Ref: BIB's (Willis); B. Warren.

Mr. Leguignon, Healer

See: Monsieur Leguignon, Guérisseur (1953).

Mister Magoo

(The Nearsighted Mister Magoo --alt.t.)

1949-- UPA (Col) color ani 1 reel series.

Prod: Stephen Bosustow.

Dir: John Hubley, Pete Burness, & others.

Voice of Magoo: Jim Backus.

F-com (adventures of a confident but nearsighted old man)

Ref: Ani/Cin p 171; It 6.

See also: Magoo. . .; Mister Magoo. . .; Ragtime Bear (1949); Trouble Indemnity (1950); Pink and Blue Blues (1952); Destination Magoo (1954); When Magoo Flew (1954); Magoo's Puddle Jumper (1956); 1001 Arabian Nights (1959); Martian Magoo (1960.

Mister Magoo in Sherwood Forest

1964 (1967) UPA color ani 83 mins.

Feature re-edited from TV series.

Voices: Jim Backus and others.

F

Ref: UPA.

See also: Robin Hood; Mister Magoo (1949-).

Mister Magoo — Man of Mystery

1964 (1967) UPA color ani 93 mins.
Feature re-edited from TV series.

Voice: Jim Backus.

F (Magoo as Sherlock Holmes, as Dr. Frankenstein, and in an adventure with Dick Tracy)

Based on the character Sherlock Holmes created by A. Conan Doyle, the novel "Frankenstein" by Mary Shelley, and the character Dick Tracy created by Chester Gould.

Ref: UPA; Ideal cat '69-70 p 109.

See also: Dick Tracy; Frankenstein; Sherlock Holmes; Mister Magoo (1949-).

Mister Magoo's Christmas Carol

1964 (1967) UPA (Maron) color ani 52 mins.

Prod: Lee Orgel.

Dir: Abe Levitow.

Adapt: Barbara Chain.

Mus: Jule Styne & Bob Merril.

Voices: Jim Backus, Morey Amsterdam, Jack Cassidy, Royal Dano, Paul Frees, Joan Gardner, John Hart, Les Tremayne.

F (Magoo, as Scrooge, is visited by three ghosts at Christmastime)

cont

Mister Magoo's Christmas Carol cont.

Ref: Collier; Ideal cat '69-70 p32, 116; UPA.

Based on short novel "A Christmas Carol" by Charles Dickens.

See also: Christmas Carol, A; Mister Magoo (1949-)

Mister Magoo's Favorite Heroes

1964 (1967) UPA color ani 90 mins.

Feature re-edited from TV series.

Voice: Jim Backus.

F-com

Ref: Ideal cat; UPA.

Based on the legend of William Tell, the poem "Gunga Din" by Rudyard Kipling, and the story "Rip Van Winkle" by Washington Irving.

See also: Rip Van Winkle; Mister Magoo (1949--).

Mister Magoo's Little Snow White

1964 (1967) UPA (Maron) color ani 52 mins.

Voices: Jim Backus & others.

F-com (Magoo plays all seven dwarfs)

Ref: UPA.

See also: Mister Magoo's Story-book (1964); Snow White; Mister Magoo (1949--).

Mister Magoo's Story Book

1964 (1967) UPA color ani 113 mins.

Feature re-edited from TV series.

Voices: Jim Backus & others.

F

Ref: UPA; Ideal cat.

Based on the story "Snow White" by Jacob & Wilhelm Grimm, the novel "Don Quixote" by Miguel de Cervantes, and the play "A Midsummer Night's Dream" by William Shakespeare.

See also: Don Quixote; Snow White; Midsummer Night's Dream, A; Mister Magoo's Little Snow White (1964); Mister Magoo (1949--).

Mister Magrooter's Marvelous Machine

n.d. (Modern Film Rentals) color ani 7.5 mins.

F (machine that removes seeds from watermelons rendered non-functional by the addition of too many impressive accouterments)

Ref: Sightlines Jan-Feb '73 p22.

Mr. Monster

1969 Iranian color ani sh.

Dir: Farshid Mesghali.

F (machine monster)

Ref: ASIFA 6.

Mr. Motorboat's Last Stand

1933 16mm? sh?

Dir: John Florey & Theodore Huff.

exp-F-com

Ref: USA Exp List; Exp/Film p 127.

Mr. Noad's Adless Day

1914 Joker (U) sil 1 reel.

F-com-dream (in dream Satan grants wish for no advertising)

Ref: MPW 22:538.

Mr. Peabody and the Mermaid

1948 Inter John Inc (U) 89 mins.

Prod & SP: Nunnally Johnson.

Dir: Irving Pichel.

Assoc Prod: Gene Fowler Jr.

Art Dir: Bernard Herzbrun.

Cin: Russell Metty.

Underwater Cin: David S. Horsley.

Edit: Marjorie Fowler.

Mus: Robert Emmett Doland.

cont

Mr. Peabody & the Mermaid cont.

Cast: William Powell, Ann Blyth [mermaid], Irene Hervey, Andrea King, Fred Clark.

F-com (Boston businessman wintering in the Caribbean catches a mermaid)

Ref: Vd & HR 8 July '48; LC; FD 13 July '48; MFB March '49 p45.

Based on novel "Peabody's Mermaid" by Guy & Constance Jones.

Mr. Peek-A-Boo

(Le Passe-Muraille)

1950 (1951) French, Cité (UA) 74 mins.

Prod: Jacques Bar.

Dir: Jean Boyer.

SP: J. Boyer & Michel Audiard.

Art Dir: Robert Giordani.

Cin: Charles Suin.

SpFX: Paul Raibaud & Henry Harris.

Mus: Georges Van Parys.

Cast: Bourvil, Joan Greenwood, Marcelle Arnold, Raymond Souplex, Gerard Oury, Henri Cremieux, Jacques Erwin, Roger Treville.

F-com (government official discovers he can walk through walls, catches a burglar, reforms an English girl)

Ref: Vd & HR 17 Sept '51; MFB June '52 p81; deGroote 160.

Based on novelet "Garou-Garou le Passe-Muraille" (The Man Who Walked through Walls) by Marcel Aymé.

See also: Man Who Walked through the Wall, The (1960).

Mr. Prokouk

See: Adventures of Mr. Prokouk (1947-58).

Mr. Robida, Prophet and Explorer of Time

See: Monsieur Robida, Prophete et Explorateur du Temps (1963).

Mr. Rossi

See: Signor Rossi (1963?. . .)

Mr. Rossi Buys a Car

(Il Signor Rossi Compera l'Automobila)

1966 Swiss/Italian (Atlantic) color ani 11 mins.

Dir: Bruno Bozzetto.

Story: Sergio Crivellaro.

Art Dir: Giovanni Mulazzani & Giancarlo Cereda.

Mus: Giampiero Boneschi.

Ani: Franco Martelli & Giuseppe Lagana.

F-com (in land where even cats chase mice by car, Mr. Rossi, thwarted at first, soon has super-defensive car)

Ref: MFB April '68 p63.

See also: Signor Rossi (1963?-).

Mr. Sardonicus

(Sardonicus --s.t.)

1961 William Castle Prods (Col) 89 mins.

Prod & Dir: William Castle.

SP: Ray Russell.

Art Dir: Cary Odell.

Makeup: Ben Lane.

Cin: Burnett Guffey.

Edit: Edwin Bryant.

Mus: Von Dexter.

Cast: Oscar Homolka, Ronald Lewis, Audrey Dalton, Guy Rolfe, Vladimir Sokoloff, Erika Peters, Lorna Hanson.

H (Sardonicus, rich man of 19th Century who, terrified when robbing his father's grave, has had his face permanently fixed in wide grin; doctor cures him, leaves, but Sardonicus' mouth will not open at all; torture by leeches)

cont

Mr. Sardonicus cont.

Ref: FD 8 Oct '61; FF '61 p243-44.

Based on short novel "Sardonicus" by Ray Russell.

Mr. Servadac's Arch

See: Na Komete (1970).

Mr. Smith Goes Ghost

1950? Toddy.

Cast: Pigmeat Markham, Lawrence Criner, Johnny Taylor.

H-com

Ref: Poster (Ackerman).

Mr. Steinway

(short story by R. Bloch)

See: Torture Garden (1967).

Mr. Stop

See: Monsieur Stop (1907).

Mr. Super Invisible

See: Invencible Hombre Invisible, El (1969).

Mr. Trumpet

1960 Polish color ani sh.

Dir: Jerzy Zitzman.

F

Ref: Ani/Cin p 114, 176.

Mr. Tvardovski

(Pan Tvardovski)

1916 Part I 1917 Part II Russian sil.

Dir: Ladislas Starevitch.

Cast: N. Saltikoff, S. Tchapelski, Z. Valevska.

F

Ref: Filmlex p929.

Based on the story by I.J. Kraszevski.

See also: Pan Tvardovski (1937).

Mister Unsichtbar

See: Invencible Hombre Invisible, El (1970).

Mr. Victor

See: Monsieur Victor (1957).

Mister Wister the Time Twister

(La Machine a Retrouve le Temps)

1956 French, Jean Image color ani 7 mins.

Dir: Jean Image.

F

Mr. Wonderbird

See: Curious Adventures of Mr. Wonderbird (1952).

Mister, You Are a Widow

See: Pane Vy Jste Vdova (1971).

Misterio de las Naranjas Azules, El

(The Mystery of the Blue Oranges; Tin Tin et les Oranges Bleues; Tin Tin and the Blue Oranges)

1965 Spanish/French color 74 mins.

Dir: Philippe Condroyer.

SP: Francisco Gozálvez, André Barret, & Antonio Gimenez Rico.

Art Dir: Ramiro Gomez & P.L. Thevenet.

Cin: Jean Badal.

Mus: Antoine Duhamel.

Cast: Jean Pierre Talbot, Jean Bouise, Felix Fernandez, Angel Alvarez.

bor-SF-com (scientist grows oranges in sand but they come out blue)

Ref: SpCin '66 p70-71; CoF 7:54; MTVM March '65.

Misterio del Rostro Palido, El

(The Mystery of the Pallid Face; The Mystery of the Ghastly Face -- ad.t?)

1935 (1937) Mexican, Alcayde.

Dir & SP: Juan Bustillo Oro.

Cin: Augustín Jiménez.

cont

Misterio del Rostro... cont.

Mus: Max Urban.

Cast: Beatriz Ramoz, Carlos Villarías, René Cardona, Joaquin Busquets, Miguel Arenas, Manuel Noriega, Natalia Ortiz.

H (man tries to find the secret of life, goes mad instead)

Ref: Aventura p429-30; Indice; NYT 4 Jan '37.

Misterios de la Magia Negra

(Mysteries of Black Magic)

1957 Mexican, Alfa (Col)

Dir: Miguel M. Delgado.

SP: Ulises Petit de Murat.

Art Dir: G. Gunther Gerszo.

Cin: Victor Herrera.

Mus: José de la Vega.

Cast: Nadia Haro Oliva, Carlos Riquelme, Aldo Monti, Lourdes Pargas, Angelines Fernandez.

F-H (woman tries to communicate spiritually with her dead husband)

Ref: PB; MM 3:9-13.

Misterios de Ultratumba

See: Black Pit of Dr. M (1959).

Misterioso Tio Sylas, El

(The Mysterious Uncle Silas)

1947 Argentine, Efa 83 mins.

Dir: Carlos Schliepper.

SP: Jorge Jantus & Leon Miralas.

Art Dir: Juan M. Concado.

Cin: J.M. Concado & Roque Funes.

Edit: José Cardella.

Mus: Juan Ehlert.

Cast: Elisa Galvé, Francisco de Paula, Elsa O'Connor, Ricardo Galache, Homero Carpena.

H

Ref: Nubila II:87, 286.

Based on novel "Uncle Silas" by J.S. Le Fanu.

See also: Inheritance, The (1947).

Mistero dei Trei Continenti, Il

(The Mystery of Three Continents; Les Mysteres d'Angkor: The Mysteries of Angkor; Herrin der Welt: Mistress of the World --US TV title of severely shortened print)

1959 Italian/French/W.German, Continenta/Franco London/CCC color Part I: 100 mins; Part II: 90 mins.

Filmed in Bangkok & France.

Dir: William Dieterle.

SP: Jo Esinger & M.G. Petersson.

Art Dir: Willy Schatz & Helmut Nentwig.

Cin: Richard Angst, Richard Oehlers, & Peter Homfeld.

Edit: Jutta Herring.

Mus: Roman Vlad.

Cast: Martha Hyer, Carlos Thompson, Micheline Prèsle, Gino Cervi, Sabu, Lino Venturi, Wolfgang Preiss, George Rivière, Carl Lange.

SF (formula for controlling gravitational & magnetic fields)

Ref: FIR April '71 p209; TVK; German Pics '63/64; Eric Hoffman.

Mistero di Atlantide, Il

See: Giant of Metropolis,The (1962).

Mistletoe Bough, The

● 1904 British, Clarendon sil 477 ft.

Dir: Percy Stow.

Mus: Henry Bishop.

F-H-seq (on wedding day game of hide & seek is played & bride vanishes; 30 years later groom has vision of her rising from chest; looks in it & finds her skeleton)

Mistletoe Bough cont.

Ref: BFI cat F.599 p79; Gifford/BFC 00958.

● (#1 in "Gems of Literature" series)

1923 British, B&C sil 2050 ft.

Prod: Edward Godol.

Dir: Edwin D. Collins.

Sc: Eliot Stannard.

Cast: John Stuart, Flora le Breton, Lionel D'Aragon, William Lugg.

Ref: Gifford/BFC 07663-64.

Based on the play by Charles Somerset.

● (Haunted Castles series)

1926 British sil 1600 ft.

Dir: Charles C. Calvert.

Cast: Gladys Jennings.

Ref: Vw 24 Feb '26; Brit Cin; Gifford/BFC 08028.

● (Ghost Tales Retold series)

1938 British, AIP 25 mins.

Dir: Widgey R. Newman.

SP: George A. Cooper.

Ref: Gifford/BFC 10525.

See also: Ghost Tales Retold (1938).

F-H
Based on the traditional British ghost story.

Mrs. Death

See: Senora Muerte (1968).

Mistress Holle

1965 E. German, DEFA

Dir: Gottfried Kolditz.

Cast: Mathilde Danegger, Karin Ugowski, Elfriede Florin.

F (fairy tale: beautiful good girl rewarded by a rain of gold)

Ref: MTVM March '65 p 19.

Mistress of Atlantis, The

See: Atlantide, L' (1932).

Mistress of the World

US TV title of severely shortened print of Mistero dei Trei Continenti, Il (1959).

Mistresses of Dr. Jekyll

See: Dr. Orloff's Monster (1964).

Misunderstood

1971? Iranian ani sh.

Dir: Farshid Mesaghali.

F

Ref: ASIFA Bltn 2, '71.

Mitten, The

1968 Soviet, color ani puppet 10 mins.

F

Ref: LA County Museum.

Mixed Master

1956 WB color ani 7 mins.

Dir: Robert McKimson.

F-com

Mo-Toy Comedies

1917 Toyland Films Corp (Peter Pan Film Corp) sil ani puppet sh series.

Goldie Locks and the Three Bears; Midnight Frolic; A Trip to the Moon; Little Red Riding Hood; Out of the Rain.

F-com

Ref: MPW 32:759, 552-53 ads.

Moby Dick

(novel by H. Melville)

See: Magoo at Sea.

Moc Osudu

(The Force of Destiny)

1969 Czech, Kratky color ani 6 mins.

Dir & Story: Jiří Brdečka.

F (soothsayer)

Ref: Mamaia '70.

Modeling

1921 ani, object ani, & live sil sh.

Prod: Max Fleischer.

Dir: Dave Fleischer.

Cin: Joe Fleischer.

Cast: Max Fleischer, Dave Fleischer.

F-com (Koko jumps off easel, Fleischers chase him, he hides in clay statue & it distorts)

Ref: Hist US Ani Prog.

See also: Out of the Inkwell (1919-23).

Modern Blue Beard, The

See: Moderno Barba-Azul, El (1947).

Modern Dr. Jekyll, The

See: Dr. Jekyll and Mr. Hyde (Selig, 1908).

Modern Fable, A

See: Moderna Basna (1965).

Modern Inventions

1937 WD color? ani 9 mins.

Prod: Walt Disney.

Voice: Clarence Nash.

F-com (Donald vs. robots)

Ref: Lighthouse 16 Oct '37.

See also: Donald Duck (1934-61).

Modern Lorelei, A

(The Lorelei of the Sea -- alt.t?)

1917 Marine Film Corp sil 7 reels.

Dir: A. Henry Otto.

Sc: Richard Willis.

Cin: James Crosby.

Cast: Tyrone Power (Sr), Frances Burnham, John Oaker, Jay Belasco.

F-dream (sea nymphs)

Ref: MPN 16:1859, 2906; WID's 6 Sept ' 17 p572.

Based on the legend.

Modern Magic

1908 French, Pathé sil 393 ft.

F (appearances, disappearances, transformations: woman into butterfly, etc.)

Ref: Views 137:10.

Modern Mother Goose

1917 Fort Dearborn Photoplays (Lea-Bel Co) sil 5 reels.

F

Ref: MPW 31:966 ad, 1048.

Modern Mystery, A

1912 British, Urban sil ani clay 290 ft.

Dir: W.R. Booth.

F ("animated clay models of conjuror, skeleton, lady")

Ref: Gifford/BFC 03395.

Modern Pirates, The

(The Raid of the Armoured Motor --1911 rr.t.)

1906 British?, Alpha sil sh.

bor-SF (armor-plated car)

Dir: Arthur Cooper.

Ref: Gifford/SF p34; Gifford/BFC 01442.

Modern Samson, A

1907 Italian, Cines sil 420 ft.

F-com (man loses super strength when wife cuts his hair)

Ref: F/A p361; MPW 1:441-42.

See also: Samson.

Modern Sculptors

1908 French, Pathé sil sh.

F

Ref: MPW 2:327.

Modern Sphinx, A

1916 American sil 3 reels.

Dir: Charles Bartlett.

Cast: Winnifred Greenwood, Edward Coxen, George Field, Charles Newton, Nan Christy, King Clark.

F (daughter of Egyptian astrologer put to sleep for 3000 years to be awakened by true love; awakens in modern time but is returned to her own era)

Ref: MPW 27:1142, 1151, 1189.

Modern Sports Coaching

(Sports Coaching --ad.t?)

1970 Hungarian color ani sh.

Dir: Béla Ternovszky.

Story: Jozsef Nepp.

.sat-F-com

Ref: IAFF '72; Filmex II; S&S Autumn '72 p204.

Modern Times

1936 Charles Chaplin Film Corp (UA) 87 mins.

Prod, Dir, SP, Edit, Mus: Charles Chaplin.

Art Dir: Charles D. Hall.

Cin: Rollie Toetheroh & Ira Morgan.

Mus Arr & Adapt: David Raskin.

Mus Dir: Alfred Newman.

Cast: Charlie Chaplin, Paulette Goddard, Henry Bergman, Chester Conklin.

sat-com; bor-SF seqs (TV used to watch employees & make boss visible almost anywhere in factory; speed-up chemical in salt shaker; machine designed to feed people is tested on Charlie)

Ref: MPH 8 Feb '36 p9; HR 6 Feb '36; FDY '37; RAF p245-46, 519; F&F April '72 p62; LC.

Modern Yarn, A

1911 French, Pathé sil 360 ft.

F (man drives car on the bottom of the sea)

Ref: Bios 30 May '12.

Moderna Basna

(A Modern Fable)

1965 Yugoslavian, Zagreb color ani 10 mins.

Dir, Design, Ani: Aleksandar Marks & Vladimir Jutriša.

Story: Šime Šimatović.

Bg: Srdjan Matić.

Mus: Miljenko Prohaska.

F-com (rabbit escapes from hunting preserve where each hunter can pick his trophy according to his wealth)

Ref: Z/Zagreb p82.

Moderno Barba-Azul, El

(The Modern Blue Beard)

1947 (1950) Mexican, Alsa (Azteca).

Dir & SP: Jaime Salvador.

Story: Victor Trivas.

Art Dir: Ramon Rodriguez.

Makeup: A. Garibay.

Cin: Augustin Jimenez.

Edit: Rafael Ceballos.

Cast: Buster Keaton, Angel Garasa (Garsa?), Virginia Serret, Luis G. Burreiro, Jorge Mondragon, Fernando Soto.

SF-com (man thinks he flies to the Moon in a rocket ship)

Ref: Gasca p 123-24; Ackerman; FM 31:19.

See also: Bluebeard.

Modesty Blaise

1966 British, Joseph Janni Prods (20th-Fox) color 119 mins.

Prod: Joseph Janni.

Dir: Joseph Losey.

SP: Evan Jones.

Art Dir: Jack Shampan.

Prod Design: Richard MacDonald.

Cin: Jack Hildyard.

Edit: Reginald Beck.

Mus: John Dankworth.

Cast: Monica Vitt, Terence Stamp, Dirk Bogarde, Harry Andrews, Michael Craig, Clive Revill.

F (secret weapons; fantastic atmosphere; inexplicable costume changes; etc.)

Ref: MFB June '66 p89; FF '66 p222; Vw 11 May '66.

Based on the comic strip by Peter O'Donnell & Jim Holdaway.

Moebius Flip

1969 Summit (Pyramid) 16mm color 28 mins.

SF (skiers suddenly find world's "polarity" reversed, so must perform strange acrobatics to return to the normal world)

Ref: Pyramid cat p 128.

Mohini Avatar

(Mohini, Incarnation of God)

1925 Indian sil.

myth-F

Ref: IndCin YB.

Moidodyr

1927 Soviet sil ani puppet.

F

Ref: Kino p274.

Based on the poem by Chukovsky.

Moine, Le

(The Monk)

1971? (1972) French/Italian, Maya & Comacico/ Peri & Tritone color 90 mins.

Dir: Ado Kyrou.

SP: Luis Buñuel, Jean-Claude Carriere, & A. Kyrou.

Cin: Sacha Vierny.

Mus: Ennio Morricone.

Cast: Franco Nero, Nathalie Delon, Nicol Williamson, Nadja Tiller, Eliana De Santis, Elisabeth Wiener.

F-H (in medieval times, girl disguised as a monk is actually the Devil's emissary; a real monk makes a deal with the Devil & becomes today's Pope)

Ref: Vw 10 Dec '69, 11 July '73 p 110; CineF series I #3.

Based on the novel by Matthew G. Lewis.

Moiré

n.d. Italian, Amateur (Film-makers' Coop) 16mm color sil 3 mins.

Made by: Bruno Munari & Marcello Piccardo.

abs-exp-F

Ref: FMC 5:245.

Mojū

(The Blind Beast)

1969 Japanese, Daiei color scope 84 mins.

Dir: Yasuzo Masumura.

SP: Yoshiro Shirasaka.

Art Dir: Shigeo Mano.

Cin: Setsuo Kobayashi.

Mus: Hikaru Hayashi.

Cast: Eiji Funakoshi, Mako Midori, Noriko Sengoku.

H (girl captured & tortured by ugly man)

Based on a story by Rampo Edogawa

Ref: MPH 26 March '69; UniJ 44:2.

Mole, The

1955?--? Czech color ani sh series.

Dir: Zdenek Miler.

F-com

Ref: MTVM Aug '69 p22.

See also: How the Mole Got His Overalls (1957); Mole and the Motorcar, The (1963); Mole and the Green Star, The (1969).

Mole, The

See: Topo, El (1971).

Mole and the Green Star, The

(Krtek a Zelena Hvezda)

1969 Czech, Kratky color ani 8 mins.

Dir & Story: Zdenek Miler.

F-com (mole finds green pebble & mobilizes animals & the Moon to place it back in the sky)

Ref: Mamaia '70.

See also: Mole, The (1955?-).

Mole and the Motorcar, The

1963 Czech ani sh.

Dir: Zdenek Miler.

F

Ref: Ani/Cin p 174.

See also: Mole, The (1955?-).

Mole Men vs. the Son of Hercules

(Maciste, l'Uomo Più Forte del Mondo: Maciste, the Strongest Man in the World; Maciste and the Night Queen --ad.t?; The Strongest Man in the World --Brit.t.)

1961 (1963?) Italian, Inter-film-Leone color scope 97 mins.

Prod: Elio Scardamaglia.

Dir & Story: Antonio Leonviola.

SP: Marcello Baldi & Giuseppe Mangione.

Art Dir: Franco Lolli.

Cin: Alvaro Mancori.

Edit: Otello Colangeli.

Mus: Armando Trovaioli.

Cast: Mark Forest, Moira Orfei, Paul Wynter, Raffaella Carra, Gianni Garko, Graziella Granta, Enrico Glori.

myth-F-H (Maciste, here called the Son of Hercules, battles Mole Men, albinos from super-scientific underground city to whom sunlight is fatal; Maciste splits the ground over their city to kill them)

Ref: MFB May '64 p 75-76; FEFN Sept '61 p50; TVK.

See also: Maciste.

Mole People, The

1956 U 78 mins.

Prod: William Alland.

Dir: Virgil Vogel.

SP: Laszlo Gorog.

Art Dir: Alexander Golitzen & Robert E. Smith.

Cin: Ellis Carter.

SpFX Cin: Clifford Stine.

Edit: Irving Birnbaum.

Mus Dir: Joseph Gershenson.

Cast: John Agar, Cynthia Patrick, Hugh Beaumont, Nestor Paiva, Alan Napier, Eddie Parker, Robin Hughes, Rodd Redwing, Frank Baxter.

SF-H (lost Sumerian city found underground, populated by albinos; mole-like quasi-human slaves; albinos killed by ordinary sunlight)

Ref: HR & Vd 26 Oct '56; deGroote 285; FD 31 Oct '56.

Molécula en Orbita

(Molecule in Orbit)

1970 Spanish, Estudios Cruz Delgado color ani 757 ft.

Dir: Cruz Delgado.

Molécula en Orbita cont.

F-com (professor given secret formula by benign aliens; monsters)

Ref: SpCin '71.

Molly Moo-Cow

1935-36 Van Beuren Corp ani sh series.

Dir: Burt Gillett & Tom Palmer.

F-com

Ref: LC.

See also: Molly Moo-Cow and Rip Van Winkle (1935); Burt Gillett's Rainbow Parade (1934-35); Rainbow Parade (1935-36).

Molly Moo-Cow and Rip Van Winkle

1935 Van Beuren Corp (RKO) ani 1 reel.

Dir: Burt Gillett & Tom Palmer.

F-com

Ref: LC.

See also: Rip Van Winkle; Molly Moo-Cow (1935-36).

Molten Meteor, The

See: Blob, The (1958).

Moment in Love, A

1956 Amateur (Contemporary) 16mm color 9 mins.

Made by: Shirley Clarke.

Choreog: Anna Sokolow & S. Clarke.

Mus: Norman Lloyd.

exp-dance-F (dancers fly through clouds, under water; appear & disappear in magic ruins)

Ref: Contemp cat p60; FMC 5:64.

Momentum

1969 Amateur 16mm color 6 mins.

Made by: Jordan Belson.

abs-F

Ref: LAFP 4 July '69; ExCin p 174-77.

See also: Kinetic Art, The (1970).

Momia, La

See: Aztec Mummy, The (1957).

Momia contra el Robot Humano, El

See: Robot vs. the Aztec Mummy, The (1959).

Momie du Roi, La

See: Mummy of the King of Ramsee, The (1909).

Mon Merle

See: Merle, Le (1958).

Mona Lisa

(painting by Da Vinci)

See: Joconde, La (1958); Why Do You Smile, Mona Lisa? (1966).

Monaco di Monza, Il

(The Monk of Monza)

1963 Italian.

Prod: Giovanni Addessi.

Dir: Sergio Corbucci.

SP: S. Corbucci & Giovanni Grimaldi.

Cin: Enzo Barboni.

Mus: Armando Trovajoli.

Cast: Toto, Nino Taranto, Erminio Macario, Lisa Gastoni, Moira Orfei.

bor-F-H-com (fake monk engineers ghosts and other weird happenings; love potion causes outlandish behavior)

Ref: Ital Prods '63 I:64-65.

Mönch mit der Peitsche, Der

(The Monk with the Whip)

1967 W. German, Rialto color.

Dir: Alfred Vohrer.

SP: Alex Berg.

Cin: Karl Löb.

Cast: Joachim Fuchsberger, Siegfried Schürenberg, Ursula Glas, Ilse Page, Grit Böttchen.

bor-H

Ref: GFN 2; Bianco Sept '68 p91 (Willis).

Based on a novel by Edgar Wallace.

Monde come il Va, Le

(by Voltaire)

See: Or et le Plomb, L' (1966).

Monde Tremblera, Le

(The World Will Shake; La Revolte des Vivants: The Revolt of the Living --alt.t? The Death Predictor --ad.t?)

1939 French, CICC 110 mins.

Dir: Richard Pottier.

SP: Henri-Georges Clouzot & J. Villard.

Art Dir: Perrier.

Cin: R. Lefevre.

Cast: Madeleine Solonge, Armand Bernard, Erich von Stroheim, Claude Dauphin, Roger Duchesne.

SF (machine which can predict death for anyone results in universal disorder, assassinations, suicides, etc.)

Ref: Gasca p82; Ackerman; Rep Gen '47.

Based on a story by Charles Robert Dumas & R.F. Didelot.

Mondo Keyhole

1968?

sex; F-H seq (Dracula sequence)

Ref: Soren.

See also: Dracula.

Monello della Strada, Il

(Street Arab)

1951 Italian, Lux.

Dir: Carlo Borghesio.

Story: Leo Benvenutti, Marcello Marchesi, Vittorio Metz, & Glauco Pellegrini.

Art Dir: Luigi Ricci.

Cin: Arturo Gallea.

Mus: Nino Rota.

Cast: Macario, Luisa Rossi, Saro Urzi, Giulio Stival, Ciccio Jacono.

F (mother comes down from Heaven to help son get a good father)

Ref: Ital Prods '50-51.

Money and Love

See: Denara e d'Amore (1936).

Money-Box Pig, A

1964 Soviet, All-Union (Sovexportfilm) color ani 17 mins.

Dir: L. Milchin.

Story: S. Runge & A. Kumm.

F (pig bank admires only the tinkle of coins)

Ref: Sovexportfilm cat 2:126.

Based on a story by Hans Christian Andersen.

Money-Go-Round

1966 British, Libertas Films for London Stock Exchange color 38 mins.

Prod: Margaret K. Johns.

Dir: Alvin Rakoff.

SP: Wolf Rilla & Ian Dawson-Shepherd.

Art Dir: Bernard Sarron.

Cin: Jean Bourgoin.

cont.

cont.

Money-Go-Round cont.

Edit: Peter Austen-Hunt.

Mus & Lyrics: Bill Martin & Phil Coulter.

Songs Sung by: The Koobas.

Cast: Sheila White, Jeremy Bulloch, Anthony Oliver, John Franklyn-Robbins, Helen Fenemore.

mus-F-doc (children transported to a fantasy world are told how the Stock Exchange works)

Ref: MFB June '67 p98.

Monitors, The

1969 USA and Bell & Howell Prod (Commonwealth United) color 92 mins.

Prod: Bernard Sahlins.

Dir: Jack Shea.

SP: Myron J. Gold.

Art Dir: Roy Henry.

Cin: William (Vilmos) Zsigmond.

Edit: Patrick Kennedy.

Mus: Fred Kaz.

Cast: Guy Stockwell, Susan Oliver, Avery Schreiber, Sherry Jackson. Sheppherd Strudwick [alien], Keenan Wynn, Ed Begley, Larry Storch, Alan Arkin, Xavier Cugat, Stubby Kaye, Jackie Vernon, Everett Dirksen.

SF-sat-com (monitors from space control mankind, not allowing humans to endanger themselves or each other)

Ref: Vw 15 Oct '69; BIB's; BO 10 Nov '69; Trieste '70.

Based on the novel by Keith Laumer.

Monk, The

See: Moine, Le (1971?).

Monk of Monza, The

See: Monaco di Monza, Il (1963).

Monk with the Whip, The

See: Mönch mit der Pfeitsche, Der (1967).

Monkey, The

(The Ape --alt.t?)

1959 Chinese ani sh.

Dir: Yang Tei.

F

Ref: Animée p 153.

Monkey

(Hsi-yu Chi; The Journey to the West --ad.t?)

1960?--?? Chinese feature series.

myth-F (half-man, half-monkey evolved from a stone can cover thousands of miles in a somersault; magic club; much other magic)

Ref: Landers.

Based on Chinese legend.

See also: Monkey God, The (1960?); Monkey Comes Again, The (1970).

Monkey, The

1961 Amateur 16mm color ani 3 mins.

Made by: Larry Jordan.

exp-F

Ref: Undrgnd p 155, 279.

Monkey Bite, A

1911 French, Pathé sil 420 ft.

F-com (monkey's bite makes people act like monkeys)

Ref: Bios 26 Oct '11.

Monkey Business

(Be Your Age --s.t?)

1952 20th-Fox 97 mins.

Prod: Sol C. Siegel.

Dir: Howard Hawks.

Story: Harry Segall.

SP: Ben Hecht, Charles Lederer, & I.A.L. Diamond.

cont.

The Monkey's Paw (1932)

Monkey Business cont.

Art Dir: Lyle Wheeler & George Patrick.

Cin: Milton Krasner.

Edit: William B. Murphy.

Mus: Leigh Harline.
Mus Dir: Lionel Newman.

Cast: Cary Grant, Ginger Rogers, Charles Coburn, Hugh Marlowe, Douglas Spencer, Marilyn Monroe, Larry Keating, George Winslow.

SF-com (formula makes people grow gradually younger, act childish)

Ref: HR & Vd 2 Sept '52; MFB Oct '52 p 144; FDY '53.

Monkey Comes Again, The

1970 Hongkong, Cathay color scope.
Cast: Tieng Ching, Elly Tam, Wendy Chin.

F (ad shows monkey god on cloud, man with pig's head)

Ref: Singapore Straits-Times 28 Jan '71.

See also: Monkey (1960?--??); Monkey God, The (1960?).

Monkey God, The

1960? Hongkong, Shaw.

F

Ref: FEFN March '60 p44.

See also: Monkey (1960?--??); Monkey Comes Again, The (1970).

Monkey Land, a Jungle Romance

1908 (1909) Vit sil 330 ft.

F-com

Ref: Views & FI IV:1:7; LC.

Monkey Man, The

1908 French sil sh.

SF

Ref: Gifford/H p27.

Monkey Planet

See: Planet of the Apes (1968).

Monkey Talks, The

1927 Fox sil 6 reels.

Prod: Arch Selwyn.

Dir: Raoul Walsh.
Sc: Gladys Unger & L.G. Rigby.

cont.

Money Talks cont.

Makeup: Jack Pierce.

Cin: William O'Connell.

Cast: Olive Borden, Jacques Lerner, Don Alvarado, Malcolm Waite, Raymond Hitchcock, Ted McNamara.

bor-H (midget impersonates monkey, saves heroine from killer chimpanzee)

Ref: AFI F2.3680 p522; LC; MPW 79:8, 85:56; FM 60:4.

Based on play "Le Singe Qui Parle" by René Fauchois.

Monkey Woman, The

See: Ape Woman, The (1963).

Monkey's Paw, The

● 1915 British, Magnet sil 2800 ft.
Dir: Sidney Northcote.

Cast: John Lawson.

Ref: Collier; Hist/Brit p 177; Gifford/BFC 05483.

cont.

Monkey's Paw cont.

Based on a play from the story by W.W. Jacobs.

● 1923 British, Artistic (Selznick) sil 5700 ft.

Dir: Manning Haynes.

Sc: Lydia Hayward.

Cin: Frank Grainger.

Cast: Moore Marriott, A.B. Imeson, Marie Ault, Charles Ashton, Johnny Butt, George Wynne, Tom Coventry.

Ref: Brit Cin p56; FDY '24.

● 1932 (1933) RKO 56 mins.

Prod: David O. Selznick.

Dir: Wesley Ruggles.

SP: Graham John.

Cin: Leo Tover.

Edit: Charles L. Kimball.

Mus Dir: Max Steiner.

Cast: C. Aubrey Smith, Ivan Simpson, Louis Carter, Bramwell Fletcher, Betty Lqwford, Herbert Bunston.

F-H-dream (the usual story, with everything turning out to have been a dream)

Ref: FIR March '64 p 151; FD 1 June '33; Vw 6 June '33.

Based on the play by Louis N. Parker from the story by W.W. Jacobs.

● 1948 British, Kay Film 64 mins.

Dir: Norman Lee.

SP: N. Lee & Barbara Toy.

Cin: Bryan Langley.

Mus Dir: Stanley Black.

Cast: Milton Rosmer, Megs Jenkins, Joan Seton, Norman Shelley, Michael Martin Harvey.

Ref: MFD July '48 p92.

F-H (couple obtains monkey's paw which grants wishes, but always at great cost: wish for wealth results in son being mangled to death & couple getting insurance money; wish for son to return brings him out of grave, still mangled; etc.)

Based on the short story by W.W. Jacobs.

See also: Spiritism (1961); Tales from the Crypt (1971).

Monkey's Teeth, The

See: Dents du Singe, Les (1960).

Monkey's Uncle, The

1965 WD (BV) color 91 mins.

Prod: Walt Disney.

Co Prod: Ron Miller.

Dir: Robert Stevenson.

Story: Bill Walsh.

SP: Tom & Helen August.

Art Dir: Carroll Clark & William H. Tuntke.

Cin: Edward Colman.

SpFX: Robert A. Mattey & Eustace Lycett.

Edit: Cotton Warburton.

Mus: Buddy Baker.

Cast: Tommy Kirk, Annette Funicello, Leon Ames, Frank Faylen, Arthur O'Connell, Leon Tyler, Norman Grabowski, Connie Gilchrist, Gage Clarke, Mark Goddard.

SF-com (college genius Merlin Jones saves football team by sleep-teaching, which has already made chimpanzee smart; drug increases strength; man-powered flying machine)

Ref: Vw 26 May '65; FD 27 July '65; MFB Aug '65 p 124-25.

Sequel to: Misadventures of Merlin Jones, The (1963).

Monolith Monsters, The

(Monolith! --s.t.)

1957 U 77 mins.

Prod: Howard Christie.

Dir: John Sherwood.

Story: Jack Arnold & Robert M. Fresco.

SP: Norman Jolley & R.M. Fresco.

Art Dir: Alexander Golitzen & Bob Smith.

Makeup: Bud Westmore.

Cin: Ellis W. Carter.

SpFX Cin: Clifford Stine.

Edit: Patrick McCormack.

Mus: Joseph Gershenson.

Cast: Grant Williams, Lola Albright, Les Tremayne, Trevor Bardette, William Flaherty, Harry Jackson, William Schallert.

SF-H (when wet, meteor crystals found to grow rapidly & absorb silicon out of living things, including people, turning them to stone; rain causes huge numbers of giant crystals to approach town; salt stops growth)

Ref: Vd 22 Oct '57; FD 28 Oct '57; SFF p 140.

Monopole Capitalism, The

(story by Baran & Sweezy)

See: Grosse Verhau, Der (1971).

Monopolist, The

1915 Pathé sil 3000 ft.

bor-SF (invention increases speed of ships)

Ref: MPN 21 Aug '15 (Willis).

Monsieur Clown chez les Lilliputiens

(Mister Clown among the Lilliputians)

1909 French, Gaum sil ani sh.

Dir: Emile Cohl.

F-com

Ref: Filmlex p 1370.

See also: Gulliver's Travels.

Monsieur Leguignon, Guérisseur

(Mr. Leguignon, Healer)

1953 French, Jason Films.

Dir: Maurice Labro.

SP: Solange Terac, Pierre Ferrari, M. Labro, & Robert Picq.

Art Dir: Jean Douarinou.

Cin: Nicolas Toporkoff.

Cast: Yves Deniaud, Jeanne (Jane) Marken, Nicole Besnard, André Brunot, Michel Roux, Paul Demange.

F-com (M. Leguignon discovers he has the power of healing)

Ref: Unifrance 5:12.

Based on the radio show by Robert Picq & Pierre Ferrari.

Monsieur Nickola Duprée

1915 Thanhouser sil 2 reels.

Cast: Ernest Ward, Florence La Badie, Morris Foster, Harris Gordon.

F (like "the Devil" but is instead agent of good)

Ref: MPW 24:1072.

Same film as God's Witness (1915)?

Monsieur Robida, Prophete et Explorateur du Temps

(Mr. Robida, Prophet and Explorer of Time)

1963 French 25 mins.

Dir: Pierre Kast.

SP: France Roche.

SF-sat (time travel)

Ref: Gasca p322; Trieste I p 19.

Monsieur Stop

(Mr. Stop)

1907 French, Gaum sil sh.

Dir: Émile Cohl.

F-com (invention immobilizes people)

Ref: F/A p420; Filmlex p 1370.

Monsieur Tête

(Mister Head)

1959 French ani sh.

Dir: Jan Lenica & Henri Gruel.

F

Ref: Ani/Cin p 101, 107-08, 170, 173.

Monsieur Victor

(Mr. Victor)

1957 French ani sh.

Prod: Jean Image.

F

Ref: Elements; Gasca p 173.

Monster, The

(Le Monstre)

1903 French, Star sil 170 ft.

Made by: Georges Méliès.

F-com (tricks in an Egyptian setting)

Ref: Sadoul/M, GM Mage; LC; Gifford/H p24; Niver p68.

Monster, The

1925 Metro-Goldwyn sil 6425 ft.

Prod & Dir: Roland West.

Sc: Willard Mack & Albert G. Kenyon.

Titles: C. Gardner Sullivan.

Cin: Hal Mohr.

Edit: A. Carle Palm.

Cast: Lon Chaney, Gertrude Olmsted, Hallam Cooley, Johnny Arthur, Charles A. Sellon, Walter James, Knute Erickson, George Austin, Edward McWade, Ethel Wales.

psy-H; bor-com (Chaney, the mad Dr. Ziska, believes he can bring the dead back to life, captures passing motorists & puts them in the dungeon of his sanitarium for use in future experiments)

Ref: AFI F2.3682 p522; LC; Vw 18 Feb '25; MPN 31:929.

Based on the play by Crane Wilbur.

Monster, The

(short story by S. Crane)

See: Face of Fire (1959).

Monster, The

See: Monstruo, El (1971).

Monster a Go-Go

(Terror at Halfday --s.t.)

1965 B.I. & L. Releasing Corp 70 mins.

Prod & Dir: Herschell Gordon Lewis (Sheldon Seymour) & Bill Rebane.

Cast: Phil Morton, June Travis, George Perry, Lois Brooks, Henry Hite [monster].

SF-H (astronaut comes back from space as 10' monster)

Ref: FM 36:9; Ackerman; PB; A. Romanoff.

Monster and a Half, A

See: Mostro. . .e Mezzo, Un (1964).

Monster and I, The

(Neman i Vi: The Monster and You)

1964 Yugoslavian, Zagreb (World Health Organization) color ani 10.9 mins.

Dir, Story, Design: Boris Kolar.

Ani: Zdenko Gašparović.

Mus: Davor Kajfes.

doc; F-seqs

Ref: Ani/Cin p 172; Z/Zagreb p75; FQ Fall '68 p49.

Monster and the Ape, The

1945 Darmour (Col) serial 15 parts 30 reels.

Prod: Rudolph C. Flothow.

cont.

Monster & the Ape cont.

Dir: Howard Bretherton.

SP: Sherman Lowe & Royal K. Cole.

Cin: L.W. O'Connell.

Edit: Dwight Caldwell & Earl Turner.

Mus: Lee Zahler.

Cast: Robert Lowery, George Macready, Ralph Morgan, Carole Mathews, Ray "Crash" Corrigan [the ape], Willie Best, Jack Ingram, Anthony Warde, Ted Mapes, Eddie Parker, Stanley Price.

SF-H (criminals after super-robot that runs on "metalogen" metal; killer ape named Thor)

Ref: MPH 21 April '45; Ser/Col; LC; FanMo 2:1:14.

Monster and the Girl, The

(D.O.A. --s.t.)

1941 Par 65 mins.

Prod: Jack Moss.

Dir: Stuart Heisler.

SP: Stuart Anthony.

Art Dir: Hans Dreier & Haldane Douglas.

Cin: Victor Milner.

Edit: Everett Douglas.

Mus Dir: Sigmund Krumgold.

Cast: Ellen Drew, Robert Paige, Paul Lukas, Onslow Stevens, George Zucco, Rod Cameron, Marc Lawrence, Phillip Terry, Gerald Mohr, Joseph Calleia.

SF-H (brain of wrongly-executed man transplanted into gorilla, which gets revenge on gang which sold dead man's sister into prostitution & arranged execution)

Ref: MFB Nov '41 p52; HR & Vd 6 Feb '41; FD 24 March '41; B Movies; Pardi.

Probably remake of Go and Get It (1920).

Monster and the Lady, The

See: Lady and the Monster, The (1944).

Monster and the Woman

Canadian title of Four-Sided Triangle (1953).

Monster and You, The

See: Monster and I, The (1964).

Monster Demolisher

(Nostradamus y el Destructor de Monstruos: Nostradamus and the Destroyer of Monsters)

1960? (1962) Mexican (Clasa-Mohme & AIP-TV) 74 mins.

Feature made from 2 episodes of series (serial?) La Maldicion de Nostradamus (El Estudiante y la Horca: The Student and the Gallows; El Ataud Vacio: The Empty Coffin)

Prod: Victor Parra.

Dir: Frederick Curiel.

Story: Charles Taboada & Alfred Ruanova.

SP: F. Curiel & C. Taboada.

Cin: Ferdinand Colin.

Edit: Joseph J. Mungala.

Mus: George Perez.

English language version Prod: K. Gordon Murray.

Dir: Stim Segar.

Cast: German Robles [vampire], Julio Alemán, Domingo Soler, Aurora Alvarado, Rogelio Jimenez Pons.

F-H (the vampire Nostradamus is finally destroyed by a stake through the heart)

Ref: PS; TVK; Willis; Photon 19:37; Azteca; FM 33:10.

Sequel to: Curse of Nostradamus, The (1960).

Monster Dog, The
See: Pet, The (1917).

Monster from a Prehistoric Planet
(Daikyajû Gappa; Gappa — Triphibian Monster --ad.t.; Gappa, Frankenstein Fliegend Monster --German t.)
1967 Japanese, Nikkatsu (AIP-TV) color scope 90 mins (85 mins).
Prod: Hideo Koi.
Dir: Haruyasu Noguchi.
SP: Iwao Yamazak & Ryuzo Nakanishi.
Art Dir: Kazumi Koike.
Cin: Muneo Ueda.
SpFX: Akira Watanabe.
Mus: Seitaro Omori.
Cast: Tamio Kawaji, Yôko Yamamoto, Tatsuya Fuji, Koji Wada, Yuji Odaka.
SF-H (giant octopus helps hatch egg on isolated island, young creature taken back to Tokyo, but its amphibious flying bird monster parents rescue it)
Ref: Vw 19 April '67; F&F Dec '69 p55; UniJ 37:32-33.

Monster from Earth's End
(novel by M. Leinster)
See: Navy vs. the Night Monsters, The (1966).

Monster from Galaxy 27, The
See: Night of the Blood Beast (1958).

Monster from Green Hell, The
1957 (1958) Grosse-Krasne (DCA) 71 mins.
Prod: Al Zimbalist.
Dir: Kenneth Crane.
SP: Louis Vittes & Endre Bohem.
Cin: Ray Flin.
SpFX: Jess Davison, Jack Rabin, & Louis DeWitt.
Cast: Jim Davis, Robert E. Griffin, Barbara Turner, Eduardo Ciannelli, Vladimir Sokoloff, Joe Fluellen.
SF-H (experimental rocket containing wasps as test animals is exposed to radiation, crashes in Africa; giant wasps result, which are destroyed by volcano)
Ref: FF '58 p285; FIR Dec '69 p641; LAT 12 Dec '58.

Monster from Mars
See: Robot Monster (1953).

Monster from the Ocean Floor
(It Stalked the Ocean Floor --e.t.; Monster Maker -- Canadian t.)
1954 Palo Alto Prods (Lippert) 64 mins.
Prod: Roger Corman.
Dir: Wyott Ordung.
SP: William Danch.
Prod Design: Ben Hayne.
Cin: Floyd Crosby.
Edit: Ed Samson.
Mus: Andre Brumer.
SF-H (giant amoeba encountered; killed by ramming it in eye with midget submarine)
Ref: MFB March '56 p33; Vd 27 May '54; FM 1:39.

Monster from the Surf
See: Beach Girls and the Monster (1964).

Monster from the Unknown World
See: Atlas Against the Cyclops (1961).

Monster Gorilla, The
See: Gekko Kamen (1959).

Monster in the Basement, The
1962 Amateur 16mm 8 mins.
Made by: Robert Kraus.
Cin: Arthur Blumenfeld & Jerry Cohen.
Cast: Lee Lorenz & Lenore Ross.
exp-SF-H
Ref: FM 19:58.

Monster in the Night
See: Monster on the Campus (1958).

Monster in the Shadow, The
See: Monstruo en la Sombra, El (1954).

Monster Maker, The
1944 Sigmund Neufeld Prods (PRC) 64 mins.
Prod: Sigmund Neufeld.
Dir: Sam Newfield.
Story: Lawrence Williams.
SP: Pierre Gendron & Martin Mooney.
Art Dir: Paul Palmentola.
Cin: Robert Cline.
Edit: Holbrook N. Todd.
Mus: Albert Glasser.
Cast: J. Carrol Naish, Ralph Morgan, Wanda McKay, Tola Birell, Glenn Strange, Terry Frost, Sam Flint.
bor-SF; H (acromegaly "germs" distort concert pianist's hands and face)
Ref: HR & Vd 6 March '44; MFB March '49 p45; LC.

Monster Maker
See: Monster from the Ocean Floor (1954).

Monster Meets the Gorilla, The
See: Bela·Lugosi Meets a Brooklyn Gorilla (1952).

Monster of Ceremonies
1966 U color ani 1 reel.
Prod: Walter Lantz.
Dir: Paul Smith.
Voice of Woody: Grace Stafford.
F-com
Ref: PopCar.
See also: Woody Woodpecker (1966).

Monster of Fate, The
See: Golem, The (1914).

Monster of Frankenstein, The
See: Mostro di Frankenstein, Il (1920).

Monster of Highgate Ponds, The
1960 British ani & live 62 mins.
Prod: John Halas.
Dir: Alberto Cavalcanti.
Story: Joy Batchelor.
SP: Mary Cathcart Borer.
Model Ani: Vic Hotchkiss.
Cin: Frank North.
Edit: Jack King & Robert Hill.
Mus: Francis Chagrin.
Cast: Roy Vincente [monster], Ronald Howard, Rachel Clay, Philip Latham, Michael Wade, Terry Raven.
F-com (monster hatches from egg from Malaya; after adventures with children, the monster returns to Malaya)
Ref: MFB June '61 p 83; Ideal '69-70 p 184.

Monster of London City, The
(Das Ungeheuer von London City)
1964 (1967) W. German, C.C.C. Prods (PRC) 90 mins (87 mins).
Prod: Artur Brauner.
Dir: Edwin Zbonek (Zebonek?).
SP: Robert A. Stemmle.
Art Dir: Hans Jurgen Kiebach & Ernst Schomer.

cont.

Monster of London City cont.
Cin: Siegfried Hold.
Edit: Walter Wischniewski.
Mus: Martin Boettcher.
Cast: Marianne Koch, Hansjörg Felmy, Dietmar Schoenherr, Hans Nielsen, Chariklia Baxevanos, Fritz Tillmann.
H (Jack-the-Ripper styled murders)
Ref: FF '67 p238; MFB April '67 p64; Vw 2 Aug '67.
Based on a story by Bryan Edgar Wallace.
See also: Jack the Ripper.

Monster of Monsters Ghidorah
See: Ghidrah, the Three-Headed Monster (1965).

Monster of Piedras Blancas, The
1958 (1959) VanWick Prods (Filmservice Distributors) 71 mins.
Prod: Jack Kevan.
Dir: Irvin Berwick.
SP: Haile Chace.
Art Dir: Walter Woodworth.
Cin: Philip Lathrop.
Edit: George Gittens.
Cast: Les Tremayne, Forrest Lewis, John Harmon, Jeanne Carmen, Don Sullivan, Frank Arvidson, Wayne Berwick, Joseph LaCava.
SF-H (man-shaped seamonster fed by lighthouse keeper; goes around ripping heads off people)
Ref: MFB April '62 p54; HR 16 April '58; FM 3:41; FF '59 p341.

Monster of Terror
See: Die Monster Die! (1965).

Monster of the Opera
See: Vampiro dell' Opera, Il (1961).

Monster of the Volcanos, The
See: Monstruo de los Volcanes, El (1962).

Monster of the Wax Museum, The
See: Nightmare in Wax (1969).

Monster of Venice, The
See: Embalmer, The (1964).

Monster on the Campus
(Monster in the Night -s.t.)
1958 U 77 mins.
Prod & Mus: Joseph Gershenson.
Dir: Jack Arnold.
SP: David Duncan.
Art Dir: Alexander Golitzen.
Makeup: Bud Westmore.
Set Dec: Russell A. Gausman & Julia Heron.
Cin: Russell Metty.
SpFX Cin: Clifford Stine.
Edit: Ted J. Kent.
Cast: Arthur Franz, Joanna Moore, Judson Pratt, Nancy Walters, Troy Donahue, Phil Harvey, Helen Westcott, Whit Bissell, Eddie Parker [apeman].
SF-H (scientist's serum turns dragonfly into primitive form, dog into dire wolf, fish into coelecanth; serum accidentally gets into pipe & when scientist smokes it turns into murderous ape-like primitive man)
Ref: FF '58 p270; Vd & HR 14 Oct '58; FM 31:54.

Monster Prince
See: Kaijû Ôji (1968).

Monster Raid
See: Dr. Terror's Gallery of Horrors (1967).

Monster Rumble
1961 Amateur 16mm color sil sh.
Prod: Don Glut.
Cast: D. Glut [8 roles].
F-H (sequel to most of Glut's films, with Frankenstein's Monster, the Teenage Frankenstein, Dracula, the Wolf Man, the Teenage Werewolf, Ygor, etc.)
Ref: D. Glut.
See also: Dracula; Frankenstein; Son of Frankenstein (1939); Wolf Man, The (1941); I Was a Teenage Frankenstein (1957); I Was a Teenage Werewolf (1957).

Monster Show, The
See: Freaks (1931).

Monster Snowman, The
See: Half Human (1955).

Monster Strikes, The
See: Pusang Itim (1959).

Monster That Challenged the World, The
1957 Gramercy (UA) 85 mins.
Prod: Arthur Gardner & Jules V. Levy.
Dir: Arnold Laven.
Story: David Duncan.
SP: Pat Fielder.
Art Dir: James Vance.
Cin: Lester White.
Underwater Cin: Scotty Welborn.
Edit: John Faure.
Mus: Heinz Roemheld.
Cast: Tim Holt, Audrey Dalton, Hans Conreid, Barbara Darrow, Casey Adams, Harlan Warde, Milton Parsons, Jody McCrea.
SF-H (earthquake releases giant caterpillar-like sea snails into Salton Sea)
Ref: Vw 22 May '57; MFB Sept '57 p 115; FD 23 May '57.

Monster Walks, The
1932 Mayfair Pictures 65 mins (57 mins).
Prod: Cliff Broughton.
Dir: Frank Strayer.
SP: Robert Ellis.
Cin: Jules Cronjager.
Edit: Byron Robinson.
Cast: Rex Lease, Vera Reynolds, Mischa Auer, Sheldon Lewis, Sidney Bracey, Martha Mattox, Sleep 'n' Eat (later Willie Best).
H (real ape suspected, but moron used for killings)
Ref: Vw 31 May '32; FD 7 Feb '32; MFB Dec '41 p 167.

Monster Wangmagwi
See: Wangmagwi (1967).

Monster with Green Eyes, The
See: Planets Against Us (1961).

Monster Yongkari
See: Yongary, Monster from the Deep (1967).

Monster Zero
(Kaiju Daisenso: Invasion of Astro-Monsters; Battle of the Astros; Godzilla Radon Kingidorah --all ad.t.s)
1965 (1970) Japanese, Toho (Maron) color 96 mins.
Prod: Tomoyuki Tanaka.
Dir: Inoshiro Honda.
SP: Shinichi Sekizawa.
Art Dir: Takeo Kita.
Cin: Hajime Koizumi.
SpFX: Eiji Tsuburaya.
Edit: Ryohei Fujii.
Mus Dir: Akira Ifukube.

cont.

Monster Zero cont.

Cast: Nick Adams, Akira Takarada, Kumi Mizuno, Jun Tazaki, Akira Kubo.

SF-H (aliens pretend to help Earth by taking Godzilla & Rodan away, but unleash instead Ghidrah; space travel; rays)

Ref: MPH 22 Dec '65 p24-25; Willis; Pardi.

See also: Godzilla, King of the Monsters (1954); Rodan (1956); Ghidrah the Three-Headed Monster (1965).

Monsters Crash Pajama Party

1965 Brandon color 45 mins.

Cast: Don Brandon.

F-H (haunted house; mad scientist; gorilla; man in werewolf mask; etc.)

Ref: Richardson.

Monsters from the Moon

See: Robot Monster (1953).

Monsters Invade Expo 70

See: Gamera vs Monster X (1970).

Monsters of Frankenstein

See: House of Freaks, The (1973).

Monsters of Terror, The

See: Hombre Que Vino del Ummo, El (1970).

Monsters of the Night

See: Navy vs. the Night Monsters (1966).

Monstre, Le

See: Monster, The (1903).

Monstre aux Yeux Verts, Le

See: Planets Against Us (1961).

Monstrosity

(The Atomic Brain --s.t?)

1963 (1964) Cinema Venture (Emerson Film Enterprises) 70 mins.

Prod: Jack Pollexfen & Dean Dillman Jr.

Dir: Joseph Mascelli.

SP: Vi Russell, Sue Dwiggens, & D. Dillman Jr.

Electrical FX: Kenneth Strickfaden.

Cin: Alfred Taylor.

Edit: Owen C. Gladden.

Mus: Gene Kauer.

Cast: Frank Gerstle, Erika Peters, Judy Bamber, Marjorie Eaton.

SF-H (human brain transplant experiments produce zombies; cat's brain transplanted into girl)

Ref: Vw 16 Dec '64; Borst; BO 18 Feb '63.

Monstruo, El

(The Monster)

1971 Spanish, Estudios Castillo color ani 9.1 mins.

Dir: Amaro Carretero.

Realisation: Vicente Rodríguez.

SF-com (giant lizard reduces things to ashes)

Ref: SpCin '72.

Monstruo de la Montaña Hueca, El

See: Beast of Hollow Mountain, The (1956).

Monstruo de los Volcanes, El

(The Monster of the Volcanos; El Fantasma de las Nieves: The Phantom of the Snows --s.t?)

1962 (1964) Mexican, Grovas (Clasa-Mohme).

Prod: Rafael Grovas.

cont.

Monstruo de los Volcanes cont.

Dir: Jaime Salvador.

SP: Federico Curiel & Alfredo Ruanova.

Art Dir: S.L. Mena.

Cin: Ezequiel Carrasco.

Cast: Joaquin Cordero, Ana Bertha Lepe, Andres Soler, Antonio Raxel, Victor Alcocer, David Hayat, José Chavez.

SF-H (hairy monster lives on volcanic mountain)

Ref: PS; MTVM May '62 p26; Indice; FDY '65.

See also: Terrible Gigante de las Nieves, El (1962).

Monstruo de la Sombra, El

(The Monster of the Shadow)

1954 (1956) Mexican, Cub-Mex (Clasa-Mohme & Azteca) 92 mins.

Dir: Zacarias Gomez Urquiza.

SP: A.P. Delgado.

Cin: Gabriel Figueroa.

Mus: G.C. Carrion.

Cast: Eduardo Noriega, Martha Roth, Jaime Fernandez, Carmen Montejo.

F-H

Ref: Indice; FM 31:22; LC.

Based on a story by Felix B. Caignet.

Monstruo Resuscitado, El

(The Resurrected Monster)

1952 (1955) Mexican, Internacional Cinematografica (Azteca)

Dir & SP: Chano Urueta.

Story: Dino Maiuri.

Art Dir: Mario Padilla & Gunter Gerszo.

Makeup: Armando Meyer.

Cin: Victor Herrera.

SpFX: Jorge Benavides.

Mus: Raul Lavista.

Cast: Miroslava, Carlos Navarro, José Maria Linares Rivas, Fernando Wagner, Alberto Mariscal.

SF-H (doctor digs up corpse, transplants brain of near-savage into body, brings it back to life)

Ref: LAT 28 Sept '55; Aventura p430; Scognamillo; Azteca.

Monstruos del Terror, Los

See: Hombre Que Vino del Ummo, El (1970).

Montana Mike

See: Heaven Only Knows (1947).

Monty Phython's Flying Circus

(BBC-TV show)

See: And Now for Something Completely Different (1971).

Mood Contrast

1954 Amateur 16mm? electronic ani sh.

Made by: Mary Ellen Bute & Ted Nemeth.

exp-F

Ref: Undrgnd p81.

Moods of Evil

See: Hidden Dangers (1920).

Moon for Your Love

1909 French, Gaum sil 424 ft.

F (witches & fairies; Moon brought to Earth)

Ref: FI IV:47:10; MPW 5:798, 820.

Moon in His Apron, The

See: Lune dans Son Tablier, La (1909).

Note: title devised by BFI.

Moon Man

1905 British sil 106 ft.

F (moon has living face)

Ref: BFI cat p80.

Note: title devised by BFI.

Moon Men

See: Jungle Moon Men (1954).

Moon of Israel

(Die Sklavenkönigin)

1924 (1927) Austrian, Sascha (FBO) sil (6680 ft).

Dir: Michael Curtiz.

Sc: Ladislaus Vajda.

Creative Sup & Titles: H. Rider Haggard.

Edit: Herbert Hoagland.

Cast: Marie Corda, Arlette Marchal, Adelqui Millar, Oscar Beregi, Ferdinand Onna, Lya de Putti.

rel-F (parting of the Red Sea)

Ref: Vw 4 Feb '25; MPW 86: 588, 87:100, 115; BFI cat p2; FD 3 July '27.

Based on the novel by H. Rider Haggard.

See also: Ten Commandments, The.

Moon of the Wolf

1972 Filmways (ABC-TV) color 80 mins approx.

Exec Prod: Edward S. Feldman.

Prod: Everett Chambers & Peter Thomas.

Dir: Daniel Petrie.

SP: Alvin Sapinsley.

Art Dir: James Hulsey.

Makeup: Tom Tuttle & William Tuttle.

Cin: Richard C. Glouner.

Edit: Richard Halsey.

Mus: Bernardo Segal.

Cast: David Janssen, Barbara Rush, Bradford Dillman [werewolf], John Beradino, Claudia McNeil, Royal Dano, John Chandler, Geoffrey Lewis, Dan Priest.

F-H (werewolf menaces modern Louisiana's bayou region)

Ref: LAT 26 Sept '72 IV:14; HR 7 July '72; TVG 23 Sept '72.

Based on the novel by Leslie H. Whitten.

See also: Wolf Man, The (1941).

Moon of Tobalito, The

See: Luna de Tobalito, La (1968).

Moon Pilot

1961 (1962) WD (BV) color 98 mins.

Prod: Walt Disney.

Co-Prod: Bill Anderson.

Dir: James Neilson.

SP: Maurice Tombragel.

Art Dir: Carroll Clark & Marvin Aubrey Davis.

Cin: William Snyder.

SpFX: Eustace Lycett.

Edit: Cotton Warburton.

Mus: Paul Smith.

Cast: Tom Tryon, Brian Keith, Edmond O'Brien, Dany Saval [alien girl], Tommy Kirk, Bob Sweeney, Kent Smith, Dick Whittinghill, Nancy Kulp.

SF-com (girl from planet Beta Lyrae comes to Earth to warn astronauts of "proton rays;" one goes to her planet at end)

Ref: FF '62 p85-86; FD 22 Jan '62; MFB May '62 p68.

Based on a novel by Robert Buckner.

Moon-Robbers, The

See: O Dwoch Takich Co Ukradli Ksiezc (1962).

Moon 69

1969 The Serious Business Co (Film-makers' Coop) 16mm color 15 mins.

Made by: Scott Bartlett.

exp-abs-SF

Ref: MFB April '71 p86; FMC 5:29.

Moon Stone, The

See: Moonstone, The.

Moon Zero Two

1969 British, Hammer (WB) color 100 mins.

Prod & SP: Michael Carreras.

Dir: Roy Ward Baker.

Story: Gavin Lyall, Frank Hardman, & Martin Davison.

Art Dir: Scott MacGregor.

Cin: Paul Beeson.

SpFX: Kit West, Nick Allder, & Les Bowie.

Edit: Spencer Reeve.

Mus: Philip Martell.

Cast: James Olson, Catherina von Schell, Warren Mitchell, Adrienne Corri, Ori Levy, Dudley Foster, Bernard Bresslaw, Neil McCallum, Michael Ripper, Sam Kydd.

SF (in 2021 hard-luck space shuttle pilot blackmailed by crooks into trying to capture sapphire asteroid; set in space & on Moon)

Ref: MFB Nov '69 p241; Vw 29 Oct '69; FD 31 Dec '69.

Moonbeam Man, The

See: Gekko Kamen (1958).

Moonbird

1959 Storyboard color ani 10 mins.

Prod & Dir: John Hubley.

Ani: Ed Smith & Robert Cannon.

Edit: Faith Hubley.

F

Ref: Ideal '69-70 p207; C-16 p23; Acad winner.

Moonchild

1972 Filmmakers Ltd color feature.

Exec Prod: Donald G. Wizeman Jr.

Assoc Exec Prod: John Mansfield.

Prod: Dick Alexander.

Assoc Prod: James Sund.

Dir & SP: Alan Gadney.

Art Dir: Richard Tamburino.

Makeup & Costumes: Jane Alexander.

Cin: Emmett Alston.

Edit: Jack H. Conrad.

Mus Prod: Kelly Gordon.

Mus: Pat Williams & Bill Byers.

Cast: Victor Buono, John Carradine, William Challee, Janet Landgard, Pat Renella, Mark Travis, Frank Corsentino, Marie Denn.

alleg-F (reincarnate forced to repeat his life every 25 years for 225 years so far; "deformed, man-made man" --CineF)

Ref: Am Cin Sept '72 p 1038+; CineF 2:3:30-31.

Moonglow

n.d. Dutch ani sh.

Dir: Martin Toonder.

F

Ref: Ani/Cin p 158.

Moonlight Fantasy

1967 Japanese, Gakken color ani 10 mins.

Dir: Tatsuo Shimamura.

F (an old lady is sold a pair of magic spectacles)

Ref: UniJ '67.

314

Moonlight Mask

See: Gekko Kamen.

Moonlight Serenade, A or The Miser Punished

(Au Clair de la Lune ou Pierrot Malheureux; Pierrot's Grief)

1903 (1904) French, Star sil 187 ft.

Made by: Georges Méliès.

F (tricks)

Ref: Sadoul/M, GM Mage; LC; Views 1:29:8; Niver p340.

Moonlight Sonata

n.d. Amateur (CFS) color ani 11 mins.

Made by: Donald Meyer & Frank Collins.

exp-abs-F

Ref: CFS cat Sept '68.

Moonplay

1962 Amateur (Film-makers' Coop) 16mm ani objects 5 mins.

Made by: Marie Menken.

exp-F

Ref: Undrgnd p 171; FMC 3:48.

Moonshine Mountain

1967? Dominant color 90 mins.

Prod & Dir: Herschell Gordon Lewis.

SP: Charles Glore.

Cin: Andy Romanoff (?).

Cast: Chuck Scott, Adam Sorg, Jeffrey Allen, Bonnie Hinson.

H-com (half-human, ape-like man provides menace)

Ref: PB; Miami Herald 16 Dec '67.

Moonshot

See: Countdown (1967).

Moonstone, The

● 1909 Selig sil 1000 ft.

F (stolen sacred stone traced by girl in trance)

Ref: FI IV-24:7.

● 1911 British, Urbanora sil 1320 ft.

Ref: Bios 28 Sept '11, 9 Oct '13.

● 1915 World Co. sil 5 reels.

Dir: Frank Crane.

Sc: E.M. Ingleton.

Cast: Eugene O'Brien, Elaine Hammerstein, William Rosell, Ruth Findlay.

Ref: MPN 26 June '15 p71; CoF 11:61; LC.

● 1934 Mono.

Prod: Paul Malvern.

Dir: Reginald Barker.

SP: Adele Buffington.

Cin: Robert Planck.

Cast: David Manners, Claude King, Phyllis Barry, Gustav von Seyffertitz, Herbert Bunston, Olaf Hytten.

Ref: HR 6 Aug '34; LC; Vw 18 Sept '34; MPH 11 Aug '34 p35.

bor-F; H-seqs (sleepwalking; 3 sinister priests follow stolen eye-of-idol diamond)

Based on the novel by Wilkie Collins.

Moonstruck

1909 French, Pathé sil colored 721 ft.

F-dream (transformations; drunk blown to Moon finds funny-looking little people)

Ref: FI IV-16:8.

Moonstruck

1962 British, Halas & Batchelor ani 7 mins.

Prod: John Halas, Joy Batchelor, & Roger Manvell.

Dir: J. Halas.

F-com (2 puppies go to the moon in a spaceship)

Ref: Gasca p322; SM 8:7.

More Fun with Liquid Electricity

See: Galvanic Fluid (1908).

More Than a Miracle

(C'Era una Volta: Once Upon a Time; Cinderella — Italian Style --Brit.t.)

1966 (1967) Italian/French, Champion/Concordia (MGM) color scope 110 mins.

Prod: Carlo Ponti.

Dir: Franceso Rosi.

Story: Tonino Guerra.

SP: F. Rosi, T. Guerra, Raffaele La Capria, & Peppino Patroni Griffi.

Art Dir: Piero Poletto.

Cin: Pasquale De Santis.

Edit: Jolanda Benvenuti.

Mus: Piero Piccioni.

Cast: Sophia Loren, Omar Sharif, Dolores Del Rio, Georges Wilson, Leslie French, Carlo Pisacane [witch], Marina Malfatti, Anna Nogara, Rita Forzano, Rosemary Martin.

F (fairy tale about peasant girl & arrogant prince; flying monk becomes an angel at end; witches cast spell)

Ref: MFB Sept '69 p 193; FF '67 p307; Time 10 Nov '67.

Morella

(short story by E.A. Poe)

See: Tales of Terror (1961).

Morgan!

(Morgan, a Suitable Case for Treatment --Brit.t.)

1966 British, Quintra (Cinema V) 97 mins.

Prod: Leon Clore.

Dir: Karel Reisz.

SP: David Mercer.

Art Dir: Philip Harrison.

Cin: Larry Pizer & Gerry Turpin.

Edit: Victor Proctor.

Mus: John Dankworth.

Cast: Vanessa Redgrave, David Warner, Robert Stephens, Irene Handl, Bernard Bresslaw, Arthur Mullard, Newton Blick, Graham Crowden.

psy-F-seq (insane artist has gorilla fixation; scenes from King Kong)

Ref: FF '66; FD 6 April '66 Gifford/BFC 13582.

Mori no Ishimatsu Yurei Dochu

(Ishimatsu Travels with Ghosts)

1959 Japanese, Toho.

Dir: Kozo Saeki.

Cast: Frankie Sakai, Kaoru Yachigusa.

F-com

Ref: Japanese Films '60.

Morianerna

See: Morianna (1965).

Morianna

(Morianerna: Blackamoors; I, the Body --a.d.t.)

1965 (1967) Swedish, Bison (Mondial) 100 mins (90 mins).

Prod: Inge Ivarson & Ewert Granholm.

Dir: Arne Matsson.

SP: A. Matsson & Per Wahlöo.

cont.

Morianna cont.

Art Dir: Doa Sivertaer.

Cin: Max Vihlen.

Edit: Lennart Waller.

Mus: Georg Ridel.

Cast: Anders Henriksson, Eva Dahlbeck, Ella Henriksson, Valter Norman, Elsa Prawitz, Erik Hell, Lotte Tarp.

bor-F-H (murders; man sees supposedly dead man return to sit in his favorite chair; "phone call from Death" -- MFB)

Ref: MFB May '66 p75; Shriek 4:49; FF '68 p 126.

Based on the novel by Jan Exström.

Morning Star

(Cholpon)

1961 Soviet, Lenfilm & Frunze color (75 mins).

Dir: Roman Tikhomirov.

SP: Isaac Menaker, Nikolai Tugelov, Appollinari Dudko, & R. Tikhomirov.

Cin: Appollinari Dudko.

Cast: Reina Chokeyeva, Uran Sarbagishev, Bibisara Beishenaliyeva [sorceress].

ballet-F

Ref: Brandon sup 2 to cat 27 p30.

Morok

1917 (1918) Italian, Pasquali sil.

F (man wanders Earth for ages)

Ref: MPW 35:866; FD 7 Feb '18; LC.

Based on novel "The Wandering Jew" by Eugene Süe.

See also: Wandering Jew, The.

Morozko

(Father Frost)

1924 Soviet, Mezhrabpom-Russ sil 4920 ft.

Dir, Sc, Cin: Yuri Scheljabuschsky (Zhelyabuzhky)

Art Dir: Victor Simov & Sergei Kozlovsky.

Cast: Klavidya Yelenskaya, Varvara Massalitinova, Vasili Toporkov, Boris Livanov.

F

Ref: Soviet Cinema p 19; Kino p428.

Based on the Russian fairy tale.

See also: Jack Frost (1965); Fire, Water and Brass Trumpets (1967).

Morpheus Mike

1917? Edison sil ani puppet sh.

Made by: Willis O'Brien.

F-com (hobo Mike smokes opium, dreams he is back in prehistoric days)

Ref: CFC 30:55.

Mort d'Arthur, Le

(work by T. Malory)

See: Knights of the Round Table (1953).

See also: Once and Future King, The.

Mort du Jules César, La

See: Shakespeare Writing Julius Caesar (1907).

Mort du Soleil, La

(The Death of the Sun)

1920 French sil.

Dir: Germaine Dulac.

exp-SF (end of the world)

Ref: Baxter/SF p 146; French Exp List.

Mort Que Tué, Le

See: Fantomas (1913-14); Dead Man Who Killed, The (1914).

Mortadelo y Filomón

1968-- Spanish, Vara color ani 1 reel series.

Prod & Dir: Rafael Vara.

F-com

Ref: SpCin '69 p244--45, '71 p240-69.

Mortadelo y Filomón en "El Yeti"

(Mortadelo and Filomon in "The Yeti")

1970 Spanish, Vara color ani 10 mins.

Prod & Dir: Rafael Vara.

F-H-com

Ref: SpCin '71.

Mortal Orbit

See: Mission Stardust (1968).

Morte Ha Fatto l'Uova, La

See: Plucked (1967).

Morte in Vacanza, La

(play by A. Casella)

See: Death Takes a Holiday.

Morte Viene dal Buio, La

See: Cauldron of Blood (1967).

Morte Viene dallo Spazio, La

See: Day the Sky Exploded, The (1958).

Mortmain

1915 Vit sil 3300 ft.

Dir: Theodore Marston.

Story: Arthur Train.

Cast: Robert Edeson, Donald Hall.

F-dream ("man dreams he loses his hand and has one grafted on in its place" --Willis)

Ref: MPN 4 Sept '15; LC.

Morty

196? Amateur stills 5 mins.

exp-F (little boy really kills when he points his finger & says "bang")

Ref: Collier.

Mosaic

(Mosaique)

1964 (1965) Canadian, NFB (CFS, Pyramid) color 7 mins.

Made by: Norman McLaren & Evelyn Lambert.

exp-abs-F

Ref: Canadian Centre Bltn '64 4:1; Ani/Cin p 174; CFS cat Sept '68.

Mosaic in Confidence

See: Mosaik im Vertrauen (1955).

Mosaik im Vertrauen

(Mosaic in Confidence)

1955 Austrian (Film-makers' Coop) 16mm color & b&w 16.5 mins.

Made by: Peter Kubelka.

exp-F

Ref: FC 44:47

Mosaique

See: Mosaic (1964).

Mose and Funny Face Make Angel Cake

1924 Red Seal sil puppet 530 ft.

Prod: Edwin Miles Fadman.

F (puppets make a giant cake which explodes)

Ref: BFI cat p257.

Moses and the Exodus from Egypt

1907 French, Pathé sil 478 ft.

rel-F (God gives Moses the Ten Commandments; manna from Heaven; etc.)

Ref: BFI cat p 19.

Based on "The Old Testament" portion of "The Bible."

See also: Ten Commandments, The.

Mosquito, The

See: How a Mosquito Operates (1910).

Most Dangerous Game, The

(The Hounds of Zaroff -- Brit.t.)

1932 RKO 78 mins (63 mins).

Exec Prod: David O. Selznick.

Prod: Merian C. Cooper & Ernest B. Schoedsack.

Dir: E.B. Schoedsack & Irving Pichel.

SP: James A. Creelman.

Art Dir: Carroll Clark.

Makeup: Wally Westmore.

Cin: Henry Gerrard.

Edit: Archie Marshek.

Mus: Max Steiner.

Cast: Joel McCrea, Fay Wray, Leslie Banks, Robert Armstrong, Noble Johnson, Hale Hamilton, Steve Clemento.

psy-H (mad Count Zaroff ship-wrecks people on his island, then hunts them to death like animals; trophy room with human heads mounted on walls)

Ref: MPH 21 May '32 p31, 30 July '32 p32; Vw 22 Nov '32; FD 10 Sept '32; Bloch.

Based on the short story by Richard Connell.

See also: Game of Death, A (1945); Black Forest, The (1954); Bloodlust (1961); Naganacz (1963?).

Most Dangerous Man Alive

(The Steel Monster --s.t?)

1958 (1961) Trans-Global Films Inc (Col) 82 mins (76 mins).

Prod: Benedict Bogeaus.

Dir: Allan Dwan.

Story: Phillip Rock & Michael Pate.

SP: James Leicester & P. Rock.

Cin: Carl Carvahal.

Edit: Carlo Lodato.

Mus: Louis Forbes.

Cast: Ron Randell, Debra Paget, Elaine Stewart, Anthony Caruso, Gregg Palmer, Morris Ankrum, Tudor Owen, Steve Mitchell, Joel Donte.

SF-H (framed convict escapes, exposed to cobalt bomb, absorbs steel & becomes steel-hard; turns to dust at climax)

Ref: Vd & HR 8 June '61; MFB Feb '62 p24; FF '61 p 156; Bogdanovich/Dwan p200.

Most Dangerous Man in the World, The

See: Chairman, The (1969).

Most Extraordinary Adventures of Farandoul, The

(novel by A. Robida)

See: Zingo, Son of the Sea (1914).

Most Fantastic and Marvelous Adventure in the Jungle (Tarzan)

See: Karzan il Favoloso Uomo della Giungla (1971).

Most Prohibited Sex

See: Sexy Probitissimo (1963).

Mostro di Frankenstein, Il [...Frakestein?]

(The Monster of Frankenstein; Frankenstein's Monster)

cont.

Mostro di Frankenstein cont.

1920 Italian, Albertini Film--UCI sil.

Dir: Eugenio Testa.

Sc: Giovanni Drovetti.

Cin: De Simone. (Segundo de Chomon?)

Cast: Luciano Alberti, Umberto Guarracino [Frankenstein's Monster].

SF-H (Frankenstein pieces together a creature out of parts of dead bodies & brings it to life)

Ref: Glut/F p67.

Based on novel "Frankenstein, or a Modern Prometheus" by Mary W. Shelley.

See also: Frankenstein.

Mostro di Venezia, Il

See: Embalmer, The (1964).

Mostro...e Mezzo, Un

(A Monster and a Half)

1964 Italian, Adelphia.

Dir: Stefano Steno.

SP: S. Steno & Continenza.

Cin: Clemente Santoni.

Mus: Franco Mannino.

Cast: Franco Franchi, Ciccio Ingrassia, Alberto Bonucci, Giuseppe Pertile, Lena von Martens, Maruska Rossetti, Margaret Lee.

H-com (professor makes thief's face look like that of a famous killer)

Ref: Ital Prods '64 p200-01.

Mosura

See: Mothra (1961).

Mosura tai Gojira

See: Godzilla vs. the Thing (1964).

Mother Gets the Wrong Tonic

1913 British, Cricks & Martin sil 420 ft.

Dir: Charles Calvert.

bor-SF-com (drinking the wrong tonic makes woman act like a horse)

Ref: Bios 28 Aug '13; Gifford/BFC 04222.

Mother Goose

1909 Edison sil 356 ft.

F-dream-com (child goes to sleep & Mother Goose jumps out of book; fairies, etc.)

Ref: MPW 5:133, 162; FI IV-31 p5, 13; LC.

See also: Mother Goose...; Mighty Mouse in Mother Goose's Party (1950).

Mother Goose Goes Hollywood

1938 RKO color ani sh. Prod: Walt Disney.

F

Ref: Acad nom.

Mother Goose Nursery Rhymes

1902 British, G.A. Smith sil sh.

Prod & Dir: G.A. Smith.

Cast: Tom Green.

F (8 seqs: "Sing a Song of Sixpence;" "Old Mother Hubbard;" "Little Miss Muffet;" "Goosey Gander;" "Jack & Jill;" "Old Woman in a Shoe;" "Hey Diddle Diddle")

Ref: Sadoul; Brit Cin; Gifford/BFC 00616.

Mother Goose Series, The

1911-12 Champion sil 950 ft series.

F

Ref: MPW 10:662, 668.

See also: First Edition of Mother Goose Rhymes (1911); Yankee Doodle (1911); Ding Dong Bell (1912).

Mother Goose Stories

1946 Bailey 16mm color ani puppet 11 mins.

Prod: Ray Harryhausen.

Assoc Prod: Fred Blasalif.

F

Ref: LC; SpFXRH 1:22.

Mother Goose's Party

See: Mighty Mouse in Mother Goose's Party (1950).

Mother, I Need You

1918 Lloyd Carleton Prods sil.

Cast: Enid Markey, Edward Coxen.

F-seq (begins in Garden of Eden, passes through Valley of Shadow, to the present)

Ref: MPN:1665 ad.

See also: Adam and Eve.

Mother-in-Law Would Fly

1909 British, Walturdaw sil 540 ft.

SF-com (motor-propelled flying bed)

Ref: Bios 9 Dec '09.

Mother Joan and Angels

See: Joan of the Angels? (1960).

Mother Joan of the Angels

See: Joan of the Angels? (1960).

Mother Machree

1922 Cardinal Films (Creston Feature Pictures) sil 7 reels approx.

Cast: Amanda Trinkle, James La Para, Jack Hopkins [Spirit of Bad Council].

alleg-F (allegorical treatment of some aspects of Irish history with spirits)

Ref: AFI F2.3710 p527.

Mother Riley in Dracula's Desire

See: My Son, the Vampire (1952).

Mother Riley Meets the Vampire

See: My Son, the Vampire (1952).

Mother Riley Runs Riot

See: My Son, the Vampire (1952).

Mother's Day

1948 Farallone Films (Film Images) 16mm 23 mins.

Dir & Sc: James Broughton.

Cin: Frank Stauffacher.

exp-sur-F

Ref: Film Images 21; C-16 p23; FC 29:20.

Mother's Spirit, A

1913 Kinemacolor sil 2 reels.

F (spirit of dead mother puts out toys for children, red rose for husband)

Ref: MPW 15:1264, 18:1584.

Mothlight

1963 Amateur (Film-makers' Coop; Pyramid) 16mm color sil 4 mins.

Made by: Stan Brakhage.

exp-abs-F

Ref: FMC 5:38; Pyramid cat.

Mothra

(Mosura)

1961 (1962) Japanese, Toho (Col) color scope 100 mins.

Prod: Tomoyuki Tanaka.

Dir: Inoshiro Honda.

SP: Shinichi Sekizawa.

Art Dir: Takeo Kita & Kimei Abe.

Cin: Hajime Koizumi.

SpFX: Eiji Tsuburaya & Hiroshi Mukouyama.

Edit: Ichiji Taira.

cont.

Mothra cont.

Mus: Yuji Koseki.

Cast: Frankie (Franky) Sakai, Hiroshi Koizumi, Ken Uehara, Kyoko Kagawa, Emi & Yumi Ito.

SF (6-inch twin girls guard giant egg worshipped by natives on island; girls taken to Japan & egg hatches, giant caterpillar emerges; later turns into giant moth & rescues the tiny girls)

Ref: FF '62 p341-42; Vd & HR 14 May '62; F.M 19:14.

See also: Godzilla vs the Thing (1964); Godzilla vs. the Sea Monster (1966); Destroy All Monsters (1968).

Mothra vs. Godzilla

See: Godzilla vs. the Thing (1964).

Motif

1956 Amateur 16mm? color stop motion painting sh.

Made by: Carmen D'Avino.

exp-F

Ref: Ani/Cin p 166.

Motion Painting No. 1

1949 Amateur 16mm color stop motion painting sh.

Made by: Oskar Fischinger.

Mus: J.S. Bach ("Brandenburg Concerto No. 3").

exp-abs-F

Ref: CFS cat Sept '68; MMA '63 p58; USA Exp List.

Motion Picture #1

See: Motion Pictures (1956).

Motion Pictures

(Motion Picture #1 --Brit.t?)

1956 Amateur 16mm collage 10 mins.

Made by: Robert Breer.

exp-F

Ref: Undrgnd p 131; BFI Dist cat sup 1:76.

Motor Car of the Future

1910 German, Messter sil 300 ft.

SF (car flies, jumps over train, goes to Saturn, etc.)

Ref: Gifford/SF p34; Bios 23 Feb '11.

Motor Chair, The

1911 Italian, Italia sil 360 ft.

bor-SF

Ref: Bios 27 July '11.

Motor Scooter, The

1963 Soviet, Tallinfilm color ani puppet 10.7 mins.

Dir: H. Pars.

Story: E. Raud.

F

Ref: Sovexport cat 1:136.

Motor Valet, The

(The New Moto(r?) Valet --alt.t.)

1906? British, Alpha sil sh.

Dir: Arthur Cooper.

SF-com (robot servant smashes furniture, then explodes)

Ref: Gifford/BFC 01307; Gifford/SF p51.

Motorist, The "?"

1906 British, R.W. Paul sil 200 ft.

Prod: R.W. Paul.

Dir: Walter R. Booth.

F-com (car drives to sun, around Saturn)

Ref: Gasca p18; Hist/Brit p80; BFI cat p81; Gifford/BFC 01438.

Moulin des Supplices, Le

See: Mill of the Stone Women (1960).

316

Mountain of Fear

See: Srecno, Kekec! (1964).

Mouse and Cat

(Myszka i Kotek; Mouse and Kitten; The Cat and the Mouse)

1958 Polish, Bielsko-Biala color ani 9 mins.

Dir: Wladyslaw Nehrebecki.

Story: Leszek Lorek & W. Nehrebecki.

Design: W. Nehrebecki & Adam Jasinski.

Mus: Tadeusz Kanski.

F-com (mechanical mouse vs. line-drawn cat)

Ref: Ani/Cin p 117; ASIFA info sheet; Polish Cin p 170.

Mouse and Garden

1960 WB color ani 7 mins.

F-com

Ref: LC; Acad nom.

See also: Sylvester P. Pussycat.

Mouse and Kitten

See: Mouse and Cat (1958).

Mouse and the Crayon, The

1958 Bulgarian ani sh.

Dir: Radka Buchvarova.

F

Ref: Ani/Cin p 167.

Mouse Cleaning

1948 MGM color ani 7 mins.

Prod: Fred Quimby.

Dir: William Hanna & Joseph Barbera.

Ani: Irven Spence, Kenneth Muse, Ed Barge, & Ray Patterson.

Mus: Scott Bradley.

F-com

Ref: Ani/Cin p 171; LC.

See also: Tom and Jerry (1940--).

Mouse for Sale

1955 MGM color ani 7 mins.

Dir: William Hanna & Joseph Barbera.

F-com

Ref: Ani/Cin p 171; LC.

See also: Tom and Jerry (1940--).

Mouse-Merized Cat, The

1946 WB color ani 7 mins.

Dir: Robert McKimson.

Story: Warren Foster.

F-com

Ref: Ani/Cin p 173; LC.

Mouse on the Moon, The

(A Rocket from Fenwick -- s.t.)

1963 British, Walter Shenson Prods (Lopert) color 85 mins.

Prod: Walter Shenson.

Dir: Richard Lester.

SP: Michael Pertwee.

Art Dir: John Howell.

Cin: Wilkie Cooper.

Edit: Bill Lenny.

Mus: Ron Grainer.

Cast: Margaret Rutherford, Bernard Cribbins, Terry-Thomas, Ron Moody, David Kossoff, June Ritchie, John Le Mesurier.

SF-sat-com (powered by wine fuel, astronaut from the Duchy of Grand Fenwick reaches the Moon before the Russians & US do, rescues their astronauts)

Ref: FF '63 p 167-68; MFB June '63 p87; FD 24 May '63.

Based on the novel by Leonard Wibberley.

Sequel to: Mouse That Roared, The (1959).

cont.

Mothra (1961) Japanese

Mouse That Roared, The

(The Day New York Was Invaded --ad.t.)

1959 British, Open Road Films (Col) color 85 mins.

Prod: Walter Shenson.

Dir: Jack Arnold.

SP: Roger MacDougall & Stanley Mann.

Art Dir: Geoffrey Drake.

Makeup: Stuart Freeborn.

Cin: John Wilcox.

Edit: Raymond Poulton.

Mus: Edwin Astley.

Cast: Peter Sellers [3 roles], Jean Seberg, David Kossoff, William Hartnell, Timothy Bateson, Monty Landis, Leo McKern.

soc-SF-com (in effort to get US foreign aid, tiny Duchy of Grand Fenwick declares war on US, invades New York with squad of longbowmen, captures new bomb, wins the war)

cont.

Mouse That Roared cont.

Ref: HR 1 Oct '59; FF '59 p291-92; FD 2 Oct '59.

Based on the novel by Leonard Wibberley.

Sequel: Mouse on the Moon, The (1963).

Mouse Trouble

1944 MGM color ani 679 ft.

Prod: Fred Quimby.

Dir: William Hanna & Joseph Barbera.

Ani: Ray Patterson, Irven Spence, Ken Muse, & Pete Burness.

Mus: Scott Bradley.

F-com

Ref: LC; Acad winner.

See also: Tom and Jerry (1940--).

Mouse That Jack Built, The

1958 (1959) WB color ani 7 mins.

cont.

Mouse That Jack Built cont.

Dir: Robert McKimson.

Voices: Jack Benny and others.

F-com (Jack Benny dreams that he is a rich, tightwad mouse)

Ref: Ani/Cin p 173; LC.

Mouse Wreckers

1949 WB color ani 7 mins.

Prod: Edward Selzer.

Dir: Chuck Jones.

Mus: Carl W. Stalling.

Voices: Mel Blanc.

F-com (Herbie & Bertie the mice drive Claude the cat mad)

Ref: LC; David Rider; Acad nom.

Mousetaken Identity

1957 WB color ani 7 mins.

Dir: Robert McKimson.

cont

Mousetaken Identity cont.

Voices: Mel Blanc.

F-com

Ref: Ani/Cin p 173; LC.

See also: Sylvester P. Pussycat.

Mousie Come Home

1946 U color ani 1 reel.

Prod: Walter Lantz.

Dir: James Culhane.

Story: Ben Hardaway & Milt Schaffer.

Ani: Pat Matthews & Paul Smith.

Mus: Darrell Calker.

F-com

Ref: LC.

See also: Swing Symphony (1941-46).

Moveite, a New Hustling Powder

1910 British, Walturdaw sil 300 ft.

SF-com (professor's powder makes burglar, sheep, workers, etc. "gyrate")

Ref: Gifford/BFC 02875; Bios 15 Dec '10.

Movement Movement, The

1969 British/French; Knight Films/Lys Prods color ani & live 26 mins.

Prod Coordinator: Edward Quinn.

Dir & SP: Bruce Parsons.

Edit: Vivienne Brander.

Mus: Tony Meehan.

Nar: George Thompson.

Cast: Julien LeParc, Victor Vasarely, Jaacov Agam, Gregorio Vardanega.

doc; abs-F-seq (fantasy seqs in doc on kinetic art movement)

Ref: MFB June '70 p 135.

Movie, A

1960 Amateur (Film-makers' Coop; C-16) 16mm 12 mins.

Made by: Bruce Conner.

exp-sur-F

Ref: FMC 3:21; FQ Spring '61 p33, 34; C-16 p23.

Movie-Go-Round

1949 British, Fama Films 45 mins.

Dir: Fred Weiss.

SP: Jim Phelan & Patrick Burke.

Cast: Donald Biset, Rene Goddard, Sam Kydd.

doc; F-dream-seq (in dream, repairman sees old & new movie projector turn into people & talk about movies)

Ref: Gifford/BFC 11329.

Movie Star, American Style or **LSD I Hate You**

1966 Albert Zugsmith (Famous Players Corp) color seq 99 mins.

Exec Prod: Arnold Stoltz.

Prod & Cin: Robert Caramico.

Dir: Albert Zugsmith.

SP: A. Zugsmith, Graham Lee Mahin, & Lulu Talmadge.

Edit: Herman Freedman.

Mus: Joe Greene.

Cast: Robert Strauss, Del Moore, T.C. Jones, Paula Lane, Steve Drexel, Steven Rogers, Richard Clair, Albert Zugsmith.

psy-F-seq (lengthy LSD "trip" is depicted)

Ref: FF '67 p434; Vw 17 Aug '66.

Movies Take a Holiday, The

1944 16mm.

Prod: Herman G. Weinberg & Hans Richter.

cont.

Movies Take a Holiday cont.

Edit: H. Richter.

exp-F

Ref: Richter index p6.

Movini's Venom

See: Night of the Cobra Woman (1972).

Moviola Blues

n.d. Amateur (CFS) 16mm? 8 mins.

Made by: Leon Ortiz.

exp-F-com

Ref: CFS cat Sept '68.

Mozart Rondo

1949 Amateur (CFS) 16mm sh color hand-manipulated cut-outs.

Made by: John Whitney.

Mus: W.A. Mozart.

exp-abs-F

Ref: Undrgnd p94, 280.

Možda Diogen

See: Diogenes Perhaps (1967).

Mrav Dobra Srca

See: Kind-Hearted Ant, The (1965).

Mrlja na Savjesti

(Stain on the Conscience)

1968 Yugoslavian, Zagreb & Dunav color live & ani 16.6 mins.

Dir & Design: Dušan Vukotić.

SP: Dejan Djurović, Vuk Babić, & Marko Babac.

Ani: Vladimir Jutriša.

Cin: Djordje Nikolić.

Mus: Tomislav Simović.

Cast: Slavko Simić.

F (man pursued by animated smear of red, representing his conscience)

Ref: Z/Zagreb p20, 94; SF Times #458:1968.

Much Ado About Murder

See: Theatre of Blood (1972).

Much Ado About Mutton

1947 Par color ani 8 mins.

Dir: Izzy Sparber.

Story: Joe Stultz & Carl Meyer.

F-com

Ref: LC.

See also: Noveltoons (1945--).

Much Ado About Nutting

1953 WB color ani 7 mins.

Dir: Chuck Jones.

F-com (a squirrel tries to crack a coconut)

Ref: LC; David Rider.

Müde Tod, Der

See: Destiny (1921).

Muenchausen

See: Baron Münchausen.

Muerte Enamorada, La

(Death in Love)

1950 Mexican, Victoria.

Dir: Ernesto Cortázar.

SP: Fernando Galiana.

Cin: Jack Draper.

Mus: Manuel Esperon.

Cast: Miroslava Stern, Fernando Fernandez, E. Issa, J. Reyes.

F (Death falls in love with a mortal girl)

Ref: Aventura (Willis).

See also: Death Takes a Holiday.

Muerte Viaja Demasiado, La

(Death Travels Too Much)

1965 Spanish/French/Italian, Época/Lux/Sagitario 105 mins.

French language credits:
Dir & SP: Claude Autant-Lara.

Italian language credits:
Dir: Giancarlo Zagni.

SP: G. Zagni & Tito Carpi.

Spanish language credits:
Dir: José M. Forqué.

SP: J.M. Forqué, J. de Armiñán, Vicente Coello, & Marcello Fondato.

Cast: Emma Penella, Leo Anchóriz, Pierre Brasseur, Alida Valli, Folco Lulli, Sylvie.

F-H-dream-seq (3-episode film, one episode, "The Crow," is fantasy: Death, in the guise of a widow, answers a man's advertisement)

Ref: SpCin '66 p 142-43.

Muerte Vivante, La

See: Snake People (1968).

Muertos de Risa

(Dead of Laughter)

1957 Mexican, Sotomayor (Col).

Prod: Jesús Sotomajor.

Dir: Adolfo Fernandez Bustamante.

SP: Fernando Galiana & Carlos Orellana.

Cin: Agustin Jimenez.

Cast: Resortes, Maria Victoria, Armando Arriola, Renée Damas, José Bigton Castro.

F-H-com (ghosts; mummies; giant spider)

Ref: PS; Ackerman; Indice.

Muertos Hablan, Los

(The Dead Speak)

1935 Mexican, J. Luis Bueno.

Dir: Gabriel Soria (or Bustillo De Oro?).

Story: Pedro Zapiin (?).

SP: Roberto Quigley.

Cin: Jack Draper.

Cast: Julian Soler, Amalia de Ilisa, Manuel Noriega.

bor-SF-H (murder victim's eye retains image of murderer)

Ref: FD 26 Nov '35 p7; NYT 25 Nov '35; Indice.

Muertos no Perdonan, Los

(The Dead Don't Forgive)

1963 Spanish, Juro.

Dir: Julio Coll.

SP: J. Coll & José German Huici.

Art Dir: José Alguero.

Cin: Manuel Rojas.

Mus: José Sola.

Cast: Javier Escriva, Luis Prendes, Francisco Moran, Alberto Dalbes, Antonio Casas, Antonio Molino, May Heatherly, Irán Eory.

F (parapsychology & ESP cards give knowledge of death before man is told of it; old legend & ESP solve murder)

Ref: SpCin '64 p 142-43; CoF 4:58; MMF 9:16, 21.

Muha

See: Fly, The (1967).

Mujer Murcielago, La

(The Bat Woman)

1967 (1968) Mexican color.

Dir: René Cardona.

Cast: Mauro Monti, Armando Silvestre, Roberto Cañedo, Hector Godoy, David Silva, Eric del Castillo.

SF-H (costumed super-heroine battles fish-man monsters)

Ref: FDY '69; PS; MMF 18, 19; LAT 22 May '67.

Mujer y la Bestia, La

(The Woman and the Beast)

1958 (1959) Mexican (Clasa-Mohme).

Dir: Alfonso Corono Blake.

Story: Oscar Brooks & F. Galiana.

Cin: Jack Draper.

Mus: Manuel Esperon.

Cast: Ana Luisa Peluffo, Carlos Cores, Ruben Rojo, Fanny Schiller, Andres Soler.

F-H

Ref: PS; Ackerman; FDY '60.

Mujeres de Dracula, Las

See: Imperio de Dracula, El (1967).

Mujeres Panteras, Las

(The Panther Women)

1966? (1967) Mexican, Cinematografica Calderon (Azteca).

Dir: René Cardona.

SP: Alfredo Salazar.

Cast: El Angel Ariadne Welter, Elizabeth Campbell, Eric del Castillo, Manuel "Loco" Valdes, Eda Lorna.

F-H (panther women invoke goddess of evil to exterminate descendants of man who destroyed their leader; they acquire power & claws of panther; leader revived with fresh blood; repelled by cross of Druids; battle wrestling women)

Ref: FDY '68; PS.

See also: Cat People, The (1942); Wrestling Women.

Mujeres Vampiro, Las

See: Samson vs. the Vampire Women (1962).

Mulher de Todes, A

(The Woman of Everyone)

1969 Brazilian, Servicine.

Dir & SP: Rogerio Sganzerla.

Cin: Peter Overbeck.

Mus: Ana Soralina.

Cast: Helena Ines, Jo Soares.

F-H (woman of title makes love in a "Draculinian way"; "vampirism" --Photon)

Ref: Vw 1 April '70; Photon 21:29.

Based on story by Egidio Eccio.

Mulino delle Donne di Pietra, Il

See: Mill of the Stone Women (1960).

Multiple Maniacs

1969? Amateur (Film-makers' Coop) 16mm 94 mins.

Made by: John Waters.

Cast: Divine, David Lochary, Mary Vivian Pearce, Mink Stole.

exp-sat-F-H-com (maniacs; freakshow of dope addicts & homosexuals; giant hallucinatory lobster; etc.)

Ref: FMC 5:328-29.

Múltiples, Número Indeterminado

(Multiples, Indeterminate Number)

1971 Spanish, Actual Films 1/2 minute loop.

Dir: Javier Aguirre.

exp-F

Ref: SpCin '72.

Multityder

(Multitudes)

1969 Danish color ani 6 mins.

Dir & Story: Mogens Zieler.

F

Ref: Mamaia '70.

Mumie Ma, Die

See: Eyes of the Mummy, The (1918).

Mûmin

1971 Japanese, Toho color ani 25 mins.

F

Ref: UniJ 53:36.

Mummy, The

1911 Thanhouser sil 1000 ft.

F (electricity brings mummy to life as beautiful Egyptian girl)

Ref: MPW 8:546, 554, 604; FIR March '64 p 151.

Mummy, The

1911 British?, Urban sil 960 ft.

F-dream (man dreams a mummy comes to life)

Ref: Bios 14 Sept '11.

Mummy, The

● 1932 U 78 mins (63 mins).

Exec Prod: Carl Laemmle Jr.

Prod: Stanley Bergerman.

Dir: Karl Freund.

Story: Nina Wilcox Putnam & Richard Schayer.

SP: John L. Balderston.

Design: Willy Pogany.

Makeup: Jack Pierce.

Cin: Charles Stumar.

Cast: Boris Karloff [mummy], Zita Johann, David Manners, Edward Van Sloan, Bramwell Fletcher, Henry Victor, Noble Johnson, Arthur Byron, Leonard Mudie.

F-H (in ancient Egypt Im-Ho-Tep is mummified alive for trying to bring dead princess back to life; in 20th Century Im-Ho-Tep is accidentally revived & seeks out reincarnation of princess; shows her their past lives in magic pool; Im-Ho-Tep turned to dust by goddess)

Ref: Vw 2 Dec '32, 10 Jan '33; MPH 3 Dec '32 p27; LC.

● 1959 British, Hammer (U) color 88 mins.

Prod: Michael Carreras.

Assoc Prod: Anthony Nelson-Keys.

Dir: Terence Fisher.

SP: Jimmy Sangster.

Art Dir: Bernard Robinson.

Makeup: Roy Ashton.

Cin: Jack Asher.

Edit: James Needs & Alfred Cox.

Mus: Frank Reizenstein.

Mus Dir: John Hollingsworth.

Cast: Peter Cushing, Christopher Lee [mummy], Yvonne Furneaux, Eddie Byrne, Felix Aylmer, Raymond Huntley, George Pastell, John Stuart, Michael Ripper, Harold Goodwin, Dennis Shaw.

F-H (in Ancient Egypt Kharis is mummified alive for trying to bring dead princess back to life; in 19th Century he is accidentally revived as walking mummy & is used as instrument of revenge by fanatic on those who desecrated princess' tomb; hero saved when mummy sees reincarnation of princess)

Ref: HR 9 July '59; FD 2 July '59; FF '59 p298.

See also other films which include walking mummies: Mummy of King Ramsees, The (1909); Kalkoot (1935); Mummy's Boys (1936); Mummy's Hand, The (1940) and sequels; Harem Alek (1953); Abbott and Costello Meet the Mummy (1955); Pharaoh's Curse,

cont.

Mummy cont.

The (1956); Isabell, a Dream (1958?); Aztec Mummy, The (1959) and sequels; Face of the Screaming Werewolf, The (1959); Kiss Me Quick (1963); Curse of the Mummy's Tomb, The (1964); Mummy's Shroud, The (1966) Orgy of the Dead; (1966); Hombre Que Vino del Ummo (1970); Samson y Blue Demon Contra los Monstruos (1970); Santo en la Venganza de la Momia (1971); Venganza de la Momia, La (1973?).

Mummy Love

1926 Standard Cinema Corp sil 2 reels.

Prod & Dir: Joe Rock.

Cast: Neely Edwards, Alice Ardell.

H-com

Ref: LC; MPW 78:797.

Mummy of the King Ramsees, The (La Momie du Roi)

1909 French, Lux sil 600 ft.

Dir: Gerard Bourgeois.

F (mummy brought to life)

Ref: Bios 22 July '09; Gifford/MM p 146.

Mummy's Boys

1936 RKO 68 mins.

Exec Prod: Samuel J. Briskin.

Assoc Prod: Lee Marcus.

Dir: Fred Guiol.

Story: Jack Townley & Lew Lipton.

SP: J. Townley, Philip G. Epstein, & Charles Roberts.

Art Dir: Van Nest Polglase.

Cin: Jack McKenzie.

SpFX Cin: Vernon Walker.

Edit: John Lockert.

Mus Dir: Roy Webb.

Cast: Bert Wheeler, Robert Woolsey, Barbara Pepper, Moroni Olsen, Willie Best, Frank Lackteen.

H-com (curse on Egyptian tomb seems to kill 10 scientists; fake walking mummy)

Ref: Vw 1 Dec '36; LC; MPH 20 June '36 p71-74.

See also: Mummy, The.

Mummy's Curse, The

1944 (1945) U 62 mins.

Exec Prod: Ben Pivar.

Assoc Prod: Oliver Drake.

Dir: Leslie Goodwins.

Story: Leon Abrams & Dwight V. Babcock.

Art Dir: John B. Goodman.

Makeup: Jack Pierce.

Cin: Virgil Miller.

SpFX Cin: John P. Fulton.

Edit: Fred R. Feitshans Jr.

Mus Dir: Paul Sawtell.

Cast: Lon Chaney (Jr) [Kharis, the Mummy], Virginia Christine, Peter Coe, Kay Harding, Martin Kosleck, Kurt Katch, Addison Richards, Holmes Herbert, William Farnum, Eddie Parker [stunts].

F-H (mummy of Princess Ananka dug out of swamp, restored to life & beauty by sun; tana leaves revive mummy of Kharis)

Ref: Vd & HR 20 Dec '44; LC; MFB Aug '46 p 112.

Sequel to: Mummy's Hand, The (1940).

Mummy's Dummies, The

1948 Col 16 mins.

Prod: Hugh McCollum.

Dir: Edward Bernds.

cont.

Mummy's Dummies cont.

SP: Elwood Ullman.

Art Dir: Charles Clague.

Cin: Allen Siegler.

Edit: Henry De Mond.

Cast: The Three Stooges (Moe Howard, Shemp Howard, Larry Fine), Vernon Dent, Ralph Dunn , Phil Van Zandt, Dee Green.

bor-F-com (set in ancient Rome with anachronistic gags)

Ref: LC; Maltin/GMS p 136; Pardi.

See also: Three Stooges, The (1934-59).

Mummy's Foot, The

1949 Marshall Grant & Realm TV Prods 16mm 2 reels.

Prod: Louis Lantz.

Dir: Sobey Martin.

SP: Stanley Rubin.

F (playwright meets 3000 year old princess)

Ref: LC.

Based on novel "The Romance of a Mummy" by Theophile Gautier.

Mummy's Ghost, The

1943 (1944) U 61 mins.

Exec Prod: Joseph Gershenson.

Assoc Prod: Ben Pivar.

Dir: Reginald Le Borg.

Story: Griffin Jay & Henry Sucher.

SP: G. Jay, H. Sucher, & Brena Weisberg.

Art Dir: John B. Goodman & Abraham Grossman.

Makeup: Jack Pierce.

Cin: William Sickner.

Edit: Saul Goodkind.

Mus Dir: H.J. Salter.

Cast: Lon Chaney (Jr) [Kharis, the Mummy], John Carradine, Ramsay Ames, Robert Lowery, Barton MacLane, Claire Whitney, George Zucco, Frank Reicher, Eddie Parker [stunts].

F-H (caretaker of Kharis the living mummy takes mummy to New England to seek reincarnation of Princess Ananka; at climax mummy walks into swamp with girl who is the reincarnation & she turns first into Ananka & then into a mummy herself)

Ref: Vd 3 May '44; MFB May '47 p66; FD 12 July '44.

Sequel to: Mummy's Hand, The (1940).

Mummy's Hand, The

1940 U 67 mins.

Prod: Ben Pivar.

Dir: Christy Cabanne.

Story: Griffin Jay.

SP: G. Jay & Maxwell Shane.

Art Dir: Jack Otterson & Ralph M. De Lacy.

Makeup: Jack Pierce.

Cin: Elwood Bredell.

Edit: Phil Cahn.

Cast: Dick Foran, Peggy Moran, Wallace Ford, Eduardo Ciannelli, George Zucco, Cecil Kellaway, Charles Trowbridge, Tom Tyler [Kharis, the Mummy], Siegfried Arno, Michael Mark.

F-H (explorers in Egypt encounter Kharis, a mummy kept alive for 3000 years by succession of priests who feed him varying numbers of tana leaves for increased activity)

Ref: Vw 25 Sept '40; HR 23 Aug '40; FD 4 Oct '40; Pardi; MFB March '41 p33-34.

Sequels: Mummy's Tomb, The (1942); Mummy's Ghost, The (1944); Mummy's Curse, The (1945).

See also: Mummy, The; Adventures of the Spirit (1963).

Mummy's Revenge, The

See: Venganza de la Momia, La (1973?).

Mummy's Shroud, The

1966 (1967) British, Hammer & 7 Arts (20th-Fox) color 84 mins.

Prod: Anthony Nelson Keys.

Dir & SP: John Gilling.

Story: John Elder (Anthony Hinds?).

Prod Design: Bernard Robinson.

Makeup: George Partleton.

Cin: Arthur Grant.

SpFX: Bowie Films.

Sup Edit: James Needs.

Edit: Chris Barnes.

Mus: Don Banks.

Nar: Peter Cushing.

Cast: André Morell, John Phillips, David Buck, Elizabeth Sellars, Maggie Kimberly, Michael Ripper, Tim Barrett, Richard Warner, Catherine Lacey, Dickie Owen, Toolie Persauld, Eddie Powell [living mummy].

F-H (in 1920's, mummy slave of mummified pharaoh brought back to life, used for revenge; mummy turns to dust at end)

Ref: FF '67 p222; FD 11 April '67; MFB June '67 p95-96.

See also: Mummy, The.

Mummy's Tomb, The

1942 U 61 mins.

Assoc Prod: Ben Pivar.

Dir: Harold Young.

Story: Neil P. Varnick.

SP: Griffin Jay & Henry Sucher.

Art Dir: Jack Otterson.

Makeup: Jack Pierce.

Cin: George Robinson.

Edit: Milton Carruth.

Mus Dir: H.J. Salter.

Cast: Lon Chaney (Jr) [Kharis, the Mummy], Turhan Bey, Wallace Ford, Dick Foran, John Hubbard, Elyse Knox, George Zucco, Janet Shaw, Glenn Strange, Rex Lease, Grace Cunard, Frank Reicher, Eddie Parker [stunts].

F-H (living mummy of Kharis is brought to the US to get revenge on the Banning family)

Ref: Vd & HR 13 Oct '42; PB; FD 19 Oct '42; LC.

Sequel to: Mummy's Hand, The (1940).

Mumsy, Nanny, Sonny and Girly

See: Girly (1969).

Münchausen

1920 German, Institut fur Kulturforschung sil ani 662 ft.

Ani: Richard Felgenauer.

F-com (Munchausen's lies depicted, including washing the Moon)

Ref: BFI cat p59.

See also: Adventures of Baron Münchausen (1943); Baron Münchausen; New Adventures of Baron Münchausen, The

Münchausen in Afrika

1958 German, CCC color 89 mins.

Dir: Werner Jacobs.

Mus: Heinz Gietz.

Cast: Peter Alexander, Anita Gutwell, Gunther Philipp, Johanna Konig.

F-com (descendant of Baron Münchausen has incredible adventures)

Ref: German Pics '58 p 136.

Based on descendant of character chronicled by R.E. Raspe.

Mundane Illusionist, The

See: Illusioniste Mondain, L' (1901).

Mundo de los Drogos, El

(The World of Drugs)

1963 (1964) Mexican (Azteca).

psy-F-H-seq

Ref: FM 33:8-10; FDY '65.

Mundo de los Muertos, El

(The World of the Dead)

1968? (1969) Mexican, Sotomayor (Clasa-Mohme & Azteca) color.

Dir: Gilberto Martinez Solares.

Cast: Santo, Blue Demon, Pilar Pellicer, Mary Montiel.

F-H (witch)

Ref: PS.

See also: Santo; Blue Demon.

Mundo de los Vampiros

See: World of the Vampires, The (1960).

Muñecos Infernales

See: Curse of the Doll People, The (1960).

Munro

1960 Rembrandt Films color ani. 9 mins.

Made in Czechoslovakia.

Prod: William L. Snyder.

Dir: Gene Deitch.

Story & Artwork: Jules Feiffer.

Voices: Howard Morris.

F-com-sat (little boy is drafted into the US Army)

Ref: FD 28 Feb '61; Acad award.

Based on the book by Jules Feiffer.

Munster, Go Home!

1966 U color 96 mins.

Prod: Joe Connelly & Bob Mosher.

Dir: Earl Bellamy.

SP: George Tibbles, J. Connelly, & B. Mosher.

Art Dir: Alexander Golitzen. & John Lloyd.

Makeup: Bud Westmore.

Cin: Benny Kline.

Edit: Bud Isaacs.

Mus: Jack Marshall.

Cast: Fred Gwynne, Yvonne De Carlo, Al Lewis, Debbie Watson, Terry-Thomas, Hermione Gingold, Butch Patrick, John Carradine.

F-H-com (Herman Munster is monster created by Dr. Frankenstein; Grandpa is a vampire, probably Dracula; Herman's son may be a werewolf, wife is vampire-like)

Ref: FF '66 p 148; MFB Jan '67 p 11; Vw 22 June '66.

Based on TV show "The Munsters."

See also: Dracula; Frankenstein; Wolf Man, The (1941).

Muraliwala

See: Kalia Mardan (1934).

Murder

See: Meurtre (1964).

Murder at Dawn

(The Death Ray --Brit.t.)

1932 Big Four 55 mins.

Prod: Burton King.

Dir: Richard Thorpe.

SP: Barry Barringer.

Cin: Edward Kull.

Edit: Fred Bain.

Cast: Jack Mulhall, Josephine Dunn, Mischa Auer, Martha Mattox, Crauford Kent, Marjorie Beebe.

SF-H (death ray machine uses sunlight; weird happenings in old house)

cont.

Murder at Dawn cont.

Ref: Vw 5 April '32; Photo April '32; Gifford/SF.

Murder at 45 R.P.M.

(Meurtre en 45 Tours)

1960 French, Cite-Films (MGM) 105 mins.

Dir: Etienne Perier.

SP: Albert Valentin, Dominique Fabre, & E. Perier.

Cin: Marcel Weiss.

Cast: Danielle Darrieux, Michael (Michel?) Auclair, Jean Servais.

myst; bor-H (dead composer seems to haunt wife)

Ref: V 15 June '60; TVG.

Murder by Proxy

(novel by B.E. Wallace)

See: Phantom of Soho, The (1963).

Murder by Television

1935 Cameo (Imperial Distributing Co) 60 mins.

Pres: William M. Pizor.

Assoc Prod: Edward M. Spitz.

Dir: Clifford Sanforth.

Idea: Clarence Hennecke & Carl Coolidge.

SP: Joseph O'Donnell.

Art Dir: Louis (Lewis?) Rachmil.

Prod Mgr: Melville Delay.

TV Technician: Milton M. Stern.

Tech Sup: Henry Spitz.

Edit: Leslie Wilder.

Mus: Oliver Wallace.

Cast: Bela Lugosi, June Collyer, Huntley (Huntly) Gordon, George Meeker, Henry Mowbray, Charles K. French, Charles Hill Mailes, Claire McDowell, Hattie McDaniel, Allan Jung, Larry Francis, Henry Hall.

SF (telephone call causes mechanism to make TV camera act as death ray)

Ref: Bizarre 24/25:63; B. Warren.

Murder by the Clock

1931 Par 74 mins.

Dir: Edward Sloman.

SP: Henry Myers.

Cin: Karl Struss.

Cast: William Boyd, Lilyan Tashman, Irving Pichel, Regis Toomey, Sally O'Neil, Blanche Friderici, Lenita Lane, Williard Robertson.

myst-H; bor-SF (drug restores man to life, but he is killed again)

Ref: Vw 21 July '31; NYT 18 July '31 16:6.

Based on the story by Rufus King and the play by Charles Beahan.

Murder Chamber, The

See: Black Magic (1944).

Murder Clinic, The

(La Lama nel Corpo: The Blade in the Body, The Knife in the Body; Les Nuits del Epouvante: The Night of Terrors --also ad.t.; The Murder Society --ad.t.; Revenge of the Living Dead --rr.t.)

1966 (1968; 1972 --rr) Italian/French, Leone Films/ Orphée Prods (Europix) color scope 86 mins (75 mins approx --rr in 1972).

Prod & Dir: Elio Scardamaglia (Michael Hamilton).

SP: Ernesto Gastaldi (Julian Berry) & Luciano Martino (Martin Hardy).

Art Dir: Alberto Salvatori.

Makeup: Massimo Giustini.

Cin: Marcello Masciocchi (Marc Lane).

cont.

Murder Clinic cont.

Edit: Alberto Gallitti (Richard Hartley).

Mus: Francesco De Masi (Frank Mason).

Cast: William Berger, Françoise Prevost, Mary Young, Barbara Wilson, Harriet White (Giuliana Raffaelli?).

bor-SF; H (doctor surgically attempts to restore face of woman he mistakenly believes he disfigured; hooded killer roams clinic for mentally ill)

Ref: FF '68 p298; Vw 9 Jan '68; MFB May '69 p 103; BO 25 June '73 p8.

Based on novel "The Knife in the Body" by Robert Williams.

Murder Czech Style

See: Vrazda po Cesky (1966).

Murder in a Gilded Cage

(novel by S. Spewack)

See: Secret Witness (1931).

Murder in the Blue Room

1944 U 61 mins.

Assoc Prod: Frank Gross.

Dir: Leslie Goodwins.

SP: I.A.L. Diamond & Stanley Davis.

Art Dir: John B. Goodman & Harold H. MacArthur.

Cin: George Robinson.

Edit: Charles Maynard.

Mus Dir: Sam Freed Jr.

Cast: Anne Gwynne, Donald Cook, John Litel, Grace McDonald, Betty Kean, June Preissler, Regis Toomey, Emmett Vogan.

myst-com; F-seq (locked-room disappearance; real ghost in comedy scenes; secret passages; sliding panels; etc.)

Ref: Vd 8 Nov '44; LC; FD 8 Nov '44.

Based on novel "Secret of the Blue Room" by Erich Philippi.

See also: Missing Guest, The (1938).

Murder in the Family

See: Crazy Knights (1944).

Murder in the Red Barn

(Maria Marten or the Murder in the Red Barn)

1935 British, Olympic 67 mins.

Dir: Milton Rosmer (George King? --Gifford)

SP: Randall (Randal?) Faye.

Edit: Charles Saunders.

Cast: Tod Slaughter, Sophie Stewart, Eric Portman, Ann Trevor, D.J. Williams, Clare Greet, Dennis Hoey, Hilary Eaves?, Noel Dainton?

psy-H (squire murders his pregnant mistress)

Ref: Vw 2 Sept '36; FD 19 Aug '36; Gifford/BFC 09763.

Based on the play.

See also: Maria Marten.

Murder Is Unpredictable

See: Mysterious Intruder, The (1946).

Murder of Dr. Devil, The

See: Vrazda Inzenyra Certa (1970).

Murder Society, The

See: Murder Clinic, The (1966).

Murder Will Out

(Le Spectre)

1899 French, Star sil 65 ft.

Made by: Georges Méliès.

F

Ref: Sadoul/M, GM Mage 184.

Murder with Noodles

1971? Hungarian ani objects sh.

Dir: Otto Foky.

F-com

Ref: Vw 12 May '71.

Murderer's Command

See: Commando de Asesinos (1966).

Murderers from Other Worlds

See: Asesinos de Otros Mundos (1971).

Murderer's Row

1966 Meadway-Claude (Col) color 108 mins.

Prod: Irving Allen.

Dir: Henry Levin.

SP: Herbert Baker.

Art Dir: Joe Wright.

Cin: Sam Leavitt.

SpFX: Danny Lee.

Edit: Walter Thompson.

Mus: Lalo Schifrin.

Cast: Dean Martin, Ann-Margret, Karl Malden, Camilla Sparv, James Gregory, Beverly Adams, Richard Eastham, Tom Reese, Marcel Hillaire.

bor-SF (helio-beam, created by harnassing the rays of the Sun, can destroy Earth)

Ref: FF '66 p353; MFB Feb '67 p28; Vw 14 Dec '66.

Based on the novel by Donald Hamilton.

See also: Matt Helm.

Murdering Mite, The

See: Tomei Ningen to Hai Otoko (1957).

Murders in the Rue Morgue, The

● 1914 Rosenberg sil sh?

Prod & Sc: Sol A. Rosenberg.

H (trained ape used as killer)

Ref: LC.

● 1932 U 75 mins (61 mins).

Prod: Carl Laemmle Jr.

Dir & Adapt: Robert Florey.

SP: Tom Reed & Dale van Every.

Addit Dialog: John Huston.

Art Dir: Charles D. Hall.

Makeup: Jack Pierce.

Cin: Karl Freund.

SpFX: John Fulton.

Edit: Milton Carruth.

Cast: Bela Lugosi, Sidney Fox, Leon Waycroff (later Leon Ames), Bert Roach, D'Arcy Corrigan, Herman Bing, Arlene Francis.

bor-SF; H (to get subjects for his attempts to cross-breed apes and humans, Dr. Mirakle uses his trained ape, which also kills people)

Ref: FD 14 Feb '32; MPH 30 Jan '32 p49, 20 Feb '32 p34, 38, 40, 41; LC.

● 1971 AIP color 87 mins.

Filmed in Spain.

Exec Prod: James H. Nicholson & Samuel Z. Arkoff.

Prod: Louis M. Heyward.

Dir: Gordon Hessler.

SP: Christopher Wicking & Henry Slesar.

Prod Design: José Luis Galicia.

Makeup: Jack Young.

Cin: Manuel Berenguer.

Edit: Max Benedict.

Mus: Waldo de los Rios.

Cast: Jason Robards (Jr), Herbert Lom, Christine Kaufmann, Adolfo Celi, Lilli Palmer, Maria Perschy, Michael Dunn, José Calvo, Peter Arne.

psy-F-dream; H (disfigured Lom carries out plan of vengeance against horror theater owner Robards in 19th Century France; dream sequences)

Ref: Vw 1 Sept '71; FF '72 p62; MFB Dec '71 p243.

Suggested by the short story by Edgar Allan Poe.

cont.

Murders in Rue Morgue cont.

See also: Sherlock Holmes in the Great Murder Mystery (1908); Raven, The (1912); Leopard Lady, The (1927); Mystery of Marie Roget, The (1942); Phantom of the Rue Morgue (1953).

Murders in the Zoo

1933 Par 66 mins (55 mins).

Dir: Edward Sutherland.

SP: Philip Wylie & Seton I. Miller.

Cin: Ernest Haller.

Cast: Charlie Ruggles, Lionel Atwill, Gail Patrick, Randolph Scott, John Lodge, Kathleen Burke, Harry Beresford, Edward McWade.

H (mad zoo keeper uses the various animals in his zoo as murder instruments)

Ref: Vw 4 April '33; MPH 11 March '33 p 19; FDY '34.

Murliwala

1951 Indian, Madhuvani Chitra 131 mins.

Dir: Vasant Painter.

Dialog: C.L. Kavish.

Cin: Pandurang Naik.

Mus Dir: Sudheer.

Cast: Vijayalaxmi, Sashi Kapoor, Gulab, Durga Khote, Chanda, Niranjan Sharma.

myth-F

Ref: Indian MPA '53 p45.

Muro, Il

(The Wall)

1972? Italian color ani sh.

F

Ref: CineF 2:3:39.

Murphy and the Mermaids

1914 Biograph sil 1/2 reel.

F-dream

Ref: MPW 22:64; LC.

Murzilka Sullosputnik

1959 Soviet ani.

Dir: A. Snezhko-Blotskoi (Snesko-Blozskiaia).

F

Ref: Gasca p242.

Muscle Beach Tom

1956 MGM scope color ani 7 mins.

Dir: William Hanna & Joseph Barbera.

F-com

Ref: Ani/Cin p 171; LC.

See also: Tom and Jerry (1940--).

Museo del Horror, El

(The Museum of Horror)

1964? Mexican, Sotomayor (CoI).

Prod: Jesús Sotomayor.

Dir: Rafael Baledon.

SP: José Unsain.

Art Dir: J. R. Granada.

Cin: Raul Martinez Solares.

Mus: Sergio Guerrero.

Cast: Julio Aleman, Patricia Conde, Joaquin Cordero, Carlos Lopez Moctezuma, Sonia Infante, David Reynoso.

H (girls made into exhibits for museum by mad ex-actor)

Ref: Heraldo 31 May '67; PB.

Museum of Horror, The

See: Museo del Horror, El (1964).

Museum Piece No. 13

(story by R. King)

See: Secret Beyond the Door (1947).

Museum Spooks

(Dreams in a Picture Gallery -- alt.t.)

1910 British?, Walturdaw sil 360 ft.

F-dream (in dream, figures in paintings get out of frames & dance)

Ref: Bios 27 Jan '10.

Music Box, The

1933 Soviet ani sh.

Dir: H. Hodatyev.

F

Ref: Ani/Cin p 147.

Music from Mars

(Music on Mars -- alt. trans?)

1954 Czech.

Dir: Jan Kadar & Elmar Klos.

Cast: Jaroslav Marvan.

SF

Ref: Collier; DdC III:147.

Music Hath Its Charms

1908 French, Pathé sil 328 ft.

F

Ref: View 125:10.

Music of Govind

See: Geet Govind (1947).

Music on Mars

See: Music from Mars (1954).

Musical Chairs, The

1969 Amateur (Film-makers' Coop) 16mm color live & object ani 16 mins.

Made by: Warren Collins.

F-com

Ref: FMC 5:67.

Musical Pig

See: Muzikalno Prase (1965).

Musical Poster Number One

1939 British 16mm ani 3 mins.

Made by: Len Lye.

abs-F

Ref: Undrgnd p82, 280; MMA '63 p56.

Musicalulu

1946 Par color ani 7 mins.

Dir: Isidore Sparber.

Story: Bill Turner & Otto Messmer.

F-com

Ref: LC.

See also: Little Lulu (1946 -48).

Musicians

1963 E. German, DEFA color ani sh.

Dir: Katja & Klaus Georgi.

F

Ref: Ani/Cin p 170.

Musicians

See: Músicos (1971).

Músicos

(Musicians)

1971 Spanish, S. Film color ani 5.5 mins.

Dir: Pablo Nuñez.

F-com (girl gets shot into space by toy rocket)

Ref: SpCin '72.

Mutation, The

1967 Belgian color? ani 12 mins.

Made by: Yvan Lemaire.

F

Ref: IAFF '72.

Mutation, The

1972 (1973) US/British, Getty Pictures Corp/Cyclone color.

Exec Prod: J. Ronald Getty.

Assoc Prod: Herbert G. Luft.

Prod: Robert Weinbach.

Dir: Jack Cardiff.

Story: R. Weinbach & Edward Mann.

SP: Garson Raye.

Art Dir: Herbert Smith.

Makeup: Charles Parker.

Cin: Paul Beeson.

Edit: John Trumper.

Cast: Donald Pleasence, Tom Baker, Scott Antony, Jill Haworth, Michael Dunn, Brad Harris, Julie Ege.

SF-H (scientist attempts to produce plant-animal mutations)

Ref: BO 6 Nov '72 p 18, 18 Dec '72 p9; HR 8 Dec '72 p 13.

Mutations

1972 Bell Telephone color computer ani 7.5 mins.

Made by: Lillian Schwartz & Ken Knowlton.

exp-F

Ref: IAFF '72.

Mutiny in Outer Space

(Space Station X --e.t.; Invasion from the Moon --e.t.; Attack from Outer Space -- s.t?)

1964 (1965) Hugo Grimaldi Prods (Woolner Bros & Crest; AA) 85 mins.

Prod: Hugo Grimaldi & Arthur C. Pierce.

Dir: H. Grimaldi.

SP: A.C. Pierce.

Art Dir: Paul Sylos.

Cin: Archie Dalzell.

Edit: George White.

Mus Dir: Gordon Zahler.

Cast: William Leslie, Dolores Faith, Pamela Curran, Richard Garland, James Dobson, Carl Crow, Harold Lloyd Jr, Glen Langan.

SF (lunar fungus which thrives on heat infests space station)

Ref: MFB March '65 p42; FF '65 p98; Vd 13 May '65.

Mutt and Jeff

1916-28 Bud Fisher (Fox and others) sil ani series 1/2 reel.

Prod & Ani: Bud Fisher.

com; F-seqs

Ref: Ani chart; BFI cat, MPN. Based on the comic strip by Bud Fisher.

See also: Harps and Halos (1917); Fisherless Cartoon, A (1918); Inventors, The (1918); Invisible Revenge, The (1925).

Muzikalno Prase

(Musical Pig)

1965 Yugoslavian, Zagreb color ani 9.6 mins.

Dir & Design: Zlatko Grgić.

Story: Z. Grgic & Borijov Dovniković.

Ani: Z. Grgić & Turido Pauš.

Bg: Pavao Štalter.

Mus: Andjelko Klobučar.

F

Ref: Z/Zagreb; Ani/Cin p135; MFB July '71 p 151.

Muzz Prvního Stoleti

See: Man in Outer Space (1961).

My Adorable Slave

See: Mi Adorable Esclava (1961).

My Adored Clementine

See: Mi Adorada Clementina (1953).

My Blood Runs Cold

1965 WB scope 104 mins.

Prod & Dir: William Conrad.

Story: John Meredyth Lucas.

SP: John Mantley.

Art Dir: LeRoy Deane.

Cin: Sam Leavitt.

Edit: William Ziegler.

Mus: George Duning.

Cast: Troy Donahue, Joey Heatherton, Barry Sullivan, Nicolas Coster, Jeanette Nolan, Russell Thorson, Ben Wright.

psy-H (psychotic killer fakes being reincarnation of heroine's ancestor's lover)

Ref: FF '65 p42-43; MFB June '65 p93; Vw 17 March '65.

My Boy Johnny

1944 Terrytoons (20th-Fox) color ani sh.

Prod: Paul Terry.

Dir: Eddie Donnelly.

Story: John Foster.

Mus: Philip A. Scheib.

F-com

Ref: LC; Acad nom.

My Bride Is a Ghost

See: Mi Novia Es un Fantasma (1944); Kaidan Botan Doro (1968).

My Brother Talks to Horses

1946 MGM 94 mins.

Prod: Samuel Marx.

Dir: Fred Zinnemann.

SP: Morton Thompson.

Art Dir: Cedric Gibbons & Leonid Vasian.

Cin: Harold Rosson.

SpFX: Warren Newcombe.

Edit: George White.

Mus: Rudolph G. Kopp.

Cast: Peter Lawford, Charles Ruggles, "Butch" Jenkins, Beverly Tyler, Edward Arnold, Spring Byington, O.Z. Whitehead.

F (boy gets tips on horse races directly from the horses)

Ref: Vd & HR 19 Nov '46; MFB March '47 p39; FDY '47.

Based on short story "Lewie, My Brother Who Talked to Horses" by Morton Thompson.

My Bunny Lies Over the Sea

1948 WB color ani 7 mins.

Dir: Chuck (Charles M.) Jones.

Story: Michael Maltese.

Ani: Ken Harris, Phil Monroe, Ben Washam, & Lloyd Vaughan.

Voices: Mel Blanc.

F-com

Ref: LC.

See also: Bugs Bunny (1938-63).

My Client Curley

(radio play by N. Corwin)

See: Once Upon a Time (1943).

My Dream Is Yours

1949 WB color ani seq 99 mins.

Prod & Dir: Michael Curtiz.

Story: Jerry Wald & P. Finder Moss.

SP: Harry Kurnitz & Dane Lussier.

Art Dir: Robert Haas.

Ani Seq Dir: I. Freleng.

Cin: Ernest Haller & Wilfred M. Cline.

SpFX: Edwin DuPar.

Edit: Folmer Blangsted.

Mus & Lyrics: Ralph Blane & Harry Warren.

Cast: Jack Carson, Doris Day, Lee Bowman, Adolphe Menjou, Eve Arden, S.Z. Sakall, Selena Royle, Edgar Kennedy, Sheldon Leonard.

cont.

My Dream Is Yours cont.

mus-com; F-dream-seq (Day & Carson, wearing bunny suits, dance with Bugs Bunny in boy's dream)

Ref: HR & Vd 15 March '49; MFB Sept '49 p 163.

See also: Bugs Bunny (1938-63).

My Friend Death

See: Yurei Hanjo-Ki (1961).

My Friend, Dr. Jekyll

See: Mio Amico Jeckyll, Il (1960).

My Friend, the Devil

1922 (1923) Fox sil 9555 ft.

Dir: Harry Millarde.

Sc: Paul H. Sloane.

Cin: Joseph Ruttenberg.

Cast: Charles Richman, Ben Grauer, William Tooker, Adolph Milar, John Tavernier, Myrtle Stewart, Peggy Shaw.
rel-F (child prays for lightning to kill evil stepfather, but it kills mother instead; as adult, he is atheistic doctor, but calls on God to save dying daughter & she is miraculously saved.

Ref: AFI F2.3728 p531; MPW 57:fp270; MPN 26:11165.

Based on novel "Le Docteur Rameau" by Georges Ohnet.

My Green Fedora

1935 WB (Vitaphone) ani 1 reel.

Prod: Leon Schlesinger.

Dir: Friz (Isadore) Freleng.

Ani: Robert Clampett & Chuck Jones.

Mus: Bernard Brown.

F-com

Ref: LC.

My Maid Is too Slow

1910 French, Eclair sil 480 ft.

SF (maid flies when battery is connected)

Ref: Bios 14 April '10.

My Son, the Hero

(Arrivano i Titani: The Titans Arrive; I Titani; Les Titans: The Titans; Sons of Thunder)

1961 (1963) Italian/French, Vides/Films Ariane & Filmsonar (UA) color 111 mins.

Prod: Franco Cristaldi.

Dir: Duccio Tessari.

SP: Ennio De Cocini & D. Tessari.

Art Dir: Ottavio Scotti.

Cin: Alfio Contini.

SpFX: Joseph Natanson.

Edit: Renzo Lucidi.

Mus: Carlo Rustichelli.

English language version
Prod: Alexander Mnouchkine.

Dialog: T. Rowe.

Cast: Pedro Armendariz, Giuliano Gemma, Antonella Lualdi, Jaqueline Sassard, Gérard Séty, Serge Nubret, Tania Lopert.

myth-F-com (much fantasy: Titan released by Jove from Underworld; Pluto's helmet of invisibility; snake-haired Gorgon; thunderbolt from Cyclops; statues come to life; invulnerability from dragon's blood; etc.)

Ref: FF '63 p217; MFB July '63 p98-99; Vw 18 Sept '63.

My Son, The Vampire

(Mother Riley Meets the Vampire; Old Mother Riley Meets the Vampire --Brit.ts; Vampire Over London --s.t.; King Robot -- re-edited US title, never completed;

My Son, the Vampire cont.

Mother Riley Runs Riot -- 8mm t.; Mother Riley in Dracula's Desire --8mm t.)

1952 (196?) British, Fernwood & Renown (Blue Chip) 74 mins.

Prod & Dir: John Gilling.

SP: Val Valentine.

Art Dir: Bernard Robinson.

Cin: Dudley Lovell.

Edit: Leo Trumm.

Mus: Lindo Southworth.

Cast: Bela Lugosi, Arthur Lucan [Old Mother Riley], Dora Bryan, Richard Wattis, Philip Leaver, Ian Wilson, Charles Lloyd-Pack.
SF-H-com (Lugosi is criminal who thinks of himself as vampire, wears cape, sleeps in coffin, etc.; has robot & machine that can explode 200 battleships; foiled by cleaning woman)

Ref: Photon 19:32; S&S Autumn '58 p295; Collier.

See also other Old Mother Riley films with fantasy content: Old Mother Riley's Ghosts (1941); Jungle Treasure (1951).

My Tail Is My Ticket

See: Rep Je Ulaznica (1959).

My Twelve Papas

1960 Czech color ani sh.

Dir: Eduard Hofman.

F

Ref: Ani/Cin p 171.

My Uncle, The Vampire

See: Uncle Was a Vampire (1959).

My Weakness

1933 Fox 75 mins.

Prod & Story: B.G. De Sylva.

Dir & Adapt: David Butler.

SP: B.G. De Sylva, Ben Ryan, Bert Hanlon, & D. Butler.

Cin: Arthur Miller.

Edit: Irene Morra.

Mus: B.G. De Sylva, Richart Whiting, & Leo Robbins.

Cast: Lilian Harvey, Lew Ayres, Harry Langdon [Cupid], Charles Butterworth, Sid Silvers, Irene Bentley, Henry Travers.

mus-com; F-seq (Langdon as Cupid has wings, sits on a cloud)

Ref: Vw 26 Sept '33; LC; FIR Oct '67 p480, 484, 478.

My Wife Is a Panther

See: Ma Femme Est une Panthère (1961).

My World Dies Screaming

See: Terror in the Haunted House (1958).

Myra Breckinridge

1970 20th-Fox color scope 94 mins.

Prod: Robert Fryer.

Dir: Michael Sarne.

SP: M. Sarne & David Giler.

Art Dir: Jack Martin Smith & Fred Harpman.

Cin: Richard Moore.

SpFX: L.B. Abbott & Art Cruickshank.

Edit: Danford B. Greene.

Mus: Lionel Newman.

Cast: Mae West, John Huston, Raquel Welch, Rex Reed, Farrah Fawcett, Roger C. Carmel, George Furth, Calvin Lockhart, Jim Backus, John Carradine, Andy Devine, Grady Sutton, Skip Ward, Kathleen Freeman.

Myra Breckinridge cont.

sex-com; psy-F-seq (man is turned into gorgeous woman by surgery; at end is turned back into a man by accident)

Ref: LAT 5 July '70, 25 June '70; Vw 24 June '70; NYT 5 July '70; F&F Feb '71 p26-27.

Based on the novel by Gore Vidal.

Myrna's

1971 Amateur? color? ani 57 seconds.

Dir: Bruce Cayard.

F

Ref: IAFF '72.

Myrte and the Demons

(Myrthe en de Demonen)

1948 British/Dutch puppet & live 73 mins.

Prod & Dir: Bruno Paul Schreiber.

Cin: Bert Haanstra.

Puppets by: Mevr Alth Bigot.

Mus: Marinus Adam.

Cast: Myrte, John Moore, Sonia Gables.

F (playmates of little girl turned to stone by wood demons)

Ref: MFB June '51 p281; F&F Oct '65 p54; S&S Sum '49 p84.

Mystère de la Villa Rose, Le

(The Mystery of the Villa Rose)

1931 (1932) French, Jacques Haik (First Division).

Prod: Jacques Haik.

Dir: Louis Mercanton & René Hervil.

SP: Louis d'Yvre.

Cin: Chasil (Basil?) Emmott.

Cast: Simone Vaudry, Leon Mathot, Helene Manso, Jean Mercanton.

bor-H (spiritualism; murders)

Ref: NYT 11 Jan '32; FD 17 Jan '32; Vw 12 Jan '32.

Based on novel "At the Villa Rose" by A.E.W. Mason.

See also: At the Villa Rose (1920).

Mystères d'Angkor, Les

See: Mistero dei Trei Continenti,Il (1959).

Mysteres de la Vie et de la Mort

(Mysteries of Life and Death)

1923 French sil.

F ("spiritualism" --Willis)

Ref: DdC II:306; Willis.

Mystères du Château du De,Les

See: Mysteries of the Chateau du De, The (1929).

Mysterians, The

(Chikyu Boeigun: Earth Defense Forces)

1957 (1959) Japanese, Toho (RKO, later MGM) color scope 89 mins.

Prod: Tomoyuki Tanaka.

Dir: Inoshiro Honda.

Story: Jojiro Okami.

Adapt: S. Kayama.

SP: Takeshi Kimura.

Art Dir: Teruaki Abe.

Cin: Hajime Koizumi.

SpFX: Eiji Tsuburaya.

Edit: Hiroichi Iwashita.

Mus: Akira Ifukube.

Cast: Kenji Sahara, Yumi Shirakawa, Akihiko Hirata, Momoko Kochi, Takashi Shimura.
SF (alien invaders land in Japan seeking women for breeding purposes; spaceships, rays, gigantic robot)

Ref: Vd & HR 19 May '59; Toho Films '58; Gasca p 196.

Mysteries from Beyond the Tomb

See: Black Pit of Dr. M (1959).

Mysteries of Angkor, The

See: Mistero dei Trei Continenti, Il (1959).

Mysteries of Black Magic

See: Misterios de la Magica Negra (1957).

Mysteries of India

See: Indian Tomb, The (1920).

Mysteries of Life and Death

See: Mystères de la Vie et de la Mort (1923).

Mysteries of Myra, The

1916 Whartons Inc (Int'l Film Service) sil serial tinted seq 15 parts 31 reels.

Dir: Theodore & Leo Wharton.

Story: Hereward Carrington.

Sc: Charles W. Goddard.

Tech Advisor: Harry Houdini.

Cast: Howard Estabrook, Jean Southern, Mike W. Rale, Allen Murname, Bessie Wharton.

F-H (black magic plant emits poison gas; thought images caught on glass plate; ghosts; elementals; "thought monster" --Gifford.

Ref: Gifford/H p44; FD 27 April '16; MPW 28:1044 etc; LC; Motog 6 May '16.

Mysteries of the Chateau du De, The

(Les Mystères du Château du De)

1929 French sil sh.

Made by: Man Ray.

exp-F

Ref: MMA p56.

Mysteries of the Orient

See: Secrets of the Orient (1928).

Mysterious Accordion, The

See: Accordeon Mysterieux, L' (1906).

Mysterious Armor, The

1907 French, Pathé sil sh.

F (suit of armor comes to life, becomes lady in medieval costume; magic tricks)

Ref: MPW 1:583-84.

Mysterious Automaton of Dr. Kempelen, The

(novel by H. Dupuy-Mazuel)

See: Chess Player, The.

Mysterious Box, The

(La Boite à Malice)

1903 French, Star sil 165 ft.

Made by: Georges Méliès.

Cast: Georges Méliès.

F (people vanish from box)

Ref: Sadoul/M, GM Mage 458-59.

Mysterious Cafe, The

1901 Edison sil 93 ft.

Dir: Edwin S. Porter.

F-com (appearances & disappearances)

Ref: Niver 69.

Mysterious Card, The

1913 IMP sil sh.

F-com

Ref: MPW 16:281.

Mysterious Contragrav, The

1915 Gold Seal sil 2 reels.

Prod & Sc: Henry McRae.

SF (antigravity device powered by "negative electricity" allows floating)

Ref: MPW 24:132; LC.

cont.

cont.

Mysterious Dislocation, A

See: Extraordinary Dislocation, An (1901).

Mysterious Dr. Fu Manchu, The

1929 Par sil & sound versions 85 mins sound (7695 ft sil).

Prod & Addit Dialog: George Marion Jr.

Dir: Rowland V. Lee.

SP: Florence Ryerson & Lloyd Corrigan.

Cin: Harry Fischbeck.

Edit (sil version): Bronson Howard.

Edit (sound version): George Nichols Jr.

Cast: Warner Oland [Fu Manchu], Jean Arthur, Neil Hamilton, O.P. Heggie, William Austin, Claude King, Noble Johnson, Tully Marshall.

bor-F-H (Chinese scientist has powers of super-hypnosis)

Ref: AFI F2.3760 p534; Vw 24 July '29; MPN 41:11:94.

Based on characters created by Sax Rohmer.

Sequels: Return of Dr. Fu Manchu, The (1930); Daughter of the Dragon (1931).

See also: Mask of Fu Manchu, The (1932); Face of Fu Manchu (1965) and sequels; Fu Manchu; Dr. No (1962).

Mysterious Dr. R

See: Man Made Monster (1941).

Mysterious Dr. Satan, The

1940 Rep serial 15 parts 31 reels.

Also edited to 100 min TV version in 1966 as Dr. Satan's Robot.

Assoc Prod: Hiram S. Brown Jr.

Dir: William Witney & John English.

SP: Franklyn Adreon, Ronald Davidson, Norman S. Hall, Joseph Poland, & Sol Shor.

Cin: William Nobles.

Edit: Edward Todd & William Thompson.

Mus: Cy Feuer.

Cast: Eduardo Ciannelli, Robert Wilcox, William Newell, C. Montague Shaw, Ella Neal, Dorothy Herbert, Charles Trowbridge, Jack Mulhall, Edwin Stanley, Walter McGrail, Bud Geary, Archie Twitchell, Kenneth Terrell, Dave Sharp, Tom Steele [robot].

SF-H (mad scientist Dr. Satan uses robot & gadgetry in attempt to conquer world, foiled by masked hero, the Copperhead)

Ref: Ser/Rep; TBC; STI 3:36; LC.

Mysterious Doll, The

1913 Eclectic sil 328 ft.

F (dolls come to life)

Ref: MPW 16:947.

Mysterious Drum, A

1959 Japanese, Puppet Film & Dentsu Film ani puppet 19 mins.

F (gods give a man power)

Ref: FEFN 12:18/19:65.

Mysterious Fine Arts, The

See: Beaux-Arts Mysterieux, Les (1910).

Mysterious Flames

1908 French, Pathé sil 311 ft.

F (Satan does magic)

Ref: MPW 2:547; Views 114:10.

Mysterious Folding Screen, The

See: Paravent Mystérieux, Le (1903).

My Son, the Vampire (1952) British

Mysterious Intruder, The

(Murder Is Unpredictable --s.t.)

1946 Col 62 mins.

Prod: Rudolph C. Flothow.

Dir: William Castle.

SP: Eric Taylor.

Art Dir: Hans Radon.

Cin: Philip Tannura.

Edit: Dwight Caldwell.

Theme of Whistler: Wilbur Hatch.

Mus Dir: Mischa Bakaleinikoff.

Cast: Richard Dix, Barton Maclane, Nina Vale, Regis Toomey, Mike Mazurki, Helen Mouery, Pamela Blake.

myst; psy-F-seqs (Whistler's voice as narrator is voice of Fate)

Ref: Vd 3 May '46; FD 10 April '46; HR 20 May '46.

Based on the CBS radio show "The Whistler."
See also: Whistler, The (1944).

Mysterious Invader, The

See: Astounding She-Monster, The (1958).

Mysterious Island

● 1929 MGM 2-color sound FX 95 mins.

Dir: Lucien Hubbard, Maurice Tourneur, & Benjamin Christiansen.

Sc: L. Hubbard.

Art Dir: Cedric Gibbons.

Cin: Percy Hilburn.

Tech FX: James Basevi, Louis H. Tolhurst, & Irving Ries.

Edit: Carl L. Pierson.

Mus: Martin Broones & Arthur Lange.

Cast: Lionel Barrymore, Pauline Starke, Karl Dane, Warner Oland, Jane Daly, Lloyd Hughes, Montague Love, Harry Gribbon, Snitz Edwards.

SF (Count Dakkar builds 2 submarines, little men live on sea bottom; underwater dragon; giant octopus)

Ref: AFI F2.3762 p534; Vw 25 Dec '29; MPN 41:11:94; FDY '30; LC.

Mysterious Island cont.

Note: filming begun in 1926; some shot in 1927; not completed until 1929.

Captain Nemo is not a character in this version.

● 1941 Soviet, Children's Film Studio.

Dir: E. Penzline & B.M. Chelintzev.

SP: B.M. Chelintzev & M.P. Kalinine.

Cin: M.B. Belskine.

SpFX: M.F. Karukov.

Cast: M.V. Commisarov, A.S. Krasnopolski, P.I. Klansky, R. Ross.

SF (Captain Nemo secretly aids castaways with help of his submarine)

Ref: MMF 15/16 p35.

● 1950 (1951) Esskay Pictures (Col) serial 15 parts 30 reels.

Prod: Sam Katzman.

Dir: Spencer G. Bennet.

Assist Dir: R.M. Andrews.

SP: Lewis Clay, Royal K. Cole, & George H. Plympton.

Cin: Fayte Browne.

Edit: Earl Turner.

Mus Dir: Mischa Bakaleinikoff.

Cast: Richard Crane, Marshall Reed, Karen Randle, Ralph Hodges, Gene Roth, Hugh Prosser, Terry Frost, Rusty Wescoatt, Bernard Hamilton, Leonard Penn [Captain Nemo].

SF (Captain Nemo aids Civil War castaways with his gadgets & submarine, can walk through stone walls; invaders from Mercury use their spaceships & ray guns)

Ref: Ser/Col; LC; FDY '58; Acad.

● 1960 (1961) British/US, Charles H. Schneer Prods (Col) color 100 mins.

Filmed in Spain and England.

Mysterious Island cont.

Prod: Charles H. Schneer.

Dir: Cy Endfield.

SP: John Prebble, Daniel Ullman, & Crane Wilbur.

Art Dir: Bill Andrews.

Cin: Wilkie Cooper.

Underwater Cin: Egil Woxholt.

SpFX: Ray Harryhausen.

Edit: Frederick Wilson.

Mus: Bernard Herrmann.

Cast: Michael Craig, Joan Greenwood, Michael Callan, Gary Merrill, Herbert Lom [Captain Nemo], Nigel Green.

SF (captives escape from Confederate prison by balloon, land on island; encounter giant crab, bee, & bird; Captain Nemo & his submarine help them; giant cephalopod)

Ref: FF '61 p311-12; MFB June '62 p82; Vd & HR 6 Dec '61; FD 14 Dec '61.

● (The Mysterious Island --ad.t.; L'Île Mysterieuse)

1972? French/Italian/US/ Spanish color.

Dir: (Spanish version) Juan Antonio Bardem & (French version) Henri Colpi.

Cast: Omar Sharif [Captian Nemo], Cyrus Smith, Philippe Nicaud, Raymond Pellegrin.

SF (the exploits of Captain Nemo & his submarine)

Ref: Vw 8 Dec '71 p24; UniFrance Jan '72.

Based on novel "L'Île Mysterieux" by Jules Verne.

See also: 20,000 Leagues Under the Sea.

Mysterious Island, The

See: Ulysses and Giant Polyphemus (1905).

Mysterious Knight, The

(Le Chevalier Mystère)

1899 French, Star sil 130 ft.

Made by: Georges Méliès.

cont.

cont.

cont.

Mysterious Knight cont.

F (transformations)

Ref: Sadoul/M, GM Mage 226-27.

Mysterious Knight

1908 French, Pathé sil
colored 459 ft.

F (knight appears in burst
of flame, calls up amazons,
appearances & disappearances)

Ref: Views 131:9.

**Mysterious Lady Baffles and
Detective Duck**

See: Lady Baffles and Detective
Duck (1915).

Mysterious Magician, The

(Der Hexer: The Magician,
The Wizard)

1965 W. German.

Dir: Alfred Vohrer.

SP: Herbert Reinecker & H.
(M.?) Petersson.

Cast: Joachim Berger, Heinz
Drache, Eddi Arent, Sophie
Hardy, Siegfried Lowitz.

H ("phantom-like avenger
seems to have returned from
the dead" --Willis)

Ref: FIR; TVK (Willis).

Based on "The Ringer" by
Edgar Wallace.

Mysterious Midgets, The

1904 Biograph sil 185
ft.

F (stop-action magic;
puppets)

Ref: LC; Niver 348.

Mysterious Mr. Chautard, The

See: Man with Two Faces (1934).

Mysterious Mr. M

1946 U serial 13 parts
26 reels.

Exec Prod: Morgan B. Cox.

Assoc Prod: Joseph O'Donnell.

Dir: Vernon Keays & Lewis
D. Collins.

SP: Joseph F. Poland, Paul
Huston, & Barry Shipman.

Cin: Gus Peterson.

Cast: Richard Martin, Pamela
Blake, Dennis Moore, Jane
Randolph, Jack Ingram,
Byron Foulger, Virginia
Brissac, Joseph Crehan,
Mauritz Hugo, Anthony Warde.

bor-SF (submarine motor
operates without batteries;
hypnotic power from injections)

Ref: FD 5 Aug '46; LC.

Mysterious Mr. Wong, The

1935 Mono 60 mins.

Prod: George Yohalem.

Dir: William Nigh.

SP: Nina Howatt.

Art Dir: E.R. Erickson.

Cin: Harry Neumann.

Edit: Jack Ogilvie.

Cast: Bela Lugosi, Wallace
Ford, Arline Judge, Lee
Shumway, Lotus Long, Robert
Emmet O'Connor.

bor-F-H (Lugosi, head of
Hatchetmen, after 12 coins,
ownership of which was pre-
dicted by Confucious to
bestow rulership of China;
tortures)

Ref: Vw 13 March '35; FD 15
Jan '35; LC; Borst.

Based on story "The Twelve
Coins of Confucious" by
Harry Stephen Keeler.

Mysterious Mrs. M, The

1916 Bluebird sil 3300 ft.

Dir: Lois Weber.

Cast: Harrison Ford, Mary
MacLaren, Willis Marks.

bor-F-H (fortuneteller predicts
death for herself & customer,
& the fortuneteller dies)

cont.

Mysterious Mrs. M. cont.

Ref: LC; MPW 31:908; MPN
15:757.

Based on the story by
Thomas Edgelow.

Mysterious Mose

1930 Par ani 8 mins.

Prod: Max Fleischer.

Dir: Dave Fleischer.

Ani: Willard Bowsky & Ted
Sears.

F-com (Betty Boop & Bimbo
in a haunted house)

Ref: CFS cat '69; LC.

See also: Betty Boop (1930-
39); Bimbo (1931-3?).

Mysterious Paper, The

(La Papier Protée)

1896 French, Star sil
65 ft.

Made by: Georges Méliès.

F

Ref: Sadoul/M, GM Mage 53.

Mysterious Portrait, A

(Le Portrait Mystérieux)

1899 French, Star sil
65 ft.

Made by: Georges Méliès.

F

Ref: Sadoul/M, GM Mage 196.

Mysterious Prince

1934 Indian, Saraswati
Cinetone.

Prod & Dir: R.G. Torney.

SP: B.V. Varerker.

Mus Dir: Annasheb Mainker.

Cast: Vithal, Salvi, Menaka.

F

Ref: MovPicM May '34 p8.

Mysterious Rabbit, The

1896 British, R.W. Paul sil
40 ft.

Cast: David Devant.

F (stage magician's act: pulls
rabbit from hat & duplicates it)

Ref: Gifford/BFC 00016.

Mysterious Retort, The

(L'Alchemiste Parafaragaramus
ou La Cornue Infernale; The
Alchemist and the Demon --alt.t?)

1906 French, Star sil 200
ft.

Made by: Georges Méliès.

F-dream (imp in dream)

Ref: Sadoul/M, GM Mage
874-76; LC; Views 1:34:5, 8.

Mysterious Satellite

(Uchujin Tokyo Arawaru:
Spacemen Arrive in Tokyo;
Warning from Space --US
TV title)

1956 (196?) Japanese, Daiei
color 87 mins.

Prod: Masaichi Nagata.

Dir: Koji Shima.

SP: Hideo Oguni.

Art Dir: Shigeo Muno.

Cin: Kimio Watanabe.

Edit: Toyo Suzuki.

Cast: Toyomi Karita, Keizo
Kawasaki, Isao Yamagati,
Shozo Nanbu, Bontaro Miake,
Mieko Nagai, Kiyoko Hirai.

SF (benign aliens from
wandering planet disguise
themselves as humans, come
to Earth to warn of H-bomb
dangers; aliens look like
giant, one-eyed starfish)

Ref: MFB May '58 p64; FEFN
8 June '56 p20, 23.

Based on novel by Gentaro
Nakajima, from Japanese
folk tale "Kaguyahime."

Mysterious Stranger, The

1911 French, Eclipse (George
Kleine) sil 610 ft.

rel-F (girl struck by lightning restored by stranger,
who turns out to be Jesus)

Ref: MPW 10:903; F/A p492;
FIR March '64 p 158.

Mysterious Stranger, The

1913 Essanay sil sh?

Cast: E.H. Calvert, Bryant
Washburn.

F (Satan-like hypnotist gives
man visions which haunt him)

Ref: MPW 16:1359.

Mysterious Uncle Silas, The

See: Misterioso Tio Sylas,
El (1947).

Mysterious Yarn

1917 Int'l Film Services
ani sh.

F-com

Ref: LC.

See also: Katzenjammer Kids
(1917).

Mystery

See: Raaz (1965).

Mystery and Terror

See: Hiwa ng Lagim (1970).

Mystery at the Villa Rose

1930 British (Harold Auten)
78 mins.

Exec Prod: Julius Hagen &
Henry Edwards.

Prod: Basil Dean.

Dir: Leslie Hiscott.

Cin: Sidney Blythe.

Cast: Austin Trevor, Richard
Cooper, Francis Lister, John
Hamilton, Amy Brandon-Thomas.

myst; bor-H (seances; mysterious
murderer)

Ref: Vw 4 June '30; NYT 2
June '30 25:4.

Based on novel "At the Villa
Rose" by A.E.W. Mason.

See also: At the Villa Rose (1920).

Mystery Film, The

(Where-U-Seer? --rr.t.)

1924 British, Int'l Cine Corp
sil 1253 ft.

Cast: Ah-Ben-Aza.

F ("magician comes from Bagdad
in a sack and reads the minds
of the cinema audience")

Ref: Gifford/BFC 07901.

Mystery in the Mine

1958 British serial 8
parts 128 mins total.

Prod: Frank A. Hoare.

Dir: James Hill.

Story: Peter Ling.

SP: Dallas Bower & J. Hill.

Cin: John Wiles.

Edit: Ernest Hilton.

Mus: Max Saunders.

Cast: Ingrid Cardon, Stewart
Guidotti, Howard Greene,
Peter Copley, Elwyn Brook-
Jones.

SF (space mirror would allow
domination of the world, but
needs rare element to operate)

Ref: MFB Oct '59 p 138; Collier.

Mystery Liner

1934 Mono 7 reels.

Prod: Paul Malvern.

Dir: William Nigh.

SP: Wellyn Totman.

Cin: Archie Stout.

Edit: Carl Pierson.

Cast: Noah Beery, Astrid
Allwyn, Gustav von Seyffertitz, Edwin Maxwell, Cornelius Keefe, Ralph Lewis,
George Cleveland, Olaf Hytten.

cont.

Mystery Liner cont.

bor-SF; myst (radio-controlled
ship; murder at sea)

Ref: Vw 10 April '34; TVG.

Based on novel "The Ghost
of John Holling" by Edgar
Wallace.

Mystery Mind, The

1920 Supreme Pictures (Pioneer)
sil serial 15 parts.

Dir: Fred W. Sittenham &
William S. Davis.

Sc: A.B. Reeve & J.W. Grey.

Cin: David(e?) Calcagini.

Cast: Violet MacMillan, J.
Robert Pauline, Peggy Shanor,
Paul Panzer, Ed Rogers,
DeSacia Saville.

SF-H (ape-man villain;
hypnotism; rays?)

Ref: Gasca p33; LC; MPW
43:929; MPN 20:2016.

Based on the novel by Arthur
B. Reeve & John W. Grey.

Mystery of Dr. Fu Manchu, The

1923 British, Stoll sil
2 reel series.

Based on characters created
by Sax Rohmer.

Ref: BFI cat; MMF 14:34;
Gifford/BFC 07683-98.

See also: Aaron's Rod;
Call of Siva, The; Clue
of the Pigtail, The; Cry of
the Nighthawk, The; Fiery
Hand, The; Fungi Cellars,
The; Knocking on the Door,
The; Man with the Limp, The;
Miracle, The; Queen of Hearts,
The; Sacred Order, The;
Scented Envelopes, The;
Shrine of the Seven Lamps, The;
Silver Buddha, The; West Case,
The.

Sequel: Further Mysteries
of Fu Manchu (1924).

See also: Fu Manchu.

Mystery of Hamlet, The

(book by E.P. Vining)

See: Hamlet (1920).

Mystery of Hidden House, The

1914 Vit sil 2 reels.

bor-F-H (girl with split
personality)

Ref: MPW 20:102.

Mystery of Islington, The

(story by A. Machen)

See: Esqueleto de la Señora
Morales, El (1959).

Mystery of Life

1931 Classic (U) 8 reels
(62 mins).

Dir: George Cochrane.

SP: H.M. Parshley.

Edit: W.W. Young.

Cast: Clarence Darrow.

doc; SF-seqs (history of
animal life & evolution;
scenes with dinosaurs?)

Ref: FD 5 July '31; MPH
18 April '31 p23, 11 July
'31 p33-34; LC.

Mystery of Lost Ranch, The

1925 Vit sil 5 reels.

Dir: Harry S. Webb & Tom
Gibson.

Story: Barr Cross.

Continuity: George Hall.

Cast: Pete Morrison.

west; SF (spies & a death
ray in a western setting)

Ref: AFI F2.3770 p535.

Mystery of Marie Roget, The

(Phantom of Paris --rr.t.)

1942 U 7 reels.

Assoc Prod: Paul Malvern.

Dir: Phil Rosen.

SP: Michel Jacoby.

Art Dir: Jack Otterson.

Cin: Woody Bredell.

Edit: Milton Carruth.

Mus: Hans J. Salter.

Cast: Maria Montez, Patric Knowles, Maria Ouspenskaya, John Litel, Charles Middleton, Lloyd Corrigan, Frank Reicher, Reed Hadley.

H (brain snatched from body in morgue; face clawed as if by animal; mystery solved by detective Dupin)

Ref: MFB June '42 p73; FD 3 April '42; HR 3 April '42.

Based on the short story by Edgar Allan Poe.

See also: Murders in the Rue Morgue, The.

Mystery of Temple Court, The

1910 Vit sil 900 ft.

F-dream (vision of a dead woman)

Ref: Bios 9 June '10.

Mystery of the Black Castle, The

See: Black Castle, The (1952).

Mystery of the Blue Oranges, The

See: Misterio de las Naranjas Azules, El (1965).

Mystery of the Fatal Pearl, The

1914 American Kineto sil 4800 ft.

F (cursed pearl stolen from temple of Buddha -- possessors die)

Ref: MPW 19:730.

Mystery of the Ganges River

See: Ganga Maiya (1953).

Mystery of the Ghastly Face, The

See: Misterio del Rostro Palido, El (1935).

Mystery of the Glass Coffin, The

1912 French, Eclair sil 3000 ft.

bor-H (man finds girl's body preserved in glass casket)

Ref: Bios (Willis).

Mystery of the Haunted Hotel, The

1913 Thanhauser sil 1020 ft.

bor-H (fake ghost)

Ref: MPW 18:420; Bios 29 Jan '14.

Mystery of the Lama Convent, The

(Dr. Nicola in Tibet)

1909 Danish, Nordisk (Great Northern) sil sh.

F (dead are returned to life)

Ref: Bios 18 Nov '09; MPW 6:186, 191, 215.

Mystery of the Marie Celeste, The

(novel by D. Clift)

See: Phantom Ship, The (1936).

Mystery of the Pallid Face, The

See: Misterio del Rostro Palido (1935).

Mystery of the Sleeping Death, The

1914 Kalem sil 2 reels.

Dir: Kenean Buel.

Sc: Doty C. Hobart.

Cast: Tom Moore, Alice Joyce, Henry Hallam.

cont.

The Mysteries of Myra (1916) Serial

Mystery of the Sleeping Death cont.

F (man cursed to sleep as if dead, reincarnated every century to relive his love)

Ref: MPW 21:1487, 1549; Blum p55.

Mystery of the Three Continents, The

See: Misterio dei Trei Continenti, Il (1959).

Mystery of the Villa Rose, The

See: Mystère de la Villa Rose, Le (1931).

Mystery of the Wax Museum, The

(Wax Museum --ad.t.)

1932 (1933) WB 2-color 78 mins.

Dir: Michael Curtiz.

SP: Don Mullaly & Carl Erickson.

Art Dir: Anton Grot.

Cin: Ray Rennahan.

Edit: George Amy.

Cast: Lionel Atwill, Fay Wray, Glenda Farrell, Frank McHugh, Allen Vincent, Holmes Herbert, Edwin Maxwell, Arthur Edmund Carew, DeWitt Jennings, Pat O'Malley.

H (fire scars wax sculptor hideously; no longer able to work as sculptor, he kills people & encases them in wax to form exhibits; wears wax mask to disguise disfigured features)

Ref: Vw 23 Dec '32, 21 Feb '33; MPH 7 Jan '33 p23; LC; AFI Report '72 #1; Pardi.

Based on play "Waxworks" by Charles S. Belden.

Remake: House of Wax (1953).

Mystery of 13, The

1919 Burston Films sil serial 15 parts 30? reels.

Prod: Louis Burston.

Dir: Francis Ford.

Story: Elsie Van Name.

Mystery of 13 cont.

Sc: John B. Clymer.

Cast: Francis Ford, Rosemary Theby, Pete Girard, Mark Fenton, Phil Ford, Jack Saville, Doris Dare, Nigel De Brulier (De Brouiller).

myst; bor-F-H

Ref: CNW 73, 197-98; LC; MPN 20:fp648.

Mystery of Tut-Ankh-Amen's Eighth Wife, The

See: King Tut-Ankh-Amen's Eighth Wife (1923).

Mystery Plane

See: Sky Pirate (1939).

Mystery Rider, The

1928 U sil serial 10 parts 20? reels.

Dir: Jack Nelson.

Cast: William Desmond, Derelys Perdue, Sid Saylor, Walter Shumway, Tom London, Bud Osborne, Red Basset, Ben Corbett.

west; bor-SF-H (formula for making rubber from mesquite sap)

Ref: CNW 126f, 145, 266; LC.

Mystery Ship, The

1917-18 U sil serial 18 parts 36 reels.

Dir: Harry Harvey & Francis Ford.

Story: Elsie Van Name.

Sc: William Parker & Blaine Pearson.

Cast: Nigel de Brulier, Ben Wilson, Neva Gerber, Kingsley Benedict, Duke Worne, Elsie Van Name.

SF-seq (light ray melts steel walls, also death ray; helmet enhances senses; ship can be run by one man)

Ref: MPW 34:885, 1408-09, 1544, 1676, 1841, 2000, 35:138, 281, 421; LC.

Mystic, The

1925 MGM sil 7 reels (5147 ft).

Dir & Story: Tod Browning.

Sc: Waldemar Young.

Sets: Cedric Gibbons & Hervey Libbert.

Cin: Ira Morgan.

Edit: Frank Sullivan.

Cast: Aileen Pringle, Conway Tearle, Mitchell Lewis, Robert Ober, Stanton Heck, David Torrence, Gladys Hulette, DeWitt Jennings.

F-H-seq (supposedly fake Hungarian mystics really raise spirit of girl's dead father)

Ref: AFI F2.3774 p536; LC; Vw 2 Sept '25; MPW 76:170.

Mystic Ball, The

1915 Selig sil 2 reels.

Dir: William Robert Daly.

Sc: Wallace C. Clifton.

Cast: George Larkin, Fritzi Brunette.

F (magic crystal ball)

Ref: MPW 25:2176; LC.

Mystic Circle Murder, The

(Religious Racketeers --alt.t?)

1939 Merit 69 mins.

Dir & SP: Frank O'Connor.

Cast: Betty Compson, Robert Fisk, Arthur Gardner, Helen Le Berthon, Madame Harry Houdini.

myst; bor-H (fake spiritualists, mediums, etc. exposed as charlatans & their tricks demonstrated)

Ref: FD 18 April '38, 13 Aug '39; FWD p 191.

Mystic Glove, The

1914 British, Bamforth sil sh.

F-dream-com (ghost gives hero magic gloves in dream which cause transformations)

Ref: BFI cat p99.

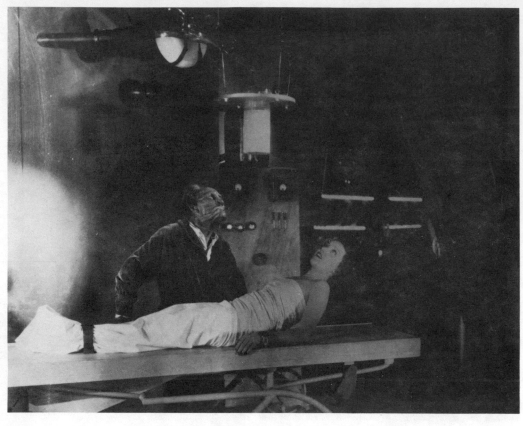

The Mystery of the Wax Museum (1932)

Mystic Manipulations

1912 British, Kinemacolour
sil 2-color sh.

F (magician's act includes
color changes)

Ref: MPW 15:81, 718; F/A
p424.

Mystic Melodies

1909 French, Gaum (Kleine)
sil 266 ft.

F (Muse of Melody transforms
room & wife)

Ref: MPW 5:655; FI IV-45:5.

Mystic Mirror, The

1928 German, UFA sil
7003 ft (67 mins).

Dir: Karl Hoffmann & Prof.
Teschner.

Sc: Robert Reinert.

Cin: K. Hoffmann & Karl
Böhm.

Cast: Fritz Rasp, Rina de
Ligoure, Felicitas Malten,
Albach Retty.

F-H (mirror shows future
during full Moon: villain
sees himself strangled)

Ref: Vw 17 Oct '28; FIR
Feb '60 p93; FD 7 Oct '28.

Mystic Moonstone, The

1913 British, Cricks & Martin
sil 365 ft.

F-com (everything vanishes)

Ref: Bios 13 March '13 p xxii,
xxxi.

Mystic Prophecies and Nostradamus

1961 Premier Prods color.

F; doc

Ref: Acad.

Mystic Re-incarnation, A

1902 Biograph sil 60 ft.

F (parts of woman appear;
magician assembles them &
she comes to life)

Ref: LC; Niver 348.

Mystic Ring, The

1912 British, Cricks & Martin
sil 467 ft.

F-dream-com (in dream the Devil
gives a man a ring of invisibility)

Ref: BFI cat p94.

Mystic Swing, The

1900 Edison sil 55 ft.

Dir: Edwin S. Porter.

F (magician; appearances &
disappearances centered around
a swing)

Ref: LC; Niver 348.

Mystical Flame, The

(La Flamme Merveilleuse)

1903 French, Star sil
120 ft.

Made by: Georges Méliès.

Cast: Georges Méliès.

F-com (appearances & disappearances)

Ref: Sadoul/M, GM Mage;
Niver 69; LC.

**Mystical Maide of Jamasha Pass,
The**

(The Myth of Jamasha Pass)

1912 American sil tinted
1000 ft.

Cast: Jessalyn Van Trump,
J. Warren Kerrigan, Jack
Richardson.

F (maid disappears through
solid rock, lures men to
their death)

Ref: MPW 12:319, 562, 630;
F/A p424.

Based on Indian legend.

Myszka i Kotek

See: Mouse and Cat (1958).

Myth of Jamasha Pass, The

See: Mystical Maide of Jamasha
Pass, The (1912).

N

N:O:T:H:I:N:G

1968 Amateur (Film-makers'
Coop) 16mm color 35 mins.

Made by: Paul Sharits.

exp-F

Ref: FC 47:9; FMC 5:291.

N.P. (— The Secret)

1971 Italian, Zeta-A-Elle
color 106 mins.

Prod: Enrico Zaccaria.

Dir & SP: Silvano Agosti.

Art Dir: Isabella Genoese.

Cin: Nicola Dimitri.

Mus: Nicola Piovani.

Cast: Francesco (Francisco?)
Rabal, Ingrid Thulin, Irene
Papas.

SF (socio-political panorama
at the close of the 20th
Century; machine-liberated
workers)

Vw 4 Aug '71, 27 Oct '71.

Nth

1970 Amateur ani sh?

Made by: Ellen Olean.

F

Ref: NYT 14 Oct '70.

N.Y., N.Y.

1952/1957 Amateur 16mm
color 15 mins.

Made by: Francis Thompson.

Mus: Gene Forrell.

exp-F (distortion by lenses:
autos swallow themselves,
buildings float, etc.)

Ref: FQ Summer '59 p52-54;
MMA '63 p58.

Na Dnu

(On the Bottom)

1969 Yugoslavian, Zagreb
color ani 6.5 mins.

Dir, SP, Design, Ani: Zlatko
Pavlinic.

Mus: Andjelko Klobucar.

F-com (man tries to get out
of hole, crawls instead into
nearby grave)

Ref: Z/Zagreb p 101.

Na Komete

(On the Comet; Mr. Servadac's
Arch --ad.t.)

1970 Czech, Barrandov color
85 mins.

Dir & SP: Karel Zeman.

Art Dir: Jiří Hlupy.

Cin: Rudolf Stahl.

Mus: Lubos Fiser.

Cast: Emil Horvath, Magda
Vasarykova, Frantisek Fili-
povsky.

SF (man swept into space on
comet, where there are prehistoric beasts)

Ref: Vw 2 Sept '70; MTVM
Dec '68.

Based on novel "Hector Servadac"
(aka "Off on a Comet" & "Career
of a Comet") by Jules Verne.

See also: Valley of the Dragons
(1961).

Na Livadi

(On a Meadow)

1957 Yugoslavian, Zagreb
color? ani 7.5 mins.

Dir: Nikola Kostelac.

SP: Vatroslav Mimica &
Vladimir Tadej.

Design & Ani: Aleksandar
Marks.

Bg: Ivo Dulčić.

Mus: Milko Kelemen.

F-H (2 boys quarrel over
a flower -- "develops into
a horror film on war" --Z/Z)

Ref: Z/Zagreb p54.

Naach Ghar

1959 Indian (in Hindi),
Kwality Pictures 135 mins.

Dir: R.S. Tara.

Cast: Shubha Khote, Anoop
Kumar, Ashok Kumar, Kamala
Laxman.

F-seq (cripple miraculously
cured)

Ref: FEFN 12:12/13:29.

Naag Rani

See: Cobra Girl (1962).

Naan Kanda Swargam

(I Discovered Heaven)

1960 Indian (in Tamil),
Bhargavi Films 179 mins.

Dir: C. Pulliah.

Cast: "Sowcar" Janaki, K.A.
Thangavelu, Sairam.

F-com (man, not dead, taken
to Kingdom of God of Death,
raises a ruckus, sent back
to Earth)

Ref: FEFN Sept '60 p27.

Nabeshima Kaibyoden

(Ghost-cat Mansion of
Nabeshima)

1949 Japanese, Shin Toho.

Dir: Kunio Watanabe.

Cast: Denjiro Okochi, Michiyo
Kogure.

F-H (ghost story about a
cat-woman)

Ref: Unij Bltn.

See also: Hiroku Kaibyoden
(1969).

Nabonga

(Gorilla; The Girl and the Gorilla --s.t?; The Jungle Woman --ad.t?; Fils de King Kong --Belgian t.)

1943 (1944) Neufeld (PRC) 73 mins.

Prod: Sigmund Neufeld.

Dir: Sam Newfield.

SP: Fred Myton.

Art Dir: Paul Palmentola.

Cin: Robert Cline.

Edit: Holbrook N. Todd.

Mus: Willy Stahl.

Cast: Buster Crabbe, Barton MacLane, Fifi D'Orsay, Julie London, Herbert Rawlinson, Bryant Washburn.

bor-F (girl grows up in jungle, has gorilla bodyguard because she nursed its wounds; she is called witch by natives)

Ref: Vw 23 Feb '44; HR & Vd 20 March '44; MFB June '44 p69.

Nache Nagin Baje Been

(Dance of Cobra to Playing of Veena)

1960 Indian (in Hindi), Janta Chitra.

Dir: Tara Harish.

Cast: Helen, Chandrasekhar.

F (girl cursed: whoever loves her will die of snakebite; boy does but is restored to life by Queen of the Snake Empire)

Ref: FEFN July '60 p53.

Nacht des Grauens

(Night of Terror; A Night of Horror --ad.t.?)

1916 German sil.

Dir: Arthur Robison.

Cast: Werner Krauss, Emil Jannings, Lupu Pick.

F-H ("a night among the 'grey people of superstition'")

Ref: Shriek 1:63; Borst; DdC III:257; F&F June '58 p 14.

Nacht des Grauens, Eine

See: Zwolfte Stunde, Die (1921).

Nachtschatten

(Nightshade)

1972 W. German, Visual Film Produktion 16mm color 96 mins.

Dir, Sp, Edit: Niklaus Schilling.

Cin: Ingo Hamer.

Mus: E.G. Bearbitung & A.E. Amalthea.

Cast: Elke Hart, John Van Dreelen (Dreelan?), Max Kurgel, Ella Timmermann.

bor-psy-F-H (expressionistic; man feels drawn to strange woman in house in the country)

Ref: Vw 6 Sept '72 p20.

Nackt Sind Seine Opfer

See: X+YY — Formel des Bosen (1969).

Nackte und der Satan, Die

See: Head, The (1959).

Nag-Aapoy na Dambana

1968? Philippine, LEA.

Dir: Luciano B. Carlos.

Story & SP: Pablo S. Gomez.

Mus: Restie Umali.

Cast: Gloria Romero, Lolita Rodriguez, Luis Gonzales, Roger Calvin, Alicia Alonzo, Matimtiman Cruz, Dante Rivero, Rosa Santos.

H

Ref: Chodkowski.

Based on the Continental Komics serial.

Nag Devta

1962 Indian, Vinod Films.

Dir: Shantilal Shoni.

Cast: Anjali Devi, Mahipal, Shashikala, B.M. Vyas, Leela Chitnis.

mus-F

Ref: MTVM April '62 p57.

Naga-Nanda

1934 Indian, Samrat.

Prod: D.G. Vanakudre.

Dir: Y.V. Rao.

Cin: Kasinath Bawadekar.

Cast: Azambai, Chitalkar, Sadolikar, Paragaonkar, Thamekar.

myth-F

Ref: Dipali Oct '34 p28, 90, 7 Dec '34 p20.

Nagagutsu o Haita Neko

See: Puss in Boots (1969).

Nagakannika

1949 Indian, Mahatma 172 mins.

Prod: D Sankar Singh.

Dir: G. Vishwanath.

myth-F

Ref: Indian MPA '53 p93.

Naganacz

1963? Polish.

Dir: Czeslaw & Eva Petelski.

H

Ref: F&F Oct '64 p51.

See also: Most Dangerous Game, The (1932).

Nagin

(Female Cobra)

1959 Pakistani, Films Hayat 118 mins.

Dir: Khalil Quaiser.

F (two dangerous supernatural reptiles disguise themselves as children)

Ref: FEFN Sept '59 p56.

Nagushacharita

See: Brahmaratham (1949).

Nagymama

(Grandmother)

1935 Hungarian, Eco.

Dir: Istavan Gyoergy.

Cast: Ilona Cs. Aczel, Laszlo Perenyi.

F-com (fairy godmother)

Ref: FD 31 Dec '35.

Naica and the Squirrel

n.d. Rumanian color ani sh.

Dir: Elisabeta Bostan.

F

Ref: LA County Museum.

Naidra, the Dream Woman

1914 Thanhouser sil.

Cast: Mignon Anderson, Riley Chamberlain.

SF-dream (man dreams he creates beautiful woman incapable of love, using old alchemist formula)

Ref: MPN 19 Dec '14 p85; MPW 22:1524, 1586.

Nailed

19?? Russian, Thiemann & Reinhardt.

Prod: Paul Thiemann & F. Reinhardt.

H (like Grand Guignol)

Ref: Kino p 59-60.

Nails

1972? Swiss ani objects color 4 mins.

Dir: Kurt Aeschbacher.

exp-F (nails form geometric patterns by stop-motion, then rust)

Ref: ASIFA 8.

Nain et Géant

See: Dwarf and the Giant, The (1901).

Naissance du Cinéma, La

(The Birth of Cinema)

1964? Belgian color ani seq 10 mins.

Dir: E. Degelin.

Ani: J. Coignon.

F-seq

Ref: Ani/Belgium p57-58.

Naked and Satan, The

See: Head, The (1959).

Naked Ape, The

1973 Playboy (U) color ani seq 85 mins.

Exec Prod: Hugh M. Hefner.

Prod: Zev Bufman.

Dir & SP: Donald Driver.

Ani Prod: Jerry Good.

Ani Dir: Charles Swenson.

Prod Design: Lawrence G. Paull.

Cin: John Alonzo.

Edit: Michael Economou.

Mus: Jimmy Webb.

Cast: Johnny Crawford, Victoria Principal, Dennis Olivieri, Diana Darrin, Norman Grabowski, John Hillerman, Helen Horowitz, Robert Ito, Marvin Miller.

doc; F-seq (animated story of evolution; other fantasy, including cavemen wading in a skyscraper's fountain)

Ref: Vw 15 Aug '73; Playboy Sept '73 p159-67.

Based on the book by Desmond Morris.

Naked Evil

1966 (1973) British, Gibraltar (Hampton Int'l & Saxton Films) color 79 mins.

Prod: Michael F. Johnson.

Dir & SP: Stanley Goulder.

Art Dir: George Provis.

cont.

Nabonga (1943)

Naked Evil cont.

Cin: Geoffrey Faithfull.

Edit: Peter Musgrave.

Mus: Bernard Ebbinghouse.

Cast: Anthony Ainley, Basil Dignam, Suzanne Neve, Richard Coleman, Ronald Bridges, Olaf Pooley.

F-H (magic bottle, obi, filled with grave dirt & feathers given to enemy -- when broken it releases spirit which kills recipient; spirit of voodoo practioner possesses man)

Ref: MFB July '69 p 148; BO 18 Dec '72 BookinGuide, 28 May '73 back cover ad.

Based on play "The Obi" by Jon Manchip White.

Naked Goddess, The

See: Devil's Hand, The (1958).

Naked Gun, The

1956 Associated Film Releasing Corp 69 mins.

Prod: Ron Ormond.

Dir: Edward Dew.

SP: R. Ormond & Jack Lewis.

Mus: Walter Green.

Cast: Willard Parker, Mara Corday, Barton MacLane, Tom Brown, Veda Ann Borg, Chick Chandler, Jody McCrea, Billy House, Morris Ankrum, Bill Phillips.

west; bor-F (western treasure cursed by Indian sorcerer)

Ref: MPH '57 p266; TVG.

Naked Jungle, The

1953 (1954) Par color 95 mins.

Prod: George Pal.

Dir: Byron Haskin.

SP: Philip Yordan & Ranald MacDougall.

Art Dir: Hal Pereira & Franz Bachelin.

Cin: Ernest Laszlo.

SpFX: John P. Fulton.

Edit: Everett Douglas.

Mus: Daniele Amfitheatrof.

Cast: Charlton Heston, Eleanor Parker, William Conrad, Abraham Sofaer, Romo Vincent, Douglas Fowley, John Dierkes, Leonard Strong.

bor-SF-H (South American plantation threatened by soldier or army ants, which eat all in their path, including people)

Ref: Vd & HR 10 Feb '54; MFB May '54 p71-72.

Based on short story "Leininger Versus the Ants" by Carl Stephenson.

Naked Vampire, The

See: Vampire Nue, La (1969).

Naked Witch, The

1966 (1967) Mishkin 80 mins.

Dir: Andy Milligan.

SP: Clay Guss.

Cast: Beth Porter, Robert Burgos, Bryarly Lee, Lee Forbes.

hist-H (witchcraft in New England; woman burned as a witch)

Ref: BO 6 March '67.

Nakurami

See: Lady and the Dragon, The (1955).

Nala Damyanti

● 1917 Indian, Madan sil.

Prod: J.F. Madan.

● 1945 Indian (in Hindi).

Ref: Filmindia Dec '45 p72.

myth-F

Name for Evil, A

(The Grove --e.t.; There Is a Name for Evil --s.t.)

1970 (1973) Penthouse (Cinerama) color.

Filmed in Canada.

Prod: Reed Sherman.

Dir & SP: Bernard Girard.

Mus: Dominic Frontiere.

Cast: Robert Culp, Samantha Eggar, Sheila Sullivan, Mike Lane, Reed Sherman, Clarence Millar, Sue Hathaway.

F-H-dream(?) (ghost of hero's evil ancestor haunts Southern mansion, induces him to kill his wife; may be a dream)

Ref: Playboy March '73 p 147-49; Photon 21:5; Locus 134:7; SF Chronicle ad; Acad.

Based on a novel by Andrew Lytle.

Name of the Game is Kill!, The

1968 Fanfare color 92 mins.

Exec Prod: Joe Solomon.

Prod: Robert Poore.

Dir: Gunnar Hellstrom.

SP: Gary Crutcher.

Art Dir: Ray Markham.

Cin: William (later Vilmos) Zsigmond.

Edit: Louis Lombardo.

Mus: Stu Phillips.

Cast: Jack Lord, Susan Strasberg, Collin Wilcox, Tisha Sterling. T.C. Jones, Mort Mills.

psy-H (father has lived for years disguised as mother; sadism; torture; family of psychotics)

Ref: MFB Nov '69 p242.

Nan in Fairyland

1912 British, Cricks & Martin sil 1250 ft.

Dir: Edwin J. Collins.

Cast: Edwin J. Collins.

F-dream (little girl dreams she is in fairyland, meets the Imp of Mischief & Puck)

Ref: BFI cat p94; Gifford/ BFC 03721.

Nan of the North

1912-22 Arrow Film Corp sil serial 15 parts 30 reels.

Prod: Ben Wilson.

Dir: Duke Worne.

Story: Karl Coolidge.

Cast: Ann (Anna?) Little, Leonard Clapham, Joseph W. Girard, Hal Wilson, Howard Crampton, J. Morris Foster, Edith Stoyart.

SF (substance "Titano" from meteorite is the source of limitless energy)

Ref: LC; CNW 100-01, 229.

Nanbanji no Semushi-Otoko

(Return to Manhood --ad.t.)

1957 Japanese, Daiei 78 mins.

Prod: Atsushi Sakai.

Dir: Torajiro Sato.

Story: Katsumi Mizoguchi.

SP: Akira Fushimi.

Cin: Hiroshi Imai.

Cast: Achako Hanabishi, Naritoshi Hayashi, Shunji Sakai, Kyu Sazanka, Tamao Nakamura.

F-com (warrior is drunkard; at last, sake makes him into deformed hunchback & he becomes bell-ringer; when he kills his enemy he regains his normal shape)

Ref: FEFN 26 July '57.

Lampoon of: Hunchback of Notre Dame, The.

Nand Kishore

1951 Indian, M&T Films 154 mins.

Prod & Dir: Vasant Joglekar.

Story: S.A. Shukla.

SP & Songs: Narendra Sharma.

Art Dir: Dalvi & Sant Singh.

Cin: Bal M. Joglekar.

Cast: Nalini Jaywant, Lalita Pawar, Baburao Pendharkar, Durga Khote, Samati Gupte, Sulochana, Surendra Kumar, Sadhana Bose.

myth-F

Ref: Indian MPA '53 p45-46.

Nand Kumar

1937 (1938) Indian, Jaishree 113 mins.

Dir: Keshavrao Dhaiber.

SP: M.G. Rangnekar.

Cin: S.K. Pai.

Edit: M.T. Limaye.

Mus: G.P. Kapur.

Cast: Mrs. Durga Khote, Govindrao Tembe, Anant Marathe, Govind Kurvalikar, Keshavrao Dhaiber, Jaishree Kamulkar.

myth-F (childhood stories of Krishna)

Ref: Dipali 15 April '38 p26; Filmindia Feb '38 p39-40; MovPicM May '38.

Based on part of "Mahabharat."

Nankai no Dai Ketto

See: Godzilla vs. the Sea Monster (1966).

Nankai no Daikaiju

See: Yog → Monster from Space (1970).

Nap es a Hold el Rablasa, A

See: Kidnapping of the Sun and the Moon, The (1969).

Naplo

n.d. Hungarian, Pannonia ani sh.

F

Ref: MTVM Nov '68 p20A.

Nara Narayan

● 1937 Indian, Wadia 122 mins.

Dir: Rangarao & Ramji.

Cin: Master & Mahomed.

Cast: Pulipath, Venkateswarlu, Tilakam, Addanki, Sreerama Murty.

Ref: Indian Cin YB '38.

● 1939 Indian, Radha.

Dir: Jyotish Banerjee.

Cin: Jotin Das.

Mus: K.C. De, Mrinal Ghose, & Dhiren Das.

Cast: Dhiraj Bhattacharya, Reunka Roy, Rani Bala, Sheila Halder, Roby Jahar, Jahar Ganguly, Ahindra Chowdhury.

Ref: 12 May '39 p28, 7 July '39, etc.

myth-F (story of Krishna)

Narad Muni

1949 Indian (in Hindi), Diljit Chitra 123 mins.

Prod: Chotubhai Punatar.

Dir: Raman B. Desai.

Story: Pt. Indra.

Art Dir: S.A. Wahab.

Cin: D.C. Mehta.

Edit: S.M. Wast.

Mus Dir: Bulo C. Rani.

Cast: Babu Raje, Lata, Poornima, Devendra, Urmilla, Kusum Thakkar, Shanti Madhok.

myth-F

Ref: Indian MPA '53 p 14.

Narad-Naradi

1941 Indian, Saraswati.

Dir: Dadasaheb Torney.

SP: S.A. Shukla.

Mus: Sadashiv Nevrekar.

Cast: Dinkar, Kamanna, Kusum, Deshpande, Kamla Barodekar, Ved Pathak.

myth-F-mus-com (Saint Narad decides to marry & raise a family)

Ref: Filmindia May '41 p34 ad.

Narcissus

1956 Gryphon 16mm 48 mins.

Dir, SP, Cin, Edit: Ben Moore & Willard Maas.

Mus: Alan Hovhaness.

exp-F (Narcissus looks in mirrors instead of a stream)

Ref: C-16 p24; FMC 5:223.

Narcissus

1966? Soviet, Gruziafilm (Sovexportfilm) color ani 20 mins.

Dir: Vaktang Bakhtadze.

Story: N. Benashvili & V. Bakhtadze.

Ani: I. Samsonadze & A. Nersesov.

myth-F (Narcissus loved by the nymph Echo; goddess Aphrodite causes him to fall in love with himself; gazes at self in river, turned into flower)

Ref: Sovexportfilm cat 3:113.

Based on the Greek myth.

Narcissus Echo

196? French color computer ani sh.

Dir: Peter Foldes.

exp-F (the Narcissus legend in computer animation)

Ref: ASIFA 7.

Nargis

1966? Soviet, Soyuzmultfilm (Sovexportfilm) color ani 20 mins.

Dir: V. Polkovnikov.

Story: Vitkovich & N. Klado.

Ani: A. Volkov.

F (flowers turn into maidens; one loves the leader of bees, who is impersonated by the Master of Storms)

Ref: Sovexportfilm cat 3:112.

Based on fairy tale "Song of Kashmir" by Sharaf Rashidov.

Narkose

(Narcosis)

1929 German, G.P. sil.

Dir: Alfred Abel.

Sc: Béla Balázs.

Art Dir: Julius von Borsody & Willy Brummer.

Cin: Günther Krampf.

SpFX: Eugen Schüfftan.

Cast: Renée Héribel, Alfred Abel, Karl Platen, Jack Trevor, Fritz Alberti, Gustav Rickelt.

sur-F-seq (expressionistic sequence)

Ref: Eisner p31, 106, 108, 352; DdC III:34, I:300.

Based on a story by Stefan Zweig.

Narsi Bhagat

1940 Indian, Prakash.

Dir: Vijay Bhatt.

Story: M.G. Dave.

Cast: Vishnupant Pagnis, Durga Khote, Pande, Ram Marathe, Vimla Vashishta, Amir Karnataki.

myth-F

Ref: Dipali 12 July '40 p23.

Narthanasala
1963 Indian, Rajam.
Dir: Kameswara Rao.
SP: Samudrala Sr.
Cast: N.T. Rama Rao, Savithri, S.V. Ranga Rao.
myth-F
Ref: Movieland 29 March '63.

Narukami
See: Bijo to Kairyu (1955).

Nashörner, Die
See: Rhinoceros (1963).

Nasibani Devi
See: Goddess of Luck (1927).

Natale Che Quasi No Fui, Il
See: Christmas That Almost Wasn't, The (1965).

Nathaniel Hawthorne's Twice Told Tales
See: Twice Told Tales (1963).

Nation's Peril, The
1915 Lubin 5 reels (3300 ft.).
Dir: George Terwilliger.
Sc: G. Terwilliger & Harry Chandlee.
Cast: Earle Metcalfe, Ormi Hawley, William H. Turner.
soc-SF (foreign power invades US in 1918; "air torpedo invention" --Willis)
Ref: LC; MPW 26:1675.

Nature Fakirs
1907 Kalem sil 480 ft.
SF-com (giant chicken-like monster, a "Dingbat", attacks a man)
Ref: MPW '07 p472, 475.

Nature Girls on the Moon
(Nudes on the Moon; Girls on the Moon --ad.ts.)
1960 Jer & Luna.
sex-SF (telepathic nudists inhabit the Moon)
Ref: MMF 8:31.

Nature in the Wrong
(Tarzan in the Wrong --s.t.)
1933 Roach (MGM) 2 reels.
Prod: Hal Roach.
Edit: William Terhune.
Cast: Charley Chase, Muriel Evans, Carlton Griffin, Nora Cecil, Mary Gordon.
bor-F-com-sat (Charley discovers he is a descendant of Tarzan)
Ref: Maltin/GMS p58, 60, 64; LC; Essoe/Tarzan p208.
See also: Charley Chase Comedy; Tarzan.

Nature's Mistakes
See: Freaks (1931).

Nature's Work Shop
1933 U ani sh.
Dir & Ani: Walter Lantz & William Nolan.
F-com
Ref: LC.
See also: Pooch the Pup (1932-33).

Naufragos de la Calle de la Providencia, Los
See: Exterminating Angel,The (1963).

Naughty
1927 Chadwick Pictures (First Division Distributors) sil 4667 ft.
Pres: I.E. Chadwick.
Dir & Sc: Hampton Del Ruth.
Titles: Jean La'Ple.
Cin: Ernest Miller.
Cast: Pauline Garon, Johnny Harron, Walter Hiers.
cont.

Naughty cont.
com; F-seq (at beginning of film fortune-teller makes predictions which come true)
Ref: AFI F2.3781 p537.

Naughty Ball, The
See: Flicek the Ball (1956).

Naughty But Mice
1939 Vitaphone (WB) color? ani 1 reel.
Prod: Leon Schlesinger.
Dir: Chuck (Charles M.) Jones.
Story: Richard Hogan.
Ani: Phil Monroe.
Mus Dir: Carl W. Stalling.
Voices: Mel Blanc.
F-com
Ref: LC.

Naughty Dr. Jekyll
(Dirty Dr. Jekyll --alt.t?)
1973?
sex-SF-H
Ref: Chicago newspaper ad.
Based on characters created by Robert Louis Stevenson.
See also: Dr. Jekyll and Mr. Hyde.

Naughty Duck, The
1950? Rumanian ani sh.
Dir: Ion Popescu Gopo.
F
Ref: Ani/Cin p 144, 174.

Naughty Girl
1934 Indian, Ranjit.
Dir & SP: Chandulal Shah.
Cast: Gohar, Ghory, Dixit.
bor-F (hypnosis)
Ref: Dipali 11 Jan '35.

Naughty Kitten, The
1953? Soviet color ani 11 mins.
Dir: Mstislav Paschenko.
F-com
Ref: MFB March '54 p44.

Naughty Owl, The
See: Uhuka (1969).

Nav Jawan
1937 Indian, Wadia 136 mins.
Dir: Aspi.
Cast: Harishchandra.
hist-H (deformed hunchback)
Ref: Lighthouse 13 March '37.
Based on novel "Notre Dame de Paris" by Victor Hugo.
See also: Hunchback of Notre Dame, The.

Nav-Jeevan
1939 Indian, Bombay Talkies.
Dir: Franz Osten.
SP: S. Bannerjee & J.S. Casshyap.
Cin: R.D. Pareenja.
Cast: Hansa, Rama Shukul, V.H. Desai, Saroj Borkar, Mumtaz Ali.
F (man dreams he is back in ancient times, awakes a new man)
Ref: Filmindia May '39 p90.
Based on novel by Munshi Prem Chand.
See also: Navjivan (1935).

Navaho Rain Chant
1971 UCLA color 16mm ani sh.
Dir: Susan Dyal.
F
Ref: Transit-Mix June '71.

Nave de los Monstruos, La
(The Ship of the Monsters)
1960 Mexican, Sotomayor (CoI).
Prod: Jesús Sotomajor.
Dir: Rogelio A. Gonzales.
Story: José Unsain.
SP: Fredo Varela Jr.
Art Dir: Javier Torres Torna.
Makeup: Rosa Guerrero.
Cin: Raul Solares.
SpFX: Juan Muñoz Ravelo.
Edit: Carlos Savage.
Cast: Lalo Gonzalez, Ana Bertha Lepe, Lorena Velaquez, Consuelo Frank, Manuel Alvarado.
SF-H-com (spaceship with robot, spider creature, many other monsters; heat ray)
Ref: FM 17:16, 30; Scogamillo.

Navigation by Wireless
1912 Danube sil 360 ft.
bor-SF (invention of wireless operated vehicles)
Ref: Bios 1 Feb '12.

Navjivan
1935 Indian, Ajanta.
Cast: Miss Nangis, W. Khan, Bai Munni Bai, Ameena, Bhudo Advani, Parashar.
F (man dreams he is back in ancient times)
Ref: MovPicM July '35 p54.
Based on a novel by Munshi Prem Chand.
See also: Nav-Jeevan (1939).

Navy vs. the Night Monsters, The
(Monsters of the Night --Brit.t.; The Night Crawlers --s.t.)
1966 Standard Club of California (Realart) color 90 mins (87 mins).
Prod: George Edwards.
Dir & SP: Michael Hoey.
Art Dir: Paul Sylos.
Makeup: Harry Thomas.
Cin: Stanley Cortez.
SpFX: Edwin Tillman.
Edit: George White.
Mus: Gordon Zahler.
Cast: Mamie Van Doren, Anthony Eisley, Pamela Mason, Bill Gray, Bobby Van, Walter Sande, Philip Terry, Russ Bender.
SF-H (trees from hot area of South Pole walk & kill people on isolated island)
Ref: MFB May '67 p78; FF '66 p315; Vw 23 Nov '66.
Based on novel "Monster from Earth's End" by Murray Leinster.

Ne Bougeons Plus
See: Don't Move (1900).

Ne Jouez Pas avec les Martians
(Don't Play with Martians, Don't Mess with the Martians; Comme Mars en Careme, Mars en Careme: Mars at Easter; Regular as Clockwork --ad.t?)
1967 (1968) French, Fildebroc & UA color 85 mins.
Dir & Mus: Henri Lanoe.
SP: H. Lanoe & Johanne Harwood.
Cin: Rene Matchin.
Cast: Jean Rochefort, Macha Meril, Andre Vallardy, Haydee Politoff, Pierre Dac.
SF-com (reporter fakes Martian landing around birth of sextuplets; aliens, not Martians, arrive & claim children; prehistoric monster)
Ref: Vw 10 April '68, 8 May '68 p 121, 24 July '68; MTVM April '67.
Based on novel "Les Sextuplets de Locqmaria" by Michel Labry.

Neal of the Navy
1915 Pathé (Balboa) serial 14 parts 28 reels.
Dir: W.M. Harvey.
Cast: Lillian Lorraine, William Courtleigh Jr., Ed Brady, Henry Stanley, William Conklin.
bor-F-H (apeman slave cuts rope ladder with his teeth)
Ref: CNW p33, 164; LC; MPW 18 Sept '15; MPN 4 Sept '15.

Neanderthal Man, The
1952 (1953) Wisberg-Pollexfen Prods (UA) 77 mins.
Prod & SP: Aubrey Wisberg & Jack Pollexfen.
Dir: E.A. DuPont.
Art Dir: Walter Koestler.
Cin: Stanley Cortez.
SpFX: Jack Rabin & others.
Edit: Fred Feitshans.
Mus: Albert Glasser.
Cast: Robert Shayne, Richard Crane, Doris Merric, Joyce Terry, Robert Long, Dick Rich.
SF-H (scientist causes cat to revert to saber-tooth cat himself to murderous Neanderthal man)
Ref: Vd 3 June '53; MFB Jan '54 p 10; HR 3 June '53.

Near-Sighted Mister Magoo, The
See: Mister Magoo (1949-).

Neat Job, The
(comic book story by W.M. Gaines & A.B. Feldstein)
See: Vault of Horror, The (1972).

Neath the Bababa Tree
1931 Harman-Ising (WB) ani sh.
Ani: Irving A. Jacoby.
Mus: Philip Scheib.
F
Ref: Ani chart L31; LC.
Based on a story by Dr. Seuss.

Nebelmorder, Der
(The Fog Murderer)
1964 W. German, Waldemar-Schweitzer, Nora 90 mins.
Dir: Eugen York.
SP: Walter Forster & Per Schwenzen.
Cin: Gunther Haase.
Mus: Herbert Jadrzyk.
Cast: Hansjorg Felmy, Ingmar Zeisberg, Ralph Persson, Elke Arendt.
myst; bor-H (fiendish killer)
Ref: German Pictures '63-64 p 158.

Nebo Zowet
(The Heavens Call)
1959 Soviet, Dovzhenko color 90 mins.
Dir: Alexandr Kozyr (Kosyr) & M. Karinkov.
SP: A. Sazanov & J. Pomieszczykov.
Cin: Nikolai Kulchitski.
Cast: A. Szworin (Shvorin), L. Lobanov (Lobandov), Ivan Pereverzev, T. Litvienenko.
SF (Soviets rescue stranded US expedition to Mars)
Ref: Gasca; SM 4:8; Scognamillo.
See also Battle Beyond the Sun (1963), US film which used much footage from Nebo Zowet.

Nebula
1968? Amateur (Center Cinema) 16mm? color 7 mins.
Made by: Robert Frerck.
exp-abs-F
Ref: CCC 2:9.

Nebula 2

1969 Amateur (Center Cinema) 16mm? color 7.5 mins.

Made by: Robert Frerck.

exp-abs-F

Ref: CCC 2:9.

Necklace of Rameses, The

1914 Edison sil 3000 ft.

Dir: Charles Brabin.

Sc: Charles Vernon.

Cast: Robert Brower, Gertrude Braun, Marc MacDermott, William Betchell, Charles Vernon, Miriam Nesbitt, Marjorie Ellison, Rex Hitchcock.

bor-F (necklace on body of Rameses' daughter is cursed if it is removed from her body; in modern times it is stolen)

Ref: EK 15 Jan '14 p9; LC; Bios 2 April '14.

Necklace of the Dead

1910 Danish, Nordisk sil 1020 ft.

H (premature burial)

Ref: Bios 1 Dec '10.

Necromancer, The

1903 Biograph sil 153 ft.

F (necromancer in trance paid to conjure up women)

Ref: Niver 69-70; LC.

Necromancers, The

(novel by H. Benson)

See: Spellbound (1940).

Necromancy

(The Toy Factory --s.t.; A Life for a Life --ad.t.)

1971 Zenith Int'l (Cinerama) color 82 mins.

Exec Prod: Sidney L. Caplan & Robert J. Stone.

Prod, Dir, SP: Bert I. Gordon.

Art Dir: Frank Sylos.

Cin: Winton Hoch.

SpFX: William Vanderbyl.

Edit: John Woelz.

Mus: Fred Karger.

Cast: Orson Welles, Pamela Franklin, Lee Purcell, Michael Ontkean, Harvey Jason, Lisa James, Sue Bernard, Terry Quinn.

F-H (Welles tries to use Franklin to bring his dead son back to life; occult rituals; at end, it was all a dream but begins occurring in life)

Ref: Vw 11 Oct '72 p 18; BO 25 Oct '71 p2 ad.

Necromancy

See: Kaibyo Yonaki Numa (1957).

Necronomicon

See: Succubus (1968).

Necrophagus

(El Descuartizador de Binbrook: The Dismemberer of Binbrook)

1971? Spanish, Int'l Films color scope 87 mins.

Prod: Tony Recorder.

Dir & SP: Miguel Madrid (Michael Skaife).

Art Dir: Barbard Hyde.

Cin: Alfonso Nieva.

SpFX: Antonio Molina.

Edit: María Luisa Soriano.

Mus: Alfonso Santisteben.

Cast: Bill Curran, Francisco (Frank) Braña, Beatriz Lacy, Victor Israel, Catherine Ellison, Yocasta Grey, J.R. Clark, Marisa Shiero.

Necrophagus cont.

SF-H (man's scientist brother becomes hairy monster, mixture of animal, mineral & vegetable, & has to be buried underground & fed fresh corpse daily)

Ref: Vw 27 Oct '71; SpCin '72 p 168-69.

Necropolis

1970 Italian, Cosmoseion & Q Prods color 120 mins.

Prod: Gianni Barcelloni & Alan Power.

Dir & SP: Franco Brocani.

Art Dir: Peter Steifel.

Cin: Ivan Stoinov.

SpFX: Alfonso Gola.

Edit: M. Ludovica Barrani.

Mus: Gavin Bryars.

Cast: Viva Auder, Tina Aumont, Carmelo Bene, Pierre Clémenti, B. Corazzari, Paul Jabara.

sur-F (plotless "statement about life;" main characters are Frankenstein's Monster, Attila the Hun, Montezuma, Countess Elizabeth Bathory, the Devil, and King Kong)

Ref: MFB March '71 p54; Vw 9 Dec '70; S&S Spring '71 p v.

See also: Countess Dracula (1970); Daughters of Darkness (1970); Frankenstein; King Kong (1933).

Nedokonceny Weekend

(Unfinished Weekend)

1971? Czech color ani sh.

Dir: Vaclav Bedrich.

F-com (spoof of horror movies)

Ref: Vw 30 June '71.

Neel Kamal

1968 Indian.

F-H (ghost returns after several hundred years to haunt reincarnation of his lover)

Ref: Shankar's Weekly 13 Oct '68.

Neelamali Thirudan

(Bandit of the Blue Mountain)

1957 Indian (in Tamil), Devar 180 mins.

Dir: Tirumugam.

Cast: Kannamba, Ranjan, Anjali, E.V. Saroja, Veerappa.

F (woman lost in woods for years rescued by her son & his magic horse & dog)

Ref: FEFN 18 Oct '57 p 17.

Neighbors

1936 Screen Gems (Col & IBM) color ani sh.

Dir: Charles B. Mintz.

F

Ref: F/A p627; LC; Fortune 13:26, May '36.

Neighbors

1952 Canadian, NFB color pixilation 10 mins.

Dir: Norman McLaren.

Cin: Wolf Koenig.

Cast: Grant Munro, Jean Paul Ladouceur.

exp-F-H-alleg (two neighbors fight over flower, turn into monsters while fighting)

Ref: Ani/Cin p70-71; C-16 p24; CFS cat.

Neither the Sea nor the Sand

1972 British, Tigon & Portland color 94 mins.

Exec Prod: Tony Tenser & Peter J. Thompson.

Prod: Jack Smith & Peter Fetterman.

Dir: Fred Burnley.

Neither the Sea nor the Sand cont.

SP: Gordon Honeycombe & Rosemary Davies.

Art Dir: Michael Bastow.

Cin: David Muri.

Edit: Norman Wanstall.

Mus: Nahum Heiman.

Cast: Susan Hampshire, Michael Petrovitch, Frank Finlay, Michael Craze, Jack Lambert, David Garth.

F-H (girl's love keeps dead lover alive & walking until he begins to rot)

Ref: MFB Dec '72 p255.

Based on the novel by Gordon Honeycombe.

Nel Paese dei Sogni

See: In Dreamland (1906).

Nel Paese del'Oro

See: In the Land of the Gold Mines (1908).

Nel Regno dei Sogni

See: In the Kingdom of Dreams (n.d.).

Nella Stretta Morsa del Ragno

(In the Grip of the Spider; E Venne l'Alba. . .Ma Tinta Dirosso: And Comes the Dawn . . .But Colored Red --e.t.; Dracula im Schloss des Schreckens: Dracula in the Castle of Terror --German t.)

1971 Italian/French/W. German color scope.

Prod: Giovanni Addessi.

Dir: Antonio Margheriti (Anthony Dawson).

SP: A. Margheriti & G. Addessi.

Cin: Sandro Mancori.

Mus: Riz Ortolani.

Cast: Anthony Franciosa, Michele Mercier, Karin Field, Klaus Kinski, Paolo Goslino, Irinia Maleva.

F-H (Poe challenges man to stay overnight in haunted castle; blood-sucking ghosts haunt the castle)

Ref: D. Klemensen; Soren; CineF 2:3:47.

Based on "Dance Macabre" by Edgar Allan Poe.

Remake of: Castle of Blood (1964).

Nelly's Folly

1961 WB color ani 7 mins.

Prod & Dir: Chuck Jones.

F-com (adventures of Nelly the Giraffe)

Ref: LC; Acad nom.

Neman i Vi

See: Monster and I, The (1964).

Nemesis

See: Eva and the Grasshopper (1927).

Neo-Impressionist Painter, The

(Le Peintre Neo-Impressioniste)

1910 French sil ani sh.

Dir: Emile Cohl.

F

Ref: Sadoul p445; Filmlex p 1370; MMA '63 p20.

Neovy Knovennyi Match

(An Unusual Match)

1955 Soviet, Soyuzmultfilm color ani 11 mins.

Dir: M. Paschenko & B. Dezhkin.

SP: M. Paschenko.

Mus: Aram Katchaturian (Khachaturian).

F (toys play soccer)

Ref: MFB April '56 p52.

Nepovodeny Panacek

(The Badly-Made Puppet; The Misfit --a.t.)

1951 Czech color ani puppet & live sh.

Dir: Hermina Tyrlova & K.M. Wallo.

SP: H. Tyrlova & L. Foman.

Mus: Zdenek Liska.

F

Ref: Montevideo '56; FEFN July '61 p 13.

Neptune and Amphitrite

(Neptune et Amphitrite)

1899 French, Star sil 65 ft.

Made by: Georges Méliès.

F

Ref: Sadoul/M, GM Mage 200.

Neptune Factor — An Undersea Odyssey, The

(Conquest of the Deeps --e.t.)

1973 Canadian, Quadrant & Bellevue-Pathé (20th Fox) color 98 mins.

Exec Prod: David M. Perlmutter & Harold Greenberg.

Prod: Sanford Howard.

Dir: Daniel Petrie.

SP Jack DeWitt (John T. Kelley?).

Prod Design: Dennis Lynton Clark & Jack McAdam.

Underwater Dir: Paul Stader.

Cin: Harry Makin.

Underwater Cin: Lamar Boren & Paul Herberman.

SpFX: Film Opticals of Canada & Lee Howard.

Edit: Stan Cole.

Mus: William McCauley.

Cast: Ben Gazzara, Yvette Mimieux, Walter Pidgeon, Ernest Borgnine, Chris Wiggins, Donnelly Rhodes, Ed McGibbon, Michael J. Reynolds.

SF (searching for lost underwater lab, submarine finds it in grotto full of giant sea creatures)

Ref: 20th-Fox notes; Vw 23 May '73; HR 8 Dec '72.

Neptune's Daughter

1912 Essanay sil 1000 ft.

Cast: Francis X. Bushman, Martha Russell, Harry Cashman, Ruth Stonehouse, William Walters.

F (Undine, daughter of Neptune, weds man & cannot return to the sea)

Ref: MPW 13:1196, 1276, 1284.

See also: Undine.

Neptune's Daughter

1914 Imp (U) sil 7 reels.

Dir: Herbert Brenon.

Sc: Leslie T. Peacocke.

Cast: Annette Kellermann, Leah Baird, William E. Shay, Herbert Brenon, Katherine Lee, William Welsh.

F

Ref: MPW 20:796-97, 1452; RAF p214, 279; F/A p424.

Neptune's Daughters

1903 Biograph sil 25 ft.

F (ghosts on ships)

Ref: LC; Niver 327.

Nestašni Robot

(The Playful Robot)

1956 Yugoslavian, Zagreb color ani 7.6 mins.

Dir: Andre Lušičić.

Dir: Dusan Vukotić.

Design: Aleksandar Marks & Boris Kolar.

---

cont.   cont.   cont.

Nestašni Robot cont.

Ani: Vladimir Jutriša & Vjekoslav Kostanjšek.

Bg: Zlatko Bourek.

Mus: Aleksandar Bubanović.

SF-com (2 baby robots created)

Ref: Z/Zagreb p 13, 53.

See also: Ludo Srce (1959).

Note: first cartoon from Zagreb studios.

Nest of Spies

See: Nido de Espias (1967).

Net, The

(novel by J. Pudney)

See: Project M-7 (1953).

Neutron

Black-masked Mexican wrestler.

See: Ladron de Cadaveres (1957); Neutron Against the Death Robots (1961); Neutron and the Black Mask (1961); Neutron Battles the Karate Assassins (1962?); Neutron vs. the Maniac (1962); Neutron vs. the Amazing Dr. Caronte (1963); Neutron Traps the Invisible Killers (1964).

Neutron Against the Death Robots

(Los Automatas de la Muerte: The Robots of Death)

1961 (1962) Mexican, Corsa (Clasa-Mohme & Azteca; Commonwealth-United TV) 5 reels.

Prod: Luis Garcia De Leon.

Dir & SP: Frederico Curiel.

Story: Alfredo Ruanova.

Cin: Fernando Colin.

Edit: J. Juan Munguia.

Mus: Enrico Cabiati.

Cast: Wolf Ruvinskis, Rosita Arenas, Julio Aleman, Armando Silvestre, Beto El Boticario.

SF-H (monster brain created from brains of 3 scientist lives on blood; human robots; neutron bomb)

Ref: Azteca files; PS; FDY'63.

See also: Neutron.

Neutron and the Black Mask

(Neutron, el Enmascarado Negro: Black-Masked Neutron)

1961 (1962) Mexican (Clasa-Mohme) 5 reels.

Prod: Luis Garcia De Leon.

Dir & SP: Federico Curiel.

Story: Alfredo Ruanova.

Cin: Fernando Colin.

Edit: J. Juan Munguia.

Mus: Enrico Cabiati.

Cast: Wolf Ruvinskis, Rosita Arenas, Julio Aleman, Armando Silvestre, Beto El Boticario.

SF-H (world's deadliest weapon)

Ref: FDY '63; BIB's.

See also: Neutron.

Neutron and the Cosmic Bomb

See: Neutron vs. the Maniac (1962).

Neutron Battles the Karate Assassins

1962? Mexican, TEC (Commonwealth-United TV) 79 mins.

Cast: Wolf Ruvinskis.

SF

Ref: BIB's (Willis).

See also: Neutron.

Neutron contra el Doctor Caronte

See: Neutron vs. the Amazing Dr. Caronte (1963).

Neutron, el Enmascarado Negro

See: Neutron and the Black Mask (1961).

Neutron Traps the Invisible Killers

1964 Mexican, TEC (Commonwealth-United TV) 78 mins.

SF

Ref: BIB's (Willis).

See also: Neutron.

Neutron vs. the Death Robots

See: Neutron Against the Death Robots (1961).

Neutron vs. the Maniac

(Neutron and the Cosmic Bomb --alt.t?)

1961 Mexican, TEC (Commonwealth-United TV) 81 mins.

Cast: Wolf Ruvinski.

SF (Neutron vs. Dr. Caronte for control of cosmic bomb)

Ref: BIB's (Willis).

See also: Neutron.

Neutron vs. the Amazing Dr. Caronte

(Neutron contra el Doctor Caronte)

1963 (1964) Mexican (Clasa-Mohme; Commonwealth-United TV).

Cast: Julio Aleman, Rosita Arenas, Wolf Ruvinskis, Armando Silvestre, Beto El Boticario.

SF-H

Ref: BIB's; CoF 10:45; PS; FDY '64.

See also: Neutron.

Never Bet the Devil Your Head

(short story by E.A. Poe)

See: Spirits of the Dead (1967).

Never Kick a Woman

1936 Par ani 1 reel.

Prod: Max Fleischer.

Dir: Dave Fleischer.

Ani: Seymour Kneitel & Roland Crandall.

F-com

Ref: LC; PopCar.

See also: Popeye the Sailor (1935-57).

Neverwhere

1968 Amateur 16mm color ani & live sh.

Prod & Ani: Richard Corben.

Dir: Michael Wadell.

F (spark shows man how to make a machine which makes him into a cartoon swordsman; fights monsters & wizard, wins princess)

Ref: SF Times 458.

Nevsky Prospect

(story by N. Gogol)

See: Overcoat, The (1926).

Nevesta

(The Bride)

1971? Yugoslavian, Zagreb (?) color ani sh.

Dir: Borislav Sajtinac.

F (witch lays egg, flies off on swan that hatches from it; apparitions)

Ref: Vw 30 June '71.

New Adam and Eve, The

1915 Gaum (Mutual) sil 3 reels.

Dir: Richard Garrick.

Cast: Groce Valentine, Charles Richmond, Mathilde Baring, Edward Craske, Elaine Ivans.

F-dream (disembodied souls wander hand in hand)

Ref: MPW 26:926, 1161, 1313, 1378.

Based on the story by Nathaniel Hawthorne.

New Adventures of Baron Münchausen, The

1915 British, Kent sil 995 ft.

Dir: F. Mai in Thornton.

F-com (Münchausen's war adventures)

Ref: Gifford/BFC 05703.

Based on character chronicled by R.E. Raspe.

New Adventures of Batman and Robin

See: Batman and Robin (1949).

New Adventures of Dr. Fu Manchu

See: Return of Dr. Fu Manchu, The (1930).

New Adventures of Tarzan, The

(Tarzan in Guatemala --s.t.; Tarzan and the Lost Goddess -s.t.)

1935 Burroughs' Tarzan Enterprises (Rep) serial 12 parts 24 reels.
Also released as 72 minute feature, rereleased in 1938 as Tarzan and the Green Goddess.
Filmed in Guatemala.

Prod: George W. Stout, Ben S. Cohen, Ashton Dearholt, & Edgar Rice Burroughs.

Dir: Edward Kull & Wilber F. McGaugh.

Adapt: Charles F. Royal & Edwin H. Blum.

SP: C.F. Royal.

Cin: E. Kull & Ernest F. Smith.

cont.

New Adventures of Tarzan cont.

Edit: Edward Schroeder & Harold Minter.

Cast: Herman Brix (later Bruce Bennett), Ula Holt, Frank Baker, Dale Walsh, Ashton Dearholt.

bor-F (Tarzan comes to South America, becomes involved with spies & secret formula for new explosive)

Ref: Vw 16 Oct '35, June '38; FD 21 May '35, 16 Oct '35; HR 26 March '35; Essoe/Tarzan p87-92.

Based on a screen treatment by Edgar Rice Burroughs.

See also: Tarzan of the Apes (1917).

New Aladdin, A

1912 British, Hepworth sil 500 ft.

Dir: Frank Wilson (?).

F-dream ("tramp finds lamp and dreams it is Aladdin's")

Ref: Gifford/BFC 03836.

See also: Aladdin.

New Creature, A

See: Nueva Criatura, Una (1971).

New Death Penalty, A

(La Nouvelle Peine de Mort)

1907 French, Star sil 525 ft (400 ft).

Made by: Georges Méliès.

F

Ref: LC; Sadoul/M, GM Mage 951-55.

New Exploits of Elaine, The

1915 Whartons (Pathé) sil serial 10 parts 20 reels.

Prod: Theodore & Leopold Wharton.

Dir: George B. Seitz.

Cast: Pearl White, Arnold Daly, Edwin Arden, Creighton Hale.

SF (ultra-powerful "Trodite")

Ref: Stringham; CNW p28, 164; LC; MPW 24:344, 986, 1340.

See also: Exploits of Elaine, The (1914-15).

New Gulliver, The

1935 Soviet, Mosfilm (Serlin-Burstyn) ani puppet & live 77 mins.

Dir: Alexander Ptushko.

cont.

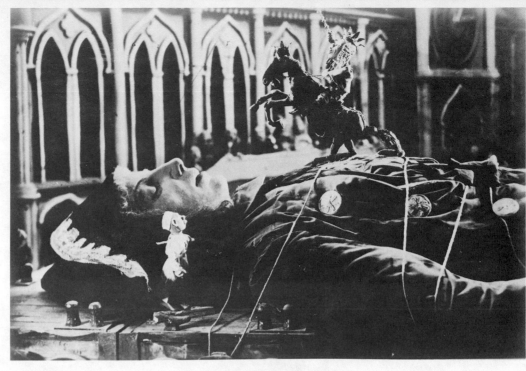

The New Gulliver (1935) Soviet

New Gulliver cont.

SP: Grigori Roshal & A. Ptushko.

Puppets Designed by: Sarra Mokel.

Cin: Alex Renkov.

Mus: Lev Schwartz.

Cast: V. Konstantinov.

F -sat (boy dreams of the land of Lilliput; workers revolt against monarchy; parodies of crooners & jazz groups, etc.)

Ref: HR 12 Oct '35; LAT 5 March '46; Ani/Cin p 147; FD 29 Oct '35; MPH 14 Oct '44.

Based on novel "Gulliver's Travels" by Jonathan Swift.

See also: Gulliver's Travels.

New Invisible Man, The

(El Hombre Que Logro Ser Invisible: The Man Who Benefits by Being Invisible; Invisible Man in Mexico --Brit.t.; H.G. Wells' New Invisible Man -- ad.t.)

1957 (1966?) Mexican, Calderon SA (Screen Gems) 94 mins (89 mins).

Prod: Guillermo Calderon Stell.

Dir: Alfredo Crevena.

SP: Alfredo Salazar.

Cin: Raúl Martinez Solares.

Mus: A.D. Conde.

Cast: Arturo de Cordova, Ana Luisa Peluffo, Augusto Benedico, Raul Meraz.

SF (drug makes hunted man invisible, but drives him mad)

Ref: MFB March '62 p40; Gasca; MMF 2:45; TVG.

See also: Invisible Man, The (1933).

New Joke with Old Iron, A

See: Gluma Nova cu Fier Vechi (1965).

New Jonah, The

1909? French, Pathé sil 420 ft.

SF-H (giant scaly monster)

Ref: Bios 14 Oct '09.

New Kind of Love, A

1963 Llenroc (Par) color 110 mins.

Prod, Dir, SP: Melville Shavelson.

Art Dir: Hal Pereira & Arthur Lonergan.

Cin: Daniel Fapp.

Edit: Frank Bracht.

Mus: Leith Stevens & Erroll Garner.

Cast: Paul Newman, Joanne Woodward, Thelma Ritter, Eva Gabor, George Tobias, Marvin Kaplan, Robert Clary, Maurice Chevalier.

com; F-seq

Ref: FF '63 p238-39; MFB Nov '63 p 159-60.

New Magic

1906 French, Pathé sil 180 ft.

F (tricks)

Ref: Views 1:18:5, 9.

New Microbe, The

1912 Italian, Cines sil 420 ft.

F (germ causes weakness)

Ref: Bios 26 Dec '12.

New Mission of Judex, The

(La Nouvelle Mission de Judex)

1917 French, Gaum sil serial 12 parts.

Dir: Louis Feuillade.

Cast: Andre Brunelle, Marcel Levesque.

cont.

New Mission of Judex cont.

bor-F (super-hypnotism)

Ref: Stringham; LC; DdC II:223, III:225; CoF 9:39.

Sequel to: Judex (1916).

New Moon, The

1970 Amateur (Center Cinema) 16mm? color 9 mins.

Made by: Charles Lyman.

exp-SF (astronaut suspended in space sees world destroyed)

Ref: CCC 2:19.

New Moto(r?) Valet, The

See: Motor Valet, The (1906?).

New One-Armed Swordsman, The

1972 Hongkong, Shaw Bros color 102 mins.

Prod: Run Run Shaw.

Dir: Chang Cheh.

SP: I. Kuang.

Art Dir: Tsao Chuang-sheng.

Cin: Kung Mu-to.

Edit: Kuo Ting-hung.

Mus: Chen Yung-huang.

Cast: Li Ching, David Chiang, Ti Lung, Ku Feng, Chen Hsing, Wang Chung, Cheng Lei, Liu Kang, Wang Kuang Yu.

F-seqs (China; one-armed hero defeats villain while juggling three swords; other mystic martial arts)

Ref: MFB Aug '73 p 173.

See also: One Armed Swordsman, The (196?....).

New Pain Killer

1909 French, Gaum (Kleine) sil 370 ft.

SF-com (spray makes hero immune to pain & damage)

Ref: FI IV-19:6.

New Recruit, The

1917 Int'l Film Service sil ani 1 reel.

F-com

Ref: LC.

See also: Happy Hooligan (1917).

New Trip to the Moon

(Voyage dans la Lune)

1909 French, Pathé sil sh.

Dir: Segundo de Chomon.

SF

Ref: Gasca p21-22; DdC.

New Wizard of Oz, The

See: His Majesty the Scarecrow of Oz (1914).

New World, The

See: RoGoPaG (1962).

New Year's Eve

1964 Polish color ani sh.

Dir: Jerzy Zitzman.

F

Ref: Ani/Cin p 114, 176.

New York Calling Superdragon

See: Secret Agent Super Dragon (1966).

New York Chiama Superdrago

See: Secret Agent Super Dragon (1966).

New York Lightboard

1960 Canadian, NFB color ani sh.

Dir: Norman McLaren.

F

Ref: Ani/Cin p 174.

New York Paris en Automobile

See: Mishaps of the New York Paris Race (1908).

New York Trip

1971 Japanese color? ani 5.5 mins.

Dir: Taku Furukawa.

F

Ref: IAFF '72.

News Hound

1955 Par color ani 1 reel.

F-com

Ref: LC.

See also: Noveltoons (1945-).

Newman's Laugh-O-Grams

1920 Newman Theater ani & live sil sh.

Ani: Walt Disney.

Cast: Walt Disney.

F-com (animated political cartoons)

Ref: Hist US Ani Prog.

See also: Laugh-O-Grams (1922-23).

Newsboy's Christmas Dream, A

1913 British, Cricks sil 1940 ft.

Dir: Edwin J. Collins.

Cast: Eileen Daybell, Leo Cauty, R. Howard Cricks.

F-dream ("orphan newsboy adopted after dreaming of wizards and dragons" --Gifford)

Ref: Gifford/BFC 04360; Bios 30 Oct '13.

Next Voice You Hear, The

1950 MGM 83 mins.

Prod: Dore Schary.

Dir: William Wellman.

Art Dir: Cedric Gibbons & Eddie Imazu.

Cin: William Mellor.

Edit: John Dunning.

Mus: David Raksin.

Cast: James Whitmore, Nancy Davis, Gary Gray, Lillian Bronson, Jeff Corey.

rel-F (God talks to small town on the radio)

Ref: MFB May '51 p259; FD & Vd 7 June '50.

Based on a story by George Sumner Albee.

Nez, Le

(The Nose; Screen of Pins --ad.t?)

1963 French pin-board ani 12 mins.

Dir: Alexandre Alexeieff & Claire Parker.

F (man's nose leaves his face & he pursues it)

Ref: Collier; FQ Spring '64 p 15; FIR Feb '64 p86.

Based on story "The Nose" by N. Gogol.

See also: Nose, The (1966).

Nez au Vent

(Nose to the Wind)

1957 French, ALKAM color ani puppet 13 mins.

Dir: Ladislas Starevitch.

F

Ref: FACSEA 14.

Ni Yaki Zakana

See: Two Grilled Fish (1967?).

Nibelungen Part I

(Whom the Gods Wish to Destroy --S.E. Asia t.)

1966 W. German/Yugoslavian, CCC/Avala color scope 195 mins.

Prod: Artur Brauner.

Dir: Harald Reinl.

SP: Harald G. Petersson, H. Reinl & Ladislas Fodor.

cont.

Nibelungen cont.

Art Dir: Isabella Schlichting, Werner Schlichting, & Alfred Schulz.

Cin: Ernst W. Kalinke.

Edit: Hermann Haller.

Mus: Rolf Wilhelm.

Cast: Uwe Beyer, Maria Marlow, Rolf Henninger, Karin Dor, Siegfried Wischnewski, Herbert Lom, Mario Girotti.

F (dragons, dwarf king, walls of fire, hood of invisibility, etc.)

Ref: MFB Sept '69 p 197; Vw 12 April '67.

Based on the ancient Teutonic epic "Das Nibelungenlieb."

See also: Siegfried; Nibelunghi, I (1910); Epopea dei Nibelunghi, L' (1913); Kriemhild's Revenge (1924); Tesoro della Foresta Pietrificata, Il (1965).

Nibelgunghi, I

(The Nibelungen)

1910 Italian, Milano sil sh?

Sc: M. Bernacchi.

See also: Nibelungen (1966).

Nichiren to Moko Daishurai

(Nichiren, Man of Many Miracles)

1958 Japanese, Daiei color 137 mins.

Dir: Kunio Watanabe.

SP: K. Watanabe & Fuji Yahiro.

Cin: Takashi Watanabe.

Cast: Kazuo Hasegawa, Raizo Ichikawa, Shintaro Katsu, Shoji Umewaka.

F (Nichiren's prayers for rain are answered)

Ref: Japanese Films '59.

Nicht Mehr Fliehen

See: No More Fleeing (1955).

Nick Carter

(character created by John Corryell)

See: License to Kill (1964); Nick Carter et le Trefle Rouge (1965).

Nick Carter and the Red Club

See: Nick Carter et le Trefle Rouge (1965).

Nick Carter et le Trefle Rouge

(Nick Carter and the Red Club)

1965 French, Chaumiane & Parc Films & Film .85 mins.

Dir: Jean-Paul Savignac.

SP: J.-P. Savignac & Paul Vecchiali.

Cin: Claude Beausoleil.

Edit: Leila Biro.

Cast: Eddie Constantine, Nicole Courcel, Jeanne Valerie, Jo Dassin, Jacques Harden.

bor-SF (new nuclear weapons)

Ref: Vw 22 Dec '65.

Based on novel by Claude Rank, from character created by John R. Corryell.

Nick Carter Va Tout Casser

See: License to Kill (1964).

Nick Winter and the Somnambulist Thief

1911 French, Pathé sil 720 ft.

bor-F (girl steals under hypnosis)

Ref: Bios 24 Aug '11.

Nicko and Sicko

1963 Soviet, Georgia color
ani puppet 20.7 mins.

Dir: S. Gedevanishvili.

Story: V. Karzanidze.

F (2 people step out
of a picture)

Ref: Sovexportfilm cat 1:136.

Nido de Espias

(Nest of Spies; Il Raggio
Infernale: The Infernal Ray)

1967 Spanish/Italian, Leda/
Meteor color 106 mins.

Dir: Gianfranco Baldanello
(Frank G. Carroll).

SP: Juano Antonio Cabezas,
Jaime Comas, & Aldo Cristiani.

Art Dir: Luis Arguello.

Cin: Manuel Hernandez Sanjuan.

Mus: Gianni Ferri.

Cast: Gordon Scott, Alberto
Dalbes, Delfy (Delph) Maurenn
(Maureen?), Man Dean, Ted
Carter, Silvia Solar.

bor-SF (advanced laser beam)

Ref: SpCin '68 p54-55.

Niebezpieczenstwo

(Danger)

1963 Polish color marionettes
7 mins.
Dir: Jerzy Kotowski.

SP: Jan Czarny.

Art Dir: Adam Kilian.

Cin: Eugeniusz Ignaciuk.

Mus: Wlodzimierz Kotonski.

F (post-bomb mechanical
animals frightened by real
egg)

Ref: MMF 9:26; Collier;
Gasca p322-23.

Niece of the Vampire, The

See: Malenka (1968).

Niemandsland

See: Hell on Earth (1931).

Night. . .a Train, A

See: Soir. . .un Train, Un
(1968).

Night after Night after Night

1969 British, Dudley Birch
Films color 88 mins.

Prod: James Mellor.

Dir: Lewis J. Force.

SP: Dail Ambler.

Art Dir: Wilfred Arnold.

Cin: Douglas Hill.

Edit: John Rushton.

Cast: Jack May, Justine
Lord, Gilbert Wynne, Linda
Marlowe, Terry Scully,
Donald Sumpter.

psy-H (psychotic killer
of women)

Ref: MFB April '70 p82-83.

Night Beauties

See: Beauties of the Night,
The (1952).

Night Before Christmas, The

● 1905 Edison sil ani
miniatures & live 800
ft.
Dir: Edwin S. Porter.

Ref: LC; FIR Dec '61 p605;
Sadoul 467.

● 1933 WD ani 1 reel.

Prod: Walt Disney.

Ref: FIR Dec '61 p604-
05; LC; Blum 74.

F (Santa Claus brings
gifts to family aboard
his flying sleigh)

Based on poem "A Visit
from St. Nicholas"
by Clement Clarke
Moore.

See also: Christmas
Visitor, The (1958).

Night Before Christmas, The

1941 MGM color ani
787 ft.

F-com

Ref: LC; Acad nom.

See also: Tom and Jerry
(1940-).

Night Before Christmas, The

1951 Soviet ani sh.

Dir: V. & L. Broumberg.

F

Ref: Ani/Cin p 167.

**Night Before Christmas Eve,
The**

See: Noc Pered Rozdestvom
(1913).

Night Blossoms

1966 Amateur (Film-makers'
Coop) 16mm color & b&w
sil 4.5 mins.
Made by: Tom S. Chomont.

F

Ref: FMC 5:61.

Night Callers, The

(novel by F. Crisp)
See: Blood Beast from
Outer Space (1965).

Night Child

See: Night Hair Child
(1971).

Night Comes too Soon, The

(The Ghost of Rashmon Hall
--rr.t.)

1947 British, British
Animated-Federated 57
mins.

Prod: Harold Baim.

Dir: Denis Kavanagh.

SP: Pat Dixon.

Cin: Ray Densham.

Cast: Valentine Dyall,
Anne Howard, Alec Faversham,
Howard Douglas, Beatrice
Marsden, Arthur Brander,
Anthony Baird.

F-H ("doctor rids old house
of the ghosts of sailor,
his wife, and her lover"
--Gifford)

Ref: MFB Feb '48 p 16-17;
Gifford/BFC 11182.

Based on play "The Haunted
and the Haunters" by
Edward G. Bulwer-Lytton.

Night Crawlers

1964 Amateur (Film-makers'
Coop) 16mm 4 mins.
Made by: Peter Emanuel
Goldman.

sur-F (optically-distorted
scenes of Times Square)

Ref: FMC 5:124; Undrgnd
p 147.

Night Crawlers, The

See: Navy vs. the Night
Monsters, The (1966).

Night Creatures

(Captain Clegg --Brit.t.;
Dr. Syn --s.t.)
1962 Hammer & Merlin &
Major (U) color 88 mins.

Prod: John Temple-Smith.

Dir: Peter Graham Scott.

SP: John Elder (Anthony
Hinds?) & Barbara S.
Harper.

Art Dir: Bernard Robinson
& Don Mingaye.

Cin: Arthur Grant.

SpFX: Les Bowie.

Edit: James Needs & Eric
Boyd-Perkins.

Mus: Don Banks.

Mus Dir: Philip Martell.

Cast: Peter Cushing, Yvonne
Romain, Patrick Allen,
Oliver Reed, Michael
Ripper, Martin Benson,
Derek Francis, Milton Reid.

cont.

Night Creatures cont.

hist; H-seq (1792- "Captain
unmasks vicar as the
'dead' pirate leader of
smugglers who pose as
ghosts" --Gifford)

Ref: FF '62 p216; Gifford/
BFC 13109.

Based on novel "Dr. Syn"
by Russell Thorndike.
Other film versions not
significant H.

Night Creatures, The

See: Last Man on Earth,
The (1963).

**Night Evelyn Came Out of the
Grave, The**

(La Notte Che Evelyn Usca'
dalla Tomba)

1971 (1972) Italian, Phoenix
Cinemat. (Phase I) color
scope 99 mins.

Dir: Emilio P. Miraglia.

SP: Fabio Pittoru, Massomo
Felisatti, & E.P. Miraglia.

Sets: Lorenzo Baraldi.

Cin: Gastone DiGiovanni.

Mus: Bruno Nicolai.

Cast: Antonio De Teffe
(Anthony Steffen), Marina
Malfatti, Rod Murdock,
Giocomo Rossi-Stuart, Umberto
Raho, Roberto Maldera.

myst-H (attempt to drive
man mad by making him think
his dead wife has come back
to life)

Ref: Vw 26 July '72 p22;
Ital Prods '72 p 144-45.

Night Full of Surprises

1967 Polish color ani
puppet sh.

Dir: Janina Hartwig.

F (toys come to life)

Ref: MTVM April '67 p28.

Night Gallery

1969 U (NBC-TV) color
95 mins.

Dir: Boris Sagal, Stephen
Spielberg, & Barry Shear.

SP & Nar: Rod Serling.

Art Dir: Howard E. Johnson.

Cin: Richard Batcheller
& William Margulies.

Mus: William Goldenberg.

Cast: Joan Crawford, Richard
Kiley, Roddy McDowall, Barry
Sullivan, Ossie Davis, George
Macready, Sam Jaffe, Tom
Bosley, Barry Atwater, Rod
Serling.

F-H (3 stories: painting seems
to haunt man to death, then his
ghost does it for real; rich
woman buys poor man's eyes
which give her 12 hours of
sight during New York power
blackout; fleeing Nazi magically
enters painting, ends up
crucified)

Ref: Willis p352.

Pilot for the TV series.

Night Hair Child

(Child of the Night; Night
Child --s.t.s)

1971 (1972) British, Leander
color 89 mins.

Filmed in Spain.

Exec Prod: Harry Alan Towers.

Prod: Graham Harris.

Dir: James Kelly.

Cin: Luis Cuadrado & Harry
Waxman.

Edit: Nicholas Wentworth.

Mus: Stelvio Cipriani.

Cast: Mark Lester, Britt
Ekland, Hardy Krüger, Lilli
Palmer, Harry Andrews,
Conchita Montez, Collette
Jack.

psy-H (child is sexual psychopath; matricide)

Ref: MFB Jan '73 p 12-13;
Dick Klemensen; BO 7 June '71.

Night Has a Thousand Eyes

1948 Par 81 mins.

Prod: Endre Bohem.

Dir: John Farrow.

SP: Barré Lyndon & Jonathan
Latimer.

Art Dir: Hans Dreier & Franz
Bachelin.

Cin: John F. Seitz.

Process Cin: Farciot Edouart.

Edit: Eda Warren.

Mus: Victor Young.

Cast: Edward G. Robinson,
Gail Russell, John Lund,
Virginia Bruce, William
Demarest, Onslow Stevens,
Richard Webb, Jerome Cowan.

F-H (vaudeville magician finds
he really is able to see the
future; foretells death, tries
to prevent it)

Ref: FD 15 July '48; Vd &
HR 12 July '48; MFB July
'48 p98.

Based on the novel by Cornell
Woolrich (George Hopley).

See also: Clairvoyant, The
(1935).

Night Has Eyes, The

See: Terror House (1942).

Night in Dreamland, A

1907 (1908) Vit sil 500
ft.

Prod & Dir: J. Stuart Blackton.

F

Ref: Filmlex p682; LC;
Views 89:7.

Night in Paradise

1946 Walter Wanger (U) color
10 reels (84 mins).

Prod: Walter Wanger.

Assoc Prod: Alexander Golitzen.

Dir: Arthur Lubin.

Adapt: Emmet Lavery.

SP: Ernest Pascal.

Art Dir: John B. Goodman &
Alexander Golitzen.

Makeup: Jack Pierce.

Cin: Hal Mohr & W. Howard
Greene.

SpFX Cin: John P. Fulton.

Edit: Milton Carruth.

Mus: Frank Skinner.

Cast: Merle Oberon, Turhan
Bey, Gale Sondergaard, Thomas
Gomez, Ray Collins, Douglass
Dumbrille, Paul Cavanaugh,
Marvin Miller, Moroni Olsen,
John Litel, Ernest Truex,
Jerome Cowan, Julie London,
Barbara Bates.

F (Sondergaard is witch with
black magic powers)

Ref: Vd 8 April '46; MFB
July '46 p98; FD 22 April '46.

Based on novel "Peacock's
Feather" by George S. Hellman.

Night in the Chamber of Horrors, A

1914 French?, Eclair sil
900 ft.

H ("Grand Guignol")

Ref: Bios 26 Feb '14.

Night Is the Phantom

See: What! (1963).

Night Key

1937 U 68 mins.

Assoc Prod: Robert Presnell.

Dir: Lloyd Corrigan.

Story: William Pierce.
SP: Tristram Tupper &
John C. Moffitt.

Art Dir: Jack Otterson.

Cin: George Robinson.

SpFX: John P. Fulton.

Edit: Otis Garrett.

Mus Dir: Lou Forbes.

Cast: Boris Karloff, Jean
Rogers, J. Warren Hull,

cont

Night Key cont.

Ward Bond, Hobart Cavanaugh, Samuel Hinds, Frank Reicher, Alan Baxter, Edwin Maxwell.

SF (inventor of burglar alarm has his invention stolen from him & so develops electronic gadget which opens doors & keeps burglar alarm from going off; electrical ray shoots at people & shocks them senseless)

Ref: HR 16 April '37; Vw & FD 21 April '37; LC.

Night Life of the Gods

(Private Life of the Gods --ad.t.)

1935 U 75 mins.

Prod: Carl Laemmle Jr.

Dir: Lowell Sherman.

SP: Barry Trivers.

Art Dir: Charles D. Hall.

Edit Sup: Maurice Pivar.

Edit: Ted Kent.

Cast: Alan Mowbray, Florine McKinney, Peggy Shannon, Phillips Smalley, Gilbert Emery, Douglas Fowley, William Boyd, Irene Ware, Richard Carle, Henry Armetta, Robert Warwick, Wesley Barry.

F-com (Mowbray gets magic ring which turns people into statues or brings statues to life; uses it on statues of Greek gods; all-a-dream ending)

Ref: Vw 27 Feb '35; MPH 8 Sept '34 p31; FD 23 Feb '35.

Based on the novel by Thorne Smith.

Night Like Any Other, A

See: Witches, The (1965).

Night Monster

(House of Mystery --Brit.t.)

1942 U 73 mins.

Prod & Dir: Forde Beebe.

Assoc Prod: Don Brown.

SP: Clarence Upson Young.

Art Dir: Jack Otterson & Richard Riedel.

Cin: Charles Van Enger.

Edit: Milton Carruth.

Mus Dir: Hans J. Salter.

Cast: Ralph Morgan, Bela Lugosi, Lionel Atwill, Don Porter, Irene Hervey, Nils Asther, Leif Erickson, Elyse Knox, Janet Shaw, Frank Reicher, Cyril Delevanti.

F-H (skeleton holding box materialized by will power; also by will power, man without legs creates monstrous-looking but usable legs for himself so he can murder)

Ref: Vd & HR 19 Oct '42; MFB April '43 p41.

Night Must Fall

1964 British, MGM 105 mins.

Exec Prod: Lawrence P. Bachman.

Prod: Albert Finney & Karel Reisz.

Dir: K. Reisz.

SP: Clive Exton.

Art Dir: Lionel Couch.

Cin: Freddie Francis.

Sup Edit: Fergus McDonnell.

Edit: Philip Barnikel.

Mus: Ron Grainer.

Cast: Albert Finney, Susan Hampshire, Mona Washbourne, Sheila Hancock, Michael Medwin, Joe Gladwin.

psy-H (charming young man is psychopathic axe-murderer)

Ref: FF '64 p92; MFB July '64 p 103; FD 19 March '64.

Based on the play by Emlyn Williams.

Note: the 1937 version is not significant H.

Night My Number Came Up, The

1955 (1956) British, Ealing Studios & J. Arthur Rank (Continental) 94 mins.

Prod: Michael Balcon.

Dir: Leslie Norman.

SP: R.C. Sherriff.

Art Dir: Jim Morahan.

Cin: Lionel Banes.

Edit: Peter Tanner.

Mus: Malcolm Arnold.

Cast: Michael Redgrave, Sheila Sim, Alexander Knox, Denholm Elliott, Ursula Jeans, Ralph Truman, Michael Hordern, Nigel Stock, George Rose, Alfie Bass, Victor Maddern.

psy-F-H-dream (man relates dream involving one of his listeners & airline crash; next day dream comes true in every detail except tragic end)

Ref: MFB May '55 p76; FD 29 Dec '55; Gifford/BFC 12082.

Night of Anubis

See: Night of the Living Dead (1968).

Night of Bloody Horror

1969 Cinema IV (Howco Int'l) color 89 mins.

Exec Prod: Albert J. Salzer.

Prod & Dir: Joy N. Houck Jr.

SP: J.N. Houck Jr. & Robert A. Weaver.

Cin & Edit: R.A. Weaver.

Makeup: Philip St. Jon.

Cast: Gerald McRaney, Gale Yellen, Evelyn Hendricks, Herbert Nelson, Lisa Dameron, Charlotte White, Nigel Strangeways.

H (bloody, brutal murders committed by psychopath)

Ref: Village Voice 19 Nov '70; PB; B. Warren.

Night of Dark Shadows

(Curse of Dark Shadows --s.t.)

1971 MGM color 97 mins.

Prod & Dir: Dan Curtis.

Story: D. Curtis & Sam Hall.

SP: S. Hall.

Assoc Prod & Art Dir: Trevor Williams.

Makeup: Reginald Tackley.

Cin: Richard Shore.

Edit: Charles Goldsmith.

Mus: Robert Cobert.

Cast: David Selby, Lara Parker [ghost], Kate Jackson, Grayson Hall, John Karlen, Nancy Barrett, Thayer David.

F-H (man possessed by ghost of executed witch, his ancestor's lover)

Ref: FF '71 p543-44; LAT 22 Sept '71; Vw 11 Aug '71.

Based on the TV series "Dark Shadows."

See also: House of Dark Shadows (1970).

Night of Horror, A

See: Nacht des Grauens (1916).

Night of Magic, A

1944 British, Berkeley Films 56 mins.

Prod: Burt Hyams.

Dir: Herbert Wynne.

SP: Ewesley Bracken.

Cin: W. Richards.

Cast: Robert Griffith, Billy Scott, Marion Olive, Dot Delavine, Vera Bradley.

mus; F-dream (in dream man finds 3000 year old princess alive)

Ref: MFB '44 p 114; Gifford / BFC 10979.

Night of Terror

1933 Col 65 mins.

Dir: Benjamin Stoloff.

SP: Beatrice Van, William Jacobs, & Lester Nielson.

Cin: Joseph A. Valentine.

Edit: Arthur Hilton.

Cast: Bela Lugosi, George Meeker, Tully Marshall, Bryant Washburn, Edwin Maxwell, Gertrude Michael, Wallace Ford, Sally Blane, Dave O'Brien.

myst; F-H-seq (fake suspended animation; maniac killer; spiritualistic trance; at end dead killer revives & warns audience not to reveal the plot)

Ref: MPH 5 August '33; FD 7 June '33; Vw 27 June '33.

Based on story "The Public Be Damned" by Willard Mack.

Night of Terror

See: Nacht des Grauens (1916).

Night of Terrors, A

See: Zwolfte Stunde, Die (1921).

Night of Terrors, The

See: Murder Clinic, The (1966).

Night of the Beast

See: House of the Black Death (1965).

Night of the Big Heat

See: Island of the Burning Damned (1967).

Night of the Blind Dead

See: Tombs of the Blind Dead (1972).

Night of the Blind Terror

See: Tombs of the Blind Dead (1972).

Night of the Blood Beast

(The Creature from Galaxy 27 --s.t.; The Monster from Galaxy 27 --s.t.)

1958 Balboa (AIP) 65 mins.

Exec Prod: Roger Corman.

Prod & Story: Gene Corman.

Dir: Bernard Kowalski.

SP: Martin Varno.

Art Dir: Daniel Haller.

Cin: John Nicholaus Jr.

Edit: Dick Currier.

Mus: Alexander Laszlo.

Cast: Michael Emmet, Angela Greene, John Baer, Ed Nelson, Tyler McVey, Ross Sturlin [alien].

SF-H (alien implants cells of its own body in astronaut's body, & embryos begin to develop)

Ref: FF '58 p274; Vd 4 Dec '58; LC.

Night of the Blood Monster

(El Proceso de las Brujas: The Trial of the Witches; El Juez Sangriento: The Bloody Judge --Brit.t.; Der Hexentoter von Blackmoor: The Witch-Killer of Blackmoor; Il Trono di Fuoco: The Throne of Fire)

1970 (1972) Spanish/German/Italian, CC Fenix/Terra Filmkunst/Prodimex (AIP) color scope 96 mins.

Prod: Harry Alan Towers & Anthony Scott Veitch.

Dir: Jesús Franco (Jess Frank).

Story: H.A. Towers (Peter Welbeck).

SP: J. Franco & E. Colombo.

Art Dir: G. Sanabria.

Cin: Manuel Merino.

Edit: Maria Luisa Soriano.

Mus: Bruno Nicolai.

cont.

Night of the Blood Monster cont.

Cast: Christopher Lee, Maria Schell, Leo Genn, Maria Rohm, Margaret Lee, Hans Hass, José Maria Prada.

hist-H (Lee is sadistic witch-hunter; torture; set in medieval(?) England)

Ref: SpCin '71 p 170; BO 15 May '72 ads.

Night of the Bloody Apes

(Horror y Sexo: Horror and Sex)

1968? (1972) Mexican, Cinematografica Calderon (Azteca --Spanish-language prints; Jerand --dubbed prints) color.

Prod: G. Calderon Stell.

Dir: Rene Cardona.

SP: R. Cardona & Rene Cardona Jr.

Cin: Raul Solares.

Edit: Jorge (George) Bustos.

Mus: Antonio Conde.

Cast: Armando Silvestre (Armand Silva), Norma Lazareno (Norma LaZar), José Elias Moreno, Carlos Lopez Moctezuma, Augustin Martinez Solares, Javier Rizo, Noelia Noel

SF-H (heart transplants: doctor puts gorilla's heart into son, replaces it with a girl's heart; boy turns into murderous, raping monster)

Ref: PB; PS; BO 6 March '72 BookinGuide p 10, 5 June '72 p89; Willis.

Night of the Cobra Woman

(Movini's Venom --ad.t.)

1972? Philippine/US, New World color 85 mins.

Prod: Kerry Magnus.

Dir: Andrew Meyer.

SP: K. Magnus & A. Meyer.

Art Dir: Ben Otico.

Cin: Nonong Rusca.

SpFX: Feling Hilario.

Cast: Joy Bang, Marlene Clark, Roger Garrett, Vic Diaz, Slash Marks, Carmen Argenziano, Charlie Kierkop.

F-H (bitten by snake, woman can turn into cobra; sucks life & vitality out of men during intercourse)

Ref: Willis.

See also: Cult of the Cobra (1955); Snake Woman, The (1972).

Night of the Damned, The

See: Notte dei Dannati, La (1971).

Night of the Demon

See: Curse of the Demon (1956).

Night of the Devils, The

See: Notte dei Diavoli, La (1971).

Night of the Doomed

See: Nightmare Castle (1965).

Night of the Eagle

See: Burn Witch, Burn (1961).

Night of the Flesh Eaters

See: Night of the Living Dead (1968).

Night of the Full Moon

See: Poonam Ki Raat (1965).

Night of the Ghouls

1959 Edward D. Wood Prods & Atomic Prods.

Prod, Dir, SP: Edward D. Wood Jr.

Cast: Criswell, Tor Johnson, Kenne Duncan, Valda Hansen, Vampira.

F-H (Criswell rises from coffin to tell story; ghosts; disfigured man; walking dead)

Ref: FM 3:44-47; Photon 19:35; Richardson.

Note: completed but apparently not released.

Night of the Hunter, The

1955 Paul Gregory Prods (UA) 93 mins.

Prod: Paul Gregory.

Dir: Charles Laughton.

SP: James Agee.

Art Dir: Hilyard Brown.

Cin: Stanley Cortez.

Edit: Robert Golden.

Mus: Walter Schumann.

Cast: Robert Mitchum, Shelley Winters, Peter Graves, Lillian Gish, James Gleason, Evelyn Varden, Don Beddoe, Gloria Castillo, Billy Chapin, Sally Jane Bruce.

psy-H (US during the depression; Mitchum, masquerading as preacher, is psychotic killer of women)

Ref: MFB Jan '56 p3-4; Vd 20 July '55; FD 3 Aug '55.

Based on the novel by Davis Grubb.

Night of the Lepus

(Rabbits --s.t.)

1972 MGM color 88 mins.

Prod: A.C. Lyles.

Dir: William F. Claxton.

SP: Don Holliday & Gene R. Kearney.

Prod Design & 2nd Unit Dir: Stan Jolley.

Cin: Ted Voigtlander.

SpFX: Howard A. Anderson Co.

Edit: John McSweeney.

Mus: Jimmie Haskell.

Cast: Stuart Whitman, Janet Leigh, Rory Calhoun, DeForest Kelley, Paul Fix, Melanie Fullerton, I. Stanford Jolley.

SF-H (in attempt to control expanding rabbit population in contemporary US Southwest hormone is used that accidentally causes rabbits to turn into wolf-sized carnivores)

Ref: Vw 5 July '72; MFB March '73 p55; BO 20 Dec '71 p 10.

Based on novel "The Year of the Angry Rabbit" by Russell Braddon.

Night of the Living Dead

(Night of the Flesh Eaters --s.t.; Night of Anubis --s.t.)

1968 Image 10 Prods (Walter Reade-Continental) 96 mins (90 mins).

Prod: Russell Streiner & Karl Hardman.

Dir & Cin: George A. Romero.

SP: John A. Russo.

SpFX: Regis Survinski & Tony Pantanello.

Cast: Duane Jones, Judith O'Dea, Russell Streiner, Karl Hardman, Keith Wayne.

SF-H (plague or radiation from space causes the recently dead to rise & eat the living)

Ref: S&S Spring '70 p 105; FF '68 p442; Vd 15 Oct '68; FD 21 Oct '68; CineF 2:3:8-15.

See also: Plan 9 From Outer Space (1956); Invisible Invaders (1959); Earth Dies Screaming, The (1964).

Night of the Silicates

See: Island of Terror (1966).

Night of the Specters, The

See: Notte degli Spettri, La (1913).

Night of the Terrors, The

See: Murder Clinic, The (1966).

Night of the Thousand Cats, The

See: Noche de los Mil Gatos, La (1972?).

Night of the Vampire

n.d. Amateur (Center Cinema) 16mm? color 9 mins.

Made by: Peter Mays.

cont.

Night Monster (1942)

Night of the Vampire cont.

F-H (nude Miss Dracula dines on blood of her victims)

Rcf: CFS cat Sept '68.

Night of the Witches

1970 Medford color.

Prod: Keith Erik Burt (Keith Larsen?) & Vincent Forte.

Dir: K.E. Burt (K. Larsen?).

Art Dir: Ted Jonson.

Cin: Herb V. Theiss.

Edit: Anthony de Laune.

Mus: Sean Bonniwell.

Cast: Keith Erik Burt (Keith Larsen?), Randy Stafford, Ron Taft, Kathryn Loder, Leon Charles, Ernest L. Rossi.

F-H (phoney, murderous preacher encounters band of homicidal witches in contemporary California; black magic)

Ref: Borst; B. Warren.

Night of Thrills, A

1914 Rex (U) sil 2 reels.

Cast: Lon Chaney.

H-com (comedy in haunted house)

Ref: Focus May'Aug '70 p32.

Night of Violence

1965 Italian.

Dir: Roberto Mauri.

SP: R. Mauri & Mulgaria.

Cin: Vitaliano Natalucci.

Cast: Alberto Lupo, Marilu Tolo, Lisa Gastoni, Helene Chanel.

H (horrifying face resulted from Hiroshima A-bomb)

Ref: Ital Prods.

Night on Bald Mountain, A

(Nuite sur la Monte Chauve)

1934 French pin-screen ani sh.

Made by: Alexandre Alexeieff & Claire Parker.

cont.

Night on Bald Mountain cont.

Mus: Moussorgsky.

F (demonic revels)

Ref: F/A p627; FC Winter-Spring '70 p48; Ani/Cin p93-94.

See also: Fantasia (1940)

Night on Bare Mountain

See: House on Bare Mountain (1962)

Night Prayer

See: Preghiere della Notte (1972?).

Night Slaves

1970 Bing Crosby Prods & WB (ABC-TV) color 72 mins approx.

Prod: Everett Chambers.

Dir: Ted Post.

SP: E. Chambers & Robert Specht.

Art Dir: Howard Hollander.

Cin: Robert Hauser.

Edit: Michael Kahn.

Mus: Bernardo Segall.

Cast: James Franciscus, Lee Grant, Scott Marlowe, Andrew Prine, Tisha Sterling, Leslie Nielsen.

SF (aliens use hypnotised inhabitants of small town to repair spaceship; hero leaves with alien he loves at end)

Ref: CineF 4:9; HR 1 Oct '70; LAT 30 Sept '70.

Based on the novel by Jerry Sohl.

Night Stalker, The

(The Kolchack Tapes --s.t.)

1971 (1972) ABC-TV color 72 mins approx.

Prod: Dan Curtis.

Dir: John Llewellyn Moxey.

SP: Richard Matheson.

Art Dir: Trevor Williams.

Makeup: Jerry Dash.

Cin: Michel Hugo.

Edit: Desmond Marquette.

Mus: Robert Cobert.

cont.

Night Stalker cont.

Cast: Darren McGavin, Carol Lynley, Simon Oakland, Ralph Meeker, Claude Akins, Charles McGraw, Barry Atwater [vampire], Kent Smith, Larry Linville, Elisha Cook Jr, Stanley Adams.

F-H (reporter tracks down & kills vampire in present-day Las Vegas)

Ref: LAT 11 Jan '72; CineF 2:3:31.

Based on a novel by Jeff Rice.

Sequel: Night Strangler, The (1972).

Night Star, Goddess of Electra

See: War of the Zombies (1963).

Night Strangler, The

(The Time Killer --s.t.)

1972 (1973) ABC-Circle Film (ABC-TV) color 74 mins.

Prod & Dir: Dan Curtis.

SP: Richard Matheson.

Prod Design: Trevor Williams.

Makeup: William J. Tuttle.

Cin: Robert Hauser.

SpFX: Ira Anderson.

Edit: Folmar Blangsted.

Mus: Robert Cobert.

Cast: Darren McGavin, Jo Ann Pflug, Simon Oakland, Scott Brady, Wally Cox, Margaret Hamilton, John Carradine, Nina Wayne, Richard Anderson [alchemist].

F-H (reporter battles century-old alchemist who needs fresh blood to maintain eternal life, strangles women by night in Seattle, lives in house beneath the city)

Ref: Matheson; Pardi; LAT 16 Jan '73 IV:12.

Based on characters created by Jeff Rice.

Sequel to: Night Stalker, The (1971).

Night the Animals Talked, The

1970 Italian, Gamma color? ani 24 mins.
Dir: Roberto Gavioli.
F
Ref: IAFF '72.

Night the Creatures Came

See: Island of Terror (1966).

Night the Silicates Came, The

See: Island of Terror (1966).

Night the Sun Came Out on Happy Hollow Lane, The

See: Watermelon Man (1970).

Night the World Exploded, The

1957 Clover (Col) 64 mins.
Prod: Sam Katzman.

Dir: Fred F. Sears.
SP: Luci Ward & Jack Natte-ford.
Art Dir: Paul Palmentola.
Cin: Benjamin H. Kline.
Edit: Paul Borofsky.
Mus Dir: Ross DiMaggio.
Cast: Kathryn Grant, William Leslie, Tristram Coffin, Raymond Greenleaf, Charles Evans, Frank Scannell, Marshall Reed, Fred Coby, Paul Savage, Terry Frost.
SF (mineral discovered which absorbs nitrogen, then explodes with great force; threatens to destroy the world)
Ref: HR & Vd 7 June '57; FD 18 June '57; deGroote 289.

Night the World Shook, The

See: Gorgo (1959).

Night They Killed Rasputin, The

(L'Ultimo Zar: The Last Czar; Les Nuits de Raspoutine: The Nights of Rasputin)
1960 (1962) Italian/French Wanguard & Faro & Explorer & C.F.P.C. & Rialto (Brigadier) color (b&w) 95 mins (87 mins).
Dir: Pierre Chenal.
Story: P. Chenal & André Tabet.
SP: Ugo Liberatore, P. Chenal, & A. Tabet.
Art Dir: Arrigo Equini.
Cin: Adalberto Albertini.
Edit: Antonietta Zita.
Mus: Angelo Francesco Lavagnino.

Cast: Edmund Purdom [Rasputin], Gianna Maria Canale, John Drew Barrymore, Jany Clair, Ugo Sasso, Giulia Rubini.
bor-F-hist-H (monk Rasputin cures czar's son in early 20th-century Russia; has hypnotic powers; very diffi-cult to kill)
Ref: MFB Oct '62 p 141; FF '62 p371; CineF Fall '70 p 16.
See also: Rasputin.

Night Tide

1961 (1963) Virgo Prods (AIP) 84 mins.
Prod: Aram Kantarian.
Dir & SP: Curtis Harrington.
Art Dir: Paul Mathison.
Cin: Vilis Lapenieks & Floyd Crosby.
Edit: Jodie Copelan.
Mus: David Raksin.
Cast: Dennis Hopper, Linda Lawson, Gavin Muir, Luana Anders, Marjorie Eaton, Cameron.
psy-F (girl believes she is one of ancient race of under-sea people; dream seqs)
Ref: FF 22 Aug '63; Photon Sept '66; MFB April '67 p61; MPH 4 Sept '63; FQ Spring '61 p 11-12.

Night unto Night

1947 (1949) WB 92 mins (84 mins).
Prod: Owen Crump.
Dir: Don Siegel.
SP: Kathryn Scola.
Art Dir: Hugh Retiker.
Cin: Peverell Marley.
SpFX: Harry Barndollar.
Edit: Hugh Reilly.
Mus: Franz Waxman.
Cast: Ronald Reagan, Viveca Lindfors, Broderick Crawford, Rosemary De Camp, Osa Massen, Art Baker, Lillian Yarbo, Erskine Sanford, Craig Stevens.
psy-F-H (girl believes the ghost of her husband haunts a house, occasionally hears his voice)
Ref: HR & Vd 19 April '49; MFB Sept '50 p 141-42.
Based on the novel by Philip Wylie.

Night Visitor, The

(Salem Come to Supper --s.t.) Filmed in Sweden.
1971 Hemisphere (UMC) color 102 mins.
Prod: Mel Ferrer.
Dir: Laslo Benedek.
SP: Guy Elmes.
Prod Design: P.A. Lundgren.
Art Dir: Viggo Bentzon.
Cin: Henning Kristiansen.
Edit: Bill Blunden.
Mus: Henry Mancini.
Cast: Max von Sydow, Trevor Howard, Liv Ullmann, Per Oscarsson, Rupert Davies, Andrew Keir.
psy-H (man falsely committed to insane asylum secretly escapes each night to kill those who wronged him, then returns to asylum; axe murders)
Ref: Vw 24 Feb '71; FF '71 p 123.
Based on a story by Samuel Rosecca.

Night Walker, The

1964 (1965) Castle Pics (U) 86 mins.
Prod & Dir: William Castle.
SP: Robert Bloch.
Art Dir: Frank Arrigo.
Makeup: Bud Westmore, Carl Silvera, & Dick Blair.
Cin: Harold Stine.
SpFX: Charles Spurgeon.
Edit: Edwin H. Bryant.
Mus: Vic Mizzy.
Cast: Barbara Stanwyck, Robert Taylor, Hayden Rorke, Lloyd Bochner, Judith Meredith, Rochelle Hudson, Jess Barker.
psy-H (attempt to drive woman insane by making her think she cannot wake up from nightmares; hideously disfigured man)
Ref: FF '65 p5, 6; HR & Vd 22 Dec '64; MFB July '65 p 111.

Night Watch

1973 British, Brut (Avco-Embassy) color 99 mins.
Prod: Martin Poll, George W. George, & Barnard S. Strauss.
Dir: Brian G. Hutton.
SP: Tony Williamson.
Addit Dialog: Evan Jones.
Art Dir: Peter Murton.
Cin: Billy Williams.
Edit: John Jympson.
Mus: John Cameron.
Cast: Elizabeth Taylor, Lawrence Harvey, Billie Whitelaw, Robert Lang, Tony Britton, Bill Dean, Michael Danvers-Walker, Rosario Serrano.
psy-H (Harvey tries to drive wife Taylor insane with visions of gory corpses, etc.)

Night Watch cont.

Ref: Vw 8 Aug '73; Vogue June '73; Acad.
Based on the play by Lucille Fletcher.

Night Watchman, The

1938 Vitaphone (WB) color ani 7 mins.
Prod: Leon Schlesinger.
Dir: Chuck (Charles M.) Jones.
Story: Ted (Tedd) Pierce.
Ani: Ken Harris.
Mus Dir: Carl W. Stalling.
Voices: Mel Blanc.
F-com
Ref: LC.

Night We Got the Bird, The

1960 British, Rix-Conyers 82 mins.
Prod: Darcy Conyers & Brian Rix.
Dir: D. Conyers.
SP: Ray Cooney, Tony Hilton, & D. Conyers.
Cin: S.D. Onions.
Edit: Thelma Connell.
Cast: Brian Rix, Dora Bryan, Ronald Shiner, Leo Franklyn, Irene Handl, Liz Fraser, Reginald Beckwith, John le Mesureir, Kynaston Reeves.
F-com (man persecuted by talking parrot which is rein-carnation of wife's first husband; parrot sent to Moon)
Ref: MFB Dec '60 p 171-72; PB.

Nightingale, The

See: Emperor's Nightingale, The (1947).

Nightingale and the Rose, The

1967 Czech ani sh.
Dir: Josef Kabrt.
F
Ref: MTVM June '67 p 17.
Based on the story by Oscar Wilde.

Nightmare, A

(Le Cauchemar)
1897 French, Star sil 65 ft.
Made by: Georges Méliès.
F-dream
Ref: Sadoul/M, GM Mage 82.

Nightmare

1956 Pine-Thomas-Shane Prods (UA) 89 mins.
Prod: William Thomas & Howard Pine.
Dir & SP: Maxwell Shane.
Art Dir: Frank Sylos.
Cin: Joseph Biroc.
Edit: George Gittens.
Mus: Herschel Burke Gilbert.
Cast: Edward G. Robinson, Kevin McCarthy, Connie Russell, Virginia Christine, Rhys Williams, Gage Clarke, Barry Atwater.
bor-ps,-F-H (in nightmare man murders another; hypno-sis used to cause murder & attempted suicide)
Ref: MPH 19 May '56 p898; FD 17 May '56; MFB June '56 p78.
Based on the story by Cornell Woolrich.
See also: Fear in the Night (1946).

Nightmare

1963 (1964) British, Hammer (U) 83 mins.
Prod & SP: Jimmie Sangster.
Dir: Freddie Francis.
Art Dir: Bernard Robinson.
Cin: John Wilcox.

Nightmare cont.

SpFX: Les Bowie.
Sup Edit: James Needs.
Mus: Don Banks.
Cast: David Knight, Moira Redmond, Brenda Bruce, Jennie Linden, George A. Cooper, Clytie Jessop.
psy-H-dream (girl has induced nightmares of insane mother calling her to join her in asylum; attempt by guardian to drive girl to psychotic homicide)
Ref: FF '64 p92; MFB June '64 p90; HR 28 April '64.

Nightmare

(story by G.P. Breakston)
See: Manster, The (1959).

Nightmare

(novel by A. Blaisdell)
See: Die! Die! My Darling! (1965).

Nightmare Alley

1947 20th-Fox 112 mins.
Prod: George Jessel.
Dir: Edmund Goulding.
SP: Jules Furthman.
Art Dir: Lyle Wheeler & J. Russell Spencer.
Cin: Lee Garmes.
SpFX: Fred Sersen.
Edit: Barbara McLean.
Mus: Cyril Mockridge.
Mus Dir: Lionel Newman.
Cast: Tyrone Power, Joan Blondell, Coleen Gray, Helen Walker, Ian Keith, Taylor Holmes, Mike Mazurki, Roy Roberts, Henry Hall, Gene Stutenroth, George Chandler.
psy-F-H-seq (carnival barker becomes famous spiritualist, fakes vision of millionaire's dead daughter)
Ref: MFB Aug '48 p 116; Agee p280-81, 381; Vd & HR 9 Oct '47; LC.
Based on the novel by William Lindsay Gresham.

Nightmare and Sweet Dream

See: Cauchemar et Doux Rêve (1908).

Nightmare Blood Bath

1971 Independent-Int'l color.
Cast: Regina Carrol, Scott Brady.
H
Ref: BO 2 Aug '71.

Nightmare Castle

(Amanti d'Oltretomba: Lovers Beyond the Tomb; The Faceless Monster --Brit.t.; Night of the Doomed --ad.t?)
1965 (1966) Italian, Cinemat. Emme Ci (AA) 105 mins (90 mins).
Prod: Carlo Caiano.
Dir: Mario Caiano (Alan Grunewald).
SP: Fabio de Agostino & M. Caiano.
Art Dir: Massimo Tavazzi.
Cin: E. Barboni.
Edit: Renato Cinquini.
Mus: Ennio Morricone.
Cast: Barbara Steele, Paul Miller, Helga Line, Laurence Clift, Giuseppe Addobbati (John McDouglas), Rik Battaglia.
F-H (scientist kills wife & her lover, uses their blood to rejuvate accomplice; ghosts of murdered couple return, get revenge -- one sucks blood of accomplice; disfigurement; hearts in urn cause nightmares)
Ref: FF '67 p435; MFB Jan '70 p 10; BO 28 Nov '66.

cont.

cont.

Nightmare in Wax

(The Monster of the Wax Museum --s.t.; Crimes in the Wax Museum --ad.t.)

1969 A&E Film Corp (Crown-Int'l) color 91 mins.

Exec Prod: Rex Carlton & Herbert Sussan.
Prod: Martin B. Cohen.

Dir: Bud Townsend.

SP: R. Carlton.

Art Dir: James Freiberg.

Makeup: Martin Varno (Martin Vernaux).

Cin: Glen Smith.

Edit: Leonard Kwit.

Mus: Igo Kantor.

Cast: Cameron Mitchell, Anne Helm, Scott Brady, Berry Kroeger, Victoria Carrol, Phillip Baird, Johnny Cardos, Hollis Morrison, James Forrest.

SF-H (makeup man, disfigured by sadistic movie producer, runs wax museum where he has embalmed missing actors alive & uses them as exhibits; at climax they return to life & toss him in vat of wax)

Ref: MFB Feb '70 p33; LAT 12 Dec '69.

Nightmare of the Glad-Eye Twins, The

(Elsie's Nightmare --rr.t.)

1913 British, Kineto sil 770 ft.

Dir: Edgar Rogers.

F-dream (in dream, girl's two dolls come to life & play)

Ref: Gifford/BFC 04080.

Nightmare Park

See: House in Nightmare Park, The (1973).

Nights in Prague

See: Prazske Noci (1968).

Nights of Dracula, The

See: Count Dracula (1970).

Nights of Rasputin

See: Night They Killed Rasputin, The (1960).

Nights of Terror

See: Twice Told Tales (1963).

Nights of the Werewolf, The

See: Noches del Hombre Lobo, Las (1968).

Nightshade

See: Nachtschatten (1972).

Nihikino Samna

See: Two Grilled Fish (1968).

Nije Bilo Uzalud

(It Was Not in Vain)

1967? Yugoslavian, Jadran.

Dir & SP: Nikola Tanhofer.

Cin: Slavko Zalar.

Mus: Milo Cipra.

Cast: Mira Nikolić, Boris Buzančić, Zvonimir Rogoz, Antun Vrdoljak.

bor-F-H ("a fortune teller rules over a swamp with curses that come true. Her son is thought to be dead & a ghost" --Willis)

Ref: Jadran Film (Willis).

Nils Holgersson's Underbararesa

See: Wonderful Adventures of Nils, The (1962).

Nine Ages of Nakedness, The

1969 British, Token Films color 95 mins.

Prod: Harry Reuben.

Dir & SP: George Harrison Marks.

Prod Design: Tony Roberts.

Cin: Terry Maher.

cont.

1984 (1955) British

Nine Ages of Nakedness cont.

Edit: Peter Mayhew.

Mus: Peter Jeffries.
Cast: George Harrison Marks, Max Wall, Max Bacon, Julian Orchard, Cardew Robinson, Big Bruno Erlington.

sex-com; psy-F-seqs (psychiatrist retrogresses photographer to recount ancestors' lives, including caveman, "Frankenstein Marks," etc.; seq in future)

Ref: MFB Oct '69 p218; Gifford/BFC 13973.

See also: Frankenstein.

Nine Chicks

1952 Czech ani sh.

Dir: Hermina Týrlová.

F

Ref: Ani/Cin p 176; FEFN July '61 p 13.

Nine Lives of a Cat

1907 Edison sil 955 ft.

F-com (cat put through sausage machine)

Ref: MPW 1:362, 622; LC.

Nine Seconds from Heaven

1922 Danish (Rialto Prods) sil (5800 ft).

English Titles: Harry Chandlee.

Cast: Charles King, Louise Reinwood.

bor-F-H (drug puts hero into death-like trance; hypnotist)

Ref: MPW 57:173.

1985

1970 CCM (University of Calif.) color 56 mins.

SF ("fictionalized news broadcast of ecological crisis of 1985 when long-predicted disasters totally devastate the environment")

Ref: Films/Future p25.

1984

1955 (1956) British, Holiday Film Prods 91 mins.

Prod: N. Peter Rathvon.

Dir: Michael Anderson.

SP: William P. Templeton & Ralph Bettinson.

Art Dir: Terence Verity.

cont.

1984 cont.

Cin: C. Pennington Richards.

SpFX: B. Langley, G. Blackwell, & N. Warwick.

Edit: Bill Lewthwaite.

Mus: Malcolm Arnold.

Cast: Edmond O'Brien, Michael Redgrave, Jan Sterling, David Kossoff, Mervyn Johns, Donald Pleasence, Michael Ripper, Patrick Allen, Ewen Solon.

SF (in totalitarian government of 1984, history reviser tries to rebel; television spy-eyes everywhere; perpetual war; super-brainwashing)

Ref: HR 13 July '56; MFB April '56 p43; Time 8 Oct '56 p 108; S&S Sept '56 p 198.

Based on the novel by George Orwell.

Note: British & US prints have different endings; in former, O'Brien shouts "Down with Big Brother" & he & lover Sterling are killed; in US prints, brainwashing worked & they part, loyal to Big Brother.

1941

1941 Amateur (C-16) 16mm color 5 mins.

Made by: Francis Lee.

abs-F

Ref: Undrgnd p83, 281; C-16 p24.

1900

n.d. Amateur (Film-makers' Coop) 16mm 9.5 mins.

Made by: David Devensky.

exp-F

Ref: FMC 5:78.

Ningen Dobutsuen

(Human Zoo; Clap Vocalism --ad.t?)

1962 Japanese, Kuri Jikken Manga Kobo color ani 2 mins.

Dir, SP, Ani: Yoji Kuri.

Mus: Toru Takemitsu.

F

Ref: MFB May '66 p77; Ani/Cin p 154-55.

Ningyo Shoten

(Mermaids and Sea Robbers)

1959 Japanese, Shochiku.

Dir: Seiichiro Uchikawa.

Cast: Kyoko Izumi, Tatsuya Mihashi.

F (mermaid runs mystery craft)

Ref: Shochiku Selected Films '59 (Willis).

Based on a novel by A. Hino.

Ninja Boy

See: Watari (1966).

Ninja Bugelijo

(A Band of Ninja)

1967 Japanese, Oshima Prods 135 mins.

Dir: Nagisa Oshima.

Drawings: Shirato Sampei.

Mus: Hiraku Haiyashi.

F (military spies in 13th Century, adept at water-walking, invisibility, etc.)

Ref: Vw 25 Jan '67.
Literally filmed comic strip, panel by panel.

Ninjutsu

See: Secret Scrolls (1957).

Ninjutsu Mushashugyo

(The Three Magicians)

1960 Japanese, Shochiku scope.

Dir: Seiichi Fukuda.

Cast: Norihei Miki, Achako Hanabishi, Junzaburo Ban.

F-com

Ref: FEFN Feb '60 p44 ad; MMF 9.

Ninth Circle

See: Deveti Krug (1961).

Ninth Guest, The

1934 Col 65 mins.

Dir: Roy William Neill.

SP: Garnett Weston.

Cin: Benjamin Kline.

Edit: Gene Milford.

Cast: Donald Cook, Genevieve Tobin, Hardie Albright, Edward Ellis, Edwin Maxwell, Vince Barnett, Samuel S. Hinds.

mystery; bor-H (8 guests at a party begin to be murdered one by one by madman)

Ref: Vw 6 March '34; Bloch; FD 3 March '34.

Based on the play by Owen Davis from novel "The Invisible Host" by Gwen Bristow & Bruce Manning.

Niobe

1915 Famous Players (Par) sil 5 reels.

Prod: Daniel Frohman.

Cast: Hazel Dawn, Charles Abbe.

F-com (statue comes to life via electrical wires)

Ref: MPW 24:986; Blum p70; MPH 7 Oct '39.

Nipote del Vampiro, La

See: Malenka (1968).

Nipper's Transformations, The

1912 British, Urbanora sil ani 325 ft.

Prod: Charles Urban.

F-com

Ref: Bios 15 Feb '12 p xix.

Nippon Tanjo

See: Three Treasures, The (1958).

Nirvana

n.d. Amateur (Film-makers Coop) super 8mm sound-on-tape color 25 mins.

Made by: Carlisle Scott.

exp-F (black boy seeks & finds Nirvana, a place)

Ref: FMC 5:287-88.

Nishithey

1963 Indian, Agragami.

Prod & Dir: Agragami.

SP: Samaresh Bose.

Cin: Ramananda Sen Gupta.

Mus: Sudhir Das Gupta.

Cast: Nandita Bose, Uttam Kumar, Supriya Chowdhury.

F-seq

Ref: Movieland 15 March '63.
Based on the short story by Tagore.

Nitwits, The

1935 RKO 81 mins.

Assoc Prod: Lee Marcus.

Dir: George Stevens.

Story: Stuart Palmer.

SP: Fred Guiol & Al Boasberg.

Cin: Edward Cronjager.

Edit: John Lockert.

Mus Dir: Roy Webb.

Cast: Bert Wheeler, Robert Woolsey, Fred Keating, Betty Grable, Evelyn Brent, Hale Hamilton, Willie Best, Arthur Treacher.

com; SF-seq (whodunit featuring electric chair for making people tell what is on their minds)

Ref: FD 5 June '35; Vw 26 June '35; LC.

Nix on Hypnotricks

1941 Par ani 1 reel.

Prod: Max Fleischer.

Dir: Dave Fleischer.

Story: Bill Turner & Cal Howard.

Ani: Dave Tendlar & John Walworth.

F-com

Ref: LC; PopCar.
See also: Popeye (1933-57).

No Barking

1954 WB color ani 7 mins.

Dir: Chuck Jones.

Ani: Ken Harris.

F-com (Claude the nervous cat vs. a frisky puppy)

Ref: LC; D. Rider.

No Blade of Grass

1970 British, Symbol (MGM) color scope 96 mins.

Prod & Dir: Cornel Wilde.

SP: Sean Forestal & Jefferson Pascal.

Art Dir: Elliot Scott.

Cin: H.A.R. Thomson.

SpFX: Terry Witherington.

Edit: Frank Clarke & Eric Boyd-Perkins.

Mus: Burnell Whibley.

Cast: Nigel Davenport, Jean Wallace, Anthony May, John Hamill, Lynne Frederick, Patrick Holt, George Coulouris, Anthony Sharp.

SF (set in near future; pollution causes mutant virus, which destroys long-bladed grass-type plants, resulting in world-wide famine & collapse of civilization)

Ref: Vw 4 Nov '70; MPH 18 Nov '70; SF Chronicle 5 Nov '70.

Based on the novel by John Christopher (C.S. Youd).

No Coffin for the Corpse

(novel by C. Rawson)

See: Man Who Wouldn't Die, The (1942).

No Credit

1947 Amateur (C-16) 16mm color ani clay sil 8 mins.

Made by: Leonard Tregillus & Ralph Luce.

exp-abs-F

Ref: C-16.

No Credits

See: Bes Naslova (1964).

No Exit

1962 Argentinian (Zenith Int'l) 85 mins.

Prod: Fernando Ayala & Hector Olivera.

Assoc Prod: James Zea.

Dir: Tad Danielewski.

SP: George Tabori.

Art Dir: Mario Vanarelli.

Cin: Ricardo Younis.

Edit: Carl Lerner.

Mus: Vladimir Ussachevsky.

Cast: Viveca Lindfors, Rita Gam, Morgan Sterne, Ben Piazza, Susan Mayo, Orlando Sacha, Manuel Roson, Mirtha Miller.

F (3 people, strangers to each other, are ushered into a hotel room -- they soon realize that they are in Hell, together for eternity)

Ref: FF '62 p328-30; Time 21 Dec '62; FD 12 Dec '62.

Based on play "Huis Clos" by Jean-Paul Sartre.

See also: Huis Clos (1954).

No Food for Thought

(teleplay by R.M. Fresco)

See: Tarantula (1955).

No Haunt for a Gentleman

1952 British, Anglo-Scottish (Apex) 58 mins.

Prod: Charles Reynolds.

Dir: Leonard Reeve.

Story: Frederic Allwood.

SP: Julian Caunter, Gerard Bryant, & Leonard Reeve.

Cast: Anthony Pendrell, Sally Newton, Jack MacNaughton, Patience Rentoul, Dorothy Summers, Peter Swanwick.

F-com ("ghost helps newly-wed frighten away mother-in-law" --Gifford)

Ref: BIB's; Gifford/BFC 11674.

No Holds Barred

1952 Mono 65 mins.

Prod: Jerry Thomas.

Dir: William Beaudine.

SP: Tim Ryan, Jack Crutcher, & Bert Lawrence.

Art Dir: Dave Milton.

Cin: Ernest Miller.

Edit: William Austin.

Mus Sup: Edward J. Kay.

Cast: Leo Gorcey, Huntz Hall, Marjorie Reynolds, Leonard Penn, Henry Kulky, David Condon, Bennie Bartlett, Sandra Gould.

F-com (magic helps boxer)

Ref: Vd & HR 18 Dec '52; Monogram production sheet.

See also: Spooks Run Wild (1941).

No Hunting

1955 WD (RKO) color ani 1 reel.

Prod: Walt Disney.

F-com

Ref: LC; Acad nom.

See also: Donald Duck (1934-61).

No Miracle at All

(Here Are Some Miracles --alt.t.)

1965 Soviet, Soyuzmultfilm (Sovexport) color ani 9.5 mins.

Dir: M. Kamenetsky & I. Uphimtsev.

Story: V. Kapninsky.

Ani: Y. Zaltsman.

F (burst waterpipe thought to be miracle)

Ref: Sovexport cat 2:116, cat 3:104.

No More Bald Heads

1908 French, Pathé sil 148 ft.

SF-com (hair-grower overdoes it)

Ref: BFI cat p23.

Note: title provided by BFI.

No More Fleeing

(Nicht Mehr Fliehen)

1955 German, Filmaufbau (C-16) 70 mins.

Dir: Herbert Vesely.

SP: H. Vesely & Hubert Aratym.

Cin: Hugo Holub.

Mus: Gerhard Rühm.

Cast: Xenia Hagman, Hector Mayro, Ditta Folda.

exp-sur-F

Ref: C-16; Classics of the Film p 132.

No Nightingales

(novel by S.J. Simon & C. Brahms)

See: Ghosts of Berkeley Square (1947).

No Orchids for Lulu

See: Lulu (1962).

No Parking Hare

1953 WB color ani 7 mins.

Dir: Robert McKimson.

F-com

Ref: Ani/Cin p 173; LC.

See also: Bugs Bunny (1938-62).

No Place Like Homicide

(What a Carve-Up! --Brit.t.)

1961 (1962) British, New World (Embassy) 88 mins.

Prod: Robert S. Baker & Monty Berman.

Dir: Pat Jackson.

SP: Ray Cooney & Tony Hilton.

Art Dir: Ivan King.

cont.

No Place Like Homicide cont.

Cin: M. Berman.

Edit: Gordon Pilkington.

Mus: Muir Mathieson.

Cast: Kenneth Connor, Sidney James, Shirley Eaton, Donald Pleasence, Dennis Price, Michael Gough, Valerie Taylor, Michael Gwynn, George Woodbridge.

H-com (in old, sinister house, madman fakes his death in effort to murder his relatives)

Ref: FF /62 p226; MFB Sept '61 p 133; FD 6 June '62.

Based on novel "The Ghoul" by Frank King & Leonard Hines.

See also: Ghoul, The (1933).

No Place to Hide

1955 US/Philippine, AA color 71 mins.

Filmed in the Philippines.

Prod, Dir, Story: Josef Shaftel.

Assoc Prod: Dan Milner.

SP: Norman Corwin.

Cin: Gilbert Warrenton.

Mus: Herschel Burke Gilbert.

Cast: David Brian, Marsha Hunt, Celia Flor, Manuel Silos, Hugh Corcoran, Ike Jarlego Jr, Eddie Infante, Lou Salvador.

bor-SF (super-bacteria strain; monster?)

Ref: Gasca p 188-89; MFB '58 p37; TVK.

No Questions on Saturday

See: Impossible on Saturday (1964).

No Survivors, Please

(Der Chef Wünscht Keine Zeugen: The Chief Wants No Survivors)

1963 W. German, Shorcht 93 mins.

Prod: Hans Albin.

Dir: Hans Albin & Peter Berneis.

SP: P. Berneis.

English Dialog: Steve Sekely (Szekely).

Art Dir: Tibor Redras.

Cin: Heinz Schnackertz.

Edit: Claus von Boro.

Mus: Hermann Ihieme.

Cast: Maria Perschy, Robert Cunningham, Uwe Friedrichsen, Rolf von Naukhaff, Karen Blaguernon, Gustavo Rojo.

SF (aliens from Orion take over bodies of Earth leaders at point of death to instigate war to wipe out human race, leaving Earth to the Orions)

Ref: TVG; MFB June '65 p90; Gasca p 331.

No Time for Love

1942 (1943) Par 8 reels.

Exec Prod: B.G. DeSylva.

Assoc Prod: Fred Kohlmar.

Dir: Mitchell Leisen.

Story: Robert Lees & Fred Rinaldo.

Adapt: Warren Duff.

SP: Claude Binyom.

Art Dir: Hans Dreier & Robert Usher.

Cin: Charles Lang Jr.

Process Cin: Farciot Edouart.

SpFX: Gordon Jennings.

Edit: Alma Macrorie.

Mus: Victor Young.

Cast: Claudette Colbert, Fred MacMurray, Ilka Chase, Richard Hayden, Paul McGrath, June Havoc, Rod Cameron.

F-dream; com (MacMurray dreams he is flying superhero)

Ref: Vd 8 Nov '43; HR 9 Nov '43; Life 5 Jan '44 p85.

No Trespassing

See: Red House, The (1946).

No Violence Between Us

See: Quem E Beta? (1973).

No, You Exaggerate

See: Non, Tu Exageres (n.d.).

Noah's Ark

● 1909 British?, Alpha sil ani puppet & live 350 ft.

Prod: Arthur Melbourne Cooper.

F-dream (in a girl's dream, her toys act out the story of the Deluge)

Ref: BFI cat p88.

● 1928 WB part talking 9507 ft; also sil, 9058 ft.

Dir: Michael Curtiz.

Story: Darryl Francis Zanuck.

SP: Anthony Coldeway.

Titles: DeLeon Anthony.

Cin: Hal Mohr & Barney McGill.

SpFX: Fred Jackman.

Technicians: Ned Mann and others.

Edit: Harold McCord.

Mus: Louis Silvers.

Cast: Dolores Costello, George O'Brien, Noah Beery, Louise Fazenda, Guinn Williams, Paul McAllister, Nigel De Brulier, Anders Randolf, Armand Kaliz, Myrna Loy, William V. Mong, Malcolm Waite, Noble Johnson, Otto Hoffman, Joe Bonomo.

rel-F-seq (story set in present day has flashbacks to story of Noah & the Deluge)

Ref: AFI F2.3865 p549-50; MPW 41:11:96; Vw 7 Nov '28.

● 1959 WB (BV) color ani 1 reel.

Prod: Walt Disney.

F

Ref: LC; Acad nom.

Based on the story of Noah and the Ark from "The Bible."

See also: Deluge, The (1911); Magoo at Sea (1964); Arche de Noe, L' (1966); Bible, (1966).

Noah's Ark

1950 (1951) French (Nayfack) 97 mins.

Dir: Henri Jacques.

Cast: Pierre Brasseur, Alerme, Armand Bernard, Georges Rollin, Claude Larue, Jacqueline Pierreux (Pierreau?), Jeanne Marken.

SF-com (inventor's auto motor uses water for fuel)

Ref: BO 9 Sept '50; FDY '51.

Nobody Works Like Father

1906 Vit sil 690 ft.

F-dream-com

Ref: Views & FI 1:10:10; LC.

Nobody's Boy

See: Chibikko Remi to Meiken Kapi (1970).

Noc Pered Rozdestvom

See: Christmas Eve (1913).

Noce au Village, Une

See: Fun in Court (1901).

Noces de Plumes

(Marriage of the Pens)

1968 Belgian, Les Prod'ns Pierre Levie 25 mins.

Dir & Mus: Patrick Ledoux.

Cin: Freddy Rents.

Cast: Laetitia Dufer, Edmond Bernhard, Kupisosnov, Max Rneard, Emile Verhaeren.

cont.

Noces de Plumes cont.

SF?

Ref: Trieste '69.

Based on a story by Eric Uytborck.

Noche de los Diablos, La

See: Notte dei Diavoli, La (1971).

Noche de los Mil Gatos, La

(The Night of the Thousand Cats)

1972? Mexican, Avant.

Dir: René Cardona.

SP: Mario Marzac.

Cin: Alex Phillips.

Cast: Anjanette Comer, Zulma Faiad, Hugo Stiglitz, Christa Linder.

H (madman millionaire keeps thousands of starved cats, feeds them human flesh; kills beautiful girls & pickles their heads; potential victim frees cats & they eat villain)

Ref: Vw 25 Oct '72 p26.

Noche de Walpurgis, La

See: Werewolf vs. the Vampire Woman, The (1970).

Noche del Terror Ciego, La

See: Tombs of the Blind Dead (1972).

Noches del Hombre Lobo, Las

(The Nights of the Werewolf)

1968 Spanish/French, Kin-Films color.

Dir: René Govar.

Story: Jacinto Molina.

SP: J. Molina, C. Beliaro, & R. Goyar (Govar?).

Cast: Paul Naschy (real name: Jacinto Molina) [werewolf], Monique Brainville, Helene Vatelle, Peter Beaumont.

F-H (mad scientist vs. a werewolf)

Ref: Vw 3 Nov '71; Eric Hoffman.

Sequel to: Frankenstein's Bloody Terror (1968).

Nocturnal Sorcery

See: Sorcellerie Nocturne, La (1903).

Nocturne

1954 French color ani sh.

Dir: Alexandre Alexeieff & George Violet.

F

Ref: Ani/Cin p95, 166.

Nocturne

(Nocturno)

1958 Yugoslavian, Zagreb color ani 9.8 mins.

Dir: Nikola Kostelac.

Story: Vatroslav Mimica & Vladimir Tadej.

Design & Ani: Vjekoslav Kostanjšek.

Bg: Zlatko Bourek.

Mus: Dragutin Savin.

F

Ref: Ani/Cin p 131, 172; Z/Zagreb p56-57.

Nocturno

See: Nocturne (1958).

Noddy in Toyland

1958 British, Bill & Michael Luckwell color 87 mins.

Prod: Kay Luckwell.

Dir: Maclean Rogers.

Cast: Colin Spaull, Gloria Johnson, Leslie Sarony, Peter Elliott.

F ("toyland boy blamed for crimes of Red Goblins")

Ref: Gifford/BFC 12569.

Based on play by Enid Blyton.

Noge

(Feet)

1967 Yugoslavian, Zagreb color ani 9.6 mins.

Dir, SP, Design, Ani: Ante Zaninović.

Bg: Zvonimir Lončarić.

Mus: Tomislav Simović.

F-com (2 men quarrel over enormous shoes; the giant owner returns & steps on the men)

Ref: Z/Zagreb p92.

Nöi Dolgok

(Eccentricities of Women)

1963 Hungarian, Pannonia 16mm color ani 10 mins.

Dir: Pál Nagy.

Story: Anna Vasvári.

Ani: Miklós Temesi, Jenö Koltai, Károlyne Kreitz, & Marfa Szilli.

Bg: Peter Szoboszlai.

Edit: János Czipauer.

Mus: József Kincses.

F-com

Ref: MFB Oct '72 p220.

Noir et Blanc

(Black and White)

1961 French ani sh.

Dir: Robert Lapoujade.

F

Ref: Ani/Cin p 98, 173.

Noise

n.d. Amateur (Film-makers' Coop) 16mm color & b&w live & ani 9 mins.

Made by: Alan Stecker.

exp-sur-F

Ref: FMC 5:311.

Noita Palaa Elämään

See: Witch, The (1952).

Nomads, The

See: Deserter and the Nomads, The (1969).

Non-Existant Knight, The

See: Cavaliere Inesistente, Il (1970).

Non Perdiamo la Testa

(Let's Not Lose Our Heads)

1959 Italian, Galatea.

Dir: Mario Mattoli.

SP: Ruggero Maccari, Giulio Scarnicci, & Renzo Tarabusi.

Cast: Ugo Tognazzi, Franca Valeri, Carlo Campanini, Xenia Valderi.

bor-H-com (man evades his benefactress's mad scientist brother who wants to kill him)

Ref: FEFN 12:16/17:41; Ital Prods '59 p22.

Non-Stop New York

1937 British, Gaum 8 reels.

Dir: Robert Stevenson.

SP: Roland Pertwee & J.O.C. Orton.

Cin: Mutz Greenbaum.

Edit: A. Barnes.

Mus Dir: Louis Levy.

SP: Kurt (later Curt) Siodmak, Roland Pertwee, J.O.C. Orton, & Derek Twist.

Cast: John Loder, Anna Lee, Francis L. Sullivan, Frank Cellier, Desmond Tester, William Dewhurst, Athene Syler.

myst; bor-SF (set slightly in future aboard non-stop trans-Atlantic & transcontinental planes)

Ref: Vw 29 Sept '37; LC; MPH 2 Oct '37; Gifford/SF p28; Gifford/BFC 10325.

Based on novel "Sky Steward" by Ken Attiwill.

Non, Tu Exageres

(No, You Exaggerate)

n.d. French sil 2 reels.

Dir: Charley Bowers (Bricolo).

Cast: Charley Bowers.

F-com

Ref: MMF 17:63.

Nonexistent Knight, The

See: Cavaliere Inesistente, Il (1970).

Nonki Ekicho

(A Happy-Go-Lucky Stationmaster)

1959? Japanese, Toei ani 16 mins.

F (stationmaster stops train wreck -- cartoon)

Ref: FEFN 12:16/17:45.

Noon to Midnight

See: Midi-Minuit (1969).

Noor-e-Arab

See: Tilasmi Talwar (1935).

Noor-e-Yaman

1935 Indian, Wadia.

Dir: J.B.H. Wadia.

Cast: Feroze Dastur, Sherifa, Muhommad, Husn Banoo.

F-H (house of a demon)

Ref: Dipali 6 Sept '35 p25-26.

See also: Lal-e-Yaman (1934).

Nora in Wonderland

1970 Philippine, Tower color.

Prod: Victor Villanueva.

Dir: Artemio Marquez.

Story: Rico Bello Omagap.

Sp Cin FX: Ricardo Marcelino.

Cast: Nora Aunor, Manny DeLeon, Ike Lozada, Bella Flores, Tessie Lagman.

F (giant, witch, fairy, etc.)

Ref: Borst.

Norliss Tapes, The

1973 Dan Curtis Prods & Metromedia (NBC-TV) color 75 mins.

Exec Prod: Charles Fries.

Prod & Dir: Dan Curtis.

Assoc Prod: Bob Singer.

SP: William F. Nolan.

Art Dir: Trevor Williams.

Makeup: Fred Phillips.

Cin: Ben Colman.

SpFX: Roger George.

Edit: John F. Link II.

Mus: Robert Cobert.

Cast: Roy Thinnes, Don Porter, Angie Dickinson, Claude Akins, Michele Carey, Vonetta McGee, Hurd Hatfield, Brian O'Byrne, Stanley Adams, Nick Dimitri [living corpse], Edmund Gilbert, Bob Schott [demon].

F-H (occult investigator vs. walking corpse who brings to life demon he has made out of clay composed largely of human blood)

Based on a story by Fred Mustard Stewart.

Pilot for TV series.

Ref: LAT 14 Jan '73.

Norman McLaren's Opening Speech

See: Opening Speech (1960).

Norwich Victims, The

(novel by F. Beeding)

See: Dead Men Tell No Tales (1938).

Nose, The

1966 Amateur ani sh.

Made by: Mordi Gerstein.

F-com (man seeks his runaway nose)

cont.

Nose cont.

Ref: Ani/Cin p95n.

Parody of the short story by N. Gogol.

See also: Nez, Le (1963).

Nose to the Wind

See: Nez au Vent (1957).

Nosferatu, the Vampire

(Nosferatu, eine Symphonies des Grauens: Nosferatu, a Symphony of Terror; The Terror of Dracula --8mm t.)

1922 (1929) German, Prana-Films (Film Arts Guild) sil (70 mins).

Dir: F.W. Murnau.

Sc: Henrik Galeen.

Art Dir: Albin Grau.

Cin: Fritz Wagner & Günter Krampf.

Edit: Symon Gould.

Mus: Hans Erdmann.

Cast: Max Schreck [vampire], Alexandr Granach, Gustav von Wangenheim, Grete Schröder, G.H. Schnell, Ruth Landshoff, John Gottowt, Gustav Botz, Max Nemtz.

F-H (Count Orlock is a vampire; destroyed by woman keeping him by her side until sunrise; where he goes rats & plague follow)

Ref: Vw 25 Dec '29; FTN p278, 636; F et R; MMF 4/5:145; F&F June '58 p34.

Based on novel "Dracula" by Bram Stoker.

See also: Dracula.

Nostradamus

1938-53 MGM 1 reel series.

Prod & Nar: Carey Wilson.

Dir: David Miller, Cyril Endfield, Paul Burnford, & others.

SP: Carl Dudley, DeVallon Scott, & others.

Edit: Tom Biggart & others.

Mus Dir: David Snell, Max Terr, Nathaniel Shilkret (Shikret?), & others.

doc; F-seqs (the prophecies of the historical Nostradamus depicted)

Ref: LC; MPH 22 Oct '38 p48.

Nostradamus

Mexican vampire series; in order of US release, see Curse of Nostradamus, The (1960); Monster Demolisher, The (1960?); Genii of Darkness (1960?); Blood of Nostradamus, The (1960).

Nostradamus y el Destructor de Monstruos

See: Monster Demolisher (1960?).

Not of This Earth

1956 Los Altos Prods (AA) 67 mins.

Prod & Dir: Roger Corman.

SP: Charles Griffith & Mark Hanna.

Assist Dir: Lou Place.

SpFX: Paul Blaisdell.

Cin: John Mescall.

Edit: Charles Gross.

Mus: Ronald Stein.

Cast: Paul Birch [alien], Beverly Garland, Morgan Jones, Jonathan Haze, Dick Miller, Ann Carroll.

SF-H (blank-eyed blood-drinking alien sent to Earth by matter-transmission; has telepathic & other psi powers; umbrella-shaped bat-like head-crushing monster)

Ref: HR & Vd 21 March '57; Corman p92; Photon 19:33.

Not too Narrow, Not too Deep

(novel by R. Sale)

See: Strange Cargo (1940).

Notes on a Triangle

(Note sur un Triangle)

1966 Canadian, NFB color ani 6 mins.

Prod: René Jodoin.

Mus: Maurice Blackburn.

abs-F

Ref: ASIFA 3; CFS cat '69; Ani/Cin p74.

Nothing

See: N:O:T:H:I:N:G (1968).

Nothing But a Nothing

1970? Soviet/Indian.

Dir: Mikhail Yuzovsky.

F (matches grant wishes; kingdom of evil magician)

Ref: MTVM 25:12::13; Soviet Film #4 '71 p20.

Nothing But the Night

1972 British, Charlemagne color 90 mins.

Exec Prod: Christopher Lee.

Prod: Anthony Nelson Keys.

Dir: Peter Sasdy.

SP: Brian Hayles.

Art Dir: Colin Grimes.

Makeup: Eddie Knight.

Cin: Ken Talbot.

SpFX: Les Bowie.

Edit: Keith Palmer.

Mus: Malcolm Williamson.

Mus Dir: Philip Martell.

Cast: Christopher Lee, Peter Cushing, Diana Dors, Georgia Brown, Keith Barron, Gwyneth Strong, Duncan Lamont, Fulton Mackay, Kathleen Byron.

SF-H (children injected with life essence of dead people have the dead people's memories, become fiendish killers)

Ref: MFB Feb '73 p32; CineF 2:3:24-25; Klemensen; Vw 3 May '72 p28; C. Lee.

Based on the novel by John Blackburn.

Nothing Venture

1947 British, Baxter 73 mins.

Dir: John Baxter.

SP: Geoffrey Orme.

Cin: Jo Jago.

Cast: The Artemus Boys, Terry Randal, Patric Curwen, Michael Aldridge, Paul Blake, Wilfred Caithness.

bor-SF ("boys save plans of professor's secret ray & catch crooks" --Gifford)

Ref: Gifford/BFC 11185; MFB '48 p30.

Notre Dame

1913 Pathéplay sil tinted 3 reels.

hist-H (France in Middle Ages: deformed hunchback bellringer loves gypsy dancer)

Ref: MPW 15:1037, 1073; Bios 16 Oct '13.

Based on novel "Notre-Dame de Paris" by Victor Hugo.

See also: Hunchback of Notre Dame, The.

Notre-Dame de Paris

1911 French, C.G.P.C. (Pathé) sil 2088 ft.

Dir: Albert Capellani.

Cast: Stacia Napierkovska, Henry Krauss, Claude Garry, René Alexandre, Georges Treville.

bor-hist-H; F-seq (France in Middle Ages; deformed hunchback bellringer loves gypsy dancer; becomes handsome when kissed; torture)

cont.

Notre-Dame de Paris cont.

Ref: MPW 10:884; BFI cat p39; Gifford/H p24, 27; F/A p318.

Based on the novel by Victor Hugo.

See also: Hunchback of Notre Dame, The.

Notte Che Evelyn Usca' Dalla Tomba, La

See: Night Evelyn Came Out of the Grave, The (1972).

Notte degli Spettri, La

(The Night of the Specters)

1913 Italian, Volsca sil sh.

F-H

Ref: Scognamillo.

Notte dei Dannati, La

(The Night of the Damned)

1971 Italian, Primax color 87 mins.

Prod Sup: Nicola Addario & Lucia Carnemolla.

Dir: Filippo Maria Ratti (Peter Rush).

SP: Aldo Marco Vecchio.

Addit Dialog: Ted Rusoff.

Art Dir: Ditta Rancati.

Makeup: Marcella Pelliccia.

Cin: Girolamo La Rosa.

SpFX: Rino Carboni.

Edit: Rolando Salvatori.

Mus: Carlo Savina.

Cast: Pierre Brice, Patrizia Viotti, Angela De Leo, Mario Carra, Antonio Pavan, Daniele D'Agostini.

F-H (woman is reincarnation of witch, kills descendants of her killers; at end she turns into dust)

Ref: MFB July '72 p 142; Vw 12 May '71.

Note: seems to exist in 2 versions, one emphasizing horror, one emphasizing sex.

Notte dei Diavoli, La

(La Noche de los Diablos: The Night of the Devils)

1971 Italian/Spanish, Filmes Cinemat. & Due Emme Cinemat./ Copercines color 88 mins.

Exec Prod: Luigi Mariani.

Dir: Giorgio Ferroni.

Adapt: Eduardo M. Brochero.

SP: E. M. Brochero, Romano Migliorini, & Giambattista Mussetto.

Art Dir: Eugenio Liverani & Cubero Y. Galicia.

Cin: Manuel Berenguer.

SpFX: Rambaldi.

Edit: Gian M. Messin.

Mus: Giorgio Gaslini.

Cast: Gianni Garko, Agostina Belli, Mark Roberts, Bill Vanders, Cinzia De Carolis, Teresa Gimpera, Luis Suarez, Umberto Raho.

psy-F-H (man meets family who on death become inhuman creatures who kill from fear of eternal loneliness; they are killed by stakes through their hearts, & decompose; all-a-delusion ending)

Ref: Ital Prods '72 p 146-47; MFB Feb '73 p32-33; MTVM 26:7:1:31.

Based on a story ("The Wurdulak"?) by A. Tolstoi.

Nouveau Monde, Le

See: RoGoPaG (1962).

Nouvelle Aventure du Lemmy Caution, Une

See: Alphaville, une Etrange Aventure du Lemmy Caution (1965).

Nouvelle Mission de Judex, La

See: New Mission of Judex, The (1917).

Nouvelle Peine de Mort, La
See: New Death Penalty, A (1907).

Nouvelles Luttes Extravagantes
See: Fat and Lean Wrestling Match (1900).

Novel Navigation
1909 French sil sh.
F-com (sail on cab makes it fly)
Ref: Bios 3 Feb '10.

Noveltoon
1945-67? Par color ani sh series.
F-com
Ref: LC.
See: Self-Made Mongrel, A (1945); Goal Rush, The (1941); Spree for All (1946); Much Ado About Mutton (1947); Santa's Surprise (1947); Land of the Lost, The (1948); There's Good Boos Tonight (1948); Leprechaun's Gold (1949); Quack a Doodle Doo (1950); Voice of the Turkey (1950); Of Mice and Magic (1953); Huey's Ducky Daddy (1953); Little Audrey Riding Hood (1955); News Hound (1955); Swab the Duck (1956); Right off the Bat (1958); Petite Parade, La (1959); Planet Mouseola, The (1960); Whiz Quiz Kid (1963); Space Kid (1966); Trip, The (1967).

Novia Ensangrentada, La
(The Bloody Bride)
1972? Spanish.
Dir: Vicente Aranda.
Assist Dir: Carlos Duran.
Cast: Alexandra Bastedo, Maribel Martin, Simon Andrev, Rosa M. Rodriguez, Dean Selmier, Montserrat Julio, Angel Lombarte.
F-H (vampires)
Ref: LSH 2.
Based on "Carmilla" by J. Sheridan Le Fanu.
See also: Vampyr (1931/32); Blood and Roses (1960); Terror in the Crypt (1963); Vampire Lovers, The (1970).

Novice at X-Rays, A
(Les Rayons X. The X Rays)
1898 French, Star sil 65 ft.
Made by: Georges Méliès.
F-com (transformations)
Ref: Sadoul/M, GM Mage 142.

Now Hear This
1962 WB color ani sh.
Prod & Dir: Chuck Jones.
F-com (Devil's horn used disastrously as trumpet)
Ref: LC; Acad nom.

Now Is the Time
1951 Canadian, NFB color 3D ani sh.
Dir: Norman McLaren & Raymond Spottiswoode.
exp-F
Ref: Ani/Cin p 174; French Ani p97.

Now We'll Tell One
1933 Roach (MGM) 2 reels.
Prod: Hal Roach.
Dir: James Chase (James Parrott).
Edit: Richard Currier.
Cast: Charley Chase, Muriel Evans, Lillian Elliot, Frank Darien, Gale Henry, Eddie Baker.
SF-com ("a belt that can transmit the personality of the wearer to anyone wearing a copy of the same belt" -- Maltin)
Ref: Maltin/GMS p58, 64; LC.
See also: Charley Chase Comedy.

Now You See Him, Now You Don't
1971 (1972) WD (BV) color 88 mins.
Prod: Ron Miller.
Assoc Prod & SP: Joseph L. McEveety.
Dir: Robert Butler.
Story: Robert L. King.
Art Dir: John B. Mansbridge & Walter Tyler.
Cin: Frank Phillips.
SpFX: Eustace Lycett & Danny Lee.
Edit: Cotton Warburton.
Mus: Robert F. Brunner.
Cast: Kurt Russell, Cesar Romero, Joe Flynn, Joyce Menges, Jim Backus, William Windom, Michael McGreevey, Richard Bakalyan, Frank Aletter, Edward Andrews.
SF-com (boy accidentally creates spray-on invisibility fluid which can be washed off with water; crooks after it)
Ref: Vw 5 July '72; LAT 12 July '72; CineF 4:45.
Sequel to: Computer Wore Tennis Shoes, The (1969).
See also: Invisible Man, The (1933).

Nuages Fous, Les
(The Mad Clouds)
1962 French color ani sh.
Dir: Henri Lacam.
F
Ref: Ani/Cin p98, 173; ASIFA Bulletin March '66.

Nude Beast, The
See: Bestia Desnuda, La (1968).

Nude in His Pocket
See: Amour de Poche, Un (1957).

Nude Vampire, The
See: Vampire Nue, La (1969).

Nudes on the Moon
See: Nature Girls on the Moon (1960).

Nudnik
1963?-- Rembrandt Films color ani 1 reel series.
Prod: William L. Snyder.
Dir: Gene Deitch.
F-com
Ref: Annecy '65; Acad nom.

Nueva Criatura, Una
(A New Creature)
1971 Spanish, Herga Films color 12 mins.
Dir: Francisco G. Ciurana.
Cin: Ricardo Abiñana Jr.
Edit: Raúl Roman.
Cast: Alexis.
F-doc (an apeman and a girl tour a real zoo)
Ref: SpCin '72.

Nuit du Cimetiere, La
(Cemetery Night)
1973? French, Films A.B.C. color.
Dir: Jean Rollin.
sex-F-H
Ref: Vw 9 May '73 p 106.

Nuit Fantastique, La
See: Fantastic Night (1942).

Nuit sur la Monte Chauve
See: Night on Bald Mountain, A (1934).

Nuit Terrible, Une
(A Terrible Night)
1896 French, Star sil 65 ft.
Made by: Georges Méliès.
F (very large beetle)
Ref: BFI cat p6; GM Mage 26.

Nuits de Dracula, Les
See: Count Dracula (1970).

Nuits de l'Epouvante, Les
See: Murder Clinic, The (1966).

Nuits de Raspoutine, Les
See: Night They Killed Rasputin, The (1960).

00-2 Agenti Segretissimi
(00-2 Secret Agents)
1964 Italian, Mega color.
Dir: Lucio Fulci.
SP: Metz, L. Fulci, Sollazzo, Vighi, Guerra.
Cin: Adalberto Albertini.
Mus: Piero Umiliani.
Cast: Franco Franchi, Ciccio Ingrassia, Ingrid Schoeller, Aroldo Tieri, Anni Gorassini.
bor-SF-com
Ref: Ital Próds '64 p 106-07.

002 Operazione Luna
See: Dos Cosmonautas a la Fuerza (1966).

087 "Missione Apocalisse"
(087 Mission Apocalypse; 087 Mision Apocalipsis)
1966 Italian/Spanish, Nike/Estela color 87 mins.
Dir: Guido Malatesta (James Reed).
SP: Arpad Sangermano (David Moreno) & G. Malatesta (J. Reed).
Art Dir: Jaime P. Cubero.
Cin: Julio Ortas.
Mus: Francesco de Masi.
Cast: Arthur Hansl, Pamela Tudor, Moa Thai, Harold N. Bradley, Eduardo Fajardo, Jorge Rigaud.
bor-SF (new bombs & atomic gas; criminal association has secret missile base)
Ref: SpCin '68 p42-43; Ital Prods 66 I:32-33.

No. 93 Lost in Action
n.d. Czech color 10 mins.
F (guardian angel becomes human, assigned to be guardian to expectant mothers)
Ref: Czech films flyer.

Number 1-13
● **Number 1-3**
1939-47 Amateur (Film-makers' Distribution Center) 16mm color 5 mins.
Made by: Harry Smith.
exp-abs-F
Ref: Undrgnd p 180, 282.
● **Number 4**
1950 Amateur (Film-makers' Distribution Center) 16mm 6 mins.
Made by: Harry Smith.
exp-abs-F
Ref: Undrgnd p 180, 281.
● **Number 5**
1947 Amateur (Film-makers' Distribution Center) 16mm color 6 mins.
Made by: Harry Smith.
exp-abs-F
Ref: SF Art Mus Prog 24 Oct '47; Undrgnd p 180.
● **Number 6**
1951 Amateur (Film-makers' Coop) 16mm 3D color 20 mins.
Made by: Harry Smith.
abs-F
Ref: SF Art Mus Prog; Undrgnd p95, 282.

cont.

Number 1 - 13 cont.
● **Number 7**
1951 Amateur (Film-makers' Distribution Center) color 16mm 15 mins.
Made by: Harry Smith.
exp-abs-F
Ref: Undrgnd p 180, 281-82.
● **Number 8-12**
1954 --8&9, 1956 --10&11; 1943-58 --12 Amateur (Film-makers' Distribution Center) 16mm 8, b&w, sil; others, color & sound; ani collage; lengths: 8, 5 mins; 9 & 10 10 mins; 11, 4mins; 12, 50 mins.
Made by: Harry Smith.
exp-sur-F
Ref: Undrgnd p 180, 281-82.
● **Number 13**
1962 Amateur (Film-makers' Distribution Center) color ani 180 mins.
Made by: Harry Smith.
F
Ref: Undrgnd p 180, 282.
Based on parts of novel "The Wizard of Oz" by L. Frank Baum.
See also: Wizard of Oz, The.
Note: this is test footage for planned but uncompleted feature cartoon version of "The Wizard of Oz."

Number III
See: III-es, A [spelled: Harmas, A].

No. 13 Demon Street
(unsold TV series)
See: Devil's Messenger, The (1962).

No. 00173
1966 (1969) Polish (Contemporary) color ani & live 9 mins.
Dir & Story: Jan Habarta.
Mus: Eugeniusz Rudnik.
F (butterfly disturbs the rhythm of a worker in a future society)
Ref: MTVM Sept '67 p21; Sightlines Jan-Feb '73 p6; Contemp cat '72-73 p335.

Numbers
See: Reign of Numbers (1966?).

Nupitae
1969 Amateur (Film-makers' Coop; Grove; Audio) 16mm color 14 mins.
Made by: James Broughton.
Cin: Stan Brakhage.
Mus: Lou Harrison.
F-seq (celebration of spiritual wedding)
Ref: FMC 5:50.

Nur Tote Zeugen Schweigen
See: Hypnosis (1962).

Nurse Mates
1940 Par ani 1 reel.
Prod: Max Fleischer.
Dir: Dave Fleischer.
Story: George Manuell.
Ani: Orestes Calpini & Louis Zukor.
F-com
Ref: LC; PopCar.
See also: Popeye the Sailor (1933-57).

Nursery Favorites
1913 Edison sound 1 reel.
F-mus (nursery characters, including Old King Cole, Giant, Miss Muffett's giant spider, etc. sing & dance)
Ref: B. Warren.

Nursery Rhymes
See: Mother Goose Nursery Rhymes (1902).

The Nutty Professor (1962)

Nursie and Knight

1912 Thanhouser sil 1020 ft.

F-dream (dragon in dream)

Ref: Bios 2 Jan '13.

Nutcracker, The

● 1965 W. German, Bavaria color 60 mins.

Prod: Karl Heinz Elsnor.

Dir: Heinz Liesendahl.

Art Dir: Rolf Zehetbauer & Herbert Strabel.

Cin: Werner Kurz, & Robert Hofer.

Choreog: Kurt Jacob.

Mus: P.I. Tchaikovsky.

Dancers: Melissa Hayden, Edward Villella, Patricia McBride, Harald Kreutzberg, Helga Heinrich.

ballet-F (girl's nutcracker present comes to life as a handsome prince & leads her into a world of magic & fairies)

Ref: MFB April '67 p62; UNESCO cat p45.

Based on the ballet by Peter Ilich Tchaikovsky from the story by .E.T.A. Hoffmann.

● (The Nut-Cracker)

1967 Polish color scope 89 mins.

Dir: Halina Bielinska.

Cast: Wienczyslaw Glinski, Barbara Wrzesinska, L. Niemczyk.

F (heroic nutcracker battles villainous mice)

Ref: MTVM June '67 p29, April '68 p42.

● n.d. KGO-TV color 60 mins.

Dir: Dave Crommie.

Choreog: Lew Christensen.

Mus: P.I. Tchaikovsky.

Dancers: Cynthia Gregory, & San Francisco Ballet Co.

cont.

Nutcracker cont.

ballet-F

Ref: UNESCO cat p88.

Based on the ballet by P.I. Tchaikovsky from the story by E.T.A. Hoffmann.

Based on short story "The Nutcracker and the King of Mice" by E.T.A. Hoffmann.

Nutcracker and the King of Mice, The

(story by E.T.A. Hoffmann)

See: Nutcracker, The.

Nutria, La

(The Otter)

1971 Spanish, Estudios Castilla color ani 8.4 mins.

Dir: Amaro Carretero.

Realisation: Vicente Rodríguez.

bor-F-doc (otter vs osprey)

Ref: SpCin '72.

Nutty, Naughty Chateau

(Château en Suede: Castle in Sweden)

1963 (1964) French, Corona & Spectacles Lubroso & Euro Int'l (Lopert) color 110 mins (102 mins).

Exec Prod: Robert Dorfmann.

Dir: Roger Vadim.

SP: R. Vadim & Claude Choblier.

Art Dir: Jean Andre.

Cin: Armand Thirard.

Edit: Victoria Mercanton.

Mus: Raymond Le Senechal.

Cast: Monica Vitti, Curt Jurgens, Suzanne Flon, Jean-Claude Brialy, Sylvie, Jean-Louis Trintignant, Françoise Hardy.

bor-H-com (insane wife thought to be a ghost)

Ref: Vw 18 Dec '63; Time 23 Oct '64; FD 13 Oct '64.

Based on play "Château en Suede" by Francoise Sagan.

Nutty Professor, The

1962 (1963) Jerry Lewis Enterprises (Par) color 107 mins.

Prod: Ernest D. Glucksman.

Dir: Jerry Lewis.

SP: J. Lewis & Bill Richmond.

Art Dir: Hal Pereira & Walter Tyler.

Cin: W. Wallace Kelley.

SpFX: Paul K. Lerpae.

Edit: John Woodcock.

Mus: Walter Scharf.

Cast: Jerry Lewis, Stella Stevens, Del Moore, Kathleen Freeman, Howard Morris, Milton Frome, Buddy Lester, Marvin Kaplan, Skip Ward, Henry Gibson, Doodles Weaver.

SF-com (awkward, ugly professor Kelp's potion turns him into dashing, handsome, malicious Buddy Love)

Ref: FF '63 p 141-42; Vd & HR 16 May '63; MFB Aug '63 p 111; FD 17 May '63.

See also: Dr. Jekyll and Mr. Hyde.

Nylon Noose, The

(Die Nylonschlinge [?])

1963 W. German, Urania 83 mins.

Dir: Rudolf Zehetgruber.

SP: Fred Ignor & Thomas Engel.

Cin: Otto Ritter.

Mus: Walter Baumgartner.

Cast: Richard Goodman, Laya Raki, Dietmar Schönherr, Helga Sommerfeld, Adi Berber, Gustav Knuth.

H (doctor trying to preserve people like mummies; catacombs)

Ref: FM 37:2; German Pictures (Willis).

Nymph of the Waves

1903 Biograph sil 25 ft.

Cast: Cathrina Bartho.

F (dancer dances on waves)

Ref: Niver 327; LC.

Nympho Werewolf

1970? Portugese.

sex-F-H (werewolf)

Ref: Richardson.

See also: Wolf Man, The (1941).

Nymphs' Bath, The

1909 French, Gaum sil 360 ft.

F (ghosts & nymphs)

Ref: Bios 9 Dec '09.

Nyoka and the Lost Secrets of Hippocrates

See: Perils of Nyoka (1942).

Nyoka and the Tiger Man

See: Perils of Nyoka (1942).

O

O

n.d. Amateur (Film-makers' Coop) 16mm 5 mins.

Made by: Paul Beattie.

F

Ref: FMC 5:31.

O Dwoch Takich Co Ukradli Ksiezc

(About Two Men Who Stole the Moon; The Moon-Robbers --ad.t?)

1962 Polish, Polski color scope 82 mins.

Prod: Franciszyc (Franciszek?) Petersile.

Dir: Jan Batory.

SP: Jan Brzechwa & J. Batory.

Cin: Boguslaw Lambach.

Mus: Adam Walacinski.

Cast: Lech Kaczynski, Jaroslaw Kaczynski, Ludwik Benoit, Helena Grossowna, Janusz Strachocki, Tadeusz Wozniak.

F-com (2 bored peasants decide to steal the moon; have many fantastic adventures)

Ref: Gasca p294-95; MMF 9:24.

Based on a novel by K.K. Makuszynski.

087 Mission Apocalypse

See: 087 "Missione Apocalisse" [spelled Nulla Otto Sette. . .] (1966)

O.K. Connery

See: Operation Kid Brother (1967).

O.K. Nero

(O.K. Nerone)

1951 (1953) Italian 84 mins.

Prod: Niccolo Theodoli.

Dir: Mario Soldati.

Story: Stefano Steno & Mario Monicelli.

SP: Age Continenza.

Art Dir: Guido Fiorini.

Cin: Mario Montuori.

Edit: Roberto Cinquini.

Mus: Mario Nascimbene.

Cast: Walter Chiari, Carlo Campanini, Silvana Pampanini, Jackie Frost, Gino Cervi.

F-com-sat (men knocked out in present day, wakes up in Nero's time)

Ref: MFB July '54 p 101; Ital Prods '50-51 p74-75.

O Lucky Man!
1973 British, Memorial Film & SAM (WB-Col) color 186 mins (176 mins).
Prod: Michael Medwin & Lindsay Anderson.
Dir: L. Anderson.
Story Idea: Malcolm McDowell.
SP: David Sherwin.
Prod Design: Jocelyn Herbert.
Art Dir: Alan Withy.
Cin: Miroslav Ondricek.
Sup Edit: Tom Priestley.
Edit: David Gladwell.
Mus: Alan Price.
Cast: Malcolm McDowell, Ralph Richardson, Rachel Roberts, Arthur Lowe, Helen Mirren, Dandy Nichols, Graham Crowden, Mona Washbourne, Vivian Pickles, Lindsay Anderson, Alan Price, Michael Medwin.
sat-com; SF-H seq (picaresque tale of young man's journey through society, treated almost surrealistically; encounters a pig with a boy's head grafted on it)
Ref: Vw 18 April '73 p30; HR 29 May '73.

O Mišu i Satovima
(Of Mice and Ben)
1969 Yugoslavian, Zagreb color ani 8.5 mins.
F-com (mouse friend of Prof. Balthasar fixes Big Ben)
Ref: Z/Zagreb p 110.
See also: Professor Balthasar (1967-69).

O Moda, Moda
(Oh Fashion, Fashion)
1969 Soviet color ani 20 mins.
Dir: Vahtang Bachtadze.
F-com (fashions through the centuries)
Ref: Mamaia '70.

007
See: James Bond.

002 Operation Moon
See: Dos Cosmonautas a la Fuerza (1966).

00-2 Secret Agents
See: 00-2 Agenti Segretissimi [spelled Nulla Nulla Due. . .] (1964).

O Rupama Čepovima
See: Of Holes and Corks (1967).

OSS 117
French spy series.
See: Shadow of Evil (1964); OSS 117 — Mission for a Killer (1965); Terror in Tokyo (1966); OSS 117 Prend des Vacances (1969?).

OSS 117 — Mission for a Killer
(Furia a Bahia pour O.S.S. 117: Trouble in Bahia for O.S.S. 117).
1965 (1966) French, P.A.C. & P.M.C. (Embassy) color scope 115 mins (84 mins).
Prod: Paul Cadeac.
Dir: André Hunebelle.
SP: Jean Halain, Pierre Foucaud, & A. Hunebelle.
Art Dir: Paul Boutie.
Cin: Marcel Grignon.
Edit: Jean Feyte.
Mus: Michel Magne.
Cast: Frederick Stafford, Mylene Demongeot, Raymond Pellegrin, Perrette Pradier, Annie Andersson, Francois Maistre, Jacques Riberolles.
cont.

OSS 117 — Mission .cont.
bor-SF (spy adventure involving drug from dried flowers which removes will power & causes victim to obey any orders)
Ref: FF '66 p266; FD 9 Sept '66; NYT 13 Oct '66.
Based on novel "Dernier Quart d'Heure" (The Last Quarter Hour) by Jean Bruce.
: See also: OSS 117.

OSS 117 Prend des Vacances
(OSS 117 Takes a Vacation)
1969? French/Brazilian, Cocinor/Films Number One & Vera Cruz color 92 mins.
Dir: Pierre Kalfon.
SP: P. Kalfon, Josette Bruce, & Pierre Philippe.
Cin: Etienne Becker.
Cast: Luc Merenda, Elsa Martinelli, Ewidge (Edwige?) Feuillere, Genevieve Grad, Norma Bengell.
bor-SF ("secret weapons")
Ref: Vw 25 Feb '70.
Based on the novel by Josette Bruce.
See also: OSS 117.

OSS 117 Takes a Vacation
See: OSS 117 Prend des Vacances (1969?).

O Slavnosti a Hostech
See: Report on the Party and the Guests, A (1966).

Obeah
1934 (1935) Arcturus Pics 75 mins.
Dir & Story: F. Herrick Herrick.
Cin: Harry W. Smith.
Edit: Leonard Weiss.
Cast: Phillips H. Lord, Jeane Kelly, Alice Wesslar.
F-H (voodoo curse)
Ref: FD 13 Feb '35.

Obedient Flame, The
1939 British, Film Centre color ani sh.
Dir: Norman McLaren.
F
Ref: Ani/Cin p 174.

Oberammergau Passion Play
(La Passion)
1897 French, Lumière sil sh? Filmed in Bavaria.
Dir: Hurd.
rel-F (the life of Jesus in Passion Play form)
Ref: Sadoul p21, 386; Rel/Cin p33.
See also: Passion Play, The.

Oberst Redls Erben
See: Brandstifter Europas, Die (1926).

Obi
(play by J.M. White)
See: Naked Evil (1966).

Object Lesson
1941 Amateur (C-16) 16mm? 12 mins.
Made by: Christopher Young.
exp-F (symbolic objects in natural landscape makes surrealistic effect)
Ref: Undrgnd p83; USA Exp List; C-16 p26.
See also: Subject Lesson (1956).

Objective Moon
(Destination Moon --alt.t?)
1962 French ani.
F
Ref: BIB's; TVG.
Based on the book "Destination Moon" by Hergé (Georges Remy).
See also: TinTin.

Oblacak i Oblaci
1962 Yugoslavian 12 mins.
Dir & Story: France Kosmac.
Mus: Alojz Srebotnjak.
SF (grandfather sees pollution, imagines future life on Earth)
Ref: Gasca p294.

Oblong Box, The
(Dance, Mephisto --e.t?)
1969 British/US, AIP color 91 mins.
Exec Prod: Louis M. Heyward.
Prod & Dir: Gordon Hessler.
SP: Lawrence Huntington & Christopher Wicking.
Art Dir: George Provis.
Cin: John Coquillon.
Edit: Max Benedict.
Mus: Harry Robinson.
Cast: Vincent Price, Christopher Lee, Alastair Williamson, Hilary Dwyer, Peter Arne, Harry Baird, Rupert Davies, Sally Geeson.
H; F-seq (Price's disfigured brother is buried alive, dug up by chance, murders conspirators; was disfigured by witch doctor's curse, which Price inherits after brother's death)
Ref: FF '69 p375; LAT 13 June '69; MFB July '70 p 148; Vw 11 June '69.
Title from short story by Edgar Allan Poe.

Obmaru
(Ombaru?)
1953 Amateur (CFS) 16mm color 4 mins.
Prod (& Dir?): Patricia Marx.
Cin: Jordan Belson.
Mus: Kaye Dunham.
exp-F
Ref: CFS cat '68; Undrgnd p95, 282.

Obras Maestras del Terror
See: Master of Horror (1960).

Obscenity of the Viper
See: Jasei no In (1920); Ugetsu (1953).

Obsession, An
1958 French color sh.
Prod: Edmonde Tamiz.
F-com (man sees the Mona Lisa everywhere)
Ref: FIR Dec '58 p604; Collier.

Obstacle of Affection, An
See: Temptation (1968).

Occhio nel Labirinto, L'
(The Eye of the Labyrinth)
1971 Italian, Transeurope color.
Prod: Nello Santi.
Dir: Mario Caiano.
SP: M. Caiano & Saguera.
Cin: Giovanni Ciarlo.
Mus: Roberto Nicolosi.
Cast: Rosemary Dexter, Adolfo Celi, Horst Frank, Franco Ressel, Sybill Danning (Dunning?), Michael Mayen, Benjamin Lev.
psy-H-dream seq (in a dream a girl sees her lover pursued by invisible killer & image turns to that of an eye in a labyrinth)
Ref: Ital Prods '72 p 150-51.

Occult, The
1913 American sil sh?
Author: Charles D. Myers.
bor-F ("hypnotic influence")
Ref: Bios 22 Jan '14; LC.

Occurrence at Owl Creek Bridge, An
(Au Coeur de la Vie)
1961 (1963) French 2 reels. One episode from 3-part French film, shown separately in US.
Prod: René Aulois.
Dir & SP: Robert Enrico.
Art Dir: Frédéric De Pascale.
Cin: Jean Boffety.
Edit: Denise de Casabianca.
Mus: Henri Lanoé.
Cast: Roger Jacquet, Anne Cornaly, Anker Larsen, Stephane Fey, Jean-Francois Zeller.
psy-F (in US Civil War, man imagines he has escaped hanging, flees captors, & makes way home to wife -- all in the split second before he dies)
Ref: MFB Nov '62 p 159; Unifrance '39; MMF 7:66-67; Acad winner.
Based on the short story by Ambrose Bierce.
See also: Spy, The (1932).

Oceans: Living in Liquid Air, The
1972 Document Associates (University of Calif) color 22 mins.
doc; SF (how man may develop artificial gills, possible human habitation of the ocean)
Ref: Films/Future p38.

Octave of Claudius, The
(novel by B. Pain)
See: Blind Bargain, A (1922).

Od Rzemyczka
(The Flight)
1961 Polish ani sh.
Dir: Miroslaw Kijowicz.
F

Odd Birds
See: Ptaci Kohaci (1965).

Odd Fellows Hall
1950 Amateur sil 16mm 10 mins.
Made by: Denver Sutton & Leonard Tregillus.
exp-F-sat-com
Ref: Film Images 16; Coronet.

Odds and Ends
1959 Amateur (C-16) 16mm color 5 mins.
Made by: Jane Belson Conger.
Mus: Henry Jacobs.
exp-F
Ref: FQ Spring '61 p34; CFS cat '68.

Odissea, L'
See: Homer's Odyssey (1911).

Odor-able Kitty, The
1944 WB color ani 7 mins.
Dir: Chuck (Charles M.) Jones.
Story: Tedd Pierce.
Ani: Robert Cannon.
Mus Dir: Carl W. Stalling.
F-com
Ref: LC.

Odyssey, The
1963 Australian?, Firebird Films 16mm ani cutouts serial 10 parts, first 12 mins, remaining 13 mins each.
Made by: Arthur & Corinne Cantrill.
myth-F
Ref: Collier.
Based on the epic poem by Homer.
See also: Return of Ulysses, The (1908); Dangerous Houses (1952); Homer's Odyssey; Ulysses.

Oedipus Rex

(Edipo Re)

1967 Italian color.

Prod: Alfredo Bini.

Dir & SP: Pier Paolo Pasolini.

Cin: Giuseppe Ruzzolini.

Cast: Franco Citti, Silvana Mangano, Alida Valli, Julian Beck, Carmelo Bene.

F-H-seq (oracle makes predictions which come true; when he learns his wife is his mother, ancient Greek Oedipus blinds himself)

Ref: Ital Prods '67 p 160-61.

See also: Oedipus the King (1967).

Oedipus the King

1967 (1968) British, Crossroads & U (U) color 97 mins.

Prod: Michael Luke.

Dir: Philip Saville.

SP: M. Luke & P. Saville.

Art Dir: Yannis Migadis.

Makeup: Ron Berkeley.

Cin: Walter Lassally.

Edit: Paul Davies.

Mus: Yannis Christou.

Cast: Christopher Plummer, Orson Welles, Lilli Palmer, Richard Johnson, Roger Livesey, Donald Sutherland, Friedrich Ledebur.

F-H-seq (oracle makes predictions which come true; when he learns his wife is his mother, ancient Greek Oedipus blinds himself)

Ref: FF '68 p372; MFB Aug '68 p 112; Vw 3 July '68.

Based on the play by Sophocles as translated by Paul Roche.

See also: Oedipus Rex (1967).

Oeuf à la Coque, L'

See: Boiled Egg (1963).

Oeuf du Sorcier, L'

See: Prolific Magical Egg, The (1901).

Oeuf Magique Prolifique, L'

See: Prolific Magical Egg, The (1901).

Oeyama Shuten Doji

(The Ogre in Mt. Oe)

1960 Japanese, Daiei color 114 mins.

Dir: Tokuzo Tanaka.

SP: Fuji Yahiro.

Cin: Hiroshi Imai.

Cast: Kazuo Hasegawa, Raizo Ichikawa, Shintaro Katsu, Kojiro Hongo, Fujiko Yamamoto, Tamao Nakamura.

F-H (apparitions; monsters & giant ox; flying goblin; witches & wizards)

Ref: UniJ 9:18.

Of-Course-I-Can Brothers, The

1913 British, Hepworth sil 575 ft.

Dir: Hay Plumb.

Cast: Harry Buss.

F-com (man experiences pain inflicted on twin)

Ref: Gifford/BFC 04129.

See also: Corsican Brothers, The.

Of Gods and the Dead

See: Os Deuses e os Mortos (1970).

Of Holes and Corks

(O Rupama Čepovima)

1967 Yugoslavian, Zagreb color ani 9.5 mins.

Dir, Story, Design, Ani: Ante Zaninović.

Bg: Pavao Štalter.

Mus: Branimir Sakač.

cont.

Of Holes and Corks cont.

F-sat-com (man corks tiny volcanoes & causes them to play tunes)

Ref: Z/Zagreb p91; Film Com Fall '68.

Of Men and Demons

1969 Hubley (Par) color ani 9 mins.

Prod: John & Faith Hubley.

Mus: Quincy Jones.

alleg-F (battle of men with his environment, conquering demons of rain, thunder & lightning, but releasing new demons of pollution & smog)

Ref: Vw 1 April '70; FIR April '70 p253; Acad nom.

Of Mice and Ben

See: O Mišu i Satovima (1969).

Of Mice and Magic

1953 Par color ani 7 mins.

F-com

Ref: LC.

See also: Noveltoons (1945-67?).

Of Stars and Men

1961 Storyboard color ani 63 mins.

Prod & SP: John & Faith Hubley.

Dir: J. Hubley.

Ani Dir: William Littlejohn & Gary Mooney.

Mus: Bach, Beethoven, Gabrieli, Handel, Mozart, Petzel, & Vivaldi.

SF-doc (man's status in the universe of electrons, atoms, protoplasm, stars, & galaxies)

Ref: Time 12 June '64; FQ Summer '62 p45-47; BO 20 July '64.

Based on the book by Dr. Harlow Shapley.

Of What Are the Young Films Dreaming?

See: À Quoi Revent les Jeuenes Films (1925).

Off on a Comet

(novel by J. Verne)

See: Valley of the Dragons (1961); Na Komete (1970).

Off to Bloomingdale Asylum

(L'Omnibus des Toqués)

1901 French, Star sil 65 ft.

Made by: Georges Méliès.

F (Negros change into clowns, then into one large Negro)

Ref: Sadoul/M, GM Mage 359.

Officer 444

1926 Davis Distributing Division (Goodwill Pics) sil serial 10 parts.

Dir: Ben Wilson & Francis Ford.

Cast: Ben Wilson, Neva Gerber, Al Ferguson, Phil Ford.

SF; H-seq (formula will allow person to rule the world; "The Radio Ray" --chapter t.)

Ref: CNW p 130, 253; Collier.

Official Secret

(play by J. Dell)

See: Spies of the Air (1939).

Offon

1968 The Serious Business Co (Film-makers' Coop; Canyon Cinema; others) 16mm color 10 mins.

Made by: Scott Bartlett.

exp-abs-F

Ref: MFB April '71 p86; CFS cat '68.

Often an Orphan

1949 WB color ani 7 mins.

Dir: Chuck (Charles M.) Jones.

Story: Michael Maltese.

Ani: Lloyd Vaughan, Ken Harris, Phil Monroe, & Ben Washam.

F-com

Ref: LC.

Ogon Batto

(Golden Bat)

1966 Japanese, Toei.

Dir: Hajime Sato.

Cast: Shinichi Chiba, Wataru Yamakawa, Hisako Tsukuba.

F (the Golden Bat wakes up from 10,000 year sleep to aid weak & just vs strong & evil)

Ref: MTVM April '67 p46; UniJ Bltn.

Based on the comic strip.

Ogon Kujyaku-jo

(Golden Peacock Castle; Adventures on the Ryukyus --ad.t.)

1961 Japanese, Toei 4 parts; pt 1, 57 mins; pt 2, 56 mins; pt 3, 57 mins; pt 4, 53 mins.

Dir: Shoji Matsumura.

SP: Shinji Kessoku.

Cin: Ko Matsui.

Cast: Tossho Sawamura, Kotaro Satomi, Shingo Yamashiro, Choichiro Kawarazaki, Hiroko Yoshikawa, Keiko Ogimachi.

F-seq (wizards; some swordsmen can become invisible)

Ref: UniJ 14:22-23; FEFN April '61 p67-68.

Ogre, The

See: Ogro, El (1969?).

Ogre in Mt. Oe, The

See: Oeyama Shuten Doji (1960).

Ogro, El

(The Ogre)

1969? (1970) Mexican, Matela (Azteca) color.

Dir: Ismael Rodriguez.

Mus: Les Baxter.

Cast: Tin-Tan, Cuitlahuac, Xanath, Tizoc, Tonatiuh.

bor-H-com (children in jungle think they meet ogre in jungle ruins)

Ref: PS.

Oh

1968 Amateur (Film-makers' Coop; Grove) 16mm color ani 10 mins.

Made by: Stan VanDerBeek.

exp-F

Ref: FMC 5:324.

Oh, Boy!

1938 British, Associated British Pathé Co. 76 mins (73 mins?).

Prod: Walter C. Mycroft.

Dir: Albert De Courville.

SP: Dudley Leslie.

Cast: Albert Burdon, Mary Lawson, Bernard Nedell, Jay Laurier, Robert Cochran, Edmon Ryan.

SF-com (potion turns timid chemist strong & confident, but also is turning him slowly into a baby)

Ref: Collier; Gifford/BFC 10427; MFB '38.

Oh Dad, Poor Dad, Mamma's Hung You in the Closet and I'm Feeling So Sad

1965 (1967) 7 Arts (Par) color 86 mins.

Prod: Ray Stark & Stanley Rubin.

cont.

Oh Dad, Poor Dad cont.

Assoc Prod: Carter De Haven.

Dir: Richard Quine.

SP: Ian Bernard.

Nar Written by: Pat McCormick & Herbert Baker.

Art Dir: Phil Jeffries.

Cin: Geoffrey Unsworth.

SpFX Cin: Farciot Edouart.

SpFX: Charles Spurgeon.

Edit: Warren Low & David Wages.

Mus: Neal Hefti.

Nar: Jonathan Winters.

Cast: Rosalind Russell, Hugh Griffith, Robert Morse, Barbara Harris, Jonathan Winters, Lionel Jeffries.

F-com-H (theater-of-the-absurd story; Winters [Dad], dead & stuffed, kept in closet, narrates & comments from Heaven as angel)

Ref: MFB April '69 p84; Vw 15 Feb '67; FF '67 p45; Time 3 March '67.

Based on the play by Arthur Kopit.

Oh Dear, Oh Dear, Oh Dear

See: Oj Oj Oj (1966).

Oh Dem Watermelons

1965 Amateur (Film-makers' Coop; Center Cinema; etc.) 16mm color 11 mins.

Made by: Robert Nelson.

Title Song: Stephen Foster & Steve Rush.

Electronic Mus: Steve Reich.

Cast: Members of the San Francisco Mime Troupe.

exp-F-sat (pixilated watermelons, representing Negroes, turn on the white race)

Ref: MFB June '71 p 129; FMC 5:253; FQ Summer '68 p51.

Oh Fashion, Fashion

See: O Moda, Moda (1969).

Oh, Grandmother's Dead!

See: To', È Morta la Nonna! (1969).

Oh, That Tonic!

1910 Italian, Lux sil 240 ft.

SF-com (potion gives woman super-speed)

Ref: Bios 199:35.

Oh What a Flash

1971? French, Marquise.

Dir: Jean-Michel Barjon.

SF (convicts sent into space)

Ref: Vw 3 May '72 p 100.

Oh! What a Lovely War

1969 British, Accord & Par (Par) color scope 144 mins.

Prod: Brian Duffy & Richard Attenborough.

Dir: R. Attenborough.

SP: Len Deighton.

Art Dir: Harry White.

Cin: Gerry Turpin.

SpFX: Ron Ballanger.

Edit: Kevin Connor.

Mus: Alfred Ralston, with traditional World War I songs.

Cast: John Mills, Vincent Ball, Pia Colombo, Paul Daneman, Isabel Dean, Robert Flemyng, Ian Holm, Joe Melia, Juliet Mills, Nanette Newman, Gerald Sim, Thorley Walters, Corin Redgrave, Dirk Bogarde, Phyllis Calvert, Jean-Pierre Cassel, John Clements, John Gielgud, Jack Hawkins, Kenneth More, Laurence Olivier, Michael Redgrave, Vanessa Redgrave, Ralph Richardson, Maggie Smith, Susannah York, Malcolm McFee, Colin Farrell, Maurice Roëves.

cont.

Oh! What a Lovely War cont.

mus-com-sat-F (World War I treated as variety show & amusement pier; much Fantasy)

Ref: MFB May '69 p93-94; FF '69 p385; SR 4 Oct '69; Gifford/BFC 13954.

Based on the play by Joan Littlewood.

Oh! What an Appetite

1908 Essanay sil sh.

SF-com (tonic makes man eat anything)

Ref: V&FI 29 Aug '08.

Oh, You Skeleton

1910 Selig sil sh.

H-com (girl medical student pursued by skeletons)

Ref: F/A p363; MPW 7:1007.

Oh! You Unbreakable Doll

1913 French, Lux sil 480 ft.

SF-com (indestructable doll)

Ref: Bios 15 May '13.

Ohatari Tankui Goten

(The Badger Palace)

1958 Japanese, Toho color scope 98 mins.

Prod: Sadao Sugihara.

Dir: Kozo Saeki.

SP: Tatsuo Nakada.

Cin: Kozo Okazaki.

Cast: Shinji Yamada, Ichiro Arishima, Yuji Nanto, Hibari Misora, Izumi Yukimura, Michiko Hamamura.

F (badgers save princess from evil spider queen)

Ref: FEFN 7 March '58 p 18.

Based on a story by Keigo Kimura.

Oil Can Harry

1933 Terrytoons (Fox) ani sh series.

Prod: Paul Terry.

Dir: P. Terry & Frank Moser.

F-com

Ref: Ani chart.

Oiley Peloso the Pumph Man

1965 Amateur (Film-makers' Coop; CFS) 16mm 14.5 mins.

Made by: Robert Nelson.

exp-F

Ref: CFS cat '68; FC 48/49: 25-26.

Oily Man, The

(Orang Minyak [?])

1958 Malayan, Keris.

F-H (magical oily man)

Ref: FEFN 28 Nov '58.

See also: Sumpah Orang Minyak (1958).

Oily Man Strikes Again, The

1958 Malayan, Keris.

F-H

Ref: FEFN 28 Nov '58.

See also: Sumpah Orang Minyak (1958).

Oiseau, L'

(The Bird)

1965 French color ani sh.

Dir: Jacques Vausseur.

F

Ref: Ani/Cin p 176.

Oiseau Bleu, L'

(play by M. Maeterlinck)

See: Blue Bird, The.

Oiseau de la Sagesse, L'

See: Bird of Wisdom (1966).

Oiseau de Sang, L'

(The Bird of Blood)

1972? French/Spanish.

Dir: Philippe Brottet.

Cast: Paul Naschy (real name: Jacinto Molina).

H; F?

Ref: LSH 2:69.

Oiseau du Paradis, L'

See: Bird of Paradise, The (1962).

Oiseau en Papier Journal, Un

(A Bird of Newspaper)

1962 French ani sh.

Dir: Julien Pappé.

F

Ref: Ani/Cin p 100, 174.

Oj Oj Oj

(Oh Dear, Oh Dear, Oh Dear; Well, Well, Well; Eller Sängen om den Eldröda Hummern: The Song of the Red Lobster)

1966 Swedish, Svensk Film-industri color.

Prod: Bengt Forslund.

Dir: Torbjorn Axelman.

SP: T. Axelman & B. Forslund.

Art Dir: Ardy Strüwer & Lars Åberg.

Makeup: Jan Garmstedt.

Cin: Gunnar Fischer.

SpFX: Bengt Lothner.

Edit: Carl-Olov Skeppstedt.

Mus: Daniel Bell, Börje Fredriksson, Lars Farnlof, & Erik Nordgren.

Nar: Olaf Thunberg.

Cast: Ardy, Lasse, Torbjorn, Lena Madsen, Sven Tumba, Signe Stade, Karin Stenback, Jan Halldoff, Alene Gebeyehou, Alan Blair.

bor-F-com-sat

Ref: Collier.

Ojo to Yubiwa

(The Princess and the Ring)

1956 Japanese, Toei Doga ani silhouette 16 mins.

myth-F (ring swallowed by great fish; prince fights demons)

Ref: ShF/J '58-59 p34.

Based on ancient Indian drama "Shakuntala" by Kalidasas.

See also: Shakuntala.

Okay, Toots!

1935 Roach (MGM) 1391 ft.

Prod: Hal Roach.

Dir: Charley Chase (Charles Parrott) & William Terhune.

Edit: Burt Jordan.

Cast: Charley Chase, Jeanie Roberts, Constance Bergen, Ferdinand Murier, Harry Bernard, Polly Chase.

F-com (Charley & wife exchange minds & voices)

Ref: Maltin/GMS p65; LC.

See also: Charley Chase Comedy.

Oklahoma!

1955 Magna Theaters Corp color Todd-AO 145 mins.

Prod: Arthur Hornblow Jr.

Dir: Fred Zinnemann.

SP: Sonya Levien & William Ludwig.

Art Dir: Joseph Wright.

Cin: Robert Surtees.

Edit: Gene Ruggiero.

Mus & Lyrics: Richard Rodgers & Oscar Hammerstein II.

Mus Arr: Robert Russell Bennett.

Mus Dir: Jay Blackton.

Bg Mus Adapt: Adolph Deutsch.

cont.

Oklahoma! cont.

Cast: Shirley Jones, Gordon MacRae, Gloria Grahame, Gene Nelson, Charlotte Greenwood, Eddie Albert, James Whitmore, Rod Steiger, Jay C. Flippen, Roy Barcroft.

mus; ballet-F-dream (musical western; in dream seq, bullets don't slow Steiger down)

Ref: FDY '56.

Based on musical play by Richard Rodgers & Oscar Hammerstein II, from play "Green Grow the Lilacs" by Lynn Riggs.

Oksigen

(Oxygen)

1970 Yugoslavian, Viba, Ljubljana IFrz 82 mins.

Dir: Matjaz Klopcic.

SP: Dimitrij Rupel & M. Klopcic.

Art Dir: Vlastimir Gavrik.

Cin: Rudi Valpotik.

Cast: Steve Zignon, Dusica Zegarac, Maugozata Braunek, Dare Ulaga.

sur-F (anti-automation film)

Ref: Vw 12 Aug '70.

Ol' Man Adam an' His Chillun

(sketches by R. Bradford)

See: Green Pastures, The (1936).

Old Czech Legends

See: Staré Pověsti Ceské (1952).

Old Dark House, The

● 1932 U 9 reels (74 mins).

Prod: Carl Laemmle Jr.

Dir: James Whale.

SP: Benn Levy.

Addit Dialog: R.C. Sherriff.

Art Dir: Charles D. Hall.

Cin: Arthur Edeson.

Edit: Clarence Kolster.

Cast: Boris Karloff, Charles Laughton, Raymond Massey, Melvyn Douglas, Gloria Stuart, Lillian Bond, Brember Wills, Ernest Thesiger, Eva Moore.

H (homicidal pyromaniac)

Ref: Vw 1 Nov '32; MPH 16 July '32 p52; FDY '33.

● 1963 US/British, Castle/ Hammer (Col) color (b&w) 86 mins.

Filmed in England.

Prod: William Castle & Anthony Hinds.

Dir: W. Castle.

SP: Robert Dillon.

Prod Design: Bernard Robinson.

Cin: Arthur Grant.

SpFX: Les Bowie.

Edit: James Needs.

Mus: Benjamin Frankel.

Title Bg: Charles Addams.

Cast: Tom Poston, Robert Morley, Janette Scott, Joyce Grenfell, Mervyn Johns, Peter Bull.

H-com (mysterious murders)

Ref: MFB Oct '66 p 155; HR & Vd 22 Oct '63; FF '63 p229.

H (stranded travelers encounter house with insane family, homicidal butler, etc.)

Based on novel "Benighted" by J.B. Priestley.

Old Doc Yak

1913-14 Selig sil live & ani 1 reel series.

Dir: Sidney Smith.

Cast: Sidney Smith.

F-com (drawings come to life)

Ref: F/A p627; MPW 17:56, 72; LC; Ani chart.

See also: Old Doc Yak and the Artist's Dream (1913).

Old Doc Yak and the Artist's Dream

1913 Selig sil ani & live 1000 ft.

Ani: Sidney Smith.

Cast: Sidney Smith.

F-dream (artist dreams drawing comes to life)

Ref: MPW 18:412.

See also: Old Doc Yak (1913-14).

Old Favourite and the Ugly Golliwog,The

1908 British, Clarendon sil 250 ft.

Dir: Percy Stow.

Sc: Langford Reed.

F (golliwog doll resent's child's new doll)

Ref: Gifford/BFC 02109.

Old Glory

1939 Vitaphone (WB) ani 1 reel.

Prod: Leon Schlesinger.

Dir: Chuck (Charles M.) Jones.

Ani: Robert McKimson.

Mus Dir: Carl W. Stalling.

Voices: Mel Blanc.

F-com

Ref: LC.

Old Hall Clock, The

1909 Lubin sil 875 ft.

F-seq (ghosts show modern couple use of secret panel behind clock)

Ref: FI IV:18:7; LC.

Old House Passing, The

1965? Amateur 16mm sh.

Made by: Larry Jordan.

Cast: John Graham.

F (ghost)

Ref: FC 52:84-86.

Old Iron, New Humor

1965 Rumanian color ani sh.

Dir: Bob Calinescu.

F

Ref: Ani/Cin p 145-46.

Old Khottabych

See: Flying Carpet, The (1960).

Old Lady and the Shoe, The

1929 WB 1 reel.

Cast: The Meglin Kiddies, including Frances Gumm (later Judy Garland).

F-mus

Ref: Film Careers 6:6.

Old Legends of Czechoslovakia

See: Staré Pověsti Ceské (1952).

Old Man and His Hen, The

See: Kobutori (1958).

Old Man and the Flower, The

1962 Pintoff Prods color ani 8 mins.

Prod, Dir, Sc: Ernest Pintoff.

Nar: Dayton Allen.

F-com

Ref: MFB Feb '65 p30.

Old Man of the Mountain, The

1933 Par ani & live 1 reel.

Prod: Max Fleischer.

Dir: Dave Fleischer.

Ani: Bernard Wolf & Thomas Johnson.

Voice of Betty Boop: May Questall.

Cast: Cab Calloway.

F-com (Betty saved from ogre by animals; songs)

Ref: LC; Hist US Ani Prog.

See also: Betty Boop (1930-39).

Old Mill, The
1937 WD (RKO) ani color
1 reel.
Prod: Walt Disney.
Ani: Josh Meador & others.
F
Ref: LC; Acad award; Hist
US Ani Prog.

Old Mill Pond, The
1936 MGM ani color sh.
Prod: Hugh Harman & Rudolph
Ising.
F-com
Ref: LC; Acad nom.

Old Monk's Tale, The
1913 Edison sil 995 ft.
rel-F
Ref: MPW 15:888; LC.

**Old Mother Riley Meets the
Vampire**
See: My Son the Vampire
(1952).

Old Mother Riley's Ghosts
1941 British, British Nat'l
82 mins.
Prod: John Baxter.
Dir: J. Baxter (Wallace
Orton?).
SP: Con West, Geoffrey Orme,
& Arthur Lucan.
Cast: Arthur Lucan, Kitty
McShane, John Stuart, A.
Bromley Davenport, Dennis
Wyndham, John Laurie, Peter
Gawthorne.
H-com ("charwoman foils
spies seeking inventor's
plans in 'haunted' castle")
Ref: Bizarre 24/25:73; Gifford/
BFC 10783; Collier.
See also: Jungle Treasure
(1951); My Son the Vampire
(1952).

**Old Mother Riley's Jungle
Treasure**
See: Jungle Treasure (1941).

Old Nip's Wedding
See: Rübezahls Hochzeit
(1916).

Old Old Fairy Tale
1969 Soviet.
F (friendly witch)
Ref: Soviet Film 8-69.

Old Play of Everyman, The
1915 Danish, Film Factory
Denmark sil.
Dir: Vilhelm Glückstadt.
alleg-F
Ref: Neergaard p46.
See also: Everyman.

Old Scientist, The
See: Vieux Savant, Le
(1964?).

Old Scrooge
1910 Italian, Cines sil
675 ft.
F-dream (old man visited
by 3 ghosts on Xmas eve)
Ref: Bios 1 Dec '10 p29.
Based on short novel "A
Christmas Carol" by Charles
Dickens.
See also: Christmas Carol,
A.

Old Shoemaker, The
1909 French, Gaum sil
840 ft.
H; psy-F-seqs ("fear &
visions of victim drive
murderer mad" --Willis)
Ref: Bios 14 Nov '09.

Old Sweethearts of Mine
1909 Vit sil 355 ft.
F-dream (visions of girls;
ani cigarette dream)
Ref: F/A p424; MPW 4:687.

Old-Time Nightmare, An
1911 Powers sil 1 reel.
F-dream (birds put boy on
trial)
Ref: MPW 9:778, 824, 10:41;
Bios 14 March '12.

Old Toymaker, The
1917 Rex (U) sil 1 reel.
Dir & Sc: Allen J. Holubar.
Story: H.A. Palowsky.
Cast: Allen J. Holubar,
Leah Baird, George C. Pearce,
Virginia Corbin.
F-dream (in dream, doll comes
to life)
Ref: MPW 31:547, 585; LC.

Old Woman Who Lived in a Shoe, The
● 1903 Lubin sil sh.
Ref: LC.

● 1920? Australian, E.J. &
Dan Carroll sil sh.
Ref: Collier.
F (lady lives in large
shoe with lots of children)
Based on the nursery rhyme.
See also: Old Lady and
the Shoe, The (1929).

Olden and New Style Conjuring
(La Magic à Travers les Âges)
1906 French, Star sil 204
ft.
Made by: Georges Méliès.
F
Ref: Sadoul/M, GM Mage 810-12.

Oldest Profession, The
(Le Plus Vieux Metier du
Mond: The Oldest Profession
in the World; L'Amore Attra-
verso i Secoli: Love Through
the Centuries)
1967 (1968) French/W German/
Italian, Les Films Gibé/
Rialto/Francoriz Rizzoli
(VIP & Jack H. Harris) color
115 mins (97 mins).
Prod: Joseph Bergholz.
Art Dir: Max Douy, Bernard
Evein, & Maurice Petri.
Six seqs; two fantastic,
as follows:
"Prehistoric Times" ("Ere
Préhistorique")
Dir: Franco Indovina.
SP: Ennio Flaiano.
Cin: Heinz Holscher.
Cast: Michele Mercier,
Enrico Maria Salerno,
Gabriele Tinti.
bor-SF (prostitution
in prehistoric times)
"Anticipation" ("L'An
2000" [The Year 2000])
Dir & SP: Jean-Luc Godard.
Cin: Pierre L'Homme.
Edit: Agnes Guillemot.
Cast: Jacques Charrier,
Anna Karina, Marilu Tolo,
Jean-Pierre Leaud.
SF-com (in year 2000,
visitor from space dis-
covers sexual & sexless
prostitution, reintroduces
the kiss & then love)
Ref: FF '68 p483-84; Vw 24
May '67; HR 17 June '68;
MFB Dec '67 p 187-88.

Ole Dole Doff
196? Swedish ani torn
paper sh.
Dir: Lars Lindberg.
F
Ref: Ani/Cin p 157.

Olvidados, Los
(The Lost Ones, The For-
gotten Ones; The Young and
the Damned --alt.t.)
1950 (1952) Mexican, Ultramar
(Mayer-Kingsley) 88 mins.
Prod: Oscar Danciger.

Olvidados, Los cont.
Dir: Luis Buñuel.
SP: L. Buñuel & Luis Alocriza.
Art Dir: Edward Fitzgerald.
Cin: Gabriel Figueroa.
Edit: Carlos Savage.
Mus: Rodolfo Halffter, from
themes by Gustavo Pitaluga.
Cast: Alfonso Mejía, Roberto
Cobo, Estela Inda, Miguel
Inclan, Hector Lopez Portillo,
Salvador Quiros, Victor Manuel
Mendoza, Alma Fuentes.
F-H-dream (story of juvenile
delinquents; in dream, boy
sees mother rise & float in
slow motion; while dying,
boy has vision of Death per-
sonified as a black dog)
Ref: Durgnat/Buñuel p60-68,
148; Kyrou/Buñuel p 197;
S&S May '51.

Olympiad
1971 Bell Telephone color
computer ani 3.5 mins.
Made by: Lillian Schwartz
& Ken Knowlton.
exp-F
Ref: IAFF '72.

Omar and the Ogres
n.d. Soviet? (Radio &
TV Packagers Inc) color
ani 17 mins.
F (boy battles pair of
ogres)
Ref: BIB's Winter-Spring
'70 pA-47.
Based on the story from
"The Jungle Book" by
Rudyard Kipling.

Ombaru
See: Obmaru (1953).

Ombre de la Pomme, L'
(The Shadow of the Apple)
1967 French ani sh.
Dir: Robert Lapoujade.
F (what happens after Adam
& Eve eat the apple)
Ref: Vw 28 June '67.
See also: Adam and Eve.

Ombro Cinema: La Danse
1968 USC color ani sh.
Made by: Herb Kosower.
F
Ref: ASIFA 5.

Omega
1970 UCLA (Pyramid) 16mm
color 13 mins.
Made by: Donald Fox.
exp-F
Ref: Vw 9 Dec '70; UCLA Prog;
Filmmakers 4:6:51-52.
See also: Genesis III (1970).

Omega Man, The
1971 Walter Seltzer (WB) color
98 mins.
Prod: Walter Seltzer.
Dir: Boris Sagal.
SP: John William & Joyce
H. Corrington.
Art Dir: Arthur Loel &
Walter M. Simonds.
Makeup Sup: Gordon Bau.
Cin: Russell Metty.
Edit: William Ziegler.
Mus: Ron Grainer.
Cast: Charlton Heston,
Anthony Zerbe, Rosalind
Cash, Paul Koslo, Lincoln
Kilpatrick, Eric Laneuville,
Brian Tochi.
SF-H (near future, in Los
Angeles: Heston thinks he
is only normal survivor
of plague war; some sur-
vivors are albino, light-
sensitive psychopaths, out
to kill him; group of
normal, young people &
way to combat plague found)

Omega Man cont.
Ref: FF '71 p493-96; WB
flyer.
Based on novel "I Am Legend"
by Richard Matheson.
See also: Last Man on Earth,
The (1963).

Omegans, The
1968
Cast: Keith Larsen, Ingrid
Pitt.
SF-H ("a strange tribe who
have become immune to radio-
active water causing dis-
figurement, death, and
life after death" --Collier)
Ref: Collier.
Note: following are credits
which were announced for
proposed production; same
as above?
1967? US/Philippine.
Prod: W. Lee Wilder & Vic
N. Nayve.
Cast: Joseph Cotten, Martha
Hyer, Ric Rodrigo, Bruno
Punzalan.
Ref: MTVM July '66 p26.

Omelette Fantastique, L'
1909 French, Gaum sil
ani sh.
Dir: Emile Cohl.
F
Ref: Filmlex p 1370.

Omicron
1963 Italian, Lux & Ultra &
Vides (Manley).
Prod: Franco Cristaldi.
Dir & SP: Ugo Gregoretti.
Cin: Carlo Di Palma.
Art Dir: Carlo Gentili.
Edit: Nino Baragli.
Mus: Piero Umiliani.
Cast: Renato Salvatori,
Rosemarie Dexter, Gaetano
Quartaro, Mara Carisi, Ida
Serasini, Calisto Calisti,
Dante di Pinto.
SF-H (factory worker taken
over by bodiless being from
another world, later decides
to have his planet invade
Venus instead of Earth)
Ref: Unitalia '63 I:132-33;
Gasca p324; CoF 4:57.

Omnibus des Toqués, L'
See: Off to Bloomingdale
Asylum (1901).

Omoo Omoo, the Shark God
1949 Esla Pics (Screen-
Guild) 58 mins.
Prod: Leonard S. Picker.
Assoc Prod & SP: George D.
Green.
Dir: Leon Leonard.
Cin: Ben Line.
Edit: Stanley Frazen.
Mus: Albert Glasser.
Cast: Ron Randell, Devera
Burton, Trevor Bardette,
Pedro DeCordoba.
bor-F (en route to South
Seas to return cursed pearls,
captain is murdered, curse
transferred to his daughter;
pearls returned to idol at end)
Ref: HR 28 June '49; Vd 29
June '49; MPH 9 July '49; LC.
Based on novel "Omoo" by Herman
Melville.

On a Clear Day You Can See Forever
1970 Par color scope 129 mins.
Prod: Howard W. Koch & Alan
Jay Lerner.
Dir: Vicente Minnelli.
SP & Lyrics: A.J. Lerner.
Prod Design: John De Cuir.
Choreog: Howard Jeffrey.
Cin: Harry Stradling.
Edit: David Bretherton.

cont.

cont

cont

On a Clear Day... cont.

Mus: Burton Lane.

Cast: Barbra Streisand, Yves Montand, Bob Newhart, Larry Blyden, Simon Oakland, Jack Nicholson, John Richardson, Roy Kinnear, John Le Mesurier, Richard Kiel.

F-mus-com (Streisand has psi powers: can make flowers grow, can sometimes read future; retrogression to past lives, progression to future life, etc.)

Ref: MFB Sept '71 p 184; CineF Winter '71 p27; Vw 17 June '70; SR 4 July '70.

Based on the musical play by Alan Jay Lerner.

On a Meadow
See: Na Livadi (1957).

On a Wall
See: Pe un Perete (1969).

On Borrowed Time
1939 MGM 100 mins (95 mins).

Prod: Sidney Franklin.

Dir: Harold S. Bucquet.

SP: Alice D.G. Miller, Frank O'Neill, & Claudine West.

Art Dir: Cedric Gibbons.

Cin: Joseph Ruttenberg.

Edit: George Boemler.

Mus: Franz Waxman.

Cast: Lionel Barrymore, Cedric Hardwicke [Death], Beulah Bondi, Una Merkel, Henry Travers, Nat Pendleton, Grant Mitchell, Ian Wolfe, Truman Bradley.

F (old man isn't ready to die, so he traps Death in an apple tree & no one dies)

Ref: Vw 5 July '39; FD 28 June '39; MPH 1 July '39 p45; LC; FIR Jan '65 p22.

Based on the play by Paul Osborn from the novel by Lawrence Edward Watkin.

On Celebrations and Guests
See: Report on the Party and the Guests, A (1966).

On Devil's Service
1972 Belgian/Italian.

H

Ref: CineF 2:3:39.

On Her Majesty's Secret Service
1969 British/US, Eon & Danilaq (UA) color scope 140 mins.

Prod: Harry Saltzman & Albert R. Broccoli.

Dir: Peter Hunt.

SP: Richard Maibaum.

Prod Design: Syd Cain.

Art Dir: Bob Laing.

Cin: Michael Reed.

SpFX: John Stears.

Edit: John Glen.

Mus: John Barry.

Cast: George Lazenby [James Bond], Diana Rigg, Telly Savalas, Ilse Steppat, Bernard Lee, Lois Maxwell, Desmond Llewelyn, Gabriele Ferzetti, Yuri Borienko, Angela Scoular, Catherine von Schell, Bessie Love, Julie Ege.

bor-SF (Bond vs Blofeld, who is engineering a bacteriological plot against various plants & animals in effort to conquer world; mental control via super-hypnotism)

Ref: MFB Feb '70 p34; LAT 18 Dec '69; Vw 17 Dec '69.

Based on the novel by Ian Fleming.

Sequel to: Dr. No (1962).
See also: James Bond.

On Parade
1936 Dutch ani puppet sh.

Dir: George Pal.

F

Ref: Ani/Cin p 174.

On the Air
See: Trouble with 2B, The (1972).

On the Beach
1959 Lomitas Prods (UA) 134 mins.

Filmed in Australia.

Prod & Dir: Stanley Kramer.

SP: John Paxton.

Prod Design: Rudolph Sternad.

Art Dir: Fernando Carrere.

Cin: Giuseppe Rotunno.

SpFX: Lee Zavitz.

Edit: Frederic Knudtson.

Mus: Ernest Gold.

Cast: Gregory Peck, Ava Gardner, Fred Astaire, Anthony Perkins, Donna Anderson, Guy Doleman, John Tate.

soc-SF (in 1964, nuclear war has created radioactive shroud gradually encircling Earth, killing all life; last to go are people in Australia)

Ref: FF '59 p299-301; FD 2 Dec '59; HR & Vd 2 Dec '59.

Based on the novel by Nevil Shute.

On the Bench
n.d. Amateur (Center Cinema) 16mm? 9 mins.

Made by: Ray Craig.

Cast: Larry Brown & Carol Zinner.

exp-SF (man meets alien)

Ref: CCC cat 2:8.

On the Bottom
See: Na Dnu (1969).

On the Brink
See: These Are the Damned (1961).

On the Comet
See: Na Komete (1970).

On the Edge
1949 Amateur (Brandon) 16mm 6 mins.

Made by: Curtis Harrington.

exp-sur-F

Ref: Brandon cat p255.

On the Edge of the Void
See: Seuil du Vide, Le (1971?).

On the Everyday Use of the Eyes of Death
1968 Amateur 16mm color sil 10 mins.

Made by: Robert Beavers.

exp-F

Ref: FC 48/49:23.

On the Planet Ygam
See: Sur le Planète Ygam (1967?).

On the Stormy Hill
See: Pokpoongea Uhunduck (1960).

On the Trail of the Lonesome Pill
1916 (1917) L-KO (U) sil 2 reels.

Dir: Phil Dunham, Lucille Hutton, Vin Moore.

F-dream-com (in dream, man visits home of magic mandarin; appearances & disappearances)

Ref: MPW 31:133-34; LC.

On These Evenings
n.d. Amateur (C-16) 16mm 23 mins.

Made by: Herbert Vesely.

cont.

On These Evenings cont.

exp-F

Based on poem by George Trakl.

See also: Death and the Maiden.

On Thursdays, a Miracle
See: Jueves, Milagro, Los (1957).

On Time
1924 Carlos Prods (Truart) sil 6 reels.

Prod: Richard Talmadge.

Dir: Henry Lehrman.

Story: Albert Cohn.

Sc: Garrett Fort.

Cin: William Marshall.

Edit: Ralph Spence.

Cast: Richard Talmadge, Billie Dove, Charles Clary, Stuart Holmes, Tom Wilson, Douglas Gerard, Fred Kirby.

bor-SF-H (demented surgeon seems to attempt to transfer brain of gorilla to hero, but is faked, attempt to see if he is capable of being movie actor)

Ref: MPN 29:1920; LC; AFI F2.3978 p565:

On to Mars
See: Abbott and Costello Go to Mars (1953).

Onan
1963 Japanese, Amateur (Film-makers' Coop) 16mm 7 mins.

Made by: Takahiko Iimura.

Mus: Yasunao Tone.

exp-F (masturbating boy gives birth to a plastic egg)

Ref: FMC 5:162.

Once and Future King, The
(novel by T.H. White)

See: Sword in the Stone, The (1963); Camelot (1967).

Once in a New Moon
1935 British, Fox British 63 mins.

Dir: Anthony Kimmins.

Cast: Eliot Makeham, Rene Ray, Morton Selten, Wally Patch, Derrick de Marney, John Clements, Mary Hinton, Gerald Barry, Richard Goolden, H. Saxon-Snell, John Turnbull.

SF ("socialist postmaster elected governor of village thrown into space when Moon collides with star" --Gifford)

Ref: Gifford/BFC 09686; Brit Cin; kerman.

Based on novel "Lucky Star" by Owen Rutter.

Once or Twice Upon a Time and Thrice Upon a Space
1965 Canadian color ani sh.

Dir: Al Sens.

F

Ref: Ani/Cin p 175.

Once There Was
(Once Upon a Time --alt.t.)
1957? Polish ani cut-outs sh.

Dir: Walerian Borowczyk & Jan Lenica.

F

Ref: Polish Cin p59f; Ani/Cin p 106, 107.

Once Upon a Time
1913 British, Folly sil 700 ft.

Dir & Sc: Fred Evans & Joe Evans.

Cast: Joe Evans, Fred Evans.

F-dream ("fairy changes yokel, tramp, farmer and daughter into first harlequinade")

Ref: Gifford/BFC 04492.

Once Upon a Time; or, Sovereign Goose Pie
1921 Czech sil 3086 ft.

Cast: Theodor Pýštěk, Zdenka Kavkova. (?)

F (fairy tale with witch, goose transformed into girl, etc.)

Ref: BFI cat p3.

Once Upon a Time
1943 (1944) Col 88 mins.

Prod: Louis F. Edelman.

Dir: Alexander Hall.

SP: Lewis Meltzer & Oscar Saul.

Art Dir: Lionel Banks & Edward Jewell.

Cin: Franz F. Planer.

Edit: Gene Havlick.

Mus: Frederick Hollander.

Mus Dir: M.W. Stoloff.

Cast: Cary Grant, Janet Blair, James Gleason, William Demarest, Ted Donaldson, Ian Wolfe, Kirk Alyn, Lloyd Bridges, John Abbott, Gabriel Heatter.

bor-F-com (dancing caterpillar)

Ref: HR & Vd 18 April '44.

Based on radio play "My Client Curley" by Norman Corwin.

Once Upon a Time
1972? Amateur 16mm (8mm?) color ani sh.

SF (age of dinosaurs)

Ref: TVG 4 June '72.

Once Upon a Time. . .
See: Once There Was (1957?); More Than a Miracle (1966).

Once Upon a Time There Was...
1907 (Miles Bros) sil 867 ft.

F (magic kettle can tell the gossip of the town)

Ref: MPW 1:442.

Once Upon a Time There Was a Dot
1964 Yugoslavian, Zagreb color ani 7.5 mins.

Dir, Story, Bg: Mladen Dejaković.

Design: Nedeljko Dragić.

Ani: Branislav Nemet.

Mus: Davor Kajfeš.

F-com

Ref: FC Fall '68; FQ Fall '68 p50; Z/Zagreb p78-79.

Ondine
See: Undine; Royal Ballet, The (1959); Sea Shadow (1965).

1
n.d. Amateur (Center Cinema) color 3.5 mins.

Made by: Grant Strombeck.

exp-abs-F

Ref: CCC cat 2:26.

One, The
See: Uno, L' (1965).

1, April 2000
See: April 1, 2000 (1953).

One Arabian Night
(Widow Twan-Kee --e.t.)
1924 British, Stoll sil 5871 ft. (6050 ft?)

Dir & Sc: Sinclair Hill.

Art Dir: Walter W. Murton.

Cin: D.P. Cooper.

Edit: H. Leslie Brittain & Rupert Hazell.

Cast: George Robey, Julia Kean (Julie Keene?), Lionelle Howard, Edward O'Neill, W. G. Saunders, Harry Agar Lyons, Basil Saunders [genie], Julie Suedo [ring fairy].

cont

One Arabian Night cont.

F (set in China; "washer-woman's son uses magic lamp [and ring] to marry princess" --Gifford)

Ref: BFI cat p 131; Gifford/BFC 07758.

Based on the story of Aladdin from "The Arabian Nights' Entertainments."

See also: Aladdin.

One Arabian Night

See: Sumurun (1920).

One Armed Swordsman, The

196?... Hongkong, Shaw Bros. color feature series.

Cast: Wang Yu (Chu).

bor-F (mystic martial arts)

Ref: Jim Landers.

See also: Zatoichi Meets His Equal (1969?); New One-Armed Swordsman, The (1972).

One Day, a Cat...

See: When the Cat Comes (1963).

One Day in Paris

1964? French, M.K. Prods 19 mins.

Dir: Sorge Korber.

Cin: Willy Gobagier.

Cast: Jean-Louis Trintignant, Anne Lewis.

F (magic umbrella flies about, bringing luck & love to each new owner)

Ref: Edinburgh '65 p22.

One Droopy Knight

1957 MGM color scope stereophonic sound ani 7 mins.

Prod & Dir: William Hanna & Joseph Barbera.

F-com

Ref: LC; Acad nom.

See also: Droopy (1943-57).

One-Eyed Soldiers, The

1965 (1967) Yugoslavian/British/US, Avala/BACO British/United Screen Arts color scope 92 mins.

Prod: Clive Sharp.

Dir & SP: Jean Cristophe.

Story: Richard Fraink.

Cin: Branko Ivatovic.

Cast: Dale Robertson, Luciana Paluzzi, Guy Deghy, Andrew Faulds, Mila Avramovic, Dragi Nikol.

H-seq (torture chamber; sadistic dwarf; "the earless monster")

Ref: MFB Sept '69 p 198; FF '67 p440.

One Froggy Evening

1955 WB color ani 7 mins.

Dir: Chuck Jones.

F-com (man finds dancing, singing frog in cornerstone; since it only dances & sings when he's alone it drives him to ruin, puts it back in cornerstone)

Ref: David Rider; LC.

One Glorious Day

(Ek --s.t.)

1922 Famous Players-Lasky (Par) sil 5100 ft.

Dir: James Cruze.

Story: A.B. Barringer & Walter Woods.

Sc: W. Woods.

Cin: Karl Brown.

Cast: Will Rogers, Lila Lee, Alan Hale (Sr), John Fox [spirit], George Nichols, Emily Rait, Clarence Burton.

F-com (Ek, spirit from Valhalla waiting to be born, takes over body of timid professor)

Ref: F/A p424; MPW 54:665; MW 5:48; AFI F2.3994 p568.

One Hour Before Dawn

1920 Pathe sil.

Dir: Henry King.

Sc: Frank Leon Smith.

Cast: H.B. Warner.

bor-F-H (man ordered by hypnosis to kill one hour before dawn; dreams of killing man who is found dead in reality)

Ref: NYT 12 July '20; LC.

Based on novel "Behind Red Curtains" by Mansfield Scott.

One Hour to Doomsday

See: City Beneath the Sea (1970).

One Hundred and One Dalmatians

1960 (1961) WD (BV) color ani 79 mins.

Prod: Walt Disney.

Dir: Wolfgang Reitherman, Hamilton S. Luske, & Clyde Geronimi.

SP: Bill Peet.

Art Dir & Prod Design: Ken Anderson.

Ani Dirs: Milt Kahl, Ollie Johnston, John Lounsbery, Marc Davis, Frank Thomas, & Eric Larson.

Prod Sup: Ken Peterson.

SpFX: Ub Iwerks & Eustace Lycett.

Mus: George Bruns.

Songs: Mel Leven.

Voices: Rod Taylor, J. Pat O'Malley, Betty Lou Gerson, Martha Wentworth, Lisa Davis, Tom Conway, Tudor Owen, Paul Wexler, Queenie Leonard, Thurl Ravenscroft.

F-mus-com (in modern London, Dalmatian dogs save their puppies & many others from evil woman who wants to make them into a fur coat)

Ref: FF '61 p31-32; HR & Vd 18 Jan '61; FD 18 Jan '61.

Based on the novel by Dodie Smith.

One Hundred Cries of Terror

See: Cien Gritos de Terror (1964).

100 Monsters

See: Yokai Hyaku Monogatari (1968).

120 Adventures of the Gullible Kid

n.d. Polish, miniature ani series.

F-com

Ref: MTVM 25:3:16.

Based on a character created by Kornel K. Makuszynski & Marian Walentynowicz.

One Hundred Years After

1911 French, Pathé sil 780 ft.

SF (scientist sleeps 100 years, awakens in 2011)

Ref: Bios 5 Oct '11.

100 Years Hence

See: Airship, The (1908).

One-Man Band, The

(L'Homme Orchestra)

1900 French, Star sil 130 ft.

Made by: Georges Méliès.

F

Ref: Sadoul/M, GM Mage 262-63.

One Man Show

n.d. Amateur (Film-makers' Coop) 16mm color & b&w 62 mins.

Made by: Maurice Amar.

8 films, 2 of which are abs-F: Love at Chrystie St.; Yellow Alley.

Ref: FMC 5:11-12.

One Man Show

1967? Amateur (Film-makers' Coop) 16mm color & b&w 50 mins.

Made by: Robert Breer.

exp-F

Ref: FMC 5:44.

See also: Jamestown Baloos (1957); Blazes (1961); Horse over Tea Kettle (1962); Breathing (1963); Fist Fight (1964); 66 (1966).

One Man's Secret!

(play by R. Weiman)

See: Possessed (1947).

One Million AC/DC

1970? NFB Films (Canyon) color.

sex-SF-com (dinosaurs vs. cavemen)

Ref: BO 31 July '72 pNE-3; Richardson.

One Million B.C.

(Cave Man --rr.t.; Man and His Mate --Brit.t.; Battle of the Giants --8mm t.)

1940 Hal Roach (UA) 85 mins (80 mins).

Prod: Hal Roach.

Assoc Prod (uncredited): D.W. Griffith.
Note: Griffith worked chiefly on the process material with the prehistoric animals.

Dir: H. Roach & Hal Roach Jr.

Story: Eugene Roche.

SP: Mickell Novak, George Baker, & Joseph Frickert.

Art Dir: Charles D. Hall.

Cin: Norbert Brodine.

SpFX: Roy Seawright.

Edit: Ray Snyder.

Mus: Werner R. Heymann.

Nar: Conrad Nagel.

Note: D.W. Griffith supposedly worked on this film, but his work is disputed.

Cast: Victor Mature, Carole Landis, Lon Chaney Jr, John Hubbard, Nigel de Brulier, Robert Kent, Ed Coxen, Creighton Hale.

SF (cavemen vs. dinosaurs; volcanic devastation)

Ref: HR 10 April '40; FD 16 April '40; MPH 6 Jan '40 p48.

See also: Son of Tor (1964); One Million Years B.C. (1966); Isla de los Dinosaurs, La (1966).

$1,000,000.00 Duck

See: Million Dollar Duck (1971).

One Million Dollars

1915 Rolfe (Metro) sil 5 reels.

Dir: John W. Noble.

Cast: William Faversham, Henry Bergman, Charles Graham.

F (astral body projection by detective)

Ref: LC; MPN 27 Nov '15.

1,000,000 Eyes of Sumuru, The

See: Million Eyes of Su-Muru, The (1967).

One Million Years B.C.

1966 (1967) British/US, Hammer/7 Arts (20th Fox) color 100 mins (91 mins).

Prod & SP: Michael Carreras.

Dir: Don Chaffey.

Story: Mickell Novak, George Baker, & Joseph Frickert.

Art Dir: Bob Jones.

Makeup: Wally Schneiderman.

Cin: Wilkie Cooper.

SpFX Dir: Ray Harryhausen.

cont.

One Million Years B.C. cont.

SpFX: George Blackwell.

Edit: James Needs & Tom Simpson.

Mus: Mario Nascimbene.

Cast: Raquel Welch, John Richardson, Robert Brown, Yvonne Horner, Percy Herbert, Martine Beswick.

SF (cavemen vs. dinosaurs; giant spider; volcanic destruction; ape-men)

Ref: Time 10 March '67; MFB Dec '66 p 180; LAT 26 July '67.

Based on film One Million B.C. (1940).

One More Time

1970 British, Chrislaw & Trace-Mark (UA) color 93 mins.

Exec Prod: Peter Lawford & Sammy Davis Jr.

Prod: Milton Ebbins.

Dir: Jerry Lewis.

SP: Michael Pertwee.

Prod Design: Jack Stevens.

SpFX: Terry Witherington.

Cin: Ernest W. Steward.

Edit: Bill Butler.

Mus: Les Reed.

Cast: Peter Lawford, Sammy Davis Jr, &*(unbilled) Christopher Lee, Peter Cushing.

com; F-H-seq (Davis encounters Dr. Frankenstein [Cushing], Dracula [Lee] & a Frankenstein Monster)

Ref: LAT 4 Nov '70; Photon 21:31.

See also: Dracula; Frankenstein.

One Never Knows

See: You Never Can Tell (1951).

One Night: ...a Train

See: Soir. ..un Train, Un (1968).

One Night, By Chance

See: Un Soir. . .Par Hazard (1964).

One Night of Fame

See: Fame and the Devil (1950).

One Night of 21 Hours

(story by R. Pestriniero)

See: Planet of the Vampires (1965).

One of Our Spies Is Missing!

1966 Arena (MGM) color 91 mins.

Exec Prod: Norman Felton.

Prod: Boris Ingster.

Dir: E. Darrell Hallenbeck.

Story: Henry Slesar.

SP: Howard Rodman.

Art Dir: George W. Davis & James W. Sullivan.

Cin: Fred Koenekamp.

Edit: Henry Berman & William B. Gulick.

Mus: Gerald Fried.

Cast: Robert Vaughn, David McCallum, Leo G. Carroll, Maurice Evans, Vera Miles, Dolores Faith, Yvonne Craig, James Doohan.

bor-SF (spies; rejuvenation serum)

Ref: MFB Aug '66 p 126.

Episodes of TV series "The Man from U.N.C.L.E." edited together for theatrical showing.

See also: Man from U.N.C.L.E., The.

One Out of Many

See: E Pluribus Unum (1969).

One Spooky Night

1923 Sennett (Pathé) sil sh.

H-com

Ref: LC.

One Glorious Day (1922)

One Spooky Night

1955 Col 2 reels.

Dir: Jules White.

Cast: Andy Clyde, Barbara Bartay, Norman Ollestad, Carol Coombs, Doyle Baker.

H-com

Ref: Maltin/GMS p 102; LC.
See also: Andy Clyde Comedy (1929-56).

One Spy too Many

1966 Arena (MGM) color 102 mins.

Exec Prod: Norman Felton.

Prod: David Victor.

Dir: Joseph Sargent.

SP: Dean Hargrove.

Art Dir: George W. Davis & Merrill Pye.

Cin: Fred Koenekamp.

Edit: Henry Berman.

Mus: Gerald Fried.

Theme: Jerry Goldsmith.

Cast: Robert Vaughn, David McCallum, Rip Torn, Dorothy Provine, Leo G. Carroll, Yvonne Craig, David Opatoshu, Cal Bolder, Teru Shimada.

bor-SF (gadgets; spies; torture via pendulum, mind-bending world gas; attempt to conquer the world; etc.)

cont.

One Spy too Many cont.

Ref: Vw 28 Sept '66; FD 29 Sept '66; F & F March '66 p5-52.
"The Alexander the Greater Affair" episodes of tv series "The Man from U.N.C.L.E." edited together for theatrical showing.
See also: Man from U.N.C.L.E., The.

One-Thousand and One Nights

See: Thousand and One Nights, A; 1001 Arabian Nights (1959).

1,000 Eyes of Dr. Mabuse

See: Thousand Eyes of Dr. Mabuse, The (1960).

One Thousand Miles an Hour

1916 (1917) Nestor (U) sil 1 reel.

Prod: Louis William Chaudet.

Sc: Bess Meredyth.

Cast: Eddie Lyons, Lee Moran, Harry Nolan, Edith Roberts.

SF-com (chemical makes super fuel for "flivver")

Ref: MPW 31:246, 275; LC.

1001 Arabian Nights

1959 UPA (Col) color ani 76 mins.

Prod: Stephen Bosustow.

Dir: Jack Kinney.

cont.

1001 Arabian Nights cont.

Story: Dick Shaw, Dick Kinney, Leo Salkin, Pete Burness, Lew Keller, Ed Nofziger, Ted Allan, Margaret & Paul Schneider.

SP: Czenzi Ormonde.

Prod Design: Robert Dranko.

Seq Dir: Rudy Larriva, Gil Turner, Osmond Evans, Tom McDonald, & Alan Zaslove.

Ani Dir: Abe Levitow.

Ani: Harvey Toombs, Phil Dunsan, Clarke Mallery, Bob Carlson, Hank Smith, Ken Hultgren, Jim Davis, Casey Onaitis, Stanford Strother, Ed Friedman, Jack Campbell, Herman Cohen, Rudy Zamora, & Stan Wilkins.

Edit: Joe Siracusa, Skip Craig, & Earl Bennett.

Mus: George Duning.

Mus Dir: Morris Stoloff.

Voices: Jim Backus, Kathryn Grant, Hans Conried, Dwayne Hickman, Herschel Bernardi, Daws Butler.

F-com (Aladdin's lamp & genie, with Magoo as Aladdin's uncle)

Ref: FF '59 p303-04; MFB Dec '59 p 156; Vd & HR 9 Dec '59; MPH 12 Dec '59.

See also: Arabian Nights, The; Mister Magoo (1949-).

1000 Years from Now

See: Captive Women (1952).

One Too-Exciting Night

1922 British, Hepworth sil 850 ft.

Prod: C.W. Hepworth.

Dir & Sc: Gaston Quiribet.

F-com (tricks)

Ref: Gifford/BFC 07601; Sus/Cin p 121.

See also: Q-Riosities by 'Q'.

One Touch of Venus

1948 U 82 mins.

Prod: Lester Cowan.

Dir: William A. Seiter.

SP: Harry Kurnitz & Frank Tashlin.

Art Dir: Bernard Herzbrun & Emrich Nicholson.

Makeup: Bud Westmore.

Cin: Frank Planer.

SpFX Cin: David S. Horsley.

Edit: Otto Ludwig.

Mus: Kurt Weill.

Cast: Robert Walker, Ava Gardner, Dick Haymes, Eve Arden, Tom Conway, Olga San Juan, James Flavin, Sara Allgood, Arthur O'Connell.

F-mus-com (statue comes to life)

cont

One Touch of Venus cont.

Ref: HR & Vd 19 Aug '48; MFB April–May '50 p60.

Based on the musical play with book & lyrics by S.J. Perelman & Ogden Nash and music by Kurt Weill.

See also: Tinted Venus, The (1921).

One, Two, Three, Four

See: Black Tights (1960).

One Way Passage

1932 WB 67 mins.

Dir: Tay Garnett.

SP: Wilson Mizner & Joseph Jackson.

Cin: Robert Kurble (Kurrle?).

Edit: Ralph Dawson.

Cast: William Powell, Kay Francis, Frank McHugh, Aline MacMahon, Warren Hymer, Frederick Burton, Douglas Gerrard, Herbert Mundin.

F-seq (at end, wine glasses broken by ghosts of dead lovers as they did for toasts in life)

Ref: Vw 18 Oct '32; Harrison Reports 17 Sept '32; Photo Oct '32.

Based on the story by Robert Lord.

See also: 'Til We Meet Again (in exclusion list).

One Way Pendulum

1964 (1965) British, Woodfall (Lopert) 90 mins.

Exec Prod: Oscar Lewenstein.

Prod: Michael Deeley.

Dir: Peter Yates.

SP: N.F. Simpson.

Prod Design: Reece Pemberton.

Cin: Denys Coop.

Edit: Peter Taylor.

Mus: Richard Rodney Bennett.

Cast: Eric Sykes, George Cole, Julia Foster, Jonathan Miller, Peggy Mount, Mona Washbourne, Douglas Wilmer.

exp-sur-F-com (peculiar family; speak-your-weight machines made to sing "Hallelujah Chorus;" etc.)

Based on the play by N.F. Simpson.

One Way Street

1925 FN sil 5596 ft.

Prod & Adapt: Earl Hudson.

Dir: John Francis Dillon.

Sc: Arthur Statter & Mary Alice Scully.

Cin: Arthur Edeson.

Cast: Ben Lyon, Anna Q. Nilsson, Marjorie Daw, Dorothy Cumming, Lumsden Hare, Mona Kingsley, Thomas Holding.

SF (woman is rejuvenated by monkey-gland treatment; becomes suddenly very old at climax)

Ref: MPN 31:1646; AFI F2. 4020 p571-72; LC.

Based on the novel by Beale Davis.

One Wish too Many

1956 British, Realist Film Unit 56 mins.

Prod: Basil Wright.

Dir: John Durst.

Story: Norah Pulling.

Adapt: Mary Cathcart Borer.

SP: John Eldridge.

Cin: Adrian Jeakins.

Edit: James Clark.

SpFX: (Les?) Bowie & Margutti.

Mus: Douglas Gamley.

Cast: Anthony Richmond, Rosalind Gourgey, John Pike, Terry Cooke.

F-com (magic marble grants wishes)

Ref: MFB Nov '56 p 141; Vw 28 April '65; TVG.

Onésime et la Maison Hantée

(Simple Simon and the Haunted House)

1913 French, Gaum sil sh.

Dir: Jean Durand.

Cast: Ernest Bourbon.

H-com

Ref: Mitry II (Willis).

See also: Onésime Horloger (1912).

Onésime et le Clubman

(Simple Simon and the Clubman)

1914 French sil 1/2 reel.

Dir: Jean Durand.

Cast: Ernest Bourbon.

H-com

Ref: Bios 5 March'14; Scognamillo.

See also: Onésime Horloger (1912).

Onésime aux Enfers

(Simple Simon in Hell; Simple Simon and the Devil --Brit.t.)

1912 French, Pathé sil 1/2 reel.

Dir: Jean Durand.

Cast: Ernest Bourbon.

F-com

Ref: Scognamillo; Bios 3 Oct '12.

See also: Onésime Horloger (1912).

Onésime Horloger

(Simple Simon Clock Maker)

1912 French, Pathé sil (5850 ft).

Dir: Jean Durand.

Cast: Ernest Bourbon, Gaston Modot.

F-com (to inherit fortune in 20 years, Onésime tampers with clock to speed up time) up time)

Ref: Scognamillo; DdC II:308; Laclos 188.

See also: Onésime aux Enfers (1912); Onésime et la Maison Hantee (1913); Onésime et le Clubman (1914); Times Are Out of Joint, The (1910).

Onibaba

(Oni Baba; The Demon; The Hole; Devil Woman --ad.t.)

1965 Japanese, Toho scope 103 mins.

Prod: Kindai Eiga Kyokai & Tokyo Eiga.

Dir, SP, Art Dir: Kaneto Shindo.

Cin: Kiyomi Kuroda.

Edit: Toshio Enoki.

Mus: Hikaru Hayashi.

Cast: Nobuko Otowa, Jitsuko Yoshimura, Kei Sato, Taiji Tonoyama, Jukichi Uno.

psy-F-H (under mask of a demon, woman's face rots; two women kill samurai to get armor by making them fall into hole)

Ref: MFB Dec '66 p 180; F&F Jan '67 p33; FD 18 Feb '65; Vw 10 Feb '65.

Onibi

(Will of the Wisp --ad.t.)

1956 Japanese, Toho 63 mins.

Cast: Daisuke Kato, Seiji Miyaguchi, Nobuo Nakamura, Sachio Sakai, Keiko Tsushima.

bor-F-H (man sees an "unearthly light" flickering over dead bodies of husband & wife)

Ref: FEFN 27 July '56 p 17.

Based on a novel by Nobuko Yoshiya.

Only a Coffin

See: Solo un Ataud (1966).

Only a Dream

1909 French, Gaum (Kleine) sil 470 ft.

F-dream

Ref: MPW 5:61, 88; FI IV-29:5.

Only One Girl; or, A Boom in Sausages

1910 British, Clarendon sil 495 ft.

Dir: Percy Stow.

F-com (small town has only one available girl, so hero makes rivals into sausages to win her)

Ref: Gifford/BFC 02808.

Only Some Steps from the Roof

See: Shag S Krishi (1966).

Only the Dead Are Silent

See: Hypnosis (1962).

Only Way Out Is Dead, The

See: Man Who Wanted to Live Forever, The (1970).

Onna Kyuketsuki

(Male Vampire; Vampire Man [sic: "Onna" means "woman " trans. t. provided in sources])

1959 Japanese, Shintoho 78 mins.

Dir: Nobuo Nakagawa.

SP: Shin Nakazawa & Katsuyoshi Nakatsu.

Cin: Yoshima Hirano.

Cast: Shigeru Amachi, Yoko Mihara, Keinosuke Wada, Junko Ikeuchi.

F-H (vampire can't stand moonlight; has pigmy, witch, monster as assistants; girl turned into wax doll)

Ref: UniJ 5:22; Photon 19:35; MMF 9:f32.

Onryo Sakura Dai-Sodo

(He Had to Die --ad.t.)

1957 Japanese, Shintoho 103 mins.

Prod: Mitsugi Okura.

Dir & SP: Kunio Watanabe.

Cin: Takashi Watanabe.

Cast: Kanjuro Arashi, Shoji Nakayama, Joji Oka, Minoru Takada, Ranko Hanai.

F-H (man pleads with Shogun to relieve taxes, is executed; his ghost haunts the Shogun's aide who ordered his execution)

Ref: FEFN 24 May '57 p22.

Based on a story by Yoshihiro Takenaka.

Onset: Variation No. 1

n.d. Amateur (Film-makers' Coop) 16mm color 4 mins.

Made by: John Gruenberger.

Mus: Ravi Shankar or The Beatles.

exp-F

Ref: FMC 5:136; CFS cat '69.

Note: two versions available, identical except for music.

Oompah-Pah

1965 Belgian ani 10 mins.

F-com

Ref: Ani/Belgium p31.

Oompahs, The

1951 (1952) UPA (Col) color ani 8 mins.

Exec Prod: Stephen Bosustow.

Prod & Dir: Robert Cannon.

Story & Design: T. Hee.

Mus: Ray Sherman.

F-com (musical instruments personified)

Ref: MFB Oct '56 p 133; LC.

Op Hop — Hop Op

1966 Canadian, NFB 16mm 4 mins.

Dir: Pierre Hébert.

abs-F

Ref: Vw 28 June '67.

Opening Night

See: Premijera (1957).

Opening Speech

(Mesdames, Messieurs; Norman McLaren's Opening Speech --alt.ts.)

1960 Canadian, NFB (Pyramid) color live & ani objects 7 mins.

Dir: Norman McLaren.

Cast: Norman McLaren.

F-com (McLaren tries to introduce film festival, but must fight with microphone)

Ref: Ani/Cin p71, 174; Pyramid cat p228.

Opera Cordis

1968 Yugoslavian, Zagreb color ani 10 mins.

Dir, Story, Design, Ani: Dusan Vukotić.

Bg: Srdjan Matić.

Mus: Tomislav Simović.

F (after operation on wife's heart husband discovers his rival in the heart, takes his place)

Ref: Mamaia '70; Trieste '69; Z/Zagreb p94.

Opera 2, 3, & 4

1923 German sil series.

Dir: Walter Ruttmann.

exp-abs-F

Ref: F/A p643.

Operacion Atlantida

See: Operation Atlantis (1965).

Operacíon Contraespionaje

See: Operazione Controspionaggio (1965).

Operacion Goldman

See: Lightning Bolt (1966).

Operation Atlantis

(Agente S03 Operazione Atlantide; Agent 003, Operacion Atlantida)

1965 Italian/Spanish, Splendor/Fisa color scope 88 mins.

Prod: Sidney Pink.

Dir: Domenico Paolella (Paul Fleming).

Story: Vinicio Marinucci (Vic Powell).

SP: Victor Auz.

Cin: Francisco Sanchez & Marcello Masciocchi.

Mus: Teo Usuelli.

Cast: John Ericson, Berna Rock, Erika Blank, Beni Deus, Maria Granada, Carlo Hinterman, José Manuel Martin.

bor-SF (secret Chinese atomic installation)

Ref: LAT Calendar 20 June '65; SpCin '67 p 14-15; Ital Prods '65 p76-77.

Operation Counterspy

See: Operazione Controspionaggio (1965).

Operation Fear

See: Kill Baby Kill (1966).

Operation Goldman

See: Lightning Bolt (1966).

Operation Goldseven

See: Operazione Goldseven (1966).

Operation Kid Brother
(O.K. Connery)
1967 Italian, Dario Sabatello Prods (UA) color 104 mins.
Prod: Dario Sabatello.
Dir: Alberto De Martino.
SP: Paul Levi, Frank Walker, & Canzio.
Art Dir: Franco Fontana.
Cin: Alejandro Ulloa.
SpFX: Gagliano.
Edit: Otello Colangeli.
Mus: Ennio Morricone & Bruno Nicolai.
Cast: Neil Connery, Daniela Bianchi, Adolfo Celi, Agata Flori, Bernard Lee, Anthony Dawson, Lois Maxwell, Yachuco Yama.
bor-SF (truth-compelling hypnosis; futuristic atomic underground city; radiation device deactivates weapons; Note: hero is implied to be James Bond's brother, & the actor is Sean Connery's brother in reality)
Ref: FF '67 p380-81; MFB May '68 p78; Vw 11 Oct '67.
See also: James Bond.

Operation Monsterland
See: Destroy All Monsters (1968).

Operation Paradise
See: Kiss the Girls and Make Them Die (1966).

Operation Poker
See: Operazione Poker (1965).

Operation: Rabbit
1951 (1952) WB color ani 7 mins.
Dir: Chuck Jones.
Story: Michael Maltese.
Layouts: Robert Gribbroek.
Bg: Philip de Guard.
Ani: Lloyd Vaughan, Ben Washam, Ken Harris, & Phil Monroe.
Mus Dir: Carl W. Stalling.
Voices: Mel Blanc.
F-com (Bugs vs. the Coyote)
Ref: LC; PopCar; David Rider.
See also: Bugs Bunny (1938-63); Road Runner and the Coyote (1948-   ).

Operation X-70
1972 Belgian ani sh.
Dir: Raoul Servais.
F-com (euphoric gas bombards country)
Ref: S&S Autumn '72 p204; CineF 2:3:39.

Operation 'Y'
See: Ypotron — Final Countdown (1966).

Operazione Controspionaggio
(Operation Counterspy; Asso di Picche; As de Pic; Ace of Spades; Operacion Controespionaje)
1965 Italian/Spanish/French, Cineproduzioni/Balcazar/Copernic color scope 111 mins.
Dir: Nick Nostro.
Story: Giuseppe Maggi.
SP: Gianni Simonelli, N. Nostro, & Alfonso Balcazar.
Art Dir: Juan Alberto Soler.
Cin: Franco Delli Colli.
Mus: Franco Pisano.
Cast: George A. Ardisson, Joaquin Diaz, Lena von Martens, Helen Chanel, Leontina Mariotti (Leontine May).
bor-SF (installation intended to destroy the world build by madman is vaporized by the hero)
Ref: SpCin '67 p28-29; Ital Prods '65.

Operazione Goldman
See: Lightning Bolt (1966).

Operazione Goldseven
(Operation Goldseven)
1966 Italian/Spanish color.
Dir: Alberto Leonardi (Albert B. Leonard).
SP: Maria del Carmen & Martinez Roman.
Cin: Alfonso Nieva.
Mus: Piero Umiliani.
Cast: Tony Russell, Erika Blanc, Conrado San Martin, Fernando Cebrian, Dianik Zurakowska, Wilbert Braley, Peter White.
bor-SF (serum immunizes against radiation)
Ref: Ital Prods '66 I:32-33.

Operazione Paradiso
See: Kiss the Girls and Make Them Die (1966).

Operazione Paura
See: Kill Baby Kill (1966).

Operazione Poker
(Operacion Poker: Operation Poker)
1965 Italian/Spanish, Wonder/Alcocer color scope 110 mins.
Dir: Osvaldo Civirana.
SP: Roberto Gianviti.
Art Dir: Teddy Villalba.
Cin: Alfonso Nieva.
Mus: Piero Umiliani.
Cast: Roger Browne, José Greci, Sancho Gracia, Carla Calo (Carol Brown), Helga Linè, Angel Ter.
SF-seq (device to see through solid objects)
Ref: MFB Aug '66 p 121; SpCin '67 p240-41; Ital Prods '65 p 184-85.

Opet Twist, I
See: Twist Again.

Opium Smoker's Dream
1906 Biograph sil 495 ft.
F-H-dream (Hell; demons)
Ref: Biograph Bulletin.

Optic Ticklers
1966? British color ani collage sh.
Dir: Stuart Wynn Jones.
F
Ref: Ani/Cin p84.

Optical Impulses in Geometric Progression
See: Impulses Ópticos en Progresión Geométrica (1971).

Optical Poem
1938 MGM ani color 650 ft.
Dir: Oskar Fischinger.
Mus Adapt: David Snell.
Mus: Franz Liszt ("The Second Hungarian Rhapsody").
Mus Orchestration: Paul Marquardt.
abs-F
Ref: Exp/Film p 140; LC; Undrgnd p81.

Opus 5
See: Three: Les Poissons, Jabberwock, Opus 5 (1962?).

Opus 3
1966 Canadian, NFB 16mm 6 mins.
Dir: Pierre Hébert.
abs-F
Ref: Canadian Centre Bltn 4.

Or, L'
See: Gold (1934).

Or et le Plomb, L'
(Gold and Lead)
1966 French.
Dir: Alain Cuniot.
Cin: Yann Le Masson.
Mus: Michel Legrand.
Cast: Alain Cuniot, Emmanuelle Riva, Max Paul Fouchet, Michel Legrand, Jean Massin.
SF-seq (man from another planet interviews people to decide if Earth is worth saving -- several stories)
Ref: CoF 10:48; F&F Oct '66; Bianco 7/8 '66 p 124.
Based on "Le Monde Comme Il Va" by Voltaire.

Ora Pro Nobis; or, The Poor Orphan's Last Prayer
(Pro Nobis: For Us)
1901 British, R.W. Paul sil (made to accompany live singer) 100 ft.
Prod: R.W. Paul.
Dir: Walter Booth.
F ("orphan dies in snow & angels bear her spirit to Heaven" --Gifford)
Ref: Hist/Brit p96; Film-Tex p420; Gifford/BFC 00436.
Based on the song & intended to be shown while it is sung.

Oracle, The
See: Horse's Mouth, The (1953).

Oracle de Delphes, L'
See: Oracle of Delphi, The (1903).

Oracle of Delphi, The
(L'Oracle de Delphes)
1903 French, Star sil 100 ft.
Made by: Georges Méliès.
F (stone sphinx comes to life; bearded figure scares thief stealing vase)
Ref: LC; Niver 75; Gifford/H p24.

Oramunde
1931 sh.
Made by: Emlen Etting.
exp-bor-F
Ref: USA Exp List; Undrgnd p79, 80.

Orang Minyak
See: Oily Man, The (1958); Sumpah Orang Minyak (1958).

Orator, The
See: Uvodni Slovo Pronese (1962).

Orbita Mortal
See: Mission Stardust (1968).

Orchestra Land
1964 Soviet, All-Union (Sovexportfilm) color ani 16 mins.
Dir: A. Karanovich.
Story: K. Rapoport.
F (instruments live in harmony, don't like false notes; saxophone cast out of the land)
Ref: Sovexportfilm cat 2:125.

Orden: FX 18 Debe Morir
(Order: FX 18 Must Die; FX 18 Secret Agent --alt.t?)
1965 Spanish/French color scope 97 mins.
Dir: Maurice Cloche.
SP: C. Plume, J. Bollo & O. Cloche.
Art Dir: Robert Giordani.
Cin: P. Gueguen & Juan Julio Baena.
Mus: Eddie Barclay.
Cast: Ken Clark, Jany Clair, Guy Delorme, Jacques Dacqmine.
cont.

Orden... cont.
bor-SF (satellite receives spy messages)
Ref: SpCin '66.
Based on novel "Coplan Tente Sa Chance" by R. Paul Kenny.
See also: Coplan.

Order and Disorder
See: Josef Killian (1963).

Order: FX 18 Must Die
See: Orden: FX 18 Debe Morir (1965).

Ordet
(The Word)
● 1943 Swedish.
Prod: Harold Molander.
Dir: Gustav Molander.
SP: Rune Lindstrom.
Cast: Victor Sjöström, Rune Lindström, Vanda Rothgardt, Stig Olin.
Ref: Sweden 2:66-67; FIR Oct '55 p428; S&S Winter '55-56 p 126.

● 1955 (1957) Danish, Palladium Film (Kinsley Int'l) 126 mins.
Prod, Dir, SP: Carl Dreyer.
Set Design: Erik Aaes.
Cin: Henning Bendtsen.
Mus: Paul Schierbeck.
Cast: Henrik Malberg, Emil Haas Christensen, Birgitte Federspiel, Preben Lerdorff Rye, Cay Kristiansen, Henry Skjaer.
Ref: FTN p749; FIR March '64 p 158; LA p253-54; FD 5 Dec '57.
rel-F (religious fanatic knows the word which raises the dead, & brings dead woman back to life)
Based on play "A Legend for Today" by Kaj Munk.

Ordinary Hour in the Extraordinary Life of Robin Beckett, An
(Life of Robin Beckett --alt.t.)
1963 Australian, Triumvir Ate Films 7 mins.
F (small businessman comes out of dustbin, goes through strange activities)
Ref: Collier.

Ördög; Vigjáték Három Felvonásban, Az
(play by F. Molnár)
See: Devil, The.

Orfeo Negro
See: Black Orpheus (1959).

Orfeu da Conceicao
(play by V. de Moraes)
See: Black Orpheus (1959).

Orfeus & Julie
1969 Danish, Bent Barfod color ani & live 7 mins.
Dir & Story: Bent Barfod.
F (dancer in midst of animated settings)
Ref: Mamaia '70.

Orgasm
See: Paranoia (1968).

Orgasmo
See: Paranoia (1968).

Orgia de los Muertos, La
(The Orgy of the Dead)
1972 Spanish/Italian, Petruka/Prodimex.
Dir: José Luis Merino.
Cast: Paul Naschy (rn Jacinto Molina), Dianik Zurakowska, Carlos Quiney.
H (Naschy plays a necrophile)
Ref: LSH 2:69; Vw 9 May '73 p 144.

Orgies du Docteur Orloff, Les
  See: Solo un Ataud (1966).

Orgies of Dr. Orloff, The
  See: Solo un Ataud (1966).

Orgueil, L'
  (Pride; Arrogance)
  1907? French, Pathé.
  Dir & Sc: M.M. Dumény & LeGrand.
  Cast: Henri Desfontaines [Mephistopheles], M. Dumény.
  F (devil visits painter at work in church)
  Ref: Collier.

Orgy of the Dead
  (Revenge of the Dead --s.t.?; Orgy of the Vampires --alt.t?)
  1966 Astra (F.O.G.) color.
  Prod: A.C. Stevens.
  SP: Edward D. Wood Jr.
  Cin: Robert Caramico.
  Cast: Criswell, Pat Barringer, Fawn Silver, William Bates, Louis Ojena, John Andrews.
  sex-F-H (ghoul; walking mummy; wolfman; giant; skeleton; zombie)
  Ref: Photon 19:43, 21:28; Richardson; Ackerman; Willis.
  See also: White Zombie (1932); Wolf Man, The (1941); Mummy, The.

Orgy of the Dead, The
  See: Orgia de los Muertos, La (1972).

Orgy of the Vampires
  See: Orgy of the Dead (1966).

Oriental Black Art
  1908 French, Star sil 472 ft.
  Made by: Georges Méliès.
  F (tree grows out of anvil; turns self into bubble)
  Ref: LC; Views '08 126:10.

Oriental Mystic, The
  1909 Vit sil 395 ft.
  Prod & Dir: J. Stuart Blackton.
  F-com (disappearances; man hides in mirror; appearances)
  Ref: Filmlex p683; FI IV-23 p 12; LC.

Origin of Man, The
  Chicago drive-in ad retitling of Lost World, The (1960).
  Ref: D. Glut.

Origin of the Ganges River
  See: Ganga Avtaran (1935).

Original Locataire, Un
  (An Eccentric Lodger; Un Inventeur Acharne: An Enthu- siastic Inventor --alt.t?)
  n.d. French sil 2 reels.
  Dir: Charley Bowers (aka Bricolo).
  Cast: Charley Bowers.
  F-com
  Ref: MMF 17:62-65.

Original Sin, The
  (Der Apfel Ist Ab: The Apple Has Been Eaten)
  1947 (1950) W. German (Lopert) 105 mins (95 mins).
  Dir: Helmut Käutner.
  Cast: Bobby Todd, Bettina Moissi, Joana Maria Gorvin, Helmut Käutner, Arno Assmann [Lucifer].
  sat-mus-com-F-dream
  Ref: Vw 26 Jan '49, 16 Aug '50; BO 9 Sept '50.
  See also: Adam and Eve.

Original Sin
  See: Pecado Original, El (1964).

Origini della Fantascienza, Le
  (The Origins of Science Fiction)
  1963 Italian 16mm color sh.
  Dir: Silvestri & Falessi.
  SF-doc
  Ref: Gasca p325; Trieste.

Origins of Science Fiction, The
  See: Origini della Fantascienza, Le (1963).

Orlac Hände
  See: Hands of Orlac, The (1925).

Orlak, el Infierno de Frankenstein
  (Orlak, the Hell of Frankenstein)
  1960 Mexican, Independiente (Col).
  Prod & Dir: Rafael Baledon.
  SP: Alfredo Ruanova & Carlos E. Taboada.
  Cin: Fernando Colin.
  Mus: Fondo Jorge Perez.
  Cast: Joaquin Cordero, Armando Calva, Rosa de Castilla, Irma Dorantes, Andres Soler, Pedro D'Aquillon.
  F-H (body brought back to life with metal, box-like head & tremendous strength; artificial face melts in heat; vampires?)
  Ref: Gasca p295; PB; SM 5:33; MM 4:26; Gifford/MM p 145.
  See also: Frankenstein.

Orloff y el Hombre Invisible
  (Orloff et l'Homme Invisible: Orloff and the Invisible Man)
  1970 Spanish/French, Mezquiriz/ Celia color 80 mins.
  Dir: Pierre Chevalier.
  SP: Juan Fortuny & P. Chevalier.
  Art Dir: Ramon Matheu.
  Cin: J. Fortuny.
  Edit: Alberto G. Nicolau.
  Mus: Camille Sauvage.
  Cast: Howard Vernon, Isabel del Rio, Francisco Valladares, Brigitte Carva, Fernando Sancho, Evane Hanska.
  SF-H (Orloff has made man invisible, & invisible man is slowly going insane)
  Ref: Vw 12 May '71 p 74, 143; SpCin '72 p48-49.
  Sequel to: Awful Dr. Orlof, The (1961).
  See also: Invisible Man, The (1933).

Orinithology
  See: Ornitologija (1970).

Ornitologija
  (Ornithology)
  1970 Yugoslavian, Zagreb color 8.4 mins.
  Dir, SP, Design, Ani: Ante Zaninović.
  Mus: Tomislav Simovič.
  F-com (series of absurdist gags about birds)
  Ref: Z/Zagreb p 104-05.

Orphan Brother, The
  See: Littlest Warrior, The (1961).

Orphan's Benefit
  1934 RKO ani 1 reel.
  Prod: Walt Disney.
  F-com
  Ref: LC.
  See also: Mickey Mouse (1928-6?).

Orpheus
  (Orphée)
  1950 French (Discina) 95 mins.
  Prod: André Paulvé.
  Assoc Prod: Emile Darbon.

Orpheus cont.
  Dir & SP: Jean Cocteau.
  Art Dir: D'Eaubonne.
  Cin: Nicholas Hayer.
  Edit: J. Sadoul.
  Mus: Georges Auric.
  Cast: Jean Marais, Francois Périer, Maria Casarès, Maria Déa, Roger Blin, Edouardo Dermithe, Henri Crémieux, Juliette Gréco.
  sur-F (in contemporary France, poet meets his own Death, per- sonified as a woman; passes through mirror into weird zone where Death dwells; car radio deliver strange messages; etc.)
  Ref: MFB June '50 p81; FIR Feb '51 p38, June-July '51 p 18; Oct '51 p59; FD 22 Nov '50; Vw 12 July '50.
  Based on the play by Jean Cocteau from Greek mythology.
  See also: Legend of Orpheus (1909); Black Orpheus (1959); Testament of Orpheus (1959); Metamorfeus (1969).

Orpheus
  1964 W. German, ZDF.
  Choreog: Alfred Rodrigues.
  Decor: Andrzej Majewski.
  Mus: Igor Stravinski.
  ballet-F (Orpheus goes into the Underworld to get by Eurydice)
  Ref: UNESCO cat p45.
  Based on the ballet choreographed by George Balanchine.

Orpheus and Eurydice
  1939 Czech ani sh?
  mus-F
  Ref: Americana V:686f.
  Based on the opera by Christoph Willibald Gluck.

Orpheon
  196? French ani sh.
  Dir: Meunier.
  F
  Ref: LAFP 22 Dec '67 ad.

Orrible Segreto del Dr. Hichcock, L'
  See: Horrible Dr. Hichcock, The (1962).

Oru Kaiju Daishingeki
  See: Godzilla's Revenge (1969).

Os Deuses e os Mortos
  (Of Gods and the Dead; The Gods and the Dead --ad.t.)
  1970 Brazilian, Daga color 129 mins.
  Prod: J. Fredy Rosenberg.
  Dir & Edit: Ruy Guerra.
  SP: R. Guerra, Paula Jose, & Flavio Imperio.
  Cin: Dib Lutfi.
  Mus: Milton Nascimento.
  Cast: Norma Bengell, Othon Bastos, Itala Nandi, Nelson Xavier, Ruy Polanah.
  F-H (supernatural creatures take the form of human beings & mingle with humans; lots of killings)
  Ref: Vw 8 July '70; AFI Prog.

Osaka 1-2-3
  1970 Amateur (Pyramid) computer ani 3 mins.
  Made by: John Whitney.
  exp-F
  Ref: Pyramid p 148.

Osakajo Monogatari
  See: Daredevil in the Castle (1961).

Oscar's Gift
  See: Cadeau d'Oscar, Le (1965).

Oskleničku Víc
  See: Drop too Much, A (1954).

Oslic, Seledka i Medla
  (The Donkey, the Herring, and the Broom)
  1969 Soviet, Talimfilm color ani puppet 15 mins.
  Dir & SP: Elbert Tuganov.
  F (magic broom)
  Ref: MTVM 25:3:5; Mamaia '70.
  Based on Indian, Estonian, and Czech fairy tales.

Osorezan no Onna
  (An Innocent Witch)
  1966 Japanese, Shochiku 98 mins.
  Dir: Heinosuke Gosho.
  SP: Hideo Horie.
  Cin: Shozaburo Shinomura.
  Cast: Jitsuko Yoshimura, Kin Sugai, Taiji Tonoyama, Keizo Kawasaki.
  F-seq (prostitute beaten to death, falsely accused of witchcraft; speaks to mother through medium)
  Ref: UniJ '67; MTVM March '66 p24.

Ostrich, The
  See: Pštros (1960).

Ostrov Zabvenya
  See: Isle of Oblivion (1917).

Osudy Dobrého Vojáka Svejka
  (The Good Soldier Schweik)
  1954 Czech color ani puppet sh.
  Dir, Sc, Art Dir: Jiří Trnka.
  Cin: E. Franek.
  Mus: Vaclav Trojan.
  F
  Ref: Trnka p262; S&S Autumn '55 p64; Montevideo '56.
  Based on the novel by Jaroslav Hasek.
  See also: Good Soldier Schweik, The (1929); Loutky Jiriho Trnky (1955).

Osvetnic
  (Revenger)
  1958 Yugoslavian, Zagreb color ani 12.8 mins. •
  Dir: Dušan Vukotić.
  SP: D. Vukotić & Branko Ranitović.
  Design: Boris Kolar.
  Ani: Zlatko Grgić.
  Bg: Zvonimir Lončarić.
  Mus: Aleksandar Bubanović.
  psy-F (cuckolded man visualizes his revenges)
  Ref: Z/Zagreb p56.
  Based on a short story by Anton Chekhov.

Oswald
  1927-38 Winkler Pictures (U) ani 1 reel series.
  Created by Walt Disney.
  After 1927, Prod: Walter Lantz.
  F-com (adventures of a rabbit)
  Ref: FD 26 March '28; LC.
  See also: Spooks (1930); Mars (U-1931); Merry Old Soul, The (1931); Mechani- cal Man (1932); Ham and Eggs (1933); Handy Man, The (1937); Voodoo in Harlem (1938).

Ot Perc Glylkossag
  See: Five Minute Thrill (1967?).

Othello
  1920 British, Hepworth sil ani sh.
  Dir & Ani: Anson Dyer.

cont.

F-com

Ref: Shake/Sil p265.

Parody of the play by William Shakespeare.

Other, The

1972 20th-Fox color 100 mins.

Exec Prod & SP: Thomas Tryon.

Prod & Dir: Robert Mulligan.

Prod Design: Albert Brenner.

Cin: Robert L. Surtees.

Edit: Folmar Blangsted & O. Nicholas Brown.

Mus: Jerry Goldsmith.

Cast: Uta Hagen, Diana Muldaur, Chris Udvarnoky, Martin Udvarnoky, Norma Connolly, Victor French, Portia Nelson.

psy-F-H (USA, in the 1930s; one of twin boys is dead, the other believes he is alive, seems to adopt dead one's ways & kills people; seems to be able to transfer mind into other people's & animal's bodies)

Ref: Vw 24 May '72 p 19; MFB Dec '72 p256; CineF 2:3:27-29.

Based on the novel by Thomas Tryon.

Other, The

See: Andere, Der.

Other Christopher, The

See: Otro Cristobal, El (1962).

Other Fu Manchu, The

See: Otro Fu Manchu, El (1945).

Other One, The

(novel by C. Turney)

See: Back from the Dead (1957)

Other Person, The

1921 British, Granger-Binger sil 5319 ft.

Dir: B.E. Doxat-Pratt.

Sc: Benedict James.

Cast: Zoe Palmer, Adelqui Migliar, Arthur Pusey, E. Story-Gofton, William Huntre, Ivo Dawson, Nora Hayden, Arthur Walcott.

F-H (ghost impells spiritualist to kill his wealthy father; this is disclosed by seance)

Ref: Gifford/BFC 07129.

Based on the novel by Fergus Hume.

Other Self, The

1915 Lubin sil 1800 ft.

Dir: Leon D. Kent.

Sc: Julian Louis Lamothe.

bor-F ("hypnosis gives girl split personality" --Willis)

Ref: MPN 29 May '15.

Other Self, The

See: Andere Ich, Das (1918).

Other Shore, The

See: Otra Orilla, La (1966).

Other Side of the Rainbow, The

1959 Soviet.

Cast: Igor Ilyinsky.

F-com (man-eating snowmen of Caucasas)

Ref: Vw 18 Nov '59.

Other Side of Underneath, The

1972 British, Jack Bond Films 16mm color 133 mins.

Prod: Jack Bond.

Assoc Prod: Prue Faull.

Dir & SP: Jane Arden.

Art Dir: Penny Slinger & Liz Danciger.

Cin: Aubrew Dewar & J. Bond.

Edit: David Mingay.

Mus: Sally Minford.

Cast: Sheila Allen, Jane Arden,

Orpheus (1950) French

Other Side of Underneath cont.

Liz Danciger, Elaine Donovan, Susanka Fraey, Penny Slinger.

psy-F (nearly-drowned girl has memories & fantasies, involving sex, self-sacrifice, gore, women as archetypes, etc.)

Ref: MFB April '73 p80.

Others' Blood, The

See: Sang des Autres, Le (1972).

Otkrovitelj

See: Discoverer (1967).

Otoko to Onno no Shinwa

(Star of Adam)

1969 Japanese, Toho.

Dir: Hideo Onchi.

SF (survivors of WWIII go to another world)

Ref: Photon 21:8; Willis.

Otra Orilla, La

(The Other Shore; From the Other Side --ad.t.)

1966 Spanish, Agrupa scope 80 mins.

Dir: José Luis Madrid.

SP: J.L. Madrid & J.L. Figueras.

Art Dir: D.M. Infiesta.

Cin: Aurelio G. Larraya.

Mus: F. Martinez Tudo.

Cast: Marisa de Leza, Luis Dávila, Antonio G. Escribano.

F (souls who died violent deaths leave their bodies; life prolonged for a while)

Ref: SpCin '67.

Based on the work by José Lopez Rubio.

Otro Cristobal, El

(The Other Christopher)

1962 Cuban 115 mins.

Dir & SP: Armand Gatti.

Cin: Henri Alekan.

Otro Cristobal cont.

Cast: Jean Bouise, Alden Knight, Bertina Acevedo.

rel-F (begins in heaven with angels; dictator in purgatory hatches plot to take over heaven, & does)

Ref: FIR June-July '63 p344-45; Vw 29 May '63.

Otro Fu Manchu, El

(The Other Fu Manchu)

1945 Spanish, Bascon Films.

Prod: Alberto A. Cienfuegos.

Dir & SP: Ramon Barreiro.

Art Dir: Lopez Rubío.

Cin: Cesar Benitez.

Edit: Sara Ontañon.

Mus: Jesús Garcia Leoz.

Cast: Rosita Yarza, Adela Esteban, Alicia Torres, Candida Lopez, Mary Gonzalez, Carlos Muños, Manuel Requena.

F-H (Chinese super-villain in pursuit of magic shell)

cont.

cont.

cont.

Otro Fu Manchu cont.

Ref: Gasca; MMF 9:14, 19, 14:37, 39.

Based on a character created by Sax Rohmer.

See also: Fu Manchu.

Ott in Space

1962 Soviet, Tallinfilm color ani puppet 22 mins.

Dir: E. Tuganov.

Story: V. Pant.

F (boy sent into space by accident, can't save himself because he was inattentive in school)

Ref: Sovexportfilm cat 1:136.

Otter, The

See: Nutria, La (1971).

Otto e Mezzo

See: 8 1/2 (1963).

Otto Luck

1915 Wallace A. Carlson (General Film Corp) sil ani (& live?) sh series.

Prod: J.R. Bray & Wallace A. Carlson.

F-com

Ref: Ani Chart.

Ouanga

See: Drums of the Jungle (1935).

Our Friend, the Atom

1956 (1957) WD color ani & live 48 mins.

Exec Prod: Walt Disney.

doc; F-seq

Ref: Films Inc p 128.

Our Gang Comedy

(Hal Roach's Our Gang Comedy)

1923-44 Hal Roach, later MGM series 2 reels, later 1 reel.

See: Lad an' a Lamp, A (1932); Mama's Little Pirates (1934); Shrimps for a Day (1935); Duel Personalities (1939); Robot Wrecks (1941).

See also: 45 Minutes from Hollywood (1926).

Our Heavenly Bodies

(Wunder der Schöpfung: Wonders of Creation, Miracles of Creation)

1925 German, UFA sil 7 reels.

Dir: Hans Walter Kornblum.

Cast: Theodor Loos, Walter Reimann.

doc-SF (tour of solar system; end of the universe)

Ref: CtoH p 152; Ackerman.

Our India

(Hindustan Hamara)

1950 Indian, Art Films of Asia 139 mins.

Prod & Dir: Paul Zils.

SP & English Dialog: S.R. Dadachanji & Evelyn Wood.

Hindi Dialog: Dewan Sharar.

Cin (interiors): Yusuf Mulji.

Cin (exteriors): Fali R. Bilimoria.

Edit: Mohammed Haji.

Mus: Vasant Desai.

Cast: Durga Khote, Tripti Mitra, Nalini Jayawant, Yashodhara Kathju, Prithviraj Kapoor, Dev Anand, Jairaj, K.N. Singh.

doc; F-seqs (the history of India; early scenes feature fantasy, gods, etc.)

Ref: Orient 26.

Based on the book by M.R. Masani.

Our Lady of Compassion

See: A Compadecida (1969).

Our Lady of the Sphere

n.d. Amateur 16mm? color ani sh?

Made by: Larry Jordan.

exp-F (girl's head floats away)

Ref: SF Chronicle & Examiner California Living Magazine.

Our Man Flint

1965 (1966) 20th-Fox color scope 107 mins.

Prod: Saul David.

Dir: Daniel Mann.

SP: Hal Fimberg & Benn Starr.

Art Dir: Jack Martin Smith & Ed Graves.

Cin: Daniel L. Fapp.

SpFX: L.B. Abbott, Howard Lydecker, & Emil Kosa Jr.

Edit: William Reynolds.

Mus: Jerry Goldsmith.

Cast: James Coburn, Lee J. Cobb, Gila Golan, Edward Mulhare, Benson Fong, Shelby Grant, Rhys Williams, Russ Conway.

bor-SF (superspy vs 3 mad scientist out to take over the world through weather control; one gadget: all-purpose cigarette lighter)

Ref: FF '66 p11; MFB March '66 p39; FD 3 Jan '66.

Sequel: In Like Flint (1967).

Based on a story by Hal Fimberg.

Our Mother's House

1967 British, Heron Films & Filmways (MGM) color 105 mins.

Exec Prod: Martin Ransohoff.

Prod & Dir: Jack Clayton.

SP: Jeremy Brooks & Haya Harareet.

Art Dir: Reece Pemberton.

Cin: Larry Pizer.

Edit: Tom Priestley.

Mus: Georges Delerue.

Cast: Dirk Bogarde, Margaret Brooks, Pamela Franklin, Louis Sheldon Williams, John Gugolka, Mark Lester, Sarah Nicholls, Gustav Henry, Arnette Carell, Yootha Joyce.

psy-H (7 children believe they communicate with dead mother whom they have buried in the back yard)

Ref: FF '67 p 311-12.

Based on the novel by Julian Gloag.

Our Red Riding Hood

1960 Czech ani sh.

Dir: Jiří Brdečka.

F-com

See also: Little Red RidingHood.

Our Town

1940 Sol Lesser (UA) 89 mins.

Prod: Sol Lesser.

Dir: Sam Wood.

SP: Thornton Wilder, Frank Craven, & Harry Chandlee.

Prod Design: William Cameron Menzies.

Cin: Bert Glennon.

SpFX: Jack Cosgrove.

Edit: Sherman Todd.

Mus: Aaron Copland.

Nar: Frank Craven.

Cast: William Holden, Martha Scott, Fay Bainter, Guy Kibbee, Thomas Mitchell, Beulah Bondi, Stuart Erwin, Frank Craven.

F-seqs (dead woman revisits the town she lived in)

Ref: FIR May '63 p288; Acad; MPH 23 March '40 p30; FD 5 May '40.

Based on the play by Thornton Wilder.

Ours, L'

(The Bear; The Talking Bear --ad.t.?)

1961 French (Embassy) color 86 mins.

Dir: Edmond Sechan.

SP: E. Sechan & Roger Mauge.

Cin: André Villard.

Edit: Jacqueline Thiedot.

Cast: Renato Rascel, Francis Blanché.

F-com (bear in Paris zoo can talk, write, etc.)

Ref: Vw 22 Feb '61; Ideal cat '69-70 p 165; CoF 5:4.

Out of an Old Man's Head

(I Huvet Paa en Gammal Gubbe: In an Old Man's Head)

1968 Swedish, Svenska Ord & GK-Film color ani & live 76 mins.

Dir: Tage Danielsson.

Ani: Per Ahlin.

Cin: Conny Marnelius, Bo Wanngaard.

Cast: Hans Alfredson.

F-dream (old sick man re-members life in cartoon form)

Ref: Vw 5 Feb '69; ASIFA info sheet; LA County Museum.

Out of Reach of the Devil

See: Where the Devil Cannot Go (1960).

Out of Step

See: Contrary Shoes (1965).

Out of the Dark

(novel by U. Curtiss)

See: I Saw What You Did (1965).

Out of the Darkness

See: Teenage Caveman (1958).

Out of the Inkwell

1919-23 Bray (Goldwyn) ani & live 1 reel series.

Prod: Max Fleischer.

F-com

Ref: MPW 40:1497; MPN 22: 2493.

See also: Invisible Ink (1921); Modeling (1921); Ko-Ko the Clown (1922-29).

Out of the Night

See: Strange Illusion (1945).

Out of the Rain

1917 Peter Pan sil ani puppet 474 ft.

F

Ref: BFI cat p235.

See also: Mo-Toy Comedies (1917).

Out of This World

1954 Roland Reed (MCA-TV) 78 mins.

Prod: Roland Reed.

Cast: Richard Crane, Ian Keith.

SF

Ref: FD 29 April '54; Willis.

See also: Rocky Jones, Space Ranger.

Out of This World

See: Hold That Hypnotist (1957).

Outer Space Jitters

1957 Col 16.5 mins.

Prod & Dir: Jules White.

SP: Jack White.

Art Dir: Walter Holscher.

Cin: William Bradford.

Edit: Harold White.

Cast: The Three Stooges (Moe Howard, Larry Fine, Joe Besser), Gene Roth, Emil Sitka, Phil Van Zandt, Joe Palma, Don (later Dan) Blocker, Harriette Tarler, Diana Darrin.

cont.

Outer Space Jitters cont.

SF-com (prehistoric man brought to life on space ship; girls on planet Zunev have electricity in their veins)

Ref: MPH 29 Nov '58 p26; LC; Pardi; Maltin/GMS p 140.

See also: Three Stooges, The (1934-59).

Outer Space Visitor

1959 Terrytoons (20th-Fox) color scope ani 1 reel.

F-com

Ref: LC.

Outlaw Planet

See: Planet of the Vampires (1965).

Outlaws IS Coming, The

1965 Normandy (Col) 89 mins.

Prod, Dir, Story: Norman Maurer.

SP: Elwood Ullman.

Art Dir: Robert Peterson.

Cin: Irving Lippman.

SpFX: Richard Albain.

Edit: Aaron Nibley.

Mus: Paul Dunlap.

Cast: The Three Stooges (Moe Howard, Larry Fine, Joe De Rita), Adam West, Nancy Kovack, Mort Mills, Don Lamond, Rex Holman, Emil Sitka, Henry Gibson.

west-com; F-seqs (Cole Younger has a magic mirror; in Old West, a tank with a modern-day machine gun; many anachronisms)

Ref: FF '65 p 108; D. Glut.

See also: Have Rocket Will Travel (1959).

Outward Bound

1930 WB 82 mins.

Prod: J.L. Warner.

Dir: Robert Milton.

SP: J. Grubb Alexander.

Cin: Hal Mohr.

Edit: Ralph Dawson.

Cast: Leslie Howard, Douglas Fairbanks Jr, Helen Chandler, Beryl Mercer, Alec B. Francis, Alison Skipworth, Lionel Watts, Montagu Love, Dudley Digges.

F (people aboard ship gradually learn they are all dead, suicides, & are on their way to be "examined;" young lovers returned to Earth)

Ref: F/A p297; Photo Nov '30 p52; AFI f2.4088 p581.

Based on the play by Sutton Vane.

See also: Between Two Worlds (1944).

Oval Portrait, The

1934 USC 16mm 2 reels.

F (life drawn from artist's wife as he paints her portrait; she dies when it is finished)

Ref: Vd 5 Oct '34.

Based on the short story by Edgar Allan Poe.

See also: Fall of the House of Usher, The (French -1928).

Over-Incubated Baby, An

1901 British, R.W. Paul sil 80 ft.

Dir: Walter Booth.

F-com (incubator ages baby into old man)

Ref: Gifford/BFC 00420.

Over the Little Dog and the Little Cat

See: Providani o Pejskovi a Kocicce (1955).

Overcharged

1912 British, Hepworth sil
350 ft.

Dir: Frank Wilson (?).

SF-com ("weak man electrified
becomes magnetic")

Ref: Gifford/BFC 03297.

Overcoat, The

● (Shinel: The Cloak)

1926 Soviet, Leningrad Kino
sil 6300 ft.

Dir: Grigori Kozintsen
(Kutznestov) & Leonid
Trauberg.

Sc: Yuri Tinyanov.

Art Dir: Yevgeni Enei.

Cin: Andrei Moskvin.

Cast: Andrei Kostrichkin,
Sergei Gerasimov, Anna
Zheimo.

F-com

Ref: Kino p202, 430; FTN
p237; LA p70.

Based on the story by N. Gogol;
three-reel prolog based on
short story "Nevsky Prospect"
also by Gogol.

● (Il Cappotto)

1952 Italian, Farro 100
mins (93 mins).

Prod: Enzo Corelli.

Dir: Alberto Lattuada.

SP: A. Lattuada & Cesare
Zavattini, Enzo Corelli,
Girogio Prosperi, Girordano
Corsi, Luigi Malerba, &
Leonardo Sinisgalli.

Art Dir: Gianni Polidori.

Cin: Mario Montouri.

Mus: Felice Lattuada.

Cast: Renato Rascel, Yvonn
Sanson, Giulio Stival, Anna
Maria Carena, Antonella
Lualdi.

Ref: Vw 4 June '52; MFB
May '55 p67; LAT 11 Sept '54.

● (Der Mantel)

1955 German color 35 mins.

Dir: Wolfgang Schleif.

Cin: E.W. Fielder.

Cast: Marcel Marceau.

Ref: Brandon cat p245.

● (Shinel)

1958 (1965) Soviet, Lenfilm
(Cinemasters Int'l) 93 mins
(78 mins).

Dir: Alexei Batalov.

SP: A. Solovyov.

Art Dir: B. Manevitch &
I. Kaplan.

Cin: G. Maranjan.

Mus: N. Sidelnikov.

Cast: Rolan Bykov, Y.
Tolubeyev, A. Ezkina
(Yezhkina), & Y. Ponsova.

Ref: Vw 2 Sept '59; FF '65
p95-96; Time 26 March '65.

F-seq (when poor clerk's
overcoat is stolen & he
dies, his ghost takes
coats from the living)

Based on story "Shinel"
(The Overcoat; The Cloak;
or The Greatcoat) by
Nikolai Gogol.

See also: Bespoke Over-
coat, The (1955); Garm
Coat (1955).

Overman

1972? Amateur 16mm color sh.

Made by: Sean Phillips.

SF (future of man)

Ref: Kodak Senior Division '73;
telecast on KCET 22 July '73.

Qvoce Stromj Rajskych Jime

(We'll Eat the Fruit of
Paradise)

1970 Czech/Belgian, Elisabeth
Films/Barrandov color 98
mins.

Dir: Vera Chytilova.

SP: V. Chytilova & Ester
Krumbachova.

Cin: Jaroslav Kucera.

Edit: Miloslav Hasek.

Mus: Zdenek Liska.

Cast: Karel Novak, Jitka
Novakova, Jan Schmid.

rel-F (starts in Garden of
Eden, switches to sanitorium
run by husband & wife)

Ref: Vw 13 May '70.

Suggested by "Book of
Genesis" in "The Bible."

See also: Adam and Eve.

Owana, the Devil Woman

1913 Nestor sil 1020 ft.

F (Indian witch changes son
of tribal chief into pony;
witch killed by good fairy
of Indians, pony turns back
into boy)

Ref: MPW 16:952, 1033;
Bios 11 Dec '13.

Owanga

See: Drums of the Jungle
(1935).

Owl and the Pussycat, The

1953 British, Halas &
Batchelor 3D color
ani 6 mins.

Dir: John Halas.

Mus: Matyas Seiber.

3D Design: Brian Borthwick.

Singer: Maurice Bevan.

F

Ref: MFB July '53 p 113;
Elements.

Oxed Men

1966? Japanese color ani
sh.

Dir: Takui Furatwa.

F

Ref: S&S Winter '68-69 p22;
ASIFA 3.

Oxygen

See: Oksigen (1970).

Ozlaté Rybee

See: Golden Fish, The
(1951).

PROBLEMS

The titles listed in this section have not been determined
beyond reasonable doubt to satisfy two conditions necessary
for inclusion in the main listings: 1) significant fantastic
content and 2) existence, at one time or another, as a film.

It is hoped that information on these films will eventually
become available so they can be entered in the main listings
or in the EXCLUSIONS which follow this list of PROBLEMS.

G

Gaibi Talwar
1946 Indian, A.M. Khan.
Prod & Dir: A.M. Khan.
rel-F (miracles)
Ref: Filmindia Oct '46 p48.
Completed?

Galaxie
n.d.
Made by: Gregory J. Markopoulos.
SF? exp-SF?
Ref: Richardson.

Galaxie
1971 French, Tanit & MRM &
Societe General de Production.
Dir: Mathias Meregny.
Cast: Marika Green, Henri Serre,
Jean Gras, Reinhardt Kollhoff.
SF? ("cybernetic spies")
Ref: Vw 3 May '72 p 100; CineF
2:3:47; Soren.

Galerie des Monstres, La
(The Gallery of Monsters)
1924 French sil.
Dir & Sc: Jacques Catelain.
Cast: Philippe Hériat, Simone
Mareuil, Lois Moran, Jean Murat.
F?
Ref: DdC I:336, III:34, 312,
409, 422.
Same as film of same title with
no date, below?

Galerie des Monstres, La
(The Gallery of Monsters)
n.d. French.
Dir: Marcel l'Herbier.
F?
Ref: MMF 2:37.
Completed? Same as film
of same title and 1924 date,
above?

Gallery of Monsters, The
See: Galerie des Monstres, La
(1924; n.d.).

Galloping Ghosts
1926 Standard Cinema sil
2 reels.
Dir: Ralph Ceder.
F-com?
Ref: LC.
Same as 1927 film of same
title, below?

Galloping Ghosts
1927 Hal Roach (Pathé) sil
2 reels.
Cast: James Finlayson, Ora
Carew, Oliver Hardy.
F-com?
Ref: DdC II:353; MPN 3 March '28;
LC.
Same as 1926 film of same
title, above?

Game of Frogs
n.d. Italian, West.
H?
Ref: Photon 21:8.
Announced; made?

Game of Hearts, A
See: Cupid's Realm (1908).

Gamera vs. Leoman
n.d. Japanese, Daiei.
SF (giant,fanged,firebreathing,
rocket-propelled turtle)
Ref: CineF 3:11.
Completed? Title change?

Garden of Allah
1936 Selznick Int'l (UA) color
9 reels.
F-seq? (real fortune-telling?)
Ref: MPW 86:582, 87:113; LC.

Garden of Dr. Kanashima
n.d. U:S./Japanese, Manley/Toho.
SF-H?
Ref: Willis.
Announced; made?

Garden of the Moon
n.d. Manley.
SF?
Ref: Willis.
Announced; made?

Garden on the Moon
n.d. Plaza Int'l.
SF
Ref: Photon 21:6.
Based on the novel by Pierre
Boulle.

Gardener, The
1973? KKI Inc.
Filmed in Puerto Rico.
Cast: Joe Dallesandro, Katherine
Houghton.
H?
Ref: LSH 2:67.
Made?

Gardiens du Phare
(Guardians of Phare)
1928 French.
Dir: Jean Gremillon.
H? ("grande guignol")
Ref: French Exp List; Willis.

Gargantua and Pantagruel
1973 Italian/British, PEA/
??.
Dir: Ken Russell.
F
Ref: Vw 9 May '73 p68.
Based on the epic poem by
Rabelais.
Announced.

Gathering of Vultures, A
1973? British, Hammer.
To shoot in Australia.
F? H?
Ref: LSH 2:60.
Announced; made?

Gato sin Botas, El
(The Cat Without Boots)
1958 (1959) Mexican (Clasa-Mohme).
Cast: Tin-Tan, Martha Valdez, Wolf
Rubinsky, Marcelo, Nono Arzu.
F-com?
Ref: Ackerman.

Gavroche et les Esprits
(Gavroche and the Ghosts)
1912 Eclair sil.
Dir: Romeo Bosetti.
F?
Ref: Mitry II.

Gay Vampires
n.d. Fanfare.
sex-F-H-com? (homosexual
vampires?)
Ref: Willis.
Announced; made? (doubtful)

Gemini --12/Cape Canaveral
n.d.
SF?
Ref: Willis.
Exists?

Gendarme
(Policeman)
1897 French sil ani 2 mins.
Prod: Emile Cohl.
F-com
Ref: John Wilson.
Exists?

Gentleman in Room Six, The
n.d. sil.
F?

Same as following film?

Gentleman in Room Six
n.d. 11 mins.
F?
Ref: Contemp p 108.
Based on the short story by
Sidney Carroll.
Same as preceding film?

Gentleman Jekyll and Driver Hyde
1950 Canadian, International
8 mins.
F-com?
Ref: MFB Sept '50 p 145.
Possibly documentary on auto
safety.

Gentlemen with Umbrellas
n.d. Rumanian.
SF? ("chemical invention")
Ref: MTVM Jan '70.

Germ in the Kiss
1914 sil sh.
SF-com?
Ref: MPW 19:594.

Geschlossene Kette, Die
See: Sappho (1921).

Get Along, Little Zombie
1946 Col 2 reels.
Dir & SP: Edward Bernds.
F-H-com?
Ref: LC.
Possibly a Three Stooges short,
later retitled.

Get Off My Foot
1935 British (FN).
Dir: Monty Banks.
SP?: Frank Launder
Cast: Max Miller, Chili Bouchier.
F-com? ("ghost" of murdered man)
Ref: Willis: Sound & Shadow 5
Dec '35; Brit Cin.

Ghaba Nus el Lail
(The Midnight Ghost)
1947 Egyptian.
Dir: Abdel Fattah Hassan.
F-H?
Ref: Arab Cin p277.

Ghalta Putla
1935 Indian, Imperial.
Dir: Sarpotdar.
Cast: Dulari, Datar.
SF-H? ("Frankenstein touch")
Ref: MovPicM July '35 p2 ad.

Ghastly Tale, A
1938?
psy-H? ("psychological murder
theme")
Ref: Willis: FD 28 June '39.

Ghost, The
1898 British sil sh.
F?
Ref: DdC II:448.

Ghost, The
1910 French, Gaum (Kleine)
sil sh.
F?
Ref: MPW 1910.

Ghost, The
See: Fantasma, El (n.d.);
Fantome, Le (1936); Revenant,
Le.

Ghost and Doña Juanita, The
See: Fantasma y Doña Juanita, El
(1944).

Ghost Baron
1927 Swedish sil.
F?
Ref: DdC I:240.

Ghost Bride, The
1971? color scope.
F?
Ref: Singapore Straits-Times
2 March '71.
Probably same as Kaidan Botan
Doro (1968, main list).

Ghost City, The
1923-24 U sil serial 15
parts.
Dir: Jay Marchant.
Cast: Pete Morrison, Margaret
Morris, Al Wilson.
F? (doubtful)
Ref: CNW p234; LC.

Ghost for Sale
See: Spoke Till Salu (1939).

Ghost from the Unknown
n.d.
Ref: Ackerman.
F?
Exists? Doubtful.

Ghost Gunman, The
See: Pistolero Fantasma, El
(1967).

Ghost House, The
See: Pueblo Fantasma, El (1965).

Ghost in Love, A
(Et Spökelse Forelsker Seg)
1947 Norwegian.
Dir: Tancred Ibsen.
F?
Ref: Scand Film p 50-51.

Ghost in the Noonday Sun
1971?
Prod: Ben Kadish.
Cast: Jack Wild.
F?
Ref: Photon 21:7.
Made? Doubtful.

Ghost in the Past
n.d.
F?
Ref: Collier.

Ghost King, The
1914 Italian sil sh.
F?
Ref: DdC II:302.

Ghost Morning
n.d.
F?
Ref: LAT March '70 (Willis).

Ghost of Algiers, The
1906 French sil sh.
Prod: Georges Méliès.
Ref: DdC III:352 (Willis).
Alternate title of another
film?

Ghost of Donkergat, The
See: Spook van Donkergat, Die
(1972).

Ghost of Elisha Doom, The
1966? Yugoslavian color.
F?
Ref: FanMo 6:41; Willis.

Ghost of Iowa, The
n.d. Japanese.
F?
Ref: MTVM April '70 p44.

Ghost of Iwojima
See: Iwojima (1959).

Ghost of Rashman, The
n.d.
F
Ref: Richardson.
Same as Night Comes too Soon
(1947, main list)?

Ghost of St. Michael's, The
1940 British, Ealing-ABFD 82
mins.
Dir: Marcel Varnel.
Cast: Peter Ustinov, Will Hay,
Claude Hulbert.
F-H-com? bor-H-com? (pipes heard
before deaths supposedly played
by a ghost)
Ref: MFB '41 p 13; Collier.

Ghost of Samara, The
See: Afrit Samara (1959).

Ghost of Sierra de Cobre
1963 85 mins.
Cast: Martin Landau.
F? ("ghost-hunting"; "Weird
happenings")
Ref: Collier.

Ghost of Sunshine Mansion, The
1965? E. German, Deutscher
Fernsehfunk 74 mins.
Dir: Gerhard Klingenberg.
Cast: Werner Senftleben, Kurt
Conradi.
F? ("thriller about strange hap-
penings in a lake district guest
house")
Ref: MTVM Aug '66 p27.

Ghost of the Canyon, The
1920 sil.
Cast: Helen Gibson.
F? (doubtful)
Ref: Collier.

Ghost of the Dead
See: Jerangkong (1957?).

Ghost of the Indian Ocean
1923 sil.
F?
Ref: Willis.

Ghost of the Oven
1957? Malayan.
F-H? ("horror")
Ref: FEFN 26 July '57.
Announced; made?

Ghost of the Past, The
1915 Danish, Nordisk sil.
F?
Ref: LC.

Ghost of Their Ancestors, The
(The Great Inheritance --alt.t.)
1915 Danish, Nordisk sil.
F?
Ref: LC.

Ghost of Tolston's Manor, The
1923 Micheaux sil.
F-H?
Ref: AFI F2.2063 p288.
All-black cast for Negro market.

Ghost of Yesterday
1918 Selig sil.
F-H? (doubtful)
Ref: Willis.

Ghost Reporter
1941 Swedish.
F?
Ref: DdC II:228.

Ghost Rider
1935 FD 56 mins.
Cast: Rex Lease, Bobby Nelson.
F? (deputy aided by "ghostly
companion")
Ref: BIB's Winter-Spring '71
p A-246.

Ghost Ship, The
1973? Spanish.
Cast: Paul Naschy (r.n. Jacinto
Molina).
F-H (werewolf threatens passengers
on a ship)
Ref: LSH 2:70.
Planned.

Ghost Standing Upside Down
See: Sakadachi Yurei (1962).

Ghost Story
1944 British.
Cast: Derek (?) Farr, Felix
Aylmer.
F?

Ghost Story
See: Bancho Sarayashiki (1957).

Ghost Tiger, The
See: Hantu Rimau (1959).

Ghost Train
n.d. Japanese.
F?
Ref: Willis.

Ghost Woman
1957? Taiwan.
Dir: Sin Ta.
Cast: Ko Yu Shia, Wong Tai
Chon.
F?
Ref: FEFN 19 July '57 p30.

Ghosts
(Who's Afraid --alt.t.)
1913 Vit sil 1 reel.
Dir: W.J. Bauman.
F?
Ref: Willis.

Ghosts, The
1914 sil sh.
Dir: Holger Madsen.
F? (probably)
Ref: DdC II:306, 315.

Ghosts, The
1960 Polish.
F?
Ref: DdC I:417.

Ghosts
See: Powrot (1960).

Ghosts and Thieves
See: Fantasmi e Ladri (1959).

Ghosts! Ghosts!
See: Spokar, Det Spokar, Det (1943?).

Ghosts in the House
See: Fantasmas en la Casa (1958).

Ghosts of Nagasaki
1967? U.S./Japanese, Ram.
F?
Ref: Richardson.
Made? Doubtful.

Ghost's Revenge
n.d. Hongkong.
F?
Ref: Willis.
Same as Ghost's Revenge, A
(1968?, main list)?

Ghouls Are Among Us, The
1971? British, Tigon-Chilton.
SP: Robert Wynne Simmons.
F-H?
Ref: CineF Fall '70 p44;
FM 97:21.
Announced; made? (doubtful)

Giant, The
Chicago drive-in ad retitling
of what film?
Ref: D. Glut.

Giant, The
See: Mared, El (1964).

Giants of the Sea
1960 Egyptian.
F?
Ref: Arab Cin p283.

Giants of the Unknown
Chicago drive-in ad retitling
of what film? Probably Giant
from the Unknown (1958, main
list).
Ref: D. Glut.

Giant's Tattoo Parlor, The
n.d. Amateur (Film-makers' Coop)
16mm color & b&w 33 1/2 mins.
Made by: Howard Bass.
Assists: Eric Saarinen & Henry
Tiffany.
Cast: Dick Lear, Sue Hoagland,
Crow Thompson.
exp-F?
Ref: FMC 5:29-30.

Giant's Three Golden Hares, The
n.d.
F?
Ref: Willis.

Gibus the Magician
n.d. Belgian ani 6 mins.
F? ("live mummy")
Ref: Willis: Belgian Film Prods.

Gift, The
1962 Herbert Danska 40 mins.
Prod & Dir: Herbert Danska.
F?
Ref: Willis.

Ginger Nutt's Forest Dragon
1950 British 7 mins.
F?
Ref: MFB '50 p94.

Gioco della Torre, Il
1965 Italian, Dolomit Cinemat.
Dir: Angelo Dorigo.
Cast: Gianni Medici, Rita Klein,
Lawrence Tierney.
F-H? ("terror tale set in ancient
castle")
Ref: MTVM July '65 p40; MMF 12:37.
Completed?

Gioconda, La
(by D'Annunzio)
See: Devil's Daughter, The (1915).

Girl and the Corpse
1919 Italian sil.
H?
Ref: DdC II:430.

Girl from Out of This World, The
See: Dreamland Capers (1958).

Girl from Pussycat, The
1970?
sex-bor-SF?
Ref: Photon 21:6.
Based on the novel by Ted Mark.
Made? Doubtful.

Girl in the Mirror
n.d.
Cast: Betty Hutton, Cesar Romero,
Tom Conway.
psy-F? (Goldie meets her "other
self")
Ref: Film catalog.

Girl of the Bersagliere
1966 Italian.
F? ('spirit')
Ref: Willis.

Girl of the Cursed Wood, The
See: Fille du Bois Maudit, La
(1937).

Girl of the Nile, The
1967 W.German/U.S., UFA/Sidney
Pink color.
Prod: Sidney Pink.
Dir: Joe Lacy.
Cast: Rory Calhoun, James
Philbrook, Nuria Torrey.
bor-F? (gods' curse fulfilled?)
Ref: MTVM June '67 (Willis).

Girls from Atlantis, The
See: Manner Sind Sum Lieben Da
(1970).

Give Me a Bit of Looove. . . !
See: ¡Dame un Poco de Amooor. . .!
(1968).

Gladiateur Magnifique, Le
n.d.
Cast: Mark Forest.
F?

French title of which
Italian film?

Glass Coffin
(The Crystal Casket --alt.t.)
1912 Eclair sil sh.
F?
Ref: LC.

Glass Eye, The
See: Ojo de Vidrio, El (196?).

Glass Tower, The
1957.
F?
Ref: CoF 10:38.

Glass Work of Telegaon, The
1915 Indian sil sh.
Prod & Dir: Dada Phalke.
F?
Ref: Lighthouse 21 Aug '37.

Glittering Curse, The
1921 Austrian sil.
bor-F-H? (cursed diamond?)
Ref: Willis.

Glorie
See: O Věcech Nadpřirozenych
(1958).

God Monster, The
1973 Dimension Pictures.
SF-H?
Ref: BO 29 Jan '73 pSW-8 ad.
Announced.

God of Vengeance, The
1914 Chariot Film Corp sil
4 reels.
F? ('weird')
Ref: MPW 20:130 ad.

Goddess of Mercy
1967 Hongkong Shaw.
F?
Ref: MTVM April '67 p40.

Goddess of War, The
(Ranchandi)
1929 Indian, Kohinoor United
Artists sil.
rel-F?
Ref: Ind Cin Yb.

Gold Ghost, The
1934 Educational 2 reels.
Cast: Buster Keaton.
F?-com
Ref: Maltin/GMS p 158.

Golden Ass -- Trial of Lucius Apulius
for Witchcraft, The
See: Asino d'Oro -- Processo per
Fatti Strani con Lucius Apuleius,
L' (1970?).

Golden Boy Subdues Monsters
1970 Mandarin color scope.
Cast: Kanie Ko, Wang Pin Pin.
F?
Ref: Singapore Straits-Times 16 Oct '70.

Golden Buddha, The
1967?
F?
Ref: Richardson.

Golden Couple, The
See: Ogon no Tozoko (1966).

Golden Dragon, The
1967? French/Italian, PEA/ Parnass.
bor-SF? (spies)
Ref: Richardson.

Golden Fleece
1946.
Cin: Thomas Bouchard.
Dancers: Hanya Holm and group.

exp-ballet-F?
Ref: USA Exp List.

Golden Fly, The
1914 German, Bioscop sil.
Dir?: Stellan Rye.
F?
Ref: LC.

Golden Goddess of Rio Beni
n.d.
Cast: Pierre Brice, Gillian Hill.
SF?
Ref: Richardson.
Made?

Golden Key, The
1922 Czech sil.
F?
Ref: Encic DS III:364.
Based on a story by Karel Capek.

Golden Lion, The
1972 Hongkong, Shaw.
Dir: Ho Meng Hua.
Cast: Li Ching, Li Kuang.
F-seq? (mystic martial arts?)
Ref: MTVM 25:11:14.
Completed?

Goldfish Bowl, The
1973? British, Hammer.
Prod, Dir, SP: Jimmy Sangster.
H?
Ref: CoF 19:50-51.
Announced.

Goldmarie in Fix and Foxi's Country
1972? Italian/W. German, Gamma/ Rolf Kauka Filmprod color ani.
Dir: Rolf Kauka.
F?
Ref: MTVM 27:2:22.
Completed?

Goliath and the Conquest of Damascus
n.d. Italian.
Cast: Rock Stevens, Anthony Steele.
F-seqs? (superstrength?)
Ref: Collier.

Good Age, The
See: Bel Age, Le (1964?).

Good Fairy
1951 Japanese.
F?
Ref: UniJ 19.

Good King Dagobert, The
See: Bon Roi Dagobert, Le (1963?).

Good Little Brownie
1920 Century sil 2 reels.
Cast: Billy Watson.
F?
Ref: LC.

Good Little Shepherdess and the Wicked Princess, The
190? French, Méliès sil sh.
Prod: Georges Méliès.
F?
Ref: B&B p40.

Good Morning, Berenger! How's Everything Today? Not Bad. That's Good!
(! --ad.t.)
n.d. Rembrandt.
F?
Ref: Photon 21:6.
Is this the same film as Kdo Chce Zabit Jessii? (1965, main list)?

Good Soldier Schweik, The
1926 sil.
F-seq? ("seance brings ghosts")
Ref: Willis.
Is this same film as the 1929 version, main list?

Goodoo of Wirreebilla, The
1971?
SP: Clarisa Bernhardt.
F?
Ref: Photon 21:8.
Announced; made?

Goofy Ghosts
1928 Par sil 2 reels.
Dir: Harold Beaudine.
Story: Sig Herzig.
F?-H?-com
Ref: LC; MPN 28 April '28.

Gopher, The
1915 Bison (U) sil 2 reels.
Prod: William Worthington.
Sc: Harvey Gates.
SF? ("scientific device")
Ref: MPN 21 Aug '15.

Gorgona, La
1914 Italian sil.
F-H?
Ref: DdC III:112.

Gorilla, The
1914 British, Big Ben sil sh.
bor-H?
Ref: Hist Brit p282.

Gothic Line, The
1971 Czech.
H?
Ref: Photon 21:45.

Goulbe, La
1972? French.
Dir: Bepi Fontana.
F? H?
Ref: Vw 20 Sept '72 p6 -- at Sitges Festival.

Gourmets, The
1972? Genini.
Prod & Dir: T.V. Mikels.
H (cannibalism)
Ref: BO 3 Jan '72 p3.
Announced; made?

Grabuge, Le
(Hung Up)
1968? 20th-Fox.
Dir: Edouard Luntz.
Cast: Patricia Gozzi, Calvin Lockhart, Julie Dassin.
F? ("adventure-fantasy")
Ref: MTVM May '68 p30.
Completed?

Grand Guignol
(Grande Guignol?)
1966?
H?
Ref: CoF 7:50.
Exists? (doubtful)

Grand-Pere Miracle
1959 Soviet.
Dir: G. Kazans.
F?
Ref: Willis.

Grande Bidule, Le
(The Great Gimmick)
1967 French, Greenwich.
Dir: Raoul Andre.
Cast: Francis Blanche, Michel Serrault, Darry Cowl.
SF-seq? (revolutionary new fuel)
Ref: MTVM June '67 p28.

Grande Frousse, La
(The Great Fear)
n.d.
F?
Ref: MMF 17:42.

Grandma's House
1965 Amateur (Film-makers' Coop) 16mm 25 mins.
Made by: Bob Fleischner.
Mus: Murray Greenberg.
Cast: Jerry Sims, Barbara Kahn.
exp-F?
Ref: FMC 3:25-26.

Grandmother's Wolf
1900 British sil.
Prod: G.A. Smith.
F?
Ref: Sadoul p362.

Granny's Darling
1909 British? sil sh.
F-com? (hypnotism)
Ref: Bios 30 Dec '09.

Graveside Story, The
1971? Magnum Prods (Cinerama).
Cast: Vincent Price, Gloria Swanson.
H?
Ref: Photon 21:5, BO 25 Oct '71 p6.
Announced; made?

Gravitation and Youthful Fantasy of Employee Boris Horvat, The
n.d. Yugoslavian.
F?
Ref: Richardson.

Great Chase, The
1962 Harvey Cort (Continental Distributing) 77 mins.
F-seqs? (this is compilation of chase scenes from silent films; may have fantasy sequences)
Ref: FF '62 p358-59; CoF 10:39.

Great Devil-Spirit
1967? Japanese.
F?
Ref: MTVM Nov '67 p 18.

Great Ganton Mystery, The
1913 Rex sil 1920 ft.
F? ("murder, hypnotism")
Ref: Bios 28 Aug '13.

Great Gimmick, The
See: Grande Bidule, Le (1967).

Great Inheritance, The
See: Ghost of Their Ancestors, The (1915).

Great Romance, The
1918 Metro sil.
bor-F? (adventures in mythical country)
Ref: FIR May '71 p295.

Great Unknown, The
1927 German sil.
F?
Ref: Willis.

Green Cockatoo, The
1937 British.
Cast: Robert Newton, John Mills.
H?
Ref: Willis.

Green Monster, The
n.d. Italian.
F-H (Dracula?)
Ref: Soren.

Green Spider, The
See: Zelyonyi Pauk (1916).

Gribli, Wind of the Sun
1971? Italian, International Movies.
SF?
Ref: Photon 21:8.
Announced; made?

Grim Reaper, The
See: Commare Seca, La (1962).

Grimaces
See: Gyermekbetegsegek (1966).

Grip of the Spider
1972? Jack Vaughan Prods.
F? H?
Ref: BO 6 March '72 pSE-2.

Grito de la Muerte, El
(The Cry of Death)
1958 Mexican, Alameda Films & César Santos Galindo color.
Dir: Fernando Mendez.
Cin: Victor Herrera.
Cast: Gaston Santos, Pedro D'Aguillon, Carlos Ancira, Carolina Barret, Antonio Raxel.
H?
Ref: Aventura p420.
Based on a short story by Ramón Obón.

Guardians of Phare
See: Gardiens du Phare (1928).

Guest of Stone
n.d. Soviet, Sovexportfilm 70mm color.
Dir: Vladimir Gorikker.
Cast: Sergei Martinson, Lidia Smirnova, Nikolai Rybnikov.
opera-F?
Ref: MTVM Nov '66 p 19.
Completed?

Gul-Bakawali
n.d. Singapore, Cathay (in Malayan).
Dir: B.N. Rao.
Cast: Latiffah Omar, Noordin Ahmad.
F? ("fantasy")
Ref: MTVM Aug '62 p21.
Completed?

Gul Baradin
1961? Indian? Pakistani?
F?
Ref: FEFN '61; Collier.

Gullible's Travels
1952.
Dir?: Felix Adler.
F?
Ref: Collier.

Made? (Doubtful)

Gullivar the Giant and the Little People
Chicago drive-in ad retitling, presumably of Three Worlds of Gulliver, The (1959, main list).
Ref: D. Glut.

Gulliver

1971? Italian, Ultra.

Dir & SP: Vittorio Gassman.

Cast: Vittorio Gassman.

F?

Ref: Photon 21:8.

Based on "Gulliver's Travels" by Jonathan Swift?

Gulliver in the Land of the Giants

n.d.

Dir: Segundo de Chomon.

F?

Rèf: Gasca p 15.

Based on "Gulliver's Travels" by Jonathan Swift?

Gullivers Reisen

(Gulliver's Travels)

1924 Austrian sil.

F?

Ref: Willis.

Based on "Gulliver's Travels" by Jonathan Swift?

Gulliver's Travels

● 1903 Lubin sil sh.

F

Ref: LC.

Sames as the 1902 film by Méliès, main list?

● 1973? British/Belgian, Valeness/Belvision live & ani color.

Exec Prod: Josef Shaftel & Raymond Ledlanc.

Prod: Derek Horne.

SP & Lyrics: Don Black.

Mus: John Barry.

Cast: Richard Harris.

F

Ref: Vw 17 Jan '73 p31; QHP 17 Feb '73 p 14.

Completed?

Based on the novel by Jonathan Swift.

See also: Gullivers Reisen (1924); Man Who Carried the Wind on His Back, The (1970?); Region of Friendly Spirits, The (1969).

Gulliver's Troubles

n.d. British? ani & live.

Prod: John & Faith Hubley.

F?

Guns of the Trees

1962? Amateur (Film-makers' Coop) 16mm 75 mins.

Dir: Jonas Mekas.

Assists: Adolfas Mekas and Sheldon Rochlin.

Poetry written & spoken by: Allen Ginsberg.

Mus: Lucia Dlugoszewski.

Cast: Ben Carruthers, Frances Stillman, Argus Speare Juillard, Adolfas Mekas, Frank Kuenstler, Leonard Hicks.

sur-com-F-seq?

Ref: FQ Summer '62 p47; FMC 5:232.

Gustave le Medium

1921 French sil.

Cast: Georges Biscot.

F?

Ref: DdC I:239.

H

Haendeligt Uheld

(One of Those Things)

1971? Danish, A/S Nordisk Film.

Cast: Judy Geeson.

psy-H?

Ref: Photon 21:8.

Made?

Hägringen

(The Mirage)

1959? Swedish (C-16) 72 mins.

Prod: Peter Weiss.

exp-F ("man against society;" "fantasy life")

Ref: C-16 p22-23; Sweden 2 p83-84.

Haine du Sorcier, La

(The Hate of the Sorcerer)

1913 French sil.

Dir: Charles Burguet.

F-H?

Ref: DdC I:287.

Hair

1974? Michael Butler Associates.

Prod: Michael Butler.

SP: Gerome Ragni & James Rado.

Mus: Galt MacDermot.

mus; F-seq

Ref: NYT 22 April '73.

Based on the rock musical by Gerome Ragni & James Rado.

Announced.

Hakuchu no Torima

(Phantom Killer)

1966? Japanese, Sozosha & Shochiku.

Dir: Nagisa Oshima.

Cast: Sae Kawaguchi, Akiko Koyama, Kei Sato.

F?

Ref: MTVM July '66 p33.

Completed?

Halaka el Safkuda, El

(The Missing Link)

1949 Egyptian.

Dir: Ibrahim Lama.

SF?

Ref: Arab Cin p278.

Halo, The

See: O Věcech Nadpřirozených (1958).

Hamati Kombola Zorria

(My Mother-in-Law Is an Atomic Bomb)

1952 Egyptian.

Dir: Hilmy Rafla.

SF-com?

Ref: Arab Cin p279.

Hamati Malak

(My Mother-in-Law is an Angel)

1960 Egyptian.

Dir: Issa Karama.

F-com?

Ref: Arab Cin p283.

Hamlet

● 1908 Vit sil sh.

Dir: J. Stuart Blackton.

Ref: Filmlex p680.

F-seq? (ghost scenes included?)

Exists? (Doubtful)

cont.

Hamlet cont.

● 1912? sil.

Cast: Alla Nazimova.

F-seq? (ghost scenes included?)

Ref: Shake/Sil p 149.

Exists? (Doubtful)

● 1943 British.

Cast: Peter Ustinov.

F-seq? (ghost scenes included?)

Ref: Collier.

Exists? (Doubtful)

● 1955? Indian.

Cast: Venus Bannerjee.

F-seq

Ref: Filmindia Jan '55.

Same as 1953 version, main list?

● 1967? Polish 41 mins.

Dir: Witold Filler.

Cast: Wieslaw Michnikowski, Magdalena Zawadzka, Bronislaw Pawlik, Stanislaw Szymanski, Jan Kobuszeski.

F-seq? (ghost scenes included?)

Ref: MTVM Aug '68 p9A.

Any theatrical showings? This was made for television.

Based on the play by William Shakespeare.

Han Robado una Estrella

1961? Spanish, P.C.M.D.

Dir: Javier Seto.

Cast: Estrellita, Spartaco Santoni.

F? ("folklore")

Ref: MTVM Oct '61 p 13.

Completed?

Hand Invisible, The

1919 World sil.

Dir: Harry O. Hoyt.

Story: Wallace C. Clifton.

Sc: Clara S. Beranger.

SF? (doubtful)

Ref: LC.

Hand of Horror, The

1914 Edison sil 2 reels.

Author?: W.H. Durham.

H?

Ref: LC.

Hand of Vengeance

1918 Gaum sil serial 10 parts 20 reels.

F? (doubtful)

Ref: MPW 36:1528; LC.

Probably same film as Man from the Dead (1918 problem list).

Hands and Feet

1925 French sil.

Dir: Nalpas.

exp-F?

Ref: French Exp List.

Hands of Man, The

n.d. Czech.

Dir: Bruno Šefranka.

F?

Ref: Czech An '61.

Hands of Space

1961? South African, Rand Films.

SF?

Ref: MTVM Nov '61 p33.

Completed?

Hands Up

1918 Astra (Pathé) sil serial 15 parts 31 reels.

Dir: James Horne.

Story: Gilson Willets.

cont.

Hands Up cont.

Sc: Jack Cunningham.

Cast: Ruth Roland, George Chesebro, George Larkin, Easter Walters.

F-seq? (chapter titles include: "The Phantom Trail" and "The Celestial Messenger")

Ref: MPW 37:881, 884; LC; CNW p v, viii, 62, 104, 186-87.

Hangman and the Witch, The

1955 French? 111 mins.

Cast: Danielle Darrieux, Paul Meurisse, Viviane Romance.

F? (witch?)

Ref: BIB's Winter-Spring '71 pA275.

Hangman of St. Marien, The

See: Henker von St.-Marien, Der (1920).

Hanno Cambiato Faccia

(They've Changed Faces)

1971 Italia, Filmsettanta color 90 mins.

Dir: Corrado Farina.

SP: C. Farina & Giulio Berruti.

Cin: Ajace Parolin.

Mus: Amedeo Tommasi.

Cast: Giuliano Disperati, Geraldine Hooper, Adolfo Celi.

F? (doubtful; film is apparently gangster version of Nosferatu [1922, main list] with vampires replaced by criminals)

Ref: Vw 1 Sept '71.

Hans Christian Andersen Story

1971? Animedia ani & live color.

Prod & Dir: Bern Wolf.

Prod Design: Joe Messerli.

F

Ref: Vd 12 March '71.

Completed?

Hans Trutz im Schlaraffenland

n.d.

Cast: Paul Wegener.

F? (Legend)

Ref: Eisner p44.

Hansel and Gretel

1919 sil.

F?

Ref: Willis.

Hantu Penanggal

1957? Hongkong/Malayan Shaw.

SP: Run Run Shaw.

F-H (living disembodied head with dangling entrails needs blood from women in labor in order to survive)

Ref: FEFN 26 July '57 p 17.

Announced; made?

Hantu Rimau

1959 Malayan, Cathay & Keris.

Dir: B. N. Rao, L. Krishnan, & Roomai Noor.

Cast: Roomai Noor.

F-H? (3 story film; third part about "tiger spirit")

Ref: FEFN Aug '59 p 16.

Happy Anniversary

1963 French 12 mins.

Prod & Dir: Pierre Etaix.

Cast: Pierre Etaix.

com; F-seq? (doubtful)

Happy Elf, The

n.d. color ani 8 mins.

Created by: Witold Giersz.

F

Ref: Ideal 69-70 p207.

Happy Forest, The
1972? Hongkong, Shaw.
Dir: Chang Cheh.
Cast: Ti Lung, Tien Ching.
F? ("Chinese legend")
Ref: MTVM 26:8:27.
Completed?

Happy Microbes
1907 French sil sh.
F-com?
Ref: HR 21 June '39.

Happy Witchery
1970? Soviet.
F?
Ref: Collier.

Harmonia
197? Silver Screen Prods color ani.
Prod: James M. Farquharson & Randy Ericson.
SP: R. Ericson.
Nar: De Veren Brookwalter.
F (history of man in warfare and music from beginning to year 2000)
Ref: BO 7 June '71 p 91.
Announced; made?

Harry Hooton
1971 Australian color ani sh.
Dir: Arthur & Corinne Cantrill.
exp-F; doc
Ref: ASIFA Info Bltn #2.
See also: Directions of Harry Hooton, The (1960?, main list).
Exists?

Hartigan
n.d. Amateur (Film-makers' Coop) 16mm color 10 mins.
Made by: Hart Perry.
Assists: Grace Hartigan Price & Tina Gram.
exp-F? ("utilizes. . .technology in the tradition of Georges Méliès")
Ref: FMC 5:265.

Hary Janos
1951 Hungarian.
F?
Ref: Shea.
Based on Kordaly's suite.

Hate of the Sorcerer, The
See: Haine du Sorcier, La (1913).

Haunt of Fear, The
1973 British, Amicus (Cinerama) color.
Prod: Max J. Rosenberg & Milton Subotsky.
F-H
Ref: LSH 2:65.
Based on comic magazine stories by William M. Gaines and Albert B. Feldstein.
Announced; not made yet.

Haunted, The
1966? Hongkong/Taiwanese.
F-H?
Ref: MTVM Jan '67.

Haunted Bedroom, The
1907 French, Urban-Eclipse sil 267 ft.
F-com?
Ref: MPW 1:622.

Haunted by Hawkeye
1913 sil sh.
F?
Ref: Bios 15 May '13.

Haunted Castle, The
1912 sil 2 reels.
F?

Haunted Castle, The
1922 Educational sil 1 reel.
F?
Ref: MPN 26:3253.

Haunted Chamber, The
1913 Anderson sil 2700 ft.
F?
Ref: Bios 4 Sept '13 p xxx.

Haunted England
1961 British.
F?
Ref: Willis.

Haunted Fright
Chicago drive-in ad retitling of what film?
Ref: D. Glut.

Haunted Heiress, A
1925 Century (U) sil 2 reels.
Story: Francis Corby.
Cast: Edna Marian.
bor-F-com? (fake haunted house)
Ref: FD 9 May '26.

Haunted Homestead, The
1927 Mustang (U) sil 2 reels.
Dir: William Wyler.
Sc: L.V. Jefferson.
F? (doubtful; probably fake ghosts)
Ref: FD 3 April '27.

Haunted Hotel, The
1913 Pathé sil 1200 ft.
F? ("strange happenings")
Ref: Bios 3 April '13.

Haunted House, The
1899 Lubin sil.
F-H-com?
Ref: LC.

Haunted House, The
190? Vit sil 100 ft.
F-H-com?
Ref: Collier.
Same film as Haunted Hotel (1907, main list)?

Haunted House, The
1917 Triangle sil sh.
F-H-com?
Ref: FD 20 Sept '17; Willis.

Haunted House
1919 sil 2 reels.
Dir: ? Cline.
H-com (fake ghosts)
Ref: Willis.

Haunted House, The
1922 Fox sil 2 reels.
Dir: Earle Kenton.
F-H-com?
Ref: LC.

Haunted House
1939 Vitaphone 12 mins.
Dir: Joseph Henabery.
SP: Burnet Hershey.
F-H (doubtful)
Ref: LC; Willis.

Haunted Island
1927-28 U sil serial 10 parts 20 reels.
Dir: Robert F. Hill.
Sc: George Morgan & Carl Krusada.
Cast: Jack Daugherty, Helen Foster.
F? H? (doubtful)
Ref: CNW p 145-46, 264-65.
Based on story "Pleasure Island" by Frank P. Adams.
Remake of Brass Bullet, The (1918, exclusion list).

Haunted Palace
1949.
Dir: Richard Fisher.
F?

Haunted Tomb
1964 Gorgon Enterprises.
F-H?
Ref: MadMon 9:9.
Exists? Doubtful.

Haunted Valley
1923 Pathé sil serial.
Dir: George Marshall.
Cast: Ruth Roland, Jack Daugherty, Larry Steers, Eulalie Jenson, Francis Ford, William Ryno, Edouard Trebeal.
F? (doubtful)
Ref: CNW p 108, 234-35.

Haunting Castle in Salzkammergut, The
See: Spukschloss im Salzkammergut (1965).

Haunting Eye
1915? sil.
F?
Ref: Motog 10 April '15.

Haunting of Silas P. Gould, The
1915 British, Ivy Close Films sil sh.
Prod: Elwin Neame.
com; F?
Ref: Collier; Hist Brit.

Haupt der Medusa, Der
(The Head of Medusa)
1919 Austrian sil.
F?
Ref: Osterr (Willis).

Hawk of the Caribbean, The
See: Sparviero dei Caraibi, La (n.d.).

Head Mistress
1967 color.
F-H ("disembodied head keeps reappearing")
Ref: Soren.

Head of Medusa, The
See: Haupt der Medusa, Der (1919).

Headfilm
n.d. Amateur (Film-makers' Coop) 16mm color & b&w 5 mins.
Made by: Standish D. Lawder.
Cast: Lon Chaney.
exp-F?
Ref: FMC 5:197.

Headless Husband, The
1971 Kirt Films Int'l.
Dir & SP: Andrew Sugarman.
Cast: Brenda Major, Duncan MacGlore.
H?
Ref: CineF 3.
Completed?

Heads for Sale
1970 color.
H?
Ref: Singapore Straits-Times 25 July '70.

Heart and Soul
1917 Fox sil 5 reels.
Dir: J. Gordon Edwards.
Sc: Adrian Johnson.
Cast: Theda Bara.
F?
Ref: MPW 32:1342, 1623, 1627; LC.
Based on novel "Jess" by H. Rider Haggard.

Heart of Jade, The
n.d. Vietnamese color 31 mins.
F? ("fairy tale")
Ref: Collier.

Heaven and Hell
See: Janna wa Narr (1953).

Heavenly Gift
1972 Israeli, Gimel Daled Ltd.
Dir: Gad Ben-Artzi.
Cast: Amos Tel-Shir, Edna Lev, Yossi Pollack, Gabi Amrani.
F?
Ref: Vw 3 Jan '73 p48.

Heba the Snake Woman
1915 Excelsior sil.
F?
Ref: Gifford/MM p 154.

Hedonist Hypnotist
1971?
sex-F? H? SF?
Ref: Photon 21:5.

Heisses Blut
(Burning Blood)
1911 German sil.
Dir: Urban Gad.
Cast: Asta Nielsen.
F?

Hekayet Nus el Lail
(A Tale of Midnight)
1964 Egyptian.
Dir: Issa Karama.
H?
Ref: Arab Cin p285.

Helen and Ferdinand and . . . .
1955? Czech.
Compiled by (Prod?): Karel Forst.
F? (probable; compilation film on history of warfare)
Ref: Collier.

Hell Ship, The
(Eld Ombord; Fire on Board)
1923 Swedish sil.
Dir: Victor Sjöström.
Cin: Julius Jaenzon.
Cast: Victor Sjöström, Matheson Lang, Jenny Hasselqvist.
F-H? ("evokes supernatural quality": B&B)
Ref: B&B p 178; MPW 43:1289; MPN 38:11:869; FIR May '60 p277, June '60 p354.

Hellish Brain, The
See: Cerebro Infernal, El (1967).

Hello Mars
1922 Century Comedies (U) sil 2 reels.
Dir & Sc: Alfred T. Goulding.
SF-com?
Ref: Collier; LC.

Hell's Illusion
1971? Danish.
Dir: Claus Oersted.
F?
Ref: Photon 21:45.
Announced; made?

Hell's Tattooers
1969 Japanese, Toei color 95 mins.
F-H? ("sadistic tortures")
Ref: MTVM April '69 p26 ad.

Hellseher, Der
(The Clairvoyant)
1933 German, AAFA.
Dir: Eugen Thiele.
Cast: Max Adalbert, Trude Berliner, Johannes Riemann, Marianne Winkelstern, Ernst Verebes, Senta Soenland, Paul Hoerbiger.
com; F? ("part-time clairvoyant")
Ref: NYT 11 Sept '33.

Help, Help, the Globolinks
n.d.
SF-opera?
Ref: Willis.
Announced; made? (doubtful)

Help, There's a Blonde in My Bed
1967? Czech? Rembrandt.
Prod: William Snyder.
SP: Stuart Hample.
Cast: Olinka Berova.
SF-com
Ref: Vw 16 Aug '67; MTVM Sept '67 p 10; Soren.
Announced; made?

Helping Hand, The
1908 sil sh.
Prod: Gaston Méliès?
F?
Ref: LC.

Hemlighetsfull X, Det
(The Mysterious X)
1913 Danish sil sh.
Dir: Benjamin Christensen.
F-H?
Ref: Collier; DdC II:8.

Henker von St. Marien, Der
(The Hangman of St. Marien)
1920 German sil.
F?
Ref: C to H p 110.

Hercules Reborn
1972
sex; F?
Ref: Vw 3 May '72 p218 ad.

Hercules, Samson, and Maciste to the Rescue
n.d. Italian.
Dir: Pietro Francisci.
F
Ref: Collier.
Exists?

Hercules vs. Maciste
(Ercole Contro Maciste)
n.d. Italian.
Dir: Carlo Campogalliani.
F
Ref: Collier.
Exists?

Heritage of Beaucitron, The
1915 Roach sil.
Prod: Hal Roach.
F?
Ref: CoF 6:31.

Heroes of the Flames
1931 U serial 12 parts 24 reels.
F? (doubtful)
Ref: LC.

Herr des Mondes, Der
(The Master of the Moons; The Man from the Moons)
1922 German? Austrian? sil.
SF?
Ref: Willis.

Herr des Todes, Der
(The Master of Death)
1914 German, Bioscop sil.
Dir: Max Obal.
F-H?
Ref: LC.
Based on a novel by Carl Rosner.

Herrenhof Saga
n.d. Swedish.
Cast: Gösta Björling.
F? ("spider spins web in man's brain")
Ref: Gerrard Pick.
Exists?

He's Dead Because of the Bunglers
n.d. Spanish.
Dir: Jesus Franco.
Cast: Fred Williams.
F-H?
Ref: Soren.

Heute Nacht Oder Nie
(Tonight or Never)
1972 Swiss, Unset color 90 mins.
Prod: Ingrid Caven.
Dir & SP: Daniel Schmid.
Cin: Renato Berta.
Edit: Ila Von Hasperg.
Cast: Ingrid Caven, Voli Geiler, Peter Chatel, Igo Jozsa, Peter Kern, Harry Baer, Beatrice Stoll, Rosemarie Haeinikel.
F-seqs? (servants change places with masters; highly symbolic but any fantasy?)
Ref: Vw 13 Sept '72 p20.

Hexe, Die
(The Witch)
1954 German.
Cast: Attila Hörbiger, Anita Björk, Karl Boehm.
F?
Ref: DdC I:239, 250, III:54.

Hexed
1971? Cambist.
F
Ref: CineF 3; Photon 21:7.
Based on novel "Night of the Warlock."
Announced; made? (doubtful)

Hexer, Der
1932 German.
Dir: Karel Lamac.
Cast: Fritz Rasp.
H?
Ref: FIR June-July '63 p 376, Feb '67 p76.
Based on play "The Ringer" by Edgar Wallace.

Hiawatha
1910 sil.
F?
Ref: Bios 21 July '10.
Based on the poem by Henry Wadsworth Longfellow?

Hidden Children, The
1917 Yorke Film Corp sil 5 reels.
Dir: Oscar Apfel.
F?
Ref: LC.
Based on the novel by Robert W. Chambers.

Hidden Enemy
n.d.
SF? F? H?
Ref: Willis.

Hidden Room, The
n.d. British.
F? H?
Ref: Willis.

High Priest of Vampires
1971? British, Hammer.
F-H
Ref: CineF 2:42.
Announced; not yet made.

Hijo del Diablo, El
(The Devil's Son, The Son of the Devil)
196? (1967) Mexican (Clasa-Mohme)
F-H?
Ref: FDY '68 p 178.

Hill of the Little Devils, The
1966? Spanish.
F?
Ref: MTVM July '66 p27.

Hilm Layla
(Dream of a Night)
1948/49 Egyptian.
Dir: Salaheddine Badrakan.
F?
Ref: Arab Cin p278.

His Pre-Historic Blunder
1922 A Star Comedy (U) sil 1000 ft.
Dir: Craig Hutchinson.
Story & Sc: Glenn Lambert.
bor-SF-com?
Ref: LC; MPW 57:454.

His Prehistoric Past
1923 Tri-Stone 2 reels.
com; bor-SF?
Ref: LC.
Is this a reissue of the 1914 Charlie Chaplin film of the same title?

Histoire de l'Oeil, L'
(The Story of the Eye)
1972? Italian/Beligan, Rolfilm/Films de l'Oeil.
Prod: Alberto Ardissone & Patrick Longchamps.
Dir: P. Longchamps.
Cast: Patrick Magee, Laura Antonelli.
sur-F? ("the prohibited surrealism of George Bataille's startling novel")
Ref: Vw 14 June '72.
Based on the novel by George Bataille.

Histoire du Futur Anterieur
(Story of Previous Future)
1969 French, Canthy Films color 18 mins.
Dir: Frank Cassendo.
Cin: Jean Pierre Baux.
Mus: Luc Ferrari & Carl Baüle.
F? SF?
Ref: Trieste '70.

Historia de la Frivolidad
(History of Frivolity, Story of Frivolity)
1967? Spanish.
com; F-seqs? (history of sexual frivolity from Adam & Eve to the future)
Ref: Collier.
Exists?

History of Frivolity
See: Historia de la Frivolidad (1967?).

Hobbit, The
197? Tomorrow Entertainment Inc.
Prod: Arthur Rankin Jr. & Jules Bass.
F
Ref: Vw 29 Nov '72.
Based on the novel by J.R.R. Tolkien.
Completed?

Hobgoblin, The
1924 German sil.
F?
Ref: Willis.

Hochtourist, Der
1961? W. German, Corona & UFA.
Dir: Ulrich Erfurth.
Cast: Willy Millowitsch, Marlies Behrens.
F? ("folklore")
Ref: MTVM Oct '61 p23.
Completed?

Hocus Pocus
n.d. German.
Cast: Felix Aylmer.
F?

Hole in the Wall, A
1930 French.
F?
Ref: DdC III:356.

Holiday in the Caribbean
1958? Spanish.
H-seq? ("voodoo ceremony")
Ref: SpCin '59 (Willis).

Holidays in Hell
See: Igaza fi Gehannam (1949).

Holy Devil, The
193? Fox?
Prod: William Fox.
Dir: Raoul Walsh.
Cast: Paul Muni.
F-H?
Exists? Doubtful.

Hombe Que Hizo el Milagro, El
(The Man Who Created a Miracle)
1958 Argentine, Sandrini 95 mins.
Prod & Dir: Luis Sandrini.
Story: Paulino Masip.
SP: Emilio Villaba Welsh & Ariel Cortazzo.
Cast: Luis Sandrini, Nelly Panizza.
F? (grotesque)
Ref: Nubila II:238, 252, 311.

Hombre y la Bestia, El
(The Man and the Beast)
1962 Mexican.
F-H?
Ref: Gifford/MM p 154.

Homme des Cinq Saisons, L'
(The Man for Five Seasons)
1972 French.
Dir: Edmond Fress.
SP: Pierre Fabre.
Cast: Philippe Noiret, Liselotte Pulver.
F-com? (man and wife take group of strange people into their home; may have fantasy or even horror sequences)
Ref: Unifrance Film News Jan '72.
Completed?

Homme du Large, L'
(The Man of the Wide-Open Spaces --?)
1920 French sil.
Dir: Marcel l'Herbier.
exp-F?
Ref: French Exp List.

Homme et la Poupee, L'
(The Man and the Doll)
1921 (1922) French, Gaum sil.
F?
Ref: LC.

Homme Qui Revient de Loin, L'
(The Man Who Returned from Afar)
1949 French.
Dir: Jean Castanier.
Cast: Maria Casarès, Paul Bernard, Annabella, Henri Crémieux.
F? H?
Ref: de Groot p 158.
Based on the novel by Gaston Leroux.

Homo Homini
n.d. Czech 10 mins.
Dir: Vaclav Bedrich.
F? ("violent bombardment with disturbing images")
Ref: Edinburgh Fest '68.

Honeymoon in a Balloon
1908 French? sil sh.
Dir: Gaston Méliès?
F?
Ref: LC.

Hoodoo Ranch
1926 Action (Weiss Artclass) sil 4414 ft.
Dir: William Bertram.
Cast: Buddy Roosevelt.
F-seqs? ("haunted ranch house")
Ref: AFI F2.2579 p362.

Hoor-E-Baghdad
1963 Indian.
Cast: Darasing, Vijaya Chowdhury.
F?
Ref: Picturepost Feb '63.

Horla, Le
n.d.
Cast: Laurent Terzieff.
F?
Ref: MMF 17:66.
Based on the short story by Guy de Maupassant?

Horrible Midnight
1958 Japanese.
F? H?
Ref: Japanese Films '60 p94.

Horrible Orgies of Count Dracula, or Black Magic -- Rites -- Reincarnations, The
1972? Italian, G.R.P.
Dir: Ralph Brown.
F-H?
Ref: MTVM 26:5:24.
Completed?

Horripilant
1972? Italian? Tarquina Int'l Cin.
Dir: Miles Deem.
Cast: Christopher Lee, Hunt Power, Red Carter, Simone Blondell.
F-H?
Ref: MTVM 27:4:16.
Announced; made?

Horripilations of the Spastic
Chicago drive-in ad retitling of what film?
Ref: D. Glut.

Horror Dream
1947 Amateur 10 mins.
Made by: Sidney Peterson & Hy Hirsh.
Mus: John Cage.
Choreog: Marian Van Tuyl.
Cast: Marian Van Tuyl and her dance troupe.
dance-F?
Ref: USA Exp List; Undrgnd p91.

Horror High
1973 James P. Graham & Jamison Film color?
Exec Prod: James P. Graham.
cont.

Horror High cont.
Prod: Tom Moore.
Dir: Larry Stouffer.
Cast: Pat Cardi, Rosey Holotik, Austin Stoker, Mike McHenry, John Niland.
F? H?
Ref: Vw 27 June '63 p 18.
In production.

Horror Hospital
1972 (1973?) British/American.
Prod: Richard Gordon.
Dir: Anthony Balch.
Cast: Michael Gough, Dennis Price, Robin Askwith, Skip Ward.
H? SF-H?
Ref: HR 26 Dec '72 p 1 & 4.
Completed?

Horror of Darkness
1965 Canadian, CBC-TV 90 mins.
Prod: Robert Allan.
Dir: Paul Almond.
Cast: Neil McCallum, Susan Clark, Jonathan White.
H? (paranoid homosexual visits a friend)
Ref: MTVM Nov '65 p 18.
Television show?

Horror of Mars
1968?
SF?
Ref: Miami Herald 5 April '68 (Willis).
Probably same film as Mission Mars (1968, main list).

Horror Syndicate
n.d.
Cast: Erika Remberg, Adrian Hoven.
H?

Horrors of the Green Macabre, The
Chicago drive-in ad retitling of what film? Possibly Monster from Green Hell (1957), Macabre (1958) or Horrors of the Black Museum (1959) (all main list).

Hot Eye of Heaven
1960.
F?
Ref: Collier.

Hot Ice
1953 British.
Cast: Barbara Murray, John Justin.
H? ("spooky mansion")
Ref: Soren.

Hot Spring Ghost
1965? Japanese.
F?
Ref: Ackerman.
Possibly retitling for ad of some unknown film in main list.

Hotel for Foreigners
1967? Spanish?
Dir: Antonin Masa.
sur-F? ("cross between Marien- bad and The Trial")
Ref: Cont FR June '67 p4 (Collier).

Hotel Indiscreet
n.d. color 3 mins.
Prod: Bill Norton & Steve Rosen.
Mus: Sagittarius.
sur- ?
Ref: CFS cat '69.

Hound of the Baskervilles, The
1932? 1934? British.
Cast: Arthur Wontner.
H
Ref: Film Collectors' Registry March-April '73 p 1.
Probably an error for the 1932 British First Division film, or for Murder at the Baskervilles (1936, exclusions), with Arthur Wontner as Sherlock Holmes.
Based on the novel by Arthur Conan Doyle.

Hour of the Unicorn, The
1971?
F?
Ref: CineF Fall '70 p44.
Based on the novel by James Parish.
Announced; made? (doubtful)

House at World's End, The
1973? British.
Prod & Dir: Byron (Bryan?) Forbes.
F?
Ref: LSH 2:65.
Planned.

House Goblin, The
1946? Swedish.
F? ('fairy tale')
Ref: S&S Winter '47-48 p 174?

House of Cards
See: Château de Cartes (19??).

House of Darkness
1913 Biograph sil sh.
Sc: J.F. Looney.
H?
Ref: Willis.

House of Darkness
193? British.
F? H?

Exists?

House of Dracula's Daughter, The
1973? First Leisure Corp (Ellman) color.
Exec Prod: Harry Hope.
Prod & SP: Peter Crowcroft.
Dir: Gordon Hessler.
Cast: Peter Lorre Jr., John Carradine, David Carradine, Lorraine Day, Broderick Crawford.
F-H
Ref: Vw 10 May '72 p 19 ad.
Planned.
Based on a character created by Bram Stoker.

House of Fear, The
See: Manoir de la Peur, Le (1927).

House of Ghosts
See: Beit al Ashbah (1951/52).

House of Glass, The
See: Casa de Cristal, La (n.d.).

House of Lost Souls, The
1967? Czech.
Dir: Jiri Hanibal.
SP: Pavel Hejcman.
F? H?

House of Madness, The
See: Mansion de la Locura, La (1972?).

House of Mystery
1920 Steiner sil.
Sc: Alexander F. Frank.
F? H?
Ref: LC.

House of Mystery, The
1922 French sil.
F? H? (doubtful)
Ref: DdC II:234.

House of 100 Horrors
1971?
Cast: Joseph Cotten.
F-H?
Ref: BO 30 Aug '71.
Announced; made? (doubtful)

House of Perdition
(Casa de Pericion)
1951 Mexican.
F? H?
Ref: Willis.

House of Spies., The
n.d. Associated Television Corp.
Prod: Julian Wintle.
bor-SF?
Ref: Richardson.
Exists?

House of the Dead
n.d. German sil.
H?
Ref: Willis.

House of the Dead
n.d.
Cast: Christopher Lee.
F-H?
Ref: Collier.
Possibly mistake for Horror Hotel (British title: City of the Dead; 1960, main list).

House of the Living Dead, The
1973 South African, Capital.
Exec Prod: Philip N. Krasne.
Prod: Matt Drucker.
Dir: Ray Austin.
SP: Marc Marais.
Cast: Mark Burns, Shirley Ann Field.
F-H?
Ref: Vw 7 Feb '73 p27.
Completed?

House of the Ravens, The
See: Casa de Cuervos, La (1941).

House of the Screaming Terror
1971? Marlene.
F-H?
Ref: Photon 21:6.
Announced; made? (doubtful)

House of the Seven Gables, The
1972 AIP.
Exec Prod: Louis M. Heyward.
Prod: Samuel Z. Arkoff & James H. Nicholson.
F?-H
Ref: Photon 21:5; BO 25 Oct '71 p6.
Announced; not yet made.
Based on the novel by Nathaniel Hawthorne.

House of the Spaniard
1936 British.
H? ("mysterious mansion")
Ref: BIB's (Willis).

House of Whispers, The
1920 Hodkinson sil.
Cast: J. W. Kerrigan.
F? (doubtful)
Ref: Willis; MPN 2 Oct '20.

House that Jack Built, The
● 1909 Lubin sil sh.
F?
Ref: LC.
● n.d. ani?
F?

House that Stood Still, The
1973? Italian.
Prod?: Luigi Cozzi.
SF
Ref: Vw 16 Aug '72 p24; FM 97:21.
Based on the novel by A.E. van Vogt.
Announced; made? (doubtful)

House Without a Key, The
1926 Pathé sil serial.
F? H?
Ref: LC.

House Without Frontiers, The
1971? Spanish.
Dir: Pedro Olea.
Cast: Geraldine Chaplin, Viveca Lindfors.
H? ("mysterious international organization which kills its employees with stilettos")
Ref: F&F p23-24.

How Bridget's Lover Escaped
(Le Mariage de Victorine)
1907 French sil 500 ft.
Prod: Georges Méliès.
F?
Ref: Sadoul; LC; GM Mage.

How Jones Lost His Roll
1905 Edison sil sh.
Dir: Edwin S. Porter.
F-com?
Ref: LC; LA p 19.

How Mice Buried the Cat
n.d. Soviet, Gruzia.
F? (based on Georgian Tegend)
Ref: MTVM 25:12:13.

How They Became Vampires
1973? Sun, Moon, Star Co.
Prod: LaMont Johnson.
Dir: Amen El-Kakim.
F-H-com?
Ref: LSH 2:66.
Announced; made?

How to Become a Vampire
n.d. Benmar.
F-com?
Ref: CineF 2:42.
Announced; made? (doubtful)

How to Get Rid of Helen
1967? Czech.
Dir: Vaclav Gajer.
H? (a strange dream and its consequences)
Ref: MTVM May '67 p40.

How to Succeed with Sex
1969? Medford color 77 mins.
Prod: Jerome F. Katzman.
Dir & SP: Bert I. Gordon.
Cin: Michel Getti.
Edit: John Bushelman.
Mus: Forest Hamilton & Sean Bonniwell.
Cast: Zach Taylor, Mary Jane Carpenter, Keith London, Bambi Allen, Victoria Bond, Luanne Roberts.
sex-bor-F? ("plotless, semi-nude fantasy" --CoF)
Ref: CoF 16:60; MFB Sept '71 p 182.

Howdy Dowdy's Magic Hat
1955 UPA.

Howl, The
n.d. Italian 99 mins.
F-H?
Ref: Chodkowski.

Huckleberry Finn
1972? Filmation ani.
Prod: Norman Prescott & Lou Scheimer.
bor-F?
Ref: Vw 3 Jan '73 p60.
Completed? Television only?
Based on the novel by Mark Twain.

Huge
1972? Amateur.
Made by: Steve Arnold.
exp-F?
Ref: California Living 11 July '72.

Hugo, the Hippo
1973? U.S./Hungarian, Brut/color ani 90 mins.
Prod: Robert Halmi.
Dir: William Feigenbaum.
Voices: Burl Ives, Paul Lynde.
F-com
Ref: MTVM 27:3:11; Vw 3 Jan '73 p60.
Completed?

Huis Clos
(play by J.-P. Sartre)
See: No Exit (n.d.).

Human Clock, The
1907 sil sh.
F?
Ref: MPW 1907 p220 (Willis).

Human Gorilla, The
n.d.
SF-H?
Possibly same film as Bela Lugosi Meets a Brooklyn Gorilla (1952, main list).

Human Terror, The
1924 Geneva Dist Corp sil 4800 ft.
Cast: Alec B. Francis, Margaret Seddon.
H?
Ref: AFI F2.2619 p368.

Human Torpedoes
1967? Japanese.
SF? (doubtful)
Ref: UniJ 40.

Humbregolo, El
1971?
Dir: Pedro Portabella.
H?
Ref: Photon 21:8.

Hunchback, The
1909 Vit sil sh.
Dir: J. Stuart Blackton.
H?
Ref: Filmlex p683; LC.

Hunchback, The
See: Ahdab, El (1946/47).

Hung Up
See: Grabuge, Le (1968?).

Hunter Baj
1947? Indian, A.M. Khan.
Prod & Dir: A.M. Khan.
rel-F?(miracles?)
Ref: Filmindia Oct '46 p48.

Hunting Instinct
n.d. WD color ani? 70 mins.
F-com?
Ref: Ideal '69-'70 p77.

Hunting the Teddy Bear
1908 sil sh.
Prod: Gaston? Georges? Méliès.
F?
Ref: LC.

Huntingtower
1928 British, Welsh-Pearson & Co (Par) sil 72 mins.
Dir: George Pearson.
Sc: Charles E. Whittaker & Ray Overbaugh.
Edit: T. Hays Hunter.
Cast: Harry Lauder, Vera Veronia.
H? F?
Ref: Collier; Vw 21 March '28.
Based on the novel by John Buchan.

Husband of Pontianak, The
1958? Malayan? Philippine?
F-H
Ref: FEFN 22 Nov '57.
Announced; made? (doubtful)

Hyacinth Child's Bedtime Story, The
1962
Dir?: Burton Rubenstein.
exp-F?
Ref: Richardson.

Hypnose
1919 Austrian sil.
bor-F?
Ref: Willis.

Hypnotic Mirror, The
1909 sil sh.
bor-F?
Ref: Bios 14 Oct '09.

Hypnotising the Hypnotist
1912 sil sh.
F?
Ref: Bios 7 March '12.
Same film as Hypnotist, The (1911, main list)?

Hypnotist, The
1913 Nordisk sil sh.
bor-F?
Ref: Bios 24 July '13.

Hypnotized Policeman, The
n.d. French, Pathé sil 1/3 reel.
F-com?
Ref: Collier.

I

I, a Marquis
n.d. Danish, Polaris.
H?
Ref: Richardson.

I Am One Possessed
See: Je Suis Une Possedee (1970).

I Crave Your Blood
1971? Marlene Prods.
Cast: Laura Latrell.
F-H?
Ref: Photon 21:44.
Announced; made? (doubtful)

I, Dorian Gray
1970 Italian.
Cast: Katarina Lidfelt.
F
Ref: Parade 15 Nov '70.
Based on "The Picture of Dorian Gray" by Oscar Wilde.
Announced; made? (Doubtful; possibly same film as Secret of Dorian Gray, The [1970, main list].)

I Dreamed of You
See: Ich Hab von Dir Geträumt (1944).

I Kill for Kicks
1971? Cinemation.
H?
Ref: Photon 21:5.
Announced; made? (doubtful)

I, Marquis De Sade
1971?
H?
Ref: LAT 6 Aug '71.

I Seed the Winds
See: Je Sème à Tout Vent (1952).

I, the Vampire
1972? Spanish, Hispamex.
Dir: Leon Klimowsky.
Cast: Paul Naschy (r.n.: Jacinto Molina), Christopher Lee.
F-H
Ref: Vw 3 Nov '71.
Announced; not made yet.

I, Vor Pittfalks, Universal Confidence Man
n.d. British color ani sh.
Dir: Richard Williams.
F?
Ref: TVG.
Theatrical?

Ice Witch, The
1965? (New Trends).
F?
Ref: New Trends.

Ich Hab von Dir Geträumt
(I Dreamed of You)
1944 German.
H? F?
Ref: UF p412.

Icy Knife of Terror, The
See: Nude Horror (1972?).

Idaho Transfer
1971 (1973?) (Cinemation?).
Prod & Dir: Peter Fonda.
SP: Thomas Matthiesen.
SF (matter-transmission)
Ref: Vw 11 Aug '71.
Completed?

Ideal Woman, The
1935 French.
Dir: Berthomieu.
F?
Ref: Willis.

Idylle sous un Tunnel
(Idyll in a Tunnel)
1901 French, Pathé sil sh.
Dir: Ferdinand Zecca.
Cast: Liezer.
F?
Ref: Sadoul p47.

If a Ghost Dies
1936? Japanese.
F?
Ref: Cinema Ybk of Japan
1936-'37.

If I Grow Up
1971? Hungarian ani.
Dir: Peter Szoboszlay.
F
Ref: Vw 12 May '71.

If We Lived on the Moon
n.d. sil colored seq sh.
Prod: Max Fleischer.
SF?
Exists?

If You Touch Me, Danger
See: Oreni Sawaruto Abunaine
(n.d.).

If Youth Only Knew
See: Si Jeunesse Savant (1948).

Igaza fi Gehannam
(Holidays in Hell)
1949 Egyptian.

Dir: Izzeddine Zulficar.
com; F-H?
Ref: Arab Cin p278.

Igorota
(The Legend of the Tree of Life)
1970 Philippine, Nepomuceno color
scope.
Prod: Luis Nepomuceno.
F?
Ref: MTVM May '70 p 14.

Ile de Calypso, L'
n.d. sil sh.
Prod: Georges? Gaston? Méliès.
F?

Ile des Filles Perdus, L'
(The Island of Lost Girls)
1961 French?
F?
Ref: MMF 12:16.

Illiad, The
1968? Italian.
Prod: Dino De Laurentiis.
F
Ref: Richardson.
Based on the epic poem by Homer.
Made for television? Exists?

Im Banne des Unheimlichen
n.d. German, Wallace.
Dir: Alf Vohrer.
H?
Ref: Film 7 '68 p3.

Ima Vamp, Fairyland, and Memories
1920 Special Pictures Corp sil
2 reels.

Dir & Sc: Ward Lascelle.
F?
Ref: LC.
Probably three different
films on 2 reels.

Image in the Snow
n.d. Amateur (Film-makers'
Coop) 16mm 29 mins.
Made by: Willard Maas & Marie
Menken.
Mus: Ben Weber.
exp-F? ("lyric landscape of a dream")
Ref: FMC 5:224; C-16 p 17;
IFC cat p75.

Image of Love
1964?
F?
Ref: CoF 7:49.

Image One: An Event
1963 Amateur (Film-makers'
Coop) 16mm sil 3 mins.
Made by: Paul J. Sharits.
exp-F? ("image-symbols")
Ref: FMC 3:55-56.

Images
1972? Canadian.
Dir: Julius Kohany.
F? H?
Ref: Vw 20 Sept '72 p6 at
Sitges festival.

Imagine Robinson
See: Tu Imagines Robinson
(1968?).

Immortal
See: Amar (1953).

Immortal Monster, The
Chicago drive-in ad retitling;
presumably of Caltiki (1959).
Ref: D. Glut.

Immortality
See: Khulud (1948).

Imp in the Body, The
See: Con el Diablo en el Cuerpo
(1955).

Impassive Footman, The
1932 British.
H?
Ref: MFB '48 p 171.

Implosion
1966 Belgian.
Dir: Marcel Fraikin.
SF?

Impossibilities
1908 Lubin sil sh.
F?
Ref: LC.

In Ancient Days
1911 French, Gaum sil sh.
F-dream?
Ref: Willis.

In Frankfurt Sind die Nacht Heiss
1966.
Dir: Rolf Olsen.
H?
Ref: MMF 12:68.

In Nome del Padre
(In the Name of the Father)
1971 Italian, Vides Cinemat. di
Franco Cristaldi color
115 mins.

Dir & SP: Marco Bellocchio.
Sets: Amadeo Sego.
Cin: Franco di Giacomo.
Edit: Franco Artalli.
Mus: Nicola Piovani.
Cast: Yves Benayton, Renato
Scarpa, Aldo Sassi, Lou
Castel.
sur-F? ("grotesques," "Grand
Guignol" set in Catholic school
for boys; "bizarre")
Ref: Vw 20 Oct '71 at New York
Film Festival.

In Secret
(novel by R.W. Chambers)
See: Black Secret, The (1919).

In the Dead o' Night
1916 Imp 2 reels sil.
Dir: Douglas Gerrard.
Sc?: Willis Woods.
F?
Ref: LC.

In the Devil's Throat
1971? Brazilian.
Dir: Walter Hugo Khouri.
F-H?
Ref: Vw 12 May '71 p201 ad.

In the Forest, in the Sites
See: Do Lesicka na Cakanou
(n.d.).

In the Future
193? Australian, Efftee Film
Prods sh.
Cast: Ada Reeve.
SF?
Ref: Collier.

In the Land of Upside Down
1909 Lubin sil sh.
F?
Ref: LC.

In the Moon's Ray
1916 Essanay sil 2 reels.
Cast: Francis X. Bushman.
F?
Ref: LC; Collier.

In the Name of the Father
See: In Nome del Padre (1971).

In the New World
See: En un Mundo Nuevo (1971).

In the Sea
1948 Amateur.
Made·by: Ernest Beadle.
exp-F?
Ref: USA Exp List.

**In the Secret Service of Her Majesty
the Queen**
1971?
Cast: Gabrielle Ferzetti.
bor-SF?
Ref: Photon 21:8.
Exists?

In the Shadow of the Past
n.d.
F?

Inbad the Sailor
● 1917 Powers (U) sil 1/2
reel.
● 1923 Pathé sil sh.
Prod: Mack Sennett.
● 1924 Fox sil 2 reels.
Dir: Ben Stoloff & Clyde
Carruth.
● 1935 Joseph Cammer 35 mins.

F? F-com?
Ref: LC; MPN 28:3000.

Incinerator of Cadavers
1971 Czech.
Dir: Juraj Herz.
H?
Ref: Soren.

Inclusive Tour
1972? Italian, Stefano.
Dir: Luciano Salce.
F-H-com? (about Italian
tourists embroiled with
black magic)
Ref: Vw 3 May '72 p50.
Announced; made?

Inconnus dans la Masion, Les
1944 French.
F?
Ref: S&S Summer '46 p51.

Incredible Creeping Monsters, The
n.d.
SF-H?
Ref: Willis.
Made? Retitling?

Incubus
See: Morte Accarezza a Mezzanotte,
La (1972).

Incubus Ritual, The
n.d. American Media Prods.
Prod & Story: Richard Alexander.
Dir & SP: Alan Gadney.
Cast: Pat Renella.
F-H?
Ref: BO 2 Aug '71.
Announced; made? (doubtful)

Indera Bangsawan
(Turn Princess)
1961? Malayan, Shaw.
Dir: Dhiresh Ghosh.
Cast: Jins Samsuddin, Saadiah.
F
Ref: FEFN Nov '60.
Completed?

Indestructable Monster
1960? Japanese.
SF-H?
Ref: FEFN Jan '61 p38.
Retitling of what film?

Indian Fantasy
1967? French ani.
Dir: Anthony Gross.
F?
Ref: MTVM Nov '68 p20A.

Indian Vampire
See: Vampira Indiana, La (1913).

Infernal Fiend, The
See: Demonio Infernal, El (1960?).

Infernal Ray, The
See: Raggio Infernale, Il (1967).

Inferno of Genghis Khan
n.d.
F? H?
Ref: Soren.

Inn of Death, The
1908 Vit sil sh.
Dir: J. Stuart Blackton.
F? H?
Ref: LC; Filmlex p683.

Inn of the Frightened People
n.d. (Hemisphere).
H?
Ref: Vw 25 Oct '72 p41.
Possibly retitling of theatrically released Hemisphere
film.

Innocence of the Devil, The
See: Innocenza del Diavolo, L'
(1970).

Innocenza del Diavolo, L'
(The Devil's Innocence; Innocence
of the Devil)
1970 Italian, Carmelo Bene Prods.
Prod & Dir: Carmelo Bene.
Cast: Carmelo Bene, Lidia
Mencinelli.
F? H?
Ref: Vw 26 Aug '70.
Completed?

Insanity
Chicago drive-in ad retitling of
what film?
Ref: D. Glut.

Insatiable Bee, The
1966? Hungarian color
ani sh.
Dir: Gyula Mackassy.
F
Ref: MTVM Nov '67 p9.

Insect Play, The
n.d. British, BBC-TV.
F?
Based on the play by Karel
Capek.
Ref: Willis.
Television only?

Insect Woman
1972? S. Korean.
Dir: Kee Yung Kim.
F?
Ref: Vw 20 Sept '72 p6 at
Sitges Festival.

Instant Film #2
n.d. Amateur 16mm? 3 mins.
Made by: Charles Brittin.
exp-sat-F-com?
Ref: CFS cat Sept '68.

Interior Mechanism
See: Mecanismo Interior (1971).

International Check
n.d.
SF? F? H?
Ref: Soren.

Interplanetary Tourists
See: Turistas Interplantarios
(1960?).

Interpol Code 8
n.d.
SF?
Ref: Soren.

Intrigues of Los Angeles
1964 Italian.
bor-SF?
Ref: Willis.

Intruder, The
1933 Allied 52 mins.
Assoc Prod: M.H. Hoffman.
Dir: Alfred Ray.
SP: Frances Hyland.
Cin: Tom Galligan.
Edit: Mildred Johnson.
Cast: Gwen Lee, Arthur Houseman,
Mischa Auer, Harry Cordling,
W.B. Davidson, Mildred Lucas.
F? H?
Ref: Vw 25 April '33; MPH 14
Jan '33; Photo May '34 -- mentions
wild man named Ingagi.

Invaded Man, The
See: Uomo Invaso, L' (1973?).

Invaders Attack, The
n.d.
SF?
Ref: Soren.

Invasion
1971? Argentine.
soc-SF? (invaders take over
an indifferent city)
Ref: CoF 14:7.

Invasion
1972? Cummings Int'l color
Prod: C.S. Cummings.
SF? ("super suspence"[sic])
Ref: BO 15 May '72 pSW-4.
Exists?

Invasion of Ghoul Circus
Chicago drive-in ad retitling of
what film?
Ref: D. Glut.

Invasion of the Night Things
1966? AIP.
F-H? SF-H?
Ref: MTVM Dec '65 p24.
Made, with title change?
(doubtful)

Invasionen
1969 Swedish, Svenska
Filminstitatet 3 mins.
Dir: Carl-Henrik Svenstedt &
Stefania Borje.
Cin: Lars Swanberg & Tony
Landberg.
Mus: Bo Anders Persson & Arne
Ericsson.
Cast: Vibeke Lökkeberg, Roberto
Panto.
SF?
Ref: Trieste '70.

Inventor Bricolo
1914 sil sh.
Prod: Hal Roach.
SF-com?
Ref: CoF 6:31.

Invincible Boxer, The
1970 Shaw? Chinese language.
F? (mystic martial arts?)
Ref: Vw 7 March '73.

Invincible Sword, The
1971? Hongkong?
F-seqs? (mystic martial arts?)
Ref: MTVM 26:8:23.

Invincible Zorro, The
n.d. Italian, Laos Film.
Dir: Guido Zurli.
Cast: Giorgia Ardisson.
F?
Ref: Richardson.

Invisible Death
1917 French sil.
F?
Ref: DdC I:316.

Invisible Family, The
See: Invisible People, The (1903).

Invisible Golden Man, The
1968? Philippine?
F?
Ref: MTVM March '68 p29.

Invisible Hand
1914 sil sh.
F? H?
Ref: BO 9 April '14.

Invisible Hand, The
1920 Vit sil serial 15
parts 31 reels.
Dir: William J. Bowman.
Story: Albert E. Smith & Cyrus
Townsend Brady.
Sc: Graham Baker.
Cast: Antonio Moreno, Pauline
Culey, Brinsley Shaw, Jay Morley,
Sam Polo, George Mellcrest.
SF?
Ref: FIR June-July '67 p339;
LC; CNW p206.

Invisible Magic Sword
1936? Japanese.
F?
Ref: Cinema YB of Japan
'36-37.

Invisible Man, The
1910 French sil sh.
SF?
Ref: Collier.
Very probably Invisible Thief,
The (1905, main list).

Invisible Man from Space, The
n.d.
SF?
Ref: Magnitude I:4:20 Winter '57.
Exists?

Invisible Men in Tokyo
See: Tokyo Ninja Butai (1966?).

Invisible Mr. Unmei
1952? Japanese/American.
F? (doubtful)
Ref: MFB '52 p 111.

Invisible People, The
(The Invisible Family --alt.t?)
1903 British, Urban sil sh.
Prod: Charles Urban.
Dir: Martin Duncan.
F?
Ref: Sadoul.

Invisible Woman, The
See: Femme Invisible, La (1932).

Invisible Worm, The
1951 Japanese.
F?
Ref: Motion Picture Feb '51
(Collier).

Invitation to Lust
1968.
sex; bor-F? (drug induces passion)
Ref: Willis.

Iolanthe
n.d.
F? (if based on the operetta
by Gilbert and Sullivan, this
has fairies)
Ref: Collier.

Irezumi
(Spider Tattoo)
1965? Japanese, Daiei color.
Dir: Yasuzo Masumura.
Cast: Ayako Wakao, Akio Hasegawa,
Manabu Yamamoto.
H? F? ("erotic terror")
Ref: MTVM Dec '65 p 11.
Completed?

Ironie du Destin, L'
1924 French sil.
Dir: Dmitri Kirsanov.
exp-F?
Ref: French Exp List.

Is There a Vampire in the House?
1972? D.D. Prods.
Prod & Dir: Eddie Saeta.
Assoc Prod: Sal Ponti.
F-H-com
Ref: Vd 13 Oct '72 p6.
Completed? (doubtful)

Is There Intelligent Life on Earth?
1964.
mus-com
Ref: Limbacher/4 p241.
3-wall rear projection show plus
live actors; probably more theatre
than cinema.

Island, The
1975? Michael Butler Asso-
ciates.
Prod: Michael Butler.
SP: Laura Huxley.
SF
Ref: NYT 22 April '73.
Based on the novel by Aldous
Huxley.
Announced.

Island of Blood
Chicago drive-in ad retitling of
what film?
Ref: D. Glut.

Island of Dr. Moreau, The
1973 Metromedia.
Prod: John Temple Smith.
SF-H
Ref: MTVM 27:5:26.
Based on the novel by H.G.
Wells.
Ref: MTVM 27:5:26.

Island of Horrors
1970 Japanese.
H?
Ref: UniJ 51.

Island of Living Horror, The
n.d. (Hemisphere).
SF-H?
Retitling of theatrically
released Hemisphere movie?

Island of Lost Girls, The
See: Ile des Filles Perdus, L'
(1961).

Island of the Lost
(Dangerous Island --s.t.; Lost
Island --s.t.)
1967 Ivan Tors color.
Exec Prod: Ivan Tors & John Florea.
Prod & Dir: Ricou Browning.
Cin: Howard Winner.
Edit: Erwin Dumbrille.
Cast: Richard Greene, Luke
Halpin, Mart Hulswit, Jose
De Vega, Robin Mattson, Irene
Tsu, Sheilah Wells.
SF? bor-SF? (mutated animals?)
Ref: HR 4 Nov '66.

Isle of Sunken Gold
1927 Mascot sil serial.
Dir: Harry Webb.
Cast: Anita Stewart, Duke
Kahanamoku.
bor-F-H? (ape villain)
Ref: CNW p259; FIR March '68
p 160-61.

Isle of the Dead
1924 French sil.
F-H?
Ref: DdC II:127.

Isle of the Doomed
n.d. color.
H
Ref: ad.

Ismail Yassine and the Ghost
See: Afritet Ismail Yassine
(1954).

Ismail Yassine at the Waxworks
1957 Egyptian.
H-com?
Ref: Arab Cin p282.

Isputnik vs Darna
1963 Philippine.
SF? (probably)
Ref: MTVM 15 Sept '63 p52.

Ispytanie
1969 Soviet, Tsentrnaug-Film..
SF?
Ref: Trieste '70.

It Ate the Town Alive
1969.
Cast: Ursula Anders, Julian
Karswell [note: this is the name
of the villain played by Niall
MacGinnis in Curse of the Demon
(1956, main list).]

16mm print of this offered for
sale; almost certainly a hoax.

It is Unbelievable
See: Eddini Akhlak (1952/53).

Item 72-D

1969 New York University color 27 mins.

Dir: Edward T. Summer.

SP: John Byrun, Harry Narunsky, & E.T. Summer.

Cin: Michael Sullivan.

Mus: Alan Leichtling.

Cast: Mark Joo Alexander, Herve Villechaize, Michael Sullivan, Shelly Desai, William Boesen, John Copeland, Ron Bowman.

SF?

Ref: Trieste '70.

It's Midnight, Throw Down the Body

1967? Italian.

SF-com? F-H-com?

Ref: Richardson.

Exists?

Ivan the Terrible

1917 sil.

H-seq?

Ref: MPW 32:1888.

Ivory Snuff Box, The

1915 World sil.

Dir: Maurice Tourneur.

Sc: E.M. Ingleton.

Cast: Holbrook Blinn, Alma Belwin, Norman Trevor, Robert Cummings.

F?

Ref: MPW 25:2197, 2078.

Based on novel by Frederic Arnold Kummer.

Iwojima

(The Ghost of Iwojima)

1959 Japanese.

F?

Ref: Japanese Films '60 p567.

J

Ja Gore

n.d. Polish "Studio" Film Unit for Polish Television. 28 mins.

Dir: Janusz Majewski.

Cin: Tadeusz Wiezan.

Mus: Andrej Kurylewicz.

Cast: Jerzy Tursk, Jerzy Wasowski, Cezary Julski, Krystyna Kolotziejezyk, Kazimiers Ruzski.

SF?

Ref: Trieste '69.

Based on a story by Henryk Rzewuski.

Jaal

1968 in Hindi color.

Cast: Mala Sinha, Biswajaet.

F-H? (ads show monstrous figure)

Ref: Singapore Straits-Times 6 June '68.

Jababira, Al

(The Colossi)

1965, Lebanese.

Dir: Hassib Chams.

F? (doubtful)

Ref: Arab Cin p272.

Jack and the Beanstalk

1970 United Int'l Films.

Prod: Martin Rude.

F

Ref: Vw 29 April '70.

Based on the fairy tale.

Announced; made? (doubtful)

Jack the Ripper Goes West

1974 British/US, Euan Lloyd/Shalako.

Prod: Euan Lloyd.

SP: Scot Finch.

Cast: Christopher Lee.

west-H (Jack the Ripper in the US Old West)

Ref: Vw 9 May '73 p 159, 163 ad.

Announced.

Jadu Nagri

1957 Pakistani.

Dir: Saglain Rizvi.

F ("magic")

Ref: FEFN 24 May '57 p 18.

Completed?

Jadugarin

(Enchantress)

1937 Indian.

Cast: Balasaheb Yadav, Zunzarrao Power, B. Nandrekar, Miss Sharda, Miss Shalini.

F?

Ref: Filmindia May '37 p 19 ad.

Jagd nach dem Glück, Die

See: Running After Luck (1929).

James Tont: Operation Goldsinger

1966 W. German.

bor-SF?

Ref: TVG.

Of which James Tont film is this the retitling?

Jane Eyre

1910 Italian sil sh?

H-seq?

Ref: Bios 23 June '10.

Based on the novel by Charlotte Brönte.

See also: Woman and Wife (1918).

Janna wa Narr

(Heaven and Hell)

1953 Egyptian.

Dir: Hussein Fawzi.

F?

Ref: Arab Cin p280.

Janwar

1965 Indian.

bor-SF? ("caveman")

Ref: Shankar's Weekly 18 April '65.

Japan Archipelago Alive

1960? Japanese, Shintoho color ani? 30 mins.

doc; SF-seqs? (dinosaurs?)

Ref: FEFN Oct '60 p22.

Japan Sinks Into the Sea

1972 Japanese, Daiei.

SP: Sakyo Komatsu.

SF

Ref: MTVM 25:12:21.

Announced; made? (doubtful)

Jardin Enfermo, El

1967? Mexican, Clasa.

F?

Ref: Richardson.

Jazz

n.d.

Dir: James Cruze.

dream seq?

Ref: FTN p203; note: no LC, no AFI listings.

Je Sème à Tout Vent

(I Seed the Winds)

1952 French.

Dir: Pierre Kast.

SP: Francois Chalais.

F?

Ref: Willis.

Je Suis Une Possedee

(I Am One Possessed)

1970 French/Italian.

Cast: Antonella Lualdi, Michel Lemoine, John Drew Barrymore.

F-H? ("sorcery and hypnotism in chateau")

Ref: Soren.

Jerangkong

(Ghost of the Dead --trans.t?)

1957? Hongkong/Malayan, Shaw.

SP: Run Run Shaw.

F (corpse returns to life when a black cat jumps over it)

Ref: FEFN 26 July '57 p 17.

Announced; made?

Jerusalem

1926 Swedish.

Dir: Gustav Molander.

F?

Ref: Sil Cin p84-85.

Based on the novel by Selma Lagerlöf.

See also: Karin Ingmarsdotter (1920).

Jess

(novel by H.R. Haggard)

See: Heart and Soul (1917).

Jesús, María y José

(Jesus, Mary and Joseph)

n.d. Mexican (Azteca).

Cast: Guillermo Murray, Gayle Bedall, Juan Miranda, Xavier Loya, Enrique Rambal, Eric Del Castillo.

rel-F? (the childhood of Jesus?)

Ref: BO 18 Dec '72 pSW-8 ad.

Jesus of Nazareth

1912 Kalem sil sh?

rel-F?

Ref: LC.

Jeu de Massacre

(Killing Game)

1966? French, Francinor & Davis.

Dir?: Alain Jessua.

Cast: Jean-Pierre Cassel, Claudine Auget (Auger?), Michel Duchaussoy.

bor-SF? (cartoonist become involved with man who dreams of experiencing adventures they invent)

Ref: Richardson; MTVM Oct '66 p 18.

Jimmy the Tiger

See: Tzimis o Tigris (n.d.).

Jinete Fantasma, El

See: Pistolero Fantasma, El (1967).

Jinkee

1969 Philippine, Sampaguita 90 mins.

Dir: Mar S. Torres.

SP: Medy Tarnate & Tony De Lumen.

Mus: Restie Umali.

Cast: Rosemarie, Ricky Belmonte, Bella Flores, Norma Blancaflor, Matimtiman Cruz, Ven Medina, Venchito Galvez.

F? (possibly Cinderella-type story)

Ref: Chodkowski.

Jodie

n.d. Dundee Prods.

Prod: Don Henderson & George E. Carey.

SP: James E. McLarty.

F-H (young boy falls in love with a girl who has made a pact with the devil and is 127 years old)

Ref: CineF 3.

Announced; made? (doubtful)

Johannisfeur

n.d. German.

F?

Ref: Acad.

Josie's Castle

1972

Cast: Tom Fielding, George Takei, Holly Mascot.

F-seq?

Ref: Acad; Bjo Trimble.

Journal of Albion Moonlight, The

1969? Amateur (AFI).

Made by: Bruce Lane.

F?

Ref: LAT 22 Oct '69.

Based on the book by Kenneth Patchen.

Announced; made?

Journey into Darkness

1967? Australian.

F?

Ref: Richardson.

Journey into Vortex

1972? Italian, Italian Int'l.

Dir: Antonio De Gregorio.

Cast: Ingrid Thulin.

SF? F? H?

Ref: Vw 3 May '72 p45.

Announced; made?

Journey of the Oceanauts

1973 20th-Fox color.

Prod: Arthur P. Jacobs.

Dir: J. Lee Thompson & Doug Trumbull.

cont.

Journey of the Oceanauts cont.

SP: Ben Maddow & Mayo Simon.

SF (3 men walk across the ocean floor in super-diving equipment)

Ref: CineF Fall '70 p44; Vw 29 Nov ''72 p 17 ad.

Based on the novel by Louis Wolfe.

Journey Through Space and Time

1939 Amusalon Inc.

Made by: Fred Waller.

SF-doc?

Ref: LC.

Journey to Cosmaton, The

n.d.

F (flight to the moon "via imagination")

Ref: Willis.

Possibly the same film as Wishing Machine, The (1967, main list).

Journey to the Moon

See: Rehla ilal Kamar (1959).

Journey Without Return Ticket

n.d. Czech.

F? (has "flashforwards" to imagined events)

Ref: Collier.

Joy of Torture

1969 Japanese, Toei color 95 mins.

H?

Ref: MTVM April '69 p26 ad.

Judgment of God, The

See: Jugement de Dieu, Le (1952).

Juellen

n.d.

F?

Based on a work by E.T.A. Hoffmann.

Jugement de Dieu, Le

(The Judgment of God)

1952 French.

Dir: Raymond Bernard.

Sc: Bernard Zimmer.

Cast: Andreé Debar, Jean-Claude Pascal, Pierre Renoir.

rel-F?

Ref: de Groot p 182.

Jula Juli Bintang Tujoh

1961? Malayan, Cathay.

Dir: B.N. Rao.

Cast: Noordin Ahmad.

F

Ref: MTVM Aug '61 p30, Sept '61 p50.

Completed?

Jules Verne

1960? Bulgarian sh.

Dir: Arcady.

doc-SF?

Ref: DdC I:108.

Julia and the Coelecanth

1961 Spanish.

SF?

Ref: SpCin '62.

Julius Caesar

1959 British, BBC kinescope 115 mins.

Dir: Peter Burge.

Cast: William Sylvester, Eric Porter, Michael Gough, Robert Percival, John Moffatt, Daphne Slater.

F-seq? (are the prophecies, dreams, and Caesar's ghost depicted?)

Ref: FIR March '73 p50-51.

Based on the play by William Shakespeare.

Jungle Book, The

1971 (Omega).

F?

Ref: Photon 21:7.

Based on the book by Rudyard Kipling?

Jungle Boy

1955 Taj Mahal Prods.

Prod: J. Manning Post.

Dir & SP: Norman A. Cerf.

bor-F?

Ref: Acad.

Jungle Gods

1927 Carl von Hoffman sil 7 reels.

F?

Ref: AFI F2.2825 p398.

Jungle Princess, The

1923 Adolph Kremnitzer sil 7 reels.

Cast: Juanita Hansen.

bor-F?

Ref: AFI F2.2826 p398.

Jungle Stories

See: Last Man, The (1924).

Jungle's Prisoner, The

See: Cautiva de la Selva (n.d.).

Junior Adventurers

1968? Soviet, Gorki 68 mins.

Dir: I. Magiton.

SP: N. Nosov.

Cin: B. Monastyrsky.

Cast: Y. Ovtchukov, S. Ryjov, O. Tsuprikov, Y. Nikulin.

F? ("pranks of fact & phantasy")

Ref: MTVM July '68 p31 ad.

Just Spooks

(Dinkey Doodle #13)

1925 Bray (Standard) sil 1 reel ani?

F?

Ref: LC; Willis.

Justice et la Vengeance Poursuivant le Crime

1905 French, Star sil sh.

Prod: Georges Méliès.

Ref: Jeanne 1:f48.

Justinian's Human Torches

(Torches Humaines)

1908 French, Star sil 246 ft. (187 ft).

Prod: Georges Méliès.

F?

Ref: Sadoul/M, GM Mage 1066-68.

Juwelen

1930 Austrian.

F?

Ref: Osterr.

Based on story by E.T.A. Hoffmann.

Jwala Dweepa Rahasyam

1965 Indian, Madhu & Madras.

Dir: Vittalacharya.

Cast: Kantha Rao, Rajanala.

F? ("folklore")

Ref: MTVM April '65 p 15.

Completed?

K

Kabinett des Dr. Segato, Das

(The Cabinet of Dr. Segato)

1924 German sil.

F?

Ref: Deutsche .

Kabir Saheb

1938 Indian, Kohinoor.

rel-F? ("religious pic")

Ref: MovPicM Nov '38.

Kahan-Hai-Manzil

1940 Indian, Wadia.

Cin: M.A. Rehman.

Cast: Illa Devi, Minoo, Radhi Rani.

myth-F?

Ref: Dipali 8 March '40.

Kain the XVIII

n.d. Soviet.

F? ("fairy tale")

Ref: Collier.

Kamale Kamini

1966? Indian, S.D. Prods.

Dir: Guru Bagchi.

myth-F? ("mythological")

Ref: MTVM Jan '66 p24.

Completed?

Kandhan Karunai

1965? Indian, AL.S.

Dir: A.P. Nagarajan.

Cast: Sivaji Ganesan, S. Varalakskmi.

myth-F? ("mythological")

Ref: MTVM Dec '65 p 11.

Completed?

Kapal Kundala

n.d. Indian.

H?

Ref: Filmindia; The Indian Film (Willis).

Kara Leken, Den

(The Beloved Game)

1959 Swedish, Nordisk Tonefilm 92 mins.

Prod: Gosta Hammarback.

Dir: Kenne Fant.

Cast: Sven Lindberg, Bibi Andersson, Lars Ekborg, Sigge Furst.

F-dream-seqs? (man dreams of his wife in many desired forms)

Ref: FEFN Nov '59 p50.

Karate in Tangiers for Agent Z7

n.d.

SF?

Ref: Soren.

Kardong Kidlat

1967? Philippine, Illang-Ilang Prods.

F?

Ref: Richardson.

Karin Ingmarsdotter

(Karin, Ingmar's Daughter)

1920 Swedish.

Dir: Victor Sjöström.

Cast: Tore Teja.

F?

Ref: FIR May '60 p26, June-July '60 p353; Sil Cin p84.

Based on chapters 3 & 4 of novel "Jerusalem" by Selma Lagerlöf.

See also: Jerusalem (1926).

Kasr el Maloun, El

(The Accursed Castle)

1962 Egyptian.

Dir: Hassan Reda.

F? H?

Ref: Arab Cin p284.

Katarsis

(Catharsis; Faust -ad.t.)

1963 Italian, Belotti 121 mins?

Dir: Joseph Vegh.

Cin: Parapetti.

Cast: Christopher Lee [Faust & Mephistopheles], Lilli Parker, Piero Vida, Bella Cortez, Giorgio Ardisson.

F (man sells soul to devil)

Ref: MMF 8:58, 14:24; CoF 12:30; FM 26:13; Christopher Lee.

Note: Christopher Lee says this film was not completed, due to death of the producer.

Kate and the Crocodile

1966? Czech, Ceskoslovensky Filmexport.

Dir: Vera Plivova-Simkova.

Cast: Yetta Hallanerova, Tomas Drbohlav, Barborka Zikova.

F-com? (children chase crocodile through Prague)

Ref: MTVM July '66 p37.

Kaya, I'll Kill You

n.d. Yugoslavian.

F?

Ref: Richardson.

Kaye

1969 French/Yugoslavian.

H? ("strange murders")

Ref: BO 7 April '69.

Kelly of the Secret Service

1936 Principal 69 mins.

Prod: Sam Katzman.

Dir: Robert Hill.

SP: Al Martin.

Cin: William Hyer.

Edit: Dan Milner.

Cast: Lloyd Hughes, Sheila Manors, Fuzzy Knight, Syd Saylor, Jack Mulhall, Forrest Taylor.

Based on story "On Irish Hill" by Peter B. Kyne.

bor-SF? ("invention to keep enemy fleets from American shores")

Ref: FD 22 July '36.

Kernel Nutt

1916 Vit sil 1 reel series.

Prod & Dir: C. Jay Williams & Charles Dickson.

Authors: Graham Baker, Ross D. Whytock, Beryl Caton, Frank Koch Jr., Charles Brown, Bide Dudley, Reginald Wright Kauffman, Mark Swan, & Mrs. L. Case Russell.

F?

Ref: LC.

Khadra wa Sindibad el Khebli

(Khadra and Sindbad the South- erner)

1952 Egyptian.

Dir: El Sayed Ziada.

F?

Ref: Arab Cin p279.

Khatem Suleiman

(Solomon's Ring)

1947 Egyptian.

Dir: Hassan Ramzi.

F?

Ref: Arab Cin p277.

Khulud

(Immortality)

1948 Egyptian.

Dir: Izzeddine Zulficar.

F?

Ref: Arab Cin p277.

Kidnapping Gorillas

1934 Kinematrade.

bor-SF-H?

Ref: FD 1 Dec '34.

Is this the same film as Ingagi (1930, main list)?

Kill and Be Killed
1966.
SF?
Ref: Richardson.

Kill Tony Falcon
n.d. Philippine, Illang-Ilang Prods.
SF?
Ref: Richardson.

Killing Game
See: Jeu de Massacre (1966?).

Kindness Abused
1910 sil sh.
F? (magic wand?)
Ref: Bios 15 Sept '10.

King Arthur
1972? Filmation ani.
Prod: Norman Prescott & Lou Scheimer.
Dir: Hal Sutherland.
F?
Ref: Vw 3 Jan '73 p60.

King Fah Fairy, The
1970 Hongkong.
F?
Ref: Singapore Straits-Times 10 Sept '70.

King Kong
1962 Indian, Santosh.
Dir: Babubhai Mistri.
Cast: Kum Kum, Dara Singh.
F? (doubtful)
Ref: MTVM Aug '62 p37.

King Lavra and the Barber
1965.
F?
Ref: NYT 28 March '65.

King of Africa
1966? Sandy Howard & NTA Harris Assoc.
F? SF?
Ref: Richardson.

King of Atlantis, The
See: Re di Atlantide, Il (1962?).

King of Kings, The
See: Král Krála (1965?).

King of the Alders, The
See: Roi des Aulnes, Le (1908).

King of the Circus
1920 U sil serial 18 parts.
Dir: J.P. McGowan.
Cast: Eddie Polo, Corinne Porter, Harry Madison, Kittoria Beveridge, Charles Forture.
F? (doubtful)
Ref: CNW p206-07.

King of the White Elephant
1940 Pridi Prods 8 reels.
F?
Ref: LC.

King Richard III
1913 Sterling sil sh?
Cast: Frederick Warde.
F-H-dream-seq?
Ref: Blum p40.
Based on play "Richard III" by William Shakespeare?

King Solomon's Mines
1918 South African sil.
Dir: H. Lucoque.
F-seq?
Based on the novel by H. Rider Haggard.

King Thrushbeard
1967 E. German, DEFA.
Dir: Walter Beck.
cont.

King Thrushbeard cont.
Cast: Manfred Krug, Karin Ugowski, Martin Floerchinger.
F?
Ref: MTVM Feb '67 p45.

King with the Elastic Head, The
See: Rey de la Cabeza Elastica, El (n.d.).

Kingdom of Youth, The
1918 Goldwyn sil 5 reels.
F? (doubtful)
Ref: LC.

Kino I
1962 German 12 mins.
abs-F?

Kismet Ka Dhani
1946 Indian.
Cast: Gulab, Agha Jan.
F? ("fantasies of fate")
Ref: Filmindia Aug '46 p54 ad.

Kiss of the Dead
1948 Italian.
F-H?
Ref: DdC I:270.

Kiss the Dead
1961.
F? H?
Ref: FDY '61.

Klabautermanden
(We Are All Demons --ad.t.)
1969 Danish/Swedish/Norwegian, Nordisk Film/Sandrews/Team Film 92 mins.
Dir & SP: Henning Carlsen & Paul Borum.
Cin: Joergen Skov.
Mus: Finn Savery.
Cast: Hans Stormoen, Lise Fjeldstad, Claus Nissen, Allan Edwall, Peter Lindgren.
F-seqs? (original title refers to demon which swims in sea, sighs when it passes doomed ship, for it knows its passing dooms the ship -- is this depicted?)
Ref: Vw 9 July '69.
Based on the novel by Aksei Sandemose.

Knife for the Ladies, A
1973 Spangler-Jolley color.
Dir: Larry G Spangler.
Cast: Jack Elam, Ruth Roman, Jeff Cooper.
H? ("an American 'Jack the Ripper' brought terror on the old West")
Ref: Vw 4 July 1973 ad.

Knight Without Armor
n.d. Bulgarian.
Cast: Oleg Kovachev.
dream seqs? (boy in modern times imagines himself as a knight, as Don Quixote, d'Artagnan, etc.)
Ref: Collier.

Knockers Up
1965?
F?
Ref: Chodkowski.

Knot in the Handkerchief, The
1960? Czech.
F?

Kodak Ghost Poems -- Part I, The Adventures of the Exquisite Corpse
1969? Amateur (Film-makers' Coop) 16mm color sil 50 mins.
Made by: Andrew Noren.
F?
Ref: FMC 5:p257-58.

Koenigsmark
1935 French.
F?
Ref: F/A p313.
Based on the novel by Pierre Benoît.

Koppelia
See: Coppelia (1912).

Kouzelný Dům
(The Enchanted House, The Magic House)
1939 Czech.
Dir: Otaka Vavra.
F?
Ref: F&F June '65 p40; Brož.
Based on the novel by K.J. Benes.

Král Králů
(The King of Kings)
1965? Czech.
Dir: Martin Frič.
Story: Jiří Weiss.
com; F?
Ref: Brož '66.

Krusenduller
(Spirals)
1969 Danish color ani 4 mins.
Dir & SP: Ib Steinaa.
F?
Ref: Mamaia '70.

Kwok Su Yueh Bears a Child in the Coffin
1957? Taiwanese.
Dir: Hu Chieh.
Cast: Yeh Luk.
F? H?
Ref: FEFN 19 July '57 p30.

Kyojinno Hoshi
(A Star of Giants)
1969? Japanese, Toho color ani.
F? SF?
Ref: MTVM Aug '69 p40.
Completed?

L

L.D. 100
1952? British, Bernard Glasser.
Prod: George O'Brien.
Cast: George O'Brien.
SF?
Completed?

LSD, a Trip to Terror
See: LSD, Viaje al Terror (1967?).

LSD, Viaje al Terror
(LSD, a Trip to Terror)
1967? Spanish/Argentinian, Hispamer/Procinsa.
psy-F-H?
Ref: Richardson.

Labyrinth
1960 German.
Dir: Rolf Thiele.
F?
Ref: DdC II:314.

Labyrinth
1967 Canadian, NFB 2-screen.
F
Ref: Time 7 July '67 at Expo '67.
Based on the legend of Theseus and the Minotaur.

Labyrinth
1968? Bing Crosby Prods.
Prod: Jack Chertok.
F?
Ref: Richardson.
Made? (very doubtful)

Laddie
See: Little Vampire, The (1969).

Lady and the Monster, The
1960.
SF-H?
Ref: Film Weekly 29 Sept '60.
Announced; made? (doubtful)

Lady from the Land of the Dead, The
1973 U (NBC-TV) color.
SP: Christopher Isherwood.
F (reincarnation)
Ref: Vw 18 April '73.
Announced.

Lady from the Moon
1953? Hongkong tinted seq.
F?
Ref: S&S Oct-Dec '54 p84.

Lady Macbeth
1917 Italian sil.
F?
Ref: Mitry V:11.
Based on play "Macbeth" by William Shakespeare?

Lady Whirlwind
1972 Hongkong, Golden Harvest.
Dir: Wang Feng.
Cast: Mao Ying, Chang I, Pai Ying.
bor-F? (mystic martial arts?)
Ref: MTVM 25:11:14.
Completed?

Laila Majunun
1962? Malayan, Cathay.
Dir: B.N. Rao.
Cast: Noordin Ahmad.
myth-F? ("legend")
Ref: MTVM March '62 p 12.
Completed?

Lailat el Kadr
(The Night of Miracles)
1952 Egyptian.
Dir: Hussein Sidky.
F?
Ref: Arab Cin p279.

Lame Devil, The
(The Limping Devil --ad.t.)
1970? Czech.
F?
Ref: Luna 18, Nov '70 at
Sitges Festival.
Is this the same film as Diablo
Conjuelo, El (1970, main list)?

Lanchang Kuning
1961? Malayan, Cathay.
Dir: M. Amin.
Cast: Noordin Ahmad, Latiffah
Omar.
myth-F? ("folklore")
Ref: MTVM Nov '61 p 13.
Completed?

Land of 1000 Monsters
1971? Filmpeople.
F-H?
Ref: Photon 21:6.
Announced; made?

Land of the Midnight Sun
n.d.
Cast: William Boyd.
F? (doubtful)
Ref: UC Berkeley.

Land of the Mist, The
1935 British.
SF
Ref: Ackerman.
Based on the novel by Arthur
Conan Doyle.
Exists? (doubtful)

Land of the Sun
1932.
Made by: Seymour Stern.
exp-F?
Ref: USA Exp List.

Land That Time Forgot, The
1974? British, Amicus.
Prod: Max J. Rosenberg &
Milton Subotsky.
SF (island where dinosaurs
still live)
Ref: Vw 9 May '73 p 159.
Based on the novel by
Edgar Rice Burroughs.
Announced.

Landru
● 1923 Austrian.
H ?
Ref: Osterr.

● 1971? Italian, Selenia Cinemat.
Dir: Mario Monicelli.
H?
Ref: Photon 21:8.
Announced; made? (doubtful)
        Based on the career of the
        French wife-murderer.

Lanka Laxmi
1927 Indian, Kanhere Prod sil.
F?
Ref: Ind Cin YB.

Lankaki Ladi
See: Fairy of Ceylon (1925).

Lankapati
(Burning of Owner)
1947 Indian, Pravin Leela.
Dir: W. Garcher.
myth-F
Ref: Filmindia Dec '46 p50 ad.
Completed?

Laser, The
1967 Ram Films.
Prod, Dir, SP: George Breakston.
SF
Ref: HR 10 Feb '67.
Announced; made? (doubtful)

Lash of the Penitentes, The
1936 (1937) Stewart Prods
(Telepictures).
Prod: Harry Revier.
Dir & SP: Zelma Carroll.
Cin: Roland Price.
Mus: Lee Zahler.
Cast: Marie De Forest, William
Marcos, Joseph Swickard.
bor-rel-H? (whippings and murders
by religious sect)
Ref: LC; HR 6 March '37.

Last Drop, The
1968? Two World Enterprises.
Prod: David L. Lewis.
F?
Ref: Richardson.
Made?

Last Goddess, The
1971 Movie Tech (United
General).
F?
Ref: Photon 21:6.
Announced; made? (doubtful)

Last Horror Film, The
1973? British, Amicus.
Prod: Max J. Rosenberg & Milton
Subotsky.
F-H (as movie studio is closing,
the famous monsters of movies
kill people)
Ref: LSH 2:65.
Announced.

Last Man, The
(Jungle Stories series)
1924 Selig sil 1706 ft.
Prod: Paul Hurst.
Dir: Bertram Bracken.
SP: B. Bracken & John T. Prince.
Cin: Eddie Beesley.
Cast: William Clifford, Oscar
Morgan, Hedda Nova, Richard
Sterling.
bor-SF? H? (crazed scientist;
caged man)
Ref: BFI cat p256.

Last Man, The
1970? Brazilian.
Dir: Fontuora y Calmon.
SF?
Ref: Luna 18 Nov '70 at
Sitges Festival.

Last Morning of Edgar Allan Poe, The
1964 French sh.
H?
Ref: Willis.

Last Night, The
See: Leila el Akhira, El (1960).

Last of the Cavewomen
Chicago drive-in ad retitling of
what film?
Ref: D. Glut.

Last of the Crazy People, The
1971? MGM.
Dir: Dan Curtis.
F? H?
Ref: Photon 21:5.
Based on the novel by Timothy
Findley.
Announced; not made yet.

Last of the Fairies, The
n.d. Gaum sil 2 reels.
F?
Ref: Collier.

Last Place Left
1970?
Prod: Charles H. Schneer.
Dir: Sam Wanamaker.
SF?
Ref: CineF Fall '70 p44.
Announced; made? (doubtful)

Last Planet, The
1971 Italian, RAI.
Dir: Gian Luigi Poli.
SF
Ref: Vw 28 Aug '71 ad.
Made?

Last Supper, The
(Assassination in Hot Blood --ad.t.)
1967? Czech.
F?
Ref: Richardson.

Last Testament, The
1973? W.German/Italian.
Prod: Alfred Leone.
Cast: John Ashley, John Marley.
F-H?
Ref: LSH 2:67.
Announced; made?

Last Three Days
1966? Indian, M.B. Films.
Dir: Prafulla Chakraborty.
Cast: Anup Kumar, Sumita Sanyal,
Gitali Ray.
SF? ("protest against atomic
threat")
Ref: MTVM Aug '66 p22.

Last Unicorn, The
1973? Balaban & Quine.
F
Ref: MTVM 27:1:22.
Based on the novel by Peter S.
Beagle.
Announced.

Last Witch, The
1957 Czech.
F? H?
Ref: Modern Czechoslovak Film.

Laughing Gas
1907 Vit sil sh.
Dir: J. Stuart Blackton.
F?
Ref: Filmlex p682.

Laughing Woman, The
1970?
H?
Ref: BO 29 June '70.
Exists?

Laughter in Paradise
1951 British, ABPC (Stratford &
Monogram) 97 mins.
Prod & Dir: Mario Zampi.
SP: Michael Pertwee & Jack Zampi.
Cin: William McLeod.
Edit: Giulio Zampi.
Mus: Stanley Black.

Cast: Alastair Sim, Fay Compton,
Guy Middleton, George Cole,
Hugh Griffith, Ernest Thesiger,
Joyce Grenfell, Audrey Hepburn.
com; F-seq? (heirs battle;
possibly title is literal with
deceased laughing at the battle)
Ref: Vw 27 June '51; Acad.

Laughter Trap, The
1967?
Prod: Paul Jacobson & Arnold
O. Leeds.
F?
Ref: Richardson.
Exists?

Laureate
1932 sh.
Made by: Emlen Etting.
exp-F?
Ref: US Exp List.

Laxmi Pooja
1957 Indian, Hemlata (in
Hindi) 133 mins.
Dir: Jayant Desai.
Cast: Nirupa Roy, Shahu Modak,
Jeevan, Babu Raje.
rel-F? ("miracles")
Ref: FEFN 25 Oct '57 p28.

League of Terror, The
1965?
H?
Ref: FM 24:13.
Based on a story by Edgar
Wallace?

League of the Phantoms
1914 Italian, Cines (George
Kleine).
F?
Ref: LC.

Leech, The
1921 Selected Pictures (Pioneer)
sil 4610 ft.
Dir: Herbert Hancock.
Cin: Alvin Knechtel.
Cast: Ray Howard, Alex Hall,
Claire Whitney, Katherine
Leon, Ren Gennard.
dream seq? (a dream convinces a
man his sweetheart was right)
Ref: AFI F2.3027 p428.
May have been made in 1919.

Legacy of Horror, The
1964 German.
Dir: F.J. Gottlieb.
SP: Jurgen Kiebach & Ernst
Schomer.
Cast: Hansjorg Felmy, Marianne
Koch.
H?
Ref: FIR '67 p84; Collier.
Based on novel by Bryan Edgar
Wallace.

Legacy of Satan
1973? Damiano Film Prods.
sex-F-H?
Ref: LSH 2:66.

Legend of Blood Mountain
1968.
F? H?
Ref: Miami Herald 5 April '68.

Legend of Horror
1966.
Cast: Fawn Silver.
F? H?
Ref: CoF 8:48.
Is this the same film as the
1968 movie of the same title,
main list?

Legend of Johnny Appleseed
n.d.
F?

Legend of Polichinelle, The
See: Légende de Polichinelle,
La (1907).

Legend of the Everglade
1913 sil sh?
F?
Ref: Bios 19 June '13.

Legend of the Tree of Life, The
See: Igorota (1970).

Legend of the Witches
n.d.
F? H?
Ref: Soren.

Légende de Polichinelle, La
(The Legend of Polichinelle)
1907 French, Pathé sil.
Dir: Ferdinand Zecca.
F?
Ref: Sadoul; The Film and the Public p320.

Leila el Akhira, El
(The Last Night)
1960 Egyptian.
Dir: Kamal El Sheikh.
F?
Ref: Willis.

Lemmy for the Women
1962 French.
Cast: Eddie Constantine?
bor-SF? ("secret laboratory")
Ref: FIR '68 (Willis).

Lena and the Geese
1912 Biograph sil 2 reels.
Dir: D.W. Griffith.
Story: Mary Pickford.
Cin: Billy Bitzer.
Cast: Mary Pickford.
F? (doubtful)
Ref: Henderson/Griffith p 134.

Leo, King of the Jungle
1971? ani feature?
Dir: Al Bisney (sic).
F
Ref: Vw 29 Dec '71 p 16.

Leon Tigre
n.d. Philippine, Illang-Ilang Prods (in Tagalog).
F?
Ref: Richardson?

Levande Mumien, Die
(The Living Mummy)
1918 Swedish sil.
Cast: John Ekman.
F?
Ref: Sweden I.

Liang Shan-Po and Chu Ying-Tai
1953 Hongkong?, Gala & Shanghai 110 mins.
Dir: Huang Sha, Sang Hu.
H? (tomb splits in storm)
Ref: MFB (Willis).

Liberator, The
(Maciste in the Liberator --alt.t.)
1918 Italian (Harry Raver Inc) sil serial 12 parts.
Cast: Ernest Pagano.
F? (statue comes to life?)
Ref: MPW 39:302, 40:785.
Based on a story by Agnes Fletcher Bain.

Liberty, a Daughter of the U.S.A.
1916 U sil serial 20 parts.
Dir: Jacques Jaccard & Henry McRae.
Cast: Marie Walcamp, Jack Holt, Neal Hart, G. Raymond Nye, L.M. Wells, Eddie Polo, Hazel Buckram.
F? (still shows strange birdlike figure)
Ref: Lahue/B&G p 163; CNW 39-40, 170-71.

Libido
1965 Italian, Imperialcine.
Dir & SP: Ernesto Gastaldi & Vittorio Salerno.
Cast: Mara Maryl, Dominique Boschero, Alan Collins, John Charle.
F?
Ref: MMF 14:67.
Based on a story by Mara Maryl.

Lick of Cream, A
1971?
F? H?
Ref: Photon 21:7.
Based on the novel by Marc Deschamps.
Announced; made? (doubtful)

Liebe Muss Verstanden Sein!
(Love Has Its Reasons!)
1933 German, UFA 84 mins.
Dir: Hans Steinhoff.
Cast: Rose Barsony, Theo Lingen.
SF? (dancing robot actually girl)
Ref: Deutscher.

Life After Death
1932? Indian.
F?
Ref: Indian Cin:157 (Willis).

Life After Death
1973?
Prod: Bill Naud & Marcus Bach.
F? H?
Ref: CineF 2:3:42.

Life in Death
n.d. Soviet, Khanzhonkov.
Dir: Baver.
SP: Valery Brysov.
Cast: Ivan Mosjoukine.
F?
Ref: Collier.

Life Is Beautiful
1957 Polish sh.
exp-F (monkey puts wreath on grave of hero)
Ref: S&S Summer '58 p233.

Life of Buddha, The
n.d. Japanese color.
Dir: Noburo Ofuji?
rel-F?
Ref: French Ani Book.

Life of Christ
1910 French, Pathé sil sh?
rel-F
Ref: MPW 7:988; F/A p491.
Probably duplicate listing of title in main list.

Light Fantastic
1964 Seneca (Embassy).
Prod: Robert Gaffney.
Dir: Robert McCarty.
SP: Joseph Hochstein.
Cin: J. Burgi Contner.
Mus: Joseph Liebman.
Cast: Dolores McDougal, Barry Bartle, Jean Shepherd, Lesley Woods, Alan Bergmann, Jane Ross.
SF-com?
Ref: Richardson.
Title change? Hoax?

Light Modulator
1948.
Made by: Elwood Dekker.
exp-F?
Ref: USA Exp List.

Light of God, The
1966 UAR.
SP: Abdel Waress & Mahamed Karim.
Cast: Faten Hammama, Ahmad Mazhar, Amina Rizk, Yahia Chahine, Mahmoud el-Miligui, Fasid Chawki.
rel-F? (depicts "spirit of Islam")
Ref: MTVM March '66 p 11.
Announced; made?

Light Out of Nowhere
1972 Israeli, Shabazi Ltd.
Prod: Jacob M. Alkow.
cont.

Light out of Nowhere cont.
Dir: Nissim Dayan.
SP: N. Dayan & J.M. Alkow.
Cast: Nisim Levi, Shlomo Basan, Abie Zaltsberg, Esther Eshed, Leon Etinger.
F?
Ref: Vw 3 Jan '73 p48.

Lighter, The
See: Tinderbox, The (1967?).

Lightning Stealers
1967 Heritage.
SF?
Ref: Richardson.

Liliom
1973 American Film Theatre.
SP: Charles Gordone.
F (updated black version)
Ref: Vw 15 Nov '72 p 18 ad.
Based on the play by Ferenc Molnar.
Announced.

Lilith and Ly
1919 Austrian sil.
Sc: Fritz Lang.
F? ("vampirismus")
Ref: Osterr.

Limping Devil, The
See: Lame Devil, The (1970).

Lion and the Mouse
n.d.
F?
Ref: Collier.

Little American
1917 Artcraft sil 6 reels.
Dir: Cecil B. DeMille.
Sc: Jeanie MacPherson.
F-seq? ("Valley of the Shadow of Death" sequence)
Ref: LC; FIR Dec '65 p651.

Little Boy Blue
n.d. AIP-TV color 100 mins.
Prod: K. Gordon Murray.
F?
Ref: MTVM Jan '66 p35.

Little Chimney Sweep
n.d.
F?
Ref: Contemp p77.

Little Conjurer
1907 French, Pathé sil 246 ft.
F?
Ref: MPW 1:622.

Little Devil
1970? Hongkong?
F?
Ref: Manila Bulletin 24 Aug '70.

Little Dick the Midget
See: Mighty Potz the Midget (1973).

Little Drummer, The
1971 Omega color ani.
F?
Ref: Photon 21:7.

Little Girl, the Dog and the Seal, The
1965? Swedish color.
Dir: Olle Hellbom.
F?
Ref: MTVM Aug '65 p 10.

Little Monster, The
See: Petit Monstre, Le (1964).

Little Mouck
n.d. Soviet ani sh.
F?
Is this the same as Geschichte vom Kleinen Muck, Die (1954, main list).

Little Negro, The
1960? Polish sh.
Dir: Danuta Kedzierzawska.
F? (actors behave like puppets)
Ref: Polish Cin p82.
Based on designs by Zbigniew Lengren.

Little Peacemaker
1908 French? sil sh.
Prod: Georges? Gaston? Méliès.
F?
Ref: LC.

Little Pete and the Looking Glass
n.d. Polish ani sh.
Dir: Waclaw Wajzer.
Design: Gwidon Miklaszewski.
F?
Ref: Polish Cin p82.

Little Puppet Seller, The
1913 Italian, Ambrosio sil sh?
F?
Ref: MPW 17:79.

Little Red Riding Hood
1917? Wholesome Film Corp.
F?
Ref: MPW 34:1422 ad.

Little Snowdrop
1903 Lubin sil sh.
F?
Ref: LC.

Little Spoon, The
(La Petite Cuillère)
1959 French (Contemporary) color 11 mins.
Prod: Carlos Vilardebo.
Mus: Beethoven.
F?
Ref: Contemp p 117.

Little Tom Thumb
1903 Lubin sil sh.
F?
Ref: LC.

Little Vampire, The
(Buebchen: Laddie)
1969 W. German, Alpha.
Dir: Roland Klick.
F? H?
Ref: Photon 21:29.
Exists?

Littlest Angel, The
1960? K. Gordon Murray 90 mins.
Nar: Hugh Downs.
F (cow needs angel's help to give milk)
Ref: CoF 14:49.
Theatrical?

Live and the Dead, The
1969? Soviet color.
F?
Ref: Collier.

Lively Pranks with a Fake Python
1908 French? sil sh.
Prod: Gaston? Georges? Méliès.
F?
Ref: LC.

Living Dead Man, The
See: Mort Vivant, Le (1912).

Living Flowers
1906 French, Pathé sil colored 344 ft.
F? (doubtful)
Ref: V&FI 1:1:12.

Living Forest, The
1958 Soviet.
Dir: S. Kaminsky & B. Asmous.
F? (doubtful)
Ref: Willis.

Living Ghost, The
1928 Japanese sil
F?
Ref: DdC III:130.

Living Mask, The
1928 Film Art Guild sil.
F?
Ref: FDY.

Living Mummy, The
See: Levande Mumien, Die (1918).

Lo Que Va de Ayer a Hoy
n.d. Mexican.
SF?
Ref: Aventura.

Loch Ness Monster, The
1964.
SF-H?
Ref: BO 23 March '64; F&F March '64; CoF 14:49.
Announced; made?

Lodger, The
See: Sublokator (1967?).

Lodger 5
n.d.
F?
Ref: Richardson.

Lorelei
n.d. Canadian, NFB sh.
F?
Ref: Collier.
Exists?

Loser
(La Chien Fou: The Mad Dog)
n.d. French/Canadian (Curtis-Rubenstein Film Associates).
H?
Ref: Richardson.

Lost City of Ceylon
1967? Italian/German.
SP: Robert Cunningham.
Cast: Robert Cunningham.
F? (doubtful)
Ref: Richardson.

Lost Civilization
Chicago drive-in ad retitling of what film? Possibly Minotaur, The (1960, main list).
Ref: D. Glut.

Lost Island
See: Island of the Lost (1967).

Lost Love
1966? Indian, Paradise Prods.
Dir: Ashim Banarji.
Cast: Nirmal Kumar, Supriya Chowdhury, Ashim Kumar.
F? ("girl hopes to prove that love outlasts death")
Ref: MTVM July '66 p34.

Lost Paradise
1973? Italian, DeLaurentiis.
Dir: Nelo Risi.
F?
Ref: Vw 9 May '73 p49.
Announced.

Lost Planet, The
1968 German.
SF? Exists?
Ref: Willis.

Lost Secret, The
1915 Pathé (Balboa) sil 2 reels.
bor-SF? ("new explosive")
Ref: MPW 25 Sept '15.

Loup des Malveneurs, Le
1942 French.
F-H? (werewolf?)

Loupe de Grandmaman, La
(Grandmother's Eyeglasses)
1901 French, Pathé sil sh.
Dir: Ferdinand Zecca.
Cast: Ferdinand Zecca.
com; F?
Ref: Filmlex p 1772-73.

Loupežník
(Brigand)
n.d. Czech.
F?
Ref: Brož p 19.
Based on the play by Karel Čapek.

Lov na Mamuta
(The Mammoth Hunt)
1965? Czech, Filmexport 96 mins.
Dir: Oldrich Danek.
Cast: Lubomir Lipsky, Milos Kopecky, Josef Kemr, Jana Houkalova.
F? SF? ("grotesque tale")
Ref: MTVM Oct '65 p 14.

Love and Death
See: Amore e Morte (1932).

Love and Molasses
1908 French? sil sh.
Prod: Georges Méliès? Gaston Méliès?
F?
Ref: LC.

Love Bite
1971?
sex-F-H (sex-mad werewolf)
Ref: Photon 21:6.
Possibly doesn't exist.

Love Has Its Reasons!
See: Liebe Muss Verstanden Sein! (1933).

Love Is My Undoing
See: E' l'Amor Che Mi Rovina (1950).

Love of the Tomb
1912 Italian sil sh?
F-H? ("guignol")
Ref: Kino p59.

Love Potion Number Nine
1969? Amateur (Film-makers' Coop) 16mm 6 mins.
Made by: Fred Safran.
exp-F-com? ("love sick young man. . .visits a gypsy fortune teller")
Ref: FMC 5:281.

Love Statue, The
1964 Vansan 85 mins.
Cast: Peter Ratray, Ondine Use.
F?
Ref: CoF 10:6.

Love Tragedy in Spain
1908 French? sil sh.
Prod: Gaston? Georges? Méliès.
F?
Ref: LC.

Love -- Vampire Style
1971 W. German, Atlas color.
Cast: Brigitte Skay, Herbert Fux, Barbara Valentin, Eva Renzi, Patrick Jordan.
F-H-com?
Ref: MTVM 25:12:11.
Completed?

Lover and the Madman, The
1905 British, Paul sil sh.
Prod: Robert W. Paul.
F? H?
Ref: Filmlex p420.

Love's Crucible
(Vem Domer?)
1921 Swedish sil.
Dir: Victor Sjöström.
Cast: Gösta Eckman, Jenny Hasselqvist.
rel-F?
Ref: Dyer.

Loves of Pharaoh, The
(Das Weib des Pharao)
1922 German, UFA sil.
Dir: Ernst Lubtisch.
Sc: Norbert Falk & Hans Kraly.
Cast: Emil Janning, Paul Wegener, Dagny Servaes, Harry Liedtke.
F? H? (doubtful)
Ref: C to H p50, 54; F&F June '58 p 15; MPW 55:79; F/A p499; LC.

Loving Touch, The
1971 Medford.
H? (rapist & murderer on loose)
Ref: Photon 21:6.
Announced; made?

Lubalang Daik
1962? Malayan, Shaw.
Dir: Jamil Sulong.
Cast: Aziz, Japar.
F? ("legend")
Ref: MTVM March '62 p 12.
Completed?

Luchador Fenómeno, El
(The Phenomenal Wrestler)
1952 Mexican.
F? (doubtful)
Ref: Aventura.

Lucifer
1921 Austrian sil.
F? (doubtful)
Ref: Osterr.

Lucifer Rising
1973? Amateur color feature.
Made in England.
Made by: Kenneth Anger.
exp-F?
Ref: Vw 9 May '73 p34.
Based on the life of Aleister Crowley.

Luna-cy
1922 sil 3D.
F?
Ref: Limbacher/4.

Luna de Miel
1959 Spanish, Suevia Films color 105 mins.
Choreog: Leonide Massine.
Decor: Ivoe Beddoes.
Libretto: Michael Powell & Luis Escobar.
Mus: Miklos Theodorakis.
Cast: Antonio, Ludmila Tcherina, Leonide Massine.
ballet-F?
Ref: UNESCO cat p65.
Excerpts from the ballet "El Amor Brujo."

Lupinek Case, The
1961 Czech.
Cast: Martin Svehla, Otto Sklencka, Karl Michalek, Eva Danielova, Zuzana Tumova.
F?
Ref: TVG.

Lure of Egypt, The
1921 Federal Photoplays of California (Pathé) sil 6 reels.
Dir: Howard Hickman.
Sc: Elliott Clawson & E. Richard Schayer.
Cin: Harry Vallejo.
Cast: Robert McKim, Claire Adams, Joseph J. Dowling, Carl Gantvoort, Maude Wayne, William Lion West.
H-seqs? (prophet knows the location of a tomb)
Ref: AFI F2.3304.
Based on novel "There Was a King in Egypt" by Norma Lorimer.

Lure of the Mask, The
1915 American-Mutual sil.
F?
Ref: FIR May '71 p292.

Lurking Peril, The
1919 Arrow (Wistaria) sil serial.
Dir: George Morgan.
Cast: Anne Luther, George Larkin, Ruth Dwyer, William Betchel, Peggy Shanor.

Lurking Vampire, The
See: Vampiro Acecha, El (1959?).

Lust of the Vampire
1967 Miracle.
F-H
Ref: Richardson.
Made? (doubtful)

M

Macabre Track, The
n.d. Mexican.
H?
Ref: LAT (Willis).
Error for possible remake
of Baul Macabro, El (The Macabre
Trunk, 1936, main list)?

Macbeth

● 1898 sil sh.
Cast: J. Forbes Robertson.
Ref: S&S Summer '60 p 149;
not in Shake/Sil.

● 1922? German, Elel-Film
sil 3000 ft.
Dir: Heinz Schall.
Sc: Fritz Kaufmann & Eugen
Klopfer.
Ref: Shake/Sil p279.
Exists?

● 1943 British.
Art Dir: John Peters.
Cast: Peter Ustinov.
Ref: Collier.
Exists? (doubtful)

F-H-seqs
Based on the play by
William Shakespeare.

Machine for Recreating Life, A
1924 French sil.
Dir: Julien Duvivier & Lepage.
doc; F-seq.
Ref: B&B p 150.
Includes sequences from Brasier
Ardent, Le (1922) & Cabinet of
Dr. Caligari, The (1919), both
in main list.

Machine that Kills Bad People, The
1948 Italian.
Dir: Roberto Rossellini.
SF?
Ref: LAT 5 Sept '48.
Completed? (doubtful)

Maciste Contra ie Fantome
n.d. Italian?
F?
Ref: Fred Clarke ad.
Exists? Retitling of another
Maciste film?

Maciste Contre la Mort
1916/20 Italian sil.
F?
Ref: DdC II:234.

Maciste Contre les Géants
(Maciste vs. the Giants)
1963 Italian.
Dir: Michele Lupo.
Cast: Mark Forest, Scilla
Gabel, José Greci, John
Chevron.
F?
Ref: Cahiers (Willis).
Possibly either Death in the
Arena (1962), or Goliath and
the Sins of Babylon (1963), both
main list.

Maciste Contro i Mongoli
1963 Italian, Jonia Film color.
Dir: Domenico Paolella.
Cast: Mark Forest, Jose Greci,
Grazia Spina, Ken Clark.
F?
Ref: MMF 12:16f.
Retitling of another Maciste
film?

Maciste Contro lo Sceicco
n.d. Italian.
Dir: Paoletta.

cont.

Maciste Contro lo Sceicco cont.
Cast: Ed Fury.
F?
Ref: F&F June '63.
Retitling of another
Maciste film?

Maciste in the Liberator
See: Liberator, The (1918).

Maciste vs. Hercules
n.d. Italian.
Cast: Mark Forest.
F?
Ref: FIR Aug-Sept '61 p444.
Same as Hercules vs. Maciste
(problem list)?

Maciste vs. the Giants
See: Maciste Contre les Géants
(1963).

Maciste vs. the Vikings
n.d. Italian?
Cast: Mark Forest.
F?
Ref: FIR Aug-Sept '61 p444;
Collier.

Maciste's Inferno
n.d. Italian?
F?
Same film as Maciste all'
Inferno (1926), or Hercules
Against the Barbarians (1964)?
(Former title from main list,
latter title from exclusions.)

Mad Dane, The
n.d. Danish.
Dir: Kirsten Stenbaek.
H?
Ref: Photon 21:45.
Exists?

Mad Dog, The
See: Loser (n.d.).

Mad Love
See: Sappho (1921).

Mad Minstrel, The
1963?
F? H?
Ref: Horror Monsters 7:43.
Exists? (doubtful)

Mad Sea
(La Mer Fou [?])
1968 French.
Cast: Dominique Boschero,
Thomas Milan.
F? (mermaid?)
Ref: Bean May '68.
Completed?

Mad Vampire
1967?
F-H (vampire repelled by
projected image of cross,
destroyed by huge cross
falling on him)
Ref: B. Warren.
Possibly film made in South-
eastern U.S., more likely
a hoax.

Mademoiselle Ange
n.d. W. German? French?
Dir: Geza von Radvany.
Cast: Romy Schneider, Henri
Vidal, Michèle Mercier, Jean-
Paul Belmondo.
F?
Ref: de Groot p373.

Madly Sad Princess, The
(Ever! So! Sad Princess --ad.t.)
1968 Czech, Filmexport.
Dir: Borivoj Zeman.
Cast: Helena Vondrackova,
Vaclav Neckar.

cont.

Madly Sad Princess, The cont.
F? ("a modern paraphrase of
the traditional fairy story")
Ref: MTVM June '68 p28.

Madman of the Movies
1973 General Film.
Filmed in England.
Prod & Dir: Pete Walker.
H?
Ref: BO 6 Nov '72 p9.
Completed?

Madmen, Maniacs and Monsters
1971? Independent Int'l.
Cast: Boris Karloff.
doc-F-H? ("horror classics" --
compilation film?)
Ref: Vw 12 May '71 p203 ad.
Completed?

Madron
n.d.
F (nun keeps coming back to
life)

Maelstrom
1972 USC 2 mins.
Made by: Larry Bock.
exp-F?
Ref: Filmex II.

Maggot Creatures, The
n.d.
SF-H?
Ref: B. Warren.
Possibly film made in South-
eastern U.S., more likely a
hoax.

Magic Beam, The
n.d. Soviet 7399 ft.
F?
Ref: Collier.

Magic Bicycle, The
See: Zaczarowany Rower (1955).

Magic City
1940 Indian, Vishnu.
Cast: Yashvant Dave, Rajkumari,
Shamim, Samson.
F?
Ref: Dipall 26 April '40 p24 ad.

Magic Dice
See: Dadi Magici (190?).

Magic Drawing Room
1907 French, Pathé sil
295 ft.
F?
Ref: MPW 1:317.

Magic Fan, The
n.d. Hongkong, Cathay.
Dir: Tang Huang.
Cast: Betty Loh Ti, Chao
Lei, Tien Ching.
F?
Ref: MTVM April '66 p30.
Completed?

Magic Fire 101
1967 Hongkong.
F?
Ref: MTVM April '67 p40.

Magic Gifts
n.d. Polish ani sh.
F?
Ref: Polish Cin p71.

Magic Hat, The
1952 Czech.
Dir: Alred Radok.
F?
Ref: Collier.

Magic House, The
See: Kouzelný Dům (1939).

cont.

Magic Medium, The
1972? Italian, Champion.
Prod: Carlo Ponti.
Dir: Roman Polanski.
Cast: Marcello Mastroianni,
Jack Nicholson.
F-com?
Ref: Vw 3 May '72 p37.
Completed? Or was the title
changed to What? ?

Magic Memories
n.d.
F?
Ref: Ackerman.

Magic of Catchy Songs
1908 French? sil sh.
Prod: Georges? Gaston? Méliès.
F?
Ref: LC.

Magic Ring, The
1922 Egyptian sil.
F?
Ref: Arab Cin p71.

Magic Ring
1964? Indian.
Prod & Dir: A.M. Khan.
Cast: Chitra, Manhar Desai,
Krishna Mumari.
F?
Ref: MTVM Oct '64 p58?
Completed?

Magic Screen, The
190? sil sh.
F?
Ref: Collier.

Magic Through the Ages
190? French, sil sh.
Prod: Georges Méliès.
F
Ref: DdC III:352.
Probably alternate trans-
lation of a Méliès film
included in the main list.

Magic Toymaker
1915 R&R Film Co sil sh?
F?
Ref: FD 2 Dec '15.

Magic Valley
See: Maya Mahal (1928).

Magic Voice
1940 Hoffberg.
F?
Ref: FDY.

Magic World of Ninjas, The
1968? color, scope.
Cast: Tombei.
F?
Ref: Singapore Straits-Times
21 June '68.
Is this the same film as Watari
in the Magic World of Ninjas
(1970?, main list)?

Magician, The
1972 Art Center College of
Design 2 mins.
Made by: Charles Krausne.
exp-F?
Ref: Filmex II.

Magician, The
See: Magicien, Le (1932).

Magician of Bengal
1936 Indian, Par.
F?
Ref: MovPicM March-April '36
p7.
Completed?

Magician of Taloo, The
1925 German sil ani silhouette.
Dir: Lotte Reiniger?
F?

Magician's Daughter, The
1938 MGM 2 reels.
Dir & Story: Felix E. Feist.
SP: Jack Woodford & Richard Goldstone.
F?
Ref: LC.

Magicien, Le
(The Magician)
1932 French.
Cast: Firmin Gémier.
F?
Ref: DdC II:428.

Magnet of Doom
See: Aine des Ferchaux, L' (n.d.).

Magnetized Man, The
1907 French, Gaum sil 467 ft.
F-com?
Ref: MPW 1:622.

Maha Sathi Anasuya
1965? Indian, Vikram.
Dir: B.S. Ranga.
Cast: Pandaribai, Rajkumar.
myth-F? ("mythological")
Ref: MTVM Dec '65 p 12.

Maid for Murder
n.d. British.
F-com? (ghosts?)
Ref: Willis.

Maid of the Mist
1915 Rex (U) sil 1 reel.
Cast: Lon Chaney.
F? H? (doubtful)
Ref: LC.

Maiden and the Monster
1952 Broadway Roadshow Prods 10 mins.
F? H?
Ref: LC.

Main du Diable, La
(The Devil's Hand)
1922 French sil.
F? H?
Ref: DdC II:27.

Make a Face
1971 Karen Sperling Prods Inc. 90 mins.
Dir: Karen Sperling & Avraham Tau.
SP: K. Sperling, Barbara Connell, & A. Tau.
Cin: Jeri Sopanen & Ken Van Sickle.
Edit: B. Connell.
Mus: Tony Cohan.
Cast: Karen Sperling, Paolo Patti, Davis Bernstein, Nicolas Surovy, Joe Horan.
psy-F? (rich girl living alone in luxurious New York apartment moves in reality, fantasy, & dreams)
Ref: Vw 25 Aug '71.

Maker of Madmen, The
1914 French, Eclair sil sh?
SF-H?
Ref: LC.

Malak el Rahma
(The Angel of Mercy)
1946-47 Egyptian.
Dir: Youssef Wahby.
F?
Ref: Arab Cin p277.

Maldicion de mi Raza, La
(The Curse of My Race)
1961 Mexican, Azteca.
F? (doubtful)
Ref: FDY.

Maldicion del Oro, La
(The Curse of Gold)
1967? (1968) Mexican, Clasa-Mohme.
F? H?
Ref: FDY '69.

Maldone
1928 French sil.
Dir: Jean Gremillion.
exp-F?
Ref: French Exp List.

Malec chez les Fantômes [sic]
1914 sil sh.
Cast: Buster Keaton.
F-com?
Ref: Willis.

Malefice, Le
1912 French sil.
Dir: Louis Feuillade.
F? H?
Ref: DdC II:338.

Malefico Anello, Il
1916 Italian sil sh?
F-H?
Ref: DdC II:302.

Malemort du Canard, La
1929 French sil sh?
Dir: Silka.
exp-F?
Ref: French Exp List.

Malia
1951 (1952) Italian, Titanus 79 mins.
Dir: Giuseppe Amato.
Cast: Rossano Brazzi.
F? (involves girl thought to be a witch?)
Ref: Acad.

Malika fi Gehennam
(Angels in Hell)
1947 Egyptian.
Dir: Hassan Ramzi.
F?
Ref: Arab Cin p277.

Malombra
1916 Italian sil.
F?
Ref: Willis.

Mammoth and Artificial Respiration, The
1967? Czech ani.
Dir?: Milos Mancourek & Stanislav Latal.
Art Dir: Jan Brychta.
F?
Ref: MTVM April '67 p32.
Completed?

Mammoth Hunt, The
See: Lov na Mamuta (1965?).

Man, The
See: Aadmi (1958).

Man and His Woman
1963 Starkey Associates.
rel-F-seqs? (modern version of Adam and Eve?)
Ref: Acad.

Man and the Beast, The
See: Hombre y la Bestia, El (1962).

Man and the Doll, The
See: Homme et la Poupée, L' (1921).

Man at the Top
1973 British, Hammer/Dutton.
Exec Prod: Roy Skeggs.
Prod: Peter Charlesworth & Jock Jacobsen.
Dir: Mike Vardy.

Man at the Top cont.
Cast: Kenneth Haigh, Harry Andrews, Nanette Newman.
SF? F-H? (doubtful)
Ref: Vw 18 April '73 p 18; LSH 2:50.
In production.

Man, Beast, and Virtue
See: Uomo, la Bestia, e la Vertu, L' (1953).

Man for Five Seasons, The
See: Homme des Cinq Saisons, L' (1972).

Man from Outer Space
1960? Japanese.
SF?
Ref: FEFN Jan '61 p38.
S.E. Asia title for a Japanese film already in main list?

Man from the Comet, The
See: Mann auf dem Kometen, Der (1924).

Man from the Dead, The
1918 Gaum sil serial 10 parts 20 reels.
F? H? (doubtful; probably Count-of-Monte-Cristo-type story)
Ref: MPW 36:1073 ad, 1316, 1528.
Probably same film as Hand of Vengeance (1918, problem list).

Man from the Grave, A
1963 S. Korean, Tongsung.
Dir: Lee Yong-Min.
Cast: Doh Keum-bong, Park Noh-sik.
F? H?
Ref: MTVM June '63 p 13.

Man, Ghost, Fox
1969 Hongkong?
F? (probable)
Ref: MTVM Nov '69 p25.

Man Hunters of the Caribbean
1938 5 mins.
H? ("voodoo ceremonial with one of their members hung on a cross as a sacrifice as the voodoo witch supervises")
Ref: FD 24 Jan '38.

Man in Space
1967? Siemens (Gamma).
SF?
Ref: Richardson.

Man in the Air, The
n.d. Czech.
Cast: Rudof Hrusinsky.
SF?
Ref: Collier.

Man-Mirror, The
1923 German sil.
F? H?
Ref: DdC I:300.

Man-Monkey
1907 French, Gaum sil 534 ft.
F?
Ref: MPW 1:127.

Man of Might, The
1918-19 Vit sil serial.
F? SF?
Ref: LC; CNW p 196.

Man of the Future, The
See: Rajul el Mostakbal (1947).

Man of the Wide-Open Spaces, The
See: Homme du Large, L' (1920).

Man Under Water
See: Clovek Pod Vodou (1960).

Man Who Carried the Wind on His Back, The
1970? British, Trickfilm color ani.
Designed by: Heinz Edelmann.
F
Ref: MPH 9 April '69.
Based on novel "Gulliver's Travels" by Jonathan Swift.
Announced; made? (doubtful)

Man Who Could Not Die
1956?
Prod: Gordon Kay.
SP: Curt Siodmak.
SF-H?
Was this finally filmed as Thing that Couldn't Die, The (1958, main list)?

Man Who Created a Miracle, The
See: Hombre Que Hizo el Miraglo, El (1958).

Man Who Et the Popomack, The
193? British.
SF-com (man becomes untouchable after eating the popomack)
Ref: Charles Higham.
Based on a radio play by W.J. Turner.
Exists?

Man Who Fell to Earth, The
n.d. Cannon Group.
Prod: Christopher Dewey.
SF (. benign alien must survive on Earth after being stranded)
Ref: Vw 14 July '71.
Based on the novel by Walter Tevis.
Announced; made? (doubtful)

Man Who Invented Gold, The
n.d. Amateur 16mm color 14 mins.
Made by: Christopher Maclain.
exp-F?
Ref: C-16.

Man Who Laughs, The
1926 sil.
Sc: Von Ludwig Nerz.
hist-H
Ref: LC.
Based on the novel by Victor Hugo.
Exists?

Man Who Returned from Afar, The
See: Homme Qui Revient de Loin, L' (1949).

Man with Icy Eyes
1971 Italian, Cinegai.
Exec Prod: Ottavio Oppo.
Dir: Alberto de Martino.
Cast: Antonio Sabato, Barbara Bouchet, Faith Domergue, Victor Buono, Keenan Wynn.
F-H? SF?
Ref: Vw 12 May '71 ad; Photon 21:6.
Completed?

Man with Nine Lives
1967? Japanese.
Dir: Saito.
SF? F? H?
Ref: Japanese Films '68 p60.

Man with the Golden Gun, The
1975? British/U.S. UA color.
Prod: Harry Saltzman & Albert R. Broccoli.
Cast: Roger Moore [James Bond].
SF-seqs?
Ref: LA Herald-Ex 7 Jan '73.
Based on the novel by Ian Fleming.
Announced.

cont.

Man with the Magnetic Eyes, The
1945 British, British Foundation
42 mins.
Dir & SP: Ron Haines.
Cin: Stanley Fletcher.
Cast: Robert Bradfield, Henry
Norman, Joan Carter.
bor-F? (super-hypnotism?)
Ref: MFB '45 p70.
Based on a novel by Roland
Daniel.

Man with the Missing Finger, The
1915-17 Danish, Nordisk sil
series 4 parts.
H?
Ref: LC.

Man with Two Faces, The
See: Zoul Wijhain (1949).

Man Without a Face, The
1927/28 Pathé sil serial
10 parts 20 reels.
Dir: Spencer Gordon Bennet.
Sc: Joseph Anthony Roach.
Cast: Allene Ray, Walter
Miller, E.H. Calvert, Sojin,
Jeanette Loff.
H? SF?
Ref: CNW p 143, 265; LC.

Mangala, Daughter of India
n.d. Indian.
Cast: Dilip Kumar, Nimmi.
F?
Ref: Soren.

Manhunt in Ceylon
n.d.
SF?
Ref: Soren.

Maniac Barber, The
n.d. French? sil sh.
Prod: Georges? Gaston? Méliès.
F?
Exists?

Manifestations of Henry Ort, The
(by E.W. Mumford)
See: Straight Is the Way (1921).

Mann auf dem Kometen, Der
(The Man from the Comet)
1924 German sil.
SF?
Ref: Deutscher.

Mannahatta
1921 sil 1 reel.
Dir: Charles Sheeler & Paul
Strand.
exp-F?
Ref: USA Exp List.

Mannequin, Alta Tension
(Mannequin, High Tension)
1966? Italian/Argentine.
SF?
Ref: Richardson.

Manner Sind Zum Lieben Da
(The Girls from Atlantis --ad.t.)
1970 W. German.
Dir: Eckardt Schmidt.
Cast: Horst Letten, Barbara
Kapel (Capell?).
SF?
Ref: CineF 2:3:47.

Mano Derecha del Diablo, La
(The Right Hand of the Devil)
1971? Spanish/Italian, Lacy
Int'l Films/Sara Films.
F-H?
Ref: Photon 21:8.
Completed?

Manoir de la Peur, Le
(The House of Fear)
cont.

Manoir de la Peur, Le cont.
1927 French sil.
Dir: Alfred Machin.
Cast: Romuald Joubé.
F? H?
Ref: DdC III:265.

Manole
1972? Rumanian, Animafilm ani.
Dir: Sabin Balasa.
F
Ref: MTVM 26:12:10.
Planned.

Mansion de la Locura, La
(The House of Madness)
1972? Mexican.
H?
Ref: Vw 9 May '73 p 124 ad.

Mansion of Evil
1972?
Prod & Dir: James Mayberry.
SP: Joel Levinson.
Cast: Leonard Barr, John Armond,
Bobby Rosenblum, Maidre Norman,
Louise Lawson, Don Blackman.
F-H (Satan reborn on Earth as
a baby)
Ref: Vw 2 Aug '72, 20 Sept '72;
CineF 2:3:43.
Completed?

Mansion of Mystery
1927 Capitol Production Exporting
Co. (States' Rights) sil serial
10 parts.
Dir: Robert J. Horner.
Cast: William Barrymore, Teddy
Reavis.
H?
Ref: CNW p260.

Many Ghosts
See: Yokai no Ranbu (n.d.).

Marble Heart, The
(The Sculptor's Dream --alt.t.)
1909 Vit sil sh.
dream seq?
Ref: LC.

Marcho di Kriminal, Il
n.d. Italian/Spanish, Filmes/
Copercines color.
Dir: Fernando Cerchio.
Cast: Armando Francioli, Helga
Line.
bor-SF?
Ref: MTVM July '67 p41.
Completed?

Marco Polo Returns
1971? Animation Int'l ani.
Prod: Sheldon Moldoff.
F?
Ref: Vw 11 Aug '71.
Completed? (doubtful)

Marco's Theme
See: Tema di Marco (1972).

Mared, El
(The Giant)
1964 Egyptian.
Dir: Sayyed Issa.
F?
Ref: Arab Cin p285.

Marguerite
1916 Danish, Nordisk sil.
F?
Ref: LC.

Marguerite
1971? color 16mm? 4 mins.
Prod: Betty Yao-Jung Chen.
F? ("a poetic progression
between two old photographs
found in a junk shop")
Ref: Genesis IV.

Marguerite and Faust
n.d. German/Austrian.
Dir: Richard Oswald?
F
Ref: Willis.
Exists?

Maria
n.d. Mexican.
F?
Ref: Ackerman.

Maria Martinez Lopez
1971 German color ani sh.
Dir: Dieter Glasmacher & Kurt
Rosenthal.
F? (probable)
Ref: Obehausen '72.

Mariage de Victorine, Le
See: How Bridget's Lover Escaped
(1907).

Mariandl
1961? W. German, Sascha &
Constantin.
Dir: Werner Jacobs.
Cast: Conny Froboess, Rudolf
Prack.
F? ("folklore")
Ref: MTVM Aug '61 p29.
Completed?

Mario and the Magician
n.d. British, Bradford Broad-
way Prods.
Dir: Abraham Polonsky.
F?
Ref: MTVM 25:12:11.
Based on the novel by Thomas
Mann.
Announced; made? (doubtful)

Marizania
See?: Witch from Beneath the
Sea (1965?).

Mark of Cancer, The
1967 Czech, Ceskoslovak Film-
export.
Dir: Juraj Herz.
Cast: Karla Chadimova, Zdenek
Stepanek, Zora Bozinova.
psy-H? ("psychological thriller")
Ref: MTVM Feb '67 p45.

Mark of the Phantom, The
1920 Hungarian sil.
Dir: Paul Fejos.
F?
Ref: DdC II:324.

Mark of the Vam re, The
See: Señal del Vampiro, La
(1943?).

Marked Victim, The
1971 Italian, Maurizia Lucidi.
F? H? ("suspense and terror")
Ref: Vw 1 Sept '71.

Marketa Lazarova
1968 Czech.
H? ("horror build-up")
Ref: S&S '68 p 185.

Marquis of Sade, The
1971 French.
Dir: Alain Resnais.
Cast: Dirk Bogarde.
H?
Ref: Photon 21:7.
Announced; made? (doubtful)

Marriage of the Swallow, The
See: Noces d'Hirondelle, Les
(1968).

Mars and Neptune
1959 French color 27 mins.
SF? F?

Martin Speaking
1966? Czech.
Dir: Milan Vosmik.
SP: Ota Hofman.
Cin: Jan Novak.
Mus: Svatopluk Havelka.
Cast: Jaroslav Vizner.
com; F-seq? (2-part children's
film; one part, "Flying Saucer,"
may be fantasy; Martin is a
detective in a children's
division in a police station)
Ref: MTVM June '66 p 16.
See also Ring Up Martin 224466
(1966).

Martyr, The
1963 Japanese, Amateur (Film-
makers' Coop) 16mm 28 mins.
Made by: Kasuhiro Tomita.
exp-F? ("dream-like")
Ref: FMC 5:318.

Martyrs of Love
1968? Czech.
Dir: Jan Nemec.
sur-F?
Ref: Cont FR Sept '69, at
Locarno Festival.

Marvelous Capillary Elixer
1901 British sil sh.
Made by: Williamson.
F?
Ref: Sadoul p389.

Marvelous Vision of Joan of Arc, The
(La Merveilleuse Vue de Jeanne
d'Arc)
190? French sil sh.
rel-F?

Marysia i Krasnoludki
(Orphan Mary and the Dwarfs)
1961 Polish, Rytm ani puppet &
live.
Dir: Jerzy Szeski & Konrad
Paradowski.
SP: J. Szeski & Zdzislaw
Skowronski.
Sets: J. Szeski.
Puppets: Jerzy Srokowski.
Cin: Stanislaw Loth.
Mus: Grazyna Bacewicz.
Cast: Malgorzata Piekarska,
Wojciech Siemion, Izabella
Olszewska.
F?
Ref: Polish Cin p 154.
Based on "About the Dwarfs and
Orphan Mary" by Maria Konopnicka.

Mas Merah
1961? Malayan, Shaw.
Dir: Dhiresh Ghosh.
Cast: Ahmad Mohamad, Saadiah.
F? ("folklore")
Ref: MTVM Sept '61 p50.
Completed?

Maschera di Mistero
(Mask of Mystery)
1916 Italian sil.
Dir: Mario Caserini.
F? H?
Ref: DdC I:331.

Mask of Horror
1912 French sil sh?
Dir & Sc: Abel Gance.
F? H?
Ref: DdC II:416.

Mask of Mystery
See: Maschera di Mistero (1916).

Mask of the Himalayas
1953 Col.
SP: Ivan Tors & Sam Meyer.
F? (weird animal god?)
Ref: Newsweek 24 Aug '53.
Is this same film as the non-
fantastic Storm Over Tibet (1952)?

Masked Menace, The
1927 Pathé sil serial 10 parts.
Dir: Arch B. Heath.
Cast: Larry Kent, Jean Arthur, Tom Holding, Laura Alberta, John F. Hamilton, Gus De Weil, Agnes Dome.
SF? F? H?
Ref: CNW p 135, 260-61; LC.

Maskelyne the Magician
1898? British, Paul sil sh.
Prod: R.W. Paul.
bor-F?
Ref: Sadoul p 360, 467.

Massacre for an Orgy
n.d. French.
H?
Ref: Richardson.

Master Man
1938 Indian.
F? ("Jekyll & Hyde? Doubt." [Willis])
Ref: The Lighthouse 21 May '38.

Master of Death, The
See: Herr des Todes, Der (1914).

Master of the Moons, The
See: Herr des Mondes, Der (1922).

Master of the World, The
1934? British?
SF (robots)
Ref: The Sketch 12 Dec '34.
Exists?

Master Over Life and Death
n.d.
Dir: Victor Vicas.
SF? F? H?
Ref: Cont FR May '64.

Master Thief, The
n.d. color ani puppet sh.
F
Ref: TVG.
Based on the fairy tale as collected by Jacob & Wilhelm Grimm.

Mat Raja Kapor
1967? Cathay, Keris.
Dir: M. Amin & Mat Sentol.
Cast: Mat Sentol, Malik Selamat, Rose Mary Cox.
SF? F? (ad shows flying phone-booth, or something similar; one of a series of "Mat Bond" adventures)
Ref: Singapore Straits-Times 1 Jan '68.

Mata Shaitan
1962? Malayan, Cathay.
Dir: Hussain Haniff.
Cast: Fatimah Ahmad, Yusoff Latiff.
H? ("horror")
Ref: MTVM Jan '62 p 14.
Completed?

Matchseller, The
1967 Amateur (Center Cin Coop) color 12.5 mins.
Made by: Laurie Lewis.
exp-F? ("color fairy tale of a girl looking for a husband")
Ref: Center Cin Coop cat #2, p 18.

Mathias Sandorf
1963 French.
F? (doubtful)
Ref: Vw 7 Nov '62, 20 March '63.

Matricule 20.007
1969 French, Les Films Armorial color 20 mins.
Dir: Robert Revol.
Cin: Rene Gosset.
SF?
Ref: Trieste '70.

Maudits, Les
See: Accursed, The (1945).

Maudits Sauvages, Les
1971? Canadian.
F?
Ref: V 9 June '71.

Mauprat
1926 French sil.
Dir & Sc: Jean Epstein.
Art Dir: Pierre Kefer.
Asst Dir: Luis Buñuel.
Cin: Duverger.
Cast: Sandra Milowanoff, Maurice Schutz, Nino Costantini, René Ferté, Alex Allin, Halma, Bondireff, Line Doré.
F?
Based on the novel by George Sand.

Max Magician
n.d. French? sil sh?
Dir: Max Linder.
F?
Ref: FIR '65 p280.

Max und Moritz
n.d. German color.
F-com?
Ref: Collier.
Based on the comic strip? by Wilhelm Busch.

May Fairy Tale
See: Pohádka Máje (1939).

Maya Mahal
(Magic Valley)
1928 Indian, Sharada sil.
F?
Ref: Ind Cin Yb.

Mean Mr. Firecracker
1970?
F (talking pelican, friendly Tobster)
Ref: Collier.
Based on a Greek legend.

Meanwhile, Back on Earth
n.d. 14 mins.
doc-SF? ("space age future")
Ref: SM 1:10.

Mechanical Horse, The
n.d. ani.
F?
Ref: MPW 57:703.
Exists?

Mechanical Principles
1930 sh?
Made by: Ralph Steiner.
exp-F?
Ref: USA Exp List.

Mecanismo Interior
(Interior Mechanism)
1971 Spanish, Escola.
Prod & Dir: Ramon Barco.
Cast: Maria Mahor, Dean Selmier.
SF?
Ref: Vw 3 May '72 p 175.

Mécano's Vacuum Cleaner
1905? French sil sh.
Dir: Lortak.
SF?
Ref: Ani/Cin p32.

Med Kaerlig Hilsen
(With Love and Kisses)
1971 Danish, Gabriel Axel & Henning Karmark color 85 mins.
Dir & SP: Gabriel Axel.
Cin: Rolf Roenne.
Edit: Anders Refn.
Mus: Bent Fabricius-Bjerre.

cont.

Med Kaerlig Hilsen cont.
Nar: Knub Poulsen.
Cast: Birte Tove, Buster Larsen, Christian Sarvig.
F-seq? (Adam & Eve & the apple throughout history)
Ref: Vw 25 Aug '71.

Medal from the Devil
See: Akuma Kara no Kunshô (1967).

Medium Spirits
1921 Reggie Morris Prods (Arrow Film Corp) sil 2 reels.
Dir: Reggie Morris.
F?
Ref: LC.

Medusa, La
1967? French.
F? H?
Ref: Richardson.
Made?

Meeting at Salzbourg
1963 French.
Cast: Curt Jurgens.
F?
Ref: Collier.

Megh Malhar
1966? Indian, Film Asia.
Dir: T. Prakash Rao.
Cast: Vyjayantimala, Bharat Bhushan.
mus-F? ("musical fantasy")
Ref: MTVM April '61 p31.
Completed?

Melchior, das Medium
1919 Austrian sil.
F?
Ref: Osterr.

Melody of Death
1917 Rex (U) sil 2 reels.
H?
Ref: LC.

Memoirs of the Dream of the Wedding of Nastala
n.d.
F? ("an electric experience")
Ref: Collier.

Memorias de una Vampiresa
1945 Mexican.
F? H? (doubtful)
Ref: Indice.

Memories of the Future
n.d. Spanish/Mexican.
Prod: Sonia Bruno.
SF?
Ref: Richardson.
Exists?

Men in the Sky
1958.
Dir: Languepin.
F? (doubtful)
Ref: Cahiers (Willis).

Menace of Frankenstein, The
1970 Gardiner Co.
Prod: Ronald Hale.
Dir: Greg Chalfin.
SP: Dan Alderson.
Cast: Linda Gray, Sanford Cohen [monster], Vanessa Meier, Ellen Fox.
SF-H (monster found in ice floe)
Ref: FM 75:13.
Completed?

Mentivendoli, I
(The Brain Merchants)
n.d. Italian, Explorer - PAC & Fiodorcinema.
Cast: Lou Castel.
SF-H?

Mephisto
1931 French.
Dir: Henri Debain & René Navarre.
Cast: Jean Gabin, René Navarre, France Dhelia.
F?
Ref: FIR April '63 p209.

Mephisto's Carnival
1919 Austrian sil.
F?
Ref: Osterr.

Mer Fou, La
See: Mad Sea (1968).

Meravigliose Avventure di Pollicino, Le
See: Tom Thumb (n.d.).

Mermaid, The
See: Arousset el Bahr (1946/47).

Mermaids and Guys
n.d. Greek.
F?
Ref: Collier.

Mermen Attack
196?
SF
Ref: Ackerman.
Exists? (doubtful)

Mermen of Tiberon
n.d.
SF?
Ref: Ackerman.
Exists? (doubtful)

Merveilleuse Vue de Jeanne d'Arc, La
See: Marvelous Vision of Joan of Arc, The (190?).

Mésaventures d'une Tête de Veau, Les
(The Misadventures of a Calf's Head)
1899 French sil sh.
Dir: Alice Guy.
F?
Ref: Sadoul p 387.

Mesmerist, The
1899 British sil sh.
Prod: J. Stuart Blackton.
F?
Ref: Filmlex p681; DdC II:448.

Message from the Sky, A
See: O-18 (1915).

Message of the Dead, The
1913 French (Eclectic) sil sh?
SF?
Ref: LC.

Messalina Against the Son of Hercules
n.d. (1965) Italian? (Embassy) color.
Cast: Richard Harrison.
F?
Ref: MTVM April '65 p 10.

Messenger from the Moon
1956 Japanese.
SF?
Ref: FEFN 22 June '56.

Meteor, The
1902 Biograph sil sh.
SF?
Ref: LC.

Meteorango Kid, Intergalactic Hero
1969 Brazilian.
SF?
Ref: V 29 April '70 p 167.

Mickey's Ape Man
1933 Empire (RKO) sh?
Dir: J.A. Duffy.
Story: Earl Montgomery.
F?
Ref: LC.

Microscopic Liquid Subway to Oblivion, The
1971? Italian, Sound Prods.
Cast: Ewa Aulin.
F?
Ref: Photon 21:8.
Completed?

Midnight Demon, The
196? French.
Cast: Daniela Bianchi.
F? H?
Ref: Collier.

Midnight Ghost, The
See: Ghaba Nus el Lail (1947).

Midnight in Bombay
1948 Indian.
H? ("pendulum torture" [Willis])
Ref: Filmindia March '48.

Midnight Man, The
1919 U sil serial 18 parts 36 reels.
Dir: James W. Horne.
Story: J.W. Horne & Frank Howard Clarke.
Sc: Harvey Gates.
Cast: James J. Corbett, Kathleen O'Connor, Orral Humphrey, Sam Polo, Joseph W. Girard, Noble Johnson.
F? H?
Ref: MPW 43:472; CNW p70-71, 197; LC.

Midsummer Night's Dream, A
● 1912 sil 3 reels.
Ref: FWD p 196.
Exists?
● 1928 Fifty-fifth St. Playhouse Group sil?
Ref: FDY.
Exists?
● n.d. UCLA Theater Arts.
F-seqs? (doubtful)
Ref: Collier.
● n.d. French, Starevitch.
Prod: Ladislas Starevitch.
Completed? (doubtful)
    Based on the play by William Shakespeare.

Mighty Potz the Midget
(Little Dick the Midget --ad.t.)
1973 Italian, Claudio Monti color ani feature.
sex-F-com
Ref: Vw 9 May '73 p68, 94 ad.
Announced.

Mighty Samson, The
See: Samsun el Kabir (1948).

Milagro a los Cobades [Cobardes?]
(Miracle of the Cowards?)
1961 Spanish, Trefilms.
Dir: Mur-Oti.
Cast: Ruth Roman, Javier Escriva.
H?
Ref: FEFN Feb '61.

Mile, Le
1932 French sh?
Dir: Lods.
exp-F?
Ref: French Exp List.

Milky Way, The
1922 Western Pictures Exploitation Co. sil 4850 ft.
Cast: David Butler.
F? (doubtful)
Ref: AFI F2.3618 p513.

Mimi, the Prophet
1972 Mexican, Churubusco.
Dir: José Estrada.
Cast: Ignacio Lopez Tarso, Ana Martin, Ofelia Guillmain, Carmen Montejo, Ernest Gomez Cruz.
F?
Ref: MTVM 27:4:8.

Mind-Sweepers
1972? Filmakers Int'l.
Exec Prod: Lamar Card.
Prod & Dir: Paul Hunt.
SP: Steve Fisher.
Cast: Michael Greene.
SF? F? H?
Ref: Vw 2 Aug '72.

Minnie the Mermaid
1942 Soundies 1 reel.
F?
Ref: LC.

Minutes Before Death
1972 Canadian, Bellevue - Pathé & Maple Leaf.
Prod: Enrique Torres Tudela.
Dir: Rogelio Gonzales.
Set Design: Mirna Sinclair.
Cin: Leon Sanchez.
Cast: Rhonda Hendrix, Giselle McKenzie, Barry Coe, Maraye Ayers, Doris Buckingham, Daphne Goldrick, Pia Shandel, Graham Crowell, Terrance Kelly.
F? H?
Ref: BO 27 March '72 p K8.
Announced; made?

Miracle, The
1913 German sil sh?
F? rel-F?
Ref: MPW 15:975.

Miracle, The
1928 Conquest sil sh?
F?

Miracle, The
See: Muageza, El (1963).

Miracle
(novel by C.B. Kelland)
See: Woman's Faith, A (1925).

Miracle at Verdun
n.d. French.
rel-F?

Miracle from Heaven, A
See: Mogezat el Samaa (1956).

Miracle Kid
1923 Associated Exhibitors.
F?
Ref: FDY.

Miracle Man
1938 Polish.
F?
Ref: FDY.

Miracle of Sister Beatrice, The
1939 Park Lane (Rico Bros) 8 reels.
Dir: Harry T. Dixon.
Author: Jacques de Baroncelli.
Mus: Alfredo Antonini.
rel-F? (probable)
Ref: LC.
Based on a legend of the 13th Century.

Miracle of the Cowards [?]
See: Milagro a los Cobades [Cobardes?] (1961).

Miracle of the White Reindeer
1964? 60 mins.
Cast: Charles Winninger, Fritz Feld, Ruthy Robinson, Dennis Holmes, Hal Smith.
F?
Ref: Vw 7 April '65.

Miracle Weaver, The
See: Trejedor de Milagros, El (1962?).

Miracles in Mud
n.d. Amateur? ani clay sh.
Made by: Willie Hopkins.
F?
Ref: Don Douglas.

Miraculous Eggs
1907 Lubin sil sh.
F-com?
Ref: LC.

Miraculous Happening
See: O Věcech Nadpřirozených (1958).

Miraculous Mandarin, The
See: Csodálatos Mandarin, A (1965).

Mirage, The
(The Death of a Dream --alt.t.)
1912 French, Eclair sil sh.
F?
Ref: LC.

Mirage, The
See: Hägringen (1959?).

Miroir de Venise, Le
See: Venetian Looking-Glass, The (1905).

Mirror of the Future, A
1910 French? sil sh.
Dir: D.W. Griffith?
F
Ref: Griffith Index.

Mirrorman, The
See: Spiegelmensch, Der (1923).

Misadventures of a Calf's Head, The
See: Mésaventures d'une Tête de Veau, Les (1899).

Mischances of a Photographer
1908 French? sil sh.
Prod: Gaston? Georges? Méliès.
F-com?
Ref: LC.

Mischief in Wonderland
n.d. AIP-TV color 100 mins.
Prod: K. Gordon Murray.
F?
Ref: MTVM Jan '66 p35.

Mise à Sac
(Torn to Bits)
1968? French sh?
Dir: Alain Cavalier.
F? SF? H?
Ref: Richardson.
Made?

Miser, The
(L'Avare)
1908 French sil 886 ft.
Prod: Georges Méliès.
F-com?
Ref: LC; Sadoul; GM Mage.

Mision Special en Caracas
1966 Spanish.
SF? ("new type bomb" [Willis])
Ref: SpCin '67.

Miss Dillinger and Miss Ripper
1973?
Sp: Philip Yordan.
H?
Ref: LSH 2:66.
Announced.

Missiles from Hell
Chicago drive-in ad retitling? Or Missile from Hell (1958, exclusions)?
Ref: D. Glut.

Missing Link, The
See: Halaka el Safkuda, El (1949).

Mission Interplan
1962 W. German.
SF?
Ref: SM 5:8.
Amateur?

Mission Lisbon
n.d.
Cast: Brett Halsey.
SF?

Mistaken Identity, A
(Quiproquo)
1908 French sil 510 ft (355 ft).
Prod: Georges Méliès.
F-com?
Ref: Sadoul; GM Mage; LC.

Mr. Atom Bomb
195?
SF-com?
Ref: N. Kagan.

Mr. Dynamite
1966? French/Italian, Parnass/PEA.
Cast: Lex Barker.
SF?
Ref: Richardson.

Mr. Tau
(Pan Tau)
1971? Czech, Barrandov serial.
Dir: Jindrich Polak.
SP: Ota Hofman.
Cast: Otto Simacek (Siamanek?).
F (Human puppet goes about righting wrongs)
Ref: Vw 30 June '71.

Mr. Tau and Claudia
1971 Czech/W. German, Barrandov/Westdeutscher Rundfunk color.
Dir: Jindrich Polak.
SP: Ota Hofman & J. Polak.
Cin: Jiri Tarantik.
Cast: Otto Siamanek (Simacek?), Jan Werich, Veronika Rencova.
F? (7th episode of series about Mr. Tau who herein introduces girl to "world of miracles and poetry")
Ref: MTVM 25:12:14.

Mr. Trull Finds Out
1940 Film Associates sh?
Dir: Henwar Rodakiewicz.
Sc: Joseph Krumgold.
Cin: Roger Barlow.
Mus: Gian-Carlo Menotti.
exp-F?
Ref: USA Exp List.

Mr. Voodoo
1933.
F-H?
Exists? (doubtful)

Mr. X
1938 Indian?
F? SF? (revival from dead?)
Ref: MovPicM Dec '38.

Misterio de la Cobra, El
(The Mystery of the Cobra)
1958 (1959) Mexican (Azteca).
Cast: Rosita Arenas, Ramon Gay, Rosa Carmina, José Galvez.
F-H?
Ref: PS.

Misterio de la Vida, El
(The Mystery of Life)
1971 Spanish, Balcazar.
Dir: Balcazar.
Cast: Dominique Simpson, Monica Randall.
F? (doubtful)
Ref: Vw 3 May '72 p 175.

Mistero di Osiris, Il
(The Mystery of the Jewels
--alt.t.)
1921 Talisman sil.
Author: Giovanni De Odota.
Pres?: Harry Houdini.
F? H?
Ref: LC.

Mrs. and Mr. Duff
1909 French? sil sh.
Prod: Georges? Gaston? Méliès.
F?
Ref: LC.

Mrs. Ward
1971?
Cast: Edwige Fenech.
H?
Ref: Photon 21:8.
Announced; made?

Mistrz Tanca
1969 Polish, Studio Film Unit
30 mins.
Dir: Jerzy Gruza .
SP: Janusz Majewski & Jerzy Merzejewski.
Cin: Marek Nowicki.
Cast: Andrzej Lapicki, Bronislaw Pawlik, Kazimierz Rudzki.
SF?
Ref: Trieste '70.
Based on "La Casa all'Angolo"
by Josef Korzeniowski.

Mix up in the Gallery, A
1906 French, Star sil 183 ft.
Prod: Georges Méliès.
F?
Ref: LC; Sadoul; GM Mage.

Mobile Composition
1930 Amateur? sh?
Dir: Lewis Jacobs, Jo Gercon, & Hershell Louis.
exp-F?
Ref: USA Exp List.

Modern Janko the Musician, The
n.d. Polish, ani sh.
Dir: Jan Lenica.
F?
Ref: Polish Cin p82.
Parody of "Janko the Musician"
by Henryk Sienkiewicz.

Modern Love Potion
1910 British sil.
SF?
Ref: Bios 15 Sept '10.

Modern Rip Van Winkle, A
1914 American sil 2 reel.
Author: M.R. McKinstry.
F?
Ref: LC.

Modern School
See: Moderne École (1909).

Moderne École
(Modern School)
1909 . French, Gaum sil sh.
Dir: Emile Cohl.
F-com?
Ref: Filmlex p 1370.

Mogezat el Samaa
(A Miracle from Heaven)

cont.

Mogezat el Samaa cont.
1956 Egyptian.
Dir: Atef Salem.
rel-F?
Ref: Arab Cin p281.

Momie, La
(The Mummy)
1913 French sil sh?
Dir: Louis Feuillade.
F?
Ref: DdC II:339.

Mon Paris
(My Paris)
1928 French.
Made by: Albert Guyet.
exp-F?
Ref: French Exp List.

Monday or Tuesday
See: Pondeljak Ili Utorak
(1966).

Monihara
1968 Indian sh.
F? ("ghost")
Ref: Link 14 Jan '68.

Monja, Casada, Virgen y Martir
(Nun, Married Woman, Virgin,
and Martyr)
1935 Mexican.
F?
Ref: Aventura.

Monkey and the Spider
1967? Hongkong.
F?
Ref: MTVM Nov '67 p 18.

Monkey into Man
1940 British 67 mins.
doc; SF? ("animal life from stone age to present"; any dinosaurs or other prehistoric beasts depicted alive?)
Ref: Vw 17 April '40; MPH 30 March '40.

Monkey's Moon
n.d. sil.
Dir: Kenneth MacPherson.
F?

Monnaie de Lapin, La
(The Rabbit's Money)
1899 French, Gaum sil 75 ft.
Dir: Alice Guy.
F?
Ref: DdC II:480.

Monsieur le Baron
190? French? sil sh.
Dir: Georges? Gaston? Méliès.
F?
Ref: Collier.
Retitling of an already listed Méliès film?

Monsieur X
n.d.
SF?

Monster, The
1927 Chinese sil.
Dir: Tan To Yu.
F? H?
Ref: DdC I:402.

Monster, The
1961? Allied Film Exchange.
Filmed in Texas.
SF?
Ref: FD; Collier.

Monster, The
1966? UAR (Filmintage).
SF? F? H?
Ref: MTVM Jan '66 p 15.

Monster, The
See: Wahsh, El (1954).

Monster and the Playgirl
1961?
Prod: George White.
SF-H?
Ref: Collier.
Made? (doubtful)

Monster Beast
1968?
SF-H? F-H?
Ref: Miami Herald 11 May '68.

Monster from Space
1971? Japanese?
SF? (probable)
Ref: CineF 2:44.
Announced.
Probably the same film as
Yog: Monster from Space
(1970).

Monster from the La Brea Tar Pits, The
n.d.
SF
Ref: J. Baxter says this was shown in England around 1952.
Very probably does not exist.

Monster I Love, The
1958.
SF?
Ref: Willis.

Monster Maker, The
n.d. French?
Dir: Alain Resnais.
SP: Stan Lee.
SF-H
Ref: F&F July '71 p 12;
Marvel Comics during 1971.
Not yet made.

Monster of Blackwood Castle, The
n.d. Sunset Int'l..
H?
Ref: BO 8 May '72 pSE-4; MTVM 26:7:25.
Is this the same film as
Hund von Blackwood Castle, Der
(1968, main list)?

Monster of Rome, The
1972 Italian, De Laurentiis.
Prod: Dino De Laurentiis.
Dir: Damiano Damiani.
Cast: Nino Manfredi, Anna Maria Pascatori, Umberto Raho, Luciano Catenacci, Mario Carotenuto.
F-H? SF-H? H?
Ref: Vw 26 July '72.
Announced; made?

Monster of the Night
1971 British, Hammer.
F-H
Ref: CineF 2:44.
Announced; not yet made.

Monster Without a Face, The
See: Monstre sans Visage, Le
(1961?).

Monsters
n.d.
SF
Ref: FM 97:21.
Based on stories by A.E. van Vogt.
Announced.

Monsters of the Moon
n.d. Amateur?
SF
Ref: Ackerman.

Monsters of the Sea
n.d.
SF? (doubtful)
Is this the same film as
Monsters of the Deep (1931, exclusions)?
Ref: FW Dir.

Monstre sans Visage, Le
(The Monster Without a Face,
The Faceless Monster)
1961? Mexican.
F-H?
Ref: MTVM April '62 p37.

Mont Maudit, Le
(The Accursed Mountain)
1920 French sil.
Cast: Adolphe Candé.
F?
Ref: DdC I:316.

Montparnasse
1929 French sil?
Made by: Eugene Deslaw.
exp-F?
Ref: French Exp List.

Moon Fairytale, The
1960? Czech.
F?
Ref: Czech An '61.

Moon Riders, The
1920 U serial 18 parts.
Dir: B. Reeves Eason & Albert Russell.
Story: William Pigott, Karl Coolidge, A. Russell, George Hively, & Theodore Wharton.
Sc: G. Hively, A. Russell, & T. Wharton.
Cast: Art Accord.
SF? F? (doubtful; however, title of Ch 7: "The Menacing Monster.")
Ref: LC; Gasca p 32-33.

Moonglow
n.d. ani.
F? ("witch")
Ref: DdC II:101

Moonlight Madness
n.d.
F?
Ref: Richardson.

Mor Vran
1931 French sil? sh?
Made by: Jean Epstein.
exp-sur-F?
Ref: French Exp List; LA County Museum.

More
n.d.
Dir: Barbet-Schroeder.
Cast: Mimsy Farmer, Klaus Grünberg.
F? H?
Ref: MMF 21:46-47.

More Poisonous than the Cobra
1971 Italian?
H? ("suspence [sic] and terror")
Ref: Vw 1 Sept '71.

Morgane, la Sirène
1920 French sil.
F?

Morpheus in Hell
1967 Amateur (Film-makers' Coop) 16mm color/b&w sil 16 mins.
Made by: Tom S. Chomont.
exp-F?
Ref: FMC 5:61.

Mort und Totschag
(Dead and Killing)
1967? W.? German.
F-H?
Ref: Richardson.

Mort Vivant, Le
(The Living Dead Man)
1912 French sil sh?
Dir: Louis Feuillade.
F? H?
Ref: DdC II:338.

Mortalized Snake Girl, The
1957? Philippine/Hongkong, Sampaguita/Golden City color.
F? (probable)
Ref: FEFN 24 May '57 p 18.
Completed?

Morte Accarezza a Mezzanotte, La
(Death Cherishes Midnight[?]; Incubus --ad.t.)
1972 Italian/Spanish, Cinecompany/ Cineriz.
Prod: Alberto Pugliese.
Dir: Luciano Ercoli.
Cast: Susan Scott, Peter Martell, Simon Andreu, Claudie Lange.
H?
Ref: Vw 3 May '72 p40 ad, 26 July '72.

Morts Reviennent-Ils, Les?
See: Drame au Château d'Acre, Un (1914).

Moschettiere Fantasma, Il
1952 Italian.
F-H?
Ref: DdC III:215.

Most Dangerous Game, The
1924 British sil.
H?
Ref: Ackerman.
Based on the short story by Richard Connell?

Mostakbel el Maghoul, El
(The Unknown Future)
1948 Egyptian.
Dir: Ahmad Salem.
SF? (doubtful)
Ref: Arab Cin p277.

Moth, The
See: Nachtfalter (1911).

Moth-err
1964 Amateur (Film-makers' Coop) 16mm color 7 mins.
Made by: Dov Lederberg.
exp-F?
Ref: FMC 3:37.

Mother Goose Rhymes
1957? Coronet 11 mins.
F?
Ref: Collier.

Motherland, The
See: Dharati-Mata (1938).

Motion
1947.
Made by: Henry E. Hird.
exp-F?
Ref: USA Exp List.

Motor Pirate, The
190? Alpha Trading Co sil.
Prod & Dir: Arthur Melbourne Cooper.
F?
Ref: Collier.

Mountain King and the Misanthropist, The
1965 Austrian.
F?
Ref: Filmkunst 48:f3.

Mourir a l'Aube
(To Die at Dawn)
n.d. French.
Dir: Jean Rollin.
F-H (vampires)
Ref: Willis.
Announced; made?

Mrtví Mezi Zivými
(Dead Among the Living)
n.d. Czech.
Dir: Elmar Klos & Bořivoj Zeman.

cont.

Mrtví Mezi Zivými cont.
F?
Ref: Broz p44.
Based on a novel by Sigurd Christiansen.

Muageza, El
(The Miracle)
1963 Egyptian.
Dir: Hassan el Imam.
rel-F?
Ref: Arab Cin p285.

Mud Cure, The
1916 sil sh?
SF?
Ref: MPN 14:1895.

Muet Mélomame, Le
1899 French, Pathé sil? sh.
Cast: Ferdinand Zecca.
F?
Ref: Sadoul.

Mujer o Fiera
(Woman or Beast)
1954 Mexican.
F-H?
Ref: LC.

Mujer sin Cabeza, La
(The Woman Without a Head)
1943 Mexican, Films Mundiales.
Dir: René Cardona.
SP: R. Cardona & Xavier Villaurrutia.
Cin: Gabriel Figueroa.
Mus: Manuel Esperón.
Cast: Fu-Man Chu, Manuel Medel, Carlos Riquelme, Angel T. Sala, Manolo Noriega.
F? H?
Ref: Aventura p431.
Based on a story by David T. Bamberg (Fu-Man-Chu).
Note: this Fu-Man-Chu is not Sax Rohmer's Oriental super-villain, but a detective instead.

Mujeres Mandan, Las
1936 Mexican.
F-H?
Ref: Aventura.

Mummies of Guanajuato, The
1973? Mexican.
F-H?
Ref: LSH 2:67.
See also: Theft of the Mummies of Guanajuato (1973?).
Made?

Mummy, The
1900? French, Gaum sil sh.
Dir: Alice Guy.
F?
Ref: FIR March '64 p 142.

Mummy, The
1923 Fox sil 2 reels.
Dir: Norman Taurog.
F?
Ref: Photon 15:11; LC.

Mummy, The
See: Momie, La (1913).

Mummy and the Curse of the Jackals, The
(The Mummy vs. the Were-Jackal --s.t.)
1967?
Cast: Anthony Eisley.
F-H
Ref: TVG; B. Warren.
Exists, but possibly is uncompleted.

Mummy Interferes, The
1967? Hungarian.
F-com? ("satire on crime drama")
Ref: MTVM May '67, Jan '68.

Mummy, Mummy
1971? British, Polytechnic of Central London's Film Section sh.
Dir & SP: J. Beech.
Cin: R. Gibb.
Edit: A. Gilliand.
sur-F? ("surrealist study" of mother trying to satisfy son's every wish; title refers to British equivalent of "Mommy," rather than a mummy)
Ref: MTVM 25:12:14 A.

Mummy vs the Were-Jackal, The
See: Mummy and the Curse of the Jackals, The (1967?).

Münchhausen
1969 EPC Coordinators ltd & Gyula Trebitsch.
Conceived by: Allan A. Buckhantz.
SP: Shepherd Mead.
F?
Ref: Vw 1 Oct '69 ad.
Based on the stories by R.E. Raspe.
Completed? (doubtful)

Mundo Salvaje de Baru, El
See: Baru's Savage World (1964?).

Murder a la Mod
1968.
H-com?
Ref: Vd 26 April '68.

Murderer from the Other World, The
(Murderer from Beyond the Grave --ad.t.)
1967? Czech, Ceskoslovensky Filmexport.
Dir: Andrej Lettrich.
Cast: Ladislav Chudik, Julius Pantik, Dana Smutna.
H? ("thriller" --MTVM)
Ref: MTVM Oct '66 p 17; Czechoslovak Film 3)
See also: Call of the Demons, The (1968).

Murders in the Moulin Rouge
1971 British, Hammer.
F-H?
Ref: CineF 2:44.
Announced; not yet made.

Museo del Crimen, El
(The Museum of Crime)
1944 Mexican, Astro.
Dir: René Cardona.
SP: R. Cardona & Ramón Pérez Peláez.
Cin: José Ortiz Ramos.
Mus: Jorge Pérez.
Cast: Fu-Man-Chu, Pituka de Foronda, Katy Jurado, Angel T. Sala, Rafael Icardo.
F? H?
Ref: Aventura p432.
Based on a story by David T. Bamberg (Fu-Man-Chu).
Note: this Fu-Man-Chu is not Sax Rohmer's Oriental super-villain, but instead a detective.

Museum of Crime, The
See: Museo del Crimen, El (1944).

Music Master, The
1908 Biograph sil 500 ft.
Dir: Allan Dwan.
Cast: D.W. Griffith.
F-dream?
Ref: Willis.

Mutano the Horrible
1961 W. German, Amateur?
Prod: Klaus Unbehaun.
F-H?
Ref: FFF p48.
Sequel: Experiments of Yalon, The (1966)

Mutilated
1973? Harvest Films.
H? SF-H? ("abominable snowman")
Ref: LSH 2:66.

My Ghost
1970 Malayan? color, scope.
F? ("a beautiful young ghost")
Ref: Bangkok Post 1 March '70.

My Green Crocodile
n.d. Soviet.
F?
Ref: LA County Museum.

My Mother-in-Law is an Angel
See: Hamati Malak (1960).

My Mother-in-Law is an Atomic Bomb
See: Hamati Kombola Zorria (1952).

My Paris
See: Mon Paris (1928).

Myortvetz
See: Dead Man, The (1915).

Myself Went Young
1948 sh?
Made by: Ernest Beadle.
exp-F?
Ref: USA Exp List.

Mystères de la Vie et de la Mort
(Mysteries of Life and Death)
1923 French sil.
F? (spiritualism?)
Ref: DdC II:306.

Mysteries of Life and Death
See: Mystères de la Vie et de la Mort (1923).

Mysteries of Souls, The
1912 Danish, Nordisk (Great Northern) sil sh?
F? (hypnosis)
Ref: MPW 12:849 ad; LC.

Mysteries of the Grand Hotel
191? sil.
F?
Ref: RAF p270.

Mysteriet Nattantill den 25:e
(The Mystery of the Night of the 25th)
1916 Swedish sil.
Dir: Af Klercker.
F? H?
Ref: Sweden 2:68-69.

Mysterious Airman, The
1928 Artclass sil serial.
Dir: Harry Revier.
Cast: Walter Miller, Eugenia Gilbert.
SF?
Ref: CNW; FDY '58.

Mysterious Astrologer's Dream, The
1903? sil sh?
F-dream?
Ref: Hist/Brit.

Mysterious Black Box, The
1914 Selig sil 1000 ft.
Prod: Norval MacGregor.
Author: W.E. Wing.
F?
Ref: LC.

Mysterious Creature, The
See: Créature Mysterieuse, La (1914).

Mysterious Hindu, A
1967? Soviet.
Dir: Petr Todorovsky.
SP: A. Volodin.
F? (doubtful)
Ref: MTVM Sept '67 p 10.

Mysterious Island, The
1956 Indian.
SF?
Ref: FEFN 27 July '56.
Based on novel "L'Île Mystérieuse" by Jules Verne?

Mysterious Lodger, The
1914 Vit sil sh?
Dir: Maurice Costello & Robert Gaillard.
H?
Ref: Willis.

Mysterious Mr. X, The
1939 German.
H?

Mysterious Pearl, The
1921 Photoplay Serials Co. sil.
Dir: Ben Wilson.
Cast: Ben Wilson, Neva Gerber.
F? H?
Ref: CNW p222-23.

Mysterious Princess
1919 sil.
Cast: Marie Doro.
F?
Ref: Blum p 176.

Mysterious Stranger, The
● 1920 Vit sil.
Dir & Sc: Jess Robbins.
Ref: Willis.

● 1925 Fox sil.
Dir: Roy Del Ruth.
Ref: Willis.

● (Mozgóképipari)
1936 Hungarian.
Ref: Willis.

Are any of the above based on the novel by Mark Twain?

Mysterious Villa, The
1913 German sil sh?
H?
Ref: DdC III:337.

Mysterious X, The
See: Hemlighetsfull X, Det (1913).

Mystery in the Convent
1973? Italian, Julia Cinema.
H?
Ref: LSH 2:66.
Made?

Mystery of Corby Castle
1914 German Biophone sil.
H?
Ref: Willis.

Mystery of Life, The
See: Misterio de la Vida, El (1971).

Mystery of the Castle
1914 Savoia (Film Releases) sil sh?
H? ("weird adventures")
Ref: Bios 18 Dec '13; LC.

Mystery of the Cobra, The
See: Misterio de la Cobra, El (1958).

Mystery of the Death Head
1914 Scandinavian Co (Monarch) sil.
H?
Ref: LC.

Mystery of the Double Cross, The
1917 Astra Film Corp (Pathé) sil serial 15 parts.
Dir: William Parke.
Cast: Molly King.
H?
Ref: CNW p50-51, 179; LC.

Mystery of the Garrison, The
1908 sil sh.
Prod: Georges? Gaston? Méliès.
F?
Ref: LC.

Mystery of the Jewels, The
See: Mistero di Osiris, Il (1921).

Mystery of the Night of the 25th, The
See: Mystèriet Nattan till den 25:e (1916).

Mystery Rider, The
1928 Associated Independent Producers sil 4500 ft.
Dir & Sc: Robert J. Horner.
Titles: Bert Ames.
Cin: Paul Allen.
Edit: Frank Penrock.
Cast: Pawnee Bill Jr., Bruce Gordon, Bud Osborne.
F?
Ref: AFI F2.3771 p535; Lahue/B&G p 162.

Mystification Amusante, La
(The Amusing Hoax)
1903 French, Pathé sil sh.
Dir: Gaston Velle.
F?
Ref: Filmlex p785.

Na Garganta do Diabo
1960 Brazilian.
Dir: Walter Khoury.
F? H?
Ref: Bianco May '62 p33.

Nachenschnur des Tot
(Necklace of the Dead)
1919 German sil.
Cast: Bela Lugosi.
F? H?
Ref: FIR Oct '64 p513; FanMo 6:36; Collier.

Nacht der Grauens
1912 German sil sh?
H?
Ref: Germany.
Possible error for Nacht des Grauens (1921, main list)?

Nacht des Schreckens
(Night of Frights)
n.d. German.
H?
Ref: Deutscher.

Nachtfalter
(The Moth)
1911 German sil.
Dir: Urban Gad.
Cast: Asta Nielsen.
H?
Ref: FIR Jan '56 p20.

Naga Salitang Kalansay
1961 Philippine.
Prod: Larry Santiago.
Dir: Pablo Santiago.
H?

Ref: MTVM June '61 p41.
Made?

Nagin
1955 Indian.
H? ("Mala has to pass through Dantesque Hell" --Willis)
Ref: Thought 15 Jan '55.

Nailcutter, The
See: Pince à Ongles, La (1970?).

Naked Terror
1961 Brenner color 74 mins.
doc; H? ("murder by witchcraft")
Ref: FF '61 p365.

Naked Witch, The
1972 Clark Rel. Co.
F-H?
Ref: BO 1 May '72 pSE-2.
Is this the same film as the 1966 movie of the same title (main list)? Or is it the same as the following title?

Naked Wytche, The
1972 Sunset Int'l.
Cast: Barbara Klingered.
F-H?
Ref: BO 13 Nov '72 p E-11.
Is this the same film as the preceding title?

Narcose
1929 sil?
Dir: Alfred Abel.
F? (doubtful)
Ref: Willis.

Narcotic Spectre, The
1914 sil sh?
F-dream? (probable)
Ref: Bios 23 April '14.

Narrow Escape
1914 sil sh?
H? ("fearsome Macbethian crone")
Ref: Bios 30 April '14.

Natale
(The Nativity)
n.d. Italian, Cines.
rel-F?
Ref: 50 Yrs Ital Cin p 19.

Nativity, The
See: Natale (n.d.).

Natur und Liebe
(Nature and Love)
1928 German, UFA sil.
F-seq? ("monumental vision of mankind's birth and rise")
Ref: C to H p 151-52.

Nature and Love
See: Natur und Liebe (1928).

Naulahka, The
1918 Pathé sil.
Cast: Doraldina, Warner Oland.
F? (doubtful)
Ref: Blum p 157.

Navarathri
1964 Indian, Sri Vijayalakshmi.
Dir: A.P. Nagarajan.
Cast: Sivaji Ganesan.
F? ("folklore")
Ref: MTVM Aug '15 '64 p42.

Neck Biters, The
n.d.
F-H?
Exists? (doubtful)

Necklace of the Dead
See: Nachenschnur des Tot (1919).

Necklace of the Mummy
n.d. Danish sil.
F?
Ref: Collier.

Ned med Vaabnene
See: Down with Weapons (1914).

Neo Cleopatra
1970? Japanese, Mushi color ani.
F? (erotic)
Ref: MTVM Oct '69 p 18, Nov '69 p20.
Probably the same film as Cleopatra, Queen of Sex (1971?, main list).

Neptune's Romance
1924 Fox sil.
Prod & Dir: Henry Otto.
F?
Ref: MPN 30:84-85; no LC; no AFI.
Exists?

Nessie Come Home
1971.
SF-com?
Ref: CineF 2:44.
Announced; made? (doubtful)

Nest of the Cuckoo Bird
1966 Williams.
F-H? (doubtful)
Ref: Willis.

Neues vom Hexer
(Again the Wizard)
1965 W. German.
Dir: Alfred Vobrer (Vohrer?).
SP: Herbert Reinecker.
Cast: Heinz Drache, Eddi Arent, Rene Dottgen, Barbara Rutting, Brigitte Horney,

cont.

Neues vom Hexer cont.

Klaus Kinsky, Karl John.
bor-H?
Ref: FIR '67 p85.
Based on short story collection "Again the Ringer" by Edgar Wallace.

Neutron contra el Creminal Sadico
n.d. Mexican.
SF?
Ref: LAT (Willis).

New Absurd Wrestling Matches
1900 French sil sh.
F? ("woman dismembered")
Ref: Willis.

New Adventures of Space Explorers
n.d. (New Trends).
SF-doc?
Ref: New Trends.

New Angels, The
1966? Promenade.
F? (motorcycle gangs?)
Ref: Richardson.

New Rocambole, The
See: Nouveau Rocambole, Le (1913).

New Year's Day: Year 2000
1968 Italian.
Prod: Angelo Rizzoli.
Dir: Luigi Comencini.
SF
Ref: Vw 8 May '68 p48.
Completed?

Nick Carter, Master Detective
1939.
F? H? SF? (doubtful)
Ref: NYT 14 Dec '39.

Nick Carter vs. Lady Lister
1966 Italian, Titanus & 7 Arts.
SF?
Ref: Richardson.

Niece of Dr. Jekyll, The
1972 Italian/U.S., Tele-Roma/ Heraldic.
Dir: Robert Mansfield.
SF-H
Ref: MTVM 26:12:6.
Based on characters created by Robert Louis Stevenson.
Announced; made?

Night Before Christmas
1962? Soviet? (Artkino).
F?
Ref: FDY '62.

Night Bird
1935 Indian.
Dir: Dhiren Ganguly.
Cin: Shailen Bose.
Cast: Mazhar Khan, Anwari, Gul Hamid, Nazir, Phalwan Indubala.
H-seqs? ("phantastic thriller" -- Dipali)
Ref: Dipali 4 Jan '35 p37, p56 ad, 21 June '35 p21.

Night Creatures Against the Son of Hercules
n.d. Italian?
Cast: Mark Forest.
F?
Ref: FFF p50.
This is probably the same film as Molemen vs. the Son of Hercules (1961, main list).

Night in the Mirror, The
See: Noche en el Espejo, La (1962).

Night Is a Sorceress, The
See: Nuit Est une Sorcière, La (1959).

Night of a Dead Woman Who Lived, The
See: Noche de una Muerta que Vivio, La (1971).

Night of All Horror, The
See: Noche de Todos los Horrores, La (1973?).

Night of Frights
See: Nacht des Schreckens (n.d.).

Night of Horror, A
190? Alpha Trading Co. sil sh.
Prod & Dir: Arthur Mebourne Cooper.
H?
Ref: Collier.

Night of Miracles, The
See: Lailat el Kadr (1952).

Night of Revenge
1915 Danish sil.
Dir: Ben Christensen.
H? (doubtful)
Ref: Willis.

Night of Terror
1914 Danish sil.
H?
Ref: Willis.

Night of the Cat
1973 Dominant.
H?
Ref: BO 22 Jan '73.
Possibly same film as Mexican film, Noche de los Mil Gatos, La (1972?, main list).

Night of the Cemetery, The
See: Nuit du Cimetiere, La (1972?).

Night of the Devil
1973 AIP.
F-H?
Ref: BO 18 Dec '72 pSE-4.
Completed?

Night of the Flowers
1971? Italian, Idi.
Prod & Dir: Gianvittorio Baldi.
Cast: Dominique Sanda, Hiram Keller, Macha Meril.
F? ("fantasy")
Ref: Vw 3 May '72 p45.

Night of the Serpents
n.d. Italian, Madison Cinemat. & Ascot Cineraid.
Dir: Giulio Petroni.
Cast: Luke Askey, Luigi Pistilli, José Torres, Gina Rovera.
Ref: F? H? (doubtful; probably western)
Ref: Vw.

Night of the Warlock
n.d. (1973) Cambist.
F-H?
Ref: Vw 3 Jan '73 p79.
Completed?

Night of the Warlock
(novel by ---?)
See: Hexed (1971?).

Night of the Witch
1971 Cannon Films.
SP: Lloyd Kaufman.
F-H?
Ref: BO 12 July '71.
Announced; made?

Night Porter, The
See: Portiere di Notte, Il (1972?).

Night that God Screamed, The
See: Nightmare House (1973?).

Night Walk, The
1973? Canadian.
Dir: Benjamin Clark.
Cast: John Marley.
F? H?
Ref: LSH 2:67.
Announced; made?

Night with Masqueraders in Paris, A
(Nuit de Carnaval)
1908 French, Star sil 470 ft (363 ft).
Prod: Georges Méliès.
F? (doubtful)
Ref: Sadoul; GM Mage; LC.

Night with the Devil, A
1945? Toddy 71 mins.
All-Negro cast.
rel-mus; F?
Ref: N. Kagan.
Based on a novel by S. Wilson & C. Grant.

Night in Transylvania, A
1941 Hungarian.
F? H? (doubtful)
Ref: Encic DS IX:1247.

Night of Haste, A
1966? Mexican.
Cast: Lon Chaney Jr.
F? H? SF?
Ref: Richardson.
Made?

Nightfall
1956.
F?
Ref: MMF 12:16f.

Nightingale
1936 Soviet 2-color.
Dir: N. Ekk.
F?
Ref: Soviet Cinema p76.

Nightmare
1967 German.
H?
Ref: Richardson.
Made?

Nightmare House
(The Night that God Screamed --e.t.)
n.d. (1973) Carlon & Lasky (Cinemation).
Prod: Ed Lasky & Gil Carlin (Carlon?).
Dir: Lee Madden.
Cast: Jeanne Crain, Alex Nicol.
F? H?
Ref: BO 6 Nov '72 p 10, 29 Jan '73 p9; MTVM 27:4:5.

Nightride
1964 Amateur (Film-makers' Coop) 16mm color sil 10 mins.
Made by: Michael Mideke.
Cast: Tracy Page.
exp-F? ("chod experiences on the Astral Plane")
Ref: FMC 5:242.

Nightscapes
n.d. Amateur (C-16) 16mm ani collage 6 mins.
Made by: Richard Preston.
exp-F? ("comment on atomic war")
Ref: FMC 3:51; C-16 p24.

Nikolai Stavrogin
1915 Russian, Yermoliev sil 7300 ft.
Dir & Sc: Yakov Protazanov.
Design: Nikolai Suvorov.

cont

Nikolai Stavrogin cont.

Cin: Yevgeni Slavinsky.
Cast: Ivan Mozhukhin, Lydia Rindina, A. Ivonin, Pyotr Starkovsky, Nikolai Panov, Vera Orlova.
F? H? (doubtful)
Ref: Kino p420.
Based on "The Devils" by Fyodor Dostoyevsky.

Nine Days in One Year
1961 Soviet 96 mins.
Dir: Mikhail Romm.
Cast: Alexei Batalov, Tamara Lavrova, Innokenty Smoktunovsky.
bor-SF? ("explores perceptively the complexities of a world where technology and humanism have not yet found a meeting place" --unidentified quote from Collier)
Ref: Baxter p 163-65; Collier.

Nine Supermen
n.d.
F?
Ref: LAT 25 May '71.

1985
1970 (CCM Films) color 56 mins.
SF?
Ref: Sightlines Jan-Feb '73 p30.

1984
n.d.
TV film also shown in theaters? Exists? Doubtful.
Based on the novel by George Orwell.

Ninjutsu Musha Shugyo
(The Stupid Sorcerer)
1956 Japanese, Daiei 44 mins.
Cast: Tony Tani, Entatsu Yokoyama, Tokiko Mita.
F? (shop owner's son believes he is "a sorcerer with supernatural powers")
Ref: FEFN 13 April '56.
Film with same title, 1960, included in main list, however, this one may not be fantastic.

No Exit
n.d. Italian.
Prod: Pierluigi Torri.
Dir: Piero Sciume.
Cast: Marisa Mell, Philippe Leroy, Lea Massari, Roger Hanin, Jorge Rigaud.
F?
Ref: Vw.
Possibly based on play "Huis Clos" by Jean-Paul Sartre.

No More Spooks
1953 Czech.
F-com?
Ref: Modern Czech Film.

No Trifling with Love
1908 French? sil sh.
Prod: Georges? Gaston? Méliès.
F?
Ref: LC.

Noces d'Hirondelle, Les
(The Marriage of the Swallow)
1968 French, Les Films del Adagio 16min.
Dir & SP: Phillipe Durand.
Cin: Pierre Montazel & Jean Dasque.
Ani: Michel Boschet.
Edit: Chantal Durand.
Cast: Juliette Villard, Monique Mélinand, Jean-Pierre Gasc, René Michaud.
F? (probable)
Ref: MMF 21:29-33.

Noche de Todos los Horrores, La
  1973? Spanish.
  Cast: Paul Naschy (r.n. Jacinto Molina).
  F-H (vampires)
  Ref: LSH 2:69.
  Planned.

Noche de una Muerta qu Vivio, La
  (The Night of a Dead Woman Who Lived)
  1971 Spanish/Italian, Balcazar/Apollo.
  Dir: Balcazar.
  Cast: José Antonio Amor, Nuria Torray, Teresa Gimpera.
  F-H?
  Ref: Vw 3 May '72 p 175.

Noche en el Espejo, La
  (The Night in the Mirror)
  1962 Argentinian, Aries.
  Dir: Fernando Ayala.
  SP: Omar del Carlo.
  F (couple fall in love because of magic)
  Ref: NYT 8 April '62.
  Made?

Noche Terrible
  (Terrible Night)
  1968? Argentinian.
  Dir: Rudolfo Kuhn.
  Cast: Susana Rinaldi, Jorge Rivera Lopez.
  F? H?
  Ref: Richardson.

Nocturnal Horror
  (Nocni Des)
  1915 Czech.
  Dir: J.A. Pallausch.
  Cin: M. Urban.
  F?
  Ref: Encic DS 3:364.

Noddy in Toyland
  1948 British.
  Dir: MacLean Rogers.
  F?
  Ref: Collier.
  Exists?

Nogent, Eldorado du Dimanche
  1929 French sil?
  Dir: Marcel Carne.
  exp-F?
  Ref: French Exp List.

Non Lieu
  1968 Belgian, Les Productions Pierre Levie 25 mins.
  Dir: Michel Stameschkine.
  Cin: Emmanuel Bonmariage.
  Cast: Georges Randax, Lucien Salkin, Georges Rossair, Piroksa Muharay, Olga.
  SF?
  Ref: Trieste '69.
  Based on a story by Thomas Owen.

Non si Sevizia un Paperino
  See: Don't Torture the Duckling (1972).

Noodnik of the North
  1924 sil 2 reels?
  Cast: Ben Turpin.
  F-com? (igloos appearing from nowhere?)

Noonday Demons
  1972? British.
  Prod: Gene Persson.
  Cast: Joe Melia.
  F?
  Ref: Photon 21:7.
  Based on the play by Peter Barnes.
  Announced; made? (doubtful)

Noose, The
  See: Petla (1958).

Norlela
  (possibly Norela)
  1962? Malayan, Shaws.
  Dir: D. Ghosh.
  Cast: Aziz Jaasar, Sarimah.
  F? ("Arabian Nights")
  Ref: MTVM June '62 p 14, Oct '62 p34.
  Completed?

Nostradamus
  1937 Mexican, Stahl.
  Dir: Juan Bastillo Oro.
  SP: J.B. Oro & Antonio Helu.
  Cin: Victor Herrera.
  Cast: Consuelo Frank, Carlos Villarias, Juan José, Martinez Casado, René Cardona.
  F-H? (vampires?)
  Ref: HR 9 Jan '37.
  Completed?

Not Guilty
  1908 French? sil sh.
  Prod: Georges? Gaston? Méliès.
  F?
  Ref: LC.

Nothing But Dreams
  1968? Yugoslavian.
  Dir: Soja Jovanovic.
  Cast: Nusa Marovic-Antonini.
  F? (man dreams of films & film stars)
  Ref: MTVM March '68 p22.

Nothing Is Impossible to the Man
  See: Rien n'Est Impossible a l'Homme (1912).

Notre Dame de Paris
  (novel by V. Hugo)
  See: Esmerelda (1905).

Nouveau Rocambole, Le
  (The New Rocambole)
  1913 French? sil sh?
  Dir: Georges Denola.
  F?
  Ref: DdC II:64.

Now I Lay Me Down to Die
  (Black Magic --s.t.)
  1971 (1972?) Clover Films 90 mins.
  Prod: Dan Cady.
  Dir & SP: John P. Hayes.
  Cast: Edmond O'Brien, Brook Mills.
  F-H ("About an Elmer Gantry type. . .whose daughter brings him back to life to kill people at her command" --BO)
  Ref: BO 30 Aug '71; 15 May '72.
  Completed? Further title changes?

Nude Horror
  (The Icy Knife of Terror -- S.E. Asia t.)
  1972? Italian, Tritone.
  H?
  Ref: LSH 2:66.

Nuit du Cimetiere, La
  (The Night of the Cemetery)
  1972? French, Films ABC.
  Dir: Jean Rollin.
  Cast: Françoise Pascal, Hughes Quester.
  F-H?
  Ref: MTVM 27:4:17.
  Completed?

Nuit de Carnaval
  See: Night with Masqueraders in Paris, A (1908).

Nuit Est une Sorcière, La
  (The Night is a Sorceress)
  1959 French, Optimax 17 mins.
  Dir: Marcel Martin.
  Libretto: André Coffraut.
  Mus: Sidney Bechet.
  Choreog: Pierre Lacotte.
  Cast: Josette Clavier, Pierre Lacotte, Gene Robinson, Doren Velikovic.
  dance-F? (somnambulist)
  Ref: UNESCO cat p36-37.

Nutcracker
  n.d. French scope.
  Mus: Tchaikovsky?
  ballet-F
  Ref: Collier.
  Completed?

O

O Dreamland
  1956 British.
  F?
  Ref: S&S Spring '63 p56.

0-18
  (A Message from the Sky --alt.t.)
  1915 British, London Film Co sil.
  SF?
  Ref: LC.

O Věcech Nadpřirozených
  (Glorie; Miraculous Happenings; The Halo)
  1958 Czech.
  Dir: Jiří Krejčík.
  Cin: Vladimir Bor.
  Cin: Vladimír Novotný.
  F?
  Ref: Broz p98.

Obsede, L'
  1957?
  F?
  Ref: Cinema '57.

Occhio Selvaggio
  (The Savage Eye)
  1966? Italian.
  F?
  Ref: Richardson.

Occurrence at Owl Creek Bridge, An
  1923? German sil 2 reels?
  Cast: Wilhelm (later William) Dieterle.
  psy-F
  Ref: Milton Lubovski.
  Based on the short story by Ambrose Bierce.
  Exists?

Oceano
  (Ocean Odyssey)
  1971?
  SF?
  Ref: Photon 21:8.
  Made?

Octamon
  See: Octoman (1971).

Octavius
  1913 sil sh.
  F? ("ghost?" --Willis)
  Ref: Bios 12 June '13.

Octoman
  (Octamon --ad.t.)
  1971 Filmers Guild.
  Prod: Harry Essex & Michael Kraike.
  Dir: H. Essex.
  Makeup Design: George Barr.
  Makeup: Ric Baker.
  Cast: Kerwin Matthews, Pier Angeli, Jeff Morrow.
  SF-H (part man, part octopus monster menaces heroine)
  Ref: Vw 11 Aug '71.
  Completed? (doubtful)

Ode to Madness
  See: Eloges de la Folie (n.d.).

Odessey of the North, An
  1915 Bosworth sil.
  Cast: Hobart Bosworth.
  bor-F?
  Ref: Blum p83.

Odyssey, The
  1968 Italian 2 hrs.
  Prod: Dino De Laurentiis.

cont.

Odyssey, The cont.
Dir: Franco Rossi.
F?
Ref: Vw 8 May '68 p48.
Based on the epic poem by Homer.

Oedipus
n.d. Amateur (C-16) 16mm 12 mins.
Made by: Robert Vickrey.
exp-sur-F
Ref: C-16 p26.

Off the Earth
1922 U sil 1 reel.
com; F?
Ref: LC.

Ogling Phantom, The
n.d.
sex-F-H?
Ref: Richardson.
Probably same film as Peeping Phantom, The (1964?, main list).

Ogon no Tozoko
(The Golden Couple)
1966 Japanese, Toei color scope 90 mins.
Dir: Tadashi Sawashima.
Story: Kazuyoshi Takasawa.
SP: Daisuke Yamazaki & Masahiro Kakefuda.
Cast: Hiroki Matsukata, Koichi Ose, Kanmi Fujiyama.
F? ("search for treasury with fantasy treatment")
Ref: Collier.

Ogre de Mecklembourg, L'
1957?
F?
Ref: Cinema '57.

Ogre of Athens, The
1955 Greek.
F? H?
Ref: DdC II:458.

Ogre's House, The
See: Casa del Ogro, La (1938).

Ogre's Kitchen, The
1908 French.
F?
Ref: DdC III:352.

Oh Mummy
1927 Par sil 2 reels.
Prod: Al Christie.
F?-com
Ref: LC.

Ohyaku the Female Demon
n.d. Japanese.
Dir: Y. Ishikawa.
F-H?
Ref: CoF 15:16.

Oiseau, L'
(The Bird)
n.d. French ani.
Dir: Jacques Vausseur.
F?

Ojo de Vidrio, El
(The Glass Eye)
196? Mexican, Masai.
F? H?
Ref: Richardson.
Made?

Ojos Azules de la Muñeca Rota, Los
(The Blue Eyes of the Broken Doll)
1973 Spanish, Profilmes.
Dir: Carlos Aured.

cont.

Ojos Azules de la Muñeca Rota, Los cont.
Cast: Paul Naschy (r.n. Jacinto Molina).
F? H?
Ref: Vw 28 Feb '73 p28.
Completed?

Old Applejoy's Ghost
(story by F. Stockton)
See: Fantasy (1927).

Old Dark House, The
n.d. British.
Dir: Walter Summers.
H?
Ref: Collier.
Based on novel "Benighted" by J.B. Priestley?
Exists?

Old Footlight Favorite
1908 French? sil sh.
Prod: Gaston? Georges? Méliès.
F?
Ref: LC.

Old Man Who Tried to Grow Young, The
1916 Selig sil 3 reels.
Dir: T.N. Heffron.
Author: Malcolm Douglas.
SF?
Ref: LC.

Old Mansion, The
See: Vieux Chateau, Le (n.d.).

Old Woman Who Lived in a Shoe, The
n.d. Australian.
F?
Ref: Collier.

Old Woodman, The
1909? sil sh.
F-seq? ("image of death")
Ref: Bios 21 Oct '09.
Same as the following film?

Old Woodman, The
1910 sil sh.
F-seq? ("devil")
Ref: Bios 13 Jan '10.
Same as the preceding film?

Olga's Girls
1964 Weiss 95 mins.
sex-H? ("torture scenes")
Ref: CoF 8:6.
Exists?

Oliver Twist
1972 Filmation ani.
Prod: Norman Prescott & Lou Scheimer.
Dir: Hal Sutherland.
F-seqs?
Ref: Vw 3 Jan '73 p60.
Based on the novel by Charles Dickens.
Completed?

Ombre Oculto, El
1970 Spanish, Mota.
Dir: Alfonso Ungria.
Cast: Carlos Otero.
SF? F?
Ref: Vw 12 May '71.

Ombres Chinoises, Les
(The Chinese Shadows)
1907 French (Pathé) sil sh.
Dir: Segundo de Chomon.
F?
Ref: DdC p43.

Ombromagie
(Shadow Magic)
1956? French, Films J.R.D. 16 mins.

cont.

Ombromagie cont.
Dir: Jean-Paul Sassy.
Cin: Georges Leclerc.
Mus: Sidney Bechet, Perez Prado, Philippe Gerard, & Guy Patrick.
Cast: Amy Aaroe, Guy Patrick, Apsita Fradet, Amadou Sissoko.
F? ("Chinese shadows")
Ref: UniF 18.

On a Silver Platter
1971? Italian.
Dir: Giorgie Capitani.
F? H?
Ref: Photon 21:8.
Announced; made?

On His Goatmobile
1916 sil ani sh.
Dir: Earl Hurd.
F?
Ref: LA County Museum.

On Irish Hill
(story by P.B. Kyne)
See: Kelly of the Secret Service (1936).

On Sundays
1961 Amateur (Film-makers' Coop) 16mm 26 mins.
Made by: Bruce Baille.
exp-F-seq? ("part fantasy" -- FMC)
Ref: FMC 5:22; Undrgnd p 113.

On the Stroke of 12
1915 sil sh.
H? SF? ("invention")
Ref: Motog 6 March '15.

On the Threshold of Space Travel
1960? Czech.
Dir: Kurt Goldberger.
doc; SF-seq?
Ref: Czech An '61.

On the Twelfth Day
1956 22 mins.
SF? F? H?
Ref: Willis.

Once It Was Human
1973 Entertainment Pyramid Inc.
SF? F? H?
Ref: BO 12 March '73 pC-4.

Once Upon a Dream
n.d. British.
Cast: Googie Withers, Griffith Jones.
F? (woman dreams of affair --did it happen?)
Ref: Collier.

Once Upon a Time
(Der Var Engang)
1922 Danish, Sophus Madsen sil.
Dir: Carl Dreyer.
Sc: C. Dreyer & Palle Rosen-krantz.
Cin: George Scheevoigt.
Cast: Clara Pontoppidan, Svend Methling, Peter Jerndorff.
F (fairy tale)
Ref: FC 35:2 & 8.
Based on the play by Holger Drachmann.
Completed? (doubtful)

Ondata di Calore
See: Dead of Summer (n.d.).

One-Armed Swordsman
n.d. Hongkong, Shaw.
F-seq? (mystic martial arts?)
Ref: MTVM Oct '67 p 19.

One Dark Night
1939 81 mins.
H? (frightens rival)
Ref: FD 1 Dec '39.

One Frightful Night
1971 Clover Films color.
F? H?
Ref: BO 6 Sept '71.
Made?

One Hamlet Less
See: Un Amleto de Meno (1973).

108 Heroes from Liang Shan, The
1972? Hongkong, Shaw.
Dir: Chang Cheh.
Cast: David Chiang, Ku Feng.
F? ("Chinese legend")
Ref: MTVM 26:8:27.

1,000,000 A.D.
1973 Cine-Fund color.
Prod: S. Lee Lieb.
Dir: Allen Baron.
SP: Shelly Silverstein & Allen Foster.
Cast: John Carradine, Anthony Eisley, Jo Morrow.
SF-H (men from today end up in the world of one million a.d.)
Ref: Vw 16 May '73 p23 ad; A. Foster.
Announced.

One Minute to Midnight
n.d. Swedish.
Cast: Lars Hansen.
SF?
Ref: Collier.

One of Those Things
See: Haendeligt Uheld (1971?).

1 + 1 = 3
1967? Yugoslavian ani acetate.
F?
Ref: Richardson.

One Step Up
1967? Italian.
Dir: Giancarlo Zagni.
Cast: Carroll Baker.
H? ("based on 'Macbeth'" -- Collier)
Ref: Cont FR Oct '67 p 13. (Collier).

1001 Nights
1967 Spanish/Italian?
Prod: Mitchell Grayson.
Dir: José Maria Ellorieta.
Cast: Luciana Paluzzi, Jeff Cooper, Ruben Rojo, Perla Cristal, Raf Vallone, Ruben Rojo, Tomas Blanco, Brigitte St. John.
F?
Ref: Vw 22 Nov '67, 11 Oct '67 ad.
Completed?

£1000 Spook, The
(The Thousand Pound Spook)
1907 British sil sh.
Dir: Walter Booth.
F-com?
Ref: Brit Cin.

Open the Door and See All the People
1964 Barney Pitkins Assocs 82 mins.
Made by: Dick Higgins.
Cin: Gayne Rescher.
Mus: Alec Wilder.
Cast: Maybelle Nash, Alec Wilder, Jeremiah Sullivan, Charles Rydell, Ellen Martin, Taylor Mead.
sur-F?
Ref: FMC 3:31.

Opera Maldita, La
   (The Accursed Opera)
   n.d. Argentinian.
   F? H?
   Ref: Willis?

Operation Abduction
   1961 French.
   SF? ("new rocket fuel")
   Ref: TVG.

Operation Diplomatic Passport
   n.d.
   SF? ("synthetic petroleum"
   -- Willis)
   Ref: BIB's (Willis).

Operation Double Cross
   1965.
   Cast: M. Mell, Vernon.
   SF? ("atomic cannon")
   Ref: BIB's (Willis).

Operation Gold Ingot
   n.d. French (AIP-TV)
   85 mins.
   Dir: Georges Lautner.
   Cast: Alberto Lionello, Felix
   Marten, Martine Carol.
   SF? (heating element strong
   enough to melt safe)
   Ref: MTVM Dec '65 p22.

Operation: Lovebirds
   1968? Emerson Film Enterprises.
   SF?
   Ref: Richardson.

Operation M
   1967? East-West Int'l Prods.
   SF?
   Ref: Richardson.
   Completed?

Operation St. Peters
   1967 Ultra & Marianne &
   Roxfilm/Par.
   SF?
   Ref: Richardson.
   Made?

Operation Top Secret
   n.d.
   SF?
   Ref: BIB's.

Operation Turntable
   1966 W. German.
   SF? ("arch-criminal Gold-
   singer")
   Ref: TVG.
   Probably the same film as
   James Tont: Operation Gold-
   singer (1966, problem list).

Operation W.E.I.R.D.
   1965? UPI Prods.
   Prod: Thomas Naud.
   Dir: Claudio Guzman.
   SF?
   Ref: Vw 13 Oct '65.

Operation Warhead
   n.d.
   SF? ("transistorized bomb"
   -- Willis)
   Ref: BIB's (Willis).

Opsteel
   1968 Italian, R.P.R. color
   15 mins.
   Dir: Emilio Marsili.
   Nar: "Nuova Conoscenza."
   SF?
   Ref: Trieste '69.

Opus One
   1972 Cal Arts 4 mins.
   Made by: Joyce Borenstein.
   exp-F?
   Ref: Filmex II.

Orchid Lady, The
   n.d.
   Cast: Corinne Griffith, Erich
   von Stroheim.
   F? (WWI story; ancestor of lady
   comes out of painting at end)
   Ref: Crackel; no Acad, no LC;
   no AFI.
   Synopsis as given probably identifies a real film; however, the
   cast and title are probably
   wrong.

Order No. ----
   1925 Soviet, Vufku sil.
   sur-F?
   Ref: Kino p8, 190.

Oreni Sawaruto Abunaine
   (If You Touch Me, Danger)
   n.d. Japanese, Nikkatsu.
   Dir: Yashuharu Hasebe.
   F? (mermaid?)
   Ref: Gasca.

Organ, The
   1965? Czech.
   Dir: Stefan Uher.
   bor-F?("beautiful, poetic
   & mystic atmosphere")
   Ref: Collier.

Orgelbauer von St. Marien, Der
   1961? W. German, Schonbrunn &
   F.T.R.
   Dir: August Rieger.
   Cast: Gerlinde Locker, Paul
   Horbiger.
   F? ("folklore")
   Ref: MTVM Aug '61 p29.
   Completed?

Orgy Story in Edo, The
   1969 Japanese, Toei color
   95 mins.
   sex-H? (sadistic tortures)
   Ref: MTVM April '69 p26 ad.

Orlando Furioso
   1964?
   Dir: Aristo.
   F?
   Ref: S&S Spring '64 p84.

Orphan Mary and the Dwarfs
   See: Marysia i Krasnoludki
   (1961).

Orpheus in the Underworld
   1909 Swedish sil.
   Dir: Charles Magnusson.
   F?
   Ref: Sweden I.

Oscuridad en el Cerebro, La
   (The Darkness in the Brain)
   1971 Spanish/Italian, Orfeo
   P.C./Queen Cine.
   Dir: Teodoro Ricci.
   Cast: Philippe Leroy, Rossana
   Yanni.
   H?
   Ref: Vw 3 May '72 p 175.

Oscuros Sueños de Agosto
   (Dark Dreams of August)
   1967? Spanish.
   Dir: Miguel Picazo.
   Cast: Viveca Lindfors, Francisco
   Rabal, Julian Mateoa, Sonia
   Bruno.
   F? H?
   Ref: Richardson.

Osterman Weekend, The
   1973? WB.
   Prod: William Castle.
   F? H?
   Ref: CoF 19:48.
   Announced; to be made.
   (Probably will not be made.)

Ostroznie Yeti
   (Beware of the Yeti)
   1958 Polish, Syrena.
   Dir: Andrzej Czekalski.
   SP: Andrzej Brzozowski & A.
   Czekalski.
   Sets: Jerzy Skrzepinski.
   Cin: Henryk Depczyk & Jan
   Janczewski.
   Mus: Lucjan M. Kaszycki.
   Cast: Jarema Stepowski, Stefan
   Bartik, Jozef Nowak, Bronislaw
   Pawlik, Wojciech Pokora, Zygmunt
   Zintel.
   SF? (abominable snowmen?)
   Ref: Polish Cin p 153.

Our Agent Tiger
   1965 Italian? color 89
   mins.
   Dir: Claude Chabrol.
   Cast: Roger Hanin, Margaret
   Lee, Michel Bouquet.
   SF?
   Ref: United Films cat '73-74
   p96.

Our Heavenly Bodies
   192? French.
   Prod: Lucien Rudaux.
   SF-doc?
   Ref: Science & Invention
   March '28.

Our Planet, the Earth
   n.d. Polish.
   Dir: Maciej Sienski.
   doc; bor-SF-seqs?
   Ref: Polish Cin p66.

Out of Evil
   1950? Israeli.
   Dir & SP: Joseph Krumgold.
   F-seq? (puppet seq)
   Ref: Collier.

Out of the Darkness
   1915 Par sil.
   F?
   Ref: Willis.

Out of the Darkness
   1921 British? Gaum sil.
   F?
   Ref: Willis.

Outer Dark
   n.d.
   Dir: Stacy Keach.
   H? (incest in Appalachia)
   Ref: Photon 21:7.
   Announced; made?

Oval Portrait, The
   1972 Canadian, Bellevue-Pathé &
   Maple Leaf Int'l.
   Prod: Enrique Torres Tudela.
   Dir: Rogelio Gonzales.
   Set Design: Mirna Sinclair.
   Cin: Leon Sanchez.
   Cast: Rhonda Henrix, Giselle
   McKenzie, Barry Coe, Maraye
   Ayers, Doris Buckingham, Daphne
   Goldrick, Pia Shandel, Graham
   Crowell, Terrance Kelly.
   F? H?
   Ref: BO 27 March '72 pK-8;
   HR 21 April '72.
   Based on the short story by
   Edgar Allan Poe?
   Completed?

Oval Portrait, The
   See: Portrait Ovale, Le (1969).

Over the Planet in a Diving Suit
   n.d. Soviet?
   F?
   Ref: Collier.

Overall 1
   1968 Germany, Edgar Reitz
   Film-Produktion color 40 mins.
   Dir, Story, Cin: Edgar Reitz.
   SF?
   Ref: Trieste '69.

Overture/Nyitany
   n.d. (Contemporary) sh.
   F?

Owl Witch, The
   1927 sil sh.
   F? ("legend")
   Ref: The Film Spectator
   19 Feb '27.

EXCLUSIONS

The titles listed in this section have been determined beyond reasonable doubt <u>not</u> to be fantastic. They were researched because their titles, casts, ads, or reported subject matter suggested they might be fantastic. Many of them have been included in other works on science-fiction, fantasy, or horror films.

The exclusions are printed here to answer, in advance, questions as to whether or not some specific title was considered for inclusion.

G

G.O.O.
(Genetic Octopodular Ooze)
n.d. AIP.
SP: Richard Matheson.
Ref: Photon 21:5; R. Matheson.
Announced, never made.

Gambler's Dream
1911 French, Pathé sil sh.
Ref: MPW 10:150; F/A p461.

Gambler's Nightmare
1906 Lubin sil 255 ft.
Ref: Views 1:13: 5, 10.

Gangway for Tomorrow
1946 RKO.
Ref: Acad.

Garden of Eden, The
1928 Feature Prods (UA) sil 7300 ft.
Ref: AFI F2.2016 p281.
Based on the work by Rudolf Bernauer & Rudolf Oesterreicher.

Garden of Eden
1957
Ref: FD 18 Dec 57.

Garments of Truth
1921 S-L Pictures (Metro) sil 4968 ft.
Ref: AFI F2.2018 p282.
Based on the story by Freeman Tilden.

Gaslight
● (Angel Street -rr.t.)
1940 British.

● 1944 MGM 114 mins.
Ref: Scognamillo; R. Warren.
Based on the play by Patrick Hamilton, presented in the United States as "Angel Street."

Gatos Negros, Los
(The Black Cats)
1964 Spanish.
Ref: SpCin 65 p 136-37.

Gavotte
n.d. French 10 mins.
Ref: S&S Spring 68 p76.

Geheimnis der Sphinx, Das
(The Secret of the Sphinx)
n.d. German.
Sc: Fritz Lang.
Ref: Fritz Lang in America p 121.
Unfilmed 3rd part of Spinnen, Die.

Geisha Girl
1953 Japanese.
Ref: V 21 May 52 p6.

Genetic Octopodular Ooze
See: G.O.O. (n.d.).

Gentle Art of Murder, The
See: Crime Does Not Pay (1962)

Germany Year Zero
n.d.
Ref: Acad.

Gespenster
(Ghosts)
1939 German.
Ref: UF p 162, 401.
Based on the play by Ibsen.
See also: Ghosts.

Get on with It
1963?
Ref: BO 24 June '63.

Ghost, The
1910 French, Pathé sil sh.
Ref: Bios 8 Sept '10.

Ghost, The
1913 Victor sil 1000 ft.
Ref: MPW 17:845.

Ghost, A
See: Revenant, Un (1948).

Ghost and the Guest, The
1943 PRC 62 mins.
Ref: MFB Dec '43 p 135; V & HR 12 July '43.

Ghost at Noon, A
(novel by A. Moravia)
See: Contempt (1963).

Ghost Camera, The
1933 British (Favorite Films) 60 mins.
Ref: V 1 Aug '33.

Ghost City
1921 Helen Holmes Prods (Associated Photoplays) sil 5 reels.
Ref: AFI F2.2061 p287.

Ghost City
1932 Mono.
Ref: MPH 6 Feb '32 p29, 9 April '32 p25.

Ghost Club, The
1913 sil.
Ref: MPW 18:1459 ad.

Ghost Comes Home, The
1940 MGM.
Ref: Ackerman.

Ghost Diver
1957 Regal (20th-Fox) scope 76 mins.
Ref: FD 4 Nov '57.

Ghost Flower, The
1918
Ref: MPW 37:1159, 1302.

Ghost Girls, The
1917 sil.
Ref: MPW 34:464, 40:580.

Ghost Guns
(Ghost of Indian Springs -alt.t.?)
1944 Mono.
Ref: MPH 18 Nov '44; Vd & HR 10 Nov '44.

Ghost in a Cab
See: Yurei Takushii (1956).

Ghost in the Garret, The
1919 (1920) New Art Film Co. (Par) sil 5 reels.
Ref: LC; FIR Aug-Sept '68 p412-13.

Ghost in Uniform, The
1913 sil.
Ref: MPW 15:930.

Ghost Murderer
See: Ginda Jumon (1957).

Ghost of Circle X Camp, The
(Ghosts at Circle X Camp -e.t.?)
1912 American Wild West sil 1140 ft.
Ref: Bios 14 Nov '12; MPW 12:1226.

Ghost of Crossbone Canyon
1953 Newhall (AA) 56 mins.
Ref: MFB '52 p 178; MPH 4 April '53.

Ghost of Hidden Valley
1947
Ref: HR 25 April '47.

Ghost of Indian Springs
See: Ghost Guns (1944).

Ghost of Monk's Island, The
1966 British, Countrywide/Chil-
dren's Film Foundation 7 parts
106 mins total.
Ref: MFB Jan '68 p9.

Ghost of Rosy Taylor
1918 Mutual sil.
Ref: MPW 37:248; Early Am Cin
p84.

Ghost of Sulphur Mountain, The
1912 Méliès sil.
Ref: MPW 12:66.

Ghost of the Hacienda
1913 sil.
Ref: F/A p395; MPW 17:1154.

Ghost of the Manor, The
(story by M. Grant)
See: Shadow Strikes, The (1937).

Ghost of the Oven
1910 Selig sil.
Ref: MPW 7:1007.

Ghost of the Rocks, The
See: Papa Gaspard (1909).

Ghost of the Vaults, The
1911 Great Northern sil.
Ref: MPW 8:1463; Bios 16 Feb '11.

Ghost of the White Lady
1914 Great Northern sil.
Ref: MPW 19:471-72.

Ghost Patrol, The
1922 (1923) U sil 5 reels.
Ref: AFI F2.2064 p288; MPN
27:472.
Based on the short story by Sinclair
Lewis.

Ghost Rider
1943 Mono 6 reels.

Ghost Riders of the West
See: Phantom Rider, The (1945-46).

Ghost That Never Returns, The
(Prividenie, Kotoroe ne voz
Vrachtchaetsia)
1929 Soviet, Sovkino sil.
Ref: Collier.
Based on "Le Rendez-vous Qui n'a
pas eu Lieu" by Henri Barbusse.

Ghost That Walks Alone
1944 Col.
Ref: Acad.
Based on "The Wedding Guest Sat
on a Stone" by R. Shattuck.

Ghost Town
1955 UA.
Ref: FD 23 Dec '55; MPA 26 March
'56.

Ghost Town, The
See: Pueblo Fantasma, El (1964?).

Ghost Train, The
1903 Biograph sil.
Ref: Niver.

Ghost Train, The
1927 (1928) British sil.
Ref: Halliwell p308; Brit Cin.

1931 British.
Ref: MPH 25 Feb '33 p40-41.

1941 British.
Ref: MFB March '41 p27.

Based on the play by Arnold
Ripley.
See also: Oh, Mr. Porter!
(1938).

Ghost Valley
1932 RKO 61 mins.
Ref: Vw 30 Aug '32; FDY.

Ghost Valley Raiders
1940 Rep 6 reels.
Ref: Willis.

Ghosts
1912 Essanay sil.
Ref: MPW 13:1300, 14:53.

Ghosts, The
1914 sil.
Ref: MPW 19:1414.

Ghosts
● 1914 British sil 1125 ft.
Ref: Hist/Brit p281; Bloch.

● 1915 Majestic (Mutual) sil
5 reels.
Ref: F/A p291; MPW 24:1439-40,
1477, 1510; Bloch.

Based on the play by Henrik
Ibsen.
See also: Gespenster (1939).

Ghosts and Flypaper
1915 Vit sil 900 ft.
Ref: Willis.

Ghosts at Circle X Camp
See: Ghost of Circle X Camp, The
(1912).

Ghunghat
See: Veil, The (n.d.).

Giant of Marathon, The
1959 (1960) Italian, Titanus-
Galatea (MGM) color 90 mins.
Dir: Jacques Tourneur.
Ref: FF '60 p 108.

Giant of the Evil Island
1964 Italian color.
Ref: Willis.

Giant Sloth, The
n.d.
Ref: Ackerman.
Announced, never made.

Giants of Rome, The
See: Gigante di Roma, I
(1964).

Gift of Gab
1934 U 70 mins.
Dir: Karl Freund.
Cast includes: Boris Karloff,
Bela Lugosi.
Ref: Acad; Ackerman.

Gift of the Fairies
1917 sil.
Ref: MPW 32:1174.

Gigante di Roma, I
(The Giants of Roma)
1964 Italian/French.
Ref: Ital Prods '64 p 118-19.

Ginda Jumon
(Ghost Murderer)
1957 Japanese, Shochiku.
Ref: FEFN 27 Sept '57.

Girl from Frisco, The
See: Treasure of Cibola, The
(1916).

Girl of the Sea
1920 Williamson sil.
Ref: MPN 20:3384; MPW 43:
2173.

Girl on the Bridge, The
1951 20th-Fox.
Ref: Vd 6 Dec '51.

Girl Who Knew Too Much, The
See: Evil Eye, The (1962).

Girl with the Skin of the Moon, The
See: Ragazza dalla Pelle di Luna, La
(1972).

Gladiatore Invincible, Il
See: Invincible Gladiator, The
(1961).

Gladiators Seven
1964 Italian/Spanish, Film Columbia/
Atenea (MGM) color scope 92 mins.
Ref: FF '64 p 109.

Glass Ceiling, The
1970 Spanish.
Ref: V 12 May '71; Willis.

Glimpses of the Moon, The
1923 Par sil 6502 ft.
Ref: AFI F2.2123 p297.
Based on the novel by Edith
Wharton.

Glut
1967 USC 16mm 15 mins.
Ref: D. Glut.

Go Get 'Em Hutch
1922 Pathé sil serial 15 parts
31 reels.
Ref: CNW p227-28.

Gobbo, Il
See: Hunchback, The (1960).

God is Dog Spelled Backwards
1967 Amateur (Film-makers' Coop)
16mm color 4 mins.
Ref: FMC 5:222.

Goha
1958 French/Tunisian color.
Ref: MFB May '59 p55.
Based on "The Diary of Goha the
Simple" by A. Ades & A. Josipovici.

Gold
1932 Majestic.
Ref: FD 5 Oct '32.

Golden Apples of the Sun
1971 Canadian.
Ref: Vw 9 June '71.

Golden Coach, The
(Le Carrose d'Or)
1954 French color.

Golden Fleece, The
1918 Triangle sil.
Ref: MPW 37:725.

Golden Fleecing, The
(play by L. Semple Jr.)
See: Honeymoon Machine, The (1961).

Golden Hands of Kurigal, The
See: Federal Agents vs. Crime, Inc.
(1948).

Golden Salamander
1951.

Golden Web, The
1926 Gotham (Lumas) sil 6224 ft.
Cast includes: Boris Karloff.
Ref: AFI F2.2178 p304-05.

Goldsnake "Anonima Killers"
1966 Italian/French.
Ref: Ital Prods '66 I p26.

Goldwyn Follies
1938 UA.
Ref: Bloch.

Golia alla Conquista di Bagdad
(Goliath at the Conquest of Bagdad)
1964 Italian, Romano color.
Ref: Ital Prods '64 p 184-85.

Golia e il Cavaliere Mascherato
See: Hercules and the Masked Rider
(1963).

Goliath and the Barbarians
(Il Terrore dei Barbari: The Terror
of the Barbarians)
1959 Italian, Standard (AIP) color
85 mins.
Ref: Unitalia '59 p 104-05; Acad.

Goliath and the Rebel Slave Girl
See: Goliath e la Schiava Ribelle
(1963).

Goliath at the Conquest of Bagdad
See: Golia alla Conquista di Bagdad
(1964).

Goliath e la Schiava Ribelle
(Goliath and the Rebel Slave Girl;
Arrow of the Avenger --Brit.t.)
1963 Italian/French, FIA/Georges
de Beauregard & Gladiator color
scope 86 mins.
Ref: MFB July '66 p 109; Unitalia
'63 p42-43.

Gone to the Dogs
1939 Australian.
Ref: Collier.

Good Fairy, The
1935 U.
Ref: MPW 9 Feb '35; F/A p291.
Based on a play by Ferenc Molnar.

Good Luck of a Souse, The
(Il y A un Dieu pour les Ivrognes)
1908 French sil 575 ft (445 ft).
Ref: MPW 2:102.

Goose Girl, The
1911 Thanhouser sil.
Ref: MPW 9:998, 1000, 10:131;
F/A p461.

Goose Girl, The
1915 Par sil.
Ref: MPN 6 Feb '15 p44; FIR Dec
'53 p554; Bloch.

Goose Woman, The
1925 U sil 7500 ft.
Ref: AFI F2.2198 p307-08; F/A
p407.
Based on the story by Rex Beach.

Gordian Knot, The
1911 Essanay sil.
Ref: MPW 9:391.

Gordon of Ghost City
1933 U serial 12 parts 24 reels.
Ref: Willis; LC.

Gorilla Girl
1956 ARC.
Ref: B. Warren.
Announced, never made.

Gorilla Man, The
1942 WB.
Ref: Vd 8 Dec '42.

Gorilla Salutes You, The
See: Gorille Vous Salue Bien, Le
(1957).

Gorilla Ship
1932 Mayfair.
Ref: FD 20 July '32.

Gorille a Mordu l'Archevêque, Le
(The Bite of the Gorilla --Brit.t.)
1962 French, Progefi 90 mins.
Ref: MFB March '66 p43.

Gorille Vous Salue Bien, Le
(The Gorilla Salutes You)
1957 French, Raoul Ploquin - S.N.
Pathé scope.
Ref: UniF 20.

Government Agents vs. the Phantom Legion
1951 Rep serial 12 parts 24 reels.
Ref: D. Glut.

Governor's Ghost, The
1914 Ramo sil sh.
Ref: MPW 19:1076; LC.

Gran Calavera, El
(The Great Madcap)
1949 Mexican, Ultramar 90 mins.
Dir: Luis Buñuel.
Ref: Aventura p420; Durgnat/Buñuel
p59; Kyrou/Buñuel p48.

Gran Golpe de Niza, El
> (Grande Colpo dei 7 Uomini d'Oro:
> Great Coup of the 7 Golden Men; Seven
> Golden Men Strike Again -ad.t.)
> 1966   Italian/Spanish.
> Ref: SpCin '68 p248-49; Ital Prods
> '66 I p40.

Grande Colpo dei 7 Uomini d'Oro
> See: Gran Golpe de Niza, El (1966).

Grande Dia, Un
> See: Miracle of the White Suit
> (1957).

Grape Dealer's Daughter, The
> 1970?   Amateur (Film-Makers' Coop)
> 16mm   color   90 mins.
> Ref: MFB Nov '72 p232-33; FMC 5:138.

Gray Ghost, The
> 1917   U   sil   serial.
> Ref: CNW p55, 176-77; LC.

Gray Wolf's Ghost, The
> 1919   R-C   sil.
> Ref: Willis.

Great Adventure, The
> (novel by A. Bennett)
> See: His Double Life (1933).

Great Blow to Her Majesty's Service
> n.d.   Spanish/Italian.
> Ref: Willis.

Great Coup of the Seven Golden Men
> See: Gran Golpe de Niza, El (1966).

Great Day, A
> See: Miracle of the White Suit
> (1957).

Great Dictator, The
> 1940   UA.
> Ref: Bloch; Collier; Scognamillo.

Great Green Og, The
> See: Naked World (n.d.).

Great Impersonation, The
> ● 1921   Famous Players-Lasky (Par)
> sil   6658 ft.
> Ref: AFI F2.2226 p312.

> ● 1942   U   8 reels.
> Ref: Willis.

>> Based on the novel by E. Phillips
>> Oppenheim.

Great Madcap, The
> See: Gran Calavera, El (1949).

Great Spy Chase, The
> (Les Barbouzes: The Private Eyes)
> 1964   (1966)   French (AIP)   84 mins.
> Ref: FF '66 p304-05.

Greater Love, The
> See: Weakness of Man, The (1916).

Green Goddess, The
> ● 1923   Distinctive (Goldwyn-Cosmo-
> politan)   sil   10 reels (8 reels).
> Ref: AFI F2.2249 p315; Bloch.

> ● 1930   WB   7 reels.
> Ref: AFI F2.2250 p315; Bloch.

>> Based on the play by William
>> Archer.

Green Hell
> 1939   U   10 reels.
> Dir: James Whale.
> Cin: Karl Freund.
> Ref: FIR May '62 p284; MPH 20
> Jan '40 p44.

Green-Eyed Monster, The
> 1912   Edison   sil   sh.
> Ref: EK 1 Oct '12.

Greene Murder Case, The
> 1929   Par   68 mins.
> Ref: AFI F2.2254 p316; Vw 14
> Aug '29.
> Based on the novel by S.S. Van Dine.

Grey Vulture, The
> 1926   Davis Distributing   sil
> 5 reels.
> Ref: AFI F2.2257 p316.

Grim Game, The
> 1919   Par   sil.
> Ref: MPN 20:2293.

Grinning Skull, The
> 1916   Selig   sil   3 reels.
> Ref: MPW 27:1498; LC.

Grounds for Marriage
> 1950   (1951)   MGM   91 mins.
> Ref: LAT 13 Jan '51; Los
> Angeles Examiner 13 Jan '51.

Groundstar Conspiracy, The
> (The Plastic Man --s.t.)
> 1971   (1972)   Hal Roach Int'l & U
> (U)   color   95 mins.
> Ref: Vw 10 May '72; Ackerman.

>> Based on novel "The Alien" by L.P.
>> Davies.

Guest in the House
> 1944   Hunt Stromberg (UA)   117 mins.
> Ref: Willis.
> Based on the play by Hagar Wilde &
> Dale Eunson.

Gypsy Blood
> 1918   (1921)   German, Asil (FN).
> Based on the opera "Carmen" by Georges
> Bizet from the novel by Prosper
> Mérimée.

H₂O
> 1929   sil.
> Ref: USA Exp List.

Habit Ne Fait Pas le Moine, L'
> See: Fake Diamond Swindler, A
> (1908).

Hagbard and Signe
> 1969?   Swedish/Danish/Icelandic.
> Ref: Collier.

Half Angel
> 1951   20th-Fox.
> Ref: Vd 9 April '51.

Half-Way to Heaven
> 1929   Par Famous Players Lasky
> 8 reels (sound; sil: 5179 ft).
> Ref: AFI F2.2298 p321-22; FD
> 8 Dec '29.
> Based on novel "Here Comes the
> Bandwagon" by Henry Leyford Gates.

Halloween
> 1905   Biograph   sil   sh.
> Ref: Niver p41; LC.

Halloween Night at the Seminary
> 1904   Edison   sil.
> Ref: Niver p41; LC.

Hamlet
> 1918   sil.
> Ref: Shake/Sil p253, 368.
> Based on the play by William
> Shakespeare.
> Does not exist.

Hampelmann, Der
> (The Puppet)
> 1931   German   67 mins.
> Ref: 13 Sept '31,

Handle with Care
> (1972)   Italian/Spanish?   (HK).
> Ref: BO 20 March '72.

Handsome Monster, A
> See: Beau Monstre, Un (1970).

Hanged Man, The
> 1964   U (NBC-TV)   color   110 mins.
> Ref: CoF 10:40.
> Based on novel "Ride the Pink Horse"
> by Dorothy B. Hughes.

Hangman of Venice, The
> See: Boia de Venezia, Il (1962).

Hard Boiled Mahoney
> 1947   Mono   63 mins.
> Ref: Acad.

Harriet and the Piper
> 1920   Anita Stewart Prods (FN)   sil
> 6 reels.
> Ref: MPN 22:3449.
> Based on the novel by Kathleen Norris.

Haunted
> 1916   E&R Jungle Film Co   sil.
> Ref: MPW 28:1946; MPN 13:2552.

Haunted Attic, The
> 1915   Lubin   sil.
> Ref: MPW 24:446.

Haunted Bachelor, The
> 1912   sil.
> Ref: MPW 13:1008.

Haunted Bell, The
> 1916   Imp (U)   sil   2 reels.
> Ref: MPW 28:648, 679-80.
> Based on a story by Jacques
> Futrelle.

Haunted Bride
> 1914   Rex   sil   935 ft.
> Ref: Bios 12 Feb '14 p xiv.

Haunted Castle, The
> 1909   French, Pathé   sil.
> Ref: MPW 5:760.

Haunted Castle, The
> See: Just William's Luck (1948).

Haunted Hat, The
> 1909   Lubin   sil.
> Ref: MPW 5:321.

Haunted Hearts
> 1915   U (Gold Seal)   sil   2 reels.
> Ref: MPN 27 Feb '15 p55.

Haunted Honeymoon, A
> (Billy Gets Married -e.t.?)
> 1925   Hal Roach (Pathé)   sil   sh.
> Ref: MPN 31:923.

Haunted Honeymoon
> (Busman's Holiday -Brit.t.?)
> 1940   British, MGM   9 reels.
> Ref: Willis.
> Based on play by Dorothy L.
> Sayers and Muriel St. Clare
> Byrne from novel "Busman's
> Holiday" by D. L. Sayers.

Haunted House, The
> 1911   Gaum   sil   780 ft.
> Ref: Bios 28 Sept '11; Willis.

Haunted House, The
> 1911   IMP   sil.
> Ref: MPW 9:548.

Haunted House, The
> 1913   (1914)   American Co.   sil
> 925 ft.
> Ref: Bios 1 Jan '14 p iii.

Haunted House, The
> 1913   Kalem   sil.
> Ref: BFI cat p 198; MPW 16:
> 403.

Haunted House, The
> 1917   Triangle   sil.
> Ref: WID's 20 Sept '17.

Haunted House, The
> 1921   Metro   sil   2 reels.
> Ref: MPN 24:416; B. Warren.

Haunted House
> (The Blake Murder Mystery -
> Brit.t.)
> 1940   Mono.
> Ref: Vd 17 July '40; MPH
> 20 July '40.

Haunted House, The
> See: Just William's Luck (1948).

Haunted House of Wild Island
> 1915   sil.
> Ref: MPW 24:616.

Haunted Lady, The
> (story by A.R. St. John)
> See: Scandal (1929).

Haunted Light, The
> (by. E.P.J. Byford)
> See: Phantom Light (1935).

Haunted Lounge
> 1908   Essanay   sil.
> Ref: FI 9 Jan '09 p6.

Haunted Manor, The
> 1916   Gaum   sil.
> Ref: MPW 27:2080.

Haunted Mine, The
> 1946   Mono   6 reels.
> Ref: HR & V 29 March '46.

Haunted Ranch
> 1943   Range Busters Inc.   6 reels.
> Ref: HR 18 May '43; LC.

Haunted Ranch, The
  See: Haunted Range, The (1926).

Haunted Range
  1912 sil.
  Ref: Bios 13 June '12; Willis.

Haunted Range, The
  (The Haunted Ranch --ad.t.)
  1926 Davis sil 5 reels.
  Ref: AFI F2.2334 p327.

Haunted Rocker, The
  1912 Vit sil.
  Ref: MPW 11:1094.

Haunted Samurai, The
  (The Hunted Samurai --ad.t.)
  1970 (1971) Japanese, Toho
  color scope 87 mins.
  Ref: Vw 2 July '71; LAT 10 July
  '71.

Haunted Ship, The
  1927 Tiffany-Stahl sil
  4752 ft.
  Ref: AFI F2.2335 p327; MPN
  37:3803.

Haunted Well
  1910 British? sil.
  Ref: Bios 15 Sept '10; Willis.

Haunting Fear
  1915 sil.
  Ref: Photo Aug '15 p 138.

Haunting Shadows
  1920 sil.
  Ref: MPW 43:632.
  Based on novel "House of a
  Thousand Candles" by Meredith
  Nicholson.
  See also: House of a Thousand
  Candles, The (1915).

Having a Wild Weekend
  (Catch Us if You Can --Brit.t.)
  1965 British, Bruton Film Prods (WB)
  91 mins.
  Ref: FDY '66; MFB '65 p 118.

Hawk Island
  (play by H. Young)
  See: Midnight Mystery (1930).

Hawk of the Hills
  1927 Pathé sil serial 10 parts
  20 reels.
  Ref: MPN 41:11:83.

He Did Not Die
  1910 British? sil.
  Ref: Bios 28 April '10; Willis.

He Lived to Kill
  n.d.
  Cast: Bela Lugosi.
  Ref: FIR Oct '64 p513.
  Does not exist.

He Who Gets Slapped
  1924 MGM sil 6953 ft.
  Cast includes: Lon Chaney.
  Ref: AFI F2.2341;
  Bloch; MPN 30:2517.
  Based on play "He, the One Who
  Gets Slapped" by Leonid Andreyev.

Head Hunters
  See: Cazadores de Cabezas (n.d.).

Hearts and Flowers
  1915 Majestic (Mutual) sil.
  Ref: MPN 4 Sept '15 p70.

Heavens Above
  1963 British, Charter 118 mins.
  Ref: MFB July '63 p95.

Heels Go to Hell
  1955 French.
  Ref: Scognamillo.

Heinze's Resurrection
  1913 sil.
  Ref: MPW 15:890.

Hell, Heaven, or Hoboken
  1959 British.
  Ref: MPH 10 Oct '59.

Hellfire Club, The
  1960 British, New World color
  93 mins.
  Cast includes: Peter Cushing.
  Ref: MFB April '61 p48; CoF 2:47.

Hello Elephant
  (Buongiorno, Elefante!)
  1951 Italian.
  Ref: MFB Feb '53 p22; Scognamillo.

Hell's Bloody Devils
  1970.
  Ref: B. Warren.

Hell's Cargo
  See: Below the Sea (1933).

Her Heart in Her Throat
  (novel by E.L. White)
  See: Unseen, The (1944).

Her Highness and the Bellboy
  1945 MGM 11 reels.
  Ref: LC.

Hercule
  n.d. French
  Cast includes: Fernandel.

Hercules and the Black Pirate
  (Sansone contro il Corsaro Nero:
  Samson vs. the Black Pirate)
  1962 (1967) Italian, Romana
  (AIP-TV) color.
  Ref: Unitalia '63 II p78; MTVM
  July '67 p47.

Hercules and the Masked Rider
  (Golia e il Cavaliere Mascherato)
  1963 (1967) Italian, Romania (Romana?)
  (AIP-TV) color 85 mins.
  Ref: MFB July '65 p 110; MTVM July
  '67 p47.

Hercules and the Princess of Troy
  1966.
  Cast: Gordon Scott.
  Ref: FM 38:66-69.
  Pilot for TV series, not treated
  as feature.

Here Comes Mr. Jordan
  1970? W7.
  Dir: Francis Ford Coppola.
  Cast: Bill Cosby.
  Ref: Vd 27 Nov '68.
  Announced, never made.

Here Comes the Bandwagon
  (novel by H.L. Gates)
  See: Half-Way to Heaven (1929).

Heroes of the Wild
  1927 Mascot sil serial 10 parts.
  Ref: CNW p259.

Hets
  See: Torment (1944).

Hiawatha
● 1913 Colonia sil 4 reels.
  Ref: MPW 15:980; LC.

● 1952 AA.
  Ref: MPH 20 Dec '52.

● 195? WD (BV).
  Exists?
    Based on the poem by Henry
    Wadsworth Longfellow.

High
  1968 Canadian.
  Ref: Vw 10 July '68.

High Season for Spies
  n.d.
  Ref: Willis.

High Spirits
  1927 Cameo-Educational sil.
  Ref: FD 20 Feb '27.

Hills of Donegal, The
  1947 British, Argyle 75 mins.
  Ref: MFB '47 p27; CoF 10:42.

Hindoo Charm, The
  1913 Vit sil 1 reel.
  Ref: BFI cat p 198; FIR Aug-
  Sept '61 p 423.

Hiroshima, Mon Amour
  1959 (1960) French/Japanese,
  Argos & Pathé/Daiei (Zenith Int'l)
  88 mins.
  Ref: FF '60 p 109-11.

His Double Life
  1933 Eddie Dowling Pictures Corp
  8 reels.
  Based on novel "Buried Alive" and
  play "The Great Adventure" by
  Arnold Bennett.

His Great Uncle's Spirit
  1912 Thanhouser sil.
  Ref: MPW 11:804.

Hole in the Wall, The
  1921 Metro sil 6100 ft.
  Ref: AFI F2.2548 p358.

Hole in the Wall, The
  1929 Par 5850 ft.
  Ref: AFI F2.2549 p358.

Hollywood Blue
  1970 Blue Lite 90 mins.
  Ref: HR 24 Nov '70.

Holt of the Secret Service
  1941 Col serial.
  Ref: Collier; D. Glut.

Holy City, The
  1912 Eclair sil.
  Ref:

Homme de Nulle Part, L'
  (The Man from Nowhere)
  1936 French.
  Ref: P.J. Dyer.
  Based on "Il Fu Mattia Pascal"
  by Luigi Pirandello.
  See also: Feu Mathias Pascal
  (1925); Late Mattia Pascal, The
  (1937).

Homme d'Istanbul, L'
  See: That Man in Istanbul (1965).

Honeymoon Machine, The
  1961 Avon (MGM) color scope
  88 mins.
  Ref: FF '61 p219-21.
  Based on play "The Golden Fleecing"
  by Lorenzo Semple Jr.

Honeymoon of Horror
  (Orgy of Golden Nudes --e.t.)
  1970? Flamingo Prod (Manson) color
  84 mins (76 mins).
  Ref: PB.

Hooded Terror, The
  (Sexton Blake and the Hooded
  Terror --Brit.t.?)
  1943 British, Eros.
  Cast includes: Tod Slaughter.
  Ref: B. Warren.

Hoodoo Alarm Clock
  1910 IMP sil.
  Ref: MPW 7:317.

Horla, The
  1957 Par VV.
  Ref: Par flyer 15 Jan '57.
  Based on the story by Guy
  de Maupassant.
  Announced, never made.
  See also: Madman, The (1962).

Hospital, The
  1971 Howard Gottfried--Paddy
  Chayefsky & Arthur Hiller (UA)
  color 103 mins.
  Ref: FF '71 p441-45; B. Warren.

Hot Ice
  1952 British, Apex & Present
  Day.
  Ref: Willis.
  Based on "A Weekend at Thrackley"
  by Alan Melville.

Hot Money
  1936 WB 7 reels.
  Ref: Acad; LC.

Hot Water
  1924 Harold Lloyd Corp (Pathé)
  sil.
  Ref: AFI F2.2596 p365.

Hôtel des Voyageurs de Commerce, L'
  See: Road Side Inn, A (1906).

Houdini
  1953 Par color 106 mins.
  Prod: George Pal.
  Ref: HR 18 May '53; MFB Dec '53
  p 177.
  Based on book by Harold Kellock.

Hour of 13
  1952 MGM.
  Ref: MPH 4 Oct '52.

House of a Thousand Candles, The
● 1915 Selig sil 5 reels.
  Ref: MPW; RAF p270.

● 1936 Rep.
  Ref: HR 27 Feb '36; MPH 7 March
  '36 p50-51.
    Based on the novel by Meredith
    Nicholson.
    See also: Haunting Shadows (1920).

House of Death
  1932 Soviet (Amkino).
  Ref: FD 13 Aug '32.

House of Fear
  1915 Pathé sil.
  Ref: MPN 11 Dec '15 p92-93;
  MPW 26:1845.

House of Fear
  1945 U.
  Cast includes: Basil Rathbone.
  Ref: B. Warren.
  Based on "The Five Orange Pips"
  by A. Conan Doyle.

House of Menace
  See: Kind Lady (1935).

House of Mystery
  1913 sil.
  Ref: MPW 1913 p843.

House of Mystery, The
  1934 French.
  Ref: Willis.

House of Mystery
  See: Making the Headlines (1938).

House of Secrets
  1956 British 60 mins.
  Ref: V; Acad.

House of Seven Joys, The
  See: Wrecking Crew, The (1968).

House of Terror, The
  1908 Lubin sil.
  Ref: FI IV:18:10.

House of Terror
  1972 (Gamalex) color 90 mins.
  Ref: BO 13 Nov '72 p 17, 22 Jan
  '73.

House that Jack Built
  1911 Lubin sil.
  Ref: MPW 10:637.

Howling in the Woods, A
 1971? (CBS-TV) color.
 Ref: Photon 21:7.

Hue and Cry
 1946 (1950) British (Fine Arts).
 Ref: FD 12 Dec '50; Vd 5 Feb '51;
 MPH 9 Dec '50.

Human Clay, The
 See: Barro Humano, El (1955).

Hunchback, The
 (Il Gobbo)
 1960 Italian.
 Ref: Unitalia '60 p212-13.

Hunchback of Soho, The
 (Der Bucklige von Soho)
 1966 German, Rialto color 92
 mins.
 Ref: Vw 7 Dec '66.
 Based on several novels by Edgar
 Wallace.

Hungarian Picture Book
 1953 Hungarian color 20 mins.
 Ref: MFB Feb '55 p27.

Hunted Samurai, The
 See: Haunted Samurai, The (1970).

Hunting the Devil
 1907 Italian, Cines sil.
 Ref: MPW 1:622.

Hurricane at Pilgrim Hill
 1949 (1953) Howco 53 mins.
 Ref: Exhibitor 8 April '53 p3498.
 Based on short story "Battle of
 Pilgrim Hill" by James Charles
 Lynch.

Hypnotized
 1932 World Wide.
 Ref: MPH 24 Dec '32 p24.

I

I Am an Elephant, Madame
 1969 German.
 Ref: MTVM Aug '69 p25-A.

I Am Legend
 (novel by R. Matheson)
 See: Je Suis une Legende (n.d.).

I Love a Mystery
 1966 (1973) (NBC-TV) color 100
 mins.
 Ref: B. Warren.

I Want What I Want
 1971? (1970) Marayan (Cinerama)
 color.
 Ref: MPH 13 Oct '71; B. Warren.
 Based on the novel by Geoff Brown.

Ice Station Zebra
 1968 MGM color Cinerama 152 mins.
 Ref: MFB May '69 p 103.
 Based on the novel by Alistair
 McLean.

Ich Wollt' Ich Ware Frankenstein
 German title of non-fantastic
 Madigan's Millions.

If a Body Meets a Body
 1945 Col 2 reels.
 Cast: The Three Stooges.
 Ref: Maltin/GMS p 135; Pardi.

Il Y a un Dieu pour les Ivrognes
 See: Good Luck of a Souse, The
 (1908).

Ilê aux Chèvres, L'
 (play by U. Betti)
 See: Possédées, Les (1955).

Illusion
 1929 Par Famous Players Lasky
 7536 ft (6972 ft - sound; sil:
 6141 ft)
 Ref: AFI F2.2672 p375; FD 29
 Sept '29.
 Based on the novel by Arthur
 Chesney Train.

Imagine
 1972 British color.
 Ref: MFB Feb '73 p29.

Immortalita
 (Immortality)
 1961 Italian.
 Ref: Vw 17 Sept '69.

Imp, The
 1920 Selznick sil.
 Ref: MPW 43:1120.

Implosion
 n.d. AIP.
 SP: Richard Matheson.
 Ref: Vd 23 Jan '69; R.
 Matheson.
 Based on the novel by D.F. Jones.
 Announced, never made.

In Search of the Castaways
 ● 1914 French, Eclair sil.
 Ref: LC.

 ● 1962 Disney (BV) color 100
 mins. Filmed in England.
 Ref: FF '62 p324-25.

   Based on novel "Les Enfants
   du Capitaine Grant" (The
   Children of Capt. Grant) by
   Jules Verne.
   See also: Captain Grant's
   Children.

In the Days of Witchcraft
 1909 Edison sil sh.
 Ref: Willis.

In the Days of Witchcraft
 1913 Selig sil sh.
 Ref: MPW 16:505, 811.

In the Haunts of Rip Van Winkle
 1906 Biograph sil sh.
 Ref: Niver 51.

In the Next Room
 1930 FN 6336 ft.
 Ref: AFI F2.2698 p379.
 Based on play by E. Robson &
 B.E. Stevenson and novel "The
 Mystery of the Boule Cabinet"
 by B.E. Stevenson.
 See also: Pursuing Vengeance,
 The (1916).

Indian Legend, An
 1911 Bison sil.
 Ref: MPW 9:646.

Indian Tomb
 1938 German.
 Ref: Vw 1 July '59; Acad.

Indische Grabmal, Der
 See: Journey to the Lost City
 (1959).

Indiscretion
 1921 A.J. Bimberg (Pioneer) sil
 6 reels.
 Cast includes: Lionel Atwill.
 Ref: AFI F2.2703 p379.

Inferno
 1953 20th-Fox color 3D 10
 reels.
 Ref: MFB Oct '53 p 143.

Infidel, The
 1922 Preferred Pictures (Associated FN Pictures) sil 5377 ft.
 Cast includes: Boris Karloff.
 Ref: AFI F2.2707 p380.

Innocent Sorcerers
 See: Niewinni Czarodzieje (1960).

Innocent Vampire, An
 1916 sil.
 Ref: MPN 13:3271; Willis.

Insane Demons of Topanga Canyon, The
 n.d.
 Ref: MadMon 9:41.
 Hoax title.

Insect Woman, The
 (Nippon Konchuki: Japanese
 Insect Story)
 1963 (1964) Japanese, Nikkatsu
 (Jerome Balsam Films) 123 mins.
 Ref: FF '64 p347-49.

International Crime, The
 (The Shadow Speaks -s.t.)
 1938 Grand National 65 mins.
 Ref: Vw 18 May '38; MPH 23 April
 '38; FD 20 April '38.
 Based on novel "The Fox Hound"
 by Maxwell Grant.

Invencibles, Los
 (The Invincible Ones)
 1964 Spanish/Italian.
 Ref: SpCin '65 p 140-41.

Invincible Gladiator, The
 (Il Gladiatore Invincible)
 1961 (1963) Italian/Spanish,
 Columbus/Atenea (Seven Arts)
 color scope 96 mins.
 Ref: FF '63 p311; MFB Dec '66
 p 186.

Invincible Sette, Gli
 (The Invincible Seven)
 1963 Italian.
 Ref: Unitalia '63 II p 130-31.

Invisible, The
 1912 French, Eclair sil 905
 ft.
 Ref: MPW 14:910; Bios 8 Aug '12
 p xv.

Invisible Black Hands
 n.d. Japanese.
 Ref: Willis: UniJ 8.

Invisible Enemy
 1938 Rep 66 mins.
 Ref: FDY '39; Acad; LC.

Invisible Informer, The
 1946 Rep.
 Ref: Vd 19 Aug '46

Invisible Menace, The
 (Without Warning -s.t.)
 1937 (1938) WB.
 Cast: Boris Karloff and others.
 Ref: Vw 26 Jan '38; MPH 23 Oct
 '37.

Invisible Power, The
 1921 Goldwyn sil 6613 ft.
 Ref: AFI F2.2727 p383.

Invisible Witness, The
 (The Witness Invisible -alt.t.)
 1914 Luna Film sil.
 Ref: LC; MPN 28 Nov '14 p47.

Invisible Woman, The
 1969 Italian, Clesi Cinemat.
 color.
 Ref: MTVM June '69 p42; Collier.

Ira di Achille, L'
 See: Achilles (1962).

Iron Man, The
 1924 U sil serial 15 parts
 30 reels.
 Ref: LC; CNW p 118, 242.

Iron Man
 ● 1931 U.
 ● 1951 U.
   Ref: FD.

Iron Test, The
 1918 (1919) Vit sil serial.
 Ref: CNW p64, 187-88.

Island of Doomed Men
 1940 Col 67 mins.
 Ref: PB; Acad.

Island of Lost Men
 1939 Par.
 Ref: Vw Aug '39.
 Remake of: White Woman (1933).

Island of Love
 1963 WB color scope 101
 mins.
 Ref: FF '63 p 124-26; Willis.

Island Woman
 1958 Security Pictures (UA)
 72 mins.
 Ref: FF '58 p297.

Istambul 65
 See: That Man in Istanbul (1965).

Italian Straw Hat, The
 (Un Chapeau de Paille d'Italie)
 1927 French, Films Albatros-
 Sequana sil 110 mins.
 Ref: Acad; FTN p646.
 Based on the play by Eugene
 Labiche & Marc Michel.

Itching Palms
 1923 R-C Pictures sil 6 reels.
 Ref: AFI F2.2770 p389-90; LC
 Based on play "When Jerry Comes
 Home" by R. Brian.

It's Hot in Hell
 See: Monkey in Winter (1969).

It's Never too Late to Mend
 1936 British, Reliable.
 Cast: Tod Slaughter and others.
 Ref: B. Warren.

It's Only Money
 1962 Par.
 Ref: V 21 Nov '62.

Ivan's Childhood
 See: My Name Is Ivan (1962).

Jade Casket, The
(Cosmos)
1929 French, Gaum sil 65 mins.
Ref: Vw 26 June '29; FDY '30.

Jaguar
1956 Rep 66 mins.
Ref: MFB March '56 p32; FDY '57.

Jaguar's Claws, The
1917 Par sil.
Ref: WID's 7 June '17.

Jamaica Inn
1939 British, Pommer-Laughton Mayflower (Par) 9 reels.
Dir: Alfred Hitchcock.
Cast: Charles Laughton and others.
Ref: B. Warren; LC.
Based on the novel by Daphne Du Maurier.

Jamaica Run
1953 Clarion (Par) color 92 mins.
Ref: Vd 8 April '53; PB.

Jamming the Blues
1944 WB sh.
Ref: USA Exp List.

Jane Eyre
● 1915 Biograph sil 3 reels.
Ref: MPW 24:1797, 25:670; MPN 31 July '15 p76.

● 1921 Hugo Ballin Prods (W.W. Hodkinson Co) sil 6550 ft.
Ref: AFI F2.2782 p391.

● 1934 Mono 7 reels.
Ref: Vw 20 Feb '35.

● 1970 British, Omnibus/Sagittarius color 110 mins.
Ref: MFB April '71 p75.
Based on the novel by Charlotte Brontë.

Japanese Insect Story
See: Insect Woman, The (1963).

Je Suis une Legende
(I Am a Legend)
n.d. French.
Dir: Claude Chabrol.
Ref: Richardson '68; B. Warren.
Based on novel I Am Legend by Richard Matheson.
Announced; never filmed.

Jean de la Lune
1932 French?
Ref: FD 13 March '32.

Jeannie
1941 British.
Ref: Vw 27 Aug '41.

Jerry Land, Cacciatore di Spie
(Jerry Land, Spy-Hunter)
1966 Italian/W. German/Spanish, PEA/Theumer/Juan De Orduna color scope.
Ref: Ital Prods I:52-53.

Jerusalem in the Time of Christ
1908 Kalem sil.

Jet Jackson, the Flying Commando
1954 Screen Gems 16mm 30 min series.
Ref: LC.
Television series.

Jigsaw
1968 U color.
Ref: LAT 18 Oct '68; Vw 29 May '68.

Jim Hood's Ghost
1926 Mustang sil 2 reels.
Ref: MPW 82:48.

Joan of Arc
See: Passion of Joan of Arc (1928).

Joanna
1968 British, Laughlin Films (20th-Fox) color scope 107 mins.
Ref: B. Warren; FDY '69.

Johnnie
1971.
Ref: BO 12 July '71.
Announced; never made.

Jonah and the Whale
1960.
Prod: Jack. H. Harris.
Ref: Acad.
Announced; never made.

Joseph Greer and His Daughter
(novel by H.K. Webster)
See: What Fools Men (1925).

Journal d'un Fou, Le
See: Diary of a Madman (1963).

Journey
(Undersky -s.t.)
1972 Canadian color.
Ref: B. Warren.

Journey into Hell
WB?
Prod: William Conrad.
Ref: Richardson.
Evidently never made.

Journey of the "Jules Verne," The
1960
Ref: HR 30 Sept '60.
Never made.

Journey to the Lost City
(Condensed version of Der Tiger von Eschnapur and Der Indische Grabmal)
1959 (1960) German (AIP) color (94 mins).
Dir: Fritz Lang.
Ref: FF '60 p287.
Based on novel by Thea von Harbou.

Journey's End
1930 British.
Ref: Vw 16 April '30, 30 April '30.

Judith of Bethulia
1914 Biograph sil 3 reels.
Ref: MPW 20:1608.

Juggernaut
1915 Vit sil.
Ref: MPW 24:870.

Juicio contra un Angel
1964 Spanish/Puerto Rican.
Ref: SpCin '65 p94-95.

Julius Caesar
● 1953 MGM 119 mins.
Ref: LC.

● 1965 British, BBC videotape 80 mins.
Ref: FIR March '73 p 157
Based on the play by William Shakespeare.

Jungle Drums of Africa
1952 (1953) Rep serial 12 parts 24 reels.
Ref: Ser/Rep; Eric Hoffman.

Jungle Goddess
1948 Screen Guild.
Ref: MFB May '51 p265-66; Acad.

Jungle Jim
● 1936-37 U serial 12 parts 24 reels.
Ref: Acad; LC.

● (Jungle Jim's Adventure -s.t.)
1948 Col 73 mins.
Ref: HR 16 Dec '48; MPH 15 Jan '49.
Based on the comic strip by Alex Raymond.

Jungle Jim's Adventure
See: Jungle Jim (1948).

Jungle Man Eaters
1954 Col.
Ref: LC.

Jungle Menace
1937 Col serial 15 parts 31 reels.
Ref: Vw 27 Oct '37; Stringham; LC.

Jungle Siren
1942 PRC 7 reels.
Ref: MFB '43 p 15; HR & Vd 12 Oct '42.

Jungle Woman, The
1926 Stolltturlez sil.

Just Like a Woman
1967 British, Dormar color 89 mins.
Ref: MFB March '67 p45; F&F May '67.

Just William's Luck
(The Haunted Castle; The Haunted House -- s.t.s?)
1948 British.
Dir: Val Guest.
Ref: FD 14 Dec '48; Vd 7 Dec '48.

K
(novel by M.R. Rinehart)
See: K — The Unknown (1924).

K — The Unknown
1924 U sil 8146 ft.
Ref: AFI F2.2910 p411; Willis.
Based on novel "K" by Mary Roberts Rinehart.

Kagi
(novel by J. Tanizaki)
See: Odd Obsession (1960).

Kala Bhut
See: Black Ghost (1937).

Kali-Yug, la Dea della Vendetta
(Kali-Yug, the Goddess of Revenge)
1962 Italian.
Ref: Unitalia '63 I p76-77.

Karma
1931 (1932) Indian, Himansurai.
Ref: MovPicM Annual '39; March '34 p 39.

Kawaii Akujo
(Lill, My Darling Witch -ad.t.)
1971 Japanese, Shochiku.
Ref: UniJ 55:4.

Kejsarn av Portugallien: en Värmlandsberättelse
(novel by S.O.L. Lagerlöf)
See: Tower of Lies (1925).

Kelly Green
1966 Hanna-Barbera.
Ref: Richardson.
Announced; never made.

Key, The
See: Odd Obsession (1960).

Keys of Heaven, The
n.d.
Ref: Collier.

Kidnapped Stockbroker, The
1915 Vit sil 2 reels.
Ref: MPW 25:1891; MPN 11 Sept '15.

Kill a Dragon
1967 Aubrey Schenck Prods (UA) color 91 mins.
Ref: FF '67 p394-95; MFB '68 p60.

Killdozer!
n.d. Italian, Cineluxor.
Ref: MTVM Oct '66 p16.
Based on the story by Theodore Sturgeon.
Announced; never made.

Killer at Large
1936 Col.
Cast includes: Lon Chaney Jr.
Ref: MPH 22 Aug '36 p33; V 28 Oct '36.

Killer Gorilla
n.d.
Ref: B. Warren.

Killer Leopard
1954 AA 70 mins.
Ref: LC.
Based on characters in the Bomba books created by Roy Rockwood.

Kind Lady
(House of Menace -s.t?)
1935 MGM 76 mins.
Ref: Vw 1 Jan '36; Acad.
Based on "Silver Mask" by Hugh Walpole.

King Arthur Was a Gentleman
   1942 British.
   Ref: Collier.

King Kong, Frankenstein's Son
   Translation of German retitling
   of King Kong Escapes (main list,
   1967).
   Ref: D. Glut; Photon 21:8.

King Must Die, The
   1960 20th Fox scope color.
   Ref: Collier.
   Based on the novel by Mary
   Renault.
   Announced; never made.

King of Atlantis
   n.d.
   Cast: Orson Welles.
   Ref: FanMo 6:41.
   Does not exist.

King of Hearts
   (Le Roi de Coeur)
   1966 (1967) French/Italian,
   Fildebroc (Lopert) color
   scope 102 mins.
   Ref: FF '67 p 181-82; FD 8
   June '67.

King of Jazz, The
   1930 U color 9100 ft.
   Ref: AFI F2.2873 p405.

King of the Damned
   1935 British.
   Ref: Vw 15 Jan '36; FD
   1 Feb '36.

King of the Forest Rangers
   1946 Rep serial 12 parts 24 reels.
   Ref: Stringham; LC.

King of the Texas Rangers
   1941 Rep serial 12 parts
   25 reels.
   Ref: Stringham; D. Glut; LC.

King Solomon's Mines
   1950 MGM color 102 mins.
   Ref: MFB June '51 p204; Vd
   26 Sept '50; FIR Nov '50 p24.
   Based on the novel by H. Rider
   Haggard.

King's Rhapsody
   1955 British.
   Ref: Collier.

Kismet
 • 1919 (1920) French sil.
   Ref: Societe des Films Mercanton;
   MPN 20:3422.

 • 1920 Brenon (Robertson-Cole)
   sil 9 reels (5 reels) .
   Ref: MPN 22:3621, 16:2670;
   Blum p 190.

 • 1930 (1931) FN 90 mins.
   Ref: MPN 42:19:46; FD 2 Nov '30.

 • 1944 MGM color 10 reels.
   Ref: FIR '54 p511, '56 p36,
   '58 p 185; LC.

 • 1955 MGM color scope 113
   mins.
   Ref: LC.
   Based on the musical play by
   Charles Lederer and Luther
   Davis.
      Based on the play by Edward
      Knoblock.

Kiss Doctor, The
   1928 Fox sil 2 reels.
   Ref: MPN 17 March '28 p897;
   LC.
   Based on "The Adventures of
   Van Bibber" by Richard Harding
   Davis.

Kiss Kiss Bang Bang
   1966 Italian/Spanish.
   Ref: SpCin '68 p 104-05; Ital
   Prods '66 p6.

Kiss My Firm But Pliant Lips
   (novel by D. Greenburg)
   See: Live a Little, Love a
   Little (1968).

Kiss of the Vampire
   1915 sil.
   Ref: Photon 19.

Kitty Foyle
   1940 (1941) RKO 108 mins.
   Ref: MFB May '41 p57; LC.

Knickerbocker Holiday
   1944 Producers Corp. of America (UA) 85 mins.
   Ref: Vd & HR 22 Feb '44; LAT
   22 Feb '44, 1 March '44.
   Based on the musical play by
   Maxwell Anderson and Kurt Weill.

Knight of the Cursed Castle
   See: Cavalier in Devil's Castle
   (1959).

Knock on Wood
   1954 Par color 103 mins.
   Ref: MFB May '54.

Kongress Tanzt, Der
   See: Congress Dances (1931).

Kriminal
   1966 Italian/Spanish color.
   Ref: Ital Prods 66 II p66-67.
   Based on the comic strip.

Kunoichi Gesho
   (The Spying Sorceress)
   n.d. Japanese, Toei.
   Ref: UniJ.

Kurotokage
   See: Black Lizard (1968).

L

Lady from Hell, The
   1926 Stuart Paton (Associated
   Exhibitors) sil 5337 ft.
   Ref: AFI F2.2930 p414.

Lady from Nowhere
   1931 British, Chesterfield.
   Ref: Vw 1 Sept '31.

Lady from Nowhere
   1936 Col.
   Ref:

Lady in the Death House
   1944 PRC.
   Cast includes: Lionel Atwill.
   Ref: HR & Vd 17 March '44; MFB
   July '44 p81.

Lancelot and Guinevere
   See: Sword of Lancelot (1963).

Lancer Spy, The
   1937 20th-Fox.
   Cast includes: Peter Lorre.
   Ref: Vw 6 Oct '37; Bloch.
   Based on a novel by Marthe
   McKenna.

Land of Prehistoric Women
   1965 AIP color.
   Ref: FDY '66 p33 ad.
   Announced; never made.

Landru
   1963 French/Italian, Paris/Rome
   (Embassy) color 114 mins.
   Dir: Claude Chabrol.
   Ref: FF '63 p82-84.

Larsan's Last Incarnation
   1914 French, Eclair (Leading
   Players Film Corp) sil.
   Ref: Scognamillo.
   Based on novel "The Perfume
   of the Lady in Black" by
   Gaston Leroux.

Last Days of Pompeii, The
 • 1908 sil.

 • 1913 Italian, Pasquali
   (Pasquali American Co.) sil.
   Ref: LC.

 • 1913 Italian, Societa Anonima
   Ambrosio (The Photo Drama Co)
   1913 sil.
   Ref: LC.

 • 1925 Italian sil.
   Ref: Halliwell.

 • 1935 RKO 10 reels.
   Prod: Merian C. Cooper.
   Dir: Ernest B. Schoedsack.
   SpFX: Willis O'Brien.
   Ref: LC.

 • (Les Dernier Jours de Pompeii)
   1950 French.
   Ref: FF '60 p 178.
   Never shown in the U.S.

 • (Ultimi Giorni di Pompeii)
   1959 (1960) Italian/Spanish,
   Cineproduzioni/Procusa (UA)
   color scope 103 mins.
   Ref: FF '60 p 178.
      Loosely based on the novel
      by Edward Bulwer-Lytton.

Last Frontier
   See: Black Ghost (1932).

Last Leaf, The
   1917 Broadway Star Features
   sil 2 reels.
   Ref: LC.
   Based on the short story by
   O. Henry.
   See also: O'Henry's Full House
   (1952).

Last Man, The
   1916 Vit sil.
   Ref: MPW 30:689.

Last Man, The
   1932 Col.
   Ref: Ackerman.

Last Man on Earth, The
   (Der Letzte Mann)
   1924 German, UFA.
   Ref: Vw 17 Dec '24.

Last Night, The
   1937 Soviet.

Last Night, The
   See: Letzte Nacht, Die (1930).

Last of the Warrens
   1936 Supreme 60 mins.
   Ref: FD 2 July '36; Willis.

Last Paradise, The
   1957 French, Paneuropa/Zenith
   (Aidart) color scope 10 reels.
   Ref: Limbacher/4; LC.
   Sequel to: Lost Continent, The
   (1957).

Last Revolution, The
   n.d.
   Prod: George Pal.
   SP: Rod Serling.
   Ref: Richardson.
   Based on the novel by Lord
   Dunsany.
   Announced; never filmed.

Late Corpse, The
   1952 Adrian Weiss Prods 16mm
   25 mins.
   Ref: LC; Stringham.
   Based on character "Craig
   Kennedy" created by Arthur B.
   Reeve.
   Episode of television series.

Late Mattia Pascal, The
   (L'Homme de Nulle Part)
   1937 Italian.
   Ref: MPH 10 April '37.
   Based on "Il Fu Mattia Pascal"
   by Luigi Pirandello.
   See also: Feu Mathias Pascal
   (1925); Homme de Nulle Part, L'
   (1936).

Latest in Vampires, The
   1916 Victor (U) sil 2 reels.
   Ref: LC; Willis.

Laugh, Clown, Laugh
   1928 MGM sil 7045 ft.
   Cast includes Lon Chaney.
   Ref: AFI F2.2990 p423.

Laughter in Hell
   1932 U.
   Ref: Ackerman; Acad.

Law and Order
 • 1932 U 7 reels.
   Ref: LC.

 • 1940 U 6 reels.
   Ref: LC.

 • 1953 U color 9 reels.
   Ref: HR & Vd 3 April '53; LC.
      Based on the novel by W.R.
      Burnett.

Law and Order
   1943 PRC 6 reels.
   Ref: LC.

Law of Fear, The
   1928 FBO sil.
   Ref: MPN 10 March '28, AFI
   F2.3003 p425.

Law of the Tong
1931 Syndicate.
Ref: FD 20 Dec '31.

Leave It to the Irish
1944 Mono 6 reels.
Ref: Acad.

Legend of Narayama
See: Narayama Bushi-Ko (1958).

Legend of the Poisoned Pool, The
1915 Lubin sil.
Ref: MPH 26:17:11.

Legend of Ursula
n.d.
Ref: Collier.

Légende d'Uylenspiegel, La
(by C. deCoster)
See: Mysterious Picture, The (1949).

Legion of Terror
1936 Col.
Ref: Acad.

Leopard Woman, The
1920 Associated Production sil 6 reels.
Ref: MPN 22:3085.
Based on the story by Stewart Edward White.

Leopardess, The
1923 Famous Players-Lasky (Par) sil 5621 ft.
Ref: AFI F2.3037 p429.

Leopard's Bride
1916 sil.
Ref: FD 20 April '16; MPW 28:514.

Let's Go Native
1930 Par-Publix Corp 9 reels.
Ref: AFI F2.3051 p431.

Let's Kill Uncle
1966 U color 92 mins.
Prod & Dir: William Castle.
Ref: FF '66 p324-26.
Based on the novel by Rohan O'Grady.

Letzte Nacht, Die
(The Last Night)
1930 German.
Ref:

Letzte Mann, Der
See: Last Man on Earth, The (1924).

Liane, Jungle Goddess
(Liane die Weisse Sklavin)
1956 W. German color.
Ref: MFB Nov '60 p 156, April '59 p46; Stringham; Richardson.

Licensed to Kill
See: Second Best Secret Agent in the Whole Wide World, The (1965).

Life and Times of Judge Roy Bean, The
1972 First Artists (National General) color.
Ref: Vw 13 Sept '72 ad; B. Warren.

Life Begins Tomorrow
1951 French.
Ref: Acad.

Life in Hell
See: Vie à l'Envers, La (n.d.).

Life's Crossroads
1928 Excellent Pictures sil 5355 ft.
Ref: AFI F2.3060 p432.

Life's Mockery
(Reform --alt.t.)
1928 Chadwick sil 5700 ft.
Ref: AFI F2.3064 p433.

Light at the Edge of the World, The
1971 U.S./Spanish/Lichtensteinian, Byrna/Jet/Triumfilm (National General) color scope 120 mins.
Ref: Acad; MFB Feb '73 p30.
Based on the novel by Jules Verne.

Lightnin'
● 1925 Fox sil 8 reels.
Ref: AFI F2.3073 p434-35; MPN 31:2905; LC.

● 1930 Fox 8500 ft.
Ref: AFI F2.3074 p435.
Based on the play by Frank Bacon.

Lightning Strikes, The
n.d. Rep serial.
Ref: Collier.
Error: this is title of first chapter of serial Fighting Devil Dogs, The (main list; 1938).

Liliom
1919 sil.
Ref: FIR Nov '70.
Based on the play by Ferenc Molnar.
Not completed.

Lill, My Darling Witch
See: Kawaii Akujo (1971).

Lilya
(Lileya -alt.t.)
n.d. (1961) Soviet color.
Ref: MPH 11 Feb '61.

Limping Man, The
● (Creeping Shadows --s.t?)
1931 British, Powers 53 mins.
Ref: Willis.

● 1936 British, Pathe British 72 mins.
Ref: V 18 Nov '36.
Based on a play by Will Scott.

Lio en el Laboratorio
1967 Spanish.
Ref: SpCin '68 p 102-03.

Lion Man, The
1919-20 U sil serial.
Ref: CNW p68-69.
Based on novel "The Strange Case of Cavendish" by Randall Parrish.

Lion's Bride, The
1913 (1914) German, Bioscop (EcTectic) sil 4 reels.
Ref: MPW 21:122; FIR May '67 p316.

Lion's Claws, The
1918 U sil serial.
Ref: CNW 62-63; Stringham.

Little Bit of Heaven, A
1940 U 10 reels.

Little Boy Blue
1912 Lubin sil.
Ref: MPW 12:398.

Little Clause and Big Claus
1914 Diana Biofilm sil sh.
Ref: LC.
Based on the story by Hans Christian Andersen.

Little Flatt in the Tempel, A
(novel by P. Wynne)
See: Devotion (1931).

Little Girl Next Door, The
1923 Blair Coan Prods sil 5950 ft.
Ref: AFI F2.3114 p441.

Little Mary Sunshine
1916 Balboa (Pathé) sil.
Ref: MPW 27:1846, 1598-99.

Little Match Seller, The
1912 Selig sil.
Ref: MPW 11:510.

Little Meg and the Wonderful Lamp
n.d. sil.
Ref: MPW 1:509.

Little Orphan Annie
1938 Par 6 reels.
Ref: HR 25 Nov '38; Vw 30 Nov '38.
Based on the comic strip by Harold Gray.

Little Orphant Annie
1919 Pioneer sil.
Ref: MPW 39:249; MPN 18:3770.
Based on the poem by James Whitcomb Riley.

Littlest Hobo, The
1958 AA 77 mins.
Ref: Acad; LC.

Live a Little, Love a Little
1968 Douglas Lawrence (MGM) color scope 90 mins.
Ref: FF '68 p512; HR 9 Oct '68.
Based on novel "Kiss My Firm But Pliant Lips" by Dan Greenburg.

Live Corpse, A
1910 Pathé sil.
Ref: MPW 6:56.

Live Ghost, A
1934 Hal Roach 2 reels.
Ref: Collier; B. Warren; LC.

Live Man's Tomb
1912 Italian, Itala sil sh.
Ref: Bios 19 Sept '12.

Living and the Dead, The
n.d. Soviet.
Ref: Collier,

Living Corpse, The
● 1913 Italian, Savoy (Warners) sil.
Ref: MPW 18:50; LC; F/A p294.

● 1915 IMP (U) sil.
Ref: MPW 26:2025.
Possibly never made.

● 1928 (1931) Soviet (Foreign Feature Films) sil.
Ref: FD 18 Jan '31.

● 1940 French? Juno Films.
Ref: MPH 28 Sept '40 p84.
Based on the play by Leo Tolstoy.
See also: Weakness of Man, The (1916).

Living Dead, The
1911 British, Gaum sil sh.
Ref: Bios 28 Sept '11.

Living Doll, The
1913 sil sh.
Ref: MPW 18:1212.

Living Dolls
1909 Pathé sil sh.
Ref: MPW 5:137.

Locked Door, The
1929 Feature Prods (UA) 6844 ft.
Ref: AFI F2.3142 p445; Acad.
Based on novel "The Sign on the Door" by Channing Pollock.

Locket, The
1946 RKO 86 mins.
Ref: HR & V 17 Dec '46; Scognamillo.

London by Night
1937 MGM 7 reels.
Ref: LC; FD 20 July '73; Vw; Acad.

Long Pants
1927 Harry Langdon Corp (FN) sil 5550 ft.
Ref: AFI F2.3177 p449.

Lord Love a Duck
1965 (1966) Charleston Enterprises (UA) 109 mins.
Ref: FF '66 p49-50.
Based on the novel by Al Hine.

Lord Maletroit's Door
1949 Marshall Grant -- Realm TV Prods 15mm 2 reels.
Ref: LC.
Based on story "The Sire de Maletroit's Door" by Robert Louis Stevenson.

Lord of the Jungle
1955 AA 69 mins.
Ref: LC.
Based on the character "Bomba" created by Roy Rockwood.

Lost City, The
1920 WB sil serial 15 parts 31 reels.
Ref: MPW 43:775; Acad; LC.

Lost Continent, The
1957 Italian (Lopert) color scope 64 mins.
Ref: FD 22 March '57.
Sequel: Last Paradise, The (1957).

Lost Eden
1966 MGM color.
Prod: George Pal.
Ref: FD 3 May '66.
Based on the novel by Paul McGinnis.
Announced; never made.

Lost in the Stratosphere
(Stratosphere --s.t.)
1934 Mono 7 reels.
Ref: MPH 27 Oct '34 p44; Acad; LC.

Lost Paradise, The
n.d. sil.
Ref: MPW 21:1495.
Based on play "Der Verlorene Paradies" by Ludwig Fulda.

Lost Patrol, The
1934 RKO 8 reels.
Cast includes: Boris Karloff.
Ref: Vw 3 April '34; Bloch; LC.

Lost Special, The
1932-33 U serial 12 parts 24 reels.
Ref: Stringham; FDY '58 p294.

Lost Volcano, The
1950 Mono 75 mins.
Ref: Acad; LC.
Based on the character "Bomba" created by Roy Rockwood.

Lotta Coin's Ghost
n.d. sil.
Ref: MPW 24:439.

Loup Garou, Le
(The Werewolf)
1932 German.
Ref: F/A p411; FIR Oct'61 p492.
Based on novel "Der Schwarze Mann" (The Wolf-Man; The Were-wolf) by Alfred Machard.

Louves, Les
See: Demoniaque (1957).

Love and the Devil
1929 FN sil w/sound FX & mus 6588 ft.
Ref: AFI F2.3212 p455; FD 23 June '29.

Love Charm, The
1921 Realart (Par) sil 4540 ft.
Ref: AFI F2.3216 p455.

Love from a Stranger
1947 Eagle Lion 81 mins.
Ref: MFB July '48 p97.
MPH 13 Feb '37 p60.
Based on the play by Frank
Vosper from a story by Agatha
Christie.

Love in a Wood
1916 British, London sil.
Ref: LC.
Based on play "As You Like It"
by William Shakespeare.

Love in Four Dimensions
See: Amore in Quattro Dimensione
(1963).

Love in Times Gone By
(Amore di Altri Tempi)
n.d. Italian.

Love-Ins, The
1967 Four Leaf (Col) color
91 mins.
Prod: Sam Katzman.
Ref: FF '67 p264-66.

Love Life of a Gorilla
1937 Jewel Prods 80 mins.
Ref: LC; Ficara; MPH 6 Nov '37
p39.

Love of Jeanne Ney, The
1927 German sil.
Ref: MMA p22; C to H.

Lover's Hazing, A
(Mariage de Raison et Mariage
d'Amour)
1908 French sil 572 ft (468 ft).
Prod: Georges Méliès.
Ref: Sadoul; Views '08 107:13.

Loves of Carmen, The
1948 Col color 98 mins.
Ref: LC.
Based on opera "Carmen" by Georges
Bizet from the novel by Prosper
Mérimée.
See also: Carmen.

Loves of Edgar Allan Poe, The
1942 20th-Fox 67 mins.
Ref: MFB Dec '42 p 158; Vd &
HR 8 July '42.

Loves of Ondine, The
1967 (1968) Warhol (Factory)
16mm color 86 mins.
Made by: Andy Warhol.
Ref: FF '68 p380.

Loving
n.d. Amateur, Brakhage 16mm.
Ref: FQ Spring '59 p53.

Lucky Star
1929 Fox sil & sound versions
8784 ft (8725 ft).
Ref: AFI F2.3298 p467; FD 28 July
'29.
Based on the short story "Three
Episodes in the Life of Timothy
Osborn" by Tristram Tupper.

Lucky Stiff, The
1949 Amusement Enterprises
(UA) 99 mins.
Ref: LC.
Based on the novel by Craig
Rice.

Lucretia Borgia
1922 German sil.
Ref: FD 6 Jan '29; Bloch;
MPH 23 Oct '37 p56.

Lucretia Borgia
(Lucrece Borgia)
1952 French/Italian, Films
Ariane & Filmsonor/Rizzoli
91 mins.
Ref: MFB May '55 p75.

M

MGM's Big Parade of Comedy
1964 Robert Youngson (MGM)
91 mins.
Ref: FF '64 p360-61.

M.M.M. 83
1965 Italian.
Ref: Soren.

Macabro
(Tabu II)
1966 (1967) Italian, Royal
(Trans America [AIP]) color
87 mins.
Ref: FF '67 p78.

Macbeth
● 1945 British sh.
Ref: Contemp p61.
Based on some scenes from
the play by William Shakespeare.

● n.d. French.
Ref: S&S Spring '57 p 186.
Stage play only.

Based on the play by William
Shakespeare.

Maciste
1918 Italian serial.
Ref: MPW 37:1283.

Macumba
1956 Favorite Films.
Ref: Collier.

Mad Wednesday
(The Sin of Harold Diddlebock
--alt.t,)
1947 UA 8 reels.
Ref: FIR Aug-Sept '62 p418, 422;
B. Warren.

Madam Satan
1913 Exclusive Supply Corp.
sil 3 reels.
Ref: MPW 18:1480.

Madam Satan
1930 MGM 10320 ft.
Ref: AFI F2.3325 p471; B. Warren.

Madame X
● 1920 Goldwyn sil 7 reels.
Ref: LC.

● 1929 MGM 8806 ft.
Ref: AFI F2.3328 p471-72.

● 1937 MGM 8 reels.
Ref: MPH 2 Oct '37 p36.

● 1966 Ross Hunter-Eltee-
Universal (U) color 99 mins.
Ref: FF '66 p 102-04.

Based on the play by
Alexandre Bisson.

Madman, The
1962 Canadian.
Ref: Collier.
Based on short story "The Horla"
by Guy De Maupassant.
Television series.

Madman's Holiday
(story by F. Brown)
See: Crack-Up (1946).

Madwoman of Chaillot, The
1969 (1970) British, Commonwealth
United (WB?) color scope 142 mins.
Ref: MFB Nov '69 p233.
Based on the play by Jean Giraudoux.

Magic Bag, The
1908 Danish? Nordisk sil.
Ref MPW 2:243.

Magic Bow, The
1947 British, Gainsborough (U)
105 mins.
Ref: LC.
Based on the novel by Manuel
Komroff on the life of Nicolo
Paganini.

Magic Carpet
1972 U (NBC-TV) color
"120 mins."
Ref: TVG; B. Warren.

Magic Cup, The
1921 Realart sil 4587 ft.
Ref: AFI F2.3339 p473; MPW
50:86.

Magic Fire
1956 Rep color 112 mins.
Is this British?
Ref: Acad.
Based on the novel by Bertita
Harding on the life of Richard
Wagner.

Magic Flame, The
1927 UA sil 8308 ft.
Ref: F2.3340 p473; Acad;
MPW 87:249.

Magic Garden
1927 Gene Stratton Porter Prods
(FBO) sil 6807 ft.
Ref: AFI F2.3341 p474.
Based on the novel by Gene Stratton
Porter.

Magic Night
1932 British, British & Dominions
(UA) 9 reels.
Ref: Vw & FD 3 Nov '32; Acad.

Magic Shoes, The
1913 Selig sil.
Ref: MPW 16:298.

Magic Village, The
See: Village Magique, Le (1953).

Magic Wand, The
1912 sil sh.
Ref: MPW 13:663.

Magical Suit of Armor
1908 Gaum sil sh.
Ref: MPW 2:496.

Magician, The
n.d. 20th-Fox.
Ref: Willis.
Announced; never made.

Magician' Apprentices of Ulm, The
1959 German 12 mins.
Ref: Collier.

Magnet, The
1950 British, Ealing (U) 78 mins.
Ref: FIR March '51 p39; LC.

Magnet of Destruction, The
1915 sil.
Ref: MPW 24:65.

Magnificent Six and 1/2, The
1967 British, Children's Film
Foundation/Century serial.
Ref: MFB '68 p 181.

Maid of Niagara
1910 Pathé sil sh.
Ref: MPW 7:1308; F/A p423.

Maid of Salem
1936 (1937) Par 85 mins.
Ref: MPH 30 Jan '37; HR 21 Jan
'37; Acad.

Mais Ne Nous Deliverez Pas du Mal
(But Do Not Deliver Us from Evil)
1971 French color.
Ref: Vw 26 May '71; Bob Greenburg.

Making the Headlines
(House of Mystery -e.t?; All Were
Guilty -e.t?)
1938 Col 60 mins.
Ref: Acad.

Malamondo
1964 Italian.
Ref: Willis.

Mammals
See: Ssaki (1962).

Mammy's Ghost
1911 Vit sil 906 ft.
Ref: Bios 8 June '11 p xiii.

Man Alive
(The Amorous Ghost -e.t?)
1945 RKO 70 mins.
Ref: HR & Vd 26 Sept '45;
NY Tribune 17 Nov '45.

Man and the Devil
See: Phantom Killer (1942).

Man Behind You, The
1934 MGM.
Ref: Willis.
Never made.

Man Between, The
(novel by W.A. Frost)
See: Black Magic (1929).

Man Bring This Up the Road
(story by T. Williams)
See: Boom! (1968).

Man Called Demon
n.d. Japanese.
Ref: FIR VIII:325.

Man Enters Cosmic Space
1966? Soviet.
Ref: MTVM April '66 p 18.

Man from Hell, The
1934.
Ref: MPH 29 Aug '34; Acad.

Man from Istanbul, The
See: That Man in Istanbul (1965).

Man from Nowhere, The
See: Homme de Nulle Part, L'
(1936).

Man from Planet Earth
n.d. Soviet.
Ref: Collier.

Man in the Iron Mask, The
1939 Edward Small (UA)
12 reels.
Dir: James Whale.
Ref: Acad; LC.
Based on the novel by Alexandre
Dumas.

Man in the Moon
1963 British.
Ref: Gasca p320-21
Stage play only.

Man of Two Worlds
1934 RKO 10 reels.
Ref: FD 13 Jan '34; LC.
Based on the novel by Ainsworth
Morgan.

Man Under Water
1961 Czech ani sh.
Ref: Ani/Cin p 126.

Man Upstairs, The
1926 WB sil 7 reels.
Ref: AFI F2.3426.
Based on the story by Earl
Derr Biggers.

Man Wanted
1922 Herbert L. Steiner (Clark-
Cornelius Corp) sil 4966 ft.
Ref: AFI F2.3427 p485-86.

Man Who Cried Wolf, The
1937 U 7 reels.
Ref: Acad; LC; FD 19 Aug '37.

Man Who Dared, The
1946 Col 7 reels.
Ref: LC.

Man Who Died Twice, The
1958 Rep 70 mins.
Ref: FF '58 p299.

Man Who Disappeared, The
1914 Edison sil serial 10
parts 10 reels.
Ref: CNW 19, 157-58.

Man Who Finally Died, The
1963 (1967).
Ref: FF '67 p44.

Man Who Married His Own Wife, The
1922 U sil 4313 ft.
Ref: AFI F2.3433 p486-87.
Based on the story by John Fleming
Wilson and Mary Ashe Miller.

Man Who Returned to Life, The
1942 Col 6 reels.
Ref: Vd 19 Feb '42; LC.

Man Who Walks on Water
1908 Pathé sil sh.
Ref: Views 91:9.

Man Who Would Not Die
1916 sil.
Ref: MPW 29:1751.

Man Who Would Not Die
1924 Pathé sil 2 reels.
Ref: MPN 29:514.

Man with a Cloak, The
1951 MGM 81 mins.
Ref: Acad; FIR Oct '61 p471;
LC.
Based on a story by John Dickson
Carr.

Man with 100 Faces
1938 British.
Ref: Acad.

Man with the Dolls
n.d. Pathé sil.
Ref: MPW 5:733.

Man with the Steel Whip
1954 Rep serial 12 parts
24 reels.
Ref: LC.

Man Without a Face, The
(novel by E. Wallace)
See: Psycho-Circus (1966);
Ratsel des Silbernen Dreiecks, Das
(1966).

Mandragola, La
1965 French/Italian.
Ref: Ital Prods p78-79.

Mandrake the Magician
1968 King Features.
Ref: B. Warren.
Announced; never made.

Manhattan Shakedown
1938 Canadian, Central (Col)
57 mins.
Ref: V 14? Oct '39; MFB '38.

Maniac
1963 British, Hammer 86 mins.
Prod & SP: Jimmy Sangster.
Ref: FD 23 Oct '63; MFB May '63
p67; B. Warren.

Marchands d'Illusions
(Vendors of Dreams)
1953 French, Vascos Films.
Ref: UniF 5.

Mariage de Raison et Mariage d'Amour
See: Lover's Hazing, A (1908).

Mariee Etait en Noir, La
See: Bride Wore Black, The (1968).

Mark of Dracula
See: Curse of the Headless Demon,
The (n.d.).

Mark of the Beast
1923 Thomas Dixon (W.W. Hodkinson
Co.) sil 5988 ft.
Ref: AFI F2.3474 p493.

Mark of the Devil
1961 Mexican.
Ref: MPH 25 March '61.

Mark of the Frog
1928 Pathé sil serial 10
parts.
Ref: CNW p 142.

Mark of the Gorilla
1950 Col sepia 68 mins.
Ref: Vd & HR 13 Jan '50;
Acad.
Based on the character "Jungle
Jim" from the comic strip by
Alex Raymond.

Mark of the Hawk, The
1957 (1958) Film Productions Int'l
(World Horizons) color scope
212 mins.
Ref: LC.

Mascara de Kriminal, La
1967 Spanish/Italian.
Ref: SpCin '68 p 144-45.

Mascara de la Muerte, La
(The Mask of Death)
1960 (1961) Mexican (Clasa-
Mohme).
Ref: FDY.

Mask of Death, The
See: Mascara de la Muerte, La
(1960).

Mask of Dimitrios, The
1944 WB 95 mins.
Ref: V 16 Oct '44; B. Warren.
Based on novel "A Coffin for
Dimitrios" by Eric Ambler.

Mask of Love, The
See: Such Men Are Dangerous (1930).

Mask of the Dragon
1951 Lippert Prods 52 mins.
Ref: HR & Vd 19 March '51; MFB
Dec '51 p376-77.

Masquerade
1965 British, Novus (UA) color
102 mins.
Ref: FF '65 p 118-20; CoF 7:46.

Mastermind
1969 UA.
Ref: MTVM Nov '69 p20.
Shooting halted.

Matrimonio Es Como el Demonio, El
(Matrimony is Like the Devil)
n.d. Mexican (Clasa Mohme/Azteca).
Ref: PS.

Medico e lo Stregone, Il
(The Doctor and the Wizard)
1957 Italian.
Ref: Unitalia '57 p 114-15.

Medium's Nemesis, The
1913 Thanhouser (Mutual) sil
1020 ft.
Ref: MPW 1913 p882; Bios 18
Dec '13.

Meet the Baron
1933 MGM 7 reels.
Ref: HR & Vd 2 Oct '33; Acad;
Bloch.

Meeting with the Devil
1959 French.
Ref: Vw 26 Aug '59; Acad.

Melting Millions
1927 Pathé serial 10 parts
20 reels.
Ref: CNW p 134.

Memento
1968 French.
Ref: Willis.

Memoiren des Satans, Die
See: Dr. Mors (1914).

Memoirs of Satan, The
See: Dr. Mors (1914).

Men of Iron
(novel by H. Fast)
See: Black Shield of Falworth,
The (1954).

Men of To-morrow
1932 (1934) British, London (Par)
89 mins.
Ref: Acad; LC.
Based on novel "Young Apollo" by
Anthony Gibbs.

Men Without Souls
1940 Col 6 reels.
Ref: Acad; LC.

Menace, The
1932 Col 7 reels.
Ref: MPH 6 Feb '32; Acad.
Based on "The Feathered Serpent"
by Edgar Wallace.

Menilmontant
1924 (1925?) French sil.
Ref: F/A p643; Acad.

Mephisto at a Masquerade
1910 Gaum sil.
Ref: MPW 6:655.

Mephistophelia
1914 Italian (French?) sil.
Ref: F/A p397; MPW 19:1686;
LC.

Mermaid, The
1910 Thanhouser sil sh.
Ref: MPW 7:267.

Mermaid, The
1913 sil.
Ref:

Message from Beyond, A
1911 Vit sil.
Ref: MPW 10:551.

Message from the Moon, A
1912 Biograph sil.
Ref: MPW 11:712.

Mexican Bus Ride
(Subida al Cielo: Ascent to
Heaven)
1951 (1954) Mexican, Isla
85 mins (73 mins).
Dir: Luis Buñuel.
Ref: Durgnat/Buñuel.

Mi Marido. . .Que Espanto de Hombre
(My Husband, What a Frightful
Creature)
n.d. Spanish/Italian, Lacy Int'l
Films/?
Ref: Photon 21:8.

Mibster and the Monster, The
n.d.
Ref: Willis.
Error for non-fantastic The
Mibster and the Mobster, which
was announced but never filmed.

Midland Bank
1966? British, Cammel, Hudson and
Brownjohn Associates color ani
2 mins.
Ref: ASIFA 3.
Advertisement for bank.

Midnight Cowboy
1969 UA color 119 mins
(111 mins).
Ref: FDY; B. Warren.

Midnight Girl, The
1925 Chadwick sil 7 reels.
Cast includes: Bela Lugosi.
Ref: AFI F2.3589 p509.

Midnight Guest, The
(One Dark Night -e.t.; Flesh -e.t.)
1923 U sil 4795 ft.
Ref: AFI F2.3590 p509-10.

Midnight Madonna
1937 Par 7 reels.
Ref: FD 8 June '37; LC.

Midnight Man, The
1917 Butterfly (U) sil 5 reels.
Ref: MPN 16:1320.

Midnight Manhunt
(One Exciting Night -s.t.)
1945 Par 81 mins.
Cast includes: George Zucco.
Ref: HR 8 June '45.

Midnight Mystery
1930 RKO 69 mins.
Ref: AFI F2.3598 p511.
Based on play "Hawk Island" by
Howard Young.

Midnight Phantom
1935 Reliable 63 mins.
Ref: HR 18 Nov '35; Willis.

Midnight Scare, A
1914 Crystal sil 480 ft.
Ref: Willis.

Midnight Sun, The
1926 U sil 8767 ft.
Ref: AFI F2.3605 p511-12; MPH
78:f294; MPW 80:23, 169.

Midwinter Night's Dream
1912 Lubin sil sh.
Ref: MPH 11:710.

Mighty Atom, The
1911 British, Banforth sil sh.

Ref: BFI cat p98-99; FilmLex
p1503.

Mighty Ursus
1961 Italian/Spanish, Cine Italia/
Atenea (UA) color 92 mins.
Ref: Acad; Collier.
See also: Ursus.

Mighty Warrior, The
See: Vendetta di Ursus, La (1961).

Milk Train Doesn't Stop Here Anymore, The
(play by T. Williams)
See: Boom! (1968).

Mille e una Donna
(A Thousand and One Women)
1963 Italian, Documento color scope.
Ref: Ital Prods '65 p224.

Million Dollar Mystery, The
1914 Thanhouser sil serial 26 parts 52 reels.
Ref: CNW p 15-16; Bloch; MPW 20:959, 1054; F/A p513.

Million Dollars for Seven Assassins, A
1966 Italian.
Ref: Willis.

Million Year Old Man, The
n.d. British, Tigon.
Ref: Richardson.
Announced; never made.

Mills of the Gods, The
1909 Biograph sil sh.
Ref: MPW 5:317.

Millstone, The
n.d. British, Amicus.
Ref: Richardson.
Announced; never made.

Mind Reader, The
1933 FN 8 reels.
Ref: MPH 25 Feb '33 p37.

Mind Thing, The
n.d.
Prod: Ivan Tors.
Ref: CineF Fall '70 p44.
Based on the novel by Frederic Brown.
Announced; never made.

Mini Weekend
1967 British, Tigon/Global 79 mins.
Ref: Collier; MFB June '67 p95.

Miracle, The
1912 Vit sil sh.
Ref: MPW 13:370.

Miracle, The
1949 Italian.
Ref: Scognamillo.

Miracle at Lourdes
1939 (1940) MGM 11 mins.
Ref: MPH 20 Jan '40.

Miracle at Viggiu
See: Miracolo a Viggiu (1950).

Miracle des Loups, Le
(The Miracle of the Wolves)
1966 French/Italian, S.N. Pathé/Dama Cinemat. color scope.
Ref: UniF cat '66.

Miracle in Harlem
1948.
Ref: MPH 14 Aug '48; Acad.

Miracle Kid
1941 PRC 7 reels.
Ref: MFB April '42 p47; FD 27 April '42; Vd 23 Jan '42.

Miracle Man, The
● 1919 Par Artcraft sil 7 reels.
Cast includes: Lon Chaney.
Ref: MPN 20:2057, 3362; FD 31 Aug '19.

● 1931 (1932) Par 9 reels.
Ref: FD 24 April '32; MPH 16 Jan '32, 30 April '32 p40.

Based on the play by George M. Cohan from the story by Frank L. Packard and Richard Harding Davis.

Miracle of Father Malachias, The
See: Wunder des Malachias, Das (1961).

Miracle of Life, The
1926 S.E.V. Taylor (Associated Exhibitors) sil 4757 ft.
Ref: AFI F2.3639 p516.

Miracle of St. Therese
1958 (1959) French.
Ref: Acad; BO 16 March '59; FD 30 Jan '59.

Miracle of the White Suit
(Un Grande Dia: A Great Day)
1957 (1962) Spanish, ASPA (Ellis Films) 94 mins.
Ref: FF '62 p369.

Miracle of the Wolves, The
(Le Miracle des Loups)
1925 French sil.
Ref: Photo May '25 p46; MPN 31:1021.
See also: Miracle des Loups, Le (1966).

Miracle on Main Street, A
1939 Col 78 mins.
Ref: Acad.

Miracle Woman, The
1931 Col 9 reels.
Ref: FD 2 Aug '31.
Based on play "Bless You Sister" by John Meehan & Robert Riskin.

Miracles
1934 Soviet (Amkino).
Ref: FD 23 Oct '34.

Miracles for Sale
1939 MGM 70 mins.
Dir: Tod Browning.
Ref: MPH 5 Aug '39 p88; Bloch.
Based on novel "Death from a Top Hat" by Clayton Rawson.

Miracolo a Viggiu
(Miracle at Viggiu)
1950 Italian.
Ref: Unitalia '50-'51 p68-69.

Mirage
1965 U scope 109 mins.
Ref: MFB Oct '65 p 151.

Mirage, The
(play by E. Selwyn)
See: Possessed (1931).

Mirror Has Two Faces, The
1959 French (Continental Distributing)
Ref: FD 21 May '59.

Mision Secreta en el Caribe
(Secret Mission in the Caribbean)
1971 Spanish/Mexican, Tusisa/Fermont color 77 mins.
Cast includes: Santo.
Ref: SpCin '72 p 148-49.
See also: Santo contra los Asesinos de la Mafia (1970).

Miss Pinkerton
1932 FN 75 mins.
Ref: Willis; FD 9 July '32.

Miss Robin Crusoe
1954 20th-Fox color 8 reels.
Ref: LC; B. Warren.

Missile from Hell
(Battle of the V. 1 --Brit.t; Unseen Heroes --alt.t.)
1958 (1961) British, George Maynard - John Bash (NTA) 104 mins (82 mins).
Ref: MPH 2 July '60.

Missing Corpse, The
1945 PRC 8 reels.
Ref: Vd 23 April '45.

Missing from St. Agil
See: Disparus de St. Agil, Les (1938).

Missing Lady, The
1946 Mono 60 mins.
Ref: LC; FD 18 Sept '46; Vd 27 Dec '46; MFB April '47 p51.
Based on the Street and Smith Magazine character "The Shadow" created by Maxwell Grant.

Missing Mummy, The
1915 Kalem sil sh.
Ref: MPW 26:2425.

Mission Bloody Mary
See: Agente 077 -- Missione Bloody Mary (1965).

Missione Speciale Lady Chaplin
(Special Mission Lady Chaplin; Operacion Lady Chaplin: Operation Lady Chaplin)
1966 Italian/French/Spanish.
Ref: Ital Prods '66 I p 126.

Mr. Emmanuel
1945 British, Two Cities (UA) 10 reels.
Ref: FD 5 Jan '45; Acad.
Based on the novel by Louis Golding.

Mister V
1941 Edward Small Prods (UA) 60 mins.
Ref: LC.

Mr. Vampire
1916 Rex (U) sil 2 reels.
Ref: LC.

Mr. Wong at Headquarters
See: Fatal Hour, The (1939).

Mr. Wong in Havana
n.d. Mono.
Ref: FD 5 May '39.
Announced; never made.

Mr. Wong in New York
n.d. Mono.
Ref: FD 5 May '39.
Announced; never made.

Mr. Wong Vanishes
n.d. Mono.
Ref: FD 5 May '39.
Announced; never made.

Mr. Wong's Chinatown Squad
n.d. Mono.
Ref: FD 5 May '39.
Announced; never made.

Mr. Wu
1927 MGM sil 7603 ft.
Cast includes: Lon Chaney.
Ref: AFI F2.3656 p519.

Mister X
1967 Italian/Spanish.
Ref: Ital Prods '67 p90.

Misteri della Giungla Nera, I
See: Mystery of Thug Island (1964).

Misterio del Cuarto Amarillo, El
(The Mystery of the Yellow Room)
1947 Argentinian, Film Andes y Pyada.
Ref: Willis.
Based on novel "Le Mystère de la Chambre Jaune" by Gaston Leroux.
See also: Mystery of the Yellow Room, The.

Mistero del Tempio Indiano, Il
(The Mystery of the Indian Temple)
1963 Italian.
Ref: Ital Prods.

Mists of Autumn
See: Brumes d'Automne (1928).

Mistress of the World, The
(Die Herrin der Welt)
1920 (1922) German, May-Film (Famous Players-Lasky) serial 8 parts (4 parts) 23 reels?
Ref: F et R p 19; LC.
Based on the novel by Karl Figdor.

Mrs. Smithers' Boarding School
1917 Biog sil sh.
Ref: MPW 1907 p62.

Moby Dick
● 1930 WB 75 mins.
Ref: AFI F2.3660 p519; Vw 20 Aug '30.

● 1956 WB color 116 mins.
SP: Ray Bradbury and John Huston.
2nd Unit Dir: Jack Clayton.
2nd Unit Cin: Freddie Francis.
Ref: MFB Dec '56 p 150; S&S Winter 56'57 p 151.

● n.d. 30 mins.
Ref: Contemp p49.

Based on the novel by Herman Melville.
See also: Sea Beast, The (1926).

Modern Cinderella, A
1910 Vit sil sh.
Ref: MPW 6:955.

Modern Cinderella
1911 Edison sil sh.
Ref: MPW 10:410.

Modern Jekyll and Hyde, A
1913 Kalem sil 2 reels.
Ref: MPW 18:1584, 19:289.

Modern Mephisto, A
(The Oath of the Bible -alt.t.)
1914 sil 6 reels.
Ref: MPW 20:122.

Modern Mystery, The
n.d.
Ref: Collier.

Modern Psyche, A
1913 Vit sil sh.
Ref: MPW 16:657, 946.

Modern Rip, A
1911 sil sh.
Ref: MPW 10:1008.

Modern Rocambole, The
See: Moderno Rocamble, Il (1918).

Moderno Rocamble, Il
(The Modern Rocambole)
1918 Italian sil.
Ref: DdC III:285.

Mon Oncle
See: My Uncle (1956).

Mondo Balordo
(Foolish World)
1967 (1968) Italian (AIP) color 86 mins.
Nar: Boris Karloff.
Ref: FF '68 p528; Willis.

Mondo Bizarro
n.d. Italian?

Mondo Freudo
n.d. Italian?

Mondo dei Miracoli, Il
(The World of Miracles)
1958 Italian.
Ref: Unitalia '59 p 152-53.

Money
See: Argent, L' (1928).

Money to Burn
1922 Fox sil 4850 ft.
Ref: AFI F2.3678 p521-22.
Based on novel "Cherub Divine" by Sewell Ford.

Monica Stop
n.d. Spanish.
Ref: Willis.
Not completed.

Monkey in Winter
(Un Singe en Hiver; It's Hot in Hell)
1962 (1963) French, Cipra -- Cite (MGM) scope 104 mins.
Ref: FF '63 p24; MFB Sept '63 p 133.

Monkeys Go Home
1967 WD (BV) color 101 mins.
Ref: Vw 13 Oct '65, 10 Nov '65; FDY '68.
Based on novel "The Monkeys" by G.K. Wilkinson.

Monocle Rit Jaune, Le
(The Monocle Gives a Sickly Smile)
1964 French, Les Films Cocinor/ Laetitia.
Cast includes: Barbara Steele.
Ref: Willis.

Monsieur Verdoux
1947 Chaplin Studios Inc. (UA) 124 mins.
Ref: Acad; MFB Nov '47 p 158; LC.

Monster, The
See: Wahsh, El (1953/54).

Monster and the Girl, The
1914 Solax sil.
Ref: MPW 19:1694, 20:518.

Monster in My Blood
See: Destroyer, The (n.d.).

Monster Kills, The
(Murder at Midnight --e.t.?)
1931 Tiffany.
Ref: MPH 18 July '31 p33 ad.

Monster of the Island, The
See: Mostro dell' Isola, Il (1953).

Monsters, The
See: Mostri, I (1963).

Monsters of the Deep
1931 Talking Picture Epics sil.
Ref: FD 24 May '31; Vw 20 May '31.

Moon Wolf
1964 (1966) AA 74 mins.
Ref: FF '66 p386.

Moonskin
See: Ragazza della Pelle di Luna, La (1972).

Moriarty
See: Sherlock Holmes (1922).

Moro Witch Doctor
1964 U.S./Philippine Hemisphere (20th-Fox) 61 mins.
Ref: FF '64 p347.

Mort du Cygne, La
(The Death of a Swan)
1937 French.
Ref: Scognamillo.
See also: Unfinished Dance, The (1947).

Mort en ce Jardin, La
(Death in the Garden)
1956 French/Mexican color.
Dir: Luis Buñuel.
Ref: MFB Nov '58 p 140.

Most Dangerous Game, The
1968 French.
Ref: MTVM March '68 p38.
Not based on the story by Richard Connell.

Most Dangerous Game, The
(short story by R. Connell)
See: Run for the Sun (1956).

Mostri, I
(The Monsters)
1963 Italian.
Ref: Unitalia '63 II p32-33.

Mostro dell' Isola, Il
(The Monster of the Island)
1953 Italian, Romano.
Cast includes: Boris Karloff.
Ref: Collier; FIR Aug-Sept '64 p412.

Mother Goose in 16th Century Theater
1912 Edison sil sh.
Ref: EK 15 Oct '12.

Mountain Witch, The
1913 Kalem sil sh.
Ref: MPW 15:704.

Mud Turtle, The
(story by B. Cohn)
See: Best Man Wins (1934).

Muerta Camina con Tacon Alto, La
(Death Walks on High Heels)
1971? Spanish/Italian, Atlantida/ Cine.
Ref: Vw 3 May '72 p 175.

Muerta Espera en Atenas, La
1966 Spanish.
Ref: Willis.

Muerto Hace las Maletas, El
(Death Packs Up; Der Todesracher: Death Avenger)
1971 Spanish/German, Fenix/Telecine Film.
Ref: Vw 3 May '72 p 175; Terror Fantastic p36.

Mujer sin Alma
(Woman Without a Soul)
1944 Mexican.

Mujer sin Cabeza
(Woman Without a Head)
1944 Mexican.
Ref: Acad; LAT 29 Aug '44.

Mulligan's Ghost
n.d. sil.
Ref: MPW 22:534.

Mumia, El
(The Mummy)
1969 UAR 102 mins.
Ref: MFB May '72 p98.

Mummy, The
1908 French, Pathé sil 344 ft.
Ref: MPW 2:190, 193.

Mummy, The
1912 Pathé sil 528 ft.
Ref: Bios 15 Feb '12 p iii.

Mummy, The
See: Mumia, El (1969).

Mummy and the Hummingbird, The
1915 Famous Players sil.
Ref: Bloch; MPN 27 Nov '15; FD 18 Nov '15.

Mummy's Secret, The
1952 Adrian Weiss Prods 16mm 3 reels.
Ref: Collier.
Based on the character "Craig Kennedy" created by Arthur B. Reeve.
TV series episode.

Mundo, Demonio y Carne
(The World, the Devil, and the Flesh)
1960 Mexican.
Ref: Acad; Vw 12 Oct '60.

Muntz TV Spot
n.d. ani 2 mins.
Ref: CFS cat '69.

Muratti Cigarette Commercial
1932 color ani 4 mins.
Ref: CFS cat '69.

Murder at Midnight
See: Monster Kills, The (1931).

Murder at the Baskervilles
(Silver Blaze --Brit.t.)
1936 (1941) British, Twickenham (Astor) 66 mins.
Ref: MPH 17 July '37 p50; FD 18 June '41.
Based on short story "Silver Blaze" by Arthur Conan Doyle.

Murder by Invitation
1941 Mono 67 mins.
Ref: V 30 July '41.

Murder in the Red Barn
See: Maria Marten (1899).

Murder in the Surgery
(novel by J.G. Edwards)
See: Mystery of the White Room, The (1939).

Murder of the Month Club
1971 AIP.
SP: Jimmy Sangster.
Ref: Photon 21:5.
Announced; not made.

Murderer of Dusseldorf, The
See: Asesino de Dusseldorf, El (1964).

Musgrave Ritual, The
● 1913 French sil sh.
Ref: LC.
● 1922 British, Stoll sil 1260 ft.
Ref: BFI cat p 117.
Based on the story by Arthur Conan Doyle.
See also: Sherlock Holmes Faces Death (1943).

My Country First
1916 sil.
Ref: FIR May '66.

My Daughter Joy
See: Operation X (1951).

My Husband, What a Frightful Creature
See: Mi Marido. . .Que Espanto de Hombre (n.d.).

My Name Is Ivan
(Detstvo Ivana: Ivan's Childhood)
1962 (1963) Soviet, Mosfilm (Sig Shore) 95 mins (84 mins).
Ref: FF '63 p 183-84; CoF 5:4.

My Uncle
(Mon Oncle)
1956 (1958) French/Italian, Spectra - Gray - Alter/Le Film del Centauro (Continental Distributing) color 110 mins.
Ref: UniF 15; FD 23 Oct '58.

Mystère de la Chambre Jaune, Le
(The Mystery of the Yellow Room)
● 1931 French, Osso.
Ref: Acad; FD 31 May '31.
● 1948 French, Cin Alcina color 90 mins.
Ref: MMF 24:49.
Based on the novel by Gaston Leroux.
See also: Mystery of the Yellow Room, The.

Mystère Saint-Val, Le
(The Saint-Val Mystery)
1945 French.
Ref: Willis.

Mystères de Paris, Les
(The Mysteries of Paris)
● 1922 French sil.
Ref: DdC III:197.
● 1935 (1937) French 85 mins.
Ref: Vw 3 Feb '37; HR 13 July '35.
● 1943 French.
Ref: DdC III:36.
● 1962 French?
Ref: Willis.
Based on the novel by Eugène Süe.
See also: Mysteries of Paris, The (1913).

Mysteries of Notre Dame
1936 Du World sil.
Ref: FD 30 Oct '36.

Mysteries of Paris, The
(Les Mystères de Paris; The Child of Fate)
1913 French, Eclectic-Pathé sil 5000 ft.
Ref: Bloch; MPW 16:1292; F/A p317.
Based on novel "Les Mystères de Paris" by Eugène Süe.
See also: Mystères de Paris, Les.

Mysterious Phonograph, The
1908 Lubin sil sh.
Ref: MPW 2:403.

Mysterious Picture, The
1949 Marshall Grant/Realm TV Prods 16mm 2 reels.
Ref: LC.
Based on an adventure in "la Legende d'Uylenspiegel" by Charles de Coster.
TV episode only.

Mysterious Pilot, The
1938 Col serial 15 parts 31 reels.
Ref: Stringham; FIR Aug-Sept '61 p 425.
Based on novel "The Silver Hawk" by William Byron Mowery.

Mysterious Stranger, The
1925 Carlos Prods (FBO) sil 5270 ft.
Ref: AFI F2.3766 p535.

Mystery Mountain
1934 Mascot serial.
Ref: D. Glut.

Mystery of Edwin Drood, The
● 1914 Shubert (World Film Corp) sil 5 reels.
Ref: MPW 22:299, 356, 410.
● 1935 U 87 mins.
Ref: MFB March '49 p46; HR 17 Jan '35; FD 20 March '35.
Based on the unfinished novel by Charles Dickens.

Mystery of Grayson Hall, The
1914 Eclair sil 1800 ft.
Ref: MPW 22:643, 714.

Mystery of Lourdes
1928 Phoenix sil.
Ref: FDY.

Mystery of Mr. X, The
1934 MGM 9 reels.
Ref: Acad.
Based on the novel by Philip MacDonald.

Mystery of Souls, The
1911 Italian, Itala sil 3000 ft.
Ref: Bios 28 Dec '11; 14 May '14.

Mystery of the Black Jungle
See: Mystery of Thug Island (1964).

Mystery of the Blue Room
See: Secret of the Blue Room (1933).

Mystery of the Boule Cabinet, The
(novel by B.E. Stevenson)
See: In the Next Room (1930);
Pursuing Vengeance, The (1916).

Mystery of the Indian Temple, The
See: Mistero del Tempio Indiano, Il (1963).

Mystery of the Red Barn, The
See: Maria Marten (1914).

Mystery of the Thirteenth Guest, The
1943 Mono 6 reels.
Ref: Vd 7 Oct '43.
Based on novel "The 13th Guest"
by Armitage Trail.
Remake without horror elements
of Thirteenth Guest, The (1932).

Mystery of the White Room, The
1939 U 6 reels.
Ref: Acad.
Based on novel "Murder in the
Surgery" by James G. Edwards
(J.W. MacQueen).

Mystery of the Yellow Room, The
● 1919 Mayflower (Realart) sil
6200 ft.
Ref: MPN 20:2684, 3347; FD 26
Oct '19.

● (Le Mystère de la Chambre Jaune)
1913 French, Eclair sil.
Ref: Bios 10 April '13; F/A p398.

Based on novel "Le Mystère de
la Chambre Jaune" by Gaston
Leroux.
See also: Misterio del Cuatro
Amarillo, El (1947); Mystère
de la Chambre Jaune, Le.

Mystery of Thug Island
(I Misteri della Giungla Nera:
The Mystery of the Black Jungle)
1964 (1966) Italian/German,
Lieber/Eichberg (Col) color
scope 96 mins.
Ref: FF '66 p382.
Based on novel "The Mystery of
the Black Jungle" by Emilio
Salgari.

Mystery Pilot
1926 Rayart sil serial 10
parts 20 reels.
Ref: CNW p252-53.

Mystery Ship
1941 Col 8 reels.
Ref: HR & Vd 29 July '41; LC.

Mystery Squadron
1933 Mascot serial 12 parts
25 reels.
Ref: Stringham; Willis.

Mystery Submarine
1950 U 78 mins.
Ref: FD 24 Nov '50; LC.

Mystic Faces
1918 sil.
Ref: MPW 37:1771.

Mystic Hour, The
1917 Apollo (Art Dramas)
sil.
Ref: MPW 32:1460; MPN 15:3622.

Mystic Hour, The
1934 Progressive Pics.
Ref: Vd 8 Sept '34.

Mystic Mountain, The
1936 French/Swiss? (Lenauer
Int'l) 80 mins.
Ref: FD 1 April '36; HR 9 April
'36.

Mystic Shriners' Day at Dreamland
1907 (1908) Actograph Co sil sh.
Ref: Views 89:7; MPW 1:62; LC.

N

Nachts, Wenn der Teufel Kam
See: Devil Strikes at Night, The
(1958).

Nada Menos Que un Arkangel
(Nothing Less than an Archangel)
1958 Spanish.
Ref: Cine Español '59 p96-97.

Naked Kiss, The
1964 AA 89 mins.
Ref: MMF 14:118.

Naked World
(The Great Green Og --e.t.)
n.d.
Announced; never made.

Namahage, the Demons
1961.
Ref: FEFN Feb '61 p57.

Nanny, The
1965 British, Hammer (20th-Fox)
93 mins.
Sp: Jimmy Sangster.
Ref: MFB Nov '65 p164.
Based on the novel by Evelyn
Piper.

Narayama Bushi-Ko
(Legend of Narayama)
1958 Japanese color 98 mins.
Ref: Vw 17 Sept '58.

Navy Spy
1937 Condor Pics (Grand
National) 6 reels.
Ref: V 24 March '37; HR 10
April '37.

Nazarin
1958 Mexican 94 mins.
Dir: Luis Buñuel.
Ref: Vw 20 May '59; FF '68
p249.
Based on the novel by Benito
Pérez Galdos.

Negatives
1968 British, Kettledrum -
Narizzano (Walter Reade-Continen-
tal) color 98 mins (90 mins).
Ref: Acad.
Based on the novel by Peter Everett.

Neptune's Daughter
1949 MGM color 93 mins.
Ref: Acad.

Nest in a Falling Tree
(novel by J. Crowley)
See: Night Digger, The (1971).

Never too Late to Mend
See: It's Never too Late to
Mend (1936).

New Babylon, The
1920 (1929) Soviet sil.
Ref: Vw 4 Dec '29; S&S Winter
'62-63 p47; FTN p237.

Next!
See: Next Victim, The (1971).

Next to No Time
1958 (1960) British, Lion color
93 mins.
Ref: FF '60 p149-50; Vw 20 Aug
'58; MPH 30 July '60.
Based on short story "The
Enchanted Hour" by Paul Gallico.

Next Victim, The
(Next! --ad.t.)
1971 Italian/Spanish, Devon/
Copercines (Maron) color
scope 81 mins.
Ref: BO 9 Aug '71.

Ni Vu, Ni Connu
1958 French.
Ref: MFB Sept '58 p116.
Based on novel "L'Affaire
Blaireau" by Alphone Allais.

Nicholas and Alexandra
1971 Horizon (Col) color scope
183 mins.
Ref: FF '71 p553-57.

Nick Carter in Panama
See: Phantom Raiders (1940).

Niente Rose per OSS 117
(Pas de Roses pour OSS 117: No
Roses for OSS 117; OSS 117
Murder for Sale --Brit.t.)
1968 Italian/French, DA.MA./PAC
color 105 mins.
Ref: MFB Aug '70 p167.

Niewinni Czarodzieje
(Innocent Sorcerers)
1960 Polish, Kadir 86 mins.
Ref: MFB March '62 p33.

Night Before Christmas, The
1912 Vit sil.
Ref: MPW 14:1108.

Night Digger, The
(The Road Builder --Brit.t.)
1971 British, Yongestreet-Tacitus
(MGM) color 110 mins.
Ref: Vw 10 May '71; FF '71
p299-300.
Based on novel "Nest in a Falling
Tree" by Joy Crowley.

Night in a Harem, A
1958 British ani silhouette
14 mins.
Ref: Collier.
Based on opera "The Abduction from the Seraglio" by
Mozart.

Night Must Fall
1937 MGM 115 mins.
Ref: MPH 10 April '37; FD 22
April '37.
Based on the play by Emlyn
Williams.

Night of Terror, A
1908 Biograph sil.
Ref: MPW 2:479.

Night of Terror, A
1911 Edison sil.
Ref: MPW 8:607.

Night of the Auk
n.d.
Ref: Collier.
Based on the play by Arch
Oboler.
No theatrical release.

Night of the Following Day, The
1969 U color 93 mins.
Ref: FF '69 p56; MFB March '69
p52.

Night World
1932 U 6 reels.
Cast includes: Boris Karloff.
Ref: Vw 31 May '32; LC.

Nightcomers, The
1971 (1972) British, Scimitar
color.
Ref: BO 28 Feb '72; HR 12
March '72; Vw 8 Sept '71;
B. Warren.
Based on characters in "The Turn
of the Screw" by Henry James.

Nightmare
1942 U 8 reels.
Ref: Vd 9 Nov '42.
Based on a story by Philip
MacDonald.

998
(novel by E. Hyams)
See: You Know What Sailors Are
(1953).

1999 1/2
n.d. Italian.
Dir: Federico Fellini.
Cast: Cary Grant.
Ref: MTVM 26:8:18.
Announced; never made.

Nippon Konchuki
See: Insect Woman, The (1963).

No Highway in the Sky
1951 20th-Fox 98 mins.
Ref: Collier; LC.

No Roses for OSS 117
See: Niente Rose per OSS 117
(1970).

Not Tonight Henry
196? color 61 mins.
Ref: Collier.

Nothing Less than an Archangel
See: Nada Menos que un Arcangel
(1958).

Notti Blanche
See: White Nights (1957).

Nuit Electrique, La
n.d.

Number Please
See: What a Night! (1928).

Nylon Moon
1966.
Ref: MTVM July '66 p37.

Dreamland
1954 British, Sequence Films
16mm 14 mins.
Ref: Collier.

Henry's Full House
1952 20th-Fox 117 mins.
Ref: MPH 22 Aug '52; FD 26
Aug '52; LC.
Based on five short stories
by O. Henry.
See also: Last Leaf, The (1917).

S.S. 117 Is Not Dead
See: O.S.S. 117 N'Est Pas Mort
(1956).

SS 117 Murder for Sale
See: Niente Rose per OSS 117
(1968).

S.S. 117 N'Est Pas Mort
(O.S.S. 117 Is Not Dead)
1956 French, Globe Omnium color
scope.
Ref: UniF 15:22.

S 77 Operazion Fioz di Loto
1965 Italian/French.
Ref: Ital Prods '65 p 162-63.

th of Stephen Huller, The
(novel by F. Holländer)
See: Variety (1925).

th of the Bible, The
See: Modern Mephisto, A (1914).

chod na Korze
See: Shop on Main Street, The
(1965).

ean Waif, The
1916 Golden Eagle sil.
Ref: MPN 14:3012.

tober Moth
1959 British, Independent
Artists 54 mins.
Ref: Collier.

tober the First Is too Late
n.d. Col.
Ref: Richardson.
Based on the novel by Fred
Hoyle.
Announced; never made.

d Obsession
(Kagi: The Key)
1960 (1961) Japanese, Daiei
(Edward Harrison) color scope
96 mins.
Ref: FF '61.
Based on novel "Kagi" by Junichiro
Tanizaki.

gi, Domani e Dopodomani
See: Paranoia (1966).

re, The
1913 sil.
Ref: MPW 15:366.

re and the Girl, The
1915 Lubin sil.
Ref: MPW 26:1714.

Men! Oh Women!
1956 20th-Fox color scope
90 mins.
Ref: Collier; LC.

! Mr. Porter
1938 British.
CoSP: Val Guest.
Ref: Halliwell.
See also: Ghost Train, The.

l's Well that Ends Well
1958 Col 2 reels.
Ref: Pardi.

Olveira Street
1934.
Ref: USA Exp List.

Omar Khayyam
1957 Par color VV 101 mins.
Ref: MFB Oct '57 p 129; HR 1
Aug '57.

Omar the Tentmaker
1922 Tully (FN) sil 8090 ft.
Ref: AFI F2.3963 p563.
Based on the play by Richard
Walton Tully.

On the Busses
1971 British, Hammer color
88 mins.
Ref: MFB '71 p 168.

On the Stroke of Twelve
1928 Trem Carr Prods (Rayart)
sil 5842 ft.
Ref: AFI F2.3975 p565.

On the Threshold of Space
1956 20th-Fox color scope
95 mins.
Ref: MFB May '56 p63.

Once in a Blue Moon
1935 (1936) Par 72 mins.
Ref: Vw 9 Dec '36; FD 3 Dec '36.

One Body too Many
1944 Par 8 reels.
Cast includes: Bela Lugosi.
Ref: Vd & HR 18 Oct '44; MPH
21 Oct '44.

One Dark Night
See: Midnight Guest, The (1923).

One Exciting Night
1922 D.W. Griffith Inc. (UA) sil
11500 ft.
Ref: AFI F2.3993 p568.

One Exciting Night
See: Midnight Manhunt (1945).

One Frightened Night
1935 Mascot 7 reels.
Ref: Willis.

One Live Ghost
1936 RKO 2 reels.
Ref: Maltin/GMS; Lighthouse
25 May '37.

One More Spring
1935 Fox 7860 ft.
Ref: Vw 27 Feb '35; FD 12 Feb
'35.
Based on the novel by Robert
Nathan.

One Mysterious Night
1944 Col 7 reels.
Ref: HR 21 Aug '44; Acad.
Based on character "Boston
Blackie" created by Jack Boyle.

One of Millions
1914 Dyreda Film Corp (World)
sil 4 reels.
Ref: MPW 22:992.

One Romantic Night
1930 UA 8 reels.
Ref: F/A p300.
Based on play "The Swan"
by Ferenc Molnar.

Only Thing, The
1925 MGM sil 6 reels.
Ref: AFI F2.4033 p573-74.

Open Window, The
1972 AFI color sh.
Ref: LAT 1 Feb '73 IV:14;
B. Warren.
Based on the short story by
Saki.

Operación Lady Chaplin
See: Missione Speciale Lady
Chaplin (1966).

Operation White Shark
See: A.D. 3 Operazione Squalo
Bianco (1966).

Operation X
(My Daughter Joy --s.t.)
1951 Col 88 mins.
Ref: Acad; LC.
Based on novel "David Golder"
by Irene Nemirovsky.

Ophelia
1962 French.
Dir: Claude Chabrol.
Ref: F&F Nov '63; Collier; Acad.
Inspired by play "Hamlet" by
William Shakespeare.

Orgy of Golden Nudes
See: Honeymoon of Horror (1970?).

Oriental Evil
1952 Japanese.
Ref: Ackerman; Vd 26 Sept '52;
HR 29 Sept '52.

Other Boarding School, The
See: Otra Residencia, La (1970).

Other Tomorrow, The
1930 FN sil & sound versions
5800 ft.
Ref: AFI F2.4050 p576.

Otra Residencia, La
(The Other Boarding School)
1970 Spanish/Italian, José
Antonio/Copercines color scope
80 mins.
Ref: Vw 12 May '71 p 143; SpCin
'71.

Out of the Fog
See: Fog for a Killer (1962).

Out of the Mist
(Der Sohn der Hagar)
1927 German, Defa sil.
Ref: C to H p 154-55; FTN p289.

Out of This World
1945 Par 10 reels.
Ref: LC.

Outback
1970 (1971) Australian, NLT
Prods -- Group W (UA) color
109 mins.
Ref: BO 18 Oct '71; MFB Dec
'71 p244.

Outer Space Daze
Apparently confusion with
Outer Space Jitters (1957).

Outrage, The
1964 MGM 97 mins.
Ref: MFB Oct '65 p 147; FF '64
p248-50.
Based on stories by Ryunosuke
Akutagawa, the film Rashomon
(1950), and play of the film by
Fay Kanin and Michael Kanin.

Outside Woman, The
1921 Realart sil 4225 ft.
Ref: AFI F2.4086 p581; MPW
29:108.
Based on play "All Night Long"
by Paul B. Sipe and Philip
Bartholomae.

Over the Moon
1940 British, London (UA) color
8 reels.
Ref: LC.

Oyster Princess, The
See: Austernprinzessin, Die (1919).

0734